W9-BWM-554

THE
HANDYBOOK
FOR
GENEALOGISTS

UNITED STATES
OF
AMERICA

TENTH EDITION

Published by

Everton Publishers
Draper, Utah

In memory of . . .

*four generations of the Everton family
whose tireless effort and years of service
have paved the way.*

In honor of . . .

Louise M. Everton

Dedicated to . . .

*all who will use this book in a
quest to seek out and make cherished
connections with their family.*

FOREWORD

In 1947, the first edition of *The Handybook for Genealogists* was published with 205 pages in a soft cover. The launch of this unique publication set a standard that resulted in the distribution of more than 1,000,000 copies through the ninth edition. And so it is that we express our gratitude for your loyalty and support. This year, we present our Tenth Edition in celebration of fifty-five years of success in helping you find the connection to your ancestors.

We can think of no better way to set off our new direction as Everton's Family History Network than to publish the finest *Handybook* ever. It is a tribute to you, our loyal employees, and hundreds of thousands of friends in the genealogy and family history community.

The *Tenth Edition Handybook*, a grand book of over nine hundred pages, is now published and presented for your use and benefit. Thousands of hours have been given to research, confirmation, data entry, update and upgrade. All this has been reviewed time and again to assure that the most accurate and useful information is contained in this marvelous book.

We proudly offer this book, filled with county, state and foreign country information, as the most complete, carefully prepared and published book ever in the genealogy and family history research field.

There is none other like it in its fullness, and none to match our objective that the book be a tribute to hundreds of thousands of you who have made a commitment to connecting your family—past and present—that you may know more fully *who you are and from whence you came*.

Sincerely,

R. Craig Hansen
Chairman and CEO

Stephen E. Featherstone
Director

PREFACE

ACKNOWLEDGMENTS

Many individuals have collected the data and prepared the material for the Tenth Edition Handybook. Countless hours were devoted to provide the most current information possible.

Everton Publishers is most grateful to those, both staff and volunteers, whose contributions over the years have made this book possible. Thanks are due to the past generations of the Everton family who created the idea and the first *Handybook* so many years ago.

My personal thanks also go to Holly T. Hansen - project manager, Gene F. Williams CGRS[sm], Tamara Pluth, Sheila Everton, Pamela Bankhead, Donna M. Brown, Jenni Johnson and the rest of the employees who have assisted in this monumental effort.

A. Lee Everton
Publisher

Introduction

Holly T. Hansen

Genealogy is fast becoming the number one hobby in the world. Today, an estimated 170 million Americans are interested in tracing their family history. The *Handybook* provides an avenue for individuals to pursue their personal heritage through the county record system of the United States.

In 1947, Everton Publishers began a unique collection of maps, addresses, land and property, vital records and other holdings for each county of the United States of America. Since that time, we have continued collecting and evaluating information to help family history researchers. Professional genealogists have invested thousands of hours checking these addresses, telephone numbers and websites to make sure that you have the most accurate information possible for contacting record keepers at the county level.

A new section in this edition illustrates the type of information contained within each record type held at the county level. Many researchers who have been actively involved with family history know what information is available in the various records, but newcomers may not have this innate knowledge.

We have also made an extensive search of available books and publications to provide a new, comprehensive bibliography for each state. Through the pages of the *Handybook*, you will find the county information that you have come to expect plus myriad pages of books and other publications that will assist you in continuing the quest for your family history.

One of the most notable changes in the *Handybook* is the inclusion of websites for every county in the United States. The arduous task of determining the best websites was necessary to give you as much contact information as possible for using the Internet in addition to the postal service and the telephone. With the research that was accomplished, we feel that you now have in your hands the most comprehensive resource for county research in the United States.

USING THE HANDYBOOK

While the excitement of finding your ancestors can send electrical charges up and down the spine, there are times when you need a little help locating records that may provide yet another spark. Often, the very roadblock you are trying to break through may become a giant stepping-stone. Paying close attention to the places where our ancestors lived, visited and traveled can help you identify information necessary to move forward in the search for that elusive individual.

Many places or localities no longer exist today, or the names may have changed. County and state boundaries have changed throughout the years. Territories became states and counties were divided. It is possible that an individual or family may have lived in five different counties without ever moving from the original homestead. All of these changes affected records and the way they were kept. This means that a diligent searcher needs to know where to find records for each county that a person may have lived in. The *Handybook* is your lifeline to solving the mysteries of your ancestor's whereabouts.

The *Handybook* begins with the United States of America, followed by information on nineteen foreign countries. Under the United States of America, information is organized alphabetically by state. Each state section contains the following general information:
- Brief History
- List of Archives, Libraries and Societies
- Bibliography of Atlases, Maps and Gazetteers
- Bibliography of family history publications and genealogy finding aids

Always consult the general information on a state before proceeding to the state and county listings that follow. Records are kept by individual jurisdictions. Each country keeps records on its citizens, and a state government holds different record types than the local county government. Using each jurisdiction will help you find your ancestors more effectively. Using the sources listed in the *Handybook* can save you hours of research.

Among the valuable resources held by national governments are census records, military service and pensions, land holdings, treaties, great historical libraries and other valuable collections that tell the story of individuals and the world in which they lived. Records held by the state include land, tax, birth, marriage and death records. Some records, such as immigration, emigration and naturalization records, can be located at all levels of jurisdiction—national, state and county. The *Handybook* gives contact information for offices that maintain records which allow you to quickly locate and request copies of valuable documents. Where known, Internet addresses have also been included.

After reading the general information for the country and state, you will find an alphabetic list for each state's counties, including counties that no longer exist. You can trace a county by its parent county or the territory from which it was created. There is an index to help you locate each county on the state county map. County creation dates are included to help you build a timeline for your research and locate the correct county records to search. These listings contain valuable data useful in helping you trace your ancestry and add life to your family tree.

Key to reading the information in the county pages:

County. This is the current name of the county (or Louisiana parish or Alaska borough). If the name has changed, the former name appears in alphabetical order with a reference to the current name. A county

County Website	Map Index	Date Created	Parent County or Territory From Which Organized Address/Details
Iron* www.co.iron.ut.us/	N2	31 Jan 1850	Original county Iron County; 68 S 100 E; PO Box 429; Parowan, UT 84761; Ph. 435.477.8341 Details: (Formerly Little Salt Lake Co. Name changed to Iron 3 Dec 1850) (Co Clk has m rec from 1887; Co Rcdr has land rec from 1852; Clk Dis Ct has div, pro & ct rec)

that has been discontinued is also noted.

*Asterisk. An asterisk (*) following a county's name indicates its inclusion in the Historical Records Survey.

Website. The URL of the official county website or USGENWEB address.

Map Index. The coordinates used to locate this county on the map.

Date Created. The date the county, parish, or borough was created or incorporated.

Parent County or Territory From Which Organized. The name of the county or counties from which this county was formed. Some counties were formed at the same time the state or territory was organized (original counties), while others were organized from previous entities such as a state or territory (in the eastern United States), or a Mexican municipality (in the American southwest).

Information on parent counties can help you know which government office has custody of records for a specific time period. Even if a family did not physically change residence, the location of records on that family could have moved as jurisdictional boundaries changed.

For example, a family living in what was to become Ford County, Illinois between 1788 and 1865, may have records in the custody of nine different offices. Working backwards, Ford County was organized in 1859 from land previously belonging to Clark County. Clark County was formed in 1819 from land previously belonging to Crawford County, which was formed in 1816 from a part of Edwards County. Edwards County was organized in 1814 from parts of both Madison and Gallatin counties. Madison had been split off of St. Clair County in 1812, while Gallatin was organized from a part of Randolph County in 1812. In turn, St. Clair County was formed from the old Northwest Territory in 1790, while Randolph County was organized from the Northwest Territory in 1795. To get all of the records on your family, you would consult the archives of all nine of these government units.

Address. The contact information including the address and phone number of the main offices of this county or parish.

Details. (Formerly Little Salt Lake Co. Name changed to Iron 3 Dec 1850) (Co Clk has m rec from 1887; Co Rcdr has land rec from 1852; Clk Dis Ct has div, pro & ct rec) Definitions: County clerk has marriage records from 1887; Co recorder has land records from 1852; Clerk of the district court has divorce, probate and court records.

For additional information on abbreviations, see "Abbreviations and Definitions" at the end of this section.

Explanation of the Historical Records Survey

When the Great Depression hit the United States in 1929, the American economy hit rock bottom. In 1933, President Franklin D. Roosevelt introduced "The New Deal," a series of new programs designed to pick America up and get the economy moving again.

The *Works Progress Administration* (WPA) was one of these programs. The WPA employed out-of-work Americans who were certified by local agencies as meeting certain qualifications.

The WPA was born in 1935. In 1939, the WPA was renamed to the *Works Projects Administration*. Over the years, the WPA would employ nearly 8.5 million Americans. Interestingly, half of those workers were employed in New York City. The WPA existed for only eight years, but provided a valuable resource for genealogists. Originally organized in 1935 as part of the *Federal Writers Project, the Historical Records Survey* (HRS) documented resources for research into American history. In 1939 it became a unit of the *Research and Records Program*.

The WPA was organized into regional, state and local divisions. Much of the work performed by the HRS was done for the *National Archives and Records Administration* (NARA), as well as state archives and state historical societies.

The HRS was responsible for creating the soundex indexes of the Federal Census. The HRS also compiled indexes of vital statistics, cemetery interments, school records, military records, maps, newspapers, and the list went on. Surveys of public record archives were conducted and inventories created in most states between the years 1936 and 1943. While few of these inventories give full transcripts, they do name the records that were available in the respective archives at the time of the survey. These inventories often give the condition of the various records, where they were stored and the dates of commencement and conclusion of the records. Microfilms of these indexes were later made by other organizations.

After the WPA was dissolved, the records, now in the hands of state archives and historical societies, were microfilmed, indexed and made available for use. However, many other records were placed into boxes and stored away. Also, a few have been destroyed, and in some cases, destroyed deliberately.

A checklist of publications was originally published by the WPA as *W.P.A. Technical Series, Research and Records Bibliography Number 7*. It has been reprinted by the Genealogical Publishing Company in Baltimore, Maryland as the *Check List of Historical Records Survey Publications, Bibliography of Research Projects Reports*, by Sargent B. Child and Dorothy B. Holmes. You may obtain a microform copy through the Family History Library in Salt Lake City, Utah. The microfilm numbers are 874,113 item 2 and a second filming numbered 9244683 item 4; and microfiche number 6016392.

ABBREVIATIONS AND DEFINITIONS

Abbreviations have been used to save space, making it possible to include more information.

appr   **Appraisement, Appraisal**
To set a price or value, to estimate the amount, quality or worth of something.

Asr   **Assessor**
An officer who assesses taxes.

Aud   **Auditor**
A person who inspects accounts.

b   **Birth Record**
Record testifying of the actual birth of a child.

bk   **Book**
A number of sheets of paper bound or stitched together.

bur   **Burial Record**
Record testifying of the burying of a dead body.

cem   **Cemetery Record**
Record testifying of the burial of the dead in a specific location.

cen   **Census**
An official numbering of the people of a country or district.

Chan   **Chancery**
A court of equity, as distinguished from a common-law court. A court of records; archives.

CH   **Courthouse**
A public building occupied by the judicial courts; a county seat.

Cir Ct   **Circuit Court**
A federal court of the United States superior to a district court: abolished 1911. A state court presided over by a circuit judge.

City Clk   **City Clerk**
An officer or employee of a city court; office.

civ   **civil**
Pertaining to citizens or to the state or between citizens, as regulated by law; distinguished from criminal, political or natural.

Clk   **Clerk**
An officer or employee of a court, legislatively body, corporation, society, or the like, charged with the care of its records, correspondence, and accounts.

Clk Chan Ct   **Clerk of Chancery Court**
An officer or employee of a Court of Equity, a court of records or archives.

Clk Cir Ct   **Clerk of Circuit Court**
An officer or employee of a Circuit Court.

Clk Cts   **Clerk of Courts**
An officer or employee of more than one court.

Clk Dis Ct   **Clerk of District Court**
An officer or employee of a District Court.

Clk Mag Cts   **Clerk of Magistrates Court**
An officer or employee of a Magistrates Court; an executive or judicial court.

Clk of Peace   **Clerk of the Peace**
An officer or employee; working with a Justice of the Peace.

Clk Sup Ct   **Clerk of Superior Court**
An officer or employee of a Superior Court.

Comm   **Commissioner, commissioners**
The head of an executive department of government.

Com Pleas Ct   **Common Pleas Court**
A common-law court of record, having original jurisdiction over civil and criminal matters. Formerly, an English court with exclusive jurisdiction in various classes of civil cases.

com   **Complete**
Having all needed parts, elements or details.

Co   **County**
A civil division of a state or kingdom, created for political, judicial and administrative purposes.

Co Asr   **County Assessor**
An officer who assesses taxes for a county.

Co Aud   **County Auditor**
A person who inspects accounts for a county.

Co Clk   **County Clerk**
An officer of the county.

Co Health   **County Health Department**
An entity connected with, or engaged in public-health work; county jurisdiction.

Co Judge   **County Judge**
An officer invested with authority to administer justice in the county.

Co Ord   **County Ordinary**
A probate judge in some jurisdictions of the United States.

Co Rcdr   **County Recorder**
An officer who records land records.

Ct   **Court**
A place where justice is judicially administered.

Ct Admin   **Court Administrator**
One commissioned by a competent court to administer upon the personal property of a deceased person. To take charge of and settle by will or official appointment; act as administrator.

crim   **Criminal**
Relating to crime, or pertaining to the administration of penal as opposed to civil law.

d   **Death Record**
Record testifying of the actual death of an individual.

Dis Ct   **District Court**
A United States court serving a Federal judicial district; also, a state court serving a state judicial district.

div   **Divorce Record**
Record testifying of the legal dissolution of a marriage relation.

FHC   **Family History Center**
Family History Centers are branch facilities of the Family History Library in Salt Lake City.

Centers provide access to most of the microfilms and microfiche in the Family History Library to help patrons identify their ancestors. Everyone is welcome to visit and use Family History Center resources.

FHL   **Family History Library**
A private library belonging to The Church of Jesus Christ of Latter-day Saints, located in Salt Lake City, Utah.

Gen Soc   **Genealogical Society**
A body of persons associated for the purpose of tracing family history.

Hist Soc   **Historical Society**
A body of persons associated for the purpose of gathering and preserving history.

hlth   **Health Record**
Record testifying of the birth, death or medical condition of an individual.

inc   **Incomplete**
Not complete; imperfect; lacking in certain parts, as a partial collection.

J P   **Justice of the Peace**
An inferior magistrate elected or appointed to prevent breaches of the peace within a county or township, to punish violators of the law and to discharge various other local magisterial duties.

land   **Land Record**
Recording of any tract of ground whatever, together with its appurtenances.

lib   **Library**
A collection of books, pamphlets, etc., kept for reading and consultation.

m   **Marriage Record**
Record testifying of marriage compact entered into by two individuals, based on mutual regard, to live together as husband and wife until separated by death.

Mag   **Magistrate**
One clothed with public civil authority; an executive or judicial officer.

mil   **Military record**
Record testifying of service pertaining to armed forces, naval, etc.: distinguished from civil.

Mil Dis Rec   **Military Discharge Record**
Records testifying to the discharge or release of an individual serving in the military.

mtg   **Mortgage**
An estate in land created by conveyance together with a condition of making null and void on the performance of some stipulated condition, as the payment of money. A lien upon land or other property as security for the performance of some obligation, to become void on such performance, as the payment of money.

nat   **Naturalization Record**
Record testifying of the act or process of admitting an alien into citizenship.

off   **Office**
A particular duty charge or trust; an employment undertaken by commission or authority. A place, a building or series of rooms in which some particular branch of the public service is conducted; as, the Patent Office, Post Office, etc.

Ord   **Ordinary**
Having immediate or ex-officio jurisdiction, as a judge.

Ord Ct   **Ordinary Court**
A section of the chancery court that handles common-law matters.

Orph Ct   **Orphans Court**
A portion of the probate court which handles estate accounts and petitions to court regarding estate matters, as in petitions for guardianship, petitions for auditors, returns of valuations and renunciations. The orphan's court records do not always relate to orphans.

Par Clk   **Parish Clerk**
An officer or employee of the parish office.

pro   **Probate Record**
Record testifying of formal, legal proof, as of the settling of an estate or will.

Pro Ct   **Probate Court**
A court having jurisdiction of the proof of wills, of guardianships and of the settlement of estates.

Pro Judge   **Probate Judge**
An officer invested with authority to administer justice in the probate court.

pub   **Public**
Pertaining to or affecting the people at large or the community: distinguished from private or personal.

Rcdr   **Recorder**
One who records. A magistrate having criminal jurisdiction in a city or borough.

Reg   **Register or Registrar**
An official record, the book containing it, or an entry therein; roll; list; schedule; a registry. The authorized keeper of a register of records.

Reg in Chan   **Register in Chancery**
An officer or clerk in the chancery court.

Reg Deeds   **Register of Deeds**
An officer or clerk in the Register of Deeds office.

Reg of Wills   **Register of Wills**
An officer or clerk in the Register of Wills office.

Rgstr   **Registrar**
The authorized keeper of a register or of records.
SupSuperiorHighest, as in court or ranking officer.

Sup Ct   **Superior Court**
In parts of the United States, a court between the inferior courts and those of last resort; in England, one of the principal courts at Westminster: King's Bench, common pleas, exchequer.

Supt   **Superintendent**
One whose function is to superintend some

particular work, office, or undertaking; as, a school superintendent, road superintendent or an overseer of wills.

Surr   **Surrogate**
A probate judge. A deputy appointed by an ecclesiastical judge to act in his place.

Terr   **Territory**
The domain over which a sovereign state exercises jurisdiction. Any considerable tract of land; a region; district.

Twn Clk   **Town Clerk**
An official who keeps the records of the town.

Treas   **Treasurer**
An officer legally authorized to receive, care for and disburse public revenues upon lawful orders; also, a similar custodian of the funds of a society or a corporation.

Unorg   **Unorganized**
Not organized.

Vit Stat   **Vital Statistics**
Public records of births, marriages, deaths, etc.

War Ser   **War Service**
Pertaining to military or naval service.

A FINAL WORD

Since 1947, *The Handybook for Genealogists* has been the "must have" tool for researchers. It contains a vast amount of information from county creation dates, to records kept at the county level, to county websites. With this latest edition, Everton's and the Family History Network invite you to move with us into the next generation of family research.

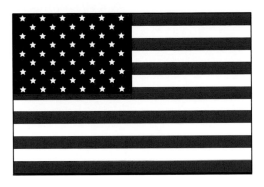

THE UNITED STATES OF AMERICA

CAPITAL: WASHINGTON, DISTRICT OF COLUMBIA

History records that the Italian Spanish navigator, Christopher Columbus, 1451-1506, sailed west across the Atlantic ocean in search of a route to Asia. He landed in the Americas instead. On 12 October 1942 two worlds met on a small island in the Caribbean Sea.

On a voyage for Spain, Columbus unintentionally discovered the Americas. He was in search of a direct sea route from Europe to Asia. The explorer made four separate voyages to the Caribbean from 1492 to 1504. However, he remained convinced that he had found the lands that Marco Polo reached in his overland travels to China at the end of the 13th century. Columbus was not the first European to reach the Americas. Vikings from Scandinavia had briefly settled on the North American coast – we know it now as Newfoundland, Canada – in the late 10th or early 11th century. However, Columbus's explorations had a major impact on the world. He had opened the door to colonization of the western hemisphere and all of the trade and commerce that came with it. He was soon followed by additional explorers.

Spanish explorer and treasure hunter, Don Juan Ponce de Leon, first sighted the mainland of the North American Continent on Easter, 27 March 1513. He claimed the land for Spain and called it La Florida, interpreted as "Land of Flowers." Between 1513 and 1563, the government of Spain launched six expeditions to settle La Florida, but all failed. Jean Ribaut a French explorer and his party built Fort Caroline in 1562 and by 1564 they had established a colony on the St. Johns River. This settlement was destroyed when the Spainard Don Pedro Menendez de Aviles, his soldiers, and settlers founded St. Augustine in 1565. St. Augustine is generally regarded as the first permanent European settlement in what is now the United States.

In 1607, Captain John Smith, accompanied by 105 settlers, established the English colony of Jamestown in what is now Virginia. This started a land rush that would last for centuries. The establishment of Plymouth Colony in 1620 followed. Peter Minuit purchased Manhattan Island in 1626. Maryland was established as a Roman Catholic colony in 1634.

Exploration, religion and the desire for land appear to be the driving factors in these first waves of migration to the New World. The French settled in the area of the Great Lakes, in what is now known as upstate New York and the province of Quebec. They also settled along the coast of the Gulf of Mexico, in what later became Mississippi and Louisiana. The Dutch established towns in New York, New Jersey, and Pennsylvania. Germans and other German-speaking groups, fleeing religious persecution, established colonies in New York, Pennsylvania, and the Carolinas. The British settled up and down the Atlantic and Gulf coasts.

The land was occupied by great numbers of Native Americans long before the arrival of explorers and those seeking new land and religious freedom. Many of the natives aided the new comers, some listened to and accepted Christianity. Many, however, were driven from their homes suffering death from warfare, slavery and European diseases. The clash of cultures that existed during the formative years of America caused long lasting effects.

The population of newcomers grew from about 4,600 in 1630 to more than 100,000 in 1670. By 1700, the population was more than a quarter of a million. When space became limited on the coasts, people of all origins moved inland. Even though each settler viewed it as a land of opportunity, the various visions of opportunity and loyalty to different political and religious systems caused friction. Eventually, major confrontations broke out between the English colonists and the French, resulting in King George's War in 1744 and the French Indian War (the Seven Years War) in 1754. The resulting treaty, in 1763, expanded British influence in areas of Canada and the lower American Colonies.

As Britain's American Colony continued to grow to more than 2 million by 1770, its citizens became increasingly uncomfortable with the absentee rule of the British Crown. A series of unpopular taxes, enacted

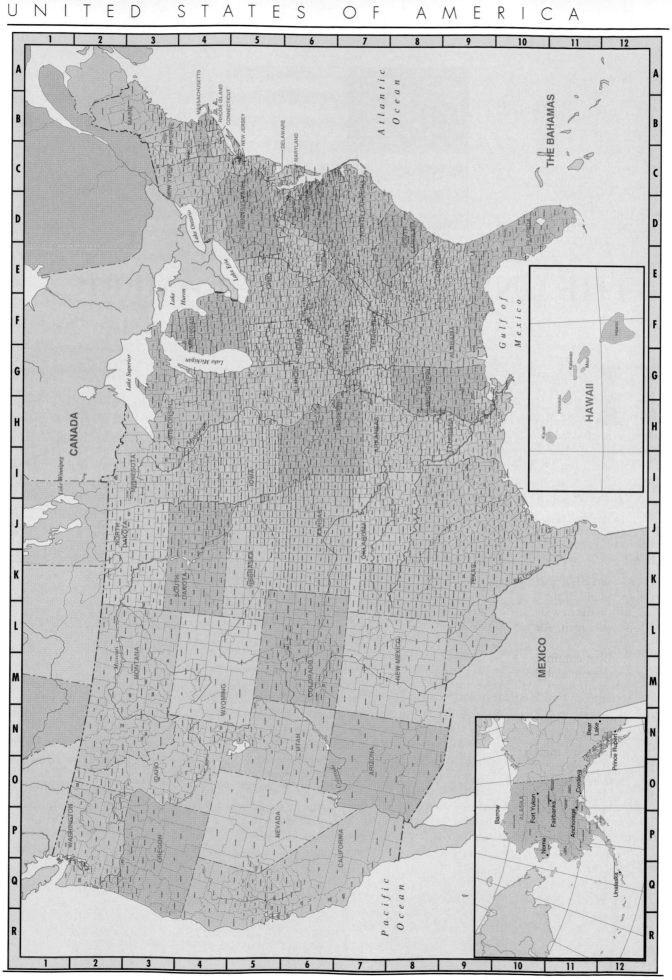

between 1764 and 1774, led to the seating of the first Continental Congress in 1774 and eventually to a Declaration of Independence by 13 colonies in 1776. A new nation was formally created. By the time the Revolutionary War came to an end in 1781, almost 250,000 men had served the American cause, with about 34,000 casualties on the American side.

The colonies of the new nation had a working agreement in the Articles of Confederation, but a more formal, binding document was needed to ensure that the various states would not disintegrate. At a convention in Philadelphia in 1787, a constitution was written and proposed to the individual states. That constitution was ratified and put into effect in 1789.

One of the provisions of the new constitution required a census of the population every 10 years beginning in 1790. That first census included only the names of the heads of households, and showed a population of 3,929,214. By the next federal census in 1800, the population count had risen to 5,308,483.

In 1803, the geographic size of the United States doubled with the purchase from France of an area stretching from the Gulf Coast to what is now Montana. Total cost for the new real estate was $15 million. In 1819, Spain ceded the Florida peninsula and Gulf coastal territory west to Louisiana to the United States.

While the country acquired land to the south and west, its citizens were fending off the British. The War of 1812 lasted until 1815, with 285,000 Americans fighting to maintain their freedom from Britain, at a cost of 7,000 casualties.

Bonds were raised to purchase land from the French. However, the United States still had difficulty raising funds for the veterans of its wars. Instead, huge tracts of western lands were opened for exclusive use as "bounties" for those who had served in U.S. military actions. The prospect of free, open land in the west lured many veterans and their families into the new states and territories of Ohio, Indiana, Illinois, Michigan, Alabama, Mississippi, Arkansas, and Missouri.

Conflict continued to smolder between settlers due to their divergent cultural backgrounds. Slavery in various states and territories was a source of conflict, and on several occasions it threatened to split the nation. Henry Clay's Missouri Compromise of 1820 set boundaries for freedom and slavery, but was only a temporary measure. In 1835, Texas declared its independence from Mexico and joined the United States in 1845. Following the war with Mexico from 1846 to 1848, Mexico ceded vast portions of the American West to the United States, including the current states of California, Arizona, New Mexico, Nevada, Utah, and part of Colorado.

The opening of these new lands, with their apparent unlimited possibilities, exacerbated the debate on the slavery issue. In 1850, Henry Clay proposed another compromise, but it could not solve the problem. By the end of the 1850's several southern states had become disenchanted with the process, and openly talked of secession from the rest of the nation.

Between 1861 and 1865, the Civil War (also known as the War Between the States, or the War of the Rebellion) r0cked the nation. More than 2 million men served in the Union forces, and more than 1 million served the Confederacy. By the end of the war, casualties among Union forces were about 360,222, with more than 258,000 suffered by the Confederacy. Some estimates place total casualties closer to 700,000 for both sides combined.

Although it would take decades for the wounds of that war to heal, westward expansion in the United States continued. To encourage settlement in new lands, the Homestead Act was passed in 1862. Free land was granted to those who would settle it. In 1867, Alaska was purchased from Russia for $7.2 million. The first transcontinental railroad was completed in 1869, allowing easier, quicker access to frontier territories.

The effect of these developments on the population of the country was dramatic. During the decade of the Civil War, the population grew from 31 million to 38 million, an increase of only 7 million. The population rose to more than 50 million by 1880, to almost 63 million by 1890, and to more than 76 million by the turn of the century.

Between 1820 and 1920, 30 million immigrants arrived on America's shores. The major ports for the immigrants were New York, Boston, Baltimore, Philadelphia, New Orleans, and San Francisco. Numerous other ports on the Atlantic, Pacific, and Gulf coasts also welcomed immigrants. Large numbers also entered overland, crossing the Canadian and Mexican borders.

Eventually, the numbers of immigrants and the cultural diversity of those already living in the United States created a backlash that caused the welcome mat to be removed. In 1921, Congress established a quota system limiting the amount of immigrants that would be accepted. This system did not undergo major modification until 1965. It vastly slowed the number of immigrants during that 45-year span. Even so, the population of the United States grew from 106 million in 1920 to almost 180 million by 1960.

In the meantime, the United States was involved in three military actions. Its participation in the First World War lasted from 1917 to 1918, involving about 5 million American servicemen. About 320,000 died. The Second World War involved 16 million Americans from 1941 to 1945, with 1 million casualties. The United States sent 6 million men to serve in the Korean War (1950-1953), with 160,000 casualties.

In 1959, Alaska was admitted to the Union as the 49th state. Hawaii followed as the 50th state later that year.

American military involvement in Vietnam between 1963 and 1973 involved 9 million servicemen who suffered 200,000 casualties. Approximately 500,000 served in the war against Iraq in 1991, with less than 300 casualties.

On 11 September 2001, the United States of America was violently launched into a new kind of war, "A War on Terrorism," declared by newly-elected President George W. Bush. The declaration came after a series of unprovoked terrorist attacks on American soil. At 8:45 a.m. (EDT), a hijacked passenger jet, American Airlines Flight 11 out of Boston, Massachusetts, crashed into the north tower of the World Trade Center in New York City. Only 18 minutes later, a second hijacked airliner, United Airlines Flight 175 from Boston, crashed into the south tower of the World Trade Center and exploded. American citizens froze as they learned of the apparent terrorist attack. At 10:05 a.m., the south tower collapsed, followed by the north tower 23 minutes later. Thousands of civilians were killed by the falling debris, smoke and fire, and as a result of attempts to escape.

At 9:43 a.m. on that same day of terror, American Airlines Flight 77 crashed into the Pentagon in Washington, DC. A portion of the Pentagon later collapsed. More innocent people died in this tragedy.

At 10:10 a.m., United Airlines Flight 93, also hijacked, crashed in Somerset County, Pennsylvania, southeast of Pittsburgh. Passengers attempted to stop the hijackers, but all aboard were killed in the crash.

The American Stock Exchange, the Nasdaq and the New York Stock Exchange closed temporarily in a scramble to spare the country's economy.

At 8:30 that evening, President George Bush addressed the nation and declared war on terrorism. He warned the world that the U.S. government would make no distinction between terrorists who committed the acts and those who harbored them.

On 13 September 2001, Secretary of State Colin Powell identified Osama bin Laden, Afghanistan, as a prime suspect and declared that the United States would respond with a sustained military campaign. The world was left wondering when the campaign would begin and where.

On 7 October 2001, American and British forces unleashed missile attacks against Taliban military targets and bin Laden's training camps inside Afghanistan. President Bush announced, "We will not waver, we will not tire, we will not falter and we will not fail."

At the time of publication, the outcome of this war, expected to last a decade, was uncertain. However, the United States had scored many victories in Afghanistan by March 2002. The scarred economy of the United States had begun to recover from a brief recession only six months later.

FEDERAL RESOURCES

Note: The federal government of the United States is not responsible for the maintenance of vital records (births, marriages, divorces and deaths). But there are several important record types in federal repositories that are valuable to family historians. Many of these are in the custody of the United States National Archives in Washington, DC and in its several regional facilities throughout the nation. A list of these archives is included in the United States section of this *Handybook*.

Following are summaries of some useful types of federal records:
- **Population Census Schedules:** By constitutional mandate, a census of the population of the United States is conducted every 10 years. These decennial censuses began in 1790 and have continued since. From 1790 through 1840 the federal censuses contained only the names of the heads of households, with a numeric breakdown of the members of the household by gender, age and race. Beginning in 1850, the federal population schedules have shown every resident of the country with his or her name, age, gender, occupation, and state or country of birth. Industry and Manufacturing schedules exist for 1850, 1860 and 1870. Mortality schedules exist for 1850, 1860, 1870 and 1880. Slave schedules are available for 1850 and 1860. Social statistics schedules are available for 1850, 1860 and 1870. More recent censuses may also show such data as literacy, parents' birthplaces, marital status, the number of years married, whether naturalized, the year of immigration to the United States, and more.

In 2002, federal population schedules became publicly available for 1790 through 1930. The 1890 federal census is available, but the original schedules were largely destroyed, with only scattered pages surviving for a small number of localities with just a few thousand residents.

These schedules were microfilmed by the National Archives staff and are widely available through the Family History Library in Salt Lake City and its 3,731 Family History Centers located throughout the world. There are additional sources, such as state libraries and archives, local libraries, and commercial interests. Some are now commercially available on CD-ROM, specifically designed for genealogical research.

These population schedules are generally arranged geographically, with each enumerator following a route designed to cover all of the residences in his or her assigned area. These enumeration districts were logically assigned, following streets, towns, townships, and county boundaries.

There are statewide indexes for a large portion of the available federal censuses, although many of these contain only the names of the heads of the households rather than all of the names that appear on the original schedules. Digital Indexes are being created constantly to help genealogists access census records quickly and efficiently.

Mortality schedules are also available from most of the same sources as the federal censuses, and all of them have been every-name indexed. Like the population schedules, the federal mortality schedules are organized geographically. Generally they show the name of each person who died 12 months prior to the census, his or her age, gender, race, marital status, occupation, month and cause of death.

- **Immigration Records:** Immigration records, commonly called "ship passenger arrival records," may provide evidence of a person's arrival in the United States as well as foreign birthplace. The National Archives and Records Administration (NARA) has immigration records for various ports for the years 1800 to 1959. Prior to 1 January 1820, the United States Federal Government did not require captains or masters of vessels to present passenger lists to U.S. officials.

Passenger lists are arranged by port, then by date, and finally by ship. Each generally shows the name of the ship, the port from which it sailed, when it arrived in the United States, and its captain. Individual data, recorded for every passenger on the ship, includes the passenger's name, age, gender, occupation, former residence, and destination. Even the names of those who were born on board or who died during the voyage should be recorded.

There are indexes to most passenger arrival lists. These lists and their indexes are available on microfilm from the National Archives, the Family History Library and its Family History Centers, some state and local libraries, and a number of commercial entities. They are increasingly published on the World Wide Web in searchable databases.

To locate other passenger lists from 1538 to 1959, consult the books dealing with immigration and ship passenger lists noted in the bibliography section of this chapter.

- **Military Records:** The United States National Archives is the official repository for records of military personnel who have been discharged from the U.S. Air Force, Army Marine Corps, and Navy. Those records, available for public examination at the National Archives, are a valuable source of information about an individual's military service, family and medical history. Because of their research value, NARA has microfilmed many of these records, primarily those created before 1900. For more information, visit NARA's catalog of microfilm publications for military service records at the following website at: <www.nara.gov/publications/microfilm/military/service.html>. Some of these records are also available at the Family History Library and its affiliated Family History Centers.

Following is a list of useful military records for genealogical research:

- **Enlistment records:** Include recruit's name, age, gender, residence, and unit. Some include the names of parents, spouse or children.
- **Service records:** Detail participation in periodic musters, battles, and other actions, as well as wounds, hospitalizations, reassignments, etc.
- **Pension applications:** Include details of service, documentation of relationships, and, in some cases, depositions made by individuals who served in the same unit giving additional details of their military service.

Societies and Repositories

Afro-American Historical and Genealogical Society, Inc., National; PO Box 73086; Washington, DC 20056-3086

American College of Heraldry; Drawer CG; University of Alabama; Tuscaloosa, Alabama 35486-2887

American Family Records Association; PO Box 15505; Kansas City, Missouri 64106

American Genealogical Lending Library; PO Box 244, Bountiful, Utah 84011

American Historical Society of Germans from Russia; 631 D. Street; Lincoln, Nebraska 68502

American Indian Institute; The University of Oklahoma; 555 Constitution St.; Suite 237; Norman, Oklahoma 73037-0005

American-Canadian Genealogical Society; PO Box 668; Manchester, New Hampshire 03105

American-French Genealogical Society; PO Box 2113; Pawtucket, Rhode Island 02861

American-Portuguese Genealogical Society, Inc.; PO Box 644; Taunton, Massachusetts 02780

American-Schleswig-Holstein Heritage Society; PO Box 21; LeClaire, Iowa 52753

Association of Professional Genealogists, 3421 M St. NW, Suite 236; Washington, DC 20007-3552

Civil War Descendants Society; PO Box 233; Athens, Alabama 35611

Colonial Dames of America in the State of New York; National Society of Library; 215 East 71st St.; New York, New York 10008

Daughters of the Union Veterans of the Civil War 1861-1865; 503 S. Walnut, Springfield, Illinois 62704

Everton Publisher's Library, 3223 S. Main; Nibley, Utah 84321

Family History Library of The Church of Jesus Christ of Latter-day Saints, 35 North West Temple, Salt Lake City, UT 84150

Federation of Genealogical Societies; PO Box 3385; Salt Lake City, Utah 84110-3385

First World War, Order of the; PO Box 7062-GH; Gainesville, Florida 32605-7062

Flemish Americans, Genealogical Society of; 18740 Thirteen Mile Road; Roseville, Michigan 48066

Genealogical Center Library; PO Box 71343; Marietta, Georgia 30007-1343

Genealogical Library of the Church of Jesus Christ of Latter-day Saints, 35 North West; Temple, Salt Lake City, Utah 84150

German American Heritage Center; PO Box 243; Davenport, Iowa 52805-0243

Hispanic Historical and Ancestral Research, Society of; PO Box 5294; 92635

Immigrant Genealogical Society; PO Box 7369; Burbank, California 91510-7369

Institute of Genealogy and History for Latin America; 316 W. 500 North, St. George, Utah 84770

International Society for British Genealogy and Family History; PO Box 20425; Cleveland, Ohio 44120

Jewish Genealogical Societies, Association of; 1485 Teaneck Road; Teaneck, New Jersey 07666

Library of Congress; Local History & Genealogy Division; Washington, DC 20540

Loyalist Descendants (American Revolution), Society of; PO Box 848, Desk 120; Rockingham, North Carolina 28379

Mayflower Descendants, General Society of; Box 3297; Plymouth, Massachusetts 02361

Mexican War Veterans, Descendants of; 1114 Pacific Drive; Richardson, Texas 75081

National Genealogical Society Library; 4527 17th St.; North, Arlington, Virginia 22207-2399; 703.525.0050, Ext. 331; <www.ngsgenealogy.org>

National Huguenot Society; 9033 Lyndale Ave. S. Suite 108; Bloomington, Minnesota 55420-3535

National Society Daughters of the American Revolution Library; 1776 D Street, N.W.; Washington, DC 20006-5303

National Society Sons of the American Revolution Library; 1000 South Fourth St.; Louisville, Kentucky 40203

New England Historic Genealogical Society; 101 Newbury St.; Boston, Massachusetts 02116

Norwegian-American Genealogical Association; c/o Minnesota Genealogy Society; PO Box 16069; St. Paul, Minnesota 55116-0069

Norwegian-American Museum, Vesterheim; 502 W. Water St.; Decorah, Iowa 52101; 319.382.9681; Fax: 319.382.9683

Orphan Train Heritage Society of America; 4453 South 48th; Springdale, Arizona 72764

Palatine Library, Palatines to America, Capital Univ.; Box 101; Columbus, Ohio 43209-2394; 614-236-8281; <genealogy.org/~palam/>

Professional Genealogists, Association of; PO Box 11601; Salt Lake City, Utah 84147

Railroad Retirement Board, United States of America; 844 Rush St., Chicago, Illinois 60611

Second World War, Order of the; PO Box 7062-GH; Gainesville, Florida 32605-7062

Southern Society of Genealogists, Inc.; Box 295; Centre, Alabama 35960

Stagecoach Library for Genealogical Research; 1840 South Wolcott Ct.; Denver, Colorado 80219; (Rental library)

Swenson Swedish Immigration Research Center; Box 175; Augustana College; Rock Island, Illinois 61201-2296

United States State Department; Washington, DC 20520;

Virginia Society of the Sons of the American Revolution; 3600 West Broad, Suite 446; Richmond, Virginia 23230-4918

White House Historical Association; 740 Jackson Place; N.W., Washington, DC 20506

National Archives

National Archives & Record Center; National Records Center Bldg.; 4205 Suitland Rd.; (Suitland, Maryland-location); Washington, DC 20409

National Archives; 24000 Avila Rd.; PO Box 6719; Laguna Niguel, California 92677

National Archives; 1000 Commodore Dr.; San Bruno, California 94066

National Archives; Bldg. 48, Denver Federal; Center, Denver, Colorado 80225

National Archives; 1557 Saint Joseph Ave.; East Point, Georgia 30344

National Archives; 7358 S. Pulaski Rd.; Chicago, Illinois 60629

National Archives; 380 Trapelo Rd., Waltham, Massachusetts 02154

National Archives Library, NNUL, Rm. 2380; 8601 Adelphi Rd.; College Park, Maryland 20740-6001

National Archives; 2306 E. Bannister Rd.; Kansas City, Missouri 64131

National Archives; 9th & Market Sts., Room 1350; Philadelphia, Pennsylvania 19144; 215.597.3000

National Archives; 501 W. Felix St.; PO Box 6216; Fort Worth, Texas 76115

National Archives; 6125 Sand Point Way, N.E.; Seattle, Washington 98115

United States National Archives & Records Administration, 700 Pennsylvania Ave. NW, Washington, DC 20408;

Archives and Libraries

American Library Directory: A Classified List of Libraries in the United States and Canada. With Personal and Statistical Data. New York: R.R. Bowker, annual.

Bentley, Elizabeth Petty, and Debra Ann Carl, comps. *Directory of 3rd ed. Turlock, California: Marietta Pub. Co., 1996. Family Associations.* 4th ed. Baltimore: Genealogical Publishing Co., Inc., 2001.

Cavanaugh, Karen B. *A Genealogist's Guide to the Ft. Wayne, Indiana, Public Library;* Owensboro, Kentucky: McDowell Publications, 1980.

Daughters of the American Revolution Library. *Library Catalog. 3 vols. Washington, D.C.: Daughters of the American Revolution, 1982-1992.*

Directory of Archives and Manuscript Repositories in the United States. 2nd ed. Phoenix Press, 1988.

Downs, Robert B. *American Library Resources: A Bibliographical Guide.* Boston: Gregg Press, 1972.

Encyclopedia of Associations. 3 vols. 32nd ed. Detroit: Gale Research Co., 1987-.

Filby, P. William. *Directory of American Libraries With Genealogy or Local History Collections.* Wilmington, Delaware: Scholarly Resources, 1988.

Guide to Genealogical Research in the National Archives. Washington, DC: National Archives Trust Fund Board, 1985.

Hereditary Register of the United States of America. Annual. Yoncalla, Ore.: Hereditary Register Publications, 1972-.

Makower, Joel and Linda Zaleskie. *The American History Sourcebook.* New York: Prentice-Hall, 1998.

Meyer, Mary K., ed. *Directory of Genealogical Societies in the U.S.A. and Canada.* 11th ed. Mt. Airy, Maryland: Mary K. Meyer, 1996.

Neagles, James C. *The Library of Congress: A Guide to Genealogical and Historical Research.* Salt Lake City: Ancestry Publishing, 1990.

Parch, Grace D., ed. *Directory of Newspaper Libraries in the United States and Canada.* New York: Project of the Newspaper Division, Special Libraries Assoc., 1976.

Parker, J. Carlyle. *Going to Salt Lake City to do Family History Research.* 3rd ed. Turlock, California: Marietta Publishing Company, 1996.

Roberts, Jayare, and Dorothy Hebertson, comps. *Register of U.S. Lineage Societies.* Salt Lake City: Family History Library, 1990.

Schaefer, Christina K. *The Center: Guide to Genealogical Research in the National Capitol Area.* Baltimore: Genealogical Publishing, 1996.

Sinko, Peggy Tuck. *Guide to Local and Family History at the Newberry Library.* Salt Lake City: Ancestry, 1987.

Szucs, Loretto Dennis, and Sandra Hargraves Luebking. *The Archives: A Guide to the National Archives Field Branches.* Salt Lake City: Ancestry, 1988.

Warren, Paula Stuart and James W. *Your Guide to the Family History Library: How to Access the World's Largest Genealogy Resource.* Cincinnati, Ohio: Betterway Books, 2001.

Wheeler, Mary Bray, ed. *Directory of Historical Organizations in the United States and Canada.* 14th ed. Nashville, Tennessee: American Association for State and Local History, 1990.

Zakailik, Joanne A., ed. *Directory of Special Libraries and Information Centers.* 17th ed. Detroit: Gale Research Co., 1994.

Bible Records

Bible Records, ca. 1747-1982. National Genealogical Society (Arlington, Virginia). (Salt Lake City: Filmed by the Genealogical Society of Utah, 1995). Bible records were collected from members of the National Genealogical Society.

Edmondson, Chan. *Revolutionary War Period Bible, Family, and Marriage Records Gleaned from Pension Applications,* 10 vol. Dallas, Tex.: C. Edmondson, 1990.

Kirkham, E. Kay. *An Index to Some of the Bibles and Family Records of the United States: 35,500 References as Taken From NSDAR Files and Elsewhere....* Logan, Utah: Everton Publishers], 1979.

Kirkham, E. Kay. *An Index to Some of the Bibles and Family Records of the United States: 45,500 References as Taken From the Microfilm at the Genealogical Society of Utah.* Logan, Utah: Everton Publishers, 1984.

Lester, Memory Aldridge. *Old Southern Bible Records: Transcriptions of Births, Marriages and Deaths from Family Bibles, Chiefly of the 18th and 19th Centuries.* Baltimore: Clearfield Co., 1990.

Biography

American Biographical Index. 6 vols. London: Bowker-Saur, 1993.

Biographical Books, 1876-1949 and 1950-1980. New York: Bowker, 1983, 1980.

Black Biography, 1790-1950: A Cumulative Index. 3 vols. Alexandria, VA: Chadwyck-Healey, 1991.

Cimbala, Diane J., Jennifer Cargill, and Brian Alley. *Biographical Sources: A Guide to Dictionaries and Reference Works.* Phoenix L Oryx Press, 1986.

Dictionary of American Biography. New York: Charles Scribner's Sons, 1928-1988.

Herbert, Mirana C., and Barbara McNeil. *Biographical and Genealogy Master Index,* 2nd ed, vols., Detroit: Gale Research, 1980-.

Herbert, Miranda C. and Barbara McNeil. *Historical and Biographical Dictionaries, Master Index: a Consolidated Index to Biographical Information Concerning Historical Personages in over 35 of the Principal Retrospective Biographical Dictionaries.* Detroit: Gale Research Co., 1980.

Index to Biographies in Local Histories in the Library of Congress. Baltimore: Magna Carta Book, [1979].

Library of Congress Index to Biographies in State and Local Histories. Baltimore: Magna Carta Book Co., 1979.

Rider, Fremont, ed. *The American Genealogical-Biographical Index to American, Biographical and Local History Materials.* (AGBI). Series 2. Middletown, Connecticut: Godfrey Memorial Library, 1952-.

Slocum, Robert B., ed. *Biographical Dictionaries and Related Works,* 2 vols. 2d ed. Detroit: Gale Research, 1986.

Cemeteries

American Blue Book of Funeral Directors. New York: Kates-Boyston Publications, 1932-.

American Blue Book of Funeral Directors. New York: The American Funeral Director, biennial.

Annese, Domenico. " Construction: Cemetery Design Standards." *Landscape Architecture* (January 1983): 85987.

Brown, John Gary. *Soul in the Stone: Cemetery Art From America's Heartland.* Lawrence, Kansas: University Press of Kansas, 1994.

Burek, Deborah, ed. *Cemeteries of the United States.* Detroit: Gale Research Co., 1994.

Cemeteries of the U.S.: A Guide to Contact Information for U.S. Cemeteries and Their Records. 1st ed. Detroit: Gale Research, 1994.

Kot, Elizabeth Gorrell and James D. Kot. *United States Cemetery Address Book, 1994-1995.* Vallejo, California Indices Publishing, 1994.

Meyer, Richard E. ed. *Cemeteries and Gravemarkers: Voices of American Culture.* Ann Arbor: UMI Research Press, 1989.

National Directory of Morticians. Youngstown, Ohio: National Directory of Morticians, 1959-.

National Yellow Book of Funeral Director. Youngstown, Ohio: Nomis Publications, c1989-.

Nishiura, Elizabeth. *American Battle Monuments: A Guide to Battlefields and Cemeteries of the United States Armed Forces.* Detroit: Omnigraphics, 1989.

Stemmons, Jack and Diane Stemmons. *Cemetery Record Compendium.* Logan, Utah: Everton Publishers, 1979.

Wallis, Charles L. *American Epitaphs: Grave and Humorous.* New York: Dover Publications, 1975.

Census Records

A Census of Pensioners for Revolutionary or Military Service. 1841, various years. Reprint, Baltimore: Genealogical Publishing. 1967.

Buckway, G. Eileen. *U.S. 1910 Federal Census: Unindexed States: A Guide to Finding Census Enumeration Districts for Unindexed*

Cities, Towns and Villages. Salt Lake City: Family History Library, 1992.

Census Enumeration Districts 1830-1890 and 1910-1950. National Archives Microfilm Publication T-1224, 146 rolls.

Davidson, Katherine H., and Charlotte Am. Ashby, comps. *Preliminary Inventory of the Records of the Bureau of the Census.* Preliminary Inventory No. 161. Washington, D.C.: National Archives and Records Service, 1964.

Dollarhide, William. *The Census Book: A Genealogist's Guide to Federal Census Facts, Schedules and Indexes.* Bountiful, Utah: Heritage Quest, 1999.

Dubester, Henry J. State Censuses: *An Annotated Bibliography of Censuses of Population Taken After the Year 1790 by the States and Territories of the United States.* Reprint. Knightstown, Indiana: Bookmark, 1975.

Hamilton, Ann B. *Researcher's Guide to United States Census Availability, 1790-1920.* Bowie, Maryland: Heritage Books, 1987.

Indexes to Manufacturers' Census of 1920: An Edited Printing of the Original Indexes and Information. Reprint. Knightstown, Ind.: Bookmark, n.d.

Jackson, Ronald V., Jr. *Early American Series.* Salt Lake City: Accelerated Indexing Systems, 1981-84.

Kemp, Thomas Jay. *The American Census Handbook.* Wilmington, Delaware: Scholarly Resources, Inc., 2001.

Konrad, J. *Directory of Census Information Sources.* Summit Publications, 1984.

Lainhart, Ann S., *State Census Records.* Baltimore: Genealogical Publishing, 1992.

National Archives and Records Administration. *Federal Population and Mortality Schedules, 1790-1910, in the National Archives and the States.* Washington, D.C.: National Archives, 1986. 2 microfiche.

National Archives and Records Administration. *Cartographic Records of the Bureau of the Census.* Preliminary Inventory No. 103. Washington, D.C.: National Archives, 1958.

National Archives Trust Fund Board. *Federal Population Census, 1790-1890: A Catalog of Microfilm Copies of the Schedules.* Rev. Washington, D.C.: National Archives Trust Fund Board, 2001.

National Archives Trust Fund Board. *Federal Population Census, 1900: A Catalog of Microfilm Copies of the Schedules.* Rev. Washington, D.C.: National Archives Trust Fund Board, 2000.

National Archives Trust Fund Board. *Federal Population Census, 1910: A Catalog of Microfilm Copies of the Schedules.* Rev. Washington, D.C.: National Archives Trust Fund Board, 2000.

National Archives Trust Fund Board. *Federal Population Census, 1920: A Catalog of Microfilm Copies of the Schedules.* Rev. Washington, D.C.: National Archives Trust Fund Board, 1992.

Parker, J. Carlyle. *City, County, Town and Township Index to the 1850 Federal Census Schedules.* Detroit: Gale Research Co., 1979.

Stephenson, Charles, "The Methodology of Historical Census Record Lineage: A User's Guide to the Soundex," *Journal of Family History* 5(1) (Spring 1980): 112-15. Reprinted in *Prolgue* 12 (2) (Fall 1980): 151-53.

Steuart, Bradley W. *The Soundex Reference Guide: Soundex Codes to Over 125,000 Surnames.* Bountiful, Utah: Precision Indexing, 1990.

Street Indexes to the 29 Largest Cities in the 1910 Census. National Archives Microfiche Publication M-1283.

Thorndale, William, and William Dollarhide. *Map Guide to the U.S. Federal Census, 1790-1920.* Baltimore: Genealogical Publishing Co., 1987.

Thorndale, William. "Census Indexes and Spelling Variants." *APG (Association of Professional Genealogists) Newsletter* 4 (5) (May 1982): 6-9. Reprinted in *The Source: A Guidebook of American Genealogy,* edited by Arlene Eakle and Johni Cerny. Salt Lake City: Ancestry, 1984, pp. 17-20.

U.S. Bureau of the Census. *200 Years of U.S. Census Taking: Population and Housing Questions, 1790-1990.* Washington, D.C.: Government Printing Office, 1989.

U.S. Congress. Senate. *The History and Growth of the United States Census.* Prepared by the Senate Committee on the Census by Carroll D. Wright. S. Doc. 194, 56 Cong., I sess., Serial 385b. Reprint. 1967.

U.S. Library of Congress. Census Library Project. *State Censuses: An Annotated Bibliography of Censuses of Population Taken After the Year 1790 by States an Territories of the United States of the Unites States.* Prepared by Henry J. Dubester. Washington, D.C.: Government Printing Office, 1948.

United States. Bureau of the Census. *Cross Index to Selected City Streets and Enumeration Districts.* Washington, D.C.: National Archives, [1984].

United States. Bureau of the Census. 11th Census, 1890. *Schedules Enumerating Union Veterans and Widows of Union Veterans of the Civil War.* Washington, D.C.: National Archives, 1948.

Wright, Carroll D. *The History and Growth of the United States Census.* Reprint. New York: Johnson, 1966.

Church Records

Ahlstrom, Sydney E. *A Religious History of the American People.* New Haven, Conn.: Yale University Press, 1972.

Allison, William H. *Inventory of Unpublished Material for American Religious History in Protestant Church Archives and Their Repositories.* Washington, D.C.: Carnegie Institute, 1910.

Check List of Historical Records Survey Publications. WPA, 1943. Reprint. Baltimore: Genealogical Publishing Co., 1969.

Church and Synagogue Libraries. Metuchen, New Jersey: The Scarecrow Press, 1980.

Ganstadt, Edwin Scott. *Historical Atlas of Religions in America.* New York: Harper & Row, 1962.

Hefner, Loretta L. *The WPA Historical Records Survey: A Guide to the Unpublished Inventories, Indexes and Transcripts.* Chicago: Society of American Archivists, 1980.

Hill, Thomas. *Monthly Meetings in North America: An Index.* 2nd ed. Cincinnati: n.p., 1993.

Hinshaw, William Wade. *Encyclopedia of American Quaker Genealogy.* 6 vols. Ann Arbor, Mich.: Edwards Brothers, 1936-1950. Reprint. Baltimore: Genealogical Publishing Co., 1973, 1994.

Jacquet, Constant H. *Yearbook of American and Canadian Churches.* Nashville: Abingdon Press, annual.

Kirkham, E. Kay. *A Survey of American Church Records.* Logan, Utah: Everton Publishers, 1978.

Mead, Frank S. *Handbook of American Denominations.* 8th ed. Nashville: Aningdon Press, 1985.

Melton, John Gordon, ed. *National Directory of Churches, Synagogues and Other Houses of Worship*. 4 vols. Detroit: Gale Research, 1994.

Melton, John Gordon. *The Encyclopedia of American Religions*. Detroit: Gale Research, 1989.

Pettee, Julia. *List of Churches: Official Forms of the Names for Denominational Bodies With Brief Descriptive and Historical Notes*. Chicago: American Library Association, 1948.

Rodda, Dorothy. *Directory of Church Libraries*. Philadelphia: Drexel Press, 1967.

Suelflow, August R. *A Preliminary Guide to Church Records Repositories*. St. Louis: Church Archives Committee, Society of American Archivists, 1969.

Sweet, William Warren. *Religion on the American Frontier, 1783-1840: A Collection of Source Materials*. New York: Cooper Square Publishers, 1940, 1964.

The Official Catholic Directory. Chicago: Hoffman Bros., 1886-1997.

Court Records

Askin, Jayne. *Search: A Handbook for Adoptees and Birthparents*. 2nd ed. Phoenix, Arizona: Oryx Press, 1992.

Bentley, Elizabeth Petty. *County Courthouse Book*. Genealogical Publishing, 1995.

Black, Henry Campbell. *Black's Law Dictionary: Definitions of the Terms and Phrases of American and English Jurisprudence, Ancient and Modern*. St. Paul: West Publishing, 1991.

Blume, William, and Elizabeth Gaspar Brown. *Digests and Lists Pertaining to the Development of Law and Legal Institutions in the Territories of the United States: 1787-1954*. 6 vols. Ann Arbor: university Microfilm, 1965-79.

BRB Publication Research and Editorial Staff. *The Sourcebook of Federal Courts, U.S. District and Bankruptcy: The Definitive Guide to Searching for Case Information at the Local Level Within the Federal Court System*. Temp, Ariz.: BRB Publications, 1993.

Burton, William C. *Burton's Legal Thesaurus*. 3rd ed. Columbus, Ohio: McGraw Hill Professional Publishing, 2001.

Eichholz, Alice, ed. *Ancestry's Red Book: American State, County & Town Sources*. Salt Lake City, Utah: Ancestry, 1992.

Evans, Barbara Jean. *The New A to Zax: A Comprehensive Genealogical Dictionary for Genealogists and Historians*. 2nd ed. Champaign, Ill.: B. J. Evans, 1990.

Hasse, Adelaide R. *Materials for a Bibliography of the Pubic Archives of the Thirteen Original States Covering Colonial Period and State period to 1789*. 1908. Reprint. New York: Argonaut Press, 1966.

Jeffrey, William, Jr. "Early New England Court Records: A Bibliography of Published Material." *Boston Public Library Quarterly* 1954, as reprinted in *American Journal of Legal History*. 1 (1957): 119-47.

Klunder, Virgil L. *Lifeline: The Action Guide to Adoption Search*. Cape Coral, Florida: Caradium Publishing, 1991.

Low, Erick Baker. *A Bibliography on the History of the Organizational and Jurisdiction of State Courts*. Williamsburg: National Center for State Courts, 1980.

McReynolds, Michael. *List of Pre-1840 Federal District Court Records Located in Federal Record Centers*. Washington, D.C.: Government Printing Office, 1972. Special List, 31.

National Association of State Libraries. *A Checklist of Legislative Journals of the States of the U.S.A*. New York: Oxford Press, 1938.

National Association of State Libraries. *Preliminary Checklists of Session Laws, to 1922*. New York: Oxford Press, 1934.

Ray, Susanne Smith, et al., comp. *A Preliminary Guide to the Pre-1904 County Records in the National Archives Branch*. Richmond: Virginia State Library and Archives, 1987.

Salmon, Marylynn. *Women and the Law of Property in Early America*. Chapel Hill: University of North Carolina Press, 1986.

Sourcebook of Federal Courts: U.S. District and Bankruptcy. Public Record Research Library. Tempe, Ariz.: BRB Publications, 1993.

Szucs, Loretto Dennis, and Sandra Hargraves Luebking. *The Archives: A Guide to the National Archives Field Branches*. Salt Lake City: Ancestry, 1988. (Extensive bibliography for Court Records, pp 232-38).

The Handybook for Genealogists, 10th ed. Logan, Utah: Everton Publishers Inc., 2002.

Tompkins, Dorothy Campbell. *Court Organizations and Administration: A Bibliography*. Berkeley: University of California Press, 1973.

Washington Division of Archives and Records Management. *Frontier Justice: Abstracts and Indexes to the Records of the Territorial District Courts, 1853-1889*. Olympia, Wash.: Secretary of State, 1987.

Dictionaries

Dictionary Catalog of the Local History and Genealogy Division. Boston: G. K. Hall, 1974.

Dictionary of American Biography. New York: Charles Scribner's Sons, 1928-1988.

Dictionary of Indian Tribes of the Americas. Newport Beach CA: American Indian Publishers, 1993.

Oxford English Dictionary. Oxford, England: Clarendon Press, 1931-86.

Directories

American Library Directory. New York: R.R. Bowker Co., annual.

Ayer Directory of Publications. Bala Cynwyd, Pennsylvania: Ayer Press, annual.

Bentley, Elizabeth Petty, and Debra Ann Carl, comps. *Directory of Family Associations*. 4th ed. Baltimore: Genealogical Publishing Co., Inc., 2001.

Bentley, Elizabeth Petty. *The Genealogist's Address Book*. 4th ed. Baltimore: Genealogical Publishing Co., Inc., 1998.

Burton, Robert E. "City Directories in the United States, 1784-1820: A Bibliography with Historical Notes." M.S. Thesis, University of Michigan, 1956.

Catalog of City, County, and State Directories Published in North America. New York North American Directory Publishers, 1967.

City Directories of the United States Pre 1860 Through 1901: Guide to the Microfilm Collection. Woodbridge, Conn.: Research Publications, 1983.

Klein, Bernard. *Guide to American Directories*. 5th ed. Englewood Cliffs, N.J.: Prentice-Hall, 1962.

National Historical Publications and Records Commission. *Directory of Archives and Manuscript Depositories in the United States.* Washington, DC.: National Archives and Records Service, 1978.

National Historical Publications and Records Commission. *Directory of Archives and Manuscript Repositories in the United States.* 2ns. Ed. Phoenix: Oryx Press, 1988.

Parch, Grace D., ed. *Directory of Newspaper Libraries in the United States and Canada.* New York: Project of the Newspaper Division, Special Libraries Assoc., 1976.

Smith, Betty P. *Directory of Historical Societies and Agencies in the United States and Canada.* 14th ed. Nashville: American Association for State and Local history, 1990.

Spear, Dorothea N. *Bibliography of American Directories Through 1860.* Worcester, Mass.: American Antiquarian Society, 1961.

Street Directory of the Principal Cities of the United States…to April 1908. 5th ed. 1908. Detroit: Gale Research Co., 1973.

Emigration, Immigration, Migration and Naturalization

Allen, James Paul, and Eugene James Turner. *We the People: An Atlas of America's Diversity.* New York: McMillian, 1988.

Anuta, Michael J. *Ships of our Ancestors.* 2nd ed. Baltimore: Genealogical Publishing Co., 1993.

Appel, John J. *Immigrant Historical Societies in the USA.* New York: Amo Press, 1980.

Appel, John J. *The New Immigration.* New York: Pitman Publishers, 1971.

Auerbach, Frank L. *Immigration Laws of the United States.* Indianapolis: Bobbs-Merrill, 1961.

Bodnar, John. *The Transplanted: A History of Immigrants in Urban America.* Bloomington: Indiana University Press, 1987.

Bolino, August C. *The Ellis Island Source Book.* Washington, D.C.: Kensington Historical Press, 1985.

Boyer, Carl. *Ship Passenger Lists, National and New England (1600-1825).* Newhall, California: C. Boyer, 1977. Covers Lancour entries 1-71.

Boyer, Carl. *Ship Passenger Lists, New York and New Jersey (1600-1825).* Newhall, California: C. Boyer, 1978. Covers Lancour entries 72-115.

Boyer, Carl. *Ship Passenger Lists, the South (1538-1825).* Newhall, California: C. Boyer, 1979. Covers Lancour entries 198E-243.

Boyer, Carol. *Ship Passenger Lists, Pennsylvania and Delaware (1641-1825).* Newhall, California: C. Boyer, 1980. Covers Lancour entries 116-197.

Buenker, John D. Nicholas C. Burckel, and Rudolph J. Vecoli. *Immigration and Ethnicity: A Guide to Information Sources.* Detroit: Gale Research Co., 1977.

Carmack, Sharon DeBartolo. *A Genealogist's Guide to Discovering Your Emigrant & Ethnic Ancestors.* Cincinnati: Betterway Books, 2000.

Coldham, Peter Wilson. *Bonded Passengers to America.* Vol. I-IX. Baltimore: Genealogical Publishing Co., 1993.

Coldham, Peter Wilson. *Emigrants in Chains.* Baltimore: Genealogical Publishing Co., 1992.

Coldham, Peter Wilson. *Supplement to The Complete Book of Immigrants in Bondage, 1614-1775.* Baltimore: Genealogical Publishing Co., 1992.

Coldham, Peter Wilson. *The Complete Book of Emigrants in Bondage, 1614-1755.* Baltimore: Genealogical Publishing Co., 1988.

Coldham, Peter Wilson. *The Complete Book of Immigrants, 1607-1660.* Baltimore: Genealogical Publishing Co., 1987.

Coldham, Peter Wilson. *The Complete Book of Immigrants, 1661-1699.* Baltimore: Genealogical Publishing Co., 1990.

Coldham, Peter Wilson. *The Complete Book of Immigrants, 1700-1750.* Baltimore: Genealogical Publishing Co., 1992.

Coldham, Peter Wilson. *The Complete Book of Immigrants, 1751-1776.* Baltimore: Genealogical Publishing Co., 1993.

Colletta, John P. *They Came in Ships.* 2nd ed. Salt Lake City, UT: Ancestry, Inc., 1993.

Cordasco, Francescoa, ed. *A Bibliography of American Immigration History.* Fairfield, N.J.: Augustus M. Kelly Publishers, 1978.

Cordasco, Francescoa, ed. *The Immigrant Woman in North America.* Metuchen, N.J.: Scarecrow Press, 1985.

Cordasco, Francescoa, ed. *The New American Immigration: Evolving Patterns of Legal and Illegal Emigration: A Bibliography of Selected References.* New York: Garland, 1987.

Douglas, Lee V. *A Select Bibliography of Works: Norwegian-American Immigration and Local History.* Research Guide No. 6. (Washington, DC: Library of Congress, Local History & Genealogy Reading Room, n.d.).

Douglass, Lee V. *Danish Immigration to America: An Annotated Bibliography of Resources at the Library of Congress.* Research Guide No. 28. (Washington, DC: Library of Congress, Local History & Genealogy Reading Room, n.d.).

Filby, P. William, ed. Passenger and Immigration Lists Bibliography, 1538-1900. 2nd ed. Detroit, MI: Gale Research Co., 1988.

Filby, P. William, et al. *Passenger and Immigration Lists Index,* 15 vols. Detroit, Gale Research Co., 1981-.

Glazier, Ira A., ed. T*he Famine Immigrants: Lists of Irish Immigrants Arriving at the Port of New York, 1846-1851.* 8 vols. Baltimore: Genealogical Publishing Co., 1983-1986.

Guillet, Edwin C. *The Great Migration: The Atlantic Crossing by Sailing Ship Since 1770.* Rev. Ed. Toronto: University Press, 1963.

Handlin, Oscar, ed. *Immigration as a Factor in American History.* Englewood Cliffs, NJ: Prentice-Hall, Inc., 1959.

Handlin, Oscar, ed. *The Uprooted: The Epic Story of the Great Migrations that Made the American People.* Reprinted, 2nd ed. Enlarged, Boston: Little Brown & Co., 1973.

History of the Immigration and Naturalization Service. Washington, D.C.: Government Printing Office, 1988.

Hoglund, A. William. *Immigrants and Their Children in the United States: A Bibliography of Doctoral Dissertations, 1885-1982.* New York: Garland, 1986.

Kennedy, John F. *A Nation of Immigrants.* New York: Harper and Row, 1964.

Konvitz, Milton R. *Civil Rights in Immigration.* Ithaca, NY: Cornell University Press, 1953.

Kraut, Alan M. *The Huddled Masses: The Immigrant in American Society.* Arlington Heights, Ill.: Harlan Davidson, 1982.

Lancour, Harold, comp. *A Bibliography of Ship Passenger Lists, 1538-1825; Being a Guide to Published Lists of Early Immigrants to North America.* 3rd ed. New York: New York Public Library, 1978.

Lind, Marilyn. *Immigration, Migration and Settlement in the United States: A Genealogical Guidebook.* Cloquet, Minn.: The Linden Ress, 1985.

Miller, Olga K. *Migration, Emigration, Immigration.* Logan, Utah: Everton Publishers, 1981.

Moody, Suzanna and Joel Wurt, eds. *The Immigration History Research Center: A Guide to Collections.* New York: Greenwood Press, 1991.

Morrison, Joan, and Charlotte Fox Zabusky. *American Mosaic: The Immigrant Experience in the Words of Those Who Lived It.* 2nd ed. Pittsburgh: University of Pittsburgh Press, 1993.

Morton Allen Directory of European Steamship Arrivals: for the Years 1890 to 1930 at the Port of New York and for the Years 1904 to 1926 at the Ports of New York, Philadelphia, Boston and Baltimore. 1931. Reprint, Genealogical Publishing, 1980, 1987.

Neagles, James C. and Lila Lee Neagles. *Locating Your Immigrant Ancestor.* Logan, Utah: Everton Publishers, 1975.

Tepper, Michael. *American Passenger Arrival Records: A Guide to the Records of Immigrants Arriving at American Ports by Sail and Stream.* 2nd ed. Baltimore: Genealogical Publishing Co., 1993.

Tepper, Michael. *Emigrants to Pennsylvania, 1641-1819: A Consolidation of Ship Passenger Lists from the Pennsylvania Magazine of History and Biography.* Baltimore: Genealogical Publishing Co., 1978.

Tepper, Michael. *Immigrants to the Middle Colonies: A Consolidation of Ship Passenger Lists and Associated Data from the New York Genealogical and Biographical Record.* Baltimore: Genealogical Publishing Co., 1978.

Tepper, Michael. *New World Immigrants: A Consolidation of Ship Passenger Lists and Associated Data from Periodical Literature.* 2 vols. Baltimore: Genealogical Publishing Co., 1988.

Tepper, Michael. *Passengers to America: A Consolidation of Ship Passenger Lists from the New England Historical and Genealogical Register.* Baltimore: Genealogical Publishing Co., 1977.

The Church of Jesus Christ of Latter-day Saints. *Research Outline: Tracing Immigrant Origins.* Salt Lake City: Family History Library, 1992.

The Great Migration Begins: Immigrants to New England 1620-1633. CD-ROM ed. Salt Lake City: Ancestry, 2000.

Wood, Virginia Steele. *Immigrant Arrivals: A Guide to Published Sources.* Rev. ed. Washington, D.C: Library of Congress, Local History & Genealogy Reading Room, n.d.

Gazetteers

Abate, Frank R., ed. *American Places Dictionary: A Guide to 45,000 Populated Places, Natural Features, and Other Places in the United States.* 4 vols. Detroit: Omnigraphics, 1994.

Abate, Frank R., ed. *Omni Gazetteer of the United States of America: Providing Name, Location, and Identification for Nearly 1,500,000 Populated Places, Structures, Facilities, Locales, Historic Places, and Geographic Features in the Fifty States...* 11 vols. Detroit: Omnigraphics, 1994.

Bahn, Gilbert S. *American Place Names of Long Ago. A Republication of the Index of Cram's Unrivaled Atlas of the World as based on the Census on 1890.* Baltimore: Genealogical Publishing Co., 1998.

Fanning's Illustrated Gazetteer of the United States. New York: Ensign, Bridgman, and Fanning, 1855.

Gannett, Henry. *The Origin of Certain Place Names in the United States.* 2nd ed. Baltimore: Clearfield Co. 1996.

Kane, Joseph Nathan. *The American Counties: A Record of the Origin of the 3,072 Counties, Dates of Creation and Organization, Area, 1960 Population, Historical Data, etc. of the 50 States.* New York: Scarecrow Press, 1962.

Seltzer, Leon E. *The Columbia-Lippincott Gazetteer of the World.* Morningside Heights, New York: Columbia University Press, 1952.

Genealogy

A Complement to Genealogies in the Library of Congress: A Bibliography. Reprint. Baltimore: Genealogical Publishing Co., Inc. 2001.

Clark, Patricia L., and Dorothy Huntsman, eds. *American Genealogical Biographical Key Title Index.* Salt Lake City: Genealogical Society of Utah, 1990.

Dictionary Catalog of the Local History and Genealogy Division. Boston: G. K. Hall, 1974.

Genealogical Index of the Newberry Library. 4 vols. Boston: G.K. Hall, 1960.

Genealogies Cataloged in the Library of Congress Since 1986. Washington, D.C.: Cataloging Distribution Service, Library of Congress, 1992.

Greenlaw, William Prescott. *The Greenlaw Index of the New England Historic Genealogical Society.* Boston: G.K. Hall, 1979.

Index to American Genealogies: And to Genealogical Material contained in all works as Town Histories, County Histories, Local Histories, Historical Society Publications, Biographies, Historical Periodicals, and Kindred Works. Baltimore: Genealogical Publishing, 1984.

Index to Personal Names in the National Union Catalog of Manuscript Collections, 1959-1984. 2 vols. Alexandria, Virginia: Chadwyck-Healey, 1988.

Index to Some of the Family Records of the Southern States: 35,000 Microfilm References from the N.S.D.A.R. Files and Elsewhere. Logan, Utah: Everton Publishers, 1979.

Kaminkow, Marion J., ed. *A Complement to Genealogies in the Library of Congress.* Baltimore: Magna Carta Book Co., 1981.

Kaminkow, Marion J., ed. *United States Local Histories in the Library of Congress, A Bibliography.* Baltimore: Magna Carta Book Co., 1972.

Kaminkow, Marion J., *Genealogies in the Library of Congress: A Bibliography.* 2 vols. 2 supplements, 1972-76, 1976-86. Baltimore: Magna Carta Book, 1972. Reprint. Baltimore: Genealogical Publishing Co., 2001.

National Union Catalog of Manuscript Collections (NUCMC). Annual. Washington, D.C.: Library of Congress, 1959–.

New York Public Library. *Dictionary Catalog of the Local History and Genealogy Division.* 18 vols. Boston: G.K. Hall, 1974.

Rider, Fremont, ed. *The American Genealogical-Biographical Index to American, Biographical and Local History Materials*. Middletown, Connecticut: Godfrey Memorial Library, 1999, 2000.

Schreiner-Yantis, Netti. *Genealogical and Local History Books in Print*. Springfield, Virginia: Genealogical Books in Print, 1976-.

Virkus, Frederick A., ed. *Abridged Compendium of American Genealogy: First Families of the United States*. 7 vols. 1925-1942. Reprint, Baltimore: Genealogical Publishing, 1987.

Handbooks and Guidebooks

American Society of Genealogists. *Genealogical Research: Methods and Sources*. 2 vols. Rev. ed. Washington, D.C.: American Society of Genealogists, 1980, 1983.

Greenwood, Val D. *The Researcher's Guide to American Genealogy*, 3rd edition. Baltimore: Genealogical Publishing Co., Inc., 2000.

Guide to Genealogical Research in the National Archives. Washington, DC: National Archives Trust Fund Board, 1985.

Hall, H. Byron, ed. *Lest We Forget: A Guide to Genealogical Research in the Nation's Capital*. Annandale, Virginia: Annandale and Oakton Stakes of the Church of Jesus Christ of Latter-day Saints, 1989, c1965.

Hefner, Loretta L. *The W.P.A. Historical Records Survey: A Guide to Unpublished Inventories, Indexes and Transcripts*. Chicago: Society of American Archivists, 1980.

Kemp, Thomas Jay. *International Vital Records Handbook*. Baltimore: Genealogical Publishing Co., Inc., 2001.

Kemp, Thomas Jay. *The American Census Handbook*. Wilmington, Delaware: Scholarly Resources, Inc., 2001.

Kirkham, E. Kay. *A Handy Guide to Record Searching in the Larger Cities of the United States, Including a Guide to Their Vital Records and Some Maps with Street Indexes with Other Information of Genealogical Value*. Logan, Utah: Everton Publishers, 1974.

Kirkham, E. Kay. *A Survey of American Church Records*. Logan, Utah: Everton Publishers, 1978.

Kirkham, E. Kay. *The Handwriting of American Records for a Period of 300 Years*. Logan, Utah: Everton Publishers, 1973.

Lackey, Richard S. *Cite Your Sources: A Manual for Documenting Family Histories and Genealogical Records*. Reprint. Jackson, MS.: University Press of Mississippi, 1986.

Makower, Joel and Linda Zaleskie. *The American History Sourcebook*. New York: Prentice-Hall, 1998.

Mead, Frank S. *Handbook of Denominations*. New York; Arlington Press, 1965.

Meyerink, Kory L. ed. *Printed Sources: A Guide to Published Genealogical Records*. Salt Lake City: Ancestry Publishing, 1998.

Mills, Elizabeth Shown, ed. *Professional Genealogy: A Manual for Researchers, Writers, Editors, Lecturers and Librarians*. Baltimore: Genealogical Publishing Co., 2001.

Mills, Elizabeth Shown. *Evidence!: Citation & Analysis for the Family Historian*. Baltimore: Genealogical Publishing Co., 2000.

Neagles, James C. *The Library of Congress: A Guide to Genealogical and Historical Research*. Salt Lake City: Ancestry, 1990.

Pfeiffer, Laura Szucs. *Hidden Sources: Family History in Unlikely Places*. Salt Lake City: Ancestry Publishing, 2000.

Rubincam, Milton. *Pitfalls in Genealogical Research*. Salt Lake City: Ancestry Pubs., 1987.

Schreiner-Yantis, Netti. *Genealogical and Local History Books in Print*. Springfield, Virginia: Genealogical Books in Print, 1981.

Stevenson, Noel C. *Evidence: A Guide to the Standard of Proof Relating to Pedigree, Ancestry, Heirship, and Family History*. Rev. ed. Lagunna Hills, Calif.: Aegean Park Press, 1989.

Stryker-Rodda, Harriet. *Understanding Colonial Handwriting*. Baltimore: Genealogical Publishing. 1986.

Szucs, Loretto Dennis and Sandra Hargreaves Luebking, eds. *The Source: A Guidebook for American Genealogy*. Rev. ed. Salt Lake City: Ancestry Incorporated, 1997.

Wright, Norman E. *Preserving Your American Heritage: A Guide to Family and Local History*. Provo, Utah: Brigham Young University Press, 1981.

Historical Geography

Adams, James Truslow. *Atlas of American History*. New York: New York: Charles Scribner's Sons, 1943.

Atlas of American History. New York: Charles Scribner's Sons, 1984.

Grim, Ronald E. *Historical Geography of the United States: A Guide to Information Sources*. Detroit: Gale Research, 1982.

Holt, Alfred. *American Place Names*. New York: Thomas Y. Crowell, 1938.

Kane, Joseph Nathan. *The American Counties: Origins of Names, Dates of Creation and Organization, Area, Population, Historical Data, and Published Sources*. 4th ed. Metuchen, N.J.: Scarecrow press, 1983.

Kirkham, E. Kay. *A Genealogical and Historical Atlas of the United States of America*. Logan, Utah: Everton Publishers, 1976.

Sealock, Richard B., ed., et al. *Bibliography of Place-Name Literature, United States and Canada*. 3rd ed. Chicago: American Library Assoc., 1982.

The Handybook for Genealogists. Logan, Utah: Everton Publishers Inc., 2002.

History

Atlas of American History. New York: Charles Scribner's Sons, 1984.

Buenker, John D., Gerald Michael Greenfield, and William J. Murin. *Urban History: A Guide to Information Sources*. Detroit: Gale Research Co., 1981.

Dictionary Catalog of the Local History and Genealogy Division. Boston: G. K. Hall, 1974.

Dictionary of American History, Revised ed., 8 vol. New York: Charles Scribner's Sons, 1976.

Douglas, Lee V. *A Select Bibliography of Works: Norwegian-American Immigration and Local History*. Research Guide No. 6. (Washington, DC: Library of Congress, Local History & Genealogy Reading Room, n.d.).

Filby, P. William. *A Bibliography of American County Histories*. Baltimore: Genealogical Publishing Co., 1985.

Handlin, Oscar, ed. *Immigration as a Factor in American History.* Englewood Cliffs, New Jersey: Prentice-Hall, Inc., 1959.

Handlin, Oscar, ed. *The Uprooted: The Epic Story of the Great Migrations that Made the American People.* Reprinted, 2nd ed. Enlarged, Boston: Little Brown & Co., 1973.

Kaminkow, Marion J., ed. *United States Local Histories in the Library of Congress, A Bibliography.* 5 vols. Baltimore: Magna Carta Book Co., 1975-76.

Schlesinger, Jr., and Arthur M. *The Almanac of American History.* Greenwich, Conn.: Bison Books, 1983.

Schreiner-Yantis, Netti. *Genealogical and Local History Books in Print.* Springfield, Virginia: Genealogical Books in Print, 1981.

United States Local Histories in the Library of Congress, A Bibliography. Baltimore: Magna Carta Book Co., 1975.

Webster's Guide to American History: A Chronological, Geographical, and Biographical Survey and Compendium. Springfield, Massachusetts: G&C Merriam, 1971.

Land and Property

Billington, Ray Allen, and Martin Ridge. *Western Expansion, A History of the American Frontier.* 5th ed. New York: Macmillan Publishing Co., 1982.

Bureau of Land Management. *Manual of Instruction for the Survey of the Public Lands of the United States.* Technical Bulletin 6. Washington, D.C.: Department of the Interior, 1973.

Bureau of Land Management. *Public Land Bibliography.* Washington, D.C.: Bureau of Land Management, 1962.

Department of the Interior. *Catalog of the United States Geological Survey Library.* 24 vols. plus a supplement of 11 vols. and a second of 4. Boston: G.K. Hall, 1964, 1972-74.

Digested Summary and Alphabetical List of Private Claims Which Have Been Presented to the House Representatives…. Baltimore: Genealogical Publishing Co., 1970.

Donaldson, Thomas. *The Public Domain: Its History with Statistics.* House Misc. Doc. 45 pt. 4, 47th Cong., 2nd Sess. 1884. Reprint. New York: Johnson Reprint, 1970.

Hibbard, Benjamin Horace. *A History of the Public Domain Policies.* New York: Peter, Smith, 1939.

Higham, John. *Strangers in the Land Patterns of American Nativism, 1860-1925.* Rutgers, NJ: Rutgers University Press, 1955. Reprint, New York: Atheneum, 1963-1981.

Hone, Wade. *Land and Property Research in the United States.* Salt Lake City: Ancestry, 1997.

Kirkham. E. Kay. *The Land Records of American and Their Genealogical Value.* Salt Lake City: Deseret Book, 1964.

Lee, Lawrence B. "American Public Land History: A Review Essay." *Agricultural History* 55 (1981): 284-99.

McMullin, Phillip W., ed. *Grassroots of America.* Reprint. Greenville, S.C.: Southern Historical Press, 1993.

National Archives. *Guide to Genealogical Research in the National Archives.* Washington, D.C.: National Archives and Records Service, 2000.

Robbins, Roy Marvin. *Our Landed Heritage: The Public Domain, 1776-1970.* 2nd ed. Lincoln: University of Nebraska Press, 1976.

Rohrbough, Malcolm J. *The Land Office Business: The Settlement and Administration of American Public Lands, 1789-1837.* Belmont, Calif.: Wadsworth Publishing Co., 1990.

Salmon, Marylynn. *Women and the Law of Property in Early America.* Chapel Hill: University of North Carolina Press, 1986.

Smith, Clifford Neal. *Federal Land Series: A Calendar of Archival Materials on the Land Patents Issued by the United States Government, with Subject, Tract and Name Indexes.* 4 vols. Reprint. Baltimore: Clearfield Co. 1999.

Stevenson, Richard W. *Land Ownership Maps.* Washington, D.C.: Library of Congress, 1967.

Treat, Payson Jackson. *The National Land System, 1785-1820.* New York: E.B. Treat, 1910.

United States Congress. *American State Papers, Class VIII,: Public Lands* and *The American State Papers, Class IX,: Claims.* 9 vols. Washington, D.C.: Gale and Seaton, 1832-61. Reprint, Greenville, S.C.: Southern Historical Press, 1994.

United States Congress. House. *Digested Summary and Alphabetical List of Private Claims Which Have Been Presented to the House of Representatives.* Washington, D.C.: Library of Congress, [19–].

Yoshpe, Harry P., and Phillip P. Brower. *Preliminary Inventory of the Land-Entry Papers of the General Land Office.* Preliminary Inventory 22 (Washington, D.C.: National Archives, 1949. Reprint. San Jose, Calif.: Rose Family Association, 1996.

Maps and Atlases

Androit, Jay. *Township Atlas of the United States.* McClean, Virginia: Documents Index, 1991.

Atlas of American History, 2nd ed., revised. New York: Charles Scribner's Sons, 1984.

Cobb, David A., comp. *Guide to U.S. Map Resources.* Chicago: American Library Association, 1986.

Geography and Map Section of the Library of Congress. "Fire Insurance Maps in the Library of Congress." Washington, D.C.: 1981.

Kirkham, E. Kay. *A Genealogical and Historical Atlas of the United States of America.* Logan, Utah: Everton Publishers, 1976.

Library of Congress. Geography and Map Division. *Land Ownership Maps.* Washington, D.C.: Library of Congress, 1983.

Library of Congress. Geography and Map Division. *Land Ownership Maps: A Checklist of Nineteenth Century United States County Maps in the Library of Congress.* Washington, D.C.: Library of Congress, 1967.

Library of Congress. *Panoramic Maps of Cities in the United States and Canada: A Checklist of Maps of the Collections of the Library of Congress, Geography and Map Division.* 2nd ed. Washington, D.C.: Library of Congress, 1984.

Long, John H., ed. *Historical Atlas and Chronology of County Boundaries, 1788-1980.* 5 vols. Boston: G. K. Hall, 1984.

Long, John H., ed., *[State] Atlas of Historical County Boundaries.* New York: Charles Scribner's sons, 1996-.

Madower, Joel, ed. *The Map Catalog.* New York: Vintage Books, 1986.

Meinig, D. W. *The Shaping of America: A Geographical Perspective on 500 Years of History.* 2 vols. New Haven, Conn.: Yale University Press, 1986.

Moffat, Riley Moore. *Map Index to Topographic Quadrangles of the United States, 1882-1940.* Occasional paper: Western Association of Map Libraries, no. 10 Santa Cruz, Calif.: Western Association of Map Libraries, 1986.

Rand-McNally Commercial Atlas and Marketing Guide. New York: Rand-McNally & Co., annual.

Shelley, Michael H. *Ward Maps of United States Cities: A Selective Checklist of Pre-1900 Maps in the Library of Congress.* Washington, D.C.: N.p., 1975.

The American Heritage Pictorial Atlas of United States History. New York: American Heritage Publishing, 1966.

Thorndale, William, and William Dollarhide. *Map Guide to the U.S. Federal Census, 1790-1920.* Baltimore: Genealogical Publishing Co., 1987.

Thrower, Norman J.W. "The County Atlases of the United States." *Surveying and Mapping* 21 (1961): 365-73.

United States. Geological Survey. *Topographic Maps of the United States.* Scale varies. Suitland, Maryland: National Archives and Records Service, 1976-.

Walsh, Jim. *Maps Contained in the Publications of the American Bibliography, 1639-1819: An Index and Checklist.* Metuchen, New Jersey: Scarecrow Press, 1988.

Ward Maps of United States Cities. Washington, D.C.: Library of Congress, [1975?].

Military Records

D.A.R. Patriot Index. Washington, DC: National Society, Daughters of the American Revolution, 1979.

Davis, Lenwood G. *Blacks in the American Armed Forces, 1776-1983: A Bibliography.* Westport, Conn.: Greenwood Press, 1985.

Deputy, Marilyn, and Pat Barben. *Register of Federal United States Military Records, A Guide to Manuscript Sources at the Genealogical Library Salt Lake City and the National Archives in Washington, DC.* 3 vols. Bowie, Maryland: Heritage Books, 1986.

Family History Library. *U.S. Military Records: Research Outline.* Salt Lake City: The Church of Jesus Christ of Latter-day Saints, 1998.

Giller, Sadye, William H. Dumont and Louise M. Dumont. *Index of Revolutionary War Pension Applications.* Washington, DC: National Genealogical Society, 1966.

Groene, Bertram H. *Tracing Your Civil War Ancestor.* Revised. Winston-Salem, North Carolina: John F. Blair, 1995.

Heitman, Francis B. *Historical Register and Dictionary of the United States Army, From Its Organization September 29, 1789 to March 2, 1903.* 2 vols. 1965. Reprint. Baltimore: Genealogical Publishing Co., 1994.

Horowita, Lois. *A Bibliography of Military Name Lists From Pre-1675 to 1900: A Guide to Genealogical Sources.* Metuchen, New Jersey: The Scarecrow Press, 1990.

Hughes, Mark, comp. *The Unpublished Roll of Honor.* Baltimore: Genealogical Publishing Co., Inc. 1996.

Index of Rolls of Honor in the Lineage Books. Washington, D.C.: DAR, 1939-.

Index to Revolutionary War Pension Applications in the National Archives. National Genealogical Society Special Publication No. 40. Washington, D.C.: NGS, 1976.

Johnson, Richard S. *How to Locate Anyone Who Is or Has Been in the Military.* 7th ed. Spartanburg, South Carolina: MIE Publishing, 1996.

Kinnell, Susan K. *Military History of the United States; an Annotated Bibliography.* Santa Barbara, California: ABC-CLIO, 1986.

Kirkham, E. Kay. *Some of the Military Records of America (Before 1900): Their Use and Values in Genealogical and Historical Research.* Salt Lake City: Deseret Book Co., 1964.

Lane, Jack C. *America's Military Past: A Guide to Information Sources.* Detroit: Gale Research, 1980.

Military Service Records: A Select Catalog of National Archives Microfilm Publications. Washington, D.C.: National Archives Trust, 1985.

Mulligan, Timothy P. comp. *Guide to Records Relating to U.S. Military Participation in World War II.* Washington, D.C.: National Archives and Records Administration, 1996.

Neagles, James C. and Lila L. Neagles. *Locating Your Revolutionary War Ancestors: A Guide to the Military Records.* Logan, Utah: Everton Publishers, 1983.

Neagles, James C., *U.S. Military Records: A Guide to Federal and State Sources, Colonial America to the Present.* Salt Lake City: Ancestry, 1994.

Patriot Index Centennial Edition. Washington, D.C.: National Society DAR, 1994.

Poulos, Paula Nassen, ed. *A Woman's War Too: U.S. Women in the Military in World War II.* Washington, D.C.: National Archives and Records Administration, 1996.

Powell, William H. *List of Officers of the Army of the United States From 1779 to 1900 Embracing a Register of All Appointments by the President of the United States in the Volunteer Service During the Civil War and of Volunteer Officers of the United States June 1, 1900.* Detroit: Gale Research Co. 1967.

Purdy, Virginia C. and Robert Gruber, comp. *American Women and the U.S. Armed Forces: A Guide to the Records of Military Agencies in the National Archives Relating to American Women.* Washington, D.C.: National Archives and Records Administration, 1992.

Reamy, Martha, and William Reamy, comps. *Index to the Roll of Honor.* Baltimore: Genealogical Publishing Co., 1995.

Ryan, Gary D., and Timothy K. Nenninge, eds. *Soldiers and Civilians: The U.S. Army and the American People.* Washington, D.C.: National Archives and Records Administration, 1987.

Tozeski, Stanley R. *Preliminary Inventory of the Records of the U.S. Military Academy.* Washington, D.C.: National Archives and Records Service, 1976.

U.S. Quartermaster's Department. *Roll of Honor.* 27 Vols. Reprint. Baltimore: Genealogical Publishing Co., Inc., 1994.

U.S. Veterans Administration. *Abstracts of Service Records of Naval Officers ("Records of Officers") 1798-1893.* M330, 19 rolls. Washington, D.C.: National Archives Microfilm Publications.

U.S. Veterans Administration. *Registers of Enlistments in the United States Army, 1789-1914.* M233, 80 rolls. Washington, D.C.: National Archives Publications, 1963.

White, Virgil D. *Genealogical Abstracts of Revolutionary War Pension Files.* 3 vol. Waynesboro, Tennessee: National Historical Publishing Co., 1990-1992.

White, Virgil D. *Index to War of 1812 Pension Files.* 2 vol. Waynesboro, Tennessee: National Historical Pub. Co., 1992.

White, Virgil D. *Index of U. S. Marshals, 1789-1960.* Waynesboro, Tennessee: National Historical Pub. Co., 1988.

White, Virgil D. *Index to Mexican War Pension Files.* Waynesboro, Tennessee: National Historical Pub. Co., 1989.

White, Virgil D. *Index to Old Wars Pension Files, 1815-1926.* Waynesboro, Tennessee: National Historical Publishing, 1993.

White, Virgil D. *Index to Pension Applications for Indian Wars Service Between 1817 and 1898.* Waynesboro, Tennessee: National Historical Pub. Co., 1997.

White, Virgil D. *Index to US Military Pension Applications of Remarried Widows for Service Between 1812 and 1911.* Waynesboro, Tennessee: National Historical Publishing Co., 1999.

White, Virgil D. *Index to Volunteer Soldiers in Indian Wars and Disturbances, 1815-1858.* Waynesboro, Tennessee: National Historical Publishing Co., 1994.

White, Virgil D. *Index to Volunteer Soldiers, 1784-1811.* Waynesboro, Tennessee: National Historical Pub. Co., 1987.

White, Virgin D. *Index to Medal of Honor Recipients, 1863-1978.* Waynesboro, Tennessee: National Historical Pub. Co., 1999.

Minorities

Archeacon, Thomas J. *Becoming American: An Ethnic History.* New York: The Free Press, 1983.

Bodnar, John. *The Transplanted: A History of Immigrants in Urban America.* Bloomington, Ind.: Indiana University Press, 1985.

Carmack, Sharon DeBartolo. *A Genealogist's Guide to Discovering Your Emigrant & Ethnic Ancestors.* Cincinnati: Betterway Books, 2000.

Ethnographic Bibliography of North America. 4th ed. 5 vols. Behavior Science Bibliographies. New Haven, Conn.: Human Relations Area Files, 1975; supplement (3 vols.), 1990.

Lieberson, Stanley. *Ethnic Patterns in American Cities.* New York: Free Press, 1963.

Mindel, Charles H. and Robert W. Habenstein. *Ethnic Families in America: Patterns and Variations.* New York: Elsevier Science Publishing Co., 1981.

Murdock, George P., and Timothy J. O'Leary, ed. *Ethnographic Bibliography of North America, 1975 and Supplement to the 1975 Edition,* 1990.

Smith, Jessie C. *Ethnic Genealogy: A Resource Guide.* Westport, Conn.: Greenwood Press, 1983.

Sowell, Thomas. *Ethnic America: A History.* New York: Basic Books, 1981.

Szucs, Loretto Dennis and Sandra Hargraves Luebking. *The Source: A Guidebook of American Genealogy.* Revised ed. Salt Lake City, Utah: Ancestry Incorporated, 1997. (Extensive bibliography on United States ethnic sources in Chapter 13, "*Immigration: Finding Immigrant Origins.*").

Thernatrom, Stephen, ed. *Harvard Encyclopedia of American Ethnic Groups.* Cambridge, Mass.: Harvard University Press, 1980.

Tracing Immigrant Origins: Research Outline. Salt Lake City: Family History Library, 1992.

Wasserman, Paul, and Alice E. Kennington. *Ethnic Information Sources of the United States: A Guide to Organizations, Agencies, Foundations, Institutions, Media, Commercial and Trade Bodies, Government Programs, Research Institutes, Libraries and Museums, Religious Organizations, Banking Firms, Festivals and Fairs, Travel and Tourist Offices, Airlines and Ship Lines, Bookdealers and Publishers' Representatives, and Books, Pamphlets, and Audiovisuals on Specific Ethnic Groups.* 2nd ed. 2 vols. Detroit: Gale Research Co., 1983.

Wynar, Lubomyr R. and Anna T. Wynar. *The Encyclopedic Directory of Ethnic Newspapers and Periodicals in the United States.* 2nd ed. Littleton, Colo.: Libraries Unlimited, 1976.

Wynar, Lubomyr R. *Encyclopedia Directory of Ethnic Organizations in the United States.* Littleton, Colorado: Libraries Unlimited, 1976.

African-Americans

African American Genealogical Sourcebook. New York: Gale Research, 1995.

Black Studies: A Select Catalog of National Archives Microfilm Publications. Washington, D.C.: National Archives, 1984.

Burkett, Randall K, Nancy Hall Burkett, and Henry Louis Gates, Jr., eds. *Black Biographical Dictionaries 1790-1950.* Alexandria, Virginia: Chadwyck-Healy, Inc., [198-].

Burroughs, Tony. *Black Roots: A Beginner's Guide to Tracing the African American Family Tree.* New York: Fireside Div. Of Simon & Schuster, 2001.

Campbell, Georgetta Merritt. *Extant Collections of Early Black Newspapers: A Research Guide to the Black Press, 1880-1915, With an Index to the Boston Guardian, 1902-1904.*

Fears, Mary Louvenis Jackson. *Slave Ancestral Research: It's Something Else.* Bowie, Maryland: Heritage Books, 1995.

Frazier, Thomas R. *Afro-American History: Primary Sources.* Chicago: The Dorsey Press, 1988.

Gutman, Herbert George. *The Black Family in Slavery and Freedom, 1750-1925.* New York: Vintage Books, 1976.

Ham, Debra Newman, and Beverly Brannan, eds. *The African-American Mosaic: A Library of Congress Resource Guide for the Study of Black History and Culture.* Washington, D.C.: Library of Congress, 1993.

Henritze, Barbara K. *Bibliographic Checklist of African American Newspapers.* Baltimore, Maryland: Genealogical Publishing Co., 1995.

Newspapers and Periodicals by and About Black People. North Carolina Central University. School of Library Science. African-American Materials Project. Boston: G.K. Hall, 1978.

Records of Ante-Bellum Southern Plantations From the Revolution Through the Civil War. Frederic, Maryland: University Publications of America, 1985-.

Rose, James and Alice Eichholz. *Black Genesis.* Detroit: Gale, Research, 1978.

Schubert, Frank N. *On the Trail of the Buffalo Soldier: Biographies of African Americans in the U.S. Army, 1866-1917.* Wilmington, Delaware: Scholarly Resources, 1995.

Streets, David H. *Slave Genealogy: A Research Guide with Case Studies*. Bowie, Maryland: Heritage, 986.

Thackery, David T. *A Bibliography of African American Family History at the Newberry Library*. Chicago: The Newberry Library, 1993.

Thackery, David T., and Dee Woodtor. *Case Studies in Afro-American Genealogy*. Chicago: The Newberry Library, 1989. Troy, New York: Whitston Publishing Co., 1981.

Wadelington, Charles Weldon. *Tips on Collecting and Preserving Black Family History: A Guide for the Beginner*. Raleigh, N.C.: North Carolina Afro-American Genealogical Society, 1986.

Woodtor, Dee Parmer. *Finding a Place Called Home: A Guide to African-American Genealogy and Historical Identity*. New York: Random House, 1999.

Young, Tommie Morton. *Afro-American Genealogy Sourcebook*. New York: Garland Publishing, Inc., 1987.

Hispanic

Byers, Paula K, ed. *Hispanic American Genealogy Sourcebook*. New York: Gale Research, 1995.

Camarillo, Albert. *Latinos in the United States: A Historical Bibliography*. Santa Barbara, California: ABC-Clio, 1986.

Codinach, Guadalupe Jiménez. *The Hispanic World, 1492-1898: A Guide to Photo Reproduced Manuscripts from Spain in the Collections of the United States, Guam and Puerto Rico – El mundo hispánico 1492-1898: guía de copias fotográficas de manuscritos españoles existentes en los Estados Unidos de América, Guam y Puerto Rico*. Washington: Library of Congress, 1994.

Fernandez-Shaw, Carlos. *The Hispanic Presence in the United States from 1492 to Today*. New York: Facts on File, 1987.

Flores, Norma, and Patsy Ludwig. *A Beginner's Guide to Hispanic Genealogy*. San Mateo, California: Western Book/Journal Press, 1993.

Hispanic American Genealogical Sourcebook. New York: Gale Research, 1995.

Platt, Lyman D. *Census Records for Latin America and Hispanic United States*. Baltimore: Genealogical Publishing Co., 1998.

Platt, Lyman D. *Spanish Surname Histories*. Orem, Utah: Automated Archives, 1984.

Ryskamp, George and Peggy Ryskamp. *A Student's Guide to Mexican American Genealogy*. Phoenix, Ariz.: Oryx Press, 1996.

Ryskamp, George R. *Finding Your Hispanic Roots*. Baltimore, Maryland: Genealogical Publishing Co., Inc., 1997.

Ryskamp, George R. *Tracing Your Hispanic Heritage*. Riverside, Calif.: Hispanic Family History Research, 1984.

Jewish Americans

Blau, Joseph Leon. *The Jews of the United States, 1790-1840: A Documentary History*. New York: Columbia University Press, 1963.

Daniels, Judith M. *The Concise Dictionary of American Jewish Biography*. 2 vols. Brooklyn: Carlson Publishing, 1994.

Dimont, Max. *The Jews in America: The Roots, History, and Destiny of American Jews*. New York: Simon and Schuster, 1978.

Diner, Hasia R. *A Time for Gathering: The Second Migration, 1820-1880*. Baltimore: Johns Hopkins University Press, 1992.

Faber, Eli, and Henry L. Feingold, ed. *A Time for Planting: The First Migration, 1654-1820*. Baltimore: Johns Hopkins University Press, 1992.

Goodstein, Nancy. *Jewish Records in the Family History Library Catalog*. 9 vols. [Salt Lake City: Family History Department, Church of Jesus Christ of Latter-day Saints, 2000].

Gorr, Samuel. *Jewish Personal Names: Their Origin, Derivation and Diminutive Forms*. Teaneck, N.J.: Avotaynu, 1992.

Guggenheimer, Heinrich W. *Jewish Family Names and Their Origins: An Etymological Dictionary*. [Hoboken, N.J.]: Ktav, 1992.

Harvey, John Frederick. *Church and Synagogue Libraries*. Metuchen, N.J.: The Scarecrow Press, 1980.

Kohn, Gary J. *The Jewish Experience: A Guide to Manuscript Sources in the Library of Congress*. Cincinnati: American Jewish Archives, 1986.

Kurzweil, Arthur. *The Encyclopedia of Jewish Genealogy*. 3 vols. Northvale, N.J.: Jason Aronson, 1991.

Marcus, Jacob Rader. *United States Jewry, 1776-1985*. 4 vols. Detroit: Wayne State University Press, 1989.

Marx, Alexander. *Studies in Jewish History and Booklore*. New York: Jewish Theological Seminary of America, 1944.

Mason, Philip P. *Directory of Jewish Archival Institutions*. Detroit: Published for the National Foundation for Jewish Culture by Wayne State University Press, 1975.

Rischin, Moses. *Jews of the American West*. Detroit: Wayne State University, 1991.

Rudd, Hynda L. *Mountain West Pioneer Jewry: An Historical and Genealogical Source Book (from origins to 1885)*. Los Angeles: Will Kramer, 1980.

Sachar, Howard M. *A History of the Jews in America*. New York: Alfred A. Knopf, 1994, c1992.

Scharfman, I. Harold. *Jews on the Frontier: An Account of Jewish Pioneers and Settlers on the American Frontier*. Malibu, Calif.: Joseph Simon/Pangloss Press, 1990, 1977.

Schleifer, Jay. *A Student's Guide to Jewish American Genealogy*. Phoenix, Ariz.: Oryx Press, 1996.

Segall, Aryeh. *Guide to Jewish Archives*. Jerusalem; New York: World Council on Jewish Archives, 1981.

Sorin, Gerald. *A Time for Building: The Third Migration, 1880-1920*. Baltimore: Johns Hopkins University, 1992.

Stern, Malcolm H. *First American Jewish Families: 600 genealogies, 1654-1988*. 3rd ed. Baltimore: Ottenheimer, 1991.

Zubatsky, David S., and Irwin M. Berebt. *Jewish Genealogy: A Sourcebook of Family Histories and Genealogies*. Reprint. Teaneck, NJ: Avotaynu, Inc., 1996.

Names

Bardsley, Charles W. *Curiosities of Puritan Nomenclature. 1880. Reprint*. Baltimore: Clearfield Co., 1996.

Baring-Gould, Sabine. *Family Names and Their Story*. Baltimore: Genealogical Publishing Co., 1968.

Bowman, William Dodgson. *The Story of Surnames*. 1932. Reprint. Detroit: Gale Research, 1968.

Hook, J. N. *Family Names: How Our Surnames Came to America*. New York: Macmillan Pub., 1982.

Latham, Edward. *A Dictionary of Names, Nicknames and Surnames of Persons, Places and Things*. Detroit: Gale Research, 1966.

Loughead, Flora Haines Apponyi. *Dictionary of Given Names with Origins and Meanings*. 2nd ed. Glendale, Calif.: Arthur H. Clark, 1974, 1933.

Moody, Sophy. *What is Your Name? A Popular Account of the Meanings and Derivations of Christian Names*. 1863. Reprint. Detroit: Gale Research, 1976.

Payton, Geoffrey. *Webster's Dictionary of Proper Names*. Springfield, Mass.: G. & C. Merriam, 1970.

Room, Adrian. *Brewer's Dictionary of Names*. Oxford: Cassell, 1992.

Rose, Christine. *Nicknames Past and Present*. 3rd ed. rev. and enl. San Jose, California: Rose Family Association, 1998.

Smith, Elsdon C. *American Surnames*. Baltimore: Genealogical Publishing Co., 1986.

Smith, Elsdon C. *New Dictionary of American Family Names*. New York: Harper & Row, 1973.

Smith, Elsdon C. *Personal Names: A Bibliography*. New York: New York Public Library, 1952.

Smith, Elsdon C. *The Story of Our Names*. New York: Harper, 1950.

Stein, Lou. *Clues to Family Names*. 2nd ed. rev. Bowie, Maryland: Heritage Books, 1988.

Surnames in the United States Census of 1790: An Analysis of National Origins of the Population. Baltimore: Genealogical Pub. Co., 1969.

Vallentine, John F. *Locality Finding Aids for United States Surnames*. Logan, Utah: Everton Publishers, 1977.

Native Races

American Indians: A Select Catalog of National Archives Microfilm Publications. Washington, D.C.: National Archives and Records Administrations, 1994.

Barr, Charles B. *Guide to Sources of Indian Genealogy*. Independence, Missouri: C.B. Barr, 1989.

Bataille, Gretchen M., editor. *Native American Women: A Bibliographical Dictionary*, Garland Publishing, New York, 1993.

Byers, Paula K., ed. *Native American Genealogical Sourcebook*. Detroit: Gale Research Inc, 1995.

Carter, Kent. *The Dawes Commission and the Allotment of the Five Civilized Tribes, 1893-1914*. Provo, Utah: Ancestry, 1999.

Champagne, Duane, ed. *The Native North American Almanac*. Detroit, Michigan: Gale Research, 1994.

Cohen, Felix. *Handbook of Federal Indian Law*. Reprint of the 1942 edition. Albuquerque: University of New Mexico Press.

D'Arcey McNickle Center for History of the American Indian. Pasadena, California: Salem Press, 1991.

Danby, James P., ed. *Native American Periodicals and Newspapers, 1828-1982; Bibliography, Publishing Record, and Holdings*. Westport, Connecticut: Greenwood Press, 1984.

Davis, Mary B., editor. *Native America in the Twentieth Century: An Encyclopedia*. New York: Garland Publishing, 1994.

Dewitt, Donald L. *American Indian Resource Materials in the Western History Collection, University of Oklahoma*. Norman: University of Oklahoma Press, 1990.

Dictionary of Indian Tribes of the Americas. 4 vols. Newport Beach California: American Indian Publishers, 1993.

Driver, Harold F. *Indians of North America*. Chicago: University of Chicago Press, 1961.

Duffy, Laurie Beth. *Who's Looking for Whom in Native American Ancestry*. 2 vols. Bowie, Maryland: Heritage Books, Inc., 1997, 1999.

Furtaw, Julia C., ed. *Native Americans Information Directory*. Detroit, Michigan: Gale Research, 1993.

Gannett, Henry A. *A Gazetteer of Indian Territory*. Washington, D.C.: Government Printing Office, 1905.

Gideon, D.C. *Indian Territory – Descriptive, Biographical and Genealogical, Including the Landed Estates, County Seats, With General History of the Territory*. Chicago: The Lewis Publishing Co., 1901.

Hill, Edward E. *Guide to Records in the National Archives of the United States Relating to American Indians*. Washington, D.C.: U.S. Government Printing Office, 1981.

Hill, Edward E. *The Office of Indian Affairs, 1824-1880: Historical Sketches*. New York: Clearwater Publishing Co., 1974.

Hirschfelder, Arlene and Martha Kreipe de Montano. *The Native American Almanac: A Portrait of Native America Today*, New York: Prentice Hall, 1993.

Hirschfelder, Arlene and Paulette Miolin. *The Encyclopedia of Native American Religions: An Introduction. Facts on File*, 1992.

Hoxie, Frederick E., and Harvey Markowitz. *Native Americans: An Annotated Bibliography*. Pasadena, California: Salem Press, 1991.

Indian Reservations: A State and Federal Handbook. Confederation of American Indians. Jefferson, North Carolina: McFarland, 1986.

Kirkham, E. Kay. *Our Native Americans: Their Records of Genealogical Value: Volume I Federal Government Records, Oklahoma Historical Society Records, Genealogical Society of Utah Listings*. Logan, Utah: Everton Publishers, 1980.

Kirkham, E. Kay. *Our Native Americans: Their Records of Genealogical Value. Volume 2*. Logan, Utah: Everton Publishers, 1984.

Leirch, Barbara. *A Concise Dictionary of Indian Tribes in North America*. Algonac, Mich.: Reference Publications, 1979.

Lipps, Oscar Hiram. *Laws and Regulations Relating to Indians and Their Lands*. Lewiston, Idaho: Lewiston Printing and Binding Co., 1913.

McDowell, Janet A. *The Dispossession of the American Indian, 1887-1834*. Bloomington: Indiana University Press, 1991.

Native American Periodicals and Newspapers, 1828-1982: A Bibliography, Publishing Records and Holdings. Westport, Connecticut: Greenwood Press, 1984.

Native American Women: Telling their Lives. Lincoln: University of Nebraska Press, 1984.

Pangburn, Richard. *Indian Blood II: Further Adventures in Finding Your Native American Ancestor.* Louisville, Kentucky: Butler Books, 1996.

Pangburn, Richard. *Indian Blood: Finding Your Native American Ancestor.* Louisville, Kentucky: Butler Books, 1993.

Russell, George L. *American Indian Digest.* Phoenix, Arizona: Thunderbird Enterprises, 1994.

Sturdevant, William C., ed, *Handbook of North American Indians.* Washington, DC.: Smithsonian Institution Press, 1978-.

Swanton, John R. *The Indian Tribes of North America.* Smithsonian Institution Press, Washington, D.C., 1979.

U.S. Department of the Interior Library. *Bibliographic and Historical Index of American Indians and Persons Involved in Indian Affairs.* 8 vols. Boston: G.K. Hall, 1966.

Waldman, Carl. *Atlas of the North American Indian.* Reprint. New York: Facts on File Publications, 1985.

Waldman, Carl. *Encyclopedia of Native American Tribes.* New York: Facts on File Publications, 1988.

Waldman, Carl. *Who Was Who in Native American History.* New York; Facts on File Publications, 1990.

Witcher, Burt Bryan. *A Bibliography of Sources for Native American Family History.* Fort Wayne, Indiana: Allen County Public Library, 1988.

Naturalization and Citizenship

Directory of Courts Having Jurisdiction in Naturalization Proceedings. United States Department of Justice, Immigration and Naturalization Service. (Washington, D.C.: Microfilmed by the Library of Congress Photoduplication Service, 1992).

Kettner, James H. *The Development of American Citizenship, 1608-1870.* Chapel Hill, North Carolina: Published for the Institute of Early American History and Culture by the University of North Carolina Press, 1978.

Neagles, James C. *Locating Your Immigrant Ancestor: A Guide to Naturalization Records.* Logan, Utah: Everton Publishers, 1986.

Newman, John J. *American Naturalization Records, 1790-1990: What They Are and How to Use Them.* Bountiful, Utah: Heritage Quest, 1998.

Schaefer, Christina K. *Guide to Naturalization Records of the United States.* Baltimore: Genealogical Publishing Co., 1997.

Smith, Darrell Hevenor. *The Bureau of Naturalization: Its History, Activities and Organization.* New York: AMS Press, 1974.

Szucs, Loretto Dennis. *They Became Americans: Finding Naturalization Records and Ethnic Origins.* Salt Lake City: Ancestry Inc., 1998.

Udell, Gilman G. *Naturalization Laws.* Washington: Government Print Office, 1968.

Newspapers

Allbaugh, Gaylord P. *History and Annotated Bibliography of American Religious Periodicals and Newspapers Established From 1730 Through 1830.* 2 vols. Worcester, Massachusetts: American Antiquarian Society, 1994.

American Newspaper Directory, (annual). 1869-1908. New York: George P. Rowell and Co.

Brigham, Clarence Saunders. *History and Bibliography of American Newspapers, 1690-1820.* 2 vols. Worcester, Massachusetts: American Antiquarian Society, 1975.

Center for Research Libraries. *The Center for Research Libraries Catalogue: Newspapers.* 2nd ed. Chicago: The Center, 1978.

Gale Directory of Publications: An Annual Guide to Newspapers, Magazines, Journals, and Related Publications; Formerly Ayer Directory of Publications; Published Annually since 1869. Detroit, Michigan: Gale Research, 1987-.

Gregory, Winifred. *American Newspapers, 1821-1936: A Union List of Files Available in the United States and Canada.* New York: H.W. Wilson Co., 1937, reprint 1967.

Guide to Microforms in Print, (annual). 1961- Munich: K.G. Saur. Annual Catalog of microform titles, including newspapers.

Heuvel, Jon Vanden. *Untapped Sources: America's Newspaper Archives and Histories.* New York: Gannett Foundation Media Center, 1991.

Lathem, Edward Connery. *Chronological Tables of American Newspapers, 1690-1820; Being a Tabular Guide to Holdings of Newspapers Published in America Through the Year 1820.* Worsester, Mass.: American Antiquarian Society, 1972.

Library of Congress Catalog Management and Publication Division. *Newspapers in Microform, United States 1948-1972.* Washington, DC: Catalog Publication Division Progressing Department, 1984.

Milner, Anita. *Newspaper Genealogical Column Directory.* Bowie, Maryland: Heritage Books, 1992.

Milner, Anita. *Newspaper Indexes: A Location and Subject Guide for Researchers.* Metuchen, New Jersey: Scarecrow Press, 1979.

Newspapers in Microform: United States, 1948-1983. 2 vols. Washington, D.C.: Library of Congress, 1984.

Parch, Grace D., ed. *Directory of Newspaper Libraries in the United States and Canada.* New York: Project of the Newspaper Division, Special Libraries Assoc., 1976.

Rowell, George Presbury. *Rowell's American Newspaper Directory: Containing a Description of all the Newspapers and Periodicals Published in the United States and Territories, Dominion of Canada and Newfoundland, and of the Towns and Cities in Which They are Published, Together With a Statement or Estimate of the Average Number of Copies....* 40 vols. New York: Geo. P. Rowell & Co., 1869-1908.

Serials and Newspapers in Microform (annual). Ann Arbor, Mich.: University Microfilms International. Annual catalog of microfilmed newspapers for sale.

Swigart, Paul E. *Chronological Index of Newspapers for the Period 1801-1952 in the Collections of the Library of Congress.* 3 vols. plus supplement. (Washington, D.C.: Microfilmed by Library of Congress Photoduplication Service, 199-?).

Union List of Serials in Libraries of the United States and Canada. 3rd ed. 5 vols. New York: H.W. Wilson, 1965.

United States Newspaper Program National Union List. 4th ed. Dublin, Ohio: Online Computer Library Center, 1993. Microfiche.

Wynar, Lubomyr Roman. *Encyclopedic Directory of Ethnic Newspapers and Periodicals in the United States*. Littleton, Colo.: Libraries Unlimited, 1976.

Obituaries

Jarboe, Betty M. *Obituaries: A Guide to Sources*. Boston: G. K. Hall, 1989.

Levy, Felice D. *Obituaries on File*. 2 vols. New York: Facts on File, 1979. (These books are a compilation of the obituaries that have appeared in Facts on File from the beginning of the journal in the late 1940's through 1978).

The New York Times Obituaries Index. New York: The Times, 1970.

Online Sources

Crowe, Elizabeth Powell. *Genealogy Online, 6th Edition*. New York: Osborne/McGraw-Hill, 2002.

Howells, Cyndi. *Cyndi's List: A Comprehensive List of 70,000 Genealogy Sites on the Internet*. Baltimore: Genealogical Publishing Co., Inc., 2001.

Schafer, Christina K. *Instant Information on the Internet: A Genealogist's No-Frills Guide to the 50 States and the District of Columbia*. Revised. Baltimore: Genealogical Publishing Company, 2000.

Periodicals - Genealogy

Everton's Family History Magazine: A Descendant of Everton's Genealogical Helper. 1947-. [Published by Everton Publishers, Inc., Logan, Utah].

Genealogical Computing. 1981-. [Published by Ancestry.com, Salt Lake City, Utah].

Genealogical Journal. 1972-. [Published by the Utah Genealogical Association, Salt Lake City, Utah].

Heritage Quest: The International Genealogy Forum. 1985-. [Published by Heritage Quest, Bountiful, Utah].

National Genealogical Society Quarterly. 1912-. [Published by the National Genealogical Society, Arlington, Virginia].

New England Historical and Genealogical Register. 1847-. [Published by the New England Historic and Genealogical Society, Boston, Massachusetts].

The American Genealogist. 1922-. [Published by Dr. David Greene. Domorest, Georgia].

Sources and Indexes

Bibliography of Genealogical and Local History Periodicals With Union List of Major U.S. Collections. Fort Wayne, Indiana: Allen Count Public Library Foundation, 1990.

Boyer, Carl III. *Donald Jacobus' Index to Genealogical Periodicals*. Newhall, Calif.: Boyer Publications, 1983.

Carson, Dina C. *Directory of Genealogical and Historical Publications in the US and Canada*. Niwot, Colorado: Iron Gate Publishing, 1992.

Genealogical Guide Master Index of Genealogy in the Daughters of the American Revolution Magazine Volumes 1-84 (1892-1950) with Supplement Volumes 85-89 (1950-66) Combined Edition. Compiled by Elizabeth Benton Chapter, NSDAR, Kansas City, Missouri, 1951. Reprint. Baltimore: Genealogical Publishing Co., 1994.

Jacobus, Donald Lines. *Index to Genealogical Periodicals*. Baltimore: Genealogical Publishing Co., 1978.

Periodical Source Index (PERSI). Ft. Wayne, Indiana: Allen County Public Library Foundation, 1987-.

Quigley, Maud. *Index to Family Names in Genealogical Periodicals*. Grand Rapids, Michigan: Western Michigan Genealogical Society, 1981.

Sperry, Kip. *Index to Genealogical Periodical Literature, 1960-1977*. Detroit: Gale Research Co., 1979.

Towle, Laird C. and Catherine M. Mayhew. *Genealogical Periodical Annual Index*. Bowie, Maryland: Heritage Books, annual.

Postal and Shipping Guides

Bowen, Eli. *The United States Post-Office Guide*. New York: Arno Press, 1976.

Bullinger's Postal and Shipping Guide for the United States and Canada, annual. Westwood, New Jersey: Bullinger's Guides, 1871-.

Conkling, Roscoe Platt. *The Butterfield Overland Mail, 1857-1869: Its Organization and Operation Over the Southern Route to 1861, Subsequently Over the Central Route to 1866, and Under Wells, Fargo and Company in 1869*. 3 vols. Glendale, Calif.: Arthur H. Clark Co., 1947.

Hafen, LeRoy R. *The Overland Mail*. Lawrence, Mass.: Quarterman Pub., 1976.

Record of Appointment of Postmasters, October 1789-1832. Washington, D.C.: The National Archives, 1980.

Simmons, Don. *Post Offices in the United States*. Melber, Ky.: Simmons Historical Publications, 1991.

United States Directory of Post Offices. Washington, DC: U.S. Postal Department, Annual.

United States Official Postal Guide. Washington: U.S. Government Printing Office, 1879-.

Webster's Atlas and Zip Code Directory. Springfield, Mass.: G. & C. Merriam, 1981. (Includes maps).

Probate Records

Carter, Fran. *Searching American Probate Records*. Bountiful, Utah: American Genealogical Lending Library, 1993.

Coldham, Peter Wilson. *American Wills & Administrations in the Prerogative Court of Canterbury, 1610-1857*. Baltimore, Maryland: Genealogical Publishing Co., 1989.

Coldham, Peter Wilson. *American Wills Proved in London, 1611-1775*. Baltimore, Maryland: Genealogical Publishing, 1992.

Dobson, David. *Scottish-American Wills, 1650-1900*. Baltimore: Genealogical Publishing, 1991.

Vital Records

Kemp, Thomas Jay. *International Vital Records Handbook*. 4th ed. Baltimore: Genealogical Publishing Co., Inc., 2000.

Stemmons, Jack and Diane Stemmons. *The Vital Records Compendium: Comprising a Directory of Vital Records and Where They May be Located*. Logan, Utah: Everton Publishers, 1979.

Notes

DISTRICT OF COLUMBIA

TERRITORY OF WASHINGTON, DC – ORGANIZED 1790 –
SEAT OF GOVERNMENT 1800

The capital of the United States covers about 70 square miles on the northeast side of the Potomac River, about 38 miles southwest of Baltimore. Maryland ceded parts of Montgomery, including Georgetown, and Prince George's County to the United States for its capital in the late 1780's. Virginia also ceded part of Fairfax County, including Alexandria. These counties continued to govern the area until about 1801. Virginia kept permanent custody of the records from Alexandria.

Congress convened for the first time in Washington in 1800 and Thomas Jefferson's inaugural in March 1801 was its first inauguration. Growth was very slow, increasing from 8,000 in 1800 to only 75,000 in 1860. In 1801, the counties of Washington and Alexandria were established in the District. The city of Washington was incorporated in 1802. The British captured Washington during the War of 1812 and burned most of the public buildings and records. During the Civil War, Washington was again threatened, but survived unscathed. Slavery was abolished in the District of Columbia in 1862.

The land ceded by Virginia for the District was returned to Virginia in 1846. The city's status was changed to that of a federal territory in 1871. Georgetown became part of the city of Washington DC in 1895. Since then, the city of Washington DC has had the same boundaries as the District of Columbia.

Look for vital records in the following locations:

- **Birth and death records:** Registration of birth and death records began in 1874, with general compliance by 1915 for births and 1880 for deaths, although some earlier death records exist. The Department of Human Services, Vital Records Section in Washington, DC is the custodian for these records.
- **Marriage records:** The Superior Court of the District of Columbia, Marriage License Bureau in Washington, DC keeps marriage records. Registration began in 1811.
- **Divorce records:** Divorce proceedings prior to September 1956 are available from the Clerk of the U.S. District in Washington, DC. Divorce docket, 1803-1848, is in the General Branch, Civil Archives Division, National Archives and Record Administration in Maryland. The administration

receives mail at the Washington, DC address noted below.
- **Court records:** The National Archives also has records for the U.S. Circuit Court for the District of Columbia and Washington County Court records. Other records include building permits for the District for 1877-1949, Internal Revenue assessment lists for 1862-1866, and other tax books for Georgetown and the city and county of Washington.
- **Wills:** Clerk of the Probate Court, U.S. Courthouse has original wills from 1801 to the present. The courts in Virginia and Maryland kept probate records prior to 1801.
- **Land records:** Recorder of Deeds in Washington, DC holds all real estate records. Prior to 1895, deeds and wills for Georgetown were registered in Montgomery County, Maryland. Some of the records for Georgetown for 1800-1879 are available from the National Archives, microfilm M605.
- **More records:** The National Society, Daughters of the American Revolution in Washington, DC, maintains a library of more than 40,000 volumes consisting of manuscripts and genealogical records, tombstone inscriptions, etc. The Genealogical Department of the Library of Congress in Washington, DC, and the National Archives are two of the richest sources of genealogical material for Washington DC and the entire United States.

Department of Human Services
Vital Records Section
Room 3007, 4265 "I" Street, N.W
Washington, DC 20001

Recorder of Deeds
Sixth and D Streets, N.W.
Washington, DC 20004

Clerk of the U.S. District
Constitution Ave. and John Marshall Place, N.W.
Washington, DC 20001
General Branch, Civil Archives Division
National Archives and Record Administration
Washington, DC 20409

Register of Wills and Clerk of the Probate Court
U.S. Courthouse
500 Indiana Avenue, N.W.
Washington, DC 20001

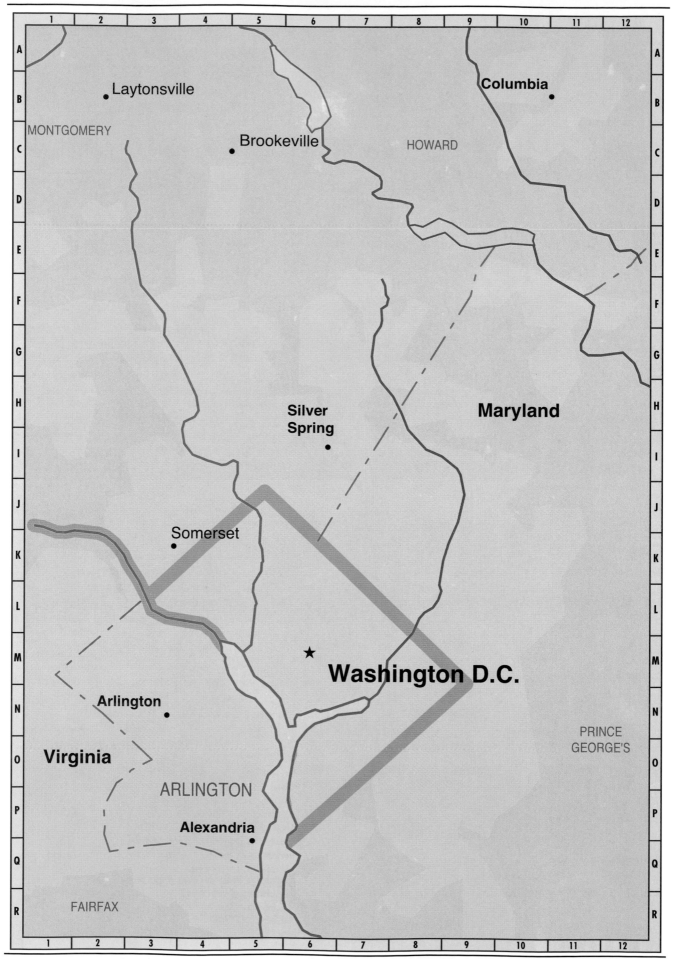

Laytonsville

Columbia

MONTGOMERY

Brookeville

HOWARD

Maryland

Silver
Spring

Somerset

Washington D.C.

★

Arlington

Virginia

PRINCE
GEORGE'S

ARLINGTON

Alexandria

FAIRFAX

Societies and Repositories

Afro-American Historical and Genealogical Society, Inc., National; PO Box 73086; Washington, DC 20056-3086

American Baptist Historical Society; 1106 South Goodman Street; Rochester, New York 14620; 716.473.1740; Fax 716.473.1740

Anderson House Library & Museum; 2118 Massachusetts Ave., N.W.; Washington, DC 20008

Arlington Fort Myers National Cemetery; Arlington, Virginia 22211; 703.697.2131

Association of Professional Genealogists; 3421 N Street NW, Suite 236; Washington, DC 20007-3552

Clerk of the Superior Court; Family Division; 500 Indiana Avenue, N.W.; Washington, DC 20001; 202.879.1418; (Divorce documents filed since 1956)

Clerk of the U.S. District Court; 3rd and Constitution Ave. N.W.; Washington, DC 20001; 202.273.0555; (Divorce proceedings prior to September 1956 are available. Some of the early divorce records are at the National Archives.)

Columbia Historical Society; 1307 New Hampshire Ave., N.W.; Washington, DC 20036; 202.785.2068; Fax 202.887.5785

Congressional Cemetery; 1801 "E" St., S.E.; Washington, DC 20003; 202.543.0539

Department of Human Services; Vital Records Division; 800 9th St. S.W.; Washington, DC 20024; 202.645.5962

District of Columbia Afro-American Historical and Genealogical Society; James Dent Walker-DC; PO Box 34683; Washington, DC 20043

District of Columbia Public Library; Information and Reference; 901 "G" Street, N.W.; Washington, DC 20001-4599; 202.727.1101; Fax 202.707.1129

District of Columbia Society, SAR; 725 15th Street, N.W., Suite 607; Washington, DC 20005; <www.sar.org/dcssar/>

Family History Library; 35 North West Temple Street; Salt Lake City, Utah 84150; 800.346.6044 or 801.240.2584; <www.familysearch.org>; Find a Family History Center near you; <www.familysearch.org/Eng/Library/FHC/frameset_fhc.asp>

Glenwood Cemetery; 2219 Lincoln Rd., N.E.; Washington, D.C. 20002; 202.667.1016; The stones were transcribed by the DAR (FHL book 975.3 V22da).

Historiographer; Archdiocese of Washington; 5001 Eastern Avenue; PO Box 29260; Washington, D.C. 20017; 301.853.4500; Fax 301.853.3246; (Roman Catholic records)

Jewish Special Interest Group; 3701 Connecticut Ave., NW #228; Washington, DC 20008

Knights of Columbus; 1275 Pennsylvania Avenue, NW; Washington, DC 20004-2404

Library of Congress; General Reference and Bibliography Division; 101 Independence Ave. at First St., S.E.; Washington, DC 20504; 202.707.5000; Fax 202.707.5844

Martin Luther King Memorial Library; 901 "G" Street, N.W.; Washington, DC 20001

Maryland State Archives; 350 Rowe Blvd.; Annapolis, MD 21401; 410.974.3914; Fax 410.974.3895

Mount Olivet Cemetery (Roman Catholic); 1300 Bladensburg Road, N.E.; Washington, D.C. 20002; 202.399.3000

Nation's Capitol area Chapter, AHSGR; 2328 19th Street, NW; Washington, DC 20009; 202.232.8827

National Archives; Pennsylvania Avenue at 8th St., N.W.; Washington, DC 20408; 202.501.5415; Fax 301.713.6740

National Society Children of the American Revolution; 1776 D Street NW Room 224; Washington, DC 20006-5392; 202.737.3162

National Society DAR Library; 1776 D Street, N.W.; Washington, DC 20006-5303

National Society Daughters of American Colonists; 2205 Massachusetts Ave. N.W.; Washington, DC 20008-2813;

Prospect Hill Cemetery; 2201 N. Capitol St., N.W.; Washington, D.C. 20002; 202.667.0676

Rock Creek Cemetery; Rock Creek Church Rd. and Webster St. N.W.; Washington, D.C. 20010; 202.829.0585; Fax 202.829.6505; The Daughters of the American Colonists have transcribed the tombstones of this cemetery (FHL book 975.3 V22d; film 874221)

St. Alban's Parish; Massachusetts and Wisconsin Ave. N.W.; Washington DC 20016-5098; 202.363.8286

Superior Court of the District of Columbia; Marriage License Bureau; 500 Indiana Ave. N.W.; Washington, DC 20001; 202.879.4840

The Episcopal Church Historian; Washington National Cathedral; Massachusetts and Wisconsin Ave. N.W.; Washington, D.C. 20016; 202.537.6200; Fax 202.364.6600

The Library of Virginia; 11th Street at Capitol Square; Richmond, Virginia 23219-3491; 804.786.8929; Fax 804.786.5855

The Oak Hill Cemetery Company; 3001 "R" St., N.W.; Washington, D.C. 20007-2923; 202.337.2835

U.S. Courthouse; 500 Indiana Ave., N.W., Rm. 5000; Washington, D.C. 20001; 202.879.1499

U.S. District Court; 3rd and Constitution Ave. N.W.; Washington, D.C. 20001; 202.273.0555

United Methodist Archives Center; Drew University Library; PO Box 127; Madison, New Jersey 07940; 201.408.3189; Fax 201.408.3909

White House Historical Association; 740 Jackson Place, N.W.; Washington, DC 20506

Bibliography and Record Sources

General Sources

Allen, Ethan. *Washington; or, the Revolution: A Drama Founded Upon the Historic Events of the War for American Independence.* Washington, D.C.: National Cash Register, 1975. 5 microfiches.

American Biographical Directories, District of Columbia... 1908-0908. *Washington, D.C.: Potomac Press, 1908.*

A Biographical Congressional Directory, 1774 to 1900: The Continental Congress: September 5, 1774, to October 21, 1788, Inclusive [and] the United States Congress: the First Congress to the Fifty-seventh Congress, March 4, 1789, to March 4, 1903, Inclusive Washington, D.C.: Government Printing Office, 1903.

American Biographical Directories, District of Columbia, 1908-1909. Washington, D.C.: Potomac Press, 1908.

Angevine, Erma Miller. *Research in the District of Columbia.* Arlington, Virginia: National Genealogical Society, 1992.

Benton, Mildred, ed. *Library and Reference Facilities in the Area of the District of Columbia.* 12th ed. American Society for Information Science, 1986.

Cook, Eleanor Mildred Vaughan. *Guide to the records of your District of Columbia ancestors.* Silver Spring, Maryland: Family Line, 1987.

Daily National Intelligencer (Washington, D.C.). – No. 1 (Oct. 31, 1800). Washington: Library of Congress, 1959.

A Directory of Churches and Religious Organizations in the District of Columbia, 1939. Washington, D.C.: District of Columbia Historical Records Survey, 1939.

Georgetown, Maryland (Montgomery County). *Property Tax Records: 1800-20, 1862-79.* Washington, D. C.: Filmed by the National Archives, 1965.

Georgetown, Maryland (Montgomery County). *Records, 1791-1878. Washington, D.C.: The National Archives, 1965.*

Green, Constance McLaughlin. Washington: A History of the Capital, 1800-1950. *Princeton: Princeton University Press, 1964.*

Hall, H. Byron. *Lest We Forget: A Guide to Genealogical Research in the Nation's Capital.* Annandale, Virginia: Annandale Stake, Church of Jesus Christ of Latter-day Saints, 1986.

Howe, Henry. *Historical Collections of Virginia: Containing a Collection of the Most Interesting Facts, Tradition, Biographical Sketches, Anecdotes, etc. Relating to its History and Antiquities, Together with Geographical and Statistical Description, to Which is Appended an Historical and Descriptive Sketch of the District of Columbia.* Charleston, S.C.: Babcock, 1845.

Inventory of Church Archives in the District of Columbia: the Protestant Episcopal Church, Diocese of Washington. 2 vols. Washington, D.C.: Historical Records Survey, 1940.

Kranz, Sharlene. *Capital Collections: Resources for Jewish Genealogical Research in the Washington DC Area.* Bethesada, Maryland: Jewish Genealogical Society of Greater Washington, 1995.

Lewis, David L. *District of Columbia: A Bicentennial History.* New York: Norton, 1976.

Mackall, S. Somervell. *Early Days of Washington.* Washington: Neale Co., 1899.

National Archives and Records Administration. *Guide to Washington National Records Center Services.* Washington: National Archives and Records Administration, [199-?].

Official Register of the United States: Containing a List of Officers and Employees in the Civil, Military, and Naval Service. Washington, D.C.: U.S. Gov't Printing Office, 1863-.

Pippenger, Wesley E. *District of Columbia Ancestors: A Guide to Records of the District of Columbia.* Westminster, Maryland: Family Line, 1997.

Porter, John Addison. *The City of Washington, Its Origin and Administration.* Baltimore: John Hopkins University, 1885.

Proctor, John Clagett. *Washington, Past and Present.* 4 vols. (New York: Lewis Historical Publishing Co., 1930.

Provine, Dorothy S. *District of Columbia Free Negro Registers, 1821-1861.* 2 vols. Bowie, Maryland: Heritage Books, 1996.

Provine, Dorothy S. *District of Columbia Indentures of Apprenticeship, 1801-1893.* Lovettsville, Virginia: Willow Bend and Family Line Publications, 1998.

Provine, Dorothy S. *Preliminary Inventory of the Records of the Government of the District of Columbia. Record Group 351.* Washington, D.C.: National Archives and Records Service, 1976.

Schaefer, Christina K.. *The Center: A Guide to Genealogical Research in the National Capitol Area.* Baltimore: Genealogical Publishing, 1996.

Smith, Chester M. *The Postal History of Maryland, the Delmarva Peninsula and the District of Columbia: The Post Offices and First Postmasters from 1775 to 1984.* Burtonsville, Maryland: The Depot, 1984.

Tindall, William. *Standard History of the City of Washington: From a Study of the Original Sources.* Knoxville, Tennessee: H.W. Crew, 1914.

Truett, Randall Bond. *Washington, D.C.: A Guide to the Nation's Capital.* New York: Hastings House, 1968.

United States. National Archives and Records Service. *Guide to Genealogical Research in the National Archives.* Washington, D.C.: National Archives and Records Service, 1985.

United States. Congress. *Federal Assessment, 1790-1805, Maryland, District of Columbia.* [Baltimore]: Maryland, Hall of Records Commission, 1965.

United States. Congress. *Official Congressional Directory. – 1865- .* Washington: U.S. Gov't Printing Office, [1865?] .

United States. National Archives and Records Service. *Preliminary Inventory of the Records of the Government of the District of Columbia, Record Group 351.* Washington: National Archives and Records Service, 1976.

U.S. Department of State. *Register of Officers and Agents, Civil, Military, and Naval, in the Service of the United States.* Washington, D.C.: Government Printing Office, 1816-. Annual.

Webb, William B. *Centennial History of the City of Washington, D.C.* Dayton, Ohio: United Brethren Publishing House, 1892.

Williamson, Stanley. *Who's Who in the Nation's Capital.* Washington, D.C.: Ransdell, Inc., Biennial.

Atlases, Maps and Gazetteers

Long, John H. *Delaware, Maryland, District of Columbia Atlas of Historical County Boundaries.* New York: Charles Scribner's Sons, Simon & Schuster Macmillan, 1996.

Martin, Joseph. *A New and Comprehensive Gazetteer of Virginia, and the District of Columbia: Containing a Copious Collection of Geographical, Statistical, Political, Commercial, Religious, Moral and Miscellaneous Information, Collected and Compiled from the Most Respectable, and Chiefly from Original Sources.* Charlottesville, Virginia: J. Martin, 1835 (Moseley & Tompkins, printers.)

National Geographic Society (United States). Cartographic Division. *Round About the Nation's Capital with Descriptive Notes.* Washington, D.C.: The Society, 1956.

Truett, Randall Bond. *Washington, D.C.: A Guide to the Nation's Capital.* Original edition 1942. New York: Hastings House, 1968.

United States. Office of Geographic Research. Branch of Geographic Names. *District of Columbia Geographic Names.* [Reston, Va.]: United States. Branch of Geographic Names, 1981. 2 microfiche.

Census Records

Available Census Records and Census Substitutes

Federal Census 1790 (with Maryland), 1800, 1810, 1820 (includes Alexandria County, Virginia), 1830 (includes Alexandria County, Virginia), 1840 (includes Alexandria County, Virginia), 1850, 1860, 1870, 1880, 1890, 1900, 1910, 1920, 1930.

Federal Mortality Schedules 1850, 1860, 1870, 1880.

Union Veterans and Widows 1890.

State/Territorial Census 1867.

Brown, Mary Ross. *An Illustrated Genealogy of the Counties of Maryland and the District of Columbia as a Guide to Locating Records: Including Detailed Maps Showing the Wards of the City of Baltimore in the Federal Censuses of 1850, 1860, 1870 & 1880.* Baltimore: French Bay Printing, 1967.

Dollarhide, William. *The Census Book: A Genealogist's Guide to Federal Census Facts, Schedules and Indexes.* Bountiful, Utah: Heritage Quest, 1999.

Kemp, Thomas Jay. *The American Census Handbook.* Wilmington, Delaware: Scholarly Resources, Inc., 2001.

Szucs, Loretto Dennis, and Matthew Wright. *Finding Answers in U.S. Census Records.* Ancestry Publishing, 2001

Thorndale, William & William Dollarhide. *Map Guide to the U.S. Federal Censuses, 1790-1920.* Baltimore: Genealogical Publishing Co., 1987.

Court Records, Probate and Wills

Abstracts of Wills in the District of Columbia, 1776-1815: Compiled from Records in the Office of the Register of Wills. 2 vols. Washington: [s.n.], 1945-1946.

Bell, Mrs. Alexander H. *Abstracts of Wills in the District of Columbia, 1776-1815,* 2 vols. Washington, D.C.: Bell, 1946.

District of Columbia. Orphans Court. *Indentures of Apprenticeship Recorded in the Orphans Court, Washington County, District of Columbia, 1802-1811.* Washington: National Archives & Records Admin., 2000.

District of Columbia. *Register of Wills. Probate Records- 1801-1930, 1801-1930.* Microfilm of originals at the Office of Public Records, Washington, D.C. (Salt Lake City: Filmed by the Genealogical Society of Utah, 1996-1997). 133 microfilm.

Hynson, Jerry M. *District of Columbia D.C. Department of Corrections Runaway Slave Book, 1848-1863: U.S. District Court for the District of Columbia Fugitive Slave Cases, 1862-1863.* Westminster, Maryland: Willow Bend Books, 1999.

Langille, Letitia A. *Wills, Book IV, Dated 1799 to 1837: As Recorded in the Office of Register of Wills, Municipal Court, Washington, D.C.* Microfilm of typescript ([50], 104 leaves) at the National Library of the D.A.R., Washington, D.C. (Salt Lake City: Filmed by the Genealogical Society of Utah, 1972).

Pippenger, Wesley E. *District of Columbia Probate Records: Will books 1 through 6, 1801-1852 and Estate Files, 1801-1852.* Westminster, Maryland: Family Line, 1996.

Provine Dorothy S. *Index to District of Columbia Wills [1801-1920].* Baltimore: Genealogical Pub. Co., 1992.

United States. Circuit Court (District of Columbia). *Habeas Corpus Case Records: 1820-1863.* Washington, D.C.: National Archives. Central Plains Region, 1963. 2 microfilm.

United States. Circuit Court (District of Columbia). *Minutes of the U.S. Circuit Court for the District of Columbia, 1801-1863.* Washington, D.C.: National Archives. Central Plains Region, 1975. 6 microfilm.

United States. District Court (District of Columbia). *Records of the United States District Court for the District of Columbia Relating to Slaves, 1851-1863.* Washington: Filmed by the National Archives, 1963. 2 microfilm.

Virginia. County Court (Alexandria County). *Will books, 1800-1878; Index to Wills, 1800-1951.* Microfilm of original records at the Alexandria City Courthouse in Alexandria, Virginia and the Arlington County Courthouse in Arlington, Virginia. (Salt Lake City:). The Genealogical Society of Utah, 1951.) 6 microfilm.

Emigration, Immigration, Migration and Naturalization

"Early Circuit Court Naturalizations." *National Genealogical Society Quarterly.* Arlington, Virginia: National Genealogical Society Quarterly, vols. 41-45.

United States. Bureau of Customs. *Copies of Lists of Passengers Arriving At Miscellaneous Ports on the Atlantic and Gulf Coasts and At Ports on the Great Lakes, 1820-1873.* Washington, D.C.: The National Archives, 1964.

United States. District Court (District of Columbia). *Records of the United States District Court for the District of Columbia Relating to Slaves, 1851-1863.* Washington: Filmed by the National Archives, 1963.

Land and Property

District of Columbia. Recorder of Deeds. *Land Records, 1792-1886; General Index to Deeds, 1792-1919.* (Salt Lake City: Filmed by the Genealogical Society of Utah, 1972).

Gahn, Bessie Wilmarth. *Original Patentees of Land at Washington Prior to 1700.* 1936, Reprint Baltimore: Genealogical Publishing Co., 1969.

Georgetown, Maryland (Montgomery County). *Property Tax Records: 1800-20, 1862-79.* Washington, D.C.: Filmed by the National Archives, 1965. 9 microfilm.

Georgetown, Maryland (Montgomery County). *Real Estate Belonging to the District of Columbia: 1860-1869.* Washington, D.C.: Filmed by the National Archives, 1965.

Montgomery County (Virginia). County Clerk. *General Index to Deeds, 1773-1933; Deeds, 1773-1868; Wills, 1773-1797.* Microfilm of original records in the District of Columbia Courthouse (Washington, D.C.). (Salt Lake City: Filmed by the Genealogical Society of Utah, 1953). 694 microfilm.

Pippenger, Wesley E. *District of Columbia Original Land Owners, 1791-1800.* Westminster, Maryland: W.E. Pippenger, 1999.

Prince George County (Virginia). Clerk of County Court. *Deed Books, 1842-1858.* (Salt Lake City: Filmed by the Genealogical Society of Utah, 1948).

Virginia. Corporation Court (Alexandria (Independent City)). *Deed Books, 1783-1865; Index, 1793-1870.* (Salt Lake City: Filmed by the Genealogical Society of Utah, 1951).

Military

Pierce, Alycon Trubey. *Selected Final Pension Payment Vouchers, 1818-1864, District of Columbia.* Leesburg, Virginia: Willow Bend and Family Line Publications, 1998.

Sluby, Paul E., comp. *Civil War Cemeteries of the District of Columbia Metropolitan Area.* Washington, D.C.: Columbian Harmony Society, 1982.

United States. Adjutant General's Office. *Index to Compiled Service Records of Volunteer Union Soldiers Who Served in Organizations from the District of Columbia.* Washington, D.C.: The National Archives, 1964.

United States. Selective Service System. *District of Columbia, World War I Selective Service System Draft Registration Cards, 1917-1918.* National Archives Microfilm Publications, M1509. Washington, D.C.: National Archives, 1987-1988.

United States, Quartermaster's Department. *Roll of Honor, Vol. 1, Names of Soldiers Who Died in Defense of the American Union: Interred in the National Cemeteries at Washington, D.C. from August 3, 1861-June 30, 1865.* Washington: Government Print Office, 1869.

Virginia. Office of the Comptroller. *Confederate Pension Applications, Virginia, acts of 1888, 1900, 1902; index, 1888-1934.* Microreproduction of original records at the Virginia State Library and Archives in Richmond, Virginia. (Salt Lake City: Filmed by the Genealogical Society of Utah, 1988). 219 microfilm.

Wells, Charles J. *Maryland and District of Columbia Volunteers in the Mexican War.* Westminster, Maryland: Family Line Pub., 1991.

Vital and Cemetery Records

Congressional Cemetery Association (Washington, D.C.). *Cemetery Records, 1820-1988.* Microfilm of original records at the Washington Congressional Cemetery Association. (Salt Lake City: Filmed by the Genealogical Society of Utah). 13 microfilm.

District of Columbia. Clerk of the Superior Court. *Marriage Records, 1811-1854, 1870-1921; Index, 1811-1986.* Microfilm of originals at the DC Records Office. (Salt Lake City: Filmed by the Genealogical Society of Utah, 1997). 98 microfilm.

District of Columbia. Clerk of the Superior Court. *Marriage Records, 1907-1950.* Microfilm of originals at the DC Records Center. (Salt Lake City: Filmed by the Genealogical Society of Utah, 1997). 38 microfilm.

District of Columbia. Health Department. *Birth Records, 1874-1897.* Microfilm of originals at the Health Department, Washington, D.C. (Salt Lake City: Filmed by the Genealogical Society of Utah, 1995). 31 microfilm.

District of Columbia. Health Department. *Death Records, 1855-1949.* Microfilm at the Health Department in Washington, D.C. (Salt Lake City: Filmed by the Genealogical Society of Utah, 1995). 180 microfilm.

District of Columbia. Health Department. *Foreign Death Certificates, 1888-1933.* Microfilm of originals at the District Records Center. (Salt Lake City: Filmed by the Genealogical Society of Utah, 1997). 14 microfilm.

District of Columbia. Health Department. *Record of Disinterment, 1912-1940.* Microfilm of originals at the DC Records Center. (Salt Lake City: Filmed by the Genealogical Society of Utah, 1997). 3 microfilm

Leach, Frank William, comp. *Extracts of Some of the Marriages and Deaths Printed in the National Intelligencer, Washington, D.C. Between the Years 1806 – 1858.* (Salt Lake City: Filmed by the Genealogical Society of Utah, 1965).

Martin, George. *Marriage and Death Notices from the National Intelligencer (Washington, D.C.) 1800-1850.* Washington, D.C.: National Genealogical Society Bookstore, 1976. 3 microfilm.

Pippenger, Wesley E. *District of Columbia Marriage Licenses: Registers.* Westminster, Maryland: Family Line, 1994-.

Register of Burials in District of Columbia Cemeteries, 1847-1938. Microreproduction of original records (6 v.) at the D.A.R. Library, Washington, D. C. (Salt Lake City: Filmed by the Genealogical Society of Utah, 1971).

Ridgely, Helen West. *Historic Graves of Maryland and the District of Columbia: With the Inscriptions Appearing on the Tombstones in Most of the Counties of the State and in Washington and Georgetown.* Baltimore: Genealogical Publishing Co., 1967.

Sluby, Paul Edward, Sr. *Blacks in the Marriage Records of the District of Columbia, Dec. 23, 1811 - June 16, 1870.* 2 vols. Washington, D.C.: Columbian Harmony Society, c1988.

Sluby, Paul E., Sr. *Civil War Cemeteries of the District of Columbia Metropolitan Area.* Washington, D.C.: Columbian Harmony Society, [1982].

Sluby, Paul E., Sr. *Selected Small Cemeteries of Washington, DC.* Washington, D.C.: Columbian Harmony Society, 1987.

United States 1691-1850 Marriage Index. Bountiful, Utah: Heritage Quest, 1998.

Walker, Homer A. *Historical Court Records of Washington, District of Columbia.* Washington: [s.n., 19–?].

Washington Hebrew Congregation (Washington, D. C.). *Interment List, 1856-1911.* Microreproduction of original records at the American Jewish Archives, Cincinnati, Ohio. (Salt Lake City: Filmed by the Genealogical Society of Utah, 1977).

Wright, F. Edward. *Marriage Licenses of Washington, D.C., 1811-1830.* Silver Spring, Maryland: Family Line Pub., 1988.

County Website	Map Index	Date Created	Parent County or Territory From Which Organized Address/Details
District of Columbia www.dchomepage.net/dchomepage/ main.htm		1790	District of Columbia; 500 Indiana Ave NW; Washington, DC 20001-2131; Ph.202.879.1010 Details: Capitol City of the United States of America.

Notes

Red Camellias

ALABAMA

CAPITAL: MONTGOMERY - TERRITORY 1817- STATE 1819 (22ND)

The Spanish explorers, Panfilo de Narvaez and Cabeza de Vaca, were among the first non-Indians to pass through this area in 1528. The first settlers were Spanish and French, perhaps arriving as early as 1699. The first community founded was Mobile in 1702, which was settled by the French. France governed the area from 1710 to 1763 when England gained control. Settlers during this period came from South Carolina and Georgia, as well as England, France, and Spain.

To avoid participation in the Revolutionary War, many British sympathizers left Georgia in 1775 to settle in the Alabama area. Planters from Georgia, Virginia, and the Carolinas followed in 1783. That same year, Britain ceded the Mobile area to Spain, leaving the remainder of present-day Alabama to Georgia. In 1795 the Alabama region became part of the Territory of Mississippi.

In the early 1800's, emigrants from the Carolinas and Virginia came to the central and western parts of Alabama, especially in areas along the Tombigbee and Black Warrior Rivers. The Scotch-Irish from Tennessee settled the Tennessee Valley district in northern Alabama in 1809. During the War of 1812, American forces captured Mobile from the Spanish and defeated the Creek Indians. This led to the removal of the Creeks and other Indian tribes and opened the area to settlement. An influx of settlers, many of whom brought slaves with them, resulted in the formation of the Alabama Territory in 1817. Seven counties were formed at that time and St. Stephens became the capital. In November of 1818, the paper city of Cahaba became capital. The physical site of Huntsville was used until Cahaba was built in 1820. Tuscaloosa became the capital in 1826, followed by Montgomery, the present capital, in 1846.

Representatives of Alabama's 22 counties gathered in Huntsville for a convention in 1819. On 14 December 1819, Alabama became the 22nd state.

Alabama seceded from the Union in 1861. About 2,500 men from Alabama served in the Union forces and an estimated 100,000 men served in the Confederate forces. Alabama was readmitted to the Union in 1868.

Look for vital records in the following locations:

- **Birth and death records:** State Department of Health Bureau of Vital Statistics. Records are incomplete prior to 1908.
- **Marriage records:** State Department of Health Bureau of Vital Statistics post 1936. Check individual county and city courthouses for prior marriages generally dating back to the formation of each county.
- **Divorce records:** Supreme Court of the Territory and General Assembly. Most divorce proceedings were filed with local Chancery courts. In 1917, the Chancery courts were merged with the Circuit Court for each county.
- **Naturalizations:** Scattered throughout court minute books, especially county circuit records.
- **Census records:** Alabama Department of Archives and History. Early census records for French settlements near Mobile are available. Incomplete territorial and state census records exist for 1816, 1818, 1820, 1831, 1850, 1855, 1860 and 1880. State census records are available. A special census of Confederate Veterans was taken in 1907, which has been abstracted, indexed, and published.

Alabama Department of Archives and History
624 Washington Avenue
Montgomery, Alabama 36130

The Bureau of Vital Statistics, Department of Health
201 Monroe Street, Suite 1140 D
Montgomery, Alabama 36104
334.206.5418

ALABAMA

Societies and Repositories

Alabama Dept. of Archives & History (AHAH); PO Box 300100; Montgomery, Alabama 36130-0100; 334.242.4363 Ext. 244; <www.archives.state.al.us>

Alabama Division, United Daughters of the Confederacy; 16149 Highway 10; East Pine Apple, Alabama 36768; <www.members.home.net/aladivudc/>

Alabama Genealogical Society, Inc.; AGS Depository & Headquarters; Samford University Library; 800 Lakeshore Dr.; Birmingham, Alabama 35229

Alabama Historical Association (AHA); c/o ADAH; 624 Washington Ave.; Montgomery, Alabama 36130

American College of Heraldry; Drawer CG; University of Alabama; Tuscaloosa, Alabama 35486-2887

Andalusia Public Library; 212 S. Three Notch St.; Andalusia, Alabama 36420

Archdiocese of Mobile Archives; Chancery Office; 400 Government Street; PO Box 1966; Mobile, Alabama 36633; 334.434.1583; Fax 334.434.1588; (Roman Catholic Church Records)

Auburn University Library; Auburn, Alabama 36830

Auburn University; Ralph Brown Draughon Library; Auburn, Alabama 36849-3501; 334.844.1700

Autauga Genealogical Society; PO Box 680668; Prattville, Alabama 36068-0668; <www.rootsweb.com/~alags/>

Baldwin Co. Gen. Soc. Library; PO Box 501; Lillian, Alabama 36549

Baldwin County Genealogical Society; PO Box 108; Foley, Alabama 36536

Barbour County Genealogy & Local Historical Society; c/o Eufaula Carnegie Library; 217 No. Eufaula Ave.; Eufaula, Alabama 36027

Birmingham Genealogical Society, Inc.; PO Box 2432; Birmingham, Alabama 35201;

Birmingham Public Library; 2020 7th Ave. N.; Birmingham, Alabama 35203

Birmingham Public Library; Tutwiler Collection of Southern History and Literature; 2100 Park Place; Birmingham, Alabama 35203; 205.226.3665; Fax 205.226.3743

Black Warrior River Chapter, SAR; 3032 Firethorne Dr.; Tuscaloosa, Alabama 35405; 205.553.1695; <members.aol.com/blkwriver/>

Bullock County Historical Society; PO Box 663; Union Springs, Alabama 36089

Butler Co. Historical Society/Library; 309 Ft. Date St.; Greenville, Alabama 36037

Butler County Historical Society/Library; 309 Ft. Dale St.; Greenville, Alabama 36037

Center for Health Statistics Record Services; State Department of Public Health; RSA Tower; 201 Monroe St. Suite 1150; Montgomery, Alabama 36104; 334.206.5418; Fax 334.262.9563; Mailing Address; PO Box 5625; Montgomery, Alabama 36103

Central Alabama Genealogical Society; PO Box 125; Selma, Alabama 36701

Charles Andrew Rush Library, Birmingham-Southern College; 900 Arkadelphia; Birmingham, Alabama 35254; 205.226.4740; Fax 205.226.4743; (Methodist Church Records)

Chattahoocee Valley Historical Society; 3419 20th Ave.; Cobb Memorial Archives; Valley, Alabama 36854

Choctaw County Genealogical Society; 691 Hwy 114; Butler, Alabama 36904; <www.rootsweb.com/~alccgs/>

Civil War Descendants Society; PO Box 233; Athens, Alabama 35611

Coosa County Historical Society; PO Box 5; Rockford, Alabama 35136

Cullman Chapter, SAR; 1468 County Road 1559; Cullman, Alabama 35058; 256.796.6859

Cullman Co. Public Library; 200 Clarke St., NE; Cullman, Alabama 35055

Dale County Genealogical and Historical Society; 320 James Street; Ozark, Alabama 36360; 334.774.0888; <web.snowhill.com/~marian/ a.society.genealogical.historical.html>

Dekalb County Genealogical Society, Inc.; PO Box 681087; Fort Payne, Alabama 35968-1612; <pages.about.com/ lanaffloyd/index.html>

Etowah Chapter, SAR; 1001 Padenreich Ave.; Gadsden, Alabama 35903; 256.546.8067

Evergreen - Conecuh Public Library; 201 Park St.; Evergreen, Alabama 36401

Family History Library; 35 North West Temple Street; Salt Lake City, Utah 84150; 800.346.6044 or 801.240.2584; <www.familysearch.org>; Find a Family History Center near you; <www.familysearch.org/Eng/Library/FHC/ frameset_fhc.asp>

Florence - Lauderdale Public Library; 218 N. Wood Ave; Florence, Alabama 35603

Genealogical Society of East Alabama, Inc.; PO Box 2992; Opelika, Alabama 36803

Genealogy Society of Washington County; PO Box 399; Chatom, Alabama 36518; <members.aol.com/ JORDANJM2/WCGS.html>

General Richard Montgomery Chapter, SAR; 3813 Marie Cook Drive; Montgomery, Alabama 36109; 334.272.2174

Harwell Goodwin Davis Library, Samford University; 800 Lakeshore Drive; Birmingham, Alabama 35229-0001; 205.870.2749; Fax 205.870.2642; (Baptist Church Records)

Houghton Memorial Library, Huntingdon College; 1500 E. Fairview Avenue; Montgomery, Alabama 36194; 334.833.4421; Fax; 334.263.4465; (Methodist Church Records)

Hueytown Historical Society; 3264 Fieldale Drive; Hueytown, Alabama 35023; 205.497.0689; <www.hueytown.org/ historical/>

Huntsville Public Library; Box 443; 108 Fountain; Huntsville, Alabama 35804

Huntsville Public Library; c/o Heritage Room; 915 Monroe St.; Huntsville, Alabama 35801

Jackson County Historical Association, Inc.; PO Box 1494; Scottsboro, Alabama 35768

Lamar County Genealogical Society; PO Box 357; Vernon, Alabama 35592; ; <www.fayette.net/carruth/ genealogysociety.htm>

Lawrence Co. Historical Commission & Lawrence Co. Archives; 698 Main St., Moulton; Moulton, Alabama 35650; <members.aol.com/carchives>

Leeds Historical Society; 2623 Madison Avenue Apt. 1282; Moody, Alabama 35004; <leedsalabama.com/ historical_society.htm>

Liles Memorial Library; Box 308; 108 E. 10th St.; Anniston, Alabama 36201

Limestone County Historical Society; PO Box 82; Athens, Alabama 35611

Lowndes County Historical & Genealogical Society; HCR 2, Box 350; Minter, Alabama 36761

Marion County Genealogical Society; PO Box 360; Winfield, Alabama 35594

Mary Wallace Cobb Memorial Library; City Hall Bldg.; PO Box 357; Vernon, Alabama 35592

Mobile Genealogical Society, Inc.; PO Box 6224; Mobile, Alabama 36606; <www.siteone.com/clubs/mgs/>

Montgomery County Historical Society; 512 South Court Street; PO Box 1829; Montgomery, Alabama 36102; <www.mindspring.com/~mchs/#menu>

Montgomery Genealogical Society, Inc.; PO Box 230194; Montgomery, Alabama 36123-0194; <www.rootsweb.com/ ~almgs/>

Natchez Trace Genealogical Society; PO Box 420; Florence, Alabama 35631

National Archives—Southeast Region; 1557 St. Joseph Avenue; East Point, Georgia 30344; 404.763.7477; Fax 404.763.7033

North Central Alabama Genealogical Society; PO Box 13; Cullman, Alabama 35056-0013; <home.hiwaay.net/ ~lthurman/society.htm>

Northeast Alabama Genealogical Society; PO Box 674; Gadsden, Alabama 35902

Ozark-Dale Co. Public Library; Jocelyn Rayford; 320 James St.; Ozark, Alabama 36360; Fax 334.774.9156

Pea River Historical and Genealogical Society; 109 Main Street; Enterprise, Alabama 36330; <www.angelfire.com/al2/ peariverhistgensoc/index.html>

Piedmont Historical and Genealogical Society; PO Box 47; Spring Garden, Alabama 36275

Pike County Historical & Genealogical Society; c/o Mrs. Clara Miller; 6754 Elba Hwy.; Troy, Alabama 36079; <www.intersurf.com/~johnjanr/hsp.htm>

Presbyterian Historical Society; 425 Lombard Street; Philadelphia, Pennsylvania 19147; 215.627.1852; 215.627.0509; (Presbyterian Church Records)

Richard Henry Lee Chapter, SAR; 869 Cary Drive; Auburn, Alabama 36830; 334.887.9661

Samford University Library/Alabama Genealogical; Society Depository and Headquarters; PO Box 2296; 800 Lakeshore Drive; Birmingham, Alabama 35229; 205.870.2749

Samford University Library; 800 Lake Shore Dr.; Birmingham, Alabama 35229

Shelby County Historical Society, Inc.; 1854 Old Courthouse; PO Box 457; Columbiana, Alabama 35051-0457; <www.rootsweb.com/~alshelby/schs.html>

Society of the Desc. of Washington's Army at Valley Forge, Alabama Brigade; 7905 Ensley Dr., SW; Huntsville, Alabama 35802-2959

Sons of the American Revolution, Alabama Society; 507 Bonnet Hill Circle; Mobile, Alabama 36609

Southeast Alabama Genealogical Society (SEAGS); PO Box 246; Dothan, Alabama 36302

Southern Society of Genealogists, Inc.; PO Box 295; Centre, Alabama 35960

St. Clair Historical Society; PO Box 125; Odenville, Alabama 35120

Steward University System Library, RFD 5; Box 109; Piedmont, Alabama 36272

Tennessee Valley Chapter, SAR; 5460 Chickasaw Drive; Guntersville, Alabama 35976-2802; 256.582.0313

Tennessee Valley Genealogical Society; PO Box 1568; Huntsville, Alabama 35807; <hiwaay.net/~white/TVGS/ sitemap.html>

Tennessee Valley Historical Society; PO Box 149; Sheffield, Alabama 35660-0149; <home.hiwaay.net/~krjohn/>

Tuscaloosa Genealogical Society, Morning Group; 2020 Third Court E, Tuscaloosa, Alabama 35401

University of Alabama; William Stanley Hoole Library; Drawer "S"; University, Alabama 35487-2909; 205.348.0500; Fax 205.348.1699

Walker County Genealogical Society; PO Box 3408; Jasper, Alabama 35502

Wallace State Community College Library; Fam. & Regional Hist. Program; Wallace State Community College, Hanceville, Alabama 35077

Washington County Historical Society; PO Box 456; Chatom, Alabama 36518

Wilcox Historical Society; PO Box 464; Camden, Alabama 36726; <www.wilcoxwebworks.com/history/>

Winston County Genealogical Society; PO Box 112; Double Springs, Alabama 35553;

Wiregrass Chapter, SAR; 200 E. Silver Oak Dr.; Enterprise, Alabama 36330; 334. 347.0661

Bibliography and Record Sources

General Sources

Abernathy, Thomas Perkins. *The Formative Period in Alabama, 1815-1828*. Tuscaloosa, Alabama; University of Alabama Press, 1990.

Alabama Genealogical Records; Alabama Genealogical Records Commission, DAR, 1964-65. Reprint. Microfilm. Salt Lake City; Genealogical Society of Utah, 1970.

Alabama Research Outline. Series US-States, No. 1. Salt Lake City; Family History Library, 1988.

Austin, Jeannette H. *Alabama Bible Records*. Riverdale, Georgia; Jeanette Austin, 1987.

Barefield, Marilyn Davis. *Researching in Alabama; A Genealogical Guide*. Easley, South Carolina; Southern Historical Press, 1987.

Brewer, W. *Alabama; Her History, Resources, War Record, and Public Men from 1540 to 1872*. (1872) Reprint 1995. Baltimore; Clearfield Co., 2001.

Daughters of the American Revolution (Alabama). *Some Early Alabama Churches, Established Before 1870*. Salt Lake City; Filmed by the Genealogical Society of Utah, 1978.

DuBose, Joel C. *Notable Men of Alabama; Personal & Genealogical*. 1904. Reprint on Microfiche. Spartanburg, South Carolina; The Reprint Co., 1976.

Elliott, Wendy L. *Research in Alabama. Bountiful*. Utah; American Genealogical Lending Library, 1987.

Foscue, Virginia O. *Place Names in Alabama*. Tuscaloosa, Alabama; University of Alabama Press, 1989.

Gandrud, Pauline M., and Kathleen P. Jones. *Alabama Records*. 244 vols. Easley, SC; Southern Historical Press, 1981.

Newspapers on Microfilm, Samford University Library Birmingham; Samford University Library, 1970.

Oliver, Lloyd F., *Index to Colonel James Edmonds Saunders' Early Settlers of Alabama*. (Tomball, Tex.; Genealogical Publications, 1978).

Owen, Thomas McAdory, *History of Alabama and Dictionary of Alabama Biography*. 4 vols. Chicago; The S.J. Clarke Publishing Co., 1921.

Rogers, William Warren, Robert David Ward, Leah Rawls Atkins, and Wayne Flynt. *Alabama; The History of a Deep South State*. Tuscaloosa, Alabama; University of Alabama Press, 1994.

Southerland, Henry Deleon Jr., and Jerry Elijah Brown. *The Federal Road Through Georgia, the Creek Nation, and Alabama, 1806-1836*. 1989. Tuscaloosa, Alabama; University of Alabama Press, 1990.

Strickland, Jean, and Patricia N. Edwards. *Residents of the Mississippi Territory*. 5 vols. Moss Point MS; J. Stickland, 1995.

Stubbs, Elizabeth Saundars Blair. *Early Settlers of Alabama; With "Notes and Genealogies."* Reprint. Baltimore; Clearfield Co., 1991.

Atlases, Maps and Gazetteers

Berney, Saffold. *Hand-book of Alabama . . .* Birmingham; Roberts and Son, 1892.

Dodd, Donald B., and Borden D. Dent. *Historical Atlas of Alabama*. University, Alabama; University of Alabama Press, 1974.

Harris, W. Stuart. *Dead Towns of Alabama*. University, Ala.; University of Alabama Press, 1977.

Long, John H., ed. *Atlas of Historical County Boundaries Alabama*. New York; Simon & Schuster, 1996.

Mason, Sara Elizabeth. *A List of Nineteenth Century Maps of the State Of Alabama*. Birmington, Alabama. Birmington Public Library, 1973.

Yesterday's Faces of Alabama; A Collection of Maps, 1822-1909. Montgomery, Alabama; Society of Pioneers of Montgomery, 1978.

Census Records

Available Census Records and Census Substitutes

Federal Census 1830, 1840, 1850, 1860, 1870, 1880, 1900, 1910, 1920, 1930.

State/Territorial Census 1816, 1818, 1820, 1831, 1850, 1855, 1866, 1880.

Early Alabama Settlers 1816.

Confederate Veterans 1907, 1921, 1927.

Federal Mortality Schedules 1850, 1860, 1870, 1880.

Alabama 1907 Census of Confederate Soldiers. Cullman, AL; Gregath Publishing Co., 1982-83.

Dollarhide, William. *The Census Book; A Genealogist's Guide to Federal Census Facts, Schedules and Indexes*. Bountiful, Utah; Heritage Quest, 1999.

Kemp, Thomas Jay. *The American Census Handbook*. Wilmington, Delaware; Scholarly Resources, Inc., 2001.

Lainhart, Ann S. *State Census Records*. Baltimore; Genealogical Publishing Co., Inc., 1992.

McMillan, James B. and William A. Read. *Indian Place Names in Alabama*. Revised ed. Tuscaloosa, Alabama; University of Alabama Press, 1984.

Owen, Marie Bankhead. *Alabama Census Returns, 1820, and an Abstract of Federal Census of Alabama, 1830*. Reprinted from the Alabama Historical Quarterly (1944) Vol. 6, No. 3. Baltimore; Genealogical Pub. Co., 1996.

Szucs, Loretto Dennis, and Matthew Wright. *Finding Answers in U.S. Census Records*. Ancestry Publishing, 2001.

Thorndale, William, and William Dollarhide. *Map Guide to the U.S. Federal Censuses, 1790-1920*. Baltimore: Genealogical Publishing Co., 1987.

Court Records, Probate and Wills

Alabama Society, Daughters of the American Revolution. *Index to Alabama Wills 1808-1870*. Reprint. Baltimore; Genealogical Publishing Co., 1977.

Emigration, Immigration, Migration and Naturalization

Connick, Lucille Mallon. *Lists of Ships' Passengers, Mobile, Alabama*. 2 vols. Mobile, AL; Lucille Connick, 1988-89.

Mitchell, Mrs. Lois Dumas. *Mobile Ship News*. (Manuscript) Mobile, AL, 1964.

United States. Bureau of Customs. *A Supplemental Index to Passenger Lists of Vessels Arriving At Atlantic & Gulf Coast Ports (Excluding New York) 1820-1874*. Washington, D.C.; Filmed by the National Archives Record Services, 1960.

United States. Bureau of Customs. *Copies of Lists of Passengers Arriving At Miscellaneous Ports on the Atlantic and Gulf Coasts and At Ports on the Great Lakes, 1820-1873*. Washington, D.C.; The National Archives, 1964.

United States. Circuit Court (Alabama, Northern District). *Declarations of Intention, Huntsville, 1875-1894*. Microfilm of originals in the National Archives Center in East Point, Georgia. (Salt Lake City ; Filmed by the Genealogical Society of Utah, 1989). Microfilm, 1 roll.

United States. Immigration and Naturalization Service. *Index* to Passenger Lists of Vessels Arriving At Miscellaneous Ports in Alabama, Florida, Georgia, and South Carolina, 1890-1924. [Washington, D.C.]; Microphotographed by Immigration and Naturalization Service, 1957.

Land and Property

Ainsworth, Fern. *Private Land Claims; Alabama, Arkansas, Florida*. Natchitoches, Louisiana; Fern Ainsworth, 1978.

Barefield, Marilyn Davis Hahn. *Old Cahaba Land Office Records and Military Warrants, 1817-1853*. Birmingham, Alabama; Southern University Press, 1986.

Cowart, Margaret Matthews. *Old Land Records of [county], Alabama*. Huntsville, Alabama; Margaret Matthews Cowart, 1980-86

De Ville, Winston. *English Land Grants in West Florida; A Register for the States of Alabama, Mississippi, and Parts of Florida and Louisiana, 1766-1776*. Ville Platte, LA; Winston De Ville, 1986.

Douthat, James L. Robert. *Armstrong's survey book of Cherokee lands ; lands granted from the treaty of 27 February 1819*. Signal Mountain, Tennessee; Institute of Historic Research, 1993.

Old Huntsville Land Office Records and Military Warrants, 1810-1854. Easley, SC; Southern Historical Press, 1985.

Old Sparta and Elba Land Office Records and Military Warrants, 1822-1860. Easley, SC; Southern Historical Press, 1983.

Old St. Stephen's Land Office Records and American State Papers, Public Lands. Easley, SC; Southern Historical Press, 1983.

Old Tuscaloosa Land Office Records and Military Warrants, 1821-1855. Easley, SC; Southern Historical Press, 1984.

United States. Bureau of Land Management *Card files*. Washington, D.C.; Bureau of Land Management, [19—]. Microfilm, 160 rolls.

United States. Department of the Interior. Bureau of Land Management. *Alabama Pre-1908 Patents; Homesteads, Cash Entry, Creek Indian Treaty and Choctaw Indian Scrip*. Springfield, Virginia; BLM Eastern States, 1996. CD-ROM.

Military

Alabama, Department of Archives and History. *Alabama State Troops (Militia), 1873-1898*. Microfilm of originals in the Alabama Department of Archives and History in Montgomery, Alabama. (Salt Lake City; Filmed by the Genealogical Society of Utah, 1986). Microfilm, 5 Rolls.

Alabama, Department of Archives and History. *Revolutionary Soldiers in Alabama, Being a List of Names Compiled from Authentic Sources, of Soldiers of the American Revolution, Who Resided in the State of Alabama*. Montgomery, Alabama; Brown Printing Co., 1967.

Barefield, Marilyn Davis Hahn. *Old Cahaba Land Office Records and Military Warrants, 1817-1853*. Birmingham, Alabama; Southern University Press, 1986.

Black, Clifford. *An Index to Alabama Society Sons of the American Revolution, Members and their Ancestors, 1903-1996*. Signal Mountain, Tennessee; Mountain Press, 1996.

Douthat, James. L. *Volunteer Soldiers In the Cherokee War – 1836-1839*. Signal Mountain, Tennessee; Mountain Press, 1995.

Fritot, Jesse R. *Pension Records of Soldiers of the Revolution Who Removed to Florida, with Record of Service*. [S.I.]; AR National Society, Jacksonville Chapter, 1946.

Old Huntsville Land Office Records and Military Warrants, 1810-1854. Easley, South Carolina; Southern Historical Press, 1985.

Old Sparta and Elba Land Office Records and Military Warrants, 1822-1860. Easley, South Carolina; Southern Historical Press, 1983.

Old Tuscaloosa Land Office Records and Military Warrants, 1821-1855. Easley, South Carolina; Southern Historical Press, 1984.

Owen, Thomas M. *Revolutionary Soldiers in Alabama*. Alabama State Archives Bulletin 5, 1911. Reprint. Baltimore;. Clearfield, Colorado, 1991.

Penny, Morris M. and J. Gary Laine, *Law's Alabama Brigade in the War between the Union and the Confederacy*. Shippensburg, Pennsylvania; White Mane Pub., 1996.

Potter, Johnny L.T.N. *First Tennessee & Alabama Independent Vidette Cavalry, 1863-1864, Roster; Companies A, B, C, D, E, F, G, H*. Chattanooga, Tennessee; Mountain Press, 1995.

Sifakis, Stewart. *Compendium of the Confederate Armies; Alabama*. Galveston, Texas; Frontier Press, 1992.

United States. Record and Pension Office. *Compiled Service Records of Volunteer Union Soldiers who Served in Organizations from the State of Alabama*. Washington, D.C.; The National Archives, 1959. Microfilm, 10 rolls.

United States. Selective Service System. *Alabama, World Ward I Selective Service System Draft Registration Cards, 1917-1918*. Washington, D.C. The National Archives, 1987-1988.

Vital and Cemetery Records

Alabama Cemetery Records. Typescript. Salt Lake City; Genealogical Society of Utah, 1942-45.

Alabama. Department of Health (Montgomery, Alabama*). Marriage Certificates, 1936-1992; Index, 1936-1959*. Salt Lake City; Filmed by the Genealogical Society of Utah, 1993. Microfilm, multiple rolls.

Bible and Cemetery Records. Birmingham, Alabama; Birmingham Genealogical Society, 1963.

Dodd, Jordan R., and Norman L. Moyes. *Alabama Marriages, Early to 1825*. Bountiful, Utah; Precision Indexing, 1991.

England, Flora Dainwood. *Alabama Notes*. 4 vols. Reprint. Baltimore; Genealogical Publishing Co., 1977.

Foley, Helen S. *Marriage and Death Notices from Alabama Newspapers and Family Records, 1819-1890*. Easley, SC; Southern Historical Press, 1981.

Gandrud, Pauline Jones. *Marriage, Death and Legal Notices from Early Alabama Newspapers, 1818-1880*. (1981) Reprint. Greenville, South Carolina; Southern Historical Press, 1994.

Marriage, Death, and Legal Notices From Early Alabama Newspapers, 1819-1893. Easley, South Carolina; Southern Historical Press, 1981.

County Website	Map Index	Date Created	Parent County or Territory From Which Organized Address/Details
Autauga www.rootsweb.com/~alautaug/	J7	21 Nov 1818	**Montgomery** Autauga County; 134 North Court St Ste 106; Prattville, AL 36067; Ph. 334.361.3725 Details: (Judge of Pro has pro, land & mil rec; Clk Cir Ct has div & ct rec; Rec Office has m rec from early 1800's; Hlth Dept has b & d rec)
Baine		7 Dec 1866	**Blount, Calhoun, Cherokee, DeKalb, Marshall, St. Clair** Details: (Abolished 3 Dec 1867. Established as Etowah Co 1 Dec 1868)
Baker		30 Dec 1868	**Autauga, Bibb, Perry, Shelby** Details: (see Chilton) Name changed to Chilton 17 Dec 1874
Baldwin www.co.baldwin.al.us/	P4	21 Dec 1809	**Washington, part of Florida** Baldwin County; 1 Court Sq; PO Box 239; Bay Mintte, AL 36507; Ph. 334.937.9561 Details: (Pro Ct has m rec from 1810, pro rec from 1809 & land rec from 1808; Clk Cir Ct has div & ct rec)
Barbour www.rootsweb.com/~albarbou/ barbour.html	L10	18 Dec 1832	**Creek Cession, part of Pike** Barbour County; 1800 Fifth Ave N; PO Box 398; Clayton, AL 36016-0398; Ph. 334.775.8371 Details: (Judge of Probate has m, pro & land rec from 1800's; Clk Cir Ct has div rec from 1860 & ct rec from 1912)
Benton		18 Dec 1832	**Creek Cession of 1832** Details: (see Calhoun) Name changed to Calhoun 29 Jan 1858
Bibb www.dbtech.net/bibbco/	H6	7 Feb 1818	**Monroe, Montgomery** Bibb County; 157 SW Davidson Dr; Centreville, AL 35042; Ph. 205.926.4747 Details: (Formerly Cahawba Co. Name changed to Bibb 2 Dec 1820) (Co Clk has m, pro & land rec from 1818; Clk Cir Ct has div & ct rec)
Blount www.rootsweb.com/~alblount/	E7	6 Feb 1818	**Cherokee Cession, Montgomery** Blount County; 220 2nd Ave E Rm 106; PO Box 45; Oneonta, AL 35121; Ph. 256.625.4160 Details: (Co Archivist has pro rec from 1824, m, land & bur rec from 1820; Clk Cir Ct has div & ct rec)
Bullock www.intersurf.com/~johnjanr/ bullock.html	K9	5 Dec 1866	**Barbour, Macon, Montgomery, Pike** Bullock County; PO Box 71; Union Springs, AL 36089; Ph. 334.738.2250 Details: (Pro Judge has pro & mil rec; Co Comm has div & land rec; Clk Cir Ct has ct rec)
Butler www.rootsweb.com/~albutler/	L7	13 Dec 1819	**Conecuh, Montgomery** Butler County; 700 Court Sq; PO Box 756; Greenville, AL 36037-0756; Ph. 334.382.3512 Details: (Courthouse burned April 1853) (Pro Judge has b & d rec 1894-1919, m, pro & land rec from 1853)
Cahawba		7 Feb 1818	**Monroe, Montgomery** Details: (see Bibb) Name changed to Bibb 4 Dec 1820
Calhoun www.rootsweb.com/~alcalhou/	F9	18 Dec 1832	**Creek Cession of 1832** Calhoun County; 1702 Noble St Ste 103; PO Box 610; Anniston, AL 36201; Ph. 256.236.8231 Details: (Formerly Benton Co. Name changed to Calhoun 29 Jan 1858) (Pro Judge has m rec 1834-1979 & land rec 1865-1979; Reg in Chan has div rec; Clk Cir Ct has ct rec)
Chambers www.rootsweb.com/~alchambe/	I10	18 Dec 1832	**Creek Cession of 1832** Chambers County; 18 Alabama Ave; Lafayette, AL 36862; Ph. 334.864.7181 Details: (Pro Office has m rec from 1833, pro & land rec from 1843; Clk Cir Ct has div & ct rec)
Cherokee www.rootsweb.com/~alcherok/	E10	9 Jan 1836	**Cherokee Cession 1835** Cherokee County; 102 W Main St; Centre, AL 35960; Ph. 256.927.3363 Details: (Rec burned in 1882) (Pro Judge has m, pro, land & mil dis rec from 1882; Clk Cir Ct has div & ct rec)

County Website	Map Index	Date Created	Parent County or Territory From Which Organized Address/Details
Chilton www.chilton.al.us/	I7	30 Dec 1868	**Autauga, Bibb, Perry, Shelby** Chilton County; PO Box 557; Clanton, AL 35045; Ph. 205.755.1555 Details: (Formerly Baker Co. Name changed to Chilton 17 Dec 1874) (Clk Cir Ct has pro & div rec, ct rec from 1868; Pro Judge has m & land rec)
Choctaw www.rootsweb.com/~alchocta/ index.htm	K3	29 Dec 1847	**Sumter, Washington** Choctaw County; 117 S Mulberry Ave; Butler, AL 36904; Ph. 205.459.2155 Details: (Co Clk has m, pro & land rec from 1873; Clk Cir Ct has ct & div rec)
Clarke www.rootsweb.com/~alclarke/ clarke.html	L4	10 Dec 1812	**Washington** Clarke County; 117 Court St; PO Box 548; Grove Hill, AL 36451; Ph. 334.275.3251 Details: (Pro Judge has m & pro rec from 1814 & land rec from 1820; Clk Cir Ct has div & ct rec; Hlth Clinic has b & d rec)
Clay www.geocities.com/sg_russell/clal.htm	G9	7 Dec 1866	**Randolph, Talladega** Clay County; PO Box 187; Ashland, AL 36251; Ph. 256.354.7888 Details: (Pro Ct has land rec from 1861, pro rec from 1865 & m rec from 1872; Co Ct has d rec 1920-1940 & voting reg 1906-1936)
Cleburne www.rootsweb.com/~alclebur/	F10	6 Dec 1866	**Calhoun, Randolph, Talladega** Cleburne County; 120 Vickery St; Heflin, AL 36264; Ph. 256.463.5655 Details: (Pro Judge has b & d rec 1911-1921, m & pro rec from 1867 & land rec from 1884)
Coffee www.rootsweb.com/~alcoffee/	M9	29 Dec 1841	**Dale** Coffee County; 230 Court St; PO Box 402; Elba, AL 36323; Ph. 334.897.2211 Details: (Pro Judge has m rec from 1877 & land rec from early 1800's; Clk Cir Ct has div & ct rec)
Colbert* www.colbertcounty.org/	C4	6 Feb 1867	**Franklin** Colbert County; 201 N Main St; Tuscumbia, AL 35674-2060; Ph. 256.386.8500 Details: (Abolished same year created, re-established 1869) (Pro Judge has m, pro & land rec; Clk Cir Ct has div rec; Co Hlth Dept has b, d & bur rec)
Conecuh* www.rootsweb.com/~alconecu/	M6	13 Feb 1818	**Monroe** Conecuh County; PO Box 347; Evergreen, AL 36401-0347; Ph. 334.578.2095 Details: (Pro Judge has m, pro & land rec)
Coosa www.rootsweb.com/~alcoosa/coosa.html	H8	18 Dec 1832	**Creek Cession of 1832** Coosa County; PO Box 10; Rockford, AL 35136; Ph. 256.377.2420 Details: (Pro Rec Off has a few b & d rec 1920-1945, m, div, pro, land & mil rec from 1834; Cir Ct Off has ct rec from 1834)
Cotaco		6 Feb 1818	**Cherokee Turkeytown Cession** Details: (see Morgan) Name changed to Morgan 14 June 1821
Covington www.rootsweb.com/~alcoving/	N8	7 Dec 1821	**Henry** Covington County; 260 Hillcrest Drive; PO Box 188; Andalusia, AL 36420; Ph. 334.428.2610 Details: (Rec burned 1895) (Pro Judge has m, pro & land rec; Clk Cir Ct has ct & div rec)
Crenshaw www.rootsweb.com/~alcrensh/	L8	24 Nov 1866	**Butler, Coffee, Covington, Lowndes, Pike** Crenshaw County; PO Box 227; Luvern, AL 36049-0227; Ph. 334.335.6568 Details: (Pro Judge has m, pro & land rec from 1866; Clk Cir Ct has div & ct rec)
Cullman* www.co.cullman.al.us/	E6	24 Jan 1877	**Blount, Morgan, Winston** Cullman County; 500 2nd Ave SW; Cullman, AL 35055-4155; Ph. 256.739.3530 Details: (Pro Judge has m, div, pro, ct & land rec from 1877, old newspapers)
Dale www.geocities.com/~rewoodham/ dale/index.html	M10	22 Dec 1824	**Covington, Henry, Pike** Dale County; 1702 Hwy 123 S; PO Box 246; Ozark, AL 36361-0246; Ph. 334.774.6025 Details: (Pro Judge has m & pro rec from 1884 & land rec; Clk Cir Ct has ct & div rec from 1885; Co Hlth Dept has b rec)
Dallas www.prairiebluff.com/algenweb/dallas/	J6	9 Feb 1818	**Montgomery, Creek Cession of 1814** Dallas County; PO Box 987; Selma, AL 36702-0997; Ph. 334.874.2560 Details: (Pro Judge has m rec from 1818, div rec from 1917, pro rec from 1821 and land rec from 1820)

County Website	Map Index	Date Created	Parent County or Territory From Which Organized Address/Details
De Kalb www.tourdekalb.com/	D9	9 Jan 1836	**Cherokee Cession of 1835** De Kalb County; 111 Grand Ave SW; Fort Payne, AL 35967-1863; Ph. 256.845.8500 Details: (Pro Judge has m, div, pro & land rec; Co Hlth Dept has b, d & bur rec; Clk Cir Ct has ct rec)
Elmore www.rootsweb.com/~alelmore/	J8	15 Feb 1866	**Autauga, Coosa, Montgomery, Tallapoosa** Elmore County; 100 Commerce St Rm 207; PO Box 338; Wetumpka, AL 36092-0338; Ph. 334.567.1159 Details: (Pro Judge has m & land rec from 1867, b & d rec 1909-1913, pro rec from 1866 & mil dis rec from 1919)
Escambia www.rootsweb.com/~alescamb/	N6	10 Dec 1868	**Baldwin, Conecuh** Escambia County; PO Box 848; Brewton, AL 36427-0848; Ph. 334.867.0208 Details: (Co Clk has m rec from 1897, pro & land rec from 1869)
Etowah www.etowahcounty.org/	E9	7 Dec 1866	**Blount, Calhoun, Cherokee, DeKalb, Marshall, St. Clair** Etowah County; 800 Forrest Ave; Gadsden, AL 35901-3641; Ph. 256.549.5300 Details: (Formerly Baine County, abolished 3 Dec 1867. Re-established as Etowah Co 1 Dec 1868) (Pro Judge has m, div, pro & land rec from 1867)
Fayette www.rootsweb.com/~alfayett/	F4	20 Dec 1824	**Marion, Pickens, Tuscaloosa** Fayette County; 103 1st Ave NW; PO Box 819; Fayette, AL 35555-0819; Ph. 205.932.4510 Details: (Pro Judge has b rec 1884-1941, d rec 1899-1941, m rec from 1866, pro rec from 1844, land rec from 1848 & mil dis rec from 1919)
Franklin www.franklinalabama.com/	D4	6 Feb 1818	**Cherokee & Chickasaw Cession of 1816** Franklin County; 410 N Jackson St; PO Box 1028; Russellville, AL 35653; Ph. 256.332.8850 Details: (Rec burned 1890) (Pro Judge has m, pro & land rec from 1890; Clk Cir Ct has ct rec from 1923 & div rec)
Geneva www.alaweb.com/~gcounty/	N9	26 Dec 1868	**Dale, Henry, Coffee** Geneva County; PO Box 430; Geneva, AL 36340-0430; Ph. 334.684.5610 Details: (Pro Judge has m rec from 1898, b rec 1909-1918, d rec 1909-1941, pro rec from 1883, land rec from1898 & mil dis rec from 1930)
Greene* home.earthlink.net/~rodbush/ GreeneHP.htm	I4	13 Dec 1819	**Marengo, Tuscaloosa** Greene County; PO Box 656; Eutaw, AL 35462-0656; Ph. 205.372.3349 Details: (Pro Judge has m rec from 1823, pro rec from 1821, land rec from 1820 & mil dis rec)
Hale* www.halecoal.org/	I5	30 Jan 1867	**Greene, Marengo, Perry, Tuscaloosa** Hale County; 1001 Main St; PO Box 396; Greensboro, AL 36744-1510; Ph. 334.624.4257 Details: (Pro Judge has m, div, pro, ct & land rec from 1868)
Hancock		12 Feb 1850	**Walker** Details: (see Winston) Name changed to Winston 22 Jan 1858
Henry www.rootsweb.com/~alhenry/	M11	13 Dec 1819	**Conecuh** Henry County; 101 Court Sq Ste A; Abbeville, AL 36310-2135; Ph. 334.585.3257 Details: (Pro Judge has m rec from 1821, land rec from 1824, b rec 1895-1922, d rec 1895-1906 & pro rec from 1839)
Houston www.houstoncounty.org/	N11	9 Feb 1903	**Dale, Geneva, Henry** Houston County; PO Box 6406; Dothan, AL 36302-6406; Ph. 334.677.4741 Details: (Hlth Dept has b, d & bur rec; Pro Off has m, pro & land rec from 1903; Clk Cir Ct has ct rec from 1903; Reg in Chan has div rec from 1903)
Jackson fly.hiwaay.net/~prm/jcalgenweb.html	C9	13 Dec 1819	**Cherokee Cession of 1816** Jackson County; 102 E Laurel St, Ste 47; PO Box 397; Scottsboro, AL 35768-0397; Ph. 256.574.9280 Details: (Pro Judge has m rec from 1851, pro rec from 1850, land rec from 1835 & 1900 Civil War Vets list; Clk Cir Ct has ct rec from 1920 & div rec from 1895; Co Hlth Dept has b & d rec; Pub Lib has cem rec)

County Website	Map Index	Date Created	Parent County or Territory From Which Organized Address/Details
Jefferson www.jeffcointouch.com/ieindex.asp	F7	13 Dec 1819	**Blount** Jefferson County; 716 Richard Arrington, Jr Blvd N; Birmingham, AL 35203; Ph. 205.325.5300 Details: (Pro Judge has m rec from 1818, pro rec from 1870 & land rec from 1820)
Jones		4 Feb 1867	**Marion, Fayette** Details: (see Lamar) Abolished 13 Nov 1867. Re-established as Sanford Co 8 Oct 1868. Name changed to Lamar 8 Feb 1877
Lamar www.lamar.net/	F3	4 Feb 1867	**Marion, Fayette** Lamar County; PO Box 338; Vernon, AL 35592; Ph. 205.695.7333 Details: (Formerly Jones Co. Abolished 13 Nov 1867 and re-established as Sanford Co 8 Oct 1868. Name changed to Lamar 8 Feb 1877) (Pro Off has m rec 1867-1997, pro and land rec; Cir Clk Off has div and ct rec)
Lauderdale* www.rootsweb.com/~allauder/index.htm	B4	6 Feb 1818	**Cherokee, Chickasaw & Choctaw Cession in 1816** Lauderdale County; PO Box 1059; Florence, AL 35631-1059; Ph. 256.760.5750 Details: (Pro Judge has m & pro rec)
Lawrence www.rootsweb.com/~allawren/	D5	6 Feb 1818	**Cherokee, Chickasaw & Choctaw Cession in 1816** Lawrence County; 750 Main St; Moulton, AL 35650-1553; Ph. 256.974.0663 Details: (Pro Judge has m, div, pro & land rec from 1810; Clk Cir Ct has ct rec)
Lee www.rootsweb.com/~allee/	J10	5 Dec 1866	**Chambers, Macon, Russell, Tallapoosa** Lee County; 215 S 9th St; PO Box 666; Opelika, AL 36801-4919; Ph. 334.745.9767 Details: (Pro Judge has m & land rec from 1867, mil dis rec from 1919 & pro rec from 1861)
Limestone www.co.limestone.al.us/	B6	6 Feb 1818	**Cherokee & Chickasaw Cession in 1816** Limestone County; 310 W Washington St; Athens, AL 35611-2597; Ph. 256.233.6400 Details: (Co Arch has b & d rec 1881-1913, m rec 1832-1900, div rec 1896-1947, pro, land & ct rec 1818-1900, tax rec 1861-1900, newspapers 1868-1985; Pro Judge has m, pro & land rec after 1900; Clk Cir Ct has ct rec after 1900 & div rec after 1947)
Lowndes* www.rootsweb.com/~allownde/	K7	20 Jan 1830	**Butler, Dallas, Montgomery** Lowndes County; PO Box 65; Hayneville, AL 36040-0065; Ph. 334.548.2331 Details: (Judge of Pro has m & land rec from 1830, b & d rec from 1879, pro rec from 1870 & mil dis rec from 1919)
Macon www.intersurf.com/~johnjanr/ macon.html	J10	18 Dec 1832	**Creek Cession of 1832** Macon County; 101 E Northside St; Tuskegee, AL 36083-1757; Ph. 334.727.5120 Details: (Pro Judge has m, pro & land rec from 1835; Clk Cir Ct has ct rec from 1868)
Madison* www.co.madison.al.us/	C7	13 Dec 1808	**Cherokee & Chickasaw Cession 1806-7** Madison County; 100 North Side Sq; Huntsville, AL 35801-4820; Ph. 256.532.3327 Details: (Pro Judge has m, pro & land rec from 1809; Clk Cir Ct has div & ct rec; Co Hlth Dept has d & bur rec)
Marengo* www.rootsweb.com/~almareng/	K4	6 Feb 1818	**Choctaw Cession of 1816** Marengo County; 101 E Coats Ave; PO Box 480715; Linden, AL 36748-1546; Ph. 334.295.2200 Details: (Pro Judge has m, pro & land rec; Reg in Chan has div rec; Clk Cir Ct has ct rec)
Marion www.rootsweb.com/~almarion/ marion1.htm	E4	13 Feb 1818	**Tuscaloosa** Marion County; PO Box 460; Hamilton, AL 35570-1595; Ph. 205.921.3172 Details: (Rec burned 1883) (Pro Judge has b & d rec 1909-1919, m rec from 1887, pro rec from 1885, land rec from 1887 & mil dis rec from 1920)
Marshall www.marshallco.org/www/	D8	9 Jan 1836	**Blount, Cherokee Cession 1835, Jackson** Marshall County; 424 Blount Ave; Guntersville, AL 35976-0000; Ph. 256.571.7701 Details: (Pro Judge has m, pro & land rec from 1836 & b & d rec from 1920)
Mobile www.mobilecounty.org/	O3	1 Aug 1812	**West Florida** Mobile County; 109 Government St; Mobile, AL 36602-3108; Ph. 334.690.8700 Details: (Pro Judge has m rec from 1813, pro rec from 1812 & land rec from 1813)

County Website	Map Index	Date Created	Parent County or Territory From Which Organized Address/Details
Monroe www.rootsweb.com/~almonroe/	**M5**	**29 Jun 1815**	**Creek Cession 1814, Washington** Monroe County; County Courthouse; PO Box 8; Monroeville, AL 36461; Ph. 334.743.4107 Details: (Courthouse fire destroyed all rec prior to 1833) (Pro Judge has m, pro & land rec from 1832; 1816 cen of Monroe Co pub by Monroe Journal, Monroeville, AL)
Montgomery www.mc-ala.org/	**K8**	**6 Dec 1816**	**Monroe** Montgomery County; PO Box 1667; Montgomery, AL 36102; Ph. 334.832.1210 Details: (Pro Judge has m rec from 1928, pro rec from 1817 & land rec from 1819; AL Dept of Arch & Hist has m rec 1817-1928; Clk of Board of Revenue has div rec from 1852 & ct rec from 1917)
Morgan www.co.morgan.al.us/	**D7**	**6 Feb 1818**	**Cherokee Turkeytown Cession** Morgan County; 302 Lee St NE; Decatur, AL 35601-1999; Ph. 256.351.4737 Details: (Formerly Cotaco Co. Name changed to Morgan 14 June 1821) (Pro Judge has m & pro rec from 1818)
Perry www.rootsweb.com/~alperry/index.htm	**I6**	**13 Dec 1819**	**Montgomery, Creek Cession of 1814** Perry County; PO Box 478; Marion, AL 36756; Ph. 334.683.2200 Details: (Co Clk has m, pro & land rec)
Pickens www.rootsweb.com/~alpicken/ pcpage.htm	**G3**	**19 Dec 1820**	**Tuscaloosa** Pickens County; PO Box 460; Carrollton, AL 35447; Ph. 205.367.2020 Details: (Pro Judge has m, pro & land rec from 1876; Clk Cir Ct has div & ct rec)
Pike www.intersurf.com/~johnjanr/pike.html	**L9**	**17 Dec 1821**	**Henry, Montgomery** Pike County; 120 W Church St; PO Box 1147; Troy, AL 36081; Ph. 334.566.6374 Details: (Pro Judge has m, pro & land rec from 1830, b rec 1881-1904, d rec 1881-1891 & 1902-1905)
Randolph www.rootsweb.com/~alrandol/	**G10**	**18 Dec 1832**	**Creek Cession 1832** Randolph County; PO Box 249; Wedowee, AL 36278; Ph. 256.357.4933 Details: (Courthouse burned 1897, rec destroyed) (Pro Judge has b & d rec from 1886, m rec from 1896, land & pro rec from 1897 & mil pensions 1904-1909)
Russell www.rootsweb.com/~alrussel/	**K11**	**18 Dec 1832**	**Creek Cession 1832** Russell County; PO Box 969; Phenix, AL 36868; Ph. 334.298.6426 Details: (Co Hlth Dept has b & d rec; Clk Cir Ct has div & ct rec; Judge of Pro has m, pro & land rec from 1833)
Sanford		**8 Oct 1868**	**Jones** Details: (see Lamar) Formed from abolished Jones Co. Name changed to Lamar 8 Feb 1877
Shelby www.shelbycountyalabama.com/ index.shtm	**G7**	**7 Feb 1818**	**Montgomery** Shelby County; Main St; PO Box 467; Columbiana, AL 35051; Ph. 205.669.3740 Details: (Pro Judge has m, pro & land rec from 1824)
St. Clair www.rootsweb.com/~alstclai/	**F8**	**20 Nov 1818**	**Shelby** St. Clair County; PO Box 397; Ashville, AL 35953-0397; Ph. 256.594.2100 Details: (Pro Judge has m, pro & land rec from 1800; Clk Cir Ct has div & ct rec)
Sumter* www.rootsweb.com/~alsumter/index.htm	**J3**	**18 Dec 1832**	**Choctaw Cession of 1830** Sumter County; Franklin St; PO Box 70; Livingston, AL 35470; Ph. 205.652.2731 Details: (Pro Judge has a few b rec 1888-1918, m & pro rec from 1833, land rec & historical voters maps)
Talladega* www.rootsweb.com/~altallad/	**G8**	**18 Dec 1832**	**Creek Cession of 1832** Talladega County; PO Box 755; Talladega, AL 35161-0755; Ph. 256.362.1357 Details: (Pro Ct has m, pro & land rec from 1833, mil dis rec from 1930; Chan Ct has div rec 1888-1892)
Tallapoosa www.intersurf.com/~johnjanr/ tallapoo.html	**I9**	**18 Dec 1832**	**Creek Cession of 1832** Tallapoosa County; 125 N Broadnax St; Dadeville, AL 36853; Ph. 256.825.4268 Details: (Pro Judge has a few b & d rec 1881-1991, m & pro rec from 1835; Clk Cir Ct has div & ct rec; 90 acres were swapped between Tallapoosa & Coosa Cos in 1963)

County Website	Map Index	Date Created	Parent County or Territory From Which Organized Address/Details
Tuscaloosa www.tuscco.com/	G5	6 Feb 1818	**Cherokee & Choctaw Cession 1816** Tuscaloosa County; 714 Greensboro Ave; Tuscaloosa, AL 35401-1895; Ph. 205.349.3870 Details: (Pro Judge has m & pro rec from 1823)
Walker www.walkercounty.com/	F5	26 Dec 1823	**Marion, Tuscaloosa** Walker County; PO Box 1447; Jasper, AL 35502; Ph. 205.384.3404 Details: (Rec burned 1877) (Pro Judge has m & pro rec)
Washington members.aol.com/JORDANJM2/ washingtn.html	M3	4 June 1800	**Mississippi Terr.** Washington County; PO Box 146; Chatom, AL, AL 36518-0146; Ph. 334.847.2208 Details: (Pro Judge has m rec from 1826, land rec from 1799, mil dis rec from 1919, b & d rec from 1920 & pro rec from 1825)
Wilcox* www.prairiebluff.com/algenweb/wilcox/	K5	13 Dec 1819	**Monroe, Dallas** Wilcox County; 12 Water St; PO Box 488; Camden, AL 36726-0656; Ph. 334.682.9112 Details: (Pro Judge has m, pro & land rec from 1819)
Winston* www.rootsweb.com/~alwinsto/	E5	12 Feb 1850	**Walker** Winston County; PO Box 147; Double Springs, AL 35553; Ph. 205.489.5026 Details: (Formerly Hancock Co. Name changed to Winston 22 Jan 1858) (Pro Judge has m, pro & land rec from 1891; Clk Cir Ct has div & ct rec)

Notes

Notes

ALASKA

CAPITAL: JUNEAU -TERRITORY 1912 -STATE 1959 (49TH)

Russians established Alaska's first permanent non-native settlement at Kodiak Island in 1784. Soon thereafter, British and American traders began to enter the area. Sitka was permanently settled by the Russians in 1804 and served as the center of government until 1906. The southern and eastern boundaries of Alaska were established by treaties with the United States and Britain between 1824 and 1828. Another boundary adjustment was made in 1903 between Alaska and British Columbia.

Alaska remained under Russian control until Russia was defeated in the Crimean War. Following this defeat, Russia sold Alaska to the United States on March 30, 1867. From 1867 to 1884, Alaska was administered first by the War Department, then by the Treasury Department, and then by the Navy Department. American settlement was sparse until the discovery of gold near Juneau in 1880. The first Organic Act, passed by Congress in 1884, provided a governor and federal courts to Alaska, with Sitka as the government's headquarters. State statute provided that persons in use of or occupying land at the beginning of civil government, May 17, 1884, would not be disturbed. The first General Land Office opened in Sitka in 1885, followed by offices in Juneau in 1902 and Nome in 1907. The Klondike strike in 1896 resulted in an influx of settlers. Further discoveries of gold at Nome in 1898 and placer fields at Fairbanks in 1902 continued the rush of settlers.

Look for vital records in the following locations:
- **Birth, death, marriage and divorce records:** The Bureau of Vital Statistics, Department of Health and Social Services in Juneau has birth, delayed birth, marriage, divorce (since 1950), and death records. State registration began in 1913 and was generally complied with by 1945.
- **Naturalizations:** Residents of Alaska in 1867 became citizens of the United States. Naturalization

records for later settlers are filed in the judicial districts. Records for some districts are at the Alaska State Archives. Old territorial records of Fairbanks, Juneau, and Nome have been transferred to the Superior Court. Naturalization records after September 1906 are at the National Archives in Seattle, Washington.
- **Land records:** The jurisdiction of Alaska's land records is either federal or state. Organized boroughs also maintain land records, but receive their information from the state. Judicial Districts were created between 1897 and 1901, covering these areas:
- First Judicial District. Provided a courthouse in Juneau and covered Southeastern Alexander Archipelago and the cities of Ketchikan, Wrangell, Sitka, and Juneau.
- Second Judicial District. Provided a courthouse in Nome and covered the northern area including Nome and Barrow.
- Third Judicial District. Provided a courthouse in Anchorage and covered the southern area including Anchorage, Kodiak and the Aleutian Islands.
- Fourth Judicial District. Provided a courthouse in Fairbanks and covered the central area including Fairbanks, Bethel and Toksook Bay.

Alaska remained a district until the Act of 1912 made Alaska a United States Territory and established the capital at Juneau. Statehood was granted in 1959. Currently, Alaska has 16 Boroughs and 11 geographical Census Areas.
- **Court records:** When researching Alaska's early court records there are three important time periods to remember:
- 1884-1912 – Alaska was a civil and judicial district; Sitka was the seat of government. Three divisions were created at Eagle City, Juneau and St. Michael.

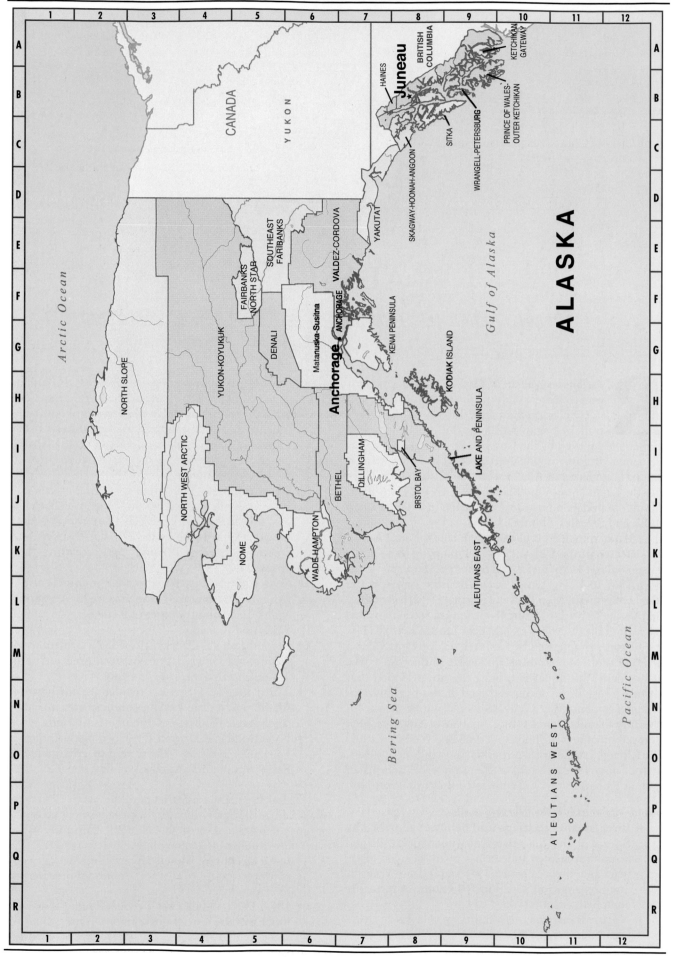

- 1912-1959 – The Federal territorial court system was implemented.
- 1959-Present – The State court system was implemented.

All records for 1884-1959 are located at the Alaska State Archives or the National Archives Pacific Region (Alaska). Some records are in manuscript collections. Generally, records from 1959 to the present are in the office of the Clerk of Court in each judicial district. Older records are periodically transferred to the Alaska State Archives.

Bureau of Vital Statistics
Department of Health and
Social Services
PO Box 110675
350 Main Street, Rm #114
Juneau, Alaska 99811
907.465.3392
Fax 907.465.3618
<www.hss.state.ak.us/dph/bvs/>

National Archives
Seattle Branch
6125 Sand Point Way NE
Seattle, Washington 98115

Alaska State Archives
141 Willoughby Avenue
Juneau, Alaska 99801
907.465.2270; Fax 907.465.2465

National Archives – Alaska Region
Federal Office Building
654 West Third Ave., Room 012
Anchorage, Alaska 99501
907.271.2441

Societies and Repositories

Alaska Division of State Libraries; Pouch G, State Capitol; Juneau, Alaska 99801

Alaska Historical Collections; State Office Building; PO Box 110571; Juneau, Alaska 99811-0571; 907.465.2910; Fax 907.465.2665

Alaska Historical Library and Museum; Juneau, Alaska 99801

Alaska Historical Society; PO Box 100299; Anchorage, Alaska 99510-0299; 907.276.1596; Fax 907.276.1596

Alaska Moravian Church; PO Box 545; Bethel, Alaska 99559

Alaska Society, Sons of the American Revolution; 3310 Checkmate Drive; Anchorage, Alaska 99508-4924; 907.333.4693

Alaska State Archives; 141 Willoughby Avenue; Juneau, Alaska 99801; 907.465.2270; Fax 907.465.2465;

Anchorage District Court, 825 West Fourth Avenue, Anchorage, AK 99501

Alaska Division of State Libraries, Pouch G, State Capitol, Juneau, AK 99801

Anchorage Genealogical Society; PO Box 242294; Anchorage, Alaska 99524-2294

Alaska Historical Society and Museum, Juneau, AK 99801

Anchorage Museum of History and Art; 121 W. 7th Ave.; Anchorage, Alaska 99501; 907.343.4326; Fax 907.343.6149

Anchorage Superior Court, 825 West Fourth Avenue, Anchorage, AK 99501

Archdiocese of Anchorage; 225 Cordova St.; Anchorage, Alaska 99501; 907.258.7898; Fax 907.279.3885

Bureau of Vital Statistics; Department of Health and Social Services; PO Box 110675; Juneau, Alaska 99811; 907.465.3038

Chancery Office; Diocese of Fairbanks; 1316 Peger Road; Fairbanks, Alaska 99701; 907.474.0753; Fax 907.474.8009

Diocese of Juneau; 419 Sixth Street; Juneau, Alaska 99801; 907.586.2227; Fax 907.463.3237; (Roman Catholic records)

Eagle Historical Society; PO Box 23; Eagle City, Alaska 99738; 907.547.2232;

Fairbanks District Court, 604 Barnette St., Fairbanks, AK 99701

Fairbanks Genealogical Society; PO Box 60534; Fairbanks, Alaska 99706-0534; <www.ptialaska.net/~fgs/>

Family History Library: 35 North West Temple Street: Salt Lake City, Utah 84150: 800.346.6044 or 801.240.2584: <www.familysearch.org>: Find a Family History Center near you: <www.familysearch.org/Eng/Library/FHC/frameset_fhc.asp>

Gastineau Genealogical Society; 3270 Nowell Ave.; Juneau, Alaska 99801

Genealogical Society of Southeastern Alaska; PO Box 6313; Ketchikan, Alaska 99901

Juneau District Court, PO Box 114100, Juneau, AK 99811

Kenai Totem Tracers; c/o Kenai Community Library; 63 Main St. Loop; Kenai, Alaska 99611

National Archives; Federal Office Bldg.; 654 W. 3rd Ave., Rm. 012; Anchorage, Alaska 99501

National Archives—Alaska Region; Federal Office Building; 654 West Third Ave.; Room 012; Anchorage, Alaska 99501; 907.271.2441

Nome District Court, PO Box 1110, Nome, AK 99762

Palmer Historical Society; PO Box 1925; Palmer, Alaska 99645

Presbyterian Historical Society; 425 Lombard Street; Philadelphia, PA 19147-1516; 215.627.1852; Fax 215.627.0509

Russian Orthodox; St. Herman's Theological Seminary; 414 Mission Rd.; Kodiak, Alaska 99615; 907.486.3524; Fax 907.486.5935

Sisters of Providence Archives; 4800 37th Avenue S.W.; Seattle, Washington 98126; 206.937.4600; Fax 206.938.6193; (Hospital records)

Sitka National Cemetery; Superintendent; PO Box 152; Sitka, Alaska 99835

Sons of the American Revolution, Alaska Society; 1925 N. Salem Dr.; Anchorage, Alaska 99504

University of Alaska, Fairbanks; Elmer E. Rasmuson Library; 310 Tanana Drive; PO Box 756800; Fairbanks, Alaska 99775-6800; 907.474.7224; Fax 907.474.6841

Wrangell Genealogical Society; PO Box 928EP; Wrangell, Alaska 99929

Bibliography and Record Sources

General Sources

Alaska Oral History Index. Fairbanks: University of Alaska Fairbanks, 1984.

The Alaska-Yukon Gold Book: A Roster of the Progressive Men and Women Who Were the Argonauts of the Klondike Gold Stampede. Seattle: Sourdough Stampede Association, 1930.

Bancroft, Hubert Howe. *History of Alaska, 1730-1885.* San Francisco: A.L. Bancroft, 1886.

Bradbury, Connie Malcolm and David Albert Hales. *Alaska Sources a Guide to Historical Records and Information Resources.* North Salt Lake: Heritage Quest, 2001.

Brooks, Maria. *Alaska Women's Oral History Collection: Catalogue with Subject Index.* Anchorage: Anchorage Community College, 1983.

De Armond, Robert N. *The Founding of Juneau.* Juneau, Alaska: Gastineau Channel Centennial Association, 1967.

Falk, Marvin W. Alaskan Maps: *A Cartobibliography of Alaska to 1900.* New York: Garland Pub., 1983.

Family History Library. *Alaska: Research Outline.* Salt Lake City: Corp. of the President of The Church of Jesus Christ of Latter-day Saints, 1988.

Ferrell, Ed. *Biographies of Alaska-Yukon pioneers.* 3 vols. 1850-1950. Bowie, Maryland: Heritage Books, c1994-1997.

Galbraith, William R. *The Alaska Newspaper Tree.* Fairbanks: Elmer Rasmuson Library, 1975.

Hone, Wade E. *Land and Property Research in the United States.* Salt Lake City: Ancestry Incorporated, 1997.

Hulley, Clarence Charles. *Alaska, 1741-1953.* Portland, Oregon: Binfords & Mort, 1953.

Hunt, William R. *Alaska, a Bicentennial History*, New York: W. W. Norton and Co., 1976.

Jackson, Ronald Vern and Gary Ronald Teeples. *Alaskan Records, 1870-1907.* North Salt Lake, Utah: Accelerated Indexing Systems International, c1976.

Lada-Mocarski, Valerian. *Bibliography of Books on Alaska Published Before 1868.* New Haven, Connecticut: Yale University Press, 1969.

MacLean, Edna A. *Genealogical Record of Barrow Eskimo Families.* Barrow, Alaska: Naval Research Laboratory, 1971.

Naske, Claus-M. and Slotnick, Herman E. *Alaska: A Picture of the 49th State.* Norman, Oklahoma: University of Oklahoma Press, 1987.

Parham, R. Bruce. *How to Find Your Gold Rush Relative: Sources on the Klondike and Alaska gold rushes (1896-1914).* Anchorage, Alaska: National Archives and Records Administration, Pacific Alaska Region, 1997.

Pierce, Richard A. *Russian America: A Biographical Dictionary.* Kingston, Ontario, Canada: Limestone Press, 1990.

Ricks, Melvin Byron. *Melvin Ricks' Alaska Bibliography: An Introductory Guide to Alaskan Historical Literature.* Portland, Oregon: Binford & Mort, 1977.

Shalkop, Antoinette. *The Alaskan Russian Church Archives: Records of the Russian Orthodox Greek Catholic Church of North America — Diocese of Alaska.* Washington: Manuscript Division, Library of Congress, 1984.

Sherwood, Morgan B. *Alaska and its History.* Seattle, Washington: University of Washington Press, 1967.

Ulibarri, George S. *Documenting Alaskan History: Guide to Federal Archives Relating to Alaska.* Fairbanks, Alaska: University of Alaska Press, 1982.

University of Washington (Seattle) Library. *The Dictionary Catalog of the Pacific Northwest Collection of the University of Washington (Seattle) Libraries.* 6 vols. Boston: G.K. Hall and Co., 1972.

Wharton, David. *The Alaska Gold Rush.* Bloomington, Indiana: Indiana University Press, 1972.

Woerner, R. K. *The Alaska Handbook.* Jefferson, North Carolina: McFarland & Co., 1986.

Atlases, Maps & Gazetteers

Alaska Atlas and Gazetteer. 4th ed. Freeport, Maine: DeLorme Mapping Co., 1995.

Baker, Marcus. *Geographic Ddictionary of Alaska.* Washington: Library of Congress Photoduplication Service, 1963. Microfilm.

Geographic Dictionary of Alaska. Washington, D.C.: Government Printing Office, 1902.

Orth, Donald J. *Dictionary of Alaska Place Names.* Washington, DC: Government Printing Office, 1902.

Phillips, James W. *Alaska-Yukon Place Names.* Seattle: University of Washington Press, 1973.

Schorr, Alan Edward. *Alaska Place Names.* Juneau, Alaska: Denali Press, 1991.

Census Records

Available Census Records and Census Substitutes

Federal Census 1900, 1910, 1920, 1930.

State/Territorial Census 1904, 1905, 1906, 1907 (partial).

Unalaska and Aleutian Villages 1878.

Dollarhide, William. *The Census Book: A Genealogist's Guide to Federal Census Facts, Schedules and Indexes.* Bountiful, Utah: Heritage Quest, 1999.

Kemp, Thomas Jay. *The American Census Handbook.* Wilmington, Deleware: Scholarly Resources, Inc., 2001.

Lainhart, Ann S. *State Census Records.* Baltimore: Genealogical Publishing Co., Inc., 1992.

Szucs, Loretto Dennis, and Matthew Wright. *Finding Answers in U.S. Census Records.* Ancestry Publishing, 2001.

Thorndale, William, and William Dollarhide. *Map Guide to the U.S. Federal Censuses, 1790-1920.* Baltimore: Genealogical Publishing Co., 1987.

Court Records, Probate and Wills

District and Territorial Court System: Record Group Inventory. [Juneau, Alaska]: State Archives, 1987.

Emigration, Immigration, Migration and Naturalization

Parham, R. Bruce. *Indexes to Naturalization Records of the U.S. District Court for the District, Territory & State of Alaska (Third Division), 1903-1991.* Seattle: National Archives and Records Administration, Pacific Alaska Region, 1997. 22 Microfilm.

Rasmussen, Janet E. *New Land, New Lives: Scandinavian Immigrants to the Pacific Northwest.* Seattle: University of Washington Press, c1993.

United States. Immigration and Naturalization Service. *Alphabetical Index of Alien Arrivals at Eagle, Hyder, Ketchikan, Nome, and Skagway, Alaska, June 1906-August 1946 : M2016.* College Park, Maryland: National Archives and Records Administration, 1997. Microfilm.

Land and Property

Alaska Department of Natural Resources. *Alaska Mining Claims Cross-Reference Index.* Juneau, Alaska: Alaska Department of Natural Resources, 2002. Online database <www.dnr.state.ak.us>.

Fisher, Raymond Henry. *Records of the Russian-American Company, 1802, 1817-1867.* Washington: National Archives, National Archives and Records Service, General Services Administration, 1971.

Russian-American Company Records, 1802-1867. 92 vols. Washington: National Archives, 1942.

U.S. Congress. House. *Message from the President of the United States in Relation to the Transfer of Territory from Russia to the United States, January 28, 1868.* 40th Cong., 2d sess. H. Exec. Doc. 125. Washington: G.PO, 1868-1912.

Military

Grant, Bruce. *American Forts Yesterday and Today.* New York: E. P. Dutton & Co., 1965.

United States. Selective Service System. *Alaska, World War I Selective Service System Draft Registration Cards, 1917-1918. National Archives Microfilm Publications, M1509.* Washington, D.C.: National Archives, 1987-1988. 4 Microfilm.

Vital and Cemetery Records

Dorosh, Elizabeth and John. *Index to Baptisms, Marriages, and Deaths in the Archives of the Russian Orthodox Greek Catholic Church in Alaska, 1900-1936.* Washington, DC: Library of Congress, 1964.

Index to Baptisms, Marriages and Deaths in the Archives of the Russian Orthodox Greek Catholic Church in Alaska, 1816-1866. Washington, DC: Library of Congress, 1973.

Index to Baptisms, Marriages and Deaths in the Archives of the Russian Orthodox Greek Catholic Church in Alaska 1867-1889. Washington, DC: Library of Congress, 1986.

County Website	Map Index	Date Created	Address/Details
Aleutians East Borough www.aleutianseast.org/	K9	—	Aleutians East Borough; PO Box 349; Sand Point, AK 99501-0349; Ph. 907.383.5334
Aleutians West Census Area	P11	—	
Anchorage Borough www.ci.anchorage.ak.us./	G7	—	Anchorage Borough; PO Box 196650; Anchorage, AK 99519-6650; Ph. 907.343.4311
Bethel Census Area future website at usgenweb.com/	J7	—	Bethel Census Area; PO Box 388; Bethel, AK 99559; Ph. 907.543.2047
Bristol Bay Borough www.theborough.com/	I8	—	Bristol Bay Borough; PO Box 189; Naknek, AK 99633-0189; Ph. 907.246.4224
Denali Borough www.mtaonline.net/~dbgovt/borough.html	G5	—	
Dillingham Census Area future website at usgenweb.com/	I7	—	Dillingham Census Area; PO Box 889; Dillingham, AK 99576; Ph. 907.842.5211
Fairbanks North Star Borough www.co.fairbanks.ak.us/	F5	—	Fairbanks North Star Borough; 809 Pioneer Rd; PO Box 71267; Fairbanks, AK 99707; Ph. 907.459.1000
Haines Borough www.haines.ak.us/	B7	—	Haines Borough; PO Box 1209; Haines, AK 99827-1209; Ph. 907.766.2711
Juneau, City and Bourough www.juneau.org/	B8	—	Juneau, City and Bourough; 155 S Seward St; Juneau, AK 99801-1332; Ph. 907.586.5240
Kenai Peninsula Borough www.borough.kenai.ak.us/	G7	—	Kenai Peninsula Borough; 144 N Binkley; Soldotna, AK 99669; Ph. 907.262.4441
Ketchikan Gateway Borough www.borough.ketchikan.ak.us/	A9	—	Ketchikan Gateway Borough; 344 Front St; Ketchikan, AK 99901-6431; Ph. 907.228.6625
Kodiak Island Borough www.kib.co.kodiak.ak.us/	H9	—	Kodiak Island Borough; 710 Mill Bay Rd; Kodiak, AK 99615; Ph. 907.486.9300
Lake and Peninsula Borough www.bristolbay.com/~lpboro/	I8	—	Lake and Peninsula Borough; PO Box 495; King Salmon, AK 99613-0495; Ph. 907.246.3421
Matanuska-Susitna Borough borough.co.mat-su.ak.us/	G6	—	Matanuska-Susitna Borough; 350 E Dahlia Ave; PO Box 1608; Palmer, AK 99645-1608; Ph. 907.745.4801
Nome Census Area future website at usgenweb.com/	K5	—	Nome Census Area; 61 Hunter Way; Nome, AK 99762; Ph. 907.443.6663
North Slope Borough www.co.north-slope.ak.us/	H2	—	North Slope Borough; PO Box 69; Barrow, AK 99723-0069; Ph. 907.852.2611
Northwest Arctic Borough future website at usgenweb.com/	J4	—	Northwest Arctic Borough; PO Box 1110; Kotzebue, AK 99752-1110; Ph. 907.442.2500

County Website	Map Index	Date Created	Address/Details
Prince of Wales-Outer Ketchika	B9		—
Sitka Borough	B8		—
www.cityofsitka.com/			Sitka Borough; 100 Lincoln St; Sitka, AK 99835-7563; Ph. 907.747.1812
Skagway-Hoonah-Angoon Census	AC8		—
Southeast Fairbanks Census Area	E5		—
Valdez Cordova Census Area	E6		—
Wade Hampton Census Area	K6		—
Wrangell-Petersburg Census Area	B9		—
Yakutat Borough	D7		—
future website at usgenweb.com/			Yakutat Borough; PO Box 160; Yukutat, AK 99689; Ph. 907.784.3323
Yukon-Koyukuk Census Area	G4		—

Notes

Saquaro

ARIZONA

CAPITAL: PHOENIX – TERRITORY 1863 – STATE 1912 (48TH)

The first explorers came to Arizona in search of gold and treasures, attracted by tales of the fabulous "Seven Cities of Cibola." European explorers came into the region as early as 1539. About 150 years later, Catholic missionaries came to proselyte the Indians. The first permanent, non-Indian settlement began in 1776 at the present site of Tucson. Arizona was under the control of Mexico in the section known as New Mexico in 1821. Early settlers generally came into the Gila Valley from the Sonora and Sinaloa states of Mexico.

Following the Mexican War, the portion of Arizona north of the Gila River became part of the United States. The lower portion of Arizona was purchased from Mexico in 1854 under terms of the Gadsden Purchase. Arizona was part of the territory of New Mexico, which was organized in 1850. Following this organization, members of The Church of Jesus Christ of Latter-day Saints began moving from Utah to settle in Arizona. In 1863, Arizona Territory was formed. Prescott was the territorial capital. During the Civil War, the New Mexico territory had about 200 soldiers fighting for the Confederacy and more than 6,000 for the Union.

From 1852 to 1863, the New Mexico district, probate, and supreme courts had jurisdiction for the Arizona area.

In 1870, Arizona had less than 10,000 residents. The population increased twenty-fold over the following 40 years. In the next half century, the population more than tripled. Phoenix became the capital in 1889. The foreign-born population of Arizona in descending order came from Mexico, Canada, England, Wales, Germany, Russia, Italy, Poland, Austria, Sweden, Greece, Ireland, Scotland, Yugoslavia, and Czechoslovakia.

Look for vital statistics in the following locations:
- **Birth and death records:** Vital Records Section,

Department of Health Service after 18 March 1909; check with county seats from 1887 to 18 March 1909.
- **Marriage records:** Clerk of the Superior Court of each county. From 1891 to 1912, clerks of probate courts issued marriage licenses.
- **Divorce records:** Clerk of the Superior Court of the county in which the license was issued. The earliest divorce records were granted by the territorial legislature and are published in the Territorial Statutes. Until 1912, the district court of each county kept these records. District courts had countywide jurisdiction over records of chancery, criminal cases, and divorces from 1864 to 1912. After 1912, superior courts had jurisdiction for most areas.
- **Naturalizations:** Filed in the district court of the county where the examination was conducted. From 1906 until 1912, the clerk of the U.S. district courts in Tucson, Tombstone, Phoenix, Prescott, and Solomonville recorded naturalizations. After 1912 (1919 for Maricopa County), naturalization records were filed in the superior courts.
- **Land records:** Office of the recorder of the county where the land is located.
- **Census records:** Incomplete territorial census records for the years 1864, 1866, 1867, 1869, 1871, 1872, and 1873 are available at the Department of Libraries, Archives and Public Records. Arizona was included in the New Mexico federal census for 1860.

Department of Libraries, Archives and Public Records
Old Capitol Building
1700 West Washington
Phoenix, Arizona 85007

Vital Records Section
Department of Health Service
PO Box 3887
Phoenix, Arizona 85030
602.255.1080

Societies and Repositories

Arizona and the West Library; 318 University of Arizona; Tucson, Arizona 85721

Arizona Chapter of the Association of Professional Genealogists; c/o Janna Larson; AzAPG Secretary/ Treasurer; 14623 N. 49th Place; Scottsdale, Arizona 85254-2207; <www.rootsweb.com/~azapg/>

Arizona Chapter, Ohio Genealogical Society; PO Box 677; Gilbert, Arizona 85299-0677

Arizona Genealogical Advisory Board; PO Box 5641; Mesa, Arizona 85211-5641;

Arizona Genealogical Computer Interest Group; PO Box 51498; Phoenix, Arizona 85076-1498; 480.759.8698;

Arizona Historical Foundation; Hayden Memorial Library; Arizona State University; Tempe, Arizona 85287; Telephone; 602.965.3283; Fax; 602.966.8331

Arizona Historical Society; 949 East Second Street; Tucson, Arizona 85719; 520.628.5774; Fax 520.628.5695; <w3.arizona.edu/~azhist/>

Arizona Pioneer's Historical Society; 949 East Second St.; Tucson, Arizona 85719

Arizona State Genealogical Society; PO Box 42075; Tucson, Arizona 85733-2075; 520.296.1498; Fax 520.885.7714

Arizona State Library, Archives and Public Records; 1700 W. Washington, Suite 200; Phoenix, Arizona 85007; 602.542.4972;

Arizona State Library, Dept. of Library, Archives & Public Records; Gen. Library, 1700 W. Washington; State Capitol; Phoenix, Arizona 85007

Arizona Sun Chapter, AHSGR; 1857 Leisure World; Mesa, Arizona 85206; 480.654.3767; <www.ahsgr.org/azsun.html>

Black Family Historical Society of Arizona; PO Box 1515; Gilbert, Arizona 85299-1515

Central Arizona Division, Arizona Historical Society; 1300 N. College Ave.; Tempe, Arizona 85281

Cherokee Family Ties; 516N. 38th St.; Mesa, Arizona 85208

Cochise Genealogical Society; PO Box 68; Pirtleville, Arizona 85626

Coconino County Genealogical Society; 649 E. Edison; Williams, Arizona 86046

Czech and Slovak Genealogical Society of Arizona; 4921 E. Exeter Blvd.; Phoenix, Arizona 85018-2942; <www.rootsweb.com/~azcsgsa/>

Daughters of The American Revolution, Arizona State; 17239 N. 59th Pl.; Scottsdale, Arizona 85254

Department of Libraries, Archives and Public Records; State Capitol Building Room 200; 1700 West Washington; Phoenix, Arizona 85007; 602.542.4035; 602.542.4972

Diocese of Phoenix; 400 East Monroe; Phoenix, AZ 85004; 602.257.0030

Family History Society of Arizona; PO Box 63094; Phoenix, Arizona 85082-3094; <www.fhsa.org/>; Fax 602.258.3425

Genealogical Society of Pinal County, Arizona, Inc.; 1107 E. 10th St.; Casa Grande, Arizona 85222

Genealogical Society of Yuma, Arizona; PO Box 2905; Yuma, Arizona 85366-2905; 928.344.2280

Genealogical Workshop of Mesa; PO Box 6052; Mesa, Arizona 85216; <members.home.net/gwom/>

Green Valley Genealogical Society; PO Box 1009; Green Valley, Arizona 85622

Jerome Historical Society; PO Box 156; Jerome, Arizona 86331; <www.jeromehistoricalsociety.org/index.html>

Jewish Historical Society of Southern Arizona, Committee on Genealogical; 4181 E. Pontatoc Canyon Dr.; Tucson, Arizona 85718

Jewish Historical Society, Arizona; 720 West Edgewood Ave.; Mesa, Arizona 85210-3513

Lake Havasu Gen. Soc. Library; 2283 Holly Ave.; Lake Havasu City, Arizona 86403; 520.855.7105

Lake Havasu Genealogical Society; PO Box 953; Lake Havasu City, Arizona 86405-0953; 928.855.5113; <www.rootsweb.com/~azlhgs/>

M.H.E. Heritage Library; 433 South Hobson; Mesa, Arizona 85204-2513

Mesa Genealogical Society; PO Box 6052; Mesa, Arizona 85216

Mohave County Genealogical Society; 400 West Beale Street; Kingman, Arizona 86401

Mohave Valley Genealogical Society; PO Box 6045; Mohave Valley, Arizona 86440

National Archives-Pacific Region (Laguna Niguel); PO Box 6719; 24000 Avila Road; Laguna Niguel, CA 92677-06719; 714.360.2641; 714.360.2644

Navajo County Genealogical Society; PO Box 1403; Winslow, Arizona 86047

Northern Arizona Genealogical Society; PO Box 695; Prescott, Arizona 86302; <www.rootsweb.com/~aznags/>

Northern Gila Co. Gen. Soc., Inc. Library; PO Box 952; Payson, Arizona 85547-0952; 520.474.2139

Oracle Historical Society; PO Box 10; Oracle, Arizona 85623; <www.ferberts.com/ohs/>

Phoenix Genealogical Society; PO Box 39703; Phoenix, Arizona 85069-8703

Presbyterian Historical Society; United Presbyterian Church in the U.S.; 425 Lombard St.; Philadelphia, PA 19147; 215.627.1852; Fax 215.627.0509

Prescott Historical Society; W. Gurley St.; Prescott, Arizona 86301

Rio Colorado Division, Arizona Historical Society; 240 S. Madison; Yuma, Arizona 85364

Roman Catholic Diocese of Tucson; 192 South Stone Ave.; PO Box 31; Tucson, AZ 85702; 520.792.3410; Fax 520.792.0291

Sedona Genealogy Club; PO Box 4258; Sedona, Arizona 86340; <fp.sedona.net/genealogy/index.htm>

Sierra Vista Genealogical Society; PO Box 1084; Sierra Vista, Arizona 85636-1084; <fp.sedona.net/genealogy/index.htm>

Sons of the American Revolution, Arizona Society; 7000 E. Berneil Dr.; Paradise Valley, Arizona 85253

Sun Cities Genealogical Society; 12600 113th Ave., Suite C-6;

PO Box 1448; Youngtown, Arizona

Tempe Historical Society; 809 E. Southern Avenue; Tempe, Arizona 85282; <www.tempe.gov/museum/ahistsoc.htm>

Tri-State Genealogical Society; PO Box 6045; Mohave Valley, Arizona 86440

University of Arizona Library; 1510 University; Tucson, Arizona 85721; 520.621.2101; Fax 520.621.9733

West Valley Genealogical Society; PO Box 1448; Sun City, Arizona 85372-1448; <www.rootsweb.com/~azwvgs/>

Bibliography and Record Sources

General Sources

A Historical and Biographical Record of the Territory of Arizona. Chicago: McFarland & Poole, 1896.

Arizona Historical Society. *Official Directory of Arizona Historical Museums and Related Support Organizations.* Tucson, Arizona: Arizona Historical Society, 1997.

Arizona History Today. Tucson, Arizona: Arizona Historical Society, 1997-. Serial.

Arizona Research Outline. Series US-States, No. 3. Salt Lake City: Family History Library, 1988.

Beers, Henry Putney. *Spanish and Mexican Records of the American Southwest: A Bibliographical Guide to Archive and Manuscript Sources.* Tucson: University of Arizona Press, 1979.

Directory of Churches and Religious Organizations in Arizona (Phoenix: Division of Professional and Service Projects, WPA, 1940).

Farish, Thomas Edwin. *History of Arizona.* 8 vols., San Francisco: Filmer Bros. Electrotype Co., 19–? Reprint of Phoenix: N.P., 1915-18.

Hayden, Carl. *Carl Hayden Biographical Files, ca. 1825-1927.* (Tempe, Arizona: Arizona State University, 19–?;).

Lutrell, Estelle. *Newspapers and Periodicals of Arizona, 1859-1911.* Tucson: University of Arizona, 1950.

Portrait and Biographical Record of Arizona. Chicago: Chapman Publishing Co., 1901.

Powell, Donald M. *Arizona Gathering II, 1950-1969: An Annotated Bibliography.* Tucson: University of Arizona Press, 1973.

Powell, Donald M. *Arizona Gathering II: An Annotated Bibliography, 1950-69.* Tucson: University of Arizona Press, 1973.

Spiros, Joyce V. Hawley. *Genealogical Guide to Arizona and Nevada.* Gallup NM: Verlene Publishing, 1983.

Surname Index for the Arizona Sentinel, 1872-1905. Yuma, Arizona: Genealogical Society of Yuma, Arizona, 1997.

Wiggins, Marvin E. *Mormons and Their Neighbors: An Index of Over 75,000 Biographical Sketches from 1820 to the Present.* 2 vols. (Provo, Utah: Brigham Young University, 1984).

Wyllys, Rufus Kay. *Arizona: The History of a Frontier State.* Phoenix: Hobson and Herr, 1950.

Atlases, Maps and Gazetteers

Barnes, Will C. *Arizona Place Names.* Revised. Tucson: University of Arizona Press, 1982.

Dreyfuss, John J. *History of Arizona's Counties and Courthouses.* Tucson: National Society of the Colonial Dames of America in the State of Arizona, 1972.

Granger, Byrd H. *Arizona's Names: X Marks the Place.* Tucson, Arizona: Falconer Pub., Co., 1983.

Herman, James E., and Barbara H. Sherman. *Ghost Towns of Arizona.* Norman, Okla.: University of Oklahoma Press, 1969.

Thoeobold, John and Lillian Theobold. *Arizona Territory: Post Offices and Postmasters.* Phoenix: Arizona Historical Foundation, 1961.

Walker, Henry P. and Don Bufkin. *Historical Atlas of Arizona.* Norman, Okla.: University of Oklahoma Press, 1979.

Census Records

Available Census Records and Census Substitutes

Federal Census 1860, 1870, 1880, 1900, 1910, 1920, 1930.

Federal Mortality Schedules 1870, 1880.

State/Territorial Census 1850, 1860, 1864, 1866, 1867, 1869.

Dollarhide, William. *The Census Book: A Genealogist's Guide to Federal Census Facts, Schedules and Indexes.* Bountiful, UT: Heritage Quest, 1999.

Kemp, Thomas Jay. *The American Census Handbook.* Wilmington, DE: Scholarly Resources, Inc., 2001.

Lainhart, Ann S. *State Census Records.* Baltimore: Genealogical Publishing Co., Inc., 1992.

Szucs, Loretto Dennis, and Matthew Wright. *Finding Answers in U.S. Census Records.* Ancestry Publishing, 2001.

Thorndale, William, and William Dollarhide. *Map Guide to the U.S. Federal Censuses, 1790-1920.* Baltimore: Genealogical Publishing Co., 1987.

United States. Bureau of the Census. *Cross Index to Selected City Streets and Enumeration Districts, 1910 Census.* Washington, D.C.: National Archives, [1984].

Court Records, Probate and Wills

A Guide to Arizona Courts. Phoenix, Arizona: Arizona Supreme Court Office of The Courts, 1997.

James, Jessamine Bland. *Will Books 1 & 2, Years 1866-1900, Pima County, Territory of Arizona.* Typescript. Salt Lake City: Filmed by the Genealogical Society of Utah, 1970.

Emigration, Immigration, Migrations and Naturalization

Arizona. Superior Court (Cochise County). *Citizenship Petitions Denied and Granted, 1929-1955.* Microfilm of original records at the Cochise County Courthouse in Bisbee, Arizona. (Salt Lake City: Filmed by the Genealogical Society of Utah, 1997). Microfilm.

United States. District Court (Arizona Territory : 2nd Judicial District*). Naturalizations, 1882-1912; Index, 1864-1911.* Microfilm of records located at the National Archives, Pacific Southwest Region, Laguna Niguel, California. (Salt Lake City: Filmed by the Genealogical Society of Utah, 1989). Microfilm, multiple rolls.

Land and Property

Miscellaneous Archives Relating to New Mexico Land Grants, 1695-1842. Albuquerque: University of New Mexico Library, 1955-1957. Text in Spanish.

New Mexico (Territory). Secretary's Office. *Records of Land Titles, 1847-1852.* Albuquerque, N.M. : University of New Mexico Library, 1955-1957.

New Mexico (Territory). Surveyor-General's Office. *Record of Private Land Claims Adjudicated By the U.S. Surveyor General, 1855-1890.* Salt Lake City: Filmed by the Genealogical Society of Utah, 1955-1957. Microfilm, multiple rolls.

Twitchell, Ralph E. *The Twitchell Archives, 1685-1898.* Albuquerque, N.M.: Filmed by the University of New Mex. Library, 1955-1957. Microfilm, 6 rolls.

United States. Land Office (Prescott, Arizona). *Land Entry Decisions by the Commission of General Land Office, Prescott, Arizona: Homestead Claims and Applications, Mineral Entries, Railroad Land Claims, etc.* Microfilm of records located at the National Archives, Pacific Southwest Region, Lugana Niguel, California. (Salt Lake City: Filmed by the Genealogical Society of Utah, 1989). Microfilm, 13 rolls.

United States. Land Office (Prescott, Arizona). *Land Records, 1847-1907.* Microfilm of records located at the National Archives Pacific Southwest Region, Lugana Niguel, California. (Salt Lake City: Filmed by the Genealogical Society of Utah, 1989). Microfilm, 3 rolls.

United States. Surveyor General (Arizona). *Records of Mineral Surveys, Homestead Surveys, and Private Land Claims.* Microfilm of records located at the National Archives, Pacific Southwest Region, Laguna Niguel, California. (Salt Lake City: Filmed by the Genealogical Society of Utah, 1989). Microfilm, 2 rolls.

Van Ness, John R., and Christine Van Ness. *Spanish and Mexican Land Grants in New Mexico and Colorado.* Manhattan, KS: Ag Press, 1981.

Vigil, Donaciano. *Vigil's Index, 1681-1846.* Albuquerque: University of New Mexico Library, 1955-1957. Text in Spanish.

Military

Alexander, David V. *Arizona Frontier Military Place Names: 1846-1912.* Las Cruces, New Mexico: Yucca Tree Press, 1998.

Altshuler, Constance Wynn. *Chains of Command : Arizona and the Army, 1856-1875.* Tucson, Arizona: Arizona Historical Society, 1981.

Arizona Pioneers' Historical Society (Tucson, Arizona). *The Army in the West, A Guide to Microfilmed Records in the Library of the Arizona Pioneers' Historical Society.* Tucson, Arizona: W.C. Cox Co., 1974.

Brandes, Ray. *Frontier Military Posts of Arizona* (Globe, Arizona: Dale S. King, 1960; Gabbert, Howard Markland.)

Hortsch, Frances A. *Arizona's Memorial to Vietnam Veterans.* Phoenix, Arizona: Phoenix Genealogical Society, 1987.

The Rough Riders: A Brief Study and Indexed Roster of the 1st Regiment, U.S. Volunteer Cavalry, 1898. Tucson, Arizona: Arizona State Genealogical Society, 1992.

United States. Adjutant General's Office. *Index to Compiled Service Records of Confederate.* Washington, D.C.: The National Archives, 1962.

United States. Adjutant General's Office. *Index to Compiled Service Records of Volunteer Union Soldiers who served in Organizations from the Territory of Arizona, 1861-1865.* Washington, D.C.: National Archives. Central Plains Region, 1964.

United States. Selective Service System. *Arizona, World War I Selective Service System Draft Registration Cards, 1917-1918.* Washington, D.C.: National Archives, 1987-1988.

Ynfante, Charles. *Arizona During the Second World War, 1941-1945, a Survey of Selected Topics.* Dissertation. (Ph.D.) Flagstaff, Arizona: Northern Arizona University, 1997.

Vital and Cemetery Records

Arizona Cemetery Records. Salt Lake City: Genealogical Society of Utah, 1959.

Arizona Death Records: An Index Compiled from Mortuary, Cemetery, Church Records. Tucson: Arizona State Genealogical Society, n.d.

Arizona Statewide Archival and Records Project, Work Projects Administration. *Guide to Public Vital Statistics Records in Arizona.* Phoenix, Arizona.: [s.n.], 1941.

ARIZONA, CA, ID, NV, 1850-1951. [S.l.]: Brøderbund, 1996. CD-ROM

Arizona. Department of Health Services. *Arizona Birth Certificates, 1855-1924.* Microfilm of original records at the Arizona Department of Library, Archives and Public Records Management Division in Phoenix, Arizona. (Salt Lake City: Filmed by the Genealogical Society of Utah, 1998-1999). Microfilm, 51 rolls.

Arizona. Department of Health Services. *Birth and Death Records for Various Arizona Counties, 1887-1912.* Salt Lake City: Filmed by the Genealogical Society of Utah, 1998.

Arizona. Department of Health Services. *Death Certificates (Arizona), ca. 1870-1949.* Microfilm of original records at the Arizona Department of Library, Archives and Public Records, Records Management Division in Phoenix, Arizona. (Salt Lake City: Filmed by the Genealogical Society of Utah, 1998-1999). Microfilm, 93 rolls.

Whiteside, Dora M. Northern *Arizona Territorial Death and Burial Records 1870-1910.* Prescott, Arizona: D. Whiteside, 1988.

County Website	Map Index	Date Created	Parent County or Territory From Which Organized Address/Details
Apache www.co.apache.az.us/	F11	14 Feb 1879	**Yavapai** Apache County; 70 West 3rd S; PO Box 428; St. Johns, AZ 85936-0428; Ph. 520.337.4364 Details: (Clk Sup Ct has m, div, pro & ct rec from 1879; Co Rcdr has land rec from 1879)
Castle Dome		1860	**Original county** Details: (see Yuma) Name changed to Yuma 21 Dec 1864
Cochise www.co.cochise.az.us/	N10	1 Feb 1881	**Pima** Cochise County; PO Box CK; Bisbee, AZ 85603-0000; Ph. 520.432.9200 Details: (Clk Sup Ct has m, div, pro & ct rec; Co Rcdr has land rec)
Coconino co.coconino.az.us/	F6	19 Feb 1891	**Yavapai** Coconino County; Flagstaff Justice Ct; 100 E Birch Ave; Flagstaff, AZ 86001-4696; Ph. 520.774.5011 Details: (Clk Sup Ct has m, div, ct & pro rec from 1891; Co Rcdr has land rec)
Ewell		1860	**Original county** Details: (see Pima) Name changed to Pima 15 Dec 1864
Gila www.rootsweb.com/~azgila/index.htm	J8	8 Feb 1881	**Maricopa, Pinal** Gila County; 1400 E Ash St; Globe, AZ 85501-1414; Ph. 520.425.3231 Details: (Co Clk has m rec from 1881, div, pro & ct rec from 1914; Co Rcdr has land rec)
Graham www.graham.az.gov/	L10	10 Mar 1881	**Apache, Pima** Graham County; 800 Main St; Safford, AZ 85546-2829; Ph. 520.428.3250 Details: (Clk Sup Ct has m, pro, div & ct rec from 1881 & nat rec 1903-1973; Co Rcdr has land rec)
Greenlee www.rootsweb.com/~azgreenl/index.html	K11	10 Mar 1909	**Graham** Greenlee County; PO Box 908; Clifton, AZ 85533; Ph. 520.865.2072 Details: (Clk Sup Ct has m, div, pro & ct rec from 1911; Co Rcdr has land rec)
La Paz www.co.la-paz.az.us/	J3	2 Nov 1982	**Yuma** La Paz County; 1108 Joshua Ave; Parker, AZ 85344-6477; Ph. 520.669.6115 Details: (Clk Sup Ct has m, div, pro & ct rec; Co Rcdr has land rec)
Maricopa* www.maricopa.gov/	K5	14 Feb 1871	**Yavapai, Yuma, Pima** Maricopa County; 301 W Jefferson; Phoenix, AZ 85003-2225; Ph. 602.506.3572 Details: (Clk Sup Ct has m rec from 1877, div rec from 1930, pro & ct rec from 1871; Co Rcdr has land rec)
Mohave www.co.mohave.az.us/	F3	21 Dec 1864	**Original county** Mohave County; 401 E Spring St; Kingman, AZ 86401; Ph. 520.753.9141 Details: (Clk Sup Ct has m rec from 1888, div, pro & ct rec from 1850; Co Rcdr has land rec)
Navajo www.co.navajo.az.us/	G9	21 Mar 1895	**Apache** Navajo County; PO Box 668; Holbrook, AZ 86025-0668; Ph. 520.524.4000 Details: (Clk Sup Ct has m, div, pro & ct rec; Co Rcdr has land rec)
Pima* www.co.pima.az.us/	M6	15 Dec 1864	**Original county** Pima County; 130 W Congress St; Tucson, AZ 85701-1333; Ph. 520.740.8661 Details: (Formerly Ewell Co. Name changed to Pima) (Clk Sup Ct has m, div, pro & ct rec from 1863)
Pinal www.co.pinal.az.us/	L8	1 Feb 1875	**Pima, Yavapai** Pinal County; 100 N Florence; Florence, AZ 85232; Ph. 520.868.6000 Details: (Clk Sup Ct has m, pro & ct rec from 1875 & div rec from 1883; Co Rcdr has land rec)
Santa Cruz* www.santacruzcountyaz.org/	N8	15 Mar 1899	**Pima, Cochise** Santa Cruz County; 2150 North Congress Dr; PO Box 1265; Nogales, AZ 85628-1265; Ph. 520.761.7800 Details: (Clk Sup Ct has m, div, pro & ct rec from 1899, mil rec 1907-1922, nat rec 1888-1985 & adoption rec from 1940)

County Website	Map Index	Date Created	Parent County or Territory From Which Organized Address/Details
Yavapai www.co.yavapai.az.us/	H5	21 Dec 1864	**Original county** Yavapai County; 1015 Fair St; Prescott, AZ 86301; Ph. 520.639.8110 Details: (Clk Sup Ct has m, div, pro & ct rec; Co Rcdr has land rec)
Yuma www.co.yuma.az.us/	L3	21 Dec 1864	**Original county** Yuma County; 168 S 2nd Ave; Yuma, AZ 85364; Ph. 520.329.2170 Details: (Formerly Castle Dome Co. Name changed to Yuma) (Clk Sup Ct has m, div, pro & ct rec from 1863)

County Website	Map Index	Date Created	Parent County or Territory From Which Organized Address/Details
Arkansas www.rootsweb.com/~ararkans/	**J8**	**31 Dec 1813**	**Original county** Arkansas County; 101 Court Sq; DeWitt, AR 72042; Ph. 870.946.4349 Details: (Co Clk has pro rec from 1809 & m rec from 1838; Clk Cir Ct has land rec, div & ct rec from 1803 & mil dis rec from 1917)
Ashley www.rootsweb.com/~arashleyl /arashley_Index1.htm	**M7**	**30 Nov 1848**	**Chicot, Union, Drew** Ashley County; 215 E Jefferson St; Hamburg, AR 71646; Ph. 870.853.2020 Details: (Co Clk has m rec from 1848, pro & land rec; Clk Cir Ct has div rec)
Baxter* www.baxtercountyonline.com/baxgen/	**D6**	**24 Mar 1873**	**Fulton, Izard, Marion, Searcy** Baxter County; Courthouse Sq; 1 E 7th St; Mountain Home, AR 72653; Ph. 870.425.3475 Details: (Co Clk has m, d, pro, div, land & ct rec)
Benton* www.co.benton.ar.us/	**D2**	**30 Sep 1836**	**Washington** Benton County; 215 E Central; Bentonville, AR 72712; Ph. 479.271.1031 Details: (Co Clk has m rec from 1861 & pro rec from 1859; Clk Cir Ct has div, ct & land rec)
Boone www.rootsweb.com/~arboone/boone.html	**D4**	**9 Apr 1869**	**Carrol, Madison** Boone County; 100 N Main St; Harrison, AR 72602; Ph. 870.741.8428 Details: (Co Clk has m & pro rec from 1869; Clk Cir Ct has div, ct & land rec)
Bradley www.rootsweb.com/~arbradle/	**L6**	**18 Dec 1840**	**Union** Bradley County; 101 E Cedar St; Warren, AR 71671-0000; Ph. 870.226.3464 Details: (Co Clk has m rec from 1846 & pro rec from 1850; Clk Cir Ct has div, ct & land rec)
Calhoun www.rootsweb.com/~arcalhou/	**L6**	**6 Dec 1850**	**Dallas, Ouachita** Calhoun County; Main St; Hampton, AR 71744; Ph. 870.798.2517 Details: (Co Clk has m & land rec from 1851, div, pro & ct rec from 1880)
Carroll* www.rootsweb.com/~arcarrol/ Carroll.html	**D3**	**1 Nov 1833**	**Izard** Carroll County; 210 W Church St; Berryville, AR 72616-4233; Ph. 870.423.2022 Details: (Co Clk has m & pro rec from 1870; Clk Cir Ct has land, ct & div rec from 1870)
Chicot www.seark.net/~sabra/chicotco.html	**M8**	**25 Oct 1823**	**Arkansas** Chicot County; 108 Main St; Lake Village, AR 71653; Ph. 870.265.8000 Details: (Co Clk has m & pro rec from 1839; Clk Cir Ct has ct rec from 1824, land & div rec)
Clark www.pastracks.com/states/arkansas/clark/	**J4**	**15 Dec 1818**	**Arkansas** Clark County; Courthouse Sq; 401 Clay St; Arkadelphia, AR 71923; Ph. 870.246.4491 Details: (Co Clk has m rec from 1821 & pro rec from 1800; Clk Cir Ct has div, ct & land rec)
Clay www.rootsweb.com/~arclay/	**D10**	**24 Mar 1873**	**Randolph, Greene** Clay County; PO Box 306; Piggott, AR 72454; Ph. 870.598.2813 Details: (Formerly Clayton Co. Name changed to Clay 6 Dec 1875; Rec burned in 1893) (Clk Cir Ct has land, div & ct rec from 1893; Co Clk has m & pro rec from 1893)
Clayton		**24 Mar 1873**	**Randolph, Greene** Details: (see Clay) Name changed to Clay 6 Dec 1875
Cleburne* www.rootsweb.com/~arclebur/	**G7**	**20 Feb 1883**	**White, Van Buren, Independence** Cleburne County; 301 W Main St; Heber Springs, AR 72543; Ph. 501.362.4620 Details: (Co Clk has m, pro, div, ct & land rec from 1883)
Cleveland* www.rootsweb.com/~arclevel/index.html	**K6**	**17 Apr 1873**	**Dallas, Bradley, Jefferson, Lincoln** Cleveland County; Main & Magnolia Sts; PO Box 348; Rison, AR 71665; Ph. 870.325.6521 Details: (Formerly Dorsey Co. Name changed to Cleveland 5 Mar 1885) (Co Clk has m rec from 1880, div, pro & ct rec)

County Website	Map Index	Date Created	Parent County or Territory From Which Organized Address/Details
Columbia www.rootsweb.com/~arcolumb/	**M4**	**17 Dec 1852**	**Lafayette, Hempstead, Ouachita** Columbia County; 1 Court Sq, #1; Magnolia, AR 71753; Ph. 870.235.3774 Details: (Co Clk has m & land rec from 1853, div & ct rec from 1860 & pro rec; Co Lib has cem rec)
Conway www.rootsweb.com/~arconway/	**G5**	**20 Oct 1825**	**Pulaski** Conway County; 117 S Moose St; Morrilton, AR 72110; Ph. 501.354.9621 Details: (Co Clk has m rec from 1858 & pro rec; Clk Cir Ct has div, ct & land rec)
Craighead www.craigheadcounty.org/	**F10**	**19 Feb 1859**	**Mississippi, Greene, Poinsett** Craighead County; 511 S Main St; Jonesboro, AR 72401; Ph. 870.933.4520 Details: (Co Clk has m & pro rec from 1878 & tax rec; Clk Cir Ct has ct & div rec from 1878 & land rec from 1900)
Crawford www.rootsweb.com/~arcrawfo/	**F2**	**18 Oct 1820**	**Pulaski** Crawford County; 300 Main St; Van Buren, AR 72956; Ph. 501.474.1312 Details: (Co Clk has m & pro rec from 1877; Clk Cir Ct has ct & land rec from 1877 & div rec)
Crittenden www.rootsweb.com/~arcritte/	**G11**	**22 Oct 1825**	**Phillips** Crittenden County; 100 Court St; Marion, AR 72364; Ph. 870.739.4434 Details: (Co Clk has m & pro rec; Clk Cir Ct has div, mil & ct rec; Co Asr has land rec)
Cross* www.rootsweb.com/~arcross/	**G10**	**15 Nov 1862**	**Crittenden, Poinsett, St. Francis** Cross County; 705 Union Ave E #8; Wynne, AR 72396; Ph. 870.238.5735 Details: (Co Clk has m & pro rec from 1863, tax & co ct rec from 1865; Clk Cir Ct has ct & land rec from 1865; Chan Cir Clk has div rec from 1866; Co Hist Soc has newspapers from 1935, cem rec & fam hist)
Dallas www.rootsweb.com/~ardallas/dallas1.htm	**K5**	**1 Jan 1845**	**Clark, Bradley** Dallas County; 206 W 3rd St; Fordyce, AR 71742; Ph. 870.352.7179 Details: (Co Clk has m rec from 1855, land rec from 1845, pro, div & ct rec)
Desha home.earthlink.net/~reitzamm/ index.html	**K8**	**12 Dec 1838**	**Arkansas, Chicot** Desha County; Robert Moore Ave; PO Box 188; Arkansas City, AR 71630; Ph. 870.877.2323 Details: (Co Clk has m rec from 1865 & pro rec; Clk Cir Ct has div, ct & land rec)
Dorsey www.rootsweb.com/~ardorsey/		**17 Apr 1873**	**Dallas, Bradley, Jefferson, Lincoln** Details: (see Cleveland) Name changed to Cleveland 5 Mar 1885
Drew members.tripod.com/~Backwards BRanch/gwdc.html	**L7**	**26 Nov 1846**	**Arkansas, Bradley** Drew County; 210 S Main St; Monticello, AR 71655; Ph. 870.460.6260 Details: (Co Clk has m & pro rec; Clk Cir Ct has div, mil & ct rec; Co Asr has land rec)
Faulkner* members.tripod.com/~Backwards BRanch/gwfc.html	**G6**	**12 Apr 1873**	**Pulaski, Conway** Faulkner County; 801 Locust St; Conway, AR 72032; Ph. 501.450.4910 Details: (Co Clk has m, pro & ct rec from 1873)
Franklin www.rootsweb.com/~arfrankl/	**F3**	**19 Dec 1837**	**Crawford** Franklin County; 211 W Commercial St; Ozark, AR 72949-0000; Ph. 501.667.3607 Details: (Co Clk has m rec from 1850, pro rec from 1838 & land rec from 1899)
Fulton www.rootsweb.com/~arfulton/	**D7**	**21 Dec 1842**	**Izard** Fulton County; PO Box 278; Salem, AR 72576-0278; Ph. 870.895.3310 Details: (Co Clk has m rec from 1887, div, land, pro & ct rec from 1891)
Garland www.garlandcounty.org/	**I4**	**5 Apr 1873**	**Saline** Garland County; 501 Ouachita Ave; Hot Springs, AR 71901; Ph. 501.622.3610 Details: (Co Clk has m & pro rec; Clk Cir Ct has div, ct & land rec)
Grant members.tripod.com/~Backwards BRanch/gwdc.html	**J6**	**4 Feb 1869**	**Jefferson, Hot Springs, Saline** Grant County; 101 W Center St #106; PO Box 364; Sheridan, AR 72150; Ph. 870.942.2551 Details: (Co Clk has m, div, pro, ct & land rec from 1877)

County Website	Map Index	Date Created	Parent County or Territory From Which Organized / Address/Details
Greene www.rootsweb.com/~argreene/ greene1.html	E10	5 Nov 1833	**Lawrence** Greene County; PO Box 62; Paragould, AR 72451-0364; Ph. 870.239.6311 Details: (Co Clk has m, pro, ct & land rec from 1876; Clk Cir Ct has div rec)
Hempstead www.rootsweb.com/~arhempst/	K3	15 Dec 1818	**Arkansas** Hempstead County; PO Box 1420; Hope, AR 71801-1420; Ph. 870.777.2241 Details: (Co Clk has m & pro rec from 1823 & land rec from 1900)
Hot Spring* www.rootsweb.com/~arhotspr/	J5	2 Nov 1829	**Clark** Hot Spring County; 210 Locust St; Malvern, AR 72104; Ph. 501.332.2291 Details: (Co Clk has m rec from 1825 & pro rec from 1834; Clk Cir Ct has ct & div rec)
Howard www.genealogyshoppe.com/arhoward/	J2	17 Apr 1873	**Pike, Hempstead, Polk, Sevier** Howard County; 421 N Main St; Nashville, AR 71852; Ph. 870.845.7502 Details: (Co Clk has m & pro rec from 1873 & some cem rec; Clk Cir Ct has div, ct & land rec from 1873)
Independence fly.hiwaay.net/~dmglenn/independ.htm	F8	23 Oct 1820	**Lawrence, Arkansas** Independence County; 192 E Main St; Batesville, AR 72501; Ph. 870.793.8828 Details: (Co Clk has m rec from 1826 & pro rec from 1839; Clk Cir Ct has div, ct & land rec; Co Lib has bur rec)
Izard* www.pastracks.com/states/arkansas/izard/	E7	27 Oct 1825	**Independence** Izard County; PO Box 327; Melbourne, AR 72556; Ph. 870.368.4328 Details: (Line between Izard & Sharp Cos changed 9 Mar 1877) (Co Clk has m, div, pro, ct & land rec from 1889)
Jackson* www.rootsweb.com/~arjackso/	F9	5 Nov 1829	**Independence** Jackson County; 208 Main St; Newport, AR 72112; Ph. 870.523.7420 Details: (Co Clk has m rec from 1843 & pro rec from 1845; Clk Cir Ct has div & ct rec from 1845 & land rec)
Jefferson www.rootsweb.com/~arjeffer/index.html	J7	2 Nov 1829	**Arkansas, Pulaski** Jefferson County; 101 W Barraque St; Pine Bluff, AR 71601; Ph. 870.541.5360 Details: (Co Clk has m rec from 1830 & pro rec from 1845; Clk Cir Ct has div, ct & land rec)
Johnson www.oklahoma.net/~pvtspark/ johnson.html	F4	16 Nov 1833	**Pope** Johnson County; 215 W Main St; PO Box 57; Clarksville, AR 72830; Ph. 501.754.3967 Details: (Co Clk has m rec from 1855 & pro rec from 1844; Clk Cir Ct has div, ct & land rec; Extension Office has bur rec)
Lafayette www.rootsweb.com/~arlafaye/	M3	15 Oct 1827	**Hempstead** Lafayette County; 2 Courthouse Sq; Lewisville, AR 71845; Ph. 870.921.4633 Details: (Co Clk has m rec from 1848 & pro rec; Clk Cir Ct has div & land rec)
Lawrence members.tripod.com/~Backwards BRanch/lc.html	E9	15 Jan 1815	**New Madrid, Mo** Lawrence County; PO Box 553, 315 W Main; Walnut Ridge, AR 72476; Ph. 870.886.1111 Details: (Co Clk has m & pro rec)
Lee www.rootsweb.com/~arlee2/lee.htm	H9	17 Apr 1873	**Phillips, Monroe, Crittenden, St. Francis** Lee County; 15 E Chestnut St; Marianna, AR 72360; Ph. 870.295.7715 Details: (Co Clk has m, pro & tax rec from 1873; Clk Cir Ct has div, mil & ct rec from 1873)
Lincoln www.rootsweb.com/~arlee2/lee.htm	K7	28 Mar 1871	**Arkansas, Bradley, Desha, Drew, Jefferson** Lincoln County; 300 S Drew St; Star City, AR 71667; Ph. 870.628.5114 Details: (Co Clk has m, pro & land rec from 1871 & tax rec)
Little River www.rootsweb.com/~arlittle/	K2	5 Mar 1867	**Hempstead** Little River County; 351 N 2nd St; Ashdown, AR 71822; Ph. 870.898.7208 Details: (Co Clk has m & pro rec from 1880; Clk Cir Ct has div & land rec)
Logan www.rootsweb.com/~arlogan/index.htm	G3	22 Mar 1871	**Pope, Franklin, Johnson, Scott, Yell** Logan County; Courthouse Sq; Paris, AR 72855; Ph. 501.963.2618 Details: (Formerly Sarber Co. Name changed to Logan 14 Dec 1875) (Co Clk has m & pro rec; Clk Cir Ct has div, ct & land rec)

County Website	Map Index	Date Created	Parent County or Territory From Which Organized Address/Details
Lonoke www.rootsweb.com/~arlonoke/	I7	16 Apr 1873	**Pulaski, Prairie** Lonoke County; 3rd & N Center St; PO Box 431; Lonoke, AR 72086-0431; Ph. 501.676.2368 Details: (Co Clk has m & pro rec) (Some rec of Lonoke Co are in Des Arc, Prairie Co, AR)
Lovely		1827	**Northwest Arkansas & Northeast Oklahoma** Details: (Lost to Oklahoma & abolished 1828)
Madison* members.aol.com/ptice/argenweb-mc.htm	E3	30 Sep 1836	**Washington** Madison County; 1 Main St; PO Box 37; Huntsville, AR 72740-0037; Ph. 501.738.6721 Details: (Co Clk has m & pro rec from 1901)
Marion www.rootsweb.com/~armarion/	E5	3 Nov 1835	**Izard** Marion County; Hwy 62; PO Box 545; Yellville, AR 72687; Ph. 870.449.6226 Details: (Formerly Searcy Co. Name changed to Marion 29 Sept 1836) (Co Clk has m, div, pro, ct & land rec from 1888)
Miller www.rootsweb.com/~armiller/	L3	Dec 1874	**Lafayette** Miller County; 400 Laurel St; Texarkana, AR 71854; Ph. 870.744.1501 Details: (Co Clk has m, pro & land rec from 1875; Clk Cir Ct has div & ct rec)
Miller, old		1 Apr 1820	**Hempstead** Details: (Abolished 1836. Re-establisted Dec 1874 from Lafayette Co)
Mississippi mcagov.missconet.com/	F11	1 Nov 1833	**Crittenden** Mississippi County; 200 W Walnut; Blytheville, AR 72315; Ph. 870.763.3212 Details: (Co Clk has m rec from 1850 & pro rec from 1865; Clk Cir Ct has div & ct rec from 1866 & land rec from 1865)
Monroe* www.rootsweb.com/~armonro2/	I9	2 Nov 1829	**Phillips, Arkansas** Monroe County; 123 Madison St; Clarendon, AR 72029-2794; Ph. 870.747.3921 Details: (Co Clk has m rec from 1850 & pro rec from 1839; Clk Cir Ct has div rec from 1839, ct rec from 1830 & land rec from 1829)
Montgomery* www.rootsweb.com/~armontgo/	I3	9 Dec 1842	**Hot Springs** Montgomery County; 1 George St; Mount Ida, AR 71957; Ph. 870.887.3521 Details: (Co Clk has m, pro, land, div & ct rec from 1845; Co Agent has bur rec)
Nevada www.rootsweb.com/~arnevada/	K4	20 Mar 1871	**Hempstead, Columbia, Ouachita** Nevada County; 215 E 2nd St S; Prescott, AR 71857; Ph. 870.887.3115 Details: (Co Clk has m & pro rec from 1871 & cem rec; Clk Cir Ct has div, ct & land rec from 1871)
Newton www.rootsweb.com/~arnewton/	E4	14 Dec 1842	**Carroll** Newton County; Court St; Jasper, AR 72641-0435; Ph. 870.446.5125 Details: (Co Clk has m & land rec from 1866, pro & ct rec from 1880)
Ouachita www.rootsweb.com/~arouachi/index.html	L5	29 Nov 1842	**Union** Ouachita County; 145 Jackson St; Camden, AR 71701; Ph. 870.837.2220 Details: (Co Clk has m & pro rec from 1875; Clk Cir Ct has div, ct & land rec)
Perry www.rootsweb.com/~arperry/	H5	18 Dec 1840	**Conway** Perry County; PO Box 358; Perryville, AR 72126-0358; Ph. 501.889.5126 Details: (Co Clk has m, div, pro, ct & land rec from 1882)
Phillips www.rootsweb.com/~arphill2/phillips.htm	I9	1 May 1820	**Arkansas, Hempstead** Phillips County; 600 Cherry St; Helena, AR 72342; Ph. 870.338.5505 Details: (Co Clk has m rec from 1831 & pro rec from 1850; Clk Cir Ct has div, ct & land rec from 1820)
Pike www.rootsweb.com/~arpike/	J3	1 Nov 1833	**Clark, Hempstead** Pike County; PO Box 219; Murfreesboro, AR 71958; Ph. 870.285.2231 Details: (Co Clk has m, div, pro, ct, land & mil dis rec from 1895)
Poinsett www.rootsweb.com/~arpoinse/	F10	28 Feb 1838	**Greene, St. Francis** Poinsett County; 401 Market St; Harrisburg, AR 72432; Ph. 870.578.4410 Details: (Co Clk has m rec from 1873 & pro rec; Clk Cir Ct has div, ct & land rec)

County Website	Map Index	Date Created	Parent County or Territory From Which Organized / Address/Details
Polk* www.rootsweb.com/~arpolk/	I2	30 Nov 1844	**Sevier** Polk County; 507 Church Ave; Mena, AR 71953; Ph. 501.394.8123 Details: (Co Clk has m rec from 1885, pro rec from 1900 & cem rec; Clk Cir Ct has div, land and ct rec from 1885 & mil rec)
Pope www.rootsweb.com/~arpope2/	G5	2 Nov 1829	**Crawford** Pope County; 100 W Main St; Russellville, AR 72801; Ph. 501.968.6064 Details: (Co Clk has m & pro rec from 1831, co ct rec from 1857, voter & d rec from 1965; Clk Cir Ct has div, land, mil & ct rec)
Prairie www.rootsweb.com/~arprairi/	H8	25 Nov 1846	**Pulaski, Monroe** Prairie County; PO Box 278; Des Arc, AR 72040-0278; Ph. 870.256.3741 Details: (Part of the county was taken from Monroe in 1869. Check Monroe Co for rec prior to this date) (Co Clk in DeValls Bluff, AR has m, div, pro, ct & land rec from 1885, nat rec 1907-1912 & mil dis rec from 1917)
Pulaski www.co.pulaski.ar.us/index.htm	H6	15 Dec 1818	**Arkansas** Pulaski County; 401 W Markham St; Little Rock, AR 72201; Ph. 501.340.8500 Details: (Co Clk has m rec from 1838, pro rec from 1820, voter reg rec from 1952, real estate tax rec from 1828, pers prop tax rec from 1869 & poll tax from 1892; Clk Cir Ct has ct, land & nat rec; Clk Chan Ct has div rec; History Commission has pro ct rec before 1920)
Randolph www.randolphchamber.com/	D9	18 Dec 1832	**Creek Cession of 1832** Randolph County; 107 W Broadway; Pocahontas, AR 72455; Ph. 870.892.5822 Details: (Co Clk has m & pro rec from 1837; Cir Clk has div, land, mil & ct rec from 1836)
Saline* www.salinecounty.org/	I5	2 Nov 1835	**Pulaski, Hempstead** Saline County; 215 North Main Ste 9; Benton, AR 72015; Ph. 501.303.5630 Details: (Co Clk has m & pro rec from 1836 & land rec from 1871)
Sarber		22 Mar 1871	**Pope, Franklin, Johnson, Scott, Yell** Details: (see Logan) Name changed to Logan 14 Dec 1875
Scott* www.rootsweb.com/~arscott/scott.htm	H2	5 Nov 1833	**Pulaski, Crawford, Pope** Scott County; 100 W 1 St Ste 1; Waldron, AR 72958; Ph. 501.637.2155 Details: (Co & Cir Clk has m, div, pro, land & ct rec from 1882)
Searcy* www.pastracks.com/states/arkansas/searcy/	F5	13 Dec 1838	**Marion** Searcy County; Courthouse Sq; PO Box 297; Marshall, AR 72650-0297; Ph. 870.448.3554 Details: (Co Clk has m, div, pro & ct rec from 1881 & land rec from 1866)
Sebastian www.rootsweb.com/~arsebast/sebast.htm	G2	6 Jan 1851	**Scott, Polk, Crawford, Van Buren** Sebastian County; 35 S 6th; Fort Smith, AR 72901; Ph. 501.782.5065 Details: (Co Clk has m rec from 1865 & pro rec from 1866; Clk Cir Ct has div, ct & land rec)
Sevier www.genealogyshoppe.com/arsevier/	J2	17 Oct 1828	**Hempstead, Miller** Sevier County; 115 N 3rd; De Queen, AR 71832; Ph. 870.642.2425 Details: (Co Clk has m & pro rec from 1829; Clk Cir Ct has div, ct & land rec)
Sharp www.sharpcounty.org/	E8	18 Jul 1868	**Lawrence** Sharp County; PO Box 307; Ash Flat, AR 72513; Ph. 870.994.7338 Details: (Line between Sharp & Izard changed 1877) (Co Clk has m, pro, div, ct & land rec from 1880)
St. Francis Check for future website at usgenweb.com/	H10	13 Oct 1827	**Phillips** St. Francis County; 313 S Izard St; Forrest City, AR 72335-3856; Ph. 870.261.1725 Details: (Co Clk has m rec from 1875, pro rec from 1910 & tax rec; Clk Cir Ct has div, ct & land rec)
Stone www.pastracks.com/states/arkansas/stone/	F6	21 Apr 1873	**Izard, Independence, Searcy, Van Buren** Stone County; HC 71 Box 1; PO Box 1427; Mountain View, AR 72560-0427; Ph. 870.269.5550 Details: (Co Clk has m & div rec from 1873; Clk Cir Ct has pro, land, mil & ct rec from 1873)

County Website	Map Index	Date Created	Parent County or Territory From Which Organized Address/Details
Union www.rootsweb.com/~arunion/	M6	2 Nov 1829	**Hempstead, Clark** Union County; 101 N Washington; El Dorado, AR 71730; Ph. 870.864.1910 Details: (Co Clk has m & pro rec from 1846; Clk Cir Ct has div, ct & land rec)
Van Buren www.rootsweb.com/~arvanbur/	F6	11 Nov 1833	**Independence, Conway, Izard** Van Buren County; Main & Griggs; Clinton, AR 72031; Ph. 501.745.4140 Details: (Co Clk has m, ct & land rec from 1859, div rec from 1874 & pro rec from 1860)
Washington www.co.washington.ar.us/	E2	17 Oct 1828	**Crawford** Washington County; 280 N College Ave #300; Fayetteville, AR 72701; Ph. 501.444.1711 Details: (Co Clk has m rec from 1845 & pro rec from 1828; Clk Cir Ct has div, ct & land rec; City Lib has cem rec)
White www.cswnet.com/~wccomp/	G7	23 Oct 1835	**Pulaski, Jackson, Independence** White County; 300 N Spruce St; Searcy, AR 72143; Ph. 501.279.6200 Details: (Co Clk has m, div, pro, ct, land, tax & misc rec)
Woodruff www.rootsweb.com/~arwoodru/	G9	26 Nov 1862	**Jackson, St. Francis** Woodruff County; 500 N 3rd St; Augusta, AR 72006-0356; Ph. 870.347.5206 Details: (Co Clk has m & pro rec from 1865; Clk Cir Ct has div, ct & land rec)
Yell www.rootsweb.com/~aryell/	H4	5 Dec 1840	**Pope, Scott** Yell County; PO Box 219; Danville, AR 72833-0219; Ph. 501.495.2630 Details: (Co Clk has m, div, pro, land & ct rec from 1865)

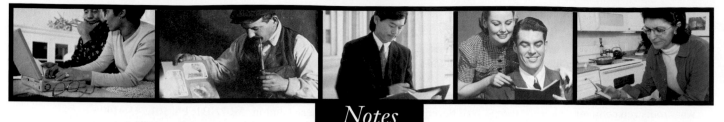

Notes

Golden Poppy

CALIFORNIA

CAPITAL: SACRAMENTO – STATE 1850 (31ST)

Juan Cabrillo discovered California in 1542. The English, due to Sir Francis Drake's visit in 1579, also laid claim to the land. However, the Spanish were first to establish settlements. San Diego was settled in 1769 and Monterey in 1770. Junipero Serra set up a chain of Franciscan missions throughout the state, which served as religious and economic centers. The Russians built Fort Ross in 1812 to serve as a trading post. In 1841 Fort Ross was abandoned. After Mexican independence in 1821, California became mainly a collection of large ranches. In 1839, a Swiss, John Augustus Sutter, established the "Kingdom of New Helvetia" in the Sacramento River Valley. Two years later Americans began traveling overland to California in significant numbers. Early in the Mexican War, American forces occupied California. John C. Fremont, the American soldier and explorer, headed a short-lived Republic of California in 1846. In 1848, California was ceded to the United States. Just nine days earlier, gold was discovered at Sutter's Mill. This discovery led to the California Gold Rush of 1849, which brought more than 100,000 people to California from all over the United States, Asia, Australia, and Europe.

The mass migration enabled California to attain the required number of inhabitants to be admitted to the Union in 1850. During the Civil War, 15,700 soldiers fought for the Union. Many Chinese immigrants who came for the gold rush helped build the transcontinental railroad, which was completed in 1869. A railroad rate war in 1884 and a real estate boom in 1885 led to another wave of immigration. Foreign-born Californians in descending order came from Mexico, Canada, Italy, England, Wales, Russia, Germany, Sweden, Ireland, Scotland, Poland, Austria, France, Denmark, Norway, Switzerland, Portugal, Greece, Yugoslavia, Hungary, Netherlands, Spain, Finland, Czechoslovakia, Romania, Lithuania, and Belgium.

Look for vital records in the following locations:

- Birth and death records: Office of Vital Records since 1905. Prior to 1 July 1905, records are available from the county recorders and the health departments of many larger cities.
- Marriage records: Office of Vital Records since 1905. Prior to 1 July 1905, records are available from the county recorders and the health departments of many larger cities.
- Divorce records: County clerks have divorce, probate, civil court and other records.
- Naturalizations: County offices of the Superior Courts and U.S. Circuit Courts in Los Angeles and San Francisco.
- Land records: Real estate deeds are filed in the County Recorder's office. Pre-statehood lists, termed padrons, of Spanish, Mexican, and Indian residents have been published.
- Census records: California State Archives has some census records for major California cities from 1897 to 1938.

Office of Vital Records
304 S. Street
Sacramento, California 94244
916.445.2684

California State Archives
Room 130, 1020 "O" Street
Sacramento, California 95814

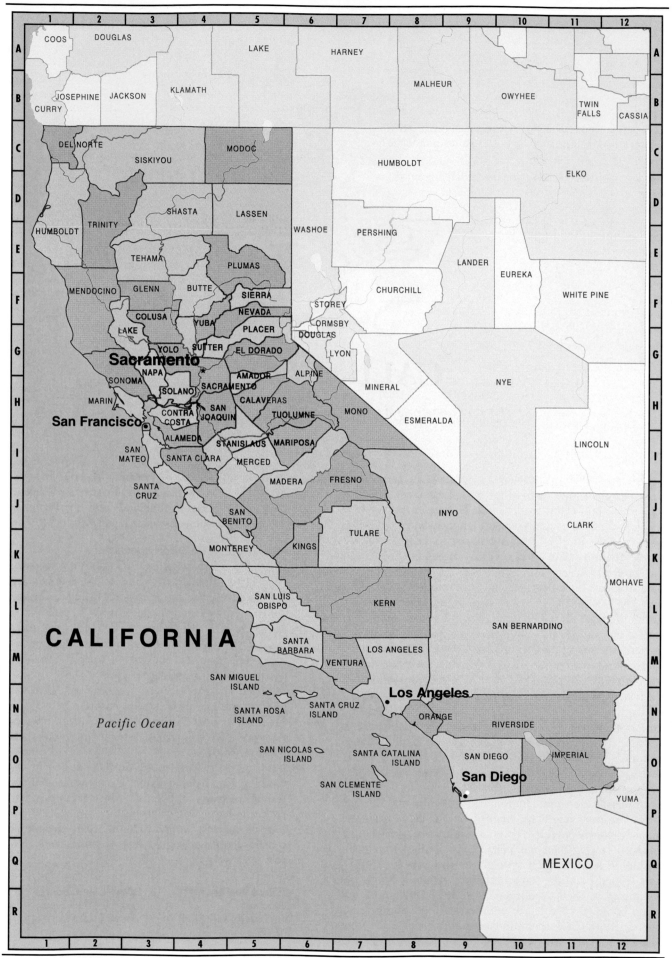

CALIFORNIA

Pacific Ocean

MEXICO

Societies and Repositories

African American Genealogical Society of Northern California; PO Box 27485; Oakland, California 94602-0985;

African-American Genealogical Society, California; PO Box 8442; Los Angeles, California 90008-0442

Afro-American Genealogical Society, California; Afro-American Museum; 600 State Dr., Exposition Park; Los Angeles, California 90037

Alameda Co. Library; 2450 Stevenson Blvd.; Fremont, California 94538-2326; 510.745.1500

Alhambra Historical Society; 1550 W. Alhambra Rd.; PO Box 6687; Alhambra, California 91802

Altadena Heritage; PO Box 218; Altadena, California 91003

Altadena Historical Society; PO Box 144; Altadena, California 91003

Amador County Friends of the Museum-Archives; PO Box 913; Jackson, California 95642

Amador County Genealogical Society; 10193 Buena Vista Dr.; Jackson, California 95642

American Historical Society of Germans from Russia, Central California Chapter, Library Museum; 3233 N. West; Fresno, California 93705; 209.229.8287

Angel Island Association; PO Box 866; Tiburon, California 94920; 415.435.2950;

Antelope Valley Genealogical Society; PO Box 1049; Lancaster, California 93534-1049; <www.qnet.com/~toiyabe/avgs/>

Augustan Soc. Library & Museum; PO Box 75; Daggett, California 92327-0075; <www.augustansociety.org>

Azusa Historical Society; City Hall Complex; 213 E. Foothill Blvd.; Azusa, California 91702

Baldwin Park Historical Society; PO Box 1; Baldwin Park, California 91706

Balkan and Eastern European American Genealogical and Historical Society; 4843 Mission St.; San Francisco, California 94112

Bancroft Library; University of California; Berkeley, California 94720

Bay Area Library & Information System (BALIS); 405 14th Street, Suite 211; Oakland, California 94612-2704

Berkeley Historical Society; PO Box 1190; Berkeley, California 94701-1190; <www.ci.berkeley.ca.us/histsoc/>

British Family Historical Society of Los Angeles; 22941 Felbar Ave.; Torrance, California 90505

British Isles Genealogical Research Association; PO Box 19775; San Diego, California 92159-0775

Burbank Historical Society; 1015 W. Olive Ave.; Burbank, California 91506

Calabasas Historical Society; PO Box 8067; Calabasas, California 91371

Calaveras County Library, Main Branch; Mountain Ranch Rd.; San Andreas, California PO Box 184; Angels Camp California 95222-0184

Calaveras Genealogical Society; PO Box 184; Angels Camp, California 95222-0184

California Genealogical Society; 1611 Telegraph Ave, Suite 200; Oakland, California 94612-2152; <www.calgensoc.com>

California Genealogical Society; 300 Brannan Street, Suite 409; PO Box 77105; San Francisco, California 94107-0105; 415.777.9936; Fax 415.777.0932

California Mennonite Historical Society; 4824 E. Butler; Fresno, California 93727-5097; <www.fresno.edu/affiliation/cmhs/>

California Mission Studies Association; PO Box 3357; Bakersfield, California 93385-3357; <www.ca-missions.org/contact.html>

California State Archives; 1020 "O" Street; Sacramento, California 95814; <www.ss.ca.gov/archives/archives.htm>

California State Genealogical Alliance; PO Box 311; Danville, California 94526-0311; <www.csga.com>

California State Library (Sutro Branch); 480 Winston Dr.; Sand Francisco, California 94132

California State Library, California Section, Rm. 304, Library and Courts Bldg.; 914 Capitol Mall; PO Box 942837; Sacramento, California 94237-0001

Carlsbad Historical Society; PO Box 252; Carlsbad, California 92018-0252; <www.carlsbad.ca.us/chs.html>

Clan Diggers Genealogical Society, Inc. of the Kern River Valley; PO Box 531; Lake Isabella, California 93240

Clayton Historical Society; PO Box 94; Clayton, California 94517-0094; <94517.com/chs/>

Colorado River-Blythe Quartzsite Genealogical Society; PO Box 404; Blythe, California 92226

ComputerRooters; PO Box 161693; Sacramento, California 95816

Conejo Valley Genealogical Society, Inc.; PO Box 1228; Thousand Oaks, California 91358-0228; <www.rootsweb.com/~cacvgs/>

Contra Costa County Genealogical Society; PO Box 910; Concord, California 94522; <www.geocities.com/Heartland/Plains/4335/cccgs/cccgs.html>

Contra Costa County Historical Society; 610 Main Street; Martinez, California 94553; 925.229.1772; <www.ccnet.com/~xptom/ccchs/>

Covina Valley Historical Society; 125 E. College St.; Covina, California 91723

Covina, Calif. Chapter, DAR; 2441 SN. Cameron Ave.; Covina, California 91724; <www.cupertino.org/update/civic/chs.htm>

Dalton Genealogical Society; 880 Ames Court; Palo Alto, California 94303

Davis Genealogical Club and Library; c/o The Davis Senior Center; 646 A Street; Davis, California; 95616-3602; <feefhs.org/ghcsv/dgc/frg-dgcl.html>

De Anza Heritage Society; PO Box 390861; Anza, California 92539

Delta Genealogical Interest Group; PO Box 157; Knightsen, California 94548

Diocese of Los Angeles; 3424 Wilshire Blvd.; Los Angeles, California 90010; 213.637.7000

Diocese of San Diego; 3888 Paducah Drive; San Diego, California 92117; 619.490.8200; Fax 619.490.8272

Downey Historical Society; PO Box 554; Downey, California 90241-0554

Duarte Historical Society; PO Box 263; Duarte, California 91009

Eagle Rock Valley Historical Society; 2035 Colorado Blvd.; Eagle Rock, California 90041

East Bay Genealogical Society; PO Box 20417; Oakland, California 94620-0417; <www.katpher.com/EBGS/ EBGS.html>

East Kern Genealogical Society; PO Box 961; North Edwards, California 93523-0961

Echo Park Historical Society; 1471 Fairbanks Pl.; Los Angeles, California 90026

El Dorado Research Society; PO Box 56; El Dorado, California 95623

El Monte Historical Society; PO Box 6307; El Monte, California 91734

Encino Historical Society; 16756 Moorpark St.; Encino, California 91436

Escondido Genealogical Society; PO Box 2190; Escondido, California 92033-2190

Eureka California Senior Center; 1910 California St.; Eureka, California 95501

Family History Library; 35 North West Temple Street; Salt Lake City, Utah 84150; 800.346.6044 or 801.240.2584; <www.familysearch.org>; Find a Family History Center near you; <www.familysearch.org/Eng/Library/FHC/ frameset_fhc.asp>

Forestville Historical Society; PO Box 195; Forestville, California 95436; <www.sonic.net/forestville/>

Fresno County Genealogical Society; PO Box 1429; Fresno, California 93716-1429

Fresno Historical Society; 7160 West Kearney Boulevard; Fresno, California 93706; 559.441.1372;

Genealogical and Historical Council of the Sacramento Valley; PO Box 214749; Sacramento, California 95821-0749; 916.682.3381; <feefhs.org/ghcsv/frgghcsv.html>

Genealogical Association of Sacramento; PO Box 292145; Sacramento, California 95829-2145

Genealogical Club of Sun City; PO Box 175; Sun City, California 92586-0175

Genealogical Society of Coachella Valley; PO Box 124; Indio, California 92202

Genealogical Society of Hispanic America of Southern California; PO Box 2472; Santa Fe Springs, California 90670

Genealogical Society of Madera; PO Box 495; Madera, California 93639

Genealogical Society of Morongo Basin; PO Box 234; Yucca Valley, California 92286; <www.yuccavalley.com/genealogy/>

Genealogical Society of North Orange County, (GSNOCC); PO Box 706; Yorba Linda, California 92885-0706

Genealogical Society of Riverside; PO Box 2557; Riverside, California 92516; <www.geocities.com/Heartland/Woods/ 6250/>

Genealogical Society of Santa Cruz County; PO Box 72; Santa Cruz, California 95063

Genealogical Society of Siskiyou County; PO Box 225; Yreka, California 96097

Genealogical Society of Stanistaus County; PO Box A; Modesto, California 95352-3660; <compuology.com/ cagenweb/gssc.html>

Genealogy Society of Vallejo-Benicia; 734 Marin Street; Vallejo, California 94590; <www.rootsweb.com/~cagsv/>

German Genealogical Society of America; 2125 Wright Ave., Ste. C-9; La Verne, California 91750

German Immigrant Genealogical Society; PO Box 7369; Burbank, California 91510-7369; 818.353.2341; 818.716 .6300; <feefhs.org/igs/frg-igs.html>

German Research Association; PO Box 11293; San Diego, California 92111

Glendale Historical Society; PO Box 4173; Glendale, California 91202

Glendora Genealogical Group; PO Box 1141; Glendora, California 91740-1141

Glendora Historical Society; 314 N. Glendora Ave.; PO Box 532; Glendora, California 91740

Glenn Genealogical Group; 1121 Marin; Orland, California 95963

Golden Gate Chapter, AHSGR; 2725 Belmont Canyon Road; Elmont, California 94002-1204; 650.591.5143

Grass Roots Genealogical Group; PO Box 98; Grass Valley, California 95945

Hayward Area Genealogical Society; PO Box 754; Hayward, California 94543

Hemet-San Jacinto Genealogical Society; PO Box 2516; Hemet, California 92343

Heritage Genealogical Society; 12056 Lomica Dr.; San Diego, California 92128

Hi-Desert Genealogical Society; PO Box 1271; Victorville, California 92393; <vvo.com/comm/hdgs.htm>

Historical Archives; 210010 Broadway; Sacramento, California 95818-2541; 916.733.0299; Fax 916.733.0215

Historical Society of Centinela Valley; 7634 Midfield Ave.; Los Angeles, California 90045

Historical Society of Long Beach; 428 Pine Ave.; PO Box 1869; Long Beach, California 90801-1869

Historical Society of Monterey Park; 781 S. Orange Ave.; PO Box 172; Monterey Park, California 91754

Historical Society of Pomona Valley; 1460 East Holt Blvd. Suite 78; Pomona, California 91767; <www.osb.net/ pomona/>

Historical Society of Southern California; 200 E. Ave. 43; Los Angeles, California 90031; 323.222.0771;

Historical Society of the Upper Mojave Desert; PO Box 2001; Ridgecrest, California 93556-2001; 760.375.7385; <www.ridgecrest.ca.us/~matmus/Hist.html>

Historical Society of West Covina; PO Box 4597; West Covina, California 91793

Holt-Atherton Church Archives; University of the Pacific; 3601 Pacific Avenue; Stockton, California 95211; 209.946.2404; Fax 209-946-2810; (Methodist Church Records)

Hugarian-American Friendship Society; c/o Doug Holmes; 1035 Starbrook Drive; Galt, California 95632; <www.dholmes.com/hafs.html>

Humboldt County Genealogical Society; 2336 G Street; Eureka, California 95501

Immigrant Genealogical Society; PO Box 7369; 1310B West Magnolia Blvd.; Burbank, California 91510-7369; 818.353.2341; <feefhs.org/igs/frg-igs.html>

Indian Wells Valley Genealogical Society; 131 Los Flores; Ridgecrest, California 93555

Jewish Genealogical Society of Los Angeles; PO Box 55443; Sherman Oaks, California 91413-0443; 818.712.9031; <www.jewishgen.org/jgsla/>

Jewish Genealogical Society of Orange County; 2370-1D Via Mariposa West; Laguna Hills, California 92653

Jewish Genealogical Society of Sacramento; 5631 Kiva Dr.; Sacramento, California 95841

Jewish Genealogical Society of San Diego; 255 South Rios Ave.; Solana Beach, California 92075

Kern County Genealogical Society; PO Box 2214; Bakersfield, California 93303

La Puente Valley Historical Society; PO Box 522; La Puente, California 91744

Lake County Genealogical Society; PO Box 1323; Lakeport, California 95453

Lake Elsinore Genealogical Society "Legs"; Box 807; Lake Elsinore, California 92531-0807

Leisure World Genealogical Workshop; c/o Leisure World Library; 2300 Beverly Manor Rd.; Seal Beach; California 90740

Livermore-Amador Genealogical Society; PO Box 901; Livermore, California 94550; <www.l-ags.org/index.html>

Lodi, California Chapter, AHSGR; 3525 Veneman Ave. No.; Modesto, California 95356-2435; 209.524.6330

Lomita Historical Society; 24016 Benhill Ave.; PO Box 549; Lomita, California 90717

Los Angeles City Historical Society; PO Box 41046; Los Angeles, California 90041

Los Angeles Westside Genealogical Society; PO Box 10447; Marina Del Rey, California 90295-6447; <www.genealogy-la.com/lawgs.shtml>

Los Banos Genealogical Society, Inc.; PO Box 2525; Los Banos, California 93635

Maidu Genealogical Society; 1550 Maidu Dr.; Roseville, California 95661

Marin County Genealogical Society; PO Box 1511; Novato, California 94949-1511;

Martinez Historical Society; PO Box 14; Martinez, California 94553; <www.martinezhistory.org/index2.html>

Mendocino Coast Genealogical Society; PO Box 762; Fort Bragg, California 95437

Mendocino County Historical Society; 603 W. Perkins St.; Ukiah, California 95482

Merced County Genealogical Society; PO Box 3061; Merced, California 95340; <www.rootsweb.com/~camcgs/home.htm>

Monterey County Genealogical Society; PO Box 8144; Salinas, California 93912-9144

Moraga Historical Society; PO Box 103; Moraga, California 94556; 925.377.0354

Moravian Heritage Society; 31910 Road 160; Visalia, California 93292; 559.798.1922; <www.czechusa.com>

Mt. Diablo Chapter, AHSGR; 11 Wandel Drive; Moraga, California 94556-1829; 510.642.6108

Mt. Diablo Genealogical Society; PO Box 4654; Walnut Creek, California 94596

Napa Valley Genealogical and Biographical Society; 1701 Menlo Ave.; Napa, California 94559; <www.napanet.net/~nvgbs/>

National Archives—Pacific Region (Laguna Niguel); 24000 Avila Road; Laguna Niguel, California 92677; 714.360.2641; Fax 714.360.2644

National Archives—Pacific Region (San Bruno); 1000 Commodore Drive; San Bruno, California 94066; 415-876-9009; Fax 415-876-9233

Native Daughters of the Golden West; 555 Baker St.; San Francisco, California 94117-1405

Native Sons of the Golden West; 414 Mason St.; San Francisco, California 94102

Nevada County Genealogical Society; PO Box 176; Cedar Ridge, California 95924; <www.rootsweb.com/~cancgs/>

North San Diego County Genealogical Society, Inc.; PO Box 581; Carlsbad, California 92008

Northern California Chapter, OGS; PO Box 60191; Sacramento, California 95960-0101

Office of Vital Records and Statistics; 304 "S" Street; PO Box 730241; Sacramento, California 94244-0241; 916.445.2684; Fax 800.858.5553

Orange County Genealogical Society; PO Box 1587; Orange, California 92856-1587;

Pacific Palisades Historical Society; PO Box 1299; Los Angeles, California 90272

Pajaro Valley Genealogical Society; 53 North Dr.; Freedom, California 95019

Palm Springs Genealogical Society; PO Box 2093; Palm Springs, California 92263-2093

Paradise Genealogical Society, Inc.; PO Box 460; Paradise, California 95967-0460; <www.jps.net/pargenso>

Pasadena Genealogical Society; PO Box 94774; Pasadena, California 91109-4774

Pasadena Heritage; 80 West Dayton; Pasadena, California 91105

Pasadena Historical Society; 470 W. Walnut St.; Pasadena, California 91103

Patterson Genies; 13218 Sycamore; Patterson, California 95363

Pico Rivera History and Heritage Society; PO Box 313; Pico Rivera, California 90666

Placer County Genealogical Society; PO Box 7385; Auburn, California 95604-7385; <www.webcom.com/gunruh/pcgs.html>

Plumas County Historical Society; PO Box 695; Quincy, California 95971

Pocahontas Trails Genealogical Society; 6015 Robin Hill Dr.; Lakeport, California 95453

Polish Genealogical Society of California; PO Box 713; Midway City, California 92655-0713; <feefhs.org/pol/pgsca/frgpgsca.html>

Pomona Valley Genealogical Society; PO Box 296; Pomona, California 91766

Questing Heirs Genealogical Society; PO Box 15102; Long Beach, California 90815-0102; 562.437.4337

Redondo Beach Historical Society; PO Box 978; Redondo Beach, California 90277; <members.aol.com/RBHistSoc/>

Redwood Genealogical Society; Box 645; Fortuna, California 95540

Renegade Root Diggers; 9171 Fargo Ave.; Hanford, California 93230

Root Diggers, Lucerne Valley Genealogical Association; c/o Lucerne Valley Library; PO Box 408; Lucerne Valley, California 92356

Roseville Genealogical Society; PO Box 459; Roseville, California 95678; <www.rootsweb.com/~carvgs/rgs.htm>

Sacramento Genealogical Society, Root Cellar; PO Box 265; Citrus Heights, California 95611-0265; <www.rootsweb.com/~carcsgs/rootcellar.html>

Sacramento German Genealogical Society; PO Box 660061; Sacramento, California 95866

Sacramento Valley Chapter, AHSGR; 624 Shangri Lane; Sacramento, California 95825-5505; 916.925.5054;

San Bernardino Valley Genealogical Society; PO Box 2220; San Bernardino, California 92405

San Clemente Historical Society; PO Box 283; San Clemente, California 92674-0283; <www.ocnow.com/community/groups/sanclemente/index.html>

San Diego Genealogical Society; 1050 Pioneer Way, Suite E; El Cajon, California 92020-1943; <www.rootsweb.com/~casdgs/>

San Diego Historical Society; PO Box 81825; San Diego, California 92138; <www.sandiegohistory.org/histsoc.html>

San Diego, California Chapter.; The National Society Daughters of the War of 1812 San Diego, California

San Fernando Valley Genealogical Society; PO Box 3486; Winnetka, California 91396-3486; <www.rootsweb.com/~casfvgs/>

San Fernando Valley Historical Society; PO Box 7039; Mission Hills, California 92346-70396

San Francisco Bay Area Jewish Genealogical Society; PO Box 471616; San Francisco, California 94147; <www.jewishgen.org/sfbajgs/>

San Francisco Public Library Gen Collection; 480 Winston Dr.; San Francisco, California 94132

San Francisco Theological Seminary Library; 2 Kensington Road; San Anselmo, California 94960; 415.258.6636; (Presbyterian Church Records)

San Gorgonio Pass Genealogical Society; 1050 Brinton Ave.; Banning, California 92220

San Joaquin Genealogical Society; PO Box 4817; Stockton, California 95204-0817; <www.rootsweb.com/~sjgs/>

San Luis Obispo Co. Gen. Soc. Library, City Administration Bldg., Rm. 104; Palma Ave. & West Mall; Atascadero, California 93423-0004

San Luis Obispo Co. Gen. Soc. Library, South County Regional Center; 800 W. Branch; Arroyo Grande, California 93420

San Luis Obispo County Genealogical Society, Inc.; PO Box 4 Atascadero, California 93423-0004

San Marino Historical Society; PO Box 80222; San Marino, California 91118-8222

San Mateo County Genealogical Society; PO Box 5083; San Mateo, California 94402-0083;

San Mateo County Historical Association; San Mateo Junior College; San Mateo, California 94402

San Ramon Valley Genealogical Society; PO Box 305; Diablo, California 94528

Santa Barbara County Genealogical Society; PO Box 1303; Goleta, California 93116-1303; <www.compuology.com/sbarbara>

Santa Clara Co. Free Library; 1095 N. 7th St.; San Jose, California 95112

Santa Clara County Historical and Genealogical Society; c/o Santa Clara City Library; 3345 Lochinvar Ave; Santa Clara, California 95051; <www.katpher.com/SCCHGS/>

Santa Clarita Valley Historical Society; 24107 San Fernando Rd.; Newhall, California 91321

Santa Cruz City-County Public Library, Central Branch; 224 Church St., Santa Cruz; Santa Cruz, California 95060

Santa Maria Public Library, Gen. Collection & Calif. Rm.; 420 S. Broadway; Santa Maria, California 93454

Santa Maria Valley Genealogical Society; PO Box 1215; Santa Maria, California 93456

Santa Monica Historical Society; 1345 3rd Street Promenade; PO Box 3059; Santa Monica, California 90408-3059

Santa Rosa-Sonoma Co. Library; Third and E. Streets; Santa Rosa, California 95404

Sequoia Genealogical Society; 113 North "F" St.; Tulare, California 93274

Shasta Genealogical Society; PO Box 994652; Redding, California 96099-4652; <www.rootsweb.com/~cascogs/>

Shields Library; University of California; Davis, California 95616

Siskiyou Co. Public Library; 719 4th St.; Yreka, California 96097

Slovak Research Center; 6862 Palmer Ct.; Chino, California 91710-7343; 909.627.2897

Society of California Pioneers; 1 Hawthorne Street; PO Box 1850; San Francisco, California 94119-1850; 415.957.9858; Fax 415.957.1849

Society of Hispanic Historical and Ancestral Research; PO Box 490; Midway City, California 92655-0490; <members.aol.com/shhar/>

Society of Mayflower Descendants in the State of California; 120 Fifteenth St., Terrace Level; Oakland, California 94612

Solano Co. Gen. Soc. Library; 620 E. Main St.; Vacaville, California PO Box 2494; Fairfield, California 94533; 707.446.6869

Solano County Genealogical Society, Inc.; PO Box 2494; Fairfield, California 94533

Sonoma County Genealogical Society; PO Box 2273; Santa Rosa, California 95405-0273;

Sons of the Revolution Library, Sons of the Revolution Bldg.; 600 S. Central Ave.; Glendale, California 91204

South Bay Cities Genealogical Society; PO Box 11069; Torrance, California 90510-1069; <www.rootsweb.com/~casbcgs/>

South Orange County Genealogical Society; PO Box 4513; Mission Viejo, California 92690-4513; <www.rootsweb.com/~casoccgs/>

Southern California Chapter, AHSGR; 16371 Silver Lane; Huntington Beach, California 92647; 714.847.6481; <www.ehrman.net/ahsgr/casocal.html>

Southern California Chapter, OGS; 14837 Los Robles Avenue; Hacienda Heights, California 91745-2615; 626.333.1194

Southern California Chapter, OGS; PO Box 5553; Whittier, California 90607-5553

Southern California Gen. Soc. Library; 417 Irving Dr.; Burbank, California 91405; 818.843.7247

Southern California Genealogical Society; 417 Irving Dr.; Burbank, California 91504-2408; 818.843.7262;

Southern California Jewish Historical Society; 6505 Wilshire Blvd.; Los Angeles, California 90048

Spanishtown Historical Society; Box 62; Half Moon Bay, California 94019

St. Ives Historical Society; 21661 Lyn St.; California City, California 93505;

Stanislaus Co. Free Library; 1500 I Street; Modesto, California 95354

Sutro Library Branch of the Calif. State Library; 480 Winston Dr.; San Francisco, California 94132

Taft Genealogical Society; PO Box 7411; Taft, California 93268

Tehama Genealogical and Historical Society; PO Box 415; Red Bluff, California 96080

Temple City Historical Society; PO Box 1379; Temple City, California 91780; <www.ci.temple-city.ca.us/comunorg/histsoc.htm>

Topanga Historical Society; PO Box 1214; Topanga, California 90290; <www.topangaonline.com/hsociety.html>

Tracy Area Genealogical Society; 1852 W. 11th St., PMB 632; Tracy, California 95376; <rootsweb.com/~catags/frmain.htm>

Triadoption Library; PO Box 5218; Huntington Beach, California 90278

TRW Genealogical Society; One Space Park S-1435; Redondo Beach, California 90279

Tulare Public Library; 113 N. F Street; Tulare, California 93274

Tule Tree Tracers; 41 W. Thurman Ave.; Porterville, California 93257

Tuolumne County Genealogical Society; PO Box 3956; Sonora, California 95370

Vandenberg Genealogical Society; PO Box 81; Lompoc, California 93438-008

Ventura Co. Genealogical Library, E.P. Foster Library; 651 E. Main; Ventura, California 93003

Ventura County Genealogical Society; PO Box 24608; Ventura, California 93002; <www.rootsweb.com/~cavcgs/>

Whittier Area Genealogical Society; PO Box 4367; Whittier, California 90607-4367

Whittier Historical Society; 6755 Newlin Ave; Whittier, California 90601; 562.945.9106; <www.whittierbiz.com/info/museum.htm>

Workman and Temple Family Homestead Museum; 15415 East Don Julian Road; City of Industry,; California 91745-1029; 626.968.2048;

Yolo County Archives; 226 Buckeye St.; Woodland, California 95695

Yolo County Historical Society; PO Box 1447; Woodland, California 95776; <www.yolo.net/ychs/>

Yorba Linda Heritage Museum and Historical Society; PO Box 396; Yorba Linda, California 92885-0396

Yucaipa Valley Genealogical Society; PO Box 32; Yucaipa, California 92399

Bibliography and Record Sources

General Sources

Bancroft, Hubert H. *California Pioneer Register and Index, 1542-1848, Including Inhabitants…1769-1800 and a List of Pioneers (1884-1901).* Reprint. Baltimore, Maryland: Clearfield Co., 1990.

Bolton, Herbert E. *The Spanish Borderlands: A Chronicle of Old Florida and the Southwest.* (1921), reprint Galveston Texas: Frontier Press, 1996.

California Genealogical Society. *Genealogy Success Stories: Personal Problem-solving Accounts that Encourage, Enlighten and Inspire You.* San Francisco, California: California Genealogical Society, 1995.

California Local History: A Bibliography and Union List of Library Holdings. 2nd ed. Stanford, California: Stanford University Press, 1970. Supplement (covering 1961 to 1970), 1976.

California Research Outline. Series US-States, No. 5. Salt Lake City: Family History Library, 1988.

Faulkinbury, Jim W. *The Foreign-Born Voters of California in 1872.* Sacramento California: Jim W. Faulkinbury, 1994.

Hunt, Rockwell Dennis, ed. *California and Californians.* Chicago: Lewis Publishing Co., 1932.

Nicklas, Laurie. *The California Locator. A Directory of Public Records for Locating People Dead or Alive in California.* Modesto California: Laurie Nicklas, 1996.

Parker, J. Carlyle. *An Index to the Biographies in 19th Century California County Histories.* (1979). Reprint, Turlock California: Marietta Pub. Co., 1994.

Phelps, Alonzo. *Contemporary Biography of California's Representative Men...*2 vols. San Francisco: A.L. Bancroft and Co., 1881.

Pompey, Sherman L. *Genealogical Records of California.* Fresno California: Sherman L. Pompey, 1968.

Smith, Clifford N. *Gold! German Transcontinental Travelers to California, 1849-1851.* McNeal AZ: Westland Publications, 1988.

Solano County Genealogical Society, Inc. *Index to the DAR "Records of the Families of the California Pioneers," Volumes 1-27.* Fairfield California: Solano Co. Gen Soc., 1988.

Southern California Genealogical Society. *Sources of Genealogical Help in California Libraries.* Rev. ed. 1996. Burbank California: The Society.

Southern California Genealogical Society. *American Indian Related Books in the SCGS Library.* Burbank California: The Society.

Southern California Genealogical Society. *UCLA Library: Sources of Genealogical Help.* Burbank California: The Society.

Atlases, Maps and Gazetteers

Beck, Warren A., and Ynez D. Haase. *Historical Atlas of California.* Norman: University of Oklahoma Press, 1974.

California City and Unincorporated Place Names. Sacramento: California Division of Highways, 1971.

Coy, Owen C. *California County Boundaries: A Study of the Division of the States into Counties and the Subsequent Changes in their Boundaries, with Maps.* Berkeley: California Historical Survey Commission, 1923. Reprint. Rev. ed. Fresno, California: Valley Publishers, 1973.

Durrennberger, Robert W. *Patterns on the Land: Geographical, Historical, and Political Maps of California.* Palo Alto, California: National Press Books, 1965.

Gudde, Erwin G. *California Place Names: The Origin and Etymology of Current Geographical Names.* 3rd ed. Rev. and Enl. Berkeley: University of California Press, 1969.

Hanna, Phil L., comp. *The Dictionary of California Land Names.* Los Angeles: Automobile Club of Southern California, 1946.

Patera, Edward L. *History of California Post Offices, 1849-1990 / H. E. Salley: Includes Branches and Stations, Rural Free Delivery Routes, Navy Numbered Branches, Highway and Railway Post Offices.* 2nd ed. [Lake Grove, Or.]: The Depot, 1991.

Preston, Ralph N. *Early California: Early Forts, Old Mines, Old Town Sites.* Northern ed. Corvallis, OR: Western Guide Publishers, 1974. Reprinted as *Early California Atlas: Northern Edition.* 2nd ed. Portland. Oregon: Binford & Mort Publishers, 1983.

Salley, Harold E. *History of California Post Offices, 1849-1976: Includes Branches and Stations, Navy Numbered Branches, Highway and Railroad Posts.* La Mesa, California: Postal History Association, 1977.

Sanchez, Nellie Van de Grift. *Spanish and Indian Place Names of California – Their Meaning and Their Romance.* San Francisco: A.M. Robertson, 1930.

Southern and Central California Atlas and Gazetteer. 3rd ed. Freeport, Maine: DeLorme Mapping Co., 1994.

United States. Geological Survey. *California, Index to Topographic and Other Map Coverage.* Reston, Virginia: United States Geological Survey. National Mapping Program, [1983].

Census Records

Available Census Records and Census Substitutes

Federal Census 1850 (except Contra Costa, San Francisco and Santa Clara Counties), 1860, 1870, 1880, 1900, 1910, 1920, 1930.

Federal Mortality Schedules 1850, 1860, 1870, 1880.

State Federal Census 1852.

Padron Census 1790.

California State Genealogical Alliance. *The California 1890 Great Register of Voters Index.* 3 vols. North Salt Lake, Utah: Heritage Quest, 2001.

Dollarhide, William. *The Census Book: A Genealogist's Guide to Federal Census Facts, Schedules and Indexes.* Bountiful, Utah: Heritage Quest, 1999.

Kemp, Thomas Jay. *The American Census Handbook.* Wilmington, Delaware: Scholarly Resources, Inc., 2001.

Lainhart, Ann S. *State Census Records.* Baltimore: Genealogical Publishing Co., Inc., 1992.

Szucs, Loretto Dennis, and Matthew Wright. *Finding Answers in U.S. Census Records.* Ancestry Publishing, 2001.

Thorndale, William, and William Dollarhide. *Map Guide to the U.S. Federal Censuses, 1790-1920.* Baltimore: Genealogical Publishing Co., 1987.

United States. Bureau of Internal Revenue. *Internal Revenue Assessment Lists for California, 1862-1866.* Washington, D.C.: The National Archives, 1988. 33 microfilm.

Court Records, Probate and Wills

California. State Archives (Sacramento). *Index to Records of Appellate Court Cases, 1900-1930.* Microfilm of original records at the State Archives, Sacramento, Calif. (Salt Lake City: Filmed by the Genealogical Society of Utah, 1975). 2 microfilm.

California. State Archives (Sacramento). *Index to Records of Supreme Court Cases, 1850-1930.* Microfilm of original records at the State Archives, Sacramento, California. (Salt Lake City: Filmed by the Genealogical Society of Utah, 1975). 2 microfilm.

California. State Archives (Sacramento). *Index to Transcripts of Court Cases in State Archives, Attorney General, State of California.* Microfilm of original records at the State Archives, Sacramento, California (Salt Lake City: Filmed by the Genealogical Society of Utah, 1975).

Dilts, Bryan Lee, comp. *1860 California Census Index: Head of Households and Other Surnames in Household Index.* 2nd ed. Bountiful, Utah: AGLL, 1984.

Nicklas, Laurie. *California County Courthouse Records: A Directory of Vital Records found in Each County Office in California.* Modesto, California: L. Nicklas, 1998.

Emigration, Immigration, Migration and Naturalization

California State Library (Sacramento). *Pioneer Index File (California), 1906-1935.* Microfilm of card file located at the California State Library, Sacramento. (Salt Lake City: Filmed by the Genealogical Society of Utah, 1991). 10 microfilm.

California. Circuit Court (Northern District). *Selected Indexes to Naturalization Records of the U.S. Circuit & District Courts, Northern, & Southern Districts of California.* Washington, D.C.: National Archives. Central Plains Region, 1984. 3 microfilm.

California. Superior Court. *Naturalization Records, 1887-1940.* Salt Lake City: Filmed by the Genealogical Society of Utah, 1987-1988). 246 microfilm.

Carr, Peter E. *San Francisco Passenger Departure Lists–Vols. I-IV.* San Luis Obispo, California: TCI Genealogical Resources, 1991-1993.

Lewis, Oscar. *Sea Routes to the Gold Fields, the Migration by Water to California in 1849-1852.* New York: Alfred A. Knopf, 1949.

United States. Bureau of Customs. *Alphabetical Index of Ships' Arrival at the Port of San Francisco, California, from ca. 1840 to 1 December 1954.* Washington, D.C.: National Archives. Central Plains Region, 1987.

United States. District Court (California: Northern District). *Declarations of Intention, 1846-1903.* Microfilm of original records at the Federal Records Center, San Bruno, California Salt Lake City: Filmed by the Genealogical Society of Utah, 1975. 4 microfilm.

United States. District Court (California: Northern District). *Index to Naturalization in the U.S. District Court for the Northern District of California, 1860-1989.* Microfilm of records located at the National Archives, Pacific Sierra Region, San Bruno, California. Salt Lake City: Filmed by the Genealogical Society of Utah, 1992-1993. 165 microfilm.

United States. District Court (California: Southern District). *Declarations of Intention, 1927-1948.* Microreproduction of the original records at the Federal Archives and Records Center, Laguna Niguel, California. Salt Lake City: Filmed by the Genealogical Society of Utah, 1978. 44 microfilm.

United States. District Court (California: Southern District: Central Division). *General Card Index to Naturalized Citizens, 1915-1978.* Microfilm of original index cards located in the National Archives, Los Angeles Branch, Laguna Niguel, California. Salt Lake City: Filmed by the Genealogical Society of Utah, 1989. 114 microfilm.

United States. District Court (California: Southern District: Central Division). *Index Cards to Overseas Military Petitions of U.S. District Court for the Southern District of California, Central Division, Laguna Niguel.* Microfilm of original index cards located in the National Archives, Los Angeles Branch, Laguna Niguel, California. Salt Lake City: Filmed by the Genealogical Society of Utah, 1989. 2 microfilm.

United States. *Immigration and Naturalization Service. Crew Lists of Vessels Arriving at San Francisco, California, 1905-1921.* Washington, D.C.: The National Archives, 1988. 35 microfilm.

United States. *Immigration and Naturalization Service. Manifests of Alien Arrivals at San Ysidro (Tia Juana) California, April 21, 1908-December 1952.* College Park, Md.: National Archives and Records Administration, 1999. 20 microfilm.

United States. Immigration and Naturalization Service. *Passenger Lists of Vessels Arriving at San Pedro/Wilmington/Los Angeles, California, June 29, 1907-June 30, 1948:* Record Group 85, M1764. Washington: National Archives and Records Administration, 1998. 18 microfilm.

United States. *Immigration and Naturalization Service. Registers of Chinese Laborers Arriving at San Francisco, 1882-1888.* Washington, D.C.: The National Archives, 1988. 12 microfilm.

Land and Property

Avina, Rose Hollenbaugh. *Spanish and Mexican Land Grants in California.* New York: Arno Press, 1976.

Bowman, J.N. *Index to the Spanish-Mexican Private Land Grant Records and Cases of California.* Bancroft Library, University of California, 1970.

California. Surveyor-general's Office. *Spanish Archives, 1833-1845.* Microfilm of original records at the State Archives, Sacramento, Calif. Salt Lake City: Filmed by the Genealogical Society of Utah, 1975. 14 microfilm.

Cowan, Robert Granniss. Ranchos of California: *A List of Spanish Concessions, 1775-1822, and Mexican Grants, 1822-1846.* Fresno California: Academy Library Guild, 1956.

Deeter, Judy A. *Veterans Who Applied for Land in Southern California 1851-1911.* The author, Mission Viejo California, 1993.

Lingenfelter Collection (California). *Northern California Bounty Land Grantees under Acts of 1847-1855.* Microfilm of originals in the Meriam Library, Special Collections, California State University, Chico, California. (Salt Lake City: Filmed by the Genealogical Society of Utah, 1990).

Shumway, Burgess McK. *California Ranchos: Patented Private Land Grants Listed by County.* Edited by Michael and Mary Burgess. Athens Georgia: Iberian Publishing Co., 1941.

United States. District Court (California: Northern District). *Private Land-Grant Case Files in the Circuit Court of the Northern District of California, 1852-1910.* Microfilm of original records located in the Bancroft Library, Berkeley, Calif. Washington, D.C.: The National Archives, 1988. 28 microfilm.

United States. Land Office (Los Angeles, California). *Land Records, 1851-1936.* Microfilm of records located at the National Archives, Pacific Southwest Region Office, Laguna Niguel, California. Salt Lake City: Filmed by the Genealogical Society of Utah, 1989. 61 microfilm.

Military

Breithaupt, Richard Hoag, Jr. *Sons of the Revolution in the State of California, Centennial Register, 1893-1993.* Universal City, Calif.: Walika, 1994.

California Adjunct General's Office. *Records of California Men in the War of the Rebellion, 1861 to 1867*. Sacramento California: State Office, 1890.

California. Adjutant General's Office. *California Military Records in the State Archives, 1858-1923*. Microfilm of original records at the State Archives, Sacramento, California Salt Lake City: Filmed by the Genealogical Society of Utah, 1975. 35 microfilm.

California. State Council of Defense. *Records of Californians Who Served in World War I*. Microfilm of original records at the California State Library. (Salt Lake City: Filmed by the Genealogical Society of Utah, 1975). 17 microfilm.

Carr, Elmer J. *Honorable Remembrance: The San Diego Master List of the Mormon Battalion* [S.l.: s.n., 1978?].

Harlow, Neal. *California Conquered: War and Peace on the Pacific, 1846-1850*. Berkeley, Calif.: University of California Press, 1982.

MacFarland, Olive K. H. *War Service Records, 1914-1919*, California Chapters, Daughters of the American Revolution. Salt Lake City: Filmed by the Genealogical Society of Utah, 1995. 14 microfiches.

Orton, Richard H. *Records of California Men in the War of the Rebellion, 1861 to 1867*. Tucson, Arizona: Filmed by W.C. Cox, 1974.

Pompey, Sherman L. *A List of Mexican War Veterans Buried in California*. Fresno California: Sherman L. Pompey, 1968.

Sánchez, Joseph P. *Spanish Bluecoats, The Catalonian Volunteers in Northwestern New Spain, 1767-1810*. Albuquerque, New Mexico: University of New Mexico Press, 1990.

Thompson, J. S. *Records of the Mormon Battalion*. Microfilm of original published: Reno, Nevada: J.S. Thompson, 1995. Salt Lake City: Filmed by the Genealogical Society of Utah, 1995.

United States. Adjutant General's Office. *Index to Compiled Service Records of Volunteer Soldiers Who Served During Indian Wars and Disturbances, 1815-1858*. Washington, D.C.: The National Archives, 1966. 42 microfilm.

United States. Army. Military department. *Records of the 10th Military Department, 1846-1851*. Washington, D.C.: The National Archives, 1955. 7 microfilm.

United States. District Court (California: Southern District: Central Division). *Index Cards to Overseas Military Petitions of U.S. District Court for the Southern District of California, Central Division, Laguna Niguel*. Microfilm of original index cards located in the National Archives, Los Angeles Branch, Laguna Niguel, California. (Salt Lake City: Filmed by the Genealogical Society of Utah, 1989). 2 microfilm.

United States. Selective Service System. *California, World War I Selective Service System Draft Registration Cards, 1917-1918*. Washington: The National Archives, 1987-1988. 158 microfilm.

Vital and Cemetery Records

Bruner, Helen Maria. *California's Old Burying Grounds: Prepared for the National Society of Colonial Dames Resident in the State of California*. Tucson, Arizona: W.C. Cox Co., 1974.

California Death Records. The California Department of Health Services Office of Health Information and Research vital Statistics Section. <vitals.rootsweb.com/ca/death/search.cgi>, 1998-2001.

California State Library (Sacramento). *List of Deaths Copied from Records in the California State Library*. Sacramento: California State Library, n.d.

California State Library (Sacramento). *Mortuary Records 1849-1900 (Northern California)*. Microfilm of card filed located in Special Collections, California State Library, Sacramento Salt Lake City: Filmed by the Genealogical Society of Utah, 1991. 13 microfilm.

California State Library (Sacramento). *Vital Statistics Index, California State Library, Sacramento, California: ca. 1800's-1920*. Microfilm of card file located in Special Collections, California State Library, Sacramento, California. Salt Lake City: Filmed by the Genealogical Society of Utah, 1991. 10 microfilm.

California State Register. *California Vital Records Indexes*. Sacramento California: Office of the State Registrar, 1983. Microfiche.

California. Department of Public Health. *California Death Index, 1940-1990*. Sacramento, California: Office of State Registrar, [1991?]. 524 microfiche.

California. State Registrar. *California Marriage Records Indexes, 1960-1985*. Sacramento, California: Office of the State Registrar, [1983?]. 664 microfiches.

California. State Registrar. *Index to Deaths, 1905-1988*. Microfilm of records located at the Office of the State Registrar, Sacramento, and at the Butte County Courthouse, Oroville. Salt Lake City: Filmed by the Genealogical Society of Utah, 1990. 7 microfilm.

Cemetery Records of California. 11 vols. Typescript. Salt Lake City: Genealogical Society of Utah, 1954-63.

Culbertson, Judi. *Permanent Californians: An Illustrated Guide to the Cemeteries of California*. Chelsea, Vermont: Chelsea Green Pub. Co., 1989.

Daughters of the American Revolution (California). *Vital Records from Cemeteries in California, to 1962*. Salt Lake City: Filmed by the Genealogical Society of Utah, 1968. 4 microfilm.

Graves and Sites on the Oregon and California Trails: A Chapter in OCTA's Efforts to Preserve the Trails. [Independence MO]: Oregon-California Trails Association, 1991.

Historical Records Survey (California*). Guide to Public Vital Statistics Records in California*. San Francisco: Northern California Historical Records Survey, 1941.

Kit, Elizabeth Gorrell, and Shirley Pugh Thompson. *California Cemetery Inscription Sources: Print and Microform*. Vallejo California; Indices Publishing, 1994.

Morebeck, Nancy Justus. *Northern California Marriage Index 1850-1860*. Vacaville California: Nancy Justus Morebeck, 1993.

Nicklas, Laurie. *California County Courthouse Records: A Directory of Vital Records Found in Each County Office in California*. Modesto, California: L. Nicklas, 1998.

Oregon-California Trails Association (Independence, Missouri). *Graves and Sites on the Oregon and California trails: A chapter in OCTA's Efforts to Preserve the Trails*. [Independence, Mo.]: Oregon-California Trails Association, 1991.

Paradise Genealogical Society. *Genealogical Library Collection Shelf List, Paradise Genealogical Society*. Paradise California: Paradise Gen. Soc., 1995.

Parker, J. Carlyle. *A Personal Name Index to Orton's Records of California Men in the War of the Rebellion, 1861 to 1867.* (1978). Reprint. Turlock California: Marietta Pub. Co., 1994.

Parker, Jimmy B. *Vital Records (Births and Deaths) of Indians of Round Valley Agency 1890-99, 1906-15, 1924.* Salt Lake City: Utah Genealogical Society, 1972.

County Website	Map Index	Date Created	Parent County or Territory From Which Organized Address/Details
Alameda* www.co.alameda.ca.us/	I4	25 Mar 1853	**Contra Costa, Santa Clara** Alameda County; 1106 Madison St; Rm 101; Oakland, CA 94607; Ph. 510.272.6362 Details: (Co Clk has m rec from 1854, pro, div, ct & land rec from 1853, b rec 1919-1988 [some from 1873] & d rec 1905-1988 [some from 1876])
Alpine www.co.alpine.ca.us/	G6	16 Mar 1864	**El Dorado, Amador, Calaveras, Mono, Tuolumne** Alpine County; 99 Water St; PO Box 158; Markleeville, CA 96120; Ph. 530.694.2287 Details: (Co Clk has b, m, d, div, pro, ct & land rec from 1900)
Amador www.co.amador.ca.us/	H5	11 May 1854	**Calaveras, El Dorado** Amador County; 500 Argonaut Ln; Jackson, CA 95642; Ph. 209.223.6468 Details: (Clk Sup Ct has div, pro & ct rec; Co Archives has nat rec; Co Clk has b & d rec from 1872)
Branciforte		18 Feb 1850	**Original county** Details: (see Santa Cruz) Name changed to Santa Cruz 5 Apr 1850
Butte www.buttecounty.net/	F4	18 Feb 1850	**Original county** Butte County; 25 County Center Dr; Oroville, CA 95965; Ph. 530.538.7691 Details: (Co Rcdr has m rec from 1851, b & d rec from 1859 & land rec; Co Clk has div, pro & ct rec from 1850; Meriam Lib, CA State Univ Chico, has div, pro & ct rec 1850-1879 & nat rec 1850-1960)
Calaveras www.co.calaveras.ca.us/	H5	18 Feb 1850	**Original county** Calaveras County; 891 Mountain Ranch Rd; San Andreas, CA 95249; Ph. 209.754.6376 Details: (Co Rcdr has b rec from 1860, m, d & div rec from 1882, pro & ct rec from 1866, land rec from 1852 & mining claims from 1850)
Colusa www.cagenweb.com/colusa/	F3	18 Feb 1850	**Original county** Colusa County; 546 Jay St; Colusa, CA 95932-2443; Ph. 530.458.0500 Details: (Colusa Co was created in 1850 but attached to Butte Co for administration until it was organized in Jan 1851) (Co Clk has b rec from 1873, m rec from 1853, d rec from 1889, pro, ct, land & assessment rolls from 1851, Great Registers from 1866 & mil rolls from 1879)
Contra Costa www.co.contra-costa.ca.us/	H3	18 Feb 1850	**Original county** Contra Costa County; 730 Las Juntas St; PO Box 350; Martinez, CA 94553; Ph. 925.646.2360 Details: (Co Rcdr has b & d rec; Co Clk has m, div, pro & ct rec)
Del Norte www.co.del-norte.ca.us/	C1	2 Mar 1857	**Klamath** Del Norte County; 981 H St; Crescent City, CA 95531; Ph. 707.464.7204 Details: (Co Clk has div, pro & ct rec from 1848; Co Rcdr has b, m & d rec from 1873, land rec from 1853, leases & agreements 1857-1954)
El Dorado www.co.el-dorado.ca.us/	G5	18 Feb 1850	**Original county** El Dorado County; 360 Fair Ln; Placerville, CA 95667; Ph. 530.621.5490 Details: (Co Clk has div, pro & ct rec; Co Rcdr has b, m, d, bur, land & mil rec)
Fresno* www.fresno.ca.gov/portal/Default.asp	J6	19 Apr 1856	**Merced, Mariposa, Tulare** Fresno County; 2221 Kern St; Fresno, CA 93721; Ph. 559.488.3003 Details: (Co Clk has b, m & d rec from 1855)
Glenn www.countyofglenn.net/	F3	11 Mar 1891	**Colusa** Glenn County; 526 W Sycamore St; PO Box 391; Willows, CA 95988; Ph. 530.934.6419 Details: (Co Clk-Rcdr has b rec from 1887, d rec from 1905, m & land rec from 1891 & mil rec from 1919; Sup Ct has pro & ct rec)
Humboldt www.co.humboldt.ca.us/	E1	12 May 1853	**Trinity, Klamath** Humboldt County; 825 5th St; Eureka, CA 95501; Ph. 707.476.2384 Details: (Co Clk has div, pro & ct rec from 1853; Co Rcdr has b, m, d, bur & land rec)
Imperial www.co.imperial.ca.us/	O11	6 Aug 1907	**San Diego** Imperial County; 940 W Main St; El Centro, CA 92243; Ph. 760.482.4220 Details: (Co Clk has m, div, pro & ct rec from 1907; Co Rcdr has b, m & d rec from 1907)

County Website	Map Index	Date Created	Parent County or Territory From Which Organized Address/Details
Inyo www.countyofinyo.org/	J8	22 Mar 1866	**Tulare, Mono** Inyo County; 168 N Edwards St; PO Box F; Independence, CA 93526; Ph. 760.878.0218 Details: (Co Clk has b & d rec from 1904, m & land rec from 1866 & mining rec from 1872)
Kern* www.co.kern.ca.us/	L7	2 Apr 1866	**Tulare, Los Angeles** Kern County; 1655 Chester Ave; Bakersfield, CA 93301; Ph. 661.868.6449 Details: (Co Clk-Rcdr has b, m, d & land rec from 1850, div, pro, ct & reg voting rec from 1866; An exchange of territory with San Bernardino Co took place in 1963)
Kings www.countyofkings.com/	K6	22 Mar 1893	**Tulare** Kings County; 1400 W Lacey Blvd; Hanford, CA 93230; Ph. 559.582.3211 Details: (Co Clk has b, m, d, div, pro. ct, land & nat rec from 1893)
Klamath		25 Apr 1851	**Original county** Details: (Dissolved 28 Mar 1874)
Lake www.co.lake.ca.us/cntyhome.html	G3	20 May 1861	**Napa** Lake County; 255 N Forbes St; Lakeport, CA 95453; Ph. 707.263.2368 Details: (Co Clk has b, m, d & land rec from 1867, mining & misc rec; Clk Sup Ct has div, pro & ct rec)
Lassen www.cagenweb.com/tp/lassen/	D5	1 Apr 1864	**Plumas, Shasta** Lassen County; 220 S Lassen St; Susanville, CA 96130; Ph. 530.251.8216 Details: (Co Clk has div, pro, ct & nat rec from 1864; Co Rcdr has m rec from 1864, land rec from 1857, b & d rec from 1907, some prior to 1907 but incomplete before 1929)
Los Angeles* www.co.la.ca.us/	M8	18 Feb 1850	**Original county** Los Angeles County; 12400 E Imperial Hwy; PO Box 1024; Norwalk, CA 90650; Ph. 562.462.2137 Details: (Co Clk has div rec from 1880, pro & ct rec from 1850; Co Rcdr has b, m, d & land rec)
Madera www.madera-county.com/	I6	11 Mar 1893	**Fresno** Madera County; 209 W Yosemite Ave; Madera, CA 93637; Ph. 559.675.7700 Details: (Co Clk has b, m, d, div, pro, ct & land rec from 1893 & some voting rec)
Marin* www.marin.org/	H3	18 Feb 1850	**Original county** Marin County; 3501 Civic Center Dr; San Rafael, CA 94903; Ph. 415.499.6094 Details: (Co Rcdr has b & d rec from 1863, m rec from 1856, land rec from 1852; Co Clk has div & ct rec from 1900 & pro rec from 1880)
Mariposa www.mariposacounty.org/	I6	18 Feb 1850	**Original county** Mariposa County; 5100 Bullion St; PO Box 35; Mariposa, CA 95338; Ph. 209.966.5719 Details: (Co Clk has div, pro & ct rec; Co Rcdr has b, m, d & bur rec)
Mendocino www.co.mendocino.ca.us/	F2	18 Feb 1850	**Original county** Mendocino County; 501 Low Gap Rd Rm 1090; Ukiah, CA 95482; Ph. 707.463.4221 Details: (Sup Ct has div & ct rec from 1858 & pro rec from 1872; Co Rcdr has b, m, d & land rec) (Some old rec in Sonoma Co)
Merced www.co.merced.ca.us/	I5	19 Apr 1855	**Mariposa** Merced County; 2222 M St; Merced, CA 95340; Ph. 209.385.7627 Details: (Co Clk has div, pro & ct rec from 1855; Co Rcdr has b, m, d & bur rec)
Modoc www.rh2o.com/modoc/	C5	17 Feb 1874	**Siskiyou** Modoc County; 204 Court St; PO Box 131; Alturas, CA 96101-0131; Ph. 530.233.6205 Details: (Co Clk has div, pro, ct & voter reg rec from 1874; Co Rcdr has b, m & d rec)
Mono* www.monocounty.org/	H7	24 Apr 1861	**Calaveras, Fresno** Mono County; Bryant Annex 2; PO Box 537; Bridgeport, CA 93517; Ph. 760.932.5241 Details: (Co Clk has b & m rec from 1861, d, bur, div, pro, ct & land rec from 1900)

County Website	Map Index	Date Created	Parent County or Territory From Which Organized / Address/Details
Monterey www.co.monterey.ca.us/	**K4**	**18 Feb 1850**	**Original county** Monterey County; 240 Church St; PO Box 29; PO Box 29, 240 Church St; Salinas, CA 93902; Ph. 831.755.5041 Details: (Co Rcdr has b & d rec & m rec from 1893; Clk Sup Ct has pro & land rec; Co Ct has div & ct rec)
Napa* www.co.napa.ca.us/internet/	**G3**	**18 Feb 1850**	**Original county** Napa County; 900 Coombs; PO Box 298; Napa, CA 94559-0298; Ph. 707.253.4246 Details: (Co Clk-Rcdr has b & d rec from 1873, m & land rec from 1850; Ct Exec Officer has div, pro & ct rec from 1850)
Nevada www.mynevadacounty.com/	**F5**	**25 Apr 1851**	**Yuba** Nevada County; 950 Maidu Ave; Nevada City, CA 95959; Ph. 530.265.1221 Details: (Co Clk has b & d rec from 1873, m & land rec from 1856, div, pro & ct rec from 1880)
Orange www.oc.ca.gov/	**N8**	**11 Mar 1889**	**Los Angeles** Orange County; 12 Civic Center Pl; Santa Ana, CA 92701; Ph. 714.834.2500 Details: (Co Rcdr has b, m, d & land rec; Co Clk has div, pro & ct rec from 1964)
Placer www.placer.ca.gov/	**G5**	**25 Apr 1851**	**Yuba, Sutter** Placer County; 2954 Richardson Dr; Auburn, CA 95603; Ph. 530.886.5600 Details: (Co Clk-Rcdr has b, m & d rec from 1873 & land rec from 1850; Co Clk has pro rec from 1851 & ct rec from 1880)
Plumas www.countyofplumas.com/	**E5**	**18 Mar 1854**	**Butte** Plumas County; 520 Main St; Quincy, CA 95971; Ph. 530.283.6218 Details: (Co Clk has div rec from 1860; Co Rcdr has b, m, d, pro, ct & land rec from 1860; Co Museum Arch has biographies and photographs)
Riverside www.co.riverside.ca.us/	**N10**	**11 Mar 1893**	**San Diego, San Bernardino** Riverside County; 4080 Lemon St 1st Fl; PO Box 12004; Riverside, CA 92502; Ph. 909.486.7000 Details: (Co Clk-Rcdr has b, m, d & land rec from 1893; Sup Ct has div, pro & ct rec from 1893)
Sacramento www.co.sacramento.ca.us/	**H4**	**18 Feb 1850**	**Original county** Sacramento County; 600 8th St; PO Box 839; Sacramento, CA 95812-0893; Ph. 916.874.6334 Details: (Co Clk has div, pro & ct rec from 1880; Co Rcdr has b, m, d & land rec)
San Benito* www.san-benito.ca.us/	**J4**	**12 Feb 1874**	**Monterey** San Benito County; 440 5th St 2nd Fl; Hollister, CA 95023; Ph. 831.636.4029 Details: (Co Clk has b, m, d, bur, land & nat rec from 1894; Sup Ct has div, pro & ct rec)
San Bernardino* www.co.san-bernardino.ca.us/	**L10**	**26 Apr 1853**	**Los Angeles, San Diego** San Bernardino County; 22 W Hospitality Ln; San Bernardino, CA 92415; Ph. 909.387.8306 Details: (Co Clk has m lic from 1887, div & pro rec from 1856, ct rec from 1853 & land rec from 1854; Co Rcdr has b & d rec from 1853 & m rec from 1857)
San Diego* www.co.san-diego.ca.us/	**O9**	**18 Feb 1850**	**Original county** San Diego County; 1600 Pacific Hwy; San Diego, CA 92101; Ph. 619.238.8158 Details: (Co Clk-Rcdr has b rec from 1857, m rec from 1856, d rec from 1873 & land rec from 1850's; Sup Ct has pro, ct & div rec)
San Francisco* www.ci.sf.ca.us/	**H3**	**18 Feb 1850**	**Original county** San Francisco County; 1 Dr Carlton B Goodlett Pl; San Francisco, CA 94102; Ph. 415.554.4950 Details: (Sup Ct Clk has div, pro & ct rec; Co Rcdr has m rec; Dept of Pub Hlth has b rec)
San Joaquin www.co.san-joaquin.ca.us/	**H4**	**18 Feb 1850**	**Original county** San Joaquin County; 24 S Hunter St #304; PO Box 1968; Stockton, CA 95201; Ph. 209.468.8075 Details: (Co Clk has div, pro & ct rec from 1851; Co Rcdr has b, m, d & land rec)

County Website	Map Index	Date Created	Parent County or Territory From Which Organized Address/Details
San Luis Obispo* www.slocounty.org/	L5	18 Feb 1850	**Original county** San Luis Obispo County; 1144 Monterey St Ste C; San Luis Obispo, CA 93408; Ph. 805.781.5080 Details: (Co Clk-Rcdr has b rec from 1873, m & d rec from 1850 & land rec from 1842; Co Clk has div, pro & ct rec)
San Mateo* www.co.sanmateo.ca.us/	I3	19 Apr 1856	**San Francisco** San Mateo County; 400 County Center; Redwood City, CA 94063; Ph. 650.363.4712 Details: (Co Clk-Rcdr has b, m & d rec from 1866, div, ct & land rec from 1880 & pro rec from 1856)
Santa Barbara* www.countyofsb.org/index.asp	M6	18 Feb 1850	**Original county** Santa Barbara County; 105 E Anapamu Rm #204; Santa Barbara, CA 93101; Ph. 805.568.2550 Details: (Sup Ct has div, pro, ct & nat rec; Co Clk-Rcdr has b, m, d & land rec from 1850)
Santa Clara* www.co.santa-clara.ca.us/	I4	18 Feb 1850	**Original county** Santa Clara County; 70 W Hedding St 1st Fl; San Jose, CA 95110-1768; Ph. 408.299.2481 Details: (Co Rcdr has b & d rec from 1873, m rec from 1850, land rec from 1846 & mil rec from 1920; Co Clk has div, pro & nat rec)
Santa Cruz www.co.santa-cruz.ca.us/	I3	18 Feb 1850	**Original county** Santa Cruz County; 701 Ocean St; Santa Cruz, CA 95060; Ph. 831.454.2800 Details: (Formerly Branciforte Co. Name changed to Santa Cruz 5 Apr 1850) (Co Rcdr has m & land rec from 1850, b & d rec from 1905 & mil rec from 1930; Clk Sup Ct has div, pro & ct rec)
Shasta www.co.shasta.ca.us/	D3	18 Feb 1850	**Original county** Shasta County; 1643 Market St; PO Box 990880; Redding, CA 96099; Ph. 530.225.5730 Details: (Co Clk has div, pro & ct rec from 1880; Co Rcdr has b, m & d rec)
Sierra www.sierracounty.ws/index.shtml	F5	16 Apr 1852	**Yuba** Sierra County; 100 Courthouse Sq Ste 11; PO Box D Ste 11; Downieville, CA 95936; Ph. 530.289.6295 Details: (Co Rcdr has b rec from 1857, m & land rec from 1852 & d rec from 1862; Sup Ct has div, pro, ct & nat rec from 1852)
Siskiyou www.co.siskiyou.ca.us/	C3	22 Mar 1852	**Shasta, Klamath** Siskiyou County; 311 Fourth St; PO Box 338; Yreka, CA 96097; Ph. 530.842.8084 Details: (Co Rcdr has b, m, d & bur rec; Ct Services has div, pro & ct rec from 1853; Co Clk has election rec, board of supervisor's minutes from 1860)
Solano www.co.solano.ca.us/	H3	18 Feb 1850	**Original county** Solano County; 701 Texas St; Fairfield, CA 94533; Ph. 707.421.6265 Details: (Co Rcdr has b, m, d & land rec; Co Clk has div, pro & ct rec from 1850)
Sonoma www.sonoma-county.org/	G2	18 Feb 1850	**Original county** Sonoma County; 2300 County Center Dr; LaPlaza Building B177; Santa Rosa, CA 95403; Ph. 707.565.3800 Details: (Co Rcdr has b, m, d, bur & land rec; Co Clk has div, pro & ct rec from 1850)
Stanislaus www.co.stanislaus.ca.us/	I4	1 Apr 1854	**Tuolumne** Stanislaus County; 1021 I St; Modesto, CA 95354; Ph. 209.525.5250 Details: (Co Clk-Rcdr has m rec from 1870, b & d rec from 1900; Clk Sup Ct has div, pro & ct rec from 1854; Co Rcdr has land rec from 1854)
Sutter www.co.sutter.ca.us/	G4	18 Feb 1850	**Original county** Sutter County; 433 2nd St; Yuba City, CA 95992; Ph. 530.822.7120 Details: (Co Clk-Rcdr has b & d rec from 1873, m, land & mil rec from 1850; Civ Division of Cts has div, pro & ct rec)
Tehama www.tehamacounty.com/	E3	9 Apr 1856	**Colusa, Butte, Shasta** Tehama County; 633 Washington St; Red Bluff, CA 96080; Ph. 530.527.3350 Details: (Co Clk has b & d rec from 1889, m rec from 1856 & mil rec from 1944)

County Website	Map Index	Date Created	Parent County or Territory From Which Organized Address/Details
Trinity www.trinitycounty.org/	E2	18 Feb 1850	**Original county** Trinity County; 101 Court St; PO Box 1258; Weaverville, CA 96093; Ph. 530.623.1215 Details: (Co Rcdr has b & d rec indexes 1873-1905, b & d rec from 1905, m rec indexes 1857-1905, m rec from 1905 & nat rec 1850-1940; Ct Services has div & ct rec from 1881, pro rec from 1887 & land rec)
Tulare www.co.tulare.ca.us/	K7	20 Apr 1852	**Mariposa** Tulare County; 221 S Mooney Blvd; Visalia, CA 93291; Ph. 559.733.6418 Details: (Co Clk-Rcdr has b & m rec from 1852, d rec from 1873 & mil rec from 1919; Clk Sup Ct has div, pro, ct & nat rec; Co Asr has land rec)
Tuolumne www.tuolumnecounty.com/	H6	18 Feb 1850	**Original county** Tuolumne County; 2 S Green St; Sonora, CA 95370-4679; Ph. 209.533.5570 Details: (Co Clk-Rcdr has b rec from 1858, m rec from 1850, d rec from 1859, bur rec from 1916, div, pro, ct & land rec from 1850 & old newspapers 1862-1948)
Ventura* www.countyofventura.org/dept.asp	M6	22 Mar 1872	**Santa Barbara** Ventura County; 800 S Victoria Ave; Ventura, CA 93009; Ph. 805.654.2267 Details: (Co Clk-Rcdr has b, m & d rec from 1873 & land rec from 1850; Clk Sup Ct has div, pro & ct rec from 1873; Some land went to Kern & Los Angeles Cos in boundary change)
Yolo www.co.yolo.ca.us/	G3	18 Feb 1850	**Original county** Yolo County; 625 Court St; PO Box 1130 zip code 95776; Woodland, CA 95695; Ph. 530.666.8130 Details: (Co Clk has b, m, d & land rec, div, pro & ct rec from 1850)
Yuba www.co.yuba.ca.us/	F4	18 Feb 1850	**Original county** Yuba County; 935 14th St; Marysville, CA 95901; Ph. 530.741.6547 Details: (Co Clk has m rec from 1865, div, pro & ct rec from 1850 & voting rec from 1866)

Notes

Columbine

COLORADO

CAPITAL: DENVER – TERRITORY 1861 – STATE 1876 (38TH)

Early Spanish explorers traveled through the Colorado area and heard exciting tales of gold and silver from the Indians. Many treasure seekers searched throughout the Southwest and Rocky Mountain areas for these elusive fortunes. Spain and France alternated control until 1803 when all areas, except those that were south and west of the Arkansas River, were sold to the United States.

In 1806, Zebulon Pike was sent to explore the area. Others such as Stephen Long in 1819 and John Fremont in 1842 also came. The remainder of present-day Colorado became part of the United States in 1848. Fur traders prospered in the area, but not until 1851 was the first town, San Luis, established. In 1854, Colorado was divided among the territories of Kansas, Nebraska, Utah, and New Mexico.

Settlement remained sparse until gold was discovered in 1858 when the Pikes Peak gold rush lured 50,000 people to Colorado. Denver, Golden, Boulder, and Pueblo were established as supply bases. The miners organized Arapaho County of the Kansas Territory in 1858. The following year the residents created the Territory of Jefferson, but Congress failed to recognize it.

The Territory of Colorado was finally organized in 1861, although some of its counties date their creation from 1859. The 1860 census for Colorado (then part of Kansas) shows 33,000 men and 1,500 women. During the Civil War, just less than 5,000 men fought for the Union.

The completion of the transcontinental railroad in 1869 linked Colorado to both coasts and provided impetus for increased migration. Colorado gained statehood in 1876. The western part of the state was officially opened to settlement in 1881. Ute Indians were moved to reservations in Utah. At the time of the last major gold strike at Cripple Creek in 1890, the state boasted a population of 400,000.

Look for vital records in the following locations:

- **Birth and death records**: Vital Records Office, Colorado Department of Health holds state records from 1907. Search county and town clerk records between January 1876 and 1907.
- **Marriage records:** Kept by the county clerks from the organization of the county.
- **Divorce records:** Kept by the county clerks from the organization of the county. Probate records and wills are also in the offices of the county clerks, except for Denver, where there is a separate probate court.
- **Land records:** The first general land office in Colorado was established in 1863. Most land office records are at the National Archives, Denver Branch. County recorders kept private land records. Spanish land grants prior to 1862 were processed in the New Mexico Office. The U.S. Surveyor processed claims from 1855 to 1890.
- **Census records:** An 1860 Territorial Census was taken in the four territories of which Colorado was a part. The Utah part was not yet settled. The Nebraska part is listed under "unorganized territory." The Kansas part is listed in the Arapahoe County schedules, and the New Mexico part is listed in the Taos and Mora county schedules.

Vital Records Office
Colorado Department of Health
4300 Cherry Creek Drive South
Denver, Colorado 80222
303.756.4464

National Archives, Denver Branch
Bldg. 48, West 6th Ave. and Kipling
Denver Federal Center
Denver, Colorado 80225

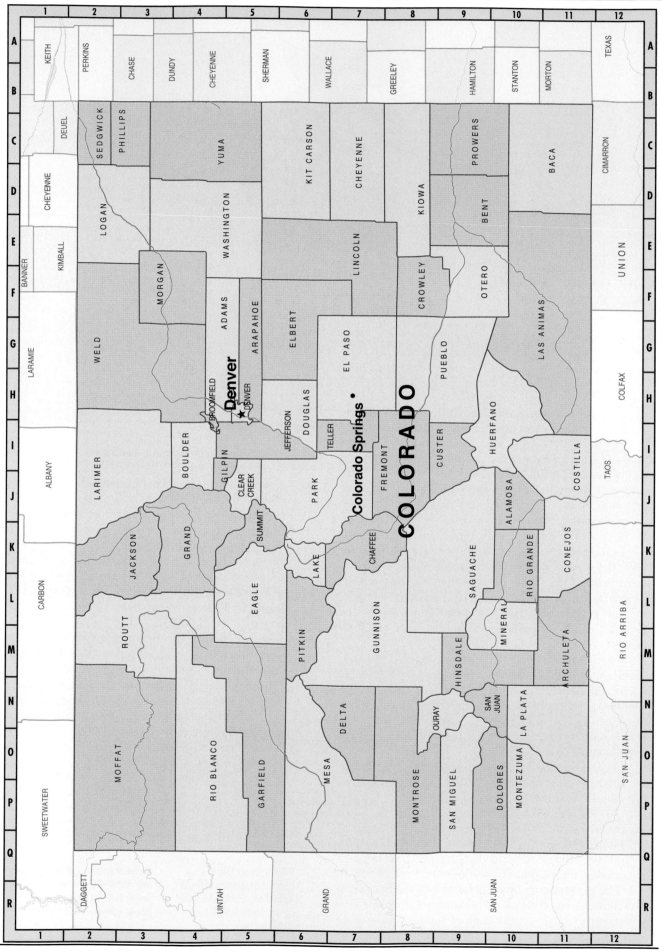

Societies and Repositories

American Baptist Historical Society; 1106 South Goodman Street; Rochester, New York 14620; 716.473.1740

Archives of the Archdiocese of Denver; 200 Josephine Street; Denver, Colorado 80206; 303.388.4411 Ext. 224; Fax 303.331.8071; (Roman Catholic Church records)

Archuleta County Genealogical Society; PO Box 1611; Pagosa Springs, Colorado 81147; <www.rootsweb.com/~cosjhs/acgs.htm>

Aspen Historical Society; 620 West Bleeker Street; Aspen, Colorado 81611

Aurora Genealogical Society of Colorado; PO Box 31732; Aurora, Colorado 80041-0732

Black Genealogical Search Group; PO Box 40674; Denver, Colorado 80204-0674

Boulder Genealogical Society; PO Box 3246; Boulder, Colorado 80307-3246; <www.rootsweb.com/~bgs/>

Boulder Public Library; 1000 Canyon Blvd.; Boulder, Colorado 80302

Boulder, Colorado Genealogical Group; 856 Applewood Dr.; Lafayette, Colorado 80026

Brighton Genealogical Society; PO Box 1005; Brighton, Colorado 80601

Bureau of Land Management, Colorado State Office; 2850 Youngfield St.; Lakewood, Colorado 80215; 303.239.3600; Fax 303.239.3933

Carnegie Branch Library; 1125 Pine St.; PO Drawer H; Boulder, CO 80306

CGS/Computer Interest Group; 6437 W. Arbor Dr.; Littleton, Colorado 80123-3927

Chancery Office; 1001 No. Grand Ave.; Pueblo, Colorado 81003; 719.544.9861; Fax 719.544.5202

Charles Leaming Tutt Library; Colorado College; Colorado Springs, Colorado 80903-2165

Colorado Association of Professional Genealogists; PO Box 740637; Arvada, Colorado 80006-0637

Colorado Chapter, OGS; PO Box 1106; Longmont, Colorado 80502-1106

Colorado Chapter, Ohio Genealogical Society; Box 1106; Longmont, Colorado 80502-1106

Colorado Committee for Women's History; PO Box 673; Denver, Colorado 80206

Colorado Cornish Cousins; 7945 S. Gaylord Way; Littleton, Colorado 80122

Colorado Council of Genealogical Societies; PO Box 24379; Denver, Colorado 80224-0379; <www.rootsweb.com/~coccgs/>

Colorado Department of Health; 4300 Cherry Creek Drive South; Denver, Colorado 80222-1530; 303.756.4464

Colorado Division of State Archives and Public Records; 1313 Sherman Street; Floor 1B, Room 20; Denver, Colorado 80203; 303.866.2358 or 303.866.2390; Fax 303.866.2257

Colorado Genealogical Society; PO Box 9218; Denver, Colorado 80209-0218; 303.571.1535

Colorado High Plains Chapter, American Historical Society of Germans from Russia; 530 Fairhurst; Sterling, Colorado 80751

Colorado Historical Society; Colorado Heritage Center; 1300 Broadway; Denver, Colorado 80203; 303.866.3392; Fax 303.866.4464

Colorado Springs Chapter, American Historical Society of Germans from Russia; 70 Watch Hill Dr. Apt. A; Colorado Springs, Colorado 80906-7935

Colorado Springs Public Library; 21 W. Kiowa St.; Colorado Springs, Colorado 80902

Colorado State Archives; 1313 Sherman Street; Room 1B-20; Denver, Colorado 80203; 303.866.2257; <www.archives.state.co.us>

Columbine Genealogical and Historical Society, Inc.; PO Box 2074; Littleton, Colorado 80161-2074; 303.841.3712; <www.rootsweb.com/~cocghs/index.htm>

Czech and Slovak Search Group; 209 S. Ogden; Denver, Colorado 80209-2321

Denver Metro Chapter, AHSGR; 13245 Grove Way; Broomfield, Colorado 80020; <www.ahsgr.org/codenver.htm>

Denver Public Library; 10 W. 14th Ave. Pkwy; Denver, Colorado 80204; 303.640.6291

Denver Public Library; Western History and Genealogy Department; 10 West 14th Avenue Parkway; Denver, Colorado 80203-2165; 303.640.6200

Diocese of Colorado; 1300 Washington; Denver, CO 80203-2008; 303-837-1173; (Episcopal Church records)

Eagle County Historical Society; PO Box 192; Eagle, Colorado 81631

Estes Park Genealogical Society; 1281 High Dr., Moraine Rt.; Estes Park, Colorado 80517

Family History Branch Library; 100 Malley Dr.; Northglenn, Colorado 80233

Family History Branch Library; 1939 E. Easter Ave; Littleton, Colorado 80122

Family History Branch Library; 2710 S. Monaco St. Pkwy.; Denver, Colorado 80237

Family History Branch Library; 6705 S. Webster; Littleton, Colorado 80123

Family History Branch Library; 701 S. Boulder Rd.; Louisville, Colorado 80027

Family History Branch Library; 7080 Independence; Arvada, Colorado 80004

Family History Library; 35 North West Temple Street; Salt Lake City, Utah 84150; 800.346.6044 or 801.240.2584; <www.familysearch.org>; Find a Family History Center near you; <www.familysearch.org/Eng/Library/FHC/frameset_fhc.asp>

Foothills Genealogical Society of Colorado, Inc.; PO Box 150382; Lakewood, Colorado 80215-0382; <www.rootsweb.com/~cofgs/>

Fore-Kin Trails Genealogical Society; 2392 E. Miami Rd.; Montrose, Colorado 81401-6007

Four Corners Genealogical Society; PO Box 2636; Durango, Colorado 81302

Fremont County Genealogical Society; Local History Center CCPL_516 Macon Ave.; Canon City, Colorado 81212

Friend Genealogy Library; 1448 Que St.; Penrose, Colorado 81240

Frontier Historical Society; 1001 Colorado Ave.; Glenwood Springs, Colorado 81601

Genealogical Research Society of Durango; 2720 Delwood; Durango, Colorado 80301

Genealogical Society of Hispanic America; PO Box 606; Denver, Colorado 80209-0606

Greeley Public Library; City Complex Bldg.; 919 7th Street; Greeley, Colorado 80631

Gunnison Co. Public Library; 307 N. Wisconsin; Gunnison, Colorado 81230

Historical and Genealogical Researchers; P.O Box 123; Trinidad, Colorado 80456; <www.usgennet.org/usa/co/town/trinidad/>

Jewish Genealogical Society of Colorado; 1982 S. Oneida St.; Denver, Colorado 80224

Lafayette-Louisville Genealogical Society; 1022 S. Pegasus Pl.; Lafayette, Colorado 80026; <www.rootsweb.com/~collgs/index.html>

Larimer County Genealogical Society; PO Box 9502; Fort Collins, Colorado 80505-9502; <jymis.com/~lcgs/index.htm>

Logan County Genealogical Society; PO Box 294; Sterling, Colorado 80751

Longmont Genealogical Society; PO Box 6081; Longmont, Colorado 80501-2077; <www.rootsweb.com/~colgs/index.htm/>

Melon Valley Chapter, American Historical Society of Germans from Russia; 708 So. 13th Street; Rocky Ford, Colorado 81067-2132; 719.254.3819

Mesa County Genealogical Society; PO Box 1506; Grand Junction, Colorado 81502-1506; <www.gj.net/mcgs/>

Montrose Public Library; City Hall; Montrose, Colorado 81401

Mountain Genealogists Society; 25 Conifer Dr.; Evergreen, Colorado 80439

National Archives and Records Administration— Rocky Mountain Region (Denver); Denver Federal Center Building 48; PO Box 25307; Denver, Colorado 80225-0307; 303.236.0817; Fax 303.236.9354

Norlin Library; University of Colorado; Boulder, Colorado 80304

Northern Colorado Chapter, American Historical Society of Germans from Russia; 1104 West Magnolia; Fort Collins, Colorado 80521; 970.484.9771; <www.ahsgr.org/conorthe.html>

Old Colorado City Historical Society; One South 24th Street; Colorado Springs, Colorado;

Palatines to America, Colorado Chapter; 7079 S. Marshall St.; Littleton, Colorado 80123-4607

Penrose Public Library; 20 North Cascade; Colorado Springs, Colorado 80902

Pikes Peak Genealogical Society; PO Box 1262; Colorado Springs, Colorado 80901

Presbyterian Historical Society; 425 Lombard Street; Philadelphia, Pennsylvania 19147; 215.627.1852; Fax 215.627.0509

Prowers County Genealogical Society; PO Box 928; Lamar, Colorado 81052-0928

Pueblo Regional Library; 100 Abriendo Ave.; Pueblo, Colorado 81005

Rio Blanco County Historical Society; 565 Park Street; Meeker, Colorado 81641; <www.rootsweb.com/~coriobla/wrm.htm>

Rocky Mountain Conference Historical Society, Ira J. Taylor Library; Iliff School of Theology; 2201 S. University Blvd.; Denver, Colorado 80210; 303.744.1287; Fax 303.777.3387 or 303.777.0164; (Methodist church records)

Rocky Mountain Jewish Historical Society; Center for Judaic Studies; 2000 East Asbury; Denver, Colorado 80208; 303.871.3037; <www.du.edu/~ctrjuds/cjsrmjhs.html>

San Juan Historical Society; PO Box 1711; Pagosa Springs, Colorado 81147; <www.rootsweb.com/~cosjhs/museum.htm>

Sedgwick County Genealogy Society; PO Box 86; Julesburg, Colorado 80737; <www.rootsweb.com/~cosedgwi/society.htm>

Sheridan Historical Society; 4101 S. Federal Blvd.; Sheridan, Colorado 80110-5399; <www.rootsweb.com/~coshs/>

Sison Memorial Library; PO Box 849; Pagosa Springs, Colorado 81147

Sons of the American Revolution, Colorado Society; 255 Moline St.; Aurora, Colorado 80010

Southeastern Colorado Genealogical Society, Inc.; PO Box 4207; Pueblo, Colorado 81003-0207

Southern Peaks Public Library; 423 Fourth St., Alamosa, Colorado 81101

Stagecoach Library; 1840 S. Wolcott Ct.; Denver, Colorado 80219

Stephen A. Hart Library, Colorado Historical Society; 1300 Broadway; Denver, Colorado 80203; 303.866.2305

Summit Historical Society; 309 N. Main; PO Box 745; Breckenridge, Colorado 80424;

Tutt Library; Colorado College; Colorado Springs, Colorado 80903

Ute Pass Historical Society; PO Box 6875; Woodland Park, Colorado 80866;

Weld Co. Library; 2227 23rd Avenue; Greeley, Colorado 80631

Weld County Genealogical Society; PO Box 278; Greeley, Colorado 80631; <www.rootsweb.com/~cowcgs/>

White River Trace Genealogical Society; 425 12th St.; Meeker, Colorado 81641

WISE Search Group; 1840 S. Wolcott Court; Denver, Colorado 80219-4309

Yuma Area Genealogical Society; PO Box 24; Yuma, Colorado 80759

Bibliography and Record Sources

General Sources

Bauer, William, and James L. Ozment and John H. Willard. *Colorado Postal History: The Post Offices*. Crete, NE:JB Publishing Co, 1971.

Bromwell, Henriette Elizabeth. *Colorado Portrait and Biography Index*. 4 vols. Denver, Colo.: Western History Dept., Denver Public Library: Dakota Microfilm Service, 1979, [1982?].

Burdick, Liz, and Kay Merrill. *Colorado Collections*. Microfilm. Salt Lake City: Genealogical Society of Utah, 1983.

Clint, Florence R. *Colorado Area Key, A Comprehensive Study of Genealogical Record Sources of CO, Including Maps and a Brief General History*. Fountain Valley, California: Eden Press, 1968.

Colorado Genealogical Society, Inc. *Surname Index to the Colorado Genealogist, Vols 1-10* (1939-1949), Parts I and II. 1969. Microfiche.

Colorado Families: A Territorial Heritage. Denver: Colorado Genealogical Society, 1981.

Colorado Research Outline. Series US-State, no. 6. Salt Lake City: Family History Library. 1988.

Donald E. Oehlerts, *Guide to Colorado Newspapers, 1859-1963*. Denver: Bibliographical Center for Research, 1964.

Genealogical Index to the Records of the Society of Colorado Pioneers. Denver: Colorado Genealogical Society, Inc., 1990.

Pioneers of the Territory of Southern Colorado. 4 vols. Monte Vista, Colorado: C.B.I. Offset Printers, 1980.

Portrait and Biographical Record of the State of Colorado: Containing Portraits and Biographies of Many Well Known Citizens of the Past and Present. 2 vol. Chicago: Chapman Pub. Co., 1899.

Subject Index to the Colorado Genealogist, Vols 1-42 (1939-1981), Parts I and II. Denver: Colorado Genealogical Society, Inc. 1982. Microfiche.

Surname Index to the Colorado Genealogist, Vols 11-20 (1950-1959), Parts I and II. Denver: Colorado Genealogical Society, Inc. 1974. Microfiche.

Surname Index to the Colorado Genealogist, Vols. 21-41 (1960-1980), Parts I and II. Denver: Colorado Genealogical Society, Inc. 1984. Microfiche.

Wynar, Bohdan S., and Roberta J. Depp, eds. *Colorado Bibliography*. Littleton, CO: Libraries Unlimited, 1980.

Atlases, Maps and Gazetteers

Bauer, William H., James L. Ozment, and John H. Willard. *Colorado Postal History: The Post Offices*. Crete, NB: J-B Publishing Co., 1971.

Crofutt, George A. *A Crofutt's Grip Sack Guide to Colorado: A Complete Encyclopedia of the State, Resources and Condensed Authentic Descriptions of Every City, Town, Village, Station, Post Office and Important Mining Camp in the State*. 1885. 2nd ed. Boulder, Colorado: Johnson Books, 1981.

Dallas, Sandra. Colorado *Ghost Towns and Mining Camps*. Norman, Oklahoma: University of Oklahoma Press, 1985.

Dawson, J. Frank. *Place Names in Colorado*. Denver: J.F. Dawson Publishing Colorado, 1954.

Eichler, George R. *Colorado Place Names: Communities, Counties, Peaks, Passes ...* Boulder, Colo.: Johnson Pub., 1980.

Gannett, Henry. *A Gazetteer of Colorado*. Washington, D.C.: Government Printing Office, 1906.

Thorndale, William, and William Dollarhide. *Map Guides to the US Federal Censuses, 1790-1920: Colorado, 1860-1920*. Baltimore: Genealogical Publishing Co., 1987.

Census Records

Available Census Records and Census Substitutes

Federal Census 1860 (with Kansas), 1870, 1880, 1900, 1910, 1920, 1930.

Federal Mortality Schedules 1870, 1880.

State/Territorial Census 1885.

Dollarhide, William. The Census Book: *A Genealogist's Guide to Federal Census Facts, Schedules and Indexes*. Bountiful, Utah: Heritage Quest, 1999.

Kemp, Thomas Jay. *The American Census Handbook*. Wilmington, Delaware: Scholarly Resources, Inc. 2001.

Lainhart, Ann S. *State Census Records*. Baltimore: Genealogical Publishing Co., 1992.

Szucs, Loretto Dennis, and Matthew Wright. *Finding Answers in U.S. Census Records*. Ancestry Publishing, 2001.

Thorndale, William, and William Dollarhide. *Map Guide to the U.S. Federal Censuses, 1790-1920*. Baltimore: Genealogical Publishing Co., 1987.

Court Records, Probate and Wills

MacDougall, Ella Ruland. *Abstracts of Early Probate Records*. n.p., n.d.

United States. Works Progress Administration (Colorado). *Inventory of Federal Archives in the States, Series 02, Federal Courts, no. 6, Colorado*. Denver, Colorado: Colorado Historical Records Survey, 1939.

Emigration, Immigration, Migration and Naturalization

Crayne-Trudell, Patricia. *Naturalization Records: Index to U.S. District Court - Denver, Colorado*. Lakewood, Colorado: Foothills Genealogical Society of Colorado, 1997.

Hafen, LeRoy R. ed. *Colorado and Its People: A Narrative and Topical History of the Centennial State*. Vol. 2. New York: Lewis Historical Publishing Co., 1948.

United States. District Court (Colorado). *Declarations of Intention, 1877-1952; Naturalization Dockets, 1906-1916; Petitions, 1906-1950; Miscellaneous Records, 1883-1922*. Washington, D.C.: National Archives. Central Plains Region, 1988. Microfilm, 79 rolls.

Land and Property

Arapahoe County (Colorado). Recorder of Deeds. *Deed Records, 1860-1934*. Microfilm of original records at the Colorado State Archives in Denver, Colorado. (Salt Lake City: Filmed by the Genealogical Society of Utah, 1992-1993). Microfilm, multiple rolls.

Beers, Henry Putney. *Spanish and Mexican Records of the American Southwest: A Bibliographic Guide to Archive and Manuscript Sources*. Tucson: University of Arizona Press, 1979.

Miscellaneous Archives Relating to New Mexico Land Grants, 1695-1842. Albuquerque, New Mexico: University of New Mexico Library, 1955-1957. Microfilm, 2 rolls.

New Mexico (Territory). Surveyor-General's Office. *Record of Private Land Claims Adjudicated by the U.S. Surveyor General, 1855-1890*. Albuquerque, New Mexico University of New Mexico Library, 1955-1957. Microfilm, 25 rolls.

New Mexico (Territory). Surveyor-General's Office. *Record of Private Land Claims Adjudicated By the U.S. Surveyor General, 1855-1890*. Albuquerque, New Mexico: University of New Mexico Library, 1955-1957.

Van Ness, John R., and Christine Van Ness. *Spanish and Mexican Land Grants in New Mexico and Colorado*. Manhattan, Kansas: AG Press, 1981.

Vigil, Donaciano. *Vigil's index, 1681-1846*. Albuquerque, New Mexico: University of New Mexico Library, 1955-1957.

Westphall, Victor. *Mercedes Reales: Hispanic Land Grants of the Upper Rio Grande Region*. Albuquerque, New Mexico: University of New Mexico Press, c1983.

Military

Colorado. National Guard. Military Affairs. *Civil War Index Cards, 1861-1865*. Microfilm of original records at the Colorado State Archives in Denver, Colorado. (Salt Lake City: Filmed by the Genealogical Society of Utah, 1992). Microfilm, 4 rolls.

Harper, Frank. *Just Outside of Manila: Letters from Members of the First Colorado Regiment in the Spanish-American and Philippine-American Wars*. Denver, Colorado: Colorado Historical Society, 1992.

Hollister, Ovando James. *Colorado Volunteers in New Mexico, 1862*. Chicago: R. R. Donnelley, 1962.

Pompey, Sherman L. *Confederate Soldiers Buried in Colorado*. Independence, California: Historical and Genealogical Publishing Co., 1965. Each soldier is listed alphabetically under the state from which he served.

United States. Adjutant General's Office. *Index to Compiled Service Records of Volunteer Union Soldiers Who Served in Organizations from the Territory of Colorado*. Washington, D.C.: National Archives. Central Plains Region, 1964. Microfilm, 3 rolls.

United States. Selective Service System. *Colorado, World War I Selective Service System Draft Registration Cards, 1917-1918*. Washington, D.C.: The National Archives, 1987-1988. Microfilm, 41 rolls.

Williams, Ellen. *Three Years and a Half in the Army, or, History of the Second Colorados*. Washington, D.C.: Filmed by Library of Congress Photoduplication Service, 1976.

Vital and Cemetery Records

Colorado. Department of Health. *Statewide Marriage Index, 1900-1939, 1975-1992*. [Denver: Colorado State Archives], [1975?]-1992. Microfilm, 106 rolls.

Guide to Vital Statistics Records in Colorado, Vol. 2. Church Archives (Denver: Colorado Historical Records Survey W.P.A., 1942.

Historical Records Survey (Colorado). *Guide to Vital Statistics Records in Colorado*. 2 vols. Denver: The Survey, 1942.

Marriages of Arapahoe County, Colorado, 1859-1901: Including Territory That Became Adams, Denver, and Other Counties. Denver: Colorado Genealogical Society, 1986.

McQueary, Lela O. *Colorado Cemetery Inscriptions*. Englewood, Colorado: K. R. Merrill, 1987.

Merrill, Kay R. *Colorado Cemetery Directory*, Denver Colorado Council of Genealogical Societies, 1985.

Territorial Vital Records: Births, Divorces, Guardianship, Marriages, Naturalization, Wills; 1800's thru 1906 Utah Territory, AZ, CO, ID, NV, WY, Indian Terr.; LDS Branches, Wards; Deseret News Vital Recs.; J.P. Marriages; Meth. Marriages. St. George, Utah: Genealogical CD Publishing, 1994. 1 CD-ROM Disc.

Wommack, Linda. *From the Grave: A Roadside Guide to Colorado's Pioneer Cemeteries*. Caldwell, Idaho: Caxton Press, 1998.

County Website	Map Index	Date Created	Parent County or Territory From Which Organized Address/Details
Adams www.co.adams.co.us/	G4	15 Apr 1901	**Arapahoe** Adams County; 450 S 4th Ave; Brighton, CO 80601-3196; Ph. 303.654.6020 Details: (Co Clk has m & land rec from 1902, some bur rec, some land rec from Arapahoe Co prior to 1901, school cen 1902-1964 & mil dis rec; 17th Jud Dist Ct Clk has div rec; Pro Ct has pro rec; Hall of Justice has ct rec)
Alamosa* www.rootsweb.com/~coalamos/index.htm	J10	8 Mar 1913	**Costilla, Conejos** Alamosa County; 402 Edison Ave; PO Box 178; Alamosa, CO 81101-2560; Ph. 719.589.6681 Details: (Co Clk has m & land rec from 1913; Clk Dis Ct has div, pro & ct rec)
Arapahoe* www.co.arapahoe.co.us/	G5	1 Nov 1861	**Original county** Arapahoe County; 5334 S Prince St; Littleton, CO 80166-0001; Ph. 303.795.4200 Details: (First formed in 1855 as Territorial Co. See Kansas 1860 for cen rec) (Co Clk has m & land rec from 1902 & bur rec to 1941; Co Ct has div, pro & ct rec)
Archuleta www.rootsweb.com/~coarchul/ archuleta.htm	M11	14 Apr 1885	**Conejos** Archuleta County; PO Box 1507; Pagosa Springs, CO 81147-1507; Ph. 970.264.5633 Details: (Co Clk has m & d rec from 1886 & land rec from 1885; Clk Dis Ct has div, pro, ct & adoption rec)
Baca www.rootsweb.com/~cobaca/	C11	16 Apr 1889	**Las Animas** Baca County; 741 Main St; Springfield, CO 81073-1548; Ph. 719.523.4372 Details: (Co Clk has m & land rec from 1889; Clk Dis Ct has div, pro & ct rec from 1910)
Bent* www.rootsweb.com/~cobent/	D9	11 Feb 1870	**Greenwood, Pueblo** Bent County; PO Box 350; Las Animas, CO 81054-0350; Ph. 719.456.1353 Details: (Co Clk-Rcdr has m & land rec from 1888 & mil dis rec; Nursing Service has b & d rec; Combine Ct has div, pro & ct rec)
Boulder www.co.boulder.co.us/	I4	1 Nov 1861	**Original county** Boulder County; 2020 13th St; PO Box 471; Boulder, CO 80302; Ph. 303.441.7770 Details: (Co Clk-Rcdr has m rec from 1863, land rec from 1864 & mil dis rec from 1917; Co Hlth Dept has b & d rec from 1872; Co Ct has pro, div & ct rec)
Broomfield www.ci.broomfield.co.us/	I4	15 Nov 2001	**Adams, Boulder, Jefferson, Weld** Broomfield County; One DesCombes Dr; Broomfield, CO 80020; Ph. 303.438.6390 Details: (Co's newest county)
Carbonate		1 Nov 1861	**Original county** Details: (see Lake Co) Name changed to Lake 10 Feb 1879
Chaffee www.chaffee-county.com/	K7	1 Nov 1861	**Original county** Chaffee County; 132 Crestone Ave; PO Box 699; Salida, CO 81201-1566; Ph. 719.539.6913 Details: (Formerly Lake Co. Name changed to Chaffee 10 Feb 1879) (Co Clk has m & land rec)
Cheyenne www.rootsweb.com/~cocheyen/index.htm	D7	25 Mar 1889	**Bent, Elbert** Cheyenne County; 615 N 5 W; PO Box 567; Cheyenne Wells, CO 80810; Ph. 719.767.5685 Details: (Rgstr has b, d & bur rec; Co Clk has m rec from 1889 & land rec from 1888; Dis Ct has div & pro rec; Co Judge has ct rec)
Clear Creek www.co.clear-creek.co.us/	J5	1 Nov 1861	**Original county** Clear Creek County; 405 Argentine St; Georgetown, CO 80444-2000; Ph. 303.679.2339 Details: (Co Clk has m & land rec from 1862)
Conejos* www.rootsweb.com/~coconejo/	K11	1 Nov 1861	**Original county** Conejos County; 6683 County Rd 13; PO Box 157; Conejos, CO 81129-0157; Ph. 719.376.5422 Details: (Formerly Guadalupe Co. Name changed to Conejos 7 Nov 1869) (Clk of Cts has pro rec; Co Clk has b, m & d rec; Co Asr has land rec)

County Website	Map Index	Date Created	Parent County or Territory From Which Organized Address/Details
Costilla* www.rootsweb.com/~cocostil/index.htm	I11	1 Nov 1861	**Original county** Costilla County; 354 Main St; PO Box 100; San Luis, CO 81152-0100; Ph. 719.672.3372 Details: (Co Clk has m & land rec from 1853; Clk Dis Ct has div, pro & ct rec)
Crowley www.rootsweb.com/~cocrowle/	F8	29 May 1911	**Bent, Otero** Crowley County; 110 E 6th St; Ordway, CO 81063-0000; Ph. 719.267.4643 Details: (Co Clk has m & land rec)
Custer www.geocities.com/Heartland/Meadows /3456/custer1.html	I9	9 Mar 1877	**Fremont** Custer County; 205 S 6th St; PO Box 150; Westcliffe, CO 81252; Ph. 719.783.0441 Details: (Co Clk has m & bur rec)
Delta www.rootsweb.com/~codelta/	N7	11 Feb 1883	**Gunnison** Delta County; 501 Palmer St; Delta, CO 81416-1753; Ph. 970.874.2150 Details: (Co Clk has b rec from 1920, m, d & land rec from 1883 & school cen 1891-1964; Clk Dis Ct has div, pro & ct rec)
Denver www.denvergov.org/	H5	18 Mar 1901	**Arapahoe** Denver County; 1437 Bannock St Ste 200; Denver, CO 80202; Ph. 303.640.3012 Details: (Has annexed terr from Arapahoe, Adams & Jefferson Cos on several occasions) (Co Clk has m rec from 1902 & land rec from 1859; Clk Dis Ct has div rec from 1967, pro & ct rec from 1858)
Dolores www.rootsweb.com/~codolore/index.html	P10	19 Feb 1881	**Ouray** Dolores County; PO Box 608; Dove Creek, CO 81324; Ph. 970.677.2383 Details: (Co Clk has b & d rec from 1894, m & land rec from 1881; Co Ct has pro & ct rec)
Douglas www.douglas.co.us/	H6	1 Nov 1861	**Original county** Douglas County; 301 Wilcox St; Castle Rock, CO 80104-2454; Ph. 303.660.7446 Details: (Co Clk has m rec from 1867 & land rec from 1864)
Eagle www.eagle-county.com/	L5	11 Feb 1883	**Summit** Eagle County; 500 Broadway; Eagle, CO 81631-0850; Ph. 970.328.8710 Details: (Co Clk has b & m rec from 1883, d & land rec; Clk Dis Ct has div, pro & ct rec)
El Paso www.co.el-paso.co.us/	G7	1 Nov 1861	**Original county** El Paso County; 200 S Cascade Ave; Colorado Springs, CO 80903-2214; Ph. 719.520.6216 Details: (Co Clk has m & land rec from 1861 & mil dis rec from 1919; Clk Dis Ct has div & pro rec; Co Ct has ct rec)
Elbert www.rootsweb.com/~coelbert/	G6	2 Feb 1874	**Douglas, Greenwood** Elbert County; 215 Comanche St; Kiowa, CO 80117-0037; Ph. 303.621.3129 Details: (Co Clk has m rec from 1893 & land rec from 1874; Clk of Combined Cts has div, pro & ct rec)
Fremont* www.fremontco.com/	I8	1 Nov 1861	**Original county** Fremont County; 615 Macon Rm 100; Canon City, CO 81212; Ph. 719.276.7330 Details: (Co Clk has m & land rec; Clk Dis Ct has div, pro & ct rec)
Garfield* www.garfield-county.com/	P5	10 Feb 1883	**Summit** Garfield County; 109 8th St Ste 200; Glenwood Springs, CO 81601; Ph. 970.945.5004 Details: (Co Clk has b, m, d & land rec from 1883 & mil rec from 1910; Dist Ct has div, pro & ct rec)
Gilpin stanwyck.com/CCGilpin/	J4	1 Nov 1861	**Original county** Gilpin County; 203 Eureka St; PO Box 366; Central City, CO 80427-0366; Ph. 303.582.5321 Details: (Co Clk has m rec from 1881 & land rec from 1861; Clk Dis Ct has div & pro rec)

County Website	Map Index	Date Created	Parent County or Territory From Which Organized Address/Details
Grand www.co.grand.co.us/	K4	2 Feb 1874	**Summit** Grand County; 308 Byers Ave; PO Box 264; Hot Sulphur Springs, CO 80451; Ph. 970.725.3347 Details: (Local Rgstr has b, d & bur rec; Co & Dis Ct has div, pro & ct rec; Co Asr has land rec; Co Clk has m rec from 1874)
Greenwood		1870	**El Paso, Pueblo** Details: (Abolished 1874. Bent and Elbert Counties formed from Greenwood)
Guadalupe		1 Nov 1861	**Original county** Details: (see Conejos) Name changed to Conejos 7 Nov 1869
Gunnison www.co.gunnison.co.us/	M7	9 Mar 1877	**Lake** Gunnison County; 200 E Virginia Ave; Gunnison, CO 81230-2297; Ph. 970.641.1516 Details: (Co Clk has m rec from 1874 & land rec from 1879; Clk Co Ct has div & pro rec from 1877 & ct rec from 1900; Gunnison Dept of Soc Serv has b, d & bur rec from 1910)
Hinsdale* www.rootsweb.com/~cohinsda/	M9	10 Feb 1874	**Conejos** Hinsdale County; 317 N Henson St; Lake City, CO 81235-0277; Ph. 970.944.2228 Details: (Co Clk has m & land rec from 1875; Co Ct has div, pro & ct rec)
Huerfano www.rootsweb.com/~cohuerfa/	I10	1 Nov 1861	**Original county** Huerfano County; 401 Main St #204; Walsenburg, CO 81089-2034; Ph. 719.738.2380 Details: (Co Clk has m & land rec; Clk Dis Ct has div, pro & ct rec)
Jackson www.rootsweb.com/~cojackso/index.htm	K3	5 May 1909	**Grand, Larimer** Jackson County; PO Box 337; Walden, CO 80480; Ph. 970.723.4334 Details: (Co Clk has m & land rec from 1909; Co Rgstr has b & d rec; Clk Dist Ct has div, pro & ct rec; Co Cem Officer has cem rec from 1909)
Jefferson 206.247.49.21/ext/index.htm	I5	1 Nov 1861	**Original county** Jefferson County; 100 Jefferson City Pkwy #2530; Golden, CO 80419-2530; Ph. 303.271.8168 Details: (Co Clk has m rec from 1868 & land rec from 1860; Co Hlth Dept has b, d & bur rec; Clk Dist Ct has div rec; Co Ct has pro & ct rec)
Kiowa www.kiowacountycolo.com/	D8	11 Apr 1889	**Cheyenne, Bent** Kiowa County; 1305 Goff; Eads, CO 81036-0000; Ph. 71.943.8521 Details: (Co Clk has m & land rec from 1889; Clk Dis Ct has div, pro & ct rec)
Kit Carson www.rootsweb.com/~cokitcar/index.htm	D6	11 Apr 1889	**Elbert** Kit Carson County; 251 16th St; Burlington, CO 80807-0249; Ph. 719.346.8638 Details: (Co Clk has m & land rec from 1889 & bur rec from 1902; Clk Dis Ct has b, d, div, pro & ct rec)
La Plata co.laplata.co.us/	N10	10 Feb 1874	**Conejos, Lake** La Plata County; 1060 E 2nd Ave; Durango, CO 81301-5157; Ph. 970.382.6219 Details: (Co Clk has m rec from 1878 & land rec from 1876; Clk Dis Ct has div & pro rec; Co Ct has ct rec; San Juan Basin Hlth Dept has b, d & bur rec)
Lake www.usgw.org/co/lake/lake.html	K6	1 Nov 1861	**Original county** Lake County; 505 Harrison Ave; Leadville, CO 80461-0917; Ph. 719.486.1410 Details: (Formerly Carbonate Co. Name changed to Lake 10 Feb 1879) (Co Clk has m rec from 1869, land rec from 1861 & some bur rec 1885-1903; Clk Dis Ct has div, pro & ct rec)
Larimer* www.co.larimer.co.us/	J2	1 Nov 1861	**Original county** Larimer County; 200 W Oak St; PO Box 1190; Fort Collins, CO 80522-1190; Ph. 970.498.7860 Details: (Co Clk has m & land rec from 1862; Co Hlth Dept has b & d rec)
Las Animas www.usroots.com/~colorado/index.htm	G10	9 Feb 1866	**Huerfano** Las Animas County; 200 E 1st St; Trinidad, CO 81082; Ph. 719.846.3314 Details: (Co Clk has m rec from 1887, land rec from 1883 & mil dis rec from 1918; Co Hlth Dept has b & d rec: Clk Dis Ct has div, pro & ct rec)

Notes

Mountain Laurel

CONNECTICUT

CAPITAL: HARTFORD – NINTH COLONY – STATE 1788 (5TH)

The Dutch seafarer, Adriaen Block, was the first European in Connecticut when he sailed up the Connecticut River in 1614. In 1633, Dutch settlers from New Amsterdam built a fort and trading post at present-day Hartford. Glowing reports from John Oldham and others, combined with disgust for the intolerance of the Massachusetts Bay Colony, led to a migration from Massachusetts to Connecticut starting about 1634. Most of the settlers of Newtown (Cambridge), Watertown, and Dorchester moved to the central part of Connecticut, establishing the towns of Wethersfield, Windsor, and Suckiang (Hartford). These towns joined together in 1639 to form the Connecticut Colony, a relatively democratic colony. Meanwhile, in 1638, a party of Puritans founded New Haven, which with Milford, Stamford, and Guilford, formed the New Haven Colony.

The New Haven Colony was theocratic and used the Old Testament as the legal code. The decade of the 1640's saw a heavy influx of settlers from England. In 1662, John Winthrop, governor of the Connecticut Colony, was granted a charter that defined the boundaries as extending from Massachusetts to Long Island Sound and from Narragansett Bay to the Pacific Ocean. The New Haven Colony finally agreed to be absorbed into the Connecticut Colony in 1665. The next forty years were marked by migration westward, sometimes entire towns moved to a new setting.

By 1740, Connecticut was settled and organized into incorporated towns. Towns have remained the basic governing unit and it is at that level where many of the records are found. Connecticut had many boundary disputes with other colonies, especially Rhode Island, Massachusetts, and New York. In 1754, Connecticut settlers colonized the Wyoming Valley in Pennsylvania. Connecticut exchanged its rights to the territory west of its present boundary for the Western Reserve in Ohio and in 1799 gave up its claims to the Wyoming Valley in Pennsylvania. In 1800, the Western Reserve was incorporated in the Northwest Territory as Trumbull County, and Connecticut's present boundaries were set.

Connecticut played an important part in the Revolutionary War. More than 40,000 of its men served in that war. In 1777, Danbury was burned, and in 1779, New Haven, Fairfield, and Norwalk were pillaged. Benedict Arnold largely destroyed New London and Groton in 1781. The 1790 Census shows a population of 223,236, most of whom came from England. Others came from Scotland, Ireland, France, and Holland.

Connecticut had more home industries than any other colony. Household gadgets invented and manufactured in the homes were carried all over the United States by "Yankee peddlars". The building of factories in the United States and the potato crop failures in Ireland brought 70,000 Irish as well as settlers from Germany, Canada, Scandinavia, Italy, Poland, Lithuania, Czechoslovakia, and Hungary. During the Civil War, Connecticut supplied about 55,000 troops to the Union Army.

Look for vital records in the following locations:
- **Birth and death records:** Connecticut State Department of Public Health, Vital Records Section. Check with town clerk records prior to 1 July 1897. Only the person, his parents, an attorney, or a member of a genealogical society in Connecticut may search birth records.
- **Marriage records:** Connecticut State Department of Public Health, Vital Records Section. Check with town clerk records prior to 1 July 1897.
- **Divorce records:** Clerk of the Superior Court. Wills, inventories, and administrations of estates are in the probate districts. The boundaries of these districts often differ from town and county boundaries. There are 118 probate districts for the 169 towns. Many probate records are now in the Connecticut State Library.
- **Naturalizations:** U.S. Circuit Court in Hartford or in the county Superior Courts.

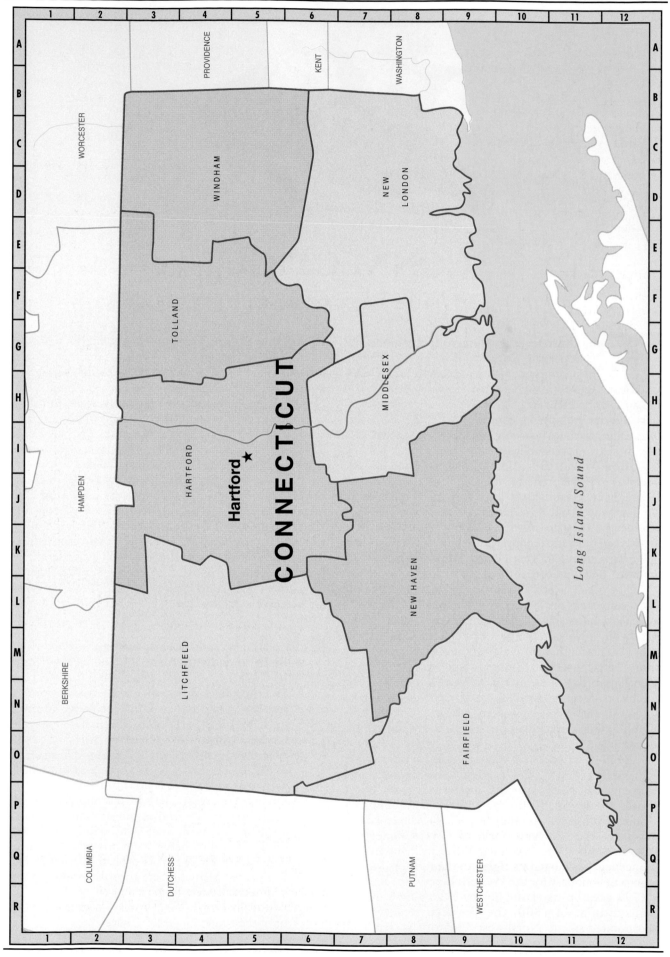

- Almost every city in the state has printed histories that contain much genealogical information, especially about early inhabitants. Many family histories exist in manuscript form only, but many of these have been indexed to facilitate research. Although libraries will not do research, they provide names of researchers or give information about indexes, if the request is accompanied by a self-addressed stamped envelope.

Connecticut State Department of Public Health Vital Records Section
150 Washington Street
Hartford, Connecticut 06106
860.509.7897

Connecticut State Library
231 Capitol Avenue
Hartford, Connecticut 06115

Societies and Repositories

Abington Social Library; Abington Four Corners; Route 97; Abington, Connecticut 06230

American Baptist - Samuel Colgate Historical Library; 1106 South Goodman Street; Rochester, New York 14620-2532; 716.473.1740; Fax 716.473.1740

Amity and Woodbridge Historical Society; c/o Thomas Darling House; 1907 Litchfield Tpke.; Woodbridge, Connecticut 06525;

Archive & Resource Center, Polish Genealogy Society Of Connecticut; 8 Lyle Rd.; New Britain, Connecticut 06053

Aspincok Historical Society of Putnam, Inc.; PO Box 465; Putnam, Connecticut 06260

Avon Historical Society, Inc.; PO Box 448; Avon, Connecticut 06001; <www.avonct.com/historicalsociety/home.htm>

Barkhamsted Historical Society; PO Box 94; Pleasant Valley, Connecticut 06063;

Beardsley & Memorial Library; Munro Place; Winsted, Connecticut 06098

Berlin Historical Society; 305 Main Street; Berlin, Connecticut 06037;

Branford Historical Society-Harrison House; 124 Main Street; Branford, Connecticut 06405

Bridgeport Public Library; 925 Broad St.; Bridgeport, Connecticut 06603

Bristol Public Library; 5 High St.; Bristol, Connecticut 06010

Brookfield, Connecticut Historical Society; PO Box 5231; Brookfield, Connecticut 06804; <www.danbury.org/org/brookhc/>

Brooklyn Historical Society; PO Box 90; Brooklyn, Connecticut 06234-0090

Burlington Historical Society; PO Box 1215; Burlington, Connecticut 06013

Canterbury Historical Society; PO Box 2; Canterbury, Connecticut 06331

Canton Historical Society; Cherry Brook Road; Canton, Connecticut 06020

Chaplin Historical Society; Chaplin Street; Chaplin, Connecticut 06235

Cheshire Historical Society; PO Box 281; Cheshire, Connecticut 06410

Chester Historical Society; 4 Liberty; Chester, Connecticut 06412; <www.wuzzup.com/lowctriver/chester/historical.html>

Colchester Historical Society; Elm Street; Colchester, Connecticut 06415

Colebrook Historical Society; PO Box 85; Colebrook, Connecticut 06021

Columbia Historical Society; 21 Edgarton Road; Columbia, Connecticut 06237

Congregational Library; 14 Beacon Street; Boston, Massachusetts 02108-3704; 617.523.0470; Fax 617.523.0491

Connecticut Ancestry Society; The Ferguson Library; One Public Library Plaza; Stamford; Connecticut 06904-1000

Connecticut College Library; Mohegan Ave.; New London, Connecticut 06320

Connecticut Historical Commission; 59 South Prospect Street; Hartford, Connecticut 06106

Connecticut Historical Society; One Elizabeth Street; Hartford, Connecticut 06105;

Connecticut League of Historical Societies; PO Box 906; Darien, Connecticut 06920

Connecticut Professional Genealogists Council; PO Box 4273; Hartford, Connecticut 06147-4273

Connecticut Society of Genealogists, Inc.; PO Box 435; Glastonbury, Connecticut 06033-0435;

Connecticut State Archives; Connecticut State Library; 231 Capitol Avenue; Hartford, Connecticut 06106; <www.cslib.org/archives.htm>

Connecticut State Library, History & Genealogy Unit; 231 Capitol Ave.; Hartford, Connecticut 06106-1537 <www.cslnet.ctstateu.edu/handg.htm>

Connecticut State Library; 231 Capitol Avenue; Hartford, Connecticut 06106; 860.566.4301; 860.566.8940; A helpful inventory of this library is *Connecticut State Library, Guide to Archives in the Connecticut State Library*, 3rd ed. (Hartford, Conn.; Connecticut State Library, 1981; FHL book 974.6 A1 No. 30).

Connecticut Trust for Historic Preservation; 940 Whitney Avenue; Hamden, Connecticut 06517-4002; 203.773.0107;

Connecticut Valley Tobacco Historical Society, Inc.; PO Box 241; Windsor, Connecticut 06095; <www.tobaccohistsoc.org/connecti.htm>

Cornwall Historical Society; 7 Pine St.; Box 115; Cornwall, Connecticut 06753

Coventry Historical Society; PO Box 534; Coventry, Connecticut 06238; <geocities.com/coventrycthistory/>

Cromwell Historical Society; 395 Main Street; Cromwell, Connecticut 06416

Cyrenius H. Booth Library; 25 Main St.; Newton, Connecticut 06470

Danbury Historical Society; 43 Main St; Danbury, Connecticut 06810;

Danbury Public Library; 170 Main St.; PO Box 1160; Danbury, Connecticut 06810

Darien Historical Society; 45 Old Kings Highway North; Darien, Connecticut 06820; <www.darien.lib.ct.us/townhall/about_darien/tour/historical_society.htm>

Deep River Historical Society; 245 Main Street; Deep River, Connecticut 06417

Department of Public Health; Vital Records Section; 410 Capitol Ave.; Hartford, Connecticut 06105; 860.509.8000; Mailing Address; PO Box 340-308 11 VRS Hartford, Connecticut 06134-0308

Derby Historical Society; 37 Elm Street; Ansonia, Connecticut 06401;

Descendants of the Founders of Ancient Windsor; PO Box 39; Windsor, Connecticut 06095-0039

Diocese of Hartford; 134 Farmington Avenue; Hartford, Connecticut 06103; 860.541.6491; Fax 860.541.6309

Diocese of Norwich; 201 Broadway; PO Box 587; Norwich, Connecticut 06360; 860.887.9294; Fax 860.886.1670; (Roman Catholic records)

East Granby Historical Society; Box 188; East Granby, Connecticut 06026; <www.eastgranby.com/HistoricalSociety/>

East Haddam Historical Society Museum; 264 Town Street; PO Box 27; East Haddam, Connecticut 06423-0027

East Hartford Public Library; 840 Main St.; East Hartford, Connecticut 06108

East Haven Historical Society; 200 Tyler St.; PO Box 120052; East Haven, Connecticut 06512

East Lyme Historical Society; Thomas Lee House; Shore Road; Niantic, Connecticut 06357

East Windsor Historical Society; PO Box 363; East Windsor Hill, Connecticut 06028;

Easton Historical Society; PO Box 121; Easton, Connecticut 06612; <www.tomorrowseaston.com/guestwebpages/historicalsociety/historicalsociety.htm>

Ellington Historical Society; PO Box 73; Ellington, Connecticut 06029

Enfield Historical Society; 1294 Enfield Street; PO Box 586; Enfield, Connecticut 06083; <home.att.net/~mkm-of-enfct/>

Episcopal Diocese of Connecticut; 135 Asylum Avenue; Hartford, Connecticut 06105-2295; 860.233.4481; Fax 860.523.1410

Essex Historical Society; PO Box 123; Essex, Connecticut 06426; <www.essexhistory.org/default.htm>

Fairfield Historical Society; 636 Old Post Rd.; Fairfield, Connecticut 06430;

Fairfield Public Library; 1080 Old Post Rd.; Fairfield, Connecticut 06430

Falls Village Depot; Railroad Street; PO Box 206; Falls Village, Connecticut 06031

Family History Library; 35 North West Temple Street; Salt Lake City, Utah 84150; 800.346.6044 or 801.240.2584; <www.familysearch.org>; Find a Family History Center near you; <www.familysearch.org/Eng/Library/FHC/frameset_fhc.asp>

Farmington Historical Society; PO Box 1645; Farmington, Connecticut 06034

Farmington Museum; 37 High St.; Farmington, Connecticut 06032

Ferguson Library; 96 Broad St.; Stamford, Connecticut 06901

Finnish American Heritage Society of Connecticut; PO Box 252; Canterbury, Connecticut 06331;

Finnish American Heritage Society; PO Box 252; Canterbury, Connecticut 06331

Franklin Historical Society; PO Box 73; Franklin, Connecticut 06254

French-Canadian Genealogical Society of Connecticut, Inc.; PO Box 928; Tolland, Connecticut 06084-0928;

Gaylordsville Historical Society; PO Box 25; Gaylordsville, Connecticut 06755;

Glastonbury Historical Society; 976 Main St.; South Glastonbury, Connecticut 06073

Godfrey Memorial Library; 134 Newfield St.; Middletown, Connecticut 06457; 860.346.4375; <www.godfrey.org>

Goshen Historical Society; 21 Old Middle Road; PO Box 457; Goshen, Connecticut 06756-0457;

Greenwich Library; 101 W. Putnam Ave.; Greenwich, Connecticut 06830

Groton Public Library; Ft. Hill Rd.; Groton, Connecticut 06340

Guilford Historical Society; 171 Boston Street; PO Box 363; Guilford, Connecticut 06437; 203.458.2797;

Haddam Historical Society; PO Box 97; Haddam, Connecticut 06438

Hamden Historical Society; PO Box 5512; Hamden, Connecticut 06518

Hampton Historical Society; PO Box 12; Hampton, Connecticut 06247

Hartford Public Library; 500 Main St.; Hartford, Connecticut 06103

Hartland Historical Society; PO Box 221; East Hartland, Connecticut 06027; 860.844.8090; <www.munic.state.ct.us/hartland/historical.htm>

Harwinton Historical Society; PO Box 84; Harwinton, Connecticut 06791

Hebron Historical Society; PO Box 43; Hebron, Connecticut 06248;

Historical Society of East Hartford; PO Box 380166; East Hartford, Connecticut 06108-0166; 860.568.7305;

Historical Society of Town of Greenwich; Bush-Holley House_39 Strickland Rd; Cos Cob, Connecticut 06878;

Indian and Colonial Research Center; Old Mystic, Connecticut 06372

Jewish Genealogical Society of Connecticut; 394 Sport Hill Rd.; Easton, Connecticut 06612

Jewish Historical Society of Greater New Haven; PO Box 3251; New Haven, Connecticut 06515-0351

Jewish Historical Society of Greater Stamford; PO Box 16918; Stamford, Connecticut 06905-8901; <www.stamfordhistory.org/jhsgs.htm>

Kent Memorial Library; 50 N. Main St.; Hartford, Connecticut 06103

Killingly Historical Society; 196 Main St.; Danielson, Connecticut 6239; <www.qvctc.commnet.edu/brian/KHS/kilz1.html>

Lebanon Historical Society; 856 Trumbull Highway; PO Box 151; Lebanon, Connecticut 06249; 860.642.6583; <www.lebanonct.org/historic_sites.html>

Litchfield Historical Society; East and South Streets; Litchfield, Connecticut 06759; <www.litchfieldct.com/twn/lhistsoc.html>

Lyme Historical Society, Inc.; Florence Griswold Museum; 96 Lyme St.; Old Lyme, Connecticut 06371

Madison Historical Society; Allis-Bushnell House; 853 Boston Post Road; Madison, Connecticut 06443

Manchester Historical Society; 106 Hartford Road; Manchester, Connecticut 6040;

Mansfield Historical Society; PO Box 145; Storrs, Connecticut 06268; 860.429.6575;

Meriden Public Library; 105 Miller St.; PO Box 868; Meriden, Connecticut 06450; 203.238.2344; Fax 203.238.3647

Middlebury Historical Society; PO Box 104; Middlebury, Connecticut 06762; <www.middlebury-ct.org/historical.shtml>

Middlefield Historical Society; 405 Main Street; Middlefield, Connecticut 06455

Middlesex County Historical Society; 151 Main St.; Middletown, Connecticut 06457

Middlesex Genealogical Society; PO Box 1111; Darien, Connecticut 06820-1111; <darien.lib.ct.us/mgs/default.htm>

Milford Historical Society; 34 High Street; Milford, Connecticut; 203.874.5789; <www.geocities.com/SiliconValley/Park/3831/>

Monroe Historical Society; Box 212; Monroe, Connecticut 06468;

Montville Historical Society; PO Box 1786; Montville, Connecticut 06353

Morris Historical Society; PO Box 234; Morris, Connecticut 06763

Mystic River Historical Society; PO Box 245; Mystic, Connecticut 06355-0245

Mystic Seaport; PO Box 6000; Mystic, Connecticut 06355-0990;

National Archives—Northeast Region (Boston); 380 Trapelo Rd.; Waltham, Massachusetts 02154; 617.647.8100; Fax 617.647.8460

Naugatuck Historical Society; PO Box 317; Naugatuck, Connecticut 06770; 203.723.8282;

New Britain Public Library; 20 High St.; PO Box 1291; New Britain, Connecticut 06050

New Canaan Historical Society; 13 Oenoke Ridge; New Canaan, Connecticut; 06480; 203.972.5917;

New England Historic Genealogical Society; 101 Newbury Street; Boston, Massachusetts 02116-3007; 617.536.5740; Fax 617.536.7307

New Fairfield Historical Society; PO Box 8156; New Fairfield, Connecticut 06812-8156

New Hartford Historical Society; PO Box 41; New Hartford, Connecticut 06057; <www.town.new-hartford.ct.us/nhhs/index.html>

New Haven Colony Historical Society; 114 Whitney Ave.; New Haven, Connecticut 06510; 203.562.2002

New Haven Public Library; 133 Elm St.; New Haven, Connecticut 06510

New London County Historical Society; Shaw Mansion; 11 Blinman St.; New London, Connecticut 06320

New Milford Historical Society; PO Box 566; 6 Aspetuck Ave.; New Milford, Connecticut 06776;

Newtown Historical Society; 6 Bari Drive; Newtown, Connecticut 06470

Noah Webster Memorial Library; 205 Main St.; West Hartford, Connecticut 06107

Noank Historical Society; 17 Sylvan St.; Box 454 Noank, Connecticut 06340

Norfolk Historical Society; 13 Village Green; PO Box 288; Norfolk, Connecticut 06058

North Haven Historical Society; 27 Broadway; North Haven, Connecticut 06473; <www.geocities.com/northhavenhistoricalsociety/home.htm>

North Stonington Historical Society Library, Inc.; PO Box 134; North Stonington, Connecticut 06359; 860.535.9448; <www.nostoningtonhistsoc.homestead.com>

North Stonington Historical Society; 1 Wyassup Rd.; PO Box 134; North Stonington, Connecticut 06359;

Norwalk Historical Society; PO Box 335; 2 East Wall Street; Norwalk, Connecticut 06852; <www.geocities.com/Heartland/Trail/8030/>

Old Saybrook Historical Society; PO Box 4; Old Saybrook, Connecticut 06475; <www.oldsaybrook.com/History/society.htm>

Old Woodbury Historical Society, Inc.; Box 705; Woodbury, Connecticut 06798

Orange Historical Society; PO Box 784; Orange, Connecticut 06477;

Otis Library; 261 Main St.; Norwich, Connecticut 06360

Phoebe Griffin Noyes Library; Lyme St.; Lyme, Connecticut 06371

Polish Genealogical Society of Connecticut and the Northeast, Inc.; 8 Lyle Rd.; New Britain, Connecticut 06053;

Portland Historical Society; Box 98; Portland, Connecticut 06480; <www.geocities.com/portlandhistsoc/>

Preston Historical Society; Town Hall; 389 Route 2; Preston, Connecticut 06365

Public Library; 63 Huntington St.; New London, Connecticut 06320

Ridgefield Historical Society; 400 Main Street; Ridgefield, Connecticut 06877;

Rocky Hill Historical Society; PO Box 185; Rocky Hill, Connecticut 06067;

Saybrook Colony Founders Association; PO Box 1635; Old Saybrook, Connecticut 06475-1000; <www.rootsweb.com/~ctscfa/>

Seymour Public Library; 46 Church St.; Seymour, Connecticut 06483

Sharon Historical Society; The Gay-Hoyt House; 18 Main Street; Sharon, Connecticut 06069; <www.sharonhist.org>

Shelton Historical Society; PO Box 2155; 70 Ripton Road; Shelton, Connecticut 06484; 203.926.9567

Silan Bronson Library; 267 Grand St.; Waterbury, Connecticut 06702; 203.574.8225

Simsbury Genealogy and Historical Research Library; 749 Hopmeadow St.; PO Box 484; Simsbury, Connecticut 06070; <www2.miracle.net/~genehist>

Society of Mayflower Descendants in Connecticut; 36 Arundel Ave.; Hartford, Connecticut 06107

Somers Historical Society, Inc.; PO Box 652; Somers, Connecticut 06071;

South Windsor Historical Society; PO Box 216; 11 Beldon Road; South Windsor, Connecticut 06074;

Southington Genealogical Society; Southington Historical Center; 239 Main St.; Southington, Connecticut 06489

Southington Historical Society; Southington, Connecticut 06489; <southington.com/History/>

Southington Public Library; 255 Main St.; Southington, Connecticut 06489

Stamford Historical Society; 1508 High Ridge Road; Stamford, Connecticut 06903; 203.322.1607;

Stonington Historical Society; 40 Palmer Street; Stonington, Connecticut 06378;

Stratford Historical Society; 967 Academy Hill; PO Box 382; Stratford, Connecticut 06497

Thompson Historical Society; PO Box 47; Thompson, Connecticut 6277;

Trinity College, Watkinson Library; 300 Summit St.; Hartford, Connecticut 06106

Trumbull Historical Society; 1856 Huntington Turnpike (Rte. 108); PO Box 312; Trumbull, Connecticut 06611-0312; <trumbull.ct.us/history/>

United Methodist Archives Center; Drew University Library; PO box 127; Madison, New Jersey 07940; 201.408.3189; Fax 201.408.3909

Vernon Historical Society; PO Box 2055; Vernon, Connecticut 06066

Wadsworth Atheneum; 600 Main St.; Hartford, Connecticut 06103

Wallingford Historical Society; PO Box 73; Wallingford, Connecticut 06492-0073

West Hartford Historical Society and Noah Webster House Museum; 227 South Main Street; West Hartford, Connecticut 06107; 860.521.4036; <www.ctstateu.edu/noahweb/>

West Hartford Public Library; 20 S. Main St.; West Hartford, Connecticut 06107

West Haven Historical Society; 219 Court Street; West Haven, Connecticut 6516

Westbrook Historical Society; 1196 Boston Post Road; Westbrook, Connecticut 06498

Weston Historical Society; PO Box 1092; Weston, Connecticut 06883; <www.wvfd.com/whs.htm>

Westport Historical Society; 25 Avery Place; Westport, Connecticut 06880; 203.221.0981;

Wethersfield Historical Society; 150 Main St.; Wethersfield, Connecticut 06109; 860.529.1905;

Whitney Library of New Haven Colony Historical Society; 114 Whitney Ave; New Haven, Connecticut 06510

Willington Historical Society; 48 Red Oak Hill; Willington, Connecticut 06279

Wilton Historical Society; Wilton Heritage Museum; 249 Danbury Rd.; Wilton, Connecticut 06897

Winchester Historical Society; 225 Prospect St.; Winsted, Connecticut 06098

Windham Historical Society; Jillson House; 627 Main St.; Windham, Connecticut 06226;

Windsor Historical Society; 96 Palisado Ave.; Windsor, Connecticut 06095; <www.townofwindsorct.com/Historic Homes.htm>

Wintonbury Historical Society; 151 School Street; Bloomfield, Connecticut 06002

Wolcott Historical Society; PO Box 6410; Wolcott, Connecticut 06716;

Woodstock Historical Society; 523 Route 169; Woodstock, Connecticut 06281; <www.uvm.edu/~histpres/vtiana/woodstockhs.html>

Yale University Library; Box 1603A, Yale Station; New Haven, Connecticut 06520

Bibliography and Record Sources

General Sources

Bailey, Frederic W. *Early Connecticut Marriages as Found on Ancient Church Records Prior to 1800.* 7 vols. New Haven: Bureau of American Ancestry for Family Research, 1896-1906.

Beardsley, E. Edwards. *The History of the Episcopal Church in Connecticut.* 2 vols. New York: Hurd and Houghton, 1865.

Bickford, Christopher P., and J. Bard McNulty. *John Warner Barber's Views of Connecticut Towns, 1834-36.* Hartford Connecticut: Connecticut Historical Society, 1990.

Bingham, Harold J. *History of Connecticut*. 4 vols. New York: Lewis Historical Publishing Company, 1962.

Bolles, J.R., and Anna B. Williams. *The Rogerenes: Some Hitherto Unpublished Annals Belonging to the Colonial History of Connecticut*. With Appendix of Rogerene writings. (1904), reprint Salem MA: Higginson Books, 1990.

Booth, Maud. *Universalist Church in Connecticut: Papers, 1791-1951*. Microreproduction of original records at the Connecticut State Library. (Salt Lake City: Filmed by the Genealogical Society of Utah, 1976).

Brown, Barbara W. *Black Roots in Southeastern Connecticut, 1650-1900*. Detroit: Gale Research Company, 1980.

Burpee, Charles W. *Burpee's The Story of Connecticut*. 4 vols. New York: American Historical Co., 1939.

Connecticut Research Outline. Series US-States, no. 7, Salt Lake City: Family History Library, 1988.

Connecticut State Library (Hartford, Connecticut). *Connecticut Archives, Indians, 1647-1789*. 2 vols. Microfilm of original published: Hartford, Connecticut: [s.n.], 1922.

Connecticut State Library, *Guide to Archives in the Connecticut State Library*. 3rd ed. Hartford, Connecticut: Connecticut State Library, 1981.

Connecticut, 1600s-1800s. [S.l.]: Brøderbund, 2000. CD ROM.

Crandall, Ralph J. ed. *Genealogical Research in New England*. Baltimore: Genealogical Publishing Co., 1984.

Cutter, William Richard, et al. *Genealogical and Family History of the State of Connecticut. A Record of the Achievements of Her People in the Making of a Commonwealth and the Building of a Nation*. In four volumes. Partially indexed. (1911) reprint, Baltimore: Clearfield Co., 1995.

Dayton, Cornelia Hughes. *Women Before the Bar: Gender, Law & Society in Connecticut: 1639-1789*. Galveston Texas: Frontier Press, 1995.

Duffy, Ward E. *Who's Who in Connecticut*. New York City: Lewis Historical Publishing Company, 1933.

Genealogical and Biographical Records of American Citizens: Connecticut. 26 vols. Hartford, CN: 1929-49.

Giles, Barbara S. *Connecticut Genealogical Resources: Including Selected Bibliographies*. Seattle, Wash.: Fiske Genealogical Foundation, 1991.

Greenlaw, William Prescott. *The Greenlaw Index of the New England Historic Genealogical Society*. 2 vols. Boston: G. K. Hall, 1979.

Guide to Vital Statistics in the Church Records of Connecticut. New Haven, Connecticut: Connecticut Historical Records Survey, 1942.

Hale, Charles R. *Hale Collection*. Microfilm of typescript at the Connecticut State Library. (Salt Lake City: Filmed by the Genealogical Society of Utah, 1949-1950).

Hall, Lu Verne V. *New England Family Historie: State of Connecticut*. Bowie, Maryland: Heritage Books, 1999.

Hart, Samuel, et al. *Encyclopedia of Connecticut Biography, Genealogical-Memorial: Representative Citizens*. 11 vols. Boston: American Historical Society, 1917-23.

Hart, Samuel. *Representative Citizens of Connecticut, Biographical, Memorial*. New York: American Historical Society, 1916.

Hinman, Royal R. *A Catalogue of the Names of the First Puritan Settlers of the Colony of Connecticut; with the Time of Their Arrival in the Colony and Their Standing in Society...* (1846) Reprint Baltimore: Clearfield Co., 1996.

Historical Records Survey (Connecticut), *Inventory of the Church Archives of Connecticut, Presbyterians*. (Salt Lake City: Filmed by the Genealogical Society of Utah, 1972).

Historical Records Survey (Connecticut). *Guide to Vital Statistics in the Church Records of Connecticut*. New Haven, Connecticut: The Survey, 1942.

Historical Records Survey (Connecticut). *Inventory of the Church Archives of Connecticut, Lutheran*. New Haven, Connecticut: The Survey, 1941.

Historical Records Survey (Connecticut). *Inventory of the Church Archives of Connecticut, Protestant Episcopal*. New Haven, Connecticut: The Survey, 1940.

Ireland, Norma Olin, and Winifred Irving. *Cutter Index: A Consolidated Index of Cutter's Nine Genealogy Series*. Fallbrook, California: Ireland Indexing Service, 197?.

Jacobus, Donald Lines. *Families of Ancient New Haven*. With an Index Vol. by Helen L. Scranton. 9 vols. in 3. Reprint, Baltimore: Genealogical Publishing, 1997.

Jacobus, Donald Lines. *Lists of Officials...of Connecticut Colony...1936 through...1677 and of New Haven Colony...[with] Soldiers in the Pequot War...*Reprint, Baltimore: Clearfield Co., 1996.

Jarvis, Lucy Cushing. *Sketches of Church life in Colonial Connecticut: Being the Story of the Transplanting of the Church of England into Forty-Two Parishes of Connecticut, with the Assistance of the Society for the Propagation of the Gospel*. New Haven: Tuttle, Morehouse & Taylor, 1902.

Kemp, Thomas J. *Connecticut Researcher's Handbook*. Detroit: Gale Research, 1981.

Lindberg, Marcia Wiswall, ed. *Genealogist's Handbook for New England Research*. 2nd ed. Boston: New England Historic Genealogical Society, 1993.

List of Church Records in the Connecticut State Library. Hartford: Connecticut State Library, 1976.

Mather, Frederick Gregory. *The Refugees of 1776 from Long Island to Connecticut*. Baltimore: Genealogical Publishing Co., 1972.

Morrison, Betty Jean. *Connecting to Connecticut*. Glastonbury: Connecticut Society of Genealogists, 1995.

New England Historic Genealogical Society. *English Origins of New England Families: from the New England Historical and Genealogical Register. First Series*. 3 vols. Baltimore: Genealogical Publishing Co., 1985.

Osborn, Norris Galpin, ed. *Men of Mark in Connecticut*. 5 vols. Hartford: Connecticut: W.R. Goodspeed, 1906-10.

Parks, Roger, ed. *Connecticut: A Bibliography of Its History*. Hanover, New Hampshire: University of New England, 1986.

Perry, Charles Edward. *Founders and Leaders of Connecticut, 1633-1783*. Boston, Massachusetts: D.C. Heath, c1934.

Report of the Temporary Examiner of Public Records (Hartford Conn.: Case, Lockwood and Brainard, 1904).

Rider, Fremont, ed. *American Genealogical- Biographical Index. Vols. 1-186*. Middletown, Connecticut: The Godfrey Memorial Library, 1952.

Savage, James. *A Genealogical Dictionary of the First Settlers of New England ...4 vols*. 1860-62. Reprint. Baltimore: Genealogical Publishing Company, 1965.

Spalding, John A. *Illustrated Popular Biography of Connecticut*. 2 vols. Hartford, Conn.: Press of the Case, Lockwood & Brainard Company, 1891.

Sperry, Kip. *Connecticut Sources for Family Historians and Genealogists*. Logan, Utah: Everton Publishers

Stone, Earle L. Historical Records Survey (Connecticut). *Inventory of the Church Archives of Connecticut, Presbyterians*. Salt Lake City: Filmed by the Genealogical Society of Utah, 1972.

The First Laws of the State of Connecticut. (1784), Reprint Wilmington, Delaware: Scholarly Resources, 1982.

The Public Records of the Colony of Connecticut (1636-1776). 15 vols. Hartford: Case, Lockwood & Brainard Co., 1850-90.

The Public Records of the State of Connecticut 1776-1792. 7 vols. Hartford: Lockwood & Brainard, 1894-1948.

Trumbull, Benjamin. *A Complete History of Connecticut, Civil and Ecclesiastical: From the Emigration of its First Planters, from England, in the Year 1630, to the Year 1764; and to the Close of the Indian Wars; with an Appendix Containing the Original Patent of New England*. 2 vols. New London, Conn.: H. D. Utley, 1898.

Ullman, Helen S. *Nutmegger Index: An Index to Non-Alphabetical Articles and a Subject Index to the Connecticut Nutmegger Volume 1-28, 1968-1996*. Rockport ME: Picton Press and Connecticut State Society of Genealogists, 1996.

Atlases, Maps and Gazetteers

Denis, Michael J. *Connecticut Towns and Counties: What was What, Where and When*. Oakland, Me.: Danbury House Books, 1985.

Gannett, Henry. *A Geographic Dictionary of Connecticut and Rhode Island*. Baltimore: Genealogical Publishing Company, 1978.

Hughes, Arthur H. *Connecticut Place Names*. Hartford: Connecticut Historical Society, 1976.

Patera, Alan H. *The Post Offices of Connecticut*. Burtonville, Maryland: The Depot, 1977.

Pease, John C. *A Gazetteer of the States of Connecticut and Rhode Island: Written with Care and Impartiality from Original and Authentic Materials, Consisting of Two Parts ... with an Accurate an Improved Map of Each State*. New Haven, Connecticut: Yale University Microfilming Unit, 1989.

Sellers, Helen Earle. *Connecticut Town Origins: Their Names Boundaries, Early Histories and First Families*. Chester, Connecticut: Pequot Press, 1973.

Town and City Atlas of the State of Connecticut. Boston: D.H. Hurd and Co., 1893.

Census Records

Available Census Records and Census Substitutes

Federal Census 1790, 1800, 1810, 1820, 1830, 1840, 1850, 1860, 1870, 1880, 1900, 1010, 1920, 1930.

State/Territorial Census 1670.

Federal Mortality Schedules 1850, 1860, 1870, 1880.

Connecticut 1670 Census. Oxford, Massachusetts: Holbrook Research Institute, 1977.

Connecticut State Library (Hartford, Connecticut). *Index of Connecticut Census Records from 1790-1850*. Microfilm of original records at the Connecticut State Library in Hartford, Connecticut. Salt Lake City: Filmed by the Genealogical Society of Utah, 1950. 95 microfilm.

Dollarhide, William. *The Census Book: A Genealogist's Guide to Federal Census Facts, Schedules and Indexes*. Bountiful, Utah: Heritage Quest, 1999.

Gannett, Henry. *A Geographic Dictionary of Connecticut and Rhode Island*. Washington: Government Printing Office, 1894. Reprint. Baltimore: Genealogical Publishing Co., 1978

Hughes, Arthur H. and Allen S. Morse. *Connecticut Place Names*. Hartford: Connecticut Historical Society, 1976.

Kemp, Thomas Jay. *The American Census Handbook*. Wilmington, Delaware: Scholarly Resources, Inc., 2001.

Szucs, Loretto Dennis, and Matthew Wright. *Finding Answers in U.S. Census Records*. Ancestry Publishing, 2001.

Thorndale, William, and William Dollarhide. *Map Guide to the U.S. Federal Censuses, 1790-1920*. Baltimore: Genealogical Publishing Co., 1987.

Court Records, Probate and Wills

Connecticut State Library (Hartford, Connecticut). *Guide to Archives in the Connecticut State Library*. 3rd Ed. Hartford, Connecticut: Connecticut State Library, 1981.

Connecticut State Library (Hartford, Connecticut). *Probate Estate Files, 1881-1915*. Microfilm of original records in the Connecticut State Library, Hartford. Salt Lake City: Filmed by the Genealogical Society of Utah, 1990-1994. 576 microfilm.

Connecticut State Library (Hartford, Connecticut). *Probate Files Collection*. Microfilm of original records in the Connecticut State Library. Salt Lake City: Filmed by the Genealogical Society of Utah, 1977-1979. 1622 microfilm.

Connecticut. Inheritance Tax Division. *Estate Record Card Index, 1915-1926*. Microfilm of original records in the Connecticut State Archives, Hartford. Salt Lake City: Filmed by the Genealogical Society of Utah, 1989. 19 microfilm.

Connecticut. Particular Court. *Records of the Particular Court of Connecticut, 1639-1663*. Bowie, Maryland: Heritage Books, 1987.

Ditz, Toby L. *Property and Kinship: Inheritance in Early Connecticut, 1750-1820*. Princeton, N. J.: Princeton University Press, 1986.

General Index to Probate Records: All Districts in Connecticut 1641-1948. Microfilm of originals in Hartford, Connecticut. Salt Lake City: Filmed by the Genealogical Society of Utah, 1957-1958. 67 microfilm.

Manwaring, Charles William, comp. *A Digest of the Early Connecticut Probate Records*. Hartford, Connecticut: R.S. Peck & Co., 1904-06. Hartford District 1635 to 1750 in three volumes. Reprint, Baltimore: Genealogical Publishing Co., 1995.

Manwaring, Charles William. *A Digest of the Early Connecticut Probate Records.* 3 vols. Reprint Baltimore: Genealogical Publishing Co., 1995.

The Public Records of The Colony of Connecticut (1636-1776). 15 vols. (Hartford, Connecticut: Case, Lockwood & Brainard Co., 1850-1890).

Emigration, Immigration, Migration and Naturalization

Filby, P. William Filby, *Passenger and Immigration Lists Index*, 15 vols. Detroit: Gale Research, 1981-United States. Bureau of Customs. *A Supplemental Index to Passenger Lists of Vessels Arriving At Atlantic & Gulf Coast Ports (Excluding New York) 1820-1874.* Washington, D.C.: Filmed by the National Archives Record Services, 1960. Microfilm.

United States. Bureau of Customs. *Copies of Lists of Passengers Arriving At Miscellaneous Ports on the Atlantic and Gulf Coasts and At Ports on the Great Lakes, 1820-1873.* Washington, D.C.: The National Archives, 1964. Microfilm.

United States. Immigration and Naturalization Service. *St. Albans District Manifest Records of Aliens Arriving from Foreign Contiguous Territory: Arrivals At Canadian Border Ports from January 1895 to June 30, 1954: Indexes (Soundex), 1895-1924.* Washington, D.C.: National Archives Records Service, 1986.

Land and Property

Burr, Jean Chandler, comp. and ed. *Lyme Records 1667-1730: A Literal Transcription of the Minutes of the Town Meetings with Marginal Notations, to which hath been Appended Land Grants and Ear Marks.* Stonington Connecticut: Pequot Press, 1968.

Colonial Land Records of Connecticut, 1640-1846. 5 vols. Microfilm of originals at the Connecticut State Library in Hartford, Connecticut. Salt Lake City: Filmed by the Genealogical Society of Utah, 1954. 3 microfilm.

Ditz, Toby L. *Property and Kinship: Inheritance in Early Connecticut, 1750-1820.* Princeton, N. J.: Princeton University Press, 1986.

Hartford (Connecticut*). Town Clerk. Land Records, 1639-1901; General Index, 1639-1865.* Microfilm of originals in the Town Hall, Hartford, Connecticut. Salt Lake City: Filmed by the Genealogical Society of Utah, 1947-1949, 1983, 1986. Microfilm.

Judd, Sylvester. *Land Lotteries and Divorces of Connecticut 1755-1789 with Index.* Microfilm of originals at the Connecticut State Library in Hartford, Connecticut. Salt Lake City: Filmed by the Genealogical Society of Utah, 1954. 2 microfilm.

Susquehanna Company. *Susquehanna Settlers [and] Western Lands.* Microfilm of original records filmed at the Connecticut State Library in Hartford, Connecticut. Salt Lake City: Filmed by the Genealogical Society of Utah, 1954. 2 microfilm.

Winthrop, Robert Charles. *Robert C. Winthrop Collection: Connecticut Manuscripts 1631-1794.* Microfilm of originals at the Connecticut State Library in Hartford, Connecticut. Salt Lake City: Filmed by the Genealogical Society of Utah, 1954.

Military

Bates, Alfred C. ed. *Rolls of the Connecticut Men in the French and Indian War, 1755-1762.* 2 vols. 1903, 1905, reprint 1997, Baltimore: Clearfield Co., 1997.

Buckingham, Thomas. *Roll and Journal of Connecticut Service in Queen Anne's War 1710-1711.* New Haven, Connecticut: Acorn Club of Connecticut, 1916.

Cemetery Inscriptions, Records of Veterans, and Other Miscellaneous Records from the Connecticut State Library. Microfilm. Salt Lake City: Genealogical Society of Utah, 1979.

Collections of the Connecticut Historical Society, vols. 9 and 10. Hartford: Connecticut Historical Society, 1905.

Connecticut Adjunct General, *Record of Service of Connecticut Men in the War of the Revolution, War of 1812, Mexican War.* Hartford, Connecticut: Case, Lockwood & Brainard, 1889.

Connecticut Adjunct General. *Catalogue of Connecticut Volunteer Organizations.* Hartford, Connecticut: adjunct general, 1869.

Connecticut Adjunct General. *Record of Service of Connecticut Men, III, Mexican War.* Hartford, Connecticut: Case, Lockwood, and Brainard, 1889.

Connecticut Adjutant General, *Records of Service of Connecticut Men in the I. War of the Revolution, II. War of 1812, III. Mexican War.* Hartford: Case, Lockwood & Brainard Co., 1889.

Connecticut Historical Society. *Rolls and Lists of Connecticut Men in the Revolution, 1775-1783.* Collections of the Connecticut Historical Society, vols. 8, 12. Hartford, Connecticut: 1901-09. Reprint, Baltimore: Heritage Books, 1996.

Connecticut Historical Society. *Rolls of Connecticut Men in the French and Indian War, 1755-1762.* 2 vols. Hartford CT: the society, 1903-05.

Connecticut Society Daughter of the American Revolution. *Connecticut Revolutionary Pensioners.* (1919) reprint Baltimore: Clearfield Co., 1997.

Connecticut State Library. *Connecticut Archives: Revolutionary War (Selected Papers), Series 1-3, 1763-1820.* Microfilm of originals at the Connecticut State Library in Hartford, Connecticut. Salt Lake City: Filmed by the Genealogical Society of Utah, 1954.

Connecticut. Governor. *Military Census Questionnaires, 1917-1918.* Microfilm of original records in the Connecticut State Archives, Hartford. Salt Lake City: Genealogical Society of Utah, 1988-1989. 454 microfilm.

Croffut, W. A. *The Military and Civil History of Connecticut during the War of 1861-65: Comprising a Detailed Account of the Various Regiments and Batteries, Through March, Encampment, Bivouac and Battle: Also Instances of Distinguished Personal Gallantry, and Biographical Sketches of Many Heroic Soldiers: Together with a Record of the Patriotic Action of Citizens at Home, and of the Liberal Support Furnished by the State in its Executive and Legislative Departments.* New York: Ledyard Bill, 1868.

Judd, Sylvester. *Connecticut Archives: War of 1812 (Selected Papers, 1812-1819.)* Salt Lake City: Filmed by the Genealogical Society of Utah, 1954. 2 microfilm.

Judd, Sylvester. *Connecticut Archives: Selected Papers of Colonial Wars*. Microfilm of originals at the Connecticut State Library in Hartford, Connecticut. Salt Lake City: Filmed by the Genealogical Society of Utah, 1954. 7 microfilm.

Record of Service of Connecticut Men in the Army and Navy of the United States During the War of the Rebellion. Hartford: Case, Lockwood & Brainard Co., 1889.

Rolls of Connecticut Men in the French and Indian War: 1755-1762. 2 vols. Hartford, Connecticut: Connecticut Historical Society, 1903-1905.

Roster of Soldiers, Sailors and Marines of the War of 1812, the Mexican War, and the War of the Rebellion. Lincoln, Neb.: Nebraska State Genealogical Society, 1988.

Shepard, James. *Connecticut Soldiers in the Pequot War of 1637*. Meriden, Connecticut: Journal Publishing Co., 1913

Society of the Colonial Wars. *Register of Pedigrees and Services of Ancestors*. Hartford, Connecticut: the society, 1941

The Public Records of the Colony of Connecticut (1636-1775), 15 vols. Hartford, Connecticut: 1850-90.

U.S. Bureau of Pensions. *Pension Records of the Revolutionary Soldiers from Connecticut*. Washington, D.C.: Government Printing Office, 1919.

United States. Selective Service System. *Connecticut World War I Selective Service System Draft Registration Cards, 1917-1918*. National Archives Microfilm Publications, M1509. Washington, D.C.: National Archives, 1987-1988.

United States. Veterans Administration. *Revolutionary War Pension and Bounty-land-warrant Application Files*. Microfilm of original records in the National Archives, Washington, D.C. Washington, D.C.: The National Archives, 1969.

White, David O. *Connecticut's Black Soldiers, 1775-1783*. Chester, Conn.: Pequot Press, 1973.

Vital and Cemetery Records

Arnold, James N. *Index to James N. Arnold Tombstone Records Collection*. Microfilm of index cards at Knight Memorial Library, Providence, Rhode Island. (Salt Lake City: Filmed by the Genealogical Society of Utah, 1992). 12 microfilm.

Bailey, Frederick. *Early Connecticut Marriages, as Found on Ancient Church Records Prior to 1800*. 1896-1906. Reprinted with integrated errata. 7 books in 1 vol. Baltimore: Genealogical Publishing Co., 1982.

Barbour, Lucius, comp. *Barbour Collection: Connecticut Vital Records Prior to 1850*. Microfilm of original records at the State Library Hartford, Connecticut. Salt Lake City: Filmed by the Genealogical Society of Utah, 1949.

Bible Records from Connecticut, Index Cards. Salt Lake City: Genealogical Society of Utah, 1949. Microfilm.

Bowman Collection: *Connecticut Vital Records in Massachusetts (1790's to Late 1800's)*. Microfilm of card file in the Connecticut State Library, Hartford, Connecticut. Salt Lake City: Filmed by the Genealogical Society of Utah, 1949. Microfilm.

Connecticut State Library (Hartford, Connecticut). *Vital Records, A-Y: An Index to the Connecticut Historical Society Bulletin, Vols. 1-8*. Microfilm of original at the State Library in Hartford, Connecticut. Salt Lake City: Filmed by the Genealogical Society of Utah, 1949. Microfilm.

Daughters of the American Revolution (Connecticut). *Genealogical Collection*. Salt Lake City: Filmed by the Genealogical Society of Utah, 1970-71.

Hale, Charles R. *Hale Collection*. Microfilm of typescript at the Connecticut State Library. Salt Lake City: Genealogical Society of Utah, 1949-50. Microfilm.

Hearn, Daniel. *Connecticut Gravestones, Early to 1800*. Microfilm. Salt Lake City: Genealogical Society of Utah, 1989.

Ledogar, Edwin Richard. *Vital Statistics of Eastern Connecticut, Western Rhode Island, South Central Massachusetts*. 2 vols. Reprint. Arvada, Colorado: Ancestors Publishers, 1995.

Slater, James A. *The Colonial Burying Grounds of Eastern Connecticut and the Men Who Made Them*. Hamden, Connecticut: Published for the Academy by Archon Books, 1987.

Torrey, Clarence Almon. *New England Marriages Prior to 1700*. Andover, Massachusetts: Northeast Document Conservation Center, [1983?].

County Website	Map Index	Date Created	Parent County or Territory From Which Organized Address/Details
Fairfield www.rootsweb.com/~ctfairfi/	O9	10 May 1666	**Original county** Fairfield County; 1061 Main St; Bridgeport, CT 06604; Ph. 203.579.6527 Details: (Twn Clks have b, m, d & land rec from 1700; Pro Judge has pro rec) Towns Organized Before 1800: Brookfield 1788, Danbury 1685, Fairfield 1639, Greenwich 1640, Huntington (Shelton) 1789, New Fairfield 1740, Newtown 1711, Norwalk 1651, Redding 1767, Ridgefield 1708, Stamford 1641, Trumbull 1798, Weston 1787.
Hartford www.rootsweb.com/~cthartfo/	J4	10 May 1666	**Original county** Hartford County; 95 Washington St; Hartford, CT 06103; Ph. 203.566.3170 Details: (Twn & City Clks have b, m, d, bur & land rec; Pro Judge has pro rec) Towns Organized Before 1800: Berlin 1785, Bristol 1785, Canton 1740, East Hartford 1783, East Windsor 1768, Enfield 1683, Farmington 1645, Glastonbury 1693, Granby 1786, Hartford 1635, Hartland 1761, Simsbury 1670, Southington 1779, Suffield 1674, Wethersfield 1634, Windsor 1633.
Litchfield www.geocities.com/TheTropics/1926/ litchfield.html	M4	14 Oct 1751	**Hartford, Fairfield** Litchfield County; PO Box 247; Litchfield, CT 06759; Ph. 203.567.0885 Details: (Clk Sup Ct has div & ct rec from 1800's; Twn Clks have b, m, d & land rec; Pro Judge has pro rec) Towns Organized Before 1800: Barkhamstead 1799, Bethlehem 1787, Canaan 1739, Colebrook 1799, Cornwall 1740, Goshen 1739, Harwinton 1737, Kent 1739, Litchfield 1719, New Hartford 1738, New Milford 1712, Norfolk 1758, Plymouth 1795, Roxbury 1796, Salisbury 1741, Sharon 1739, Torrington 1740, Washington 1779, Warren 1768, Watertown 1780, Winchester 1771, Woodbury 1673.
Middlesex www.rootsweb.com/~ctmiddle/ midlsxco.htm	H7	2 May 1785	**Hartford, New London, New Haven** Middlesex County; 265 DeKoven Dr; Middletown, CT 06457; Ph. 860.344.2966 Details: (Twn Clks have b, m, d & land rec; Clk Sup Ct has div & ct rec from 1800; Pro Judge has pro rec) Towns Organized Before 1800: Chatham 1767, Durham 1704, East Haddam 1734, Haddam 1668, Killingsworth 1667, Middletown 1651, Saybrook 1635.
New Haven www.geocities.com/TheTropics/1926/ newhaven.html	K8	10 May 1666	**Original county** New Haven County; 235 Church St; New Haven, CT 06510; Ph. 203.787.7908 Details: (Twn Clks have b, m, d & land rec; Co Clk has div & ct rec; Pro Ct has pro rec) Towns Organized Before 1800: Branford 1639, Cheshire 1780, East Haven 1785, Guilford 1639, Hamden 1786, Meriden 1796, Millford 1639, New Haven 1638, North Haven 1786, Oxford 1798, Seymour 1672, Southbury 1787, South Derby 1675, Wallingford 1670, Waterbury 1686, Wolcott 796, Woodbridge 1784.
New London www.rootsweb.com/~ctnewlon/index.htm	D7	10 May 1666	**Original county** New London County; 181 State St; New London, CT 06320; Ph. 860.447.5204 Details: (Clk Sup Ct has div rec; Twn Clks have b, m, d & land rec from 1659 & bur rec from 1893; Pro Judge has pro rec) Towns Organized Before 1800: Bozrah 1786, Colchester 1698, Franklin 1786, Groton 1705, Lebanon 1700, Lisbon 1786, Lyme 1665, Montville 1786, New London 1646, Norwich 1659, Preston 1687, Stonington 1649, Voluntown 1721.
Tolland users.rcn.com/lmerrell/tolland.html	G4	13 Oct 1785	**Windham** Tolland County; 69 Brooklyn St; Rockville, CT 06066-3643; Ph. 860.875.6294 Details: (Twn Clks have b, m, d & land rec; Pro Judge has pro rec; Clk Sup Ct has ct rec) Towns Organized Before 1800: Bolton 1730, Coventry 1712, Ellington 1786, Hebron 1708, Mansfield 1702, Somers 1734, Stafford 1719, Tolland 1715, Union 1734, Vernon 1716, Willington 1727.
Windham users.rcn.com/lmerrell/windham.html	D4	12 May 1726	**Hartford, New London** Windham County; 155 Church St; Putnam, CT 06260; Ph. 860.928.2779 Details: (Twn Clks have b, m, d & land rec from 1692 & bur rec from 1900; Pro Judge has pro rec; Clk Sup Ct has div rec) Towns Organized Before 1800: Ashford 1714, Brooklyn 1786, Canterbury 1703, Hampton 1786, Killingly 1708, Plainfield 1699, Pomfret 1713, Sterling 1794, Thompson 1785, Windham 1692, Woodstock (New Roxbury) 1686.

Notes

Peach
Blossom

DELAWARE

CAPITAL: DOVER – FIRST STATE – STATE 1787 (1ST)

Henry Hudson discovered Delaware in 1609 while in the service of the Dutch East India Company searching for the Northwest Passage. From information provided by Hudson and other Dutch navigators, the Dutch West India Company was formed in 1621. In 1629, this company adopted a charter to grant land in the New World. They bought land adjoining the Delaware River and in 1631 David Pietersen de Vries established a camp on Lewes Beach, which failed. In 1638, the New Sweden Company outfitted an expedition to establish the first permanent settlement in Delaware at Wilmington. It was called Fort Christina.

The Dutch seized Fort Christina in 1655, making it part of New Netherland. The following year, the first Finnish colonists came to Delaware. In 1664, the English conquered New Netherland. Many English settlers came shortly afterward, mainly from Virginia, Maryland, New Jersey, New York, and Europe, and mingled with the Dutch and Swedes. In 1682, Delaware was granted to William Penn, but the people in Delaware objected so strongly that they were granted their own assembly in 1703. Meanwhile, Maryland claimed the southern and western parts of Delaware from 1684 to 1763, when Mason and Dixon established the western boundary of Delaware as well as the boundary between Pennsylvania and Maryland.

Delaware was a colony of great religious diversity. The Swedes brought their religion, as did the Dutch. Irish settlers brought the Presbyterian faith after 1698. Roman Catholics, as early as 1730, settled in the northern part of Delaware. French Catholics came from the West Indies in 1790.

Many of the settlers of the northern part of Delaware moved on to Pennsylvania, Maryland, and New Jersey. Delaware was on the front line of the Revolutionary War for nearly a year. This necessitated changing the capital from New Castle to Dover. Delaware became the first state to ratify the Constitution on 7 December 1787. Although Delaware was a slave state during the Civil War, it overwhelmingly supported the Union. Over 16,000 men served the Union, while only several hundred served the Confederacy.

Due to slow transportation in its early days, Delaware's counties were divided into districts, called hundreds. These correspond to townships. Emigrants came primarily from Italy, Poland, Russia, Ireland, Germany, and England.

Look for vital records in the following locations:
- **Birth and death records:** Statewide registration of births began in 1861, stopped in 1863, and resumed in 1881. The Delaware Office of Vital Statistics in Dover, Delaware has birth and death records from 1861. Since all records are filed by year, it is necessary to have the year before a search can be initiated.
- **Marriage records:** State registrations of marriages began in 1847 and are also available from the Bureau of Vital Statistics. Counties began keeping marriage records as early as 1832.
- **Land records:** County recorders have deeds, mortgages, and leases from the late 1600's to the present.
- **Wills and probate records:** The Registrar of Wills has kept probate records from 1682 to the present. Some probate records are at the Bureau of Archives and Records Management, Hall of Records. The Bureau also has documents from the Swedish colonial period, the Dutch settlement, the Duke of York regime, and the Penn proprietorship. Most of its records date from statehood, including probate records; state, county, and municipal records; business records; and many others. Some early colonial records are in the archives of the states of New York and Pennsylvania.

Delaware Office of Vital Statistics Box 637 Dover, Delaware 19903 302.739.4721	**Bureau of Archives and Records Mgmt** Hall of Records Dover, Delaware 19902

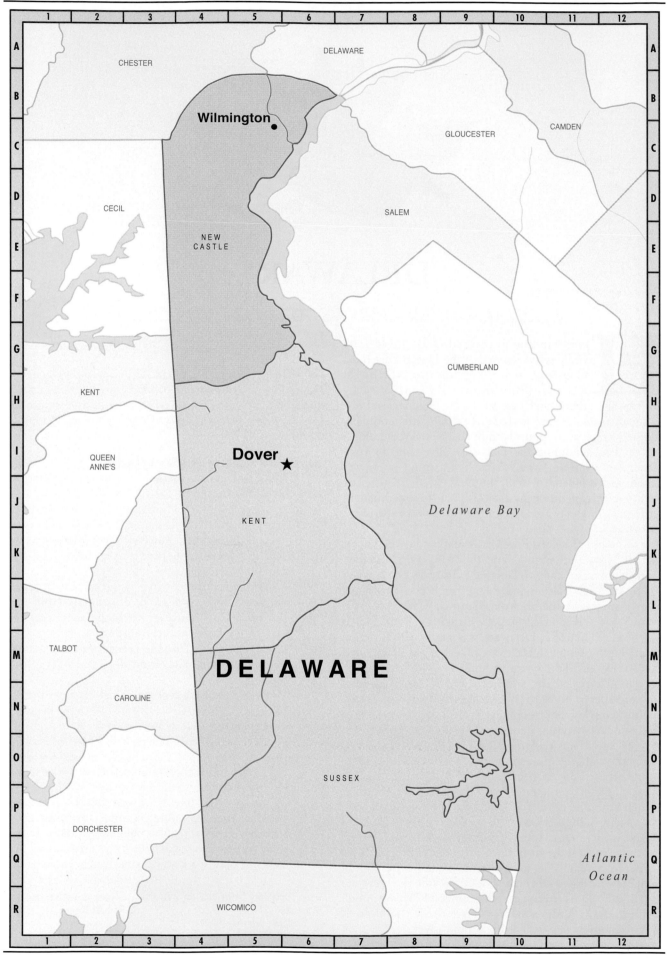

Societies and Repositories

American Baptist-Samuel Colgate Historical Library; 1106 South Goodman Street; Rochester, New York 14620; 716.473.1740

Delaware Bureau of Vital Statistics; Jesse S. Cooper Memorial Building; William Penn Street; Dover, Delaware 19901

Delaware Genealogical Society; 505 Market Street Mall; Wilmington, Delaware 19801;

Delaware Genealogical Society; 505 Market Street Mall; Wilmington, Delaware 19801-3091

Delaware Legislative Council; Legislative Hall; PO Box 1401; Dover, Delaware 19901

Delaware Public Archives; 121 Duke of York Street; Dover, Delaware 19901; <www.state.de.us/sos/dpa/>

Delaware Public Archives; Hall of Records; Dover, Delaware 19901; 302.739.5318; Fax 302.739.2578

Diocese of Wilmington Archives; PO Box 2247; Greenville, Delaware 19807; 302.655.0597 (Tuesdays 10:00 a.m. to 3:00 p.m.) (Roman Catholic Records)

Division of Historical and Cultural Affairs; Dept. of State Hall of Records; Dover, Delaware 19901

Family History Library; 35 North West Temple Street; Salt Lake City, Utah 84150; 800.346.6044 or 801.240.2584; <www.familysearch.org>; Find a Family History Center near you; <www.familysearch.org/Eng/Library/FHC/frameset_fhc.asp>

Fort Delaware Society; PO Box 553; Delaware City, Delaware 19706; 302.836.7256; <www.del.net/org/fort/>

Genealogical Society of Pennsylvania; 1305 Locust Street; Philadelphia, Pennsylvania 19107; 215.545.0391; Fax 215.545.0936

Hagley Museum and Library; PO Box 3630; Wilmington, Delaware 19807-0630; 302.658.2400; Fax 302.658.0568

Historical Society of Delaware; 505 Market Street Mall; Wilmington, Delaware 19801-3091; 302.655.7161; Fax 302.655.7844

Historical Society of Delaware; 505 Market Street; Wilmington, Delaware 19801;

Historical Society of Pennsylvania; 1300 Locust Street; Philadelphia, Pennsylvania 19107-5699; 215.732.6201; Fax 215.732.2680

Jewish Federation of Delaware; 100 W. 10thStreet, Suite 301; Wilmington, Delaware 19801-1628

Jewish Historical Society of Delaware; 505 Market Street Mall; Wilmington, Delaware 19801; <hsd.org/jhsd.htm>

Major Robert Kirkwood Chapter, DESSAR; Delaware; <www.sar.org/dessar/kirkwood.htm>

National Archives—Mid-Atlantic Region; 900 Market Street; Philadelphia, Pennsylvania 19107; 215.597.3000; Fax 215.597.2303

Presbyterian Church (U.S.A.), Dept. of History Library; 425 Lombard Street; Philadelphia, Pennsylvania 19147-1516; 215.627.1852; Fax 215.627.0509

Public Archives Commission; Hall of Records; Dover, Delaware 19901

Society of Friends (Quaker); Friends Historical Library; Swarthmore College; 500 College Avenue; Swarthmore, Pennsylvania 19081-1399; 610.328.8496

United Methodist Archives Center; Drew University; Madison, New Jersey 07940-4007; 201.408.3125

University Library; University of Delaware; Newark, Delaware 19711

University of Delaware Library; Newark, Delaware 19717-5267; 302.831.2231

Wilmington Institute Free Library; 10th and Market Streets; Wilmington, Delaware 19801

Bibliography and Record Sources

General Sources

Arellano, Fay Louise Smith. *Delaware Trails: Some Tribal Records 1842-1907*. Reprint, Baltimore: Clearfield Co., 1997.

Bendler, Bruce A. *Colonial Delaware Assemblymen, 1682-1775*. Westminster, Maryland: Family Line Publications, 1989.

Bendler, Bruce. *Colonial Delaware Records 1681-1713*. Westminster, Maryland: Family Line Publications, 1992.

Biographical and Genealogical History of the State of Delaware: Containing Biographical and Genealogical Sketches of Prominent and Representative Citizens, and Many of the Early Settlers. Tucson, Arizona: Filmed by W. C. Cox, 1974.

Burr, Horace. *The Records of Holy Trinity (Old Swedes) Church, Wilmington, Delaware, for 1697-1773*. Wilmington, Delaware: Historical Society of Delaware, 1890.

Clark, Allen B. *This Is Good Country: A History of the Amish of Delaware, 1915-1988*. Gordonville, Pennsylvania: Gordonville Print Shop, 1989.

Clark, Patricia L., and Dorothy Huntsman, ed. *American Genealogical Biographical Key Title Index*. Salt Lake City: Genealogical Society of Utah. 1990.

Clark, Raymond B. *Delaware Church Records: A Collection of Baptisms, Marriages, Deaths and Other Records and Tombstone Inscriptions, From 1686-1880; Five Important Religious Groups: Baptist, Episcopal, Methodist, Presbyterian and Quaker with Historical Sketches of the Churches or Groups ....* St. Michaels, Maryland: R. B. Clark, 1986.

Coghlan, Gladys M. *Index to History of Delaware, 1609-1888*. Wilmington, Delaware: Historical Society of Delaware, 1976.

Daughters of the American Revolution (DAR), Delaware. *Old Bible Records*. 13 vols. Newark, Delaware: n.p., 1944-73.

Delaware Genealogical Research Guide. Delaware Genealogical Society, 1989.

Delaware Public Archives Commission. *Delaware Archives*. 3 vols. Wilmington, Delaware: James and Walls, Printers, 1875.

Directory of Churches and Religious Organizations in Delaware. Dover, Delaware: Historical Records Survey, 1942.

Doherty, Thomas P., ed. *Delaware Genealogical Research Guide*. Delaware Genealogical Society, 1997.

Eckert, Jack. *Guide to the Records of Philadelphia Yearly Meeting*. Philadelphia, Pa.: Haverford College, Records Committee of Philadelphia Yearly Meeting, Swarthmore College, 1989.

Ferris, Benjamin. *A History of the Original Settlements on the Delaware...& A History of Wilmington.* Wilmington, Delaware: Wilson & Heald, 1846.

Frech, Mary L. *Chronology and Documentary Handbook of the State of Delaware.* Dobbs Ferry, New York: Oceana Publications, 1973.

Giles, Barbara S. comp. *Selected Delaware Bibliography and Resources.* Seattle: B.S. Giles, 1990.

Hart, Matilda Spicer. *The Delaware Historical and Genealogical Recall.* 1936. Reprint, Wilmington Delaware: Delaware Genealogical Society, 1984.

Hartford Times Scrapbooks Index. Microreproduction of original ms. and typescript at the Public Library, Grand Rapids, Michigan. Salt Lake City: Filmed by the Genealogical Society of Utah, 1974. 8 microfilm.

Historical Records Survey (Delaware). *Inventory of the County Archives of Delaware. No. 1. New Castle County.* Dover, Delaware: The Public Archives Commission, 1941.

Holley, Barbara Ann, ed. *Directory of Libraries and Information Sources in the Philadelphia Area (Eastern Pennsylvania, Southern New Jersey, and Delaware).* Philadelphia: Special Libraries Association, Philadelphia Chapter, 1977.

Hugh M. Morris Library, Reference Dept. *Bibliography of Delaware, 1960-1974.* Newark: University of Delaware, 1976.

Johnson, Amandus. *The Swedish Settlements on the Delaware, 1638-1664.* 2 vols. 1911. Reprint, Baltimore: Genealogical Publishing Co., 1969.

Mattern, Joanne, and Harold B. Hancock, comps. *A Preliminary Inventory of the Older Records in the Delaware Archives.* Dover, Delaware: Delaware Public Archives, 1978.

Mattsson, Algot. *New Sweden the Dream of an Empire.* Goteborg: Tre Bocker, 1987.

Nelson, Ralph D. *Delaware 1782 Tax Assessment and Census.* Wilmington, Delaware: Delaware Genealogical Society, 1994.

Public Archives Commission. *Delaware Archives.* 5 vols. Wilmington, Delaware: the commission, 1911—.

Redden, Robert, ed. *Delaware Genealogical Society Surname Index.* Wilmington, Delaware: Delaware Genealogical Society, 1995.

Reed, Henry Clay, and Marion Bjhomason Reed, comps. *A Bibliography of Delaware through 1960.* Newark: University of Delaware Press for the Institute of Delaware History and Culture, 1966.

Reed, Henry Clay, and Marion Bjhomason Reed, comps. *Delaware, A History of the First State.* 3 vols. New York: Lewis Historical Publishing Company, 1947.

Rider, Fremont, ed. *American Genealogical- Biographical Index.* Vols. 1-186+. Middletown, Connecticut: Godfrey Memorial Library, 1952-.

Riggs, John Beverley. *A Guide to Manuscripts in the Eleutherian Mills Historical Library* . . . Greenville, Delaware: Eleutherian Mills Historical Library, 1970.

Rising, Johan Claesson. *The Rise and Fall of New Sweden: Governor Johan Rising's Journal 1654-1655.* Stockholm: Almqvist & Wiksell International, 1988. Uddevalla: Bohus Laningens boktr.

Scharf, John Thomas. *History of Delaware, 1609-1888.* 2 vols. Tucson, Arizona: W. C. Cox, 1974.

Scott, Kenneth, and Janet Clarke. *Abstracts from the Pennsylvania Gazette, 1748-1755.* Baltimore: Genealogical Publishing, 1977.

Special Libraries Association. Philadelphia Chapter. *Directory of Libraries and Information Sources in the Philadelphia Area (Eastern Pennsylvania, Southern New Jersey and Delaware).* Philadelphia: [s.n.], 1977.

Todd, Robert W. *Methodism of the Peninsula, or, Sketches of Notable Characters and Events in the History of Methodism in the Maryland and Delaware Peninsula.* Philadelphia: Methodist Episcopal Book Rooms, 1886.

Turner, Joseph Brown. *Genealogical Collection of Delaware Families.* Salt Lake City: Genealogical Society of Utah, 1948.

United States. Bureau of Internal Revenue. *Internal Revenue Assessment Lists for Delaware, 1862-1866.* Washington, D.C.: National Archives, 1988.

Virdin, Donald Odell. *Delaware Family Histories and Genealogies.* St. Michaels, Maryland: Raymond B. Clark, 1984.

Weis, Fredrick Lewis. *The Colonial Clergy of Maryland, Delaware, and Georgia.* Baltimore: Genealogical Publishing, 1978.

Williams, E. Melvin. *History of Delaware, Past and Present.* 4 vols. New York: Lewis Historical Pub., 1929.

Wright, F. Edward. *Colonial Families of Delaware.* Westminster, Md.: Willow Bend and Family Line Publications, 1998, 1999, 2000.

Atlases, Maps and Gazetteers

Beers, Daniel G. *Atlas of the State of Delaware...* Philadelphia: Pomeroy and Beers, 1868.

Bounds, Harvey C. *A Postal History of Delaware.* Newark, Delaware: Press of Kells, 1938.

Heck, L. W. *Delaware Place Names.* Washington, D.C.: U.S. Government Printing Office, 1966.

Gannett, Henry. *A Gazetteer of Maryland and Delaware.* Baltimore: Genealogical Publishing Co., 1976.

Long, John H., ed. *Delaware, Maryland, District of Columbia Atlas of Historical County Boundaries.* New York: Charles Scribner's Sons, Simon & Schuster Macmillan, 1996.

Maryland-Delaware Atlas & Gazetteer. Freeport, Maine: DeLorme Mapping, 1993.

Scott, Joseph. *A Geographical Description of the States of Maryland and Delaware: Also of the Counties, Towns, Rivers, Bays and Islands with a List of the Hundreds in Each County.* Kimber, Conrad, 1807.

Smith, Chester M. *The Postal History of Maryland, the Delmarva Peninsula and the District of Columbia: The Post Offices and First Postmasters from 1775 to 1984.* Burtonsville, Maryland: The Depot, 1984.

United States. Geological Survey. *Delaware Geographic Names: Alphabetical Finding List.* Reston, Virginia: U.S.G.S. Topographic Division, [1981].

U.S. Geological Survey. *National Gazetteer of the United States: Delaware 1983.* Washington, D.C.: Government Printing Office, 1984.

Census Records

Available Census Records and Census Substitutes

Federal Census 1800, 1810, 1820, 1830, 1840, 1850, 1860, 1870, 1880, 1900, 1910, 1920, 1930.

Federal Mortality Schedules 1870, 1880.

Reconstructed State Census 1782.

Residents 1693.

Militia Rolls 1803-1807.

Tax Lists 1681-1713.

Quit Rents 1702-1713.

Rent Rolls 1681-1688.

Adams Apple Press. *The First Tax List for the Province of Pennsylvania and the Three Lower Counties, 1693.* Bedminster, Pennsylvania: The Press, 1994.

Craig, Peter Stebbins. *The 1693 Census of the Swedes on the Delaware.* Winter Park, FL: SAG Publications, 1993.

DeValinger, Leon, Jr. *Reconstructed Census of Delaware.* Arlington VA: National Genealogical Society, n.d.

Dollarhide, William. *The Census Book: A Genealogist's Guide to Federal Census Facts, Schedules and Indexes.* Bountiful, Utah: Heritage Quest, 1999.

Hancock, Harold B. *The Reconstructed Delaware Census of 1782.* Wilmington, Delaware: Delaware Genealogical Society, 1973.

Jackson, Ronald Vern, and Gary Ronald Teeples. *Early Delaware Census Records, 1665-1697.* Bountiful, Utah: Accelerated Indexing Systems, 1977.

Lainhart, Ann S. *State Census Records.* Baltimore: Genealogical Publishing Co., Inc., 1992.

Kemp, Thomas Jay. *The American Census Handbook.* Wilmington, Delaware: Scholarly Resources, Inc., 2001.

Szucs, Loretto Dennis, and Matthew Wright. *Finding Answers in U.S. Census Records.* Ancestry Publishing, 2001

Thorndale, William, and William Dollarhide. *Map Guide to the U.S. Federal Censuses, 1790-1920.* Baltimore: Genealogical Publishing Co., 1987.

Court Records, Probate and Wills

Many records for the Courts of Delaware are found in the collections of the Delaware Public Archives, Dover, Delaware. The collection includes: dockets, calendars, petitions, sessions, orphan court minutes, appearance dockets, case files, court records, chancery records, miscellaneous records, etc. The collection inventory is online at <www.state.de.us/sos/dpa/collections/guideintro.htm>.

DeValinger, Leon, Jr. *Calendar of Kent County, Delaware, Probate Records, 1680-1850.* Dover Delaware: Public Archives Commission, 1944.

DeValinger, Leon, Jr., *Calendar of Sussex County Delaware, Probate Records, 1680-1850.* Dover DE: Public Archives Commission, 1964.

Documents Relating to the Colonial History of the State of New York. Albany, New York: The Argus Co., 1877.

Gehring, Charles T. *Delaware Papers.* 2 vols. Baltimore, Maryland: Genealogical Publishing Co., 1977-1981.

Historical Research Committee. Delaware Society of the Colonial Dames of America. *A Calendar of Wills, New Castle County, 1682-1800.* New York: 1911. Reprint. Baltimore: Genealogical Publishing Co., 1969.

Smith, Carl T. *Philadelphia Administrations, 1683-1744 [abstracts].* Microfilm of original 2 vol. work at the Historical Society of Pennsylvania. Salt Lake City: Filmed by the Genealogical Society of Utah, 1964.

The First Laws of the State of Delaware 4 vols. (1797) Reprint Wilmington Delaware: Scholarly Resources.

Virdin, Donald O. *Colonial Delaware Wills and Estates to 1880; An Index.* Bowie, Maryland: Heritage Books, 1994.

Emigration, Immigration, Migration and Naturalization

Boyer, Carl. *Ship Passenger Lists: Pennsylvania and Delaware (1641-1825).* Newhall California: the compiler, 1980.

Coldham, Peter Wilson. *The Complete Book of Emigrants, 1607-1776 and Emigrants in Bondage, 1614-1775.* Novato, Calif.: Brøderbund Software, 1996.

Delaware. Superior Court. *Naturalization Papers, Transcripts and Originals, A-Z.* Microfilm of the original records from the Hall of Records in Dover, Delaware. Salt Lake City: Genealogical Society of Utah, 1949.

Filby, P. William. *Philadelphia Naturalization Records.* Detroit: Gale Research, 1982.

United States. Bureau of Customs. *Copies of Lists of Passengers Arriving at Miscellaneous Ports on the Atlantic and Gulf Coasts* National Archives Microfilm Publication.

United States. Bureau of Customs. *A Supplemental Index to Passenger Lists of Vessels Arriving At Atlantic & Gulf Coast Ports (Excluding New York) 1820-1874.* Washington, DC: Filmed by the National Archives Record Services, 1960.

United States. District Court (Delaware). *Naturalization Records, 1795-1932.* Microfilm of original records at the National Archives Branch, Philadelphia Branch. Salt Lake City: Genealogical Society of Utah, 1990. Microfilm, 27 rolls.

Land and Property

Bendler, Bruce A. *Colonial Delaware Records 1681-1713.* Westminster, Md.: Family Line Publications, 1990.

Delaware Fugitive Records: An Inventory of the Official Land Grant Records Relating to the Present State of Delaware. Dover: Department of State, Division of Historical and Cultural Affairs, 1980.

Hone, Wade E. *Land and Property Research in the United States.* Salt Lake City: Ancestry Incorporated, 1997.

Kent County (Delaware). Recorder of Deeds. *Deed Record of Kent County, Delaware, 1680-1850; General Index, 1680-1873.* Salt Lake City: Filmed by the Genealogical Society of Utah, 1948.

Myers, Albert Cook, ed. *Walter Wharton's Land Survey Register, 1675-1679.* Wilmington, Delaware: The Historical Society of Delaware, 1955.

Notes

Orange Blossom

FLORIDA

CAPITAL: TALLAHASSEE – TERRITORY 1822 – STATE 1845 (27TH)

Ponce de Leon the Spanish explorer landed on the Florida coast in 1513. He was searching for gold and the legendary fountain of youth. Early settlements by both the Spanish and French failed, but subsequent attempts succeeded. The French settled Fort Caroline in 1564 and the Spanish settled St. Augustine in 1565. The Spanish subsequently destroyed the French settlement, making St. Augustine the first permanent non-native settlement in North America. Pensacola was settled in 1698.

Meanwhile, the British, Scotch, and Irish were settling the colonies and slowly encroaching on Florida territory. In 1762, during the Seven Years' War, the British captured Havana and Cuba. By the Treaty of Paris in 1763, Spain agreed to trade Florida for Havana.

By proclamation in 1763, the King of England established East and West Florida, divided by the Chattahoochee and Apalachicola Rivers. The largest settlement during the next twenty years was at New Smyrna in 1767. Up to 1,500 colonists from Italy, Greece, and the island of Minorca settled here. In 1783, Great Britain returned Florida to Spain in exchange for some islands in the West Indies.

In 1810 and 1812, the United States annexed portions of West Florida to Louisiana and the Mississippi Territory. Unable to govern the area, Spain ceded the remainder of West Florida and all of East Florida to the United States in 1819. Only about 5,000 non-native settlers lived in Florida at the time. In 1822, Florida was organized into a territory and in 1824 Tallahassee was laid out as the capital. Early settlers were predominantly Irish. Other early settlers included the Greeks from Southern Greece and the Dodecanese Islands, who worked as sponge divers and were affiliated with the Orthodox Greek Catholic Church. Former Virginians and Carolinians settled the middle section of Florida in the 1820's.

The Seminole Wars (1835-1842) brought about by poor treatment of the Indians, resulted in removal of the Indians to present-day Oklahoma. Growth really began in the 1840's as the population grew 56 percent. Most of the growth in East Florida during this time was from Georgia, Alabama, North Carolina and South Carolina. Florida became a state on 3 March 1845.

By 1860, the population had grown to 78,000. Half of the people were native-born while 22 percent came from Georgia, 11 percent from South Carolina and 5 percent from North Carolina. Florida seceded from the Union in 1861. Over 1,000 men fought for the Union and an estimated 20,000 fought for the Confederacy. Florida was readmitted into the Union 1868. A post-Civil War boom lasted to the turn of the century due to the building of railroads and resorts. Another boom occurred from 1921 to 1925 resulting in the formation of Florida's last 13 counties.

Look for vital records in the following locations:
- **Birth and death records:** Statewide registration of births and deaths began in 1899, with general compliance by 1920. The Office of Vital Statistics in Jacksonville holds incomplete records of deaths from 1877 to 1917 and complete records since then. Some birth and death records are in city or county health departments. Jacksonville has birth and death records from 1893 to 1913, Pensacola from 1897 to 1916, and St. Petersburg prior to 1917.
- **Marriage and divorce records, wills:** The Office of Vital Statistics in Jacksonville has records of marriages from June 1927 to date as well as divorce records. Marriage records prior to June 1927 are in the office of the County Judge, generally in the county of the bride's residence. County judges also have the records of wills. Divorce records prior to 1927 are filed in the Circuit Court Clerk's office where the divorce was granted.

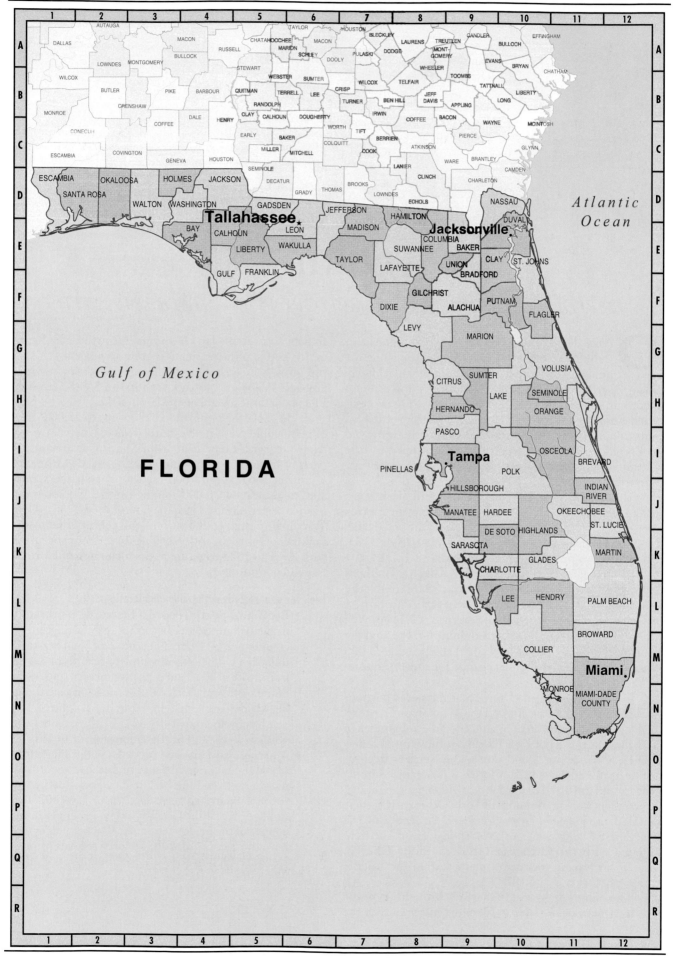

The Office of Vital Statistics
PO Box 210
Jacksonville, Florida 32231
904.359.6900

Florida State Archives,
Florida Division of Archives
History and Records Management
R.A. Gray Building
Pensacola and Bronough Streets
Tallahassee, Florida 32201

Societies and Repositories

Adjutant General, Department of Military Affairs, Attn.: M.I.L.P.; PO Box 1008; St. Augustine, Florida 32085-1008; 904.823.0315; Fax 904.823.0309

Afro-American Historical and Genealogical Society, Central Florida Chapter; PO Box 1347; Orlando, Florida 32802-1347; <www.rootsweb.com/~flcfaahg/member.html>

Alachua County Genealogical Society; PO Box 12078; Gainesville, Florida 32604; <www.afn.org/~acgs/>

Amelia Island Genealogical Society; PO Box 6005; Fernandina Beach, Florida 32035-6005; 904.261.2139; <www.net.magic.net/biz.directory/genelogy.htm>

Apalachicola Historical Society, Inc; PO Box 75; Apalachicola, Florida 32329; <mailer.fsu.edu/~rthompso/fchs_adr.html>

Archer Historical Society; PO Box 1850; Archer, Florida 32618; 352.495.1044; <www.afn.org/~archer/index.html>

Baker County Historical Society; PO Box 856; MacClenny, Florida 32063; <rootsweb.com/~flbaker/books.html>

Bay County Genealogical Society; PO Box 662; Panama City, Florida 32402-0662; <www.rootsweb.com/~flbay/genealogical.htm>

Bay County Public Library (Hdq. of Northwest Regional Library System); 25 W. Government St.; Caller Box 2625; Panama City, Florida 32402

Big Lake Family History Society; PO Box 592; Okeechobee, Florida 34973-0592

Bonita Springs Genealogy Club; PO Box 366471; Bonita Springs, Florida 34136

Bonita Springs Public Library; 26876 Pine Ave.; Bonita Springs, Florida 33923

Bowling Green Historical Council; PO Box 478; Bowling Green, Florida 33834

Boynton Beach Historical Society; Boynton Beach, Florida; <www.gopbi.com/community/groups/BBHS/index.html>

Brevard Chapter, SAR; 467 Bridgetown Ct.; Satellite Beach, Florida 32937-3813; 321.773.8369

Brevard Community College Library; 1519 Clearlake Rd.; Cocoa, Florida 32922; 321.639.2960

Brevard Genealogical Society, Inc.; PO Box 1123; Cocoa, Florida 32923-1123; 321.635.8758; <www.rootsweb.com/~flbgs/>

Broward County Genealogical Society, Inc.; PO Box 485; Ft. Lauderdale, Florida 33302; <www.rootsweb.com/~flgsbc/index.html>

Broward County Historical Commission; 151 S.W. 2nd Street; Fort Lauderdale, Florida 33301; <www.co.broward.fl.us/history.htm>

Burdick International Ancestry Library; 2317 Riverbluff Pkwy. #249; Sarasota, Florida 34231-5032

Cape Canaveral Chapter (TROACC); PO Box 254186; PAFB, Florida 32925-4186; 321.768.2194; <www.brevardelderlaw.com/troaccfam.htm>

Cape Coral Public Library; 921 SW 39th Terrace; Cape Coral, Florida 33914

Central Florida Chapter, SAR; PO Box 1015; Longwood, Florida 32750-1015; 407.767.5101

Central Florida Genealogical Society, Inc.; PO. Box 536309; Orlando, Florida 32853.6309; <www.geocities.com/Heartland/Ranch/4580/>

Central Florida, Afro-American Historical and Genealogical Society; PO Box 5742; Deltona, Florida 32728

Charlotte Chapter, SAR; 4220 Pinecress Drive; Punta Gorda, Florida 33982-1829; 941.639.7264

Charlotte County Genealogical Society; PO Box 2682; Port Charlotte, Florida 33949.2682

Citrus County Genealogical Society; PO Box 2211; Inverness, Florida 4451-2211

Citrus Springs Genealogical Society; 1826 W. Country Club Blvd; Citrus Springs, Florida 34434

Clay County Genealogical Society; PO Box 1071; Green Cove Springs, Florida 32043

Clearwater Chapter, SAR; 16135 4th St.E.; Redington Beach, Florida 33708; 727.319.6385

Cocoa Public Library; 430 Delannoy Ave.; Cocoa, Florida 32922

Collier Co. Public Library; 650 Central Ave.; Naples, Florida 34102; 941.261.8208; <www.collier-lib.org>

Cooper Memorial Library; 620 Montrose St.; Clermont, Florida 34711

Daytona,Ormond Chapter, SAR; 20 Lazy Eight Drive; Daytona Beach, Florida 32124-6776; 386.788.0074

Deland Chapter, SAR; PO Box 466; Deland, Florida 32721; 904.738.7462

DeLand Public Library; 130 East Howry Ave.; DeLand, Florida 32724

Descendants of the Knights of the Bath; PO Box 7062 GH; Gainesville, Florida 32605-7062

DeSoto Correctional Institution Library; PO Box 1072; Arcadia, Florida 33821

DeSoto County Historical Society; PO Box 1824; Arcadia, Florida 34265

Dixie County Historical Society; PO Box 928; Cross City, Florida 32628

East Hillsborough Historical Society; Quintilla Geer Bruton Archives Center; 605 N. Collins St.; Plant City, Florida 33566

Elmer's Genealogy Library; 200 East Rutledge St.; Madison, Florida 32340-2440; 850.973.3282; fax: 850.929.2970; <www.elmerslibrary.com>

Emerald Coast Chapter, SAR; 31 Emory Street; Mary Esther, Florida 32569-2009; 850.243.2879

Englewood Genealogical Society; PO Box 795; Englewood, Florida 34295

St. Augustine Historical Society (Florida). *Biographical Card Index*. Salt Lake City: Filmed by the Genealogical Society of Utah, 1974. Microfilm, 18 rolls.

Taylor, Anne Wood, and Mary lee Barnes Harrell. *Florida Connections Through Bible Records, Volume I*. Tampa, Florida: Florida State Genealogical Society, 1993.

Taylor, Anne Wood. *Florida Pioneers and Their Descendants*, Vol I. Florida State Gen. Soc., 1992.

Thomas, David Hurst. *Missions of Spanish Florida*. New York: Garland, 1991.

Thrift, Charles Tinsley (Jr). *The Trail of the Florida Circuit Rider: An Introduction to the Rise of Methodism in Middle and East Florida*. Lakeland, Florida: The Florida Southern College Press, 1944.

United States. Department of State. *Territorial Papers of Florida, 1777-1824*. Washington, D.C.:National Archives and Records Administration, 1946. 11 microfilm.

Wolfe, William A., and Janet Bingham Wolfe. *Names and Abstracts from the Acts of the Legislative Council of the Territory of Florida*. Tampa, Florida: Florida State Genealogical Society, 1991.

Atlases, Maps and Gazetteers

Bradbury, Alford G. *A Chronology of Florida Post Offices*. Sewall's Point, Fla.: Florida Classics Library, 1993.

Cline, Howard F. *Provisional Historical Gazeteer [sic] with Locational Notes on Florida Colonial Communities*. New York: Garland Pub., 1974.

Florida Atlas and Gazetteer. Freeport, Me.: DeLorme Mapping, c1987.

Florida Gazetteer and Business Directory. Jacksonville, Florida: R.L. Polk & Co., 1908.

Long, John H., ed. *Atlas of Historical County Boundaries: Florida*. New York: Simon& Schuster, 1996.

Morris, Allen Covington. *Florida Place Names*. Coral Gables, Florida: University of Miami Press, 1974.

Puetz, C.J., comp. *Florida County Maps*. Lyndon Station, Wisconsin: Thomas Publishing Co., 1988.

Census Records

Available Census Records and Census Substitutes

Federal Census 1830, 1840, 1850, 1860, 1870, 1880, 1900, 1910, 1920, 1930.

Colonial/State/Territorial Census 1783, 1786, 1790, 1793, 1814, 1825, 1837, 1845, 1855, 1865, 1868, 1875, 1885, 1895, 1935.

Federal Mortality Schedules 1850, 1860, 1880.

Dollarhide, William. *The Census Book: A Genealogist's Guide to Federal Census Facts, Schedules and Indexes*. Bountiful, UT: Heritage Quest, 1999.

Florida. Department of Education. *Census of School Age Youth (6-21 years of age), 1896-1924*. Microfilm of records located at state archives, Tallahassee, Florida. Salt Lake City: Filmed by the Genealogical Society of Utah, 1990. 2 microfilm.

Florida. Division of Elections. *Florida Territorial and State Election Records, 1826-1865*. Microfilm of records located at state archives, Tallahassee, Florida. Salt Lake City: Filmed by the Genealogical Society of Utah, 1990. 9 microfilm.

Florida. Secretary of State. *Voter Registration Rolls, 1867-1905*. Microfilm of records at Bureau of Archives and Records Management, Tallahassee, Florida. Salt Lake City: Filmed by the Genealogical Society of Utah, 1990. 2 microfilm.

Florida. Tax Commission. *Tax Rolls of Florida Counties, Some are Incomplete, 1839-1891*. Salt Lake City: Filmed by the Genealogical Society of Utah, 1956. 66 microfilm.

Kemp, Thomas Jay. *The American Census Handbook*. Wilmington, DE: Scholarly Resources, Inc., 2001.

Lainhart, Ann S. *State Census Records*. Baltimore: Genealogical Publishing Co., Inc., 1992.

Michaels, Brian E. *Voters in the First Statewide Election, May 26, 1845*. Tampa, Florida: Florida Genealogical Society, 1987.

Mills, Donna Rachael. *Florida's First Families: Translated Abstracts of Pre-1821 Spanish Censuses*. Tuscaloosa, Fla.: Mills Historical Press, 1992.

Szucs, Loretto Dennis, and Matthew Wright. *Finding Answers in U.S. Census Records*. Ancestry Publishing, 2001

Tallahassee Genealogical Society, Inc. *Florida Voter Registration Lists 1867-68*. Tallahassee Genealogical Society, 1992.

Thorndale, William, and William Dollarhide. *Map Guide to the U.S. Federal Censuses, 1790-1920*. Baltimore: Genealogical Publishing Co., 1987.

Court Records, Probate and Wills

County clerk is the custodian of the court, probate and will records. Refer to each county for those records.

Historical Records Survey (Florida). *Inventory of Federal Archives in the States, Series 02, Federal Courts; no. 09, Florida*. Jacksonville, Fla.: Historical Records Survey, 1940.

United States. District Court (Florida: Southern District). *Admiralty Final Records of the U.S. District Court for the Southern District of Florida*. Microfilm of original records in the Regional Archives Branch of the Federal Archives and Records center, Atlanta, Georgia. Washington: National Archives and Records Service, 1984. 13 microfilm.

Emigration, Immigration, Migration and Naturalization

García, María Cristina. *Havana, USA; Cuban Exiles and Cuban Americans in South Florida, 1959-1994*. Berkeley, Calif.: University of California Press, 1996.

United States. Bureau of Customs. *A Supplemental Index to Passenger Lists of Vessels Arriving At Atlantic & Gulf Coast Ports (Excluding New York) 1820-1874*. Washington, D.C.: Filmed by the National Archives Record Services, 1960.

United States. Bureau of Customs. *Copies of Lists of Passengers Arriving At Miscellaneous Ports on the Atlantic and Gulf Coasts and At Ports on the Great Lakes, 1820-1873*. Washington, D.C.: The National Archives, 1964.

United States. District Court (Alabama: Southern District). *Declarations of Intentions, Naturalizations, and Petitions, 1855-1960*. Microfilm of originals at the National Archives in East Point, Georgia. Salt Lake City: Filmed by the Genealogical Society of Utah, 1987-1989. 9 microfilm.

United States. Immigration and Naturalization Service. *Index to Passenger Lists of Vessels Arriving At Miscellaneous Ports in Alabama, Florida, Georgia, and South Carolina, 1890-1924.* Washington, D.C.: Microphotographed by Immigration and Naturalization Service, 1957.

United States. Immigration and Naturalization Service. *Passenger Lists of Vessels Arriving At Key West, 1898-1920.* Washington, D.C.: Immigration and Naturalization Service, 1946.

Land and Property

Ainsworth, Fern. *Private Land Claims: Alabama, Arkansas, Florida.* Natchitoches, LA: the author, 1978.

Davidson, Alvie L. *Florida Land: Records of the Tallahassee and Newnansville General Land Office, 1825-1892.* Bowie, Md.: Heritage Books, 1989.

DeVille, Winston. *English Land Grants in West Florida: A Register for the States of Alabama, Mississippi, and Parts of Florida and Louisiana, 1766-1776.* Ville Platte LA: the author, 1986.

East Florida. Governor. *Spanish Land Grant Archives, 1764-1844.* Salt Lake City: Filmed by the Genealogical Society of Utah, 1977.

Florida. Division of State Lands. *Homestead Application Files, 1881-1905.* Microfilm of records at Florida State Archives, Tallahassee, Florida. Salt Lake City: Filmed by the Genealogical Society of Utah, 1990. 6 microfilm.

Florida. Division of State Lands. *Homestead Swampland Claim Files, 1846-1918; Index, 1846-1853.* Microfilm of records located at state archives, Tallahassee, Florida. Salt Lake City: Filmed by the Genealogical Society of Utah, 1990. 3 microfilm.

Historical Records Survey, Division of Professional and Service Projects. Works Progress Administration. *Spanish Land Grants in Florida: Briefed Translations from the Archives of the Board of Commissioners for Ascertaining Claims and Titles to Land in the Territory of Florida.* 5 vols. Tallahassee, Florida: State Library Board, 1940-41.

Hone, Wade E. *Land and Property Research in the United States.* Salt Lake City: Ancestry Incorporated, 1997.

McMullin, Phillip W. *Grassroots of America.* Salt Lake City: Gendex Corp., 1972.

Snider, Billie Ford. *Spanish Plat Book of Land Records of the District of Pensacola, Province of West Florida, British and Spanish Land Grants, 1763-1821.* Pensacola, Florida: Antique Compiling, 1994.

Spanish Florida Land Records, 1764-1849. Microfilm of records at Florida State Archives, Tallahassee, Florida, [n.d.].

Spanish Land Grants in Florida: Briefed Translations from the Archives of the Board of Commissioner. 5 vols. Tallahassee: Historical Records Survey, 1940-1941.

United States. Commissioners for ascertaining claims to lands and titles in East Florida. *Land Claims, 1824-1828.* Salt Lake City: Filmed by the Genealogical Society of Utah, 1977.

Military

Chatelain, Verne Elmo. *The Defenses of Spanish Florida, 1565 to 1763.* Baltimore, Md.: Baltimore Press, 1941.

Davis, T. Frederick. "Florida's Part in the War with Mexico." *Florida Historical Quarterly* 20 (January 1941): 235-39

Florida State Militia, State Troops and National Guard, 1870-1918. Microfilm of records located at state archives, Tallahassee, Florida. Salt Lake City: Filmed by the Genealogical Society of Utah, 1990. 7 microfilm.

Florida. Comptroller's Office. *Pension Claims of Confederate Veterans and Their Widows Beginning 1885- 1955.* Salt Lake City: Filmed by the Genealogical Society of Utah, 1955.

Hartman, David W., and David Coles. *Biographical Rosters of Florida's Confederate & Union Soldiers 1861-1865.* 6 vols. Wilmington NC: Broadfoot Publishing, 1995.

National Archives and Records Service. *Compiled Service Records, Volunteer Soldiers, Florida Indian Wars, 1835- 1858* Washington, D.C.: Filmed by the National Archives, 1979.

Robertson, Fred L. *Soldiers of Florida in the Seminole Indian–Civil and Spanish-American Wars.* Bethesda, Md.: University Publications of America, 1990.

Sifakis. *Compendium of the Confederate Armies: Florida and Arkansas.* Galveston TX: Frontier Press, 1992.

Soldiers of Florida in the Seminole Indian Civil and Spanish-American Wars. Live Oak, Florida: Democrat Book and Job Print, 1909.

United States. Adjutant General's Office. *Compiled Service Records of Confederate Soldiers Who Served in Organizations from the State of Florida, 1861-1865.* Washington: National Archives, 1955, 1959.

United States. Adjutant General's Office. *Index to Compiled Service Records of Volunteer Soldiers Who Served During Indian Wars and Disturbances, 1815-1858.* Washington, D.C.: The National Archives, 1966.

United States. Adjutant General's Office. *Index to Compiled Service Records of Volunteer Union Soldiers Who Served in Organizations from the State of Florida.* Washington, D.C.: The National Archives, 1958.

United States. Adjutant General's Office. *World War I Navy Card Roster, 1917-1920 (Florida).* Microfilm of records located at state archives, Tallahassee, Florida. Salt Lake City: Filmed by the Genealogical Society of Utah, 1990. 4 microfilm.

United States. Record and Pension Office. *Compiled Service Records of Volunteer Union Soldiers Who Served in Organizations from the State of Florida.* Washington, D.C.: The National Archives, 1962.

United States. Selective Service System. *Florida, World War I Selective Service System Draft Registration Cards, 1917-1918.* National Archives Microfilm Publications, M1509. Washington, D.C.: National Archives, 1987-1988.

United States. Veterans Administration. *Pension Index File, Alphabetical; have the Veterans Administrative Contact and Administrative Services, Administrative Operations Services, 1861-1934.* Washington: Veterans Administration, Publications Service, 1953.

United States. Veterans Administration. *Pension Index Files, Indian Wars, 1892-1926.* Washington: Veterans' Administration, 1959.

United States. War Department. *World War II Honor List of Dead and Missing, State of Florida.* (Salt Lake City: Filmed by the Genealogical Society of Utah, 1976).

White, Virgil D. *Register of Florida CSA Pension Applications.* Waynesboro, Tenn.: National Historical Pub. Co., 1989.

Vital and Cemetery Records

A. P. Boza Funeral Home (Tampa, Florida). *Funeral Home Records, 1929-1965.* (Salt Lake City: Filmed by the Genealogical Society of Utah, 1975).

Cemetery Records of Florida and Georgia (Compiled by Members of the Florida Stake). Salt Lake City: Genealogical Society of Utah, 1960. Microfilm, 16 rolls.

Florida Combined Death Index, 1877-1969. Microfilm of records at Florida Dept. of Health and Rehabilitative Services, Jacksonville, Florida. (Salt Lake City: Filmed by the Genealogical Society of Utah, 1992). 305 microfiche.

Florida Combined Marriage Index, 1927-1969. Microfilm of records at Florida Dept. of Health and Rehabilitative Services, Jacksonville, Florida. (Salt Lake City: Filmed by the Genealogical Society of Utah, 1991). 471 microfiche.

Florida. State Board of Health. Bureau of Vital Statistics. *Florida Combined Divorce and Annulment Index, 1927-1969.* Microfilm of original records at Florida Dept. of Health and Rehabilitative Services, Jacksonville, Florida. Salt Lake City: Filmed by the Genealogical Society of Utah, 1991. 143 microfiche.

Florida. State Board of Health. Bureau of Vital Statistics. *Report of Divorce Granted and Report of Marriage Annulled, 1927-1950.* Jacksonville, Fla.: Filmed by the Florida Vital Statistics Office, [199-?]. 141 microfilm.

Hayes, E.H. *Cemetery Records of Florida.* 9 vols. Typescript. Salt Lake City: Genealogical Society of Utah, 1946.

Historical Records Survey (Florida). *Guide to Public Vital Statistics Records in Florida.* Jacksonville, Fla.: Florida Historical Records Survey, 1941.

Historical Records Survey (Florida). *Guide to the Supplementary Vital Statistics from Church Records in Florida.* 3 vols. Jacksonville: Historical Records Survey, 1942.

Jacksonville Branch Genealogical Library (Florida). *Vital Records Card File for Northern Florida and Southern Georgia, 1895-1945.* Microfilm of records in the Jacksonville Branch Genealogical Library, Jacksonville, Florida. (Salt Lake City: Genealogical Society of Utah, 1977). 17 microfilm.

Veterans Graves Registration Project. *Register of Deceased Veterans, Florida.* Salt Lake City: Genealogical Society of Utah, 1953.

County Website	Map Index	Date Created	Parent County or Territory From Which Organized Address/Details
Alachua www.co.alachua.fl.us/index_layers.html	F9	29 Dec 1824	**Duval, St. Johns** Alachua County; 201 E University Ave; PO Box 600; Gainesville, FL 32601; Ph. 352.374.3636 Details: (Co Clk has incomplete m rec from 1837, pro rec from 1840, land rec from 1848 & ct rec)
Baker www.nefcom.net/users/bcbcc/	E9	8 Feb 1861	**New River** Baker County; 339 E MacClenny Ave; MacClenny, FL 32063-2100; Ph. 904.259.3121 Details: (Co Judge has m & pro rec; Clk Cir Ct has div & ct rec from 1880)
Bay www.bocc.co.bay.fl.us./	E4	24 Apr 1913	**Calhoun** Bay County; 300 E 4th St; PO Box 2269; Panama City, FL 32402; Ph. 850.763.9061 Details: (Hlth Dept has b & d rec; Clk Cir Ct has m, pro, div, ct & land rec from 1913)
Benton		24 Feb 1843	**Alachua** Details: (see Hernando) Formerly Hernando Co. Name changed to Benton 6 Mar 1844. Name changed back to Hernando 24 Dec 1850.
Bradford www.rootsweb.com/~flbradfo/	F9	21 Dec 1858	**Columbia** Bradford County; PO Box B; Starke, FL 32091-1286; Ph. 904.964.6280 Details: (Formerly New River Co. Name changed to Bradford 6 Dec 1861) (Co Clk has m rec from 1875, pro & ct rec from 1892 & land rec from 1876)
Brevard manatee.brev.lib.fl.us/	I11	14 Mar 1844	**Mosquito** Brevard County; 400 S St; Titusville, FL 32780; Ph. 321.633.1924 Details: (Formerly St. Lucie Co. Name changed to Brevard 6 Jan 1855) (Clk Cir Ct has m rec from 1868, land rec from 1871, div & ct rec from 1879, pro rec from 1917 & mil dis rec from 1919; Co Hlth Dept has d rec from 1985 & b rec; some rec prior to 1885 destroyed
Broward www.co.broward.fl.us/	M11	30 Apr 1915	**Dade, Palm Beach** Broward County; 201 SE 6th St; Fort Lauderdale, FL 33301; Ph. 954.765.4578 Details: (Clk Cir Ct has m, pro, div, ct & land rec from 1915)
Calhoun www.rootsweb.com/~flcalhou/index.htm	E4	26 Jan 1838	**Franklin** Calhoun County; 425 E Central Ave; Blountstown, FL 32424-2242; Ph. 850.674.4545 Details: (Co Judge has m & pro rec; Co Clk has div, ct & land rec)
Charlotte* www.co.charlotte.fl.us/	K9	23 Apr 1921	**DeSoto** Charlotte County; 350 E Marion Ave; PO Box 511687; Punta Gorda, FL 33950; Ph. 941.637.2199 Details: (Clk Cir Ct has m, div, pro, ct & land rec from 1921)
Citrus www.bocc.citrus.fl.us/	H9	2 June 1887	**Hernando** Citrus County; 111 W Main St; Inverness, FL 34450; Ph. 352.637.9470 Details: (Off of Hist. Resources has m rec 1887-1945, cem, pro, land & ct rec from 1887 & mil dis rec 1919-1969; Co Hlth Dept has b & d rec)
Clay* www.claycountygov.com/	E9	31 Dec 1858	**Duval** Clay County; PO Box 698; Green Cove Springs, FL 32043-0698; Ph. 904.284.6317 Details: (Clk Cir Ct has m, pro, ct & land rec from 1872 & div rec from 1859; Co Hlth Dept has b & d rec from 1973)
Collier* www.co.collier.fl.us/	M10	8 May 1923	**Lee** Collier County; 3301 Tamiami Trail E; Naples, FL 33962-4902; Ph. 941.732.2646 Details: (Co Judge has m & pro rec; Clk Cir Ct has div, ct & land rec from 1923)
Columbia www.columbiacountyfla.com/	E8	4 Feb 1832	**Alachua** Columbia County; 145 N Hernando St; PO Box 2069; Lake City, FL 32055; Ph. 386.758.1041 Details: (Clk Cir Ct has b rec from 1943, m & land rec from 1875, div & ct rec from 1892 & pro rec from 1895; Co Pub Hlth Unit has b, d & bur rec)
Dade		4 Feb 1836	**Monroe** Details: (See Miami-Dade) Name changed to Miami-Dade 2 Dec 1997
De Soto co.desoto.fl.us/	K9	19 May 1887	**Manatee** De Soto County; 115 Oak St; Arcadia, FL 33821; Ph. 863.993.4876 Details: (Co Judge has pro rec from 1887; Clk Cir Ct has div, ct & land rec from 1887)

County Website	Map Index	Date Created	Parent County or Territory From Which Organized Address/Details
Dixie www.dixie-county.com/	F7	25 Apr 1921	**Lafayette** Dixie County; PO Box 1206; Cross City, FL 32628; Ph. 352.498.1200 Details: (Clk Cir Ct has m rec from 1973, div, pro, ct & land rec)
Duval* www.coj.net/	E10	12 Aug 1822	**St. Johns** Duval County; 330 E Bay St; Jacksonville, FL 32202; Ph. 904.630.2028 Details: (Clk Cir Ct has div, ct & land rec from 1921; Co Judge has m & pro rec)
Escambia www.co.escambia.fl.us/	D1	21 Jul 1821	**One of two original counties** Escambia County; 223 S Palafox Pl.; Pensacola, FL 32501; Ph. 850.595.4310 Details: (Clk Co Ct has m, pro & ct rec from 1821; Co Hlth Dept has b & d rec; Comptroller has land rec from 1821)
Flagler* flaglercounty.org/county1.htm	F10	28 Apr 1917	**St. Johns** Flagler County; 200 E Moody Blvd.; Bunnell, FL 32110; Ph. 386.437.7414 Details: (Clk Cir Ct has m, div, pro, ct & land rec from 1917)
Franklin www.franklincountyflorida.com/	F5	8 Feb 1832	**Jackson** Franklin County; 33 Market St; Apalachicola, FL 32320; Ph. 850.653.8861 Details: (Co Judge has m & pro rec; Clk Cir Ct has div, ct & land rec)
Gadsden www.rootsweb.com/~flgadsde/	D5	24 Jun 1823	**Jackson** Gadsden County; 10 E Jefferson St; PO Box 1799; Quincy, FL 32351; Ph. 850.875.8622 Details: (Co Judge has m & pro rec; Clk Cir Ct has div, ct & land rec)
Gilchrist www.co.gilchrist.fl.us/	F8	4 Dec 1925	**Alachua** Gilchrist County; 112 S Main St; Trenton, FL 32693; Ph. 352.463.3170 Details: (Clk Cir Ct has m, div, pro & ct rec from 1926)
Glades www.geocities.com/Heartland/ Prairie/6173/glades.html	K10	23 Apr 1921	**DeSoto** Glades County; PO Box 10; Moore Haven, FL 33471; Ph. 863.946.0361 Details: (Clk of Cts has m, div, land, pro & ct rec from 1921 & bur rec from 1925; Co Hlth Dept has b & d rec from 1921)
Gulf www.gulfcountybusiness.com/	F4	6 Jun 1925	**Calhoun** Gulf County; 1000 Cecil G Costin Sr Blvd; Port St. Joe, FL 32456; Ph. 850.229.6112 Details: (Clk Cir Ct has m, pro, div, ct, land & mil dis rec from 1925)
Hamilton www.rootsweb.com/~flhamilt/ hamilton.html	D8	26 Dec 1827	**Jefferson** Hamilton County; 207 NE 1st St; Jasper, FL 32052; Ph. 904.792.1288 Details: (Co Judge has m & pro rec; Clk Cir Ct has div & ct rec from 1881 & land rec from 1837)
Hardee* www.hardeecounty.net/start.html	J9	23 Apr 1921	**DeSoto** Hardee County; 412 W Orange St; Wauchula, FL 33873; Ph. 863.773.4174 Details: (Clk Cir Ct has m, d, div, pro, ct & land rec from 1921)
Hendry* www.hendryfla.net/	L10	11 May 1923	**Lee** Hendry County; 25 E Hickpochee Ave; PO Box 1760; LaBelle, FL 33975; Ph. 863.675.5217 Details: (Clk Cir Ct has m, div, land, pro & ct rec from 1923 & bur rec from 1953; Co Hlth Dept has b & d rec)
Hernando www.co.hernando.fl.us/	H9	24 Feb 1843	**Alachua** Hernando County; 20 N Main St; Brooksville, FL 34601; Ph. 352.754.4201 Details: (Name changed to Benton 6 Mar 1844. Name changed back to Hernando 24 Dec 1850) (Clk Co Ct has m rec; Clk Cir Ct has div, pro, ct & land rec from 1877)
Highlands www.heartlineweb.org/highlandsbcc/	K10	23 Apr 1921	**DeSoto** Highlands County; 590 S Commerce Ave; Sebring, FL 33870; Ph. 863.402.6565 Details: (Clk Cir Ct has m, div, pro, ct & land rec from 1921)
Hillsborough www.hillsboroughcounty.org/	I9	25 Jan 1834	**Alachua** Hillsborough County; 419 N Pierce St; Tampa, FL 33602; Ph. 813.276.8100 Details: (Co Judge has m & pro rec; Clk Cir Ct has div & land rec)

County Website	Map Index	Date Created	Parent County or Territory From Which Organized Address/Details
Holmes www.rootsweb.com/~flholmes/holmes.htm	**D3**	**8 Jan 1848**	**Jackson** Holmes County; 201 N Oklahoma St; Bonifay, FL 32425; Ph. 850.547.1100 Details: (Clk Cir Ct has m, pro, div, ct & land rec)
Indian River www.myfloridacounty.com/mfcTemplate/ view.jsp?countyid=INDIANRIVER	**J11**	**30 May 1925**	**St. Lucie** Indian River County; 1840 25th St; Vero Beach, FL 32960; Ph. 561.567.8000 Details: (Clk Cir Ct has m, div, pro, ct & land rec from 1925; Co Hlth Dept has b & d rec)
Jackson members.aol.com/BettyMaeS/index.html	**D4**	**12 Aug 1822**	**Escambia** Jackson County; 2864 Madison St; PO Box 510; Marianna, FL 32447; Ph. 850.482.9552 Details: (Clk Cir Ct has m rec from 1845, land rec from 1824, div, pro, mil & ct rec from 1900)
Jefferson www.co.jefferson.fl.us/	**D6**	**6 Jan 1827**	**Leon** Jefferson County; Courthouse #10; PO Box 547; Monticello, FL 32344; Ph. 850.342.0218 Details: (Clk Cir Ct has m rec from 1840, div rec from 1900, pro & ct rec from 1850 & land rec from 1827)
Lafayette www.rootsweb.com/~fllafaye/ lafayette.html	**E7**	**23 Dec 1856**	**Madison** Lafayette County; Main St; PO Box 88; Mayo, FL 32066; Ph. 904.294.1600 Details: (Co Judge has m & pro rec; Clk Cir Ct has div rec from 1902, ct rec from 1907 & land rec from 1893)
Lake www.lakegovernment.com/	**H10**	**27 May 1887**	**Orange** Lake County; 315 W Main St; PO 7800; Tavares, FL 32778; Ph. 352.742.4100 Details: (Clk Cir Ct has m, div, ct & land rec from 1887, pro rec from 1893 & adoption rec; Co Hlth Dept has d rec)
Lee www.lee-county.com/	**L10**	**13 May 1887**	**Monroe** Lee County; 2115 2nd St; Fort Myers, FL 33901; Ph. 941.335.2283 Details: (Clk Cir Ct has m, div, pro, ct & land rec)
Leon* www.co.leon.fl.us/leon.htm	**E6**	**29 Dec 1824**	**Gadsden** Leon County; 301 S Monroe St; PO Box 726; Tallahassee, FL 32302; Ph. 850.577.4000 Details: (Clk Cir Ct has m, div, pro, ct & land rec from 1825 & mil dis rec from 1914; Co Hlth Dept has b, d & bur rec)
Levy www.rootsweb.com/~fllevy/	**G8**	**10 Mar 1845**	**Alachua** Levy County; 355 Court St; Bronson, FL 32621; Ph. 352.486.5229 Details: (Clk Cir Ct has m, div, pro, ct & land rec from 1850)
Liberty www.geocities.com/PicketFence/ Street/2205/	**E5**	**15 Dec 1855**	**Gadsden** Liberty County; Hwy 20; PO Box 399; Bristol, FL 32321; Ph. 850.643.2237 Details: (Co Judge has m & pro rec; Clk Cir Ct has div, ct & land rec)
Madison www.madisonfl.org/	**E7**	**26 Dec 1827**	**Jefferson** Madison County; PO Box 237; Madison, FL 32341; Ph. 850.973.1500 Details: (Clk Cir Ct has m, pro & ct rec from 1838, land rec from 1831 & div rec)
Manatee www.co.manatee.fl.us/	**J9**	**9 Jan 1855**	**Hillsborough** Manatee County; 1115 Manatee Ave W; PO Box 25400; Bradenton, FL 34206; Ph. 941.749.1800 Details: (Clk Cir Ct has m, div, pro, ct & land rec from 1857)
Marion www.rootsweb.com/~flmarion/index.html	**G9**	**14 Mar 1844**	**Alachua** Marion County; 110 NW 1st Ave (zip 34475); PO Box 1030; Ocala, FL 34478; Ph. 352.620.3904 Details: (Recording Office has land, div, pro & ct rec; Clk of Cts has m rec; Co Hlth Dept has b & d rec)
Martin www.martin.fl.us/	**K12**	**30 May 1925**	**Palm Beach** Martin County; 2401 SE Monterey Rd; Stuart, FL 34995; Ph. 561.288.5576 Details: (Clk Cir Ct has m, div, pro, ct & land rec from 1925; Co Hlth Dept has b, d & bur rec)

County Website	Map Index	Date Created	Parent County or Territory From Which Organized Address/Details
Miami-Dade miamidade.gov/	N11	13 Nov 1997	**Monroe, Dade** Miami-Dade County; 111 NW First St Ste 220; Miami, FL 33128; Ph. 305.375.5124 Details: (Formerly Dade County named changed to Miami-Dade 2 Dec 1997)(Co Judge has m & pro rec; Clk Cir Ct has div & land rec from 1890)
Monroe www.co.monroe.fl.us/	N11	3 July 1823	**St. Johns** Monroe County; 500 Whitehead St; Key West, FL 33040; Ph. 305.292.3540 Details: (Clk Cir Ct has m, div, pro, ct & land rec from 1853)
Mosquito		29 Dec 1824	**St Johns** Details: (see Orange) Name changed to Orange 30 Jan 1845
Nassau www.nassauclerk.org/	D10	29 Dec 1824	**Duval** Nassau County; PO Box 456; Fernandina Beach, FL 32034; Ph. 904.321.5700 Details: (Clk Cir Ct has m, div, pro, ct & land rec from 1800's)
New River		21 Dec 1858	**Columbia** Details: (see Bradford) Name changed to Bradford 6 Dec 1861
Okaloosa* www.co.okaloosa.fl.us/	D2	3 Jun 1915	**Santa Rosa** Okaloosa County; 101 E James Lee Boulevard; Crestview, FL 32536; Ph. 850.689.5800 Details: (Co Judge has m & pro rec; Clk Cir Ct has div, ct & land rec from 1915)
Okeechobee www.rootsweb.com/~flokeech/index.html	J11	8 May 1917	**Brevard** Okeechobee County; 304 NW 2nd St; Okeechobee, FL 34972; Ph. 863.763.6441 Details: (Clk Cir Ct has m, div, pro & ct rec from 1917 & land rec from 1880's; Co Hlth Dept has b & d rec)
Orange www.orangecountyfl.net/Default.asp	H10	29 Dec 1824	**St. Johns** Orange County; 425 N Orange Ave; Orlando, FL 32801-3547; Ph. 407.863.6321 Details: (Formerly Mosquito Co. Name changed to Orange 30 Jan 1845) (Clk Cir Ct has m rec from 1890, ct & pro rec from 1869)
Osceola www.osceola.org/	I11	12 May 1887	**Brevard** Osceola County; 2 Courthouse Sq Ste 2000; Kissimmee, FL 34741-5188; Ph. 407.343.3500 Details: (Clk Cir Ct has m, div, pro & land rec from 1887)
Palm Beach www.co.palm-beach.fl.us/	K12	30 Apr 1909	**Dade** Palm Beach County; 301 N Olive Ave; West Palm Beach, FL 33401-4705; Ph. 561.355.2754 Details: (Co Judge has m & pro rec; Clk Cir Ct has div, ct & land rec)
Pasco www.pascocounty.com/	I8	2 Jun 1887	**Hernando** Pasco County; 38053 Live Oak Ave; New Port Richey, FL 33523; Ph. 352.521.4545 Details: (Clk Cir Ct has div, ct & land rec from 1887, m & pro rec)
Pinellas* www.co.pinellas.fl.us/bcc/	I8	23 May 1911	**Hillsborough** Pinellas County; 315 Ct St; Clearwater, FL 34616-5165; Ph. 727.464.3377 Details: (Clk Cir Ct has m, div, pro, ct & land rec from 1912)
Polk www.polk-county.net/	I10	8 Feb 1861	**Brevard** Polk County; 255 N Broadway Ave; Bartow, FL 33830-3912; Ph. 863.534.4540 Details: (Boundaries changed 1871) (Clk Cir Ct has m, div, pro, ct & land rec from 1861)
Putnam www.co.putnam.fl.us/	F10	13 Jan 1849	**Alachua** Putnam County; 410 St Johns Ave; PO Box 758; Palatka, FL 32178; Ph. 386.329.0361 Details: (Clk Cir Ct has m, div, pro, ct & land rec from 1849, nat rec 1849-1914, misc rec from 1800, cem rec survey)
Santa Rosa www.co.santa-rosa.fl.us/	D2	18 Feb 1842	**Escambia** Santa Rosa County; 6865 Caroline St; Milton, FL 32570; Ph. 850.623.0135 Details: (Courthouse burned in 1869) (Co Archives has m, div, pro & ct rec from 1869; Deed Room, Main Courthouse has land records from 1869)

County Website	Map Index	Date Created	Parent County or Territory From Which Organized Address/Details
Sarasota* www.co.sarasota.fl.us/	K9	14 May 1921	**Manatee** Sarasota County; 2000 Main St; Sarasota, FL 34237; Ph. 941.362.4066 Details: (Clk Cir Ct has m, pro, ct & land rec from 1921 & div rec from 1945; Co Hlth Dept has b & d rec)
Seminole www.co.seminole.fl.us/	H10	25 Apr 1913	**Orange** Seminole County; 301 N Park Ave; Sanford, FL 32771; Ph. 407.665.4330 Details: (Co Judge has m & pro rec; Clk Cir Ct has div, ct & land rec from 1915)
St. Johns www.co.st-johns.fl.us/	E10	21 Jul 1821	**One of two original cos** St. Johns County; 4010 Lewis Speedway Blvd; PO Box 300; Saint Augustine, FL 32085; Ph. 904.823.2333 Details: (Clk Cir Ct has div rec from 1900, ct & land rec from 1821, m & pro rec)
St. Lucie www.stlucieco.gov/	J12	24 May 1905	**Brevard** St. Lucie County; 2300 Virginia Ave; Fort Pierce, FL 34982; Ph. 561.462.1400 Details: (Clk Cir Ct has m, pro, div, ct & land rec from 1905; Co Hlth Dept has d & bur rec)
Sumter bocc.co.sumter.fl.us/	H9	8 Jan 1853	**Marion** Sumter County; 209 N Florida St; Bushnell, FL 33513-9402; Ph. 352.793.0200 Details: (Clk Cir Ct has m & land rec from 1853, pro rec from 1856, div rec from 1900, ct rec from 1913 & delayed b rec 1943-1972)
Suwannee www.rootsweb.com/~flsuwann/ suwannee.htm	E8	21 Dec 1858	**Columbia** Suwannee County; 224 Pine Ave; Live Oak, FL 32060; Ph. 940.364.3450 Details: (Clk Cir Ct has m, div, land, pro, mil dis & ct rec from 1859; Co Health Dept has d rec)
Taylor perry.gulfnet.com/new_perry/taylor.htm	E7	23 Dec 1856	**Madison** Taylor County; PO Box 620; Perry, FL 32348; Ph. 850.838.3500 Details: (Clk Cir Ct has m rec from 1908, div rec from 1898, land rec from 1857, pro rec from 1941, ct rec from 1946 & mil dis rec from 1914)
Union www.rootsweb.com/~flunion/index.htm	E9	20 May 1921	**Bradford** Union County; 15 NE First St; Lake Butler, FL 32054-1600; Ph. 904.496.4241 Details: (Clk Cir Ct has div & ct rec)
Volusia www.volusia.org/	G11	29 Dec 1854	**Orange** Volusia County; 123 W Indiana; De Land, FL 32720; Ph. 904.736.5920 Details: (Clk Cir Ct has m, div, ct, pro & land rec)
Wakulla* mailer.fsu.edu/~rthompso/wakulla.html	E6	11 Mar 1843	**Leon** Wakulla County; Hwy 319; Crawfordville, FL 32327-0337; Ph. 850.926.0905 Details: (Courthouse burned in 1896) (Clk Cir Ct has m, div, pro, ct & land rec from 1896; Co Hlth Dept has some b rec)
Walton www.rootsweb.com/~flwalton/walton.htm	D3	29 Dec 1824	**Escambia** Walton County; 571 East Nelson Ave; PO Box 1260; De Funiak Springs, FL 32433-0000; Ph. 850.892.8118 Details: (Clk Cir Ct has m rec from 1885, pro rec from 1882, div, ct & land rec, newspaper rec from 1905; Co Hlth Dept has b & d rec)
Washington www.rootsweb.com/~flwashin/	D4	9 Dec 1825	**Jackson** Washington County; 711 3rd St; Chipley, FL 32428; Ph. 850.638.6200 Details: (Clk Cir Ct has m, div, pro, land & ct rec from 1890)

Notes

Cherokee Rose

GEORGIA

CAPITAL: ATLANTA – STATE 1788 (4TH)

From its discovery in 1540 by Hernando de Soto until 1732, the Spanish and English had sporadic disputes over the future state of Georgia. In 1732, King George II granted the land between the Savannah and Altamaha Rivers to prominent Englishmen. One of these Englishmen was James Oglethorpe, who came to Georgia to help achieve the goals of the new colony. Residents set out to provide a buffer between the Carolinas and Florida and establish a refuge for those who would otherwise be sent to debtors' prison. In 1733, Oglethorpe and 35 families settled Savannah. The next year Augusta was established and a group of Protestant refugees from Salzburg settled Ebenezer, in present-day Effingham County. Other settlers arrived from Switzerland, Germany, Italy, the Scottish Highlands, and Moravia in the next five years. In 1740, Georgia was divided into two counties. Savannah County was north of the Altamaha and Frederica County was south of the Altamaha. Many of the Moravians, who had come from North Carolina, moved from Georgia to Bethlehem and Nazareth, Pennsylvania when their efforts to convert the Indians failed.

In 1752, Georgia's charter was surrendered and Georgia became a crown colony, claiming all the land between North Carolina and Florida and the Atlantic Ocean to the Mississippi. From 1758 to 1777, Georgia was divided into the following 12 parishes: St. James, St. Matthew, St. John, St. Paul, St George, St. Andrew, St. Philip, St. David, St. Patrick, St. Thomas, St. Mary, and Christ Church. These parishes were formed into seven large counties in 1777. Georgia gained statehood in 1788. In a dispute over states' rights in the 1790's, Georgia refused to carry out a Supreme Court decision against it, which led to the passage of the 11th amendment in 1798. That same year, the Territory of Mississippi, which later became the states of Alabama and Mississippi, was created from the western half of Georgia. Georgia's present boundaries were set in 1802.

Many families were drawn to Georgia in the early 1800s by land lotteries. Families who had lived in the territory for at least one year were allowed to draw for land areas as large as 400 acres. These lotteries were held in 1805, 1807, 1820, 1821, 1827, and 1832. Lists of lottery participants are held in the office of the Secretary of State. Some of these lists have been microfilmed and are available through the Family History Library in Salt Lake City, Utah.

Georgia seceded from the Union in 1861. More than 100,000 men fought for the Confederacy. More than 12,000 Union soldiers died as prisoners in Anderson, Georgia and are buried in a national cemetery in Sumter County. A published cemetery list by the Quartermaster General's Office entitled "Roll of Honor, Volume 3" is available.

Look for vital records in the following locations:

- **Birth and death records:** Vital Records Service, State Department of Human Resources in Atlanta, Georgia has birth and death records from 1919 to the present. Certified copies of birth records are issued at county and state offices to the person, a parent, or a legal representative. The index is closed to the public. Many earlier birth records are available from county offices at Atlanta, Savannah, and Macon. Death certificates are also issued at county and state offices. Indexes are closed to the public. Marriage records available from County Clerks or the County Clerk of the Ordinary Court.
- **Marriage records:** Clerk of the Court of Ordinary.
- **Divorce and civil court records:** The Superior Court Clerk keeps divorce and civil court records.
- **Naturalization records:** Shown in the minutes of the Superior, District, or City Court where the hearing was held. Also on microfilm at the Georgia Department of Archives and History in Atlanta, Georgia.
- **Land records:** Land deeds are recorded in the office of the Court of Ordinary as well as on microfilm and printed abstract form. The same

court also holds records of homesteads, land warrants, licenses, indentures and pauper registers.

- **Wills:** The Clerk of the Court of Ordinary has wills from 1777 to 1798 and after 1852.
- **Voter registration records:** Clerk of the Court of Ordinary.
- **Census records:** State censuses taken for various years from 1786 to 1890 have survived for some counties and are located at the Georgia Department of Archives and History. Indexes to many state censuses have been published. Some county census records are also available for the years 1827 to 1890.
- **Military records:** A published roster of Georgia Confederate infantry soldiers compiled by Lillian Henderson and entitled *Roster of the Confederate Soldiers of Georgia, 1861-65*, is available in six volumes through the Family History Library in Salt Lake City and its Family History Centers. The original Georgia pension records for Confederate veterans and index are at the Georgia Department of Archives and History in Atlanta, Georgia.

Vital Records Service, State Department of Human Resources
47 Trinity Avenue, S.W. Room 217-H
Atlanta, Georgia 30334
404.656.4750

Georgia Department of Archives and History
330 Capitol Avenue, S.E.
Atlanta, Georgia 30334

Societies and Repositories

Abraham Baldwin Chapter, GASSAR; 314 W. Residence Ave.; Albany, Georgia 31701-2319; 229.439.9489

African-American Family Historical Association, Inc.; PO Box 115268; Atlanta, Georgia 30310

Alma-Bacon County Historical Society; 406 Mercer St.; Alma, Georgia 31510

Alpharetta Historical Society, Inc.; PO Box 1386; 1835 Old Milton Pkwy.; Alpharetta, Georgia 30009-1386

Altamaha Chapter, GASSAR; 1381 Odum Hwy; Jesup, Georgia 31545-6947; 912.427.3123

American Cherokee Confederacy, Inc.; 619 Pine Cove Rd.; Albany, Georgia 31705-6906

Ancestors Unlimited. Inc.; PO Box 1507; Jonesboro, Georgia 30336

Andrew College Archives; Pitts Library; 413 College St.; Cuthbert, Georgia 31740

Appling County Heritage Center, Inc.; PO Box 87; Baxley, Georgia 31513

Ashantilly Center; PO Box 1449; Darien, Georgia 31305

Athens Chapter, GASSAR; 1541 Arrowhead Rd.; Greensboro, Georgia 30642-2001; 706.453.7193

Athens Historical Society; PO Box 7745; Athens, Georgia 30604-7745

Athens-Clarke Co. Library; 130 w. Paces Ferry Rd., N.W.; Atlanta, Georgia 30305-1366; 404.814.4000; <www.athist.org>

Atlanta Chapter, GASSAR; 1475 Mt. Paran Rd.,N.W.; Atlanta, Georgia 30327-3749; 404.233.1330

Atlanta Historical Society; 130 West Paces Ferry Rd. N.W.; Atlanta, Georgia 30305.1366

Atlanta History Center; 130 West Paces Ferry Rd.; Atlanta, Georgia 30305; <www.atlantahistorycenter.com>

Atlanta Public Library, I. Margaret Mitchel Square; Carnegie Way & Forsythe; Atlanta, Georgia 30303

Augusta Genealogical Society; PO Box 3743; Augusta, Georgia 30914-3743;

Augusta Museum of History; 560 Reynolds St.; Augusta, Georgia 30901; <www.augustamuseum.org>

Augusta-Richmond Co. Public Library; 902 Greene St.; Augusta, Georgia 30901

Augusta-Richmond County Historical Society; 2500 Walton Way; Augusta, Georgia 30904-2200

Banks County Historical Society; PO Box 473; Homer, Georgia 30547-0473; <www.rootsweb.com/~gabchs/html/>

Barnesville-Lamar County Historical Society; PO Box 805; Barnesville, Georgia 30204

Bartow County Genealogical Society; PO Box 993; Cartersville, Georgia 30120-0993; <www.geocities.com/Heartland/Park/9465/bartowcoga.html>

Blue Ridge Mountain Chapter, GASSAR; 1781 Possum Trot Place; Blairsville, Georgia 30512-6010; 706.745.9513

Bonaventure Historical Society; 1317 East 55th St.; Savannah, Georgia 31404.4515; <www.home.earthlink.net/~bonaventur>

Bradley Memorial Library; Bradley Dr.; Columbus, Georgia 31906

Brantley County Historical and Preservation Society; PO Box 1096; Nahunta, Georgia 31553

Brunswick Regional Library; 208 Gloucester; St. Brunswick, Georgia 31521

Bulloch County Historical Society; PO Box 42; Statesboro, Georgia 30458

Burke County Genealogical Society; 183 Knight Rd.; Waynesboro, Georgia 30830; <members.aol.com/J2525/gen.htm>

Button Gwinnett Chapter, GASSAR; 2674 Conifer Green Way; Dacula, Georgia 30019-3126; 770.338.0495

Byron Area Historical Society; PO Box 755; Byron, Georgia 31008

Candler County Historical Society; PO Box 325; Metter, Georgia 30439

Captain John Collins Chapter, GASSAR; 4531 Paper Mill Rd.; Marietta, Georgia 30067-402; 770.955.1303

Carroll County Genealogical Society; PO Box 576; Carrollton, Georgia 10117;

Carroll County Historical Society; PO Box 1308; Carrollton, Georgia 30117

Casimir Pulaski Chapter, GASSAR; 842 Old Center Point Rd.; Carrollton, Georgia 30117-6728; 770.834.7594

Catoosa Co. Library; 108 Catoosa Circle; Ringgold, Georgia 30707; 706.965.3600

Catoosa County Historical Society; PO Box 113; Ringgold, Georgia 30736

Central Georgia Genealogical Society; PO Box 2024; Warner Robins, Georgia 31093;

Chattahoochee Valley Historical Society; 1213 Fifth Avenue; West Point, Georgia 31833

Chattooga County Historical Society; PO Box 626; Summerville, Georgia 30747

Cherokee County Historical Society; PO Box 1287; Canton, Georgia 30114; <www.rockbarn.org/society.htm>

Cherokee County, Georgia Historical Society; PO Box 1287; Canton, Georgia 30114; <www.rockbarn.org/index.htm>

Cherokee Regional Library, LaFayette-Walker Co. Library, Georgia Hist. & Gen. Rm.; 305 S. Duke St.; PO Box 707; LaFayette, Georgia 30728

Chestatee Regional Library; 127 N. Main; Gainesville, Georgia 30501

Clan Buchanan Society in America; c/o Odom Library; PO Box 1110; Moultrie, Georgia 31776

Clark Oconee Genealogical Society of Athens, Georgia; PO Box 6403; Athens, Georgia 30604

Clay County Library; PO Box 275; Fort Gaines, Georgia 31751-0275

Clayton Co. Georgia Public Library; 865 Battlecreek Rd.; Jonesboro, Georgia 30236; 770.473.3850 ;

Coastal Georgia Historical Society; PO Box 21136; St. Simons Is., Georgia 31522; <www.saintsimonslighthouse.org.>

Cobb Co. Public Library System, Georgia Rm.; 266 Roswell St.; Marietta, Georgia 30060-2004; 770.528.2318; Fax 770.528.2349; ;

Cobb County Genealogical Society, Inc.; PO Box 1413; Marietta, Georgia 30061.1413; <www.rootsweb.com/~gaccgs/>

Cobb Landmarks and Historical Society, Inc.; 145 Denmead St.; Marietta, Georgia 30060

Colquitt-Thomas Regional Library; PO Box 1110; Moultrie, Georgia 31768

Coweta Charter Genealogical and Historical Society; Hwy. 54, Rt. 1; Sharpsburg, Georgia 30277; <members.tripod.com/~CowetaGS/>

Coweta County Genealogical Society, Inc.; PO Box 1014; Newnan, Georgia 30264

Coweta Falls Chapter, GASSAR; 4143 Spirea Dr.; Columbus, Georgia 31907-2643; 706.561.5347

Crawford County Historical Society; PO Box 394; Roberta, Georgia 31078

Dade County Historical Society; PO Box 512; Trenton, Georgia 30752-0512

Dalton Chapter, GASSAR; 620 Emmons Dr.; Dalton, Georgia 30720-3915; 706.278.7616

Decatur County Genealogical Society; PO Box 7492; Bainbridge, Georgia 31718

Decatur County Historical Society; PO Box 682; Bainbridge, Georgia 31718

Decatur-DeKalb Library; 215 Sycamore St.; Decatur, Georgia 30030

DeKalb Historical Society; Old Courthouse on the Square; 101 E. Court Square; Decatur, Georgia 30030; 404.373.8287;

Delta Genealogical Society; c/o Rossville Public Library; 504 McFarland Ave.; Rossville, Georgia 30741-1255; <www.rootsweb.com/~gadgs/>

Dodge Historical Society, Inc; 407 Eastman Way; Eastman, Georgia 31023

Douglas County Genealogical Society; PO Box 5667; Douglasville, Georgia 30154;

Early County Historical Society; PO Box 564; Blakely, Georgia 31723

East Georgia Genealogical Society; PO Box 117; Winder, Georgia 30680; <www.rootsweb.com/~gaeggs/>

Eatonton-Putnam County Historical Society; 104 Church St.; Eatonton, Georgia 31024

Echols County Historical Society; Rt. 2 Box 966; Lake Park, Georgia 31636

Edward Telfair Chapter, GASSAR; 1 Washington Ave.; Savannah, Georgia 31405-3104; 912.238.1201

Elbert County Historical Society; PO Box 1033; Elberton, Georgia 30635; 706.283.1185

Ellen Payne Odom Genealogy Library c/o Moultrie-Colquitt Co. Library; 204 5th St., S.E.; PO Box 1110; Moultrie, Georgia 31768

Emanuel County Historic Preservation Society; PO Box 353; Swainsboro, Georgia 30401

Etowah Valley Historical Society; PO Box 1886; Cartersville, Georgia 30120;

Evans County Historical Society, Inc.; PO Box 6; Claxton, Georgia 30417

Fairfax Resolves Chapter, SAR; 12147 Holly Knoll Circle; Great Falls, Georgia 22066; 703.430.6745

Family History Library: 35 North West Temple Street: Salt Lake City, Utah 84150: 800.346.6044 or 801.240.2584: <www.familysearch.org>: Find a Family History Center near you: <www.familysearch.org/Eng/Library/FHC/frameset_fhc.asp>

Fannin County Ancestral Hunters; Georgia; <homepages.rootsweb.com/~fcgs/>

Fayette County Historical Society; PO Box 421; Fayetteville, Georgia 30214;

Flowery Branch Chapter of the Hall County Historical Society; PO Box 1994; Flowery Branch, Georgia 30542

Franklin County Historical Society; PO Box 541; Carnesville, Georgia 30521

Genealogical Center Library; Box 71343; Marietta, Georgia 30007-1343

Genealogical Society of Muscogee County, Original; W.C. Bradley Memorial Library; 120 Bradley Dr.; Columbus, Georgia 31906

Genealogy Unlimited; 2511 Churchill Dr.; Valdosta, Georgia 31602

George Walton Chapter, GASSAR; 3166 Floyd St.; Covington, Georgia 30014-2421; 770.787.3495

Georgia Genealogical Society; PO Box 54575; Atlanta, Georgia 30308-0575;

Georgia Historical Society; 501 Whitaker Street; Savannah, Georgia 31401; (912) 651.2831;

Georgia State Archives; 330 Capitol Avenue S.E.; Atlanta, Georgia 30334; <www.sos.state.ga.us/archives/>

Georgia State University Archives; 104 Decatur St., S.E.; Atlanta, Georgia 30334

Gordon County Historical Society; PO Box 342; Calhoun, Georgia 30701

Grady County Historical Society; PO Box 586; Cairo, Georgia 31728

Greene County Historical Society; PO Box 238; Greensboro, Georgia 30642

Griffin-Spalding Historical Society; PO Box 196; Griffin, Georgia 30224

Guale Historical Society; PO Box 398; St. Mary, Georgia 31558

Gwinnett Historical Society, Inc.; PO Box 261; Lawrenceville, Georgia 30246; 770.237.5616;

Gwinnett History Center, Gwinnett Historic Courthouse; PO Box 261; 185 Crogan St.; Lawrenceville, Georgia 30046; 707.822.5174; < www.adsd.com/ghs/>

Hall County Historical Society; PO Box 2999; Gainesville, Georgia 30501; <www.hallcountyhistoricalsociety.org>

Hart County Historical Society; PO Box 96; Hartwell, Georgia 30643

Historical Society of Forsyth County, Inc; PO Box 1334; Cumming, Georgia 30028; <www.angelfire.com/ga3/hsofci/>

Historical Society of the Georgia National Guard, Inc.; 201 Spring Hill Terrace; Roswell, Georgia 30075;

Huxford Genealogical Society; PO Box 595; Homerville, Georgia 31634; 912.487.3881;

Jefferson County Historical Society, Inc.; PO Box 491; Louisville, Georgia 30434

Jewish Genealogical Society of Georgia; 245 Dalrymple Rd.; Atlanta, Georgia 30328; <www.jewishgen.org/ajgs/jgsg/>

John E. Ladson, Jr. Gen. Library; PO Box 584; 119 Church St.; Vidalia, Georgia 30474

John Milledge Chapter, GASSAR; PO Box 824; Milledgeville, Georgia 31061-0824; 478.452.3710

Johnson County Historical Society; PO Box 15; Wrightsville, Georgia 31096

Joseph Habersham Chapter, GASSAR; 452 River Forest Run; Cleveland, Georgia 30528-2578; 706.865.3345

Kennesaw Historical Society, Inc.; c/o Kennesaw Civil War Museum; 2829 Cherokee St.; Kennesaw, Georgia 30144; <www.mindspring.com/~robertcjones/khs/khs.htm>

Kennesaw Mountain Historical Association; 900 Kennesaw Mountain Dr.; Kennesaw, Georgia 30152

LaGrange Chapter, GASSAR; 503 Merrill Lane; LaGrange, Georgia 30241-1488; 706.882.2372

Lake Blackshear Regional Library; 307 E. Lamar St.; Americus, Georgia 31709

Lake Lanier Regional Library; Pike Street; Lawrenceville, Georgia 30245

Lake Park Area Historical Society; PO Box 803; Lake Park, Georgia 31636.0803; <www.datasys.net/lakepark>

Laurens County Historical Society, Inc.; PO Box 1461; Dublin, Georgia 31040; <organizations.nlamerica.com/historical/>

Lee County Historical Society; PO Box 393; Leesburg, Georgia 31763

Liberty County Historical Society; PO Box 982; Hinesville, Georgia 31310

Lincoln Co. Library; PO Box 310; 181 Peachtree St.; Lincolnton, Georgia 30817; 706.359.4014

Lincoln County Historical Society; PO Box 869; Lincolnton, Georgia 30817

Lower Altamaha Historical Society; PO Box 1405; Darien, Georgia 31305

Lowndes County Historical Society & Museum; PO Box 434; 305 W. Central Avenue; Valdosta, Georgia 31603; 229.247.2840

Lyman Hall Chapter, GASSAR; 110 Saddlehorn Court; Woodstock, Georgia 30188-2055; 678.493.2400

Macon County Historical Society; PO Box 571; Montezuma, Georgia 31063

Marble Valley Historical Society; PO Box 815; Jasper, Georgia 30143;

Marshes of Glynn Chapter, GASSAR; 105 Jackson Court St.; Simons Is., Georgia 31522-9771; 912.634.6269

McIntosh Chapter, GASSAR; 51st Ave.; East Newnan, Georgia 30265-1743; 770.253.7852

Meriwether Historical Society; PO Box 741; Greenville, Georgia 30222

Middle Georgia Chapter, GASSAR; PO Box 4261 St.; Simons Is., Georgia 31522-4261; 912.375.9373

Middle Georgia Historical Society, Inc.; PO Box 13358; Macon, Georgia 31208-3358

Middle Georgia Railroad Association; 111 Blake Terrace; Warner Robins, Georgia 31088

Mill Creek Chapter, GASSAR; 308 Savannah Ave.; Statesboro, Georgia 30458-5259

Morgan County Historical Society; 277 S. Main St.; Madison, Georgia 30650

Murrell Memorial Library; Box 606; 207 5th Ave., N.E.; Eastman, Georgia 31203

Muscogee Genealogical Society; PO Box 761; Columbus, Georgia 31902;

Newnan-Coweta Historical Society; PO Box 1001; Newnan, Georgia 30264; <www.newnan.com/nchs/index.html>

Newton County Historical Society; PO Box 2415; Covington, Georgia 30015-2415

Northeast Georgia Historical and Genealogical Society; PO Box 907643; Gainesville, Georgia 30501

Northwest Georgia Historical and Genealogical Society; PO Box 5063; Rome, Georgia 30162.5063; <www.rootsweb.com/~ganwhags/>

Ocmulgee Chapter, GASSAR; 902 Westwood Dr.; Warner Robins, Georgia 31088-5869; 478.953.3838

Oconee Co. Library; Watkinsville, Georgia 30677

Okefenokee Historical and Genealogical Society, Inc.; 1617 Ball Street; Waycross, Georgia 31503; 912.283.6612

Okefenokee Regional Library; Box 1669; 401 Lee Ave; Waycross, Georgia 31501

Old Capital Historical Society; PO Box 4; Milledgeville, Georgia 31061-0004

Old Clinton Historical Society; 154 Randolph St.; Gray, Georgia 31032

Orphans Cemetery Assciation, Inc.; PO Box 4411; Eastman, Georgia 31023

Paulding County Historical Society; PO Box 333; Dallas, Georgia 30132

Peach County Historical Society; 201 Miller Street; Fort Valley, Georgia 31030; <www.rootsweb.com/~gapchs/>

Piedmont Chapter, GASSAR; 120 Cannonade Dr.; Alpharetta, Georgia 30004-4096; 770.475.1463

Piedmont Regional Library; Winder, Georgia 30680

Pierce County Historical and Genealogical Society; PO Box 443; Blackshear, Georgia 31516; <piercecounty.www.50megs.com>

Pine Log Historical Society; 106 N. Bartow St.; Cartersville, Georgia 30120; <www.geocities.com/Heartland/Park/9465/bartowcoga.html>

Pine Mountain Regional Library; Box 508; 218 Perry St.; Manchester, Georgia 31816

Polk County Historical Society; PO Box 203; Cedartown, Georgia 30125

Prater's Mill Foundation; PO Drawer H; Varnell, Georgia 30756; <www.pratersmill.org>

Rabun County Historical Society, Inc.; PO Box 921; Clayton, Georgia 30525; <www.rootsweb.com/~garchs>

Richmond Hill Historical Society, Inc.; PO Box 381; Richmond Hill, Georgia 31324; <www.richmondhillga.com>

Rockdale County Genealogical Society; c/o Nancy Guinn Library; 864 Green St; Conyers, Georgia 30012

Rockdale County Historical Society; PO Box 351; Conyers, Georgia 30012; <www.geocities.com/Yosemite/Trails/3379/rchs.htm>

Rome Area Heritage Foundation, Inc.; PO Box 6181; Rome, Georgia 30161

Rome Chapter, GASSAR; 76 Acorn Road, SE; Rome, Georgia 30161-7707; 706.235.5713

Roopville Historical Society & Archive; PO Box 285; Roopville, Georgia 30170

Roswell Historical Society; PO Box 1636; Roswell, Georgia 30077; <www.accessatlanta.com/community/groups/roswellhistory/>

Samuel Butts Chapter, GASSAR; 1648 Old Conyers Rd.; Stockbridge, Georgia 30281-2748; 770.474.8088

Samuel Elbert Chapter, GASSAR; 2072 Pulliam Mill Rd.; Dewey Rose, Georgia 30634-2704; 706.283.0629

Sara Hightower Regional Library; 606 West, First Street; Rome, Georgia 30161

Satilla Regional Library; 617 E. Ward St.; Douglas, Georgia 31533

Savannah Area Genealogical Society; PO Box 15385; Savannah, Georgia 31416

Savannah Public Chatham, Effingham Liberty Regional Library; 2002 Bull St.; Savanna, Georgia 31401

Savannah River Valley Genealogical Society; PO Box 895; Hartwell, Georgia 30643;

Smyrna Historical & Genealogical Society; 2861 Atlanta Street; Smyrna, Georgia 30082; <www.rootsweb.com/~gashgs/>

Sons of the American Revolution, Georgia Society; 2869 Reese Rd.; Columbus, Georgia 31907

South Georgia Genealogical Society; PO Box 3307; Thomasville, Georgia 31799.3307

Southwest Georgia Genealogical Society; PO Box 4672; Albany, Georgia 31706;

Southwest Georgia Regional Library; Shotwell at Monroe; Bainbridge, Georgia 31717

Sparta-Hancock County Historical Society; 353 E. Broad St.; Sparta, Georgia 31087

Statesboro Regional Library; 124 S. Main St.; Statesboro, Georgia 30458

Stephens County Historical Society; PO Box 125; Toccoa, Georgia 30577

Taliaferro County Historical Society; PO Box 32; Crawfordville, Georgia 30631

Tattnall County Historical Society; PO Box 2012; Reidsville, Georgia 30453

Taylor County Historical.Genealogical Society; PO Box 1925; Butler, Georgia 31006

Terrell County Historic Preservation Society; PO Box 63; Dawson, Georgia 31742

The Genealogical Society of Henry & Clayton Counties, Inc.; PO Box 1296, 71 Macon St.; McDonough, Georgia 30253; <www.rootsweb.com/~gagshcc/>

The Historical Society of Colquitt County, Inc.; PO Box 1961; Moultrie, Georgia 31776-1961

The Historical Society of Douglas County, Inc.; PO Box 2018; Douglasville, Georgia 30133; 770.942.0395

The Historical Society of Walton County, Inc.; PO Box 1733; Monroe, Georgia 30655

Thomas County Historical Society; PO Box 1922; Thomasville, Georgia 31799; 229.226.7466; <www.rose.net/~history/index.htm>

Thomaston-Upson Archives; PO Box 1137; Thomaston, Georgia 30286.0015; <alltel.net/~tuarch>

Thomasville Gen., Hist. & Fine Arts Library, Inc.; PO Box 1597; 135 N. Broad St.; Thomasville, Georgia 31799; 912.226.9640; Fax 912.226.3199

Thronateeska Heritage Center; 100 Roosevelt Ave.; Albany, Georgia 31701; <www.heritagecenter.org>

Toombs County Historical Society; PO Box 2825; Vidalia, Georgia 30474

Treutlen County Historical Society, Inc.; 206 Second St., S.; Soperton, Georgia 30457

Troup County Historical Society; 136 Main Street; PO Box 1051; LaGrange, Georgia 30241;

Tybee Island Historical Society; PO Box 366; Tybee Island, Georgia 31328

Union County Historical Society; PO Box 35; Blairsville, Georgia 30514.0035; <www.ngeorgia.com/uchs.html>

Upson Historical Society; PO Box 363; Thomaston, Georgia 30296; <www.rootsweb.com/~gauhs/>

Valdosta Chapter, GASSAR; 2520 Jerry Jones Dr.; Valdosta, Georgia 31602-1645; 229.242.5087

Vienna Historic Preservation Society; 1321 E. Union St.; Vienna, Georgia 31092; <www.historicvienna.or>

Walker County Historical Society; PO Box 707; Lafayette, Georgia 30728

Washington County Historical Society; PO Box 6088; Sandersville, Georgia 31082

Washington Memorial Library; 1180 Washington Ave; Macon, Georgia 31201

Wayne County Historical Society; 125 N. East Broad St.; Jesup, Georgia 31546

West Georgia Genealogical Society; c/o Troup County Archives; PO Box 1051; LaGrange, Georgia 30241

White County Historical Society; PO Box 1139; Cleveland, Georgia 30528

Whitfield-Murray Historical Society; Crown Garden and Archives; 715 Chattanooga Ave.; Dalton, Georgia 30720

Wilkinson County Historical Society; PO Box 159; Gordon, Georgia 31031

William Few Chapter, GASSAR; 4850 Wrightsboro Road; Grovetown, Georgia 30813; 706.860.2205

William Miller Chapter, GASSAR; 1200 Pruitt Dr.; Waycross, Georgia 31501-6065; 912.283.4071

Wiregrass Genealogical Society; 45 25th Street; Eastman, Georgia 31023; 478.272.5424; <www.rootsweb.com/~gawgs/>

Worth County Historical Society; PO Box 5073; Sylvester, Georgia 31791

Bibliography and Record Sources

General Sources

Adams, Marilyn. *Georgia Local and Family History Sources in Print.* Clarkston, Georgia: Heritage Research, 1982.

Alexander, Adele Logan. *Ambiguous Lives: Free Women of Color in Rural Georgia, 1789-1879.* Fayetteville, Ark.: University of Arkansas Press, 1991.

An Index to Georgia Tax Digests. 5 vols. Spartanburg, South Carolina: The Reprint Co., 1986.

Austin, Jeanette H. *Georgia Bible Records.* Baltimore: Genealogical Publishing Co., 1985.

Austin, Jeanette Holland. *Georgia Institute Records.* Baltimore: Genealogical Publishing Co., 1986.

Austin, Jeanette Holland. *The Georgians: Genealogies of Pioneer Families.* (1984), Reprint, Baltimore: Genealogical Publishing, 1986.

Biographical Souvenir of the States of Georgia and Florida. Chicago: F.A. Battey and Co., 1889.

Blair, Ruth. *Some Early Tax Digests of Georgia.* (1926) Reprint, Greenville, South Carolina: Southern Historical Press, 1971.

Bragg. *Joe Brown's Army: The Georgia State Line, 1862-1865.* 1987. Galveston, Texas: Frontier Press, 1987.

Brandenburg, John David, and Rita Binkley Worthy. *Index to Georgia's 1867-1868 Returns of Qualified Voters and Registration Oath Books (White).* 1995. Atlanta, Georgia: the authors, 1995.

Bryan, Mary G. *Passports Issued by Governors of Georgia, 1785-1809.* Arlington, Virginia: National Genealogical Society, n.d.

Bryan, Mary G., and William H. Dumont. *Passports Issued by Governors of Georgia, 1810 to 1829...* Arlington VA; National Genealogical Society, n.d.

Campbell, Jesse H. *Georgia Baptists: Historical and Biographical* (1847) Reprint, Greenville, South Carolina: Southern Historical Press, 1993.

Candler, Allen D., et al. *The Colonial Records of the State of Georgia, 1732-1784.* 32 vols. Atlanta, Georgia: State Printers, 1904-89.

Coleman, Kenneth. *Dictionary of Georgia Biography.* Athens: University of Georgia Press, 1983.

Coulter, E. Merton, and Albert B. Saye. *A List of the Early Settlers of Georgia.* (1949, 1967) 2nd ed. Baltimore: Clearfield Co., 1996.

Davis, *The Fledgling Province: Social and Cultural Life in Colonial Georgia, 1733-1776.* Galveston, Texas: Frontier Press, 1976.

Davis, Robert Scott, Jr. *A Researcher's Library of Georgia History, Genealogy, and Records Sources, Volt I.* Greenville, South Carolina: Southern Historical Press, 1987.

Davis, Robert Scott, Jr. *A Researcher's Library of Georgia History, Genealogy, and Records Sources, Vol. II.* Greenville, South Carolina: Southern Historical Press, 1991.

Davis, Robert Scott, Jr. *Research in Georgia: With a Special Emphasis Upon the Georgia Department of Archives and History.* (1981) Greenville, South Carolina: Southern Historical Press, 1991.

Davis, Robert Scott, Jr. *The Georgia Black Book, Volume I: Morbid, Macabre, and Disgusting Records of Genealogical Value.* (1982) Reprint, Greenville, South Carolina: Southern Historical Press, 1992.

Davis, Robert Scott, Jr. *Research in Georgia.* Easley, S.C.: Southern Historical Press, 1981.

Davis, Robert Scott. *A Guide to Native American (Indian) Research Sources at the Georgia Department of Archives and History.* Jasper, Georgia: R.S. Davis, 1985.

Davis, Robert Scott. *Georgians Past: Special Files of Georgia Settlers and Citizens, Subjects and Counties, 1733-1970s.* Milledgeville, Georgia: Boyd Pub., 1997.

Dorsey, James E. *Georgia Genealogy and Local History: A Bibliography.* Spartanburg, South Carolina: Reprint Co., 1983.

Dumont, William H. *Colonial Georgia Genealogical Data 1748-1783.* Arlington, Virginia: National Genealogical Society, n.d.

Early Georgia settlers, 1700s-1800s. [S.l.]: Brøderbund, 2000. CD ROM.

Fries, Adelaide L. *The Moravians in Georgia, 1735-1740.* (1905) Reprint. Baltimore, Maryland: Clearfield Co., 1993.

Genealogical Material from Legal Notices in Early Georgia Newspapers. Greenville, South Carolina: Southern Historical Press, 1989.

Gentry, Lelia Thornton. *Historical Collections of the Georgia Chapters Daughters of the American Revolution. Volt 4: Old Bible Records and Land Lotteries.* (1932) Reprint. 1995. Baltimore, Maryland: Clearfield Co., 1995.

Georgia Biographical Dictionary: People of All Times and Places Who Have Been Important to the History and Life of the State. New York: Somerset Pub., 1994.

Georgia Department of Archives and History. *A Preliminary Guide to Eighteenth-Century Records Held by the Georgia Department of Archives and History.* Atlanta: The Department, 1976.

Georgia Newspapers on Microfilm at the UGA Libraries: A Listing of Georgia Newspaper Holdings on Microfilm in the University of Georgia Libraries. (n.p.: 1978.)

Georgia Pioneers. 23 vols. Albany, Georgia: Georgia Pioneers Genealogical Society, 1964-1987.

Georgia Research Outline. Series US-States., no. 11. Salt Lake City: Family History Library, 1988.

Georgia. State Tax Commissioner. *Index to Tax Digests, 1787-1899.* Salt Lake City: Filmed by the Genealogical Society of Utah, 1947.

Gilmer, Gov. George R. *Gilmer's Georgians (Sketches of Early Settlers of Upper Georgia, the Cherokees and the Author).* (1855, 1926) Reprint. Athens, Georgia: Iberian Publishing,

Grice, Warren. *Georgia Through Two Centuries.* 3 vols. New York: Lewis Historical Pub. Co., [1966].

Harwell, Richard Barksdale, comp. *Confederate Imprints at the Georgia Historical Society.* Savannah, *Georgia:* Georgia Historical Society, 1975.

Hawes, Lilla M., and Karen E. Osvald, comps. *Checklist of Eighteenth Century Manuscripts in the Georgia Historical Society.* Savannah, Georgia: Georgia Historical Society, 1976.

Hawes, Lilla Mills, and Albert S. Britt, Jr., eds. *The Search for Georgia's Colonial Records.* Savannah, Georgia: Georgia, 1976.

Higgins, Margaret Elliott, ed. *Georgia Genealogical Gems.* Arlington, Virginia; National Genealogical Society.

Historical Collections of Georgia Chapters Daughters of the American Revolution, Vol. 1: Seventeen Georgia Counties. (1926, 1931). Reprint. Baltimore: Clearfield Co., 1995.

History of the Baptist Denomination in Georgia. Atlanta: J.P. Harrison & Co., 1881.

Hollingsworth, Leon S. *Leon S. Hollingsworth Genealogical Card File.* Atlanta, Georgia: R.J. Taylor, Jr. Foundation, 1980.

Howell, Clark. *History of Georgia.* 4 vols. Chicago: S.J. Clarke Pub. Co., 1926.

Huxford, Folks. *Pioneers of Wiregrass Georgia.* 9 vols. Homerville, Georgia: F. Huxford, 1951-93.

Inventory of the Church Archives of Georgia: Atlanta Association of Baptist Churches. Atlanta: Georgia Historical Records Survey, 1941.

Jones, George F. *The Germans of Colonial Georgia, 1733-1783.* Rev. ed., Baltimore: Clearfield Company, 1996.

Knight, Lucian Lamar. *A Standard History of Georgia and Georgians.* 6 vols. Chicago: Lewis Publishing Co., 1917.

Lawrence, Harold. *Methodist Preachers in Georgia 1783-1900.* Tignall, Georgia: Boyd Pub., 1984.

Lucas, Silas Emmett, Jr. *Some Georgia County Records.* 7 vols. Reprint. Greenville, South Carolina: Southern Historical Press, 1991-94.

Memoirs of Georgia: Containing Historical Accounts of the State's Civil, Military, Industrial and Professional Interests, and Personal Sketches of Many of Its People. 2 vols. Atlanta: Southern Historical Association, 1895.

Miller, Zell. *Great Georgians.* Franklin Springs, Georgia: Advocate Press, 1983.

Northen, William J. *Men of Mark in Georgia: A Complete and Elaborate History of the State from its Settlement to the Present Time, Chiefly Told in Biographies and Autobiographies of the Most Eminent Men of Each Period of Georgia's Progress and Development.* 7 vols. 1907-12. Reprint, Spartanburg, South Carolina: The Reprint Co., 1974.

Robertson, David H. *Georgia Genealogical Research: A Practical Guide.* Stone Mountain, Georgia: David H. Robertson, 1989.

Rowland, Arthur Ray, and James E. Dorsey. *A Bibliography of the Writings on Georgia History 1990-1970.* Rev. ed. Spartanburg, South Carolina: The Reprint Company Publishers, 1978.

Schweitzer, George K. *Georgia Genealogical Research.* Knoxville, Tennessee: George K. Schweitzer, 1987.

Simpson, John Eddins. *Georgia History: A Bibliography.* Metuchen, NJ: Scarecrow Press, 1976.

Smith, George Gillman. *The Story of Georgia and the Georgia People, 1732 to 1860.* 2nd ed. (ca.1901) Reprint. Baltimore: Clearfield Co., 1968.

Southerland, Henry Deleon, Jr., and Jerry Elijah Brown. *The Federal Road Through Georgia, the Creek Nation, and Alabama, 1806-1836.* Galveston, Texas: Frontier Press, 1989.

Strobe, P.A. *Saltzbergers and Their Descendants, Being the History of a Colony of German, Lutheran, Protestants Who Emigrated to Georgia in 1734.* (1855) Reprint. Greenville, South Carolina: Southern Historical Press, 1980.

Subject and Surname Index to Newspapers (Daily Georgian, Etc.). Atlanta, Georgia: Department of Archives and History. Salt Lake City: Filmed by the Genealogical Society of Utah, 1960.

Warnock, Robert Holcomb. *Georgia Sources for Family History.* Atlanta, Georgia: Georgia Genealogical Society, 1995.

Warren, Mary Bondurant, and Eve B. Weeks. *Whites Among the Cherokees.* Athens, Georgia: Iberian Publishing Co., n.d.

Warren, Mary Bondurant, and Jack Moreland Jones. *Georgia Governor and Council Journal, 1761-1767.* Athens, Georgia: Iberian Publishing Co., 1992.

White, George. *Historical Collections of Georgia. Containing the Most Interesting Facts, Traditions, Biographical Sketches, Etc., Relating to its History and Antiquities, from its First Settlement to the Present Time.* 3rd Edition. Reprint. Baltimore: Clearfield Co., 1996.

Williams. *The Georgia Gold Rush; Twenty-Niners, Cherokees, and Gold Fever.* Galveston, Texas: Frontier Press, 1993.

Wood, Virginia Steele, and Ralph Van Wood, eds. *The Reuben King Journal, 1800-1806.* 1971. Savannah, Georgia: The Georgia Historical Society, 1971.

WPA Georgia: *The WPA Guide to its Town and Countryside.* Galveston, Texas: Frontier Press, n.d.

Wylly, Charles Spalding. *The Seed that Was Sown in the Colony of Georgia: The Harvest and the Aftermath, 1740-1870.* New York and Washington: Neale Publishing, 1910.

Atlases, Maps and Gazetteers

Blake, Janice Gayle. *Pre-Nineteenth Century Maps in the Collection of the Georgia Surveyor General Department.* Atlanta: Surveyor General Department, 1976.

Bonner, James C. *Atlas for Georgia History.* Milledgeville, Georgia: Georgia College Duplicating Department, 1969.

Bryant, Pat. *Georgia Counties: Their Changing Boundaries,* 2d ed. Atlanta: State Printing Office, 1983.

Candler, Allen D. Georgia: *Comprising Sketches of Counties, Towns, Events, Institutions, and Persons, Arranged in Cyclopedic Form.* 4 vols. Atlanta: State Historical Assoc., 1906.

Georgia. Surveyor General. *Surveyor-General's Maps and Maps of Counties of Georgia, Arranged in Alphabetical Order.* Atlanta: Georgia Department of State, Microfilm division, [19–].

Goff, John H. *Placenames of Georgia.* Athens, Georgia: University of Georgia Press, 1975.

Hall. *Original County Map of Georgia: Showing Present and Original Counties and Land Districts.* Atlanta: Hall Brothers, 1895.

Hemperley, Marion R. *Cities, Towns, and Communities of Georgia Between 1847-1962: 8,500 Places and the County in Which Located.* Easley, South Carolina: Southern Historical Press, 1980.

Hemperley, Marion R. *Georgia Early Roads and Trails Circa 1730-1850.* Atlanta: Georgia Surveyor General Department, 1979.

Hemperley, Marion R. *Map of Colonial Georgia, 1773-1777.* Atlanta: Georgia Surveyor General Department, 1979.

Hodler, Thomas W., and Howard A. Schretter. *The Atlas of Georgia.* Athens, Georgia: Institute of Community and Area Development, 1986.

Johnsen, Margaret A. *Nineteenth Century Maps in the Collection of the Georgia Surveyor General Department.* Atlanta: Surveyor General Department, 1981.

Krakow, Kenneth K. *Georgia Place-Names.* Macon, Georgia: Winship Press, 1975.

Long, John H. *Atlas of Historical County Boundaries: Georgia.* New York: Simon & Schuster, 2001.

Sherwood, Adiel. *A Gazetteer of the State of Georgia Containing a Particular Description of the State, Its Resources, counties, Towns, Villages and Whatever is Usual in Statistical Works.* 4th ed. Rev. and corrected. Atlanta: Cherokee Printing Co., 1970.

Census Records

Available Census Records and Census Substitutes

Federal Census 1820 (except Franklin, Rabun and Twiggs Counties), 1830, 1840, 1850, 1860, 1870, 1880, 1900, 1910, 1920, 1930.

Federal Mortality Schedules 1850, 1860, 1870, 1880.

Early Settlers 1733-1742.

Land Allotments 1741-1754.

Land Lottery 1805, 1807, 1820, 1821, 1827, 1832.

Reconstructed Census 1790.

Cornell, Nancy J. *1864 Census for Reorganizing the Georgia Militia.* Baltimore: Genealogical Publishing Co., 2000.

De Lamar, Marie, and Elisabeth Rothstein. *The Reconstructed 1790 Census of Georgia.* (1976), Reprint, Baltimore: Genealogical Publishing, 1989.

Dollarhide, William. *The Census Book: A Genealogist's Guide to Federal Census Facts, Schedules and Indexes.* Bountiful, Utah: Heritage Quest, 1999.

Kemp, Thomas Jay. *The American Census Handbook.* Wilmington, DE: Scholarly Resources, Inc., 2001.

Lainhart, Ann S. *State Census Records.* Baltimore: Genealogical Publishing Co., Inc., 1992.

Substitutes for Georgia's Lost 1790 Census. Albany, Georgia: Delwyn Assoc., 1975.

Szucs, Loretto Dennis, and Matthew Wright. *Finding Answers in U.S. Census Records.* Ancestry Publishing, 2001.

Taylor, R. J., Jr. *An Index to Georgia Tax Digests.* 5 vols. Spartanburg, South Carolina: The Reprint Co., 1986, 1986.

Thorndale, William, and William Dollarhide. *Map Guide to the U.S. Federal Censuses, 1790-1920.* Baltimore: Genealogical Publishing Co., 1987.

Court Records, Probate and Wills

Abstracts of Colonial Wills of the State of Georgia, 1733-1777. Spartanburg, South Carolina: The Reprint Co., 1981.

Austin, Jeanette Holland. *Index to Georgia Wills.* (1976) Reprint. Greenville, South Carolina: Southern Historical Press, 1985.

Austin, Jeanette Holland. *Georgia Intestate Records.* (1986) Reprint. Baltimore: Genealogical Publishing., 1995.

Brooke, Ted O. *In the Name of God, Amen: Georgia Wills, 1733-1860: An Index.* Atlanta: Pilgrim Press, 1976.

Candler, Allen D. *Statutes Enacted by the Royal Legislature of Georgia From Its First Session in 1754 to 1768.* Atlanta: The Legislature, 1910.

Early Colonial Records of Georgia: Including Wills, Letters of Administration, Inventories of Estates, Letters of Guardianship, Probate and Administration Letters, Minutes, Appraisements, etc., 1754-1778. Microreproduction of original ms. at the State Archives, Atlanta, Georgia. Salt Lake City: Filmed by the Genealogical Society of Utah, 1957. 7 microfilm.

Early Georgia Wills. Salt Lake City: American Heritage Research, 1976.

Geiger, Linda A. Woodward. *Index to Georgia's Federal Naturalization Records to 1950 (Excluding Military Petitions).* Atlanta, Georgia: Georgia Genealogical Society, 1996.

Index to Probate Records of Colonial Georgia, 1733-1778. Atlanta: R.J. Taylor, Jr., Foundation, 1983.

Lane, Jane Warren Hollingsworth. *Court Records, Georgia Counties.* Salt Lake City: Filmed by the Genealogical Society of Utah, 1940, 1971.

Thaxton, Donna B. *Georgia Indian Depredation Claims.* Americus, Georgia: Thaxton Company, 1988.

Emigration, Immigration, Migration and Naturalization

Bryan, Mary. *Passports Issued by Georgia Governors, 1785-1809, and 1810-1820.* 2 vols. Washington, D.C.: National Genealogical Society, 1959, 1964.

Hemperley, Marion. "Federal Naturalization Oaths: Savannah Georgia, 1790-1860." *Georgia Historical Quarterly,* 51, no. 4 (1967): 454-87.

Immigrants from Great Britain to the Georgia Colony. Morrow, Georgia: Genealogical Enterprises, 1970.

Miller, Stephen Franks. *The Bench and Bar of Georgia: Memoirs and Sketches with an Appendix, Containing a Court Roll From 1790 to 1857, etc.* 2 cols. Philadelphia: J.B. Lippincott, 1858.

United States. Circuit Court (Georgia). *Minutes, 1790-1842 ; Index to Plaintiffs and Defendants, 1790-1860.* Microreproduction of original records which are part of the Records of District Courts of the United States, Record Group 21, and are housed in the Federal Archives and Records Center, Atlanta, Georgia. Washington: National Archives and Record Service, [198-?]. 3 microfilm.

United States. District Court (Alabama: Southern District*).* *Declarations of Intentions, Naturalizations, and Petitions, 1855-1960.* Microfilm of originals at the National Archives in East Point, Georgia. Salt Lake City: Filmed by the Genealogical Society of Utah, 1987-1989. 9 microfilm.

United States. District Court (Georgia: Northern District: Atlanta). *Naturalization Certificate Stubs, 1907-1926.* Microfilm of original housed at the National Archives in East Point, Georgia. Salt Lake City: Filmed by the Genealogical Society of Utah, 1989.

United States. District Court (Georgia: Savannah District*).* *Index to Aliens Admitted to Citizenship, 1906-1989.* Microreproduction of original records filmed at the U. S. Courthouse, Savannah, Georgia. Salt Lake City: Filmed by the Genealogical Society of Utah, 1989. 2 microfilm.

United States. District Court (Georgia: Southern District). *General Index Books, 1789-1928 ; Minute Books and Bench Dockets, 1789-1870.* Microreproduction of original records which are part of the Records of District Courts of the United States, Record Group 21, and are housed in the Atlanta Regional Branch of the National Archives, East Point, Georgia. Washington: National Archives and Record Service, 1981. 3 microfilm.

United States. District Court (Georgia: Southern District). *Naturalization Records, 1790-1940.* Microreproduction of original records filmed at the United States Courthouse, Savannah, Georgia. Salt Lake City: Filmed by the Genealogical Society of Utah, 1990. 7 microfilm.

United States. Immigration and Naturalization Service. *Index to Passenger Lists of Vessels Arriving At Miscellaneous Ports in Alabama, Florida, Georgia, and South Carolina, 1890-1924.* Washington, D.C.: Microphotographed by Immigration and Naturalization Service, 1957.

United States. Immigration and Naturalization Service. *Savannah Passenger Lists* [United States]: Microphotographed by Immigration and Naturalization Service, 1946.

Land and Property

Bryant, Pat. *Entry of Claims for Georgia Landholders, 1733-1755.* Atlanta: State Printing Office, 1975.

Cadle, Farris W. *Georgia Land Surveying History and Law.* Athens, Georgia: University of Georgia Press, 1991.

Davis, Robert S., Jr., and Silas E. Lucas, comps. *The Georgia Land Lottery Papers, 1805-1914: Genealogical Data from the Loose Papers Filed in the Georgia Surveyor General Office Concerning the Lots Won in the State Land Lotteries and the People Who Won Them.* Easley, S.C. Southern Historical Press, 1979.

Davis, Robert Scott, Jr., *The 1833 Land Lottery of Georgia and Other Missing Names of Winners in the Georgia Land Lotteries.* Greenville, South Carolina: Southern Historical Press, 1991.

Georgia (Colony). Governor. *Colonial Records of Georgia, 1750-1829.* Microreproduction of original ms. at the State Archives, Atlanta, Georgia. (Salt Lake City: Filmed by the Genealogical Society of Utah, 1957). 25 microfilm.

Georgia, Department of Archives and History. *Revolutionary Soldiers Receipts for Georgia Bounty Grants.* Atlanta, Georgia: Foote and Davies Co., 1928.

Georgia, Secretary of State. *Authentic List of All Land Lottery Grants Made to Veterans of the Revolutionary War by the State of Georgia, Taken from Official State Records in the Surveyor-General Department, Housed in the Georgia Department of Archives and History, Atlanta, GA, 1955.* 2nd ed. Atlanta, Georgia: Secretary of State, 1966.

Georgia. Department of State. *Land Office Records, Index.* Atlanta: Georgia Department of State, Microfilm Division, [19–].

Georgia. Surveyor General *Land Lottery Records, 1841-1870; Surveyor's Filed Notes, 1806-1860.* Atlanta: Georgia Dept. of Archives and History, [1967].

Georgia. Surveyor General. *Headrights and Land Grants of Georgia, 1756-1939.* Atlanta: Georgia Department of State, Microfilm Division, 1953-1954.

Georgia. Surveyor General. *Land Lottery Surveys.* Atlanta: Georgia Dept. Archives and History, [1967].

Georgia. Surveyor General. *Reverted Lottery Land Records, 1815-1872; Register of Grants, 1834-1847.* Atlanta: State Dept. of Archives and History, 1967.

Georgia. Surveyor General. *Surveyor-General's Records, Headright Surveys.* Atlanta: Georgia Department of State, Microfilm Division, [19–].

Hemperley, Marion R. *The Georgia Surveyor General Department: A History and Inventory of Georgia's Land Office.* Atlanta: State Printing Office, 1982.

Hone, Wade E. *Land and Property Research in the United States.* Salt Lake City: Ancestry Incorporated, 1997.

Houston, Martha Lou. *Reprint of Official Register of Land Lottery of Georgia 1827.* (1928) Reprint. Baltimore: Clearfield Co., 1992.

Index to the Headright and Bounty Grants of Georgia 1756-1909. Vidalia, Georgia: Georgia Genealogical Reprints, 1970.

Lucas, Silas Emmett, Jr. *Index to the Headright and Bounty Grants in Georgia from 1756-1909.* Revised Edition. Greenville, South Carolina: Southern Historical Press, 1992.

Lucas, Silas Emmett, Jr. *The 1827 Land Lottery of Georgia.* (1975) Reprint. Greenville, South Carolina: Southern Historical Press, 1986.

Lucas, Silas Emmett, Jr. *The 1832 Gold Lottery of Georgia: Containing a List of the Fortunate Drawers in Said Lottery.* Easley, South Carolina: Southern Historical Press, 1976.

Lucas, Silas Emmett, Jr. *The Fourth or 1821 Land Lotteries of Georgia.* (1973), Reprint. Greenville, South Carolina: Southern Historical Press, 1986.

Lucas, Silas Emmett, Jr. *The Second or 1807 Land Lottery of Georgia.* (1968) Reprint, Greenville, South Carolina: Southern Historical Press, 1987.

Lucas, Silas Emmett, Jr. *The Third or 1820 Land Lotteries of Georgia.* (1983) Reprint. Greenville, South Carolina: Southern Historical Press, 1986.

Lucas, Silas Emmett, Jr., and Robert Scott Davis, Jr. eds. *The Georgia Land Lottery Papers, 1805-1914.* (1979) Reprint. Greenville, South Carolina: Southern Historical Press, 1987.

Mathews, Nathan, and Kaydee Mathews. *Abstracts of Georgia Land Plat Books A & B.* Fayetteville, Georgia: Nathan and Kaydee Mathews, 1995.

Richardson, Marian M., and Jessie J. Mize. *1832 Cherokee Land Lottery, Index to Revolutionary Soldiers, Their Widows and Orphans Who Were Fortunate Drawers.* Danielsville, Georgia: Heritage Press, 1969.

Sears, Joan N. *The First One Hundred Years of Town Planning in Georgia.* Atlanta: Cherokee Pub. Co., 1979.

Smith, James F. *The 1832 Cherokee Land Lottery of Georgia.* (1838) Reprint. Greenville, South Carolina: Southern Historical Press, 1991.

Southern California Genealogical Society. *Land! Georgia Land Lotteries: Oregon Donation Land: Oregon Donation Land: Oklahoma Land Rushes.* Burbank CA: Southern California Genealogical Society, n.d.

Warren, Mary Bondurant. *1832 Cherokee Gold Lottery.* Athens, Georgia: Iberian Publishing Co., n.d.

Wood, Ralph V., and Virginia S. Wood. *The 1805 Land Lottery of Georgia.* Cambridge MA: Greenwood Press, 1964.

Military

Arnold, H. Ross, and Hank Burnham, comps. *Georgia Revolutionary War Soldiers' Graves.* 2 vols. Athens, Georgia: Iberian Publishing Co., 1993.

Boss, Bert E. *The Georgia State Memorial Book* (n.p.: 1921.)

Brightwell, Juanita S. *Index to the Confederate Records of Georgia.* Spartanburg, South Carolina: Reprint Co., 1982.

Candler, Allen D. *The Confederate Records of the State of Georgia.* Atlanta, Georgia: C.P. Byrd, state printer, 1909-11.

Candler, Allen D. *The Revolutionary Records of the State of Georgia.* 3 vols. Atlanta, Ga.: The Franklin-Turner Co., 1908.

Clark, Murtie June. *Colonial Soldiers of the South, 1732-1774.* Baltimore: Genealogical Publishing Co., 1983.

Davis, Robert Scott, Jr. *Georgia Citizens and Soldiers of the American Revolution.* (1979). Greenville, South Carolina: Southern Historical Press, 1983.

Georgia Adjutant Generals Office. *Military Records, 1782-1899.* 6 vols. [n.p.]. (Salt Lake City: Filmed by the Genealogical Society of Utah, 1957).

Georgia Executive Department. *Military Commissions in the State Militia, 1798-1860.* Microfilm of originals in the state archives at Atlanta, Georgia. (Salt Lake City: Filmed by the Genealogical Society of Utah, 1957). 18 microfilm.

Georgia, 1851-1900. [S.l.]: Brøderbund, 1998. CD ROM.

Georgia, State Division of Confederate Pensions and Records. *Roster of the Confederate Soldiers of Georgia 1861-1865.* Reprint, Hapeville, Georgia: Logina & Porter, 1959-64.

Georgia. Department of Archives and History. *Confederate Pension Rolls.* Atlanta: Filmed by the State of Georgia Department of Archives and History, 1963. Microfilm, 634 rolls.

Georgia. Department of Health and Vital Statistics (Atlanta, Georgia). *Death index, 1919-1993.* (Salt Lake City: Filmed by the Genealogical Society of Utah, 1995). 381 microfiche.

Georgia. Department of Health and Vital Statistics (Atlanta, Georgia). *Divorce Register Index, 1965-1992.* (Salt Lake City: Filmed by the Genealogical Society of Utah, 1995). 149 microfiche.

Georgia. Department of Health and Vital Statistics (Atlanta, Georgia). *Marriage Register Index, 1964-1992.* Salt Lake City: Filmed by the Genealogical Society of Utah, 1995. 341 microfiche.

Georgia. Secretary of State. *Georgia Military Records, 1779-1842.* Microfilm of originals in the state archives at Atlanta, Georgia. (Salt Lake City: Filmed by the Genealogical Society of Utah, 1947)s. 3 microfilm.

Hemperley, Marion R. *Military Certificates of Georgia, 1776-1800.* Atlanta: State Printing Office, 1983.

Hendersen, Lillian, comp. *Roster of the Confederate Soldiers of Georgia, 1861-65,* 6 vols. Hapeville, Georgia: Longino & Porter, Inc., 1960-64.

Houston, Martha Lou. *Six Hundred Revolutionary Soldiers and Widows of Revolutionary Soldiers Living in Georgia, 1827-1828.* Athens, Georgia: Heritage Press, 1965.

Index to the Headright Bounty Grants, 1756-1909. Rev. ed. Greenville, South Carolina: Southern Historical Press, 1992.

Jackson, Ronald Vern. *Georgia 1860 Mortality.* North Salt Lake, Utah: Accelerated Indexing Systems International, 1986.

Jackson, Ronald Vern. *Mortality Schedule Georgia 1850.* Bountiful, Utah: Accelerated Indexing Systems, 1979.

Johnson, James M. *Militiamen, Rangers, and Redcoats: The Military in Georgia, 1754-1776.* Macon, Georgia: Mercer University Press, 1992.

Johnson. *Militiamen, Rangers, and Redcoats; The Military in Georgia, 1754-1776.* Galveston, Texas: Frontier Press, 1992.

Knight, Lucian L. *Georgia's Roster of the Revolution. Containing a List of the State Defenders: Officers and Men; Partisans and Regulars; Whether Enlisted from Georgia or Settled in Georgia After the Close of Hostilities.* (1920) Reprint. Baltimore: Clearfield Co, 1996.

Kratovil, Judy Swaim. *Index to War of 1812 Service Records for Volunteer Soldiers from Georgia.* Atlanta, Georgia: J. S. Kratovil, 1986, 1986.

McCall, Mrs. Howard H. *Roster of Revolutionary Soldiers in Georgia.* 3 vols. Reprint. Baltimore: Clearfield Co., 1996.

Miles, Jim. *Georgia Civil War Sites: A Comprehensive Guide to 300 Civil War Battlefields, Forts, Museums, and Cemeteries in Georgia.* Warner Robins, Georgia: J & R Graphics, c1987.

Revolutionary Soldier's Receipts for Georgia Bounty Grants. Atlanta: Foote and Davies Co., 1928.

Sifakis. *Compendium of Confederate Armies: South Carolina and Georgia.* Galveston, Texas: Frontier Press, 1995.

Thaxton, Carlton J. *A Roster of Spanish-American War Soldiers for Georgia.* Americus, Georgia: Carlton Thaxton, 1984.

United States. Selective Service System. *Georgia, World War I Selective Service System Draft Registration Cards, 1917-1918.* National Archives Microfilm Publications, M1509. Washington, D.C.: National Archives, 1987-1988.

United States. War Department. Office of Adjutant General. *Georgia World War I Statement of Service Summary Card Files, ca. 1920-1929.* Microreproduction of originals housed in the Department of Archives and History in Atlanta, Georgia. (Salt Lake City: Filmed by the Genealogical Society of Utah, 2001). 7 microfilm.

Volunteer Soldiers in the Cherokee War–1836-1839. Signal Mountain TN: Mountain Press, n.d.

Vital and Cemetery Records

Austin, Jeanette Holland. *30,638 Burials in Georgia.* Baltimore: Genealogical Publishing, 1995.

Brooke, Ted O. *Georgia Cemetery Directory and Bibliography of Georgia Cemetery Reference Sources.* Marietta, Georgia: T.O. Brooke, 1985.

Cemetery Records of Georgia, 16 vols. Salt Lake City: Genealogical Society of Utah, 1946-52

Georgia Department of Archives and History, Atlanta, Georgia. *Marriages, 1805-1866; Marriage Index, 1805-1866.* Microfilm of originals at the state archives in Atlanta, Georgia. Salt Lake City: Filmed by the Genealogical Society of Utah, 1957. 3 microfilm.

Georgia Society of the Colonial Dames of America. *Some Early Epitaphs in Georgia.* Foreword and sketches by Mrs. Peter W. Meldrim. Durham, NC: Seeman Printery, 1924.

Guide to Public Vital Statistics Records in Georgia. Atlanta: Historical Records Survey, 1941.

Ingmire, Frances T. *Colonial Georgia Marriage Records from 1760-1810.* St. Louis Frances T. Ingmire, 1895.

Jacksonville Branch Genealogical Library (Florida). *Vital Records Card File for North Florida and South Georgia, 1895-1945.* Microfilm of records in the Jacksonville Branch Genealogical Library, Jacksonville, Florida. (Salt Lake City: Filmed by the Genealogical Society of Utah, 1977, 1980). 17 microfilm.

Lane, Mrs. Julian C., comp. *Marriage Records of Effingham County, Georgia, 1780-1875.* Statesboro, Georgia: Mrs. Julian C. Lane, 1940.

Liahona Research. *Georgia Marriages, 1801-1825: A Research Tool.* Bountiful, Utah: Precision Indexing, 1992.

Liahona Research. *Georgia Marriages, Early to 1800: A Research Tool.* Bountiful, Utah: Precision Indexing, 1990.

Maddox, Joseph T. *37,000 Early Georgia Marriages.* Irwinton, Georgia: Joseph T. Maddox, 1976.

Maddox, Joseph T. *Early Georgia Marriage Round-up.* Irwinton, Georgia: Joseph T. Maddox, 1975.

Maddox, Joseph T. *Early Georgia Marriages.* Irwinton, Georgia: Joseph T. Maddox, 1980.

Maddox, Joseph T., and Mary Carter. *40,000 Early Georgia Marriages.* Irwinton, Georgia: Joseph T. Maddox, 1977.

Marriages and Obituaries from Early Georgia Newspapers. Greenville, South Carolina: Southern Historical Press, 1989.

Overby, Mary McKeown. *Obituaries Published by "The Christian Index," 1822-1899.* Macon, Georgia: Georgia Baptist Historical Society, 1975, 1982.

Rocker, Willard. *Marriages and Obituaries from the Macon Messenger, 1818-1865.* Greenville, South Carolina: Southern Historical Press, 1988.

Shaw, Aurora. *1850 Georgia Mortality Schedule or Census.* Reprint. Greenville, South Carolina: Southern Historical Press, 1982.

United States Quartermaster's Department. *Roll of Honor: Names of Soldiers Who Died in Defense of the American Union, Interred in...* 27 vols. Government Printing Office, 1865-1871. Salt Lake City: Filmed by the Genealogical Society of Utah, 1981. 3 microfilm.

United States. Works Progress Administration (Georgia). *General Index to Savannah Newspapers, Savannah, Georgia, 1763-1845.* (Salt Lake City: Filmed by the Genealogical Society of Utah, 1959, 1989).

Warren, Mary B. *Marriages and Deaths 1763-1820. Abstracted from Extant Georgia Newspapers.* 2 vols. Danielsville, Georgia: Heritage Papers, 1968.

Warren, Mary B., ed. *Georgia Marriages 1811 Through 1820 Prepared from Extant Legal Records and Published Sources.* Danielsville, Georgia: Heritage Papers, 1988.

Warren, Mary Bondurant, and Sarah Fleming White. *[Georgia] Marriages and Deaths, 1820 to 1830, Abstracted from Extant Newspapers.* (1972). Reprint. Athens, Georgia: Iberian Publishing Co., 1893.

County Website	Map Index	Date Created	Parent County or Territory From Which Organized Address/Details
Appling plant.sgc.peachnet.edu/~jbellis/ genweb/appling/appling.html	**L9**	**15 Dec 1818**	**Creek Indian Lands** Appling County; 83 S Oak St; Baxley, GA 31513-2097; Ph. 912.367.8100 Details: (Rec begin 1879, some 1859; Pro Ct has b, m, d & bur rec: Clk Sup Ct has div, pro & ct rec)
Atkinson www.geocities.com/Heartland/Lane/3390/	**M7**	**15 Aug 1917**	**Coffee, Clinch** Atkinson County; PO Box 518; Pearson, GA 31642-0518; Ph. 912.422.3391 Details: (Clk Sup Ct has div, pro & ct rec from 1919; Pro Ct has b & d rec from 1929, m & land rec from 1919)
Bacon www.rootsweb.com/~gabacon/bchom.htm	**L8**	**27 Jul 1914**	**Appling, Pearce, Ware** Bacon County; 301 N Pierce St; PO Box 356; Alma, GA 31510-1957; Ph. 912.632.4915 Details: (Clk Sup Ct has div, ct & land rec from 1915; Pro Ct has b, m, d & pro rec from 1915)
Baker www.rootsweb.com/~gabaker/	**M4**	**12 Dec 1825**	**Early** Baker County; 1 Baker Pl; PO Box 607; Newton, GA 31770-0000; Ph. 912.734.3007 Details: (Pro Ct has b & d rec from 1930, m & pro rec from 1875; Clk Sup Ct has land, div & ct rec)
Baldwin www.genealogy-quest.com/ Georgia/Baldwin/	**H7**	**11 May 1803**	**Creek Indian Lands** Baldwin County; 121 N Wilkinson; Milledgeville, GA 31061-3346; Ph. 912.445.4791 Details: (Pro Ct has b, m, d, bur & pro rec; Co Clk has div, ct & land rec from 1861)
Banks www.rootsweb.com/~gabanks/	**D6**	**11 Dec 1858**	**Franklin, Habersham** Banks County; PO Box 130; Homer, GA 30547-0130; Ph. 706.677.2320 Details: (Pro Ct has b, m & pro rec; Clk Sup Ct has ct & land rec)
Barrow www.rootsweb.com/~gabarrow/	**E6**	**7 Jul 1914**	**Jackson, Walton, Gwinnett** Barrow County; 233 E Broad St; Winder, GA 30680-1973; Ph. 770.307.3005 Details: (Pro Ct has b, m, d, bur & pro rec; Clk Sup Ct has div, ct & land rec from 1915)
Bartow www.geocities.com/Heartland/Park/ 9465/bartowcoga.html	**E3**	**3 Dec 1832**	**Cherokee** Bartow County; 135 W Cherokee Ave; PO Box 543; Cartersville, GA 30120-0543; Ph. 770.387.5030 Details: (Formerly Cass Co. Name changed to Bartow 6 Dec 1861) (Pro Ct has b, m & pro rec; Clk Sup Ct has div rec from 1862, ct rec from 1869, land rec from 1837 & mil dis rec)
Ben Hill www.benhillcounty.com/	**L7**	**31 Jul 1906**	**Irwin, Wilcox** Ben Hill County; 401 E Central Ave; Fitzgerald, GA 31750; Ph. 229.426.5135 Details: (Co Clk has div, ct & land rec from 1907; Pro Judge has b, m, d, bur & pro rec)
Berrien www.rootsweb.com/~gaberrie/	**M7**	**25 Feb 1856**	**Lowndes, Coffee, Irwin** Berrien County; 105 E Washington Ave; PO Box 446; Nashville, GA 31639; Ph. 912.686.5421 Details: (Clk Sup Ct has div & ct rec from 1856 & land rec; Pro Ct has b & d rec from 1919, m & pro rec from 1856)
Bibb www.rootsweb.com/~gabibb/bibb.htm	**I5**	**9 Dec 1822**	**Jones, Monroe, Twiggs, Houston** Bibb County; 601 Mulberry St; Macon, GA 31201-2672; Ph. 912.749.6527 Details: (Co Hlth Dept has b, d & bur rec; Pro Ct has m & pro rec; Co Clk has div, ct & land rec from 1823)
Bleckley www.rootsweb.com/~gableckl/	**J6**	**30 Jul 1912**	**Pulaski** Bleckley County; 306 2nd St SE; Cochran, GA 31014-1633; Ph. 912.934.3200 Details: (Clk Sup Ct has div, pro, ct & land rec)
Brantley www.rootsweb.com/~gabrantl/	**N9**	**14 Aug 1920**	**Charlton, Pierce, Wayne** Brantley County; PO Box 398; Nahunta, GA 31553-0398; Ph. 912.462.5256 Details: (Clk Sup Ct has b, div, pro & ct rec from 1921)

County Website	Map Index	Date Created	Parent County or Territory From Which Organized / Address/Details
Brooks personal.mia.bellsouth.net/mia/ m/i/miamibig/brooks/	N6	11 Dec 1858	**Lowndes, Thomas** Brooks County; Hwy 76 & Hwy 33; PO Box 272; Quitman, GA 31643-0000; Ph. 912.263.5561 Details: (Clk of Cts has land rec from 1800's, div & ct rec; Pro Ct has m & pro rec; Co Hlth Dept has b & d rec)
Bryan www.rootsweb.com/~gabryan/	K11	19 Dec 1793	**Chatham** Bryan County; PO Box 430; Pembroke, GA 31321-0000; Ph. 912.653.3839 Details: (Pro Judge has m, pro, b & some d rec; Co Clk has div rec from 1920, ct & land rec from 1793)
Bulloch www.rootsweb.com/~gabulloc/	J10	8 Feb 1796	**Bryan, Screven** Bulloch County; 1 Courthouse Sq; PO Box 347; Statesboro, GA 30459; Ph. 912.764.6245 Details: (Pro Ct has b, m & pro rec; Clk Sup Ct has div & ct rec from 1891 & land rec from 1876)
Burke members.aol.com/J2525/index.html	H10	5 Feb 1777	**Original county organized from St. George Parish** Burke County; 111 E 6th St; PO Box 89; Waynesboro, GA 30830-0000; Ph. 706.554.2324 Details: (Courthouse burned in Jan 1856. All rec prior to that date destoryed) (Pro Ct has b & d rec from 1927, m & pro rec from 1856)
Butts www.lofthouse.com/USA/ga/butts/	G5	24 Dec 1825	**Henry, Monroe** Butts County; 25 Third St; PO Box 320; Jackson, GA 30233-0320; Ph. 770.775.8200 Details: (Pro Ct has b, m, d & pro rec; Clk Sup Ct has div, ct & land rec from 1825)
Calhoun members.tripod.com/~rakmun/	L3	20 Feb 1854	**Baker, Early** Calhoun County; 111 School St; PO Box 111; Morgan, GA 31766; Ph. 912.849.4835 Details: (Clk Sup Ct has div, land, mil & ct rec from 1854; Pro Ct has b, m, d, bur & pro rec)
Camden www.rootsweb.com/~gacamden/	N10	5 Feb 1777	**Original county organized from St. Thomas & St. Mary Parishes** Camden County; 4th St & Courthouse Sq; PO Box 99; Woodbine, GA 31569-0000; Ph. 912.576.5601 (Fire 1870, few rec lost) (Clk Sup Ct has div, ct & land rec; Pro Ct has b, m, d & pro rec)
Campbell www.rootsweb.com/~gacampbe/		20 Dec 1828	**Carroll, Coweta, De Kalb, Fayette** Details: (see Fulton) Merged into Fulton Co 1 Jan 1932
Candler www.rootsweb.com/~gacandle/	J9	18 Feb 1854	**Bulloch, Emanuel, Tattnall** Candler County; 705 N Lewis St; Metter, GA 30439-0000; Ph. 912.685.2835 Details: (Co Clk has b, m & d rec from 1915, div, ct & land rec from 1914)
Carroll carrollcountyga.com/	G2	11 Dec 1826	**Creek Indian Lands** Carroll County; 423 College St; PO Box 338; Carrollton, GA 30117; Ph. 770.830.5801 Details: (Clk Sup Ct has div rec from 1900, land & ct rec from 1828; Pro Ct has m & pro rec from 1827; Co Hlth Dept has b & d rec)
Cass www.geocities.com/Heartland/Park/ 9465/bartowcoga.html		3 Dec 1832	**Cherokee** Details: (see Bartow) Name changed to Bartow 6 Dec 1861
Catoosa www.catoosa.com/	B2	5 Dec 1853	**Walker, Whitfield** Catoosa County; 7694 Nashville St; Ringgold, GA 30736-1799; Ph. 706.965.2500 Details: (Clk Sup Ct has ct & div rec from 1853 & land rec; Pro Ct has m & pro rec from 1853)
Charlton www.rootsweb.com/~gacharlt/	N9	18 Feb 1854	**Camden** Charlton County; 100 Third St; Folkston, GA 31537-0000; Ph. 912.496.2549 Details: (Courthouse burned in 1877) (Pro Judge has b, m, d, bur & pro rec; Clk Sup Ct has div, ct & land rec from 1877)
Chatham www.co.chatham.ga.us/	K11	5 Feb 1777	**Original county organized from St. Phillip & Christ Church Parishes** Chatham County; 133 Montgomery St; Savannah, GA 31401-3230; Ph. 912.652.7127 Details: (Pro Ct has b, m, d & pro rec; Clk Sup Ct has div & ct rec from 1783, land rec from 1785 & nat rec from 1801)

County Website	Map Index	Date Created	Parent County or Territory From Which Organized Address/Details
Chattahoochee www2.netdoor.com/~cch/CHA/	J3	13 Feb 1854	**Muscogee, Marion** Chattahoochee County; PO Box 299; Cusseta, GA 31805-0000; Ph. 706.989.3602 Details: (Pro Ct has m & pro rec from 1854, b & d rec from 1919; Clk Sup Ct has div, ct & land rec from 1854)
Chattooga www.rootsweb.com/~gachatto/	D2	28 Dec 1838	**Floyd, Walker** Chattooga County; PO Box 211; Summerville, GA 30747-0211; Ph. 706.857.0700 Details: (Clk Cts has div rec from early 1900's & ct rec; Ord Office has b, m, d, bur & pro rec)
Cherokee www.rootsweb.com/~gacherok/	D4	26 Dec 1831	**Cherokee Lands** Cherokee County; 90 N St; Canton, GA 30114-2794; Ph. 770.479.1953 Details: (Clk Sup Ct has div, ct & land rec from 1833; Pro Ct has b, m, d, bur & pro rec)
Christ Church		1758	**Creek Cession of 1733** Details: (see Chatham) Organized as an early parish & became part of Chatham Co 5 Feb 1777
Clarke www.athensclarkecounty.com/	E6	5 Dec 1801	**Jackson** Clarke County; 325 E Washington St Rm 200; PO Box 1868; Athens, GA 30601; Ph. 706.613.3031 Details: (Clk Sup Ct has div, land & ct rec from 1801 & mil rec from 1922; Co Hlth Dept has b & d rec from 1919; Pro Ct has m & pro rec from 1801)
Clay www.fortgaines.com/	L3	16 Feb 1854	**Early, Randolph** Clay County; 210 S Washington; PO Box 550; Fort Gaines, GA 31751-0550; Ph. 912.768.3238 Details: (Clk Sup Ct has div & land rec)
Clayton www.co.clayton.ga.us/	F4	30 Nov 1858	**Fayette, Henry** Clayton County; 9151 Tara Blvd; Jonesboro, GA 30236-3694; Ph. 770.477.4565 Details: (Pro Ct has b, m, d & pro rec; Clk Sup Ct has div & land rec from 1859 & ct rec from 1964)
Clinch* www.rootsweb.com/~gaclinch/	N8	14 Feb 1850	**Ware, Lowndes** Clinch County; 100 Court Sq; Homerville, GA 31634-1400; Ph. 912.487.2667 Details: (All rec burned in 1856 & 1867) (Pro Ct has b & d rec from 1919, m & pro rec from 1867; Clk Sup Ct has div & ct rec from 1867, land rec from 1868, voters list from 1890 & old co newspapers from 1895)
Cobb co.cobb.ga.us/	E3	3 Dec 1832	**Cherokee** Cobb County; 100 Cherokee St; Marietta, GA 30060; Ph. 770.528.3300 Details: (Fire in 1864; rec lost) (Pro Ct has m, d & pro rec from 1865; Clk Sup Ct has land & div rec; Magistrate Ct has ct rec)
Coffee www.geocities.com/Heartland/ Prairie/5941/	L7	9 Feb 1854	**Clinch, Irwin, Ware, Telfair** Coffee County; 101 So Peterson Ave; Douglas, GA 31533; Ph. 912.384.4799 Details: (Clk Sup Ct has div, ct & land rec from 1854 & some mil dis rec from 1919; Pro Ct has m & pro rec; Co Hlth Dept has b & d rec)
Colquitt www.rootsweb.com/~gacolqu2/	M5	25 Feb 1856	**Lowndes, Thomas** Colquitt County; 1220 S Main St; PO Box 517; Moultrie, GA 31768; Ph. 912.891.7400 Details: (Fire in 1881; rec lost) (Pro Ct has b, m, d & pro rec; Clk Sup Ct has div, ct & land rec)
Columbia www.co.columbia.ga.us/	F9	10 Dec 1790	**Richmond** Columbia County; PO Box 498; Evans, GA 30809; Ph. 760.868.3300 Details: (Clk of Cts has land rec from 1700's, ct rec from 1900's & div rec from 1945; Pro Ct has b, m, d & pro rec)
Cook* www.rootsweb.com/~gacook/	M6	30 Jul 1918	**Berrien** Cook County; 212 N Hutchinson Ave; Adel, GA 31620; Ph. 912.896.2266 Details: (Clk Sup Ct has div, land & ct rec from 1919; Pro Ct has b, m, d & pro rec from 1918)

County Website	Map Index	Date Created	Parent County or Territory From Which Organized Address/Details
Coweta www.coweta.ga.us/	G3	11 Dec 1826	**Creek Indian Lands** Coweta County; 200 Court Sq; Newnan, GA 30263; Ph. 770.254.2690 Details: (Pro Ct has b & d rec from 1919, m & pro rec from 1828; Clk Sup Ct has div, ct & land rec from 1828)
Crawford www.rootsweb.com/~gacrawfo/ gacrawford.htm	I5	9 Dec 1822	**Houston** Crawford County; PO Box 1059; Roberta, GA 31078; Ph. 912.836.3782 Details: (Clk Sup Ct has div & ct rec from 1850 & land rec)
Crisp www.rootsweb.com/~gacrisp/	K5	17 Aug 1905	**Dooly** Crisp County; 210 7th St S; Cordele, GA 31015; Ph. 912.276.2672 Details: (Clk Sup Ct has div, ct & land rec from 1905; Pro Ct has m & pro rec; Co Hlth Dept has b & d rec)
Dade www.rootsweb.com/~gadade/index.htm	C1	25 Dec 1837	**Walker** Dade County; PO Box 613; Trenton, GA 30752-0000; Ph. 706.657.4625 Details: (Co Clk has div, ct & land rec)
Dawson www.dawsoncounty.org/	D4	3 Dec 1857	**Lumpkin, Gilmer** Dawson County; PO Box 192; Dawsonville, GA 30534-0192; Ph. 706.265.3164 Details: (Clk Sup Ct has div, ct & land rec from 1857; Pro Ct has b, m, d, bur & pro rec from 1858)
De Kalb www.rootsweb.com/~gadekalb/	F4	9 Dec 1822	**Fayette, Gwinett, Henry** De Kalb County; 1300 Commerce Dr; Decatur, GA 30030-3356; Ph. 404.371.2881 Details: (Courthouse burned 1842 & 1916) (Clk Sup Ct has div, ct & land rec from 1842; Pro Ct has m & pro rec from 1842)
Decatur www.rootsweb.com/~gadecatu/	N3	8 Dec 1823	**Early** Decatur County; 1400 E Shotwell St; PO Box 735; Bainbridge, GA 31717-0735; Ph. 229.248.3030 Details: (Pro Ct has m rec from 1823 & pro rec; Clk Sup Ct has div, ct & land rec from 1823)
Dodge plant.sgc.peachnet.edu/~jbellis/ genweb/dodge/dodge.html	J7	26 Oct 1870	**Montgomery, Pulaski, Telfair** Dodge County; 407 Anson Ave; PO box 818; Eastman, GA 31023-0818; Ph. 478.374.4361 Details: (Pro Ct has b, m, d & pro rec; Clk Sup Ct has div, ct & land rec)
Dooly www.rootsweb.com/~gadooly/	K5	15 May 1821	**Creek Indian Lands** Dooly County; PO Box 348; Vienna, GA 31092-0322; Ph. 912.268.4228 Details: (Fire destroyed early rec) (Clk Sup Ct has div & ct rec from 1846 & land rec from 1850; Pro Ct has b, m, d, bur & pro rec)
Dougherty* www.albany.ga.us/doughertycounty.htm	M4	15 Dec 1853	**Baker** Dougherty County; 222 Pine Ave; Albany, GA 31703-5301; Ph. 912.431.2198 Details: (Clk Sup Ct has div & ct rec from 1856 & land rec from 1854; Pro Ct has b, m, d & pro rec)
Douglas www.co.douglas.ga.us/	F3	17 Oct 1870	**Carroll, Campbell** Douglas County; 8700 Hospital Dr; Douglasville, GA 30134-4501; Ph. 770.920.7252 Details: (Pro Ct has b, m, d & pro rec; Clk Sup Ct has div, ct & land rec from 1870)
Early www.rootsweb.com/~gaearly/	M3	15 Dec 1818	**Creek Indian Lands** Early County; PO Box 849; Blakely, GA 31723; Ph. 229.723.3033 Details: (Many rec lost, first m bk, 1854) (Clk of Ct has cem, div, land, mil & ct rec)
Echols* www.rootsweb.com/~gaechols/index.html	O7	13 Dec 1858	**Clinch, Lowndes** Echols County; PO Box 190; Statenville, GA 31648-0190; Ph. 229.559.5642 Details: (Most rec burned 1897) (Clk Sup Ct has div, ct & land rec)
Effingham www.effga.com/	J11	5 Feb 1777	**Original county organized from St. Mathew & St. Phillip Parishes** Effingham County; 901 N Pine St; Springfield, GA 31329-0000; Ph. 912.754.2101 Details: (Some rec lost in Civil War & fire 1890) (Pro Ct has b & d rec from 1927, m & pro rec from 1790; Clk Sup Ct has div & ct rec from 1777)

County Website	Map Index	Date Created	Parent County or Territory From Which Organized Address/Details
Elbert www.arches.uga.edu/~laaron/	E7	10 Dec 1790	**Wilkes** Elbert County; 10 W Church St; Elberton, GA 30635-1498; Ph. 706.283.2005 Details: (Clk Sup Ct has div, ct, land & cem rec from 1790 & mil rec from 1922; Pro Ct has b, m, d, bur & pro rec)
Emanuel www.rootsweb.com/~gaemanue/	I9	10 Dec 1812	**Montgomery, Bulloch** Emanuel County; 201 N Main St; PO Box 787; Swainsboro, GA 30401-2042; Ph. 912.237.8911 Details: (Pro Ct has b, m, d & pro rec; Clk Sup Ct has div, ct & land rec from 1812)
Evans www.rootsweb.com/~gaevans/	K10	11 Aug 1914	**Bulloch, Tattnall** Evans County; 3 Freeman St; Claxton, GA 30417-0000; Ph. 912.739.3868 Details: (Pro Ct has b, m, d, bur & pro rec; Clk Sup Ct has div, ct & land rec from 1915)
Fannin www.fannincounty.org/	B4	21 Jan 1854	**Gilmer, Union** Fannin County; 420 W Main St; PO Box 487; Blue Ridge, GA 30513-0487; Ph. 706.632.2203 Details: (Pro Ct has b, m, d & pro rec; Clk Sup Ct has div, ct & land rec from 1854)
Fayette admin.co.fayette.ga.us/	G4	15 May 1821	**Creek Indian Lands** Fayette County; 200 Courthouse Sq; Fayetteville, GA 30214-2198; Ph. 770.461.6041 Details: (Pro Ct has b, m, d & pro rec; Clk Sup Ct has div, ct & land rec)
Floyd www.floydcountyga.org/	E2	3 Dec 1832	**Cherokee** Floyd County; 3 Government Plaza; Rome, GA 30161; Ph. 706.291.5190 Details: (Pro Ct has m & pro rec; Clk Sup Ct has div, ct & land rec from 1883)
Forsyth www.co.forsyth.ga.us/	D4	3 Dec 1832	**Cherokee** Forsyth County; 100 W Courthouse Sq; Cumming, GA 30040-0128; Ph. 770.781.2120 Details: (Clk of Cts has land rec from 1830's, div & ct rec; Pro Ct has b, m, d & pro rec)
Franklin www.rootsweb.com/~gafrankl/	D6	25 Feb 1784	**Cherokee Indian Lands** Franklin County; Courthouse Sq; PO Box 159; Carnesville, GA 30521-0000; Ph. 706.384.2483 Details: (Clk Sup Ct has div & ct rec from 1900 & land rec from 1860; some rec prior to 1850 in GA Archives)
Fulton www.co.fulton.ga.us/	F3	20 Dec 1853	**DeKalb, Campbell, Milton** Fulton County; 136 Pryor St SW; Atlanta, GA 30303-3405; Ph. 404.730.5300 Details: (Pro Ct has m & pro rec; Clk Sup Ct has div, ct & land rec from 1854)
Gilmer www.rootsweb.com/~gagilmer/	C4	3 Dec 1832	**Cherokee** Gilmer County; 1 Westside Sq; Elllijay, GA 30540; Ph. 706.635.4361 Details: (Pro Ct has b & d rec from 1927, m rec from 1835 & pro rec; Clk Sup Ct has div rec from 1909, land rec from 1833, mil rec from 1902 & ct rec from 1900)
Glascock www.rootsweb.com/~gaglasco/	G8	19 Dec 1857	**Warren** Glascock County; 62 E Main St; Gibson, GA 30810-0231; Ph. 706.598.2084 Details: (Pro Ct has b, m, d & pro rec; Clk Sup Ct has div, ct & land rec)
Glynn www.glynncounty.org/	M11	5 Feb 1777	**Original county organized from St. David & St. Patrick Parishes** Glynn County; 701 H St; Brunswick, GA 31520-6750; Ph. 912.554.7272 Details: (Pro Ct has m rec from 1845 & pro rec from 1792; Clk Sup Ct has div & ct rec from 1792 & land rec 1824-1829 burned, all rec to 1818 damaged)
Gordon www.gordoncounty.org/	D3	13 Feb 1850	**Cass, Floyd** Gordon County; 101 Boston Rd; Calhoun, GA 30701-2244; Ph. 706.629.3795 Details: (Rec destroyed 1864) (Clk Sup Ct has div & ct rec from 1864 & land rec; Pro Ct has b, m, d, bur & pro rec)
Grady www.rootsweb.com/~gagrady/	O4	17 Aug 1905	**Decatur, Thomas** Grady County; 250 N Broad St; Cairo, GA 31728-4101; Ph. 912.377.2912 Details: (Clk Sup Ct has div, ct & land rec from 1906)

County Website	Map Index	Date Created	Parent County or Territory From Which Organized Address/Details
Greene www.rootsweb.com/~gagreene/	F7	3 Feb 1786	**Washington** Greene County; 113 N Main; Greensboro, GA 30642-1109; Ph. 706.453.7716 Details: (Pro Ct has m, d & pro rec; Clk Sup Ct has div rec from 1790, ct & land rec from 1785; Co Hlth Dept has b rec from 1927)
Gwinnett www.co.gwinnett.ga.us/cgi-bin/Gwinnett bvgwin/egov/page.jsp	E5	15 Dec 1818	**Cherokee & Creek Indian Lands** County; 75 Langley Dr; PO Box 880; Lawrenceville, GA 30046; Ph. 770.822.8100 Details: (Courthouse burned 1871; few rec saved) (Clk Sup Ct has div, ct & land rec)
Habersham www.co.habersham.ga.us/	C6	15 Dec 1818	**Cherokee Indian Lands** Habersham County; 555 Monroe St #35; Clarkesville, GA 30523-0227; Ph. 706.754.6264 Details: (Pro Ct has m & pro rec from 1819, b & d rec from 1940; Clk Sup Ct has div, ct & land rec from 1819)
Hall www.hallcounty.org/	D5	15 Dec 1818	**Cherokee Indian Lands** Hall County; 116 Spring St E; Gainesville, GA 30501-3765; Ph. 770.531.7025 Details: (Tornado destroyed courthouse in 1936; most rec lost, except deeds) (Clk Sup Ct has div & ct rec from 1900 & land rec from 1819; Pro Ct has m & pro rec)
Hancock www.rootsweb.com/~gahancoc/index.html	G7	17 Dec 1793	**Greene, Washington** Hancock County; Courthouse Sq; Sparta, GA 31087-0000; Ph. 706.444.6644 Details: (Pro Ct has b & d rec from 1927, m rec from 1805 & pro rec; Clk Sup Ct has div & ct rec from 1919 & land rec from 1794)
Haralson www.rootsweb.com/~gaharals/	F2	26 Jan 1856	**Carroll, Polk** Haralson County; PO Box 489; Buchanan, GA 30113-0488; Ph. 770.646.2002 Details: (Pro Ct has b, m, d, bur & pro rec; Clk Sup Ct has div, ct & land rec)
Harris www.rootsweb.com/~gaharris/index.html	I3	14 Dec 1827	**Muscogee, Troup** Harris County; PO Box 528; Hamilton, GA 31811-0528; Ph. 706.628.4944 Details: (Pro Ct has m & pro rec; Clk Sup Ct has land rec from 1827, div & ct rec from 1927; Co Hlth Dept has b & d rec)
Hart www.geocities.com/RainForest/ 9478/hartcoga.html	D7	7 Dec 1853	**Elbert, Franklin** Hart County; PO Box 279; Hartwell, GA 30643-0279; Ph. 706.376.2024 Details: (Pro Ct has b, m, d, bur & pro rec; Clk Sup Ct has div, ct & land rec from 1856)
Heard www.rootsweb.com/~gaheard/	G2	22 Dec 1830	**Carroll, Coweta, Troup** Heard County; PO Box 40; Franklin, GA 30217-0040; Ph. 770.675.3821 Details: (Fire in 1894) (Pro Ct has b & d rec from 1927, m & pro rec from 1894)
Henry www.co.henry.ga.us/	G4	15 May 1821	**Creek Indian Lands** Henry County; 345 Phillips Dr; McDonough, GA 30253-3425; Ph. 770.954.2400 Details: (Clk Sup Ct has div, ct & land rec from 1821)
Houston www.rootsweb.com/~gahousto/	J6	15 May 1821	**Creek Indian Lands** Houston County; 200 Carl Vinson Pkwy; Perry, GA 31088-5808; Ph. 478.542.2105 Details: (Pro Ct has b & d rec from 1927, m rec from 1833 & pro rec from 1827; Clk Sup Ct has div, ct & land rec from 1822)
Irwin www.geocities.com/gholback_1999/ gairwin.html	L6	15 Dec 1818	**Creek Indian Lands** Irwin County; 207 S Irwin Ave; PO Box 186; Ocilla, GA 31774-1098; Ph. 229.468.5356 Details: (Clk Sup Ct has div, land & ct rec from 1821 & mil rec from 1900; Pro Ct has b, m, d & bur rec from 1920 & pro rec from 1850)
Jackson www.rootsweb.com/~gajackso/	E6	11 Feb 1796	**Franklin** Jackson County; 67 Athens St; PO Box 68; Jefferson, GA 30549-0068; Ph. 706.367.6360 Details: (Clk Sup Ct has land & pro rec from 1796, m rec from 1803, b rec from 1919, d rec from 1927 & tax rec from 1800)

County Website	Map Index	Date Created	Parent County or Territory From Which Organized Address/Details
Jasper www.rootsweb.com/~gajasper/	G5	10 Dec 1807	**Baldwin** Jasper County; Courthouse on the Sq; Monticello, GA 31064; Ph. 706.468.4901 Details: (Formerly Randolph Co. Name changed to Jasper 10 Dec 1812) (Clk Sup Ct has land rec from 1808, div, mil & ct rec from 1900)
Jeff Davis plant.sgc.peachnet.edu/~jbellis/ genweb/jeffdavis/jd.html	L8	18 Aug 1905	**Appling, Coffee** Jeff Davis County; Jeff Davis St; PO Box 602; Hazlehurst, GA 31539-0000; Ph. 912.375.6611 Details: (Clk Sup Ct has div, ct & land rec from 1905)
Jefferson* members.aol.com/J2525/jeff.htm	H8	20 Feb 1796	**Burke, Warren** Jefferson County; 202 E Broad St; PO Box 658; Louisville, GA 30434-1622; Ph. 478.625.7922 Details: (Rec not complete; Clk of Cts has land & ct rec from 1865, div rec from 1900's & m rec; Pro Ct has pro rec; Co Hlth Dept has b & d rec)
Jenkins www.rootsweb.com/~gajenkin/	I10	17 Aug 1905	**Bullock, Burke, Emanuel, Screven** Jenkins County; Harvey St; PO Box 797; Millen, GA 30442-0797; Ph. 478.982.4683 Details: (Pro Ct has m & pro rec; Clk Sup Ct has div, ct & land rec from 1905)
Johnson www.rootsweb.com/~gajohnso/	I8	11 Dec 1858	**Emanuel, Laurens, Washington** Johnson County; PO Box 269; Wrightsville, GA 31096-0269; Ph. 912.864.3388 Details: (Clk Sup Ct has div, ct & land rec from 1858)
Jones www.rootsweb.com/~gajones/	H6	10 Dec 1807	**Baldwin** Jones County; PO Box 1359; Gray, GA 31032-1359; Ph. 478.986.6671 Details: (Pro Ct has b & d rec from 1924, m & pro rec from 1811; Clk Sup Ct has land & ct rec)
Kinchafoonee		16 Dec 1853	**Stewart** Details: (see Webster) Name changed to Webster 21 Feb 1856
Lamar www.rootsweb.com/~galamar/	H4	17 Aug 1920	**Monroe, Pike** Lamar County; 326 Thomaston St; Barnesville, GA 30204-1616; Ph. 770.358.5145 Details: (Clk Sup Ct has div, ct & land rec from 1921)
Lanier www.flash.net/~miamibig/lanier/	N7	7 Aug 1920	**Berrien, Lowndes, Clinch** Lanier County; 100 W Main St; Lakeland, GA 31635; Ph. 912.482.2088 Details: (Clk Sup Ct has div & ct rec from 1921 & land rec; Pro Ct has b, m, d & pro rec from 1921)
Laurens www.rootsweb.com/~galauren/	J7	10 Dec 1807	**Wilkinson** Laurens County; 101 N Jefferson St; Dublin, GA 31021-6198; Ph. 478.272.3210 Details: (Pro Ct has m & pro rec; Clk Sup Ct has div, ct & land rec from 1807; Co Hlth Dept has b & d rec)
Lee* www.lee.ga.us/	L4	11 Dec 1826	**Creek Indian Lands** Lee County; PO Box 889; Leesburg, GA 31763-0056; Ph. 912.759.6000 Details: (Courthouse fire 1858; all rec lost) (Clk Sup Ct has m, div & ct rec)
Liberty www.petersnn.org/libertyco/	L11	5 Feb 1777	**Original county organized from St. Andrew, St. James & St John Parishes** Liberty County; Courthouse Sq; PO Box 829; Hinesville, GA 31313-3240; Ph. 912.876.2164 Details: (Pro Judge has m & pro rec from late 1700's, b rec from 1919 & d rec from 1927; Clk of Cts has div, ct & land rec from 1756; some early rec lost)
Lincoln www.rootsweb.com/~galincol/index.html	F8	20 Feb 1796	**Wilkes** Lincoln County; 210 Humphrey St; PO Box 340; Lincolnton, GA 30817-0000; Ph. 706.359.4444 Details: (Pro Ct has b rec from 1920, m rec from 1810, d rec from 1930 & pro rec from 1796; Clk Sup Ct has div & ct rec from 1796 & land rec from 1790)
Long www.rootsweb.com/~galong/index.html	L10	14 Aug 1920	**Liberty** Long County; McDonald St; Ludowici, GA 31316-0000; Ph. 912.545.2123 Details: (Pro Ct has b, m, d, bur & pro rec; Clk Sup Ct has div, ct, land & adoption rec from 1920)

County Website	Map Index	Date Created	Parent County or Territory From Which Organized Address/Details
Lowndes www.lowndescounty.com/	N7	23 Dec 1825	**Irwin** Lowndes County; 325 W Savannah Ave; PO Box 1349; Valdosta, GA 31601; Ph. 229.333.5127 Details: (Pro Ct has m & pro rec; Clk Sup Ct has div, ct & land rec from 1858)
Lumpkin www.rootsweb.com/~galumpki/	C5	3 Dec 1832	**Cherokee, Habersham, Hall** Lumpkin County; 99 Courthouse Hill Ste A; Dahlonega, GA 30533-1167; Ph. 706.864.3742 Details: (Pro Ct has b, m, d, bur & pro rec; Clk Sup Ct has div, ct & land rec from 1833)
Macon www.rootsweb.com/~gamacon/index.html	J5	14 Dec 1837	**Houston, Marion** Macon County; Sumter St; PO Box 297; Oglethorpe, GA 31068-0000; Ph. 912.472.7021 Details: (Courthouse burned 1857; all rec lost) (Clk Sup Ct has div, ct & land rec; Pro Ct has m & pro rec from 1857, b & d rec from 1927)
Madison www.rootsweb.com/~gamadiso/	E7	5 Dec 1811	**Clarke, Elbert, Franklin, Jackson, Oglethorpe** Madison County; 91 Albany Ave; Danielsville, GA 30633-0147; Ph. 706.795.3352 Details: (Pro Ct has b, m, d, bur & pro rec; Clk Sup Ct has div, ct & land rec from 1812)
Marion www.rootsweb.com/~gamarion/	J3	14 Dec 1827	**Lee, Muscogee** Marion County; Courthouse Sq; Buena Vista, GA 31803-0000; Ph. 912.649.2603 Details: (Courthouse fire 1845; all rec lost) (Clk Sup Ct has div, ct & land rec)
McDuffie www.co.mcduffie.ga.us/	G8	18 Oct 1870	**Columbia, Warren** McDuffie County; 337 Main St; PO Box 158; Thomson, GA 30824-0028; Ph. 706.595.2134 Details: (Pro Ct has b, m, d & pro rec from 1872; Clk Sup Ct has div rec from 1872, ct rec & land rec from 1870)
McIntosh www.gabooks.com/genmain.htm	L11	19 Dec 1793	**Liberty** McIntosh County; PO Box 584; Darien, GA 31305-0584; Ph. 912.437.6671 Details: (Many rec lost during Civil War; Courthouse fire 1931) (Clk Sup Ct has div, ct, pro & land rec)
Meriwether personal.atl.bellsouth.net/atl/m/s/ msaffold/meriweth.htm	H3	14 Dec 1827	**Troup** Meriwether County; PO Box 428; Greenville, GA 30222-0428; Ph. 706.672.1314 Details: (Pro Ct has b rec from 1927, m rec from 1828, d rec from 1929 & pro rec from 1838; Clk Sup Ct has div, ct & land rec from 1827 & mil dis rec)
Miller www.rootsweb.com/~gamiller/	M3	26 Feb 1856	**Baker, Early** Miller County; 155 S 1st St Ste 2; Colquitt, GA 31737-1284; Ph. 912.758.4104 Details: (Courthouse fire 1873; all rec lost) (Pro Ct has b rec from 1919, m rec from 1904, d rec from 1950 & pro rec from 1900; Clk Sup Ct has land, div & ct rec)
Milton* www.mindspring.com/~ednab/		18 Dec 1857	**Cherokee, Cobb, Forsyth** Milton County; GA Details: (see Fulton) Merged into Fulton Co 1 Jan 1832
Mitchell www.rootsweb.com/~gamitche/ index.html	M4	21 Dec 1857	**Baker** Mitchell County; PO Box 187; Camilla, GA 31730-0000; Ph. 912.336.2000 Details: (Courthouse fire 1869; Sup Ct rec and some other rec were saved) (Clk Sup Ct has div rec from 1857 & ct rec from 1847)
Monroe www.rootsweb.com/~gamonroe/index.html	H5	15 May 1821	**Creek Indian Lands** Monroe County; PO Box 189; Forsyth, GA 31029-0189; Ph. 912.994.7000 Details: (Pro Ct has m & pro rec from 1824, b rec from 1927 & d rec from 1940; Clk Sup Ct has ct & land rec from 1821 & div rec)
Montgomery plant.sgc.peachnet.edu/~jbellis/genweb/ montgomery/montgomery.html	J8	19 Dec 1793	**Washington** Montgomery County; Railroad Ave; PO Box 295; Mount Vernon, GA 30445-0000; Ph. 912.583.2363 Details: (Pro Ct has b & d rec from 1918, m rec from 1807 & pro rec from 1793; Clk Sup Ct has div & ct rec from 1800 & land rec from 1793; most original rec prior to 1890 are in State Archives)

County Website	Map Index	Date Created	Parent County or Territory From Which Organized Address/Details
Morgan www.morgan.public.lib.ga.us/county/	F6	10 Dec 1807	**Baldwin** Morgan County; PO Box 168; Madison, GA 30650-0168; Ph. 706.342.0725 Details: (Co Hlth Dept has b rec; Pro Ct has m, d, bur & pro rec; Clk Sup Ct has div, ct & land rec from 1807)
Murray www.rootsweb.com/~gamurray/index.htm	C3	3 Dec 1832	**Cherokee** Murray County; 101 N 3rd Ave; Chatsworth, GA 30705-0000; Ph. 706.695.2932 Details: (Pro Ct has b & d rec from 1924, m rec from 1842 & pro rec from 1890; Clk Sup Ct has ct rec from 1834)
Muscogee* www.rootsweb.com/~gamuscog/ muscogee.htm	I3	11 Dec 1826	**Creek Indian Lands** Muscogee County; 100 10th St; PO Box 1340; Columbus, GA 31902; Ph. 706.653.4013 Details: (Clk Sup Ct has div, ct & land rec from 1838)
Newton www.co.newton.ga.us/	G5	24 Dec 1821	**Henry, Jasper, Walton** Newton County; 1113 Usher St; Covington, GA 30014; Ph. 770.784.2000 Details: (Clk Sup Ct has div, ct & land rec from 1822 & mil rec from 1917)
Oconee www.oconeecounty.com/	F6	25 Feb 1875	**Clarke** Oconee County; 23 N Main St; PO Box 1099; Watkinsville, GA 30677-2438; Ph. 706.769.3940 Details: (Pro Ct has b, m, d & pro rec; Clk Sup Ct has div, ct & land rec from 1875)
Oglethorpe www.rootsweb.com/~gaogleth/	F7	19 Dec 1793	**Wilkes** Oglethorpe County; PO Box 261; Lexington, GA 30648-0261; Ph. 706.743.5270 Details: (Courthouse fire 1941) (Pro Ct has b, m, d & pro rec; Clk Sup Ct has div, ct & land rec from 1794)
Paulding www.paulding.gov/	E3	3 Dec 1832	**Cherokee** Paulding County; 11 Courthouse Sq; Dallas, GA 30132-1401; Ph. 770.445.7527 Details: (Clk Sup Ct has div & ct rec from 1876 & land rec from 1848)
Peach www.rootsweb.com/~gapeach/	I5	18 Jul 1924	**Houston, Macon** Peach County; 205 W Church St; PO Box 468; Fort Valley, GA 31030-4155; Ph. 912.825.2535 Details: (Pro Ct has b, m, d & pro rec from 1925; Clk Sup Ct has div, ct & land rec from 1925)
Pickens www.rootsweb.com/~gapicken/	D4	5 Dec 1853	**Cherokee, Gilmer** Pickens County; 52 N Main St; Jasper, GA 30143-0000; Ph. 706.692.2014 Details: (Pro Ct has b, m, d, bur & pro rec; Clk Sup Ct has div, ct & land rec from 1854)
Pierce personal.jax.bellsouth.net/jax/r/s/ rskhdr/Pierce/pierce.htm	M9	18 Dec 1857	**Appling, Ware** Pierce County; PO Box 679; Blackshear, GA 31516-0679; Ph. 912.449.2022 Details: (Courthouse fire 1874) (Pro Ct has b rec from 1926, m rec from 1875, d rec from 1924 & pro rec; Clk Sup Ct has div & ct rec from 1875 & land rec)
Pike www.rootsweb.com/~gapike/index.htm	H4	9 Dec 1822	**Monroe** Pike County; PO Box 377; Zebulon, GA 30295-0377; Ph. 706.567.3406 Details: (Clk Sup Ct has ct & land rec from 1823)
Polk www.rootsweb.com/~gapolk/	E2	20 Dec 1851	**Paulding, Floyd** Polk County; PO Box 268; Cedartown, GA 30125-0268; Ph. 770.749.2100 Details: (Pro Ct has b, m, d & pro rec; Clk Sup Ct has div, ct & land rec from 1852)
Pulaski www.rootsweb.com/~gapulask/index.htm	J6	13 Dec 1808	**Laurens** Pulaski County; PO Box 29; Hawkinsville, GA 31036-0029; Ph. 912.783.4154 Details: (Clk Sup Ct has div & ct rec from 1850 & land rec from 1810; Pro Ct has m & pro rec from 1810, b rec from 1935 & d rec from 1920)
Putnam www.rootsweb.com/~gaputnam/index.html	G6	10 Dec 1807	**Baldwin** Putnam County; 100 S Jefferson Ave; Eatonton, GA 31024; Ph. 706.485.4501 Details: (Clk Sup Ct has div & ct rec from 1807; Pro Ct has b rec from 1866, m & pro rec from 1808, d rec from 1919 & tax digest 1812-1848)

County Website	Map Index	Date Created	Parent County or Territory From Which Organized / Address/Details
Quitman home.earthlink.net/~bwjohnson/ quit_mn.htm	K2	10 Dec 1858	**Randolph, Stewart** Quitman County; PO Box 114; Georgetown, GA 31754-0114; Ph. 912.334.2578 Details: (Courthouse burned) (Clk Sup Ct has b rec from 1927, m rec from 1919, d rec, div & ct rec from 1923 & land rec from 1879)
Rabun www.usgennet.org/usa/region/ southeast/garabun/	C6	21 Dec 1819	**Cherokee Indian Lands** Rabun County; 25 Courthouse Sq #7; Clayton, GA 30525-0925; Ph. 706.782.3615 Details: (Pro Ct has m & pro rec; Clk Sup Ct has div, ct & land rec)
Randolph home.earthlink.net/~bwjohnson/ rand_mn.htm	L3	20 Dec 1828	**Lee** Randolph County; 208 Court St; Cuthbert, GA 31740-0000; Ph. 229.732.6440 Details: (Pro Ct has m & pro rec from 1835; Clk Sup Ct has div, ct & land rec from 1835)
Randolph, old		10 Dec 1807	**Baldwin** Details: (see Jasper) Name changed to Jasper 10 Dec 1812
Richmond* augusta.co.richmond.ga.us/	G9	5 Feb 1777	**Original county org. from St. Paul Parish** Richmond County; 530 Green St; Augusta, GA 30911-0001; Ph. 760.821.2460 Details: (Clk Sup Ct has land rec from 1778 & ct rec; Pro Ct has m & pro rec)
Rockdale www.rockdalecounty.org/dale.cfm?pid=1	F5	18 Oct 1870	**Henry, Newton** Rockdale County; 922 Court St NE; Conyers, GA 30207-4540; Ph. 770.929.4021 Details: (Pro Ct has m & pro rec from 1870 & d rec from 1930; Clk Sup Ct has land, div & ct rec)
Schley www.rootsweb.com/~gaschley/schley.htm	J4	22 Dec 1857	**Marion, Sumter** Schley County; PO Box 352; Ellaville, GA 31806-0000; Ph. 912.937.2609 Details: (Pro Ct has b, d & bur rec from 1927, m rec from 1858 & pro rec; Clk Sup Ct has div, ct & land rec from 1857)
Screven www.rootsweb.com/~gascreve/	I10	14 Dec 1793	**Burke, Effingham** Screven County; 216 Mims Rd; Sylvania, GA 30467-0159; Ph. 912.564.2622 Details: (Pro Ct has b & d rec from 1927, m & pro rec from 1817; Clk Sup Ct has div & ct rec from 1816 & land rec from 1790)
Seminole www.rootsweb.com/~gasemino/index.html	N3	8 July 1920	**Decatur, Early** Seminole County; 200 S Knox Ave; Donalsonville, GA 31745; Ph. 912.524.2525 Details: (Pro Ct has b, m, d & pro rec; Clk Sup Ct has div, ct & land rec from 1921)
Spalding www.rootsweb.com/~gaspaldi/	G4	20 Dec 1851	**Fayette, Henry, Pike** Spalding County; 132 W Solomon St; Griffin, GA 30223-3312; Ph. 770.467.4745 Details: (Clk Sup Ct has div, ct & land rec from 1852)
St. Andrew Parish		1758	**Creek Cession of 1733** Details: (see Liberty) Organized as an early parish & became part of Liberty Co 5 Feb 1777
St. David Parish		1765	**Creek Cession of 1763** Details: (see Glynn) Organized as an early parish & became part of Glynn Co 5 Feb 1777
St. George Parish		1758	**Creek Cession of 1733** Details: (see Burke) Organized as an early parish & became Burke Co. 5 Feb 1777
St. James Parish		1758	**Creek Cession of 1733** Details: (see Liberty) Organized as an early parish & became part of Liberty Co 5 Feb 1777
St. John Parish		1758	**Creek Cession of 1733** Details: (see Liberty) Organized as an early parish & became part of Liberty Co 5 Feb 1777
St. Mary Parish		1765	**Creek Cession of 1763** Details: (see Camden) Organized as an early parish & became part of Camden Co 5 Feb 1777
St. Matthew Parish		1758	**Creek Cession of 1733** Details: (see Effingham) Organized as an early parish & became part of Effingham Co 5 Feb 1777

County Website	Map Index	Date Created	Parent County or Territory From Which Organized Address/Details
St. Patrick Parish		1765	**Creek Cession of 1763** Details: (see Glynn) Organized as an early parish & became part of Glynn Co 5 Feb 1777
St. Paul Parish		1758	**Creek Cession of 1733** Details: (see Richmond) Organized as an early parish & became Richmond Co 5 Feb 1777
St. Philip Parish		1758	**Creek Cession of 1733** Details: (see Chatham & Effingham) Organized as an early parish & became part of Chatham & Effingham Cos 5 Feb 1777
St. Thomas Parish		1765	**Creek Cession of 1763** Details: (see Camden) Organized as an early parish & became part of Camden Co 5 Feb 1777
Stephens www.rootsweb.com/~gastephe/	D6	18 Aug 1905	**Franklin, Habersham** Stephens County; 150 W Doyle St; PO Box 386; Toccoa, GA 30577-0000; Ph. 706.886.9496 Details: (Co Hlth Dept has b & d rec; Pro Ct has m & pro rec; Clk Sup Ct has div, ct & land rec from 1906)
Stewart home.earthlink.net/~bwjohnson/ stew_mn.htm	K2	23 Dec 1830	**Randolph** Stewart County; PO Box 157; Lumpkin, GA 31815-0157; Ph. 912.838.6220 Details: (Pro Ct has b, d & bur rec from 1927, m rec from 1828 & pro rec; Clk Sup Ct has div, ct & land rec from 1830)
Sumter www.sumter-ga.com/	K4	26 Dec 1831	**Lee** Sumter County; PO Box 295; Americus, GA 31709-0295; Ph. 912.924.3090 Details: (Co Hlth Dept has b, d & bur rec; Pro Ct has m & pro rec; Clk Sup Ct has div, ct & land rec from 1831)
Talbot www.rootsweb.com/~gatalbot/	I3	14 Dec 1827	**Muscogee** Talbot County; Courthouse Sq; PO Box 155; Talbotton, GA 31827-0000; Ph. 706.665.3220 Details: (Pro Ct has b, m, d & pro rec; Clk Sup Ct has div, ct & land rec)
Taliaferro web.infoave.net/~taliaferro/	F7	24 Dec 1825	**Green, Hancock, Oglethorpe, Warren, Wilkes** Taliaferro County; 113 Monument St SE; PO Box 114; Crawfordville, GA 30631-0000; Ph. 706.456.2123 Details: (Pro Ct has b rec from 1927, d rec from 1920, m & pro rec from 1826, land grants from 1750 & church rec from 1802; Clk Sup Ct has div & ct rec from 1826)
Tattnall www.tattnall.com/	K9	5 Dec 1801	**Montgomery** Tattnall County; Main & Brazell Sts; Reidsville, GA 30453-0000; Ph. 912.557.6761 Details: (Pro Ct has b, m, d & pro rec; Clk Sup Ct has div rec from 1880, ct & land rec)
Taylor www.rootsweb.com/~gataylor/gataylor.htm	I4	15 Jan 1852	**Macon, Marion, Talbot** Taylor County; 1 Courthouse Sq; PO Box 536; Butler, GA 31006; Ph. 478.862.5594 Details: (Pro Ct has m & pro rec from 1852; Clk Sup Ct has div & land rec from 852, mil dis rec from 1922 & ct rec)
Telfair plant.sgc.peachnet.edu/~jbellis/ genweb/telfair/telfair.html	K7	10 Dec 1807	**Wilkinson** Telfair County; 713 Telfair Ave; McRae, GA 31055-0000; Ph. 229.868.6525 Details: (Pro Judge has m & pro rec; Clk Sup Ct has div, ct & land rec; Co Hlth Dept has b & d rec)
Terrell home.earthlink.net/~bwjohnson/ terr_mn.htm	L4	16 Feb 1856	**Lee, Randolph** Terrell County; 235 E Lee St; Dawson, GA 31742-2100; Ph. 229.995.2631 Details: (Clk Sup Ct has div, ct & land rec from 1856)
Thomas www.thomascountyboc.org/	N5	23 Dec 1825	**Decatur, Irwin** Thomas County; 225 N Broad St; Thomasville, GA 31792; Ph. 229.225.4108 Details: (Co Hlth Dept has b & d rec; Pro Ct has m & pro rec; Clk Sup Ct has div & ct rec from 1919 & land rec from 1826)

County Website	Map Index	Date Created	Parent County or Territory From Which Organized / Address/Details
Tift www.tiftcounty.org/	**M6**	**17 Aug 1905**	**Berrien, Irwin, Worth** Tift County; 225 N Tift Ave; Tifton, GA 31794-4463; Ph. 229.386.7810 Details: (Pro Ct has m & pro rec; Clk Sup Ct has div, ct & land rec from 1905)
Toombs plant.sgc.peachnet.edu/~jbellis/ genweb/toombs/toombs.html	**K9**	**18 Aug 1905**	**Emanuel, Tattnall, Montgomery** Toombs County; 100 Courthouse Sq; Lyons, GA 30436-0000; Ph. 912.526.3501 Details: (Pro Ct has b, m, d, bur & pro rec from 1905; Clk Sup Ct has div, ct & land rec from 1905)
Towns www.rootsweb.com/~gatowns/	**B5**	**6 Mar 1856**	**Rabun, Union** Towns County; 48 River St Ste E; Hiawassee, GA 30546-0178; Ph. 706.896.2130 Details: (Pro Ct has b & d rec from 1927, m rec from 1885 & pro rec; Clk Sup Ct has div, land & mil rec from 1865)
Treutlen www.rootsweb.com/~gatreutl/	**J8**	**21 Aug 1917**	**Emanuel, Montgomery** Treutlen County; 200 Georgia Ave; Soperton, GA 30457-0000; Ph. 912.529.4215 Details: (Pro Ct has b, m, d & pro rec from 1919; Clk Sup Ct has div, ct & land rec from 1919)
Troup www.troupcountyga.org/	**H2**	**11 Dec 1826**	**Creek Indian Lands** Troup County; 118 Ridley Ave; PO Box 1051; LaGrange, GA 30240; Ph. 706.883.1740 Details: (Co Archives has m, bur, div, land, pro & ct rec from 1827, mil rec 1890-1936 & nat rec 1843-1908; Co Hlth Dept has b & d rec from 1919)
Turner www.rootsweb.com/~gaturner/	**L6**	**18 Aug 1905**	**Dooly, Irwin, Wilcox, Worth** Turner County; 219 E College Ave; Ashburn, GA 31714-1275; Ph. 229.567.2011 Details: (Clk Sup Ct has div & ct rec from 1906 & land rec; Pro Ct has b, m, d, bur & pro rec)
Twiggs www.rootsweb.com/~gatwiggs/index.htm	**I6**	**14 Dec 1809**	**Wilkinson** Twiggs County; PO Box 202; Jeffersonville, GA 31044; Ph. 478.945.3350 Details: (Clk Sup Ct has land, ct & div rec; Pro Ct has b, m, d & pro rec)
Union www.ancestraldesigns.com/union/	**C5**	**3 Dec 1832**	**Cherokee** Union County; 114 Courthouse St; Blairsville, GA 30512; Ph. 706.745.2611 Details: (Pro Ct has b, m, d & pro rec; Clk Sup Ct has div, ct & land rec)
Upson www.rootsweb.com/~gaupson/ gaupson.htm	**H4**	**15 Dec 1824**	**Crawford, Pike** Upson County; PO Box 889; Thomaston, GA 30286-0889; Ph. 706.647.7012 Details: (Pro Ct has m rec from 1825 & pro rec from 1920; Clk Sup Ct has div, ct & land rec from 1825 & newspaper files from 1870)
Walker www.co.walker.ga.us/	**C2**	**18 Dec 1833**	**Murray** Walker County; 103 S Duke St; Lafayette, GA 30728-0445; Ph. 706.638.1742 Details: (Courthouse fire 1883) (Clk Sup Ct has div, ct & land rec from 1883; Pro Judge has m & pro rec; Co Hlth Dept has b & d rec)
Walton www.waltoncountyga.org/	**F5**	**15 Dec 1818**	**Creek Indian Lands** Walton County; PO Box 585; Monroe, GA 30655-0585; Ph. 770.267.1301 Details: (Pro Ct has m & pro rec from 1819; Clk Sup Ct has land rec from 1819 & div rec from 1900; Magistrate Ct has ct rec from 1900; Co Hlth Dept has b & d rec from 1919)
Ware www.rootsweb.com/~gaware/	**N8**	**15 Dec 1824**	**Appling** Ware County; 800 Church St; Waycross, GA 31501-3501; Ph. 912.287.4340 Details: (Rec burned 1854) (Pro Ct has m & pro rec from 1874; Clk of Cts has land & ct rec)
Warren www.rootsweb.com/~gawarren/	**G8**	**19 Dec 1793**	**Columbia, Richmond, Wilkes, Hancock** Warren County; 100 Warren St; Warrenton, GA 30828-0000; Ph. 706.465.2262 Details: (Pro Ct has b, m, d & pro rec; Clk Sup Ct has div, ct & land rec)
Washington www.rootsweb.com/~gawashin/ washingtoncounty001.htm	**H8**	**25 Feb 1784**	**Creek Indian Lands** Washington County; PO Box 271; Sandersville, GA 31082-0271; Ph. 912.552.2325 Details: (Pro Ct has b, m & pro rec; Clk Sup Ct has div, ct & land rec from 1865)

County Website	Map Index	Date Created	Parent County or Territory From Which Organized Address/Details
Wayne www.co.wayne.ga.us/	L10	11 May 1803	**Creek Indian Lands** Wayne County; 242 E Walnut St; PO Box 918; Jesup, GA 31598; Ph. 912.427.5930 Details: (Pro Ct has b, m, d & pro rec; Clk Sup Ct has div, ct & land rec)
Webster www.rootsweb.com/~gawebste/	K3	16 Dec 1853	**Stewart** Webster County; Washington St & Hwy 280 ; PO Box 29; Preston, GA 31824-0000; Ph. 229.828.3525 Details: (Formerly Kinchafoonee Co. Name changed to Webster 21 Feb 1856) (Pro Ct has b, m, d, bur & pro rec; Clk Sup Ct has div, ct & land rec)
Wheeler www.rootsweb.com/~gawebste/	K8	14 Aug 1912	**Montgomery** Wheeler County; 209 W Forest Ave; Alamo, GA 30411-0000; Ph. 912.568.7137 Details: (Co Hlth Dept has b & d rec from 1927; Pro Ct has m & pro rec from 1913; Clk Sup Ct has div, ct & land rec from 1913)
White www.rootsweb.com/~gawhite/	C5	22 Dec 1857	**Habersham** White County; 59 S Main St #B; Cleveland, GA 30528-0185; Ph. 706.865.2613 Details: (Pro Ct has b, m, d & pro rec; Clk Sup Ct has div, ct & land rec from 1858 & mil dis rec)
Whitfield www.geocities.com/Heartland/ Plains/3242/whtfld.htm	C3	30 Dec 1851	**Murray** Whitfield County; 300 W Crawford St; PO Box 248; Dalton, GA 30722-0248; Ph. 706.275.7451 Details: (Pro Ct has b & d rec from 1927, m & pro rec from 1852; Clk Sup Ct has div, ct & land rec from 1852)
Wilcox www.rootsweb.com/~gawilcox/	K6	22 Dec 1857	**Dooly, Irwin, Pulaski** Wilcox County; 103 N Broad St; Abbeville, GA 31001; Ph. 912.467.2737 Details: (Pro Ct has b & d rec from 1927, m rec from 1886 & pro rec; Clk Sup Ct has land rec from 1870, div & ct rec from 1900 & mil rec from 1917)
Wilkes www.rootsweb.com/~gawilkes/	F8	5 Feb 1777	**Original county-Creek & Cherokee Indian Lands** Wilkes County; 23 E Court St Rm 205; Washington, GA 30673-1570; Ph. 706.678.2423 Details: (Pro Ct has b, m, d & pro rec from 1792; Clk Sup Ct has div & ct rec from 1778, land rec from 1777 & mil dis rec)
Wilkinson www.accucomm.net/~wilcoboc/	I7	11 May 1803	**Original county-Creek Indian Lands** Wilkinson County; PO Box 250; Irwinton, GA 31042; Ph. 478.946.2221 Details: (Courthouse burned in 1852 & 1924; land rec were not burned in 1924) (Clk Sup Ct has some div rec & land rec from 1852)
Worth www.rootsweb.com/~gaworth/	M5	20 Dec 1853	**Dooly, Irwin** Worth County; 201 N Main St; Sylvester, GA 31791-2178; Ph. 229.776.8205 Details: (Pro Ct has b rec from 1897, m rec from 1854, d rec from 1919 & pro rec from 1880; Clk Sup Ct has div, ct & land rec)

Notes

Hibiscus

HAWAII

CAPITAL: HONOLULU – TERRITORY 1900 – STATE 1959 (50TH)

Captain James Cook discovered the Hawaiian Islands in 1778 and named them the Sandwich Islands. The 390-mile chain of islands includes the following eight main islands: Hawaii, Kahoolawe, Maui, Lanai, Molokai, Oahu, Kauai, and Nihau. Between 1782 and 1810, King Kamehameha extended his rule over all the islands. The dynasty he established lasted until 1872. Weakened by political strife and foreigners' desire for freedom, the kingdom was abolished in 1893 when Queen Liliuolalani was deposed.

Protestant missionaries from New England began arriving in Hawaii in 1820. Settlers and laborers started coming about a decade later, mostly from the Orient. Booms in sandalwood, whaling, and sugar continued the influx of foreigners to the turn of the century, when the pineapple industry exploded.

On 4 July 1894, the Republic of Hawaii was established. It continued until 1898, when residents ceded Hawaii to the United States. Two years later, the Territory of Hawaii was organized. On August 21, 1959, Hawaii became America's 50th state.

Look for vital records in the following locations:

- **Birth, death, marriage and divorce records:** Statewide registration of births began in 1842, but few records exist until 1896. General compliance was not reached until 1929. Copies of birth, death, marriage, and divorce records are available through Vital Statistics, State Department of Health in Honolulu.
- **Court records:** Circuit courts have probate records from the 1840s. Microfilms of probates from 1845 to 1900 are at the Hawaii State Archives, Iolani Palace Grounds in Honolulu.
- **Census records:** Colonial census records exist for some parts of Hawaii for 1866, 1878, 1890, and 1896. The last three are at the Hawaii State Archives. Also at the Archives are two "census files," 1840 to 1866 and 1847 to 1896, which contain miscellaneous

records such as school census records, population lists, and vital record summaries.

Vital Statistics, State Department of Health
PO Box 3378
1520 Punchbowl Street
Honolulu, Hawaii 96801
808.586.4533

Hawaii State Archives
Iolani Palace Grounds
Honolulu, Hawaii 96813

Societies and Repositories

Bernice P. Bishop Museum Library; 1525 Bernice St; Honolulu, Hawaii 96817-0916

Bishop Museum & Bishop Museum Library; PO Box 19000.A; Honolulu, Hawaii 96817.0916; 808.841.8968;

Bishop Museum Library; 1525 Bernice Street; Honolulu, Hawaii 96817-0916; 808.848.4148; Fax 808.845.4133

Bureau of Conveyances; 1151 Punchbowl Street Room 123, PO Box 2867; Honolulu, Hawaii 96803; 808.587.0151; Fax 808.587.0136

DAR Memorial Library; Makiki Hts. Dr; Honolulu, Hawaii 96822

Daughters of the American Revolution Aloha Chapter House; 1914 Makiki Heights Drive; Honolulu, Hawaii 96822

Hamilton Library, Hawaii Collection; 2550 The Mall; Honolulu, Hawaii 96822; 808.956.7214, 808.956.7205; Fax 808.956.5968

Hawaii Chinese History Center; 111 North King Street Room 410; Honolulu, Hawaii 96817; 808.521.5948

Hawaii County Genealogical Society; PO Box 931; Keaau, Hawaii 96749

Hawaii Mission Children's Society Library; 553 South King Street; Honolulu, Hawaii 96813

Hawaii State Archives; Iolani Palace Grounds; Honolulu, Hawaii 96813; 808.586.0330

Hawaii State Library; 478 South King Street; Honolulu, Hawaii 96813; 808.586.3500; Fax 808.586.3584

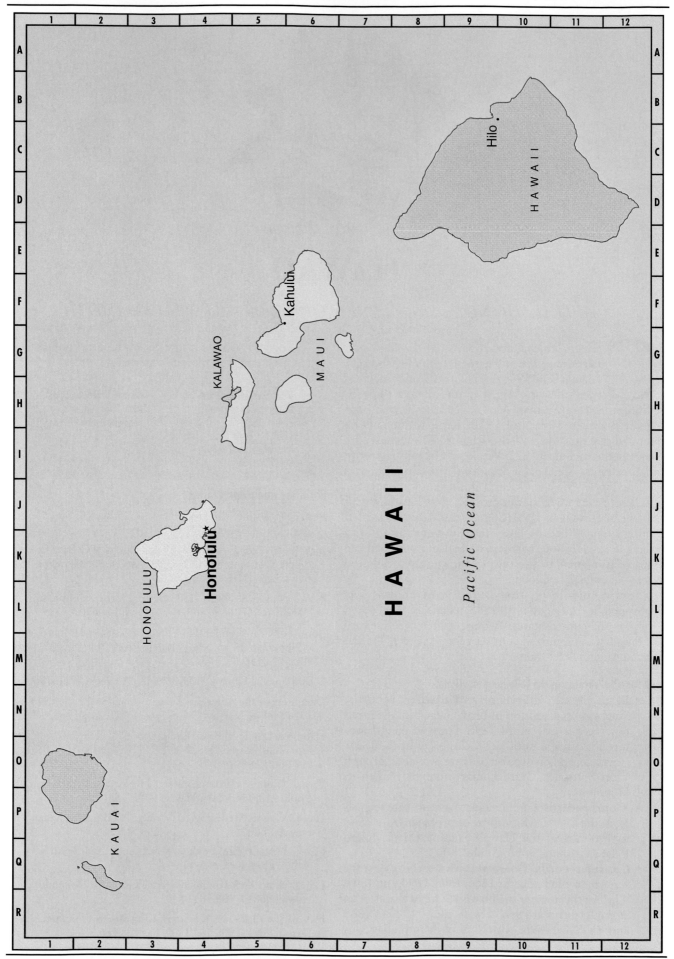

KALAWAO

Kahului

MAUI

HAWAII

Hilo

HAWAII

HAWAII

Pacific Ocean

HONOLULU

Honolulu

KAUAI

Hawaiian Historical Society; 560 Kawaiahao St.; Honolulu, Hawaii 96813;

Immigration and Naturalization Service; 595 Ala Moana Blvd.; Honolulu, Hawaii 96813; 808.532.3721

Kona Historical Society; PO Box 398; Captain Cook, Hawaii 96704;

Laie-Hawaii Stake Gen. Library, BYU Univ., Hawaii Campus; Laie; Oahu, Hawaii 96762

Library of Hawaii King & Punchbowl Sts.; Honolulu, Hawaii 96813;

Library of the Univ. of Hawaii at Manoa; 2550 The Mall; Honolulu, Hawaii 96822

Lyman House Memorial Museum; 276 Haili Street; Hilo, Hawaii 96720

Maui Genealogical Society; 38A Alania Place; Kihei, Hawaii 96753 <www.maui.net/~mauifun/mgs.htm>

Maui Historical Society; 2375-A Main Street; Wailuku, Hawaii 96793

National Archives Pacific Region; 560 Kawaiahao Street; Honolulu, Hawaii 96813; 808.537.6271

National Memorial Cemetery of the Pacific; 2177 Puowaina Dr.; Honolulu, Hawaii 96813; 808.541.1427; Fax 808.541.3546

Portuguese Genealogical Society of Hawaii; 810 N. Vineyard Blvd. Room 11; Honolulu, Hawaii 96817 <www.lusaweb.com/genealogy/html/phgs.cfm>

Research and Statistics Office, State Department of Health; PO Box 3378, 1250 Punchbowl Street; Honolulu, Hawaii 96801; 808.586.4533

Roman Catholic Diocese of Honolulu, Chancery Office; 1184 Bishop Street; Honolulu, Hawaii 96813; 808.533.1791; Fax 808.521.8428

Sandwich Islands Genealogical Society; PO Box 235039; Honolulu, Hawaii 96823.3500; <www.hpcug.org/ancestors/sigs.html>

Sons of the American Revolution, Hawaii Society; 1564 Piikea St.; Honolulu, Hawaii 96819

United Puerto Rican Association of Hawaii, Inc.; 1249 N. School St.; Honolulu, Hawaii 96817

Bibliography and Record Sources

General Sources

Alcantara, Ruben R. *The Filipinos in Hawaii: An Annotated Bibliography*. Honolulu, Hawaii: Social Science Research Institute, University of Hawaii, 1972.

Britsch, R. Lanier. *Moramona: the Mormons in Hawaii*. Laie, Hawaii: Institute for Polynesian Studies, 1989.

Chinese in Hawaii. Records from various sources: Hawaiian Archives – Extracts from "The Friend" – Cemetery inscriptions – Church records. (Salt Lake City: Filmed by the Genealogical Society of Utah, 1982).

Cole, William A. and Elwin W. Jensen. *The Cole-Jensen Collection: Oral Genealogies and Genealogical Information Collected from the Polynesian Peoples and from the Pacific Islands.* (Salt Lake City: Filmed by the Genealogical Society of Utah, 1984).

Conrad, Agnes C. *"Family History Sources in Hawaii," Hawaii Library Association Journal, 33 June 1974, p. 3-10*. Honolulu: Hawaii Library Association.

Conrad, Agnes C. *Genealogical Sources in Hawaii*. Honolulu, Hawaii: Hawaii Library Association, 1987.

Day, Arthur Grove. *History Makers of Hawaii: A Biographical Dictionary*. Honolulu, Hawaii: Mutual Publishing of Honolulu, 1984.

Freitas, Joaquim Francisco de. *Portuguese-Hawaiian Memories*. Honolulu, Hawaii: J. F. Freitas, 1930.

Gardner, Arthur L. *The Koreans in Hawaii: An Annotated Bibliography*. Honolulu, Hawaii: University of Hawaii, Social Science Research Institute, 1970.

Hawaii Research Outline. Series US States, no. 12. Salt Lake City: Family History Library, 1988.

Hawaiian Journal of History. Honolulu: Hawaiian Historical Society, 1967- (Hong Kong: Libra Press).

Hawaiian Mission Children's Society (Honolulu, Hawaii). *Portraits of American Protestant Missionaries to Hawaii*. Washington: Microfilmed by the Library of Congress Photoduplication Service, 1992.

Hilleary, Perry Edward. *Men and Women of Hawaii: 1954, A Biographical Encyclopedia of Persons of Notable Achievement and Historical Account of the Peoples Who Have Distinguished Themselves Through Personal Success and Through Public Service*. Honolulu, Hawaii: Business Consultants, 1954.

Hunter, Louise H. *Buddhism in Hawaii*. Honolulu, Hawaii: University of Hawaii Press, 1971.

Judd, Bernice. *Voyages to Hawaii before 1860: A Record, Based on Historical Narratives in the Libraries of the Hawaiian Mission Children's Society and the Hawaiian Historical Society, Extended to March 1860*. Reprint. Honolulu: University Press of Hawaii, 1974.

Judd, Henry Pratt. *Men and Women of Hawaii: 1954*. Honolulu: Business Consultants, 1954.

Kaina, Maria. *Target Your Hawaiian Genealogy and Others as Well: A Family Guide Provided by the Hawaii State Public Library System*. Honolulu: Hawaii State Public Library System, 1991.

Kuykendall, Ralph S. *The Hawaiian Kingdom*. 3 vols. Honolulu: University of Hawaii Press, 1966-1968.

Langdon, Robert. *Where the Whalers Went: An Index to the Pacific Ports and Islands Visited by American Whalers (and some other ships) in the 19th Century*. Canberra: Pacific Manuscripts Bureau, 1984.

Lind, Andrew W. *Hawaii's People*. Honolulu, Hawaii: University Press of Hawaii, [1974].

Lueras, Leonard. *Kanyaku imin: A Hundred Years of Japanese Life in Hawaii*. Honolulu, Hawaii: International Savings and Loan Association, 1985.

Luster, Arlene D. C. *A Directory of Libraries and Information Sources in Hawaii and the Pacific Islands*. Rev. ed. Honolulu: Hawaii Library Association, 1972.

Mardfin, Jean K.. *Hawaiian Genealogy Project; Directory of Secondary Sources*. Honolulu, Hawaii: Office of Hawaiian Affairs, 1995?.

Matsuda, Mitsugu. *The Japanese in Hawaii, 1868-1967: A Bibliography of the First Hundred Years*. Honolulu, Hawaii: University of Hawaii, 1968.

McGuire, Mrs. Elwood J. *Descendants of New England Protestant Missionaries to the Sandwich Islands (Hawaiian Islands), 1820-1900: An Alphabetically Arranged Copy of Births, Marriages, and Deaths from the Records of the Hawaiian Mission Children's Society Library, Honolulu, Hawaii.* Honolulu, Hawaii: Privately Printed, Hawaii State Regent, NSDAR, 1984.

McKinzie, Edith Kawelohea. *Hawaiian Genealogies: Extracted from Hawaiian Language Newspapers.* 2 vols. Honolulu: Brigham Young University–Hawaii, 1983-6.

Mellen, Kathleen Dickenson. *An Island Kingdom Passes: Hawaii Becomes American.* New York: Hastings House, 1958.

Mookini, Esther T. *The Hawaiian Newspapers.* Honolulu: Topgallant Publishing Co., 1974.

Mulholland, John F. *Hawaii's Religions.* Rutland, VT: Charles E. Tuttle Co., 1970.

Nordyke. Eleanor C. *The Peopling of Hawaii.* Honolulu: University Press of Hawaii, 1989.

Nupepa Kuokoa (Honolulu, Hawaii). Honolulu: Univ. of Hawaii Library, Archives of Hawaii, [19—?].

Ohai, Jean B. *Chinese Genealogy and Family Book Guide: Hawaiian and Chinese Sources.* Honolulu, Hawaii: Hawaii Chinese History Center, 1975.

Oliver, Douglas L. *The Pacific Islands.* Honolulu, Hawaii: University Press of Hawaii, 1961.

Oukah, Oukah. *Hawaiian Royal and Noble Genealogies.* 2nd ed. Dallas: Triskelion Press, 1998.

Peterson, Barbara Bennett. *Notable Women of Hawaii.* Honolulu, Hawaii: University of Hawaii Press, 1984.

Siddall, John William. *Men of Hawaii: Being A Biographical Reference Library, Complete and Authentic, of the Men of Note and Substantial Achievement in the Hawaiian Islands.* 5 vols. Honolulu, Hawaii: Honolulu Star-Bulletin, 1917-1930, 1936.

Taylor, Albert Pierce. *Under Hawaiian Skies: A Narrative of the Romance, Adventure and History of the Hawaiian Islands, A Complete Historical Account...* Honolulu, Hawaii: Advertiser Pub. Co., Ltd., 1926.

Young, Nancy Foon. *The Chinese in Hawaii: An Annotated Bibliography.* Honolulu, Hawaii: Social Science Research Institute, University of Hawaii, [n.d.].

Atlases, Maps and Gazetteers

Alexander, W.D., comp. *Hawaiian Geographic Names.* Washington, D.C.: United States Coast and Geodetic Survey, 1902.

Armstrong, R. Warwick. *Atlas of Hawaii.* 2nd ed. Honolulu, Hawaii: University Press of Hawaii, 1983.

Coulter, John W., comp. *A Gazetteer of the Territory of Hawaii.* Research Publications, no. 11. Honolulu: University of Hawaii, 1935. Reprint. Ann Harbor, Michigan: University Microfilm.

Fitzpatrick, Gary L., comp. *Hawaii: A List of Early Maps in the Library of Congress and a Summary of Services of Current Maps and Cartographic Information.* Washington, D.C.: Library of Congress, 1980.

Lindsey, Jessie H. *District and County Guide of the Territory of Hawaii.* n.p., 1947.

Pukui, Mary Kawena. *Place Names of Hawaii.* Honolulu: University Press of Hawaii, 1974.

United States. Board on Geographic Names. *Hawaiian Islands: Official Standard Names.* Washington, D.C.: Government Printing Office, 1956.

Census Records

Available Census Records and Census Substitutes

Federal Census 1900 (incomplete), 1910, 1920, 1930.

Island Census 1890.

State/Colonial Census 1866, 1896, 1840-1866, 1847-1896.

Dollarhide, William. *The Census Book: A Genealogist's Guide to Federal Census Facts, Schedules and Indexes.* Bountiful, Utah: Heritage Quest, 1999.

Kemp, Thomas Jay. *The American Census Handbook.* Wilmington, Delaware: Scholarly Resources, Inc., 2001.

Lainhart, Ann S. *State Census Records.* Baltimore: Genealogical Publishing Co., Inc., 1992.

Szucs, Loretto Dennis, and Matthew Wright. *Finding Answers in U.S. Census Records.* Ancestry Publishing, 2001.

Thorndale, William, and William Dollarhide. *Map Guide to the U.S. Federal Censuses, 1790-1920.* Baltimore: Genealogical Publishing Co., 1987.

Court Records, Probate and Wills

Hawaii. Circuit Courts. *Probate Records, 1848-1916.* Microfilms of original records in the Archives of Hawaiian Islands. (Salt Lake City: Filmed by the Genealogical Society of Utah, 1976). 3 microfilm.

Hawaiian Islands. Circuit Court. *Probate Records, 1845-1900.* (Salt Lake City: Filmed by the Genealogical Society of Utah, 1977).

Emigration, Immigration, Migration and Naturalization

Hawaii. Department of the Interior. *Letters of Denization, 1846-1898.* (Salt Lake City: Filmed by the Genealogical Society of Utah, 1977).

Hawaii. Department of the Interior. *List of British Subjects Who Have Received Special Rights of Citizenship [ca. 1892-1898].* (Salt Lake City: Filmed by the Genealogical Society of Utah, 1977).

Hawaii. Supreme Court. *Naturalization Records, 1874-1904.* (Salt Lake City: Filmed by the Genealogical Society of Utah, 1977).

Index to Naturalization Records, 1840-1892. Microfilm of original records at the State Archives of Hawaii (Iolani Palace Grounds) in Honolulu. (Salt Lake City: Filmed by the Genealogical Society of Utah, 1999).

Judd, Bernice. *Voyages to Hawaii Before 1860: A Record, Based on Historical Narratives in the Libraries of the Hawaiian Mission Children's Society and the Hawaiian Historical Society, Extended to March 1860.* Honolulu, Hawaii: University Press of Hawaii, 1974.

Portugal. Consulado Geral (Honolulu). *Ship Passenger Lists, 1878-1913.* (Salt Lake City: Filmed by the Genealogical Society of Utah, 1977). (online database - ftp://ftp.rootsweb.com/pub/usgenweb/hi/shiplists/portug.txt)

United States. District Court (Hawaii). *Index to Naturalizations [petitions] in the U.S. District Court for the District of Hawaii, 1900-1975*. Washington: National Archives and Records Administration, 1996. 23 microfilm.

Land and Property

British Commission Land Claims, 1843. Honolulu: Pau Hana Press. 1995.

Chinden, Jon J. *The Great Mahele: Hawaii's Land Division of 1848*. Honolulu: University Press of Hawaii, ca. 1958.

Chinen, Jon J. *Original Land Titles in Hawaii*. n.p., 1961.

Hawaii, Registrar of Bureau of Conveyances. *Deeds and Other Records, 1844-1900*. Honolulu: Department of Land and Natural Resources, ca. 1970. 108 microfilm.

Hawaii. Department of Land and Natural Resources. *Award Books, 1836-1855*. (Salt Lake City: Filmed by the Genealogical Society of Utah, 1964). 12 microfilm.

Hawaii. Department of Land and Natural Resources. *Foreign Testimony, 1846-1862*. (Salt Lake City: Filmed by the Genealogical Society of Utah, 1964). 4 microfilm.

Hawaii. Department of Land and Natural Resources. *Native Registers, 1846-1848*. (Salt Lake City: Filmed by the Genealogical Society of Utah, 1964). 4 microfilm.

Hawaii. Department of Land and Natural Resources. *Native Testimony, 1844-1854*. (Salt Lake City: Filmed by the Genealogical Society of Utah, 1864). 4 microfilm.

Hawaii. Department of Land and Natural Resources. *Patents Upon Confirmation of Land Commission, 1847-1961*. (Salt Lake City: Filmed by the Genealogical Society of Utah, 1964). 19 microfilm.

Hone, Wade E. *Land and Property Research in the United States*. Salt Lake City: Ancestry Incorporated, 1997.

Office of the Commissioner of Public Lands of the Territory of Hawaii. *Indices of Awards Made by the Board of Commissioners to Quiet Land Titles in the Hawaiian Islands*. Honolulu: Hawaii Territorial Office, 1929.

Parker, Linda S. *Native American Estate: The Struggle Over Indian and Hawaiian Lands*. Honolulu, Hawaii: University of Hawaii Press, 1989.

Military

Duus, Masayo Umezawa. *Unlikely Liberators: The Men of the 100th and the 442nd*. Honolulu, Hawaii: University of Hawaii Press, 1987.

Leslie's Official History of the Spanish-American War: A Pictorial and Descriptive Record of the Cuban Rebellion, The Causes That Involved the United States, And A Complete Narrative of Our Conflict with Spain on Land and Sea, Supplemented with Fullest Information Respecting Cuba, Puerto Rico, the Philippines and Hawaii. Washington: [Leslie's Weekly], 1899.

United States Department of the Interior. National Park Service, USS Arizona Memorial. *A Comprehensive List of the Names of All Civilians and Military Personnel Killed in the Attack on Pearl Harbor, Dec 7, 1941, Honolulu, Hawaii*. (online database - <ftp://ftp.rootsweb.com/pub/usgenweb/hi/military/pearl.txt>)

United States. Selective Service System. *Hawaii, World War I Selective Service System Draft Registration Cards, 1917-1918*. National Archives Microfilm Publications, M1509. Washington, D.C.: National Archives, 1987-1988.

Vital and Cemetery Records

Arnold, Barry. *Hawaii Birth Register*. North Sydney, NSW: CD-ROM Services, 1995. CD-ROM.

Hawaii (Kingdom). Board of Health. *Reports of Burials, Kingdom of Hawaii, 1861-1892*. Microfilm of originals at the State Dept. of Health, Honolulu. (Salt Lake City: Filmed by the Genealogical Society of Utah, 1978).

Hawaii (Territory). Board of Health. *Birth Records, 1896-1903*. Microfilm of originals in the State Department of Health, Honolulu. (Salt Lake City: Filmed by the Genealogical Society of Utah, 1978). 17 microfilm.

Hawaii (Territory). Board of Health. *Death Records, 1904-1909*. Microfilm of original records at the State Department of Health in Honolulu, Hawaii. (Salt Lake City: Filmed by the Genealogical Society of Utah, 1994).

Hawaii (Territory). Board of Health. *Death Records, 1909-1925; Index 1909-1949*. Microfilm of original records at the Department of Health, Honolulu. (Salt Lake City: Filmed by the Genealogical Society of Utah, 1991). 74 microfilm.

Hawaii (Territory). Board of Health. *Death Registers, 1896-1903*. Microfilm of originals in the State Department of Health, Honolulu. (Salt Lake City: Filmed by the Genealogical Society of Utah, 1978). 17 microfilm.

Hawaii (Territory). Board of Health. *Delayed Birth Records, 1904-1925*. Microfilm of original records at the State Department of Health, Honolulu. (Salt Lake City: Filmed by the Genealogical Society of Utah, 1993-1994). 132 microfilm.

Hawaii (Territory). Board of Health. *Marriage Records, 1904-1909*. Microfilm of original records at the State Department of Health in Honolulu, Hawaii. (Salt Lake City: Filmed by the Genealogical Society of Utah, 1994).

Hawaii (Territory). Board of Health. *Marriage Records, 1909-1925; Indexes 1909-1949*. Microfilm of original records at the State Department of Health, Honolulu. (Salt Lake City: Filmed by the Genealogical Society of Utah, 1991). 61 microfilm.

Hawaii Cemetery Records. 2 vols. Typescript. Salt Lake City: Mrs. Jessie H. Lindsay and the Genealogical Society of Utah, 1942-54.

Hawaii. Circuit Courts. *Divorce Records, 1849-1915*. Microfilm of originals made at Archives of Hawaii in Honolulu. (Salt Lake City: Filmed by the Genealogical Society of Utah, 1977). 34 microfilm.

Hawaii. Circuit Courts. *Divorce Records, 1849-1915*. Microfilm of original records in the Archives of Hawaii in Honolulu. (Salt Lake City: Filmed by the Genealogical Society of Utah, 1977). 141 microfilm.

Hawaii. Department of Health. *Restricted. Divorce Records Index, 1951-1990*. Microfilm of original records at the State Department of Health in Honolulu. (Salt Lake City: Filmed by the Genealogical Society of Utah, 1996). 3 microfilm.

Index to Archives of Hawaii Collection of Marriage Records, 1826-1910. Honolulu, Hawaii: Bishop Museum. (Salt Lake City: Filmed by the Genealogical Society of Utah, 1979).

Index to Births, Marriages, and Deaths in Hawaii Newspapers Prior to 1950. Microfilm. 6 reels. (Salt Lake City: Filmed by the Genealogical Society of Utah, 1977).

Zabriskie, George Olin. *Tombstone Inscriptions from the Royal Mausoleum*. The author, 1969.

County Website	Map Index	Date Created	Parent County or Territory From Which Organized Address/Details
Hawaii www.hawaii-county.com/	D10	1905	**Hilo** Hawaii County; 25 Aupuni St; Hilo, HI 96720; Ph. 808.961.8255 Details: (State Health Dept has m, d, b, wills, probate and land records.)
Honolulu www.co.honolulu.hi.us/	J4	1905	**Honolulu** Honolulu County; 530 S King St; Honolulu, HI 96813; Ph. 808.523.4352 Details: (State Health Dept has m, d, b, wills, probate and land records.)
Kalawao Future website at www.rootsweb.com/ ~higenweb/hawaii.htm	H5	1905	**Maui** Kalawao County; Isle of Molokai; Kalaupapa, HI; Ph. 808.553.5800 Details: (State Health Dept has m, d, b, wills, probate and land records.)
Kauai www.kauaigov.org/	O1	1905	**Lihue** Kauai County; 4963 Rice St; Lihue, HI 96766; Ph. 808.241.6371 Details: (State Health Dept has m, d, b, wills, probate and land records.)
Maui www.co.maui.hi.us/	F6	1905	**Wailuku** Maui County; 200 S High St; Wailuku, HI 96793; Ph. 808.270.7748 Details: (State Health Dept has m, d, b, wills, probate and land records.)

Syringa

IDAHO

CAPITAL: BOISE — TERRITORY 1863 — STATE 1890 (43RD)

The first explorers to travel to Idaho were Lewis and Clark in 1805. Fur traders followed. The fur traders built Fort Hall trading post in 1834 on the Snake River. Outposts near present-day Pocatello and Fort Hall served as important stopping points on the Oregon Trail. In 1848, Idaho became part of the Oregon Territory. In 1859, it became part of the Washington Territory.

The southern part of the state was settled first. Mormon immigrants from Northern Europe founded Franklin, in Cache Valley in 1860. A series of gold rushes in the river valleys of northern Idaho between 1860 and 1863 led to a mining boom. On 3 March 1863, the Idaho Territory was formed from the Washington and Dakota Territories. The Idaho Territory included all of Montana and nearly all of Wyoming in addition to Idaho. With the organization of the Montana Territory in 1864 and the Wyoming Territory in 1868, Idaho took on its present shape. Indian conflicts hampered settlement until the 1880's, when the Native Americans moved to reservations. Another mining boom and the coming of railroads brought more settlers in the 1880's. In about 1910, large irrigation systems and districts were constructed around the Snake River. This opened up new areas for farming and brought many western and mid-western farmers to the area.

Members of the Church of Jesus Christ of Latter-day Saints, also known as Mormons, originally settled Idaho. Other religions soon followed, particularly Catholic and Protestant.

Look for vital records in the following locations:

- **Birth and death records:** The first birth records came from midwives in the 1870's. Midwives sent their reports to county clerks. Counties were required to keep birth and death records between January 1907 and July 1911. Since then statewide birth and death records have been kept at the Idaho Center for Vital Statistics in Boise.
- **Marriage and divorce records:** Idaho Center for Vital Statistics has marriage and divorce records from 1947. County recorders have records of marriages. No licenses were required before 11 March 1895.
- **Wills and probate records:** County clerks' offices.
- **Land records:** County recorder.
- **Census records:** Idaho settlers were included in the Oregon Territorial census of 1850, Washington Territory in 1860, and Idaho Territory in 1870 and 1880. The 1860 Census of Idaho County is included in the Spokane County, Washington enumeration. Parts of southern Idaho were included in the 1860 and 1870 census records of Cache County, Utah. Statewide indexes and mortality schedules are available for the census of 1870 and 1880.

Idaho Center for Vital Statistics
450 West State Street
Boise, Idaho 83702

Societies and Repositories

Adams County Historical Society; PO Box 352; New Meadows, Idaho 93654

Bonner County Genealogical Society; PO Box 27; Dover, Idaho 83827-0027

Bonneville County Historical Society; PO Box 1784; Idaho Falls, Idaho 83401

Boundary County Historical Society; PO Box 809; Bonners Ferry, Idaho 83805

Caldwell, Idaho Genealogical Group; c/o Carol Murphy; 3504 S. Illinois; Caldwell, Idaho 83605

Camas County Historical Society; Fairfield, Idaho 83327

Canyon County Historical Society; PO Box 595; Nampa, Idaho 83651

Caribou County Historical Society; County Courthouse; Soda Springs, Idaho 93276

Cascade Public Library; 105 N. Front St., PO Box 697; Cascade, Idaho 83611

Clearwater County Historical Society; PO Box 1454; Orofino, Idaho 83544

College of Idaho Library; Caldwell, Idaho 83605

College of St. Gertrude Library; Cottonwood, Idaho 83522

Eagle Rock Railroad Historical Society, Inc.; PO Box 2685; Idaho Falls, Idaho 83404; 208.522.4242; <www.ida.net/org/errhsi/>

Elmore County Historical Foundation; PO Box 204; Mountain Home, Idaho 93647

Family History Library: 35 North West Temple Street: Salt Lake City, Utah 84150: 800.346.6044 or 801.240.2584: <www.familysearch.org>: Find a Family History Center near you: <www.familysearch.org/Eng/Library/FHC/frameset_fhc.asp>

Family Scanner Chapter, IGS; PO Box 581; Caldwell, Idaho 83605

Fremont County Historical Society; St. Anthony, Idaho 83445

Gooding County Genealogical Society; 1918 Whipkey Dr.; Gooding, Idaho 83330

Gooding County Historical Society; PO Box 580; Gooding, Idaho 83330

Idaho County Chapter, IGS; Grangeville Centennial Library; 215 W. North; Grangeville, Idaho 83530

Idaho Department of Health and Welfare; 450 W. State St. Statehouse Mail; Boise, Idaho 83720-9990; 208.334.5988; Fax 208.389.9096;

Idaho Genealogical Library; 325 W. State; Boise, Idaho 83702

Idaho Genealogical Society, Inc.; PO Box 1854; Boise, Idaho 83701-1854; 208.345.8838; <www.lili.org/idahogenealogy/>

Idaho Historical Society; 325 State St.; Boise, Idaho 83702

Idaho State Historical Society/Genealogical Society; 450 N. 4th St., 4620 Overland Rd. Rm #204; Boise, Idaho 83705-2867; 208.334.3356; Fax 208.334.3198

Idaho State Historical Society; 1109 Main Street, Suite 250; Boise, Idaho 83702; <www2.state.id.us/ishs/>

Idaho State Library; 325 West State Street; Boise, Idaho 83702; 208.334.4016; <www.lili.org/isl/>

Idaho State Office of the Bureau of Land Management; 1387 So. Vinnell Way; Boise, Idaho 83709-1657; 208.373.4000; Fax 208.373.3888;

Idaho State University Library; Pocatello, Idaho 83209

Ilo-Vollmer Historical Society; PO Box 61; Craigmont, Idaho 83523

Kamiah Genealogical Society; Box 322; Kamiah, Idaho 83536

Kootenai County Genealogical Society; Hayden Lake Library; 8385 North Government Way; Hayden, Idaho 83835; <www.usgennet.org/usa/id/county/kootenai/kcgs/>

Latah County Historical Society; 327 East 2nd Street; Moscow, Idaho 83843; <users.moscow.com/lchs/>

Lewis County Historical Society; Rt. 2, Box 10; Kamiah, Idaho 83536

Lewis-Clark State College Library; Lewiston, Idaho 83501

Lewiston-Nez Perce Co. Library; 533 Thain Rd.; Lewiston, Idaho 83501

Luna House Historical Society; 0310 Third St.; Lewiston, Idaho 83501

Minidoka County Historical Society; PO Box 21; Rupert, Idaho 93350

National Archives and Records Administration-Pacific Northwest Region; 6125 Sand Point Way NE; Seattle, Washington 98115; 206.526.6507; Fax 206.526.4344

Nez Perce Historical Society; PO Box 86; Nez Perce, Idaho 83542

North Idaho College Library; Coeur d'Alene, Idaho 83814

Northwest Nazarene College Library; Nampa, Idaho 83651

Old Fort Boise Historical Society; Parma, Idaho 93660

Payette County Historical Society; PO Box 476; Payette, Idaho 83661

Pocatello Branch Genealogical Society; PO Box 4272; Pocatello, Idaho 83201

Presbyterian Historical Society, United Presbyterian Church in U.S.; 425 Lombard St.; Philadelphia, Pennsylvania 19147; 215.627.1852; Fax 215.627.0509

Pullman, Washington Branch Genealogical Library; 865 Bitterroot; Moscow, Idaho 84843

Ricks College Library Special Collections Area; Rexburg, Idaho 83460-0405; 208.356.2354; Fax 208.356.2390

Roman Catholic Chancery Office Diocese of Boise; 303 Federal Way; Boise, Idaho 83705; 208.342.1311; Fax 208.342.0224

Shoshone County Genealogical Society; PO Box 183; Kellogg, Idaho 83837

South Bannock County Historical Society & Museum; PO Box 387, 110 E. Main St.; Lava Hot Springs, Idaho 83246

South Custer County Historical Society; PO Box 355; Mackay, Idaho 83251

Spirit Lake Historical Society; Spirit Lake, Idaho 83869

Treasure Valley Chapter, IGS; 325 W. State Street; Boise, Idaho 83702

Twin Rivers Genealogical Society; PO Box 386; Lewiston, Idaho 83501

United Methodist Archives Center Drew University Library; PO Box 127; Madison, New Jersey 07940; 215.408.3189; Fax 201.408.3909

University of Idaho Special Collections Library; Moscow, Idaho 83843-4198; 208.885.6534; Fax 208.885.6817

Upper Snake River Valley Historical Society; PO Box 244; Rexburg, Idaho 83440

Valley County Genealogical Society; PO Box 697; Cascade, Idaho 83611

Bibliography and Record Sources

General Sources

An Illustrated History of North Idaho: Embracing Nez Perce, Idaho, Latah, Kootenai and Shoshone Counties, State of Idaho. Spokane, Washington: Western Publishing Company, 1903.

An Illustrated History of the State of Idaho: Containing A History of the State of Idaho from the Earliest Period of its Discovery to the Present Time, Together with Glimpses of its Auspicious Futures; Illustrations...and Biographical Mention of Many Pioneers and Prominent Citizens of Today. 4 vols. in 2. Chicago: Lewis Publishing Co., 1899.

Arnold, Royal Ross. *Indian Wars of Idaho.* Caldwell, Id., The Caxton Printers, Ltd., 1932.

Arrington, Leonard J. *History of Idaho.* 2 vols. Moscow [Idaho]: University of Idaho Press; Idaho State Historical Society, 1994.

Attebery, Louie W. *Idaho Folk Life: Homesteads to Headstones.* Salt Lake City: University of Utah Press, 1985.

Battien, Pauline. *The Gold Seekers: ...A 200 Year History of Mining in Washington, Idaho, Montana & lower British Columbia.* [Washington?: s.n.], c1989 (Colville, Wash.: Statesman-Examiner).

Beal, Merrill D. *A History of Southeastern Idaho: An Intimate Narrative of Peaceful Conquest by Empire Builders… .* Caldwell, Idaho: Caxon Printers, Ltd., 1942.

Beal, Merrill D. and Merle W. Wells. *History of Idaho.* 3 vols. New York: Lewis Historical Publishing Co., 1959.

Bieter, Pat. *The Basques in Idaho.* Boise: Idaho State Historical Society, 197?.

Brooks, Juanita. *History of the Jews in Utah and Idaho.* Salt Lake City: Western Epics, 1973.

Buckendorf, Madeline, and Elizabeth P. Jacox. *Directory of Oral History Resources in Idaho.* [S.l.: Idaho State History Society, 1982].

Catholic Church. Church of the Blessed Sacrament (Montpelier, Idaho). *Church Records, 1897-1985.* (Salt Lake City: Filmed by the Genealogical Society of Utah, 1986-87). 2 microfilm.

Church of Jesus Christ of Latter-day Saints. Cassia Stake (Idaho). *The First One Hundred Years: Cassia-Oakley Idaho Stake, 1887-1987.* [S.n.: Church of Jesus Christ of Latter-day Saints. Cassia Stake (Idaho), n.d.]

Daughters of the American Revolution. Alice Whitman Chapter (Lewiston, Idaho). *Idaho Genealogical Records.* Microfilm of original records in the D.A.R. Library in Washington, D.C. (Salt Lake City: Filmed by the Genealogical Society of Utah, 1970).

Defenbach, Byron. *Idaho, The Place and Its People: A History of the Gem State from Prehistoric to Present Day.* 3 vols. Chicago: American Historical Society, Inc., 1933.

Directory of Churches and Religious Organizations of Idaho. Boise, Idaho: Historical Records Survey, 1940.

Drexler, Joan, comp. *Blackrobes Journey, 1840-1990: To the Loving Memory of the Devoted Pioneer Catholic Clergy and to the Priests, Sisters and Laity of the Current Church Community.* [S.l.: s.n.], 1990.

Etulain, Richard W. *Idaho History: A Bibliography.* Rev. ed. Pocatello: Idaho State University Press, 1979.

Forbush, Harold Sanford. *Education in the Upper Snake River Valley: The Public Schools, 1880-1950.* Rexburg, Idaho: H.S. Forbush, 1992 (Ricks College Press).

French, Hiram Taylor. *History of Idaho: A Narrative Account of its Historical Progress, Its People and Its Principal Interests.* 3 vols. Chicago: Lewis Pub., 1914.

Gobble, John R. *Lineages of the Members (Past and Present), Idaho Society, Sons of the American Revolution, 1909 through 1961… .* Idaho Falls, Idaho: J.R. Gobble, 1962.

Hailey, John. *The History of Idaho.* Boise, Idaho: Syms-York Co., 1910.

Hawley, James H. *History of Idaho: The Gem of the Mountains.* 4 vols. Chicago: S.J. Clarke Publishing Co., 1920.

Hill, Lila . *Early Methodism in Idaho: Extracts from News Articles and Historical Notes; Oregon-Idaho Conference of the United Methodist Church.* Salem, Or.: United Methodist Church. Oregon-Idaho Conference. Commission on Archives and History, 1996.

Howell, Erle. *Methodism in the Northwest.* [S.N.: n.p., n.d.]

Hult, Ruby El. *Steamboats in the Timber.* 2d ed. Portland, Or.: Binfords & Mort, 1968.

Idaho Ethnic Heritage. 3 vols. [S.l.]: Idaho Centennial Commission and Idaho State Historical Society, 1990.

Idaho Genealogical Society (Boise, Idaho). *Roman Catholic Diocese of Boise, Catholic Chancery Records of Idaho, Master Index.* 25 – vols. [Boise, Idaho: Idaho Genealogical Society, 198-?].

Idaho Genealogical Society. *Footprints Through Idaho.* 3 vols. Boise, Idaho: Idaho Genealogical Society, 1989- (Boise, Idaho: Williams Printing).

Idaho Local History: A Bibliography with a Checklist of Library Holdings. Moscow, Idaho: University Press of Idaho, 1976.

Idaho Research Outline. Series US-States, no. 13. Salt Lake City: Family History Library, 1988.

Indian Peoples of Idaho. 2d ed. Boise, Idaho: Boise State University Press, 1979.

Jensen, Dwight William. *Discovering Idaho, A History.* Caldwell, Idaho: Caxton Printers, 1977.

Kestler, William. John Meyers, and James L. Holloway. *Scattered Graves.* [S.l.: s.n.], 1998.

Kirk, John Ohara. *Idaho 100: Stories from Idaho Century Citizens.* Helena, Montana: Falcon Press, 1989.

L. D. S. Individual Histories (Idaho). 2 vols. [S.l.: s.n., 1900?].

Lawless, Elaine J. *Guide to the Idaho Folklore Archives*. Boise, Idaho: Idaho Folklife Center, Idaho State Historical Society, [1983?].

Miller, Donald C. *Ghost Towns of Idaho*. Boulder, Colo.: Pruett Pub. Co., 1976.

Nelson, Milo G., and Charles A. Webbert. *Idaho Local History: A Bibliography With a Checklist of Library Holdings*. Moscow, Idaho: University Press of Idaho, 1976.

Newspapers in the Idaho Historical Society Microfilm Collection. Boise, Idaho: Idaho State Historical Society, 1999?.

Osborn-Ryan, Sharon E. *Cumulative Baptism Index to the Catholic Church Records of the Pacific Northwest*. [S.l.]: Oregon Heritage Press, 1999.

Penson-Ward, Betty. *Idaho Women in History*. Boise, Idaho: Northwest Printing, 1991-.

Powell, Barbara V. *Citizens of North Idaho*. Medical Lake, Washington: B.V. Powell, 1986.

Quinn, Larry D. *A History of Magic Valley*. Twin Falls, Idaho: Publishing West Associates, 1996.

Sappington, Roger Edwin. *The Brethren Along the Snake River: A History of the Church of the Brethren in Idaho and Western Montana*. Elgin, Ill.: Brethren Press, 1966.

Schmick, Judy. *Idaho Surname Index*. Boise, Idaho: Idaho Genealogical Society, 1989.

Schoenberg, Wilfred P. *A History of the Catholic Church in the Pacific Northwest, 1743-1983*. Washington, D.C.: Pastoral Press, 1987.

Simpson, Claude. *Panhandle Personalities, Biographies From The Idaho Panhandle*. Moscow, Idaho: University of Idaho Press, 1984.

Sketches of the Inter-Mountain States: Together with Biographies of Many Prominent and Progressive Citizens Who Have Helped in the Development and History-Making of this Marvelous Region, 1847, 1909, Utah, Idaho, Nevada. Salt Lake City: Salt Lake Tribune, 1909.

Smith, Lorayne Orton. *Zest for Living: Southern Idaho Senior Profiles*. Dallas, Texas: Taylor Publishing, 1991.

Southern California Genealogical Society. *Sources of Genealogical Help in Idaho*. Burbank, California: Southern California Genealogical Society, [n.d.].

Swetnam, Susan Hendricks. *Lives of the Saints in Southeast Idaho: An Introduction to Mormon Pioneer Life Story Writing*. Moscow, Idaho: University of Idaho Press and Idaho State Historical Society, 1991.

The Mining Industry in Idaho: A Short Bibliography of Sources on Mines and Mining in the Idaho State Historical Society Library and Archives. Boise: The Historical Society, 1992.

Thousands of Idaho Surnames: Abstracted From Rejected Federal Land Applications. 5 vols. Portland, OR: Genealogical Forum of Portland, Oregon, 1980-87.

University of Idaho. *Idaho State Documents Catalog Contains 22,632 Catalog Cards on 38 Microfiche Cards and Provides Bibliographic Information on Idaho State Documents from the Territorial Period to 1980*. Boise, Idaho, Mountain States Microfilm, n.d.

Walker, Deward Edgar. *Indians of Idaho*. Moscow: University Press of Idaho, 1978.

Wiggins, Marvin E. *Mormons and Their Neighbors: An Index of Over 75,000 Biographical Sketches from 1820 to the Present*. 2 vols. Provo, UT: Harold B. Lee Library, Brigham Young University, 1984.

Writers' Program (Idaho). *The Idaho Encyclopedia*. Tucson, Ariz.: W. C. Cox Co., 1974.

Atlases, Maps and Gazetteers

An Atlas of Idaho Territory, 1863-1890. [Boise, ID]: Idaho Historical Society, 1978.

Boone, Lalia Phipps. *Idaho Place Names: A Geographical Dictionary*. Moscow, Idaho: University of Idaho Press, 1988.

Gazetteer of Cities, Villages, Unincorporated Communities, and Landmark Sites in the State of Idaho. 3rd ed. Idaho Department of Highways, 1966.

Kramer, Fritz L. "Idaho Town Names." *State Historical Department Biennial Report 23* (1951-52): 14-114.

Patera, Alan H., and John S. Gallagher. *A Checklist of Idaho Post Offices*. Burtonsville, Maryland: The Depot, c1984 (Lake Oswego, Oregon: Raven Press).

Preston, Ralph N. *Maps of Early Idaho*. Corvallis, Oregon: Western Guide Publishers, 1972.

Randall, Art. *A Short History and Postal Records of Idaho Towns: Ada County Through Washington County*. [S.l.]: A. Randall, 1994.

Route of the Oregon Trail in Idaho: From Thomas Fork Valley at the Wyoming State Line Westward to Fort Boise at the Oregon State Line. Boise, Idaho: Idaho Dept. of Highways, 1963.

Schell, Frank R. *Ghost Towns and Live Ones: A Chronology of the Post Office Dept. in Idaho, 1861-1973*. Twin Falls, Idaho, 1973.

Wells, Merle William. *An Atlas of Idaho Territory, 1863-1890*. Boise, Idaho: Idaho Historical Society, 1978.

Census Records
Available Census Records and Census Substitutes

Federal Census 1870, 1880, 1900, 1910, 1920, 1930.

Federal Mortality Schedules 1870, 1880.

Dollarhide, William. *The Census Book: A Genealogist's Guide to Federal Census Facts, Schedules and Indexes*. Bountiful, Utah: Heritage Quest, 1999.

Kemp, Thomas Jay. *The American Census Handbook*. Wilmington, DE: Scholarly Resources, Inc., 2001.

Lainhart, Ann S. *State Census Records*. Baltimore: Genealogical Publishing Co., Inc., 1992.

Pompey, Sherman Lee. *1863 Census of Some Prominent Men in the Idaho Territory*. (Salt Lake City: Filmed by the Genealogical Society of Utah, 1970).

Szucs, Loretto Dennis, and Matthew Wright. *Finding Answers in U.S. Census Records*. Ancestry Publishing, 2001.

Thorndale, William, and William Dollarhide. *Map Guide to the U.S. Federal Censuses, 1790-1920*. Baltimore: Genealogical Publishing Co., 1987.

Upper Snake River Valley Family History Center. *1910 Idaho Census Index*. 1993. Bountiful, UT. AGLL.

Williams, Gene F., comp. *Idaho Territorial Voters Poll Lists, 1863*. Boise, Idaho: Williams Printing, 1996.

Court Records, Probate and Wills

Carl F. Bianchi, Carl F. *Justice For The Times: A Centennial History of the Idaho State Courts*. Boise, Idaho: Idaho Law Foundation, Inc., 1990.

Idaho State Supreme Court Justices, 1890-1970, and Idaho District Judges, 1890-1989. Boise: Idaho Historical Society, 1971-[1989].

Minutes of the Idaho Territorial Supreme Court, 1866-1891. (Boise; Filmed by the Idaho Historical Society, 1961).

U. S. District Court, Idaho Territory, 1866-1890. Moscow, Idaho: University of Idaho Law Library. [n.d.] 11 microfilm.

Emigration, Immigration, Migration and Naturalization

Route of the Oregon Trail in Idaho: From Thomas Fork Valley at the Wyoming State Line Westward to Fort Boise at the Oregon State Line. Boise, Idaho: Idaho Dept. of Highways, 1963.

United States. Bureau of Land Management. *Emigrant Trails of Southeastern Idaho*. Boise, Idaho: U.S. Dept. of the Interior, Bureau of Land Management, 1976.

United States. District Court (Idaho). *Naturalization Records, Central District, Moscow, Idaho, 1892-1935*. Microfilm of originals in the Federal courthouse in Boise, Idaho. (Salt Lake City: Filmed by the Genealogical Society of Utah, 1987).

United States. District Court (Idaho). *Naturalization Records, Eastern District, Pocatello, Idaho, 1893-1945*. Microfilm of originals in the Federal courthouse in Boise, Idaho. (Salt Lake City: Filmed by the Genealogical Society of Utah, 1987). 4 microfilm.

United States. District Court (Idaho). *Naturalization Records, Northern District, Coeur d'Alene, Idaho, 1909-1929*. Microfilm of originals in the Federal courthouse in Boise, Idaho. (Salt Lake City: Filmed by the Genealogical Society of Utah, 1987). 3 microfilm.

United States. District Court (Idaho). *Naturalization Records, Southern District, Boise, Idaho, 1891-1934*. Microfilm of originals in the Federal courthouse in Boise, Idaho. (Salt Lake City: Filmed by the Genealogical Society of Utah, 1987). 4 microfilm.

Land and Property

Note: Early homestead, timber culture act, reclamation land, and mining claim records for Idaho are found at the Bureau of Land Management and the Idaho Historical Society Archives in Boise, Idaho. Additionally, land and mining entries are found in the individual county records.

Avery, J. A. *Stockman's Guide [Southeastern Idaho]*. Idaho: Downey Idahoan, 1913.

Genealogical Forum of Portland, Oregon. *Thousands of Idaho Surnames: Abstracted From Rejected Federal Land Applications*. 5 vols. Portland, Oregon: Genealogical Forum of Portland, Oregon, 1980-1987.

Hone, Wade E. *Land and Property Research in the United States*. Salt Lake City: Ancestry Incorporated, 1997.

Idaho Genealogical Society (Boise, Idaho). *Idaho State Brand Records and Indexes*. 4 vols. Boise, Idaho: The Society, 1988?.

United States. Land Office (Idaho). *Land Records, 1868-1913*. (Salt Lake City: Filmed by the Genealogical Society of Utah, 1989). 23 microfilm.

Military

Haulsee, W. M. et al. *Soldiers in the Great War*. 3 vols. Washington, D.C.: Soldiers Record Publishing Assoc., 1920.

Holloway, James Lafayette. *We Served in the Military, World War II*. (Salt Lake City: Filmed by the Genealogical Society of Utah, 1998).

United States Selective Service System. *Registration Cards of Men Born Between April 1877 and February 1897 (4th Draft Registration), Record Group 147*. Seattle, Washington: National Archives Record's Administration, Pacific Alaska Region, 1940-47.

United States. Adjutant General's Office. *Index to Compiled Service Records of Volunteer Union Soldiers Who Served in Organizations From The Territory of Washington*. Washington, D.C.: The National Archives, 1964.

United States. Selective Service System. *Idaho, World War I Selective Service System Draft Registration Cards, 1917-1918*. National Archives Microfilm Publications, M1509. Washington, D.C.: National Archives, 1987-1988.

World War II Military Records of Pocatello and Surrounding Areas. (Salt Lake City: Filmed by the Genealogical Society of Utah, 1990). 4 microfilm.

Vital and Cemetery Records

AZ, CA, ID, NV, 1850-1951. [S.l.]: Brøderbund, c1996. CD-ROM.

Cemetery Records of Idaho. 12 vols. Originals located in the Idaho Historical Society Genealogical Collection, Boise, Idaho. (Salt Lake City: Genealogical Society of Utah, 1952-1968.)

Church of Jesus Christ of Latter-day Saints. Genealogical Society. *Cemetery Records of Idaho Index*. 2 vols. Salt Lake City: The Society, 1954-1955.

Guide to Public Vital Statistics Records In Idaho, State and County. Boise, Idaho: Historical Records Survey, 1942.

Idaho. Department of Health and Welfare. *Death Certificates, 1911-1937; Index, 1911-1932*. Microfilm of originals at the Department of Health and Welfare in Boise, Idaho. (Salt Lake City: Filmed by the Genealogical Society of Utah, 1988). 63 microfilm.

Miscellaneous Marriage Records Index. (Salt Lake City: Filmed by the Genealogical Society of Utah, 1972). 19 microfilm.

Western States Historical Marriage Index. Rev. Rexburg, Idaho: BYU Idaho, 2002. Online database <abish.byui.edu/special Collections/fhc.gbsearch.htm>.

Woolf, Kathleen. *Death and Burial Records Compiled from Headstones, Sexton Records, Burial Permits, Early Ward Records, and Some Immediate Family Sources*. Microfilm of records at Family History Center, Idaho Falls, Idaho. (Salt Lake City: Filmed by the Genealogical Society of Utah, 1994). 58 microfilm.

County Website	Map Index	Date Created	Parent County or Territory From Which Organized Address/Details
Ada www.adaweb.net/	N3	22 Dec 1864	**Boise** Ada County; 650 Main St; Boise, ID 83702-5986; Ph. 208.383.4417 Details: (Co Clk has m, div, pro, ct & land rec from 1864)
Adams www.co.adams.id.us/	J2	3 Mar 1911	**Washington** Adams County; 107 Michigan Ave; Council, ID 83612-0048; Ph. 208.583.4561 Details: (Co Clk has m, div, pro, ct & land rec from 1900)
Alturas		1864	**Original county** Details: (see Blaine) Abolished 1895 to create Blaine & Lincoln Cos
Bannock www.co.bannock.id.us/	P10	6 Mar 1893	**Bear Lake** Bannock County; 624 E Center St; Pocatello, ID 83201-6274; Ph. 208.236.7340 Details: (Co Clk has b & d rec from 1902, m rec from 1893, div, pro & ct rec)
Bear Lake www.oregontrailcenter.org/bearlakeco.html	P11	5 Jan 1875	**Oneida** Bear Lake County; 7 E Center St; Paris, ID 83261-0000; Ph. 208.945.2212 Details: (Co Clk has b rec 1907-1911, d rec 1907-1915, m & land rec from 1875 & div rec from 1884)
Benewah www.rootsweb.com/~idbenewa/ ben_indx.htm	E2	23 Jan 1915	**Kootenai** Benewah County; 701 College Ave; Saint Maries, ID 83861-0000; Ph. 208.245.2234 Details: (Co Clk has m, bur, div, pro, ct & land rec from 1915)
Bingham* www.co.bingham.id.us/	N10	13 Jan 1885	**Oneida** Bingham County; 501 N Maple St; Blackfoot, ID 83221-1700; Ph. 208.785.8040 Details: (Co Clk has m & land rec from 1885, div & ct rec from 1900, pro rec from 1892, nat rec, Comm minutes from 1855 & school cen 1898-1933)
Blaine www.co.blaine.id.us/	N7	5 Mar 1895	**Alturas** Blaine County; 206 1st Ave S; PO Box 400; Hailey, ID 83333-0400; Ph. 208.788.5500 Details: (Co Clk has b & d rec 1907-1911, m, div, pro, ct & land rec from 1885)
Boise www.co.boise.id.us/	L3	4 Feb 1864	**Original county** Boise County; 420 Main St; Box BC; Idaho City, ID 83631-0157; Ph. 208.392.4431 Details: (Co Clk has m rec from 1868, div rec from 1904, pro & land rec from 1865 & ct rec from 1867; some rec are not complete due to fires)
Bonner www.co.bonner.id.us/	C2	21 Feb 1907	**Kootenai** Bonner County; 215 S 1st Ave; Sandpoint, ID 83864-1392; Ph. 208.265.1434 Details: (Co Clk has b & d rec 1907-1911, m, div & ct rec from 1907, pro rec from 1890 & land rec from 1889)
Bonneville www.co.bonneville.id.us/	N11	7 Feb 1911	**Bingham** Bonneville County; 605 N Capital Ave; Idaho Falls, ID 83402-3582; Ph. 208.529.1350 Details: (Co Clk has m, div, land, pro & ct rec from 1911)
Boundary* www.boundary-idaho.com/	B2	23 Jan 1915	**Bonner, Kootenai** Boundary County; PO Box 419; Bonners Ferry, ID 83805; Ph. 208.267.2242 Details: (Co Clk has m, land, pro & ct rec, some b, d, div & mil rec)
Butte www.rootsweb.com/~idbutte/	M8	6 Feb 1917	**Bingham** Butte County; 248 W Corand; PO Box 737; Arco, ID 83213-0737; Ph. 208.527.3021 Details: (Co Clk has m, bur, div, pro & school rec from 1917, ct rec from 1895 & land rec from 1890)
Camas www.rootsweb.com/~idcamas/	N5	6 Feb 1917	**Blaine** Camas County; 501 Soldier Rd; PO Box 430; Fairfield, ID 83327-0430; Ph. 208.764.2242 Details: (Co Clk has m, div & ct rec from 1917 & incomplete bur rec; Pro Ct has pro rec from 1890)
Canyon www.canyoncounty.org/	M2	7 Mar 1891	**Owyhee, Ada** Canyon County; 1115 Albany; Caldwell, ID 83605-3542; Ph. 208.454.7504 Details: (Co Clk has some b & d rec 1907-1911, m rec from 1895 & land rec from 1892; Dis Ct has div rec from 1892; Mag Ct has pro & ct rec from 1892)

County Website	Map Index	Date Created	Parent County or Territory From Which Organized Address/Details
Caribou www.rootsweb.com/~idcaribo/	O11	11 Feb 1919	**Bannock** Caribou County; 159 S Main St; PO Box 775; Soda Springs, ID 83276-0775; Ph. 208.547.4324 Details: (Co Clk has m rec from 1919, div, pro, ct & land rec)
Cassia www.cassiacounty.org/	P7	20 Feb 1879	**Oneida** Cassia County; 1459 Overland Ave; Burley, ID 83318; Ph. 208.878.5240 Details: (Co Rcdr has b & d rec from 1907-1911; Co Clk has m, div, pro, land, mil & ct rec from 1879 & some nat rec)
Clark* rootsweb.com/~idclark/clark.htm	L9	1 Feb 1919	**Fremont** Clark County; 320 W Main St; PO Box 205; Dubois, ID 83423-0205; Ph. 208.274.5304 Details: (Co Clk has m, div, ct & land rec from 1919)
Clearwater www.geocities.com/jcolleenfranklin/ ClearwaterCounty.html	G3	27 Feb 1911	**Nez Perce** Clearwater County; 150 Michigan Ave; PO Box 586; Orofino, ID 83544-0586; Ph. 208.476.5596 Details: (Co Clk has pro, div & ct rec from 1911; Co Rcdr has m, land & mil rec from 1911)
Custer www.co.custer.id.us/	L6	8 Jan 1881	**Alturas, Lemhi** Custer County; 801 Main St; PO Box 385; Challis, ID 83226; Ph. 208.879.2360 Details: (Co Clk has m, div, ct & land rec from 1872; Pro Ct has pro rec)
Elmore www.rootsquest.com/~idaho/elmore/	N4	7 Feb 1889	**Alturas, Ada** Elmore County; 150 S 4th E St; Mountain Home, ID 83647-3028; Ph. 208.287.2133 Details: (Co Clk has b & d rec 1907-1911, m, div, pro, ct & land rec from 1889)
Franklin www.rootsweb.com/~idfrankl/	Q10	30 Jan 1913	**Oneida** Franklin County; 39 W Oneida St; Preston, ID 83263-1234; Ph. 208.852.1090 Details: (Co Clk has m rec from 1913, ct & land rec)
Fremont www.co.fremont.id.us/	L11	4 Mar 1893	**Bingham, Lemhi** Fremont County; 151 W 1st N; St. Anthony, ID 83445; Ph. 208.624.7332 Details: (Co Clk has b & d rec 1907-1911, m, div, pro, land, ct & nat rec from 1893 & mil rec from 1919)
Gem www.co.gem.id.us/	M2	19 Mar 1915	**Boise, Canyon** Gem County; 415 E Main St; Emmett, ID 83617; Ph. 208.365.4561 Details: (Co Clk has m, div, ct, land & mil rec from 1915; Co Mag has pro rec)
Gooding www.rootsweb.com/~idgoodin/	N5	28 Jan 1913	**Lincoln** Gooding County; 624 Main St; PO Box 417; Gooding, ID 83330-0417; Ph. 208.934.4841 Details: (Co Clk has m, div, pro, ct & land rec from 1913)
Idaho www.rootsquest.com/~idaho/idaho/	I4	4 Feb 1864	**Original county** Idaho County; 320 W Main St Rm 5; Grangeville, ID 83530-1948; Ph. 208.983.2751 Details: (Co Rcdr has b & d rec 1907-1911 & m rec from 1868; Co Clk has land rec from 1862, div & ct rec from 1888)
Jefferson www.co.jefferson.id.us/	M9	18 Feb 1913	**Fremont** Jefferson County; 134 N Clark St; Rigby, ID 83442; Ph. 208.745.7756 Details: (Co Clk has m, div, pro, ct & land rec from 1914)
Jerome www.co.jerome.id.us/	O6	8 Feb 1919	**Gooding, Lincoln** Jerome County; 300 N Lincoln Ave; Jerome, ID 83338-2344; Ph. 208.324.8811 Details: (Co Clk has m, div, pro, ct & land rec from 1919)
Kootenai www.co.kootenai.id.us/	D2	22 Dec 1864	**Nez Perce** Kootenai County; 501 N Government Way; Coeur d'Alene, ID 83814-2990; Ph. 208.769.4447 Details: (Created in 1864, but not organized until 1881) (Co Clk has b & d rec 1907-1912, m, div, pro & ct rec from 1881)

County Website	Map Index	Date Created	Parent County or Territory From Which Organized Address/Details
Latah www.latah.id.us/	F2	22 Dec 1864	**Nez Perce** Latah County; 522 S Adams; PO Box 8068; Moscow, ID 83843; Ph. 208.882.8580 Details: (Created & organized by U.S. congressional enactment, said to be the only Co in the U.S. so created) (Co Clk-Rcdr has b & d rec 1907-1911, m, land & mil dis rec from 1888 & nat rec 1845-1898; Dis Ct has pro rec from 1896, ct rec from 1891 & div rec from 1940)
Lemhi* www.rootsweb.com/~idlemhi/	J6	9 Jan 1869	**Idaho** Lemhi County; 206 Courthouse Dr; Salmon, ID 83467; Ph. 208.756.2815 Details: (Co Clk-Rcdr has b & d rec 1907-1911, m, pro, land, div, mil, ct & nat rec from 1869)
Lewis www.rootsquest.com/~idaho/lewis/	G3	3 Mar 1911	**Nez Perce** Lewis County; 510 Oak St; Nezperce, ID 83543-0000; Ph. 208.937.2661 Details: (Co Clk has m, div, pro, ct & land rec from 1911)
Lincoln www.rootsweb.com/~idlincol/	O6	18 Mar 1895	**Alturas** Lincoln County; 111 W B St; Shoshone, ID 83352-0000; Ph. 208.886.7641 Details: (Co Clk has some b & d rec 1895-1913, m, div, pro, ct & land rec from 1895 & some school rec)
Madison www.co.madison.id.us/	M11	18 Feb 1913	**Fremont** Madison County; 134 E Main; PO Box 389; Rexburg, ID 83440-0389; Ph. 208.356.3662 Details: (Co Clk has m, div, pro, ct & land rec from 1914)
Minidoka* www.minidoka.id.us/	O7	28 Jan 1913	**Lincoln** Minidoka County; 715 G St; Rupert, ID 83350-0000; Ph. 208.436.9511 Details: (Co Clk has m, div, pro, ct & land rec from 1913)
Nez Perce* www.co.nezperce.id.us/	H2	4 Feb 1864	**Original county** Nez Perce County; 1230 Main St; PO Box 896; Lewiston, ID 83501-0896; Ph. 208.799.3090 Details: (Co Clk has b & d rec 1900-1911, m, div, pro, ct & land rec from 1860)
Oneida www.rootsweb.com/~idoneida/	P9	22 Jan 1864	**Original county** Oneida County; 10 Court St; Malad City, ID 83252; Ph. 208.766.4116 Details: (Co Clk has b & d rec 1907-1911, m rec from 1866, mil rec from 1919, nat rec from 1869, div, pro, ct & land rec)
Owyhee owyheecounty.net/	P3	31 Dec 1863	**Original county** Owyhee County; Hwy 78; Murphy, ID 83650-0128; Ph. 208.495.2421 Details: (Co Clk has b & d rec 1907-1913, m rec from 1895, div & ct rec from 1864 & nat rec 1893-1911)
Payette www.rootsquest.com/~idaho/payette/	L2	28 Feb 1917	**Canyon** Payette County; 1130 3rd Ave N; Payette, ID 83661; Ph. 208.642.6000 Details: (Co Clk has m, div, pro, ct & land rec from 1917 & mil dis rec from 1919)
Power* www.rootsweb.com/~idpower/index.html	O9	30 Jan 1913	**Bingham, Blaine, Oneida** Power County; 543 Bannock Ave; American Falls, ID 83211-1200; Ph. 208.226.7611 Details: (Co Clk has m rec from 1914 & div rec from 1916; Pro Ct has pro rec; Mag Ct has ct rec; Asr Office has land rec)
Shoshone www.rootsweb.com/~idshosho/	E3	4 Feb 1864	**Original county** Shoshone County; 700 Bank St; Wallace, ID 83873-1049; Ph. 208.752.3331 Details: (Co Clk has b & d rec 1907-1911, m rec from 1875, div rec from 1887, pro rec from 1885, ct rec from 1884 & land rec from 1871)
Teton* homepages.rootsweb.com/~bar19/teton.htm	M11	26 Jan 1915	**Madison, Fremont, Bingham** Teton County; 89 N Main St; PO Box 756; Driggs, ID 83422-0756; Ph. 208.354.2905 Details: (Co Clk has m, div, pro, ct & land rec from 1916)

County Website	Map Index	Date Created	Parent County or Territory From Which Organized Address/Details
Twin Falls www.rootsweb.com/~idtwinfa/	P5	21 Feb 1907	**Cassia** Twin Falls County; 425 Shoshone St N; PO Box 126; Twin Falls, ID 83303-0126; Ph. 208.736.4000 Details: (Co Clk-Rcdr has b & land rec from 1907 & mil rec from 1919; Ct Services has div, pro & ct rec from 1907)
Valley www.infowest.com/personal/w/ wcraig/valleycounty/index.html	K4	26 Feb 1917	**Boise, Idaho** Valley County; 219 N Main St; PO Box 737; Cascade, ID 83611; Ph. 208.382.4297 Details: (Co Rcdr has m rec from 1929 & land rec from 1904; Co Clk has div rec from 1950, pro rec from 1934, mil & ct rec from 1917)
Washington www.ruralnetwork.net/~wcassr/	L2	20 Feb 1879	**Boise** Washington County; 256 E Court St; Weiser, ID 83672-0670; Ph. 208.549.2092 Details: (Co Clk has b & d rec 1907-1911, m, div, pro, ct & land rec from 1879)

Violet

ILLINOIS

CAPITAL: SPRINGFIELD — TERRITORY 1809 — STATE 1818 (21ST)

In 1673, Jacques Marquette and Louis Joliet became the first to explore Illinois. The French established permanent settlements in 1699 at Cahokia and 1703 at Kaskaskia. The Illinois area was ceded to Great Britain in 1763 after the French and Indian War. Many French settlers fled to St. Louis, Natchez, and other towns at this time. Virginians began to move into the region about 1769. The area was attached to Quebec in 1774.

During the Revolutionary War, George Rogers Clark captured Kaskaskia and Cahokia, securing the lands north of the Ohio River for the United States. Virginia claimed all the land north of the Ohio River for itself, but ceded it to the United States in 1784. In 1787, Illinois became part of the Northwest Territory. Three years later, Illinois became part of the Indiana Territory. The Illinois Territory was formed in 1809, with the Wisconsin region being transferred to the Michigan Territory in 1818.

The first settlers came by way of the Ohio River from North Carolina, Tennessee, Virginia, Kentucky, Maryland, and Pennsylvania. They settled in the southern part of the state. At the time of statehood in 1818, most of the population still resided in the southern part of the state. In about 1825, settlers from the New England states and New York came on the Erie Canal, the Great Lakes, or the National Road to settle the northern portion of the state. Industrial growth in the 1830's and 1840's brought thousands of Irish, southern Europeans, and Germans to man the factories around Lake Michigan. The expulsion of Sauk and Fox warriors in 1832 ended the last Indian threats to settlement. Transportation improvements between 1838 and 1856 stimulated migration into the state. The National Road, reached Vandalia in 1838; the Illinois-Michigan Canal opened in 1848; and the Illinois Central Railroad was completed in 1856. Members of The Church of Jesus Christ of Latter-day Saints, also known as Mormons, came to Illinois in 1839 and founded Nauvoo on the Mississippi River. At one time it was the state's most populous city. Illinois sent about 255,000 men to fight the Confederacy.

Look for vital records in the following locations:
- **Birth and death records:** Division of Vital Records, State Department of Public Health, Springfield, Illinois. Statewide registration of births and deaths began in 1916. Certified copies are issued only to legally authorized (related) persons. Uncertified copies are issued for genealogical purposes. Some county clerks have birth and death records from 1877 to 1916, with a few as early as 1838.
- **Marriage and divorce records:** County clerks. Marriage licenses were not required until 1877, but some counties have records as early as 1790. Divorces were granted by the legislature and the circuit courts in the early 1800's. The Superior Court of Cook County in Chicago has custody of divorces and the county court clerks have custody of the divorce records.
- **Court and real estate records:** Counties with a population of more than 70,000 had probate courts prior to 1960. Counties with fewer people handled probate matters in the county court. Since 1960, probate matters have been handled by the circuit court. The court recorder of deeds handles all matters pertaining to real estate.
- **Census records:** Territorial and state censuses were taken in 1810, 1818, 1820, 1825, 1835, 1840, 1845, 1855, and 1865. Some residents were also listed in the 1807 Indiana Territorial census.
- **Military records:** Department of Veterans Affairs, Springfield, Illinois. VA maintains files with names of about 600,000 veterans buried in Illinois. They are listed in alphabetical order. A cemetery listing, by county, notes veteran burials. An index file of peacetime soldiers and those with unknown service is also available. Soldiers' discharge records are available at county courthouses. The State Archivist, Archives Building in Springfield might also have useful records.

Illinois State Archives
Norton Bldg.
Springfield, Illinois 62756
217.785.1266;

Societies and Repositories

Afro-American Historical and Genealogical Society of Chicago, Inc.; PO Box 37-7651; Chicago, Illinois 60637

Afro-American Historical and Genealogical Society, Little Egypt; 703 S. Wall St. #5; Carbondale, Illinois 62901

Afro-American Historical and Genealogical Society; 12516 S. Lowe St.; Chicago, Illinois 60628

Alliance Chapter, Illinois NSDAR; Urbana-Champaign, Illinois; <www.rootsweb.com/~ilacdar/>

American Baptist Historical Society (Illinois); 1106 South Goodman St.; Rochester, New York 14620; 716.473.1740

American Bicentennial Chapter, ILSSAR; 657 Darien Court; Hoffman Estates, Illinois 60194-2573; 847.884.7751

Archives of the American Lutheran Church Wartburg Theological Seminary (Illinois); 333 Wartburg Place; Dubuque, Iowa 52001

Arlington Heights Memorial Library; 500 N. Dunton Ave.; Arlington Heights, Illinois 60004; 708.392.0100; Fax 708.392.0136

Assenisipia Chapter, ILSSAR; PO Box 663; Manteno, Illinois 60950-0663

Assumption Public Library; 131 N. Chestnut, PO Box 227; Assumption, Illinois 62510-0227

Balzekas Museum of Lithuanian Culture; 6500 S. Pulaski; Chicago, Illinois 60632

Belleville Public Library; 121 E. Washington St.; Belleville, Illinois 62220; 618.234.0441; Fax 618.234.9474

Blackhawk Genealogical Society; PO Box 3912; Rock Island, Illinois 61204-3912

Bloomington-Normal Genealogical Society; PO Box 489; Normal, Illinois 61761-0488

Bond County Genealogical Society; PO Box 172; Greenville, Illinois 62246

Brookfield Historical Society; 8820. ^{1}/$_2$ Brookfield Avenue; Brookfield, Illinois 60513-1670; <www.gailla.com/bhs/>

Bryan-Bennett Library; 402 S. Broadway; Salem, Illinois 62881

Bureau County Genealogical Society; PO Box 402; Princeton, Illinois 61356-0402; <www.rootsweb.com/~ilbcgs/>

Carnegie Public Library; 6th and Van Buren Sts.; Charleston, Illinois 61920

Carroll County Genealogical Society; PO Box 347; Savanna, Illinois 61074; <www.internetni.com/~ahaliotis/index2.html>

Cass County Historical/Genealogical Society; PO Box 11; Virginia, Illinois 62691; <www.rootsweb.com/~ilcchgs/>

Champaign Genealogical Society; c/o Champaign County Historical Archives; 201 S. Race St.; Urbana, Illinois 61801-3283

Chicago Branch, National Archives; 7358 S. Pulaski Rd.; Chicago, Illinois 60629

Chicago Genealogical Society; PO Box 1160; Chicago, Illinois 60690

Chicago Historical Society; North Ave. and Clark St.; Chicago, Illinois 60614

Chicago Municipal Reference Library; City Hall-Room 1004, 121 N. LaSalle St.; Chicago, Illinois 60602

Chillicothe Historical Society; PO Box 181; Chillicothe, Illinois 61523-0181;

Christian Co. Genealogical Library; Junction of Rts. 48 & 49 East; Taylorville, Illinois 62568

Christian County Genealogical Society; PO Box 28; Taylorville, Illinois 62568; 287.7719; <www.homepage.macomb.com/~tkuntz/christianco.htm>

Clay County Genealogical Society; Box 94; Louisville, Illinois 62858

Clinton County Historical Society; 1091 Franklin St.; Carlyle, Illinois 62231; 618.594.2683; <www.carlyle.il.us/mus.htm>

Colchester Area Historical Society; 3975 E. 650th St.; Colchester, Illinois 62326

Coles County Illinois Genealogical Society; PO Box 592; Charleston, Illinois 61920; <www.rootsweb.com/~ilcoles/ccgs.htm>

Cook Memorial Library; 413 N. Milwaukee Ave.; Libertyville, Illinois 60048

Crawford County Historical Society and Museum; PO Box 554; Robinson, Illinois 62454-0554; 618.592.3310; <www.rootsweb.com/~ilcchs/>

Cumberland and Coles County of Illinois Genealogical Society; Rt. 1, Box 141; Toledo, Illinois 62468

Cumberland County Historical and Genealogical Society of Illinois; Greenup, Illinois 62428

Czech & Slovak American Genealogy Society of Illinois; PO Box 313; Sugar Grove, Illinois 60554;

Czech & Slovak Gen. Library; T. G. Masaryk School, 5701 22nd Place; Cicero, Illinois 60804

Danville Public Library; 307 N. Vermilion St.; Danville, Illinois 61832

Decatur (Macon County) Genealogical Society; PO Box 1548; Decatur, Illinois 62525.1548; <www.rootsweb.com/~ildcgs/>

Decatur Genealogical Library; 356 N. Main St.; Decatur, Illinois 62523

Des Plaines Historical Society; 789 Pearson St.; Des Plaines, Illinois 60016

DeWitt County Genealogical Society; Box 329; Clinton, Illinois 61727

Douglas County Illinois Genealogical Society; PO Box 113; Tuscola, Illinois 61953

Dundee Township Historical Society; 426 Highland Ave.; Dundee, Illinois 60118

Dunton Genealogical Society; 500 North Dunton; Arlington Heights, Illinois 60004

DuPage Co. Historical Museum; 103 E. Wesley St.; Wheaton, Illinois 60187

DuPage County Genealogical Society; PO Box 133; Lombard, Illinois 60148

DuPage County Genealogical Society; PO Box 3; Wheaton, Illinois 60189-0003;

Eastern Illinois University; Booth Library, 600 Lincoln Ave.; Charleston, Illinois 61920; 217.581.6093;

Edgar County Genealogical Society; PO Box 304; Paris, Illinois 61944-0304

Edgar County Historical Society; 408 North Main; Paris, Illinois 61944-1549

Edgewater Historical Society; 5555 N. Sheridan Rd. #1203; Chicago, Illinois 60640;

Edwards County Historical Society; 212 W. Main Street; Albion, Illinois 62806; <www.rootsweb.com/~iledward/ehistsoc.html>

Effingham County Genealogical Society; PO Box 1166; Effingham, Illinois 62401; <www.rootsweb.com/~ieffing/lookups.htm>

Ela Historical Society; 95 E. Main Street; Lake Zurich, Illinois 60047; <www.lzarea.org/ehs/>

ELCA Archives; 321 Bonnie Lane; Elk Grove Village, Illinois 60007; 847.690.9410;

Elgin Area Historical Society; 360 Park Street; Elgin, Illinois 60120;

Elgin Genealogical Society; PO Box 1418; Elgin, Illinois 60121.1418; <nsn.nslsilus.org/elghome/egs/index.html>

Ellwood House Museum (DeKalb Co.); 509 N. First St.; DeKalb, Illinois 60115

Essley Noble Museum, Mercer Co. Historical Society; 1406 SE 2nd Ave.; Aledo, Illinois 61231; 309.582.2280 309.584.4820

Evangelical Lutheran Church in America (ELCA) Archives; 8765 W. Higgins Rd.; Chicago, Illinois 60631-4198; 773.380.2818; Fax 773.380.2977

Evans Public Library; 215 S. 5th St.; Vandalia, Illinois 62471

Evanston Historical Society; 225 Greenwood; Evanston, Illinois 60201;

Family Archives c/o Audrey R. Miller; 2222 E. State St., G-18; Rockford, Illinois 61104

Fayette County Genealogical Society; Box 177; Vandalia, Illinois 62471

Fellowship of Brethren Genealogists; 1451 Dundee Ave.; Elgin, Illinois 60120

Forest Park Historical Society, c/o Forest Park Library; 7555 Jackson Ave.; Forest Park, Illinois 60130

Fort LaMotte Genealogical and Historical Society, c/o LaMotte Twp. Library; Palestine, Illinois 62451

Fox Lake Area Historical Society; PO Box 4; Fox Lake, Illinois 60020; <www.rootsweb.com/~ilflahs/histsoc.html>

Fox Valley Genealogical Society; PO Box 5435; Naperville, Illinois 60567-5435; <members.aol.com/fvgs1/index.html/>

Frankfort Area Genealogical Society; PO Box 463; West Frankfort, Illinois 62896

Freeburg Historical and Genealogical Society; Box 69; Freeburg, Illinois 62243

Freeport Public Library; 314 W. Stephenson St.; Freeport, Illinois 61032

Fulton County Historical and Genealogical Society; PO Box593; Canton, Illinois 61520

Gail Borden Public Library; 200 N. Grove Ave.; Elgin, Illinois 60120

Galena Historical Museum (Jo Daviess Co.); 211 S. Bench St.; Galena, Illinois 61036

Garrett Evangelical Theological Seminary; 2121 Sheridan Road; Evanston, Illinois 60201; 847.866.3909; Fax 708.866.3957

Genealogical Forum of Elmhurst, Illinois; 120 E. Park; Elmhurst, Illinois 60126

Genealogical Society of DcKalb County, Illinois; PO Box 295; Sycamore, Illinois 60178

Genealogical Society of Southern Illinois, c/o John A. Logan College; Rt. 2 Box 145; Carterville, Illinois 62918-9599

Genealogy Society of Southern Illinois; Carterville, Illinois; <www.jal.cc.il.us/Gssi_org.html>

Glen Ellyn Historical Society; PO Box 283; Glen Ellyn, Illinois 60138; <www.glen.ellyn.com/historical/>

Glenview Public Library; 1930 Glenview Rd.; Glenview, Illinois 60025

Golden Historical Society, Inc.; Box 148; Golden, Illinois 62339; 217.696.2360;

Great River Genealogical Society, c/o Quincy Public Library; 526 Jersey St.; Quincy, Illinois 62301.3996; <www.outfitters.com/~grgs/>

Greater Harvard Area Historical Society; 301 Hart Blvd.; PO Box 505; Harvard, Illinois 60033

Greene County Historical and Genealogical Society; PO Box 137; Carrollton, Illinois 62016; <www.rootsweb.com/~ilgreene/gcgs.htm>

Greenville Public Library; 414 E. Main; Greenville, Illinois 62246

Hancock County Historical Society; Carthage, Illinois 62361

Harold Washington Library Center, Chicago Public Library, 6N-5, Social Sciences Division, History Section; 400 State St.; Chicago, Illinois 60605

Henry County Genealogical Society; PO Box 346; Kewanee, Illinois 61443; <www.rootsweb.com/~ilhcgs/index.html>

Henry Historical and Genealogical Society; 610 North St.; Henry, Illinois 61537

Historical Society of OPRF; PO Box 771; Oak Park, Illinois 60303-0771; <www.oprf.com/oprfhist/>

Ida Public Library; 320 N. State St.; Belvidere, Illinois 61008; 815.544.3838;

Illiana Genealogical and Historical Society; PO Box 207; Danville, Illinois 61834-0207

Illiana Genealogical Library; 19 E. North St.; Danville, Illinois 61832

Illinois Jewish Genealogical Society; 404 Douglas; Park Forest, Illinois 60466

Illinois Regional Archives Depository System (IRAD); Archives Building; Springfield, Illinois 62756; 217.782.4682

Illinois Regional Archives Depository, North-eastern Illinois Univ., Ronald Williams Library; 5500 N. St. Louis Ave.; Chicago, Illinois 60625-4699

Illinois State Archives Margaret Cross Norton Building; Springfield, Illinois 62756; 217.782.3492; Fax 217.524.3930

Illinois State Archives; Norton Building, Capitol Complex; Springfield, Illinois 62756; 217.524.3930; <www.cyberdriveillinois.com/departments/archives/archives.html>

Illinois State Genealogical Society; PO Box 10195; Springfield, Illinois 62791-0195; 217.789.1968; <www.rootsweb.com/~ilsgs/; <www.tbox.com/isgs>

Illinois State Historical Society; Old State Capitol; Springfield, Illinois 62701-1503; 217.782.4836

Illinois State University; Williams Hall, Campus Box 5500; Normal, Illinois 61790-5500; 309.452.6027

Illinois Veterans' Home Library; 1707 North 12th, Quincy; Quincy, Illinois 62301

Iroquois County Genealogical Society; Old Courthouse Museum; 103 W. Cherry St.; Watseka, Illinois 60970; <www.rootsweb.com/~ilicgs/>

Jackson County Historical Society; 1616 Edith Street; Murphysboro, Illinois 62966; <home.globaleyes.net/loganmus/JCHSEgypt.htm>

Jacksonville Area Genealogical and Historical Society; 416 S. Main St.; Jacksonville, Illinois 62650.2904

Jasper County Genealogical and Historical Society; c/o Newton Public Library; Newton, Illinois 62448

Jefferson County Genealogical Society; PO Box 1131; Mt. Vernon, Illinois 62864; <www.rootsweb.com/~iljeffer/gensociety.htm>

Jersey County Genealogical Society; PO Box 12; Jerseyville, Illinois 62052; <www.jvil.com/~jchs/>

Jewish Genealogical Society of Illinois; PO Box 515; Northbrook, Illinois 60065.0515; 847.509.0201; <www.jewishgen.org/jgsi/>

John Mosser Public Library; 106 W. Meek St.; Abingdon, Illinois 61410

Johnson County Genealogical and Historical Society; PO Box 1207; Vienna, Illinois 62995;

Joiner History Room, Sycamore Public Library; 103 E. State St.; Sycamore, Illinois 60178

Kane County Genealogical Society; PO Box 504; Geneva, Illinois 60134; <www.rootsweb.com/~ilkcgs/>

Kankakee Valley Genealogical Society; PO Box 442; Bourbonnais, Illinois 60914; <www.kvgs.org/index.html>

Kendall Co. Hist. Soc.; PO Box 123; Yorkville, Illinois 60560; 630.553.6777;

Kendall County Genealogical Society; PO Box 1086; Oswego, Illinois 60543

Kendall County Historical Society; PO Box 123; Yorkville, Illinois 60560; Ph. 630.553.6777

Kishwaukee Genealogists; PO Box 5503; Rockford, Illinois 61125-0503

Knox County Historical Society; PO Box 1757; Galesburg, Illinois 61402.1757;

Knox County Illinois Genealogical Society; PO Box 13; Galesburg, Illinois 61402-0013

LaGrange Public Library; 10 W. Cossitt; LaGrange, Illinois 60525

LaHarpe Historical and Genealogical Society; Box 289; LaHarpe, Illinois 61450

Lake County, Illinois Genealogical Society; PO Box 721; Libertyville, Illinois 60048-0721; <www.rootsweb.com/~illcgs/>

LaSalle County Genealogical Guild; 115 West Glover St.; Ottawa, Illinois 61350; <www.rootsweb.com/~illcgg/>

Lawrence County Genealogical Society; R #1, Box 44; Bridgeport, Illinois 62417

Lee County Genealogical Society; PO Box 6; Dixon, Illinois 61021-0063; <www.rootsweb.com/~illee/>

Lemont Area Historical Society; PO Box 126; Lemont, Illinois 60439; <www.township.com/lemont/historical/>

Lewis and Clark Genealogical Society; PO Box 485; Godfrey, Illinois 62035

Lexington Genealogical and Historical Society; 318 W. Main St.; Lexington, Illinois 61753

Litchfield Carnegie Library (Montgomery Co. Gen. Soc.); PO Box 212; Litchfield, Illinois 62056-0212

Lithuanian American Genealogy Society; c/o Balzekas Museum of Lithuanian Culture; 6500 Pulaski Road; Chicago, Illinois 60629-5136; <feefhs.org/baltic/lt/frg.lags.html>

Little Rock Township Public Library; N. Center Street; Plano, Illinois 60545

Logan County Genealogical Society; PO Box 283; Lincoln, Illinois 62656

Lyons Public Library; 4209 Joliet Ave.; Lyons, Illinois 60534

Macoupin County Genealogical Society; PO Box 95; Staunton, Illinois 62088-0095; <www.rootsweb.com/~ilmacoup/m_gensoc.htm>

Madison Co. Gen. Soc. Library, Edwardsville Public Library; 112 S. Kansas St.; Edwardsville, Illinois 62025

Madison Co. Historical Museum and Library; 715 N. Main St.; Edwardsville, Illinois 62025

Madison County Genealogical Society; PO Box 631; Edwardsville, Illinois 62025.0631

Marion County Genealogical and Historical Society; PO Box 342; Salem, Illinois 62881

Marissa Historical and Genealogical Society; PO Box 27; Marissa, Illinois 62257

Marshall County Historical Society; 566 N. High St.; Lacon, Illinois 61540

Mascoutah Historical Society; Mascoutah, Illinois 62258; <www.mascoutah.com/Historical/WEBPG.HTM>

Mason County Genealogical & Historical Society; PO Box 446; Havana, Illinois 62644.0446; <www.havana.lib.il.us/community/mcghs.html>

Mason County LDS Genealogical Project; R 1, Box 193; Havana, Illinois 62644

Massac County Genealogical Society; PO Box 1043; Metropolis, Illinois 62960; <www.rootsweb.com/~ilmcgs/>

Mattoon Public Library; Charleston Ave. and 17th St.; Mattoon, Illinois 61938

McDonough County Genealogical Society; PO Box 202; Macomb, Illinois 61455; <www.macomb.com/mcgs/>

McHenry County Historical Society; PO Box 434; Union, Illinois 60180; <www.crystallakenet.org/mchs/>

McHenry County Illinois Genealogical Society; PO Box 184; Crystal Lake, Illinois 60039.0184;

McHenry Library; PO Box 184; Crystal Lake, Illinois 60014-0184

McLean Co. Gen. Soc. Library; The Old McLean Co. Courthouse; Bloomington, Illinois 61701

McLean County Genealogical Society; PO Box 488; Normal, Illinois 61761

Mennonite Historical and Genealogical Society, Illinois; PO Box 819; Metamora, Illinois 61548

Mercer County Historical Society; Essley-Noble Museum; 1406 SE 2nd Ave.; Aledo, Illinois 61231; <www.rootsweb.com/~ilmercer/mchs.htm>

Methodist, Illinois Great Rivers Conference Historical Society; 1211 North Park Street; Bloomington, Illinois 61701; 309.828.5092

Metropolis Public Library; 317 Metropolis St.; Metropolis, Illinois 62960

Monroe County Genealogical Society; PO Box 381; Columbia, Illinois 62236; <www.rootsweb.com/~ilmonroe/gs.htm>

Montgomery County Genealogical Society; PO Box 212; Litchfield, Illinois 62056

Morgan Area Genealogical Association; Waverly Genealogical & Historical Society; PO Box 84; Jacksonville, Illinois 62651; <www.rootsweb.com/~ilmaga/index.html>

Moultrie County Historical and Genealogical Society; PO Box 588; Sullivan, Illinois 61951.0588; <www.354.com/bethany/genealogy.htm>

Mount Prospect Historical Society; 101 South Maple Street; Mount Prospect, Illinois 60056.3203; (847) 392.8995; <www.mphist.org/mphshome.htm>

Mount Pulashi Township Historical Society; 104 E. Cooke St.; Mt. Pulashi, Illinois 62548

National Archives-Great Lakes Region; 7358 South Pulaski Road; Chicago, Illinois 60629; 773.581.7816

Newberry Library; 60 W. Walton St; Chicago, Illinois 60610-3380, 231.943.9090, <www.newbery.org>

North Central Illinois Genealogical Society; PO Box 4635; Rockford, Illinois 61110.4635

North Suburban Genealogical Society; Winnetka Public Library; 768 Oak St.; Winnetka, Illinois 60093

Northeastern Illinois University, Ronald Williams Library; 5500 N. St. Louis Ave.; Chicago, Illinois 60625-4699; 773.794.6279;

Northern Illinois Chapter, AHSGR; 208 Cold Spring Ct.; Palatine, Illinois 60067; (847) 397.7604; <www.ahsgr.org/ilnorthe.html>

Northwest Suburban Council of Genealogists; PO Box AC; Mt. Prospect, Illinois 60056

Odell Historical and Genealogical Society; PO Box 82; Odell, Illinois 60460

Office of Vital Records State Department of Public Health; 605 West Jefferson Street; Springfield, Illinois 62702

Ogle County Historical Society; 6th and Franklin Streets; Oregon, Illinois 61061

Ogle County Illinois Genealogical Society; PO Box 251; Oregon, Illinois 61061

Ostfriesian Heritage Society of East Central Illinois; 3154 CR 2000E; Rantoul, Illinois 61866; 217.892.4776

Palatines to America, Illinois Chapter; PO 9638; Peoria, Illinois 61612-9638

Peoria County Genealogical Society; PO Box 1489; Peoria, Illinois 61655-1489; <www.usgennet.org/usa/il/county/peoria/pcgs.html>

Peoria Public Library; 107 N.E. Monroe St.; Peoria, Illinois 61602

Perry County Historical Society; PO Box 1013; DuQuoin, Illinois 62832

Piatt County Historical and Genealogical Society.; PO Box 111; Monticello, Illinois 61856

Pike and Calhoun Counties Genealogical Society; PO Box 104; Pleasant Hill, Illinois 62366; <www.intersurf.com/~johnjanr/hsp.htm>

Polish Genealogical Society of America; 984 N. Milwaukee Ave.; Chicago, Illinois 60622;

Polish Museum of America; 984 N. Milwaukee Ave.; Chicago, Illinois 60622<www.PolishRoots.org>

Pontiac Public Library; 211 E. Madison; Pontiac, Illinois 61764

Putnam County Historical Society; PO Box 74; Hennepin, Illinois 61327; <www.rootsweb.com/~ilputnam/pchs.htm>

Randolph County Genealogical Society; 600 State St., Room 306; Chester, Illinois 62233; <www.rootsweb.com/~ilrcgs/index.htm>

Regenstein Library, Slavic & East European Studies, June Pachuta Farris; Room 263, 1100 E. 57th St.; Chicago, Illinois 60637

Richland County Genealogical and Historical Society; Box 202; Olney, Illinois 62450

Rock Island County Historical Society; 822 11th Avenue; Moline, Illinois 61265-1221; <www.netexpress.net/~richs/>

Rockford Public Library; 215 N. Wyman St.; Rockford, Illinois 61101

Rogers Park / West Ridge Historical Society; 6424 N. Western; Chicago, Illinois 60645-5422; 773.764.2824; <www.wecaretoo.com/Organizations/IL/rpwrhs.html>

Roman Catholic Archives of the Archdiocese of Chicago; St. Mary of the Lake Seminary; Mundelein, Illinois 60060; 312.831.0711

Saline County Genealogical Society; PO Box 4; Harrisburg, Illinois 62946

Sangamon County Genealogical Society; PO Box 1829; Springfield, Illinois 62705.1829; <www.rootsweb.com/~ilsangam/scgs/scgs.htm>

Schuyler Co. Hist. Museum & Gen. Center; Madison & Congress, PO Box 96; Rushville, Illinois 62681

Schuyler Jail Museum Genealogical and Historical Society; 2005 Congress; Rushville, Illinois 62681

Shawnee Library System, C. E. Brehm Memorial Public Library District; 101 S. Seventh St.; Mt. Vernon, Illinois 62864; 618.242.6322; Fax 618.242.0810;

Shelby County Historical and Genealogical Society; 151 South Washington; Shelbyville, Illinois 62565;

Society of Colonial Wars in the State of Illinois; 25 N. Halsted St. Suite #302; Chicago, Illinois 60661; <www.execpc.com/~sril/ilcw.html>

Sons of the American Revolution (SAR), Illinois Society; PO Box 2314; Naperville, Illinois 60567

Sons of Union Veterans of the Civil War, Illinois Dept.; PO Box 2314; Naperville, Illinois 60567

South Suburban Gen. & Hist. Soc. Research Library; Roosevelt Center, 320 E. 161st Pl.; South Holland, Illinois 60473

South Suburban Genealogical and Historical Society; PO Box 96; South Holland, Illinois 60473-0096; <www.rootsweb.com/~ssghs/ssghs.htm>

Southern Illinois University, c/o Special Collections; Morris Library-6632; Carbondale, Illinois 62901; 618.453.3040;

St. Clair County, Illinois Genealogical Society; PO Box 431; Belleville, Illinois 62222-0431; <www.compu.type.net/rengen/stclair/stchome.htm>

Stark County Genealogical Society; PO Box 83; Toulon, Illinois 61483

Stark County Historical Society; West Jefferson; Toulon, Illinois 61483

Staunton Public Library, George & Santina Sawyer Genealogy Rm.; 306 W. Main; Staunton, Illinois 62088

Stephen Decatur Chapter, NSDAR; Decatur, Illinois; <www.rootsweb.com/~ilsdcdar/>

Stephenson County Genealogical Society; PO Box 514; Freeport, Illinois 61032

Stephenson County Historical Society; 110 Coates Place; Freeport, Illinois 61032

Sterling-Rock Falls Historical Society; 1005 E. 3rd St.

Swedish American Historical Society; 5125 No. Spaulding Ave.; Chicago, Illinois 60625,

Swen Parson Hall, c/o Regional History Center; Northern Illinois University; DeKalb, Illinois 60115; 815.753.1779;

Swenson Swedish Immigration Center, Augustana College; 639 38th St.; Rock Island, Illinois 61201-2296

Tazewell County Genealogical & Historical Society; PO Box 312; 719 N. 11th St.; Pekin, Illinois 61555.0312; <www.rootsweb.com/~iltcghs>

Thornton Township Historical Society/Genealogical Society; 154 E. 154th St.; Harvey, Illinois 60426

Three Rivers Public Library District-Local Hist. Collection; PO Box 300; Channahon, Illinois 60410

Tinley Moraine Genealogists; PO Box 521; Tinley Park, Illinois 60477

Tree Climbers Society; 906 Dove St.; Rolling Meadows, Illinois 60008

Tri-County Genealogical Society; PO Box 355; Augusta, Illinois 62311

Union County Genealogical / Historical Research Committee; 101 East Spring St.; Anna, Illinois 62906.

United States of America Railroad Retirement Board; 844 Rush St.; Chicago, Illinois 60611;

University of Illinois at Springfield; LIB 144, PO Box 19243; Springfield, Illinois 62794-9243; 217.206.6520;

Urbana Free Library; 201 So. Race St.; Urbana, Illinois 61801-3283

Vogel Gen. Research Library; 305 1st Street, Box 132; Holcomb, Illinois 61043

Warren Co. Library; 60 West Side Square; Monmouth, Illinois 61462

Warren County Illinois Genealogical Society; PO Box 761; Monmouth, Illinois 61462

Waukegan Historical Society; PO Box 857; Waukegan, Illinois 60079; <www.waukeganparks.org/index.html>

Waverly Genealogical and Historical Society; Waverly, Illinois 62692

Western Illinois University, University Library; 1 University Cir.; Macomb, Illinois 61455-1390; 309.298.2716;

Wheaton Public Library; 225 N. Cross St.; Wheaton, Illinois 60187; 630.668.1374, 630.668.3097; Fax 630.668.1465;

White County Historical Society; PO Box 121; Carmi, Illinois 62821; <www.rootsweb.com/~ilwcohs/>

Whiteside County Genealogists; Box 145; Sterling, Illinois 61081

Will-Grundy Counties Genealogical Society; PO Box 24; Wilmington, Illinois 60481

Williamson County Historical Society; 105 South Van Buren St.; Marion, Illinois 62959; <www.thewchs.com/index.htm>

Winnebago and Boone Counties Genealogical Society; PO Box 10166; Rockford, Illinois 61131-0166

Winnetka Historical Society; PO Box 365; Winnetka, Illinois 60093; 847.501.3221; <www.northstarnet.org/wnkhome/history/index.html>

Winnetka Public Library; 768 Oak St.; Winnetka, Illinois 60093

Withers Public Library; 202 East Washington; Bloomington, Illinois 61701

Zion Genealogical Society; c/o the Zion Benton Public Library; 2400 Gabriel Ave.; Zion, Illinois 60099; <nsn.nslsilus.org/wkkhome/zion/index.html>

Bibliography and Record Sources

General Sources

American State Papers: Documents, Legislative and Executive of the Congress of the United States. Salt Lake City; La Crosse, Wisconsin: Brookhaven Press. (Salt Lake City: Filmed by the Genealogical Society of Utah, 1959, 1975, 1977).

Bailey, Robert E. *A Summary Guide to Local Governmental Records in the Illinois Regional Archives.* Springfield, Ill.: Ill. State Archives, Office of the Secretary of State, 1992.

Bailey, Robert E. *Descriptive Inventory of the Archives of the State of Illinois.* 2nd ed. Springfield, Ill.: Office of the Secretary of State, Ill. State Archives, 1997.

Bateman, Newton, and Paul Selby. *Historical Encyclopedia of Illinois.* 2 vols. Chicago, Illinois: Munsell, 1913

Beckstead, Gayle, and Mary Lou Kozub. *Searching in Illinois: A Reference Guide to Public and Private Records.* Costa Mesa, California: ISC Publications, 1984.

Buck, Solon Justus. *Travel and Description, 1765-1865: Together With a List of County Histories, Atlases and Biographical Collections and a List of Territorial and State Laws.* Springfield, Illinois: Trustees of the Ill. State Historical Library, 1914.

Carrier, Lois A. *Illinois: Crossroads of a Continent.* 1993. Galveston, Texas. Frontier Press, 1993

Church of Jesus Christ of Latter-day Saints. Historical Department. *Index to Journal History.* (Salt Lake City: Filmed by the Historical Dept., 1973). 58 microfilm.

Clayton, John. *The Illinois Fact Book and Historical Almanac, 1673-1968.* Carbondale, Ill.: Southern Illinois University Press, [1970].

Coffey, Achilles. *A Brief History of the Regular Baptists, Principally of Southern Illinois.* Elizabethtown, Illinois: Nelson Pub., 1984.

Davidson, Alexander, and Bernard Stuve. *A Complete History of Illinois from 1673 to 1884.* Springfield, IL: H. W. Roker, 1884.

Dunne, Edward Fitzsimons. *Illinois, The Heart of the Nation.* 5 vols. Chicago: Lewis Pub., 1933.

Eddy, Thomas Mears. *The Patriotism of Illinois: A Record of the Civil and Military History of the State in the War for the Union, With a History of the Campaigns in Which Illinois Soldiers Have Been Conspicuous, Sketches of Distinguished Officers, The Roll of the Illustrious Dead, Movements of the Sanitary and Christian Commissions.* 2 vols. Chicago: Clarke, 1865.

Encyclopedia of Biography of Illinois. 3 vols. Chicago: Century Publishing and Engraving Co., 1892-1902.

Ford, Governor Thomas. *A History of Illinois from Its Commencement as a State in 1818 to 1847.* (1854) Reprint. Galveston, Texas: Frontier Press, 1995.

Genealogical Index of the Newberry Library, Chicago. 4 vols. Boston: G.K. Hall, 1960.

Genealogical Sources in Chicago, Illinois 1835-1900. Chicago: Chicago Genealogical Society, 1982.

Gilman, Agness Geneva. *Who's Who in Illinois, Women, Makers of History.* Chicago: The Eclectic Publishers, 1927.

Gooldy, Pat, and Ray Gooldy. *Manual for Illinois Genealogical Research.* Indianapolis, IN: Ye Olde Genealogie Shoppe, 1994.

Hastings, Robert J. ed. *We Were There: An Oral History of the Illinois Baptist State Association, 1907-1976.* Springfield, Ill.: The Association, c1976.

Haynes, Nathaniel Smith,. *History of the Disciples of Christ in Illinois, 1819-1914.* Cincinnati: Standard Pub. Co., [1915].

Heckman, John. *Brethren in Northern Illinois and Wisconsin.* Elgin, Ill.: Brethren Publishing House, 1941.

Historical Records Survey (Illinois). *Guide to Church Vital Statistics Records in Illinois.* Chicago: The Survey, 1942.

Historical Records Survey (Illinois*). Guide to Depositories of Manuscript Collections in Illinois (preliminary edition).* Chicago: Illinois Historical Records Survey Project, 1940.

Hoffmann, John. *A Guide to the History of Illinois.* New York: Greenwood Press, 1991.

Howard, Richard P. *Illinois: A History of the Prairie State.* Grand Rapids, MI: William B. Eerdmans Publishing Co., 1972.

Illinois Biographical Dictionary: People of All Times and All Places Who Have Been Important to The History and Life of The State. Reprint. New York: Somerset, 1993.

Illinois Libraries: Newspapers in the Illinois State Historical Library. Springfield, IL: Illinois State Library, 1979-91.

Illinois Quaker Meeting Records. Kokomo, Indiana: Shelby Pub. and Printing, 1996.

Illinois Research Outline. Series US-States, no. 14. Salt Lake City: Family History Library, 1988.

Illinois State Genealogical Society. *Guide to Illinois Researchers & Local Societies.* Springfield, IL: Illinois State Genealogical Society, 1996.

Illinois State Genealogical Society. *Illinois Libraries with Genealogical Collections.* Reprint. Springfield, IL: Illinois State Genealogical Society, 1993.

Illinois State Genealogical Society. *Prairie Pioneers.* Springfield, IL. Illinois State Genealogical Society.

Irons, Victoria, and Patricia C. Brennan. *Descriptive Inventory of the Archives of the State of Illinois.* Springfield, IL: Illinois State Archives, 1978.

Kimball, Stanley B. *Sources of Mormon History in Illinois, 1839-48: An Annotated Catalog of The Microfilm Collection at Southern Illinois University.* 2nd ed. Carbondale, Ill.: Central Publications, Southern Ill. University, 1966.

Lunde, Mrs. O. B. *Illinois State Genealogical Society Surname Index.* Decatur, IL: Illinois State Genealogical Society, 1981.

McCormick, Henry. *The Women of Illinois.* Ill.: Pantograph Printing and Stationery, 1913.

Melton, J. Gordon. Log Cabins to Steeples: *The Complete Story of the United Methodist Way in Illinois Including All Constituent Elements of the United Methodist Church.* [Illinois]: Commissions on Archives and History; Northern, Central and Southern Illinois Conferences, 1974.

Men of Illinois. Chicago: Halliday Witherspoon, 1902.

Newspapers in the Illinois State Historical Library. Springfield, Ill.: Ill. State Historical Library, 1964-1970?.

Norton, Augustus T. *History of the Presbyterian Church in the State of Illinois: vol. 1.* St. Louis: W.S. Bryan, 1879, 1879.

Notable Men of Illinois and Their State. [Chicago]: Chicago Daily Journal, 1912.

O'Hara, Margaret. *Finding Your Chicago Ancestor ...* n.p.: M. O'Hara, 1981.

Pease, Theodore Calvin. *The County Archives in the State of Illinois.* Springfield, Illinois: Trustees of the Illinois State Historical Library, 1915.

Pease, Theodore Calvin. *The Frontier State (IL), 1818-1848.* Springfield [Ill.]: Illinois Centennial Commission, 1918.

Pennewell, Almer M. *The Methodist Movement in Northern Illinois.* Sycamore, Ill.: The Sycamore Tribune, 1942.

Plains people; the Midwest (Indiana, Illinois, Iowa, Missouri): Research Sources and Bibliographies. Seattle, Wash.: Fiske Genealogical Foundation, 1990.

Records Relating to the Mormons in Illinois, 1839-1848 (dated 1840-1852) and Memorials of Mormons to Congress, 1840-1844. Washington: National Archives. Central Plains Region, 1964.

Robson, Charles. The Biographical Encyclopedia of Illinois of the Nineteenth Century.: Philadelphia: Galaxy Pub. Co., 1875.

Schweitzer, George K. Illinois Genealogical Research. Knoxville, TN: George K. Schweitzer, 1996.

Scott, Franklin William. Newspapers and Periodicals of Illinois, 1814-1879. Springfield, Ill.: Trustees of the Ill. State Historical Library, 1910.

Smith, George Washington. History of Illinois and Her People. 6 vols. Chicago: American Historical Society, 1927.

Smith, Willard H. Mennonites in Illinois. Scottdale, Pa.: Herald Press, 1983.

Szucs, Loretto D. Chicago and Cook County: A Guide to Research. Salt Lake City: Ancestry, 1996.

The United States Biographical Dictionary and Portrait Gallery of Eminent and Self-made Men: Illinois Volume. 2 vols. Chicago and New York: American Biographical Publishing Co., 1876.

Tregillis, Helen Cox. The Indians of Illinois: A History and Genealogy. Decorah, IA: Anundsen Publishing Co., 1983.

Turnbaugh, Roy C. A Guide to County Records in the Illinois Regional Archives. Springfield, IL: Illinois State Archives, 1983.

Volkel, Lowell M. Illinois Libraries with Genealogical Collections. Springfield, Ill.: Illinois State Genealogical Society, 1992.

Volkel, Lowell M., and Marjorie Smith. How to Research a Family with Illinois Roots. Indianapolis: Ye Olde Genealogie Shoppe, 1977.

White, Elizabeth Pearson. "Illinois Settlers and Their Origins." National Genealogical Society Quarterly, vol. 74, no. 1 (March 1986), pp. 7-17.

Wolf, Joseph C. A Reference Guide for Genealogical and Historical Research in Illinois. Detroit: Detroit Society for Genealogical Research, 1967.

Atlases, Maps and Gazetteers

Adams, James N., comp. Illinois Place Names. Springfield, Ill.: Illinois State Historical Society, 1989.

Beck, Lewis Caleb. A Gazetteer of the States of Illinois and Missouri… 1823. Reprint. New York: Arno Press, 1975.

Carpentier, Charles F. Counties of Illinois: Their Origin and Evolution... . Springfield: State Journal Co., 1919.

Illinois Atlas & Gazetteer. Freeport, Me.: DeLorme Mapping, 1991.

Kelly, Sheila. County and Township Gazetteer; Notes on the Location of Illinois County Seats. Springfield, Ill.: Illinois State Archives, 1988.

Maps of Illinois Counties in 1876: Together with the Plat of Chicago and Other Cities. 1876. Reprint. Knightstown, IN: Mayhill Pub, 1972.

Origin and Evolution of Illinois Counties. [S.l.]: State of Illinois, 1989.

Peck, J. M. A Gazetteer of Illinois in Three Parts: Containing a General View of the State, A General View of Each County, and a Particular Description of Each Town, Settlement, Stream, Prairie, Bottom, Bluff, etc. Alphabetically Arranged. 2nd ed. Entirely rev., corrected and enl. Philadelphia: Grigg & Elliott, 1837. Reprint with a new place-name and index. Bowie, Maryland: Heritage Books, 1993.

Powell, Paul. Counties of Illinois: Their Origin and Evolution with Twenty-Three Maps Showing the Original and the Present Boundary Lines of Each County of the State. Springfield, Illinois: Secretary of State, 1972.

Vogel, Virgil J. Indian Place Names in Illinois. [Springfield, Ill.]: Ill. State Historical Library, 1963.

Warner and Beers. Maps of Illinois Counties in 1876, Together with the Plan of Chicago and Other Cities and a Sampling of Illustrations. Chicago: Union Atlas Co., 1876. Reprinted as Atlas of the State of Illinois to Which Are Added Various General Maps and Illustrations. Knightstown, Indiana: Mayhill Publications, 1972.

Census Records

Available Census Records and Census Substitutes

Federal Census 1820, 1830, 1840, 1850, 1860, 1870, 1880, 1900, 1910, 1920, 1930.

Federal Mortality Schedules 1850, 1860, 1870, 1880.

State/Territorial Census 1810, 1818, 1820, 1825, 1835, 1845, 1855, 1865.

Dollarhide, William. The Census Book: A Genealogist's Guide to Federal Census Facts, Schedules and Indexes. Bountiful, Utah: Heritage Quest, 1999.

Genealogical Research Series Pamphlet No. 5 State Census Records. Springfield, Illinois: Illinois State Archives [n.d.] online at - <www.sos.state.il.us/departments/archives/research_series/rseries5.html>

Kemp, Thomas Jay. The American Census Handbook. Wilmington, DE: Scholarly Resources, Inc., 2001.

Lainhart, Ann S. State Census Records. Baltimore: Genealogical Publishing Co., Inc., 1992.

Name Index to Early Illinois Records. Springfield, IL: Illinois State Archives, 1975. 248 microfilm.

Szucs, Loretto Dennis, and Matthew Wright. Finding Answers in U.S. Census Records. Ancestry Publishing, 2001.

Thorndale, William, and William Dollarhide. Map Guide to the U.S. Federal Censuses, 1790-1920. Baltimore: Genealogical Publishing Co., 1987.

Court Records, Probate and Wills

Clayton, John. The Illinois Fact Book and Historical Almanac, 1673-1968. Carbondale, IL: Southern Illinois University Press, 1970.

Crossley, Frederic Bears. Courts and Lawyers. 3 vols. Chicago: American Historical Society, 1916.

Edgar, Jim. Illinois Probate Act and Related Laws, Effective January 5, 1988. Rev. St. Paul, MN: West Publishing Co., 1988.

Genealogical Research Series Pamphlet No. 2 Probate Records. Springfield, Illinois: Illinois State Archives, [n.d.]. online at - <www.sos.state.il.us/departments/archives/research_series/rseries2.html>

Palmer, John. *The Bench and Bar of Illinois: Historical and Reminiscent.* 2 vols. Chicago: Lewis Pub., 1899.

Rubincam, Milton. "Migrations to Illinois, 1673-1860." In *Illinois State Genealogical Society Quarterly, vol. 4, no. 3 (October 1972), pp. 127-34.* Springfield, IL: The Society, 1969-.

Territory of Illinois. County Court. *Court Records, 1796-1818.* Springfield, IL: Office of the Secretary of State, Micrographics Division, Source Documents Unit, 1986

Emigration, Immigration, Migration and Naturalization

United States. Circuit Court (Illinois: Northern District). *Oaths of Allegiance, 1872-1906.* Microfilm of original records housed in the Chicago Branch of the National Archives, Chicago, Illinois. (Salt Lake City: Filmed by the Genealogical Society of Utah, 1985).

United States. Circuit Court (Illinois: Northern District). *Petitions for Naturalization, 1906-1911.* Microfilm of original records housed in the Chicago Branch of the National Archives, (Salt Lake City: Filmed by the Genealogical Society of Utah, 1985). 10 microfilm.

United States. Circuit Court (Illinois: Southern District). *Naturalization Records, 1856-1903.* Microfilm of original records housed in the Chicago Branch of the National Archives, Chicago, Illinois. (Salt Lake City: Filmed by the Genealogical Society of Utah, 1986).

United States. District Court (Illinois: Eastern District). *Naturalization Records, 1906-1932.* Microfilm of original records housed in the Chicago Branch of the National Archives, Chicago, Illinois. (Salt Lake City: Filmed by the Genealogical Society of Utah, 1986). 4 microfilm.

United States. District Court (Illinois: Northern District). *Declarations of Intentions, 1903-1931; Index, 1906-1930.* Microfilm of original records housed in the Chicago Branch of the National Archives, Chicago, Illinois. (Salt Lake City: Filmed by the Genealogical Society of Utah, 1985). 45 microfilm.

United States. District Court (Illinois: Northern District). *Naturalization Petitions, 1872-1902.* Microfilm of original records housed in the Chicago Branch of the National Archives, Chicago, Illinois. (Salt Lake City: Filmed by the Genealogical Society of Utah, 1985).

United States. District Court (Illinois: Northern District). *Oaths of Allegiance, 1872-1903.* Microfilm of original records housed in the Chicago Branch of the National Archives, Chicago, Illinois. (Salt Lake City: Filmed by the Genealogical Society of Utah, 1985).

United States. District Court (Illinois: Northern District). *Soundex Index to Naturalization Petitions for U.S. District & Circuit Courts, Northern District of Illinois and Immigration and Naturalization Service District 9, 1840-1950.* (Salt Lake City: Filmed by the Genealogical Society of Utah, 1988). 183 microfilm.

United States. District Court (Illinois: Northern District: Eastern Division). *Records of Naturalizations and Name Changes; First set, 1926-1980; Second Set, 1980-1988.* Microreproduction of original manuscripts at the United States District Court, Chicago, Illinois. (Salt Lake City: Filmed by the Genealogical Society of Utah, 1991-1992). 149 microfilm.

United States. District Court (Illinois: Southern District: Peoria). *Declarations of Intention, 1907-1936; Petitions for Naturalization, 1908-1930; Index, 1905-1954.* Microfilm of original records housed in the Chicago Branch of the National Archives, Chicago, Illinois. (Salt Lake City: Filmed by the Genealogical Society of Utah, 1986). 13 microfilm.

United States. District Court (Illinois: Southern District: Springfield). *Naturalization Records, 1906-1952.* Microfilm of original records housed in the Chicago Branch of the National Archives, Chicago, Illinois. (Salt Lake City: Filmed by the Genealogical Society of Utah, 1986). 3 microfilm

Land and Property

Carlson, Theodore Leonard. *The Illinois Military Tract: A Study of Land Occupation, Utilization and Tenure.* Urbana: University of Illinois Press, 1951.

Genealogical Research Series Pamphlet No. 1, Land Sale Records. Springfield, Illinois: Illinois State Archives, [n.d.] online at - <www.sos.state.il.us/departments/archives/research_series/rseries1.html>

Hone, Wade E. *Land and Property Research in the United States.* Salt Lake City: Ancestry Incorporated, 1997.

Illinois State Genealogical Society. *Hames Collection: Pre-Statehood Land Records.* Springfield, IL: Illinois State Genealogical Society.

Illinois. Auditor's Office. *Early Illinois Land Records, 1829-1865.* Springfield, Ill.: Office of the Secretary of State, Micrographics Division, Documents Unit, 1960.

Murphy, Charla, , Mary Jo Moore, and Jean Burke, comps. *Original Lands Grants, 1824-1870.* Marion, Ill.: Williamson County Historical Society, 1997.

Record of the Services of Illinois Soldiers... . Springfield, IL: H. W. Rokker, 1882.

United States. Bureau of Land Management. *Card Files.* Microfilm of original card files located at the Bureau of Land Management's Eastern States Office in Alexandria, Virginia. (Washington, D.C.: Bureau of Land Management, [19–].) 160 microfilm.

United States. General Land Office. *Federal Land Records, Tract Books of Illinois, 1826-1873.* Springfield, IL: (Filmed by Office of the Secretary of State, Record Management Division, 1966). 19 microfilm.

United States. General Land Office. *Public Domain Sales Land Tract Record Listing, 1814-1925 (Index).* Springfield, IL: Illinois State Archives, 1984.

United States. Veterans Administration. *War of 1812, Military Bounty Land Warrants, 1815-1858.* Washington D.C.: The National Archives, 1971.

Volkel, Lowell M. *War of 1812 Bounty Land Patents in Illinois.* Thompson, IL: Heritage House, 1977.

Walker, James D. *War of 1812 Bounty Lands in Illinois.* Thomson, Ill.: Heritage House, 1977.

Military

Barnet, James. *The Martyrs and Heroes of Illinois in the Great Rebellion: Biographical Sketches.* Reprint. Bethesda, Md.: University Publications of America, 1993.

Fighting Men of Illinois: An Illustrated Historical Biography. Reprint. Tucson, Ariz.: W. C. Cox, 1974.

Genealogical Research Series Pamphlet No. 3, Military Records. Springfield, Illinois: Illinois State Archives, [n.d.]. online at - <www.sos.state.il.us/departments/archives/research_series/rseries3.html>.

Hicken. *Illinois in the Civil War.* Galveston, Texas: Frontier Press, 1991.

Illinois Adjutant General's Office. *Record of the Service of Illinois Soldiers in the Black Hawk War, 1831-32, and the Mexican War, 1846-48.* Springfield, IL: H. W. Q. Rokker, 1882.

Illinois Soldier's and Sailor's Home at Quincy. 2 vols. Thomson, Illinois: Heritage House, 1980.

Illinois State Genealogical Society. *Remembering Illinois Veterans.* Springfield, Illinois: Illinois State Genealogical Society, 1992.

Illinois. Adjutant General. *Report of the Adjutant General of the State of Illinois.* Springfield, Illinois: Rokker, 1886.

Illinois. Assessors. *Militia Rolls, 1862-1863.* (Salt Lake City: Filmed by the Genealogical Society of Utah, 1977).

Publishers Subscription Co., ed. *Fighting Men of Illinois: An Illustrated Historical Biography.* Tucson, Arizona: W. C. Cox, 1974.

Roster of Men from Illinois Who Served in the United States Navy During the War of the Rebellion, 1861-1866. Salt Lake City: Genealogical Society of Utah, 1974, 1975.

Smith, John H. *Illinois Regiment.* Indianapolis, Indiana: Ye Olde Genealogie Shoppe.

Soldiers' and Patriots' Biographical Album: Containing Biographies and Portraits of Soldiers and Loyal Citizens in the American Conflict, Together with the Great Commanders of the Union Army, Also a History of the Organizations Growing Out of the War: Union Veteran Publishing Co., 1892.

Soldiers Burial Places in State of Illinois for Wars, 1774-1898. Microfilm of original record in Springfield, Illinois at the Illinois Veterans Commission. (Salt Lake City: Filmed by the Genealogical Society of Utah, 1975). 31 microfilm.

Soldiers of the American Revolution Buried in Illinois. Springfield, IL: Illinois State Genealogical Society, 1975.

United States. Selective Service System. *Illinois, World War I Selective Service System Draft Registration Cards, 1917-1918.* National Archives Microfilm Publications, M1509. Washington, D.C.: National Archives, 1987-1988.

Walker, Harriet J. *Revolutionary Soldiers Buried in Illinois.* (1918) Reprint. Baltimore: Clearfield Company, 1992.

Walker, Harriet J. *Soldiers of the American Revolution Buried in Illinois: From the Journal of the Illinois State Historical Society.* Baltimore: Genealogical Publishing Co., 1967.

White, Virgil D., trans. *Index to War of 1812 Pension Files.*1st Ed. Waynesboro, TN: National Historical Pub. Co., 1989.

Wilson, James Grant. *Biographical Sketches of Illinois Officers Engaged in the War Against the Rebellion of 1861.* Chicago: James Barnet, 1862.

Vital and Cemetery Records

Cemetery Records of Illinois. 13 vols. Typescript. Salt Lake City: Genealogical Society of Utah, 1960-1966.

Cole, Arthur Charles. *The Era of the Civil War: 1848-1870.* (1919) Reprint, Galveston, Texas: Frontier Press, 1987.

Department of Veterans Affairs. *Veterans National Cemetery Records, Illinois.* (Salt Lake City: Filmed by the Genealogical Society of Utah, 1981).

Guide to Public Vital Statistics Records in Illinois. 1941. Reprint. Thompson, IL: Heritage House, 1976.

Illinois State Genealogical Society. Devanny, Mrs. John S., comp. *Soldiers of the American Revolution Buried in Illinois.* Springfield, IL: 1975.

Illinois State Genealogical Society. *Illinois Marriage Records Index: 1763-1916.* (Springfield, Ill.: Filmed by the Archives and the Society, 1994?). 94 microfiche.

Illinois Veterans Commission (Springfield, Illinois). *Soldier's Burial Places in the State of Illinois for Wars, 1774-1898.* Springfield: Illinois Veterans Commission, 1975. Microfilm, 31 rolls.

Illinois. Department of Public Health. State Registrar. *Illinois Births, Prior to Act, Excluding Chicago: 1842, 1849-1872.* Microreproduction of original manuscripts at the Public Board of Health, Springfield, Illinois. (Salt Lake City: Filmed by the Genealogical Society of Utah, 1995). 6 microfilm.

Illinois. Public Board of Health. Archives. *Death Certificates for the State of Illinois, 1916-1945, Excluding Chicago with the Exception of Stillbirths: Index, 1916-1938.* Microreproduction of original at the Public Board of Health, Archives, Springfield, Illinois. (Salt Lake City: Filmed by the Genealogical Society of Utah, 1988-1992). 666 microfilm.

Index of Illinois Marriages, Earliest to 1900. Springfield, Ill.: Illinois State Genealogy Society, 1997. CD-ROM.

Mortality Schedules of Illinois, 1850-1880. Microfilm copy of original records located at the National Archives, Washington D.C. ([Illinois]: Records Management Division, Secretary of State's Office, 1967.) 7 microfilm.

Newbill, Leona Hopper. *Cook County, Illinois Marriage License Records, 1870-1880* (Salt Lake City: Filmed by the Genealogical Society of Utah, 1970).

Newspaper Research Committee, comp. *Vital Records from Chicago Newspapers* Chicago: Chicago Genealogy. Society, 1971-.

Sanders, Walters. *Marriages from Illinois Counties.* 6 vols. Litchfield, IL: Walter Sanders, 1976.

Soldiers Burial Places in State of Illinois for Wars, 1774-1898. Salt Lake City: Filmed by the Genealogical Society of Utah, 1975.

Vangeison, Aaron. *Guide to Public Vital Statistics Records in Illinois.* Thomson, Ill.: Heritage House, 1976.

Vital Records from Chicago Newspapers, Volume 1-7, 1833-1848. Chicago: Chicago Genealogical Society, Newspaper Research Committee, 1971.

Volkel, Lowell. *Illinois 1850 Mortality Schedule with Index.* 3 vols. Thomson, Ill.: Heritage House, 1977, 1972.

Volkel, Lowell. Illinois *1870 Mortality Schedule with Index.* 5 vols. Indianapolis, Ind.: Heritage House, 1985-[1987?].

Walker, Mrs. Harriet J. *Revolutionary Soldiers Buried in Illinois.* Los Angeles: Standard Printing Co., 1917. Reprint. Baltimore: Genealogical Publishing Co., 1967.

County Website	Map Index	Date Created	Parent County or Territory From Which Organized Address/Details
Adams* www.co.adams.il.us/	I2	13 Jan 1825	**Pike** Adams County; 507 Vermont St; Quincy, IL 62301-2934; Ph. 217.277.2150 Details: (Co Clk has b & d rec from 1878 & m rec from 1825; Clk Cir Ct has div, pro & ct rec)
Alexander www.rootsweb.com/~ilalexan/ alexander.htm	Q7	4 Mar 1819	**Johnson** Alexander County; 2000 Washington Ave; Cairo, IL 62914-1717; Ph. 618.734.7000 Details: (Co Clk has b & d rec from 1878, m & land rec from 1819; Clk Cir Ct has div, pro & ct rec)
Bond www.rootsweb.com/~ilbond/	L7	4 Jan 1817	**Madison** Bond County; 203 W College; Greenville, IL 62246-0407; Ph. 618.664.0449 Details: (Co Clk has b & d rec from 1877, m rec from 1817, land rec from 1870 & mil dis rec; Clk Cir Ct has div, pro & ct rec)
Boone www.rootsweb.com/~ilboone/boone.htm	B8	4 Mar 1837	**Winnebago** Boone County; 601 N Main St; Belvidere, IL 61008-2600; Ph. 815.544.3103 Details: (Co Clk has b, m & d rec from 1877 & land rec from 1838; Clk Cir Ct has div, pro & ct rec)
Brown* www.rootsweb.com/~ilbrown/brown.htm	I3	1 Feb 1839	**Schuyler** Brown County; 1 Court St; Mount Sterling, IL 62353-1241; Ph. 217.773.3421 Details: (Co Clk has b rec from 1860, m rec from 1841, d rec from 1878, land rec from 1817 & mil dis rec from 1918; Clk Cir Ct has div, pro, ct & nat rec)
Bureau www.rootsweb.com/~ilgenweb/lists/ bureaulist.htm	D6	28 Feb 1837	**Putnam** Bureau County; 700 S Main St; Princeton, IL 61356; Ph. 815.875.3239 Details: (Co Clk has b & d rec from 1878, m & land rec from 1837 & mil rec from 1865; Clk Cir Ct has div, pro, ct & nat rec)
Calhoun www.rootsweb.com/~ilcalhou/	K3	10 Jan 1825	**Pike** Calhoun County; 102 County Rd; Hardin, IL 62047-0000; Ph. 618.576.2351 Details: (Co Clk has b & d rec from 1877, m & land rec from 1825)
Carroll* www.serve.com/bmosher/ilcr/carroll.htm	C5	22 Feb 1839	**Jo Daviess** Carroll County; Rt 78 & Rapp Rd; Mount Carroll, IL 61053-0000; Ph. 815.244.0221 Details: (Co Clk has b & d rec from 1877, m rec from 1839 & land rec)
Cass www.rootsweb.com/~ilcass/cass.htm	I4	3 Mar 1837	**Morgan** Cass County; 100 E Springfield St; Virginia, IL 62691-0000; Ph. 217.452.7217 Details: (Co Clk has b rec from 1860, m rec from 1837, d rec from 1878 & land rec; Clk Cir Ct has div, pro & ct rec)
Champaign* node-02.advancenet.net/~coclerk/	I10	20 Feb 1833	**Vermilion** Champaign County; 1776 E Washington St; Urbana, IL 61802; Ph. 217.384.3720 Details: (Co Clk has b & d rec from 1878 & m rec from 1833; Clk Cir Ct has div, pro & ct rec; Rcdr of Deeds has land & mil rec)
Christian www.rootsweb.com/~ilchrist/	J7	15 Feb 1839	**Sangamon, Shelby** Christian County; 101 S Main St; Taylorville, IL 62568-1599; Ph. 217.824.4969 Details: (Formerly Dane Co. Name changed to Christian 1 Feb 1840) (Co Clk has b & d rec from 1878, m rec from 1840 & land rec from 1856; Clk Cir Ct has div, pro & ct rec from 1875)
Clark* www.clarkcountyil.org/	K10	22 Mar 1819	**Crawford** Clark County; 501 Archer Ave; Marshall, IL 62441; Ph. 217.826.8311 Details: (Co Clk has b & d rec from 1877, m rec from 1819 & land rec from 1818; Clk Cir Ct has div, pro & ct rec)
Clay www.rootsweb.com/~ilclay/	L9	23 Dec 1824	**Wayne, Lawrence, Fayette** Clay County; County Courthouse; PO Box 160; Louisville, IL 62858-0000; Ph. 618.665.3626 Details: (Co Clk has b, d & bur rec from 1878, m rec from 1824, land rec from 1825 & mil dis rec; Clk Cir Ct has div, pro & ct rec)

County Website	Map Index	Date Created	Parent County or Territory From Which Organized Address/Details
Clinton www.rootsweb.com/~ilclint2/	**M6**	**27 Dec 1824**	**Washington, Bond, Fayette, Crawford** Clinton County; 851 Franklin; PO Box 308; Carlyle, IL 62231-0000; Ph. 618.594.2464 Details: (Co Clk has b & d rec from 1877, m rec from 1825 & land rec from 1818; Clk Cir Ct has div, pro & ct rec)
Coles www.rootsweb.com/~ilcoles/coles.htm	**J9**	**25 Dec 1830**	**Clark, Edgar** Coles County; 6th & Monroe St; PO Box 227; Charleston, IL 61920-0207; Ph. 217.348.0501 Details: (Co Clk has b & d rec from 1878, m & land rec from 1830)
Cook www.co.cook.il.us/	**C11**	**15 Jan 1831**	**Putnam** Cook County; PO Box 642570; Chicago, IL 60664; Ph. 312.603.5656 Details: (Co Vit Rec has b, m & d rec from 1872)
Crawford www.rootsweb.com/~jadmire/ilcrawf/	**L11**	**31 Dec 1816**	**Edwards** Crawford County; One Courthouse Sq; Robinson, IL 62454-2146; Ph. 618.546.1212 Details: (Co Clk has b & d rec from 1877, m rec from 1817, land rec from 1816 & bur rec from 1975; Clk Cir Ct has div, pro & ct rec, phys cert, old school rec & tax rec)
Cumberland* www.rootsweb.com/~ilcumber/	**K9**	**2 Mar 1843**	**Coles** Cumberland County; PO Box 146; Toledo, IL 62468-0000; Ph. 217.849.2631 Details: (Co Clk has b, m, d, bur & land rec from 1885; Clk Cir Ct has div, pro & ct rec from 1885)
Dane		**15 Feb 1839**	**Sangamon, Shelby** Details: (see Christian) Name changed to Christian 1 Feb 1840
De Kalb www.dekalbcounty.org/	**C8**	**4 Mar 1837**	**Kane** De Kalb County; 110 E Sycamore St; Sycamore, IL 60178-1497; Ph. 815.895.7149 Details: (Co Clk has incomplete b & d rec 1878-1916, complete from 1916, m & land rec from 1837, nat rec from 1850 & poll rec 1858-1872; Clk Cir Ct has div & ct rec from 1850 & pro rec from 1859)
De Witt* www.rootsweb.com/~ildewitt/	**H8**	**1 Mar 1839**	**Macon, McLean** De Witt County; 201 W Washington St; Clinton, IL 61727-1639; Ph. 217.935.2119 Details: (Co Clk has b, d & bur rec from 1877, m & land rec from 1839; Clk Cir Ct has div, pro & ct rec from 1839)
Douglas* www.rootsweb.com/~ildougla/douglas.htm	**I10**	**8 Feb 1859**	**Coles** Douglas County; 401 S Center St; Tuscola, IL 61953-1603; Ph. 217.253.2411 Details: (Co Clk has b, m, d & land rec from 1859, some bur rec & mil dis rec; Clk Cir Ct has div, pro & ct rec)
Du Page www.dupageco.org/	**C10**	**9 Feb 1839**	**Cook** Du Page County; 421 N County Farm Rd; Wheaton, IL 60187-3978; Ph. 630.682.7035 Details: (Co Clk has b & d rec from 1879, m rec from 1839, pro & ct rec; Co Rcdr has land rec)
Edgar www.rootsweb.com/~iledgar/edgar.htm	**J10**	**3 Jan 1823**	**Clark** Edgar County; 115 W Court St; Paris, IL 61944; Ph. 217.466.7433 Details: (Co Clk has b & d rec from 1877, m rec from 1823, pro & land rec from 1827; Clk Cir Ct has div & ct rec)
Edwards www.rootsweb.com/~iledward/	**M10**	**28 Nov 1814**	**Madison, Gallatin** Edwards County; 50 E Main St; Albion, IL 62806-1262; Ph. 618.445.2115 Details: (Co Clk has b & d rec from 1877, m & land rec from 1815; Clk Cir Ct has div, pro & ct rec)
Effingham* www.co.effingham.il.us/	**L8**	**15 Feb 1831**	**Fayette, Crawford** Effingham County; 101 N 4th St PO Box 628; Effingham, IL 62401; Ph. 217.342.6535 Details: (Co Clk has b & d rec from 1878 [incomplete prior to 1916], m & land rec from 1833 & mil rec from 1919; Clk Cir Ct has div, pro & ct rec)
Fayette* www.rootsweb.com/~ilfayett/ilfayette.htm	**L8**	**14 Feb 1821**	**Bond, Wayne, Clark, Jefferson** Fayette County; PO Box 401; Vandalia, IL 62471; Ph. 618.283.5000 Details: (Co Clk-Rcdr has b & d rec from 1877, m & land rec from 1821 & mil rec from 1917; Clk Cir Ct has div, pro & ct rec)

County Website	Map Index	Date Created	Parent County or Territory From Which Organized Address/Details
Ford www.prairienet.org/fordiroq/ford.htm	G9	17 Feb 1859	**Clark** Ford County; 200 W State St Rm 101; Paxton, IL 60957; Ph. 217.379.2721 Details: (Co Clk has b & d rec from 1878, m & land rec from 1859; Clk Cir Ct has div, pro & ct rec)
Franklin* www.rootsweb.com/~ilfrankl/index2.html	O8	2 Jan 1818	**White, Gallatin** Franklin County; PO Box 607; Benton, IL 62812-2264; Ph. 618.438.3221 Details: (Co Clk has b & d rec from 1877 & m rec from 1836; Clk Cir Ct has pro & ct rec from 1843)
Fulton www.outfitters.com/illinois/fulton/	G5	28 Jan 1823	**Pike** Fulton County; 100 N Main St; Lewistown, IL 61542-1445; Ph. 309.547.3041 Details: (Co Clk has b & d rec from 1878, m rec from 1824 & land rec from 1823; Clk Cir Ct has div, pro & ct rec)
Gallatin www.rootsweb.com/~ilgalla2/	O9	14 Sep 1812	**Randolph** Gallatin County; W Lincoln Blvd; Shawneetown, IL 62984-0550; Ph. 618.269.3025 Details: (Co Clk has b & d rec from 1878, m rec from 1830 & land rec from 1800; Clk Cir Ct has pro rec from 1860)
Greene www.rootsweb.com/~ilgreene/green.htm	K4	20 Jan 1821	**Madison** Greene County; 519 N Main St; Carrollton, IL 62016; Ph. 217.942.5443 Details: (Co Clk has b & d rec from 1877, m & land rec from 1821 & mil rec from 1862; Clk Cir Ct has div, pro, ct & nat rec)
Grundy www.rootsweb.com/~ilgrundy/	E9	17 Feb 1841	**LaSalle** Grundy County; 111 E Washington St; Morris, IL 60450-2268; Ph. 815.941.3222 Details: (Co Clk has b rec from 1877, d rec from 1878, m & land rec from 1841 & bur rec from 1976; Clk Cir Ct has div, pro & ct rec from 1841)
Hamilton www.rootsweb.com/~ilhamilt/	N9	8 Feb 1821	**White** Hamilton County; Courthouse; McLeansboro, IL 62859-1489; Ph. 618.643.2721 Details: (Co Clk has b & d rec from 1878, m rec from 1821, land rec from 1835 & mil rec from 1865)
Hancock www.rootsweb.com/~ilhancoc/	G2	13 Jan 1825	**Pike, Unorg. Terr.** Hancock County; Box 39; Carthage, IL 62321; Ph. 217.357.3519 Details: (Co Clk has b & d rec from 1914 & m rec from 1829; Co Rcdr has land & mil rec from 1829; Clk Cir Ct has div, pro, ct & nat rec)
Hardin www.rootsweb.com/~ilhardi2/	P9	2 Mar 1839	**Pope** Hardin County; Main St; Elizabethtown, IL 62931; Ph. 618.287.2251 Details: (Co Clk has b, m, d & land rec from 1884; Clk Cir Ct has div, pro & ct rec from 1970)
Henderson www.outfitters.com/illinois/henderson/	F3	20 Jan 1841	**Warren** Henderson County; PO Box 308; Oquawka, IL 61469-0308; Ph. 309.867.2911 Details: (Co Clk has b, m & d rec from 1878 & land rec from 1841; Clk Cir Ct has div, pro & ct rec from 1841)
Henry www.henrycty.com/	E5	13 Jan 1825	**Fulton** Henry County; 307 W Center St; Cambridge, IL 61238; Ph. 309.937.3575 Details: (Co Clk has incomplete b & d rec from 1877, m rec from 1837 & land rec from 1835; Clk Cir Ct has div, pro & ct rec from 1880 & nat rec 1870-1940)
Iroquois www.prairienet.org/fordiroq/iroquois.htm	G10	26 Feb 1833	**Vermilion** Iroquois County; 1001 E Grant St; Watseka, IL 60970-1810; Ph. 815.432.6960 Details: (Co Clk has b & d rec from 1878, m rec from 1868 & land rec from 1835; Clk Cir Ct has div & ct rec from 1855 & pro rec from 1865; Old Courthouse Museum may have some rec)
Jackson* www.co.jackson.il.us/	O6	10 Jan 1816	**Randolph, Johnson** Jackson County; 1001 Walnut St; Murphysboro, IL 62966-2177; Ph. 618.687.7360 Details: (Co Clk has b, d & bur rec from 1872, m rec from 1842 & land rec; Clk Cir Ct has div, pro & ct rec)

County Website	Map Index	Date Created	Parent County or Territory From Which Organized
			Address/Details
Jasper www.rootsweb.com/~iljasper/	**L10**	**15 Feb 1831**	**Clay, Crawford** Jasper County; 100 W Jourdan St; Newton, IL 62448-1973; Ph. 618.783.3124 Details: (Co Clk has b & d rec from 1877, m & land rec from 1835; Clk Cir Ct has div, pro & ct rec)
Jefferson www.rootsweb.com/~iljeffer/	**N8**	**26 Mar 1819**	**Edwards, White** Jefferson County; 100 S 10th St; Mount Vernon, IL 62864-4086; Ph. 618.244.8020 Details: (Co Clk has b rec from 1878, d rec from 1877, m & land rec from 1819)
Jersey www.rootsweb.com/~iljersey/	**L4**	**28 Feb 1839**	**Greene** Jersey County; 102 W Pearl St; Jerseyville, IL 62052-1675; Ph. 618.498.5571 Details: (Co Clk has b & d rec from 1878, m & land rec from 1839, div rec from 1840, pro rec from 1850 & ct rec from 1845)
Jo Daviess* www.rootsweb.com/~iljodavi/index.html	**B5**	**17 Feb 1827**	**Henry, Mercer, Putnam** Jo Daviess County; 330 N Bench St; Galena, IL 61036-1828; Ph. 815.777.0161 Details: (Co Clk has b & d rec from 1877 with a few earlier & m rec from 1830; Clk Cir Ct has pro rec from 1830, div & ct rec from 1850 & land rec from 1828)
Johnson www.rootsweb.com/~iljohnso/	**P8**	**14 Sep 1812**	**Randolph** Johnson County; 400 Court Sq; Vienna, IL 62995-0096; Ph. 618.658.3611 Details: (Co Clk has b & d rec from 1878, m rec from 1834 & land rec from 1815; Clk Cir Ct has div, pro & ct rec)
Kane www.rootsweb.com/~ilkane/	**C9**	**16 Jan 1836**	**LaSalle** Kane County; 719 S Batavia Ave; Geneva, IL 60134; Ph. 630.232.5951 Details: (Co Clk has b & d rec from 1878 & m rec from 1836; Clk Cir Ct has div & ct rec; Pro Ct has pro rec; Supervisor of Assessments has land rec)
Kankakee www.co.kankakee.il.us/	**E10**	**11 Feb 1853**	**Iroquois, Will** Kankakee County; 189 E Court St; Kankakee, IL 60901-3997; Ph. 815.937.2990 Details: (Co Clk has b & d rec from 1878 & m rec from 1853; Clk Cir Ct has div, pro, ct & nat rec; Co Rcdr has land & mil rec)
Kendall www.rootsweb.com/~ilkendal/	**D9**	**19 Feb 1841**	**LaSalle, Kane** Kendall County; 111 W Fox St; Yorkville, IL 60560; Ph. 630.553.4183 Details: (Co Clk has b & d rec from 1877, m & land rec from 1841; Clk Cir Ct has div, pro, ct & nat rec)
Knox* www.outfitters.com/illinois/knox/knox.html	**F5**	**13 Jan 1825**	**Fulton** Knox County; 200 S Cherry St; Galesburg, IL 61401-4991; Ph. 309.345.3815 Details: (Co Clk has b & d rec from 1878 & m rec from 1830)
La Salle www.outfitters.com/illinois/lasalle/	**D8**	**15 Jan 1831**	**Putnam, Vermilion** La Salle County; 707 E Etna Rd; Ottawa, IL 61350; Ph. 815.434.8202 Details: (Co Clk has b & d rec from 1877 & m rec from 1832; Clk Cir Ct has div & ct rec; Pro Office has pro rec; Rcdr of Deeds has land rec)
Lake www.lakecountyfl.com/	**B10**	**1 Mar 1839**	**McHenry** Lake County; 18 N County St; Waukegan, IL 60085-4339; Ph. 847.360.3610 Details: (Co Clk has b rec from 1871, m rec from 1839 & d rec from 1877; Clk Cir Ct has div, pro & ct rec; Rcdr of Deeds has land rec)
Lawrence www.rootsweb.com/~illawren/index.htm	**M10**	**16 Jan 1821**	**Crawford, Edwards** Lawrence County; 1100 State St; Lawrenceville, IL 62439-0000; Ph. 618.943.2346 Details: (Co Clk has b rec from 1877, d rec from 1878, m & land rec from 1821 & cem book; Clk Cir Ct has div, pro & ct rec; City Clks have bur rec)
Lee www.outfitters.com/illinois/lee/	**D7**	**27 Feb 1839**	**Ogle** Lee County; 112 E 2nd St; Dixon, IL 61021; Ph. 815.288.3309 Details: (Co Clk has b rec from 1858, m rec from 1839, d rec from 1877, bur, land & mil rec; Clk Cir Ct has div, pro, ct & nat rec)
Livingston* www.crtelco.com/~annette1/	**F8**	**27 Feb 1837**	**LaSalle, McLean** Livingston County; 112 W Madison St; Pontiac, IL 61764; Ph. 815.844.2006 Details: (Co Clk has b rec from 1878 with a few 1856-1877, d & bur rec from 1878, m & land rec from 1837 & mil dis rec from 1861; Clk Cir Ct has div, pro & ct rec)

County Website	Map Index	Date Created	Parent County or Territory From Which Organized Address/Details
Logan*	**H6**	**15 Feb 1839**	**Sangamon**

www.rootsweb.com/~illogan/loindex.htm Logan County; 601 Broadway St; Lincoln, IL 62656; Ph. 217.732.4148
Details: (Co Clk has b & d rec from 1879, m rec from 1859 & land rec from 1849; Clk Cir Ct has div, pro & ct rec; City Clk has bur rec)

Macon*	**I8**	**19 Jan 1829**	**Shelby**

www.rootsweb.com/~ilmacon/ Macon County; 141 S Main St; Decatur, IL 62523; Ph. 217.424.1305
Details: (Co Clk has b rec from 1850, m rec from 1829, d rec from 1877 & bur rec from 1964; Clk Cir Ct has div, pro & ct rec)

Macoupin*	**K5**	**17 Jan 1829**	**Madison, Greene**

www.rootsweb.com/~ilmacoup/
macoupin.htm Macoupin County; 233 E 1st S St; Carlinville, IL 62626-0000; Ph. 217.854.3214
Details: (Co Clk has b & d rec from 1877, m & land rec from 1829; Clk Cir Ct has div, pro & ct rec)

Madison	**L6**	**14 Sep 1812**	**St. Clair**

www.co.madison.il.us/ Madison County; 155 N Main St; Edwardsville, IL 62025-1999; Ph. 618.692.6290
Details: (Co Clk has b rec from 1860, m rec from 1813 & d rec from 1878; Clk Cir Ct has div, pro & ct rec)

Marion	**M8**	**24 Jan 1823**	**Fayette, Jefferson**

www.rootsweb.com/~ilmarion/
marionco.htm Marion County; 100 E Main St; Salem, IL 62881-0000; Ph. 618.548.3400
Details: (Co Clk has b rec from 1878, m rec from 1821, d rec from 1877 & land rec from 1823; Clk Cir Ct has div & ct rec from 1858 & pro rec from 1840)

Marshall	**F7**	**19 Jan 1839**	**Putnam**

www.rootsweb.com/~ilmarsha/index.htm Marshall County; 122 N Prairie St; Lacon, IL 61540; Ph. 309.246.6325
Details: (Co Clk has b rec from 1878, m & land rec from 1839, d rec from 1877, cem rec from 1857 & mil rec from 1861; Clk Cir Ct has div, pro & ct rec)

Mason	**H5**	**20 Jan 1841**	**Tazewell, Menard**

www.outfitters.com/~masonch/ Mason County; PO Box 77; Havana, IL 62644; Ph. 309.543.6661
Details: (Co Rcdr has b & d rec from 1878, m & land rec from 1841, mil rec from 1860 & cem rec; Clk Cir Ct has div, pro, ct & nat rec from 1841)

Massac	**Q8**	**8 Feb 1843**	**Pope, Johnson**

www.rootsweb.com/~ilmassac/ Massac County; PO Box 429; Metropolis, IL 62960-0429; Ph. 618.524.5213
Details: (Co Clk has b rec from 1858, m rec from 1843, d rec from 1878, land rec from 1855 & mil rec; Clk Cir Ct has div, pro, ct & nat rec)

McDonough	**G3**	**25 Jan 1826**	**Schuyler**

www.outfitters.com/illinois/mcdonough/ McDonough County; 1 Courthouse Sq; Macomb, IL 61455; Ph. 309.833.2474
Details: (Co Clk has b rec from 1858, m rec from 1830, d rec from 1877 & land rec from 1812; City Clk has bur rec; Clk Cir Ct has div, pro & ct rec)

McHenry	**B9**	**16 Jan 1836**	**Cook**

www.co.mchenry.il.us/ McHenry County; 2200 N Seminary Ave; Woodstock, IL 60098; Ph. 815.334.4242
Details: (Co Clk has b & d rec from 1877 & m rec from 1837; Rcdr of Deeds has land rec from 1841 & mil rec; Clk Cir Ct has div & ct rec from 1836 & pro rec from 1840)

McLean	**G8**	**25 Dec 1830**	**Tazewell, Unorg. Terr**

www.mclean.gov/ McLean County; 104 W Front St; Bloomington, IL 61702; Ph. 309.888.5190
Details: (Co Clk has b rec from 1860, m rec from 1830 & d rec from 1878; Clk Cir Ct has div, pro & ct rec; Co Rcdr has land rec)

Menard*	**I6**	**15 Feb 1839**	**Sangamon**

www.rootsweb.com/~ilmenard/index.html/ Menard County; 102 S 7th St; PO Box 456; Petersburg, IL 62675-0456;
Ph. 217.632.2415
Details: (Co Clk has b & d rec from 1877, m & land rec from 1839; Clk Cir Ct has div, pro & ct rec from 1839)

Mercer	**E3**	**13 Jan 1825**	**Unorg. Terr., Pike**

www.rootsweb.com/~ilmercer/ Mercer County; 100 SE 3rd St; PO Box 66; Aledo, IL 61231; Ph. 309.582.7021
Details: (Co Clk has b rec from 1857, m rec from 1835, d rec from 1877 & mil rec from 1866; Co Rcdr has land rec from 1833; Clk Cir Ct has div, pro, ct & nat rec from 1835)

County Website	Map Index	Date Created	Parent County or Territory From Which Organized Address/Details
Monroe www.rootsweb.com/~ilmonroe/	**N5**	**6 Jan 1816**	**Randolph, St. Clair** Monroe County; 100 S Main St; Waterloo, IL 62298; Ph. 618.939.8681 Details: (Co Clk has b & d rec from 1878, m & land rec from 1816; Clk Cir Ct has pro rec from 1845, ct rec from 1843, nat & div rec)
Montgomery* www.rootsweb.com/~ilmontgo/	**K6**	**12 Feb 1821**	**Bond, Madison** Montgomery County; 1 Courthouse Sq; Hillsboro, IL 62049; Ph. 217.532.9530 Details: (Co Clk has b & d rec from 1878, m & land rec from 1821; Clk Cir Ct has div, pro & ct rec)
Morgan* www.rootsweb.com/~ilmorgan/ morgan.htm	**J5**	**31 Jan 1823**	**Sangamon** Morgan County; 300 W State St; Jacksonville, IL 62650; Ph. 217.245.4619 Details: (Co Clk has b, d & bur rec from 1878, m rec from 1827, div rec from 1831, pro rec from 1836 & ct rec from 1828)
Moultrie* www.rootsweb.com/~ilmoult2/	**J8**	**16 Feb 1843**	**Shelby, Macon** Moultrie County; 10 S Main St; Sullivan, IL 61951-0000; Ph. 217.728.4389 Details: (Co Clk has b rec from 1859, m & land rec from 1840, d rec from 1877 & bur rec from 1961; Clk Cir Ct has div, pro & ct rec)
Ogle* www.oglecounty.org/	**C7**	**16 Jan 1836**	**Jo Daviess** Ogle County; 4th & Washington St; Oregon, IL 61061; Ph. 815.732.1110 Details: (Co Clk has b rec from 1860, d rec from 1878, m & land rec from 1837; Clk Cir Ct has div, pro & ct rec)
Peoria* www.co.peoria.il.us/	**F6**	**13 Jan 1825**	**Fulton** Peoria County; 324 S Main St Rm 101; Peoria, IL 61604; Ph. 309.672.6059 Details: (Co Clk has b & d rec from 1877 & m rec from 1825; Clk Cir Ct has div, pro & ct rec; Rcdr of Deeds has land rec; Peoria twp cen taken 1888 & 1899)
Perry www.rootsweb.com/~ilperry/	**N6**	**29 Jan 1827**	**Randolph, Jackson** Perry County; RR 1; Pinckneyville, IL 62274-0000; Ph. 618.357.5116 Details: (Co Clk has incomplete b rec 1879-1916, complete from 1916, incomplete m rec from 1827 & d rec from 1879; Clk Cir Ct has div, pro & ct rec from 1827)
Piatt* www.co.piatt.il.us/	**I8**	**27 Jan 1841**	**DeWitt, Macon** Piatt County; 101 W Washington St; Monticello, IL 61856; Ph. 217.762.9487 Details: (Co Clk has b & d rec from 1877, m rec from 1841 & land rec from 1852; Clk Cir Ct has div, pro & ct rec from 1841)
Pike* www.pikeil.org/	**J3**	**31 Jan 1821**	**Madison, Bond, Clark** Pike County; 100 E Washington St; Pittsfield, IL 62363-0000; Ph. 217.285.6812 Details: (Co Clk has b & d rec from 1877, m rec from 1827 & land rec from 1821; Clk Cir Ct has div, pro & ct rec)
Pope www.rootsweb.com/~ilpope/	**P9**	**10 Jan 1816**	**Gallatin, Johnson** Pope County; 400 Main St; PO Box 216; Golconda, IL 62938; Ph. 618.683.4466 Details: (Co Clk has b rec from 1877, some from 1862, d rec from 1878, m & land rec from 1816, pro rec 1816-1950, mil dis rec from 1865, militia roll 1861-1862, 1845 & 1865 state cen; Clk Cir Ct has pro rec from 1950, ct rec from 1816, div & nat rec)
Pulaski www.rootsweb.com/~ilpulask/pulaski.htm	**Q7**	**3 Mar 1843**	**Johnson** Pulaski County; 2nd & High St; Mound City, IL 62963-0218; Ph. 618.748.9360 Details: (Co Clk has b rec from 1866, m rec from 1861, d rec from 1882, bur rec from 1950 & tax rec from 1851; Clk Cir Ct has div, pro & ct rec)
Putnam www.rootsweb.com/~ilputnam/index.htm	**E7**	**13 Jan 1825**	**Fulton** Putnam County; 120 N 4th St; Hennepin, IL 61327; Ph. 815.925.7016 Details: (Co Clk has b & d rec from 1878, m, pro & ct rec from 1831)
Randolph www.rootsweb.com/~ilrandol/	**O6**	**5 Oct 1795**	**NW Territory, St. Clair** Randolph County; 1 Taylor St; Chester, IL 62233; Ph. 618.826.2510 Details: (Co Clk has b rec from 1857, d rec from 1877, m rec from 1804, land rec from 1768 & bur rec; Clk Cir Ct has pro & ct rec from 1809)

County Website	Map Index	Date Created	Parent County or Territory From Which Organized Address/Details
Richland www.rootsweb.com/~ilrichla/index.htm	M10	24 Feb 1841	**Clay, Lawrence** Richland County; 103 W Main St; Olney, IL 62450-0000; Ph. 618.392.3111 Details: (Co Clk has b & d rec from 1878 & m rec from 1841; Clk Cir Ct has div, pro & ct rec)
Rock Island* www.co.rock-island.il.us/	E3	9 Feb 1831	**Jo Daviess** Rock Island County; 1504 3rd Ave; Rock Island, IL 61201-8646; Ph. 309.786.4451 Details: (Co Clk has b rec from 1877, m rec from 1833 & d rec from 1878; Clk Cir Ct has div, pro, ct & nat rec; Rcdr of Deeds has land rec)
Saline* www.rootsweb.com/~ilsaline/	O9	25 Feb 1847	**Gallatin** Saline County; 10 W Poplar St; Harrisburg, IL 62946; Ph. 618.253.8197 Details: (Co Clk has b rec from 1877, d rec from 1878, m & land rec from 1848; Clk Cir Ct has div, pro & ct rec; City Clk has bur rec)
Sangamon* www.co.sangamon.il.us/	J6	30 Jan 1821	**NW Territory** Sangamon County; 200 S 9th St; Springfield, IL 62701-1629; Ph. 217.753.6700 Details: (Co Clk has b & d rec from 1877 & m rec from 1821; Clk Cir Ct has div, pro & ct rec; Supervisor of Assessments has land rec; Rcdr of Deeds has mil rec)
Schuyler www.rootsweb.com/~ilschuyl/	H3	13 Jan 1825	**Pike, Fulton** Schuyler County; RR 1; PO Box 43E; Rushville, IL 62681; Ph. 217.322.4734 Details: (Co Clk has b & d rec from 1877, m & land rec from 1825 & mil rec; Clk Cir Ct has div, pro, ct & nat rec; Schuyler Co Jail Museum has cem, cen, school, tax & fam rec)
Scott* www.rootsweb.com/~ilscott/scott.htm	J4	16 Feb 1839	**Morgan** Scott County; 23 E Market St; Winchester, IL 62694; Ph. 217.742.3178 Details: (Co Clk has b rec from 1860, d rec from 1877, m & land rec from 1839; Clk Cir Ct has div, pro & ct rec)
Shelby* www.rootsweb.com/~ilshelb2/shelby.htm	K8	23 Jan 1827	**Fayette** Shelby County; 301 E Main St; Shelbyville, IL 62565; Ph. 217.774.5220 Details: (Co Clk has b rec from 1848, m rec from 1827, d rec from 1878 & land rec from 1833; Clk Cir Ct has pro rec)
St. Clair* www.frontiernet.net/~jimbridg/stclair.htm	M5	27 Apr 1790	**NW Territory** St. Clair County; 10 Public Sq; Belleville, IL 62220; Ph. 618.277.6600 Details: (Co Clk has b, m, d & bur rec)
Stark www.outfitters.com/illinois/stark/	F6	2 Mar 1839	**Knox, Putnam** Stark County; 130 W Main St; PO Box 97; Toulon, IL 61483-0000; Ph. 309.286.5911 Details: (Co Clk has b rec from 1855, m rec from 1839 & d rec from 1878; Clk Cir Ct has div, pro & ct rec)
Stephenson* www.rootsweb.com/~ilstephe/	B6	4 Mar 1837	**Jo Daviess, Winnebago** Stephenson County; 15 N Galena Ave; Freeport, IL 61032; Ph. 815.235.8289 Details: (Co Clk has b & d rec from 1878, m & land rec from 1837, pro & ct rec from 1894)
Tazewell www.usgennet.org/usa/il/county/ tazewell/index.html	G6	31 Jan 1827	**Sangamon** Tazewell County; 11 S 4th St; Pekin, IL 61554-0000; Ph. 309.477.2264 Details: (Co Clk has b & d rec from 1878 & m rec from 1827; Clk Cir Ct has bur, div, pro & ct rec; Rcdr of Deeds has land rec)
Union www.hostville.com/ilun/	P7	2 Jan 1818	**Johnson** Union County; 311 W Market St; Jonesboro, IL 62952-0000; Ph. 618.833.5711 Details: (Co Clk has b rec from 1862, d rec from 1877, m & land rec from 1818)
Vermilion* www.co.vermilion.il.us/	H11	18 Jan 1826	**Unorg. Terr., Edgar** Vermilion County; 6 N Vermilion St; Danville, IL 61832; Ph. 217.431.2615 Details: (Co Clk has b rec from 1858, m rec from 1826 & d rec from 1877; Clk Cir Ct has div, pro, ct & nat rec; Rcdr of Deeds has land & mil rec)
Wabash www.rootsweb.com/~ilwabash/	M10	27 Dec 1824	**Edwards** Wabash County; 401 N Market St; Mount Carmel, IL 62863; Ph. 618.262.4561 Details: (Co Clk has b & d rec from 1877, m & land rec from 1857, pro & ct rec 1857-1965, cem & nat rec; Clk Cir Ct has div rec)

County Website	Map Index	Date Created	Parent County or Territory From Which Organized Address/Details
Warren www.outfitters.com/illinois/warren/	G4	13 Jan 1825	**Pike** Warren County; 100 W Broadway; Monmouth, IL 61462; Ph. 309.734.8592 Details: (Co Clk has b & d rec from 1877, m & land rec from 1833 & mil rec; Clk Cir Ct has div, pro, ct & nat rec from 1825)
Washington mypage.direct.ca/m/mid/northam.html	N6	2 Jan 1818	**St. Clair** Washington County; 101 E St Louis St; Nashville, IL 62263-1599; Ph. 618.327.8314 Details: (Co Clk has b, d & bur rec from 1877, m rec from 1832 & land rec from 1818; Clk Cir Ct has div, pro & ct rec)
Wayne www.rootsweb.com/~ilwayne/index.htm	M9	26 Mar 1819	**Edwards** Wayne County; 301 E Main St; Fairfield, IL 62837-2013; Ph. 618.842.5182 Details: (Co Clk has b, m, d & bur rec from 1886 & land rec; Clk Cir Ct has pro, div & ct rec)
White www.rootsweb.com/~ilwhite2/	N10	9 Dec 1815	**Gallatin** White County; PO Box 187; Carmi, IL 62821; Ph. 618.382.7211 Details: (Co Clk has b & d rec from 1878 & m rec from 1816; Clk Cir Ct has div rec from 1840 & pro rec from 1818)
Whiteside www.whiteside.org/	D5	16 Jan 1836	**Jo Daviess, Henry** Whiteside County; 200 E Knox St; Morrison, IL 61270; Ph. 815.772.5189 Details: (Co Clk has b & d rec from 1878, m rec from 1839, mil rec 1861-1865 & tax rec from 1840; Clk Cir Ct has div, pro & ct rec; Co Rcdr has land rec)
Will www.willcountyillinois.com/	E10	12 Jan 1836	**Cook, Iroquois, Unorg. Terr.** Will County; 302 N Chicago St; Joliet, IL 60432; Ph. 815.740.4615 Details: (Co Clk has b & d rec from 1877 & m rec from 1836; Clk Cir Ct has div, pro, ct & nat rec; Co Treas has land rec; Rcdr of Deeds has mil rec)
Williamson www.people.ku.edu/~place/williamson.html	P8	28 Feb 1839	**Franklin** Williamson County; 200 W Jefferson St; Marion, IL 62959; Ph. 618.997.1301 Details: (Co Clk has b rec from 1876, m rec from 1839, d rec from 1877 & land rec; City Clk has bur rec; Clk Cir Ct has div, pro & ct rec)
Winnebago www.rootsweb.com/~ilwinneb/ winncnty.htm	B7	16 Jan 1836	**Jo Daviess** Winnebago County; 400 W State St; Rockford, IL 61101; Ph. 815.987.3050 Details: (Co Clk has b & d rec from 1876 & m rec from 1839; Clk Cir Ct has div, pro & ct rec; Co Rcdr has land rec)
Woodford www.rootsweb.com/~ilwoodfo/	F7	27 Feb 1841	**Tazewell, McLean** Woodford County; 115 N Main St; Eureka, IL 61530-1273; Ph. 309.467.2822 Details: (Co Clk has b & d rec from 1871 & m rec from 1841; Co Rcdr has land rec from 1832; Clk Cir Ct has div, pro & ct rec)

Notes

Peony

INDIANA

CAPITAL: INDIANAPOLIS – TERRITORY 1800 – STATE 1816 (19TH)

The French explor er, La Salle, first enter ed Indiana in 1679. Between 1700 and 1735, the French built Fort Miami near Fort Wayne. They also built Fort Ouiatenon, on the Wabash River, and Vincennes, on the lower Wabash, to protect their trading interests. Only Vincennes became a permanent settlement. In 1763, the area became British, but Indian uprisings made settlement difficult. During the Revolutionary War, George Rogers Clark captured Vincennes from the British and helped to end the Indian troubles. With the end of the war, Clarksville, opposite Louisville, Kentucky, was settled in 1784. Following establishment of the Northwest Territory, land was opened to Revolutionary War veterans and others.

Indiana Territory was organized in 1800. Michigan Territory was taken from it in 1805 and Illinois Territory in 1809. The last Indian resistance was finally overcome at the battle of Tippecanoe in 1811. Statehood was granted in 1816. The first counties to be settled were Knox, Harrison, Switzerland, and Clark. Most of the settlers in these counties came from Virginia, Kentucky, and the Carolinas. A group of Swiss immigrants settled in the southeast part of the state. Many Germans and Irish came to Indiana around 1830. New Englanders flocked to the state around 1850, settling in the northern counties. Quakers left Tennessee and the Carolinas to establish themselves in Wayne and Randolph counties away from slavery. Factory growth in the Calumet area attracted many central Europeans to the northwest part of Indiana. Indiana remained in the Union during the Civil War and furnished about 196,000 soldiers to the cause.

Look for vital records in the following locations:

- **Birth and death records:** Birth records from October 1907 are located at the Indiana State Depar tment of Health, Division of V ital Statistics in Indianapolis. General compliance didn' t occur until 1917. Death records date from 1900. Prior to 1900, birth and death records are located in the local health of fice of each county , generally beginning about 1882.

- **Marriage and divorce records:** County clerk' s office prior to 1958 where the license was issued. Divorces were granted by the state legislature from 1817 to 1851. Since 1853, the court of common pleas in each county has divorce jurisdiction.

- **Court records:** Only Marion and St. Joseph Counties presently have probate courts. The other county records are kept by the clerk of the circuit court or the county clerk. Early probate records are in the court of common pleas, circuit courts, or probate courts (generally between 1829 and 1853).

- **Land records:** County r ecor der. The earliest land records, from 1789 to 1837, are published and indexed. Land records prior to 1807 were handled in Cincinnati, Ohio.

- **Census records:** State or territorial censuses were taken in some areas in 1807, 1810, and 1820. A few fragments of county and state census records exist for 1853, 1856, 1857, and 1877. These are available at the Indiana State Library in Indianapolis.

Indiana State Department of Health
Division of Vital Statistics
PO Box 7125
Indianapolis, Indiana 46206
317-233-2700

Indiana State Library
140 North Senate Avenue
Indianapolis, Indiana 46204

Societies and Repositories

Adams County Historical Society; Box 262; Decatur, Indiana 46733

African-American Historical and Genealogical Society, Indiana; 502 Clover Terrace; Bloomington, Indiana 47404.1909

Alexander Hamilton Chapter, INSSAR; 7135 Koldyke Dr; Fishers, Indiana 46038

Alexandria Monroe Township Historical and Genealogical Society; RR 1 Box 402; Alexandria, Indiana 46001

Allen Co. Public Library; PO Box 2270; Fort Wayne, Indiana 46801

Allen County Genealogical Society of Indiana; PO Box 12003; Ft. Wayne, Indiana 46862; <www.ipfw.edu/ipfwhist/historgs/acgsi.htm>

Allen County Public Library; 900 Webster Street; Fort Wayne, Indiana 46802; 219.424.7241; Fax 219.422.9688

American Legion Nat'l Headquarters Library; 700 N. Pennsylvania St.; Indianapolis, Indiana 46204

Anderson Public Library; 111 E. 12th Street; Anderson, Indiana 46016

Anthony Halberstadt Chapter, INSSAR; Ft Wayne, Indiana 46815.6727; (219) 484.2745

Bartholomew County Genealogical Society; 524 Third St.; PO Box 2455; Columbus, Indiana 47202

Benton County Historical Society; 404 E. 6th St, PO Box 431; Fowler, Indiana 47944

Blackford County Historical Society; PO Box 264; Hartford City, Indiana 47348;

Blair Society for Genealogical Research; 20 Parkwood Drive; Brownsburg, Indiana 46211-1922; (317) 852.5078;

Bloomfield Carnegie Public Library; S. Franklin St.; Bloomfield, Indiana 47424

Boone County Historical Society; PO Box 141; Lebanon, Indiana 46052

Brown County Genealogical Society; PO Box 1202; Nashville, Indiana 47448.1202; <www.rootsweb.com/~inbcgs/title.htm>

Brown County Historical Society, Inc.; PO Box 668; Nashville, Indiana 47448

Carrol County Historical Society; PO Box 277; Delphi, Indiana 46923

Carroll County Historical Society; Ground Floor Court House; PO Box 277; Delphi, Indiana 46923; 765.564.3624; <dcwi.com/~cchs/cchs.html>

Cass County Genealogical Society; PO Box 373; Logansport, Indiana 46947

Clarence Cook Chapter, INSSAR; 809 N. East Street; Indianapolis, Indiana 46202-3424; (317) 917.0238 ; <www.geocities.com/inssar.south/clarcook.html>

Clark County Historical Society; PO Box 606; Jeffersonville, Indiana 47130

Clay County Genealogical Society, Inc.; PO Box 56; Center Point, Indiana 47840-0056; <www.ccgsilib.org>

Clinton County Genealogical Society; c/o Frankfort Community Public Library; 209 W. Clinton St.; Frankfort, Indiana 46041

Clinton County Historical Society, Inc. and Historical Museum; 301 E. Clinton St.; Frankfort, Indiana 46041

Commission on Public Records, Indiana States Archives Division; 140 North Senate Avenue, Room 117; Indianapolis, Indiana 46204; 317.232.3660; Fax 317.233.1085

Continental Chapter, INSSAR; 1611 N. Tillotson Ave; Muncie, Indiana 47304.2500; <www.geocities.com/inssar.south/cont.html>

Crawford County, Indiana Historical & Genealogical Society; PO Box 139; Leavenworth, Indiana 47137

Daniel Guthrie Chapter, INSSAR; 4630 Chatham Dr.; Bloomington, Indiana 47404-1319; <www.geocities.com/inssar.south/daniguth.html>

Danville Public Library; 101 S. Indiana St.; Danville, Indiana 46122

David Benton Chapter, INSSAR; PO Box 101; Brownstown, Indiana 47220; <www.geocities.com/inssar.south/dbc.htm>

DcKalb County Genealogical Society; c/o Eckhart Public Library; 603 S. Jackson St.; Auburn, Indiana 46706

DeKalb County Historical Society; Box 66; Auburn, Indiana 46706

Delaware County Historical Alliance; 120 E. Washington St.; Muncie, Indiana 47305.1734

Disciples of Christ Christian Theological Seminary Library; 1000 W. 42nd St.; Indianapolis, Indiana 46208; 317.924.1331; Fax 317.923.1961

Dubois County Genealogical Society; PO Box 84; Ferdinand, Indiana 47532.0084

Eckhart Public Library; 603 S. Jackson St.; Auburn, Indiana 46706

Elkhart County Genealogical Society; PO Box 1031; Elkhart, Indiana 46515.1031

Elwood-Pipecreek Genealogical Society; c/o Elwood Public Library; 1600 Main St.; Elwood, Indiana 46036

Family Tree and Crests; 6233 Carrollton Ave.; Indianapolis, Indiana 46220

Fort Wayne and Allen Co. Public Library; 900 Webster; Fort Wayne, Indiana 46802

Fountain County Genealogical Society; 2855 S. Kingman Rd.; Kingman, Indiana 47952

Fountain County Historical Society; Box 148; Kingman, Indiana 47952

Frankfort Community Public Library; 208 W. Clinton St.; Frankfort, Indiana 46401; 765.654.8746; <www.accs.net/fcpl>

Fulton Co. Public Library; 320 W. 7th St.; Rochester, Indiana 46975-1332; 219.223.2713; <www.fulco.lib.in.us>

Fulton County Historical Society, Genealogical Section; 37 E. 375 N.; Rochester, Indiana 46975; <icss.net/~fchs/index.htm>

Genealogical Society of Marion County; PO Box 2292; Indianapolis, Indiana 46206-2292; <www.rootsweb.com/~ingsmc/>

Genealogical Society of Whitley County; PO Box 224; Columbia City, Indiana 46725-0224; 260.691.2241; <home.whitleynet.org/genealogy/>

General Thomas Posey Chapter, INSSAR; 624 W. 6th St; Mount Vernon, Indiana 47620; (812)838.5960 ; <www.geocities.com/inssar.south/thospose.htm>

George Rogers Clark Chapter, INSSAR; 2816 Avondale Road; Vincennes, Indiana 47591; <www.geocities.com/inssar.south/georclar.html>

Gibson Historical Society; PO Box 516; Princeton, Indiana 47670

Greene County Genealogical Society; PO Box 164; Bloomfield, Indiana 47424

Hamilton County Historical Society; PO Box 397; Noblesville, Indiana 46060

Hancock County Historical Society, Inc.; PO Box 375; Greenfield, Indiana 46140-0375

Harrison County Historical Society; 117 W. Beaver St.; Corydon, Indiana 47112

Hendricks County Genealogical Society; 101 South Indiana St.; Danville, Indiana 46122

Hendricks County Historical Society; PO Box 128; Danville, Indiana 46122

Henry County Historical Society; 606 South 14th St.; New Castle, Indiana 47362

Henry F. Schricker Library, c/o The Starke Co. Gen. Soc. of Indiana; 152 W. Culver Rd.; Knox, Indiana 46534

Historical Committee and Archives of the Mennonite Church; 1700 S. Main Street; Goshen, Indiana 46526; 219.535.7293

Hoosier Pioneer Patriots Chapter, INSSAR; 733 Pennsylvania Ave; Sellersburg, Indiana 47172; 812.246.2066; <www.geocities.com/inssar.south/hoospion.html>

Howard County Genealogical Society; PO Box 2; Oakford, Indiana 46965; <www.rootsweb.com/~inhoward/hcgs/index.html>

Howard County Historical Society; 1200 West Sycamore; Kokomo, Indiana 46901;

Huntington City-Township Public Library; 200 W. Market St.; Huntington, Indiana 46750

Huntington County Genealogical Society, Huntington City Twp. Public Library; 200 W Market St.; Huntington, Indiana 46750

Indiana Baptist Collection; Franklin College Library; Franklin, Indiana 46131; 317.738.8164; Fax 317.738.8787

Indiana Genealogical Society; PO Box 10507; Fort Wayne, Indiana 46852.0507; 219.424.7241, <www.indgensoc.org>

Indiana Historical Society, William Henry Smith Memorial Library, 450 W. Ohio St., Indianapolis, IN 46202-3269

Indiana Historical Society Genealogical Section; 450 West Ohio Street; Indianapolis, Indiana 46202; 317.232.1882; Fax 317.232.3109

Indiana State Archives; 6440 E. 30th St.; Indianapolis, Indiana 46219; <www.state.in.us/icpr/webfile/archives/homepage.html>

Indiana State Library, Genealogy Division; 140 North Senate Avenue, Room 250; Indianapolis, Indiana 46204; 317.232.3689; Fax 317.232.3728

Jackson County Genealogical Society; 415 1/2 S. Poplar St.; Brownstown, Indiana 47220

Jasper County Historical Society; Augusta St.; Rensselaer, Indiana 47971

Jay County Genealogical Society; 109 S. Commerce St. Suite E; Portland, Indiana 47371; 219.726.4323

Jay County Historical Society; PO Box 1292; Portland, Indiana 47371

Jefferson County Historical Society; 615 West First Street; Madison, Indiana 47250; 812.273.5023; <www.seidata.com/~jchs/jchs.htm>

Jennings County Genealogical Society; PO Box 863; North Vernon, Indiana 47265

John Hay Chapter, INSSAR; 4913 W Luther Rd; Floyds Knobs, Indiana; 812.923.8586; <www.geocities.com/inssar.south/johnhay.html>

John Martin Chapter, INSSAR; 76 S. Thorpe Place; West Terre Haute, Indiana 47885; 812.533.2319; <www.geocities.com/inssar.south/johnmart.html>

Johnson County Historical Society; 150 West Madison St.; Franklin, Indiana 46131

Kokomo / Howard Co. Public Library; 220 N. Union St.; Kokomo, Indiana 46901-4614; 765.457.3242; <www.kokomo.lib.in.us>

Kosciusko County Historical Society; Genealogical Section; PO Box 1071; Warsaw, Indiana 46580

La Porte Co. Public Library; 904 Indiana Ave.; La Porte, Indiana 46350

La Porte County Genealogical Society; 904 Indiana Ave.; La Porte, Indiana 46350

La Porte County Historical Society; LaPorte County Complex; 809 State Street; La Porte, Indiana 46350-3329;

LaGrange County Historical Society, Inc.; R.R 1; LaGrange, Indiana 46761

Lewis Historical Collections Library; Vincennes, Indiana 47591

Lexington Historical Society, Inc.; 5764 South State Rd. 203; Lexington, Indiana 47138

Logansport Public Library; 616 E. Broadway; Logansport, Indiana 46947

Madison County Historical Society, Inc.; PO Box 523; Anderson, Indiana 46015

Madison-Jefferson Co. Public Library; 420 W. Main St.; Madison, Indiana 47250

Marion County Historical Society; 140 N. Senate; Indianapolis, Indiana 46204

Marion Public Library, Indiana Rm.; 600 S. Washington St.; Marion, Indiana 46953

Marion-Adams Genealogical Society; 309 Main St.; Sheridan, Indiana 46069

Marshall Co. Historical Center; 123 N. Michigan St., Plymouth, IN 46563; 219.936.2306

Martin County Historical Society, Inc.; PO Box R4; Shoals, Indiana 46504

Mennonite Hist. Library, Goshen College; 1700 S. Main St.; Goshen, Indiana 46526; 219.535.7418; Fax 219.535.7438

Merrillville-Ross Township Historical Society; 13 W. 73rd Avenue; Merrillville, Indiana 46410; <www.rootsweb.com/~inlake/ross.htm>

Methodist Archives of DePauw University and Indiana United Methodism; Roy O. West Library DePauw University; Greencastle, Indiana 46135; 317.658.4434; Fax 317.658.4445

Miami County Genealogical Society; PO Box 542; Peru, Indiana 46970; <www.rootsweb.com/~inmiami/gensoc.html>

Miami County Historical Society; 51 North Broadway; Peru, Indiana 46970; 765.473.3880; <www.netusa1.net/~mchs/index.html>

Michigan City Public Library; 100 E. Fourth St.; Michigan City, Indiana 46360

Middletown Public Library; Box 36, 554 Locust St.; Middletown, Indiana 47356

Mishawaka-Penn Public Library; 209 Lincoln Way East; Mishawaka, Indiana 46544-2084; 219.259.5277; <www.mppl.lib.in.us>

Monroe Co. Library; 303 E. Kirkwood Ave.; Bloomington, Indiana 47408

Monroe County Historical/Genealogical Societies; 202 E. 6th St.; Bloomington, Indiana 47408

Montgomery County Historical Society, Genealogy Section, c/o Crawfordsville Dist. Public Library; 222 So. Washington St.; Crawfordsville, Indiana 47933

Morgan Co. Public Library; 110 S. Jefferson St.; Martinsville, Indiana 46151

Morgan County History & Genealogical Association; PO Box 1012; Martinsville, Indiana 46151-0012; 765.349.2985; <www.rootsweb.com/~inmchaga/mchagai.html>

National Archives-Great Lakes Region; 7358 South Pulaski Road; Chicago, Illinois 60629; 773.581.7816; Fax 312.353.1294

Noble County Genealogical Society; 813 E. Main St.; Albion, Indiana 46701

Noblesville Southeastern Public Library; One Library Plaza; Noblesville, Indiana 46060; 317.773.1384

North Central Indiana Genealogical Society; 2300 Canterbury Dr.; Kokomo, Indiana 46901

Northern Indiana Historical Society; 112 So. Lafayette Blvd.; South Bend, Indiana 44601

Northwest Indiana Genealogical Society; c/o Valparaiso Public Library 103 Jefferson St.; Valparaiso, Indiana 46383

Northwest Indiana Genealogical Society; PO Box 595; Griffith, Indiana 46319; <www.rootsweb.com/~inlake/nwigs.htm>

Northwest Territory Genealogical Society; Lewis Historical Society. LRC 22; Vincennes University; Vincennes, Indiana 47591

Ohio County Historical Society; PO Box 194; Rising Sun, Indiana 47040; <www.risingsun.cc/comm/HistSociety.html>

Orange County Genealogical Society; PO Box 344; Paoli, Indiana 47454; <www.usgennet.org/usa/in/county/orange/gensoc.htm>

Owen County Historical & Genealogical Society; PO Box 569; Spencer, Indiana 47460; <www.owen.in.us/owenhist/owen.htm>

Owen County Public Library; Montgomery St.; Spencer, Indiana 47460

P. H. Sullivan Museum & Gen. Library; 225 W. Hawthorne St., PO Box 182; Zionsville, Indiana 46077

Palatines to America, Indiana Chapter; PO Box 40435; Indianapolis, Indiana 46240.0435

Paoli Public Library; NE Court; Paoli, Indiana 47454

Perry County Historical Society; c/o Mrs. James J. Groves; Rome, Indiana 47574

Plainfield Public Library, Guilford Township Hist. Collection; 1120 Stafford Rd.; Plainfield, Indiana 46168-2230; 317.839.6602

Plymouth Public Library; 201 N. Center St.; Plymouth, Indiana 46563

Porter County Public Library; 103 Jefferson St.; Valparaiso, Indiana 46383

Posey County Historical Society; PO Box 171; Mt. Vernon, Indiana 47620

Posey-Vanderburg Chapter, INSSAR; 612 Drexel Dr; St Phillips, Indiana; 812.985.3421 ; <www.geocities.com/inssar.south/posevand.html>

Pulaski Co. Public Library; 121 S. Riverside Dr.; Winamac, Indiana 46996

Pulaski County Genealogical Society; R.R. 4, Box 121; Winamac, Indiana 46996.

Randolph County Genealogical Society; R.R. 3 Box 61; Winchester, Indiana 47394

Randolph County Historical Society; Rt. 3, Box 60A; Winchester, Indiana 47394

Ripley County Historical Society, Inc.; 125 Washington Street; PO Box 525; Versailles, Indiana 47042; <www.seidata.com/~rchslib/>

Rockville Public Library; 106 N. Market St.; Rockville, Indiana 47872

Roman Catholic University of Notre Dame Archives; PO Box 513; Notre Dame, Indiana 46556; 219.631.5252; Fax 219.631.6772

Saint Joseph Co. Public Library, Local Hist. / Gen. Rm.; 304 S. Main St.; South Bend, Indiana 46601

Scott County Genealogical Society; 5764 S. State Rd. 203; Lexington, Indiana 47139

Seth Jewel Chapter, INSSAR; 1106 Greg St.; Auburn, Indiana 46706.1507; <www.geocities.com/inssar.south/sethjewe.html>

Shelby County Historical Society; Box 74; Shelbyville, Indiana 46176

Shelbyville-Shelby Co. Public Library; 57 W. Broadway; Shelbyville, Indiana 46176; 317.398.7121; 317.835.2653; Fax 317.398.4430

Simon Kenton Chapter, INSSAR; 470 E Amsler Rd; Rensselaer, Indiana 47978; 219.886.5200; <www.geocities.com/inssar.south/simokent.html>

Society of Indiana Pioneers; 450 West Ohio Street; Indianapolis, Indiana 46202;

Sons of the American Revolution, Indiana Society; 5401 Central Ave.; Indianapolis, Indiana 46220

South Bend Area Genealogical Society; c/o The Mishawaka. Penn Public Library 209 Lincoln Way E; Mishawaka, Indiana 46544; <www.rootsweb.com/~insbags/index.htm>

Southern Indiana Genealogical Society; PO Box 665; New Albany, Indiana 47151-0665; <www.rootsweb.com/~insigs/>

Spencer-Owen Public Library; 110 E. Market St.; Spencer, Indiana 47460

Spencer County Historical Society; Walnut St.; Rockport, Indiana 47635

Starke County Genealogical Society; c/o Henry F. Schricker Library 152 W. Culver Road; Knox, Indiana 46534; <www.maplewoodfarm.com/strkctygen.htm>

Steuben County Genealogical Society; Carnegie Library; 322 S. Wayne; Angola, Indiana 46703

Sullivan County Historical Society; PO Box 326; Sullivan, Indiana 47882

Switzerland Co. Public Library; 205 Ferry St., PO Box 133; Vevay, Indiana 47043; 812.427.3363; Fax 812.427.3654

Tippecanoe County Area Genealogical Society; 909 South St.; Lafayette, Indiana 47901

Tippecanoe County Historical Association; 1001 South Street; Lafayette, Indiana 47901; (765) 476.8414;

Tipton Co. Public Library, Gen. / Local History; 127 E. Madison St.; Tipton, Indiana 46072

Tri-County Genealogical Society; 23184 Pocket Rd. W.; Batesville, Indiana 47006

Tri-State Genealogical Society; c/o Willard Library; 21 First Avenue; Evansville, Indiana 47710; <www.rootsweb.com/~intsgs>

Twin Oaks Genealogical Society; 1371 E. 400 N.; Bluffton, Indiana 46714

Union City Library; North Columbia St.; Union City, Indiana 47390

Union Co. Public Library; 2 E. Seminary; Liberty, Indiana 47353

Union County Historical Society; 6 E. Seminary St.; Liberty, Indiana 47353

Valparaiso Public Library; 103 Jefferson St.; Valparaiso, Indiana 46383

Vigo County Historical Society; 1411 So. 6th St.; Terre Haute, Indiana 47802; <web.indstate.edu/community/vchs/home.html>

Vital Records Section State Board of Health; PO Box 1964,1330 West Michigan St.; Indianapolis, Indiana 42606-1964; 317.383.6100

Wabash Carnegie Public Library Genealogy Dept.; 188 W. Hill St.; Wabash, Indiana 46992

Wabash County Genealogical Society; PO Box 825; Wabash, Indiana 46992; <www.rootsweb.com/~inwabash/wcgs.html>

Wabash County Historical Society; Wabash County Museum; 89 W. Hill St.; Wabash, Indiana 46992

Wabash Valley Genealogical Society; PO Box 85; Terre Haute, Indiana 47808

Warren County Historical Society; PO Box 176; Williamsport, Indiana 47993

Warsaw Public Library; 315 E. Center St.; Warsaw, Indiana 46580

Washington County Historical Society; 307 E. Market St.; Salem, Indiana 47904

Washington Township Public Library; North Main St.; Lynn, Indiana 47355

Wayne County Genealogical Society; PO Box 2599; Richmond, Indiana 47375

Wayne County Historical Society; 1150 North A St.; Richmond, Indiana 47374

Wells County Historical Society; PO Box 143; Bluffton, Indiana 46714-0143; <www.wchs.museum.org/wchsociety.htm>

White County Genealogical Society; 101 South Bluff St.; Monticello, Indiana 47960

Willard Library of Evansville; 21 1st Ave.; Evansville, Indiana 47710

William Henry Harrison Chapter, INSSAR; 1733 Shenandoah Dr; Lafayette, Indiana 47905-4041; 765.447.5973; <www.geocities.com/inssar.south/willharr.html>

William Knight Chapter, INSSAR; 94 Pin Oak Road; Greencastle, Indiana 46135; 765.653.6834

William Van Gordon Chapter, INSSAR; 3047 Lake Side Dr; Highland, Indiana 46322; 219.924.0416; <www.geocities.com/inssar.south/willgord.html>

Winchester Public Library; East North St.; Winchester, Indiana 47394

Bibliography and Record Sources

General Sources

A Biographical History of Eminent and Self-made Men of the State of Indiana. 2 vols. Cincinnati: Western Biographical Publishing Co., 1880.

A Directory of Churches and Religious Organizations in Indiana. 3 vols. Indianapolis: Historical Records Survey, 1941.

Beatty, John D. *Research in Indiana.* Arlington, Virginia: National Genealogical Society, 1992.

Bender, Harold S. *The Mennonites of Indiana, 1835-1929.* (Salt Lake City: Filmed by the Genealogical Society of Utah, 1990).

Blanchard, Charles. *History of the Catholic Church in Indiana.* 2 vols. Logansport, Indiana: A.W. Bowen & Co., 1898.

Buley, R. Carlyle. *The Old Northwest: Pioneer Period, 1815-1840.* Indianapolis: Indiana Historical Society, 1950.

Caby, John Frank. *The Origin and Development of the Missionary Baptist Church in Indiana.* Franklin, Indiana: Franklin College, 1942.

Carty, Mickey Dimon. *Searching in Indiana: A Reference Guide to Public and Private Records.* Costa Mesa, California: ISC Pub., 1985.

Cavanaugh, Karen B. *A Genealogist's Guide to the Ft. Wayne, Indiana, Public Library.* Owensboro, Kentucky: McDowell Pub., 1980.

Clayton, Ellen Cox. *Memories of Yesterday in Indiana: A Brief History of the Early Days of the Church of Jesus Christ of Latter-Day Saints in Indiana*. [S.l.: s.n., 196-].

Cumback, Will. *Men of Progress, Indiana: A Selected List of Biographical Sketches and Portraits of the Leaders in Business, Professional and Official Life, Together with Brief Notes on the History and Character of Indiana*. Indianapolis: The Indianapolis Sentinel, 1899.

Dillon, John B. *A History of Indiana*. Indianapolis: Bingham and Doughty, 1859.

Dorrel, Ruth, and Thomas D. Hamm. *Abstracts of the Records of the Society of Friends in Indiana*, Vol. 1. Rev. ed. Indianapolis: Indiana Historical Society, 1996.

Dorrel, Ruth. *Indiana Source Book VI; Genealogical Material from the Hoosier Genealogist, 1982-1981*. Indianapolis: Indiana Historical Society, 1992.

Dorrel, Ruth. *Indiana Source Book VII; Genealogical Material from The Hoosier Genealogist, 1989-1990*. Indianapolis: Indiana Historical Society, 1994.

Dorrel, Ruth. *Pioneer Ancestors of Members of The Society of Indiana Pioneers*. Indianapolis: Indiana Historical Society, 1983.

Dunn, Jacob Piatt. *Indiana and Indianans*. 5 vols. Chicago and New York: The American Historical Society, 1919.

Dunn, Jacob Piatt. *Memorial and Genealogical Record of Representative Citizens of Indiana*. A.W. Bowen, 1914.

Esarey, Logan. *History of Indiana from Its Exploration to 1922*. 3 vols. Dayton, Ohio: Dayton Historical Society, 1923.

Esarey, Logan. *The Indiana Home*. (1953) Reprint. Galveston, Texas: Frontier Press, 1976.

Franklin, Charles. *Indiana Territorial Pioneer Records, 1801-1820*. [S.l.]: Heritage House, 1983-1985.

Fraustein, Rebah M., and Willard Heiss. *Indiana Source Book IV; Genealogical Material from the Hoosier Genealogist, 1979-1981*. Indianapolis: Indiana Historical Society, 1986.

Fraustein, Rehab M. *Indiana Source Book V; Genealogical Material from the Hoosier Genealogist, 1982-1984*. Indianapolis: Indiana Historical Society, 1990.

Gibbs. *Indiana's African American Heritage*. Galveston, Texas: Frontier Press, 1993.

Gooldy, Pat, and Charles M. Franklin. *Indiana Wills Phase I (to 1850) and Phase II (1851-1898)*. Indianapolis: Ye Olde Genealogie Shoppe.

Gooldy, Pat, and Ray Gooldy. *Manual for Indiana Genealogical Research*. Indianapolis: Ye Olde Genealogie Shoppe, 1991.

Griffis, Joan A. Illiana. *Ancestors Volume 5, 1993, 1994, 1995, Genealogy Column in the Commercial News, Danville, Illinois*. Danville, IL: Joan A. Griffis, 1996.

Harter, Stuart. *Indiana Genealogy and Local History Sources Index*. Fort Wayne, IN: Stuart Harter, 1985.

Heiss, William. *Indiana Source Book I; Genealogical Material from the Hoosier Genealogist, 1961-1966*. Indianapolis: Indiana Historical Society, 1977.

Heiss, William. *Indiana Source Book II: Genealogical Material from the Hoosier Genealogist, 1967-1972*. Indianapolis: Indiana Historical Society, 1981.

Heiss, William. *Indiana Source Book III; Genealogical Material from the Hoosier Genealogist, 1973-1979*. Indianapolis: Indiana Historical Society, 1982.

Hine, Darlene Clark. *The Black Women in the Middle West Project: A Comprehensive Resource Guide, Illinois and Indiana; Historical Essays, Oral Histories, Biographical Profiles, and Document Collections*. Indianapolis, Indiana: Indiana Historical Bureau, 1986.

Hinshaw, Gregory P. *Indiana Friends Heritage 1821-1996, The 175th Anniversary History of Indiana Yearly Meeting of Friends (Quakers)*, [n.p.] 1996.

Index to Encyclopedia of American Quaker Genealogy by William Wade Hinshaw. [S.l.]: Genealogical Pub. Co., 1999.

Indiana Biographical Index. West Bountiful, Utah: Genealogical Indexing Associates. 1983.

Indiana Research Outline. Series US-States, no. 15. Salt Lake City: Family History Library, 1988.

Indiana Source Book: Genealogical Material from The Hoosier Genealogist, 1979-1981. Indianapolis: Indiana Historical Society, 1987.

Men of Indiana: In Nineteen Hundred and One. Indianapolis: Benesch, 1901.

Miller, Carolynne L. *Aids for Genealogical Searching in Indiana: A Bibliography*. Detroit: Detroit Society for Genealogical Research, 1970.

Miller, Carolynne L. *Indiana Sources for Genealogical Research in the Indiana State Library*. Indianapolis: Indiana Historical Society, 1984.

Miller, John W. *Indiana Newspaper Bibliography: Historical Accounts of all Indiana Newspapers Published from 1804 to 1980 and Locational Information for all Available Copies, Both Original and Microfilm*. Indianapolis, Indiana: Indiana Historical Society, 1982.

Newhard, Malinda E. E. *A Guide to Genealogical Records in Indiana*. Harlan, IN: M. Newhard, 1979.

Parker, Jimmy B. and Lyman de Platt. *Indiana Biographical Index*. West Bountiful, UT: Genealogical Indexing Associates, 1983.

Pumroy, Eric, and Paul Brockman. *A Guide to Manuscript Collections of the Indiana Historical Society and Indiana State Library*. Indexed. Indianapolis: Indiana Historical Society, 1986.

Reed, George Irving. *Encyclopedia of Biography of Indiana*. Chicago: Century Publishing, 1895.

Rehmer, R. F. *Lutherans in Pioneer Indiana*. Lafayette, Indiana: Commercial Print., 1972.

Riker, Dorothy. *Genealogical Sources Reprinted from the Genealogical Section, Indiana Magazine of History*. Indianapolis: Indiana Historical Society, 1979.

Riker, Dorothy. *Indiana Source Books Index, Vols. 1-3*. Indianapolis: Indiana Historical Society, 1983.

Robbins, Coy D. *Indiana Negro Registers, 1852-1865*. Bowie, MD: Heritage Books, 1994.

Robinson, Mona. *Who's Your Hoosier Ancestor? Genealogy for Beginners*. Bloomington, IN: Indiana University Press, 1992.

Rudolf, L. C. and Judith E. Endelman. *Religion in Indiana, A Guide to Historical Resources*. Indiana University Press, 1986.

Rudolph. *Hoosier Faiths: A History of Indiana's Churches and Religious Groups.* Galveston, Texas: Frontier Press, 1995.

Scheiber, Harry N. *The Old Northwest: Studies in Regional History, 1787-1910.* Lincoln [Neb.]: University of Nebraska Press, 1969.

Schweitzer, George K. *Indiana Genealogical Research.* Knoxville, TN: George K. Schweitzer, 1996.

Smith, John L. *Indiana Methodism: A Series of Sketches and Incidents, Grave and Humorous Concerning Preachers and People of the West; with an Appendix Containing Personal Recollections, Public Addresses and other Miscellany.* Valparaiso, Indiana: J.L. Smith, 1892.

Southern California Genealogical Society. *Sources of Genealogical Help in Indiana.* Burbank, California: Southern California Genealogical Society.

Stott, W. T. *Baptist Church History, Indiana.* [S.l.: s.n., 1908].

Taylor, Robert M., Jr., Connie A. McBirney, eds. *Peopling Indiana: The Ethnic Experience.* Galveston, Texas: Frontier Press, 1996.

Thompson, Donald E. *Preliminary Checklist of Archives and Manuscripts in Indiana Repositories.* Indianapolis: Indiana Historical Society, 1980.

Thornbrough, Emma Lou. *The Negro in Indiana Before 1900: A Study of a Minority.* Bloomington, Indiana: Indiana University Press, 1993.

Wedel, Carolynne L. *Aids for Genealogical Searching in Indiana: A Bibliography.* Rev. ed. Detroit: Detroit Society for Genealogical Research, 1970.

Woollen, William Wesley, and Jacob Platt Dunn. *Executive Journal of Indiana Territory.* (1900) Reprint. Indianapolis: Indiana Historical Society, 1985.

Woollen, William Wesley. *Biographical and Historical Sketches of Early Indiana.* Indianapolis: Hammond, 1883.

Atlases, Maps and Gazetteers

Atlas of Indiana, 92 County Maps. Includes detailed maps of individual counties, all the back roads, streams, lakes, towns, etc. Galveston, Texas. Frontier Press, [n.d.].

Baker, J. David. *The Postal History of Indiana.* 2 vols. Louisville, Kentucky: Leonard H. Hartman, 1976.

Baker, Ronald L., and Marvin Carmony. *Indiana Place Names.* Bloomington, IN: Indiana University Press, 1975.

Ball, T. H. *Northwestern Indiana, from 1800 to 1900: A View of Our Region Through the Nineteenth Century.* Chicago: Donohue & Hanneberry, 1900.

Chamberlain, E. *The Indiana Gazetteer, or, Topographical Dictionary of the State of Indiana.* Indianapolis: E. Chamberlain, 1849.

Franklin, Charles. *Genealogical Atlas of Indiana.* Indianapolis, Indiana: Heritage House, 1985.

Illustrated Historical Atlas of the State of Indiana. Chicago: Baskin, Forster, 1876.

Indiana Gazetteer, or Topographical Dictionary of the State of Indiana. 3rd ed. (1850) Reprint, Salem, Massachusetts: Higginson Book Co., 1993.

List of Indiana Post Offices. Microfilm of originals (3 x 5 cards) at the Indiana State Library in Indianapolis, Indiana. (Salt Lake City: Filmed by the Genealogical Society of Utah, 1986).

Maps of Indiana Counties in 1876. (1968) Reprint. Indianapolis: Indiana Historical Society, 1979.

New Topographical Atlas and Gazetteer of Indiana. 1871. Reprint. Evansville, Indiana: Unigraphic, Inc., 1975.

Pence, George, and Nellie C. Armstrong. *Indiana Boundaries: Territorial, State, and County.* (1933) Reprint. Indianapolis: Indiana Historical Society, 1967.

Scott, John. *The Indiana Gazetteer or Topographical Dictionary.* 1826. Reprint. Indianapolis: Indiana Historical Society, 1954.

Sinko, Peggy Tuck. *Indiana Atlas of Historical County Boundaries.* John H. Long, editor. Charles Scribners Sons, 1996.

Wilson, George R. *Early Indiana Trails and Surveys.* (1919) Reprint. Indianapolis: Indiana Historical Society, 1991.

Census Records

Available Census Records and Census Substitutes

Federal Census 1820, 1830, 1840, 1850, 1860, 1870, 1880, 1900, 1910, 1920, 1930.

State/Territorial Census 1807, 1853, 1856, 1857, 1859, 1866, 1871, 1877.

Federal Mortality Schedules 1850.

Voters 1809.

Revolutionary War Pensioners 1835.

Dollarhide, William. *The Census Book: A Genealogist's Guide to Federal Census Facts, Schedules and Indexes.* Bountiful, Utah: Heritage Quest, 1999.

Franklin, Charles M. *Indiana Territorial Pioneer Records, 1801-1820.* [S.l.]: Heritage House, c1983-1985.

Fraustein, Rebah M. *Census of Indiana Territory for 1807.* (1980) Reprint. Indianapolis: Indiana Historical Society, 1990.

Heiss, Willard. *1820 Federal Census for Indiana.* (1966) Reprint. Indianapolis: Indiana Historical Society, 1975.

Indiana. Adjutant General. *Enrollment of the Late Soldiers, Their Widows and Orphans of the Late Armies of the United States, Residing in the State of Indiana for the Year 1886-1894.* Microfilm of records located at the Indiana State Library, Indianapolis. (Salt Lake City: Filmed by the Genealogical Society of Utah, 1988-1990). 89 microfilm.

Kemp, Thomas Jay. *The American Census Handbook.* Wilmington, DE: Scholarly Resources, Inc., 2001.

Lainhart, Ann S. *State Census Records.* Baltimore: Genealogical Publishing Co., Inc., 1992.

Szucs, Loretto Dennis, and Matthew Wright. *Finding Answers in U.S. Census Records.* Ancestry Publishing, 2001.

Thorndale, William, and William Dollarhide. *Map Guide to the U.S. Federal Censuses, 1790-1920.* Baltimore: Genealogical Publishing Co., 1987.

United States. Bureau of Internal Revenue. *Internal Revenue Assessment Lists for Indiana, 1862-1866.* Washington, D.C.: The National Archives, 1987. 42 microfilm.

Court Records, Probate and Wills

Franklin, Charles M. *Index to Indiana Wills: Phase 1, Through 1850 and Phase 2, 1850 Through 1880.* 2 Vols. Indianapolis: Heritage House, 1986-87.

Griffin, Warren B. *Preliminary Inventory: Records of the U.S. Courts for the District of Indiana.* Chicago: Federal Record Center, 1967.

Howe, Daniel Wait. *The Laws and Courts of Northwest and Indiana Territories.* Indiana Historical: Bowen-Merrill Co., 1886.

Moudy, Vera Mae. *Directory, Wills and Estates Information in Genealogy Dept., Indiana State Library.* Indianapolis, Indiana: Ye Olde Genealogie Shoppe, 1981.

Newman, John J. *Research in Indiana Courthouses: Judicial and Other Records.* (1981) Reprint Indianapolis: Indiana Historical Society, 1990.

Taylor, Charles W. *Biographical Sketches and Review of the Bench and Bar of Indiana: Containing Biographies and Sketches of Eminent Judges and Lawyers of Indiana, Together With a History of the Judiciary of the State and Review of the Bar from the Earliest Times to the Present with Anecdotes, Reminiscences, etc. …* 2 vols. Indianapolis, Indiana: Bench and Bar Pub. Co., 1895.

The Laws of Indiana Territory, 1801-1809. Springfield, Illinois: Trustees of the Ill. State Historical Library, 1930.

United States. National Archives and Records Service. *Preliminary Inventory, Records of the United States Courts for the District of Indiana, (Record Group 21).* Chicago: Federal Records Center, 1967.

Emigration, Immigration, Migration and Naturalization

An Index to Indiana Naturalization Records Found in Various Order Books of the Ninety-two Local Courts Prior to 1907. Indianapolis: Indiana Historical Society, 1981.

Burns, Lee. *The National Road in Indiana.* Indianapolis: C.E. Pauley, 1920?.

Enochs, Richard A. *From A to B: Migration Research: Birds of a Feather.* Fort Wayne, Ind.: Indiana Genealogical Society, 1994.

Indiana State Archives. (Indianapolis). *Indiana Naturalization Records Prior to 1951.* Indianapolis, Indiana: Indiana State Archives, 2002. Online database - <www.state.in.us/serv/icpr_naturalization>.

United States. District Court (Illinois: Northern District). Soundex Index to Naturalization Petitions for U.S. District & Circuit Courts, Northern District of Illinois and Immigration and Naturalization Service District 9, 1840-1950. (Salt Lake City: Filmed by the Genealogical Society of Utah, 1988). 183 microfilm.

Land and Property

Cowan, Janet C. *Jeffersonville Land Entries 1808-1818.* Indianapolis: the author, 1984.

Hone, Wade E. *Land and Property Research in the United States.* Salt Lake City: Ancestry Incorporated, 1997.

Indiana Historical Society (Indianapolis, Indiana). *This Land of Ours: The Acquisition and Disposition of the Public Domain; Papers Presented at an Indiana American Revolution Bicentennial Symposium, Purdue University, West Lafayette, Indiana, April 29 and 30, 1978.* Indianapolis, Indiana: The Society, 1978.

Indiana State Archives. (Indianapolis). *Land and Homestead Records.* Indianapolis, Indiana: Indiana State Archives, 2002. Online database -<www.state.in.us/icpr/webfile/archives/homepage.html>.

Lux, Leonard. *The Vincennes Donation Lands.* Indianapolis: Indiana Historical Society, 1949.

McMullin, Phillip W., ed. *Grassroots of America.* Salt Lake City: Gendex Corp., 1972.

Smith, Clifford N., ed. *French and British Land Grants in the Post Vincennes (Indiana) District, 1750-1784.* Selections from The American State Papers. McNeal, Arizona: Westland Publications, 1996.

This Land of Ours: The Acquisition and Disposition of the Public Domain. Indianapolis: Indiana Historical Society, 1978.

Waters, Margaret R. *Indiana Land Entries.* 2 Vols. Reprint. Knightstown, Indiana: Bookmark, 1977. Index of land entries for the Cincinnati Land District, 1801 to 1840, and Vincennes Land District, 1807 to 1877.

Military

Dorrel, Ruth. *Index to Admission Book, Indiana Soldiers and Sailors Home, 1868 through 1995.* Indianapolis, Indiana: Indiana Historical Society, 1997.

Franklin, Charles W. *Indiana, War of 1812 Soldiers: Militia.* Indianapolis: Ye Olde Genealogie Shoppe, 1984.

General Assembly of Indiana, *Record of Indiana Volunteers in the Spanish-American War 1898-1899.* Indianapolis: W. B. Burford, 1900.

Index to Indiana Enrollments of Soldiers, Their Widows and Orphans, 1886, 1890 and 1894. Microfilm of index cards located at the Indiana State Library, Indianapolis. (Salt Lake City: Filmed by the Genealogical Society of Utah, 1988). 13 microfilm.

Index to Indiana Volunteers in the Mexican War. Microfilm of index cards located at the Indiana State Library, Indianapolis. (Salt Lake City: Filmed by the Genealogical Society of Utah, 1988).

Indiana Adjutant General's Office. *Indiana in the War of the Rebellion.* 8 vols. Indianapolis: W.H.H. Terrell, 1869.

Indiana Historical Commission (Indianapolis). *Gold Star Honor Roll: A Record of Indiana Men and Women Who Died in the Service of the United States and the Allied Nations in the World War, 1914-1918.* Microfilm of original published: Indianapolis: Indiana Historical Commission, 1921. (Salt Lake City: Filmed by the Genealogical Society of Utah, 1990).

Indiana Records of Soldier Births, Enlistments, Discharges, Some Deaths, etc., ca. 1869-1964. Microreproduction of index cards at the Northern Indiana Historical Society Museum, South Bend, Indiana. (Salt Lake City: Filmed by the Genealogical Society of Utah, 1990).

Indiana State Archives. *Indianapolis Civil War Resources.* Indianapolis, Indiana: Indiana State Archives, 2002. Online database - <www.state.in.us/icpr/webfile/archives/homepage.html>.

Indiana. Adjutant General. *Report.* Indianapolis: Adjutant General, 1865-1869.

Perry, Oran. *Indiana in the Mexican War.* Indianapolis: W.B. Burford, contractor for state printing, 1908.

Record of Indiana Volunteers in the Spanish-American War, 1898-1899. Indianapolis: W. B. Burford, 1900.

Terrell, W. H. H., comp. *Report of the Adjutant General of the State of Indiana*. 8 vols. Indianapolis: Indiana Adjutant General's Office, 1869.

Trapp, Glenda K. *Index to the Report of the Adjutant General of the State of Indiana*. Evansville, IN: the author, 1986.

United States. Adjutant General's Office. *Muster Pay and Receipt Rolls of Indiana Territory Volunteers or Military of the Period of the War of 1812*. 4 Vols. Washington, D.C.: Adjutant General. n.d.

United States. Adjutant General's Office. *Index to Compiled Service Records of Volunteer Union Soldiers Who Served in Organizations from the State of Indiana, 1861-1865*. Washington, D.C.: The National Archives, 1964.

United States. Selective Service System. *Indiana, World War I Selective Service System Draft Registration Cards, 1917-1918. National Archives Microfilm Publications, M1509*. Washington, D.C.: National Archives, 1987-1988.

United States. War Department. The Adjutant General's Office. *World War I Indiana Enrollment Cards, 1919*. Microfilm of originals in the Indiana State Archives in Indianapolis, Indiana. (Salt Lake City: Filmed by the Genealogical Society of Utah, 1990). 35 microfilm.

Waters, Margaret R. *Revolutionary Soldiers, Buried in Indiana [Bound with:] Supplement*. 2 Vols. In 1 (1949, 1954). Reprint. Baltimore: Clearfield Company, 1992.

Wolfe, Barbara. *Index to Revolutionary Soldiers in Indiana*. Indianapolis: Ye Olde Genealogie Shoppe, n.d.

World War I Nurses Enrollment Cards, Indiana. Microfilm of card file located at the Indiana State Archives, Indianapolis. (Salt Lake City: Filmed by the Genealogical Society of Utah, 1991).

Vital and Cemetery Records

Cemetery Records of Indiana. 6 vols. Salt Lake City: Genealogical Society, 1954-64.

Cox, Carroll O. *Cemetery Records (Illinois and Indiana)*. (Transcript). Salt Lake City: Genealogical Society of Utah, 1983. 2 microfiche.

Dodd, Jordan R., and Norman L. Moyes, comps. *Indiana Marriages, Early to 1825*. Bountiful, Utah: Precision Indexing, Inc., 1991.

Guide to Public Vital Statistics Records in Indiana. Indianapolis: Historical Records Survey, 1941.

Historical Records Survey (Indiana*). Miscellaneous Records of Indiana, 1827-1922*. [S.l.: s.n.], 1968. 10 microfilm.

Indiana State Library Genealogy Division. *Cemetery Database*. Indianapolis, Indiana: Indiana State Library Genealogy Division, 2002. Online Database - <www.statelib.lib.in.us/WWW/INDIANA/GENEALOGY/links.HTML#databases>

Indiana, 1851-1900. [S.l.]: Brøderbund, 1998. CD ROM.

Indiana State Library. Genealogy Division. *Database to an Index of Indiana Marriages Through 1850*. Indianapolis, Indiana: Indiana State Library Genealogy Division, 2002. Online database - <www.statelib.lib.in.us/WWW/INDIANA/GENEALOGY/links.HTML#databases>.

Indiana State Library, Genealogical Division. *Cemetery Locator File*. Microfilm of original records in the Indiana State Library, Indianapolis, Indiana. (Salt Lake City: Filmed by the Genealogical Society of Utah, 1980). 4 microfilm.

Slater-Putt, Dawne Lisa. *Pre-1882 Indiana Births, From Secondary Sources*. Fort Wayne, Indiana: Heritage Pathways, Inc., 1999.

Vincent, Stephen A. *Southern Seed, Northern Soil: African-American Farm Communities in the Midwest 1765-1900*. Bloomington, Indiana: Indiana University Press, 1999.

Volkel, Lowell. *Indiana 1850 Mortality Schedule*. 3 vols [S.l.]: L. M. Volkel, 1971.

Volkel, Lowell. *Illinois Mortality Schedule, 1860*. Indianapolis, Indiana: Heritage House, 1979.

Volkel, Lowell. *1870 Illinois Mortality Schedules*. Indianapolis, Indiana: Heritage House, 1985-[1987?].

County Website	Map Index	Date Created	Parent County or Territory From Which Organized Address/Details
Adams www.rootsweb.com/~inadams/	**F11**	**7 Feb 1835**	**Allen, Randolph** Adams County; 112 S 2nd St; Decatur, IN 46733; Ph. 219.724.2600 Details: (Co Clk has m, div, pro & ct rec)
Allen* www.indico.net/counties/ALLEN/	**D11**	**17 Dec 1823**	**Unorganized Territory, Randolph** Allen County; 715 S Calhoun St #200; Fort Wayne, IN 46802; Ph. 219.449.7424 Details: (Clk Cir Ct has m rec from 1824, div, pro & ct rec from 1823; Co Rcdr has land rec; Co Board of Hlth has b, d & bur rec)
Bartholomew www.rootsweb.com/~inbartho/barth.html	**L8**	**8 Jan 1821**	**Unorganized Territory, Jackson** Bartholomew County; 440 3rd St; PO Box 924; Columbus, IN 47202-0924; Ph. 812.379.1600 Details: (Co Clk has m, div, pro & ct rec from 1821, some nat, cem & mil rec; Co Rcdr has land rec from 1821; Vit Stat has b & d rec from 1882)
Benton www.bentoncounty.org/	**F3**	**18 Feb 1840**	**Jasper** Benton County; 706 E 5th St Ste #12; Fowler, IN 47944-1556; Ph. 765.884.0320 Details: (Clk Cir Ct has m rec from 1841, div & ct rec from 1800's, pro rec from 1852 & nat rec; Co Rcdr has land & mil rec; Co Hlth Dept has b & d rec from 1882)
Blackford* www.rootsweb.com/~inblackf/index.htm	**G10**	**15 Feb 1838**	**Jay** Blackford County; 110 W Washington St; Hartford City, IN 47348; Ph. 765.348.1620 Details: (Co Clk has m, div, pro & ct rec from 1839; City & Co Hlth Officers have b & d rec; Co Rcdr has land rec; Co Coroner has bur rec)
Boone* www.bccn.boone.in.us/	**H6**	**29 Jan 1830**	**Hendricks, Marion** Boone County; 212 Courthouse Sq; Lebanon, IN 46052-2150; Ph. 765.482.3510 Details: (Co Clk has m rec from 1831, div, pro & ct rec from 1830; Co Hlth Dept has b & d rec; Co Rcdr has land rec)
Brown www.browncounty.org/	**L7**	**4 Feb 1836**	**Monroe, Bartholomew, Jackson** Brown County; Main St and Van Buren St; Nashville, IN 47448; Ph. 812.988.5510 Details: (Some rec lost in 1873 fire) (Co Hlth Dept has b & d rec from 1882; Co Clk has m, pro & ct rec from 1836, div rec from 1850, ct ordered b rec from 1942; Co Rcdr has land rec from 1874)
Carroll www.carlnet.org/	**F6**	**7 Jan 1826**	**Unorganized Territory** Carroll County; 101 W Main St; Delphi, IN 46923; Ph. 765.564.4485 Details: (Co Clk has m, div, pro & ct rec from 1828; Co Hlth Officer has b, d & bur rec from 1882; Co Rcdr has land rec from 1828; Pub Lib in Delphi has newspapers from 1841; Co Hist Soc has bur rec)
Cass www.rootsweb.com/~incass/county.html	**E7**	**18 Dec 1828**	**Carroll** Cass County; 103 Cass County Government Bldg; Logansport, IN 46947-3114; Ph. 219.753.7740 Details: (Co Hlth Dept has b & d rec; Co Clk has m & pro rec from 1892, div & ct rec from 1894; Co Aud has land rec)
Clark www.rootsweb.com/~inclark/	**O9**	**3 Feb 1801**	**Knox** Clark County; City Court Bldg 501 E Ct Ave; Jeffersonville, IN 47130; Ph. 812.285.6244 Details: (Co Clk has m & pro rec from 1850 & ct rec; Co Rcdr has land rec; Co Hlth Dept has b & d rec)
Clay* www.claycountyin.org/	**K4**	**12 Feb 1825**	**Owen, Putnam, Vigo, Sullivan** Clay County; 609 E Nation Ave; Brazil, IN 47834-2797; Ph. 812.448.9024 Details: (Co Hlth Dept has b & d rec; Co Clk has m, div, pro & ct rec from 1851; Co Rcdr has land rec from 1825, some nat & bur rec)
Clinton www.rootsweb.com/~inclinto/	**G6**	**29 Jan 1830**	**Tippecanoe** Clinton County; 265 Courthouse Sq; Frankfort, IN 46041; Ph. 765.659.6335 Details: (Co Hlth Dept has b & d rec; Co Clk has m & pro rec from 1830, div & ct rec from 1888; Co Rcdr has land rec)
Crawford www.rootsweb.com/~incrawfo/	**P6**	**29 Jan 1818**	**Orange, Harrison, Perry** Crawford County; 316 S Ct; English, IN 47118-0375; Ph. 812.338.2565 Details: (Co Clk has m rec from 1818, div, pro & ct rec from 1860; Co Hlth Dept has b & d rec; Co Rcdr has land rec)

County Website	Map Index	Date Created	Parent County or Territory From Which Organized Address/Details
Daviess www.indico.net/counties/DAVIESS/	**N4**	**24 Dec 1816**	**Knox** Daviess County; County Courthouse; PO Box 739; Washington, IN 47501; Ph. 812.254.8664 Details: (Co Clk has m, div, pro & ct rec from 1817)
De Kalb www.dekalbnet.org/	**C11**	**7 Feb 1835**	**Allen, La Grange** De Kalb County; 100 S Main St; PO Box 810; Auburn, IN 46706; Ph. 219.925.2112 Details: (Co Hlth Dept has b & d rec; Co Clk has m & ct rec from 1837, pro rec from 1855 & school rec 1903-1932; Co Rcdr has land rec)
Dearborn www.dearborncounty.org/	**L11**	**7 Mar 1803**	**Clark** Dearborn County; 215-B W High St; Lawrenceburg, IN 47025; Ph. 812.537.8867 Details: (Clk Cir Ct has m rec from 1826, div, pro & ct rec; Co Hlth Officer has b & d rec; Co Rcdr has land rec)
Decatur www.indico.net/counties/DECATUR/	**L9**	**31 Dec 1821**	**Unorganized Territory** Decatur County; 150 Courthouse Sq Ste 5; Greensburg, IN 47240; Ph. 812.663.8223 Details: (Co Clk has m rec from 1822, div, pro & ct rec; Board of Hlth has b & d rec)
Delaware* www.dcclerk.org/	**G10**	**26 Jan 1827**	**Randolph** Delaware County; 100 W Main St; Muncie, IN 47305; Ph. 765.747.7726 Details: (Co Clk has m, div, pro & ct rec from 1827)
Dubois www.rootsweb.com/~indubois/dubgen.htm	**O5**	**20 Dec 1817**	**Pike** Dubois County; 1 Courthouse Sq; Jasper, IN 47546; Ph. 812.481.7035 Details: (Rec Library has m, div, pro, land, ct & nat rec from 1839 & mil rec from 1864; Co Hlth Dept has b & d rec from 1882)
Elkhart www.elkhartcountygov.org/	**B8**	**29 Jan 1830**	**Allen, Cass** Elkhart County; Courthouse Sq; Goshen, IN 46526-3297; Ph. 219.535.6430 Details: (Co Hlth Dept has b & d rec; Co Clk has m, div, pro & ct rec from 1830; Co Rcdr has land rec)
Fayette www.indico.net/counties/FAYETTE/	**J10**	**28 Dec 1818**	**Wayne, Franklin** Fayette County; 401 N Central Ave; PO Box 607; Connersville, IN 47331-0607; Ph. 765.825.1813 Details: (Clk Cir Ct has m, pro, div & ct rec from 1819 & nat rec from 1924)
Floyd www.rootsweb.com/~infloyd/floydigw.html	**O8**	**2 Jan 1819**	**Harrison, Clarke** Floyd County; 311 W 1st St; New Albany, IN 47150-3501; Ph. 812.948.5413 Details: (Co Hlth Dept has b & d rec; Co Clk has m rec from 1819, div & ct rec from 1863 & pro rec from 1819)
Fountain glenmar.com/~emoyhbo/	**H3**	**20 Dec 1825**	**Montgomery** Fountain County; 301 4th St; PO Box 183; Covington, IN 47932; Ph. 765.793.2192 Details: (Co Hlth Dept has b & d rec from 1885; Co Clk has m rec from 1827, div, pro & ct rec from 1830; Co Rcdr has land rec from 1828)
Franklin www.rootsweb.com/~infrankl/	**K11**	**27 Nov 1810**	**Clark, Dearborn, Jefferson** Franklin County; 634 Main St; Brookville, IN 47012-1405; Ph. 765.647.3322 Details: (Co Clk has m, div, pro & ct rec from 1811; Co Rcdr has land rec from 1811; Co Hlth Dept has b & d rec from 1882; Pub Lib has cem rec from 1817 & nat rec from 1820)
Fulton* www.fultoncounty-in.org/	**D7**	**7 Feb 1835**	**Allen, Cass, St. Joseph** Fulton County; 815 Main St; Rochester, IN 46975; Ph. 219.223.2911 Details: (Co Clk has m, div, pro & ct rec from 1836; Co Hlth Dept has b & d rec; Co Rcdr has land rec)
Gibson www.usroots.com/~jmurphy/gibson/ gibson.htm	**P3**	**9 Mar 1813**	**Knox** Gibson County; 101 N Main St; Princeton, IN 47670; Ph. 812.386.8401 Details: (Co Hlth Dept has b & d rec; Co Clk has m rec from 1813, div, pro & ct rec from 1820)
Grant ww1.comteck.com/~tdtw98a/grant.htm	**G9**	**10 Feb 1831**	**Delaware, Madison, Cass** Grant County; County Courthouse; Marion, IN 46953; Ph. 765.668.8121 Details: (Co Hlth Dept has b & d rec; Co Clk has m, div, pro & ct rec from 1831; Co Aud has land rec)

County Website	Map Index	Date Created	Parent County or Territory From Which Organized

Greene*   M4   5 Jan 1821   **Daviess, Sullivan**
www.in-map.net/counties/GREENE/
Greene County; PO Box 229; Bloomfield, IN 47424; Ph. 812.384.8532
Details: (Co Clk has m, div & ct rec from 1821, pro rec from 1823 & nat rec 1854-1906; Co Rcdr has land rec from 1824, mil rec & some cem rec; Co Hlth Dept has b rec from 1885 & d rec from 1893)

Hamilton   H8   8 Jan 1823   **Unorganized Territory, Marion**
www.co.hamilton.in.us/
Hamilton County; Public Sq; Noblesville, IN 46060; Ph. 317.776.9629
Details: (Co Hlth Dept has b & d rec; Co Clk has m, div, pro & ct rec from 1833; Co Rcdr has land rec)

Hancock   I8   26 Jan 1827   **Madison**
www.hccn.org/
Hancock County; 9 E Main St; Greenfield, IN 46140; Ph. 317.462.1109
Details: (Co Clk has m, div, pro & ct rec from 1828; Co Rcdr has land rec; Co Hlth Dept has b & d rec from 1882)

Harrison   P7   11 Oct 1808   **Knox, Clark**
www.jbntelco.com/~straub/
Harrison County; 300 N Capitol Ave; Corydon, IN 47112-1139; Ph. 812.738.4289
Details: (Co Hlth Dept has b & d rec from 1882; Co Clk has m, pro & ct rec from 1809, div rec from 1815 & land rec from 1807)

Hendricks   J6   20 Dec 1823   **Unorganized Territory, Putnam**
www.indico.net/counties/HENDRICKS/
Hendricks County; PO Box 599; Danville, IN 46122-1993; Ph. 317.745.9231
Details: (Co Hlth Dept has b & d rec from 1882; Co Clk has m, div, pro & ct rec from 1823; Co Aud has land rec)

Henry   I10   31 Dec 1821   **Unorganized Territory**
www.indico.net/counties/HENRY/
Henry County; 101 S Main St; New Castle, IN 47362; Ph. 765.529.6401
Details: (Co Hlth Dept has b & d rec from 1882; Co Clk has m, div, pro & ct rec from 1822; Co Rcdr has land rec from 1823 & cem deeds from 1925)

Howard*   G8   15 Jan 1844   **Carroll, Cass, Miami, Grant, Hamilton**
www.co.howard.in.us/
Howard County; 104 N Buckeye St; PO Box 9004; Kokomo, IN 46904; Ph. 765.456.2204
Details: (Formerly Richardville Co. Name changed to Howard 28 Dec 1846) (Co Clk has m, div, pro & ct rec from 1844; Co Rcdr has land rec; Co Hlth Dept has b, d & bur rec)

Huntington   E9   2 Feb 1832   **Allen, Grant**
www.huntington.in.us/
Huntington County; 201 N Jefferson St Rm 103; Huntington, IN 46750; Ph. 219.358.4819
Details: (Co Hlth Dept has b & d rec from 1882; Co Clk has m rec from 1847, ct rec from 1840, pro & div rec from 1850; Co Rcdr has land rec from 1834)

Jackson   M7   18 Dec 1815   **Washington, Clark, Jefferson**
www.rootsweb.com/~injackso/
Jackson County; 111 S Main St; Brownstown, IN 47220; Ph. 812.358.6116
Details: (Co Hlth Dept has b & d rec; Co Clk has m, div, pro & ct rec from 1816; Co Aud has land rec)

Jasper   D4   7 Feb 1835   **White, Warren**
www.lanewood.com/
Jasper County; 115 W Washington; Rensselaer, IN 47978; Ph. 219.866.4927
Details: (Courthouse burned in 1862; all rec destroyed) (Co Hlth Dept has b & d rec; Co Clk has m & div rec from 1865, pro & ct rec from 1864)

Jay*   G11   7 Feb 1835   **Randolph, Delaware**
www.rootsweb.com/~injay/
Jay County; Main & Walnut; Portland, IN 47371; Ph. 219.726.4951
Details: (Co Hlth Dept has b & d rec from 1882; Co Clk has m rec from 1843, div rec from 1882, pro rec from 1836 & ct rec from 1837; Co Aud has land rec from 1836)

Jefferson   M10   23 Nov 1810   **Dearborn, Clark**
www.indico.net/counties/JEFFERSON/
Jefferson County; 300 E Main St #203; Madison, IN 47250; Ph. 812.265.8921
Details: (Co Hlth Dept has b, d & bur rec; Co Clk has m, div, pro & ct rec; Co Rcdr has land rec)

County Website	Map Index	Date Created	Parent County or Territory From Which Organized Address/Details
Jennings www.rootsweb.com/~injennin/	**L9**	**27 Dec 1816**	**Jefferson, Jackson** Jennings County; 275 E Main St; N. Vernon, IN 47265; Ph. 812.346.5907 Details: (Co Clk has m & pro rec; Co Rcdr has land rec; Co Hlth Dept has b & d rec)
Johnson www.rootsweb.com/~injohnso/johnson.html	**K7**	**31 Dec 1822**	**Unorganized Territory** Johnson County; County Courthouse 1st Floor; Franklin, IN 46131; Ph. 317.736.3708 Details: (Co Hlth Dept has b, d & bur rec from 1882; Co Clk has m, div, pro & ct rec from 1830; Co Rcdr has land rec)
Knox www.accessknoxcounty.com/	**N3**	**20 Jun 1790**	**Northwest Territory** Knox County; 101 N 7th St; Vincennes, IN 47591; Ph. 812.885.2521 Details: (Co Clk has m rec from 1807, div rec, pro rec from 1806 & ct rec from 1790; Co Rcdr has land rec; Co Hlth Dept has b & d rec)
Kosciusko www.rootsweb.com/~inkosciu/	**C8**	**7 Feb 1835**	**Elkhart, Cass** Kosciusko County; 121 N Lake St; Warsaw, IN 46580; Ph. 219.372.2331 Details: (Co Hlth Dept has b & d rec from 1882; Co Clk has m, div, pro & ct rec from 1836; Co Rcdr has land rec; Twp Trustees have bur rec)
La Grange www.lagrangecounty.org/	**B10**	**2 Feb 1832**	**Elkhart, Allen** La Grange County; 105 N Detroit St; La Grange, IN 46761-1853; Ph. 219.463.6371 Details: (Co Hlth Dept has b & d rec from 1882; Co Clk has m, div, pro & ct rec from 1832; Co Rcdr has land rec from 1832)
La Porte* www.lc-link.org/	**B5**	**9 Jan 1832**	**St. Joseph** La Porte County; 813 Lincoln Way; La Porte, IN 46350; Ph. 219.326.6808 Details: (Co Clk has m rec from 1832, div, pro & ct rec from 1834; Co Rcdr has land rec; Co Hlth Dept has b, d & bur rec)
Lake www.lakecountyin.com/	**C3**	**28 Jan 1836**	**Porter, Newton** Lake County; 2293 N Main St; Crown Point, IN 46307; Ph. 219.755.3440 Details: (Co Hlth Dept has b & d rec; Clk Cir Ct has m, div, pro & ct rec from 1837; Co Rcdr has land rec)
Lawrence www.rootsweb.com/~inlawren/ lawrengw.htm	**M6**	**7 Jan 1818**	**Orange** Lawrence County; County Courthouse; Bedford, IN 47421; Ph. 812.275.7543 Details: (Co Clk has m, pro, div & ct rec from 1818; Co Hlth Dept has b & d rec; Co Rcdr has land rec from 1818 & mil rec)
Madison www.rootsweb.com/~inmadiso/index.htm	**H9**	**4 Jan 1823**	**Unorganized Territory, Marion** Madison County; 16 E 9th; Anderson, IN 46016; Ph. 765.641.9457 Details: (Co Hlth Dept has b rec from 1891 & d rec from 1895; Co Clk has m rec from 1884, div, pro & ct rec from 1880; Co Aud has land rec from 1867; Co Board of Hlth has school rec 1904-1932)
Marion* www.indygov.org/	**J7**	**31 Dec 1821**	**Unorganized Territory** Marion County; 200 E Washington; Indianapolis, IN 46204; Ph. 317.327.4740 Details: (Co Clk has m & div rec; Co Rcdr has b, d & land rec; Pro Ct has pro rec)
Marshall* www.co.marshall.in.us/	**C7**	**7 Feb 1835**	**St. Joseph, Elkhart** Marshall County; 211 W Madison St; Plymouth, IN 46563-1762; Ph. 219.936.8922 Details: (Co Hlth Dept has b, d & bur rec from 1882; Co Clk has m, div, pro & ct rec from 1836; Co Rcdr has land rec)
Martin www.rootsweb.com/~inmartin/index.htm	**N5**	**17 Jan 1820**	**Daviess, Dubois** Martin County; Capitol St; PO Box 120; Shoals, IN 47581-0170; Ph. 812.247.3651 Details: (Co Hlth Dept has b & d rec; Co Clk has m & pro rec from 1820, div & ct rec from 1842; Co Rcdr has land rec)
Miami www.rootsweb.com/~inmiami/index.html	**E8**	**2 Feb 1832**	**Cass** Miami County; 21 Court St; PO Box 184; Peru, IN 46970; Ph. 756.472.3901 Details: (Co Hlth Dept has b, d & bur rec; Co Clk has m, div, pro & ct rec from 1843)

County Website	Map Index	Date Created	Parent County or Territory From Which Organized Address/Details
Monroe* www.co.monroe.in.us/	L6	14 Jan 1818	**Orange** Monroe County; 100 W 5th St; PO Box 547; Bloomington, IN 47402-0547; Ph. 812.349.2600 Details: (Co Clk has m, div & ct rec from 1818 & pro rec from 1831; Co Hlth Dept has b, d & bur rec from 1882; Co Rcdr has land rec)
Montgomery www.wico.net/~zacho/montco/	H5	21 Dec 1822	**Parke, Putnam** Montgomery County; 100 E Main St; Crawfordsville, IN 47933-1715; Ph. 765.364.6400 Details: (Co Hlth Dept has b & d rec from 1882; Co Clk has m, div, pro & ct rec from 1823 & some nat rec; Co Rcdr has land rec from 1823; Pub Lib has cem rec from 1823)
Morgan* scican2.scican.net/Home/scican_home.htm	K6	31 Dec 1821	**Unorganized Territory** Morgan County; PO Box 1556; Martinsville, IN 46151; Ph. 765.342.1025 Details: (Co Clk has m, pro & ct rec; Co Rcdr has land rec; Board of Hlth has b & d rec)
Newton www.rootsweb.com/~innewton/	D3	7 Feb 1835	**Unorganized Territory** Newton County; Courthouse Sq; PO Box 49; Kentland, IN 47951; Ph. 219.474.6081 Details: (Attached to St. Joseph, Warren & White Cos before re-creation & organization from Jasper Co 8 Dec 1859) (Co Clk has m, div, pro & ct rec from 1860; Co Hlth Dept has b & d rec from 1882; Co Rcdr has land rec from 1860)
Noble www.usgennet.org/usa/in/county/noble/	C10	7 Feb 1835	**Elkhart, LaGrange, Allen** Noble County; 101 N Orange St; Albion, IN 46701-1097; Ph. 219.636.2736 Details: (Co Hlth Dept has b & d rec; Co Clk has m, div, pro & ct rec from 1859; Co Aud has land rec; City Clk has bur rec)
Ohio www.rootsweb.com/~inohio/	M11	4 Jan 1844	**Dearborn** Ohio County; 413 Main St; Rising Sun, IN 47040; Ph. 812.438.2610 Details: (Co Clk has m, div, pro & ct rec from 1844)
Orange www.co.orange.in.us/	O6	26 Dec 1815	**Washington, Knox, Gibson** Orange County; Court St; Paoli, IN 47454; Ph. 812.723.2649 Details: (Co Hlth Dept has b rec from 1882, d & bur rec; Co Clk has m, div, pro & ct rec from 1816; Co Rcdr has land rec from 1816)
Owen www.owencounty.org/index.html	K5	21 Dec 1818	**Daviess, Sullivan** Owen County; Main St; PO Box 146; Spencer, IN 47460; Ph. 812.829.5015 Details: (Co Hlth Dept has b & d rec from 1882; Co Clk has m & ct rec from 1819, div rec from 1832 & pro rec from 1833; Co Rcdr has land rec from 1819)
Parke www.rootsweb.com/~inparke/	J4	9 Jan 1821	**Unorganized Territory, Vigo** Parke County; 116 W High St #204; Rockville, IN 47872; Ph. 765.569.5132 Details: (Co Hlth Dept has b rec from 1902 & d rec from 1882; Co Aud has m, div, pro & ct rec from 1833; Co Rcdr has land rec from 1833)
Perry www.usroots.com/~jmurphy/perry/ 　perry.htm	P6	7 Sept 1814	**Warrick, Gibson** Perry County; 2219 Payne St; Tell City, IN 47586; Ph. 812.547.3741 Details: (Co Clk has m, div, pro & ct rec from 1813; Co Rcdr has land rec from 1813; Co Hlth Dept has b & d rec from 1890)
Pike www.rootsweb.com/~inpike/Pikegen.htm	O4	21 Dec 1816	**Gibson, Perry** Pike County; 801 Main St; Petersburg, IN 47567; Ph. 812.354.6025 Details: (Co Clk has m, div & ct rec from 1817 & pro rec from early 1800's; Co Hlth Dept has b & d rec; Co Rcdr has land rec)
Porter www.porterco.org/	B4	7 Feb 1835	**St. Joseph** Porter County; 16 E Lincolnway #209; Valparaiso, IN 46383; Ph. 219.465.3450 Details: (Attached to St. Joseph Co prior to organization 6 Feb 1836) (Co Hlth Dept has b & d rec; Co Clk has m, div, pro & ct rec from 1836; Co Aud has land rec)
Posey* www.rootsweb.com/~inposey/	P2	7 Sept 1814	**Warrick, Knox, Gibson** Posey County; PO Box 606; Mt. Vernon, IN 47620; Ph. 812.838.1306 Details: (Co Clk has m, div, pro & ct rec from 1815; Co Hlth Dept has b & d rec from 1882; Co Rcdr has land rec from 1815 & some mil dis rec)

County Website	Map Index	Date Created	Parent County or Territory From Which Organized
			Address/Details
Pulaski www.rootsweb.com/~inpulask/	**D5**	**7 Feb 1835**	**Cass, St. Joseph** Pulaski County; 112 E Main St; Winamac, IN 46996-1344; Ph. 219.946.3313 Details: (Co Clk has m, div, pro & ct rec from 1839; Co Rcdr has b & d rec from 1882 & land rec)
Putnam www.rootsweb.com/~inputnam/	**J5**	**31 Dec 1821**	**Unorganized Territory, Vigo, Owen** Putnam County; 1 Courthouse Sq St; PO Box 546; Greencastle, IN 46135-0546; Ph. 765.653.2648 Details: (Co Hlth Dept has b & d rec; Co Clk has m rec from 1822, div & pro rec from 1825 & ct rec from 1828; Co Rcdr has land rec)
Randolph www.rootsweb.com/~inrandol/	**H11**	**10 Jan 1818**	**Wayne** Randolph County; County Courthouse #307; Winchester, IN 47394; Ph. 765.584.7070 Details: (Co Hlth Dept has b & d rec; Co Clk has m, div, pro & ct rec; Co Rcdr has land rec from 1818 & newspapers from 1876)
Richardville		**15 Jan 1844**	**Carroll, Cass, Miami, Grant, Hamilton** Details: (see Howard) Name changed to Howard 28 Dec 1846
Ripley www.seidata.com/~ripleych/	**L10**	**27 Dec 1816**	**Dearborn, Jefferson** Ripley County; PO Box 177; Versailles, IN 47042; Ph. 812.689.6115 Details: (Co Hlth Dept has b & d rec; Co Clk has m, div, pro & ct rec from 1818; Co Rcdr has land rec)
Rush www.rootsweb.com/~inrush/	**J9**	**31 Dec 1821**	**Unorganized Territory** Rush County; PO Box 429; Rushville, IN 46173-0429; Ph. 765.932.2086 Details: (Co Hlth Dept has b, d & bur rec from 1882; Co Clk has m, div, pro & ct rec from 1822; Co Rcdr has land rec)
Scott www.scottcounty.org/	**N9**	**12 Jan 1820**	**Clark, Jefferson, Jennings** Scott County; 1 E McClain Ave; Scottsburg, IN 47170-1848; Ph. 812.752.8420 Details: (Co Hlth Dept has b & d rec; Co Clk has m, div, pro & ct rec from 1820; Co Rcdr has land rec)
Shelby* www.shelbynet.net/scoinfo.htm	**K8**	**31 Dec 1821**	**Unorganized Territory** Shelby County; 407 S Harrison St; PO Box 198; Shelbyville, IN 46176-2161; Ph. 317.392.6320 Details: (Co Hlth Dept has b, d & bur rec; Co Clk has m, div, pro & ct rec; Co Aud has land rec)
Spencer www.spencerco.org/	**Q4**	**10 Jan 1818**	**Warrick, Perry** Spencer County; 200 Main St; Rockport, IN 47635-1478; Ph. 812.649.6027 Details: (Co Hlth Dept has b rec from 1882 & d rec from 1830; Cem trustees have bur rec; Co Clk has m rec from 1818, div & ct rec from 1883, pro rec from 1848 & nat rec 1852-1929; Co Rcdr has land rec)
St. Joseph* www.rootsweb.com/~instjose/	**B7**	**29 Jan 1830**	**Cass** St. Joseph County; 101 S Main St; South Bend, IN 46601; Ph. 219.235.9635 Details: (Co Hlth Dept has b, d & bur rec; Co Clk has m, div, pro & ct rec; Co Asr has land rec)
Starke www.rootsweb.com/~instarke/	**C6**	**7 Feb 1835**	**St. Joseph** Starke County; PO Box 395; Knox, IN 46534; Ph. 219.772.9128 Details: (Co Clk has m, div, pro & ct rec from 1850; Co Aud has land rec from 1850; Co Hlth Dept has b & d rec)
Steuben www.indico.net/counties/STEUBEN/	**B10**	**7 Feb 1835**	**LaGrange** Steuben County; 55 Public Sq; Angola, IN 46703; Ph. 219.668.1000 Details: (Co Hlth Dept has b & d rec; Co Clk has m, div, pro & ct rec from 1837 & land rec from mid-1800's)
Sullivan www.rootsweb.com/~insulliv/	**L3**	**30 Dec 1816**	**Knox** Sullivan County; 100 Courthouse Sq #304; Sullivan, IN 47882; Ph. 812.268.4657 Details: (Co Clk has m, div, pro & ct rec from 1850)
Switzerland myindianahome.net/gen/switz/index.html	**M11**	**7 Sep 1814**	**Dearborn, Jefferson** Switzerland County; 212 W Main St; Vevay, IN 47043; Ph. 812.427.3175 Details: (Co Hlth Dept has b, d & bur rec; Co Clk has m, div, ct & pro rec from 1814; Co Rcdr has land rec)

County Website	Map Index	Date Created	Parent County or Territory From Which Organized Address/Details
Tippecanoe* www.county.tippecanoe.in.us/	G5	20 Jan 1826	**Unorganized Territory, Parke** Tippecanoe County; 301 Main St; Lafayette, IN 47901; Ph. 765.423.9326 Details: (Clk Cir Ct has m rec from 1830, d rec, div rec from 1850, pro & ct rec from 1832 & nat rec)
Tipton* www.rootsweb.com/~intipton/index.htm	G8	15 Jan 1844	**Hamilton, Cass, Miami** Tipton County; 101 E Jefferson; Tipton, IN 46072; Ph. 765.675.2795 Details: (Co Clk has m rec from 1844, div, pro & ct rec from 1850)
Union www.geocities.com/Heartland/ Woods/9061/	J11	5 Jan 1821	**Wayne, Franklin, Fayette** Union County; 26 W Union St; Liberty, IN 47353; Ph. 765.458.6121 Details: (Clk Cir Ct has m, div, pro & ct rec from 1821; Co Hlth Dept has b rec from 1882 & d rec from 1907)
Vanderburgh* www.vanderburghgov.org/	P2	7 Jan 1818	**Gibson, Posey, Warrick** Vanderburgh County; Cir Center Cts Bldg Rm 216; PO Box 216; Evansville, IN 47732; Ph. 812.435.5160 Details: (Co Clk has m rec from 1916, div rec from 1969, pro rec from 1850 & ct rec from 1877; Co Hlth Dept has b & d rec from 1882; Co Rcdr has land rec from 1818 & mil rec from 1865; Willard Library has many of the older rec)
Vermillion www.rootsweb.com/~invermil/	I3	2 Jan 1824	**Parke** Vermillion County; Courthouse Sq; Newport, IN 47966-0008; Ph. 765.492.3500 Details: (Co Hlth Dept has b & d rec from 1882; Co Clk has m, div, pro & ct rec from 1824; Co Rcdr has land rec)
Vigo www.vigocountyin.com/	K3	21 Jan 1818	**Sullivan** Vigo County; 333 Wabash Ave; PO Box 8449; Terre Haute, IN 47808; Ph. 812.462.3214 Details: (Co Clk has m, pro & ct rec from 1818 & div rec from 1825)
Wabash www.rootsweb.com/~inwabash/	E8	2 Feb 1832	**Cass, Grant** Wabash County; 1 W Hill St; Wabash, IN 46992; Ph. 219.563.0661 Details: (Co Clk has m, div, pro & ct rec from 1835; Co Hlth Dept has b & d rec; Co Rcdr & Museum has bur rec)
Warren www.warrenco.net/	G3	19 Jan 1827	**Fountain** Warren County; 125 N Monroe St; Williamsport, IN 47993; Ph. 765.762.3510 Details: (Co Clk has m & div rec from 1827, pro rec from 1829 & ct rec from 1828; Co Rcdr has land rec from 1827; Co Hlth Dept has b & d rec from 1882)
Warrick* www.indico.net/counties/WARRICK/	P3	9 Mar 1813	**Knox** Warrick County; 107 W Locust St; Boonville, IN 47601; Ph. 812.897.6160 Details: (Co Hlth Dept has b, d & bur rec; Co Clk has m rec from 1819, div, ct & pro rec from 1813; Co Rcdr has land rec)
Washington 165.138.44.13/washington/	N7	21 Dec 1813	**Clark, Harrison, Jefferson** Washington County; 99 Public Sq; Salem, IN 47167; Ph. 812.883.5748 Details: (Co Hlth Dept has b & d rec from 1882; Co Clk has m, div, pro & ct rec from 1814 & newspapers from 1891; Co Rcdr has land rec; Co Hist Soc has many family rec)
Wayne www.co.wayne.in.us/	I11	27 Nov 1810	**Clark, Dearborn** Wayne County; 301 E Main; Richmond, IN 47374; Ph. 765.973.9220 Details: (Co Clk has m rec from 1810, div & ct rec from 1873 & pro rec from 1818; City-Co Hlth Officer has b, d & bur rec)
Wells* www.rootsweb.com/~inwells/	E10	7 Feb 1835	**Allen, Delaware, Randolph** Wells County; 102 W Market St; Bluffton, IN 46714; Ph. 219.824.6479 Details: (Co Hlth Dept has b & d rec; Co Clk has m, div & ct rec from 1837 & pro rec from 1838; Co Rcdr has land rec)
White www.rootsweb.com/~inwhite/	E5	1 Feb 1834	**Carroll** White County; 110 North Main St; PO Box 350; Monticello, IN 47960; Ph. 219.583.7032 Details: (Co Clk has m, div, pro & ct rec from 1834; Co Rcdr has land rec; Co Hlth Dept has b, d & bur rec)

County Website	Map Index	Date Created	Parent County or Territory From Which Organized Address/Details
Whitley www.indico.net/counties/WHITLEY/	D9	7 Feb 1835	Elkhart, Allen Whitley County; 101 W Van Buren St; Columbia City, IN 46725; Ph. 219.248.3102 Details: (Co Clk has m rec from 1836, div & ct rec from 1853 & pro rec; Co Hlth Dept has b & d rec from 1882; Co Rcdr has land rec)

Notes

Notes

Wild Rose

IOWA

CAPITAL: DES MOINES – TERRITORY 1838 – STATE 1846 (29TH)

Iowa was discovered by Marquette and Joliet after Native American tribes were well established there. The occasional fur trapper wandered through the country, too. However, it was Julien Dubuqe who came in 1788 and began negotiating with Indians to develop the area's resources. Through the permission of the Fox Indians, Dubuque established a mining settlement near the present-day city that bears his name. With the Louisiana Purchase in 1803, the United States acquired the territory and built Fort Madison and Fort Armstrong. Dubuque was abandoned following its founder's death in 1810. Little further settlement occurred until the Fox and Sauk tribes were forced to cede more than 9,000 square miles of Iowa territory in 1833. With the opening of this land, settlers flocked to the area. The first settlers came from the eastern and southern states, the majority of whom originally came from the British Isles.

Iowa was part of the Territory of Indiana immediately after its purchase, then part of the Territory of Louisiana. From 1812 to 1821, Iowa was part of the Missouri Territory. When Missouri became a state in 1821, Iowa was left without government and remained so until 1834. In 1838, Iowa became a territory, following two years each as a part of the Michigan and Wisconsin Territories. In 1846, Iowa became a state with Iowa City as its capital. Des Moines became the capital in 1857.

Immediately prior to and after statehood, thousands of immigrants flocked to Iowa.

The principal groups were:

- Scandinavians, to the central and western sections
- Hollanders, to the south central section
- Germans, along the Mississippi River
- Scottish and Welsh, to the mining towns of the southern counties
- Czechs to the east central section

Iowa sided with the Union in the Civil War, sending more than 76,000 men to serve in the Union army.

Look for vital records in the following locations:

- **Birth and death records:** Some counties began keeping birth and death records as early as 1870. It was not required until 1880, and general compliance did not occur until 1924. Delayed registration of births also took place by 1940. The clerk of the district court keeps these files. The Bureau of Vital Records, Iowa State Department of Public Health in Des Moines, has birth, marriage, and death records after July 1, 1880. Copies are available only to immediate family members, so relationship and reason for seeking information must be stated when writing. Statewide indexes by year are available. The birth index begins July 1, 1880. The death index begins January 1891. Parentage is not listed on any death record until July 1904.

- **Marriage and divorce records:** Marriage records from as early as 1850 can be obtained from county clerks. Many are transcribed and published. Early divorce records are located in the district courts. Transcribed copies were sent to the state beginning in 1906. The State Historical Society of Iowa in Des Moines has additional information.

- **Court records and wills:** Probate courts were created when Iowa became a territory. These were eventually discontinued and probate matters assigned to the district court. Copies of wills and probates can be obtained from district court clerks.

- **Census records:** Territorial censuses were taken in 1836, 1838, 1844, and 1846. However, copies exist for only a few counties. State censuses were taken in 1847, 1849, 1851, 1852, 1853, 1854, 1856, 1885, 1895, 1905, 1915, and 1925. A few town censuses were also taken in the 1880's and 1890's.

Bureau of Vital Records
Iowa State Department of
Public Health
Lucas State Office Building, First Floor
Des Moines, Iowa 50319
515.281.4944

State Historical Society of Iowa
East 12th and Grand Avenue
Des Moines, Iowa 50319

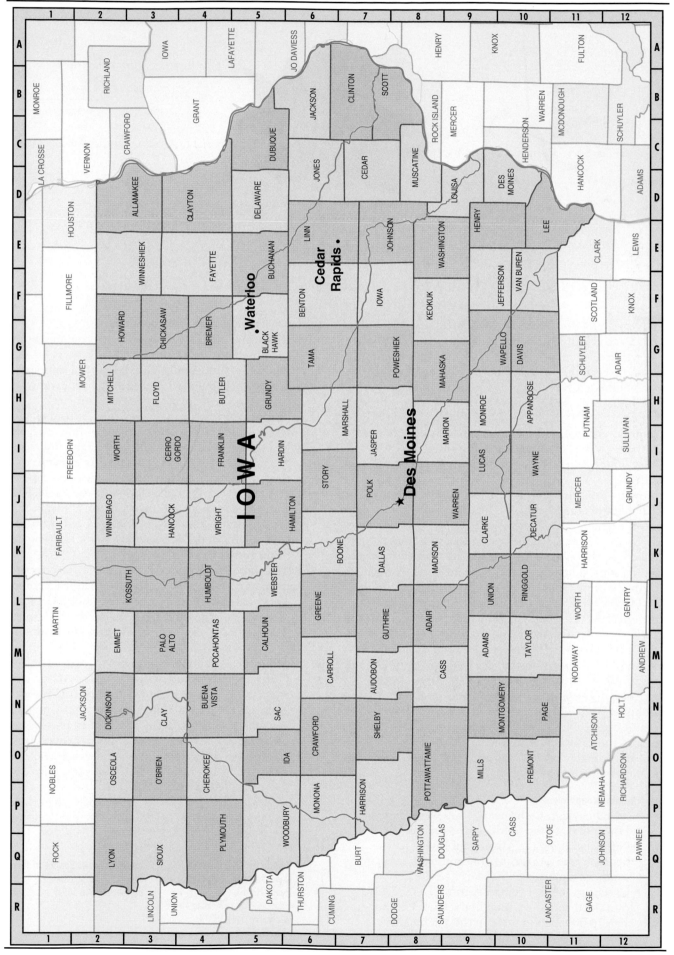

Societies and Repositories

Adair County Anquestors Genealogical Society; c/o Greenfield Public Library; PO Box 328; Greenfield, Iowa 50849-0328; <www.rootsweb.com/~iaadair/society.htm>

Adams County Genealogical Society; PO Box 117; Prescott, Iowa 50859-0177

Allamakee County Historical Society; PO Box 95; Waukon, Iowa 52172; <www.rootsweb.com/~iaachs/>

American. Schleswig-Holstein Heritage Society; PO Box 506; Walcott, Iowa 52773-0506; 507.645.9161 563.284.4184;

Ankeny Genealogical Chapter; 1110 N. W. 2nd St.; Ankeny, Iowa 50021-2320

Appanoose County Iowa Genealogical Society; 1601 S 16th St; Centerville, Iowa 52544-3040; <www.usgennet.org/usa/ia/county/appanoose/acgs.html>

Audubon County Genealogical Society; 505 Brayton St; Audubon, Iowa 50025-1301

Benton County Genealogical Society; c/o Donnette Gossen; 1808 9th Ave.; Belle Plaine, Iowa 52208; <www.rootsweb.com/~iabenton/bcgs.htm>

Benton County Historical Society; PO Box 22; Vinton, Iowa 52349; <www.rootsweb.com/~iabenton/bchs/bchs.htm>

Benton County Railway, Agricultural, Industrial Lineage Society (Rails); PO Box 196; Vinton, Iowa 52349-0186; <www.rootsweb.com/~iabenton/rails/index.htm>

Boone County Genealogical Society; PO Box 453; Boone, Iowa 50036; <www.rootsweb.com/~iabcgs/index.htm>

Boone County Historical Society; 602 Story Street; Boone, Iowa 50036

Botna Valley Genealogical Society, East Pottawattamie County; PO Box 633; Oakland, Iowa 51560-0633

Bremer County Genealogical Society; 1378 Badger Ave.; Plainfield, Iowa 50666-9772; <www.rootsweb.com/~iabremer/gensoc.html>

Buchanan County Genealogical Society; 103 4th Ave. SE, Box 4; Independence, Iowa 50644

Buena Vista Co. Genealogical Library; 221 W. Railroad St.; Storm Lake, Iowa 50588

Buena Vista County Historical Society; Box 882; Storm Lake, Iowa 50598

Buena Vista Genealogical Society; 221 W. Railroad St.; Storm Lake, Iowa 50599

Burlington Public Library; 501 N. Fourth St.; Burlington, Iowa 52601

Butler County Genealogical Society; Clarksville Public Library; 103 W. Greene St.; Clarksville, Iowa 50619; <www.pafways.org/genealogy/societies/butler.htm>

Calhoun County Genealogical Society; 426 5th St; Rockwell City, Iowa 50579-1415

Carroll County, Iowa Genealogical Society; PO Box 21; Carroll, Iowa 51401-0021

Cass County, Iowa Genealogical Society; 507 Poplar St. c/o Atlantic Public Library; Atlantic, Iowa 50022-1241

Cedar County Genealogical Society; PO Box 52; Tipton, Iowa 52772-0052; <www.rootsweb.com/~iacedar/ccgs.htm>

Cedar County Historical Society; 409 Sycamore St.; Tipton, Iowa 52772-1649

Central Community Historical Society; R. R. 2, Box 98; DeWitt, Iowa 52742; <www.rootsweb.com/~iaclinto/gensoc/cencomm.htm>

Central Iowa Genealogical Society; Box 945; Marshalltown, Iowa 50158-0945; <www.marshallnet.com/~manor/genea/cigs.html>

Charlotte Brett Memorial Collection, Spencer Public Library; 21 E. 3rd St.; Spencer, Iowa 51301

Charter-Pierce Memorial Internet Genealogical Society; 3221 Villa Vista Dr.; Des Moines, Iowa 50316-1338; <www.rootsweb.com/~iapcmigs/cpmigsl.htm>

Cherokee County Historical Society; PO Box 247; Clegborn, Iowa 51014-0247

Chickasaw County Genealogical Society; PO Box 434; New Hampton, Iowa 50659; <www.rootsweb.com/~iachicka/CK_CCGS.htm>

Clarke County Genealogical Society; c/o Osceola Public Library; 300 S. Fillmore; Osceola, Iowa 50213-1414; <www.rootsweb.com/~iaclarke/ccgs.html>

Clarke County Historical Society; Hwy. 69 South; Osceola, Iowa 50213; <www.rootsweb.com/~iaclarke/hissoc.html>

Clayton County Genealogical Society; Box 846; Elkader, Iowa 52043-0846; <www.rootsweb.com/~iaccgs/>

Clinton County Genealogical Society; Box 2062; Clinton, Iowa 52732-2062

Conrad Public Library, Grundy Co. Gen. Soc; Box 189, 102 Grundy; Conrad, Iowa 50621

Crawford County Genealogical Society; PO Box 26; Vail, Iowa 51465

Cresco Public Library (Howard & Winneshiek Cos.); 320 N. Elm; Cresco, Iowa 52136

Dallas County Genealogical Society; Box 264; Dallas Center, Iowa 50063-0264

Danish American Heritage Society; 4105 Stone Brooke Road; Ames, Iowa 50010; <www.dana.edu/dahs/>

Danish Immigrant Museum; 2212 Washington St., PO Box 470; Elk Horn, Iowa 51531-0470; <dkmuseum.org>

Daughters of Union Veterans, Iowa Dept.; R 1, Box 23; Menlo, Iowa 50164

Decorah Genealogical Association; c/o Decorah Public Library (East Entrance); 202 Winnebago; Decorah, Iowa 52101-1812; <www.harveyshobbyhut.com/genealogy/>

Decorah Public Library, Decorah Gen. Assoc.; 202 Winnebago St., Lower Level; Decorah, Iowa 52101; 319.382.8559;

Delaware County Genealogical Society; 300 N. Franklin St.; Manchester, Iowa 52057-1520

Des Moines County Genealogical Society; PO Box 493; Burlington, Iowa 52601-0493

Donnellson Public Library, Family History Dept.; 500 Park St., PO Box 290; Donnellson, Iowa 52625

Dubuque County-Key City Genealogical Society; PO Box 13; Dubuque, Iowa 52004-0013; <www.rootsweb.com/~iadckcgs/>

Dyersville Area Historical Society Library; 120 3rd SW; Dyersville, Iowa 52040

Eisenhower, Mamie Doud, Birthplace, Museum & Library; PO Box 55, 709 Carroll St.; Boone, Iowa 50036

Elliott Public Library; Box 306; Elliott, Iowa 51532

Emmet County Genealogical Society; Estherville Public Library; 613 Central Ave.; Estherville, Iowa 51334-2294

Emmetsburg Public Library; East 10th St.; Emmetsburg, Iowa 50536

Ericson Public Library; 702 Greene St.; Boone, Iowa 50036

Evangelical Lutheran Church of America, Wartburg Theological Seminary; 333 Wartburg Place; Dubuque, Iowa 52003; 319.589.0200; Fax 319.589.0333

Fairfield Public Library; 104 W. Adams; Fairfield, Iowa 52556

Family History Library: 35 North West Temple Street: Salt Lake City, Utah 84150: 800.346.6044 or 801.240.2584: <www.familysearch.org>: Find a Family History Center near you: <www.familysearch.org/Eng/Library/FHC/frameset_fhc.asp>

Fayette County Genealogical Society; 100 N Walnut; West Union, Iowa 52175-1347; <www.rootsweb.com/~iafayett/iafirst6.htm>

Franklin County Genealogical Society; c/o Hampton Iowa Public Library; 4 Federal St.; South Hampton, Iowa 50441-1934

Free Public Library, Family History Dept.; 8th and Braden; Chariton, Iowa 50049

Fremont County Historical Society; Box 671; Sidney, Iowa 51652-0337

Gateway Genealogical Society; 618 14th Ave.; Camanche, Iowa 52730

German American Heritage Center; PO Box 243; Davenport, Iowa 52805-0243

Gibson Memorial Library; 310 North Maple; Creston, Iowa 50801

Glenwood Public Library; 109 N. Vine St.; Glenwood, Iowa 51534-1516; 712.527.5252

Greater Sioux County Genealogical Society; c/o Sioux Center Public Library; 327 First Ave. N.E.; Sioux Center, Iowa 51250-1801; <www.rootsweb.com/~iasioux/gscgs.htm>

Greene County, Iowa Genealogical Society; PO Box 133; Jefferson, Iowa 50129-0133; <www.rootsweb.com/~iagreene/>

Grundy County Genealogical Society; 708 West St.; Reinbeck, Iowa 50669-1365

Guthrie County Genealogical Society; PO Box 96; Jamaica, Iowa 50128-0096

Hamilton (Co) Heritage Hunters; 943 1st St; Webster City, Iowa 50595-2001

Hampton Public Library; 4 Federal St. South; Hampton, Iowa 50441

Hancock County Genealogical Society; Box 81; Klemme, Iowa 50449-0081; 641.587.2324; <www.pafways.org/genealogy/societies/hancock.htm>

Hardin County, Iowa Genealogical Society; PO Box 252; Eldora, Iowa 50627

Harrison County, Iowa Genealogical Society; 2810 190th Trail; Woodbine, Iowa 51579; <www.rootsweb.com/~iaharris/hcgs.htm>

Henry County Genealogical Society; PO Box 81; Mt. Pleasant, Iowa 52641-0081

Howard-Winneshiek Genealogy Society; PO Box 362; Cresco, Iowa 52136; <www.pafways.org/genealogy/societies/howard_winneshiek.htm>

Humboldt County Genealogical Society; 30 6th St. North; Humboldt, Iowa 50548; <www.pafways.org/genealogy/societies/humboldt.htm>

Ida County Genealogical Society; 506 Moorehead St; Ida Grove, Iowa 51445-1631

Ida County Historical Society; 501 Zobel Lane; Ida Grove, Iowa 51445; <www.rootsweb.com/~iaida/directory/idahis.htm>

Iowa City Genealogical Society; PO Box 822; Iowa City, Iowa 52244-0822; <www.rootsweb.com/~iajohnso/icgensoc.htm>

Iowa County Historical Society; PO Box 288; Marengo, Iowa 52301

Iowa Department of Public Health, Vital Records Section; Lucas State Office Building; Des Moines, Iowa 50319; 515.281.4944; Fax 515.281.4529

Iowa Genealogical Society; 6000 Douglas; PO Box 7735; Des Moines, Iowa 50322-7735; 515.727.1824;

Iowa Lakes Genealogical Society; 601 Monroe St.; Emmetsburg, Iowa 50536

Iowa State Archives; Capital Complex, 600 East Locust; Des Moines, Iowa 50319; 515.281.3007; Fax 515.282.0502

Jackson County Genealogical Chapter; Box 1065; Maquoketa, Iowa 52060-1065; <www.rootsweb.com/~iajackso/JCGenie.html>

Jasper County Genealogical Society; PO Box 163; Newton, Iowa 50208

Jefferson County Genealogical Society; 2791 240th St.; Fairfield, Iowa 52556-8518; <www.rootsweb.com/~iajeffer/JCGS.htm>

Johnson County Historical Society; PO Box 5081; Coralville, Iowa 51141

Jones County Genealogical Society; PO Box 174; Anomosa, Iowa 52205-0174; <www.rootsweb.com/~iajones/research/research.htm#jcgs>

Keo-Mah Genealogical Society; PO Box 616; Oskaloosa, Iowa 52577-0616; 641.673.4373; <www.geocities.com/Heartland/Acres/2263/>

Keosauqua Public Library; First & Van Buren; Keosauqua, Iowa 52565; 319.293.3766; <showcase.netins.net/web/keolibrary>

Lee County Genealogical Society; PO Box 303; Keokuk, Iowa 52632-0303; <www.rootsweb.com/~ialeecgs/>

LeMars Public Library; 46 First St.; LeMars, Iowa 51031

Lime Creek / Winnebago County Genealogical Society; 135 N 11th Street; Forest City, Iowa 50436-1630; 641.585.2584; <www.pafways.org/genealogy/societies/winnebago.htm>

Linn County, Iowa Genealogical Society; 813 1st Ave. S.E.; PO Box 175; Cedar Rapids, Iowa 52406-0175

Louisa County Genealogical Society; PO Box 202; Wapello, Iowa 52653; <www.rootsweb.com/~ialcgs/>

Lucas County Genealogical Society; c/o Chariton Public Library; 803 Braden Avenue; Chariton, Iowa 50049-1742; <www.rootsweb.com/~ialucas/Lucasinfor.htm>

Madison County Genealogical Society; PO Box 26; Winterset, Iowa 50273-0026

Marion County Genealogical Society; PO Box 395; Knoxville, Iowa 50138; <www.rootsweb.com/~iamcgs/Index.html>

Marshalltown Public Library; 36 N. Center St.; Marshalltown, Iowa 50158

Mason City Public Library; Mason City, Iowa 50401

Methodist, Iowa Wesleyan College Library; Mt. Pleasant, Iowa 52641; 319.385.6317; Fax 319.385.6324

Mid-America Genealogical Society; PO Box 316; Davenport, Iowa 52801

Mills County Genealogical Society; c/o Glenwood Public Library; 109 N. Vine St.; Glenwood, Iowa 51534-1516

Monona County Genealogical Society; Box 16; Onawa, Iowa 51040-0016

Monroe County Genealogical Society; c/o Albia Public Library; 203 Benton Ave. E.; Albia, Iowa 52531

Montgomery County Genealogical Society; 320A Coolbaugh; Red Oak, Iowa 51566-2416

Montgomery County Iowa Historical Society; 2700 N 4th Street; PO Box 634; Red Oak, Iowa 51566; 712.623.3708; <www.rootsweb.com/~iamontgo/montcent.htm>

Muscatine County Genealogical Society; 323 Main; Muscatine, Iowa 52761-2867

Museum of History & Science; Park Ave. at South St.; Waterloo, Iowa 50701

National Archives-Central Plains Region; 2312 East Bannister Road; Kansas City, Missouri 64131-3060; 816.926.6920; Fax 816.926.6982

Nishnabotna Genealogical Society; 1028 Road M 56; Harlan, Iowa 51537-6020; <www.rootsweb.com/~iashelby/scgs.htm>

North American Baptist Conference; 1 South 210 Summit Ave.; Oakbrook Terrace, Illinois 60181; 630.495.2000; Fax 630.495.3301

North Central Iowa Genealogical Society; PO Box 237; Mason City, Iowa 50402-0237; <www.pafways.org/genealogy/societies/northcentraliowa/index.htm>

Northeast Iowa Genealogical Society; c/o Grout Museum of History and Science; 503 South St.; Waterloo, Iowa 50701-1517

Northeastern Iowa Genealogical Society; 503 South Street; Waterloo, Iowa 50701-1517; <iowa.counties.com/blackhawk/gene.htm>

Northwest Iowa Genealogical Society; c/o LeMars Public Library; 46 First St. S.W.; LeMars, Iowa 51031

Norwegian-American Museum, Vesterheim; 502 W. Water St.; Decorah, Iowa 52101; 319.382.9681; Fax 319.382.9683

Oelwein Area Genealogical Society; PO Box 389; Oelwein, Iowa 50662-0389; <www.rootsweb.com/~iaoags/>

Oelwein Area Historical Society; 900 2nd Avenue SE; Oelwein, Iowa; <www.rootsweb.com/~iaoahs/>

OHS Ostfriesian Heritage Society; 18419 205th St.; Grundy Center, Iowa 50638

Old Fort Genealogical Society; PO Box #1; Fort Madison, Iowa 52627-0001; <freepages.genealogy.rootsweb.com/~oldfort/>

Oskaloosa Public Library; S. Market and Second St.; Oskaloosa, Iowa 52577

Ostfriesland Society of Iowa, Inc.; 519 E. Ramsey St.; PO Box 317; Bancroft, Iowa 50517-0317

Page County Genealogical Society; Rural Route 2, Box 236; Shenandoah, Iowa 51610

Palo Alto County Genealogical Society; c/o Emmetsburg Public Library; 707 N. Superior; Emmetsburg, Iowa 50536-2410

Pioneer Sons and Daughters Genealogical Society; PO Box 2103; Des Moines, Iowa 50310

Pocahontas County Genealogical Society; c/o Pocahontas Library; 14 2nd Ave. NW; Pocahontas, Iowa 50574-1611

Pocahontas Library; 14 2nd Ave. N.W.; Pocahontas, Iowa 50574

Pottawattamie County Genealogical Society; PO Box 394; Council Bluffs, Iowa 51502-0394; <www.rootsweb.com/~iapottaw/PCGS.htm>

Poweshiek County Historical & Genealogical Society; Box 280; Montezuma, Iowa 50171-0280; <showcase.netins.net/web/powshk/index.htm>

Ringgold County Genealogical Society; c/o Betty Jo Ruby; 202 Adams St; Diagonal, Iowa 50845-1001

Roman Catholic, Diocese of Davenport; 2706 N. Gaines St.; Davenport, Iowa 52804; 319.324.1911; Fax 319.324.5842

Roman Catholic, Diocese of Des Moines; 610 Grand Ave.; Des Moines, Iowa 50309; 515.243.7653; Fax 515.237.5070;

Roman Catholic, Diocese of Sioux City; 1821 Jackson Street; Sioux City, Iowa 51105; 712.255.7933; Fax 712.233.7598

Sac County Genealogical Society; PO Box 54; Sac City, Iowa 50583-0054; <www.rootsweb.com/~iasac/gensociety/gensoc.htm>

Scott County Iowa Genealogical Society; PO Box 3132; Davenport, Iowa 52808-3132

Sherry Foresman Library; R 1, Box 23; Menlo, Iowa 50164

Sioux City Public Library; Sixth & Jackson Sts.; Sioux City, Iowa 51101

Sons of the American Revolution, Iowa Society; 403 S. Walnut; Mt. Pleasant, Iowa 52641

Spencer Public Library; 21 E. Third St.; Spencer, Iowa 51301

State Historical Society of Iowa Library, State of Iowa Historical Building; 600 East Locust; Des Moines, Iowa 50319; 515.281.3007, 515.281.6200; Fax 515.282.0502

State Historical Society of Iowa, Library and Archives Bureau; Centennial Building, 402 Iowa Avenue; Iowa City, Iowa 52240-1806; 319.335.3916; Fax 319.335.3935 <www.iowahistory.org/library/index.html>

Federal Mortality Schedules 1850, 1860, 1870, 1880.

State/Territorial Census 1836, 1838, 1840-1849, 1851, 1852, 1854, 1856, 1859, 1885, 1895, 1905, 1915, 1925.

Sac and Fox Indian Census 1847.

Dollarhide, William. *The Census Book: A Genealogist's Guide to Federal Census Facts, Schedules and Indexes.* Bountiful, UT: Heritage Quest,1999.

Kemp, Thomas Jay. *The American Census Handbook.* Wilmington, DE: Scholarly Resources, Inc., 2001.

Lainhart, Ann S. *State Census Records.* Baltimore: Genealogical Publishing Co., Inc., 1992.

Szucs, Loretto Dennis, and Matthew Wright. *Finding Answers in U.S. Census Records.* Ancestry Publishing, 2001.

Thorndale, William, and William Dollarhide. *Map Guide to the U.S. Federal Censuses, 1790-1920.* Baltimore: Genealogical Publishing Co., 1987.

United States. Bureau of Internal Revenue. *Internal Revenue Assessment Lists For Iowa, 1862-1866.* Washington, D.C.: The National Archives, 1988. 16 microfilm.

Court Records, Probate and Wills

Note: Court records, wills and probate records are found in the individual county offices. Many have been transferred to the Iowa State Archives in Des Moines. See the county pages for further information.

Daughters of the American Revolution (Iowa*). Iowa Grave Records And Genealogical Data, 1800-1900.* Microfilm Made From Originals At The Iowa State Historical Department In Des Moines, Iowa. (Salt Lake City: Filmed by the Genealogical Society of Utah, 1978). 4 microfilm.

Daughters of the American Revolution. Independence Pioneers Chapter (Missouri). *Wills, 1655-1871, 1891*Independence, Mo.: The D.A.R. chapter, 1970-1971.

Emigration, Immigration, Migration and Naturalization

Palen, Margaret Krug. *German Settlers of Iowa: Their Descendants and European Ancestors.* Bowie, Maryland: Heritage Books, 1994.

Stellingwerff, J. *Amsterdamse Emigranten: Onbekende Brieven Uit De Prairie Van Iowa, 1846-1873.* Amsterdam: Buijten & Schipperheijn, 1975.

Land and Property

Hone, Wade E. *Land and Property Research in the United States.* Salt Lake City: Ancestry Incorporated, 1997.

Iowa American Revolution Bicentennial Commission. *Century Farm Applications.* Microfilm made from originals at the Iowa State Historical Department in Des Moines. (Salt Lake City: Filmed by the Genealogical Society of Utah, 1978). 8 microfilm.

Iowa. Land Department. *Abstract of Lands in Iowa Counties, Which Were Entered, or Sold At the Land Offices.* Microfilm of originals at the Iowa State Historical Department. (Salt Lake City: Filmed by the Genealogical Society of Utah, 1978). 5 microfilm.

Iowa. Land Department. *Des Moines River Lands, 1847-1904.* Microfilm of typescript and original copy in the office of Secretary of State, Des Moines, Iowa. (Salt Lake City: Filmed by the Genealogical Society of Utah, 1977). 6 microfilm.

Iowa. Land Department. *Miscellaneous Land Records, 1839-1930.* Microfilm of typescript and originals in office of Secretary of State, Des Moines, Iowa. (Salt Lake City: Filmed by the Genealogical Society of Utah, 1977). 6 microfilm.

Iowa. Land Department. *School Land Grants, 1849-1917.* Microfilm of original copies at the office of Secretary of State, Des Moines, Iowa. (Salt Lake City: Filmed by the Genealogical Society of Utah, 1977). 19 microfilm.

Iowa. Land Department. *Swamp Land Records, 1859-1921.* Microfilm of the typescript in the office of Secretary of State, Des Moines, Iowa. (Salt Lake City: Filmed by the Genealogical Society of Utah, 1977). 3 microfilm.

Iowa. Land Department. *Tract Books of Iowa Land Districts, 1838-1910.* Microfilm of the original. (Salt Lake City: Filmed by the Genealogical Society of Utah, 1977). 45 microfilm.

Lokken, Roscoe L. *Iowa: Public Land Disposal.* Iowa City: State Historical Society of Iowa, 1942.

Swierenga, Robert P. *Pioneers and Profits: Land Speculation on the Iowa Frontier.* Ames, IA: Iowa State University Press, 1968.

Military

Iowa. Adjutant General. *List of Ex-Soldiers, Sailors and Marines Living in Iowa.* Des Moines, Iowa: adjutant general. 1886.

Iowa. War records survey. Graves Registration Division. *Iowa Veterans Buried Out Of State: Graves Registration Service, A Division Of The Adjutant General's Department.* Microfilm of original records in the Iowa State Historical Department, Des Moines. (Salt Lake City: Filmed by the Genealogical Society of Utah, 1978). 11 microfilm.

Iowa And The Civil War: A Reference Guide. Iowa City, Iowa: State Historical Society of Iowa, [199-?]

Roster and Record of Iowa Soldiers in the War of the Rebellion. Des Moines, Iowa: state printer, 1908-11.

Roster of Soldiers, Sailors and Marines of the War Of 1812, the Mexican War, and the War of the Rebellion... Lincoln, Neb.: Nebraska State Genealogical Society, 1988.

Swisher, Jacob A. *The Iowa Department Of The Grand Army Of The Republic.* Iowa City, Iowa: State Historical Society of Iowa, 1936.

The Northern Border Brigade: A Story of Military Beginnings. (Salt Lake City: Filmed by the Genealogical Society of Utah, 1976).

United States. Record and Pension Office. *Compiled Service Records of Volunteer Soldiers Who Served During the Mexican War in Mormon Organizations.* Washington, D.C.: National Archives. Central Plains Region, 1961. 3 microfilm.

United States. Selective Service System. *Iowa, World War I Selective Service System Draft Registration Cards, 1917-1918.* National Archives Microfilm Publications, M1509. Washington, DC: National Archives, 1987-1988.

Vital and Cemetery Records

Dolan, John P., and Lisa Lacher. *Guide to Public Records of Iowa Counties*. Des Moines: Connie Wimer, 1986.

Fretwell, Sheila S. *Iowa Marriages Before Statehood, 1835-1846*. Waterloo, Iowa: Sheila S. Fretwell, 1985

Guide to Public Vital Statistics in Iowa. Des Moines: Historical Records Survey, 1941.

Iowa Cemetery and Grave Records by the Grave Registration Project of the Works Progress Administration and the Daughters of the American Revolution. Microfilm made from originals at the Iowa State Historical Department in Des Moines. (Salt Lake City: Genealogical Society of Utah, 1978.) Microfilm, 21 rolls.

Iowa. State Department of History and Archives. *Iowa Cemeteries*. Microfilm made from originals at the Iowa State Historical Department in Des Moines. (Salt Lake City: Filmed by the Genealogical Society of Utah, 1978). 7 microfilm.

Iowa. State Department of History and Archives. *Iowa Cemetery and Grave Records By Grave Registration Project of the W.P.A. and D.A.R.* Microfilm made from originals at the Iowa State Historical Department in Des Moines. (Salt Lake City: Filmed by the Genealogical Society of Utah, 1978). 21 microfilm.

Iowa. State Department of History and Archives. *Iowa Marriages, Ca. 1844-1900*. Microfilm made from originals at the Iowa State Historical Department in Des Moines. (Salt Lake City: Filmed by the Genealogical Society of Utah, 1978).

Liahona Research. *Iowa Marriages, Early to 1850*. Bountiful, UT: AGLL, 1990.

Work Projects Administration (Iowa War Records Survey). *Iowa Veterans Buried Out of State General's Department*. Microfilm of original records in the Iowa State Historical Department, Des Moines. (Salt Lake City: Filmed by the Genealogical Society of Utah, 1978). 11 microfilm.

County Website	Map Index	Date Created	Parent County or Territory From Which Organized Address/Details
Clayton www.rootsweb.com/~iaclayto/index.html	D4	21 Dec 1837	**Dubuque** Clayton County; 111 High St SE; Elkader, IA 52043; Ph. 319.245.2204 Details: (Clk Dis Ct has b & div rec from 1880, m rec from 1848, d rec 1880-1921 & from 1941, pro & ct rec from 1840 & nat rec from 1858; Co Rcdr has land rec from 1839)
Clinton www.clintoncountyiowa.com/	B7	21 Dec 1837	**Dubuque** Clinton County; 1900 N 3rd St; PO Box 157; Clinton, IA 52732-0157; Ph. 319.243.6210 Details: (Attached to Scott Co prior to organization 5 Jan 1841) (Clk Dis Ct has b & d rec 1880-1935 & from 1941, m & pro rec from 1840, div & ct rec from mid-1800's; Co Rcdr has land rec from 1840)
Cook		7 Dec 1836	**Des Moines** Details: (Attached to Muscatine. Eliminated 18 Jan 1838 to Muscatine)
Crawford www.rootsweb.com/~iacrawfo/	O6	1 Jan 1851	**Pottawattamie, Unorganized Territory** Crawford County; 1202 Broadway; PO Box 546; Denison, IA 51442; Ph. 712.263.2242 Details: (Attached to Shelby Co prior to organization 3 Sep 1855) (Co Rcdr has b & d rec from 1880, m rec from 1855, land rec from 1859 & mil rec; Clk Cts has div rec from 1906, pro rec from 1869, ct rec from 1866 and some nat rec)
Crocker		12 May 1870	**Kossuth** Details: (Eliminated 11 Dec 1871 to Kossuth)
Dallas www.co.dallas.ia.us/	K7	13 Jan 1846	**Unorganized Territory** Dallas County; 801 Court St; PO Box 38; Adel, IA 50003; Ph. 515.993.5804 Details: (Attached to Polk & Mahaska Cos prior to organization 1 Mar 1847) (Clk Dis Ct has b & d rec from 1880, m rec from 1850, div rec from 1881, pro rec from 1863 & ct rec from 1860; Co Rcdr has land rec)
Davis www.rootsweb.com/~iadavis/davis.htm	G10	17 Feb 1843	**Unorganized Territory** Davis County; 100 Courthouse Sq; Bloomfield, IA 52537-1600; Ph. 515.664.2011 Details: (Attached to Van Buren Co prior to organization 1 Mar 1844) (Clk Dis Ct has b & d rec from 1880, m rec from 1844, div, pro & ct rec from 1844)
Decatur www.rootsweb.com/~iadecatu/	J10	13 Jan 1846	**Unorganized Territory** Decatur County; 207 Main St; Leon, IA 50144-1647; Ph. 515.446.4331 Details: (Attached to Davis Co prior to organization 6 May 1850; Courthouse burned in 1874) (Co Clk has b, d, div & pro rec from 1880, m & land rec from 1874 & some mil dis & cem rec)
Delaware www.rootsweb.com/~iadelawa/	D5	21 Dec 1837	**Dubuque** Delaware County; 301 E Main; PO Box 527; Manchester, IA 52057-0527; Ph. 319.927.4942 Details: (Organized 19 Nov 1841) (Clk Dis Ct has b & d rec from 1880, m, div & ct rec from 1851 & pro rec from 1849; Co Rcdr has land rec)
Des Moines www.rootsweb.com/~iadesmoi/	D10	1 Oct 1834	**Michigan Territory** Des Moines County; 513 Main St; PO Box 158; Burlington, IA 52601; Ph. 319.753.8262 Details: (Clk Dis Ct has b rec from 1880, d rec 1880-1921 & from 1941, m, div, pro & ct rec from 1835 & nat rec from 1840)
Dickinson www.co.dickinson.ia.us/	N2	15 Jan 1851	**Unorganized Territory** Dickinson County; 18th & Hill County Courthouse; Spirit Lake, IA 51360; Ph. 712.336.1138 Details: (Attached to Woodbury Co prior to organization 3 Aug 1857) (Clk Dis Ct has b, m, d, bur, div, pro & ct rec from 1880; Co Rcdr has land rec)
Dubuque www.rootsweb.com/~iadubuqu/	C5	1 Oct 1834	**Michigan Territory** Dubuque County; 720 Central Ave; Dubuque, IA 52001; Ph. 319.589.4418 Details: (Clk Dis Ct has b & d rec from 1880, m rec from 1840, div rec from 1900, pro rec from 1835 & ct rec from 1836; Co Rcdr has land rec from 1836)

County Website	Map Index	Date Created	Parent County or Territory From Which Organized Address/Details
Emmet www.emmet.org/pmc/	**M2**	**15 Jan 1851**	**Unorganized Territory** Emmet County; 609 1st Ave N; Estherville, IA 51334; Ph. 712.362.3325 Details: (Attached to Boone & Webster Cos prior to organization 7 Feb 1859) (Clk Dis Ct has b rec from 1883, m & d rec from 1890, div rec from 1915 & pro rec from 1885)
Fayette www.rootsweb.com/~iafayett/	**E4**	**21 Dec 1837**	**Dubuque** Fayette County; 114 N Vine St; West Union, IA 52175; Ph. 319.422.3234 Details: (Attached to Clayton Co prior to organization 26 Aug 1850) (Co Rcdr has b & d rec from 1880, m rec from 1851 & land rec from 1855; Clk Cts has div rec from 1897, pro rec from 1869, ct rec from 1852 & nat rec)
Floyd www.rootsweb.com/~iafloyd/	**H3**	**15 Jan 1851**	**Unorganized Territory** Floyd County; 101 S Main St; Charles City, IA 50616-2756; Ph. 515.228.7111 Details: (Attached to Fayette & Chickasaw Cos prior to organization 4 Sep 1854) (Clk Dis Ct has b & d rec from 1880, m & div rec from 1860, pro & ct rec from 1854)
Fox		**15 Jan 1851**	**Unorganized Territory** Details: (see Calhoun) Name changed to Calhoun 22 Jan 1853
Franklin www.pafways.org/iagenweb/franklin/	**I4**	**15 Jan 1851**	**Unorganized Territory** Franklin County; 12 1st Ave NW; Hampton, IA 50441; Ph. 515.456.5626 Details: (Attached to Chickasaw, Fayette & Hardin Cos prior to organization 3 Mar 1856) (Clk Cir Ct has b & d rec from 1880, m rec from 1855, pro rec from 1864, div & ct rec from 1869; Co Rcdr has land rec)
Fremont www.rootsweb.com/~iafremon/	**P10**	**24 Feb 1847**	**Unorganized Territory** Fremont County; PO Box 549; Sidney, IA 51652-0549; Ph. 712.374.2031 Details: (Attached to Appanoose Co prior to organization 10 Sep 1849) (Clk Dis Ct has b & d rec from 1880, except 1935-1941, limited m rec from 1848, div, pro & ct rec; Co Rcdr has land rec)
Greene www.jeffersoniowa.com/	**L6**	**15 Jan 1851**	**Unorganized Territory** Greene County; County Courthouse; Jefferson, IA 50129-2294; Ph. 515.386.2516 Details: (Attached to Dallas Co prior to organization 25 Aug 1853) (Clk Dis Ct has b, d, div & ct rec from 1880, m & pro rec from 1854; Co Rcdr has land rec)
Grundy www.rootsweb.com/~iagrundy/ grundy.html	**H5**	**15 Jan 1851**	**Unorganized Territory** Grundy County; 706 G Ave; Grundy Center, IA 50638-1440; Ph. 319.824.5229 Details: (Attached to Buchanan & Black Hawk Cos prior to organization 25 Dec 1856) (Clk Dis Ct has b, div & ct rec from 1880, m rec from 1856, d rec from 1881 & pro rec from 1870; Co Rcdr has land rec)
Guthrie www.rootsweb.com/~iaguthri/html/ index.html	**L8**	**15 Jan 1851**	**Unorganized Territory** Guthrie County; 200 N 5th St; Guthrie Center, IA 50115-1331; Ph. 515.747.3415 Details: (Clk Dis Ct has b & d rec from 1880, m rec from 1852, div rec from 1883, pro rec from 1881 & ct rec from 1916)
Hamilton www.hamiltoncounty.org/	**J5**	**8 Jan 1857**	**Webster** Hamilton County; County Courthouse; Webster City, IA 50595-3158; Ph. 515.832.4640 Details: (Clk Dis Ct has b, m, d, div, pro & ct rec from 1880)
Hancock www.pafways.org/iagenweb/hancock/	**J3**	**15 Jan 1851**	**Unorganized Territory** Hancock County; 855 State St; Garner, IA 50438-1645; Ph. 515.923.2532 Details: (Attached to Boone & Webster Cos prior to organization 25 Nov 1858) (Clk Dis Ct has b, m, d, bur & div rec from 1880, pro & ct rec from 1856)
Hardin www.co.hardin.ia.us/	**I5**	**15 Jan 1851**	**Unorganized Territory** Hardin County; Edgington Ave; Eldora, IA 50627-1741; Ph. 515.858.3461 Details: (Attached to Marshall Co prior to organization 2 Mar 1853) (Clk Dis Ct has b & d rec from 1880, m rec from 1864, div rec from 1889, pro, ct & land rec from 1853)
Harrison www.rootsweb.com/~iaharris/	**P7**	**15 Jan 1851**	**Pottawattamie** Harrison County; 113 N 2nd Ave; Logan, IA 51546-1331; Ph. 712.644.2665 Details: (Organized 7 Mar 1853) (Clk Dis Ct has b & d rec from 1880, m & div rec from 1853, pro rec from 1869, ct rec from 1850 & some bur rec)

County Website	Map Index	Date Created	Parent County or Territory From Which Organized Address/Details
Van Buren www.800-tourvbc.com/	F10	7 Dec 1836	**Des Moines** Van Buren County; 4th St & Dodge St; PO Box 475; Keosauqua, IA 52565-0475; Ph. 319.293.3129 Details: (Clk Dis Ct has b & d rec from 1880, m, div, pro & ct rec from 1837)
Wahkaw		15 Jan 1851	**Unorganized Territory** Details: (see Woodbury) Name changed to Woodbury 22 Jan 1853
Wapello www.rootsweb.com/~iawapell/	G10	17 Feb 1843	**Unorganized Territory** Wapello County; 4th & Court Sq; Ottumwa, IA 52501-2599; Ph. 515.683.0060 Details: (Attached to Jefferson Co prior to organization 1 Mar 1844) (Clk Cts has div, pro & ct rec from 1844; Co Rcdr has b, m, d & land rec)
Warren www.rootsweb.com/~iawarren/	J9	13 Jan 1846	**Unorganized Territory** Warren County; PO Box 379; Indianola, IA 50125-0379; Ph. 515.961.1033 Details: (Attached to Mahaska Co prior to organization 10 Feb 1849) (Clk Dis Ct has b, d, div, pro & ct rec from 1880 & m rec from 1850)
Washington co.washington.ia.us/	E8	18 Jan 1838	**Henry, Louisa, Muscatine** Washington County; PO Box 391; Washington, IA 52353-0391; Ph. 319.653.7741 Details: (Formerly Slaughter Co. Name changed to Washington 25 Jan 1839) (Clk Dis Ct has b & d rec from 1880, m rec from 1844, div, pro & ct rec from 1836 & some nat rec; Co Rcdr has land rec)
Wayne www.rootsweb.com/~iawayne/	I10	13 Jan 1846	**Unorganized Territory** Wayne County; 100 S Franklin; PO Box 424; Corydon, IA 50060-0424; Ph. 515.872.2264 Details: (Attached to Davis Co prior to organization 27 Jan 1851) (Clk Dis Ct has b & d rec from 1880, m rec from 1851, div rec from 1906, pro rec from 1891 & ct rec from 1875)
Webster www.webstercountyia.org/	L5	15 Jan 1851	**Yell, Risley** Webster County; 703 Central Ave; Fort Dodge, IA 50501; Ph. 515.576.7115 Details: (Formerly Risley & Yell Cos. Name changed to Webster 22 Jan 1853) (Clk Dis Ct has b rec from 1876, m rec from 1853, d & ct rec from 1860, div rec from 1870 & pro rec from 1855; Co Aud has land rec)
Winnebago www.rootsweb.com/~iawinneb/index.htm	J2	15 Jan 1851	**Unorganized Territory** Winnebago County; 126 S Clark St; Forest City, IA 50436-1793; Ph. 515.582.4520 Details: (Attached to Boone & Webster Cos prior to organization 1 Nov 1857) (Clk Cts has b & d rec from 1880, m, div, pro & ct rec from 1865; Co Regstr has bur rec)
Winneshiek www.rootsweb.com/~iawinnes/index.htm	F3	20 Feb 1847	**Unorganized Territory** Winneshiek County; 201 W Main St; Decorah, IA 52101-1775; Ph. 319.382.2469 Details: (Attached to Clayton Co prior to organization 1 Mar 1851) (Clk Dis Ct has b & d rec from 1880, m rec from 1851, div & ct rec from 1855 & pro rec from 1853)
Woodbury www.woodbury-ia.com/	P5	15 Jan 1851	**Unorganized Territory** Woodbury County; 101 Court St; Sioux City, IA 51101-1909; Ph. 712.279.6616 Details: (Formerly Wahkaw Co. Name changed to Woodbury 22 Jan 1853. Organized 7 Mar 1853) (Clk Dis Ct has b & d rec from 1880, m rec from 1880 & some from 1854, div rec from 1857, pro rec from 1868, ct rec from 1850 & adoption rec from 1920)
Worth www.rootsweb.com/~iaworth/	I2	15 Jan 1851	**Unorganized Territory** Worth County; 1000 Central Ave; Northwood, IA 50459-1523; Ph. 515.324.2840 Details: (Attached to Fayette, Chickasaw, Floyd & Mitchell Cos prior to organization 13 Oct 1857) (Clk Dis Ct has incomplete b rec from 1880, m rec from 1858, d rec 1880-1919, div rec from 1879, pro & ct rec from 1857 & nat rec; Co Aud has land rec)
Wright www.wrightcounty.org/	J4	15 Jan 1851	**Unorganized Territory** Wright County; PO Box 306; Clarion, IA 50525-0306; Ph. 515.532.3113 Details: (Attached to Boone & Webster Cos prior to organization 1 Oct 1855) (Clk Dis Ct has b, d & pro rec from 1880, m rec from 1860, div & ct rec from 1873 & nat rec 1857-1929; Co Rcdr has land rec; City Clks & libraries have bur rec)
Yell		15 Jan 1851	**Unorganized Territory** Details: (see Webster) Lost to Webster Co 22 Jan 1853

Notes

Notes

Sunflower

KANSAS

CAPITAL: TOPEKA – TERRITORY 1854 – STATE 1861 (34TH)

Kansas was part of the Louisiana Purchase in 1803. Government expeditions to the area reported it to be a desert, starting the myth of the Great American Desert. Indians from the East were moved into the area to brave what was believed to be a harsh desert. The relationship was hostile between Native Americans and would-be settlers. The hostility increased when the Santa Fe Trail traversed the state beginning in 1821. To protect travelers, forts were established along the trail, beginning with Fort Leavenworth in 1827. Later, the Oregon Trail crossed northeastern Kansas.

Kansas remained unorganized territory until 1854 when the Kansas-Nebraska Act created the Kansas and Nebraska territories. Kansas had the same boundaries as today except that its western boundary was the "summit of the Rocky Mountains." The Kansas-Nebraska Act also stipulated that the people of a territory would decide by majority vote whether Kansas would be a free or a slave state. This act stimulated migration to Kansas as both pro and antislavery forces tried to gain the upper hand. The violence that marked the years from 1854 to statehood in 1861 led to the term "Bleeding Kansas." Kansas ultimately voted to be a free state. The population in 1861 was 10,000, consisting primarily of Southerners and New Englanders, along with others from Illinois, Indiana, Ohio, and Kentucky.

During the Civil War, Kansas had more than 20,000 Union soldiers. Its men suffered the highest mortality rate of any state in the Union. Many of the remaining Indian tribes in the state moved to Oklahoma by 1867. The few that refused to go fought against other settlers until 1878. A post-Civil War boom occurred due to the Homestead Act and railroad growth. Many Civil War veterans took up homesteads in the state and other settlers came from Germany, Russia, Sweden, England, and Mexico.

Look for vital records in the following locations:

- **Birth and death records:** Office of Vital Statistics, Kansas State Department of Health in Topeka has birth and death records since 1 July 1911. A few counties began keeping birth and death records in 1885. These can be obtained from county clerks. Some cities also have birth and death records from 1910 to 1940.
- **Marriage and divorce records:** Office of Vital Statistics, Kansas State Department of Health, has marriage records from 1 May 1913, and divorce records from 1 July 1951. County clerks and probate court clerks also kept marriage records. Divorces prior to 1951 are on file with the district court.
- **Court records and wills:** After July 1951, probate judges began handling probate matters, wills, and in most counties civil court records.
- **Land records:** County recorders and county assessors keep real estate records.
- **Census records:** State and territorial censuses exist for 1855, 1865, 1875, 1885, 1895, 1905, 1915, and 1925. All censuses are available at the Kansas State Historical Society in Topeka. Some counties have voter censuses for 1856, 1857, and 1859.

Office of Vital Statistics
Kansas State Department of Health
900 Soutwest Jackson Street, Room 151
Topeka, Kansas 66612
785.296.1400

Kansas State Historical Society
120 West Tenth
Topeka, Kansas 66612-1291

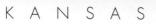
Topeka ★

Wichita •

KANSAS

Societies and Repositories

American Baptist-Samuel Colgate Historical Society; 1106 South Goodman St.; Rochester, New York 14620-2532; 716.473.1740; Fax 716.473.1740

Anderson County Genealogical Society; PO Box 194; Garnett, Kansas 66032; <kanza.net/~swguinn/acgs.html>

Arkansas City Public Library; 213 W. 5th Ave.; Arkansas City, Kansas 67705

Atchison County Kansas Genealogical Society; c/o Atchison Library; PO Box 303; Atchison, Kansas 66002; 913.367.2717; <skyways.lib.ks.us/genweb/society/atchison/ackgs.htm>

Barton County Genealogical Society; Box 425; Great Bend, Kansas 67530

Bluestem Genealogical Society; Box 582; Eureka, Kansas 67045

Branches and Twigs Genealogical Society; 455 North Main; Kingman, Kansas 67068; <skyways.lib.ks.us/genweb/kingman/branches.html>

Brown County Genealogical Society, Research Center and Library; 116 S. 7th St.; Hiawatha, Kansas 66434-2307; 785.742.7511;<bcgs@jbntelco.com>

Chanute Genealogical Society; 800 W. 14th St.; Chanute, Kansas 66720-2699; <www.rootsweb.com/~kscgs/>

Chautauqua County Historical and Genealogical Society; PO Box 227; Sedan, Kansas 67361; <freida.wells.tripod.com/ChautauquaCountyKansas/>

Cherokee County Kansas Genealogical/Historical Society, Inc.; 100 South Tennessee, PO Box 33; Columbus, Kansas 66725-0033; 316.429.2992; <skyways.lib.ks.us/kansas/genweb/cherokee/society/cckghs.html>

Cloud County Genealogical Society; Rt. #3; Concordia, Kansas 66901; <www.dustdevil.com/towns/concordia/history/ccgs/>

Cowley County Genealogical Society; 1519 E. 12th.; Winfield, Kansas 67156-3923

Crawford County Genealogical Society; c/o Pittsburg Public Library; 308 N. Walnut; Pittsburg, Kansas 66762

Decatur County Genealogical Society; 307 N. Rodehaver; Oberlin, Kansas 67749

Disciples of Christ Historical Society; 1101 19th Avenue South; Nashville, Tennessee 37212; 615.327.1444; Fax 615.327.1445

Douglas County Historical Society; Watkins Community Museum of History; 1047 Massachusetts St.; Lawrence, Kansas 66044-2923

Family History Library: 35 North West Temple Street: Salt Lake City, Utah 84150: 800.346.6044 or 801.240.2584: <www.familysearch.org>: Find a Family History Center near you: <www.familysearch.org/Eng/Library/FHC/frameset_fhc.asp>

Finney County Genealogical Society; PO Box 592; Garden City, Kansas 67846

Flint Hills Genealogical Society; PO Box 555; Emporia, Kansas 66801-0555; <skyways.lib.ks.us/genweb/society/emporia/index.html>

Flinthills Genealogical Society; PO Box 555; Emporia, Kansas 66901

Fort Hays, Kansas Genealogical Society; c/o Forsyth Library; FHS University; Hays, Kansas 67601

Frank Carlson Library, Cloud Co. Gen. Soc.; 701 Broadway St.; Concordia, Kansas 66901

Franklin County Genealogical Society; PO Box 353; Ottawa, Kansas 66067; <www.ukans.edu/~hisite/franklin/fcgs/>

Garden City Public Library; 210 N. 7th, Garden City; Garden City, Kansas 67846

Genealogical Society of Douglas County; PO Box 3664; Lawrence, Kansas 66046-0664; <skyways.lib.ks.us/kansas/genweb/douglas/dckgs.htm>

Girard Public Library; 128 W. Prairie Ave.; Girard, Kansas 66743

Golden Wheat Chapter, AHSGR; 2029 University; Wichita, Kansas 67213-3375; 316.283.3129; <www.ahsgr.org/ksgolden.html>

Greenwood Co. Historical Society, 120 West 4th, Eureka, Kansas, 67045-1445

Halstead Historical Society; PO Box 88; 116 East First; Halstead, Kansas 67056; <www.halsteadkansas.com/historical.html>

Hamilton Co. Library; 102 E. Hwy 50, Syracuse, KS 67878; 316.384.7496

Hamilton County Historical Society; 108 E. Hwy. 50, Syracuse, KS 67878; 316.384.7496

Harper County Genealogical Society; Harper Public Library; 10th and Oak; Harper, Kansas 67058; 620.962.5211; <skyways.lib.ks.us/kansas/genweb/society/harper/>

Heart of America Chapter, AHSGR; 117 E. Minneapolis Street; Salina, Kansas 67401-6024; 913.827.0782

Hereditary Order of the Descendants of the Loyalists & Patriots of the American Revolution; 608 South Overlook Drive; Coffeyville, Kansas 67337-2531; 316.251.2383

Heritage Seekers of SW Kansas Chapter, AHSGR; 511 Baughman; Ulysses, Kansas 67880; 316.356.2228

Historical Society of the Downs Carnegie Library; South Morgan Ave.; Downs, Kansas 67437

Hodgeman County Genealogical Society; PO Box 441; Jetmore, Kansas 67954

Iola Public Library; 218 E. Madison Ave.; Iola, Kansas 66749

Jefferson County Genealogical Society; PO Box 174; Oskaloosa, Kansas 66066-0174; <skyways.lib.ks.us/kansas/genweb/jefferso/jfcogen.html>

Johnson Co. Gen. Soc. Resource Center; "Old Jefferson Town", PO Box 174; Oskaloosa, Kansas 66066-0174

Johnson County Genealogical Society; PO Box 12666; Shawnee Mission, Kansas 66292-2666; <history.cc.ukans.edu/heritage/society/jcgs/jcgs_main.html>

Kansas City Area Chapter, AHSGR; 4441 W 52nd Terrace; Roeland Park, Kansas 66205; 913.362.7635

Kansas Council of Genealogical Societies, Inc.; PO Box 3859; Topeka, Kansas 66604-6858

Kansas Gen. Soc. Library, Village Square Mall- Lower level; PO Box 103, 2601 Central Ave.; Dodge City, Kansas 67801-0103; <www.dodgecity.net/kgs/>

Kansas Society, DAR; 1000 W. 55th St. S.; Wichita, Kansas 67217

Kansas State Historical Society; 6425 SW 6thAve.; Topeka, Kansas 66615-1099; 785.272.8682; <www.kshs.org/archives/>

Kansas State Library, State Capitol Bldg.; 300 SW 10th, Room 343 N; Topeka, Kansas 66612-1593; 913.296.3296; Fax 913.296.6650

Labette County Genealogical Society; c/o Mrs. Tina Rice; PO Box 544; Parsons, Kansas 67357; <skyways.lib.ks.us/kansas/genweb/society/parsons/>

Larabee Memorial Library; 108 N. Union; Stafford, Kansas 67578; 316.234.5762; <skyways.lib.ks.us/towns/Stafford/library>

Leavenworth County Genealogical Society, Inc.; PO Box 362; Leavenworth, Kansas 66048

Liberal Area Genealogical Society; PO Box 1094; Liberal, Kansas 67905-1094

Linn County Historical Society; Box 137; Pleasanton, Kansas 66075

Lyon County Historical Society; 118 E. 6th Street; Emporia, Kansas 66801

Marion County Genealogical Society; 401 S. Cedar; Marion, Kansas 66861-1331; <skyways.lib.ks.us/genweb/society/marion/>

Marshall County Historical Society; 1207 Broadway; Marysville, Kansas 66508

Mennonite Library & Archives, Bethel College; 300 E. 27th St.; North Newton, Kansas 67117

Methodist, Baker University Library; 606 Eighth Street; Baldwin City, Kansas 66006; 913.594.8414; Fax 913.594.6721

Methodist, Southwestern College, Memorial Library; 100 College Street; Winfield, Kansas 67156; 316.221.8225; Fax 316.221.2499

Miami County Genealogical Society; PO Box 123; Paola, Kansas 66071

Midwest Hist. & Gen. Library; 1203 N. Main, Box 1121; Wichita, Kansas 67201-1121; 316.264.3611; <skyways.lib.ks.us/genweb/mhgs/index.html>

Midwest Historical and Genealogical Society, Inc.; PO Box 1121; Wichita, Kansas 67201-1121; <skyways.lib.ks.us/kansas/genweb/mhgs/index.html>

Montgomery County Genealogical Society; PO. Box 444; Coffeyville, Kansas 67337; <www.rootsweb.com/~ksmontgo/>

Morris County Genealogical Society; Box 42.A, R. Rt. 2; White City, Kansas 66872

Nemaha County Genealogical Society; 6th and Nemaha; Seneca, Kansas 66538

North Central Kansas Genealogical Society; Box 251; Cawker City, Kansas 67430; <skyways.lib.ks.us/kansas/towns/Cawker/library.html#soci>

Northeast Kansas Chapter, AHSGR; 4625 NW Geronimo Trail; Topeka, Kansas 66618; 785.246.2821; <www.ahsgr.org/ksnorthe.html>

Northwest Kansas Genealogical & Historical Society; 700 W. 3rd; Oakley, Kansas 67748

Norton County Genealogical Society; 101 E. Lincoln; Norton, Kansas 67654

Office of Vital Statistics, Kansas Department of Health and Environment; 900 Jackson St; Topeka, Kansas 66612-1290; 913.296.1400

Old Fort Genealogical Society of Southeast Kansas; 502 S. National Ave.; Fort Scott, Kansas 66701; <skyways.lib.ks.us/kansas/genweb/society/ftscott/>

Osage County Historical Society; PO Box 361; Lyndon, Kansas 66451;

Osborne County Genealogical and Historical Society Inc.; 929 North 2nd St.; Osborne, Kansas 67473-1629

Phillips County Genealogical Society; PO Box 114; Phillipsburg, Kansas 67661; <skyways.lib.ks.us/genweb/phillips/plgensoc.html>

Pittsburg Public Library; 211 West 4th St.; Pittsburg, Kansas 66762

Post Rock Chapter, AHSGR; 18350 Homer Rd; Russell, Kansas 67665; 785.483.3976

Presbyterian Historical Society, United Presbyterian Church in the U.S.A.; 425 Lombard St.; Philadelphia, Pennsylvania 19147; 215.627.1852; Fax 215.627.0509

Public Library; Sixth & Minnesota Sts.; Kansas City, Kansas 66101

Rawlins County Genealogical Society; PO Box 203; Atwood, Kansas 67730; <skyways.lib.ks.us/genweb/rawlins/rawgenesoc.html>

Reno County Genealogical Society; PO Box 5; Hutchinson, Kansas 67504-0005;

Republic County Genealogical Society; Rt. 1; Belleville, Kansas 66935

Riley County Genealogical Society; 2005 Claflin Rd.; Manhattan, Kansas 66502-3415;

Roman Catholic, Archdiocese of Kansas City in Kansas, Chancery Office; 12615 Parallel Pkwy; Kansas City, Kansas 66109; 913.721.1570; Fax 913.721.1577

Santa Fe Trail Genealogical Society; PO Box 1049; Syracuse, Kansas 67878

Sherman County Historical and Genealogical Society; PO Box 684; Goodland, Kansas 67735; <skyways.lib.ks.us/genweb/sherman/shchs.html>

Smoky Valley Gen. Soc. & Library, Inc.; 211 W. Iron, Suite 205; Salina, Kansas 67401; 785.825.7573; <skyways.lib.ks.us/kansas/genweb/ottawa/smoky.html>

Southeast Kansas Genealogical Society; PO Box 393; Iola, Kansas 66749-0671

St. Marys Historical Society; 710 Alma St.; St. Marys, Kansas 66536

Stafford County Historical and Genealogical Society; 201 S. Park; Stafford, Kansas 67578

Stanton County Historical Society; 104 E. Highland, Johnson, Kansas 67855; 316.492.1526

Stevens County Genealogical Society; HC 01, Box 12; Hugoton, Kansas 67951

Sumner County Historical & Genealogical Society; PO Box 402; Wellington, Kansas 67152; <www.rootsweb.com/~ksscgs/>

Sunflower Chapter, AHSGR; 874 Samara; Munjor, Kansas 67601; (785) 625.6411; <www.ahsgr.org/kssunflo.html>

Topeka Kansas Genealogical Society; PO Box 4048; 2717 S.E. Indiana St.; Topeka, Kansas 66604-0048; <www.networksplus.net/donno/>

Topeka Public Library; 1515 West 10th; Topeka, Kansas 66604

University of Kansas; Spencer Research Library-Kansas Collections; Lawrence, Kansas 66045-2800; 913.864.4274; Fax 913.864.5803

Western Kansas Archives; Forsyth, Library; Hay, Kansas 67601

Wichita County Genealogical Society; 201 N. Fourth; PO Box 1561; Leoti, Kansas 67861; <wichitacountymuseum.org/gensociety.htm>

Wichita Genealogical Society; PO Box 3705; Wichita, Kansas 67201-3705; <kuhttp.cc.ukans.edu/kansas/wgs/wgs.html>

Wichita Public Library; 223 So. Main St.; Wichita, Kansas 67202; 316.261.8500; <www.wichita.lib.ks.us>

Wyandotte County Genealogical Society; PO Box 4228; Kansas City, Kansas 66104-0228

Wyandotte County Historical Society & Museum; 631 N. 126th St.; Bonner Springs, Kansas 66012; <www.kumc.edu/wcedc/museum/wcmuseum.html>

Bibliography and Record Sources

General Sources

A Biographical History of Central Kansas. 2 vols. New York: Lewis Pub. Co., 1902.

Adams, F. G. *Homestead Guide of Kansas and Nebraska.* Waterville, Kansas: 1873.

Anderson, Eileen. *Kansas Newspapers: A Directory of Newspaper Holdings In Kansas.* Topeka, Kansas: The Board, 1984.

Anderson, Lorene, and Alan W. Farley. "Bibliography of Town and County Histories of Kansas." *Kansas Historical Quarterly* 21 (Autumn 1955): 513-51.

Anderson, Robert D., ed. "Searching in Kansas." *Journal of Genealogy.* vol. 2 (May 1977). Omaha, Nebraska: Anderson Publishing Co.

Andreas, A. T. *History of The State of Kansas: Containing a Full Account of Its Growth From an Uninhabited Territory to a Wealthy and Important State, of Its Early Settlement, a Supplementary History and Description of Its Counties, Cities, Towns and Villages, Their Advantages, Industries and Commerce, to Which are Added Biographical Sketches and Portraits of Prominent Men and Early Settlers.* 2 vols. [Marceline, Mo.: Walsworth Pub. Co.], 1976.

Baldwin, Sara Mullin. *Illustriana Kansas: Biographical Sketches of Kansas Men and Women of Achievement Who Have Been Awarded Life Membership in Kansas Illustriana Society.* Hebron, Nebraska: Illustriana Inc., 1933.

Barry, Louise. *The Beginning of The West: Annals of the Kansas Gateway to the American West, 1540-1854.* Topeka: Kansas State Historical Society, 1972.

Berckefeldt, Denis. *Kansas County Records.* [Kansas?]: A Pathfinders Publication, [19–?].

Blackmar, Frank Wilson. *Kansas: A Cyclopedia of State History, Embracing Events, Institutions, Industries, Counties, Cities, Towns, Prominent Persons, Etc... With a Supplementary Volume Devoted to Selected Personal History and Reminiscence..* 3 vols. in 4. Chicago: Standard Pub. Co., 1912.

Bright, John D., ed. *Kansas: The First Century.* 4 vols. New York: Lewis Historical Publishing Co., 1956.

Burton, Arthur T. *Black, Buckskin and Blue: African American Scouts and Soldiers on the Western Frontier.* Austin, Texas: Eaton Press, 1999.

Connelley, William Elsey. *A Standard History of Kansas and Kansans.* 5 vols. Chicago: Lewis Pub. Co., 1918.

Correll, Charles M. *A Century of Congregationalism in Kansas, 1854-1954.* Topeka, Kansas: The Kansas Congregational and Christian Conference, c1953 (Wichita, Kansas: McCormick-Armstrong Co.)

Craik, Elmer LeRoy. *A History of The Church of the Brethren in Kansas.* Mc Pherson, Kansas: E. Craik, 1972.

Curtis, Mary B. "Bibliography of Kansas: The Formative Years." *Magazine of Bibliographies* 1 (2 December 1972).

DeZurko, Edward R. *Early Kansas Churches.* Manhattan, Kansas: Kansas State College, 1949.

Dick, Everett. *The Sod House Frontier, 1854-1890: A Social History of the Northern Plains From the Creation of Kansas & Nebraska to the Admission of the Dakotas.* Lincoln, Neb.: University of Nebraska, 1979, 1954.

Fitzgerald, Mary Paul. *Beacon On The Plains.* Leavenworth, Kansas: Saint Mary College, c1939.

Gordon, Jacob U. *Narratives of African Americans in Kansas, 1870-1992: Beyond the Exodus Movement.* Lewiston, N.Y.: E. Mellen Press, 1993.

Graves, William Whites. *The First Protestant Osage Missions, 1820-1837.* Oswego, Kansas: Carpenter Press, 1949.

Guide to Public Vital Statistics Records in Kansas. Topeka: Historical Records Survey, 1942.

Harper, Katherine C. *List Of Books and Manuscripts in Kansas State DAR Library.* Mullinville, Ks.: Dodge City Chapter, DAR, 1972.

Haury, David A. *Guide to the Microfilm Collections of the Kansas State Historical Society.* Topeka, Kansas: Kansas State Historical Society, 1991.

Hinshaw, William Wade. *The William Wade Hinshaw Index to Kansas Quaker Meeting Records.* 4 vols. Kokomo, Ind.: Selby Pub. & Printing, 1991.

Historical and Descriptive Review of Kansas: With Special Reference to the Advantages of the Towns Named in the Index, Their Prosperous Institutions and Progressive Men. 3 vols. Topeka: Jno. Lethem, 1890-1891.

Hodge, Robert A. *Kansas Orphan Train Riders – These We Know.* Emporia, Kansas: R.A. Hodge, [1996?].

Johnson, Samuel A. *The Battle Cry of Freedom: The New England Emigration Aid Company in the Kansas Crusade.* Westport, Conn.: Greenwood Press, 1977.

Kansas Pioneers. Topeka, Kansas: Topeka Genealogical Society, 1976.

Kansas Research Outline. Series US-States, no 17. Salt Lake City: Family History Library, 1988.

Kansas State Historical Society (Topeka, Kansas). *History of Kansas Newspapers: A History of the Newspapers and Magazines Published in Kansas from the Organization of Kansas Territory, 1854, to January 1, 1916 Together With Brief Statistical Information of the Counties, Cities and Towns of the State.* Topeka, Kansas: Kansas State Printing Plant, 1916.

Miner, H. Craig. *West of Wichita: Settling the High Plains of Kansas, 1865-1890.* Lawrence: University Press of Kansas, 1986.

Pioneer Women: Voices From the Kansas Frontier. New York: Simon and Schuster, 1981.

Portrait and Biographical Record of Southeastern Kansas: Containing Biographical Sketches of Prominent and Representative Citizens of the Counties, Together With Biographies and Portraits of all The Presidents of the United States and the Governors of the State of Kansas. Chicago: Biographical Pub. Co., 1894.

Roenigk, Adolph. *Pioneer History of Kansas.* Lincoln, Kansas: A. Roenigk (Denver: The Great Western Pub. Co.), 1933.

Rooney, Doris Dockstader, et al. *Kansas Genealogical Society Six-Generation Ancestor Tables.* Dodge City, Kansas: Kansas Genealogical Society, 1976.

Scheck, Floyd. *Genealogy Records of Families of Germans From Russia.* (Salt Lake City: Filmed by the Genealogical Society of Utah, 1992). 7 microfilm.

Shortridge, James R. *Peopling the Plains: Who Settled Where in Frontier Kansas.* Lawrence, Kansas: University Press of Kansas, 1995.

Smith, Patricia D. *Kansas Biographical Index: Statewide and Regional Histories.* Garden City, Kansas: Patricia D. Smith, 1994.

Sweet, William Henry. *A History of Methodism in Northwest Kansas.* [Kan.?]: Kansas Wesleyan University, 1920.

Taylor, Blanche Mercer. *Plenteous Harvest: The Episcopal Church in Kansas, 1837-1972.* [Kansas?]: The Diocese, c1973 (Topeka, Kansas: Printed by Josten's/American Yearbook Co.).

The Forgotten Settlers of Kansas. Vols. 1-17. Topeka: Kansas Council of Genealogical Societies, 1983.

The United States Biographical Dictionary: Kansas. Chicago and Kansas City: S. Lewis & Co., 1879.

Tuttle, Charles Richard. *A New Centennial History of the State of Kansas: Being a Full and Complete Civil, Political and Military History of the State, From Its Earliest Settlement to the Present Time.* Madison, Wis.: Inter-state Book Co., 1876.

United States. Department of State. *Territorial Papers of Kansas, 1854-1861.* Microfilm of originals in the National Archives in Washington, D.C., Washington, D.C.: The National Archives, 1953. 2 microfilm.

Unrau, William E. *The Kansas Indians, A History of the Wind People, 1673-1873.* Norman, Okla.: University of Oklahoma Press, 1971.

Atlases, Maps and Gazetteers

Baughman, Robert W. *Kansas in Maps.* Topeka: Kansas State Historical Society, 1961.

Baughman, Robert W. *Kansas Post Offices, May 29, 1828-Aug. 3, 1961.* Topeka: Kansas Postal History Society, 1961.

Gannett, Henry A. *A Gazetteer of Kansas.* Washington, D.C.: U.S. Government Printing Office, 1898.

Gill, Helen G. *The Establishment of Counties in Kansas, 1855-1903.* Kansas historical Society Collections 8. n.p., 1904.

Graden, Debra. *Kansas Towns & Cities as of 1912: Includes a List of Extinct Towns [and a] Bonus Index of Biographies from Volumes 1, 2 & 3 Extracted from "Kansas".* Leavenworth, Kansas: Grey Ink, c1997.

Kansas Atlas and Gazetteer. Freeport, Maine: DeLorme Mapping Co., 1997.

McCoy, Sondra Van Meter. *1001 Kansas Place Names.* Lawrence, Kansas: University Press of Kansas, 1989.

Official State Atlas of Kansas, Compiled from Government Surveys, County Records and Personal Investigations. LH Leverts and Co. (1887). Reprint by Kansas Council of Genealogical Societies, 1982.

Rydjord, John. *Kansas Place-Names.* Norman, OK: University of Oklahoma Press, 1972.

Socolofsky, Homer E., and Huber Self. *Historical Atlas of Kansas.* Norman, OK: University of Oklahoma Press, 1972.

Some Lost Towns of Kansas: and Extinct Geographical Locations. n.p.: Reprint of Kansas Historical Collections, vol. 12.

Census Records

Available Census Records and Census Substitutes

Federal Census 1860, 1870, 1880, 1900, 1910, 1920, 1930.

Federal Mortality Schedules 1860, 1870, 1880.

State/Territorial Census 1855, 1856, 1857, 1858, 1859, 1865, 1875, 1885, 1895, 1905, 1915, 1925.

Dollarhide, William. *The Census Book: A Genealogist's Guide to Federal Census Facts, Schedules and Indexes.* Bountiful, UT: Heritage Quest, 1999.

Kemp, Thomas Jay. *The American Census Handbook.* Wilmington, DE: Scholarly Resources, Inc., 2001.

Lainhart, Ann S. *State Census Records.* Baltimore: Genealogical Publishing Co., Inc., 1992.

Szucs, Loretto Dennis, and Matthew Wright. *Finding Answers in U.S. Census Records.* Ancestry Publishing, 2001

Thorndale, William, and William Dollarhide. *Map Guide to the U.S. Federal Censuses, 1790-1920.* Baltimore: Genealogical Publishing Co., 1987.

United States. Bureau of Internal Revenue. *Internal Revenue Lists For Kansas, 1862-1866.* Microfilm of originals in the National Archives in Washington, D.C.. Washington, D.C.: National Archives. Central Plains Region, 1985. 3 microfilm.

Court Records, Probate and Wills

Note: Court, probate and will records are found in the individual county court houses. Refer to the county information pages for further information.

Berckefeldt, Denis. *Kansas County Records.* [Kansas?]: A Pathfinders Publication, [19–?].

United States. District Court (Kansas). *Slave Compensation Records, 1866-1867.* Microfilm of originals in the National Archives Branch in Kansas City, Missouri. (Salt Lake City: Filmed by the Genealogical Society of Utah, 1991)

Emigration, Immigration, Migration and Naturalization

Carman, J. Neale. *Foreign-Language Units of Kansas.* Lawrence, Kansas: University of Kansas Press, 1962.

Robertson, Clara H. *Kansas Territorial Settlers of 1860 Who Were Born in Tennessee, Virginia, North Carolina and South Carolina.* Baltimore: Genealogical Publishing Co., 1976.

United States. District Court (Kansas). *Index to Naturalizations, 1856-1897; Declaration Of Intention 1862-1897.* Microfilm of originals in the National Archives Branch in Kansas City, Missouri. (Salt Lake City: Filmed by the Genealogical Society of Utah, 1990). 2 microfilm.

United States. District Court (Kansas: First Division). *Declarations of Intention, 1908-1942; Naturalizations, 1865-1984.* Microfilm of originals in the National Archives Branch in Kansas City, Missouri. (Salt Lake City: Filmed by the Genealogical Society of Utah, 1990). 13 microfilm.

United States. District Court (Kansas: Second Division). *Declarations of Intention, 1909-1947; Naturalizations, 1909-1979.* Microfilm of originals in the National Archives Branch in Kansas City, Missouri. (Salt Lake City: Filmed by the Genealogical Society of Utah, 1990). 14 microfilm.

United States. District Court (Kansas: Third Division). *Declarations of Intention, 1915-1964; Naturalizations, 1916-1966.* Microfilm of originals in the National Archives Branch in Kansas City, Missouri. (Salt Lake City: Filmed by the Genealogical Society of Utah, 1990). 2 microfilm.

Land and Property

Adams, F. G. *Homestead Guide of Kansas and Nebraska.* Waterville, Kansas: 1873.

Hone, Wade E. *Land and Property Research in the United States.* Salt Lake City: Ancestry Incorporated, 1997.

United States. General Land Office. *Field Notes From Selected General Land Office Township Surveys.* [Washington, D.C.: The National Archives, 1979]. 281 microfilm.

Military

Decker, Eugene Donald. *A Selected, Annotated Bibliography of Sources in the Kansas State Historical Society Pertaining to Kansas in the Civil War.* Emporia, Kansas: State Teacher's College. 1961.

Kansas Adjutant General's Office. *Report of the Adjutant General, C. K. Holliday, December 31, 1864.* Leavenworth, KS: Adjutant General. 1865.

Kansas Adjutant General's Office. *Report of the Adjutant General, T. J. Anderson, of the State of Kansas in 1861-1865.* 2 Vols. Topeka, Kansas: adjutant general, 1967-1870.

Kansas. Adjutant General's Office. *Kansas Troops in the Volunteer Service of the United States in the Spanish and Philippine Wars, Mustered in Under the First and Second Calls of the President of the United States: May 9, 1898-October 28, 1899.* (Washington, D.C.: Filmed by the Library of Congress, Photoduplication Service, 1989).

Loosbrock, Richard J. *The History of the Kansas Department of the American Legion.* Topeka, [Kan.]: Kansas Dept. of the American Legion, 1968.

Ostertag, John A.. *Fighting Twentieth, History and Official Souvenir: An Account of the Kansas Volunteers in the Spanish American War, 1898-1899.* [St. Joseph, Mo.?: J.A. Ostertag?], 1989.

Pompey, Sherman Lee. *An Honor Roll of Kansas Civil War Veterans.* Kingsburg, CA: Pacific Specialists, 1972.

United States. Adjutant General's Office. *Index to Compiled Service Records of Volunteer Union Soldiers Who Served in Organizations from the State of Kansas.* Washington, DC: The National Archives, 1964.

United States. Bureau of Indian Affairs. Potawatomi Agency. *Records Of Indians In World War I.* Kansas City, Mo.: Federal Archives and Records Center, 1977.

United States. Selective Service System. *Kansas, World War I Selective Service System Draft Registration Cards, 1917-1918.* National Archives Microfilm Publications, M1509. Washington, DC: National Archives, 1987-1988.

Vital and Cemetery Records

Cemetery Records in Southeastern Kansas and Southwestern Missouri. Microfilm. Salt Lake City: Genealogical Society of Utah, 1984.

Cemetery Records of Kansas (Compiled by Members of the Kansas Mission). 18 Vols. Typescript. Salt Lake City: Genealogical Society of Utah, 1956-.

Ford, Don L. *Abandoned and Semi-Active Cemeteries of Kansas. 3 Vols.* Decorah, IA: Anundsen Publishing, 1983-1985.

Historical Records Survey (Kansas). *Guide To Public Vital Statistics Records In Kansas.* Topeka, Kansas: The Survey, 1942.

Jackson, Ronald Vern. *Kansas 1860 Mortality Schedule.* Bountiful, Utah: Accelerated Indexing Systems, 1980.

Jackson, Ronald Vern. *Mortality Schedule, Kansas 1870.* Bountiful, Utah: Accelerated Indexing Systems, 1979.

Jackson, Ronald Vern. *Mortality Schedule, Kansas 1880.* Bountiful, Utah: Accelerated Indexing Systems, 1979.

Ostertag, John A.. *Births, Marriages, Deaths And Other News Items And Events.* 11 vols. St. Joseph, Mo.: J.A. Ostertag, 1989-1999.

County Website	Map Index	Date Created	Parent County or Territory From Which Organized Address/Details
Allen www.allencounty.org/	B9	30 Aug 1855	**Original county** Allen County; 1 N Washington St; Iola, KS 66749-2841; Ph. 316.365.7491 Details: (Clk Dis Ct has m rec from 1856, div, pro & ct from 1860 & nat rec 1871-1929; Reg of Deeds has land & mil rec from 1860)
Anderson skyways.lib.ks.us/genweb/anderson/ index.html	B8	30 Aug 1855	**Original county** Anderson County; 100 E 4th Ave; Garnett, KS 66032; Ph. 913.448.6841 Details: (Clk Dis Ct has m, div, pro & ct rec from 1857; Co Appraiser has land rec from 1900)
Arapahoe		1855	**Original county** Details: (Disorganized) Became Colorado Terr. in 1861
Atchison skyways.lib.ks.us/genweb/atchison/ index.html	C4	30 Aug 1855	**Original county** Atchison County; 423 N 5th St; Atchison, KS 66002; Ph. 758.367.1653 Details: (Co Clk has b rec 1891-1906 & d rec 1891-1911; City Clk has b & d rec from 1911; Clk Dis Ct has div rec; Mag Ct has pro rec; Reg of Deeds has land rec)
Barber skyways.lib.ks.us/genweb/barber/ index.html	J11	26 Feb 1867	**Marion** Barber County; 120 E Washington Ave; Medicine Lodge, KS 67104-1421; Ph. 316.886.3961 Details: (Pro Ct has pro rec; Reg of Deeds has land rec; Co Clk has b, m & d rec)
Barton www.bartonks.com/	J7	26 Feb 1867	**Marion** Barton County; 1400 Main St; PO Box 1089; Great Bend, KS 67530-1089; Ph. 316.793.1870 Details: (Co Clk has b & d rec 1892-1911 & cem rec; Reg of Deeds has land, school & mil dis rec; Clk Dis Ct has m, pro & nat rec)
Billings		7 Feb 1859	**Original county** Details: (see Norton) Org. as Oro Co. Name changed to Norton 26 Feb 1867. Name changed to Billings 6 Mar 1873. Name changed back to Norton 19 Feb 1874.
Bourbon www.bourboncountyks.org/	B8	30 Aug 1855	**Original county** Bourbon County; 210 S National Ave; Fort Scott, KS 66701-1328; Ph. 316.223.3800 Details: (Clk Ct has div rec from 1870; Pro Judge has m & pro rec from 1870 & ct rec from 1963)
Breckenridge		17 Feb 1857	**Original county** Details: (see Lyon) Name changed to Lyon 5 Feb 1862
Brown skyways.lib.ks.us/genweb/butler/ index.html	C4	30 Aug 1855	**Original county** Brown County; 601 Oregon St; Hiawatha, KS 66434; Ph. 785.742.2581 Details: (Clk Dis Ct has div, pro & ct rec from 1800's & m rec; Reg of Deeds has land rec from 1857)
Buffalo		1873	**Unorganized Territory** Details: (see Gray, old) Became Gray Co 1881, disappeared 1883 to Gray & Finney Cos
Butler www.bucoks.com/	F9	30 Aug 1855	**Original county** Butler County; 200 W Central Ave; El Dorado, KS 67042; Ph. 316.322.4232 Details: (Co Clk has b & d rec 1887-1912 & land rec from 1887; Clk Dis Ct has m, div, pro & ct rec)
Calhoun		30 Aug 1855	**Original county** Details: (see Jackson) Name changed to Jackson 11 Feb 1859
Chase skyways.lib.ks.us/genweb/chase/index.html	E8	11 Feb 1859	**Butler, Wise** Chase County; Courthouse Sq; Cottonwood Falls, KS 66845; Ph. 316.273.6423 Details: (Co Clk has b rec 1886-1911 & d rec 1886-1910; Reg of Deeds has land rec; Pro Judge has pro rec)
Chautauqua skyways.lib.ks.us/genweb/chautauq/ index.html	E11	3 Mar 1875	**Howard** Chautauqua County; 215 N Chautauqua; Sedan, KS 67361; Ph. 316.725.3282 Details: (Reg of Deeds has d & bur rec from 1871, land rec from 1870 & mil rec from 1940; Pro Judge has m & pro rec; Clk Dis Ct has div & ct rec)

County Website	Map Index	Date Created	Parent County or Territory From Which Organized Address/Details
Cherokee skyways.lib.ks.us/genweb/cherokee/ index.html	B10	30 Aug 1855	**Unorganized Territory** Cherokee County; 300 E Maple; Columbus, KS 66725; Ph. 316.429.2159 Details: (Formerly McGee Co. Name changed to Cherokee 18 Feb 1860) (Reg of Deeds has land rec from 1866, Pro Ct has pro rec from 1870; Co Clk has b, m & d rec)
Cheyenne skyways.lib.ks.us/genweb/cheyenne/ index.html	Q3	6 Mar 1873	**Unorganized Territory** Cheyenne County; PO Box 985; St. Francis, KS 67756-0646; Ph. 785.332.2401 Details: (Clk Dis Ct has m rec from 1886, div, ct & pro rec from 1892; Reg of Deeds has land rec from mid-1800's & mil dis rec from 1919)
Clark skyways.lib.ks.us/genweb/clark/index.html	M10	7 Mar 1885	**Ford** Clark County; 913 Highland St; Ashland, KS 67831; Ph. 316.635.2753 Details: (Co Clk has b rec 1904-1910; City Clk has b & bur rec from 1910; Pro Judge has m & pro rec; Clk Dis Ct has div & ct rec; Reg of Deeds has land rec)
Clay skyways.lib.ks.us/genweb/clay/index.html	G5	20 Feb 1857	**Original county** Clay County; 712 5th St; PO Box 98; Clay Center, KS 67432-0098; Ph. 785.632.2552 Details: (Co Clk has b, m & d rec 1885-1911; Clk Dis Ct has div, pro & ct rec; Reg of Deeds has land rec)
Cloud www.dustdevil.com/towns/ concordia/courthouse/	H5	27 Feb 1860	**Original county** Cloud County; 811 Washington St; Concordia, KS 66901-3415; Ph. 785.243.4319 Details: (Formerly Shirley Co. Name changed to Cloud 26 Feb 1867) (Co Clk has b, m & d rec 1885-1910; Clk Dis Ct has div rec; Pro Judge has pro & ct rec; Reg of Deeds has land rec)
Coffey www.coffeycountyks.org/	C8	30 Aug 1855	**Original county** Coffey County; 6th & Neosho; Burlington, KS 66839; Ph. 316.364.2191 Details: (Clk Dis Ct has b & d rec 1892-1910, m rec from 1855, div, pro & ct rec from 1857; Reg of Deeds has land rec from 1857; Hist Soc & Pub Lib have cem books)
Comanche skyways.lib.ks.us/genweb/comanche/ index.html	L11	26 Feb 1867	**Marion** Comanche County; 201 S New York; PO Box 397; Coldwater, KS 67029-0397; Ph. 316.582.2361 Details: (Co Clk has b & d rec 1891-1911; Mag Judge has m rec 1891-1912, pro & ct rec; Clk Dis Ct has div rec; Reg of Deeds has land rec)
Cowley www.cowleycounty.org/	F10	26 Feb 1867	**Butler** Cowley County; 311 E 9th Ave; Winfield, KS 67156; Ph. 316.221.4066 Details: (City Clk has b rec; Pro Ct has m, div & pro rec from 1870 & d rec; Clk Dis Ct has ct rec; Appraisers Office has land rec)
Crawford www.crawfordcountykansas.org/	B9	13 Feb 1867	**Bourbon, Cherokee** Crawford County; PO Box 249; Girard, KS 66743-0249; Ph. 316.724.6115 Details: (Co Clk has b & d rec 1886-1911 & bur rec 1860's-1976; Clk Dis Ct has m, div, pro, ct & nat rec; Reg of Deeds has land rec from 1869 & mil rec)
Davis		30 Aug 1855	**Original county** Details: (see Geary) Name changed to Geary 28 Feb 1889
Decatur skyways.lib.ks.us/genweb/decatur/ index.html	N4	6 Mar 1873	**Unorganized Territory** Decatur County; 120 E Hall; PO Box 89; Oberlin, KS 67749; Ph. 785.475.8102 Details: (Clk Dis Ct has b, m & d rec 1885-1913, div & ct rec from 1881, pro rec from 1891 & nat rec from 1880; Reg of Deeds has land rec from 1878 & mil dis rec from 1862)
Dickinson www.dkcoks.com/	G6	20 Feb 1857	**Davis, Unorganized Territory** Dickinson County; 109 E 1st St; Abilene, KS 67410-0248; Ph. 785.263.3774 Details: (Co Clk has incomplete b rec from 1892, m & d rec from 1892)
Doniphan skyways.lib.ks.us/genweb/doniphan/ index.html	B4	30 Aug 1855	**Original county** Doniphan County; Main St; Troy, KS 66087; Ph. 785.985.3513 Details: (Clk Dis Ct has b & d rec 1898-1910, m, div, pro & ct rec from 1856; Reg of Deeds has land rec from 1858; A yearly co cen is taken)
Dorn		30 Aug 1855	**Original county** Details: (see Neosho) Name changed to Neosho 3 Jun 1861

County Website	Map Index	Date Created	Parent County or Territory From Which Organized Address/Details
Douglas www.douglas-county.com/	**C6**	**30 Aug 1855**	**Original county** Douglas County; 111 E 11th; Lawrence, KS 66044; Ph. 785.841.7700 Details: (Clk Dis Ct has pro & ct rec from 1863 & nat rec 1867-1953; Reg of Deeds has land rec; Spencer Research Lib has m rec 1863-1912)
Edwards skyways.lib.ks.us/genweb/edwards/ index.html	**L9**	**7 Mar 1874**	**Kiowa** Edwards County; 312 Massachusetts Ave; Kinsley, KS 67547-1099; Ph. 316.659.3121 Details: (Pro Judge has m, div, pro & ct rec from 1874; Reg of Deeds has land rec from 1874)
Elk skyways.lib.ks.us/genweb/elk/index.html	**E10**	**3 Mar 1875**	**Howard** Elk County; 127 N Pine St; Howard, KS 67349; Ph. 316.374.2490 Details: (Courthouse burned in 1906) (Clk Dis Ct has b & d rec 1885-1911, m & pro rec from 1875, div & ct rec from 1906 & land rec from 1871)
Ellis www.ellisco.org/	**L6**	**26 Feb 1867**	**Unorganized Territory** Ellis County; 1204 Fort St; Hays, KS 67601; Ph. 785.628.8410 Details: (Co Clk has b, m & d rec 1886-1911; Clk Dis Ct has div, pro, ct & nat rec; Reg of Deeds has land, mil dis & school rec)
Ellsworth skyways.lib.ks.us/genweb/ellswort/ index.html	**I7**	**26 Feb 1867**	**Marion, Unorganized Territory** Ellsworth County; 210 N Kansas Ave; PO Box 396; Ellsworth, KS 67439; Ph. 785.472.3022 Details: (Pro Judge has m & pro rec; City Clk has d & bur rec; Clk Dis Ct has div rec; Co Ct has ct rec; Reg of Deeds has land rec)
Finney www.finneycounty.org/	**O8**	**6 Mar 1873**	**Marion** Finney County; 3119 N 9th St; PO Box M; Garden City, KS 67846-0450; Ph. 316.272.3051 Details: (Formerly Sequoyah Co. Name changed to Finney 21 Feb 1883) (Pro Judge has m & pro rec from 1885; Clk Dis Ct has div & ct rec from 1885)
Foote		**1873**	**Marion** Details: (see Gray, old) Became Gray Co 1881 & disappeared 1883
Ford www.fordcounty.net/	**M9**	**6 Mar 1873**	**Unorganized Territory, Marion** Ford County; 100 Gunsmoke; Dodge City, KS 67801; Ph. 316.277.3184 Details: (City Clk has b, d & bur rec; Pro Judge has m, pro & ct rec; Clk Dis Ct has div rec; Co Clk has land rec)
Franklin* www.co.franklin.ks.us/	**B7**	**30 Aug 1855**	**Original county** Franklin County; 315 S Main; Ottawa, KS 66067; Ph. 785.242.1471 Details: (Clk Dis Ct has m, div, pro & ct rec; Reg of Deeds has land & mil rec)
Garfield		**5 Mar 1887**	**Finney, Hodgeman** Details: (see Finney) Annexed to Finney, 1893
Geary skyways.lib.ks.us/genweb/geary/index.html	**F6**	**30 Aug 1855**	**Original county** Geary County; 8th & Franklin; Junction City, KS 66441; Ph. 785.238.3912 Details: (Formerly Davis Co. Name changed to Geary 28 Feb 1889) (Pro Ct has m & pro rec from 1860; Clk Dis Ct has div rec from 1860; Co Ct has ct rec from 1937; Reg of Deeds has land rec from 1858)
Godfrey		**30 Aug 1855**	**Original county** Details: (see Seward, old) Name changed to Seward 3 Jun 1861
Gove* skyways.lib.ks.us/genweb/gove/index.html	**N6**	**2 Mar 1868**	**Unorganized Territory** Gove County; 520 Washington St; PO Box 128; Gove, KS 67736-0128; Ph. 785.938.2300 Details: (Reg of Deeds has land rec; Pro Ct has pro rec)
Graham skyways.lib.ks.us/genweb/graham/ index.html	**M5**	**26 Feb 1867**	**Unorganized Territory** Graham County; 410 N Pomeroy; Hill City, KS 67642-1645; Ph. 785.674.5433 Details: (Pro Judge has m & pro rec; Clk Dis Ct has div & ct rec; Reg of Deeds has land rec)

County Website	Map Index	Date Created	Parent County or Territory From Which Organized Address/Details
Grant www.grantcoks.org/	P10	6 Mar 1873	**Unorganized Territory** Grant County; 108 S Glenn; Ulysses, KS 67880-2551; Ph. 316.356.1335 Details: (Pro Judge has m rec; Clk Dis Ct has div, pro & ct rec; Reg of Deeds has land rec; City Clk has cem rec; local census taken every year)
Gray* skyways.lib.ks.us/genweb/gray/index.html	N9	5 Mar 1887	**Finney, Ford** Gray County; PO Box 487; Cimarron, KS 67835-0487; Ph. 316.855.3618 Details: (Pro Judge has m rec from 1887 & pro rec from 1885; Clk Dis Ct has div rec from 1887; Reg of Deeds has land rec from 1887; Co Clk has tax roll cen from 1889 & school rec)
Gray, old		1881	**Foote, Buffalo** Details: (Disappeared in 1883; Reorg. 5 Mar 1887)
Greeley skyways.lib.ks.us/genweb/greeley/ index.html	Q7	6 Mar 1873	**Unorganized Territory** Greeley County; 208 Harper St; PO Box 277; Tribune, KS 67879-0277; Ph. 316.376.4256 Details: (City Clk has b rec; Pro Judge has m & pro rec; Co Ct has ct rec; Reg of Deeds has land rec)
Greenwood* skyways.lib.ks.us/genweb/greenwoo/ index.html	E9	30 Aug 1855	**Original county** Greenwood County; 311 N Main; PO Box 268; Eureka, KS 67045-1321; Ph. 316.583.7421 Details: (Co Clk has b rec 1885-1947, m rec 1885-1911 & d rec 1885-1965; Clk Dis Ct has div, pro & ct rec; Reg of Deeds has land & mil rec)
Hamilton skyways.lib.ks.us/genweb/hamilton/ index.html	Q9	6 Mar 1873	**Unorganized Territory** Hamilton County; 219 N Main St; Syracuse, KS 67878; Ph. 316.384.5629 Details: (Pro Judge has m & pro rec from 1886; City Clk has d & bur rec; Clk Dis Ct has div rec; Co Clk has land rec from 1884)
Harper www.harpercounty.org/	I11	26 Feb 1867	**Marion** Harper County; 200 N Jennings Ave; Anthony, KS 67003; Ph. 316.842.5555 Details: (Pro Judge has m & pro rec; Clk Dis Ct has div & ct rec; Reg of Deeds has land rec)
Harvey skyways.lib.ks.us/genweb/harvey/ index.html	H8	29 Feb 1872	**McPherson, Sedgwick, Marion** Harvey County; 800 N Main; Newton, KS 67114; Ph. 316.284.6840 Details: (Pro Ct has m rec from 1800's; Clk Dis Ct has div, pro & ct rec from 1872; Reg of Deeds has land rec from 1800's)
Haskell www.haskellcounty.org/	O10	5 Mar 1887	**Finney** Haskell County; PO Box 518; Sublette, KS 67877-0518; Ph. 316.675.2263 Details: (Dept of Legal Stat has b & d rec; Pro Judge has m & pro rec; Clk Dis Ct has div rec)
Hodgeman skyways.lib.ks.us/genweb/hodgeman/ index.html	M8	26 Feb 1867	**Marion** Hodgeman County; 500 Main St; PO Box 247; Jetmore, KS 67854-0247; Ph. 316.357.6421 Details: (City Clk has b, d & bur rec from 1911; Pro Judge has m & pro rec from 1887; Clk Dis Ct has div & ct rec from 1887; Reg of Deeds has land rec from 1879)
Howard		30 Aug 1855	**Original county** Howard County; KS Details: (see Elk & Chautauqua) (Org. as Godfrey Co. Name changed to Seward, old, 3 Jun 1861. Name changed to Howard 26 Feb 1867. Howard divided to form Elk & Chautauqua Cos 11 Mar 1875)
Hunter		30 Aug 1855	**Original county** Details: (see Butler) Name changed to Butler 1861
Jackson skyways.lib.ks.us/genweb/jackson/ index.html	D5	30 Aug 1855	**Original county** Jackson County; 400 New York Ave; Holton, KS 66436; Ph. 785.364.2891 Details: (Formerly Calhoun Co. Name changed to Jackson 11 Feb 1859) (Co Clk has b & d rec 1903-1911; Pro Judge has m rec from 1867, pro rec from 1857 & ct rec from 1900; Clk Dis Ct has div rec; Reg of Deeds has land rec from 1858)

County Website	Map Index	Date Created	Parent County or Territory From Which Organized Address/Details
Jefferson skyways.lib.ks.us/genweb/jefferso/ index.html	C5	30 Aug 1855	**Original county** Jefferson County; 300 W Jefferson St; PO Box 321; Oskaloosa, KS 66066-0321; Ph. 785.863.2272 Details: (Pro Judge has m & pro rec; Clk Dis Ct has div rec; Reg of Deeds has land rec)
Jewell* skyways.lib.ks.us/genweb/jewell/ index.html	I4	26 Feb 1867	**Unorganized Territory** Jewell County; 307 N Commercial; Mankato, KS 66956-2025; Ph. 785.378.3121 Details: (Clk Dis Ct has m, pro, div & ct rec; Reg of Deeds has b, m & d rec 1886-1894, cem rec from 1860's, land rec from 1871, mil rec from 1889, yearly census assessment rolls 1871-1908 & school rec from 1884)
Johnson* www.jocoks.com/	A6	30 Aug 1855	**Original county** Johnson County; 111 S Cherry; Olathe, KS 66061; Ph. 913.764.8484 ext. 5335 Details: (Clk Dis Ct has div & ct rec from 1861; Pro Ct has m & pro rec)
Kansas		1873	**Unorganized Territory** Details: (see Morton) Disappeared 1883. Reorganized 18 Feb 1886 as Morton Co.
Kearny skyways.lib.ks.us/genweb/kearny/ index.html	P8	6 Mar 1873	**Unorganized Territory** Kearny County; 305 N Main St; Lakin, KS 67860; Ph. 316.355.6422 Details: (Co Clk has b, m & d rec 1900-1910; Clk Dis Ct has div & ct rec from 1894 & pro rec from 1895; Reg of Deeds has land rec from 1894; Co Clk & Co Hist Soc have newsprs; Co Appraiser has local cen from 1913)
Kingman skyways.lib.ks.us/genweb/kingman/ index.html	I10	29 Feb 1872	**Reno** Kingman County; 130 N Spruce St; Kingman, KS 67068; Ph. 316.532.2521 Details: (Co Clk has d rec & local census; Clk Dis Ct has m, div, pro & ct rec; Co Appraiser has land rec)
Kiowa skyways.lib.ks.us/genweb/kiowa/ index.html	L10	10 Feb 1886	**Comanche, Edwards** Kiowa County; 211 E Florida; Greensburg, KS 67054; Ph. 316.723.3366 Details: (Clk Dis Ct has m, pro & nat rec; Reg of Deeds has land rec from 1886 & mil dis rec)
Kiowa, old		26 Feb 1867	**Marion** Details: (Kiowa Co absorbed by Edwards & Comanche Cos in 1875. Kiowa recreated 10 Feb 1886, being formed from parts of Edwards & Comanche)
Labette www.labettecounty.com/	C11	7 Feb 1867	**Neosho** Labette County; 501 Merchant St; PO Box 387; Oswego, KS 67356; Ph. 316.795.2138 Details: (Co Clk has b rec 1885-1896 & d rec 1885-1889; Pro Judge has m & pro rec from 1870; Clk Dis Ct has div & ct rec from 1870; Reg of Deeds has land rec from 1875; A yearly co cen taken 1915-1979)
Lane trails.net/laneco/	N7	6 Mar 1873	**Unorganized Territory** Lane County; 144 S Ln; PO Box 788; Dighton, KS 67839; Ph. 316.397.5552 Details: (Mag Ct has m, div, pro & ct rec; Reg of Deeds has land rec; City of Dighton has bur rec)
Leavenworth www.leavenworthcounty.org/	B5	30 Aug 1855	**Original county** Leavenworth County; 601 S Third St Ste 3051; Leavenworth, KS 66048-2781; Ph. 913.684.0700 Details: (Pro Judge has m & pro rec from 1855; Reg of Deeds has land rec; Clk Dis Ct has ct & nat rec from 1855)
Lincoln skyways.lib.ks.us/genweb/lincoln/ index.html	I6	26 Feb 1867	**Unorganized Territory** Lincoln County; 216 E Lincoln; Lincoln, KS 67455-2097; Ph. 785.524.4757 Details: (Co Clk has some cem, land & ct rec & some local cen rec from 1913; Clk Dis Ct has m, div, pro, ct & nat rec from 1870; Reg of Deeds has land rec from 1870 & mil dis rec from 1880)
Linn skyways.lib.ks.us/genweb/linn/index.html	B8	30 Aug 1855	**Original county** Linn County; PO Box B; Mound City, KS 66056-0601; Ph. 913.795.2668 Details: (Clk Dis Ct has pro & ct rec from 1855; Reg of Deeds has land rec & mil rec from 1900; Co Lib/Museum has b, m & d rec from 1855, div rec, cem rec from 1910, mil rec 1861-1865 & newspapers from 1864)

County Website	Map Index	Date Created	Parent County or Territory From Which Organized Address/Details
Logan skyways.lib.ks.us/genweb/logan/index.html	P6	4 Mar 1881	**Wallace** Logan County; 710 W 2nd; Oakley, KS 67748; Ph. 785.672.3654 Details: (Formerly St. John Co. Name changed to Logan 24 Feb 1887) (City Clk has b, d & bur rec; Pro Judge has m & pro rec; Clk Dis Ct has div & ct rec; Co Clk has land rec from 1885)
Lykins		30 Aug 1855	**Original county** Details: (see Miami) Name changed to Miami 3 June 1861
Lyon www.lyoncounty.org/	D8	17 Feb 1857	**Original county** Lyon County; 402 Commercial; Emporia, KS 66801-4000; Ph. 316.342.4950 Details: (Formerly Breckenridge Co. Name changed to Lyon 5 Feb 1862) (Clk Dis Ct has m rec from 1861, div rec from 1860, pro rec from 1859 & ct rec from 1858; Reg of Deeds has land rec from 1856; City Clk has b & d rec)
Madison		1855	**Original county** Details: Divided to Greenwood & Lyon Cos, 1862
Marion skyways.lib.ks.us/genweb/marion/ index.html	G8	1855	**Original county** Marion County; 204 S 4th St; PO Box 219; Marion, KS 66861; Ph. 316.382.2185 Details: (Co Clk has b & d rec 1885-1911; Clk Dis Ct has m rec from 1800's, div, pro & ct rec; Reg of Deeds has school rec 1873-1964 & land rec)
Marshall skyways.lib.ks.us/genweb/marshall/ index.html	E4	30 Aug 1855	**Original county** Marshall County; 1201 Broadway; Marysville, KS 66508-1844; Ph. 785.562.5361 Details: (Co Clk has b rec 1885-1911 & d rec 1889-1911; Clk Dis Ct has m, div, pro & ct rec; Reg of Deeds has land rec)
McGee		30 Aug 1855	**Unorganized Territory** Details: (see Cherokee) Name changed to Cherokee 18 Feb 1860
McPherson skyways.lib.ks.us/genweb/mcpherso/ index.html	H7	26 Feb 1867	**Marion** McPherson County; 117 N Maple St; PO Box 425; McPherson, KS 67460; Ph. 316.241.3656 Details: (Co Clk has b rec 1874-1911, m rec 1887-1911, d rec 1886-1911 & local cen 1932; Clk Dis Ct has div & ct rec from 1873, pro rec from 1870 & nat rec; Reg of Deeds has land rec)
Meade skyways.lib.ks.us/genweb/meade/ index.html	N11	8 Jan 1873	**Unorganized Territory** Meade County; 200 N Fowler St; PO Box 278; Meade, KS 67864; Ph. 316.873.8700 Details: (Reorganized 7 Mar 1885) (Pro Judge has b, m, pro & ct rec; City Clk has bur rec; Clk Dis Ct has div rec; Reg of Deeds has land rec)
Miami www.miamicountyks.org/	B7	30 Aug 1855	**Original County** Miami County; 201 S Pearl St Ste 102; Paola, KS 66071; Ph. 913.294.3976 Details: (Formerly Lykins Co. Name changed to Miami 3 June 1861) (Reg of Deeds has land rec from 1857; Pro Ct has pro & m rec from 1857, b & d rec; Clk Dis Ct has ct & nat rec)
Mitchell skyways.lib.ks.us/genweb/mitchell/ index.html	I5	26 Feb 1867	**Unorganized Territory** Mitchell County; 111 S Hersey Ave; Beloit, KS 67420; Ph. 785.738.3652 Details: (Pro Judge has m & pro rec; Clk Dis Ct has div rec; Reg of Deeds has land rec)
Montgomery* skyways.lib.ks.us/genweb/montgome/ index.html	D10	26 Feb 1867	**Wilson** Montgomery County; 217 E Myrtle; PO Box 446; Independence, KS 67301; Ph. 316.330.1200 Details: (Co Clk has b & d rec 1886-1911; Pro Ct has m & pro rec from 1870; Clk Dis Ct has div & ct rec from 1870; Reg of Deeds has land rec from 1870)
Morris* skyways.lib.ks.us/genweb/morris/ index.html	F7	30 Aug 1855	**Original county** Morris County; 501 W Main St; Council Grove, KS 66846; Ph. 316.767.5518 Details: (Formerly Wise Co. Name changed to Morris 11 Feb 1859) (Pro Judge has m & pro rec; City Clk has bur & d rec; Clk Dis Ct has div & ct rec; Reg of Deeds has land rec)

County Website	Map Index	Date Created	Parent County or Territory From Which Organized Address/Details
Morton skyways.lib.ks.us/genweb/morton/ index.html	Q10	18 Feb 1886	**Kansas** Morton County; 1025 Morton St; PO Box 1116; Elkhart, KS 67950-1116; Ph. 316.697.2157 Details: (Created as Kansas Co 1873. Reorganized as Morton Co 18 Feb 1886) (Co Clk has m rec from 1887, div & ct rec from 1900 & land rec from 1887)
Nemaha skyways.lib.ks.us/genweb/nemaha/ index.html	D4	30 Aug 1855	**Original county** Nemaha County; 607 Nemaha St; Seneca, KS 66538; Ph. 785.336.2146 Details: (Co Clk has b, m & d rec 1885-1911; Clk Dis Ct has m, pro & ct rec from 1857)
Neosho skyways.lib.ks.us/genweb/neosho/ index.html	C10	30 Aug 1855	**Original county** Neosho County; 100 S Main St; PO Box 237; Erie, KS 66733; Ph. 316.244.3293 Details: (Formerly Dorn Co. Name changed to Neosho 3 Jun 1861) (Pro Ct has pro rec from 1866 & m rec from 1864; Clk Dis Ct has nat rec from 1868; Reg of Deeds has land rec from 1866)
Ness skyways.lib.ks.us/genweb/ness/index.html	M7	26 Feb 1867	**Unorganized Territory** Ness County; 202 W Sycamore St; Ness City, KS 67560-1558; Ph. 785.798.2401 Details: (Pro Judge has m & pro rec; Clk Cts has div rec; City Clk has ct rec; Reg of Deeds has land rec)
Norton skyways.lib.ks.us/genweb/norton/ index.htm	M4	26 Feb 1867	**Unorganized Territory** Norton County; 101 S Kansas Ave; Norton, KS 67654-0070; Ph. 785.877.5710 Details: (Name changed to Billings 6 Mar 1873. Name changed back to Norton 19 Feb 1874) (Clk Dis Ct has m & div rec; Pro Ct has pro & ct rec; Reg of Deeds has land rec from 1874 & some cem rec; City Clks have b & d rec)
Oro		7 Feb 1859	**Original county** Oro County; KS Details: (see Norton & Billings) (Name changed to Norton 26 Feb 1867. Name changed to Billings 6 Mar 1873. Name changed back to Norton 19 Feb 1874)
Osage* www.osageco.org/	C7	30 Aug 1855	**Original county** Osage County; 717 Topeka Ave; Lyndon, KS 66451-0226; Ph. 785.828.4812 Details: (Formerly Weller Co. Name changed to Osage 11 Feb 1859) (Co Clk has b rec 1886-1921, m rec 1885-1911 & d rec 1885-1909; Clk Dis Ct has div rec from 1863; Co Ct has ct rec from 1929; Reg of Deeds has land rec from 1858)
Osborne skyways.lib.ks.us/genweb/osborne/ index.html	J5	26 Feb 1867	**Unorganized Territory** Osborne County; 423 W Main St; Osborne, KS 67473; Ph. 785.346.5911 Details: (Pro Judge has m, pro & ct rec, div rec from 1872; Reg of Deeds has land rec)
Otoe		16 Feb 1860	**Marion** Details: (see Butler) Became part of Butler Co, 1861
Ottawa* skyways.lib.ks.us/genweb/ottawa/ index.html	H5	27 Feb 1860	**Unorganized Territory** Ottawa County; 307 N Concord; Minneapolis, KS 67467; Ph. 785.392.2279 Details: (Co Clk has m, div & pro rec; City Officers have b rec from 1911 & d rec; Reg of Deeds has land rec)
Pawnee skyways.lib.ks.us/genweb/pawnee/ index.html	L8	26 Feb 1867	**Marion** Pawnee County; 715 Broadway; Larned, KS 67550; Ph. 316.285.3721 Details: (Clk Dis Ct has m rec from 1873, div, pro, ct & nat rec; Reg of Deeds has land rec; City Clk has b & d rec 1897-1911 & bur rec from 1886; cen taken in 1886)
Phillips* skyways.lib.ks.us/genweb/phillips/ index.html	L4	26 Feb 1867	**Unorganized Territory** Phillips County; 301 State St; Phillipsburg, KS 67661; Ph. 785.543.5513 Details: (Pro Judge has m & pro rec; City Clk has d & bur rec; Clk Dis Ct has div & ct rec; Co Clk has land rec)
Pottawatomie www.pottcounty.org/	E5	20 Feb 1857	**Riley, Calhoun** Pottawatomie County; 207 N First; Westmoreland, KS 66549-0187; Ph. 785.457.3314 Details: (Co Clk has b, m & d rec 1885-1910; Unified Ct System has div, pro & ct rec; Reg of Deeds has land rec)

County Website	Map Index	Date Created	Parent County or Territory From Which Organized Address/Details
Pratt www.prattcounty.org/	K9	26 Feb 1867	**Marion** Pratt County; 300 S Ninnescah St; Pratt, KS 67124; Ph. 316.672.7761 Details: (Clk Dis Ct has m, div, pro & ct rec; Reg of Deeds has land & mil rec)
Rawlins skyways.lib.ks.us/genweb/rawlins/ index.html	P4	6 Mar 1873	**Unorganized Territory** Rawlins County; 607 Main St; Atwood, KS 67730-1896; Ph. 785.626.3351 Details: (Reg of Deeds has land rec; Pro Ct has pro rec)
Reno www.rngov.reno.ks.us/	E5	26 Feb 1867	**Marion** Reno County; 206 W First; Hutchinson, KS 67501-5245; Ph. 316.665.2934 Details: (Co Clk has b & d rec 1890-1910 & cem rec 1865-1978; Clk Dis Ct has div rec; Pro Judge has pro rec)
Republic skyways.lib.ks.us/genweb/republic/ index.html	H4	27 Feb 1860	**Original county** Republic County; 1815 M St Rt 1; Belleville, KS 66935; Ph. 785.527.5691 Details: (Reg of Deeds has land rec; Pro Ct has pro rec)
Rice skyways.lib.ks.us/genweb/rice/index.html	I7	26 Feb 1867	**Marion** Rice County; 101 W Commercial St; Lyons, KS 67554; Ph. 316.257.2232 Details: (Clk Dis Ct has m rec from 1872, div, pro & ct rec; Reg of Deeds has land rec from 1871; City Clk has b rec 1895-1910 & bur rec)
Richardson		30 Aug 1855	**Original county** Details: (see Wabaunsee) Name changed to Wabaunsee 11 Feb 1859
Riley www.co.riley.ks.us/	F4	30 Aug 1855	**Original county** Riley County; 110 Courthouse Plaza; Manhattan, KS 66502-6018; Ph. 785.537.0700 Details: (Co Clk has b & d rec 1885-1886 & 1892-1909; City Clk has b & d rec from 1910; Pro Ct has pro rec; Reg of Deeds has land rec)
Rooks skyways.lib.ks.us/genweb/rooks/index.html	L5	26 Feb 1867	**Unorganized Territory** Rooks County; 115 N Walnut St; Stockton, KS 67669-1663; Ph. 785.425.6718 Details: (Clk Dis Ct has b & d rec 1888-1905, m & div rec from 1888, pro rec from 1881 & ct rec; Reg of Deeds has land rec)
Rush skyways.lib.ks.us/genweb/rush/index.html	L7	26 Feb 1867	**Unorganized Territory** Rush County; 715 Elm St; La Crosse, KS 67548; Ph. 785.222.2731 Details: (City Clk has b, d & bur rec; Pro Judge has m rec from 1876, pro & ct rec; Clk Dis Ct has div rec; Reg of Deeds has land rec)
Russell skyways.lib.ks.us/genweb/russell/ index.html	J6	26 Feb 1867	**Unorganized Territory** Russell County; 401 N Main St; Russell, KS 67665; Ph. 785.483.4641 Details: (Co Clk has m, pro & ct rec from 1876 & div rec)
Saline www.co.saline.ks.us/	H6	15 Feb 1860	**Original county** Saline County; 300 W Ash; Salina, KS 67401; Ph. 785.827.1961 Details: (Pro Judge has m & pro rec; Reg of Deeds has land rec)
Scott skyways.lib.ks.us/genweb/scott/index.html	O7	6 Mar 1873	**Unorganized Territory** Scott County; 303 Court St; Scott City, KS 67871-1122; Ph. 316.872.2420 Details: (City Clk has b & d rec; Pro Judge has m & pro rec; Co Clk has bur rec; Clk Cts has div & ct rec)
Sedgwick www.sedgwick.ks.us/	H9	26 Feb 1867	**Butler, Marion** Sedgwick County; 525 N Main St; Wichita, KS 67203; Ph. 316.383.7666 Details: (Dis Pro Ct has m & pro rec from 1870; Dis Civ Ct has ct rec; Co Clk has land rec from 1887; Community Hlth Dept (1900 E. 9th, Wichita, KS 67214) has b & d rec)
Sequoyah		1873	**Marion** Details: (see Finney) Name changed to Finney 21 Feb 1883
Seward* skyways.lib.ks.us/genweb/seward/ index.html	S10	1873	**Unorganized Territory** Seward County; 415 N Washington; Liberal, KS 67901; Ph. 316.626.0211 Details: (City Clk has b, d & bur rec; Pro Judge has m & pro rec; Clk Dis Ct has div & ct rec; Reg of Deeds has land rec; Co Clk has newspapers from 1873)

Notes

KENTUCKY

CAPITAL: FRANKFORT – STATE 1792 (15TH)

Long before explorers helped open the way for settlers in Kentucky, the entire area was claimed by Virginia as part of Augusta County. Dr. Thomas Walker explored the eastern part of Kentucky around 1750. Daniel Boone followed in 1767. The first permanent settlement took place at Harrodsburg in 1774. The next year, Colonel Richard Henderson of North Carolina formed the Transylvania Company. He purchased almost half of Kentucky from Indian tribes. This purchase included all of the land between the Kentucky River in the central part of the state and the Cumberland River in the extreme western part. Daniel Boone settled Boonesboro in 1775. In 1776, the Kentucky area was taken away from Fincastle County, Virginia. It became Kentucky County, Virginia. In 1780, Kentucky County was divided into three counties; Fayette, Jefferson, and Lincoln; which were in turn divided into nine counties within a decade.

This early period of settlement was one of much bloodshed and danger as the Indians tried to protect their lands. Early settlers came mainly from Maryland, North Carolina, Pennsylvania, Tennessee, and Virginia. They were mainly of German, English, Irish, and Scottish descent.

Kentucky became a state on 1 June 1792. After the Louisiana Purchase in 1803, migration and settlement in Kentucky increased. Immigrants from Russia, Italy, Poland, and Austria came to the area. The War of 1812 involved many Kentucky men. Although neutral in the Civil War, more than 75,000 Kentucky men fought for the Union and 35,000 to 60,000 fought for Confederate forces.

The extreme western tip of Kentucky is sometimes referred to as the Jackson Purchase Region since it was purchased in 1818 from the Chickasaw Indians during Andrew Jackson's presidency. It includes Calloway, Marshall, McCracken, Graves, Fulton, Hickman, Carlisle, and Ballard counties.

Look for vital records in the following locations:
- **Birth and death records:** Office of Vital Statistics, Department of Health Services in Frankfort, Kentucky beginning on 1 January 1911. Prior to 1911 the following birth and death records are also located there including the following:
  City of Louisville - birth records from 1898, death records from 1866
  City of Lexington - birth records from 1906, death records from 1898
  City of Covington - birth records from 1896, death records from 1880
  City of Newport - birth records from 1890, death records from 1880
  Records of births and deaths from some counties as early as 1851 are held by the Kentucky Historical Society in Frankfurt.
- **Marriage and divorce records:** Counties generally have marriage records from within a few years of their organization. Statewide collection of marriage and divorce records began on 1 June 1958. Divorces prior to 1849 were granted by the state legislature. From 1849 to 1959, divorces were usually recorded by the circuit court and were often interfiled with other court matters.
- **Wills and court records:** County clerks keep wills and other probate records. Copies are also available at the Department of Libraries and Archives, Public Records Division in Frankfort and through the Kentucky Historical Society.
- **Naturalization records:** Filed in the district courts in Bowling Green, Catlettsburg, Covington, Frankfort, London, Louisville, Owensboro, and Paducah. The office of the Clerk of the Circuit Court also has these records.

Green County Historical Society; PO Box 276; Greensburg, Kentucky 42743

Greenup Co. Public Library; 203 Harrison St.; Greenup, Kentucky 41144

Harlan County Genealogical Society; PO Box 1499; Harlan, Kentucky 40831

Harlan Heritage Seekers; PO Box 853; Harlan, Kentucky 40931

Harrodsburg Historical Society, Genealogical Committee; Box 316; Harrodsburg, Kentucky 40330

Hart County Historical Society; PO Box 606; Munfordville, Kentucky 42765

Henderson County Historical and Genealogical Society; 132-B South Green Street; PO Box 303; Henderson, Kentucky 42429-0303

Henderson Public Library; 101 S. Main St.; Henderson, Kentucky 42420

Hickman County Historical Society; Rt. 3, Box 255; Clinton, Kentucky 42031

Hopkins County Genealogical Society; PO Box 51; Madisonville, Kentucky 42431; <www.rootsweb.com/~kyhopkin/hcgs/index.html>

Jewish Genealogical Society of Louisville; Israel T. Namani Library; 3600 Dutchmans Ln.; Louisville, Kentucky 40205

John Fox Memorial Library; D. A. Shrine, Duncan Tavern St.; Paris, Kentucky 40361

John L. Street Memorial Library; Rt. 6, Box 278A; Cadiz, Kentucky 42211

John Manire Chapter, SAR; 112 Cox Mill Ct.; Hopkinsville, Kentucky 42240

John Weaver Chapter, SAR; 1239 State St.; Bowling Green, Kentucky 42101

Johnson County Historical /Genealogical Society; PO Box 798; Paintsville, Kentucky 41240

Kenton County Public Library; 5th and Scott; Covington, Kentucky 41011

Kentucky Baptist Historical Society; 10701 Shelbyville Road; Middletown, Kentucky 40243-0433; 502.245.4101; Fax 502.244.6469

Kentucky Baptist Historical Society; PO Box 43433; Louisville, Kentucky 40253-0433

Kentucky Department for Libraries and Archives; 300 Coffee Tree Road; PO Box 537; Frankfurt, Kentucky 40602-0537; 502.564.5773;

Kentucky Genealogical Society; PO Box 153; Frankfort, Kentucky 40602-0153; 502.564.8300, Ext. 347;

Kentucky Historical Society; 300 West Broadway, PO Box H; Frankfort, Kentucky 40602-2108; 502.564.3016; Fax 502.564.4701

Kentucky Historical Society; PO Box H; Frankfort, Kentucky 40602-2108

Kentucky History Center; 100 W. Broadway; Frankfort, Kentucky 40601; 877.564.1792

Kentucky Library; Western Kentucky University, 1 Big Red Way; Bowling Green, Kentucky 42101; 502.745.5083; Fax 502.745.6264

Kentucky Society of Pioneers; 1129 Pleasant Ridge Rd.; Utica, Kentucky 42376

Kentucky State Library & Archives, Public Records Division, Archives Research; PO Box 537, 300 Coffee Tree Rd.; Frankfort, Kentucky 40602-0537

Knott County Historical & Genealogical Society & Library; PO Box 1023; Hindman, Kentucky 41822; 606.785.0700; <www.geocities.com/Athens/Oracle/5468/>

Knox County Historical Society, Inc.; PO Box 528; Barbourville, Kentucky 40906

Lafayette Chapter, SAR; 405 E. Main; Georgetown, Kentucky 40324

Laurel Co. Public Library; 116 E. 4th St.; London, Kentucky 40741

Laurel County Historical Society; PO Box 816; London, Kentucky 40743; <www.users.kih.net/~lchistsoc/histsoc/index.htm>

Leslie Co. Public Library; PO Box 498; Hyden, Kentucky 41749

Letcher County Historical and Genealogical Society; PO Box 312; Whitesburg, Kentucky 41858; <www.home.mpinet.net/bcaudill/kygenweb/lchgs.htm>

Lewis County Historical Society; PO Box 212; Vanceburg, Kentucky 41179

Lexington Public Library; 2nd & Market Streets; Lexington, Kentucky 40507

Library Louisville Presbyterian Seminary; 1044 Alta Vista Road; Louisville, Kentucky 40205; 502.895.3411; Fax 502.895.1096

Lieutenant Robert Moseley Chapter, SAR; 2786 Russell RD.; Utica, Kentucky 42376

Logan Co. Archives, c/o Circuit Court Clerk; West 4th St.; Russellville, Kentucky 42276; 502.726.8179

Logan County Genealogical Society, Inc.; PO Box 853; Russellville, Kentucky 42276-0853

Louisville Free Public Library; 4th and York Sts.; Louisville, Kentucky 40203

Louisville Genealogical Society; PO Box 5164; Louisville, Kentucky 40255-0164

Louisville Thruston Chapter, SAR; PO Box 496; Peewee Valley, Kentucky 40056

Lyon County Historical Society; PO Box 994; Eddyville, Kentucky 42038

Magoffin County Historical Society; PO Box 222; Salyersville, Kentucky 41465; 606.349.1353; <www.rootsweb.com/~kymhs/>

Margaret I. King Library-North, Department of Special Collections and Archives, University of Kentucky; 110 King Library-North; Lexington, Kentucky 40506-0039; 606.257.8611; Fax 606.257.8379

Marshall County, Kentucky Genealogical Society; PO Box 373; Benton, Kentucky 42025

Mason Co. Museum and Library; 215 Sutton St.; Maysville, Kentucky 41056; 606.564.5865; Fax 606.564.4372; <webpages.maysvilleky.net/masonmuseum>

Mason County Genealogical Society; PO Box 266; Maysville, Kentucky 41056

McCracken County Genealogical Society; 4640 Buckner Lane; Paducah, Kentucky 42001

Metcalfe County Historical Society; Rt. 1, Box 371; Summer Shade, Kentucky 42166

Methodist, Kentucky Annual Conference; 4010 Dupont Circle Suite 264; Louisville, Kentucky 40207; 502.893.6715; Fax 502.893.6753

Methodist, Redbird Missionary Conference; 6 Queendale Center; Beverley, Kentucky 40913; 606.598.5915; Fax 606.598.6405

Muhlenberg County Genealogical Society; Public Library; Broad St.; Central City, Kentucky 42330

National Archives-Southeast Region (Atlanta); 1557 St. Joseph Avenue; East Point, Georgia 30344; 404.763.7477; Fax 404.763.7033

National Society Daughters of the Union 1861-1865, Inc.; PO Box 7041; Louisville, Kentucky 40257-7041

Nelson County Genealogical Roundtable; PO Box 409; Bardstown, Kentucky 40004

Office of Vital Statistics, Department for Health Services; 275 East Main Street; Frankfort, Kentucky 40621-0001; 502.564.4212

Owensboro-Daviess Co. Public Library, Kentucky Rm. Local Hist. & Gen.; 450 Griffith Ave.; Owensboro, Kentucky 42301

Pendleton County Historical and Genealogical Society; Rt. 5, Box 290; Falmouth, Kentucky 41040

Perry Co. Public Library; High St.; Hazard, Kentucky 41701

Pike County Society for Historical and Genealogical Research; PO Box 97; Pikeville, Kentucky 41502; 606.432.8698; <www.rootsweb.com/~kypike/pikesociety.htm>

Pikeville Public Library; 210 Pike Ave.; Pikeville, Kentucky 41501

Pulaski County Historical Society; Public Library Bldg.; Somerset, Kentucky 42501

Rockcastle County Historical Society; PO Box 930; Mt. Vernon, Kentucky 40456

Roman Catholic, Archdiocese of Louisville; 212 East College Street; Louisville, Kentucky 40203; 502.585.3291

Roman Catholic, Diocese of Covington; PO Box 18548; Erlanger, Kentucky 41018-0548; 606.283.6210; Fax 606.283.6334

Rowan County Historical Society; 236 Allen Ave.; Morehead, Kentucky 40351

Russell County Historical Society; PO Box 544; Jamestown, Kentucky 42629

SAR National Society Library; 1000 So. 4th St.; Louisville, Kentucky 40203

Scott County Genealogical Society; c/o Scott County Public Library East Main; Georgetown, Kentucky 40324; <home.netcom.com/~jog1/schistsoc.html>

Simpson Co. Archives & Museum, Simpson Co. Hist. Soc., Inc.; 206 N. College St.; Franklin, Kentucky 42134

Southern Historical Association; c/o Univ. of Kentucky; Lexington, Kentucky 40506

Southern Kentucky Genealogical Society; PO Box 1782; Bowling Green, Kentucky 42102-1782; <members.aol.com/kygen/skgs/>

Spencer County Historical and Genealogical Society; PO Box 266; Taylorsville, Kentucky 40071

The Campbell County Historical and Genealogical Society; 19 East Main Street; Alexandria, Kentucky 41001; <www.rootsweb.com/~kycchgs/>

Vanlear Historical Society; PO Box 12; Vanlear, Kentucky 41265

Wayne Co. Public Library; 159 So. Main St.; Monticello, Kentucky 42633

Webster County Historical & Genealogical Society; PO Box 215; Dixon, Kentucky 42409-0215; <www.rootsweb.com/~kywebste/wch_gs.htm>

West-Central Kentucky Family Research Association; PO Box 1932; Owensboro, Kentucky 42302

Winchester Public Library; 109 S. Main St.; Winchester, Kentucky 40391

Woodford County Historical Society; 121 Rose Hill; Versailles, Kentucky 40383; 859.873.6786; <www.rootsweb.com/~kywchs/woodfordpage.htm>

Bibliography and Record Sources

General Sources

Allen, William B. *A History of Kentucky*. 1872, Reprint. Ann Arbor, MI: University Microfilms, 1973.

Ardery, Julia Hoge Spencer. *Ardery Collection, Ca. 1750-1970*. (Salt Lake City: Filmed by the Genealogical Society of Utah, 1970).

Barton, E. E. *Barton Collection of Northern Kentucky Families*. (Salt Lake City: Filmed by the Genealogical Society of Utah, 1963).

Coleman, John Winston. *A Bibliography of Kentucky History*. Lexington: University of Kentucky Press, 1949.

Cook, Michael Lewis. *Kentucky Index of Biographical Sketches in State, Regional, and County Histories*. Evansville, Indiana: Cook Publications, 1986.

Cox, Mrs. Edgar L., and Thomas W. Westerfield. *Kentucky Family Records*. 19 vols. Owensboro, Kentucky: West-Central Kentucky Family Research Association, 1970-95.

Daughters of the American Revolution (Kentucky). *Genealogical Collection*. (Salt Lake City: Filmed by the Genealogical Society of Utah, 1971).

Draper, Lyman Copeland, 1815-1891. *Draper Manuscript Collection*. (Chicago: Filmed by the University of Chicago Library, [197-?]).

Dunnigan, Alice Allison. *The Fascinating Story of Black Kentuckians: Their Heritage and Traditions*. Washington, D.C.: Associated Pub., 1982.

Early Kentucky Settlers, 1700s-1800s. [S.l.]: Brøderbund, 2000. CD-ROM.

Early Kentucky Tax Records: From the Register of the Kentucky Historical Society. Baltimore: Genealogical Publishing Company, 1984.

Elliott, Sam. Carpenter. *1792 To 1892: The Illustrated Centennial Record, of the State of Kentucky: Containing a Complete List of the Executive, Judicial and Legislative Departments of the State, and Kentuckians Who Have Occupied High Official Positions Under the United States a nd State Governments Since 1792:* Louisville, Kentucky: Geo. G. Fetter Print. Co., 1892.

Fowler, Ila Earle. *Kentucky Pioneers and Their Descendants.* Genealogical Pub. Co., (1967).

Genealogies of Kentucky Families: From the Filson Club History Quarterly. Baltimore: Genealogical Publishing Co., 1981.

Genealogies of Kentucky Families: From the Register of the Kentucky Historical Society. 2 vols. Baltimore: Genealogical Publishing Co., 1981.

Gresham, John M. *Biographical Cyclopedia of the Commonwealth of Kentucky.* Chicago: J.M. Gresham, 1896.

Hathaway, Beverly W. *Inventory of County Records of Kentucky.* Salt Lake City: Accelerated Indexing Systems, 1974.

Hathaway, Beverly W. *Kentucky Genealogical Research Sources.* West Jordan, UT: Allstate Research Co., 1974.

Hogan, Roseann Reinemuth. *Kentucky Ancestry: A Guide to Genealogical and Historical Research.* Salt Lake City: Ancestry, 1992.

Inside Kentucky: Containing a Bibliography of Source Materials on Kentucky. Frankfort, Kentucky: 1974.

J. M. Armstrong Company. *The Biographical Encyclopedia of Kentucky, of the Dead and Living Men of the Nineteenth Century.* (1876) Reprint. Greenville, SC: Southern Historical Press, 1980.

Johnson, W. D. *Biographical Sketches of Prominent Negro Men and Women of Kentucky: With Introductory Memoir of the Author, nd Prefatory Remarks Showing the Difference Between American and British Slave Holders; also Opinions of Leading Thinkers of The Race.* (Lexington, Kentucky: Filmed by the Margaret I. King Library, University of Kentucky, 1953).

Kentucky Historical Society (Frankfort, Kentucky). *Bibliography of County Resources.* 3 vols. [Frankfort, Kentucky: Kentucky Historical Society, 1990].

Kentucky Historical Society Index to Tax List[s]. Frankfort, Kentucky: The Society: 1973.

Kentucky Research Outline. Series US-States, no. 18. Salt Lake City: Family History Library, 1988.

Kozee, William Carlos. *Early Families of Eastern and Southeastern Kentucky, and Their Descendants.* Strasburg, Virginia: Shenandoah Publishing House, 1961.

McDowell, Samuel R. *Who's Who in Kentucky Genealogy: A Biographical and Professional Profile of 595 Prominent Researchers in Kentucky Genealogy, With Over 6550 Surnames in Which They are Particularly Interested.* Utica, Kentucky: McDowell Publications, 1985.

Perrin, William Henry. *Kentucky; A History of the State: Embracing a Concise Account of the Origin and Development of the Virginia Colony; Its Expansion Westward, and the Settlement Of The Frontier Beyond The Alleghenies; The Erection Of Kentucky as an Independent State And Its Subsequent Development.* 7 vols. Easley, South Carolina: Southern Historical Press, 1979.

Polk, Johnson E. *A History of Kentucky and Kentuckians: The Leaders A=and Representative Men in Commerce, Industry and Modern Activities.* 3 vols. Chicago, New York: Lewis, 1912.

Schweitzer, George K. *Kentucky Genealogical Research.* Knoxville: George K. Schweitzer, 1983.

Shane Manuscript Collection. (Salt Lake City: Filmed by the Genealogical Society of Utah, 1966-1967).

Smith, Zachary F. *The History of Kentucky: From Its Earliest Discovery and Settlement, to the Present Date ... Its Military Events and Achievements, and Biographic Mention of its Historic Characters.* Louisville, Kentucky: Courier Journal, 1886.

Southard, Mary Young. *Who's Who in Kentucky: A Biographical Assembly Of Notable Kentuckians.* Louisville, Kentucky: Standard Print, 1936.

Spencer, John H. *A History of Kentucky Baptists: From 1769 to 1885, Including More Than 800 Biographical Sketches.* Cincinnati: J.R. Baumes, [1886].

Teague, Barbara. *Guide to Kentucky Archival and Manuscript Collections.* Frankfort, Kentucky: Kentucky Department for Libraries and Archives, Public Records Div., 1988-.

The Biographical Encyclopedia of Kentucky. 1 vol. in 2. Cincinnati: J.M. Armstrong, 1878.

Van Meter, Benjamin Franklin. *Genealogies and Sketches of Some old Families Who Have Taken Prominent Part in the Development of Virginia and Kentucky Especially: And Later Of Many Other States of this Union.* Louisville, Kentucky: J.P. Morton, 1901.

Walker, Emma Jane, et al. *Kentucky Bible Records.* 6 Vols. Lexington: Kentucky Society, Daughters of the American Revolution, 1962-1981.

Wallis, Frederick A. *A Sesqui-Centennial History of Kentucky: A Narrative Historical Edition, Preserving the Record of the Growth and Development of the Commonwealth, and Chronicling the Genealogical and Memorial Records of Its Prominent Families and Personages.* 4 Vols. Hopkinsville, Kentucky: Historical Record Association, 1945.

Webb, Benjamin J. *The Centenary of Catholicity in Kentucky.* 1884. Reprint (Utica, Kentucky: McDowell Publications, [198-].

Westerfield, Thomas W., and Samuel McDowell. *Kentucky Genealogy and Biography.* 9 vols. Owensboro, Kentucky: Genealogical Reference, 1969–.

Wilson, Samuel M. *Collection of Samuel M. Wilson of Lexington, Kentucky.* (Salt Lake City: Filmed by the Genealogical Society of Utah, 1958).

Atlases, Maps and Gazetteers

Atlas of Kentucky. Galveston, Texas: Frontier Press.

Clark, Thomas D.. *Historic Maps of Kentucky.* Lexington, Kentucky: University Press of Kentucky, 1979.

Field, Thomas P. *A Guide to Kentucky Place Names.* Lexington, Kentucky: University of Kentucky, 1961.

Kentucky Places and People. 1895-96. Reprint of R.L. Polk and Company's "Kentucky State Gazetteer and Business Directory." Utica, Kentucky: McDowell Publications, [1984].

Kleber, John E. *The Kentucky Encyclopedia.* Lexington, Kentucky: University Press of Kentucky, 1992.

Long, John H. *Kentucky: Atlas of Historical County Boundaries.* New York: Charles Scribner's Sons, 1995.

Murphy, Thelma M. *Kentucky Post Offices, 1794-1819.* [Indianapolis: s.n., 1975?].

Patera, Alan H. *A Checklist of Kentucky Post Offices.* Lake Grove, Or.: The Depot, 1989.

Rennick, Robert M. *Kentucky's Bluegrass: A Survey of the Post Offices.* Lake Grove, Oregon: Depot, 1993-.

Rennick, Robert M. *Kentucky Place Names.* Lexington: University Press of Kentucky, 1984.

Rone, Wendell Holmes. *An Historical Atlas of Kentucky and Her Counties: Davies County, 1850-1965.* Owensboro, Kentucky: Progress Printing Co., 1965.

United States. Office of Geographic Research. Branch of Geographic Names. *Kentucky Geographic Names.* [Reston, VA.]: United States. Branch of Geographic Names, 1981.

Census Records

Available Census Records and Census Substitutes

Federal Census, 1810, 1820, 1830, 1840, 1850, 1860, 1870, 1880, 1900, 1910, 1920, 1930.

Federal Mortality Schedules 1850, 1860, 1870, 1880.

Tax Lists 1790, 1795, 1800.

Union Veterans and Widows 1890.

Non-resident Tax Lists 1794-1805.

School Census 1870-1932.

Dollarhide, William. *The Census Book: A Genealogist's Guide to Federal Census Facts, Schedules and Indexes.* Bountiful, Utah: Heritage Quest, 1999.

Jacobs, Curtis. *The Jacobs Collection.* Microfilm of manuscripts housed at the Beauregard Parish Library, De Ridder, Louisiana. (Salt Lake City: Filmed by the Genealogical Society of Utah, 1990). 20 microfilm.

Kemp, Thomas Jay. *The American Census Handbook.* Wilmington, Delaware: Scholarly Resources, Inc., 2001.

Kentucky Historical Society. Microfilm Department. *Kentucky Historical Society Index To Tax List.* [Frankfort, Kentucky: The Society], 1973.

Lainhart, Ann S. *State Census Records.* Baltimore: Genealogical Publishing Co., Inc., 1992.

Schreiner-Yantis, Netti. *The 1787 Census Of Virginia: An Accounting of the Name of Every White Male Tithable Over 21 Years, the Number of White Males Between 16 & 21 Years, the Number of Slaves Over 16 & Those Under 16 Years, Together with a Listing Of Their Horses, Cattle & Carriages, and also the Names of All Persons tso Whom Ordinary Licenses And Physician's Licenses Were Issued.* 3 vols. Springfield, Virginia: Genealogical Books in Print, 1987.

Szucs, Loretto Dennis, and Matthew Wright. *Finding Answers in U.S. Census Records.* Ancestry Publishing, 2001.

Thorndale, William, and William Dollarhide. *Map Guide to the U.S. Federal Censuses, 1790-1920.* Baltimore: Genealogical Publishing Co., 1987.

Court Records, Probate and Wills

Cook, Michael L. *Virginia Supreme Court District of Kentucky: Order Books, 1783-1792.* Evansville, Indiana: Cook Publications, 1988.

Davis, Virginia. "McLean County Administrators Bonds-1867-1800." *Bluegrass Roots* 18 (1): 13-20 (Spring 1991).

Griffin, Warren B. *Preliminary Inventory Records of The United States Courts from the District of Kentucky, Record Group 21.* Chicago: Federal Records Center, 1968.

Ireland, Robert M. *The County Courts in Antebellum Kentucky.* Lexington: The University Press of Kentucky, 1972.

Jackson, Ronald Vern. *Index to Kentucky Wills to 1851, the Testators.* Bountiful, UT: Accelerated Indexing Systems, 1977.

Jillson. Willard Rouse. *Old Kentucky Entries and Deeds: A Complete Index to All of the Earliest Land Entries. Military Warrants. Deeds and Wills of the Commonwealth of Kentucky.* Louisville: Standard Printing Co., (1926). Reprint. Baltimore: Genealogical Publishing Co., 1987.

King, Junie Estelle Stewart. *Abstract [sic] of Early Kentucky Wills and Inventories.* 1933. Reprint. Baltimore: Genealogical Publishing Co., 1969.

McAdams, Ednah Wilson. *Kentucky Pioneer and Court Records.* 1929. Reprint. Baltimore: Genealogical Publishing Company, 1981.

Warrants. *Deeds and Wills of the Commonwealth of Kentucky.* Louisville: Standard Printing Co., (1926). Reprint. Baltimore: Genealogical Publishing Co., 1987.

Emigration, Immigration, Migration and Naturalization

Eakle, Arlene H., ed. *Kentucky Early Settlers and Stations.* Salt Lake City, Utah: [Family History World], 1990.

Jillson, Willard Rouse. *Pioneer Kentucky: An Outline of Its Exploration and Settlement, Its Early Cartography And Primitive Geography, Coupled with a Brief Presentation of the Principal Trails, Traces, Forts, Stations, Springs, Licks, Fords and Ferries Used Prior to the Year 1800.* Frankfort, Kentucky: The State journal company, 1934.

O'Mallory, Nancy. *Stockading Up: A Study of Pioneer Stations in the Inner Bluegrass Region of Kentucky.* Lexington, Kentucky: Program for cultural resources assessment, Dept. of Anthropology, University of Kentucky, 1987.

Tachau, Mary K. Bonsteel. *Federal Courts in the Early Republic: Kentucky 1789-1816.* Princeton, N.J.: Princeton University Press, 1978.

United States. District Court (Alabama: Southern District). *Declarations Of Intentions, Naturalizations, and Petitions, 1855-1960.* Microfilm of originals at the National Archives in East Point, Georgia. (Salt Lake City: Filmed by the Genealogical Society of Utah, 1987-1989). 9 microfilm.

Land and Property

Brookes-Smith, Joan. *Index for Old Kentucky Surveys and Grants; Index for Tellico Surveys and Grants.* Frankfort: Kentucky Historical Society, 1975.

Cook, Michael L. and Bettie A. Cook. *Kentucky Court of Appeals Deed Books, 1780-1835*. 4 vols. Evansville, IN: Cook Publishing, 1985.

Hone, Wade E. *Land and Property Research in the United States*. Salt Lake City: Ancestry Incorporated, 1997.

Jillson, Willard Rouse. *Kentucky Land Grants*. Genealogical Publishing Co., 1972.

Jillson, Willard Rouse. *Old Kentucky Entries and Deeds: A Complete Index to All of the Earliest Land Entries, Military Warrants, Deeds and Wills of the Commonwealth of Kentucky*. 1926. Reprint. Baltimore: Genealogical Publishing Co., 1978.

Jillson, Willard Rouse. *The Kentucky Land Grants: A Systematic Index to All of the Land Grants Recorded in the State Land Office at Frankfort, Kentucky, 1782-1924*. Louisville: Standard Printing Co., 1925.

Jillson, Willard. *Old Kentucky Entries and Deeds*. Filson Club Publication no. 35. Louisville, Kentucky: (1926). Reprint. Baltimore: Genealogical Publishing Co., 1969.

Kentucky. Governor. *County Court Orders, 1836-1955*. Microreproduction of mss., originals in the Kentucky Land Office, Frankfort, Kentucky. (Salt Lake City: Filmed by the Genealogical Society of Utah, 1962). 64 microfilm.

Kentucky. Governor. *Grants South of Green River, 1797-1866*. Microreproduction of mss., originals in the Kentucky Land Office, Frankfort, Kentucky. (Salt Lake City: Filmed by the Genealogical Society of Utah, 1962). 15 microfilm.

Kentucky. Governor. *Grants West of Tennessee River, 1820-1900*. Microreproduction of mss., originals in the Kentucky Land Office, Frankfort, Kentucky. (Salt Lake City: Filmed by the Genealogical Society of Utah, 1962). 4 microfilm.

Kentucky. Governor. *Kentucky Land Warrants, 1816-1873; Index, 1812-1836*. Microfilm of original at the state land office in Frankfort, Kentucky. (Salt Lake City: Filmed by the Genealogical Society of Utah, 1962). 9 microfilm.

Kentucky. Governor. *Old Kentucky Grants, 1793-1856*. Microreproduction of mss., originals in the Kentucky Land Office, Frankfort, Kentucky. (Salt Lake City: Filmed by the Genealogical Society of Utah, 1962). 9 microfilm.

Kentucky. State Land Office. *Tellico Land Grants, 1803-1853, V. 1-2*. Microfilm of original at Frankfort, Franklin County, Kentucky. (Salt Lake City: Filmed by the Genealogical Society of Utah, 1962). 1 microfilm.

Taylor, Philip Fall, and Samuel M. Wilson. *Kentucky Land Warrants, for the French and Indian Revolutionary Wars: A Calendar of Warrants for Land in Kentucky. Granted for Service in the French and Indian Wars; and Land Bounty Land Warrants Granted for Military Service in the War for Independence*. (1913) Reprint. Greenville, SC: Southern Historical Press, 1917.

Taylor, Philip Fall. *A Calendar of the Warrants for Land In Kentucky. Granted for Service in the French And Indian War*. (1917) Reprint. Baltimore, Maryland: Clearfield Company, 1995.

Virginia. Governor. *Virginia Grants, 1782-1792*. Microreproduction of mss., originals in the Kentucky Land Office, Frankfort, Kentucky. (Salt Lake City: Filmed by the Genealogical Society of Utah, 1962). 9 microfilm.

Warrants. The Kentucky Land Grants: A Systematic Index to All of the Land Grants Recorded in the State Land Office at Frankfort, Kentucky, 1782-1924. 1 Vol. In 2. Baltimore: Genealogical Publishing Co., 1971. Originally published as Filson Club Publication no. 33. (Louisville: Standard Printing Co., 1925).

Military

Adjutant General State of Kentucky. *Kentucky Soldiers of the War of 1812* (1891) Reprint. Greenville, South Carolina: Southern Historical Press, 1992.

Adjutant General's Office. *Index to Veterans of America Wars from Kentucky*. Frankfort: Kentucky Historical Society, 1966.

Adjutant General's Office. *Kentucky Soldiers of the War of 1812*. Baltimore: Genealogical Publishing Co., 1969.

Clift, G. Glenn. *The Cornstalk Militia of Kentucky, 1792-1811*. (1957) Reprint. Greenville, South Carolina: Southern Historical Press, 1982.

Coleman, J. Winston. *The British Invasion of Kentucky: With an Account of the Capture of Ruddell's and Martin's Stations, June 1780*. Lexington, Kentucky: Winburn Press, 1951.

Eckenrode, H. J. *List of the Revolutionary Soldiers of Virginia*. n.p., 1912.

Index to Veterans of American Wars from Kentucky. Frankfort, Kentucky: Kentucky Historical Society, 1966.

Kentucky Adjutant General. *Report of the Adjutant General of the State of Kentucky: Mexican War Veterans (1846-1847*. Frankfort, Kentucky: Capital Office, 1889.

Kentucky Adjutant General's Office. *Report of the Adjutant General of Kentucky Soldiers of the War of 1812*. Frankfort, Kentucky: 1891.

Kentucky Adjutant General's Office. *Report of the Adjutant General of the State of Kentucky: Kentucky Volunteers, War with Spain 1898-1899*. Frankfort, Kentucky: Globe Printing, 1908.

Kentucky. Confederate Pension Board. *Civil War Pension Application*. [Frankfort: Kentucky Historical Society, 19–].

Lafferty, Maude. *The Destruction of Ruddle's and Martin's Forts in the Revolutionary War*. Privately printed, Kentucky Historical Society, Frankfort. 1957

Lindsay, Kenneth G. *Kentucky's Revolutionary War Pensioners, Under the Acts of 1816, 1832*. Evansville, Maryland: Kenman Publishing Co., 1977.

Quisenberry, Anderson C. *Kentucky in the War of 1812*. (1915), Clearfield Co. Reprint, 1989.

Quisenberry, Anderson C. *Revolutionary Soldiers in Kentucky*. Excerpted from the Year Book, Kentucky Society, Sons of the American Revolution (1896). Baltimore: Genealogical Publishing Co., 1959.

Report of the Adjutant General of the State of Kentucky. *Confederate Kentucky Volunteers, War of 1861-1865*. Frankfort, Kentucky: state printer, 1915.

Simpson, Alicia. *Kentucky Confederate Veteran and Widows Pension Index*. Hartford, Kentucky: Cook and McDowell, 1979.

Speed, Thomas, et al. *The Union Regiments of Kentucky*. 1897. Reprint. Dayton, OH: Morningside House, [1984].

United States. Selective Service System. *Kentucky, World War I Selective Service System Draft Registration Cards, 1917-1918.* National Archives Microfilm Publications, M1509. Washington, DC: National Archives, 1987-1988.

Volunteer Officers and Soldiers of the Spanish American War, 1898-1899. Frankfort, Kentucky: Kentucky Historical Society, 1966.

Wilder, Minnie S. *Kentucky Soldiers of the War of 1812.* Baltimore: Genealogical Publishing Co., 1969.

Vital and Cemetery Records

Ardery, Julia H. *Kentucky Records: Early Wills and Marriages Copied from Court House Records by Regents, Historians and the State Historian, Old Bible Records and Tombstone Inscriptions, Records from Barren, Bath, Bourbon, Clark, Daviess, Fayette, Harrison, Jessamine, Lincoln, Madison, Mason, Montgomery, Nelson, Nicholas, Ohio, Scott, and Shelby Counties.* 2 Vols. Baltimore: Southern Book Co., 1958.

Ardery, Julia H.. *Kentucky [Court and Other] Records [Vol. I]. Early Wills and Marriages, Old Bible Records and Tombstone Inscriptions.* (1926) Reprint. Baltimore, Maryland: Genealogical Publishing Co, 1986.

Cemetery Records of Kentucky, 2 vols. Salt Lake City: Genealogical Society, 1962-68.

Clift, Garrett G. *Kentucky Obituaries, 1787-1854.* Baltimore: Genealogical Publishing Co., 1977.

Daughters of the American Revolution. Fincastle Chapter (Louisville, Kentucky). *Kentucky Wills, Inscriptions, Marriages, and Miscellaneous Records.* Microfilm. Salt Lake City: Genealogical Society of Utah, 1971.

Dodd, Jordan R. *Kentucky Marriages, Early To 1800: A Research Tool.* Bountiful, Utah: Precision Indexing, 1990.

Duff, Jeffrey M. *Inventory of Kentucky Birth, Marriage, and Death Records, 1852-1910.* Rev. ed. Frankfort, Kentucky: Department for Libraries and Archives, 1982.

Green, Karen Mauer, ed. *The Kentucky Gazette…. Genealogical and Historical Abstracts.* 2 vols. Baltimore: Gateway Press, Inc., 1983-85.

Guide to Public Vital Statistics Records in Kentucky. Louisville: Historical Records Survey, 1942.

Johnson, Robert Foster. *Wilderness Road Cemeteries in Kentucky, Tennessee and Virginia.* Owensboro, Kentucky: McDowell Publications, 1981.

Kentucky Death records from 1911 thru 2000. Provo, Utah: MyFamily.com Inc., 1998-2002. online database - <vitals.rootsweb.com/ky/death/search.cgi>

Kentucky Marriage Records from the Register of the Kentucky Historical Society. Baltimore: Genealogical Publishing Co., 1983.

Kentucky Office of Vital Statistics. *Births and Deaths Index, 1911-1954.* Microreproduction of original in Louisville, Kentucky. (Salt Lake City: Genealogical Society of Utah, 1960.) 92 microfilm.

Kentucky Office of Vital Statistics. *Kentucky Death Index, 1911-1986.* Frankfurt: Kentucky Office of Vital Statistics, 1988. 183 microfiche.

Kentucky. Office of Vital Statistics . *Birth Indexes, 1911-1995.* Frankfort, Kentucky: Kentucky Office of Vital Statistics, 1997. 1038 microfiche.

Kentucky. Office of Vital Statistics. *Divorce Indexes, 1972-1990.* Frankfort, Kentucky: Kentucky Office of Vital Statistics, 1991.

Kentucky. Office of Vital Statistics. *Marriage Indexes, 1973-1995.* Frankfort, Kentucky: Office of Vital Statistics, 1997. 173 microfiche.

County Website	Map Index	Date Created	Parent County or Territory From Which Organized / Address/Details
Adair columbia-adaircounty.com/	I8	11 Dec 1801	**Green** Adair County; 424 Public Sq; Columbia, KY 42728-1451; Ph. 270.384.2801 Details: (Co Clk has m, land, pro & mil rec from 1802; Clk Cir Ct has div & ct rec)
Allen www.rootsweb.com/~kyallen/	J9	11 Jan 1815	**Barren, Warren** Allen County; PO Box 336; Scottsville, KY 42164; Ph. 270.237.3706 Details: (Co Clk has m & pro rec from 1902; Clk Cir Ct has div rec from 1902)
Anderson* members.aol.com/cbc174/anderson.htm	H5	16 Jan 1827	**Franklin, Mercer, Washington** Anderson County; 151 S Main St; Lawrenceburg, KY 40342; Ph. 502.839.3041 Details: (Co Clk has m, pro & land rec from 1827 & school rec; Clk Cir Ct has ct rec from 1857)
Ballard www.ballardconet.com/	Q8	15 Feb 1842	**Hickman, McCracken** Ballard County; 424 Court St; PO Box 145; Wickliffe, KY 42087-0145; Ph. 270.335.5168 Details: (Courthouse burned in 1880) (Co Clk has m & land rec from 1880; Clk Cir Ct has div & pro rec)
Barren www.rootsweb.com/~kybarren/	J8	20 Dec 1798	**Green, Warren** Barren County; County Courthouse 1st Fl; Glasgow, KY 42141-2812; Ph. 270.651.3783 Details: (Co Clk has m, land & pro rec from 1798; Clk Cir Ct has div & ct rec)
Bath www.mindspring.com/~kyblue/bath/	E5	15 Jan 1811	**Montgomery** Bath County; PO Box 609; Owingsville, KY 40350; Ph. 606.674.2613 Details: (Co Clk has m, pro & land rec from 1811 & mil dis rec; Clk Cir Ct has div & ct rec; Co Hlth Dept has b & d rec from 1915)
Bell www.rootsweb.com/~kybell/	E8	28 Feb 1867	**Knox, Harlan** Bell County; Courthouse Sq FL 1; PO Box 156; Pineville, KY 40977; Ph. 606.337.6143 Details: (Co Clk has m & land rec)
Boone www.boonecountyky.org/	G3	13 Dec 1798	**Campbell** Boone County; 2950 E Washington Sq; Burlington, KY 41005; Ph. 606.334.2112 Details: (Co Clk has m & pro rec from 1799)
Bourbon www.parisky.com/	F5	17 Oct 1785	**Fayette** Bourbon County; 310 Main St; Paris, KY 40361; Ph. 606.987.2142 Details: (Co Clk has m & pro rec from 1786; Clk Cir Ct has ct rec from 1786 & div rec)
Boyd www.rootsweb.com/~kyboyd/	C4	16 Feb 1860	**Carter, Lawrence, Greenup** Boyd County; 2800 Louisa St; Catlettsburg, KY 41129; Ph. 606.739.5116 Details: (Co Clk has m, land & mil rec from 1860; Clk Cir Ct has div, pro & ct rec)
Boyle www.danville-ky.com/	H6	15 Feb 1842	**Mercer, Lincoln** Boyle County; 321 W Main St #123; Danville, KY 40422; Ph. 606.238.1110 Details: (Co Clk has m, pro, land & mil rec from 1842; Clk Cir Ct has div & ct rec)
Bracken www.rootsweb.com/~kybracke/brec1/html	F4	14 Dec 1796	**Campbell, Mason** Bracken County; 116 W Miami St; PO Box 147; Brooksville, KY 41004; Ph. 606.735.2952 Details: (Co Clk has m, pro & land rec from 1797)
Breathitt www.breathittcounty.com/Breathitt1.html	D7	8 Feb 1839	**Clay, Estill, Perry** Breathitt County; 1127 Main St; Jackson, KY 41339-1194; Ph. 606.666.3810 Details: (Co Clk has m, pro & land rec from 1875; Clk Cir Ct has div & ct rec)
Breckinridge* www.geocities.com/dabugman.geo/	K6	9 Dec 1799	**Hardin** Breckinridge County; Courthouse Sq; PO Box 538; Hardinsburg, KY 40143; Ph. 270.756.2246 Details: (Co Archives has some m rec from 1800, some b rec 1853-1969, some d rec 1853-1993 & land rec from 1800; Clk Cir Ct has pro & ct rec)

County Website	Map Index	Date Created	Parent County or Territory From Which Organized Address/Details
Bullitt www.ltadd.org/bullitt/	I5	13 Dec 1796	**Jefferson, Nelson** Bullitt County; 149 N Walnut St; Shepherdsville, KY 40165; Ph. 502.543.2262 Details: (Co Clk has m rec from 1795, land rec from 1796 & mil dis rec 1921-1997; Clk Cir Ct has div & ct rec; Clk Dis Ct has pro rec)
Butler www.rootsweb.com/~kybutler/	K7	18 Jan 1810	**Logan, Ohio** Butler County; 110 N Main St; Morgantown, KY 42261-0448; Ph. 270.526.5676 Details: (Co Clk has m & land rec from 1810; Clk Cir Ct has div & ct rec)
Caldwell home.hiwaay.net/~woliver/caldwell.html	N7	31 Jan 1809	**Livingston** Caldwell County; 100 E Market St Rm 3; Princeton, KY 42445-1675; Ph. 270.365.6754 Details: (Co Clk has m, land & pro rec from 1809 & mil dis rec; Clk Cir Ct has div & ct rec)
Calloway users.arn.net/~billco/calloway.html	O9	19 Dec 1821	**Hickman** Calloway County; 101 S 5th St; Murray, KY 42071; Ph. 270.767.0429 Details: (Co Clk has m, pro, land & mil dis rec, minister bonds & election rec; Clk Cir Ct has div rec)
Campbell www.campbellcountyky.org/	F3	17 Dec 1794	**Harrison, Mason, Scott** Campbell County; 340 York St; Newport, KY 41071; Ph. 606.292.3850 Details: (Co Clk has m, pro & land rec from 1785)
Carlisle* www.ballardconet.com/GenWeb/ carlisle.html	Q8	3 Apr 1886	**Ballard** Carlisle County; W Court St; Bardwell, KY 42023; Ph. 270.628.3233 Details: (Co Clk has m, pro & land rec)
Carroll gallatinky.tripod.com/Carroll/Carroll.html	H4	9 Feb 1838	**Gallatin** Carroll County; 440 Main St; Carrollton, KY 41008; Ph. 502.732.7036 Details: (Co Clk has m, pro & land rec from 1838; Clk Cir Ct has div & ct rec)
Carter www.rootsweb.com/~kycarter/	D4	9 Feb 1838	**Greenup, Lawrence** Carter County; 300 W Main St; Grayson, KY 41143; Ph. 606.474.5188 Details: (Co Clk has b & d rec 1911-1954 & m rec from 1838; Clk Cir Ct has div, pro & ct rec)
Casey www.rootsweb.com/~kycasey/ caseypge.htm	H7	14 Nov 1806	**Lincoln** Casey County; PO Box 310; Liberty, KY 42539-0310; Ph. 606.787.6471 Details: (Co Hlth Dept has b & d rec; Co Clk has m, pro & land rec from 1806; Clk Cir Ct has pro rec from 1978, div & ct rec)
Christian www.kyseeker.com/christian/index.html	N8	13 Dec 1796	**Logan** Christian County; 511 S Main St; Hopkinsville, KY 42240-2300; Ph. 270.887.4105 Details: (Co Clk has m, pro & land rec from 1797; Clk Cir Ct has pro rec from 1978, div & ct rec)
Clark www.clarkco.net/	F5	6 Dec 1792	**Bourbon, Fayette** Clark County; 34 S Main St Rm 103; Winchester, KY 40391-2600; Ph. 606.745.0282 Details: (Clk Cts has m, land & pro rec from 1793; Clk Cir Ct has div & ct rec)
Clay www.rootsweb.com/~kyclay/clay.html	E7	2 Dec 1806	**Madison, Floyd, Knox** Clay County; 316 Main St Ste 143; Manchester, KY 40962; Ph. 606.598.2544 Details: (Co Clk has m rec from 1807 & land rec; Clk Cir Ct has div rec from 1955 & pro rec from 1977)
Clinton www.rootsweb.com/~kyclinto/	H9	20 Feb 1836	**Wayne, Cumberland** Clinton County; 212 Washington; Albany, KY 42602; Ph. 606.387.5234 Details: (Co Clk has m, land & pro rec from 1865)
Crittenden home.hiwaay.net/~woliver/crittenden.html	O7	26 Jan 1842	**Livingston** Crittenden County; 107 S Main St; Marion, KY 42064; Ph. 270.965.3403 Details: (Co Clk has m, pro, land & ct rec, election returns from 1842; Clk Cir Ct has div rec)

County Website	Map Index	Date Created	Parent County or Territory From Which Organized Address/Details
Cumberland www.geocities.com/Heartland/Trail/1794/	I8	14 Dec 1798	**Green** Cumberland County; PO Box 275; Burkesville, KY 42717-0275; Ph. 270.864.3726 Details: (Co Clk has some m rec 1882-1923 & from 1927, pro rec from 1815 & land rec from 1799; Clk Cir Ct has pro rec from 1968, div & ct rec)
Daviess www.geocities.com/gsdownr_2000/ daviess1.html	M6	14 Jan 1815	**Ohio** Daviess County; 212 St Ann St; Owensboro, KY 42303; Ph. 270.685.8434 Details: (Co Clk has m & land rec from 1815 & pro rec; Clk Cir Ct has div & ct rec)
Edmonson users.rootsweb.com/~kyedmons/	K7	12 Jan 1825	**Grayson, Hart, Warren** Edmonson County; Main & Cross St; Brownsville, KY 42210; Ph. 270.597.2624 Details: (Co Clk has m rec from 1840)
Elliott home.zoomnet.net/~cbarker/elliott.htm	D5	26 Jan 1869	**Carter, Lawrence, Morgan** Elliott County; Main St; PO Box 225; Sandy Hook, KY 41171-0225; Ph. 606.738.4462 Details: (Co Clk has m rec from 1934, pro rec from 1957 & land rec from 1869; Clk Cir Ct has div rec from 1957 & ct rec; Co Hlth Dept has b & d rec)
Estill www.estill.net/	F6	27 Jan 1808	**Clark, Madison** Estill County; 130 Main St; Irvine, KY 40336-1098; Ph. 606.723.5156 Details: (Co Clk has m, bur, pro & land rec from 1808; Clk Cir Ct has div & ct rec)
Fayette* www.lfucg.com/	G5	1 May 1780	**Kentucky Co., Virginia** Fayette County; 162 E Main St; Lexington, KY 40507-1363; Ph. 859.253.3344 Details: (Co Clk has m rec from 1795, pro & land rec from 1794; Clk Cir Ct has div & ct rec)
Fleming www.flemingcounty.org/	E4	10 Feb 1798	**Mason** Fleming County; Courthouse Sq; Flemingsburg, KY 41041-1399; Ph. 606.845.8461 Details: (Co Clk has m, pro & land rec from 1798)
Floyd www.kymtnnet.org/floyd.html	C7	13 Dec 1799	**Fleming, Mason, Montgomery** Floyd County; 3rd Ave; Prestonburg, KY 41653; Ph. 606.886.3816 Details: (Co Clk has m & land rec from 1800)
Franklin www.rootsweb.com/~kyfrankl/ franklin.htm	H5	7 Dec 1794	**Woodford, Mercer, Shelby** Franklin County; PO Box 338; Frankfort, KY 40602-0338; Ph. 502.875.8702 Details: (Co Clk has m, pro, land & ct rec from 1795, Confederate Pension Applications; Clk Cir Ct has div rec)
Fulton www.rootsweb.com/~kyfulton/5642.html	Q9	15 Jan 1845	**Hickman** Fulton County; 201 Moulton St; Hickman, KY 42050; Ph. 270.236.2061 Details: (Co Clk has m, pro & land rec from 1845; Clk Cir Ct has div & ct rec)
Gallatin gallatinky.tripod.com/Gallatin.html	H3	14 Dec 1798	**Franklin, Shelby** Gallatin County; 100 Main; PO Box 616; Warsaw, KY 41095-0616; Ph. 859.567.5411 Details: (Co Clk has m, pro & land rec from 1799; Clk Cir Ct has div & ct rec)
Garrard www.angelfire.com/ar2/apeebles/ garrard/index.htm	G6	17 Dec 1796	**Madison, Lincoln, Mercer** Garrard County; Public Sq; Lancaster, KY 40444; Ph. 859.792.3071 Details: (Co Clk has m, pro & land rec from 1797; Clk Cir Ct has ct rec from 1813)
Grant grantco.org/	G4	12 Feb 1820	**Pendleton** Grant County; Courthouse Basement; PO Box 469; Williamstown, KY 41097-0469; Ph. 859.824.3321 Details: (Co Clk has m, pro & land rec from 1820)
Graves www.rootsweb.com/~kygraves/graves.htm	P9	1823	**Hickman** Graves County; 201 E College St; Mayfield, KY 42066; Ph. 270.247.1733 Details: (Co Clk has m, pro, ct & land rec from 1888; Clk Cir Ct has div rec)
Grayson www.graysoncounty.com/	K7	25 Jan 1810	**Hardin, Ohio** Grayson County; 10 Public Sq; Leitchfield, KY 42754; Ph. 270.259.5295 Details: (Co Clk has m, land & mil rec from 1896; Clk Cir Ct has pro, div & ct rec)
Green www.rootsweb.com/~kygreen/	I7	20 Dec 1792	**Lincoln, Nelson** Green County; 203 W Court St; Greensburg, KY 42743-1522; Ph. 270.932.5386 Details: (Co Clk has m, land, pro & ct rec from 1793; Clk Cir Ct has div rec; Co Hlth Office has b & d rec)

County Website	Map Index	Date Created	Parent County or Territory From Which Organized / Address/Details
Greenup www.rootsweb.com/~kygreen2/	C4	12 Dec 1803	**Mason** Greenup County; Main & Harrison; Greenup, KY 41144-1055; Ph. 606.473.7394 Details: (Co Clk has m rec from 1803, pro rec from 1837, b & d rec 1911-1949; Clk Cir Ct has div & ct rec from 1803)
Hancock www.geocities.com/gsdownr_2000/ hancock1.html	L6	3 Jan 1829	**Daviess, Ohio, Breckinridge** Hancock County; 225 Main Cross St; PO Box 146; Hawesville, KY 42348; Ph. 270.927.6117 Details: (Co Clk has m, pro & land rec from 1829; Clk Cir Ct has div & ct rec)
Hardin www.geocities.com/dabugman.geo/ hardin.html	J6	15 Dec 1792	**Nelson** Hardin County; 14 Public Sq; Elizabethtown, KY 42701; Ph. 270.765.2171 Details: (Co Clk has m & land rec)
Harlan www.rootsweb.com/~kyharlan/	D8	28 Jan 1819	**Knox, Floyd** Harlan County; 205 Central St; PO Box 956; Harlan, KY 40831-0956; Ph. 606.573.3636 Details: (Co Clk has m & land rec from 1820; Clk Cir Ct has div & ct rec)
Harrison home.netcom.com/~jog1/harrison.html	F4	21 Dec 1793	**Bourbon, Scott** Harrison County; 315 Oddville Ave; Cynthiana, KY 41031; Ph. 859.234.7130 Details: (Co Clk has m, pro & land rec from 1794; Clk Cir Ct has div & ct rec)
Hart www.hartcounty.com/	J7	28 Jan 1819	**Hardin, Barren** Hart County; Main St; Munfordville, KY 42765; Ph. 270.524.2751 Details: (Co Clk has b, m, d, land, pro & ct rec)
Henderson www.go-henderson.com/	N6	21 Dec 1798	**Christian** Henderson County; 232 1st St; PO Box 374; Henderson, KY 42420-3146; Ph. 270.827.5671 Details: (Co Clk has b & d rec 1911-1949, m rec from 1806, land rec from 1797 & pro rec from 1800; Clk Dis Ct has pro rec from 1979; Clk Cir Ct has div & ct rec)
Henry www.henryweb.com/	H4	14 Dec 1798	**Shelby** Henry County; 30 N Main St; PO Box 615; New Castle, KY 40050-0202; Ph. 502.845.5705 Details: (Co Clk has m rec from 1799, pro, land & ct rec; Clk Cir Ct has div rec)
Hickman www.rootsweb.com/~kyhickma/	Q9	19 Dec 1821	**Caldwell, Livingston** Hickman County; 110 E Clay St; Clinton, KY 42031; Ph. 270.653.2131 Details: (Co Clk has some b rec 1854-1909, some d rec 1856-1909, tax lists 1825-1829, pro & land rec; Clk Cir Ct has div & ct rec)
Hopkins www.rootsweb.com/~kyhopkin/	N7	9 Dec 1806	**Henderson** Hopkins County; 10 S Main St; PO Box Drawer 737; Madisonville, KY 42431-2064; Ph. 270.821.7361 Details: (Co Clk has m, pro, ct & land rec)
Jackson www.rootsweb.com/~kyjackso/	F7	2 Feb 1858	**Rockcastle, Owsley, Madison, Clay, Estill, Laurel** Jackson County; Main St; McKee, KY 40447; Ph. 606.287.7811 Details: (Co Clk has b, m, d & land rec)
Jefferson www.co.jefferson.ky.us/	I5	1 May 1780	**Kentucky Co, Virginia** Jefferson County; 527 W Jefferson St; Louisville, KY 40202-2814; Ph. 502.574.5700 Details: (Co Clk has m & pro rec from 1781; Clk Cir Ct has div rec from 1850; Archivist has ct rec from 1780)
Jessamine* www.jessaminecounty.org/	G6	19 Dec 1798	**Fayette** Jessamine County; 400 Park Dr; Nicholasville, KY 40356-0036; Ph. 859.885.9464 Details: (Co Clk has m, pro & land rec from 1799; Clk Cir Ct has div rec)
Johnson www.rootsweb.com/~kyjohnso/ johnson.htm	C6	24 Feb 1843	**Floyd, Morgan, Lawrence** Johnson County; Court St; Paintsville, KY 41240; Ph. 606.789.2550 Details: (Co Clk has b, m, d, pro & land rec from 1843; Clk Cir Ct has ct rec)
Kenton www.kentoncounty.org/	G3	29 Jan 1840	**Campbell** Kenton County; 303 Courthouse; PO Box 1109; Covington, KY 41012; Ph. 859.491.0702 Details: (Co Clk has m, land & pro rec from 1860; Clk Cir Ct has div & ct rec)

County Website	Map Index	Date Created	Parent County or Territory From Which Organized Address/Details
Knott www.rootsweb.com/~kyknott/	C7	5 May 1884	**Perry, Breathitt, Floyd, Letcher** Knott County; Main St; Hindman, KY 41822-0446; Ph. 606.785.5651 Details: (Co Clk has m, ct & land rec from 1886)
Knox* www.rootsweb.com/~kyknox/	E8	19 Dec 1799	**Lincoln** Knox County; 401 Court Sq #102; Barbourville, KY 40906-0105; Ph. 606.546.3568 Details: (Co Clk has m & land rec)
Larue www.rootsweb.com/~kylarue/larue4.htm	I7	4 Mar 1843	**Hardin** Larue County; 209 W High St; Hodgenville, KY 42748; Ph. 270.358.3544 Details: (Co Clk has m & land rec from 1843 & pro rec 1843-1979; Clk Cir Ct has div rec, pro rec from 1979)
Laurel* www.rootsweb.com/~kylaurel/	F8	12 Dec 1825	**Whitley, Clay, Knox, Rockcastle** Laurel County; 101 S Main St; London, KY 40741; Ph. 606.864.5158 Details: (Co Clk has m, land, pro & ct rec from 1826)
Lawrence www.rootsweb.com/~kylawren/ lawrence.html	C5	14 Dec 1821	**Floyd, Greenup** Lawrence County; 122 S Main Cross St; Louisa, KY 41230; Ph. 606.638.4102 Details: (Co Clk has m & land rec from 1822 & pro rec 1822-1977; Clk Cir Ct has div rec)
Lee www.usgennet.org/usa/ky/county/ lee/index.html	E6	29 Jan 1870	**Owsley, Breathitt, Wolfe, Estill** Lee County; Main St Room 11; PO Box 551; Beattyville, KY 41311; Ph. 606.464.4115 Details: (Co Clk has m, pro & land rec from 1870; Clk Cir Ct has div & ct rec)
Leslie www.rootsweb.com/~kyleslie/	D8	29 Mar 1878	**Clay, Harlan, Perry** Leslie County; 22010 Main St; PO Box 916; Hyden, KY 41749; Ph. 606.672.2193 Details: (Co Clk has m, pro & land rec; Clk Cir Ct has div & ct rec)
Letcher www.rootsweb.com/~kyletch/letcher.htm	C8	3 Mar 1842	**Perry, Harlan** Letcher County; 101 W Main St; PO Box 58; Whitesburg, KY 41858-0058; Ph. 606.633.2432 Details: (Co Clk has m & land rec from 1842 & pro rec)
Lewis www.rootsweb.com/~kylewis/	D4	2 Dec 1806	**Mason** Lewis County; 514 Second St; Vanceburg, KY 41179; Ph. 606.796.3062 Details: (Co Clk has m & land rec from 1807, pro rec from 1806 & ct rec)
Lincoln www.rootsweb.com/~kylincol/	G7	1 May 1780	**Kentucky Co., Virginia** Lincoln County; 102 E Main St; Stanford, KY 40484; Ph. 606.365.4570 Details: (Co Clk has m, div, pro & ct rec from 1792)
Livingston home.hiwaay.net/~woliver/livingston.html	O7	13 Dec 1798	**Christian** Livingston County; 335 Court St; PO Box 400; Smithland, KY 42081-0400; Ph. 270.928.2162 Details: (Co Clk has m rec from 1799, pro & land rec from 1800; Clk Cir Ct has div & ct rec; rec through 1865 have been microfilmed)
Logan www.rootsweb.com/~kylogan/	L8	28 Jun 1792	**Lincoln** Logan County; 229 W 3rd St; Russellville, KY 42276; Ph. 270.726.6621 Details: (Co Clk has m, pro, land & ct rec from 1792)
Lyon home.hiwaay.net/~woliver/lyon.html	O8	14 Jan 1854	**Caldwell** Lyon County; 200 W Dale Ave; PO Box 698; Eddyville, KY 42038; Ph. 270.388.2331 Details: (Co Clk has b rec 1912-1932, m & land rec from 1854; Clk Cir Ct has div rec)
Madison www.rootsweb.com/~kymadiso/ madison.html	F6	17 Oct 1785	**Lincoln** Madison County; 101 W Main St; Richmond, KY 40475-1415; Ph. 859.624.4707 Details: (Co Clk has m & land rec from 1787 & pro rec 1850-1977; Clk Dis Ct has pro rec from 1978; Clk Cir Ct has div & ct rec)
Magoffin www.rootsweb.com/~kymagoff/	D6	22 Feb 1860	**Floyd, Johnson, Morgan** Magoffin County; Court St; Salyersville, KY 41465; Ph. 606.349.2216 Details: (Co Clk has m rec from 1860)

County Website	Map Index	Date Created	Parent County or Territory From Which Organized / Address/Details
Marion www.rootsweb.com/~kymarion/	16	25 Jan 1834	**Washington** Marion County; 120 W Main; Lebanon, KY 40033; Ph. 270.692.2651 Details: (Co Hlth Dept has b & d rec; Co Clk has m & land rec from 1863 & pro rec 1863-1978; Clk Cir Ct has pro rec from 1979, div & ct rec)
Marshall home.hiwaay.net/~woliver/marshall.html	O8	12 Feb 1842	**Calloway** Marshall County; 1101 Main St; Benton, KY 42025-1498; Ph. 270.527.4740 Details: (Co Clk has m & land rec from 1848)
Martin www.kymtnnet.org/martin.html	B6	10 Mar 1870	**Lawrence, Floyd, Pike, Johnson** Martin County; Main St; Inez, KY 41224; Ph. 606.298.2810 Details: (Co Clk has b rec 1903-1949, m rec from 1883 & d rec 1911-1949; Clk Cir Ct has div, pro & ct rec)
Mason www.rootsweb.com/~kymason/mason.htm	E4	5 Nov 1788	**Bourbon** Mason County; 219 Stanley Reed Ct; Maysville, KY 41056-0234; Ph. 606.564.3341 Details: (Co Clk has m, pro & land rec from 1789; Clk Cir Ct has div rec from 1929 & ct rec from 1792)
McCracken www.co.mccracken.ky.us/	P8	17 Dec 1824	**Hickman** McCracken County; 132 S 4th St; Paducah, KY 42001; Ph. 270.335.5168 Details: (Co Clk has m, pro & land rec from 1825)
McCreary* www.pastseeker.com/mccreary/index.html	G9	12 Mar 1912	**Wayne, Pulaski, Whitley** McCreary County; Main St; PO Box 699; Whitley City, KY 42653; Ph. 606.376.2411 Details: (Co Clk has m rec from 1912, rec 1923-1927 burned & land rec)
McLean lecgbeatlcom.net.home.mindspring.com/	M7	6 Feb 1854	**Muhlenberg, Daviess, Ohio** McLean County; 210 Main St; Calhoun, KY 42327-0057; Ph. 270.273.3082 Details: (Co Clk has m, land & mil rec from 1854; Clk Cir Ct has pro rec from 1854, div & ct rec)
Meade* www.rootsweb.com/~kymeade/	K5	17 Dec 1823	**Hardin, Breckinridge** Meade County; PO Box 614; Brandenburg, KY 40108-0614; Ph. 270.422.2152 Details: (Co Clk has m rec from 1967, some m, land & pro rec from 1824, recent tax rec; Clk Cir Ct has div & pro rec)
Menifee www.rootsweb.com/~kymenife/	E5	10 Mar 1869	**Powell, Wolfe, Bath, Morgan, Montgomery** Menifee County; County Courthouse; PO Box 123; Frenchburg, KY 40322; Ph. 606.768.3512 Details: (Co Clk has m rec from 1869; Clk Cir Ct has div rec from 1869)
Mercer www.rootsweb.com/~kymercer/	H6	17 Oct 1785	**Lincoln** Mercer County; 235 S Main St; PO Box 426; Harrodsburg, KY 40330-1696; Ph. 606.734.6310 Details: (Co Clk has m, pro & land rec from 1786 & mil dis rec from 1919; Clk Cir Ct has div & ct rec)
Metcalfe www.rootsweb.com/~kymetca2/	18	1 Feb 1860	**Monroe, Adair, Barren, Cumberland, Green** Metcalfe County; PO Box 850; Edmonton, KY 42129; Ph. 270.432.4821 Details: (Co Clk has m & land rec)
Monroe www.geocities.com/Heartland/Plains/ 4335/Monroeco/monroe.html	J9	19 Jan 1820	**Barren, Cumberland** Monroe County; PO Box 188; Tompkinsville, KY 42167; Ph. 270.487.5505 Details: (Co Clk has m, pro & land rec from 1863; Clk Cir Ct has div & ct rec)
Montgomery www.rootsweb.com/~kymontgo/ montgo.html	E5	14 Dec 1796	**Clark** Montgomery County; 1 Court St; PO Box 414; Mount Sterling, KY 40353; Ph. 859.498.8700 Details: (Co Hlth Dept has b & d rec; Co Clk has m rec from 1864, pro rec from 1797 & land rec; Clk Cir Ct has div & ct rec)
Morgan www.rootsweb.com/~kymorgan/ morgan2.htm	D5	7 Dec 1822	**Floyd, Bath** Morgan County; 450 Prestonburg St; PO Box 26; West Liberty, KY 41472-1162; Ph. 606.743.3949 Details: (Co Clk has b rec 1911-1949, m, pro & land rec)

County Website	Map Index	Date Created	Parent County or Territory From Which Organized / Address/Details
Muhlenberg www.geocities.com/Heartland/Park/5159/	M7	14 Dec 1798	**Christian, Logan** Muhlenberg County; 100 S Main St; PO Box 525; Greenville, KY 42345-0525; Ph. 270.338.1441 Details: (Co Clk has m & land rec; Clk Cir Ct has pro & div rec)
Nelson bsd.pastracks.com/states/kentucky/nelson/	I6	18 Oct 1784	**Jefferson** Nelson County; 113 E Stephen Foster Ave; Bardstown, KY 40004; Ph. 502.348.1820 Details: (Co Clk has m & pro rec from 1784)
Nicholas brush-arbor.com:8080/jhagee/nichco.html	F5	18 Dec 1799	**Bourbon, Mason** Nicholas County; Main St; Carlisle, KY 40311-0329; Ph. 859.289.3730 Details: (Co Clk has m, pro & land rec from 1800; Clk Cir Ct has div & ct rec)
Ohio www.1bigparty.com/h/myfamily/ ohioco.html	L7	17 Dec 1798	**Hardin** Ohio County; Main St; PO Box 85; Hartford, KY 42347-0085; Ph. 270.298.4422 Details: (Co Hlth Dept has d rec from 1911; Co Clk has m & land rec from 1799, pro rec from 1801 & mil dis rec from 1861; Clk Cir Ct has div rec, pro rec from 1978)
Oldham oldhamcounty.state.ky.us/	I4	15 Dec 1823	**Henry, Shelby, Jefferson** Oldham County; 100 W Jefferson St; La Grange, KY 40031; Ph. 502.222.9311 Details: (Co Clk has m, pro & land rec from 1824; Clk Cir Ct has div & ct rec)
Owen www.rootsweb.com/~kyowen2/ owen.html	G4	6 Feb 1819	**Scott, Franklin, Gallatin** Owen County; Madison & Seminary St; PO Box 338; Owenton, KY 40359; Ph. 502.484.2213 Details: (Co Clk has b & d rec 1911-1949, m, pro & land rec from 1819; Clk Cir Ct has div & ct rec at State Archives-Frankfort)
Owsley www.rootsweb.com/~kyowsley/owsley.html	E7	23 Jan 1843	**Clay, Estill, Breathitt** Owsley County; 154 Main St; Booneville, KY 41314; Ph. 606.593.5735 Details: (Co Clk has m, pro & land rec from 1929; Clk Cir Ct has div & ct rec)
Pendleton www.rootsweb.com/~kypendle/	F3	4 Dec 1798	**Bracken, Campbell** Pendleton County; 223 Main St; PO Box 112; Falmouth, KY 41040; Ph. 859.654.3347 Details: (Co Clk has m rec from 1799, pro rec from 1800 & land rec; Clk Cir Ct has div & ct rec)
Perry www.rootsweb.com/~kyperry/	D7	2 Nov 1820	**Clay, Floyd** Perry County; Main St; Hazard, KY 41701; Ph. 606.436.4614 Details: (Co Clk has m & land rec from 1821; Clk Cir Ct has div rec; Clk Dis Ct has pro & ct rec)
Pike www.rootsweb.com/~kypike/	B7	19 Dec 1821	**Floyd** Pike County; 324 Main St; Pikeville, KY 41501-0631; Ph. 606.432.6211 Details: (Co Clk has b & d rec 1911-1949, m & land rec from 1824, pro rec from 1822 & school rec 1895-1934)
Powell www.usgennet.org/usa/ky/county/powell/	E6	7 Jan 1852	**Clark, Estill, Montgomery** Powell County; 140 Washington St; PO Box 548; Stanton, KY 40380; Ph. 606.663.6444 Details: (Co Clk has m, land & mil rec from 1864; Clk Cir Ct has div, pro & ct rec)
Pulaski www.rootsweb.com/~kypulask/	G8	10 Dec 1798	**Green, Lincoln** Pulaski County; PO Box 724; Somerset, KY 42501-0724; Ph. 606.679.2042 Details: (Co Clk has m, pro & land rec from 1799; Clk Cir Ct has div & ct rec)
Robertson brush-arbor.com:8080/jhagee/robco.html	F4	11 Feb 1867	**Nicholas, Bracken, Mason, Harrison** Robertson County; PO Box 75; Mount Olivet, KY 41064; Ph. 606.724.5212 Details: (Co Clk has m & land rec from 1867; Clk Cir Ct has div, pro & ct rec from 1867)
Rockcastle www.rootsweb.com/~kyrockca/rock.htm	F7	8 Jan 1810	**Pulaski, Lincoln, Madison, Knox** Rockcastle County; 205 W Main St; Mount Vernon, KY 40456-0365; Ph. 606.256.2831 Details: (Co Clk has m & land rec from 1873; Clk Cir Ct has div rec from 1873, pro & ct rec)

County Website	Map Index	Date Created	Parent County or Territory From Which Organized Address/Details
Rowan www.rootsweb.com/~kyrowan/	D5	15 Mar 1856	**Fleming, Morgan** Rowan County; 627 E Main St; Morehead, KY 40351; Ph. 606.784.5212 Details: (Co Clk has m, pro & land rec from 1890; Clk Cir Ct has div rec; Co Judge has ct rec)
Russell www.rootsweb.com/~kyrussel/russell.html	H8	14 Dec 1825	**Cumberland, Adair, Wayne** Russell County; 101 Monument Sq; PO Box 579; Jamestown, KY 42629-0579; Ph. 270.343.2125 Details: (Co Clk has m, pro, ct & land rec from 1826; Clk Cir Ct has div rec)
Scott home.netcom.com/~jog1/ScottCo.html	G5	22 Jun 1792	**Woodford** Scott County; 101 E Main St; Georgetown, KY 40324; Ph. 502.863.7875 Details: (Co Clk has m & land rec from 1837 & pro rec from 1796; Clk Cir Ct has div & ct rec)
Shelby www.shelbyvilleky.com/	H5	23 Jun 1792	**Jefferson** Shelby County; 501 Main St; Shelbyville, KY 40065-1133; Ph. 502.663.4410 Details: (Co Clk has b rec 1911-1948, m & pro rec)
Simpson simpsonco.bizland.com/index.html	K9	28 Jan 1819	**Allen, Logan, Warren** Simpson County; 103 W Cedar St; Franklin, KY 42134-0268; Ph. 270.586.8161 Details: (Co Clk has m & land rec from 1882)
Spencer www.rootsweb.com/~kyspence/ kyspenc.htm	I5	7 Jan 1824	**Shelby, Bullitt, Nelson** Spencer County; 2 Main St; Taylorsville, KY 40071; Ph. 502.477.3215 Details: (Co Clk has m rec from 1852, pro & land rec from 1824; Clk Cir Ct has div & ct rec)
Taylor www.rootsweb.com/~kytaylor/	I7	13 Jan 1848	**Green** Taylor County; 203 N Court St; Campbellsville, KY 42718; Ph. 270.465.6677 Details: (Co Clk has m, pro & land rec from 1848, b & d rec; Clk Cir Ct has ct rec from 1848)
Todd www.usgennet.org/usa/ky/county/ todd/index.htm	M8	30 Dec 1819	**Christian, Logan** Todd County; PO Box 307; Elkton, KY 42220-0157; Ph. 270.265.2363 Details: (Co Clk has m, div, pro, ct & land rec)
Trigg www.kyseeker.com/trigg/index.html	N9	27 Jan 1820	**Christian, Caldwell** Trigg County; 41 Main St; PO Box 1310; Cadiz, KY 42211-0609; Ph. 270.552.6661 Details: (Co Hlth Dept has b & d rec; Co Clk has m & land rec from 1820 & pro rec 1820-1977; Clk Cir Ct has div & ct rec)
Trimble www.kyseeker.com/trigg/index.html	I4	9 Feb 1837	**Henry, Oldham, Gallatin** Trimble County; 30 Hwy 42 E; Bedford, KY 40006; Ph. 270.639.7006 Details: (Co Clk has b rec 1911-1950, m rec from 1865 & land rec from 1837)
Union www.ole.net/~maggie/trimble/	O6	15 Jan 1811	**Henderson** Union County; Courthouse; PO Box 119; Morganfield, KY 42437; Ph. 270.389.1334 Details: (Co Clk has m, pro & land rec from 1811)
Warren www.rootsweb.com/~kywarren/	K8	14 Dec 1796	**Logan** Warren County; 429 E 10th St; Bowling Green, KY 42101-2250; Ph. 270.842.9416 Details: (Co Clk has b, m & land rec from 1797, pro rec 1797-1978 & mil dis rec from 1917)
Washington bsd.pastracks.com/states/kentucky/ washington/	H6	22 Jun 1792	**Nelson** Washington County; PO Box 446; Springfield, KY 40069-0446; Ph. 859.336.5425 Details: (Co Clk has m, pro & land rec from 1792 & school census 1893-1917; Clk Cir Ct has div & ct rec from 1792, some nat rec & mil dis rec)
Wayne www.rootsweb.com/~kywayne/wayne.html	G9	18 Dec 1800	**Pulaski, Cumberland** Wayne County; 109 N Main St; Monticello, KY 42633; Ph. 606.348.6661 Details: (Co Clk has m & land rec from 1800 & pro rec 1800-1978)
Webster www.rootsweb.com/~kywebste/	N7	29 Feb 1860	**Hopkins, Union, Henderson** Webster County; 25 Main St; Dixon, KY 42409-0155; Ph. 270.639.7006 Details: (Co Clk has m & land rec from 1860 & pro rec 1860-1977; Clk Cir Ct has div & ct rec & pro rec from 1978)

County Website	Map Index	Date Created	Parent County or Territory From Which Organized Address/Details
Whitley www.craftheadquartersonline.com/ WhitleyCo/Whitley.html	F8	17 Jan 1818	**Knox** Whitley County; Main St; PO Box 8; Williamsburg, KY 40769; Ph. 606.549.6002 Details: (Co Clk has b rec 1915-1949, m & pro rec from 1865 & land rec from 1818)
Wolfe wolfe.archland.com/	E6	5 Mar 1860	**Owsley, Breathitt, Powell, Morgan** Wolfe County; PO Box 400; Campton, KY 41301-0400; Ph. 606.668.3771 Details: (Co Clk has m rec from 1913 & land rec from 1860; Clk Cir Ct has div, pro & ct rec)
Woodford home.netcom.com/~jog1/woodford.html	G5	12 Nov 1788	**Fayette** Woodford County; 103 S Main St; Versailles, KY 40383; Ph. 859.873.3421 Details: (Co Clk has m, pro & land rec from 1789; Clk Cir Ct has div & ct rec)

Notes

Notes

Magnolia

LOUISIANA

CAPITAL: BATON ROUGE – TERRITORY 1805 – STATE 1812 (18TH)

Louisiana was discovered early in the 1500's. However, it wasn't settled until 1774 when the French settled Natchitoches on the Red River. The first organized migration from France was between 1717 and 1722 under the control of the Compagnie des Indes and a Scottish entrepreneur, John Law. Jean Baptiste Le Moyne, sieur De Bienville, sometimes called the "father of Louisiana," founded New Orleans in 1718 and became the capital in 1722. Other early settlers came from German-speaking areas of Europe, while some were brought from Africa to serve as slaves.

In 1755, the British expelled the French settlers of Acadia, and later, Nova Scotia. As many as 5,000 of these French Acadians, who became known as Cajuns, settled in Louisiana. Descendants of the older French and Spanish settlers became known as Creoles. In 1763, Spain was given all of Louisiana east of the Mississippi, except the area around New Orleans. Taking control of the area in 1769, the Spanish began keeping records in earnest.

During the Revolutionary War, some British sympathizers moved into the area to avoid the conflict. In 1800, Spain ceded Louisiana to the French, although they continued to administer the area until about 1803.

The Louisiana Purchase in 1803 made Louisiana part of the United States. The next year, Louisiana was divided into two sections, the District of Louisiana north of the 33rd parallel, and the Territory of Orleans south of the 33rd parallel. Immediately thereafter, large numbers of Americans from south of the Ohio River moved into the area. In 1805, Louisiana was divided into 12 counties, but smaller civil divisions, called parishes, gradually took over the functions of the counties. By 1807 the Territory of Orleans consisted of 19 parishes, which followed the boundaries of the Old Spanish ecclesiastical parishes. Parishes in Louisiana serve the same function as counties do in other states.

English-speaking settlers occupied Spanish West Florida, between the Mississippi and Pearl rivers, including Baton Rouge, in 1810. When Louisiana was admitted to the Union in 1812, the area was included as part of the state. Baton Rouge became the capital in 1849. Louisiana seceded from the Union in 1861. In May 1862, Union naval forces occupied New Orleans, cutting off nearly all trade. The situation caused severe hardships throughout the state. A military government was established and the courts reorganized. Louisiana furnished more than 77,000 soldiers to the Confederacy and 5,000 to the Union. In 1867, Louisiana became part of the Fifth Military District under General Philip Henry Sheridan. Louisiana was readmitted to the Union in 1868.

Look for vital records in the following locations:

- **Birth and death records:** Vital Records Registry in New Orleans, Louisiana has records of births and deaths since 1914. Delayed registration of births since 1939 are also available.
- **Marriage records:** Colonial marriages were recorded in the judicial records of the French Superior Council and the Spanish Cabildo. Originals are at the Louisiana Historical Center Library and State Museum in New Orleans. They are also kept by royal notaries. Contact the Custodian of Notarial Records in New Orleans. No statewide registration of marriages exists. The parishes keep all marriage records.
- **Court records, wills, deeds and divorce records:** Write to the clerk of each parish.
- **Census records:** Various military and local censuses were taken between 1699 and 1805. A special census of New Orleans was taken in 1805. Most of these census records have been published.

Vital Records Registry
751 Chartres Street
New Orleans, Louisiana 70112
504.568.5391
Mailing address: PO Box 60630
New Orleans, Louisiana 70160

Notarial Records
421 Loyola Avenue, Room B-4
New Orleans, Louisiana 70112

Louisiana Historical Center Library and State Museum
400 Esplanade Avenue
New Orleans, Louisiana 7011

LOUISIANA

Gulf of Mexico

Societies and Repositories

Alexandria Historical & Genealogical Library; 503 Washington; Alexandria, Louisiana 71301

Allen Genealogical & Historical Society; PO Box 789; Kinder, Louisiana 70648-0789

Amite Genealogy Club; 200 East Mulberry St; Amite, Louisiana 70422-2524

Ark-La-Tex Genealogical Association; PO Box 4462; Shreveport, Louisiana 71134-0462; <www.softdisk.com/comp/aga>

Ascension Heritage Association; PO Box 1085; Donaldsonville, Louisiana 70346-1085

Association for Preservation and Promotion of Iberville; 602 Main St.; Plaquemine, Louisiana 70764

Attakapas Historical Association; PO Box 43010, USL; Lafayette, Louisiana 70504-3010

Baptist Historical Commission, Southern Baptist Convention; 901 Commerce Street; Nashville, Tennessee 37203-3630; 615.244.0344; Fax 615.782.4821

Baton Rouge Genealogical & Historical Society; PO Box 80565 SE Station; Baton Rouge, Louisiana 70898-0565

Beauregard Historical Society; PO Box 658; De Ridder, Louisiana 70634-0658

Bienville Historical Society; Rt 1, Box 9; Bienville, Louisiana 71008-9653

Bluebonnet Regional Branch Library; 9200 Bluebonnet Blvd; Baton Rouge, Louisiana 70810

Bossier Restoration Foundation; 231 Mercy Lane; Benton, Louisiana 71006

Brimstone Historical Society; PO Box 242; Sulphur, Louisiana 70663

Broadmoor Public Library; 1212 Captain Shreve; Shreveport, Louisiana 71105; 318.219.3468; <www.shreve-lib.org>

Calcasieu Historical Preservation Society; 1635 Hodges St.; Lake Charles, Louisiana 70601-6016

Cameron Parish Historical & Genealogical Society; PO Box 1107; Cameron, Louisiana 70631

(Canary Island) Los Isleos de Galvez Heritage& Cultural Society; 7437 Meadowbrook Ave.; Baton Rouge, Louisiana 70810-2014

Central Louisiana Genealogical Society; PO Box 12206; Alexandria, Louisiana 71315-2006

Central Louisiana Historical Society; PO Box 841; Alexandria, Louisiana 71301-0841

Christmas History of Louisiana; 7024 Morgan Rd.; Greenwell Spr., Louisiana 70739

Claiborne Historical Association; 931 N. Main St.; Homer, Louisiana 71040

Comitt Louisiane Frantais; 2717 Massachusetts; Metairie, Louisiana 70003

Commission des La Avoyelles; PO Box 29; Hamburg, Louisiana 71339-0028

Czech Heritage Association, Inc.; 14 Locker Rd.; Deville, Louisiana 71329-9318

Daughters of the American Revolution, Louisiana; 2564

Donald Dr.; Baton Rouge, Louisiana 70809

Desoto Historical Society, Inc.; PO Box 925; Mansfield, Louisiana 71052.0925; <www.rootsweb.com/~ladesoto/society.htm>

Diocese of Baton Rouge, Archives Department; PO Box 2028; Baton Rouge, Louisiana 70821

Division of Archives, Records Management, and History; 3851 Essen Lane; Baton Rouge, Louisiana 70809; 504.922.1207; Fax 504.922.0002

Division of Historical Preservation; PO Box 44247; Baton Rouge, Louisiana 70804-4247

Dorcheat Historical Association, Webster Parish; PO Box 774; Minden, Louisiana 71055-0774

East Ascension Genealogical & Historical Society; PO Box 1006; Gonzales, Louisiana 70707-1006

East Baton Rouge Parish Library, Bluebonnet Regional Branch; 9200 Bluebonnet Blvd.; Baton Rouge, Louisiana 70810

Edward Livingston Historical Association; PO Box 67; Livingston, Louisiana 70754-0067

Erbon and Marie Wise Gen. Library, Louisiana State Archives; 3851 Essen Ln.; Baton Rouge, Louisiana 70804

Evangeline Genealogical & Historical Society; PO Box 664; Ville Platte, Louisiana 70586-0664

Family History Library: 35 North West Temple Street: Salt Lake City, Utah 84150: 800.346.6044 or 801.240.2584: <www.familysearch.org>: Find a Family History Center near you: <www.familysearch.org/Eng/Library/FHC/frameset_fhc.asp>

Feliciana (East) Historical Committee; PO Box 834 1; Clinton, Louisiana 70722

Feliciana (West) Historical Society; PO Box 338; St. Francisville, Louisiana 70775

Foundation for Historical Louisiana, Inc.; 900 North Blvd.; Baton Rouge, Louisiana 70802-5728

Founders of Natchitoches; PO Box 3; Natchitoches, Louisiana 71457-0003

Francaise Comite Louisiana; 2717 Massachusetts; Metairie, Louisiana 70003-5213

Franklin Parish Genealogical & Historical Society; Rt. 4, Box 150; Winnsboro, Louisiana 71295

French Settlement Historical Society; General Delivery; French Settlement, Louisiana 70733-9999

Friends of Genealogy; PO Box 17935; Shreveport, Louisiana 71138-7835

Friends of the Archives of Louisiana; PO Box 51213; New Orleans, Louisiana 70151-1213

Genealogical Research Society of New Orleans; PO Box 51791; New Orleans, Louisiana 70151; <www.rootsweb.com/~lagrsno/>

Genealogy West, Inc.; West Bank of the Mississippi River; 5644 Abby Dr.; New Orleans, Louisiana 70131-3808

General Philemon Thomas Chapter, SAR; 10547 Ridgely; Baton Rouge, Louisiana 70809; 225.293.2381;

German.Acadian Coast Historical & Genealogical Society; PO

Box 517; Destrehan, Louisiana 70047-0517; 504.652.6077; <www.rootsweb.com/~lastjohn/geracadn.htm>

Germantown Commission Association; PO Box 399; Minden, Louisiana 71055-0389

Grant Genealogical Society; 300 Main St.; Colfax, Louisiana 71417

Gretna Historical Society; PO Box 115; 104 Leighton St.; Gretna, Louisiana 70054-0115

Hill Memorial Library; Louisiana State University; Baton Rouge, Louisiana 70803-3300; 504.388.6551; Fax 504.344.6773

Historic New Orleans Collection, William Research Center; 410 Charter Street; New Orleans, Louisiana 70130; 504.598.7171; Fax 504.598.7166

Historical New Orleans Collection; 533 Royal St.; New Orleans, Louisiana 70130-2113

Historical Preservation of Shreveport; PO Box 857; Shreveport, Louisiana 71162-0857

Historical Society of North Caddo; PO Box 31; 100 SW Front Street; Vivian, Louisiana 71082; <pages.prodigy.net/scollier/hsnc/>

Howard Tilton Library Manuscripts & Rare Books, The Map & Genealogy Rm.; Tulane University, 7001 Freret Street; New Orleans, Louisiana 70118; 504.865.5131; Fax 504.865.6773

Iberia Cultural Resources; 924 E. Main St.; New Iberia, Louisiana 70560-3866

Jackson Assembly of the Felicianas; PO Box 494; Jackson, Louisiana 70748-0494

Jefferson Genealogical Society, Inc.; PO Box 961; Metairie, Louisiana 70004-0961; <gnofn.org/~jgs>

Jefferson Parish Library; 3420 N. Causeway; Metairie, Louisiana 70002

Jennings Genealogical Society; 136 Greenwood Dr.; Jennings, Louisiana 70546

Jewish Genealogical Society of New Orleans; PO Box 7811; Metairie, Louisiana 70010; <www.jewishgen.org/jgsno/>

L.D.S. Family History Center, Denham Spr. LA Stake; 7024 Morgan Rd; Greenwell Spr., Louisiana 70739

La Societe Des Cajuns; Rt. 1 Box 581; Golden Meadow, Louisiana 70357

Lafayette Genealogical Society; PO Box 30293; Lafayette, Louisiana 70593-0293

Lafayette Historical Society; 324 North Sterling; Lafayette, Louisiana 70501

Lafourche Heritage Society; PO Box 567; 412 Menard St.; Thibodaux, Louisiana 70392-0567

Lake Providence Historical Society; 1002 S. Lake St.; Lake Providence, Louisiana 71254-2428

Le Comite des Archives de la Louisiane; PO Box 44370; Baton Rouge, Louisiana 70804-4370; <sec.state.la.us/archives/archives/archives.comite.htm>

LeCircle Historique; 734 West Main St.; New Roads, Louisiana 70760-3522

Lincoln Parish Library; Box 637; 509 W. Alabama; Ruston, Louisiana 71270

Lobby Library; 3420 N. Causeway; Metairie, Louisiana 70002

Louisiana Genealogical & Historical Society; PO Box 82060; Baton Rouge, Louisiana 70884-2060; <www.rootsweb.com/~la.lghs/>

Louisiana Genealogical and Historical Society; PO Box 82060; Baton Rouge, Louisiana 70884-2068; 504.766.3018

Louisiana Genealogical Seminar; Rt. 4, Box 478; Opelousas, Louisiana 70750

Louisiana Historical Association, Univ. of Southwestern Louisiana; 929 Camp Street; New Orleans, Louisiana 70130; 318.482.6871; Fax 318.482.6028

Louisiana Historical Association, Univ. of Southwestern Louisiana; PO Box 42808; Lafayette, Louisiana 70504

Louisiana Historical Association; PO Box 40931; Lafayette, Louisiana 70504-0831

Louisiana Historical Society; 5801 St. Charles Ave.; New Orleans, Louisiana 70115-5053; <www.acadiacom.net/lahistsoc/>

Louisiana State Archives; PO Box 94125; Baton Rouge, Louisiana 70804-9125;225.922.0433; <www.sec.state.la.us/archives/archives/archives.index.htm>

Louisiana State Library; 760 Third Street; Baton Rouge, Louisiana 70802; 504.342.4913; Fax 504.342.3547

Louisiana State Library; PO Box 131; Baton Rouge, Louisiana 70821-0131

Louisiana State Library; State Capitol Ground; Baton Rouge, Louisiana 70804

Louisiana State Museum/Louisiana Historical Center Library; 400 Esplanade Avenue; New Orleans, Louisiana 70176-2448; 504.568.8214; Fax 504.568.4995

Lutheran, University of New Orleans, Earl K. Long Library; Archives and Manuscripts Div., Lake Front; New Orleans, Louisiana 70148; 504.286.6556; Fax 504.286.7277

Madison Parish Historical Society; 100 South Chestnut St.; Tallulah, Louisiana 71282-4202

Methodist, Centenary College of Louisiana; Magale Library, Cline Room, PO Box 41188; Shreveport, Louisiana 71134-1188; 318.869.5170; Fax 318.869.5004

Mississippi Memories Society; PO Box 18991; Shreveport, Louisiana 71138

Mt. Lebon Historical Society; General Delivery; Gibsland, Louisiana 71208-9999

Natchitoches Genealogical & Historical Association; PO Box 1349; Natchitoches, Louisiana 71458-1349; <www.rootsweb.com/~lanatchi/ngl.htm>

National Archives-Southwest Region (Fort Worth); 501 West Felix Street Building 1, Dock 1; Fort Worth, Texas 76115-0216; 817.334.5525; Fax 817.334.5621

National Archives-Southwest Region (Fort Worth); PO Box 6216; Fort Worth, Texas 76115-0216

New Orleans Public Library; 219 Loyola Avenue; New Orleans, Louisiana 70140-1016; 504.596.2612; Fax 504.596.2609

North Louisiana Genealogical Society; PO Box 324; Ruston, Louisiana 71273-0324

North Louisiana Historical Association; PO Box 6701; Shreveport, Louisiana 71106-6701

Orleans Parish Notarial Archives; Civil Courts Building, 421 Loyola AvenueRoom B-4; New Orleans, Louisiana 70112; 504.568.8578; Fax 504.568.8599

Ouachita Genealogical Society; 221 Riverbend; WestMonroe, Louisiana 71291

Ouachita Parish Public Library; 1800 Stubbs Ave.; Monroe, Louisiana 71201

Plaquemines Deep Delta Genealogical & Historical Society; 203 Hwy. 23; South Buras, Louisiana 70041

Pointe Coupee Historical Society; PO Box 462; New Roads, Louisiana 70760

Pointe Coupee Parish; Le Circle Historique; 734 Main St.; New Roads, Louisiana 70760

Pointe Coupee Museum & Tourist Center; Hwy. 1; New Roads, Louisiana 70760

Pointe de l'Eglise Historical & Genealogical Society; PO Box 160; Church Point, Louisiana 70525-0160

Rapides Parish Library; 411 Washington St.; Alexandria, Louisiana 71301

Red River Heritage; Rt. 4, Box 363; Coushatta, Louisiana 71019-8729

River Road Historical Society; PO Box 5; Destrehan, Louisiana 70047-0005

Roman Catholic, Archdiocese of New Orleans Archives; 7887 Walmsley Ave.; New Orleans, Louisiana 70125-3496; 504.861.9521; Fax 504.866.2906

Roman Catholic, Diocese of Alexandria-Shreveport; 4400 Coliseum Blvd.; Alexandria, Louisiana 71303; 318.445.2401; Fax 318.448.6121

Roman Catholic, Diocese of Baton Rouge Archives; 1800 South Acadian Thruway; Baton Rouge, Louisiana 70808; 504.387.0561; Fax 504.336.8789

Roman Catholic, Diocese of Baton Rouge Archives; PO Box 2028; Baton Rouge, Louisiana 70821-2028

Saint Domingue Special Interest Group; 1514 Saint Roch Ave.; New Orleans, Louisiana 70117-8347; 504.943.8150

Shreve Memorial Library, Gen. Dept.; 424 Texas St., PO Box 21523; Shreveport, Louisiana 71120

Society of the Sons & Daughters of The Province and Republic of West Florida 1763-1910; 13727 N. Amiss Rd.; Baton Rouge, Louisiana 70810-5042

Sons of the American Revolution, Louisiana Society; 3059 Belmont Ave.; Baton Rouge, Louisiana 70808

Southeast Louisiana Historical Society; PO Box 789; Hammond, Louisiana 70402-0789

Southwest Louisiana Gen. & Hist. Library; 411 Pujo St.; Lake Charles, Louisiana 70601-4254; 318. 437.3490

Southwest Louisiana Genealogical Society, Inc.; PO Box 5652; Lake Charles, Louisiana 70606-5652

Southwest Louisiana Historical Association; 4201 Alma Lane; Lake Charles, Louisiana 70605

St. Bernard Genealogical Society, Inc.; PO Box 271; Chalmette, Louisiana 70044; <www.rootsweb.com/ ~lastbern/stbgs.htm>

St. Helena Historical Society; Rt. 1, Box 131; Amite, Louisiana 70422-9415

St. Mary Genealogical & Historical Society; PO Box 662; Morgan City, Louisiana 70381-0662

St. Tammany Genealogical Society Library; 310 West 21st Ave.; Covington, Louisiana 70433

St. Tammany Genealogical Society; PO Box 1001; Mandeville, Louisiana 70470-1001

St. Tammany Historical Society; 129 Lamarque St.; Mandeville, Louisiana 70448

State Land Office; 625 N. 4th Street, Box 44124; Baton Rouge, Louisiana 70804; 504.342.4586; Fax 504.342.5458

Tangipahoa Parish Historical Society; 77139 North River Rd.; Kentwood, Louisiana 70444

Tangipahoa Parish Library; 200 E. Mulberry St.; Amite, Louisiana 70422-2524

Terrebonne Genealogical Society; PO Box 295, Station 2; Houma, Louisiana 70360-0295; <www.rootsweb.com/ ~laterreb/tgs.htm>

Vermillion Genealogical Society; PO Box 117; Abbeville, Louisiana 70511-0117

Vermillion Historical Society; PO Box 877; Abbeville, Louisiana 70510-0877

Vernon Historical & Genealogical Society & Library; Hwy. 121, Box 3713; Leesville, Louisiana 71440-0310

Vital Records Registry Office of Public Health; PO Box 60630; New Orleans, Louisiana 70160; 504.568.5152

West Bank Genealogy Society; PO Box 872; Harvey, Louisiana 70059-0872; <www.rootsweb.com/~lajeffer/wbgs.html>

West Bank Regional Library, Genealogy and Louisiana Special Collections; 2751 Manhattan Blvd.; Harvey, Louisiana 70058-6144

West Baton Rouge Genealogical Society; PO Box 1126; Port Allen, Louisiana 70767-1126

West Baton Rouge Historical Society; 845 N. Jefferson Ave.; Port Allen, Louisiana 70767-2417

West Feliciana Historical Society; PO Box 338; St. Francisville, Louisiana 70775-0338

West Florida Society, The Sons and Daughters of the Province and Republic of 1763-1810; 13727 N. Amiss Rd.; Baton Rouge, Louisiana 70810-5042

Westbank Genealogical Society; PO Box 872; Harvey, Louisiana 70058-0872

Winn Parrish Genealogical & Historical Association; PO Box 652; Winnfield, Louisiana 71483-0652; <www.rootsweb.com/~lawpgha/>

Winnfield Historical Society; PO Box 1039; Winnfield, Louisiana 71483-1039

Bibliography and Record Sources

General Sources

Adams, Donna Burge. *Women in the Florida Parishes*. 5 vols. Baton Rouge, Louisiana: D.B. Adams, 1985-1991.

Arsenault, Bona. *L'Acadie des Ancetres: Avec la Généalogie des Premières Familles Cadiennes*. Québec: Le Conseil de la vie française en Amérique, 1955.

Arthur, Stanley Clisby. *Old Families of Louisiana, 1608-1929, Volume I.* (1931) Reprint. Baltimore: Clearfield Co., 1997.

Arthur, Stanley Clisby. *Index to the Archives of Spanish West Florida, 1782-1810.* New Orleans, Louisiana: Polyanthos, 1975.

Baudier, Roger. *The Catholic Church in Louisiana.* New Orleans: Louisiana Library Association, Public Library Section, 1972.

Beers, H.P. *French and Spanish Records of Louisiana: A Bibliographical Guide to Archive and Manuscript Sources.* Baton Rouge: Louisiana State University Press, 1989.

Biographical and Historical Memoirs of Louisiana: Embracing an Authentic and Comprehensive Account of the Chief Events in the History of the State, A Special Sketch of Every Parish and a Record of the Lives of Many of the Most Worthy and Illustrious Families and Individuals. 2 vols. Chicago: Goodspeed Publishing Co., 1892.

Boling, Yvette G. *A Guide to Printed Sources for Genealogical and Historical Research in the Louisiana Parishes.* Jefferson, Louisiana: the author, 1985.

Bolton, Herbert E. *The Spanish Borderlands: A Chronicle of Old Florida and the Southwest.* (1921) Reprint. Galveston, Texas: Frontier Press.

Brasseaux, Carl A. *Founding of New Acadia: The Beginning of Acadian Life in Louisiana, 1765-1803.* Baton Rouge: Louisiana State University Press, 1987.

Brasseaux, Carl A. *Acadian to Cajun: Transformation of a People, 1803-1877.* Jackson, Miss.: University Press of Mississippi, 1992.

Brasseaux, Carl A., Keith P. Fontenot and Claude F. Oubre. *Creoles of Color in the Bayou Country.* Jackson, Mississippi: University Press of Mississippi, 1994.

Conrad. *The Louisiana Purchase Bicentennial Series in Louisiana History, Volume I: The French Experience in Louisiana.* Galveston, Texas: Frontier Press, 1995.

Courts, Kitty. *Down the Old Spanish Trail.* New Iberia, Louisiana: K. Courts, [1999?].

Cummins, Light Townsend, and Glen Jeansonne, eds. *A Guide to the History of Louisiana.* Westport, Connecticut: Greenwood Press, 1982.

Davis, Edwin Adams. *Louisiana: A Narrative History.* 2d ed. Baton Rouge: Claitor's Book Store, 1965.

Davis, Ellis Arthur. *The Historical Encyclopedia of Louisiana.* 2 vols. [Baton Rogue?]: Louisiana Historical Bureau, [19–?].

Deiler, J. Hanno. *A History of the German Churches in Louisiana (1823-1839).* Translated and edited by Marie Stella Condon. (1894, 1983) Reprint. Baltimore: Clearfield, 1995.

DeVille, Winston. *Gulf Coast Colonials. A Compendium of French Families in Early Eighteenth Century Louisiana.* (1968) Reprint. Baltimore: Clearfield Co., 1995.

Dictionary of Louisiana Biography. 2 vols. New Orleans: Louisiana Historical Association, 1988.

Din, Gilbert C. *The Canary Islanders of Louisiana.* Baton Rouge: Louisiana State University Press, 1988.

Eakin, Sue. *Louisiana, The Land and Its People.* 2nd ed. Gretna, Louisiana: Pelican Pub. Co., 1986.

Early Louisiana Settlers, 1600s-1800s. [S.l.]: Brøderbund, 2000. CD-ROM.

Fortier, Alcee. *A History of Louisiana.* 4 vols. New York: Manzi, Joyant, and Co., 1903.

Hall, Gwendolyn Midlo. *Africans in Colonial Louisiana: The Development of Afro-Creole Culture in the Eighteenth Century.* Baton Rouge: Louisiana State University Press, 1992.

Hamer, Collin B. Jr., *Genealogical Materials in the New Orleans Public Library.* New Orleans: Friends of the New Orleans Public Library, 1984.

Hebert, Donald J. *Guide to Church Records in Louisiana.* Eunice, Louisiana, 1976.

Hébert, Donald J. *A Guide to Church Records in Louisiana, 1720-1975.* [Eunice, Louisiana: s.n.], 1975.

Hebert, Donald J. *South Louisiana Records.* 12 vols. Cecilia, Louisiana: D.J. Hebert, 1978-1985.

Hebert, Donald J. *Southwest Louisiana Records: Church and Civil Records.* 40 vols. Eunice, Louisiana: D.J. Hebert, 1974-1985.

Hebert, Donald J. *Acadian-Cajun Genealogy: Step by Step.* Galveston, Texas: Frontier Press, 1993.

Hirsch, Arnold R., ed. *Creole New Orleans: Race and Americanization.* Baton Rouge: Louisiana State University Press, 1992.

Historical Records Survey (Louisiana). *Inventory of the Church and Synagogue Archives of Louisiana: Jewish Congregations and Organizations.* University, Louisiana: Dept. of Archives, L.S.U., 1941.

Inventory of the Louisiana Historical Association Collection on Deposit in the Howard-Tilton Memorial Library, Tulane University. Galveston, Texas: Frontier Press.

Kniffen, Fred B. *Historic Indian Tribes of Louisiana: From 1542 to the Present.* Reprint. Baton Rouge: Louisiana State University Press, 1994.

Labbe, Dolores Egger. *The Louisiana Purchase and Its Aftermath, 1800-1830.* Lafayette, Louisiana: Center for Louisiana Studies, University of Southwestern Louisiana, 1998.

Louisiana Colonials: Soldiers and Vagabonds. (1963), Reprint. Baltimore: Clearfield Co., 1995.

Louisiana History Association. *Louisiana History: The Journal of the Louisiana Historical Association.* Vols. 1-25, 1960-84. Vols. 26-30, 1985-89. Galveston, Texas: Frontier Press.

Louisiana Research Outline. Series US States, no. 19, Salt Lake City: Family History Library, 1988.

Louisianans and Their State: A Historical and Biographical Text Book of Louisiana. New Orleans: Louisiana Historical and Biographical Association, 1919.

Malone. *Sweet Chariot: Slave Family and Household Structure in Nineteenth Century Louisiana.* 1992. Galveston, Texas: Frontier Press, 1992.

Martin, François Xavier. *The History of Louisiana, From the Earliest Period.* 2 vols. New Orleans,: Lyman and Beardslee, 1827-29.

McAvoy, Thomas Timothy. *Guide to the Microfilm Edition of the Records of the Diocese of Louisiana and the Floridas, 1576-1803.* Notre Dame, Indiana: University of Notre Dame Archives, 1967.

Menn, Joseph Karl. *The Large Slaveholders of the Deep South, 1860.* Ann Arbor, Michigan: UMI Dissertation Services, 1964.

Mills, Gary B. *Forgotten People: Cane River's Creole of Color.* Baton Rouge: Louisiana State University Press, 1977.

Newspaper Files in Louisiana State University Library. Baton Rouge: Louisiana State University, 1961.

Nolan, Charles E. *A Southern Catholic Heritage.* New Orleans: Archdiocese of New Orleans, 1976.

Perkins, A. E. *Who's Who in Colored Louisiana.* Baton Rouge, Louisiana: Douglas Loan Co., 1930.

Perrin, William Henry. *Southwest Louisiana: Biographical and Historical.* Reprint. Baton Rouge: Claitor's Pub. Div., 1971.

Poret, George C. *Vignettes of Louisiana Church History.* [Mansura, La.?]: G. C. Poret, 1985.

Post, Lauren C. *Cajun Sketches from the Prairies of Southwest Louisiana.* Baton Rouge: Louisiana State University Press, 1990.

Resources in Louisiana Libraries: Public, Academic, Special and in Media Centers. Baton Rouge: Louisiana State Library, 1971.

Robichaux, Albert J., Jr. *German Coast Families: European Origins and Settlement in Colonial Louisiana.* Rayne, Louisiana: Hébert Publications, 1997.

Seebold, Herman Boehm de Bachellé. *Old Louisiana Plantation Homes and Family Trees.* 2 vols. [New Orleans: Pelican Press, 1941].

Sterkx, H. E. *The Free Negro in Ante-Bellum Louisiana.* Rutherford, New Jersey: Fairleigh Dickinson University Press, 1972.

Tanguay, Cyprien. *Dictionnaire Généalogique des Familles Canadiennes Depuis la Fondation de la Colonie jusqu'à nos jours.* 7 vols. New York: Ams Press, 1969.

United States. Bureau of Refugees, Freedmen, and Abandoned Lands. *Records of the Assistant Commissioner for the State of Louisiana, Bureau of Refugees, Freedmen, and Abandoned Lands, 1865-1869.* Washington, D.C.: The National Archives, 1976. 36 microfilm.

Usner, Daniel H. *Indians, Settlers & Slaves in a Frontier Exchange Economy: The Lower Mississippi Valley Before 1783.* Galveston, Texas: Frontier Press, 1992.

West, Robert C. *An Atlas of Louisiana Surnames of French and Spanish Origin.* Baton Rouge: Geoscience Pub., L.S.U. 1986.

Whittington, Hattie, and Gladys Sandefur. *Louisiana Ahnentafels, Ancestor Charts and Family Group Sheets.* Natchitoches, Louisiana: Natchitoches Genealogical and Historical Association, 1982.

Who's Who in Louisiana and Mississippi: Biographical Sketches of Prominent Men and Women of Louisiana and Mississippi. New Orleans: Times-Picayune, 1918.

Williams, Mary Eleanor. *Black Names in Louisiana.* [S.l.: s.n.], 1992.

Willie, Leroy Ellis. *German Ancestors and Patriots of Louisiana, 1722-1803.* [S.l.: s.n.], 1996.

Winzerling, Oscar William. *Acadian Odyssey.* Eunice, Louisiana: Hebert Publications, 1981.

Wood, Gregory. *A Guide to the Acadians in Maryland in the 18th and 19th Centuries.* 1995. Wheaton, Maryland: Maryland Acadian Studies, 1995.

Yoes, Henry E., 3rd, comp. *Biography of Louisiana Materials.* Hohnville, Louisiana, 1973.

Atlases, Maps and Gazetteers

County Parish Boundaries in Louisiana. New Orleans: Historical Records Survey, 1939.

Germann, John J. *Louisiana Post Offices.* Lake Grove, Oregon: The Depot, 1990.

Gibson, Dennis A., ed. *Index to Louisiana Place Names Mentioned in the War of the Rebellion: A Compilation of the Official Records of the Union and Confederate Armies.* Lafayette: University of Southwestern Louisiana, 1975.

Goins, Charles Robert, and John Michael Caldwell. *Historical Atlas of Louisiana.* 1995. Galveston, Texas: Frontier Press, 1995.

Hansen, Harry, ed. *Louisiana: A Guide to the State.* New York: Hastings House, 1971.

Historical Records Survey (Louisiana). *County Parish Boundaries in Louisiana.* New Orleans: LSU, 1939.

Newton, M. B. *Louisiana, A Geographical Portrait.* Baton Rouge: Geoforensics, 1987.

Spillman, Danell Strickland. *Louisiana Parish Map History.* Baton Rouge, Louisiana: D. Spillman, 1989.

Census Records

Available Census Records and Census Substitutes

Federal Census 1810, 1820, 1830, 1840, 1850, 1860, 1870, 1880, 1900, 1910, 1920, 1930.

Federal Mortality Schedules 1850, 1860, 1870, 1880.

Union Veterans and Widows 1890.

French Colonial Census 1699-1732.

State/Territorial Census 1706, 1721, 1726.

Confederate Veterans and Widows 1911.

Burns, Loretta E., comp. *Louisiana 1911 Census Confederate Veterans or Widows.* The author, 1995.

Dollarhide, William. *The Census Book: A Genealogist's Guide to Federal Census Facts, Schedules and Indexes.* Bountiful, Utah: Heritage Quest, 1999.

Kemp, Thomas Jay. *The American Census Handbook.* Wilmington, Delaware: Scholarly Resources, Inc., 2001.

Lainhart, Ann S. *State Census Records.* Baltimore: Genealogical Publishing Co., Inc., 1992.

Maduell, Charles R., Jr. *The Census Tables for the French Colony of Louisiana from 1699 Through 1732.* (1972) reprint, Baltimore: Clearfield Co., 1995.

Robichaux, Albert J., Jr. *Louisiana Census and Militia Lists 1770-1789.* 2 vols. Harvey, Louisiana: A. J. Robichaux, 1973 and 1974.

Szucs, Loretto Dennis, and Matthew Wright. *Finding Answers in U.S. Census Records.* Ancestry Publishing, 2001.

Thorndale, William, and William Dollarhide. *Map Guide to the U.S. Federal Censuses, 1790-1920.* Baltimore: Genealogical Publishing Co., 1987.

Court Records, Probate and Wills

Daughters of the American Revolution. Louisiana. *Genealogical Records Committee. Early Court Records and Wills.* Typescript. 1967-68.

English Language Summaries of the Records of the French Superior Council and the Judicial Records of the Spanish Cabildo, 1714-1800. N.p.: Works Project Administration, n.d.

Gianelloni, Elizabeth Becker. *Calendar of Louisiana Colonial Documents.* 3 vols. [S.l.]: The Commission, 1961-[1967?].

Louisiana (Province). Cabildo. *Inventory of the Records of the French Superior Council and Judicial Records of the Spanish Cabildo 1702-1803.* Microfilm of original records in the New Orleans Public Library. (Salt Lake City: Filmed by the Genealogical Society of Utah, 1981).

Louisiana (Province). Cabildo. *Judicial Records, 1769-1804.* Microfilm of original records filmed in the Louisiana Historical Center, New Orleans. (Salt Lake City: Filmed by the Genealogical Society of Utah, 1979-80). 239 microfilm.

Louisiana (Province). Conseil Superieur. *Records of the French Superior Court, 1679-1803. Name Card Index to Records of the French Superior Council and Judicial Records of the Spanish Cabildo.* Microfilm of original records in the Louisiana Historical Center, New Orleans. (Salt Lake City: Filmed by the Genealogical Society of Utah, 1981). 9 microfilm

Louisiana. District Court (Fifth District). *Index to Defendant and Plaintiff Dockets, 1846-1880.* Microfilm copy of original records located at the New Orleans Public Library, New Orleans, Louisiana. (Salt Lake City: Filmed by the Genealogical Society of Utah, 1985). 4 microfilm.

Louisiana. Judicial District Court (First District). *1st Judicial District Court Records, 1822-1846.* Microfilm copy of original records located at the New Orleans Public Library, New Orleans, Louisiana. (Salt Lake City: Filmed by the Genealogical Society of Utah, 1985). 3 microfilm.

National Archives Records Administration. Southwest Region in Fort Worth. *Louisiana, Eastern District, 1806-1982; Western District, 1832-1966; Louisiana, Middle District, 1971-1993; Louisiana, Western District, 1832-1961.* Fort Worth, Texas: National Archives Records Administration. Online database –<www.nara.gov/regional/findaids/ftwguid1.html#21>

Emigration, Immigration, Migration and Naturalization

Brasseaux, Carl A. *The "Foreign French": Nineteenth-Century French Immigration into Louisiana.* 3 vols. Lafayette: Center for Louisiana Studies, University of Southwestern Louisiana, 1900-93. Vol 1, 1820-39; vol. 2, 1840-48; vol 3, 1849-52.

Brasseaux, Carl A. *A Refuge For All Ages, Immigration In Louisiana History.* Lafayette, Louisiana: Center for Louisiana Studies, University of Southwestern Louisiana, 1996.

Conrad, Glen R. *The First Families of Louisiana.* 2 vols. Baton Rouge: Claitor's Pub. Division, 1970.

Early Louisiana settlers, 1600s-1800s. [S.l.]: Brøderbund, 2000. CD-ROM.

Hébert, Donald J. *Immigration Files Of Southwest Louisiana (1840-1929): Naturalization Records.* Mire, Louisiana: Hebert Pub., 1990.

Passage Index, Louisiana, 1718-1724. Miroreproduction of original published: Center Louisiana State Museum in New Orleans, Louisiana. New Orleans: Center Louisiana State Museum, 1980. 2 microfilm.

Rieder, Milton P., and Norma Gaudet Rieder, eds. *The Acadian Exiles in the American Colonies, 1755-1768.* Metairie, Louisiana: the editors, 1977.

Riviere, Mary Ann. *From Palermo to New Orleans.* [New Orleans?: M. Riviere], 1987.

Robichaux, Albert J., Jr. *German Coast Families: European Origins And Settlement In Colonial Louisiana.* Rayne, Louisiana: Hébert Publications, 1997.

United States. Circuit Court (Louisiana: Eastern District). *Naturalization Records, 1906-1912.* Microfilm copy of original records located at the district clerks office, New Orleans, Louisiana. (Salt Lake City: Filmed by the Genealogical Society of Utah, 1985). 5 microfilm.

United States. District Court (Louisiana: Eastern District). *Naturalization Record, Declaration of Intent.* (Salt Lake City: Filmed by the Genealogical Society of Utah, 1981). 7 microfilm.

United States. District Court (Louisiana: Eastern District). *Naturalization Records, 1906-1932.* Microfilm copy of original records located at the district clerk's office, New Orleans, Louisiana. (Salt Lake City: Filmed by the Genealogical Society of Utah, 1985). 30 microfilm.

United States. Immigration and Naturalization Service. *Crew Lists of Vessels Arriving at New Orleans, Louisiana, 1910-1920.* Washington, D.C.: The National Archives, 1987. 48 microfilm.

United States. Immigration and Naturalization Service. *Passenger Lists of Vessels Arriving at New Orleans, 1820-1921; Index to Passenger Lists of Vessels Arriving in New Orleans, 1853-1952.* (Washington DC: Filmed by the National Archives Record Service, 1947, 1957-1958).

United States. Immigration and Naturalization Service. *Quarterly Abstracts of Passenger Lists of Vessels Arriving At New Orleans, 1820-1875.* (Washington, DC: Filmed by the National Archives Record Service, 1959).

Viller'ae, Sidney Louis. *The Canary Islands Migration to Louisiana, 1778-1783: The History and Passenger Lists of the Islenos Volunteer Recruits and Their Families.* Baltimore: Genealogical Publishing Co., 1972.

Land and Property

Deville, Winston. *English Land Grants in West Florida: A Register for the States of Alabama, Mississippi, and Parts of Florida and Louisiana, 1766-1776.* Ville Platte, Louisiana: Winston Deville, 1986.

Exhibit Of Private Land Claims. Microfilm copy of original records located at the Division of State Lands office, Baton Rouge, Louisiana. (Salt Lake City: Filmed by the Genealogical Society of Utah, 1983).

First Settlers of the Louisiana Territory: Orleans Territory Grants from American State Papers, Class viii, Public Lands. 2 vols. Nacogdoches, Texas: Ericson Books, and St. Louis: Ingmire Publications, 1983.

Historical Records Survey (Louisiana). *Survey of Federal Archives in Louisiana: From U.S. Land Office Archives.* (Baton Rouge, Louisiana: Filmed by Archives and Records Service, [19–]).

Historical Records Survey, Division of Professional and Service Projects. Works Progress Administration. *Survey of Federal Archives in Louisiana; Land Claims and Other Documents, ca. 1800-1860.* Baton Rouge; Archives and Records Service, n.d.

Hone, Wade E. *Land and Property Research in the United States.* Salt Lake City: Ancestry Incorporated, 1997.

Lowrie, Walter, ed. *Land Claims in the Eastern District of the Orleans Territory. Communicated to the House of Representatives, January 9, 1812*. (1834) reprint Greenville, SC: Southern Historical Press, 1986.

Maudell, Charles R. *Federal Land Grants in the Territory of Orleans: The Delta Parishers*. New Orleans: Polyanthos, 1975.

McMullin, Phillip W., ed. *Grassroots of America: A Computerized Index to the American State Papers: Land Grants and Claims (1789-1837) With Other Aids to Research (Government document serial set numbers 28 through 36)*. Greenville, South Carolina: Southern Historical Press, 1994, 1990.

Pintado, Vincente Sebastian. *Pintado Papers, 1795-1842*. Baton Rouge; Archives and Records Service, n.d.

Poret, Ory Gerard,. *Louisiana Land Titles: An Inventory of State Land Office Records from the Early Nineteenth Century on File at the State Archives of Louisiana*. Ville Platte, Louisiana: Provincial Press, c1998.

Tipton, Ennis Mayfield. *Index To U.S. Tract Books, Northwestern Land District, Old Natchitoches District, In The Louisiana State Land Office*, Baton Rouge, Louisiana. Bossier City, Louisiana: Tipton Printing & Pub., 1980.

United States. District Land Office (New Orleans, Louisiana). *Surveys Of Land Claims, 1806-1813 And 1832-1834 ; Land Records, 1860- 1916; Certificates Of Location, 1858-1907*. Microfilm copy of original records located at the Division of State Lands Office, Baton Rouge, Louisiana. (Salt Lake City: Filmed by the Genealogical Society of Utah, 1983). 3 microfilm.

United States. District Land Office (Opelousas, Louisiana). *Land Records, 1805-1860*. Microfilm copy of original records located at the Division of State Lands Office, Baton Rouge, Louisiana. (Salt Lake City: Filmed by the Genealogical Society of Utah, 1983). 6 microfilm.

United States. District Land Office (St. Helena, Louisiana*). Land Records, 1803-1875*. Microfilm copy of original records located at the Division of State Lands Office, Baton Rouge, Louisiana. (Salt Lake City: Filmed by the Genealogical Society of Utah, 1983). 7 microfilm.

United States. Land Office (Baton Rouge, Louisiana). *Tract Books, 1807-1870*. (Salt Lake City: Filmed by the Genealogical Society of Utah, 1983). 24 microfilm.

Military

Adjunct General's Office. *The Compiled Service Records of Louisianans in the War of 1812*. Baton Rouge: Adjunct General's Office, n.d.

Allardice, Bruck. *Other Generals in Gray*. Baton Rouge: Louisiana State University Press, n.d.

Bartlett, Napier. *Military Record of Louisiana: Including Biographical and Historical Papers Relating to the Military Organizations of the State*. 1875. Reprint. Baton Rouge: Louisiana State University Press, 1964.

Bergeron, Arthur W. Jr. *Guide to Louisiana Confederate Military Units, 1861-1865*. Baton Rouge: Louisiana State University Press, 1989.

Booth, Andrew B. *Records of Louisiana Confederate Soldiers and Louisiana Confederate Commands*. (1920, 1984) Reprint. Spartanburg, SC: Reprint Co., 1996.

Casey, Powell A. *Louisiana in the War of 1812*. Baton Rouge: Casey, 1963.

Cunningham, H.H. *Doctors in Gray: The Confederate Medical Service*. Reprint. Baton Rouge: Louisiana State University Press, 1993.

DeVille, Winston. *Louisiana Troops, 1720-1770*. (1965) Reprint. Baltimore: Clearfield Co., 1994.

Enumeration of Ex-Confederate Soldiers and Widows of Deceased Soldiers of Louisiana, Made in 1911. (Salt Lake City: Filmed by the Genealogical Society of Utah, 1966).

España. Secretaría de Estado y del Despacho de Guerra. *Hojas de Servicios Militares de América: Floridas Y Luisiana, 1787-1794*. Madrid: Filmado por el Servicio Nacional de Microfilm, 1971.

Gaines, W. Craig. *Confederate Cherokees: John Drew's Regiment of Mounted Rifles*. Baton Rouge: Louisiana State University Press, 1989.

List of Men Who Died While Serving as Officers in the World War, Louisiana. (Salt Lake City: Filmed by the Genealogical Society of Utah, 1990).

Louisiana State Archives. *Confederate Pension Applications Index Database*. Baton Rouge, Louisiana: Louisiana State Archives 2002. Online database - <www.sec.state.la.us/archives/gen/cpa-index.htm>.

Louisiana. National Guard (New Orleans). *National Guard Records, 1717-1955*. Microreproduction of originals housed at the Louisiana National Guard, New Orleans, Louisiana. (Salt Lake City: Filmed by the Genealogical Society of Utah, 1990). 6 microfilm.

Pierson, M.J.B. *Louisiana Soldiers in the War of 1812*. Baton Rouge: Louisiana Genealogical and Historical Society, 1963.

Sifakis, Stewart. *Compendium of the Confederate Armies: Louisiana*. Galveston, Texas: Frontier Press, 1995.

United States Selective Service System, Louisiana. *World War I Selective Service System Draft Registration Cards, 1917-1918*. National Archives Microfilm Publications, M1509. Washington, D.C.: National Archives, 1987-1988.

United States. Adjutant General's Office. *Index to Compiled Service Records of Volunteer Soldiers Who Served During the Florida War in Organizations from the State of Louisiana*. Washington, D.C.: National Archives, 1957.

United States. Adjutant General's Office. *Index to Compiled Service Records of Volunteer Soldiers Who Served During the Mexican War*. Washington, D.C.: The National Archives, 1965.

United States. Adjutant General's Office. *Index to Compiled Service Records of Volunteer Soldiers Who Served During the War of 1812 in Organizations from the State of Louisiana 1812-1815*. Washington, D.C.: The National Archives, 1955.

United States. Adjutant General's Office. *Index to Compiled Service Records of Volunteer Soldiers Who Served During the War with Spain in Organizations from the State of Louisiana*. Washington, D.C.: The National Archives, 1957.

Warner, Ezra J. *Generals in Blue: Lives of the Union Commanders*. Louisiana State University Press, 1964.

Warner, Ezra J. *Generals in Gray: Lives of the Confederate Commanders*. Louisiana State University Press, 1959.

Wiley, Bell Irvin. *Life of Billy Yank: The Common Soldier of the Union*. Reprint. Baton Rouge: Louisiana State University Press, 1971.

Wiley, Bell Irwin. *Life of Johnny Reb: The Common Soldier of the Confederacy.* (1943) Reprint. Baton Rouge: Louisiana State University Press, 1971.

Wright, Nancy Lowrie, and Cathy Dantin Shannon. *Louisiana Volunteers In The War Of 1898.* Houma, Louisiana: Wright Shannon Publications, 1989.

Vital and Cemetery Records

Be It Known and Remembered: Bible Records, 4 vols. Baton Rouge: Louisiana Genealogical and Historical Society, 1960.

Bourgard, Shirley Chaisson. *Marriage Dispensations in the Diocese of Louisiana and the Floridas: 1786-1803.* New Orleans; Polyanthos, 1980.

Daughters of the American Revolution. Louisiana (New Orleans). *Louisiana Tombstone Inscriptions.* 22 vols. Salt Lake City: Genealogical Society of Utah, 1970.

DeVille, Winston. *The New Orleans French, 1720-1733, A Collection of Marriage Records Relating to the First Colonists of the Louisiana Province.* Baltimore: Genealogical Publishing Co., 1973.

Forsyth, Alice Daly. *Louisiana Marriage Contracts: A Compilation of Abstracts From Records of the Superior Council of Louisiana During the French Regime, 1725-1769.* 2 vols. New Orleans: Polyanthos, 1980.

Frazier, John Purnell. *Tombstone Inscriptions of Northwest Louisiana Cemeteries.* Pittsburg, Texas: John Purnell Fraizer, 1986.

Guide to Public Vital Statistics Records in Louisiana. New Orleans: Historical Records Survey, 1942.

Guide to Vital Statistics Records of Church Archives in Louisiana. New Orleans: Louisiana State Board of Health, 1942.

Hebert, Donald J. *South Louisiana Records.* 12 vols. Cecilia, Louisiana: Donald J. Herbert, 1978.

Louisiana Tombstone Inscriptions. 11 vols. Louisiana Society. Daughters of the American Revolution, 1957.

Marriage Records Index And Contracts (Louisiana), 1718-1900. Microreproduction of original published: Center Louisiana State Museum of New Orleans. New Orleans: Center Louisiana State Museum, 1980.

Mayers, Brenda L., and Gloria L. Kerns. *Death Notices from Louisiana Newspapers, 1811-1919.* vols. 1-6. Baker, Louisiana: Folk Finders, 1984.

Southwest Louisiana Records: Church and Civil Records. 33 vols. Eunice, Louisiana: Donald J. Herbert, 1974-85.

United States. Bureau of the Census. *Federal Mortality Census Schedules And Related Indexes: Louisiana; 1850; 1860; 1870; 1880.* Washington, D.C.: National Archives and Record Service, 1962. 5 microfilm.

County Website	Map Index	Date Created	Parent County or Territory From Which Organized Address/Details
Acadia County		10 Apr 1805	**Original county** Details: (Discontinued. Became Ascension & St. James Parishes 31 Mar 1807)
Acadia Parish www.rootsweb.com/~lapehgs/	L4	30 Jun 1886	**St. Landry** Acadia Parish; PO Box 922; Crowley, LA 70527-0922; Ph. 337.788.8881 Details: (Par Clk has m, div, pro & ct rec from 1886)
Allen Parish* www.rootsweb.com/~laallen/	K3	12 Jun 1912	**Calcasieu** Allen Parish; PO Box G; Oberlin, LA 70655-2007; Ph. 337.639.2803 Details: (Par Clk has m, div, pro & ct rec from 1913)
Ascension Parish www.ascensionparish.net/	M8	31 Mar 1807	**Acadia County** Ascension Parish; Houmas St; PO Box 192; Donaldsonville, LA 70346; Ph. 225.773.9866 Details: (Par Clk has m rec from 1763, div, pro & ct rec from 1800 & land rec from 1770)
Assumption Parish* www.rootsweb.com/~laassump/	M7	31 Mar 1807	**Lafourche** Assumption Parish; 105 Dr Martin Luther King Dr; PO Box 249; Napoleonville, LA 70390; Ph. 985.369.6653 Details: (Par Clk has m rec from 1800, pro rec from 1841, land rec from 1788, div & ct rec from 1868)
Attakapas County		10 Apr 1805	**Original parish** Details: (Created as Attakapas Co. Attakapas Parish created 31 Mar 1807. Discontinued & divided into St. Martin & St. Mary 17 Apr 1811, Lafayette 17 Feb 1823 & Vermilion 25 Mar 1844)
Avoyelles Parish www.mindspring.com/~jwbarron/ avoyeles.htm	J5	31 Mar 1807	**Original Parish** Avoyelles Parish; 312 N Main St; Marksville, LA 71351; Ph. 318.253.9208 Details: (Par Clk has m & land rec from 1908, pro rec from 1925, ct rec from 1929, div rec from 1939 & mil rec from 1886)
Baton Rouge Parish		31 Mar 1807	**Pointe Coupee** Details: (see West Baton Rouge) Created as Baton Rouge Parish & became West Baton Rouge)
Beauregard Parish* www.rootsweb.com/~labeaure/ beaurega.htm	K2	12 Jun 1912	**Calcasieu** Beauregard Parish; 412 Mayeaux Dr; De Ridder, LA 70634-0310; Ph. 337.463.6146 Details: (Par Clk has m, div, pro, ct & land rec from 1913)
Bienville Parish www.rootsweb.com/~labienvi/	G3	14 Mar 1848	**Claiborne** Bienville Parish; 300 Courthouse Sq; PO Box 746; Arcadia, LA 71001; Ph. 318.263.2123 Details: (Par Clk has m, div, pro & ct rec from 1848)
Bossier Parish* www.mybossier.com/index.htm	F2	24 Feb 1843	**Claiborne** Bossier Parish; PO Box 369; Benton, LA 71006; Ph. 318.965.2336 Details: (Par Clk has m, div, pro, land & ct rec from 1843 & mil rec from 1917)
Caddo Parish www.caddo.org/Parish_Commission/ default.htm	F1	18 Jan 1838	**Natchitoches** Caddo Parish; 501 Texas St; Shreveport, LA 71101; Ph. 318.226.6911 Details: (Par Clk has m, div, pro, ct & land rec from 1835)
Calcasieu Parish* www.cppj.net/	L2	24 Mar 1840	**St. Landry** Calcasieu Parish; PO Box 1030; Lake Charles, LA 70602-1030; Ph. 337.437.3550 Details: (Par Clk has m, div, pro, ct & land rec from 1910)
Caldwell Parish www.rootsweb.com/~lacaldwe/	H5	6 Mar 1838	**Catahoula, Ouachita** Caldwell Parish; Main St; Columbia, LA 71418; Ph. 318.649.2681 Details: (Par Clk has m, div, pro, ct & land rec from 1838)
Cameron Parish www.cameronparish.net/	M3	15 Mar 1870	**Calcasieu, Vermilion** Cameron Parish; 119 Smith Rdg; Cameron, LA 70631-0549; Ph. 337.775.5316 Details: (Par Clk has m, div, pro, ct & land rec from 1870 & mil dis rec from 1918)

County Website	Map Index	Date Created	Parent County or Territory From Which Organized Address/Details
Carroll Parish		14 Mar 1832	**Concordia, Ouachita**
			Details: (see East & West Carroll) Divided into East & West Carroll 28 Mar 1877
Catahoula Parish www.geocities.com/robertce/ catahoula/index.html	H6	23 Mar 1808	**Rapides** Catahoula Parish County; 301 Bushley St; PO Box 198; Harrisonburg, LA 71340-0198; Ph. 318.744.5497 Details: (Par Clk has m rec from 1830, bur, pro & div rec from 1800's, land rec from 1808 & mil rec)
Claiborne Parish www.rootsweb.com/~laclaib2/claibla.htm	E3	13 Mar 1828	**Natchitoches** Claiborne Parish; 512 E Main St; Homer, LA 71040; Ph. 318.927.9601 Details: (Courthouse burned 1849) (Par Clk has m, div, pro, ct & land rec from 1850)
Concordia Parish www.rootsweb.com/~laconcor/	I6	10 Apr 1805	**Original parish** Concordia Parish; 4001 Carter St, PO Box 790; Vidalia, LA 71373-0790; Ph. 318.336.4204 Details: (Par Clk has m rec from 1840, div, pro, ct & land rec from 1850)
DeSoto Parish www.rootsweb.com/~ladesoto/index.htm	G1	1 Apr 1843	**Natchitoches, Caddo** DeSoto Parish; Parish Courthouse; Mansfield, LA 71052; Ph. 318.872.3110 Details: (Par Clk has m & land rec from 1843, div, pro & ct rec)
East Baton Rouge Parish www.ci.baton-rouge.la.us/	K7	22 Dec 1810	**Feliciana** East Baton Rouge Parish; 222 St Louis St; Baton Rouge, LA 70802-5817; Ph. 225.383.0378 Details: (Par Clk has m rec from 1840, div, pro, ct & land rec from 1782)
East Carroll Parish www.eastcarroll.net/home.htm	F7	28 Mar 1877	**Carroll** East Carroll Parish; 400 1st St; Lake Providence, LA 71254-2616; Ph. 318.559.2399 Details: (Par Clk has m, pro & land rec)
East Feliciana Parish www.rootsweb.com/~laeastfe/ eastfeliciana.htm	K7	17 Feb 1824	**Feliciana** East Feliciana Parish; 12305 St Helena St; PO Drawer 599; Clinton, LA 70722; Ph. 225.683.5145 Details: (Par Clk has m, div, pro, ct & land rec from 1824)
Evangeline Parish www.evangelineparish.com/	K4	15 Jun 1910	**St. Landry** Evangeline Parish; 200 Court St; Ville Platte, LA 70586; Ph. 337.363.5671 Details: (Par Clk has m, div, pro, ct & land rec from 1911)
Feliciana Parish		7 Dec 1810	**Spanish West Florida** Details: (see East & West Feliciana) Dissolved to form parishes of East & West Feliciana 17 Feb 1824)
Franklin Parish www.rootsweb.com/~lafrankl/index.htm	G6	1 Mar 1843	**Catahoula, Ouachita, Madison** Franklin Parish ; 210 Main St; Winnsboro, LA 71295; Ph. 318.435.9429 Details: (Par Clk has m, div, pro, ct & land rec from 1843)
German Coast County		10 Apr 1805 Original county	Details: (Discontinued. Divided to form parishes of St. Charles & St. John the Baptist 31 Mar 1807)
Grant Parish* www.rootsweb.com/~lagrant/	I4	4 Mar 1869	**Rapides, Winn** Grant Parish; Main St; Colfax, LA 71417; Ph. 318.627.3157 Details: (Par Clk has m, div, land, pro, mil & ct rec from 1878)
Iberia Parish www.intersurf.com/~johnjanr/iberia.htm	M6	30 Oct 1868	**St. Martin, St. Mary** Iberia Parish County; 300 Iberia St Ste 400; New Iberia, LA 70560; Ph. 337.365.3221 Details: (Par Clk has m, div, pro & land rec from 1868)
Iberville Parish www.parish.iberville.la.us/	L7	10 Apr 1805	**Original parish** Iberville Parish; PO Box 423; Plaquemine, LA 70765-0423; Ph. 225.687.5160 Details: (Par Clk has m & land rec from 1770, div, pro & ct rec from 1807)
Jackson Parish www.rootsweb.com/~lajackso/ jacksonIndex.htm	G4	27 Feb 1845	**Claiborne, Ouachita, Union** Jackson Parish; 500 E Court St; PO Box 730; Jonesboro, LA 71251; Ph. 318.259.2424 Details: (Par Clk has m, div, land, pro, mil & ct rec from 1880)

County Website	Map Index	Date Created	Parent County or Territory From Which Organized Address/Details
Jefferson Davis Parish www.rootsweb.com/~lajeffda/	L3	12 Jun 1912	**Calcasieu** Jefferson Davis Parish; PO Box 1409; Jennings, LA 70546-1409; Ph. 337.824.1161 Details: (Par Clk has m, div, pro, ct & land rec from 1913)
Jefferson Parish* www.jeffparish.net/	N9	11 Feb 1825	**Orleans** Jefferson Parish; 200 Derbigny St; Gretna, LA 70053; Ph. 504.364.2800 Details: (Par Clk has m rec from 1863, div, pro & ct rec from 1825 & land rec from 1827)
La Salle Parish www.rootsweb.com/~lalasall/	H5	3 Jul 1908	**Catahoula** La Salle Parish; PO Box 1372; Jena, LA 71342-0057; Ph. 318.992.2101 Details: (Par Clk has m, div, pro, ct & land rec from 1910)
Lafayette Parish* www.lafayettegov.org/index.cfm	M5	17 Jan 1823	**St. Martin, Attakapas** Lafayette Parish; PO Box 4508; Lafayette, LA 70502-4508; Ph. 337.291.6400 Details: (Par Clk has m, div, pro, ct & land rec from 1823)
Lafourche Parish* www.lapage.com/parishes/lafou.htm	N8	10 Apr 1805	**Original parish** Lafourche Parish; 309 W 3rd St; Thibodaux, LA 70301-3021; Ph. 985.447.4841 Details: (Par Clk has b, m, div, pro, ct & land rec from 1808)
Lincoln Parish www.lincolnparish.org/	F4	27 Feb 1873	**Bienville, Jackson, Union, Clairborne** Lincoln Parish; 100 W Texas Ave; Ruston, LA 71270; Ph. 318.255.3663 Details: (Par Clk has m, div, pro & ct rec from 1873)
Livingston Parish www.lapage.com/parishes/livin.htm	K8	10 Feb 1832	**St. Helena** Livingston Parish; 20180 Iowa St; PO Box 427; Livingston, LA 70754; Ph. 225.686.2266 Details: (Par Clk has m, div, pro, ct & land rec from 1875)
Madison Parish www.rootsweb.com/~lamadiso/index.htm	G7	19 Jan 1838	**Concordia** Madison Parish; 100 N Cedar St; Tallulah, LA 71282; Ph. 318.574.0655 Details: (Par Clk has m rec from 1866, div & land rec from 1839, pro rec from 1850 & ct rec from 1882)
Morehouse Parish* www.rootsweb.com/~lamoreho/ morehouse.htm	E6	25 Mar 1844	**Ouachita** Morehouse Parish; 125 E Madison St; Bastrop, LA 71221; Ph. 318.281.3343 Details: (Par Clk has m, div, pro & ct rec from 1870, land rec from 1844 & cem abstract 1867-1957)
Natchitoches Parish* www.rootsweb.com/~lanatchi/index.htm	I3	10 Apr 1805	**Original parish** Natchitoches Parish; PO Box 799; Natchitoches, LA 71458-0799; Ph. 318.352.2714 Details: (Clk Ct has m rec from 1780, div, pro & ct rec)
Opelousas County		10 Apr 1810	**Original county** Details: (see St. Landry) St. Landry formed from Opelousas Co 31 Mar 1807
Orleans Parish* www.nocitycouncil.com/content/	M10	10 Apr 1805	**Original parish** Orleans Parish; 1300 Perdido St; New Orleans, LA 70112; Ph. 504.568.5152 Details: (Clk Civ Dis Ct has div, pro & ct rec from 1805; Reg of Conveyances has and rec from 1832; Pub Lib has voter registration rec 1895-1941, city directories from 1805 & precinct bks 1895-1952)
Ouachita Parish* www.bayou.com/~suelynn/ouachita.html	G5	10 Apr 1805	**Original parish** Ouachita Parish; 300 St John St; Monroe, LA 71201; Ph. 318.327.1444 Details: (Par Clk has m rec from 1800's, div, ct & pro rec from 1900, land rec from 1790's & some mil rec)
Plaquemines Parish* www.rootsweb.com/~laplaque/ laplaque.htm	O11	31 Mar 1807	**Orleans** Plaquemines Parish; Hwy 39; Pointe a la Hache, LA 70082-9999; Ph. 504.333.4343 Details: (Par Clk has m rec from 1809, div, pro, ct & land rec from 1800)

County Website	Map Index	Date Created	Parent County or Territory From Which Organized Address/Details
Pointe Coupee Parish www.pcpolicejury.org/	K6	10 Apr 1805	**Original parish** Pointe Coupee Parish; 160 E Main St; New Roads, LA 70760; Ph. 225.638.9596 Details: (Clk Ct has m rec from 1735, div rec from 1800, pro, ct & land rec from 1780)
Rapides Parish www.rppj.com/	J4	10 Apr 1805	**Original parish** Rapides Parish; 700 Murray St; PO Box 952; Alexandria, LA 71301; Ph. 318.473.8153 Details: (Par Clk has m, div, pro, ct & land rec from 1864)
Red River Parish www.rootsweb.com/~laredriv/index.htm	G2	2 Mar 1871	**Caddo, Bienville, Bossier, DeSoto, Natchitoches** Red River Parish; 615 E Carroll St; Coushatta, LA 71019; Ph. 318.932.6741 Details: (Clk Ct has m & pro rec from 1871, div & ct rec from 1904)
Richland Parish www.rootsweb.com/~larichla/home.html	G6	29 Sep 1868	**Ouachita, Carroll, Franklin, Morehouse** Richland Parish; 108 Courthouse Sq; PO Box 119; Rayville, LA 71269; Ph. 318.728.4171 Details: (Par Clk has m, div, pro, ct & land rec from 1869)
Sabine Parish* www.pastracks.com/states/louisiana/sabine/	I2	7 Mar 1843	**Natchitoches** Sabine Parish; 400 Court St; PO Box 419; Many, LA 71449-0419; Ph. 318.256.6223 Details: (Par Clk has m, div, land, pro & ct rec from 1843)
St. Bernard Parish* www.st-bernard.la.us/	M10	31 Mar 1807	**Original parish** St. Bernard Parish; 8201 W Judge Perez Dr; Chalmette, LA 70043; Ph. 504.278.1500 Details: (Clk Ct has m, pro, ct & land rec)
St. Charles Parish* www.st-charles.la.us/	N9	31 Mar 1807	**German Coast** St. Charles Parish; PO Box 302; Hahnville, LA 70057-0302; Ph. 985.783.6632 Details: (Par Clk has m, pro, land & ct rec)
St. Helena Parish www.rootsweb.com/~lasthele/index.htm	K8	27 Oct 1810	**Spanish West Florida** St. Helena Parish; Court Sq; Greensburg, LA 70441; Ph. 225.222.4521 Details: (Par Clk has rec from 1804)
St. James Parish www.stjamesla.com/	M8	31 Mar 1807	**Original parish** St. James Parish; River Rd, PO Box 106; Convent, LA 70723; Ph. 225.562.7497 Details: (Par Clk has m rec from 1846, div, pro & ct rec from 1809)
St. John the Baptist Parish www.sjbparish.com/	M8	31 Mar 1807	**German Coast** St. John the Baptist Parish; 2393 Hwy 18; La Place, LA 70049; Ph. 985.497.3331 Details: (Par Clk has m, div, pro, ct & land rec)
St. Landry Parish www.slpolicejury.org/	K5	31 Mar 1807	**Opelousas** St. Landry Parish; Court & Landry St; Opelousas, LA 70570; Ph. 337.942.5606 Details: (Par Clk has m rec from 1808, div & ct rec from 1813 & pro rec from 1809)
St. Martin Parish www.intersurf.com/~johnjanr/stmartin.htm	M6	17 Apr 1811	**Attakapas** St. Martin Parish; County Courthouse; PO Box 9; Saint Martinville, LA 70582; Ph. 337.332.4136 Details: (Par Clk has m, pro, ct & land rec)
St. Mary Parish www.parish.st-mary.la.us/	N7	17 Apr 1811	**Attakapas** St. Mary Parish; 101 Wilson St; Franklin, LA 70538; Ph. 337.828.4238 Details: (Par Clk has m, div, pro, ct & land rec from 1800)
St. Tammany Parish www.rootsweb.com/~lasttamm/ sttammany.htm	L10	27 Oct 1810	**Spanish West Florida** St. Tammany Parish; 510 E Boston St; PO Box 1090; Covington, LA 70434-1090; Ph. 985.646.4077 Details: (Par Clk has m, div, pro & ct rec from 1812, land rec from 1810, tax rec from 1880 & mil dis rec)

County Website	Map Index	Date Created	Parent County or Territory From Which Organized Address/Details
Tangipahoa Parish www.tangicouncil.com/	K9	6 Mar 1869	**Livingston, St. Tammany, St. Helena, Washington** Tangipahoa Parish; 110 N Bay St; Amite, LA 70422-0215; Ph. 985.748.8015 Details: (Par Clk has m, div, pro, ct & land rec from 1869)
Tensas Parish www.rootsweb.com/~latensas/index.html	H7	17 Mar 1843	**Concordia** Tensas Parish; Courthouse Sq; PO Box 78; Saint Joseph, LA 71366; Ph. 318.766.3921 Details: (Par Clk has m, div, pro & ct rec from 1843)
Terrebonne Parish* www.terrebonneparish.com/	O8	22 Mar 1822	**Lafourche** Terrebonne Parish; 301 Goode St; Houma, LA 70360-4513; Ph. 985.868.5660 Details: (Par Clk has m, land & pro rec)
Union Parish www.pastracks.com/states/louisiana/ union/	E4	13 Mar 1839	**Ouachita** Union Parish; Courthouse Bldg; 100 E Bayou St; Farmerville, LA 71241; Ph. 318.368.3055 Details: (Par Clk has m, div & pro rec from 1839 & ct rec)
Vermilion Parish www.vermilion.org/	N4	25 Mar 1844	**Lafayette** Vermilion Parish; 100 N State St; PO Box 790; Abbeville, LA 70510; Ph. 337.898.1992 Details: (Par Clk has m, div, pro, ct & land rec from 1885)
Vernon Parish www.rootsweb.com/~lavernon/ vernon.htm	J3	30 Mar 1871	**Natchitoches, Rapides, Sabine** Vernon Parish; 201 S 3rd St; PO Box 40; Leesville, LA 71496-0040; Ph. 337.238.1384 Details: (Par Clk has m rec from 1890, div, pro & ct rec from 1871)
Washington Parish* www.rootsweb.com/~lawashin/	K9	6 Mar 1819	**St. Tammany** Washington Parish; Courthouse; Franklinton, LA 70438; Ph. 985.839.4663 Details: (Par Clk has m, div, pro, ct & land rec from 1897)
Webster Parish www.rootsweb.com/~lawebste/ webster.html	E2	27 Feb 1871	**Claiborne, Bienville, Bossier** Webster Parish; 410 Main St; PO Box 370; Minden, LA 71058-0370; Ph. 318.371.0366 Details: (Par Clk has m, div, pro, ct & land rec from 1871)
West Baton Rouge Parish www.wbrcouncil.org/	L7	31 Mar 1807	**Pointe Coupee** West Baton Rouge Parish; PO Box 107; Port Allen, LA 70767-0757; Ph. 225.383.0378 Details: (Created as Baton Rouge Parish) (Clk Ct has b, m, pro & land rec)
West Carroll Parish www.westcarrollweb.com/	F6	28 Mar 1877	**Carroll** West Carroll Parish; PO Box 630; Oak Grove, LA 71263-0630; Ph. 318.428.3390 Details: (Par Clk has m rec from 1877, div, pro, ct & land rec from 1833)
West Feliciana Parish www.pastracks.com/states/ Louisiana/wfeliciana/	K7	17 Feb 1824	**Feliciana** West Feliciana Parish; 4789 Prosperity St; Saint Francisville, LA 70775; Ph. 225.635.3794 Details: (Par Clk has m rec from 1879, div, pro & ct rec from 1900 & land rec rom 1811)
Winn Parish* www.rootsweb.com/~lawinn/	H4	24 Feb 1852	**Natchitoches, Catahoula, Rapides** Winn Parish; PO Box 951; Winnfield, LA 71483-0951; Ph. 318.628.3515 Details: (Par Clk has m, div, pro, ct & land rec from 1886)

Notes

White Pine

MAINE

CAPITAL: AUGUSTA – STATE 1820 (23RD)

Vikings and other explorers may have sighted the coast of Maine as early as 1000 AD. The first explorers known to have definitely explored this coast were John and Sebastian Cabot in 1498. Over the next century, English, Portuguese, French, and Spanish expeditions visited the area. Attempts at settlement were made between 1607 and 1625, but all proved unsuccessful. In 1625, the English made the first permanent settlement at Permaquid. Other settlements followed rapidly including York, Saco, Biddeford, Cape Elizabeth, Falmouth (present-day Portland), and Scarboro. Two members of the Plymouth Colony, Sir Ferdinando Gorges and Captain John Mason, were granted the land between the Merrimack and Kennebec rivers in 1622. In 1629, they divided their lands, with Gorges taking the present state of Maine and Mason, New Hampshire. France likewise claimed the area. Indians sided with the French, which resulted in the French and Indian Wars from about 1632 until 1759.

Massachusetts purchased the province of Maine from Gorges' heirs in 1677 and set up a government in the area. After the death of King Charles in 1685, Massachusetts lost all of its legal standings, forcing landholders to re-secure their land at high fees. These land titles were recorded in Boston; Maine also kept a special land office at York. The area was called the Province of Maine of the Massachusetts Bay Colony until 1779, when it became the District of Maine. Following the Revolution, in which Maine suffered more damage than any other New England area, settlement increased rapidly. The biggest deterrent to settlement was the difficulty of travel in the area, as roads were extremely poor. During the War of 1812, the British captured several Maine cities and the eastern part of Maine came under British control. Desires for separation from Massachusetts intensified, which resulted in statehood as part of the Missouri Compromise of 1820.

The Aroostook War in the 1830's brought approximately 10,000 troops into the area in 1838-1839, but no actual fighting occurred. The War ended in 1842 when a treaty settled the boundary between Maine and New Brunswick. During the Civil War, Maine supplied over 70,000 men to the Union armies. Early settlers were mainly English, Scotch-Irish, and Huguenots. From 1740 to 1800, some German families came to Waldoboro. About 15 percent of the current population descends from two early French groups: the Acadians came from Nova Scotia to the Saint John Valley after 1763 and French Canadians came from Quebec after the Civil War. Artisans from England, Scotland, and Scandinavia came to work in factories and shipyards during the nineteenth century. About 1870, a large number of Swedes settled in the northeast corner of Maine, organizing such cities as New Sweden, Stockholm, Jemtland, and Linneus.

Look for vital records in the following locations:

- **Birth, deaths and marriages:** Very early in their history, Maine towns began keeping records of births, deaths, and marriages. This continued until state registration began in 1892. Selectmen or town clerks kept these records. Many of these records have been printed, while the rest are available for searching in city offices. State records are kept at the Office of Vital Statistics Department of Human Services, State House in Augusta, Maine.
- **Histories:** Town histories have also been published for the large majority of Maine cities and usually contain genealogical information about early settlers.
- **Adoption records:** Adoption decrees are at the Probate or Superior Court where the adoption was granted. They are sealed after 8 August 1953.
- **Land records:** Land records are in the 16 offices of court clerks. The 16 registrars of probate have settlements of estates.
- **Military records:** War service records, including grave registrations, are at the office of the Adjutant General in Augusta. Since Maine was part of Massachusetts until 1820, soldiers might be listed

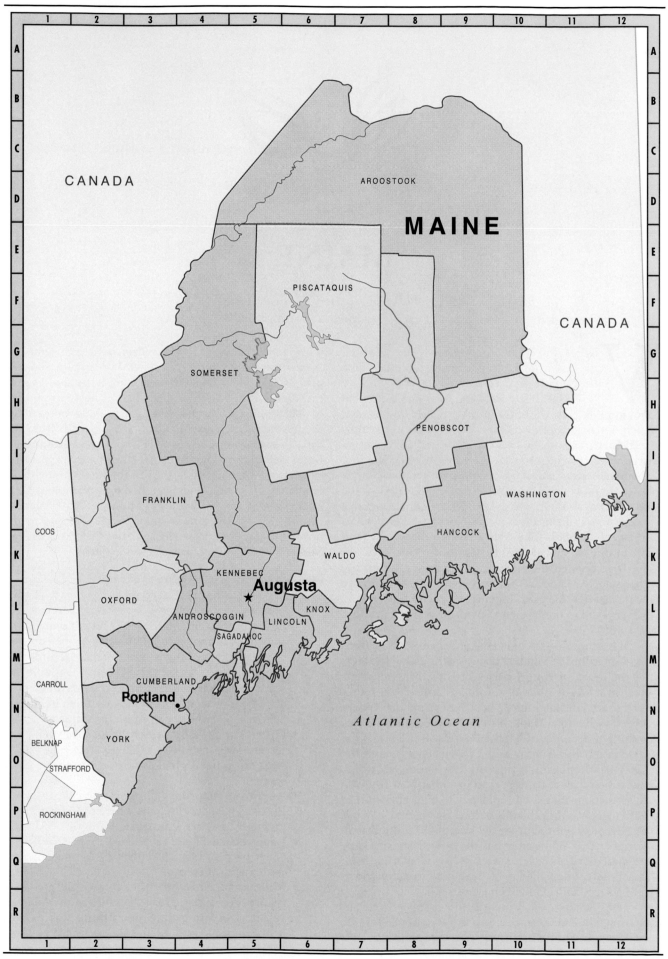

CANADA

AROOSTOOK

MAINE

PISCATAQUIS

CANADA

SOMERSET

PENOBSCOT

FRANKLIN

COOS

WASHINGTON

HANCOCK

WALDO

KENNEBEC

Augusta

OXFORD

KNOX

ANDROSCOGGIN

LINCOLN

SAGADAHOC

CARROLL

CUMBERLAND

Portland

Atlantic Ocean

BELKNAP

YORK

STRAFFORD

ROCKINGHAM

with Massachusetts' military records. Lists of many pension and bounty records have also been published.

- **Census records:** In 1827, a state census was taken, returns exist for only a few areas, including Portland, Bangor, and some unincorporated areas. These returns are available at the Maine State Archives. The returns for Eliot are at the Maine Historical Society, 435 Congress Street, Portland, Maine 04101.

**Office of Vital Statistics
Department of Human Services**
State House, Station 11
Augusta, Maine 04333

Maine State Archives Building
State House, Station 11
Augusta, Maine 04333
207.287.3181

Maine Historical Society
435 Congress Street
Portland, Maine 04101

Societies and Repositories

Acton-Shapleigh Historical Society; PO Box 545; Acton, Maine 04001-0545; <www.actonmaine.com/histscty/histscty.htm>

Albion Historical Society; PO Box 68; Albion, Maine 04910;

Allagash Historical Society; Allagash, Maine; <aroostook.me.us/allagash/historical.html>

Androscoggin Historical Society; Court Street Door; County Building; Auburn, Maine 04210-5978; <www.rootsweb.com/~meandrhs/>

Arnold Expedition Historical Society; RR 4, Box 6895; Gardiner, Maine 04345-9112; <www.rootsweb.com/~aehs/aehs.htm>

Auburn Public Library; Court & Spring Sts.; Auburn, Maine 04210

Bangor Public Library; 145 Harlow Street; Bangor, Maine 04401; 207.947.8336; Fax 207.945.6694

Baptist, American Baptist Samuel Colgate Historical Society; 1106 South Goodman Street; Rochester, New York 14602; 716.473.1740; Fax 716.473.1740

Bath Historical Society; Sagadahoc History and Genealogical Rm.; Patten Free Library; 33 Summer St.; Bath, Maine 04530-2687

Bath, Patten Free Library; Maine Hist. & Gen. Rm., 33 Summer St; Bath, Maine 04530

Bethel Historical Society; PO Box 12; Bethel, Maine 04217; 207.824.0882;

Bridgton Historical Society; PO Box 44; Bridgton, Maine 04009; <www.megalink.net/~bhs/index.html>

Buckfield Historical Society; c/o Mary Young; R.R. 4, Box 780; Turner, Maine 04282-9604

Camden Historical Society; 80 Mechanic St.; Camden, Maine 04843

Camden-Rockport Historical Society; PO Box 747; Rockport, Maine 04856; <members.mint.net/chmuseum/>

Cherryfield-Narraguagus Historical Society; PO Box 96; Cherryfield, Maine 04622

Cushing Historical Society, Inc.; PO Box 110; Cushing, Maine 04563; <www.rootsweb.com/~usgenweb/me/knox/cushing.htm>

Department of Human Services, Office of Vital Statistics; State House, Station #11; Augusta, Maine 04330; 207.287.3184

Dexter Historical Society; PO Box 481; Dexter, Maine 04930; <www.dextermaine.org/museum/index.html>

Episcopal, Archives of the Diocesan House, Attn: Archivist; 143 State Street; Portland, Maine 04101; 800.244.6062

Falmouth Historical Society; Falmouth Memorial Library; 5 Lunt Road; Falmouth, Maine 04105; <www.falmouth.lib.me.us/historical.html>

Finn-Am Society of Mid-Coast Maine; PO Box 488; Warren, Maine 04864

Finnish American Heritage Society of Maine; PO Box 294; West Paris, Maine 04289

Gorham Historical Society; 28 School Street; Gorham, Maine 04038; <www.gorhamcu.com/ghs/home.html>

Gray Historical Society; PO Box 544; Gray, Maine 04039; <www.graymaine.org/history.htm>

Hancock Genealogical Society; PO Box 243; Bass Harbor, Maine 04653; <ellsworthme.org/hcgs/>

Hiram Historical Society; 158 Sebago Road; Hiram, Maine 04041; 207.625.4663; <www.rootsweb.com/~mechiram>

Kennebeck Historical Society; PO Box 5582; Augusta, Maine 04332-5582;

Kennebunk Free Library; 112 Main St.; Kennebunk, Maine 04043

Kennebunkport Historical Society; PO Box 1173; Kennebunkport, Maine 04046; 207.967.1205;

Madison (Maine) Historical and Genealogical Society; 165 Main St.; Madison, Maine 04950; <members.mint.net/laton/mh&gsoc.htm>

Maine Franco-American Genealogical Society; Fr. Leo E. Begin Library; 115 High St.; Auburn, Maine 04210; 207.782.7939; <www.avcnet.org/begin/>

Maine Genealogical Society; PO Box 221; Farmington, Maine 04938

Maine Historical Society; 489 Congress St.; Portland, Maine 04111; 207.775.4301;

Maine Mayflower Society; PO Box 622; Yarmouth, Maine 04096-1164

Maine State Archives; 84 State House Station; Augusta, Maine 04333-0084; 207.287.5739; <www.state.me.us/sos/arc/>

Maine State Library; State House Station #64; Augusta, Maine 04333; 207.289.5600; Fax 207.287.5615

Methodist, Boston University School of Theology Library; 745 Commonwealth Ave.; Boston, Massachusetts 02215; 617.353.3034; Fax 617.353.3061

Milo Historical Society; 12 High Street; Milo, Maine 04463; 207.943.2268; <www.kynd.com/~milohist/>

Mount Desert Island Historical Society; PO Box 653; Mount Desert, Maine 04660; <ellsworthme.org/mdihsociety/>

National Archives-New England Region; 380 Trapelo Road; Waltham, Massachusetts 02154; 617.647.8100; Fax 617.647.8460

New England Historic Genealogical Society; 101 Newbury Street; Boston, Massachusetts 02116-3007; 617.536.5740, 1.888.286.3447; Fax 617.536.7307

Oakland Area Historical Society; Macartney House Museum; Main Street; Oakland, Maine; 207.465.7549; <www.rootsweb.com/~mecoakla/>

Old Broad Bay Family History Association; PO Box 1242; Waldoboro, Maine 04572; <www.rootsweb.com/~meobbfha/>

Old York Historical Society Library; PO Box 312; 207 York Street; York, Maine 03909; 207.363.4621; Fax 207.363.4974 <http:www.oldyork.org>

Otisfield Historical Society; c/o Ethel Turner; 105 Cape Road; Otisfield, Maine 04270; 539.2521; <www.rootsweb.com/~mecotisf/otis8.htm>

Patton Free Library; 33 Summer St.; Bath, Maine 04530; 207.443.5141

Pejepscot Chapter Maine Genealogical Society; 35 Grove St; Lisbon Falls, Maine 04252-1328

Pejepscot Historical Society; 159 Park Row; Brunswick, Maine 04011; 207.729.6012; <www.curtislibrary.com/pejepscot.htm>

Piscataqua Pioneers; 38 Mendum Avenue; Kittery, Maine 03904

Roman Catholic, The Archives of the Diocese of Portland; PO Box 11559, 510 Ocean Avenue; Portland, Maine 04104-7559; Fax 207.773.0182

Scarborough Historical Society; PO Box 156; Scarborough, Maine 04070-0156; <www.scarboroughmaine.com/historical/>

Society of Colonial Wars in the State of Maine; <www.acadia.net/sotcw/>

Sons of the American Revolution, Maine Society; Thing's Corner; PO Box 67; Limerick, Maine 04048

Stephen Phillips Memorial Library, Penobscot Marine Museum; PO Box 498; Searsport, Maine 04974; 207.548.2529; Fax 207.548.2520

Sullivan & Sorrento Historical Society; PO Box 44; Sullivan, Maine 04664; <ellsworthme.org/sshs/>

Sunrise Research Institute; PO Box 156; Whitneyville, Maine 04692

The Sandy River Valley Chapter of the Maine Genealogical Society; Farmington Public Library; 2 Academy Street; Farmington, Maine 04938; <www.rootsweb.com/~mesrvmgs/>

Thomaston Historical Society; PO Box 384; Thomaston, Maine 04861; <www.mint.net/thomastonhistoricalsociety/>

Union Historical Society; PO Box 154; Union, Maine 04862; <www.midcoast.com/comespring/>

University of Maine at Orono, Raymond H. Fogler Library, Special Collections; PO Box 5729; Orono, Maine 04469-5729; 207.581.1686; Fax 207.581.1653

Vinalhaven Historical Society; PO Box 339; Vinalhaven, Maine 04863; <www.midcoast.com/~vhhissoc/home.html>

Walker Memorial Library; 800 Main St.; Westbrook, Maine 04092

Washington Co. Genealogical Society; RR 1, Box 28 Shore Rd.; Perry, Maine 04667

Windham, Maine Historical Society; Windham, Maine; <www.rootsweb.com/~mewhs/>

Woolwich Historical Society; PO Box 98; Woolwich, Maine 04579;

Bibliography and Record Sources

General Sources

American Historical Association. *Annual Report of the American Historical Association for the Year 1908.* Washington, D.C.: Government Printing Office, 1909.

Anderson, Joseph C. II. *Maine Families in 1790, Volume 5.* 1996.

Banks, Ronald F. *Maine Becomes a State: The Movement to Separate Maine from Massachusetts, 1785-1820.* Middletown, Connecticut: Published for the Maine Historical Society by Wesleyan University Press, 1970.

Bibliography of the State of Maine. 2 vols. (1896) Reprint. Rockport, Maine: Picton Press, 1985.

Burrage, Henry Sweetser. *Genealogical and Family History of the State of Maine.* 4 vols. New York: Lewis Historical Publishing Company, 1909.

Chase, Henry. *Representative Men of Maine: A Collection of Portraits with Biographical Sketches of Residents of the State, Who Have Achieved Success...to Which is Added the Portraits and Sketches of all the Governors Since the Formation of the State....* Portland, Maine: Lakeside Press, 1893.

Committee for a New England Bibliography. *Maine, A Bibliography of Its History.* Boston: G. K. Hall, 1977.

Crandall, Ralph J., ed. *Genealogical Research in New England.* Baltimore: Genealogical Publishing Co., 1984.

Cutter, William Richard. *New England Families: Genealogical and Memorial.* 4 vols. New York: Lewis Historical Publishing, 1914.

Daughters of the American Revolution (Maine). *Genealogical and Miscellaneous Records Collected 1925-1972.* Microfilm of typescript material at the D.A.R. Library in Washington, D.C. (Salt Lake City: Genealogical Society of Utah, 1971-72). 18 microfilm.

Daughters of the American Revolution. Frances Scott Chapter (District of Columbia). *Maine Records.* Salt Lake City: Genealogical Society of Utah, 1958.

Davis, Walter Goodwin. *Massachusetts and Maine Families.* Baltimore: Genealogical Pub. Co., 1996.

Directory of Maine Pioneer Ancestors. n.p., 198–?

Dormer, Mary H. *Directory of Maine Pioneer Ancestors.* [S.l.: s.n., 198-?].

Early New England Settlers, 1600s-1800s. [S.l.]: Brøderbund, 1999. CD-ROM.

English Origins of New England Families: From the New England Historical and Genealogical Register. Second series, 3 vols. Baltimore: Genealogical Publishing, 1985.

Estes, Marie. *Name Index to Maine Local Histories.* Portland: Maine Historical Society, 1985.

French, W. R. *Record of Marriages, 1841-1893, asnd Funerals, 1840-1893.* (Salt Lake City: Filmed by the Genealogical Society of Utah, 1953).

Frost, John Eldridge. *Maine Genealogy: A Bibliographical Guide.* 1985. Rev. ed. Portland, Maine: Maine Historical Society, 1985.

Genealogies of Maine families. 3 vols. Microfilm of original records at the Maine Historical Society in Portland. (Salt Lake City: Filmed by the Genealogical Society of Utah, 1956).

Gorn, Michael H., ed. *An Index and Guide to the Microfilm Edition of the Massachusetts and Maine Direct Tax Census of 1798.* Boston: New England Historic Genealogical Society, 1979.

Gray, Philip Howard. *Penobscot Pioneers.* 4 vols. Camden, Maine: Penobscot Press, 1992-1994.

Greenlaw, William Prescott. *The Greenlaw Index of the New England Historic Genealogical Society.* 2 vols. Boston: G. K. Hall, 1979.

Greenleaf, Jonathan. *Sketches of the Ecclesiastical History of the State of Maine from the Earliest Settlement to the Present Time.* Portsmouth [N.H.]: H. Gray, 1821.

Hall, Lu Verne V. *New England Family Histories: States of Maine and Rhode Island.* Bowie, Md.: Heritage Books, 2000.

Haskell, John D., Jr., ed. *Maine: A Bibliography of Its History.* Boston: G.K. Hall, 1977.

Hatch, Louis Clinton, ed. *Maine: A History.* 5 vols. New York: American Historical Society, 1919.

Herdon, Richard, et al. *Men of Progress: Biographical Sketches and Portraits of Leaders in Business and Professional Life in and of the State of Maine.* Boston: New England Magazine, 1897.

Historical Records Survey (Maine). *Directory of Churches and Religious Organizations in Maine.* Portland: Maine Historical Records Survey Project, 1940.

Historical Records Survey (Maine). *Town Government in Maine.* Portland, Maine: The Survey, 1940.

Hodgkins, Theodore Roosevelt. *Brief Biographies, Maine: A Biographical Dictionary of Who's Who in Maine, Vol. 1.* Lewiston, Maine: Lewiston Journal, 1926-1927.

Kohl, J. G.. *A History of the Discovery of Maine.* Portland, Maine: Maine Historical Society, 1869.

Lawton, R. J. *Franco-Americans of the State of Maine, U.S.A., and Their Achievements: Historical, Descriptive and Biographical.* Lewiston, Maine: H.F. Roy, 1915.

Lindberg, Marcia Wiswall. *Genealogist's Handbook for New England Research.* 3rd ed. Boston, Massachusetts: New England Historic Genealogical Society, 1993.

Little, George Thomas. *Genealogical and Family History of the State of Maine.* 4 vols. New York: Lewis Historical Publishing, 1909.

Maine & New Hampshire Settlers, 1600s-1900s. [S.l.]: Brøderbund, 2000. CD-ROM.

Maine Families in 1790. 6 vols. Camden, Maine: Picton Press, 1988-1998.

Maine Research Outline. Series US States, no. 20. Salt Lake City: Family History Library, 1988.

Maine State Archives. *Agencies of State Government, 1820-1971, Parts I and II.* Augusta, Maine: Maine State Archives, n.d.

Maine State Archives. *Public Record Repositories in Maine.* Augusta, Maine: Maine State Archives, n.d.

Massachusetts & Maine Genealogies, 1650s-1930s: From The Genealogical Publishing Co., Inc.. [S.l.]: Brøderbund, 1998. CD-ROM

Moody, Robert Earle. *The Maine Frontier, 1607 to 1763.* Ann Arbor, Mich.: University Microfilms, 1980.

Moulton, Augustus F. *Maine Historical Sketches.* [Lewiston, Me.]: Printed for the State, Lewiston Journal Printshop, 1929.

Noyes, Benjamin Lake. *Vital Records Copied from Town, Churches & Cemeteries Records in Various Towns and Counties Of Maine Along the Atlantic Seaboard.* 2 vols. Washington, D.C.: D.A.R. Library.

Noyes, Sybil, Charles T. Libby, and Walter G. Davis. *Genealogical Dictionary of Maine and New Hampshire.* (1928-1939) Reprint. Baltimore: Genealogical Publishing, 1996.

Pioneers of Maine. Microfilm of original records (2v) in the Bangor Public Library. (Salt Lake City: Genealogical Society of Utah, 1956).

Piscataqua Pioneers. Applications for Membership, 1908-1990. Salt Lake City: Genealogical Society of Utah, 1978, 1980-1990.

Pope, Charles Henry. *The Pioneers of Maine and New Hampshire, 1623-1660.* (1908). Reprint. Baltimore: Clearfield Co., 1997.

Public Record Repositories in Maine. Augusta, Maine: Maine State Archives, 1976.

Ray, Roger B. *The Indians of Maine and the Atlantic Provinces: A Bibliographical Guide.* Portland, Maine: Maine Historical Society, 1977.

Rider, Fremont, ed. *American Genealogical-Biographical Index. Vols. 1-186+.* Middletown, CT: Godfrey Memorial Library, 1952-.

Ring, Elizabeth. *[Bibliographical] Reference List of Manuscripts Relating to the History of Maine.* (1938). Reprint. Salem, Massachusetts: Higginson Books, 1992.

Savage, James. *A Genealogical Dictionary of the First Settlers of New England Showing Three Generations of Those Who Came Before May 1692, on the Basis of Farmer's Register.* 4 vols. 1860-62. Reprint. Baltimore: Genealogical Publishing, Co., 1969.

Sawtelle, William Otis. *Historic Trails and Waterways of Maine.* Augusta, Maine: Maine Development Commission, 1932.

Sewall, R. K. *Ancient Dominions of Maine: Embracing the Earliest Facts ...* Bowie, Maryland: Heritage Books, 1998.

Spencer, Wilbur D. *Pioneers on Maine Rivers. With Lists to 1651.* (1930) Reprint. Baltimore: Clearfield Co., 1995.

Sylvester, Herbert Milton. *Maine Pioneer Settlements.* 5 vols. Boston, Massachusetts: W.B. Clark, 1909.

Taylor, Alan. *Liberty Men and Great Proprietors: The Revolutionary Settlement on the Maine Frontier, 1760-1820.* Galveston, Texas: Frontier Press, 1990.

United States. Commissioner of Internal Revenue. *Internal Revenue Assessment Lists for Maine, 1862-1866.* Washington, D.C.: National Archives and Records Service, 1970.

Wedda, John. *New England Worships: 100 Drawings Of Churches And Temples With Accompanying Text.* New York: Random House, 1965.

Jordan, William B., comp. *Maine in the Civil War: A Bibliographical Guide*. Portland, Maine: Maine Historical Society, 1976.

Jordan, William B., Jr. *Red Diamond Regiment: The 17th Maine Infantry, 1862-1865*. GalvestonTexas: Frontier Press, 1995.

Maine State Archives. *Dubros Times: Depositions of Revolutionary War Veterans*. Augusta, Maine: Maine State Archives, n.d.

Maine State Archives. *Military Records and Related Sources*. Augusta, Maine: Maine State Archives, 2000. <www.state.me.us/sos/arc/archives/military/military.htm>

Maine. Adjunct General. *Annual Report*. Augusta, Maine: state printer, 1862-67.

Maine. Adjutant General. *Report of the Adjutant General of the State of Maine for the Period of the World War, 1917-1919*. Augusta, Maine: Published under the direction of James W. Hanson, the Adjutant General, 1929.

Maine. Adjutant General. *Roster of Maine in the Military Service of the United States and Allies in the World War, 1917-1919*. 2 vols. Augusta, Maine: Published under the direction of James W. Hanson, the Adjutant General, 1929.

Maine. Adjutant General. *Supplement to the Annual Reports of the Adjutant General of the State of Maine for the Years 1861, '62, '63, '64, '65 and 1866*. Augusta, Maine: Stevens & Sayward, 1867.

Society of Colonial Wars. *Register of the Officers and Members of the Society of the Colonial Wars in the State of Maine: also History, Roster and Record of Colonel Jedidiah Preble's Regiment. Campaign of 1758: Together with Capt. Samuel Cobb's Journal*. Portland, Oregon: Marks Printing House, 1905.

United States. Adjutant General's Office. *General Index to Compiled Military Service Records of Revolutionary War Soldiers*. Washington, D.C,: National Archives, 1942.

United States. Adjutant General's Office. *General Index to Compiled Service Records of Volunteer Soldiers Who Served During the War with Spain*. Washington, D.C.: National Archives, 1971.

United States. Adjutant General's Office. *Index to Compiled Service Records of Volunteer Soldiers Who Served during the War of 1812*. Washington, D.C.: National Archives, 1965.

United States. Adjutant General's Office. *Index to Compiled Service Records of Volunteer Union Soldiers Who Served in Organizations from the State of Maine*. Washington, D.C.: National Archives, 1964.

United States. Selective Service System. Maine. *World War I Selective Service System Draft Registration Cards, 1917-1918*. Washington, D.C.: National Archives, 1987-1988.

United States. Veterans Administration. *Index to War of 1812 Pension Application Files*. Washington, D.C.: National Archives, 1960.

United States. Veterans Administration. *Registers Of Veterans At The National Home For Disabled Volunteer Soldiers, Eastern Branch In Togus, Maine, 1866-1934*. Microfilm of original records at the National Archives in Washington, D.C. (Salt Lake City: Genealogical Society of Utah, 1988). 18 microfilm.

United States. Veterans Administration. *Revolutionary War Pension and Bounty-Land-Warrant Application Files*. Washington, D.C.: National Archives, 1969.

United States. Veterans Administration. *Selected Records from Revolutionary War Pension & Bounty-Land-Warrant Application Files*. Washington, D.C.: National Archives, 1969.

White, Virgil D. *Genealogical Abstracts of the Revolutionary War Pension Files*. 4 vols. Waynesboro, Tennessee: National Historical Publishing, 1990.

White, Virgil D. *Index to Revolutionary War Service Records*. 4 vols. Waynesboro, Tennessee: National Historical Publishing, 1995.

White, Virgil D. *Index to War of 1812 Pension Files*. 2 vols. Waynesboro, Tennessee: National Historical Publishing Co., 1992.

Whitman, William E.S., and Charles H. True. *Maine in the War for the Union*. Lewiston, Maine: Nelson Dingley, Jr., 1865.

Vital and Cemetery Records

Daughters of the American Revolution (Massachusetts). *Grave Locations of Revolutionary Soldiers and Sailors of Maine and Massachusetts*. Salt Lake City: Genealogical Society of Utah, 1991.

Frost, John. *Guide to Maine Vital Records in Transcript*. n.p., 1963.

Maine Division of Vital Statistics. *Index to Vital Records, 1892-1907*. Microfilm of original records in the State Board of Health, Division of Vital Statistics, Augusta, Maine. Salt Lake City: Genealogical Society of Utah, 1954). 184 microfilm.

Maine Old Cemetery Association. *MOCA Revolutionary War Soldiers: Burial Places*. [n.p.], 1987.

Maine Old Cemetery Association. *MOCA Revolutionary War Soldiers*. [n.p.], 1986.

Maine Old Cemetery Association. *MOCA Revolutionary War Soldiers: Birthplaces*. [n.p.], 1987.

Maine State Archives. *Cemetery Index of Veterans*. Photographic Science Corporation. 1975. 11 microfilm.

Maine State Archives. *Maine Town Microfilm List: Town and Vital Records, and Census Reports*. Augusta, Maine: Maine State Archives, n.d.

Maine State Archives. *Delayed Return for Births, Deaths, and Marriages, ca. 1670-1891*. Microfilm of original records in the Maine State Archives. (Salt Lake City: Genealogical Society of Utah, 1954). 109 microfilm.

Maine State Archives. *Index to Maine Deaths, 1960-1996*. Augusta, Maine: Maine State Archives, 2002. online database <www.state.me.us/sos/arc/geneology/homepage.html>

Maine State Archives. *Index to Maine Marriages, 1892-1966, 1976-1996*. Augusta, Maine: Maine State Archive, 2002. online database - <www.state.me.us/sos/arc/geneology/homepage.html>

Maine State Archives. *Veterans Cemetery Records*. Microfilm. Photographic Science Corporation, 1975. 15 microfilm.

Maine State Archives. *Vital Records (Births, Marriages, Deaths) before 1892*. Augusta, Maine: Maine State Archives, 2002. Online database <www.state.me.us/sos/arc/geneology/homepage.html>

Maine State Archives. *Vital Records from 1892-1922*. Augusta,
Maine: Maine State Archives, 2002. Online database
<www.state.me.us/sos/arc/geneology/homepage.html>

Maine State Archives. *Vital Records, 1923- Present*. Augusta,
Maine: Maine State Archives, 2002. Online database -
<www.state.me.us/sos/arc/geneology/homepage.html>

Maine. Division of Vital Statistics. *Deaths of World War II
Veterans of Maine*. Microfilm of original records at Augusta,
Maine. Salt Lake City: Genealogical Society of Utah, 1954.

Maine. Division of Vital Statistics. *Index to Vital Records Prior to
1892 of Eighty Towns*. Microfilm of original records in the
State Board of Health, Division of Vital Statistics, Augusta,
Maine. (Salt Lake City: Genealogical Society of Utah,
1953). 141 microfilm.

Maine. Division of Vital Statistics. *Index to Vital Records, 1908-
1922*. Microfilm of original records in the State Board of
Health, Division of Vital Statistics, Augusta, Maine. Salt
Lake City: Genealogical Society of Utah, 1954). 148
microfilm.

Maine. Division of Vital Statistics. *Index to Vital Records: Bride
Index to Marriages, 1895-1953*. Microfilm of original records
in the State Board of Health, Division of Vital Statistics,
Augusta, Maine. (Salt Lake City: Genealogical Society of
Utah, 1954). 111 microfilm.

MOCA Cemetery Inscription Project (MIP): Series One. Bangor,
Maine: Northeast Reprographics, 198-?

Nathan Hale Cemetery Collection, Surname Index, Series 2.
Microfilm of original record in the Maine State Library,
Augusta, Maine. (Salt Lake City: Filmed by the
Genealogical Society of Utah, 1982). Microfilm, 17 rolls.

Nathan Hale Cemetery Collection, Surname Index. Microfilm of
original record in the Maine State Library, Augusta, Maine.
(Salt Lake City: Filmed by the Genealogical Society of
Utah, 1982). Microfilm, 210 rolls.

Noyes, Benjamin L. *Vital Records Copied from Town, Church, and
Cemetery Records in Various Towns and Counties of Maine Along
the Atlantic Coast*. (Salt Lake City; Genealogical Society of
Utah, 1971). 2 microfilm.

Rohrbach, Lewis Bunker, ed. *Maine Marriages 1892-1966: A
Complete List*. Rockport, Maine: Picton Press. 1996. CD-
ROM.

The Maine Historical and Genealogical Recorder, 9 vols. Portland,
Oregon: S.M. Watson, 1884-98.

Torrey, Clarence Almon. *New England Marriages Prior to 1700*.
Baltimore: Genealogical Publishing Company, c1985.

Townsend, Charles D., ed., *Cemetery Inscriptions and Odd
Information of Various Town in the State of Maine: In the
Counties of Lincoln, Oxford, Penobscot, Somerset, Waldo*.
Sarasota, Florida: Aceto Bookmen, 1995.

Trickey, Katherine W. *Maine Old Cemetery Association Cemetery
Inscription Project: Series One, Two and Three*. Bangor, Maine:
Northeast Reprographics, 198(?), 1982, 1987(?).

Young, David C. and Elizabeth Keene Young. *Vital Records from
Maine Newspapers 1785-1820*. 2 vols. Bowie, Maryland:
Heritage Books, 1993.

County Website	Map Index	Date Created	Parent County or Territory From Which Organized Address/Details
Androscoggin www.rootsweb.com/~meandros/	**L4**	**18 Mar 1854**	**Cumberland, Oxford, Kennebec, Lincoln** Androscoggin County; 2 Turner; Auburn, ME 04210; Ph. 207.784.8390 Details: (Clk Sup Ct has div & ct rec from 1854; City Clk has b, m, d & bur rec; Reg of Pro has pro rec; Reg of Deeds has land rec) Towns Organized Before 1800: Durham 1789, Greene 1788, Lewiston 1795, Lisbon 1799, Livermore 1795, Turner 1786
Aroostook www.aroostook.me.us/	**D8**	**16 Mar 1839**	**Washington, Penobscot** Aroostook County; County Courthouse; 144 Swenden St; Caribou, ME 04736; Ph. 207.493.3318 Details: (Co Clk has div & ct rec from 1839; Twn Clks have b, m, d & bur rec; Pro Ct has pro rec; Reg of Deeds has land rec)
Cumberland www.cumberlandcounty.org/	**M3**	**28 May 1760**	**York** Cumberland County; 142 Federal St; Portland, ME 04101-4151; Ph. 207.871.8380 Details: (Co Clk has d, pro & land rec from 1760; City or Twn Clks have b, m, d & bur rec) Towns Organized Before 1800: Bridgton 1794, Brunswick 1739, Cape Elizabeth 1765, Falmouth 1718, Freeport 1789, Gorham 1764, Gray 1778, Harpswell 1758, New Gloucester 1774, North Yarmouth 1732, Otisfield 1798, Portland 1786, Scarborough 1658, Standish 1785, Windham 1762
Franklin www.rootsweb.com/~mefrankl/start.htm	**J3**	**20 Mar 1838**	**Kennebec, Oxford, Somerset** Franklin County; 38 Main St; Farmington, ME 04938; Ph. 207.778.6614 Details: (Twn Clks have b, m, d & bur rec; Clk Sup Ct has div rec from 1852 & ct rec; Reg of Deeds has land rec; Pro Judge has pro rec) Towns Organized Before 1800: Farmington 1794, Jay 1795, New Sharon 1794
Hancock www.co.hancock.me.us/	**K9**	**25 Jun 1789**	**Lincoln** Hancock County; 50 State St; Ellsworth, ME 04605; Ph. 207.667.9542 Details: (Twn Clks have b, m & d rec; Clk Sup Ct has div & ct rec; Pro Office has pro rec; Reg of Deeds has land rec; Co Clk has m rec 1789-1891) Towns Organized Before 1800: Bar Harbor 1796, Blue Hill 1789, Bucksport 1792, Castine 1796, Deer Isle 1789, Gouldsboro 1789, Mount Desert 1789, Penobscot 1787, Sedgwick 1789, Sullivan 1789, Trenton 1789
Kennebec www.rootsweb.com/~mekenneb/	**K5**	**20 Feb 1799**	**Lincoln, Cumberland** Kennebec County; 95 State St; Augusta, ME 04330-5611; Ph. 207.622.0971 Details: (Reg of Deeds has land rec from 1799; Pro Ct has pro rec from 1799; Twn Clks have b, m & d rec) Towns Organized Before 1800: Augusta 1797, Belgrade 1796, China 1796, Clinton 1795, Fayette 1795, Hallowell 1771, Litchfield 1795, Monmouth 1792, Mount Vernon 1792, Pittsdon 1779, Readfield 1791, Sidney 1792, Vassalboro 1771, Wayne 1798, Winslow 1771, Winthrop 1771
Knox members.aol.com/vsena/knox/ KnoxGenWeb.html	**L6**	**9 Mar 1860**	**Lincoln, Waldo** Knox County; 62 Union St, PO Box 885; Rockland, ME 04841-0885; Ph. 207.594.9379 Details: (Twn Clks have b, m & d rec; Clk Sup Ct has div & ct rec; Pro Ct has pro rec from 1860; Reg of Deeds has land rec from 1860) Towns Organized Before 1800: Camden 1791, Cushing 1789, Thomaston 1777, Union 1786, Vinalhaven 1789, Warren 1776
Lincoln www.rootsweb.com/~melincol/index.htm	**L5**	**28 May 1760**	**York** Lincoln County; County Courthouse; High St; PO Box 249; Wiscasset, ME 04578-0000; Ph. 207.882.6311 Details: (Clk Cts has m, pro & land rec from 1860 & ct rec from 1861; Clk Sup Ct has pro rec from 1760) Towns Organized Before 1800: Alno 1794, Boothbay 1764, Bristol 1765, Dresden 1794, Newcastle 1753, Nobleboro 1788, Waldoboro 1773, Wiscasset 1760

County Website	Map Index	Date Created	Parent County or Territory From Which Organized Address/Details
Oxford www.rootsweb.com/~meoxford/	L2	4 Mar 1805	**York, Cumberland** Oxford County; 26 Western Ave; PO Box 179; South Paris, ME 04281; Ph. 207.743.6359 Details: (Twn Clks have b, m & d rec; Clk Cts has m rec 1877-1897, div & ct rec from 1930, pro & land rec from 1805) Towns Organized Before 1800: Bethel 1796, Buckfield 1793, Buxton 1772, Fryeburg 1777, Hartford 1798, Hebron 1792, Norway 1797, Paris 1793, Sumner 1798, Waterford 1797
Penobscot www.rootsweb.com/~mepenobs/ mepenobs.htm	H8	15 Feb 1816	**Hancock** Penobscot County; 97 Hammond St; Bangor, ME 04401; Ph. 207.942.8535 Details: (Clk Cts has div rec from 1900 & ct rec from 1821; Pro Ct has pro rec; Reg of Deeds has land rec) Towns Organized Before 1800: Hampden 1794, Orrington 1788
Piscataquis www.rootsweb.com/~mepiscat/	F6	23 Mar 1838	**Penobscot, Somerset** Piscataquis County; 51 E. Main St; Dover-Foxcroft, ME 04426; Ph. 207.564.2161 Details: (Twn Clks have b, m & d rec; Clk Sup Ct has div & ct rec; Pro Ct has pro rec; Reg of Deeds has land rec)
Sagadahoc www.rootsweb.com/~mesagada/index.htm	M5	4 Apr 1854	**Lincoln** Sagadahoc County; PO Box 246; Bath, ME 04530-0246; Ph. 207.443.8200 Details: (Twn Clks have b, m & d rec; Clk Dis Ct has div rec; Clk Sup Ct has ct rec; Reg of Pro has pro rec from 1854; Reg of Deeds has land rec from 1854) Towns Organized Before 1800: Bath 1781, Bowdoin 1788, Bowdoinham 1762, Georgetown 1716, Topsham 1764, Woolwich 1759
Somerset www.rootsweb.com/~mesomers/	H4	1 Mar 1809	**Kennebec** Somerset County; Court St; Skowhegan, ME 04976; Ph. 207.474.9861 Details: (Clk Cts has some m rec from 1800's & pro rec from 1809) Towns Organized Before 1800: Canaan 1788, Cornville 1798, Fairfield 1788, Norridgewock 1788, Starks 1795
Waldo www.rootsweb.com/~mewaldo/index.htm	K7	7 Feb 1827	**Hancock** Waldo County; 73 Church St; Belfast, ME 04915-1705; Ph. 207.338.3282 Details: (Co Clk has m rec 1828-1887, div & ct rec from 1828; City or Twn Clks have b, m, d & bur rec; Pro Ct has pro rec; Reg of Deeds has land rec) Towns Organized Before 1800: Belfast 1773, Frankfort 1789, Northport 1796, Prospect 1794
Washington www.rootsweb.com/~mewashin/	J10	25 Jun 1789	**Lincoln** Washington County; PO Box 297; Machias, ME 04654-0297; Ph. 207.255.3127 Details: (Twn Clks have b, m, d & bur rec; Clk Cts has div & ct rec from 1931, pro rec from 1785, land rec from 1783 & nat rec from 1854; Maine State Archives, Augusta, Maine has div & ct rec before 1931) Towns Organized Before 1800: Addison 1797, Columbia 1796, Eastport 1798, Harrington 1797, Machias 1784, Steuben 1795
York(shire) www.raynorshyn.com/megenweb/york/	N2	20 Nov 1652	**Original county** York(shire) County; 45 Kennebank Rd; Alfred, ME 04002; Ph. 207.324.1571 Details: (Twn Clks have b, m, d & bur rec; Clk Cts has div & ct rec; Reg of Pro has d & pro rec from 1637; Reg of Deeds has land rec from 1636) Towns Organized Before 1800: Berwick 1713, Biddeford 1718, Cornish 1794, Hollis 1798, Kennebunkport 1653, Kittery 1652, Lebanon 1767, Limington 1792, Lyman 1778, Newfield 1794, Parsonfield 1785, Saco 1762, Sanford 1768, Shapleigh 1785, Waterboro 1787, Wells 1653, York 1652

Notes

Black-eyed Susan

MARYLAND

CAPITAL: ANNAPOLIS – STATE 1788 (7TH)

In 1524, Giovanni de Verrazano, an Italian navigator who sailed for the French government, became the first European to set foot on Maryland soil. In 1608, Captain John Smith explored the area and made maps of it. The first settlement was on Kent Island, where William Claiborne set up a trading post. Several years later, in 1632, George Calvert and Lord Baltimore, secured land from Charles I on both sides of Chesapeake Bay north of Virginia to the 40th parallel. Lord Baltimore, however, died before the charter could be signed. His son, Cecilius Calvert, the second Lord Baltimore, received the grant in his place and began efforts to colonize the area as a haven for persecuted Catholics and those of other religions. The first emigrants left in 1634. There were twenty Catholics and about 200 Protestants. They purchased land from the Indians and settled St. Mary's. The colony experienced great growth, partly due to the passage of the Act Concerning Religion, which outlawed any intolerance of any person professing a belief in Christ. Among the groups attracted by this religious freedom was a large group of Puritans. The Puritans settled Anne Arundel County. Meanwhile, conflicts between Claiborne's group and those controlled by Lord Baltimore led to almost continuous warfare. Not until Claiborne's death in 1677 did hostilities cease.

Settlements during the first century of Maryland's colonization were confined to areas by rivers, streams, and bays. Water provided practically the only efficient means of transportation. Baltimore was founded in 1729. It soon became a major port and commercial center. The Appalachian section of Maryland was not settled until about 1740, when English, Scottish, and Scotch-Irish migrated from St. Mary's, Charles, and Prince George's Counties. Not long afterward, Germans from Pennsylvania also came into the area. The influx of settlers was so great that by 1748 Frederick County was organized in the northwest section of Maryland. Many Acadians driven from Nova Scotia came to Baltimore in 1755. Race riots in Santo Domingo brought about a thousand more French to Baltimore in 1793. Canal diggers from Ireland swelled Baltimore's population between 1817 and 1847. They became farmers and miners in the Appalachians. Baltimore also provided refuge to thousands of Germans who fled their country after the Revolution of 1848.

Maryland adopted a Declaration of Rights in 1776 as well as a state constitution. In 1788, Maryland ratified the Constitution and became the seventh state in the Union. The British ravaged Chesapeake Bay during the War of 1812, but were unable to take Baltimore. Their failed attempt to capture Fort McHenry was the inspiration for Francis Scott Key to write "The Star Spangled Banner." The National Road was completed from Cumberland to Wheeling in 1818. During the Civil War, soldiers from Maryland fought for both sides. More than 46,000 men fought for the Union, while more than 5,000 fought for the Confederacy.

Look for vital records in the following locations:

- **Birth and death records:** Division of Vital Records in Baltimore, Maryland. Civil registration of births and deaths began in 1898, except for Baltimore City, where records began in 1875. Only the individual himself, a parent, or an authorized representative has access to these records if the event occurred within the last 100 years. The Maryland State Archives, Hall of Records in Annapolis, Maryland also has many birth and death records. A few counties have pre-1720 births and deaths in county land records.
- **Marriage records:** The clergy has kept marriage banns and registers since 1640. County clerks have been required to issue marriage licenses since 1777 and to issue ministers' returns since 1865. The circuit court clerk of each county and the State Archives

Historical Society of Carroll County, Maryland, Inc.; 210 E. Main St.; Westminster, Maryland 21157;

Historical Society of Cecil County; 135 East Main St.; Elkton, Maryland 21921;

Historical Society of Frederick County, Inc.; 24 E. Church St.; Frederick, Maryland 21701; <www.fwp.net/hsfc/>

Historical Society of Talbot County; 29 S. Washington St.; Easton, Maryland 21601; 410.822.7911;

Howard County Genealogical Society; Box 274; Columbia, Maryland 21045

Jewish Genealogical Society of Greater Washington DC; PO Box 31122; Bethesda, Maryland 20824-1122; <www.jewishgen.org/jgsgw/>

Jewish Historical Society Library of Maryland; 15 Lloyd St.; Baltimore, Maryland 21202

Jewish Historical Society of Maryland; 2707 Moores Valley Dr.; Baltimore, Maryland 21209;

Jewish Special Interest Group, Gesher Galicia; 3128 Brooklawn Terrace; Chevy Chase, Maryland 20815

John Paul Jones, SAR; Maryland; <eorr.home.netcom.com/ JPJ/index.html>

Johns Hopkins University, George Peabody Library; 17 East Mount Vernon Place; Baltimore, Maryland 21202; 410.659.8179; Fax 410.659.8137

Kent County Historical Society; Church Alley; Chestertown, Maryland 21620

Lower Delmarva Genealogical Society; PO Box 3602; Salisbury, Maryland 21802-3602; <bay.intercom.net/ldgs/ index.html>

Lutheran, Archives of the Delaware-Maryland Synod Evangelical Lutheran Church in America; 7604 York Road; Towson, Maryland 21204-7570; 410.825.9520; Fax 410.825.6745

Maryland Genealogical Society; 201 W Monument St.; Baltimore, Maryland 21201; 410.685.3750, Ext. 360

Maryland Historical Society Library; 201 West Monument Street; Baltimore, Maryland 21201; 410.685.3750, Ext. 359; Fax 410.385.2105

Maryland State Archives, Hall of Records Building; 350 Rowe Boulevard; Annapolis, Maryland 21401; 410.974.3915; Fax 410.974.3895; <www.mdarchives.state.md.us/msa/ homepage/html/homepage.html>

Maryland State Law Library, Courts of Appeal Building; 361 Rowe Boulevard; Annapolis, Maryland 21401-1697; 410.974.3395; Fax 410.974.2063

Methodist, United Methodist Historical Society; Lovely Lane Museum Library, 2200 St. Paul Street; Baltimore, Maryland 21218-5897; 410.889.4458; Fax 410.889.1501

Mid-Atlantic Germanic Society; PO Box 2642; Kensington, Maryland 20891-2642; <www.rootsweb.com/~usmags/>

Montgomery County Historical Society; 103 W. Montgomery Ave.; (Beall-Dawson House); Rockville, Maryland 20850; 301.340.2825;

National Archives and Records Administration, National Archives Library; Pennsylvania Avenue at Eighth Street NW; Washington, D.C. 20408; 202.501.5415; Fax 202.501.7006

National Archives Library; NNUL, Rm. 2380, 8601 Adelphi Rd.; College Park, Maryland 20740-6001

National Archives-Mid-Atlantic Region; 5000 Wissahickon Avenue; Philadelphia, Pennsylvania 19107; 215.597.3000; Fax 215.597.2303

National Capital Buckeye, Chapter OGS; PO Box 105; Bladensburg, Maryland 20710-0105

Presbyterian Church (U.S.A.), Department of History; 318 Georgia Terrace, PO Box 849; Montreat, North Carolina 28757; 704.669.7061; Fax 704.669.5369

Prince George's County Genealogical Society; Box 819; Bowie, Maryland 20718.0819; <his.com/~krutar/PGCGS/>

Prince George's County, Afro-American Historical and Genealogical Society; PO Box 44722; Ft. Washington, Maryland 20744.9998

Prince George's Historical Society; 5626 Bell Station Rd.; Glenn Dale, Maryland 20769

Protestant Episcopal, Archives of the Episcopal Church; PO Box 2247; Austin, Texas 78768; 512.472.6816

Queene Anne's County Historical Society; Wright's Chance; Commerce St.; Centreville, Maryland 21617

Roman Catholic, Archives of Archdiocese of Baltimore; 320 Cathedral Street; Baltimore, Maryland 21201; 410.547.5443

Saint Mary's City Historical Society; 11 Courthouse Dr.; PO Box 212; Leonardtown, Maryland 20650

Saint Mary's County Genealogical Society, Inc.; PO Box 1109; Leonardtown, Maryland 20650-1109; <www.pastracks.com/ smcgs/>

Silver Spring Historical Society; PO Box 1160; Silver Spring, Maryland 20910-1160; <www.homestead.com/ silverspringhistory/>

Smithsburg Historical Society; Smithsburg, Maryland; <pilot.wash.lib.md.us/smithsburg/HIST.HTM>

Society for the History of Germans in Maryland; PO Box 22595; Baltimore, Maryland 22585

Somerset County Historical Society; Treackle Mansion; Princess Anne, Maryland 21853

Sons of the American Revolution, Maryland Society; PO Box 92; Woodstock, Maryland 21163-0082

United Baptist Missionary Convention (African American); 940 Madison Avenue; Baltimore, Maryland 21201; 410.523.2950; Fax 410.523.0250

United Methodist Historical Society, Inc.; Lovely Lane United Methodist Church; 2200 St. Paul St.; Baltimore, Maryland 21218

University of Maryland College Park Libraries; Theodore R. McKeldin Library; College Park, Maryland 20742; 301.314.9428; Fax 301.314.9408

Upper Shore Genealogical Society of Maryland; Box 275; Easton, Maryland 21601; <www.chronography.com/usgs/>

Washington County Historical Society; PO Box 1281; Hagerstown, Maryland 21741-1281; <www.rootsweb.com/ ~mdwchs/>

Washington, D.C. Temple Branch Gen. Library; PO Box 49, 1000 Stoneybrook Dr.; Kensington, Maryland 20895

Worcester Room, c/o Worcester Co. Library; 307 N. Washington St.; Snow Hill, Maryland 21863

Bibliography and Record Sources

General Sources

A Guide to Historic Episcopal Churches of Southern Maryland, 1634-1984. Leonardtown, Md.: Printing Press, [199-].

Andrusko, Samuel M. *Maryland Biographical Sketch Index.* Silver Spring, Maryland: Samuel M. Adrusko, 1983.

Barnes, Robert W., and F. Edward Wright. *Colonial Families of the Eastern Shore of Maryland, Vol. 2.* Westminster, Maryland: Family Line Publications. 1996.

Barnes, Robert. *British Roots of Maryland Families.* Baltimore: Genealogical Publishing Co., 1999.

Biographical Cyclopedia of Representative Men of Maryland and District of Columbia. Baltimore: National Biographical Publishing Co., 1879.

Bozeman, John Leeds. *The History of Maryland, from Its First Settlement in 1633 to the Restoration in 1660, Vol. 1.* (1837). Reprint. Baltimore: Heritage Books, Inc., 1990.

Brugger, Robert J. *Maryland: A Middle Temperament, 1634-1980.* (1988). Reprint. Galveston, Texas: Frontier Press. 1990.

Brumbaugh, Gaius Marcus. *Maryland Records: Colonial, Revolutionary, County and Church from Original Sources.* 2 vols. (1915, 1928). Reprint. Baltimore: Genealogical Publishing Co., 1993.

Callcott. *Mistress of Riversdale: The Plantation Letters of Rosalie Stier Calvert, 1795-1821.* Galveston, Texas: Frontier Press. 1991.

Carr, Menard, and Walsh. *Robert Cole's World: Agriculture & Society in Early Maryland.* Galveston, Texas: Frontier Press. 1991.

Carr, Morgan, and Russo, eds. *Colonial Chesapeake Society.* Galveston, Texas: Frontier Press. 1988.

Caruthers, Bettie S., comp. *Maryland Oaths of Fidelity.* (1989). Reprint. Westminster, Maryland: Family Line Publications, 1995.

Chapelle, Suzanne Ellery Greene, ed. *Maryland, A History of Its People.* Baltimore: Johns Hopkins University Press, 1986.

Coldham, Peter Wilson. *Settlers of Maryland.* 5 vols. Baltimore: Genealogical Publishing Co., 1995-1996.

Cox, Richard J., and Larry E. Sullivan, eds. *Guide to the Research Collections of the Maryland Historical Society.* Baltimore: Maryland Historical Society, 1981.

Dobson, David. *Scots on the Chesapeake, 1607-1830.* Baltimore: Genealogical Publishing Co., 1985.

Ellis, Donna M., and Karen A. Stuart. *The Calvert Papers: Calendar and Guide to the Microfilm Edition.* Baltimore: Maryland Historical Society, 1973.

Forbush, Bliss. *A History of Baltimore Yearly Meeting of Friends: Three Hundred Years of Quakerism in Maryland, Virginia, the District of Colombia, and Central Pennsylvania.* Sandy Spring, Maryland: Baltimore Yearly Meeting of Friends, 1972.

Genealogical Council of Maryland. *Inventory of Maryland Bible Records.* Westminster, Maryland: Family Line Publications, 1989.

Giles, Barbara S. *Selected Maryland Bibliography And Resources.* 2 vols. [Seattle]: B.S. Giles, c1988-1989.

Green, Karen M. *The Maryland Gazette, 1727-1761: Genealogical and Historical Abstracts.* Galveston, Texas: Frontier Press, 1990.

Hanson, George A. *Old Kent: The Eastern Shore of Maryland.* (1876) Reprint. Baltimore: Clearfield Company, 1996.

Heisey, John W. *Maryland Genealogical Library Guide.* Morgantown, Pa.: Masthof Press, 1998.

Heisey, John W. *Maryland Research Guide.* Indianapolis: Heritage House, 1986.

Henry, J. Maurice. *History of the Church of the Brethren in Maryland.* Elgin, Ill.: Brethren Publishing, 1936.

Hofstetter, Eleanor O. *Newspapers in Maryland Libraries: A Union List.* Baltimore: Division of Library Development Services, Maryland State Department of Education, 1977.

Holdcraft, Jacob Mehrling. *Obituaries, Bible Records, Church Records, Family Genealogies, County Records, etc. for Frederick County, Maryland, 1800-1977.* Salt Lake City: Genealogical Society of Utah, 1975, 1977. Microfilm, 59 rolls.

Inventory of Maryland Bible Records. Westminster, Maryland: Family Line Publications, 1989.

Inventory of the Church Archives of Maryland: Protestant Episcopal Diocese of Maryland. Baltimore: Historical Records Survey, 1940.

Jacobsen, Phebe R. *Quaker Records in Maryland.* Annapolis, Maryland: Hall of Records Commission, 1966.

Jordan, Elise Greenup. *Early Families of Southern Maryland.* 5 vols. (1993-96) Reprint. Westminster, Maryland: Family Line Publications, 1995.

Kanely, Edna A., comp. *Directory of Maryland Church Records.* Westminster, Maryland: Family Line Publications, 1987.

Kanely, Edna Agatha. *Directory of Ministers and the Maryland Churches They Served, 1634-1990,* 2 vols. Westminster, Maryland: Family Line Publications, 1991.

Kulikoff. *Tobacco and Slaves: The Development of Southern Cultures in the Chesapeake, 1680-1800.* Galveston, Texas: Frontier Press, 1986.

Kummer, Frederic Arnold. *The Free State of Maryland: A History of the State and Its People, 1634-1941. A Narrative Historical Edition Preserving The Record of the Growth and Development of the State, Together with Genealogical and Memorial Records of Its Prominent Families asnd Personages.* 4 vols. [Ft. Wayne: Allen County Public Library, 198-].

Long, Helen R. *General History Section Index of Scharf's History of Western Maryland.* Manhattan, KS: Helen R. Long, 1992.

Maryland Genealogies. (1980) Reprint. Baltimore: Genealogical Publishing Co., Inc., 1997.

Maryland Hall of Records. *Calendar of Maryland State Papers: No. 1—The Black Books.* (1942) Reprint. Baltimore: Clearfield Company, 1995.

Maryland Research Outline. Series US-States, no. 21. Salt Lake City: Family History Library, 1988. Maryland State Archives. *Archives of Maryland (original Series).* 72 vols. Annapolis, Maryland: Maryland State Archives Publications.

Maryland. Provincial Court. *Judicial and Testamentary Business of the Provincial Court: 1637-1683*. Archives of Maryland. Court Series, vols. 1-4, 8, 10-15. Baltimore: Maryland Historical Society, 1887-1964.

Maryland. Provincial Court. *Provincial Court Judgements*. Annapolis: Hall of Records Commission, 1947.

Owen, David R., and Michael C. Tolley. *Courts of Admiralty in Colonial America: The Maryland Experience, 1634-1776*. Baltimore: Maryland Historical Society.

Papenfuse, Edward C. *A Guide To The Maryland Hall Of Records: Local, Judicial And Administrative Records On Microform*. Annapolis: Archives Division, Hall of Records Commission, 1978.

Radoff, Morris Leon, et al. *The County Courthouses and Records of Maryland, Part Two: The Records*. Annapolis, Maryland: Hall of Records Commission, 1963.

Skinner, Vernon L. *Abstracts of the Inventories and Accounts of the Prerogative Court* of Maryland. Westminster, Maryland: Family Line Publications, 1988-91.

United States. Circuit Court (Maryland). *Minutes, 1790-1911*. Washington, DC: National Archives, 1973.

Wright, F. Edward. *Maryland Calendar of Wills, Vol. 10: 1748-1753*. Westminster, Maryland: Family Line Publications, 1988.

Wright, F. Edward. *Maryland Calendar of Wills, Vol. 11: 1753-1760*. Westminster, Maryland: Family Line Publications, 1988.

Wright, F. Edward. *Maryland Calendar of Wills, Vol. 9: 1744-1749*. Westminster, Maryland: Family Line Publications, 1988.

Wright, F. Edward. *Maryland Calendar of Wills: From 1744-1779*. 8 vols. Westminster, Maryland: Family Line Publications, 1988.

Emigration, Immigration, Migration and Naturalization

Campbell, Penelope. *Maryland In Africa: The Maryland State Colonization Society, 1831-1857*. Urbana: University of Illinois Press, 1971.

Coldham, Peter Wilson. *The King's Passengers To Maryland And Virginia*. Westminster, Maryland: Family Line, 1997.

Hargreaves-Mawdsley, R. *Bristol and America, a Record of the First Settlers in the Colonies of North America, 1654-1685: Including the Names with Places of Origin of More than 10,000 Servants to Foreign Plantations Who Sailed from the Port Bristol to Virginia, Maryland, and Other Parts of the Atlantic Coast, and also to the West Indies From 1654 to 1685*. Reprint. Baltimore: Genealogical Publishing Co., 1978.

Mortan Allan Directory of European Passenger Steamship Arrivals. 1931. Reprint. Baltimore: Genealogical Publishing Co., 1980.

Oszakiewski, Robert A. *Maryland Naturalization Abstracts, Volume 2*. Westminster, Maryland: Family Line Publications. 1996.

Peden, Henry C., Jr. *Marylanders to Carolina: Migrations of Marylanders to North and South Carolina Prior to 1800*. Westminster, Maryland: Family Line Publications. 1994.

Reamy, Bill, and Martha Reamy. *Immigrant Ancestors of Marylanders as Found in Local Histories*. n. p., 1993.

Skordas, Gust. *The Early Settlers of Maryland: An Index to the Names of Immigrants Compiled from Records of Land Patents, 1633-1680, in the Hall of Records, Annapolis, Maryland*. Reprint. Baltimore: Genealogical Publishing Co.,1986.

United States. Bureau of Customs. *Copies of Lists of Passengers Arriving at Miscellaneous Ports on the Atlantic and Gulf Coasts and At Ports on the Great Lakes, 1820-1873*. Washington, DC: The National Archives, 1964.

United States. Bureau of Customs. *Index (Soundex) to Passenger Lists of Vessels Arriving At Baltimore, 1897-1952*. Washington, DC: National Archives, 1956.

United States. Bureau of Customs. *Passenger Lists of Vessels Arriving At Baltimore, 1820-1921; Quarterly Abstracts of Passenger Lists of Vessels Arriving At Baltimore, 1820-1869*. Washington, DC: The National Archives, 1956, 1959, 1969.

United States. Circuit Court (Maryland). Clerk. *Indexes to Naturalization Petitions to the U.S. Circuit and District Courts for Maryland: 1797-1951*. Microfilm of originals at the Federal Archives Records Center, Philadelphia. Washington, D.C.: National Archives. Central Plains Region, 1982. 25 microfilm.

United States. Circuit Court (Maryland). *Naturalization Records, 1906-1911*. Microfilm of records at the National Archives Mid-Atlantic Region, Philadelphia. (Salt Lake City: Filmed by the Genealogical Society of Utah, 1991).

United States. District Court (Maryland). *Naturalization Records, 1792-1931*. Microfilms of the originals at the Philadelphia Branch-National Archives. (Salt Lake City: Filmed by the Genealogical Society of Utah, 1990-1991). 67 microfilm.

Wood, Gregory A. *A Guide to the Acadians in Maryland in the 18th and 19th Centuries*. Wheaton, Maryland: Maryland Acadian Studies, 1995.

Wright, F. Edward. *Citizens of the Eastern Shore of Maryland, 1659-1750*. Westminster, Maryland: Family Line Publications, 1986.

Wyand, Jeffrey A., and Florence L. Wyand. *Colonial Maryland Naturalizations*. Reprint. Baltimore: Genealogical Publishing Co., 1986.

Land and Property

Coldham, Peter Wilson. *Settlers of Maryland. [1679- 1783]*. 5 vols. Baltimore: Genealogical Publishing Company, 1995-1996.

Hartsook, Elisabeth, and Gust Skordas. *Land Office and Prerogative Court Records of Colonial Maryland*. (1968) Reprint. Baltimore: Clearfield Company, 1996.

Hone, Wade E. *Land and Property Research in the United States*. Salt Lake City: Ancestry Incorporated, 1997.

Maryland State Archives. *Land Records at the Maryland State Archives*. Annapolis, Maryland: Maryland State Archives, 2002. Online guide - <www.mdarchives.state.md.us/msa/homepage/html/refserv.html>.

Papers Relating To The Boundary Dispute Between Pennsylvania And Maryland, 1734-1760. Microfilm of original published: Harrisburg, Pa.: C.M. Busch, 1896. (Salt Lake City: Filmed by the Genealogical Society of Utah, 1969).

Patents Series: of the Maryland Land Office. Microfilm copy of original records at Hall of Records, Annapolis, Maryland. (Salt Lake City: Filmed by the Genealogical Society of Utah, 1947). 81 microfilm.

Sioussat, Annie Middleton. *Old Manors in the Colony of Maryland.* 2 vols. [Ft. Wayne: Allen County Public Library, 198-].

Military

Brumbaugh, Gaius Marcus. *Revolutionary Records of Maryland.* Washington, DC: Rufus H. Darby, 1924. Reprint. Baltimore: Clearfield Co., 1996.

Callum, Agnes Kane. *Colored Volunteers of Maryland Civil War, 7th Regiment, United States Colored Troops, 1863-1866.* Baltimore: Mullac Publishers, 1990.

Clark, Murtie June. *Colonial Soldiers of the South, 1732-1774.* Baltimore: Genealogical Publishing Co., 1983.

Clark, Murtie June. *Loyalists in the Southern Campaign of the Revolutionary War.* Baltimore: Genealogical Publishing Company, 1981.

Clements, S. Eugene. *The Maryland Militia in the Revolutionary War.* Westminster, Maryland: Family Line Publications, 1987

Eisenberg, Gerson G. *Marylanders Who Served the Nation: A Biographical Dictionary of Federal Officials from Maryland.* Annapolis, Maryland: Maryland State Archives Publications, 1992.

Goldsborough, William W. *The Maryland Line in the Confederate Army, 1861-1865.* 1900. Reprint, Gaithersburg, Maryland: Olde Soldier Books, 1987.

Hartzler, Daniel D. *Marylanders in the Confederacy.* Silver Spring. Maryland: Family Line Publications, 1986.

Huntsberry, Thomas V. and Joanne M. *Dartmoor Prison.* Baltimore: J. Mart Publishers, 1984.

Huntsberry, Thomas V., and Joanne M. Huntsberry. *Maryland in the Civil War.* 2 vols. Edgemere, Maryland: J. Mart Publishers, 1985.

Kilbourne, John Dwight. *A Short History of the Maryland Line in the Continental Army.* Baltimore: The Society of the Cincinnati of Maryland, 1992.

Marine, William M. *The British Invasion of Maryland: 1812-1815.* Baltimore, 1913. Reprint. Baltimore: Genealogical Publishing Co., 1977.

Maryland Hall of Records Commission. *Index to the Maryland Line in the Confederate Army, 1867-1865.* Publication no. 3. Annapolis, Maryland:

Maryland Historical Society. *Muster Rolls and Other Records of Service of Maryland Troops in the American Revolution, 1775-1783.* Archives of Maryland, vol. 18. Baltimore. 1900. Reprint. Baltimore: Genealogical Publishing Co., 1972.

Maryland Muster Rolls, Fort Cumberland, 1757-58. (Salt Lake City: Filmed by the Genealogical Society of Utah, 1949).

Maryland War Records Commission. *Maryland in the World War I, 1917-19. Military and Naval Service Records.* 2 vols. Baltimore: Maryland War Records Commission, 1933.

Maryland. Treasurer's Office. *A List of Invalid Pensioners.* Annapolis, Maryland: J. Hughes, Printer, 1822.

McGhee, Lucy K. *Maryland Revolutionary War Pensions, Revolutionary, 1812, and Indian Wars.* Washington, D.C.: Library of Congress Photoduplication Service, 1987.

Meyer, Mary K. *Westward of Fort Cumberland Military Lots Set Off for Maryland's Revolutionary Soldiers: With an Appended List of Revolutionary Soldiers Granted Pensions by the State of Maryland.* Finksburg, Maryland: Pipe Creek Publication, Inc., 1993.

Muster Rolls and Other Records of Service of Maryland Troops in the American Revolution: 1775-1783. Archives of Maryland. Vol. 18. Baltimore: Maryland Historical Society, 1900.

Newman, Harry Wright. *Maryland Revolutionary Records: Data Obtained from 3,050 Pension Claims and Bounty Land Applications, Including 1,000 Marriages of Maryland Soldiers and a List of 1,200 Proved Services of Soldiers and Patriots of Other States.* Reprint. Baltimore: Genealogy Publishing Co., 1993.

Register of the Commissioned and Warrant Officers of the Navy of the Confederate States: to January 1, 1863. [S.l.: s.n., 1863?].

Retzer, Henry J. *German Regiment of Maryland and Pennsylvania.* Westminster, Maryland: Family Line Publications. 1991. Rev. ed. 1996.

Roster of the Soldiers and Sailors Who Served in Organizations from Maryland During the Spanish-American War. Reprint. Westminster, Maryland: Family Line Publications, 1990.

Sifakis, Stewart. *Compendium of the Confederate Armies: Kentucky, Maryland, Missouri, the Confederate Units and the Indian Units.* 10 vols. New York: Facts on File, c1992-1995.

United States. Adjutant General's Office. *Index to Compiled Service Records of Volunteer Union Soldiers Who Served in Organizations from the State of Maryland.* Washington, DC: The National Archives, 1962.

United States. Record and Pension Office. *Compiled Service Records of Confederate Soldiers Who Served in Organizations from the State of Maryland.* Washington, DC: The National Archives, 1960. Microfilm, 22 rolls.

United States. Record and Pension Office. *Compiled Service Records of Volunteer Union Soldiers Who Served in Organizations from the State of Maryland.* Washington, DC: The National Archives, 1962. Microfilm, 238 rolls.

United States. Selective Service System. *Maryland, World War I Selective Service System Draft Registration Cards, 1917-1918.* Washington, D.C.: National Archives, 1987-1988.

United States. Veterans Administration. *Pension Index File, Alphabetical; of the Veterans Administrative Contact and Administrative Services, Administrative Operations Services, 1861- 1934.* Washington: Veterans Administration, Publications Service, 1953.

Wells, Charles J. *Maryland and District of Columbia Volunteers in the Mexican War.* Westminster, Maryland: Family Line Publications, 1991.

Wilmer, L. Allison. *History and Roster of Maryland Volunteers, War of 1861-5.* Reprint. Silver Spring, Maryland: Family Line Publications, 1987.

Wright, F. Edward. *Maryland Militia, War of 1812.* 8 vols. Silver Spring MD: Family Line Publications. 1979-92.

County Website	Map Index	Date Created	Parent County or Territory From Which Organized Address/Details
Howard* co.ho.md.us/	H4	4 Jul 1851	**Anne Arundel** Howard County; 3430 Courthouse Dr; Ellicott City, MD 21043-4300; Ph. 410.992.2025 Details: (Clk Cir Ct has m, div, ct & land rec; Reg of Wills has pro rec)
Kent www.kentcounty.com/	E4	2 Aug 1642	**St. Mary's** Kent County; 103 N Cross St; Chestertown, MD 21620; Ph. 410.778.7460 Details: (Clk Cir Ct has m rec from 1796, div rec from 1867, land rec from 1656 & ct rec from early 1800's)
Montgomery* www.co.mo.md.us/	J5	6 Sep 1776	**Frederick** Montgomery County; 101 Monroe St; Rockville, MD 20850-0000; Ph. 240.777.9466 Details: (Clk Cir Ct has m rec from 1799, div, ct & land rec from 1776) (1830 cen missing)
Patuxent		3 Jul 1654	**St. Mary's** Details: (see Calvert) Formerly Calvert Co. Name changed to Patuxent 31 Oct 1654. Name changed back to Calvert 31 Dec 1658
Prince George's www.goprincegeorgescounty.com/ index.html	H7	20 May 1695	**Charles** Prince George's County; 14735 Main St; Landover, MD 20772; Ph. 301.350.9700 Details: (Clk Cir Ct has land & ct rec; Reg of Wills has pro rec) (1830 cen missing)
Queen Anne's www.qac.org/	E6	18 Apr 1706	**Kent** Queen Anne's County; 107 N Liberty; Centreville, MD 21617; Ph. 410.758.1773 Details: (Clk Cts has m, div, ct & land rec; Orphan's Ct has pro rec) (1830 census missing)
Somerset skipjack.net/le_shore/visitsomerset/	C9	22 Aug 1666	**Kent** Somerset County; 21 Prince William St; Princess Anne, MD 21853-0000; Ph. 410.651.1555 Details: (Clk Cir Ct has m, div, ct & land rec from 1666; Reg of Wills has pro rec) (1830 cen missing)
St. Mary's www.win.net/~ehayden/states/ maryland/stmary/	G9	9 Feb 1637	**Original county** St. Mary's County; 23150 Leonard Hall Dr; Leonardtown, MD 20650; Ph. 301.475.4567 Details: (Clk Cir Ct has m & land rec; Reg of Wills has pro rec) (1830 census missing)
Talbot www.talbgov.org/	E6	18 Feb 1662	**Kent** Talbot County; 11 N Washington St; Easton, MD 21601-0000; Ph. 410.822.2401 Details: (Clk Cir Ct has m rec from 1794, div rec from 1908, ct rec from 1818 & land rec from 1662; Reg of Wills has pro rec)
Washington* pilot.wash.lib.md.us/washco/	L3	6 Sep 1776	**Frederick** Washington County; Summit Ave; Hagerstown, MD 21740; Ph. 301.790.7991 Details: (Clk Cir Ct has m rec from 1799, div & land rec from 1776, ct rec from 1797 & mil dis rec; other rec may be found at Washington Co Free Library, Hagerstown, MD)
Wicomico* www.co.wicomico.md.us/	C9	17 Aug 1867	**Somerset, Worcester** Wicomico County; PO Box 198; Salisbury, MD 21803; Ph. 410.548.4801 Details: (Clk Cir Ct has m, div, land, mil & ct rec from 1867)
Worcester www.worc.lib.md.us/	B10	29 Oct 1742	**Somerset** Worcester County; 1 W Market St; Snow Hill, MD 21863; Ph. 401.632.1194 Details: (Clk Cir Ct has m rec from 1866, div rec from 1900 & ct rec from 1916; Reg of Wills has pro rec)

Mayflower

MASSACHUSETTS

CAPITAL: BOSTON – STATE 1788 (6TH)

The first settlement in Massachusetts was at Plymouth where the Pilgrims from the Mayflower settled in 1620. The Puritans followed within a decade, establishing Salem in 1628 under John Endecott and Boston in 1630 under John Winthrop. The Massachusetts Bay Colony, founded in 1630, provided for a large amount of self-government. Within the next decade, more than 20,000 immigrants, almost entirely British, came to Massachusetts. Religious intolerance in Massachusetts led many to settle elsewhere, such as Rhode Island, Connecticut, New Hampshire, and Maine. In 1691, Plymouth Colony was joined to the Massachusetts Bay Colony, along with parts of Maine and Nova Scotia.

Massachusetts played a prominent role in the Revolutionary War from the Boston Tea Party to Lexington and Concord and the Battle of Bunker Hill. A state constitution was adopted in 1780 and Massachusetts became the sixth state to ratify the United States Constitution, with the proviso that the Bill of Rights be added.

In 1786, the Ohio Land Company was formed, which led many Massachusetts residents to migrate to Ohio. New immigrants, primarily from England, continued to come to Massachusetts for at least two centuries. Maine was separated from Massachusetts in 1819 and became a state in 1820. In the 1830's, factory development began and the demand for workers stimulated renewed immigration. Around mid-century, emigrants from Ireland, Germany and France came to escape disasters and political turmoil in their countries. A few years later, Italians, Russians, Poles, and Portuguese came to work in the factories, mills, and fisheries. During the Civil War, Massachusetts furnished 146,000 men to the Union forces.

Look for vital records in the following locations:

- **Birth, marriage and death records:** Statistics have been kept throughout Massachusetts since the earliest days. To assist researchers, each town has published these records. Statewide registration began in 1841. Early records are available at the Massachusetts State Archives in Boston. A search of town records can yield additional information. Vital records after 1890 are available from the Registrar of Vital Statistics in Boston. You will be asked to state your relationship to the person for whom you seek records and the reason for wanting the records.
- **Divorce records:** Divorce records from 1738 to 1888 are filed in the county court, the governor's council records, the superior court, or the supreme judicial court. After 1888, divorce proceedings were usually filed at the county probate court and superior court.
- **Wills, deeds and land transaction records:** Inquire at county offices. City or county assessors have kept tax records; some are published.
- **Military records:** All war service records following the Revolutionary War are at the office of the Adjutant General in Boston.
- **Naturalization records:** Filed in the various county and district courts. These were copied and indexed in the 1930's for the years 1791 to 1906. The copies and indexes are at the National Archives, Boston Branch, in Waltham, Massachusetts. For records after 1906, contact the National Archives, Boston Branch, or Immigration and Naturalization Service in Boston.
- **Census records:** State censuses were taken in 1855 and 1865. The originals are at the Massachusetts State Archives.

Massachusetts State Archives
Columbia Point
220 Morrissey Boulevard
Boston, Massachusetts 02125

Registrar of Vital Statistics
470 Atlantic Avenue, Second Floor
Boston, Massachusetts 02210
617.753.8600

Naturalization Service,
U.S. Department of Justice
JFK Federal Building, Government Center
Boston, Massachusetts 02203

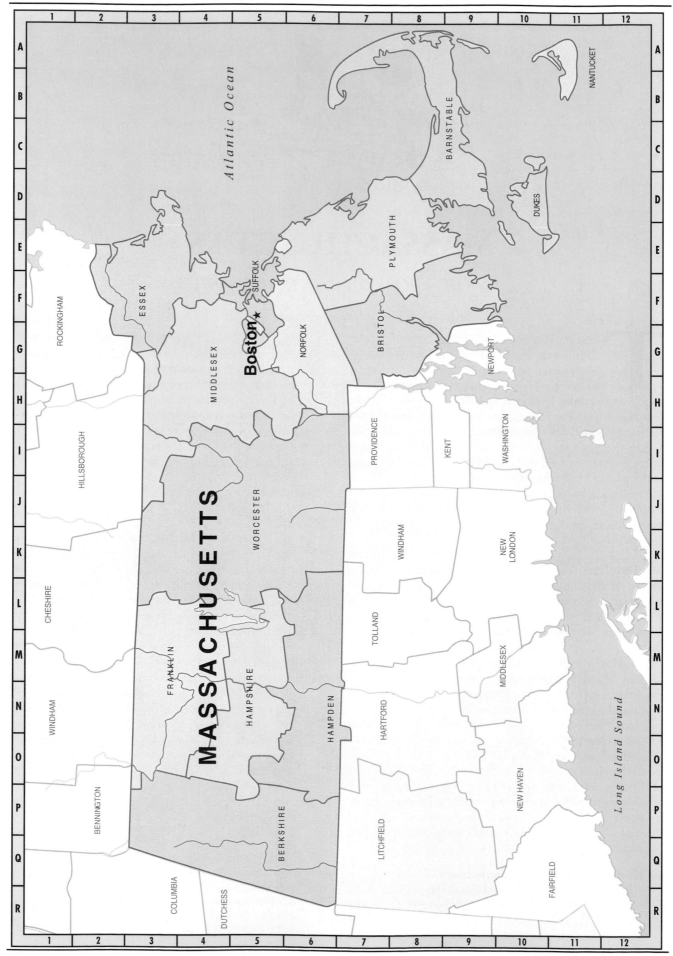

Atlantic Ocean

NANTUCKET

BARNSTABLE

DUKES

PLYMOUTH

ROCKINGHAM

ESSEX

SUFFOLK

Boston ★

MIDDLESEX

NORFOLK

BRISTOL

NEWPORT

HILLSBOROUGH

PROVIDENCE

KENT

WASHINGTON

MASSACHUSETTS

WORCESTER

WINDHAM

NEW
LONDON

CHESHIRE

FRANKLIN

TOLLAND

MIDDLESEX

WINDHAM

HAMPSHIRE

HAMPDEN

HARTFORD

Long Island Sound

BENNINGTON

BERKSHIRE

LITCHFIELD

NEW HAVEN

FAIRFIELD

COLUMBIA

DUTCHESS

Societies and Repositories

American Jewish Historical Society; 2 Thornton Rd.; Waltham, Massachusetts 02154

American-Portuguese Genealogical Society, Inc.; PO Box 644; Taunton, Massachusetts 02780

Andover Historical Society; 97 Main Street; Andover, Massachusetts 01810; 978.470.2741; <www.ultranet.com/~andhists/>

Association for Gravestone Studies; 278 Main Street, Suite 207; Greenfield, Massachusetts 01301;

Baptist, American Baptist Historical Society; 1106 S. Goodman Street; Rochester, New York 14620; 716.474.1740

Berkshire County Historical Society; 780 Holmes Road; Pittsfield, Massachusetts 01201; 413.443.1449;

Beverly Historical Society; 117 Cabot Street; Beverly, Massachusetts 01915; 978.922.7387;

Boston Chapter, MASSAR; Massachusetts; <www.massar.org/boston.htm>

Boston Public Library; Copley Square; Boston, Massachusetts 02117; 617.536.5400; Fax 617.536.4306

Braintree Historical Society; 31 Tenney Rd.; Braintree, Massachusetts 02184; 781.380.0731;

Brockton Historical Society; 216 No. Pearl Street; Brockton, Massachusetts 02301; <www.brocktonma.com/bhs/bhs_mus.html>

Canton Historical Society; 1400 Washington Street; Canton, Massachusetts 02021;

Cape Cod Genealogical Society; PO Box 1394; E. Harwich, Massachusetts 02645-6394

Congregational Christian Historical Society; 14 Beacon St.; Boston, Massachusetts 02108

Danvers Historical Society; Danvers, Massachusetts 01923

Dedham Historical Society; PO Box 215; Dedham, Massachusetts 02027; <www.dedhamhistorical.org/index.shtml>

Eastham Historical Society, Inc.; PO Box 8; Eastham, Massachusetts 02642

Easton Historical Society; PO Box 3; North Easton, Massachusetts 02356;

Episcopal, The Diocesan Library and Archives, The Episcopal Diocese of Massachusetts; 138 Tremont Street; Boston, Massachusetts 02108; 617.482.4826, Ext. 504; Fax 617.482.8431;

Essex Institute; 132 Essex St.; Salem, Massachusetts 01970

Essex Society of Genealogists, Inc; PO Box 313; Lynnfield, Massachusetts 01940-0313

Falmouth Genealogical Society; PO Box 2107; Teaticket, Massachusetts 02536-2107

Family History Library: 35 North West Temple Street: Salt Lake City, Utah 84150: 800.346.6044 or 801.240.2584: <www.familysearch.org>: Find a Family History Center near you: <www.familysearch.org/Eng/Library/FHC/frameset_fhc.asp>

Finlandia Foundation, Boston Chapter; 266 Sudbury Street; Marlboro, Massachusetts 01752

Finnish American Society of Cape Cod; PO Box 220; West Barnstable, Massachusetts 02668

Genealogical Roundtable; PO Box 654; Concord, Massachusetts 01742-0654

General Society of Colonial Wars; 1316 7th St.; New Orleans, Louisiana 70115; 504.895.5013

General Society of Mayflower Descendants; Box 3297; Plymouth, Massachusetts 02361-3297; 508.746.3188

Greater Lowell Genealogy Club; 325 Mammoth Road #2; Lowell, Massachusetts 01854

Harwich Historical Society; PO Box 17; Harwich, Massachusetts 02645

Irish Ancestral Research Association (TIARA); PO Box 619; Sudbury, Massachusetts 01776

Italian Genealogical Society of America; PO Box 3572; Peabody, Massachusetts 01961-3572

Jamaica Plain Historical Society; PO Box 2924; Jamaica Plain, Massachusetts 02130-0024; <www.geocities.com/jphistoricalsociety/>

Jewish Genealogical Society of Greater Boston; PO Box 610366; Newton, Massachusetts 02461-0366;

Jewish, American Jewish Historical Society; 2 Thornton Road; Waltham, Massachusetts 02154; 617.891.8110; Fax 617.899.9208

Knights and Ladies of Kaleva; PO Box 620; Maynard, Massachusetts 01752

Lutheran, New England Lutheran Archives, Trinity Lutheran Church; 292 Orange Street; New Haven, Conneticut 06510; 203.787.6521

Martha's Vineyard Historical Society; PO Box 1310; Edgartown, Massachusetts 02539; 508.627.4436;

Massachusetts Archives; 220 Morrissey Blvd.; Boston, Massachusetts 02125; 617.288.8429; <www.state.ma.us/sec/arc/arcgen/genidx.htm>

Massachusetts Genealogical Council; PO Box 5393; Cochituate, Massachusetts 01778-5393

Massachusetts Historical Society Library; 1154 Boylston Street; Boston, Massachusetts 02215; 617.536.1608; Fax 617.536.1608

Massachusetts Society of Genealogists, Inc.; PO Box 215; Ashland, Massachusetts 01721-0215; <www.rootsweb.com/~masgi/msog/>

Massachusetts Society of Mayflower Descendants; 376 Boylston Street; Boston, Massachusetts 02116; 617.266.1624

Massachusetts State Archives at Columbia Point; 220 Morrissey Boulevard; Boston, Massachusetts 02125; 617.727.2816

Medford Historical Society; 10 Governors Ave.; Medford, Massachusetts 02155

Methodist, Boston University School of Theology Library; 745 Commonwealth Ave.; Boston, Massachusetts 02215; 617.353.3034; Fax 617.353.3061

Middleborough Historical Association, Inc.; Jackson St.; Middleboro, Massachusetts 02346

Natick Historical Society; 58 Eliot Street; South Natick, Massachusetts 01760; <www.ultranet.com/~elliot/>

National Archives-New England Region, Immigration and Naturalization Service, U.S. Department of Justice; JFK Federal Building, Government Center; Boston, Massachusetts 02203; 617.565.3879

National Archives-New England Region; 380 Trapelo Road; Waltham, Massachusetts 02154; 617.647.8100; Fax 617.647.8460

National Society of the Daughters of the American Revolution; 1776 D Street, N.W.; Washington, D.C. 20006-5392; 202-879-3263

Needham Historical Society; 53 Glendoon Road; Needham, Massachusetts 02192; <www.needhamonline.com/HistoricalSociety/home.html>

New England Historic Genealogical Society; 101 Newbury Street; Boston, Massachusetts 02116; 617.536.5740; Fax 617.536.7307

Old Colony Historical Society; 66 Church Green; Taunton, Massachusetts 02780

Peabody Essex Museum; 132 Essex Street; Salem, Massachusetts 01970; 508.744.3390; Fax 508.744.0036

Peabody Historical Society; 35 Washington St.; Peabody, Massachusetts 01960

Pilgrim Society; 75 Court Street; Plymouth, Massachusetts 02360; 508-746-1620; Fax 508-747-4228

Plymouth County Genealogists, Inc.; PO Box 7025; Brockton, Massachusetts 02401-7025

Plympton Historical Society; 189 Main Street; Plympton, Massachusetts 02367; <www.geocities.com/PicketFence/Garden/2578/>

Presbyterian Historical Society; 425 Lombard Street; Philadelphia, Pennsylvania 19147; 215.627.1852; Fax 215.627.0509

Quincy Historical Society; 8 Adams Street; Quincy, Massachusetts 02169; <www.key.biz.com/ssn/Quincy/hist_soc.html>

Registrar of Vital Statistics; 470 Atlantic Ave.; Boston, Massachusetts 02110; 617-753-8600;

Roman Catholic, Archives of the Archdiocese of Boston; 2121 Commonwealth Avenue; Brighton, Massachusetts 02135; 617.254.0100, Ext. 108; Fax 617.783.5642

ROOTS Users Group of Cape Cod; PO Box 906; Brewster, Massachusetts 02631

Saugus Historical Society; PO Box 1209; Saugus, Massachusetts 01906-1209; <www.saugus.net/HistoricalSociety/>

Sheffield Historical Society; Mark Dewey Research Center; Box 747; Sheffield, Massachusetts 01257-0747

Shirley Historical Society; 182 Center Road; PO Box 217; Shirley, Massachusetts 01464-0217

Society of Friends (Quakers), Rhode Island Historical Society; 121 Hope Street; Providence, Rhode Island 02906; 401.331.8575; Fax 401.751.7930

Sons of the American Revolution, Massachusetts Society; 101 Tremont St., Suite 608; Boston, Massachusetts 02108

South Shore Genealogical Society; PO Box 396; Norwell, Massachusetts 02061-0396

Southborough Historical Society; PO Box 364; Southborough, Massachusetts 01772; <www.ultranet.com/~sobohist/index.html>

State Library of Massachusetts; State House, Room 341, Beacon Street; Boston, Massachusetts 02133; 617.727.2590; Fax 617.727.5819

Supreme Lodge Knights of Pythias; 59 Coddington Street, Suite 202; Quincy, Massachusetts 02169-4150;

Swedish Ancestry Research Society (SARA); PO Box 70603; Worcester, Massachusetts 01607-0603; <www.members.tripod.com/~SARAssociation/sara/SARA_Home_Page.htm>

Unitarian/Universalist, Harvard Divinity School Library; 45 Francis Avenue; Cambridge, Massachusetts 02138; 617.495.5770; Fax 617.495.9489

Walpole Historical Society; Deacon Willard Lewis House; 33 West St.; Walpole, Massachusetts 02081; <www.walpole.ma.us/hhistoric.htm>

War Records Office of the Adjutant General; Room 1000, 100 Cambridge Street; Boston, Massachusetts 02202; 617.727.2964

Western Massachusetts Genealogical Society; PO Box 206; Forest Park Station; Springfield, Massachusetts 01108-0206; <www.rootsweb.com/~mawmgs/>

Winchester Historical Society; PO Box 127; Winchester, Massachusetts 01890-0127;

Bibliography and Record Sources

General Sources

American Historical Society. *Encyclopedia of Massachusetts, Biographical-Genealogical*. 13 vols. New York: The American Historical Society, ca. 1916.

Bacon, Edwin Monroe. *Men of Progress: One Thousand Biographical Sketches and Portraits of Leaders in Business and Professional Life in the Commonwealth of Massachusetts*. Boston: New England Magazine, 1894.

Banks, Charles Edward. *The English Ancestry and Homes of the Pilgrim Fathers Who Came to Plymouth on the 'Mayflower' in 1620, the 'Fortune' in 1621, and the 'Anne' and the 'Little James' in 1623*. (1929). Reprint. Baltimore: Genealogical Publishing Co., 1989.

Banks, Charles Edward. *The Planters of the Commonwealth in Massachusetts, 1620-1640*. (1930) Reprint. Baltimore: Genealogical Publishing, 1996.

Barber, John W. *Historical Collections…Relating to the History and Antiquities of Every Town in Massachusetts. With Geographical Descriptions Illustrated by 200 Engravings*. (1839, 1844) Reprint, Baltimore: Clearfield Co., 1995.

Bowman, George Ernest. *The Mayflower Reader. A Selection of Articles from 'The Mayflower Descendant.' (1899-1905)*. Reprint. Baltimore: Clearfield Co., 1996.

Bowman, George Ernest. *Massachusetts Society of Mayflower Descendants: The Bowman Files*. Boston: Massachusetts Society of Mayflower Descendants, 1983.

Brush, John Woolman. *Baptists in Massachusetts*. Valley Forge, Pennsylvania: Judson Press, 1970.

Bushman. *King and People in Provincial Massachusetts*. Galveston, Texas: Frontier Press, 1992.

Catalog of Manuscripts of the Massachusetts Historical Society. 7 vols. Boston: G.K. Hall and Co., 1969.

Central Massachusetts Genealogical Society (Westminster, Massachusetts). *A Guide to Genealogical and Historical Holdings of Massachusetts Libraries*. Rev. ed. Westminster, Massachusetts: Central Massachusetts Genealogical Society, 1997.

Colburn, Jeremiah. *Bibliography of the Local History of Massachusetts*. Ann Arbor, Mich.: University Microfilms, 1989.

Colonial Society of Massachusetts. *Medicine in Colonial Massachusetts, 1620-1820*. Galveston, Texas: Frontier Press, 1980.

Colonial Society of Massachusetts. *Seafaring in Colonial Massachusetts*. Galveston, Texas: Frontier Press, 1980.

Corbin, Walter E. *Corbin Manuscript Collection in New England Historic Genealogical Society*. [S.l.: s.n.], 1982.

Crandall, Ralph J., ed. *Genealogical Research in New England*. Baltimore: Genealogical Publishing, 1984.

Cutter, William Richard. *Genealogical and Personal Memoirs Relating to the Families of the State of Massachusetts*. 4 vols. New York: Lewis Historical Publishing, 1910.

Duffy, Mark J., ed. *The Episcopal Diocese of Massachusetts 1784-1984*. [Boston]: Episcopal Diocese of Massachusetts, 1984.

Eliot, Samuel Atkins. *Biographical History of Massachusetts*. 10 vols. Boston: Massachusetts Biographical Society, 1911-18.

Flagg, Charles Allcott. *A Guide to Massachusetts Local History: Being a Bibliographic Index to the Literature of the Towns, Cities and Counties of the State, Including Books, Pamphlets, Articles in Periodicals and Collected Works, Books In Preparation, Historical Manuscripts, Newspaper Clippings, Etc*. Salem, Massachusetts: The Salem Press Company, 1907.

Forbes, Abner. *The Rich Men Of Massachusetts: Containing a Statement of the Reputed Wealth of About Fifteen Hundred Persons, With Brief Sketches of more than One Thousand Characters*. Boston: Fetridge and Company, 1851.

Genealogies of Mayflower Families: From the New England Historical and Genealogical Register. 3 vols. Baltimore: Genealogical Publishing, 1985.

Goodwin, John A. *The Pilgrim Republic: An Historical Review of the Colony of New Plymouth, with Sketches of Other New England Settlements, the History of Congregationalism, and the Creeds of the Period*. Boston: Tickner, 1888.

Green, Samuel Abbott. *Centennial Bibliography*. Ann Arbor, Mich.: University Microfilms, 1989.

Greenlaw, William Prescott. *The Greenlaw Index of the New England Historic Genealogical Society*. 2 vols. Boston: G. K. Hall, 1979.

Hallowell, Richard P. *The Quaker Invasion of Massachusetts*. Boston: Houghton Mifflin, 1883.

Hart, Albert Bushnell, ed. *Commonwealth History of Massachusetts: Colony, Province, and State*. 5 vols. New York: The States History, 1927-30.

Haskell, John D., Jr., ed. *Massachusetts: A Bibliography of Its History*. Hanover, NH: University Press of New England, 1983.

Historical Records Survey. *Preliminary Edition of Guide to Depositories of Manuscript Collections in Massachusetts*. Boston: Historical Records Survey, 1939.

Jacobson, Judith. *Massachusetts Bay Connections*. (1992). Reprint, Baltimore: Clearfield Co., 1994.

Kaufman, Martin, John W. Ifkovic, and Joseph Carvalho. *A Guide To The History Of Massachusetts*. New York: Greenwood Press, 1988.

Lewis, Ella May Swint. *Bible Records for Massachusetts Families*. Springfield, Massachusetts: Lewis, 1960.

Lindberg, Marcia Wiswall, ed. *Genealogist's Handbook for New England Research*. 3rd ed. Boston: New England Historic Genealogical Society, 1993.

Longver, Phyllis O., and Pauline J. Oesterlin. *Surname Guide to Massachusetts Town Histories*. Bowie, MD: Heritage Books, 1993.

Massachusetts and Maine Families in the Ancestry of Walter Goodwin Davis. 3 vols. (1916-63). Reprint. Baltimore: Genealogical Publishing Co., 1996.

Massachusetts Biographical Dictionary: People of All Times and all Places Who have been Important to the History and Life of the State. Wilmington, Del.: American Historical Publications, 1988.

Massachusetts Research Outline. Series US-States, no. 22. Salt Lake City: Family History Library, 1988.

Massachusetts, 1620-1930. [S.l.]: Brøderbund, 1998. CD-ROM.

Massachusetts. State Archives. *Card Index to the Massachusetts Archives*. (Salt Lake City: Filmed by the Genealogical Society of Utah, 1972-1973). Microfilm, 57 rolls.

New England Genealogical Society (Boston, Massachusetts). *Genealogical Card Catalog, A-Z*. Microreproduction of ms. and typescript at the New England Historic Genealogical Society. (Salt Lake City: Genealogical Society of Utah, 1970.) 19 microfilm.

New England Historic Genealogical Society. *English Origins of New England Families: from the New England Historical and Genealogical Register*. First Series, 3 vols. 1984. Second Series, 3 vols., 1985. Baltimore: Genealogical Publishing.

Northend, William Dummer. *The Bay Colony: A Civil, Religious and Social History of the Massachusetts Colony and Its Settlements From the Landing at Cape Ann in 1624 to the Death of Governor Winthrop in 1650*. Boston: Estes and Lauriat, 1896.

Pilgrim Genealogies and Histories. [S.l.]: Brøderbund, 1999. CD ROM

Pope, Charles Henry. *The Pioneers of Massachusetts 1620-1650*. (1900). Reprint. Baltimore: Genealogical Publishing Co., 1990.

Pope, Charles Henry. *The Plymouth Scrap Book: The Oldest Original Documents Extant in Plymouth Archives Printed Verbatim*. Boston: C.E. Goodspeed, 1918.

Harris, Ruth-Ann, and Donald M. Jacobs, eds. *The Search for Missing Friends: Irish Immigrant Advertisements Placed in the Boston Pilot* Boston. 5 vols. New England Historic Genealogical Society, 1989, 1991, 1993, 1995, 1996.

Massachusetts. Secretary of the Commonwealth. *Indexes to Returns of Naturalization, 1920–1923, 1924–1925.* Microreproduction of card index at Massachusetts State Archives, Boston, Massachusetts. (Salt Lake City: Genealogical Society of Utah, 1994.) 7 microfilm.

Massachusetts. Secretary of the Commonwealth. *Returns of Naturalization Before Various Massachusetts Courts, 1885–1931.* Microreproduction of documents at Massachusetts State Archives, Boston, Massachusetts. (Salt Lake City: Genealogical Society of Utah, 1993). 9 microfilm.

Munroe, J.B. *A List of Alien Passengers, Bonded from January 1, 1847 to January 1, 1851, for the Use of the Overseers of the Poor in the Commonwealth of Massachusetts.* (1851) Reprint. Baltimore: Genealogical Publishing Co., 1991.

Thayer, Mrs. Nathaniel. *"The Immigrants (1830-1929)" Commonwealth History of Massachusetts*, vol. 4. New York: The States History Company, 1930.

United States, Bureau of Customs. *A Supplemental Index to Passenger Lists of Vessels Arriving at Atlantic & Gulf Coast Ports (excluding New York) 1820–1874.* Washington, DC: National Archives Records Services, 1960.

United States, Bureau of Customs. *Passenger Lists of Vessels Arriving at Boston, 1820–1891: with index 1848–1891.* Washington, DC: National Archives Record Service, 1959–1960.

United States, District Court (Massachusetts). *Naturalization Index Cards, 1790–1926.* Microfilm of original records in the offices of the U.S. District Court, Boston, Massachusetts. (Salt Lake City: Genealogical Society of Utah, 1985.) 17 microfilm.

United States, Immigration and Naturalization Services. *St. Albans District Manifest Records of Aliens Arriving from Foreign Contiguous Territory.* Washington, DC: National Archives Records Service, 1986.

United States. District Court (Massachusetts). *Naturalization Records, 1906–1917.* Washington, DC: National Archives, 1988.

United States. Immigration and Naturalization Service. *Index To New England Naturalization Petitions, 1791-1906.* Washington: National Archives. Central Plains Region, 1983. 117 microfilm.

United States. Immigration and Naturalization Service. *Index to Passenger Lists of Vessels Arriving At Boston, Jan. 1, 1902-Dec.31, 1920; Passenger Lists of Vessels Arriving At Boston, Aug. 1, 1891- 1935; Book Indexes to Boston Passenger Lists, 1899-1940.* Washington, DC: National Archives and Records Service, 1944-1945, 1956.

Whitmore, William H. *Port Arrivals and Immigrants to the City of Boston 1715-1716.* (1900) Reprint. Baltimore: Genealogical Publishing, 1989.

Land and Property

Church of Jesus Christ of Latter-day Saints. Genealogical Society. Cataloging Section. *Registry of Deeds, Etc. from the Various Counties of Massachusetts, a Register of Contents.* (Salt Lake City: Filmed by the Genealogical Society of Utah, 1969).

Hone, Wade E. *Land and Property Research in the United States.* Salt Lake City: Ancestry Incorporated, 1997.

Judd, Sylvester, comp. *Judd Manuscripts (Connecticut).* Microfilm of manuscript at Forbes public library, Northampton, Hampshire County, Massachusetts. (Salt Lake City: Filmed by the Genealogical Society of Utah, 1960). 5 microfilm.

Massachusetts Archives. *Land Court Registration Decreases.* Boston: Massachusetts Archives, 2002. online at - <www.state.ma.us/sec/arc/arcgen/genidx.htm>

Roser, Susan E. *Mayflower Deeds & Probates: From the Files of George Ernest Bowman at the Massachusetts Society of Mayflower Descendants.* Baltimore, Maryland: Genealogical Publishing co., 1994.

Shaw, Hubert Kinney. *Plymouth Colony Wills And Inventories: Taken From The Mayflower Descendant.* Typescripts. [n. p.]

Shurtleff, N. B. and David Pulsifer, eds. *Records of the Colony of New Plymouth in New England.* 12 vols. Boston: William White, 1855-61.

Shurtleff, Nathaniel B. *Records of the Governor and Company of the Massachusetts Bay in New England.* 5 vols. Boston: W. White, 1853-54.

Military

Note: Military records for Massachusetts from the Seventeenth through the Twentieth Centuries can be found at the Massachusetts State Archives. For descriptions of collections search online at - <www.state.ma.us/sec/arc/arcgen/genidx.htm#military>

Adjutant General of Massachusetts. *Massachusetts Soldiers, Sailors, and Marines of the Civil War.* 9 vols. Norwood, Massachusetts: Norwood Press, 1931–1935.

Adjutant General of Massachusetts. *Records of the Massachusetts Volunteer Militia.* [Boston?]: Gardner W. Pearson, 1913. Boston: Wright and Potter Printing, 1913.

Allen, Gardner, Weld. *Massachusetts Privateers of the Revolution.* [Boston]: Massachusetts Historical Society, 1927.

Broadfoot Publishing Company. *Papers of the Military Historical Society of Massachusetts.* 15 vols. Wilmington, NC: Broadfoot Pub., n.d.

Budge, George Madison. *Soldiers in King Phillip's War. Official Lists of the Soldiers of Massachusetts Colony Serving in Philip's War; and Sketches of the Principal Officers, Copies of Ancient Documents and Records Relating to the War.* (1906) Reprint, Baltimore: Clearfield Co., 1995.

Doeskin, Carole. *Massachusetts Officers and Soldiers of the Seventeenth Century Conflicts.* Boston: Society of Colonial Wars, 1982.

Donahue, Mary E. *Massachusetts Officers and Soldiers 1702-1722: Queen Anne's War to Dimmer's War.* Boston: Society of Colonial Wars, 1980.

Higginson, Thomas W. *Massachusetts in the Army and Navy during the War of 1861-1865.* 2 vols. Boston: Wright and Potter, 1895-96.

Jones, Alfred E. *The Loyalists of Massachusetts: Their Memorials, Petitions and Claims.* (1930) Reprint. Baltimore: Clearfield Co., 1995.

MacLean, John P. *Historical Account of the Settlements of Scotch Highlanders in America Prior to the Peace of 1783.* Baltimore: Genealogical Publishing Co., 1968

Massachusetts Adjunct General's Office. *Record of Massachusetts Volunteers, 1861-1865.* 2 vols. Boston, Massachusetts: Adjutant General's Office, 1868-70.

Massachusetts Colonial Wars Database. Boston Society of Colonial Wars in the Commonwealth of Massachusetts, 2002. Online database – <www.newenglandancestors.org/research/database/>.

Massachusetts, Adjunct General. *Massachusetts Soldiers, Sailors and Marines in the Civil War.* Brookline, Massachusetts: Adjutant General's Office, 1931-35.

Massachusetts, Department of the State Secretary. *Massachusetts Soldiers and Sailors of the Revolutionary War.* Boston: Wright & Potter, 1896-1908.

McKay, Robert E. *Massachusetts Soldiers in the French and Indian Wars, 1744-1755.* Boston: Society of Colonial Wars, 1978.

Pearson, Gardner W. *Records of the Massachusetts Volunteer Militia Called Out by the Governor of Massachusetts to Suppress a Threatened Invasion during the War of 1812-1814.* (1913) Reprint. Baltimore: Clearfield Co., 1993.

Pierce, Ebenezer Weaver. *Pierce's Colonial Lists, Civil, Military and Professional Lists of Plymouth and Rhode Island Colonies...1621-1700.* (1881) Reprint. Baltimore: Clearfield Co., 1995.

Stachiw, Myron O. *Massachusetts Officers and Soldiers, 1723-1743: Dummer's War to the War of Jenkin's Ear.* Boston: Society of Colonial Wars in the Commonwealth of Massachusetts and The New England Historic Genealogical Society, 1979.

Stark, J.H. *The Loyalists of Massachusetts, and the Other Side of the American Revolution.* (1910) Reprint. Salem, Massachusetts: Higginson Books, 1990.

United States Veterans Administration. *Index to War of 1812 Pension Application Files.* Washington, DC: National Archives, 1960.

United States. Adjutant General's Office. *General Index to Compiled Military Service Records of Revolutionary Ward Soldiers.* Washington, DC: National Archives, 1942.

United States. Army. Massachusetts Infantry. "Casualties from Massachusetts in World War I, 1918," *Enlistments, Enrollments, Medical Examinations, Detachments, Oaths, Rosters, Election Returns, Discharges, Desertions, Resignations, Etc.* Microfilm of originals in the National Guard Supply Depot in Natick, Massachusetts. (Salt Lake City: Filmed by the Genealogical Society of Utah, 1988-1991). 120 microfilm.

United States. Selective Service System. *Massachusetts, World War I Selective Service System Draft Registration Cards, 1917–1918.* Washington, D.C.: National Archives, 1987–1988.

United States. Veterans Administration. *Revolutionary War Pension and Bounty-Land-Warrant Application Files.* Washington, DC: National Archives, 1969.

United States. Veterans Administration. *Selected Records from Revolutionary War Pension & Bounty-Land-Warrant Application Files.* Washington, DC: National Archives, 1969.

Voye, Nancy S., ed. *Massachusetts Officers in the French and Indian Wars 1748-1763.* Boston Society of Colonial Wars 1748-1763. Boston Society of Colonial Wars, 1975.

White, Virgil D. *Genealogical Abstracts of the Revolutionary War Pension Files.* 4 vols. Waynesboro, Tennessee: National Historical Publishing, 1990.

White, Virgil D. *Index to Revolutionary War Service Records.* 4 vols. Waynesboro, Tennessee: National Historical Publishing, 1995.

White, Virgil D., trans. *Index to War of 1812 Pension Files.* Waynesboro, Tennessee: National Historical Publishing Co., 1992.

Vital and Cemetery Records

American Antiquarian Society. *Index of Marriages in Massachusetts Centinel and Columbian Centinel, 1784 to 1840.* Boston: G.K. Hall and Co., 1961.

Bailey, Frederick W. *Early Massachusetts Marriages Prior to 1800: With the Addition of Plymouth Colony Marriages, 1692-1746.* 3 vols in 1. Baltimore: Genealogical Publishing Co., 1968.

Boston Athenaeum. *Index of Obituaries in Boston Newspapers, 1704-1800.* Boston: G. K. Hall and Co., 1968.

Daughters of the American Revolution. *Grave Locations of Revolutionary Soldiers and Sailors of Maine and Massachusetts.* Microfilm of original card index (396 cm., ca., 2500 cards.). (Salt Lake City: Genealogical Society of Utah, 1991.) 2 microfilm.

Holbrook, Jay Mack. *Bibliography of Massachusetts Vital Records 1620-1905.* Microfiche. Oxford, Massachusetts: Archive Publishing/Microform Books, 1996.

Holbrook, Jay Mack. *Massachusetts Birth, Marriage, & Death Indexes, 1841-1895.* Microfiche. Archive Publishing/Microform Books, 1989.

Holbrook, Jay Mack. *Massachusetts Cemetery Records: Quabbin Park 1741-1984.* Microfiche. Archive Publishing/Microform Books, 1985.

Landis, John T. *Mayflower Descendants and Their Marriage for Two Generations After the Landing.* (1922). Reprint. Baltimore: Clearfield Co., 1990.

Ledogar, Edwin Richard. *Vital Statistics of Eastern Connecticut, Western Rhode Island, South Central Massachusetts.* 2 vols. 1995. Reprint on microfiche. Arvada, Colorado: Ancestor Publishers, 1995.

Massachusetts, Secretary of the Commonwealth. *Births, Marriages (1841-1895), And Deaths (1841-1899); Indexes To Births And Marriages (1841-1905), Deaths (1841-1971).* Microfilm of original records in the Division of Vital Statistics, State House, Boston, Massachusetts. (Salt Lake City: Filmed by the Genealogical Society of Utah, 1974, 1985). 398 microfilm.

Massachusetts, Secretary of the Commonwealth. *Divorce Index, 1952–1970.* Microreproduction of original records at the State House in Boston, Massachusetts. (Salt Lake City: Genealogical Society of Utah, 1974.) 2 microfilm.

Mayflower Source Records: Primary Data Concerning Southeastern Massachusetts, Cape Cod, and the Islands of Nantucket and Martha's Vineyard. Baltimore: Genealogical Publishing Co., 1986.

Stevens, C.J. *The Massachusetts Magazine: Marriage and Death Notices, 1789-1796.* Lambertville, New Jersey: Hunterdon House, 1978.

Torrey, Clarence Almon. *New England Marriages Prior to 1700.* Andover, Massachusetts: Genealogical Publishing Co., 1985.

Vital Records of [town], Massachusetts, to the Year 1850. Boston: New England Historic Genealogical Society, 1902-ca. 1920. (Series of records for approximately 200 towns.)

County Website	Map Index	Date Created	Parent County or Territory From Which Organized / Address/Details

Barnstable   C9   2 Jun 1685   **New Plymouth Colony**
www.barnstablecounty.org/
Barnstable County; 3195 Main St; Barnstable, MA 02630; Ph. 508.362.2511
Details: (Clk Cir Ct has div & ct rec from 1828; Reg of Deeds has land rec; Pro Judge has pro rec)
Towns Organized Before 1800: Barnstable 1638, Chatham 1712, Dennis 1793, Eastham 1646, Falmouth 1694, Harwich 1694, Mashpee 1763, Orleans 1797, Provincetown 1727, Truro 1709, Wellfleet 1763, Yarmouth 1639

Berkshire   Q5   28 May 1760   **Hampshire**
www.rootsweb.com/~maberksh/
Berkshire County; 76 East St; Pittsfield, MA 01201; Ph. 413.448.8424
Details: (Clk Cts has div rec 1761-1922 & ct rec from 1761; Pro Judge has div rec from 1922 & pro rec from 1761; Reg of Deeds has land rec)
Towns Organized Before 1800: Adams 1778, Alford 1773, Becket 1765, Cheshire 1793, Clarksburg 1798, Dalton 1784, Egremont 1760, Great Barrington 1761, Hancock 1776, Lanesborough 1765, Lee 1777, Lenox 1767, Mount Washington 1779, New Ashford 1781, New Marlborough 1759, Otis 1773, Peru 1771, Pittsfield 1761, Richmond 1765, Savoy 1797, Sheffield 1733, Standisfield 1762, Stockbridge 1739, Tyringham 1762, Washington 1777, West Stockbridge 1774, Williamstown 1765

Bristol   G7   2 Jun 1685   **New Plymouth Colony**
www.bristol-county.org/bristol_home.htm
Bristol County; 9 Court St; Taunton, MA 02780-3223; Ph. 508.824.9681
Details: (Clk Cts has ct rec from 1796 & nat rec; Twn Clks have b, m & d rec; Pro Ct has div rec from 1921 & pro rec)
Towns Organized Before 1800: Attleboro 1694, Berkley 1735, Dartmouth 1652, Dighton 1712, Easton 1725, Freetown 1683, Mansfield 1770, New Bedford 1787, Norton 1710, Raynham 1731, Rehoboth 1645, Sandwich 1638, Somerset 1790, Swansea 1667, Taunton 1639, Westport 1787

Dukes   E10   22 Jun 1695   **(Martha's Vineyard)**
www.vineyard.net/vineyard/history/dukes/
Dukes County; PO Box 190; Edgartown, MA 02539; Ph. 508.627.5535
Details: (Clk Cts has div & ct rec from 1859; Pro Ct has pro rec; Twn Clks have b, m, d & bur rec)
Towns Organized Before 1800: Chilmark 1694, Edgartown 1671, Tisbury 1671

Essex*   F3   10 May 1643   **Original county**
www.essexcountyma.org/
Essex County; 36 Federal St; Salem, MA 01970; Ph. 978.741.0200
Details: (Pro Ct has pro rec; Reg of Deeds has land rec from 1640; Co Clk has b, m & d rec)
Towns Organized Before 1800: Amesbury 1668, Andover 1646, Beverly 1668, Boxford 1694, Danvers 1752, Hamilton 1793, Haverhill 1641, Ipswich 1634, Lynn 1635, Lynnfield 1782, Manchester 1645, Marblehead 1633, Methuen 1725, Middleton 1728, Newbury 1635, Newburyport 1764, Rowley 1639, Salem 1630, Salisbury 1639, Topsfield 1648, Wenham 1643

Franklin   N3   24 Jun 1811   **Hampshire**
www.rootsweb.com/~mafrankl/
Franklin County; 425 Main St; Greenfield, MA 01301-3313; Ph. 413.774.7011
Details: (Clk Cts has div & ct rec from 1811; Reg of Pro has pro rec; Reg of Deeds has land rec)
Towns Organized Before 1800: Ashfield 1765, Bernardston 1762, Buckland 1779, Charlemont 1765, Colrain 1761, Conway 1767, Deerfield 1677, Gil 1793, Greenfield 1753, Hawley 1792, Heath 1785, Leverett 1774, Leyden 1784, Montague 1754, New Salem 1753, Northfield 1714, Orange 1783, Rowe 1785, Shelburne 1768, Shuetesbury 1761, Sunderland 1714, Warwick 1763, Wendell 1781, Whately 1771, Williamsburg 1771

Hampden   N6   25 Feb 1812   **Hampshire**
www.rootsweb.com/~mafrankl/
Hampden County; 50 State St; Springfield, MA 01103; Ph. 413.748.7759
Details: (Clk Cts has div rec 1812-1932 & ct rec; Pro Judge has pro rec; Reg of Deeds has land rec)
Towns Organized Before 1800: Blandford 1741, Brimfield 1714, Chester 1765, Granville 1754, Holland 1783, Longmeadow 1783, Monson 1760, Montgomery 1780, Palmer 1752, Southwick 1770, springifeld 1641, Wales 1762, West sprigfield 1774, Westfield 1669, Wilbraham 1763

County Website	Map Index	Date Created	Parent County or Territory From Which Organized / Address/Details
Hampshire www.rootsweb.com/~mahampsh/	N5	7 May 1662	**Middlesex** Hampshire County; 33 King St; Northampton, MA 01060; Ph. 413.586.8500 Details: (City Clks have b, m & d rec; Pro Ct has pro & div rec; Dis Ct has ct rec; Reg of Deeds has land rec from 1600's) Towns Organized Before 1800: Amherst 1759, Belchertown 1761, Chesterfield 1762, Cummington 1779, Easthampton 1785, Goshen 1781, Granby 1768, Hadley 1661, Middlefield 1783, Northampton 1656, Pelham 1743, Plainfield 1785, Russell 1792, South Hadley 1753, Southampton 1753, Ware 1761, Westhampton 1778, Worthington 1768
Middlesex www.rootsweb.com/~mamiddle/	H4	10 May 1643	**Original county** Middlesex County; 208 Cambridge St; East Cambridge, MA 02141; Ph. 617.494.4533 Details: (Clk Cts has b rec 1632-1745, m rec 1651-1793, d rec 1651-1689, div rec from 1888 & ct rec from 1648; Rcdr Deeds, PO Box 68, E. Cambridge, MA 02141 has land rec 1632-1855 & for southern dis from 1855; Reg of Deeds, 360 Gorham St., Lowell, MA 01852 has land rec for northern dis from 1855) Towns Organized Before 1800; Acton 1735, Ashby 1767, Bedford 1729, Billerica 1655, Boxborough 1783, Burlington 1799, Cambridge 1631, Carlisle 1780, Chelmsford 1655, Concord 1635, Dracut 1702, Dunstable 1673, Framingham 1675, Groton 1655, Holliston 1724, Hopkinton 715, Lexington 1713, Lincoln 1754, Littleton 715, Malden 1649, Marlborough 1660, Medford 1630, Natick 1650, Newton 1691, Pepperell 1753, Reading 1644, Sherborn 1674, Shirley 1753, Stoneham 1725, Stow 1683, Sudbury 1639, Tewksbury 1734, Townsend 1732, Tyngsboro 1789, Waltham 1738, Watertown 1630, Wayland 1780, Westford 1729, Weston 1713, Wilmington 730, Woburn 1642
Nantucket www.rootsweb.com/~manantuc/ nantuckt.htm	B11	22 Jun 1695	**Original county** Nantucket County; Town and County Bldg, Broad St; Nantucket, MA 02554; Ph. 508.228.7229 Details: (Twn Clks have b, m, d & bur rec from 1600's; Pro Ct has pro & div rec; Reg of Deeds has land rec; Dis Ct has ct rec) Towns Organized Before 1800: Nantucket 1687
Norfolk www.rootsweb.com/~manorfol/ manorfol.htm	G6	26 Mar 1793	**Suffolk** Norfolk County; 650 High St; Dedham, MA 02026-1855; Ph. 781.461.6105 Details: (Pro Judge has div & pro rec; Clk Cts has ct rec from 1928; Reg of Deeds has land rec) (Originally part of the northeastern section of Mass & some towns now part of NH; The old rec are now at Salem in Essex Co which originally included most of Norfolk Co) Towns Organized Before 1800: Bellingham 1719, Braintree 1640, Brookline 1705, Canton 1797, Cohasset 1770, Dedham 1636, Dover 1784, Franklin 1778, Medfield 1650, Milton 1662, Needham 1711, Quincy 1792, Randolph 1793, Sharon 1765, Walpole 1724, Weymouth 1635, Wrentham 1673
Plymouth www.plymouth-1620.com/	E7	2 Jun 1685	**New Plymouth Colony** Plymouth County; County Courthouse; 11 S Russell St; Plymouth, MA 02360; Ph. 781.830.9100 Details: (Twn Clks have b, m, d & bur rec; Pro Ct has pro & div rec; Co Comm have land, pro & ct rec 1620-1692; Reg of Deeds has land rec) Towns Organized Before 1800: Abinton 1712, Bridgewater 1656, Carver 1790, Duxbury 1637, Halifax 1734, Hanover 1727, Hingham 1635, Hull 1644, Kingston 1726, Marshfield 1640, Middleborough 1669, Pembroke 1712, Plymouth 1620, Plympton 1707, Rochester 1686, Scituate 1633, Wareham 1739
P Suffolk www.geocities.com/masuffolk/	F5	10 May 1643	**Original county** Suffolk County; 1 City Hall Sq; Boston, MA 02201; Ph. 617.725.8000 Details: (Town & City Clks have b, m & d rec; Clk Cts has div rec; Reg of Pro has pro & ct rec; Reg of Deeds has land rec; part of 1800 cen missing) Towns Organized Before 1800: Boston 1630, Chelsea 1739, Dorchester 1630, Roxbury 1630

County Website	Map Index	Date Created	Parent County or Territory From Which Organized Address/Details
Worcester www.rootsweb.com/~maworces/	**K5**	**5 Apr 1731**	**Suffolk, Middlesex**

Worcester County; 2 Main St; Worcester, MA 01608-1116; Ph. 508.770.0825
Details: (Reg of Deeds has land rec; Pro Ct has pro rec from 1731; Twn Clks have b, m & d rec)
Towns Organized Before 1800: Ashburnham 1765, Athol 1762, Auburn 1778, Barre 1753, Berlin 1784, Bolton 1738, Boylston 1786, Brookfield 1673, Charlton 1754, Douglas 1746, Fitchburg 1764, Gardner 1785, Grafton 1735, Greenwich 1754, Hardwick 1739, Harvard 1732, Hubbardston 1767, Lancaster 1653, Leicester 1714, Leominister 1740, Lunenburg 1728, Mendon 1667, Milford 1780, New Braintree 1751, Northborough 1766, Northbridge 1772, Oakham 1762, Oxford 1693, Paxton 1765, Petersham 1754, Phillipston 1786, Princeton 1759, Royalston 1765, Rutland 1714, Shrewsbury 1720, Southborough 1727, Spencer 1753, Sterling 1781, Sutton 1714, Templeton 1762, Upton 1735, Uxbridge 1742, Warren 1742, Westbourough 1717, Westminister 1759, Winchendon 1762, Worcester 1684.

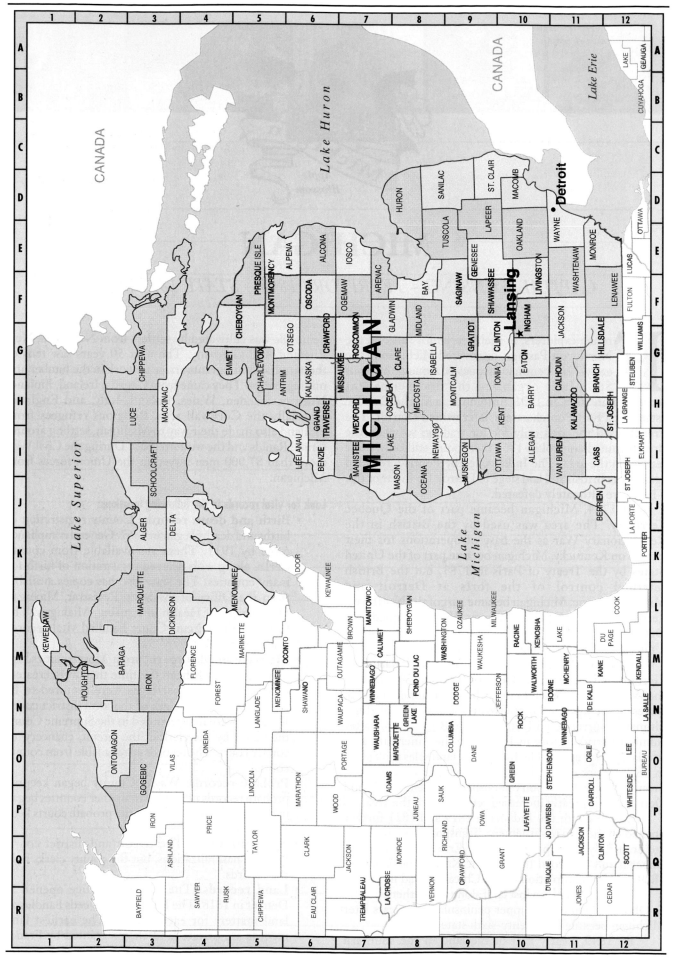

and England. These records are at the National Archives, Chicago Branch in Chicago, Illinois. Claims for 1790 to 1837 have been transcribed, indexed, and published. The Michigan State Archives, Department of State in Lansing also has many land and tax records.

- **Census records:** More than 20 early territorial censuses were taken in various areas of Michigan from 1810 to 1830 and are available in published form. Other territorial and state enumerations were made between 1827 and 1904.

Office of the State Registrar, Michigan Department of Health
PO Box 30195
Lansing, Michigan 48909
517.335.8666

Michigan State Archives, Department of State
3405 North Logan Street
Lansing, Michigan 48198

Societies and Repositories

Albion Historical Society; Gardner House Museum; 509 S. Superior St.; Albion, Michigan 49224

Archdiocese of Detroit; 1234 Washington Blvd.; Detroit, Michigan 48226; 313.237.5800; Fax 313.237.4642

Bay City Branch Library; 708 Center Ave.; Bay City, Michigan 48706

Bay County Genealogical Society; PO Box 1366; Bay City, Michigan 48706-0366; <community.mlive.com/cc/baygenealogy>

Bergen County Genealogical Society; PO Box 8808; Benton Harbor, Michigan 49023-8808; <w3.qtm.net/bcgensoc/>

Bigelow Genealogical Society; PO Box 4115; Flint, Michigan 49504

Branch County Genealogical Society; PO Box 443; Coldwater, Michigan 49036; <www.geocities.com/TheTropics/1050/Gensociety.html>

Branch County Historical Society; PO Box 107; Coldwater, Michigan 49036

Burton Historical Collection, Detroit Public Library; 5201 Woodward Avenue; Detroit, Michigan 48202; 313.833.1480

Cadillac Area Genealogical Society; 411 S. Lake Street; Cadillac, Michigan 49601;

Calhoun County Genealogical Society; PO Box 879; Marshall, Michigan 49068; <www.rootsweb.com/~micalhou/ccgs.htm>

Cass District Library, Local History Branch; 319 M-62 North; Cassopolis, Michigan 49031-1099; 616.445.3400

Cass River Genealogy Society; 359 S. Franklin; Frankenmuth, Michigan 48734; <www.frankenmuthcity.com/library/genealogy.htm>

Cedar Springs Historical Society; 60 Cedar Street; PO Box 296; Cedar Springs, Michigan 49319

Cedar Springs Museum; PO Box 296; Cedar Springs, Michigan 49319; 616.696.3335

Central Archives of Polonia, The Orchard Lake Schools; 3535 Indian Trail; Orchard Lake, Michigan 48324

Central Michigan University Library; Mt. Pleasant, Michigan 48858

Charlevoix County Genealogical Society; 201 E. Main St.; Boyne City, Michigan 49712

Charter Township of Redford Genealogical Society; 12259 Beech Daly; Redford, Michigan 48239-9998

Cheboygan County Genealogical Society; PO Box 51; Cheboygan, Michigan 49721; <www.rootsweb.com/~miccgs/CCGSmainx.html>

Chippewa County Genealogical Society; PO Box 1686; Sault Ste. Marie, Michigan 49783-1686; <www.rootsweb.com/~michcgs/index.html>

Chippewa County Historical Society; PO Box 342; Sault Ste. Marie, Michigan 49783

Dearborn Genealogical Society; PO Box 1112; Dearborn, Michigan 48121-1112; <www.rootsweb.com/~midgs/index.htm>

Delta County Genealogical Society; Box 442; Escanaba, Michigan 49829-0442; <grandmastree.com/society/>

Detroit Health Department; 1151 Taylor Street; Detroit, Michigan 48202; 313.876.4133

Detroit Public Library; 5201 Woodward Ave.; Detroit, Michigan 48202; <www.members.tripod.com/FCHS_FC/index.htm>

Detroit Society for Genealogical Research, Inc.; Detroit Public Library; 5201 Woodward Ave.; Detroit, Michigan 48202;

Dickinson County Genealogical Society; c/o Dickinson County Library; 401 Iron Mountain Street; Iron Mountain, Michigan 48901-3435

Diocese of Grand Rapids; 660 Burton St. S.E.; Grand Rapids, Michigan 49507; 616.243.0491; Fax 616.243.4910

Diocese of Lansing; 300 West Ottawa; Lansing, Michigan 48933; 517.342.2440; Fax 517.343.2515

Diocese of Saginaw; 5800 Weiss St.; Saginaw, Michigan 48603-2799; 517.799.7910; Fax 517.797.6670

Downriver Gen. Soc. Library; 1335 Southfield Rd.; Lincoln Park, Michigan 48146; 313.381.0507; <www.rootsweb.com/~midrgs/drgs.html>

Downriver Genealogical Society; 1394 Cleophus, Box 476; Lincoln Park, Michigan 49146

Eaton County Genealogical Society; PO Box 337; Charlotte, Michigan 48813-0337; 517.543.6999; <userdata.acd.net/mmgs/ecgs.html>

ELCA Archives, Methodist, Shipman Library; Adrian College, 110 South Madison Street; Adrian, Michigan 49221; 517.265.5161; Fax 517.264.3331

Ellis Reference & Information Center, Monroe Co. Library System; 3700 S. Custer Rd.; Monroe, Michigan 48161-9732

Evangelical Lutheran Church in America (ELCA Archives); 8765 West Higgins Road; Chicago, Illinois 60631-4198; 312.380.2818; Fax 312.380.2977

Family History Library: 35 North West Temple Street: Salt Lake City, Utah 84150: 800.346.6044 or 801.240.2584: <www.familysearch.org>: Find a Family History Center near you: <www.familysearch.org/Eng/Library/FHC/frameset_fhc.asp>

Farmington Genealogical Society; Farmington Community Library; 23500 Liberty Street; Farmington, Michigan 48335-3570; <www.metronet.lib.mi.us/FCL/genealsoc.html>

Finnish American Historical Society of Michigan; 19995 Melrose; Southfield, Michigan 49075

Flat River Historical Society; PO Box 19R; Greenville, Michigan 49838

Flint Genealogical Society; PO Box 1217; Flint, Michigan 48501-1217; <www.rootsweb.com/~mifgs/>

Flint Michigan Chapter, AHSGR; 4167 W Four Lakes Dr.; Linden, Michigan 48451; 810.629.8710

Flint Public Library; 1026 E. Kearsley; Flint, Michigan 48502

Ford Genealogy Club; PO Box 1652; Dearborn, Michigan 48121-1652; <www.wwnet.com/~krugman1/fgc/>

Four Flags Area Genealogical Society; PO Box 414; Niles, Michigan 49120-0414

Fred Hart Williams Genealogical Society - Detroit Burton Historical Collection; Detroit Public Library; 5201 Woodward Ave.; Detroit, Michigan 48202

French Canadian Heritage Society of Michigan; c/o Gail F. Moreau; 9513 Whipple Shores Drive; Clarkston, Michigan 48348; <habitant.org/fchsm/>

French-Canadian Heritage Society of Michigan; c/o Library of Michigan; PO Box 30007; Lansing, Michigan 48909

French-Canadian Heritage Society of Michigan; c/o Mt. Clemens Public Library; PO Box 10028; Lansing, Michigan 48901-0028

Friends of the Mitchell Public Library Research Committee; 22 N. Manning St., PO Box 873; Hillsdale, Michigan 49242

Gaylord Fact Finders Genealogical Society; PO Box 1524; Gaylord, Michigan 49734-5524

Genealogical Society of Flemish Americans; 18740 Thirteen Mile Rd.; Roseville, Michigan 48066; <www.rootsweb.com/~gsfa/>

Genealogical Society of Isabella County; 523 N. Fancher; Mount Pleasant, Michigan 48858

Genealogical Society of Monroe County, Michigan; PO Box 1428; Monroe, Michigan 48161-1428; <www.tdi.net/havekost/gsmc.htm>

Genealogical Society of Washtenaw County, Michigan, Inc.; PO Box 7155; Ann Arbor, Michigan 48107-7155; <www.hvcn.org/info/gswc/>

Genealogists of the Clinton County Historical Society; PO Box 23; St. Johns, Michigan 48879-2312; <userdata.acd.net/mmgs/gofcchs.html>; <www.sojourn.com/~mmgs/gofcchs.html>

Grace A. Dow Memorial Library; 1710 W. St. Andrews; Midland, Michigan 48657; 517.837.3430; <www.gracedowlibrary.org>

Grand Haven Genealogical Society; c/o Loutit Library; 407 Columbus Street; Grand Haven, Michigan 49417

Grand Rapids Public Library; 111 Library St., N.E; Grand Rapids, Michigan 49502

Grand Traverse Area Genealogical Society; PO Box 2015; Traverse City, Michigan 49685-2015; <www.rootsweb.com/~migtags/gtag.htm>

Gratiot County Historical and Genealogical Society; PO Box 73; Ithaca, Michigan 48847-0073; <www.rootsweb.com/~migratio/gchgs/index.html>

Harrison Area Genealogy Society; PO Box 796; Harrison, Michigan 48625; <www.rootsweb.com/~miclare/harrison.htm>

Herrick Public Library; 300 River Ave.; Holland, Michigan 49423

Hillsdale County Genealogical Society; 22 N. Manning Street; Hillsdale, Michigan 49242

Holland Genealogical Society; c/o Herrick Public Library; 300 River Avenue; Holland, Michigan 49423

Huron County Genealogical Society; c/o Marilyn Hebner; 2843 Electric Avenue; Port Huron, Michigan 48060

Huron Shores Genealogical Society; c/o Robert J. Parks Public Library; Oscoda, Michigan 48750-1577

Huron Valley Genealogical Society; 1100 Atlantic Street; Milford, Michigan 48381; 248.684.5622; <milford.lib.mi.us/MCIN/groups/hvgs.htm>

Ingham County Genealogical Society; PO Box 85; Mason, Michigan 48854; <userdata.acd.net/mmgs/icgs.html>

Ionia County Genealogical Society; 13051 Ainsworth Road, Rt. 3; Lake Odessa, Michigan 48849-9406; <www.rootsweb.com/~miionia/icgshome.htm>

Irish Genealogical Society of Michigan; c/o Gaelic League / Irish-American Club; 2068 Michigan Avenue; Detroit, Michigan 48216; <www.rootsweb.com/~miigsm/>

Isabella County Genealogical Society; 523 N. Faucher St.; Mt. Pleasant, Michigan 48858

Jackson County Genealogical Society; c/o Jackson District Library; 244 W. Michigan Avenue; Jackson, Michigan 49201; <www.rootsweb.com/~mijackso/jcgs.htm>

Jackson Public Library; 244 W. Michigan Ave.; Jackson, Michigan 49201

Jewish Genealogical Society of Michigan; 8050 Lincoln Dr.; Huntington Woods, Michigan 48070

Jewish Genealogical Society of Michigan; PO Box 251693; West Bloomfield, Michigan 48325-1693;

John M. Longyear Research Library, c/o Marquette Co. Hist. Soc.; 213 N. Front St.; Marquette, Michigan 49855

Kalamazoo College, Upjohn Library; 1200 Academy St.; Kalamazoo, Michigan 49006; 616.337.7153; Fax 616.337.7143; (Baptist church records)

Kalamazoo Valley Genealogical Society; PO Box 405; Comstock, Michigan 49041; <www.rootsweb.com/~mikvgs/>

Kalkaska Genealogical Society; PO Box 353; Kalkaska, Michigan 49646-0353; <hometown.aol.com/fiddlerben/kasgensoc.html>

Kinseekers; 5697 Old Maple Trail; Grawn, Michigan 49637

Lapeer Co. Library; 201 Village West Dr.; Lapeer, Michigan 48446-1699

Lapeer County Genealogical Society; 921 West Nepessing Street; Lapeer, Michigan 48446

Lenawee County Family Researchers; c/o Corresponding Secretary; 519 Company Street; Adrian, Michigan 49221; <people.mw.mediaone.net/coslund/lcfr/index.html>

Lenawee County Genealogical Society; PO Box 511; Adrain, Michigan 49221

Library of Michigan; 717 West Allegan Street, PO Box 30007; Lansing, Michigan 48909; 517.373.1300

Livingston County Genealogical Society; PO Box 1073; Howell, Michigan 48844-1073; <www.livgenmi.com/lcgslogo.htm>

Livonia Historical Society; 39125 Eight Mile Rd.; Livonia, Michigan 48152

Log Cabin Genealogical Society; 103 North Third Street; Manistique, Michigan 49854-1018

Luce-Mackinac County Genealogical Society; PO Box 113; Engadine, Michigan 49827-0113; <www.rootsweb.com/~miluce/luce.mac.htm>

Lyon Township Genealogical Society; c/o Lyon Township Public Library; 27025 Milford Rd.; New Hudson, Michigan 48165

Macomb County Genealogical Group; c/o Mt. Clemens Public Library; 150 Cass Avenue; Mt. Clemens, Michigan 48043; <www.libcoop.net/mountclemens/>

Marquette County Genealogical Society; 217 N. Front Street; Marquette, Michigan 49855-3710; <members.aol.com/MQTCGS/MCGS/mcgs.html>

Mason Co. Gen., Hist. Resource Center, c/o Rose Hawley Museum; PO Box 549; 305 E. Filer St.; Ludington, Michigan 49431

Mason County Historical Society; Rose Hawley Museum; 115 W. Loomis St.; Ludington, Michigan 49431

Mason Library - CADL (Bingham Co. Gen. Soc.); 145 Ash St.; Mason, Michigan 48854 <userdata.acd.net/mmgs/icgs.html>

Mecosta County Genealogical Society; PO Box 1068; Big Rapids, Michigan 49307

Michigan Department of Public Health; 3423 North Logan Street, PO Box 30035; Lansing, Michigan 48909; 517.335.8000

Michigan Genealogical Council; PO Box 80953; Lansing, Michigan 48908-0953

Michigan Historical Commission; 505 State Office Bldg.; Lansing, Michigan 48913

Michigan Society, Order of Founders & Patriots of America; 2961 Woodcreek Way; Bloomfield Hills, Michigan 48304-1974

Midland County Historical Society; c/o Midland Center for the Arts; 1901 W. St. Andrews Dr.; Midland, Michigan 48640

Midland Genealogical Society; c/o Grace A. Dow Library; 1710 W. St. Andrews Dr.; Midland, Michigan 48640; <users.tm.net/brauschj/mgs/>

Mid-Michigan Genealogical Society; PO Box 16033; Lansing, Michigan 48901-6033; <userdata.acd.net/mmgs/mmgssoc.html>

Monroe County, Genealogical Society of Michigan; PO Box1429; Monroe, Michigan 48161

Mt. Clemens Public Library; 150 Cass Ave.; Mt. Clemens, Michigan 48043

Muskegon County Genealogical Society; c/o Hackley Library; 316 W. Webster Avenue; Muskegon, Michigan 49440; <www.rootsweb.com/~mimcgs/>

National Archives and Records Administration-Chicago Branch; 7358 South Pulaski Road; Chicago, Illinois 60629; 312.581.7816

Newaygo County Society of History and Genealogy; PO Box 68; White Cloud, Michigan 49349-0068; 616.689.6699; <www.rootsweb.com/~minewayg/society.html>

North Oakland Genealogical Society; c/o Orion Township Library; 825 Joslyn Road; Lake Orion, Michigan 48362; <www.pontiac.lib.mi.us/genealog.htm>

Northeast Michigan Genealogical Society; c/o Jesse Besser Museum; 491 Johnson Street; Alpena, Michigan 49707; <members.aol.com/alpenaco/migenweb/>

Northville Genealogical Society; PO Box 932; Northville, Michigan 48167-0932; <www.rootsweb.com/~mings/>

Northwest Oakland County Historical Society; 306 South Saginaw St.; Holly, Michigan 48442; <www.pontiac.lib.mi.us/genealog.htm>

Northwestern Michigan College; Mark Osterlin library; 1704 E. Front St.; Traverse City, Michigan 49684

Northwestern Michigan Gen. Soc., Mark Osterlin Library; 1704 E. Front St.; Traverse City, Michigan 49684

Oakland County Genealogical Society; PO Box 1094; Birmingham, Michigan 48012-1094; <www.metronet.lib.mi.us/ROCH/OCGS/>

Oceana County Genealogical Chapter; 114 Dryden St.; Hart, Michigan 49420

Ogemaw District Library; 107 West Main Box 427; Rose City, Michigan 48654

Ogemaw Genealogical and Historical Society; c/o West Branch Public Library; West Branch, Michigan 49661

Onaway Library; PO Box 742; Onaway, Michigan 49765

Orion Township Public Library; 825 Joslyn; Lake Orion, Michigan 48362

Osceola County Genealogical Society; PO Box 27; Reed City, Michigan 49677-0027

Palatines to America, Michigan Chapter; 968 Beechwood St. N.E.; Grand Rapids, Michigan 49505-3783

Polish Archives, St. Mary's College; Orchard Lake, Michigan 48033

Polish Genealogical Society of Michigan; c/o Burton Historical Collection; Detroit Public Library; 5201 Woodward Avenue; Detroit, Michigan 48202-4007

Pontiac Area Historical and Genealogical Society; PO Box 901; Pontiac, Michigan 48056

Presque Isle County Genealogical Society; c/o Onaway Library; PO Box 742; Onaway, Michigan 49765-0742

Reed City Area Genealogical Society (Osceola County); 4918 Park St.; PO Box 27; Reed City, Michigan 49677

Rockwood Area Historical Society; PO Box 68; Rockwood, Michigan 48171

Roman Catholic, Diocese of Marquette; 444 South Fourth Street, PO Box 550; Marquette, Michigan 49855; 906.225.1141; Fax 906.225.0437

Rose City Area Historical Society, Inc.; c/o Ogemaw District Library+107 W. Main, Box 427; Rose City, Michigan 48654

Roseville Historical and Genealogical Society; c/o Roseville Public Library; 29777 Gratiot Avenue; Roseville, Michigan 48066-4196

Sage Branch Library; 100 E. Midland St.; Bay City, Michigan 48706

Saginaw Genealogical Society; c/o Saginaw Public Library; 505 Janes Avenue; Saginaw, Michigan 48607

Saginaw Valley Chapter, AHSGR; 6910 Trowbridge Circle; Saginaw, Michigan 48603; 517.799.4266; <www.ahsgr.org/saginaw.html>

Shiawassee County Genealogical Society; PO Box 841; Owosso, Michigan 49967; <www.shianet.org/community/orgs/scgs/index.html>

Sons of the American Revolution, Michigan Society; 2031 L'Anse; St. Clair Shore, Michigan 48081

South Side Branch Library; 311 Lafayette St.; Bay City, Michigan 48706

Southern Michigan Genealogical Society; 239 E Chicago Road; Allen, Michigan 49227

Southwest Michigan Chapter, AHSGR; 1468 St. Joseph Cir; St. Joseph, Michigan 49085-9707; <www.ahsgr.org/misouthw.html>

St. Clair Co. Library; PO Box 611493; 210 McMorran Blvd.; Port Huron, Michigan 48060

St. Clair County Family History Group; PO Box 611483; Port Huron, Michigan 48061-1483

St. Joseph Genealogical Society; PO Box 486; White Pigeon, Michigan 49099; <members.tripod.com/~tfred/sjgc.html>

State Archives of Michigan; Michigan Library and Historical Center 717 West Allegan Street; Lansing, Michigan 48909-8240; <www.sos.state.mi.us/history/archive/archive.html>

Sterling Heights Genealogical and Historical Society; PO Box 1154; Sterling Heights, Michigan 48311-1154; <www.rootsweb.com/~mishghs/>

Sturgis Public Library; N. Nottawa at West St.; Sturgis, Michigan 49091

Then & Now Historical & Genealogical Society of E. Allegan County; 532 N. Main; Wayland, Michigan 49348-1043

Three Oaks Township Library; 102 Oak St.; Three Oaks, Michigan 49128; 616.756.5621

Three Rivers Genealogical Society; 13724 Spence Rd.; Three Rivers, Michigan 49093

Tri-State Genealogical Society; c/o Sturgis Public Library; 255 North Street; Sturgis, Michigan 49091; <www.rootsweb.com/~intsgs/>

Union City Genealogical Society; 680 M-60; Union City, Michigan 49094

University of Michigan; 1150 Beal Avenue; Ann Arbor, Michigan 48109-2113; 313.764.3482

Van Buren District Library; 200 N. Phelps St.; Decatur, Michigan 49045; 616.423.4771

Van Buren Regional Genealogical Society; PO Box 143; Decatur, Michigan 49045; 423.8045; <www.woodlands.lib.mi.us/van/vbrgs.htm>

Vicksburg District Library; 215 S Michigan; Vicksburg, Michigan 49097

Vicksburg Historical Society; 7683 East YZ Ave.; Vicksburg, Michigan 49097

Waterford Township Public Library; 5168 Civic Center Dr.; Waterford, Michigan 48329; 248.674.4831; <waterford.lib.mi.us>

Webster Memorial Library; 200 Phelps St.; Decatur, Michigan 49045

Western Michigan Genealogical Society; c/o Grand Rapids Public Library; 111 Library Street NE; Grand Rapids, Michigan 49503-3268;

Western Wayne County Genealogical Society; PO Box 63; Livonia, Michigan 49152

Westland Michigan Genealogical Library; PO Box 70; Westland, Michigan 48185

Wexford Co. Public Library; 411 S. Lake St.; Cadillac, Michigan 4960; 231.775.6541

White Pine Library Cooperative; 1840 N. Michigan, Suite 114; Saginaw, Michigan 48602-5590

Willard Library; 7 W. Van Buren St.; Battle Creek, Michigan 49017; 616.968.8166

Ypsilanti Historical Society Museum; 220 North Huron St.; Ypsilanti, Michigan 48197

Bibliography and Record Sources

General Sources

American Biographical History of Eminent and Self-Made Men: Michigan Volume. Cincinnati, Ohio: Western Biographical Pub. Co., 1878.

Anderson, Alloa Caviness. *Genealogy in Michigan: What, When, Where,* 2nd ed. Ann Arbor, Michigan: A. Anderson, P. Bender, 1978.

Callard, Carole, ed. *Sourcebook of Michigan Census, County Histories, and Vital Records.* Lansing, Michigan: Library of Michigan, 1986.

Centennial Family Certificate Application Files: A Project of the Michigan Genealogical Council. Salt Lake City: Genealogical Society of Utah, 1983. Microfilm, 81 rolls.

Church Record Index. 2 vols. Grand Rapids: The Society, 1993.

DeZeeuw, Donald J., ed. *The Michigan Surname Index.* Lansing, Michigan: Michigan Genealogical Council, 1984.

Fuller, George Newman, *Michigan, A Centennial History of the State and Its People.* 5 vols.: Lewis Publishing Co., 1939.

Genealogist's Guide to Southwestern Michigan. Grawn, Michigan: Kinseeker Publications, 1987.

Genealogist's Guide to the Middle of Michigan. Grawn, Michigan: Kinseeker Publications, 1987.

Genealogist's Guide to the Thumb Area of Michigan. Grawn, Michigan: Kinseeker Publications, 1987.

Genealogist's Guide to Northeastern Michigan. Grawn, Michigan: Kinseeker Publications, 1987.

Genealogist's Guide to Upper Peninsula Michigan. Grawn, Michigan: Kinseeker Publications, 1987.

Hinz, Nelda M. *Genealogical Materials in the Eddy Historical Collection of the Public Libraries of Saginaw*. Saginaw, Michigan: Public Libraries, 1975.

Historical Records Survey (Michigan) *Inventory of the Church Archives of Michigan, The Roman Catholic Church, Archdiocese of Detroit*. Detroit: Michigan Historical Records Survey, 1941.

Kellogg, Lucy Mary. *A Guide to Ancestral Trails in Michigan*. 4th ed. Detroit, Michigan: Detroit Society for Genealogical Research, 1975.

Lanman, Charles. *The Red Book of Michigan: A Civil, Military, and Biographical History*. Detroit: E. B. Smith, 1871.

Library of Michigan (Lansing, Michigan). *Michigan Biographies*. Lansing, Michigan: Microform Systems, Inc., [198-?]. 24 microfiche.

Library of Michigan (Lansing, Michigan). *Michigan Centennial File Index*. Lansing, Michigan: Microform System, Inc., [198-?]. 19 microfiches.

Library of Michigan (Lansing, Michigan). *Michigan Surname Index*. Lansing, Michigan: Microform System, Inc., [198-?]. 136 microfiches.

Loomis, Frances. *Michigan Biography Index*. Detroit Public Library, 1946. Microfilm, 4 rolls.

McGinnis, Carol. *Michigan Genealogy Sources and Resources*. Baltimore: Genealogical Publishing Co., 1987.

Men of Progress: Embracing Biographical Sketches of Representative Michigan Men, With an Outline History of the State: Detroit: Evening New Assoc., 1900.

Michigan Biographies, Including Members of Congress, Elective State Officers, Justices of the Supreme Court, Members of the Michigan Legislature, Board of Regents of the University of Michigan, State Board of Agriculture and State Board of Education. (1924). Reprint, Baltimore: Clearfield Co., 1999.

Michigan Biographies. Lansing, Michigan: Microform Systems, Inc., 198-?

Michigan Bureau of Library Services. *Michigan County Histories: A Bibliography*. Lansing: Michigan Department of Education, Bureau of Library Services, 1978.

Michigan Centennial File Index. Lansing, Michigan: Microform System, Inc., [198-?].

Michigan Genealogical Council (Lansing, Michigan). *Guide to the Michigan Genealogical and Historical Collections at the Library of Michigan and the State Archives of Michigan*. Lansing, Michigan: Michigan Genealogical Council, 1996.

Michigan Pioneer Records, 1800–1900. Salt Lake City: Genealogical Society of Utah, 1973, 1974, 1976.

Michigan Research Outline. Series US-States, no. 23. Salt Lake City: Family History Library, 1988.

Michigan Sesquicentennial Pioneer Files and Indexes, ca. 1986–1988. Salt Lake City: Genealogical Society of Utah, 1994.

Michigan State Historical Society. *Michigan Historical Collections*. 40 vols. Lansing [Mich.]: W.S. George & Co., 1877-1929.

Michigan. State Library (Lansing, Michigan). *Card File Index to Manuscripts in the Vault, Michigan State Library*. (Salt Lake City: Filmed by the Genealogical Society of Utah, 1976). 2 microfilm.

Michigan. State Library (Lansing, Michigan). *Index to Manuscript Materials in the Michigan State Library*. (Salt Lake City: Filmed by the Genealogical Society of Utah, 1974). 2 microfilm.

Michigan. State Library (Lansing, Michigan). *Manuscript Index in the Library of Michigan*. Lansing, Michigan: Microform Systems, Inc., [198-?]. 9 microfiche.

Michigan. State Library. *Link Collection*. Lansing, Michigan: State Library, 1973.

Michigan. State Library. *Pioneer Family Collection*. Salt Lake City: Genealogical Society of Utah, 1973.

Midwest Pioneers, 1600s-1800s. [S.l.]: Brøderbund, 1999. CD-ROM.

Moore, Charles. *History of Michigan*. 4 vols. Lewis Pub. Co., 1915.

Pilcher, Rev. E.H. *Protestantism in Michigan. Being a Special History of the Methodist Episcopal Church*. Detroit, Michigan. (1878) Reprint, 1st Methodist Church, 1984.

Portrait and Biographical Record of Northern Michigan: Containing Portraits and Biographical Sketches of Prominent and Representative Citizens, Together with Biographies and Portraits of All the Presidents of the United States: Chicago: Record Pub., 1895.

Powers, Perry F. *A History of Northern Michigan and Its People*. 3 vols. Chicago: Lewis Pub. Co, 1912.

Quigley, Maud. *Index to Family Names in Genealogical Periodicals*. Grand Rapids: Western Michigan Genealogical Society, 1981.

Quigley, Maud. *Index to Michigan Research Found in Genealogical Periodicals*. Grand Rapids: Western Michigan Genealogical Society, 1979.

Sawyer, Alvah Littlefield. *A History of the Northern Peninsula of Michigan and Its People, Its Mining, Lumber and Agricultural Industries*. 3 vols. Chicago: Lewis Publishing Co., 1911.

Sourcebook of Michigan Census, County Histories, and Vital Records. Lansing, Michigan: Library of Michigan, 1986.

Sprenger, Bernice Cox. *Guide to the Manuscripts in the Burton Historical Collection*. Detroit: Detroit Public Library, 1985.

Stevens, Wystan. *Directory of Historical Collections and Societies in Michigan*. Ann Arbor: Historical Society of Michigan, 1973.

Tolzman, Don Heinrich. *Michigan's German Heritage, John Russell's History of the German Influence in the Making of Michigan*. Bowie, Maryland: Heritage Books, 1994.

Tuttle, Charles Richard. *General History of the State of Michigan: With Biographical Sketches, Portrait Engravings and Numerous Illustrations; A Complete History of the Peninsular State from Its Earliest Settlement to the Present Time*. Detroit: R.D.S. Tyler, 1873.

United States. Works Progress Administration (Michigan). *Historical Records Survey. Survey of Records*. Bowling Green, Ohio: Bowling Green University, 1989. 51 microfilm.

Vander Hill, C. Warren. *Settling the Great Lakes Frontier: Immigration to Michigan, 1837–1924*. Lansing: Michigan Historical Commission, 1970.

Warner, Robert M. *Guide to Manuscripts in the Michigan Historical Collections of the University of Michigan*. Ann Arbor: [s.n.], 1963.

Welch, Richard Warren. *County Evolution in Michigan, 1790–1897*. Lansing: Department of Education, 1972.

Western Michigan Genealogical Society (Grand Rapids, Michigan). *Surname Index, 1600s–1900s*. Salt Lake City: Genealogical Society of Utah, 1976.

Wilson, Victoria. *Genealogist's Guide to the Capitol Region of Michigan*. Grawn, Michigan: Kinseeker Publications, 1987.

Atlases, Maps and Gazetteers

Blois, John T. *Gazetteer of the State of Michigan*. Detroit: S.L. Rood, 1939.

Bowen, B. F. *Bowen's Michigan State Atlas: Containing a Separate Map of Each County, Showing Section, Township and Range Lines, Railroad and Interurban Lines...* Indianapolis: B.F. Bowen, 1916.

Ellis, David M. *Michigan Postal History: The Post Offices, 1805-1986*. Lake Grove, Oregon: The Depot, 1993.

Long, John H., ed. *Historical Atlas and Chronology of County Boundaries, 1788-1980. Scale: 1:633,600. Vol. 1-5*. Boston, Massachusetts: G.K. Hall, 1984.

Meints, Graydon M. *Along the Tracks: A Directory of Named Places on Michigan Railroads*. Mount Pleasant, Michigan: Central Michigan University, Clarke Historical Library, 1987.

Michigan Gazetteer. Wilmington, Delaware: American Historical Publications, 1991.

Miles, William. *Michigan Atlases and Plat Books: A Checklist, 1872–1973*. Lansing: State Library Service, 1975.

Puetz, C. J. *Michigan County Map Guide*. Lyndon Station, Wisconsin: Thomas Publications, [199-?].

Romig, Walter. *Michigan Place Names: The History of the Founding and the Naming of More Than Five Thousand Past and Present Michigan Communities*. Grosse Pointe, Michigan: Romig, [197-?].

Sinko, Peggy Tuck. *Michigan; Atlas of Historical County Boundaries*. New York: Charles Scribner's Sons, 1997.

Taylor, William J. *Upper Michigan Postal History and Postmarks*. Lake Grove, Oregon: The Depot, 1988.

Vogel, Virgil J. *Indian Names in Michigan*. Ann Arbor: The University of Michigan Press, 1986.

Walling, H. F., comp. *Atlas of Michigan...Gazetteer of Places, Railroad Stations, Post Offices, Landings, Lakes, Rivers, Islands, Cities, Towns, Villages, Individual Map and Every County....* Detroit: R.M. & S.T. Tackabury, 1873. Reprinted as the *1873 Atlas of Michigan....* Knightstown, Indiana: Bookmark, 1977.

Welch, Richard W. *County Evolution in Michigan, 1790-1897*. Occasional Paper no. 2 Lansing, Michigan: State Library Services, 1972.

Census Records

Available Census Records and Census Substitutes

Federal Census 1820, 1830, 1840, 1850, 1860, 1870, 1880, 1900, 1910, 1920, 1930.

Federal Mortality Schedules 1850, 1860, 1870, 1880.

Union Veterans and Widows 1890.

State/Territorial Census 1884, 1894, 1904.

Dollarhide, William. *The Census Book: A Genealogist's Guide to Federal Census Facts, Schedules and Indexes*. Bountiful, Utah: Heritage Quest, 1999.

Kemp, Thomas Jay. *The American Census Handbook*. Wilmington, Delaware: Scholarly Resources, 2001.

Lainhart, Ann S. *State Census Records*. Baltimore: Genealogical Publishing Co., Inc., 1992.

McGlynn, Estelle A., ed. *Index to 1840 Federal Population Census of Michigan*. Detroit: Detroit Society for Genealogical Research, 1977.

Michigan Veterans Serving with Allied Forces, 1917-1919: Census of World War I Veterans. Microfilm of original records at the Michigan State Archives in Lansing. (Salt Lake City: Filmed by the Genealogical Society of Utah, 1996). 5 microfilm.

Russell, Donna Valley. *Michigan Censuses 1710-1830 Under the French, British, and Americans*. Detroit: Detroit Society for Genealogical Research, 1982.

Szucs, Loretto Dennis, and Matthew Wright. *Finding Answers in U.S. Census Records*. Ancestry Publishing, 2001

Thorndale, William, and William Dollarhide. *Map Guide to the U.S. Federal Censuses, 1790-1920*. Baltimore: Genealogical Publishing Co., 1987.

United States. Bureau of Internal Revenue. *Internal Revenue Assessment Lists of Michigan, 1862-1866*. Washington, D.C.: The National Archives, 1973. 15 microfilm.

Court, Probate and Wills

Note: Individual county clerks keep court records. See each county listing for further information. Federal district court records are located in the Great Lakes Branch of the National Archives. Their holdings include: Michigan, Eastern District, Bay City, 1894-1973: Michigan, Eastern District, Detroit, 1837-1998; Michigan, Eastern District, Flint, 1895-1975; Michigan, Western District, Grand Rapids, 1863-1978; Michigan, Western District, Kalamazoo, 1967-69; Michigan, Western District, Marquette, 1878-1969; Michigan, Territorial Court, 1815-1837. For additional information online at - <www.nara.gov/regional/findaids/chiguid1.html#21>

Michigan. Supreme Court. *Court Records, 1819–1857: Index to Cases, 1805-1857*. Microfilm of original records in the Bentley Library, University of Michigan. (Salt Lake City: Genealogical Society of Utah, 1974).

Reed, George Irving. *Bench and Bar of Michigan: A Volume of History and Biography*. Century Pub. and Engraving, c1897.

United States. Territorial Court (Michigan). *Records of the Territorial Court, Michigan, 1816–1836*. National Archives Microfilm Publication M1111. Washington, D.C.: National Archives, 1988.

Emigration, Immigration, Migration and Naturalization

Indexes to Naturalization Records in the State Archives of Michigan. Lansing, Michigan: State Archives of Michigan, 2002. Online database at - <www.sos.state.mi.us/history/archive/naturalization/index.html>

Florer, Warren Washburn. *Early Michigan Settlements*. 3 vols. Ann Arbor: W. W. Florer, c1941-1953.

United States. District Court. (Michigan: Eastern District). *Declarations of Intentions, 1911–1930.* Microfilm of original records housed in the Chicago Branch of the National Archives, Chicago, Illinois. (Salt Lake City: Genealogical Society of Utah, 1986). Microfilm, 54 rolls.

United States. District Court. (Michigan: Eastern District). *Naturalization Records, 1913–1928.* Microfilm of original records housed in the Chicago Branch of the National Archives, Chicago, Illinois. (Salt Lake City: Genealogical Society of Utah, 1986). 129 microfilm.

United States. District Court. (Michigan: Western District: Northern Division). *Naturalization Records, 1887–1915.* Microfilm of original records housed in the Chicago Branch of the National Archives, Chicago, Illinois. (Salt Lake City: Genealogical Society of Utah, 1986).

United States. District Court. (Michigan: Western District: Southern Division). *Naturalization Records, 1907–1930.* Microfilm of original records housed in the Chicago Branch of the National Archives, Chicago, Illinois. (Salt Lake City: Genealogical Society of Utah, 1986). 4 microfilm.

United States Immigration and Naturalization Services. *Detroit District Manifest Records of Aliens Arriving from Foreign Contiguous Territory: Arrivals at Detroit, Michigan, 1906–1954.* Washington, D.C.: Immigration and Naturalization Services, [195?]. Microfilm, 117 rolls.

Land and Property

Ainsworth, Fern. *Private Land Claims, Illinois, Indiana, Michigan and Wisconsin.* Natchitoches, Louisiana: Fern, Ainsworth, 1985.

Land Records: AL, AR, FL, LA, MI, MN, OH, WI. [S.l.]: Brøderbund, 1996. CD ROM.

McMullin, Phillip W. *Grassroots of America.* Salt Lake City: Gendex Corp., 1972.

United States. Bureau of Land Management. *Card Files.* Washington, D.C.: Bureau of Land Management, [19–]. 160 microfilm.

United States. Congress. *American State Papers.* Salt Lake City; La Crosse, Wisconsin: Genealogical Society of Utah: Brookhaven Press, 1959, 1975, 1977.

United States. Department of State. *Territorial Papers of the United States.* 26 vols. Washington, D.C.: Government Printing Office, 1934–1962.

United States. Department of the Interior. Bureau of Land Management. *Michigan Cash and Homestead Entries, Cadastral Survey Plats.* Version 7.3. Springfield, Virginia: BLM Eastern States, 1994.

Military

Grand Army of the Republic. Department of Michigan. *Records of Posts and Index, 1876–1945.* Microfilm of original records at State Archives of Michigan, Lansing, Michigan. (Salt Lake City: Genealogical Society of Utah, 1973, 1991). 90 microfilm.

Landrum, Charles H. *Michigan in the World War: Military and Naval Honors of Michigan Men and Women.* [S.l.]: Michigan Historical Commission, [1924].

Michigan Adjutant General. *Record of Service of Michigan Volunteers in the Civil War. Indexed in Alphabetical General Index to Public Library Sets of 85,271 Names in the Civil War.* Lansing: Michigan Secretary of State, 1915.

Michigan Adjutant General's Office. *Annual Report of the Adjutant General 1865-1866.* 3 vols. Lansing, Michigan: John A. Kerr & Co., 1866.

Michigan County War Records, 1917-1919: Census of Men Serving in U.S. Forces. Microfilm of original records at the Michigan State Archives in Lansing. (Salt Lake City: Filmed by the Genealogical Society of Utah, 1996). 266 microfilm.

Michigan. Adjutant General's Office. *Michigan Volunteers Descriptive Roll, First Regiment, 1847–1848.* Microfilm of originals at the State Archives in Lansing, Michigan. (Salt Lake City: Genealogical Society of Utah, 1972).

Michigan. Adjutant General's Office. *Michigan Volunteers Descriptive Rolls, 1861–1866; Index to Michigan Volunteers, 1861–1865.* Microfilm of manuscript (handwritten) at the State Archives, Lansing, Michigan. (Salt Lake City: Genealogical Society of Utah, 1972). 5 microfilm.

Michigan. Adjutant General's Office. *Michigan Volunteers, Spanish American War, 1898–1899.* Microfilm of manuscript (handwritten) at the State Archives, Lansing, Michigan. (Salt Lake City: Genealogical Society of Utah, 1973). 5 microfilm.

Michigan. Adjutant General's Office. *Records of Michigan Volunteers Mustered into the Service of the United States, 1861–1866.* Microfilm of manuscript (handwritten) at the State Archives, Lansing, Michigan. (Salt Lake City: Genealogical Society of Utah, 1973). 7 microfilm.

Michigan. National Guard. *Descriptive Rolls, 1838-1901.* Microfilm of original records at the State Archives, Lansing, Michigan. (Salt Lake City: Filmed by the Genealogical Society of Utah, 1972). 4 microfilm.

Michigan. State Archives (Lansing, Michigan). *Deserters >From Draft Index, 1917-1918.* Microfilm of original records at the State Archives of Michigan, Lansing, Michigan. (Salt Lake City: Filmed by the Genealogical Society of Utah, 1991). 4 microfilm.

Michigan. State Archives (Lansing, Michigan). *Mexican Border Veterans Index, ca.1916-1917.* Microfilm of original records at the State Archives of Michigan, Lansing, Michigan. (Salt Lake City: Filmed by the Genealogical Society of Utah, 1991). 2 microfilm.

Michigan. State Archives (Lansing, Michigan). *United Spanish War Veterans Master Index, ca.1890-1984.* (Salt Lake City: Filmed by the Genealogical Society of Utah, 1991). 3 microfilm.

Miller, Alice Turner. *Soldiers of the War of 1812, Who Died in Michigan.* Ithaca, Michigan: Alice Turner Miller, 1962.

Record of Service of Michigan Volunteers in the Civil War, 1861–1865. 46 vols. Kalamazoo, Michigan: Ihling Bros. & Everard, 1905.

Robertson, John. *Michigan in the War,* Revised. Lansing, Michigan: W.S. George, 1882.

Selective Service System. *"Registration Card" for men born between April 28, 1877, and February 16, 1897 ("Fourth Registration"), for Illinois, Indiana, Michigan, Ohio, and Wisconsin.* Record Group 147. Chicago: National Archives Records Administration, Great Lakes Region, 1940-

Silliman, Sue. *Michigan Military Records*. Baltimore, Maryland: Genealogical Publishing Co., 1969.

Soldiers' Home (Grand Rapids, Michigan). *Historical Register of Inhabitants, 1885-1927*. Microreproduction of original typescript and ms. at the State Archives, Lansing Michigan. (Salt Lake City: Filmed by the Genealogical Society of Utah, 1972). 10 microfilm.

United States Civil War Soldiers Living in Michigan in 1894. St. Johns, Michigan: Genealogists of Clinton County Historical Society, 1988.

United States. Adjutant General's Office. *Index to Compiled Service Records of Volunteer Soldiers Who Served from the State of Michigan for the Patriot War, 1838–1839*. Washington, D.C.: The National Archives, 1965.

United States. Selective Service System. *Michigan, World War I Selective Service System Draft Registration Cards, 1917–1918, M1509*. Washington, D.C.: National Archives, 1987–1988.

United States. War Department. Bureau of Public Relations. *World War II Honor List of Dead and Missing, State of Michigan*. District of Columbia: War Dept. Bureau of Public Relations, 1946.

Welch, Richard Warren. *Michigan in the Mexican War*. [S.l.: s.n.], 1967.

World War I Card Index for Michigan. Microfilm of original records at State Library and Archives of Lansing, Michigan. (Salt Lake City: Genealogical Society of Utah, 1976). 37 microfilm.

Vital and Cemetery Records

Burton, Ann and Conrad. *Michigan Quakers, Abstracts of Fifteen Meetings of the Society of Friends 1831-1860*. Glyndwr Resources, 1989.

Grand Army of the Republic (Michigan). *Cemetery Index, 1800s–1900s*. Microfilm of typescripts housed in Grand Rapids, Michigan. (Salt Lake City: Genealogical Society of Utah, 1976). 3 microfilm.

Grand Rapids (Michigan). Public Library. *Cemetery Records of Michigan Soldiers, 1770–1930*. Microfilm of typescript in Grand Rapids, Michigan. (Salt Lake City: Genealogical Society of Utah, 1976). 3 microfilm.

Har-Al, Inc. *Michigan Cemetery Compendium*. Spring Arbor, Michigan: Har-Al, 1979.

Historical Records Survey (Michigan). *Vital Statistics Holdings by Government Agencies in Michigan; Birth Records*. Detroit, Michigan: The Project, 1941.

Historical Records Survey (Michigan). *Vital Statistics Holdings by Government Agencies in Michigan; Death Records*. Detroit, Michigan: The Project, 1942.

Historical Records Survey (Michigan). *Vital Statistics Holdings by Government Agencies in Michigan; Marriage Records*. Detroit, Michigan: The Project, 1941.

Library of Michigan (Lansing, Michigan). *Michigan Cemetery Source Book: Companion Volume to the Michigan Cemetery Atlas*. Lansing, Michigan: Library of Michigan, [1994?].

Link, Muriel. *Obituaries Index, 1933–1948*. Salt Lake City: Genealogical Society of Utah, 1976.

Michigan. Civil War Centennial Observance Commission. Committee on Civil War Grave Registration. *Civil War Graves Registration Index Cards, ca. 1861–1930*. Microfilm of original records at State Archives of Michigan, Lansing, Michigan. (Salt Lake City: Genealogical Society of Utah, 1994). 22 microfilm.

Michigan. Department of Community Health. *Michigan Death Index, 1867-1874*. 3 vols. [Lansing, Mich.]: Michigan Dept. of Community Health, [1997].

Mohnecke, Edward H. *Cemetery Inscriptions. Michigan*. 3 vols. Grand Rapids, Michigan: Edward H. Mohnecke, 1939-44.

State Library of Michigan. *Michigan Cemetery Source Book*. Lansing: State Library of Michigan, 1994.

The Historical Records Survey (Michigan). *Vital Records from the Detroit Free Press 1831–1868*. Microfilm of typescript at the State Library in Lansing, Michigan. (Salt Lake City: Genealogical Society of Utah, 1973). 3 microfilm.

County Website	Map Index	Date Created	Parent County or Territory From Which Organized Address/Details
Aishcum		1 Apr 1840	**Mackinac** Details: (see Lake) Name changed to Lake 8 Mar 1843
Alcona www.rootsweb.com/~mialcona/index.htm	E6	1 Apr 1840	**Mackinac, Unorganized Territory** Alcona County; 106 5th St; Harrisville, MI 48740; Ph. 517.724.5374 Details: (Formerly Neewago Co. Name changed to Alcona 8 Mar 1843. Attached to Mackinac, Cheboygan, Iosco & Alpena Cos prior to organization 12 Mar 1869) (Co Clk has b, m, d, div, ct & nat rec from 1869 & mil rec from 1900; Pro Ct has pro rec; Reg of Deeds has land rec)
Alger* www.markovich.info/michigan/ algercounty/	J3	17 Mar 1885	**Schoolcraft** Alger County; 101 Court St; Munising, MI 49862; Ph. 906.387.2076 Details: (Co Clk has b, d & land rec from 1884, m rec from 1887, div & ct rec from 1885; Pro Ct has pro rec)
Allegan www.allegancounty.org/	I10	2 Mar 1831	**Barry** Allegan County; 113 Chestnut St; Allegan, MI 49010-1362; Ph. 616.673.0450 Details: (Organized 7 Sep 1835) (Co Clk has b & d rec from 1867, m rec from 1835, div, ct & land rec from 1836 & mil dis rec; Pro Ct has pro rec from 1836)
Alpena* www.alpenacounty.org/alpcnty/index.htm	E6	1 Apr 1840	**Mackinac, Unorganized Territory** Alpena County; 720 W Chisholm St; Alpena, MI 49707; Ph. 517.356.0115 Details: (Formerly Anamickee Co. Name changed to Alpena 8 Mar 1843. Attached to Mackinac & Cheboygan Cos prior to organization 7 Feb 1857) (Co Clk has b rec from 1869, m, d, div & ct rec from 1871; Pro Judge has pro rec; Reg of Deeds has land rec)
Anamickee		1 Apr 1840	**Mackinac, Unorganized Territory** Details: (see Alpena) Name changed to Alpena 8 Mar 1843
Antrim www.antrimcounty.org/	H5	1 Apr 1840	**Mackinac** Antrim County; 208 E Cayugoa St; PO Box 520; Bellaire, MI 49615-0520; Ph. 616.533.8607 Details: (Formerly Meegisee Co. Name changed to Antrim 8 Mar 1843. Attached to Mackinac & Grand Traverse Cos prior to organization 11 Mar 1863) (Co Clk has b, m, d, div & ct rec from 1867 & mil dis rec; Pro Judge has pro rec from 1863; Reg of Deeds has land rec)
Arenac www.rootsweb.com/~miarenac/index.htm	F7	21 Apr 1883	**Bay** Arenac County; 120 N Grove St; PO Box 747; Standish, MI 48658; Ph. 517.846.4626 Details: (Co Clk has b, m, d, div & ct rec from 1883 & bur rec from 1952)
Arenac, old		2 Mar 1831	**Unorganized Territory** Details: (Attached to Saginaw. Absorbed by Bay Co 20 Apr 1857. Recreated 21 Apr 1883)
Baraga* www.rootsweb.com/~mibaraga/	M2	19 Feb 1875	**Houghton** Baraga County; 16 N 3rd St; L'Anse, MI 49946; Ph. 906.524.6183 Details: (Co Clk has b, m, d, div, ct & land rec from 1875 & bur rec from 1950)
Barry www.barrycounty.org/	H10	29 Oct 1829	**Unorganized Territory** Barry County; 220 W State St; Hastings, MI 49058; Ph. 616.948.4810 Details: (Attached to St. Joseph & Kalamazoo Cos prior to organization 15 Mar 1839) (Co Clk has b & d rec from 1867, m rec from 1839, div rec from 1869 & ct rec from 1845; Pro Ct has pro rec; Reg of Deeds has land rec)
Bay* www.rootsweb.com/~mibay/	F8	20 Apr 1857	**Saginaw, Midland, Arenac** Bay County; 515 Center Ave; Bay City, MI 48708-5941; Ph. 517.892.3528 Details: (Co Clk has b rec from 1868, m rec from 1857, d rec from 1867, div rec from 1883 & ct rec from 1965; Pro Ct has pro rec; Reg of Deeds has land rec)
Benzie grandtraverseregion.com/benzie/	I6	27 Feb 1863	**Leelanau** Benzie County; 448 Court Pl; PO Box 398; Beulah, MI 49617; Ph. 616.882.9671 Details: (Attached to Grand Traverse Co prior to organization 30 Mar 1869) (Co Clk has b & d rec from 1868, m & ct rec from 1869, div & pro rec from 1870, nat rec from 1871 & bur rec from 1934)

County Website	Map Index	Date Created	Parent County or Territory From Which Organized Address/Details
Berrien www.berriencounty.org/	J11	29 Oct 1829	**Unorganized Territory** Berrien County; 701 Main St; St. Joseph, MI 49085-1114; Ph. 616.983.7111 Details: (Attached to Cass Co prior to organization 1 Sep 1831) (Co Clk has b & d rec from 1867, m rec from 1831, nat rec 1835-1985 & mil rec from 1918; Pro Ct has pro rec from 1832; Reg of Deeds has land rec from 1831; Clk Cir Ct has div & ct rec from 1835)
Bleeker		15 Mar 1861	**Unorganized Territory** Details: (see Menominee) Name changed to Menominee 19 Mar 1863
Branch co.branch.mi.us/	H11	29 Oct 1829	**Lenawee, Unorganized Territory** Branch County; 31 Division St; Coldwater, MI 49036; Ph. 517.279.4306 Details: (Attached to St. Joseph Co prior to organization 1 Mar 1833) (Co Clk has b & d rec from 1867, m rec from 1833, div rec, ct rec from 1848 & nat rec from 1847; Pro Ct has pro rec; Reg of Deeds has land rec; City & Twn Clks have bur rec)
Calhoun* www.calhoun-mi.com/home.htm	G11	29 Oct 1829	**Unorganized Territory** Calhoun County; 315 W Green St; Marshall, MI 49068-1585; Ph. 616.781.0730 Details: (Attached to St. Joseph & Kalamazoo Cos prior to organization 1 Apr 1833) (Co Clk has b, m, d, div & ct rec from 1867, bur rec from 1952, nat rec from 1918, mil dis rec from 1919 & election rec from 1972; Pro Ct has pro rec)
Cass casscountymi.org/	I11	29 Oct 1829	**Unorganized Territory** Cass County; 120 N Broadway; PO Box 355; Cassopolis, MI 49031; Ph. 616.445.8621 Details: (Co Clk/Register has b & d rec from 1867, m rec from 1837, div & ct rec from 1831, land rec from 1832 & nat rec 1924-1941; Pro Ct has pro rec from 1829)
Charlevoix www.multimag.com/county/mi/charlevoix/	G5	2 Apr 1869	**Emmet, Antrim, Otsego** Charlevoix County; 203 W Antrim St; Charlevoix, MI 49720; Ph. 616.547.7200 Details: (Co Clk has b rec from 1867, m & d rec from 1868, div, ct & land rec from 1869 & pro rec from 1881)
Charlevoix, old		1 Apr 1840	**Mackinac** Details: (Formerly Keskkauko Co. Name changed to Charlevoix 8 Mar 1843. Attached to Mackinac. Eliminated 29 Jan 1853. Recreated 2 Apr 1869)
Cheboygan* www.rootsweb.com/~micheboy/ micheboy.htm	G4	1 Apr 1840	**Mackinac** Cheboygan County; 870 S Main St; PO Box 70; Cheboygan, MI 49721; Ph. 616.627.8808 Details: (Attached to Mackinac Co prior to organization 29 Jan 1853) (Co Clk has b, m & d rec from 1867, div & ct rec from 1884; Reg of Pro has pro rec from 1854; Reg of Deeds has land rec from 1854)
Cheonoquet Future website at www.rootsweb.com/ ~migenweb/county_list.htm		1 Apr 1840	**Mackinac** Details: (see Montmorency) Name changed to Montmorency 8 Mar 1843
Chippewa www.sault.com/~chippewa/	G3	1 Feb 1827	**Mackinac** Chippewa County; 319 Court St; Sault Sainte Marie, MI 49783-2183; Ph. 906.635.6300 Details: (Co Clk has b rec from 1869, m rec from 1868, d rec from 1870, div rec from 1891 & ct rec; Pro Ct has pro rec; Reg of Deeds has land rec)
Clare www.rootsweb.com/~miclare/index.htm	G8	1 Apr 1840	**Mackinac** Clare County; 225 W Main St; PO Box 438; Harrison, MI 48625-0438; Ph. 517.539.7131 Details: (Formerly Kaykakee Co. Name changed to Clare 8 Mar 1843. Attached to Saginaw, Midland, Isabelle & Mecosta Cos prior to organization 13 Mar 1871) (Co Clk has b, m, d, bur, div, ct & land rec)
Clinton www.clinton-county.org/		2 Mar 1831	**Unorganized Territory** Clinton County; 100 E State St; PO Box 69; St. Johns, MI 48879-1571; Ph. 517.224.5140 Details: (Attached to Kent & Shiawassee Cos prior to organization 12 Mar 1839) (Co Clk has b & d rec from 1867, m rec from 1839, div rec from early 1800's & ct rec)

County Website	Map Index	Date Created	Parent County or Territory From Which Organized Address/Details
Crawford www.rootsweb.com/~micrawfo/	G6	1 Apr 1840	**Mackinac** Crawford County; 200 W Michigan Ave; Grayling, MI 49738-1745; Ph. 517.348.3200 Details: (Formerly Shawano Co. Name changed to Crawford 8 Mar 1843. Attached to Mackinac, Cheboygan, Iosco, Antrim & Kalkaska Cos prior to organization 22 Mar 1879) (Co Clk has b & pro rec from 1879, m, d & div rec from 1878, ct rec from 1881 & land rec from 1863)
Delta grandmastree.com/migenweb/	J3	9 Mar 1843	**Mackinac, Unorganized Territorys** Delta County; 310 Ludington St; Escanaba, MI 49829-4057; Ph. 906.789.5105 Details: (Attached to Mackinac Co prior to organization 12 Mar 1861) (Co Clk has b, m, d, div, ct, pro & land rec from 1867)
Des Moines*		1 Oct 1834	**Unorganized Territory** Details: (Disorganized 3 Jul 1836 to Wisconsin Terr.)
Dickinson www.geocities.com/dickinsonco/	L3	21 May 1891	**Marquette, Menominee, Iron** Dickinson County; 705 S Stephenson Ave; PO Box 609; Iron Mountain, MI 49801-0609; Ph. 906.774.0988 Details: (Co Clk has b, m, d, div, ct & nat rec from 1891; Pro Ct has pro rec; Reg of Deeds has land rec)
Eaton www.co.eaton.mi.us/	G10	29 Oct 1829	**Unorganized Territory** Eaton County; 1045 Independence Blvd; Charlotte, MI 48813; Ph. 517.543.7500 Details: (Attached to St. Joseph & Kalamazoo Cos prior to organization 29 Dec 1837) (Co Clk has b & d rec from 1867, m rec from 1838, div & ct rec from 1847 & some nat rec; Pro Ct has pro rec; Reg of Deeds has land rec)
Emmet members.tripod.com/~deemamafred/ miemmet.html	G4	1 Apr 1840	**Mackinac** Emmet County; 200 Division St; Petoskey, MI 49770; Ph. 616.348.1744 Details: (Formerly Tonedagana Co. Name changed to Emmet 8 Mar 1843. Attached to Mackinac prior to organization 29 Jan 1853) (Co Clk has b, m & d rec from 1867, div rec from 1875, ct & nat rec from 1800's & some mil rec)
Genesee* co.genesee.mi.us/	E9	28 Mar 1835	**Lapeer, Saginaw, Shiawassee** Genesee County; 900 S Saginaw St; Flint, MI 48502; Ph. 810.257.3225 Details: (Co Clk has b & d rec from 1867, m & ct rec from 1835 & div rec from 1890; Pro Judge has pro rec; Cem custodians have bur rec)
Gladwin www.rootsweb.com/~migladwi/	F7	2 Mar 1831	**Unorganized Territory** Gladwin County; 401 W Cedar Ave; Gladwin, MI 48624-2023; Ph. 517.426.7351 Details: (Attached to Saginaw & Midland Cos prior to organization 18 Apr 1875) (Co Clk has b, m, d, div & ct rec from 1875 & mil rec from 1917; Pro Ct has pro rec from 1875; Reg of Deeds has land rec; Co Library has obituary file)
Gogebic www.rootsweb.com/~migogebi/ gogebic.htm	O3	7 Feb 1887	**Ontonagon** Gogebic County; 200 N Moore St; Bessemer, MI 49911; Ph. 906.663.4518 Details: (Co Clk has b, m, d, div & ct rec from 1887 & mil rec; Pro Ct has pro rec from 1887; Reg of Deeds has land rec from 1887)
Grand Traverse www.grandtraverse.org/	H6	7 Apr 1851	**Omeena** Grand Traverse County; 400 Boardman Ave; Traverse City, MI 49684; Ph. 231.922.4760 Details: (Co Clk has b & d rec from 1867, m rec from 1853, div & ct rec from 1882; Townships have bur rec; Reg of Deeds has land rec)
Gratiot www.gratiot.com/	G9	2 Mar 1831	**Unorganized Territory** Gratiot County; 214 E Center St; Ithaca, MI 48847; Ph. 517.875.5215 Details: (Attached to Saginaw & Clinton Cos prior to organization 3 Feb 1855) (Co Clk has b, d, div & ct rec from 1867 & m rec from 1855; Pro Ct has pro rec; Reg of Deeds has land rec)
Hillsdale www.co.hillsdale.mi.us/	G12	29 Oct 1829	**Unorganized Territory** Hillsdale County; County Courthouse; 29 N Howell St; Hillsdale, MI 49242-1865; Ph. 517.437.3391 Details: (Attached to Lenawee Co prior to organization 11 Feb 1835) (Co Clk has b & d rec from 1867, m rec from 1835, div & ct rec from 1845; Pro Ct has pro rec; Reg of Deeds has land rec)

Notes

Lady's Slipper

MINNESOTA

CAPITAL: ST. PAUL – TERRITORY 1849 – STATE 1858 (32ND)

French fur traders and missionaries preceded settlers in Minnesota. Among the early explorers was Daniel Greysolon, Sieur Du Lhut (Duluth), who built a fort on the shores of Lake Superior and claimed the region for France. Father Louis Hennepin explored the upper Mississippi River in 1680. There he discovered the Falls of St. Anthony, where Minneapolis is today. Eastern Minnesota was given to the British in 1763 and fur trading was taken over by the Northwest Company. This area became part of the United States in 1783 and part of the Northwest Territory in 1787. The land west of the Mississippi River became part of the United States with the Louisiana Purchase in 1803. Zebulon Pike was sent to explore the area and set up Fort Anthony, later called Fort Snelling, at the junction of the Minnesota and Mississippi rivers. Fort Snelling became the first large settlement, located near present-day St. Paul. By 1823, steamboats were coming up the Mississippi to the fort. The American Fur Company took over the fur trading industry in 1815, ending British control of the area.

In 1836, Minnesota was part of the Wisconsin Territory. The next year, the Sioux and Chippewa Indians sold their claim to the St. Croix Valley, opening the area to lumbering. Real settlement began in earnest with settlers from the eastern United States coming to the eastern part of the state. In 1849, Minnesota became a territory. Further treaties with the Indians between 1851 and 1855 opened up western Minnesota to settlement. Immigration increased with completion of the railroad to the Mississippi River. An 1862 Sioux rebellion that killed more than 500 settlers resulted in the Indians relinquishing the last of their claims.

During the Civil War, Minnesota furnished about 24,000 men to the Union. After the war Minnesota boomed due to its timber, mines, mills, and agriculture. Homesteaders moved into the western and southwestern sections primarily from Germany, Sweden, and Norway. Poland, Lithuania, and the Balkan States furnished much of the labor for the packing plants around the Twin Cities at the turn of the century. Other ethnic groups to come to the state include Danes, Canadians, English, Finns, and Russians.

Look for vital records in the following locations:

- **Birth and death records:** State registration of births began in 1900. Registration of deaths began in 1908. These records are available from the Minnesota Department of Health, Section of Vital Statistics in Minneapolis, Minnesota. Records prior to 1900 are in the offices of the District Court clerks.
- **Marriage and divorce records:** Registration began within a decade of each county's formation. District court administration offices have marriage and divorce records, except for Hennepin County. Hennepin County records are at the State Department of Health.
- **Probate records:** Probate records are at the Probate Court clerk's office.
- **Land records:** The first general land office was established in Wisconsin in 1848, but was transferred to Stillwater, Minnesota in 1849. These early books and township plats are at the Land Bureau in St. Paul Minnesota. The National Archives, Chicago Branch in Chicago, Illinois has land entry case files. The registrar of deeds in each county keeps mortgages and deeds.
- **Census records:** Minnesota was included in the Wisconsin and Iowa Territorial censuses in 1836 and 1840. Minnesota Territorial censuses exist for 1849, 1850, 1855, and 1857. State censuses were taken in 1865, 1875, 1885, and 1905.

Minnesota Department of Health,
Section of Vital Statistics
PO Box 9441
717 Delaware Street S.E.
Minneapolis, Minnesota 55414
612.623.5120

Land Bureau
658 Cedar Street
St. Paul, Minnesota 55101

National Archives
Chicago Branch
7358 South Pulaski Road
Chicago, Illinois 60629

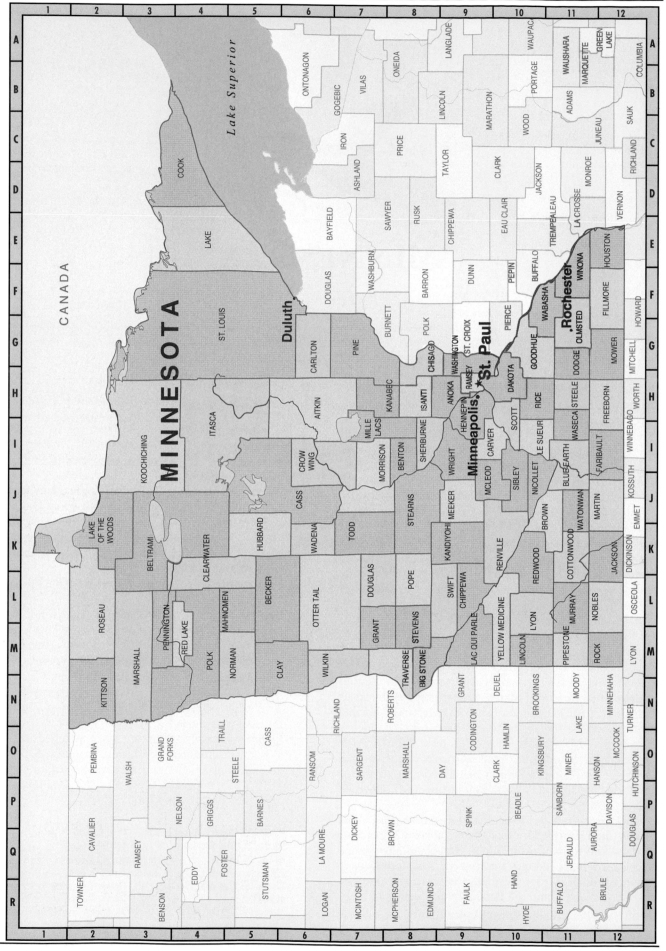

Societies and Repositories

Adolphus College; St. Peter, Minnesota 56082

Aitkin County Historical Society; PO Box 215; Aitkin, Minnesota 56431; <www.aitkin.com/achs/>

American Swedish Institute; 2600 Park Ave.; Minneapolis, Minnesota 55407; 612.871.8682;

Anoka County Genealogical Society; PO Box 48126; Coon Rapids, Minnesota 55448-0126; <freepages.genealogy.rootsweb.com/~relativememory/>

Anoka County Historical Society; 2135-3rd Ave., No.; Anoka, Minnesota 55303-2421; <www.rootsweb.com/~mnachs/>

Archives of the American Lutheran Church, Wartburg Theological Seminary; 333 Wartburg Place; Dubuque, Indiana 52003; 319.589.0200; Fax 319.589.0333

Becker County Historical Society and Museum; 714 Summit; PO Box 622; Detroit Lakes, Minnesota 56502; 218.847.5048; <www.angelfire.com/mn/bchs39/index.html>

Benton County Historical Society; Box 312; Sauk Rapids, Minnesota 56379

Blue Earth County Historical Society; 415 E. Cherry St.; Mankato, Minnesota 56001; <www.bushelboy.com/reg9/bechs/>

Brown County Historical Society; 2 North Broadway; New Ulm, Minnesota 56073; 507.354.1068;

Bureau of Land Management Eastern States Office; 7450 Boston Blvd.; Springfield, Virginia 22153; 703.440.1523; Fax 703.440.1599

Carver County Historical Society; 555 West First Street; Waconia, Minnesota; 952.442.3025; <www.co.carver.mn.us/HistoricalSociety/HistSoc.htm>

Chippewa County Genealogical Society; 151 Pioneer Dr.; PO Box 303; Montevideo, Minnesota 56265

Chippewa County Historical Society; Junction Hwy 7 & Hwy 59; Montevideo, Minnesota 56265; <www.montechamber.com/cchs/cchshp.htm>

Clearwater County Historical Society; PO Box 241; Bagley, Minnesota 56621; <www.rrv.net/bagleymn/histSoc.htm>

Crow River Genealogical Society; 380 School Road North; Hutchinson, Minnesota 55350

Crow Wing County Historical Society; PO Box 722; Brainerd, Minnesota 56401; <www.mjpdan.com/genweb/crowwing/general.htm>

Crow Wing County Minnesota Genealogical Society; 2103 Graydon Ave.; Brainerd, Minnesota 56401; <www.mjpdan.com/genweb/crowwing/general.htm>

Cuyuna Country Heritage Preservation Society; PO Box 68; Ironton, Minnesota 56455;

Czechoslovak Gen. Soc. International Library, c/o Minnesota Gen. Soc. Library; 5768 Olson Memorial Hwy.; Golden Valley, Minnesota 55422; 612.595.7799; 612.595.9347

Czechoslovak Genealogical Society International; PO Box 16225; St. Paul, Minnesota 55116-0225;

Dakota County Genealogical Society; 130 Third Avenue N.; South St. Paul, Minnesota 55075; <www.geocities.com/Heartland/Flats/9284/>

Danish American Fellowship; 4200 Cedar Ave.S.; Minneapolis, Minnesota 55407;

Danish American Genealogy Group Minnesota Genealogical Society; 5768 Olson Memorial Hwy.; Golden Valley, Minnesota 55422; <www.mtn.org/mgs/branches/danish.html>

Diocese of New Ulm; 1400 6th St. N.; New Ulm, Minnesota 56073-2099; 507.359.2966; Fax 507.354.3667; (Roman Catholic Church records)

Dodge County Genealogical Society; Box 683; Dodge Center, Minnesota 55927-0683; <www.rootsweb.com/~mndodge/resources.htm>

Dodge County Historical Society; PO Box 433; Mantorville, Minnesota 55955; <www.rootsweb.com/~mndodge/resources.htm>

Douglas County Genealogical Society; PO Box 505; Alexandria, Minnesota 56308; <www.mtn.org/mgs/branches/douglas.html>

Douglas County Historical Society; 1219 Nokomis Street; Alexandria, Minnesota 56308; 320.762.9062; <www.rea.alp.com/~historic/index.html>

Evangelical Lutheran Church of America, Region 3; 2481 Como Ave.; St. Paul, Minnesota 55108; 612.641.3205

Family History Library: 35 North West Temple Street: Salt Lake City, Utah 84150: 800.346.6044 or 801.240.2584: <www.familysearch.org>: Find a Family History Center near you: <www.familysearch.org/Eng/Library/FHC/frameset_fhc.asp>

Fillmore County Historical Center; Fountain, Minnesota 55935

Fort Snelling National Cemetery; 7601 34th Ave. South; Fort Snelling, Minnesota 55111; 612.726.1127;

Freeborn Co. Hist. Soc. Library; 1031 No. Bridge Ave.; Albert Lea, Minnesota 56007; 507.373.8003; <www.smig.net/fchm>

Freeborn County Genealogical Society; 1033 Bridge Ave.; Albert Lee, Minnesota 56007-2205

Genealogical Society of Carlton County; PO Box 204; Cloquet, Minnesota 55720

German-Bohemian Heritage Society; 311 Linden Street; New Ulm, Minnesota 56073-1519; <www.rootsweb.com/~gbhs/>

Germanic Genealogy Society; PO Box 16312; Saint Paul, Minnesota 55116-0312; <www.mtn.org/mgs/german/>

Goodhue County Family Tree Club; c/o Goodhue County Historical Society; 1166 Oak St.; Red Wing, Minnesota 55066

Great Northern Railway Historical Society; Minnesota;

Heart O'Lakes Genealogical Library; PO Box 622; 714 Summit Ave.; Detroit Lakes, Minnesota 56501; <www.angelfire.com/mn/HOLGS/index.html>

Heritage Searchers of Kandiyohi County; PO Box 175; Willmar, Minnesota 56201

Hubbard County Genealogical Society; PO Box 361; Park Rapids, Minnesota 56470; <www.rootsweb.com/~mnhgs/>

Icelandic Genealogy Group, Minnesota Genealogical Society; 5769 Olson Memorial Hwy.; Golden Valley, Minnesota 55422

Irish Genealogical Society, Int'l; PO Box 16585; St. Paul, Minnesota 55116-0585; <www.rootsweb.com/~irish/>

Iron Range Historical Society; PO Box 786; Gilbert, Minnesota 55741.0786; <www.homestead.com/gilbertmn/files/IronRangeHistoricalSociety.html>

Itasca Genealogical Club; PO Box 261; Bovey, Minnesota 55709-0261

Jewish Historical Society of the Upper Midwest; Sholom Home East; 1554 Midway Parkway; St. Paul, Minnesota 55108; <www.hamline.edu/~jhsum/>

Kanabec County Historical Society & History Center; PO Box 113, West Forest Ave.; Mora, Minnesota 55051

Kandiyohi County Historical Society; 617 NE Hwy 71; Willmar, Minnesota 56201; <freepages.genealogy.rootsweb.com/~kchs123/index.html>

Laird Lucas Library, Winona County Hist. Soc., Inc., Archives Library; 160 Johnson St.; Winona, Minnesota 55987; 507.454.2723

Le Sueur County Historical Society; PO Box 240; Elysian, Minnesota 56028;

Maplewood Area Historical Society; 2516 E. Idaho St.; Maplewood, Minnesota 55109; <www.geocities.com/CapeCanaveral/Hall/3649/mahs.html>

Martin County Genealogical Society; 208 West Second St., Room 104B; Fairmont, Minnesota 56031; <www.geocities.com/Heartland/Hills/4091/>

McLeod Co. Hist. Soc. Library; 380 School Rd. No.; Hutchinson, Minnesota 55350; 320.587.2107

Military Historical Society of Minnesota; 15000 Highway 115; Little Falls, Minnesota 56345-4173; 320.632.7702; <www.dma.state.mn.us/cpripley/SpecFeatures/muse1.htm>

Minneapolis Public Library; 300 Nicolet Ave.; Minneapolis, Minnesota 55401

Minnesota Department of Health, Birth and Death Records; PO Box 9441, 717 Delaware Street S.E.; Minneapolis, Minnesota 55440; 612.623.5121; Fax 612.331.5776

Minnesota Gen. Soc. Library; 5768 Olson Memorial Hwy.; Golden Valley, Minnesota 55422; 612.595.9347

Minnesota Genealogical Society; 1101 Fort Rd., PO Box 16069; St. Paul, Minnesota 55116; 612.645.3671

Minnesota Historical Depository, United Methodist Conference; 122 West Franklin Avenue; Minneapolis, Minnesota 55404; 612.870.0058 ext. 249;

Minnesota Historical Society, Research Center; 345 Kellogg Blvd., W.; St. Paul, Minnesota 55102-1906; 612.296.2143; Fax 612.297.1345

Minnesota State Archives; 345 W. Kellogg Blvd.; St. Paul, Minnesota 55102-1906; 651.296.9961; <www.mnhs.org/preserve/records/>

Minnetonka Historical Society; 13209 E. McGinty Road; Minnetonka, Minnesota 55305;

MinnKota Genealogical Society; PO Box 126; East Grand Forks, Minnesota 56721; <www.rootsweb.com/~minnkota/>

Morrison County Historical Society; PO Box 239; 2151 South Lindberg Drive; Little Falls, Minnesota 56345; <www.upstel.net/~johns/History/MorrisonCo.html>

Mower County Genealogical Society; PO Box 145; Austin, Minnesota 55912

Mower County Historical Society; PO Box 804; Austin, Minnesota 55912; <www2.smig.net/mchistory/>

National Archives-Central Plains Region (Kansas City); 2306 East Bannister Road; Kansas City, Missouri 64131; 816.926.7271

National Archives-Great Lakes Region (Chicago); 7358 South Pulaski Road; Chicago, Illinois 60629; 773.581.7816

National Bygdelag Council, Marilyn Somdahl, Pres.; 10129 Goodrich Circle; Bloomington, Minnesota 55437; 612.831.4409;

Nicollet County Historical Society and Museum; PO Box 153; St. Peter, Minnesota 56082

Nobles County Genealogical Society; Suite 2, 407 12th St.; Worthington, Minnesota 56187-2411

Nobles County Historical Society; 219 11th Ave.; Worthington, Minnesota 56187

Norman County Genealogical Society; 100 1st St. E. Apt. 202; Ada, Minnesota 56510; <www.rootsweb.com/~mnnorman/NCGenSoc.html>

North Star of Minnesota Chapter, AHSGR; 2479 Churchill St.; Roseville, Minnesota 55113; 612.787.0408; <www.ahsgr.org/mnnostar.html>

Northwest Territory Canadian and French Heritage Center; PO Box 29397; Brooklyn Center, Minnesota 55429-0397

Norwegian-American Genealogical Association; c/o Minn. Genealogical Society; 5768 Olson Memorial Hwy.; Golden Valley, Minnesota 55422

Norwegian-American Historical Association; 1510 St. Olaf Avenue; Northfield, Minnesota 55057-1097;

Olmsted Co. Historical Soc. Library; 1195 County Rd. #22 S.W.; Rochester, Minnesota 55902

Olmsted County Genealogical Society; PO Box 6411; Rochester, Minnesota 55903; <www.olmstedhistory.com/ocgs.htm>

Ostfriesen Genealogical Society of Minnesota; Box 474; Wyoming, Minnesota 55092; <www.rootsweb.com/~mnogsm/>

Otter Tail County Genealogical Society; 1110 Lincoln Ave. W.; Fergus Falls, Minnesota 56537

PO Box 836; Watertown, Minnesota 55388-0836; <home.earthlink.net/~lahtinen/wahs.htm>

Pennington County Historical Society; PO Box 127; Thief River Falls, Minnesota 56701

Pipestone County Genealogical Society; 113 South Hiawatha; Pipestone, Minnesota 56164

Polish Genealogical Society of Minnesota; 2217 Wight Bay; Brooklyn Park, Minnesota 55443; <www.rootsweb.com/~mnpolgs/pgs.mn.html>

Prairieland Genealogical Society Historical Center; Room 141-Social Science Building; Southwest State University; Marshall, Minnesota 56258; <freepages.genealogy.rootsweb.com/~cmolitor/>

Public Health Center (Ramsey Co.); 555 Cedar Street; St. Paul, Minnesota 55101; 612.292.7728

Ramsey County Historical Society; 323 Landmark Center; 75 West Fifth Street; Saint Paul, Minnesota 55102; 651.223.8539;

Range Genealogical Society; PO Box 388; Chisholm, Minnesota 55768

Red River Valley, Kittson Co. Library; 704-228th Ave. NE, #232; Sammamish, Washington 98074; 425.868.8868; <mytown.koz.com/community/redrive>

Redwood County Genealogical Society; 217 West Flynn Street; Redwood Falls, Minnesota 56283; <freepages.genealogy.rootsweb.com/~corder/RCGS/>

Renville County Genealogical Society; Box 331; 22 N. Main St.; Renville, Minnesota 56284; <ci.renville.mn.us/rcgs/>

Renville County Historical Society and Museum; 411 North Park Drive; PO Box 266; Morton, Minnesota 56270; <www.rootsweb.com/~mnrenvil/mus.rchs.htm>

Rice County Genealogical Society; 408 Division St.; Northfield, Minnesota 55057

Rice County Historical Museum and Genealogical Research Center; 1814 Second Ave.; Faribault, Minnesota 55021

Rochester Public Library; Broadway at First Street, S.E; Rochester, Minnesota 55901

Rolvaag Memorial Library; St. Olaf College; Northfield, Minnesota 55057

Roman Catholic, Archdiocese of St. Paul; 226 Summit Avenue; St. Paul, Minnesota 55102; 612.291.4400; Fax 612.290.1629;

Roman Catholic, Diocese of Duluth; 2830 East 4th St.; Duluth, Minnesota 55812; 218.724.9111

Roman Catholic, Diocese of St. Cloud; 214 South 3rd Ave., PO Box 1248; St. Cloud, Minnesota 56302; 320.251.2340; Fax 218.724.1056

Roman Catholic, Diocese of Winona; 55 West Sanborn St., PO Box 588; Winona, Minnesota 55987; 507.454.4643; Fax 507.454.8106

Roseau County Historical Society; 110 2nd Ave NE; Roseau, Minnesota 56751; 218.463.3795; <www.angelfire.com/mn/rchistsocmuseum/>

Sherburne County Historical Society; 13122 First St.; Becker, Minnesota 55308; 763.261.4437; <www.rootsweb.com/~mnschs/home.htm>

Sibley County Historical Society; PO Box 407; Henderson, Minnesota 56044; <history.sibley.mn.us/index.htm>

Sons of Norway; 1455 W. Lake St.; Minneapolis, Minnesota 55408-2666; 800.945.8851; Fax 612.827.0658;

Sons of the American Revolution, Minnesota Society; 2546 Cedar Ave.; Minneapolis, Minnesota 55404

St. Cloud Area Genealogists, Inc.; PO Box 213; St. Cloud, Minnesota 56302-0213; <www.rootsweb.com/~mnscag/SCAG/Activities.htm>

St. Paul Public Library; 90 West 4th; St. Paul, Minnesota 55102

Stearns County Historical Society (Scandinavian Resources); PO Box 702; 235 S. 33rd Ave.; St. Cloud, Minnesota 56302-0702

Swedish Genealogical Society of Minnesota; 5768 Olson Memorial Highway; Golden Valley, Minnesota 55422; <www.mtn.org/mgs/sweden/>

Swift County Historical Society; Box 39; Benson, Minnesota 56215

Twin Ports Genealogical Society; PO Box 16895; Duluth, Minnesota 55816-0895

University of Minnesota Library; Minneapolis, Minnesota 55455

Upsala Area Historical Society; Box 35; Upsala, Minnesota 56384; <www.upstel.net/~johns/History/>

Verndale Historical Society; Verndale, Minnesota 56481

Veterans Service Building; 20 West 12th Street; St. Paul, Minnesota 55155; 612.296.2562; Fax 612.296.3954;

Vital Records Office (Hennepin Co.); Public Service Level Gov. Center, 300 So. 6th St.; Minneapolis, Minnesota 55487; 612.348.8241; Fax 612.348.8677

Waseca Area Genealogical Society, Inc.; PO Box 314; Waseca, Minnesota 56093

Waseca County Historical Society; PO Box 314; Waseca, Minnesota 56093;

Washington County Historical Society; PO Box 167; Stillwater, Minnesota 55082;

Watertown Area Historical Society; 309 Lewis Avenue South; PO Box 836; Watertown, MN 55388-0836

White Bear Lake Genealogical Society; PO Box 10555; White Bear Lake, Minnesota 55110

Winona County Genealogical Roundtable; PO Box 363; Winona, Minnesota 55987

Winona County Historical Society; 160 Johnson Street; Winona, Minnesota 55987; 507.454.0006; <www.winona.msus.edu/historicalsociety/>

Wright County Genealogical Society; 911 2nd Ave. South; Buffalo, Minnesota 55313

Yankee Genealogical Society of Minnesota; 5768 Olson Memorial Highway; Golden Valley, Minnesota 55422; <www.mtn.org/mgs/branches/yankee.html>

Ylvisaker Library; Minneapolis, Minnesota 55455

Bibliography and Record Sources

General Sources

Bakeman, Mary Hawker. *Early Presbyterian Church Records from Minnesota 1835-1871 (Including the Church at Fort Snelling).* Roseville, Minnesota: Park Genealogical Books, 1992.

Barnquist, Joseph Alfred Arner. *Minnesota and Its People.* 4 vols. Chicago: S.J. Clarke, 1924.

Bible, Genealogical, Vital Records and Pioneer Stories of Minnesota. Duluth: s.l., s.n., 1946-47.

Björnson, Val. *The History of Minnesota.* 4 vols. West Palm Beach, Florida: Lewis Historical Pub., Co., 1969.

Blatti, Jo. *Women's History in Minnesota: A Survey of Published Sources and Dissertations.* St. Paul: Minnesota Historical Society Press, 1993.

Blegen, Theodore C. *Minnesota: A History of the State.* 2nd ed. Minneapolis: University of Minnesota Press, 1975.

Brook, Michael. *Reference Guide to Minnesota History.* St. Paul: Minnesota Historical Society, 1974.

Castle, Henry Anson. *Minnesota: Its Story and Biography*. 3 vols. Chicago: Lewis Publishing Co., 1915.

Clark, Clifford Edward. *Minnesota in a Century of Change: The State and Its People Since 1900*. St. Paul: Minnesota Historical Society Press, 1989.

Commemorative Biographical Record of the Upper Lake Region: Containing Biographical Sketches of Prominent and Representative Citizens and Many of the Early Settled Families. Chicago: J. H. Beers, 1905.

Compendium of History and Biography of Central and Northern Minnesota, Containing a History of the State of Minnesota…and a Compendium of Biography. (1904) Reprint, Salem, Massachusetts: Higginson Books, 1995.

Compendium of History and Biography of Northern Minnesota. Containing a History of the State of Minnesota. (1902) Reprint. Salem, Massachusetts: Higginson Books, 1994.

Daughters of the American Revolution (Minnesota). *Genealogical Collection*. Microfilm. Salt Lake City: Genealogical Society of Utah, 1971.

Directory of Churches and Religious Organizations in Minnesota. Madison, WI: Historical Records Survey, 1941.

Easton, Augustus B., et al., eds. *History of the St. Croix Valley*. 2 vols. (1909) Reprint. Salem, Massachusetts: Higginson Books, 1996.

Edwards, Rev. Maurice Dwight. *History of the Synod of Minnesota—Presbyterian Church USA*. Introduction by Rev. Robt. Jeambey. (1927) Reprint. Roseville, Minnesota: Park Genealogical Books, 1993.

Folsom, W.H.C. *Fifty Years in the Northwest. With an Introduction and Appendix Containing Reminiscences, Incidents and Notes*. (1888) Reprint. Salem, Massachusetts: Higginson Books, 1994.

Gaynon, D. *A Bibliography of Books and Pamphlets Held in the Northeast Minnesota Historical Center*. Duluth, Minn.: St. Louis County Historical Society, 1981.

Genealogical Resources of the Minnesota Historical Society, A Guide. Minnesota Historical Society Press, 1989.

Great Northern Railway Company. Personnel Department. *Index to Personnel Files*. Microreproduction of original records at the Minnesota Historical Society in St. Paul, Minnesota. St. Paul: Minnesota Historical Society, 1980. 4 microfilm.

Hage, Anne A. *Church Records in Minnesota: A Guide to Parish Records of Congregational, Evangelical, Reformed, and United Church of Christ Churches, 1851-1981*. Minneapolis: Minnesota Conference, United Church of Christ, 1983.

Hage, George Sigrud. *Newspapers on the Minnesota Frontier, 1849-1860*. [St. Paul]: Minnesota Historical Society, 1967.

Hamer, Maryanna. *History of the Church of the Brethren on the Northern Plains*. [S.l.: s.n.], 1977.

Historical Records Survey (Minnesota). *Guide to Depositories of Manuscript Collections in the United States: Minnesota*. Saint Paul, Minnesota: Historical Records Survey, 1941.

Historical Records Survey (Minnesota). *Guide to Public Vital Statistics Records in Minnesota*. St. Paul: The Survey, 1941.

Hobart, Chauncey. *History of Methodism in Minnesota*. Introduction by Thelma Boeder. (1887) Reprint. Roseville, Minnesota: Park Genealogical Books, 1992.

Holmquist, June Drenning. *They Chose Minnesota: A Survey of the State's Ethnic Groups*. St. Paul: Minnesota Historical Society, 1981.

Hubbard, Lucius Frederick. *Minnesota in Three Centuries, 1655 – 1908*. 4 vols. New York: Pub. Society of Minnesota, 1908.

Hyde, C. W. G. *History of the Great Northwest and Its Men of Progress: A Select List of Biographical Sketches and Portraits of the Leaders in Business, Professional and Official Life*. Minneapolis: Minneapolis Journal, 1901.

Illustrated Album of Biography of the Famous Valley of the Red River of the North and the Park Regions…Containing the Biographical Sketches of Hundreds of Prominent Old Settlers and Representative Citizens… (1889) Reprint. Salem, Massachusetts: Higginson Books, 1996.

Illustrated Historical Atlas of the State of Minnesota. Chicago: A.T. Andreas, 1874.

Jerabek, Esther. *A Bibliography of Minnesota Territorial Documents*. Saint Paul, Minnesota: Minnesota Historical Society, 1936.

Jerabek, Esther. *Check List of Minnesota State Documents, 1858-1923*. St. Paul: Minnesota Historical Society, 1972.

Kane, Lucille M. *Guide to the Public Affairs Collection of the Minnesota Historical Society*. St. Paul: Minnesota Historical Society, 1968.

Kirkeby, Lucille L. *Holdings of Genealogical Value in Minnesota's County Museums*. Brainerd, Minn.: L. Kirkeby, 1986.

Lareau, Paul J. and Elmer Courteau. *French-Canadian Families of the North Central States: A Genealogical Dictionary, 8 vols*. St. Paul, Minnesota: Northwest Territory French and Canadian Heritage Institute, 1980.

Lass, William E. *Minnesota: A Bicentennial History*. New York: W.W. Norton & Co., 1977.

Lind, Marilyn. *Continuing Your Genealogical Research in Minnesota*. Cloquet, Minnesota: The Linden Tree, 1986.

Marquis, Albert Nelson. *The Book of Minnesotans: A Biographical Dictionary of Leading Living Men of the State of Minnesota*. Chicago: A.N. Marquis, 1907.

Memorial Record of Southwestern Minnesota. (1897), Reprint. Salem, Massachusetts: Higginson Books, 1994.

Minnesota Historical Society (St. Paul, Minnesota*). Chippewa and Dakota Indians: A Subject Catalog of Books, Pamphlets, Periodical Articles, and Manuscripts in the Minnesota Historical Society*. St. Paul: Minnesota Historical Society, 1969.

Minnesota Historical Society (St. Paul, Minnesota). *Genealogical Resources of the Minnesota Historical Society: A Guide*. 2nd ed. St. Paul: Minnesota Historical Society Press, 1989, 1993.

Minnesota Historical Society (St. Paul, Minnesota). *Historic Resources in Minnesota: A Report on Their Extent, Location, and Need for Preservation*. St. Paul: The Society, 1979.

Minnesota Historical Society (St. Paul, Minnesota). *Minnesota Historic Resources Survey: Manuscripts: Collection Information Forms, 1973-1979*. Microreproduction of original records at the Division of Archives and Manuscripts, Minnesota Historical Society in St. Paul, Minnesota. St. Paul: Minnesota Historical Society, 1980. 7 microfilm.

Minnesota Historical Society (St. Paul, Minnesota). *Minnesota Historical Society Holdings of Newspapers on Master Negative Microfilm*. St. Paul: Minnesota Historical Society, 1987.

Minnesota Historical Society (St. Paul, Minnesota). *The Oral History Collections of the Minnesota Historical Society*. St. Paul: Minnesota Historical Society Press, 1984.

Minnesota Historical Society. Division of Archives and Manuscripts. *Minnesota State Archives Preliminary Checklist*. [St. Paul]: Minnesota Historical Society, Division of Archives and Manuscripts, 1979.

Minnesota Research Outline. Series US-States, no. 24. Salt Lake City. Family History Library, 1988.

Moody, Suzanna. *Guide to the Minnesota Finnish American Family History Collection*. [S.l.: s.n., 1981?].

Neill, Rev. Edward D. *History of the Upper Mississippi Valley, Including Explorers and Pioneers of Minnesota, Outlines of the History of Minnesota, Exploration and Development Above the Falls of St. Anthony*. (1881) Reprint. Salem, Massachusetts: Higginson Books, 1994.

Neill, Rev. Edward D., and Charles S. Bryant. *History of the Minnesota Valley, Including the Explorers and Pioneer of Minnesota and History of the Sioux Massacre*. (1882) Reprint. Salem, Massachusetts: Higginson Books, 1994.

Northern Pacific Railway Company. Personnel Department. *Index to Personnel Files*. Microreproduction of original records at the Minnesota Historical Society in St. Paul, Minnesota. St. Paul: Minnesota Historical Society, 1980. 3 microfilm.

Northwest Minnesota Historical Center (Moorhead, Minnesota). *Guide to the Northwest Minnesota Historical Center Collections*. Moorhead, Minnesota: Livingston Lord Library, Moorhead State University, 1988.

Offermann, Glenn W. *Missouri in Minnesota: Centennial History of the Minnesota South District, The Lutheran Church Missouri Synod, 1882-1982*. [Minnesota]: The Minnesota South District, the Lutheran Church - Missouri Synod, 1982.

Peterson, Ann H. *Every Name Index to Pioneer Chronicles, Stories of Minnesota Territorial Pioneers*. St. Paul: Warren Research & Marketing, 1990.

Pope, Wiley R. *Minnesota Genealogical Index*. St. Paul: Minnesota Family Trees, 1984.

Pope, Wiley R., and Aliss L. Wiener. *Tracing Your Ancestors in Minnesota, A Guide to Sources*. St. Paul, Minnesota: Minnesota Family Trees, 1984.

Porter, Robert B. Porter. *How to Trace Your Minnesota Ancestors*. Center City, Minnesota: Porter Publishing Co., 1985.

Richardson, Antona Hawkins, ed. *Directory of Churches and Religious Organizations in Minnesota. Minnesota Historical Records Survey—Works Progress Administration, 1942*. St. Paul, Minnesota: Paduan Press, 1977.

Shutter, Marion Daniel. *Progressive Men of Minnesota: Biographical Sketches and Portraits of the Leaders in Business, Politics and the Professions; Together with an Historical and Descriptive Sketch of the State*. Minneapolis: The Minneapolis Journal, 1897.

Strand, A.E. *History of the Swedish-Americans of Minnesota*. 3 vols. (1910) Reprint. Salem, Massachusetts: Higginson Books, 1994.

Stuhler, Barbara. *Women of Minnesota: Selected Biographical Essays*. St. Paul: Minnesota Historical Society Press, c1977, corr. reprint 1979.

Taylor, David Vassar. *Blacks in Minnesota: A Preliminary Guide to Historical Sources*. St. Paul: Minnesota Historical Society, 1976.

The United States Biographical Dictionary and Portrait Gallery of Eminent and Self-Made Men: Minnesota Volume: New York: American Biographical Pub. Co., 1879.

Upham, Warren, comp. *Minnesota Biographies, 1655-1912*. Collections of the Minnesota Historical Society vol. 14. St Paul: Minnesota Historical Society, 1912.

Warren, Paula Stewart. *An Introduction to Minnesota Research Sources*. Minnesota Genealogical Society, 1988.

Warren, Paula Stewart. *Minnesota Genealogical Reference Guide*. St. Paul, Minnesota: Warren Research & Publishing, 1994.

Warren, Paula Stewart. *Research in Minnesota*. Arlington, VA: National Genealogical Society, 1992.

Wasastjerna, Hans R.. *History of the Finns in Minnesota*. Duluth, Minnesota: Minnesota Finnish-American Historical Society, 1957.

Atlases, Maps and Gazetteers

Andreas, Alfred T. *Illustrated Historical Atlas of the State of Minnesota*. 1874. Reprint. Evansville, Indiana: Unigraphic, 1976.

Atlas of the State of Minnesota: Containing a Map of Each County, Minnesota and the U.S.... Fergus Falls, Minn.: Thomas O. Nelson Co., 1982.

Bakeman, Mary Hawker. *Comprehensive Index to A.T. Andreas' Illustrated Historical Atlas of Minnesota—1874*. Roseville, Minnesota: Park Genealogical Books, 1992.

Finnell, Arthur Louis. *Minnesota Genealogical Periodical Index*. Marshall, Minnesota: Finnell Richter and Assoc., 1980.

Hage, George Sigrud. *Newspapers on the Minnesota Frontier, 1849-1860*. St. Paul: Minnesota Historical Society, 1967.

Lass, William E. *Minnesota's Boundary with Canada: Its Evolution since 1783*. St. Paul: Minnesota Historical Society Press, 1980.

Leighton, Hudson. *Gazetteer of Minnesota Railroad Towns, 1861-1997*. Roseville, Minnesota: Park Genealogical Books, 1992.

Lewis, Mary Ellen. *The Establishment of County Boundaries in Minnesota*. Master's Thesis, University of Minnesota, 1946.

Minnesota Atlas and Gazetteer. 2nd ed. Freeport, Maine: DeLorme Mapping Co., 1995.

Ostendorf, Paul J. *Every Person's Name Index to An Illustrated Atlas of the State of Minnesota*. Winona, Minnesota: St. Mary's College, 1979.

Patera, Alan H., and John S. Gallagher. *The Post Offices of Minnesota*. Burtonville, MD: The Depot, 1978.

Rippley, LaVern J. *German Place Names in Minnesota—Deutsche Ortsnamen in Minnesota*. Northfield, Minn.: St. Olaf College, 1989.

Treude, Mai. *Windows to the Past: A Bibliography of Minnesota County Atlases*. Minneapolis: Center for Urban and Regional Affairs, University of Minnesota, 1980.

Upham, Warren. *Minnesota Geographic Names: Their Origin and Historic Significance*. Minnesota Historical Society 17 (1920). Reprint. St. Paul: Minnesota Historical Society, 1969.

Census Records

Available Census Records and Census Substitutes

Federal Census 1850, 1860, 1870, 1880, 1900, 1910, 1920, 1930.

Federal Mortality Schedules 1850, 1860, 1870, 1880, 1900.

Union Veterans and Widows 1890.

State/Territorial Census 1836, 1849, 1857, 1865, 1875, 1885, 1895, 1905.

Bakeman, Mary Hawker. *Guide to the Minnesota State Census Microfilm*. Roseville, Minnesota: Park Genealogical Books, 1992.

Dollarhide, William. *The Census Book: A Genealogist's Guide to Federal Census Facts, Schedules and Indexes*. Bountiful, Utah: Heritage Quest, 1999.

Kemp, Thomas Jay. *The American Census Handbook*. Wilmington, Delaware: Scholarly Resources, Inc., 2001.

Lainhart, Ann S. *State Census Records*. Baltimore: Genealogical Publishing Co., 1992.

Szucs, Loretto Dennis, and Matthew Wright. *Finding Answers in U.S. Census Records*. Ancestry Publishing, 2001.

Thorndale, William, and William Dollarhide. *Map Guide to the U.S. Federal Censuses, 1790-1920*. Baltimore: Genealogical Publishing Co., 1987.

Court Records, Probate and Wills

Note: Probate records are found in individual county court records. Other court records may be found in the Minnesota State Historical Society collections. District court records are found at the National Archives Great Lakes Region Branch, in Chicago.

Green, Stina B. *Adoptions & Name Changes: Minnesota Territory & State, 1851-1881*. Roseville, Minnesota: Park Genealogical Books, 1994.

National Archives Record Administration. Great Lakes Region (Chicago). *Records of the District Courts of the United States, Record Group 21: Minnesota, Third Division, St. Paul, 1861-1979; Minnesota, Fourth Division, Minneapolis, 1966-69; Minnesota, Fifth Division, Duluth, 1890-1981; Minnesota, Sixth Division, Fergus Falls, 1890-1978*. Chicago: National Archives Record Administration. Great Lakes Region (Chicago). <www.nara.gov/regional/findaids/chiguid1.html#21>

Emigration, Immigration, Migration and Naturalization

Erickson, James E. *Declarations of Intention (1847-1852) of 262 Minnesota Pioneers*. Roseville, Minnesota. Roseville, Minnesota: Park Genealogical Books, 1997.

Holmquist, June D., ed., *They Chose Minnesota: A Survey of the State's Ethnic Groups*. St. Paul: Minnesota Historical Society, 1981.

Ljungmark, Lars. *For Sale - Minnesota: Organized Promotion of Scandinavian Immigration, 1866-1873*. Chicago: Swedish Pioneer Historical Society, 1971.

United States. Circuit Court (Minnesota: First Division). *Naturalizations, 1897-1899; Declarations of Intentions, 1910*. Microfilm of originals in the National Archives Branch in Kansas City, Missouri. (Salt Lake City: Filmed by the Genealogical Society of Utah, 1991). 2 microfilm.

United States. Circuit Court (Minnesota: Fourth Division). *Naturalizations, 1890-1911; Declarations of Intention, 1890-1911*. Microfilm of originals in the National Archives Branch in Kansas City, Missouri. (Salt Lake City: Filmed by the Genealogical Society of Utah, 1991). 6 microfilm.

United States. Circuit Court (Minnesota: Second Division). *Naturalizations, 1897-1911; Declarations of Intention, 1900-1911*. Microfilm of originals in the National Archives Branch in Kansas City, Missouri. (Salt Lake City: Filmed by the Genealogical Society of Utah, 1991). 2 microfilm.

United States. Circuit Court (Minnesota: Sixth Division). *Naturalizations, 1897-1911*. Microfilm of originals in the National Archives Branch in Kansas City, Missouri. (Salt Lake City: Filmed by the Genealogical Society of Utah, 1991).

United States. Circuit Court (Minnesota: Third Division). *Naturalizations, 1875-1911; Declarations of Intention, 1875-1911*. Microfilm of originals in the National Archives Branch in Kansas City, Missouri. (Salt Lake City: Filmed by the Genealogical Society of Utah, 1991).

United States. District Court (Minnesota: First Division). *Naturalizations, 1896-1924*. Microfilm of originals in the National Archives Branch in Kansas City, Missouri. (Salt Lake City: Filmed by the Genealogical Society of Utah, 1990).

United States. District Court (Minnesota: Fourth Division: Minneapolis). *Naturalizations, 1897-1936*. Microfilm of originals in the National Archives Branch in Kansas City, Missouri. (Salt Lake City: Filmed by the Genealogical Society of Utah, 1990-1991). 25 microfilm.

United States. District Court (Minnesota: Second Division). *Declarations of Intention, 1906-1940; Naturalizations, 1897-1944*. Microfilm of originals in the National Archives Branch in Kansas City, Missouri. (Salt Lake City: Filmed by the Genealogical Society of Utah, 1990). 4 microfilm.

United States. District Court (Minnesota: Sixth Division). *Naturalizations, 1896-1936; Declarations of Intention, 1896-1936*. Microfilm of originals in the National Archives Branch in Kansas City, Missouri. (Salt Lake City: Filmed by the Genealogical Society of Utah, 1991). 3 microfilm.

United States. District Court (Minnesota: Third Division). *Declarations of Intention, 1872-1955; Naturalizations, 1859-1954*. Microfilm of originals in the National Archives Branch in Kansas City, Missouri. (Salt Lake City: Filmed by the Genealogical Society of Utah, 1990). 32 microfilm.

Land and Property

Bakeman, Mary Hawker. *Minnesota Land Owner Maps and Directories*. Roseville, Minnesota: Park Genealogical Books, 1994.

Hone, Wade E. *Land and Property Research in the United States*. Salt Lake City: Ancestry Incorporated, 1997.

Iowa. Surveyor General. *Iowa and Minnesota Boundary Records, 1852*. Microfilm made from the originals in the Office of Secretary of State, Des Moines, Iowa. (Salt Lake City: Filmed by the Genealogical Society of Utah, 1977). 2 microfilm.

Kinney, Gregory. *A Guide to the Records of Minnesota's Public Lands*. St. Paul: Minnesota Historical Society, 1985.

Land Records: AL, AR, FL, LA, MI, MN, OH, WI. [S.l.]:
Brøderbund, 1996. CD-ROM.

National Archives Record Administration. Great Lakes Region
(Chicago). *The General Land Office Records, Minnesota, 1855-
1882.* Chicago: National Archives Record Administration.
Great Lakes Region (Chicago). <www.nara.gov/regional/
findaids/chiguid1.html>

Orfield, Matthias N. *Federal Land Grants to the States with
Special Reference to Minnesota.* University of Minnesota
Studies in the Social Sciences. Minneapolis: the author,
1915.

United States. Bureau of Land Management. *Card Files.*
Microfilm of original card files located at the Bureau of
Land Management's Eastern States Office in Alexandria,
Virginia. (Washington, D.C.: Bureau of Land Management,
[19-]). 160 microfilm.

United States. Department of the Interior. Bureau of Land
Management. *Minnesota, 1820-1908: Cash and Homestead
Entries.* Springfield, Va.: BLM Eastern States, 1995. CD-
ROM.

Military

Brown, Alonzo L. *History of the Fourth Regiment of Minnesota
Infantry Volunteers During the Great Rebellion.* (1892) Reprint.
Salem, Massachusetts: Higginson Books, 1995.

Finnell, Arthur Louis. *Known War of 1812 Veterans Buried in
Minnesota*: Bloomington, Minnesota: A.L. Finnell, 1996.

Holbrook, Franklin F. *Minnesota in the Spanish-American War
and the Philippine Insurrection.* Saint Paul: Minnesota War
Records Commission, 1923.

Minnesota in the Civil and Indian Wars, 1861-1865. St. Paul:
Pioneer Press, 1890-93.

Minnesota State Historical Society. *Civil and Dakota Wars
Collection.* St. Paul, Minnesota: Minnesota State Historical
Society, 2000. Online database - <www.mnhs.org/library/
collections/manuscripts/wars.html>.

Minnesota's World War II Army Dead. Roseville, Minnesota:
Park Genealogical Books, 1994.

Minnesota's World War II Navy Casualties. Roseville, Minnesota:
Park Genealogical Books, 1996.

*Pensioners on the Rolls as of 1 January 1883 (Living in Minnesota)
with Every Name Index.* (1883) Reprint. Roseville,
Minnesota: Park Genealogical Books, 1994.

Richardson, Antona Hawkins. *Minnesotans in the Spanish-
American War and the Philippine Insurrection, April 21, 1898—
July 4, 1902.* St. Paul, Minnesota: Paduan Press, 1998.

United States. Navy. *Minnesota's W. W. II Combat Connected
Naval Casualties (Navy, Marine Corps, Coast Guard).*
Roseville, Minnesota: Park Genealogical Books, 1996.

United States. Selective Service System. *Minnesota, World War
I Selective Service System Draft Registration Cards, 1917-1918.*
National Archives Microfilm Publications, M1509.
Washington, D.C.: National Archives, 1987-1988.

Vital and Cemetery Records

*Guide to Church Vital Statistics Records in Minnesota: Baptisms,
Marriages, Funerals.* St. Paul: Historical Records Survey,
1942.

Guide to Public Vital Statistics Records in Minnesota. St. Paul:
Historical Records Survey, 1941.

Hage, Anne A. *Church Records in Minnesota: Guide to Parish
Records of Congregational, Evangelical, Reformed & United
Church of Christ Churches 1851-1891.* Roseville, Minnesota:
Park Genealogical Books, 1983.

Pond Brothers. *Early Presbyterian Church Records from Minnesota
1825-1871.* Transcribed by Mary Hawker Bakeman.
Roseville, Minnesota: Park Genealogical Books, 1992.

Pope, Wiley R. *Minnesota Cemeteries in Print: A Bibliography of
Minnesota Published Cemetery Inscriptions, and Burials, Etc.* 1st
ed. St. Paul: Minnesota Family Trees, 1986.

County Website	Map Index	Date Created	Parent County or Territory From Which Organized Address/Details
Aitkin* www.co.aitkin.mn.us/	H6	23 May 1857	Pine, Ramsey Aitkin County; 209 2nd St NW; Aitkin, MN 56431-1297; Ph. 218.927.7336 Details: (Attached to Crow Wing & Morrison Cos prior to organization 6 Feb 1885) (Clk Dis Ct has b rec from 1883, m rec from 1885, d rec from 1887, div rec from 1886, pro, ct & nat rec from 1885; Co Rcdr has land rec)
Andy Johnson		18 Mar 1858	Pembina Details: (see Wilkin) Formerly Toombs Co. Name changed to Andy Johnson 8 Mar 1862. Name changed to Wilkin 6 Mar 1868
Anoka* www.co.anoka.mn.us/	H9	23 May 1857	Ramsey Anoka County; 325 E Main St; Anoka, MN 55303-2479; Ph. 763.422.7399 Details: (Clk Dis Ct has b & d rec from 1870, m rec from 1865, div, ct & land rec from 1866; Pro Judge has pro rec)
Becker www.co.becker.mn.us/	L5	18 Mar 1858	Cass, Pembina Becker County; 913 Lake Ave; PO Box 702; Detroit Lakes, MN 56501-0787; Ph. 218.846.7304 Details: (Attached to Stearns, Crow Wing & Douglas Cos prior to organization 1 Mar 1871) (Co Rcdr has b, m & d rec from 1871, div, pro & ct rec from 1940)
Beltrami* www.rootsweb.com/~mnbeltra/	K3	28 Feb 1866	Unorganized Territory, Itasca, Pembina, Polk Beltrami County; 619 Beltrami Ave NW; Bemidji, MN 56601-3041; Ph. 218.759.4174 Details: (Attached to Becker Co prior to organization 6 Apr 1897) (Ct Administrator Customer Serv has b, m & d rec from 1896; Clk Cts has div rec from 1951, pro & ct rec; Rcdr Off has mil rec; Hist Soc has land rec prior to 1969)
Benton* www.rootsweb.com/~mnbenton/	I8	27 Oct 1849	St. Croix Benton County; 531 Dewey St; PO Box 129; Foley, MN 56329; Ph. 320.968.5037 Details: (Co Rcdr has b rec from 1870, m rec from 1887, d rec from 1871 & land rec from 1850; Ct Administrator has div & ct rec from 1900 & pro rec from 1850)
Big Sioux		23 May 1857	Brown Details: (see South Dakota) Attached to Pipestone Co. Eliminated 11 May 1858 when Minn. state was created)
Big Stone* www.rootsweb.com/~mnbigsto/ index.html	M8	20 Feb 1862	Pierce Big Stone County; 20 SE 2nd St; Ortonville, MN 56278-1544; Ph. 320.839.2308 Details: (Attached to Renville & Stevens Cos prior to organization 8 Feb 1881) (Co Rcdr has b, m, d & land rec from 1881, div & ct rec from 1885; Ct Judge has pro rec)
Blue Earth* www.co.blue-earth.mn.us/	J11	5 Mar 1853	Unorganized Territory, Dakota Blue Earth County; 204 S 5th St; PO Box 3524; Mankato, MN 56001-4585; Ph. 507.389.8343 Details: (Clk Dis Ct has b & d rec from 1870, m rec from 1865, div & ct rec from 1854 & pro rec from 1858; Reg of Deeds has land rec)
Breckenridge		18 Mar 1858	Pembina Details: (see Clay) Name changed to Clay 6 Mar 1862
Brown willow.internet-connections.net/ web2/brown/	K11	20 Feb 1855	Blue Earth Brown County; Center & State Sts; PO Box 248; New Ulm, MN 56073; Ph. 507.233.6657 Details: (Organized 11 Feb 1856) (Co Rcdr has b & d rec from 1870, m rec from 1857 & land rec; Clk Dis Ct has div & pro rec from 1856 & ct rec from 1885; MN Hist Soc has nat rec)
Buchanan		23 May 1857	Pine Details: (see Pine) Attached to Chisago & St. Louis Cos. Eliminated & absorbed by Pine Co 8 Oct 1861
Carlton www.mjpdan.com/genweb/carlton/ carlton.htm	G6	23 May 1857	Pine, St. Louis Carlton County; 301 Walnut Ave; Carlton, MN 55718; Ph. 218.384.9195 Details: (Organized 18 Feb 1870) (Clk Dis Ct has b, m, d, bur, div, pro, ct, land & nat rec from 1872)

County Website	Map Index	Date Created	Parent County or Territory From Which Organized Address/Details
Carver www.rootsweb.com/~mncarver/	**I9**	**20 Feb 1855**	**Hennepin, Sibley** Carver County; 600 E 4th St; Chaska, MN 55318; Ph. 612.361.1930 Details: (Ct Administrator has div, pro & ct rec from 1856; Co Rcdr has b, m, d & land rec from 1870)
Cass* www.mncounties.org/cass/	**J6**	**31 Mar 1851**	**Dakota, Pembina, Mahkato, Wahrahta** Cass County; 300 Minnesota Ave; PO Box 3000; Walker, MN 56484; Ph. 218.547.7247 Details: (Attached to Benton, Stearns, Crow Wing & Morrison Cos prior to organization 4 May 1872) (Co Treas has b & d rec from 1896 & m rec from 1897; Clk Dis Ct has div rec from 1899, ct rec from 1898, pro & nat rec; City or Twn Clks have bur rec)
Chippewa* www.frontiernet.net/~kmenning/	**L9**	**20 Feb 1862**	**Pierce, Davis** Chippewa County; 629 N 11th St; Montevideo, MN 56265; Ph. 320.269.9431 Details: (Attached to Renville Co prior to organization 9 Jan 1869) (Clk Dis Ct has b, m, d, div, pro & ct rec from 1870; Co Rcdr has land rec from 1870; City Clks have bur rec)
Chisago www.co.chisago.mn.us/	**G8**	**31 Mar 1851**	**Washington, Ramsey** Chisago County; 313 N Main St; Center City, MN 55012; Ph. 612.213.0438 Details: (Organized 1 Jan 1852) (Clk Dis Ct has b & d rec from 1870, m rec from 1852, ct rec from 1880 & div rec; Pro Judge has pro rec; Reg of Deeds has land rec)
Clay www.rootsweb.com/~mnclay/	**M6**	**18 Mar 1858**	**Pembina** Clay County; 807 11th St; Moorhead, MN 56561; Ph. 218.299.5031 Details: (Formerly Breckenridge Co. Name changed to Clay 6 Mar 1862. Attached to Stearns, Crow Wing, Douglas & Becker Cos prior to organization 27 Feb 1872) (Co Rcdr has b, m, d & land rec from 1872 & mil rec from 1917; Ct Admin has div & ct rec from 1931 & pro rec from 1885)
Clearwater www.co.clearwater.mn.us/	**L4**	**20 Dec 1902**	**Beltrami** Clearwater County; 213 Main Ave N; Bagley, MN 56621; Ph. 218.694.6129 Details: (Co Rcdr has b, m, d, land & mil rec from 1903; Ct Admin has div, pro, ct & nat rec)
Cook www.co.cook.mn.us/	**D4**	**3 Nov 1874**	**Lake** Cook County; PO Box 1150; Grand Marais, MN 55604; Ph. 218.387.3000 Details: (Attached to Lake & St. Louis Cos prior to organization 6 Apr 1897) (Co Rcdr has b & d rec from 1900, m rec from 1901, land rec from 1886 & mil rec from 1919; Ct Admin has div, ct & pro rec)
Cottonwood www.rrcnet.org/~cotton/index.html	**K11**	**23 May 1857**	**Brown** Cottonwood County; 900 3rd Ave; Windom, MN 56101; Ph. 507.831.1458 Details: (Attached to Brown, Redwood & Watonwan Cos prior to organization 4 Jul 1873) (Clk Dis Ct has b, m, d, div & ct rec from 1871)
Crow Wing www.co.crow-wing.mn.us/	**I6**	**23 May 1857**	**Ramsey** Crow Wing County; 326 Laurel St; Brainerd, MN 56401; Ph. 218.824.1300 Details: (Co Treas has b rec from 1873, m rec from 1871 & d rec from 1874; Ct Admin has div, pro & ct rec; Co Rcdr has land rec from 1867 & mil dis rec from 1919)
Dakota* www.co.dakota.mn.us/	**H10**	**27 Oct 1849**	**Unorganized Territory** Dakota County; 1560 Hwy 55 W; Hastings, MN 55033; Ph. 612.438.4313 Details: (Attached to Ramsey Co prior to organization 5 Mar 1853) (Clk Dis Ct has Sb & d rec from 1870, m rec from 1857, div & ct rec from 1853)
Davis		**20 Feb 1855**	**Cass, Nicollet, Pierce, Sibley** Details: (Attached to Stearns Co. Eliminated 20 Feb 1862. Lost to Chippewa & Lac Qui Parle Cos)
Dodge* www.rootsweb.com/~mndodge/	**H11**	**20 Feb 1855**	**Rice, Unorganized Territory** Dodge County; 22 E 6th St PO Box 128; Mantorville, MN 55955-0038; Ph. 507.635.6250 Details: (Clk Dis Ct has b, d, div & ct rec from 1870, m rec from 1865, pro rec from 1858 & school rec from 1917)

The HANDYBOOK for Genealogists

County Website	Map Index	Date Created	Parent County or Territory From Which Organized Address/Details
Doty		20 Feb 1855	**Itasca** Details: (see St. Louis) Name changed to Newton 3 Mar 1855. Eliminated to St. Louis Co 1 Mar 1856
Douglas* www.co.douglas.mn.us/	L7	8 Mar 1858	**Cass, Pembina** Douglas County; 305 8th Ave W; Alexandria, MN 56308; Ph. 320.762.3877 Details: (Co Rcdr has b, m & d rec from 1890, land rec from late 1800's & mil rec; Clk of Cts has div, pro & ct rec)
Faribault www.co.faribault.mn.us/index.cfm	I12	20 Feb 1855	**Blue Earth** Faribault County; N Main St; Blue Earth, MN 56013; Ph. 507.526.6252 Details: (Attached to Blue Earth Co prior to organization 1 May 1857) (Ct Administrator has b, m, d, div & pro rec from 1870, ct rec from 1950 & nat rec; Reg of Deeds has land rec)
Fillmore* www.co.fillmore.mn.us/	F12	5 Mar 1853	**Wabasha** Fillmore County; 101 Filmore St; Preston, MN 55965; Ph. 507.765.4701 Details: (Ct Administrator has b & d rec from 1870, m rec from 1865, div & ct rec from 1885 & pro rec from 1858; Co Rcdr has land rec)
Freeborn* www.albertlea.org/	H12	20 Feb 1855	**Blue Earth, Rice** Freeborn County; 411 S Broadway Ave; Albert Lea, MN 56007; Ph. 507.377.5153 Details: (Organized 6 Mar 1857) (Clk Dis Ct has b & d rec from 1870, m & ct rec from 1857; Co Rcdr has land rec from 1854; Pro Office has pro rec from 1866)
Goodhue* www.co.goodhue.mn.us/	G10	5 Mar 1853	**Wabasha, Dakota** Goodhue County; 509 5th St W; Red Wing, MN 55066; Ph. 651.385.3148 Details: (Attached to Wabasha Co prior to organization 15 Jun 1854) (Ct Administrator has b & d rec from 1870, m & pro rec from 1854, div & ct rec from 1951; MN Hist Soc has div & ct rec 1854-1950)
Grant* www.rootsweb.com/~mngrant/	M7	6 Mar 1868	**Stevens, Wilkin, Traverse** Grant County; County Courthouse; Elbow Lake, MN 56531; Ph. 218.685.4520 Details: (Attached to Douglas Co prior to organization 1 Mar 1883) (Clk Dis Ct has b & d rec from 1877, m rec from 1869, div & ct rec from 1883; Pro Judge has pro rec; Reg of Deeds has land rec)
Hennepin www.co.hennepin.mn.us/welcome.html	I9	6 Mar 1852	**Dakota** Hennepin County; 300 S 6th St; Minneapolis, MN 55487-0001; Ph. 612.348.8241 Details: (Clk Dis Ct has b & d rec from 1870, m, div & ct rec from 1853)
Houston* www.geocities.com/houstoncountymn/ HC.html	E12	4 Apr 1854	**Fillmore** Houston County; 304 S Marshall St; Caledonia, MN 55921; Ph. 507.724.5813 Details: (Clk Dis Ct has b & d rec from 1870, m rec from 1854, ct rec from 1856 & div rec; Pro Judge has pro rec; Reg of Deeds has land rec)
Hubbard* www.co.hubbard.mn.us/	K5	26 Feb 1883	**Cass** Hubbard County; 301 Court St; Park Rapids, MN 56470; Ph. 218.732.3552 Details: (Attached to Wadena Co prior to organization 3 Mar 1887) (Co Rcdr has b, d & land rec; License Center has m rec; Clk Dis Ct has div, pro & ct rec)
Isanti www.rootsweb.com/~mnisanti/Isanti/	H8	13 Feb 1857	**Ramsey** Isanti County; 555 18th Ave SW; Cambridge, MN 55008; Ph. 763.689.1191 Details: (Clk Dis Ct has b rec from 1869, m rec from 1871, d rec from 1873, bur rec 1900-1908 & 1941-1979, div & ct rec from 1872 & pro rec from 1892; Co Rcdr has land rec)
Itasca www.co.itasca.mn.us/	I4	27 Oct 1849	**Unorganized Territorys** Itasca County; 123 4th St NE; Grand Rapids, MN 55744; Ph. 218.327.2856 Details: (Attached to Washington, Benton & Chisago Cos prior to organization 6 Mar 1857) (Co Rcdr-Rgstr has b & m rec from 1891, d rec from 1894, bur rec from 1900, land rec from 1883 & mil rec from 1919; Ct Admin has pro rec from 1896, div & ct rec from 1950; MN Hist Soc has div & ct rec to 1950)

County Website	Map Index	Date Created	Parent County or Territory From Which Organized Address/Details

Jackson* K12 **23 May 1857** **Brown**
www.rootsweb.com/~mnjackso/
Jackson County; 405 4th St; PO Box 209; Jackson, MN 56143; Ph. 507.847.2580
Details: (Ct Administrator has b, d, div, pro & ct rec from 1870 & m rec from 1868;
Co Rcdr has land rec from 1870)

Kanabec* H8 **12 Oct 1858** **Pine**
www.rootsweb.com/~mnkanabe/
Kanabec County; 18 Vine St N; Mora, MN 55051; Ph. 320.679.6466
Details: (Attached to Pine Co prior to organization 4 Nov 1881) (Clk Dis Ct has b & d
rec from 1883, m, div & ct rec from 1882 & pro rec from 1891; Co Rcdr has land rec;
Mora City Hall has bur rec)

Kandiyohi K9 **20 Mar 1858** **Meeker, Renville, Pierce, Davis, Stearns**
www.co.kandiyohi.mn.us/
Kandiyohi County; 400 Benson Ave SW; Willmar, MN 56201-3281; Ph. 320.231.6532
Details: (Clk Dis Ct has b, m, d, div & ct rec from 1870)

Kittson N2 **27 Oct 1849** **Unorganized Territory**
www.rootsweb.com/~mnkittso/
Kittson County; 410 S 5th St; PO Box 39; Hallock, MN 56728; Ph. 218.843.3632
Details: (Formerly Pembina Co. Name changed to Kittson 9 Mar 1878. Attached to
Benton prior to organization 4 Mar 1852. Disorganized 5 Mar 1853. Recreated 24 Apr
1862 from Benton. Attached to Benton, Morrison, Crow Wing, Douglas, Becker, Clay
& Polk Cos prior to organization 6 Apr 1897) (Clk Dis Ct has b, m, d, div, pro & ct rec
from 1880's; Co Rcdr has land rec; MN Hist Soc has nat rec)

Koochiching I3 **19 Dec 1906** **Itasca**
www.rootsweb.com/~mnkoochi/
Koochiching County; 715 4th St; International Falls, MN 56649; Ph. 218.283.6260
Details: (Clk Dis Ct has b, m, d, div, ct & pro rec from 1907)

Lac Qui Parle M9 **7 Nov 1871** **Redwood**
www.rootsweb.com/~mnlacqui/index.htm
Lac Qui Parle County; 600 6th St; Madison, MN 56256; Ph. 320.598.3724
Details: (Attached to Redwood Co prior to organization 7 Jan 1873) (Co Rcdr has
b, m, d & mil rec; Ct Admin has div, pro & ct rec; Co Asr has land rec)

Lac Qui Parle, old **20 Feb 1862** **Davis, Pierce**
Details: (Attached to Renville Co. Eliminated 3 Nov 1868 & absorbed by
Chippewa Co)

Lake E4 **20 Feb 1855** **Itasca**
www.lakecnty.com/
Lake County; 601 3rd Ave; Two Harbors, MN 55616; Ph. 218.834.8347
Details: (Formerly Superior Co. Name changed to St. Louis, old 3 Mar 1855. Name
changed to Lake 1 Mar 1856. Attached to Benton & St. Louis Cos prior to
organization 27 Feb 1891) (Co Rgstr has b rec from 1898, m & d rec from 1891, div &
ct rec from 1892; Pro Judge has pro rec; city Clk has bur rec)

Lake of the Woods K2 **28 Nov 1922** **Beltrami**
www.rootsweb.com/~mnlakeof/
Lake of the Woods County; 206 SE 8th Ave; PO Box 808; Baudette, MN 56623;
Ph. 218.634.1902
Details: (Ct Admin has b, m, d, div, pro & ct rec from 1923)

Le Sueur I10 **5 Mar 1853** **Dakota**
www.co.le-sueur.mn.us/
Le Sueur County; 88 S Park Ave; Le Center, MN 56057; Ph. 507.357.2251
Details: (Clk Dis Ct has b & d rec from 1870, m rec from 1854, div & ct rec from
1880 & some school rec 1920-1945; Pro Judge has pro rec from 1855; Reg of Deeds
has land rec from 1850)

Lincoln* M10 **4 Nov 1873** **Lyon**
www.rootsweb.com/~mnlincol/
Lincoln County; 319 N Rebecca; Ivanhoe, MN 56142; Ph. 507.694.1360
Details: (Attached to Lyon & Redwood Cos prior to organization 9 Feb 1881) (Clk Dis
Ct has b & m rec from 1879, d & ct rec from 1880 & div rec from 1891; Pro Judge has
pro rec from 1877; Reg of Deeds has land rec from 1873)

Lincoln, old **8 Oct 1861** **Renville**
Details: (Attached to McLeod Co. Eliminated 3 Nov 1868 to Renville Co)

Lyon M10 **2 Nov 1869** **Redwood**
www.lyonco.org/
Lyon County; 607 W Main; Marshall, MN 56258-3021; Ph. 507.537.6722
Details: (Organized 12 Apr 1870) (Clk Dis Ct has b & d rec from 1874, m rec from
1872, div, pro & ct rec from 1880; Co Rcdr has land rec)

County Website	Map Index	Date Created	Parent County or Territory From Which Organized Address/Details
Mahnomen www.rootsweb.com/~mnmahnom/	L5	27 Dec 1906	**Norman** Mahnomen County; PO Box 379; Mahnomen, MN 56557; Ph. 218.935.2251 Details: (Clk Dis Ct has b, m, d, div & ct rec from 1908)
Mankahto		27 Oct 1849	**Unorganized Territorys** Details: (Attached to Ramsey. Eliminated 1 Sep 1851. Lost to Cass & Pembina Cos)
Manomin		23 May 1857	**Ramsey** Details: (Eliminated 2 Nov 1869 to Anoka Co)
Marshall* www.rootsweb.com/~mnmarsha/	M3	25 Feb 1879	**Kittson** Marshall County; 208 E Colvin Ave; Warren, MN 56762; Ph. 218.745.4816 Details: (Attached to Polk Co prior to organization 11 Mar 1881) (Ct Admin has b, m & d rec from 1882, div & pro rec from 1891 & ct rec; Co Rcdr has land rec from 1883 & mil rec from 1919)
Martin* www.co.martin.mn.us/	J12	23 May 1857	**Faribault, Brown** Martin County; 201 Lake Ave; Fairmont, MN 56031-1845; Ph. 507.238.3213 Details: (Co Rcdr has b rec from 1874, m rec from 1864, d rec from 1879 & land rec; Ct Admin has div, pro & ct rec)
McLeod www.co.mcleod.mn.us/	J9	1 Mar 1856	**Carver, Sibley** McLeod County; 830 11th St; PO Box 127; Glencoe, MN 55336; Ph. 320.864.1216 Details: (Co Rcdr has b & d rec from 1870, m rec from 1865, school cen & land rec; Co Admin has div, pro & ct rec; Veterans Service has mil rec)
Meeker* www.co.meeker.mn.us/	J9	23 Feb 1856	**Davis** Meeker County; 325 N Sibley Ave; Litchfield, MN 55355; Ph. 320.693.5345 Details: (Clk Dis Ct has b, m, d, div & ct rec from 1870, pro rec from 1858, school rec, nat rec from 1884; Co Rcdr has land rec)
Mille Lacs* www.co.mille-lacs.mn.us/	I7	23 May 1857	**Ramsey** Mille Lacs County; 635 2nd St SE; Milaca, MN 56353; Ph. 320.983.8308 Details: (Attached to Morrison Co prior to organization 30 Apr 1860) (Co Rcdr has b, m, d & land rec; Ct Admin has div, pro & ct rec)
Monongalia		8 Mar 1861	**Davis, Pierce** Details: (Discontinued 8 Nov 1870 & became part of Kandyohi Co)
Morrison* www.rootsweb.com/~mnmorris/	J7	25 Feb 1856	**Benton** Morrison County; 213 1st Ave SE; Little Falls, MN 56345; Ph. 320.632.1045 Details: (Co Rcdr has b, m, d & some cem rec, land & mil rec; Ct Admin has div, pro & ct rec)
Mower www.rootsweb.com/~mnmower/	G12	20 Feb 1855	**Rice** Mower County; 201 1st St NE; Austin, MN 55912; Ph. 507.437.9456 Details: (Organized 1 Mar 1856) (Clk Dis Ct has b & d rec from 1870, m rec from 1865, div & ct rec from 1900 & pro rec from 1856; Co Rcdr has land rec)
Murray* murray-countymn.com/	L11	23 May 1857	**Brown** Murray County; 2500 28th St; Slayton, MN 56172; Ph. 507.836.6148 Details: (Attached to Brown, Redwood, Watonwan & Cottonwood Cos prior to organization 5 Mar 1879) (Clk Dis Ct has b, m, d, div, pro & ct rec; Co Rcdr has land rec)
Newton		20 Feb 1855	**Itasca** Details: (Formerly Doty Co. Name changed to Newton 3 Mar 1855. Eliminated to St. Louis Co 1 Mar 1856)
Nicollet* www.co.nicollet.mn.us/	J10	5 Mar 1853	**Dakota** Nicollet County; 501 S Minnesota Ave; PO Box 493; St. Peter, MN 56082; Ph. 507.931.6800 Details: (Clk Dis Ct has b & d rec from 1870, m rec from 1856, div, pro & ct rec from 1853; Co Rcdr has land rec)

County Website	Map Index	Date Created	Parent County or Territory From Which Organized Address/Details

Nobles   L12   23 May 1857   **Brown**
www.co.nobles.mn.us/
Nobles County; 315 10th St; Worthington, MN 56187; Ph. 507.372.8263
Details: (Attached to Brown & Martin Cos prior to organization 19 Oct 1870) (Co Rcdr has b, m & d rec from 1872 & land rec; Ct Admin has div rec from 1882, ct rec from 1874 & pro rec)

Norman   M5   8 Nov 1881   **Polk**
www.rootsweb.com/~mnnorman/
Norman County; 16 E 3rd Ave; Ada, MN 56510; Ph. 218.784.7131
Details: (Clk Dis Ct has b & d rec from 1881, m rec from 1882, some div & ct rec; Pro Judge has pro rec)

Olmsted*   G11   20 Feb 1855   **Fillmore, Wabasha, Rice**
www.olmstedcounty.com/
Olmsted County; 151 SE 4th St; Rochester, MN 55904; Ph. 507.287.1444
Details: (Clk Dis Ct has incomplete b & d rec from 1871, m rec from 1855, div rec from 1860 & ct rec from 1858; Co Ct has pro rec; Coroner & Dept of Hlth have bur rec)

Otter Tail*   L6   18 Mar 1858   **Pembina, Cass**
www.co.otter-tail.mn.us/mainmenu.asp
Otter Tail County; 121 W Junis Ave; Fergus Falls, MN 56537; Ph. 218.739.2271
Details: (Attached to Stearns, Crow Wing & Douglas Cos prior to organization 28 Feb 1870) (Clk Dis Ct has b & d rec from 1870, m rec from 1869, div rec from 1897, pro & ct rec from 1872)

Pembina   27 Oct 1849   **Unorganized Territory**
Details: (see Kittson) Name changed to Kittson 9 Mar 1878

Pennington   M3   23 Nov 1910   **Red Lake**
www.rootsweb.com/~mnpennin/mnpennin.htm
Pennington County; 101 Main Ave; PO Box 616; Thief River Falls, MN 56701; Ph. 218.681.2522
Details: (Co Rcdr has b, m, d, bur, land & mil rec from 1910; Ct Admin has div, pro & ct rec)

Pierce   5 Mar 1853   **Dakota**
Details: (Eliminated 20 Feb 1862 to Big Stone, Chippewa, Lac Qui Parle, Pope, Stevens & Traverse Cos)

Pine   G7   1 Mar 1856   **Chisago, Ramsey**
www.pinecounty.com/
Pine County; 315 6th St; Pine City, MN 55063; Ph. 320.629.5662
Details: (Organized 1 Apr 1857) (Clk Dis Ct has b rec from 1874, d rec from 1879, m, div & ct rec from 1871; Pro Judge has pro rec; Reg of Deeds has land rec)

Pipestone*   M11   23 May 1857   **Brown**
www.mncounties.org/pipestone/
Pipestone County; 416 S Hiawatha; Pipestone, MN 56164-1562; Ph. 507.825.6755
Details: (Attached to Big Sioux, Brown, Redwood, Watonwan, Rock & Cottonwood Cos prior to organization 27 Jan 1879) (Clk Dis Ct has b, m, d, div, pro & ct rec from 1877; Co Rcdr has land rec)

Polk   M4   20 Jul 1858   **Pembina**
www.rootsweb.com/~mnpolk/
Polk County; 612 N Broadway; Crookston, MN 56716; Ph. 218.281.3464
Details: (Attached to Crow Wing, Douglas, Becker & Clay Cos prior to organization 27 Feb 1879) (Ct Admin has b, m, d, pro & ct rec from 1875; Co Rcdr has land rec)

Pope   L8   20 Feb 1862   **Pierce, Cass, Unorganized Territory**
www.mncounties.org/pope/
Pope County; 130 Minnesota Ave E; Glenwood, MN 56334; Ph. 320.634.5723
Details: (Organized 28 Feb 1866) (Clk Dis Ct has b, m & d rec from 1870, div & ct rec from 1880 & pro rec from 1867)

Ramsey   H9   27 Oct 1849   **St. Croix**
www.co.ramsey.mn.us/
Ramsey County; 15 Kellogg Blvd W; St. Paul, MN 55102; Ph. 651.266.4444
Details: (Clk Dis Ct has b & d rec from 1870, m rec from 1850, div & ct rec from 1900 & pro rec from 1849; Hist Soc has ct rec 1858-1899 & land rec)

Red Lake   M4   24 Dec 1896   **Polk**
www.rootsweb.com/~mnredlak/mnredlak.htm
Red Lake County; 124 Langevin Ave; PO Box 3; Red Lake Falls, MN 56750; Ph. 218.253.2997
Details: (Organized 6 Apr 1897) (Ct Admin has b, m, d, div, pro & ct rec from 1897 &

County Website	Map Index	Date Created	Parent County or Territory From Which Organized Address/Details
			school rec 1900-1955; Co Rcdr has land rec)
Redwood* www.rrcnet.org/~redwood/index.html	K10	4 Nov 1862	**Brown** Redwood County; PO Box 130; Redwood Falls, MN 56283; Ph. 507.637.4032 Details: (Attached to Brown Co prior to organization 23 Feb 1865) (Ct Admin has b, m & d rec from 1865, div rec from 1871, pro rec from 1877 & ct rec from 1867; Co Rcdr has land rec)
Renville* www.co.renville.mn.us/	K10	20 Feb 1855	**Nicollet, Pierce, Sibley** Renville County; 500 DePue Ave E; Olivia, MN 56277; Ph. 320.523.3669 Details: (Attached to Nicollet Co prior to organization 31 Jul 1866) (Clk Dis Ct has b, m & d rec from 1870, div, pro & ct rec; Co Rcdr has land rec)
Rice* www.co.rice.mn.us/	H10	5 Mar 1853	**Dakota, Wabasha** Rice County; 320 NW 3rd St; Faribault, MN 55021-5146; Ph. 507.332.6114 Details: (Attached to Dakota Co prior to organization 9 Oct 1855) (Clk Dis Ct has b, d, div, pro & ct rec from 1870, m rec from 1856 & bur rec; Co Rcdr has land rec)
Rock* www.co.rock.mn.us/	M12	23 May 1857	**Brown** Rock County; 204 E Brown; PO Box 509; Luverne, MN 56156-0509; Ph. 507.283.5060 Details: (Attached to Brown, Martin & Nobles Cos prior to organization 7 Feb 1874) (Co Aud/Treas has b, m & d rec from 1875; Clk Dis Ct has div & ct rec from 1872)
Roseau www.rootsweb.com/~mnroseau/	M2	28 Feb 1894	**Kittson, Beltrami** Roseau County; 606 5th Ave SW Rm 20; Roseau, MN 56751; Ph. 218.463.2541 Details: (Organized 6 Apr 1896) (Clk Dis Ct has b, m, d, div, ct & pro rec from 1895; Reg Deeds has land rec)
Scott* www.co.scott.mn.us/xpedio/groups/public/ documents/web_files/ scottcountywebframe.hcsp	I10	5 Mar 1853	**Dakota** Scott County; 428 S Holmes St; Shakopee, MN 55379; Ph. 952.496.8150 Details: (Co Rcdr has b & d rec from 1871, m rec from 1856, land rec from 1850's & mil dis rec from 1950; Clk Cts has div & pro rec from 1850's & ct rec from 1880)
Sherburne* www.co.sherburne.mn.us/	I8	25 Feb 1856	**Benton** Sherburne County; 13880 Hwy 10; Elk River, MN 55330-4601; Ph. 763.241.2915 Details: (Attached to Benton Co prior to organization 6 Mar 1862) (Ct Admin has b & d rec from 1870, m rec from 1858, div rec from 1884, pro rec from 1893 & ct rec from 1877; Co Rcdr has land rec)
Sibley www.co.sibley.mn.us/	J10	5 Mar 1853	**Dakota** Sibley County; 400 Court St; PO Box 44; Gaylord, MN 55334; Ph. 507.237.4080 Details: (Attached to Hennepin Co prior to organization 10 Oct 1854) (Ct Admin has b, d & div rec from 1860, m rec from 1856, pro & ct rec from 1870; Co Rcdr has land rec from 1855)
St. Croix		3 Aug 1840	**Wisconsin Territorys** Details: (Eliminated to Benton, Ramsey & Washington Cos 27 Oct 1849)
St. Louis www.co.st-louis.mn.us/	G4	1 Mar 1856	**Itasca, Newton** St. Louis County; 100 N 5th Ave W; Duluth, MN 55802-1202; Ph. 218.726.2559 Details: (Attached to Benton Co prior to organization 23 May 1857) (Clk Dis Ct has b, d & m rec from 1870, bur permits from 1938, div, ct & land rec from 1859; Co Ct has pro rec)
St. Louis, old		20 Feb 1855	**Itasca** Details: (Formerly Superior Co. Name changed to St. Louis, old 3 Mar 1855. Abolished 1 Mar 1856 & became part of Lake Co)
Stearns* www.co.stearns.mn.us/	J8	20 Feb 1855	**Cass, Nicollet, Pierce, Sibley** Stearns County; 705 Courthouse Sq; St. Cloud, MN 56303; Ph. 320.656.3855 Details: (Ct Admin has div, pro & ct rec; Co Rcdr has land rec; License Center has b, m & d rec)
Steele www.co.steele.mn.us/	H11	20 Feb 1855	**Rice, Blue Earth, LeSueur** Steele County; 111 E Main St; Owatonna, MN 55060; Ph. 507.444.7450 Details: (Organized 29 Feb 1856) (Clk Dis Ct has b & d rec from 1870, m rec from 1855, div, pro & ct rec from 1858; Co Rcdr has land rec from 1858)

County Website	Map Index	Date Created	Parent County or Territory From Which Organized Address/Details
Stevens www.co.stevens.mn.us/	**M8**	**20 Feb 1862**	**Pierce, Unorganized Territory** Stevens County; 400 Colorado Ave; PO Box 530; Morris, MN 56267; Ph. 320.589.7414 Details: (Attached to Stearns, Douglas & Pope Cos prior to organization 31 Dec 1871) (Clk Dis Ct has b & d rec from 1872, m rec from 1869, div & ct rec from 1873 & pro rec from 1901; Co Rcdr has land rec from 1871)
Superior www.co.todd.mn.us/		**20 Feb 1855**	**Itasca** Details: (see Lake) Name changed to Saint Louis, old 3 Mar 1855. Name changed to Lake 1 Mar 1856
Swift www.rootsweb.com/~mnswift/	**L9**	**8 Nov 1870**	**Chippewa** Swift County; 301 14th St N; PO Box 50; Benson, MN 56215; Ph. 320.843.3377 Details: (Attached to Pope & Chippewa Cos prior to organization 6 Apr 1897) (Co Treas has b rec from 1870, m rec from 1871 & d rec from 1872; Clk Cts has div, ct & pro rec; Co Rcdr has land rec)
Todd www.co.todd.mn.us/	**K7**	**20 Feb 1855**	**Cass** Todd County; 215 1st Ave S; Long Prairie, MN 56347; Ph. 320.732.4428 Details: (Attached to Stearns & Morrison Cos prior to organization 21 Feb 1873) (Clk Dis Ct has div rec from 1880, ct rec from 1874 & pro rec; Co Rcdr has b & d rec from 1870, m rec from 1867, land rec, school cen from 1914)
Toombs		**18 Mar 1858**	**Pembina** Details: (see Wilkin) Name changed to Andy Johnson 8 Mar 1862. Name changed to Wilkin 6 Mar 1868
Traverse* www.rootsweb.com/~mntraver/index.html	**M8**	**20 Feb 1862**	**Pierce, Unorganized Territory** Traverse County; 702 2nd Ave N; PO Box 487; Wheaton, MN 56296; Ph. 320.563.4266 Details: (Attached to Stearns, Douglas, Pope & Stevens Cos prior to organization 14 Feb 1881) (Clk Dis Ct has b, m, d, div, pro, ct & land rec from 1881)
Wabasha* www.co.wabasha.mn.us/	**F11**	**27 Oct 1849**	**Unorganized Territory** Wabasha County; 625 Jefferson Ave; Wabasha, MN 55981; Ph. 651.565.3018 Details: (Attached to Washington Co prior to organization 5 Mar 1853) (Co Rcdr has b & d rec from 1870, m rec from 1865 & land rec from 1855; Ct Admin has div, pro & ct rec from 1858; Veterans Service Off. has mil rec)
Wadena www.co.wadena.mn.us/	**K6**	**11 Jun 1858**	**Cass, Todd** Wadena County; 415 S Jefferson; PO Box 415; Wadena, MN 56482; Ph. 218.631.7622 Details: (Attached to Crow Wing & Morrison Cos prior to organization 17 Feb 1881) (Clk Dis Ct has b, m & d rec from 1873, div & ct rec from 1881)
Wahnata		**27 Oct 1849**	**Unorganized Territory** Details: (Eliminated 1 Sep 1851 to Cass, Dakota & Pembina Cos)
Waseca www.rootsweb.com/~mnwaseca/	**I11**	**27 Feb 1857**	**Steele** Waseca County; 307 N State St; Waseca, MN 56093; Ph. 507.835.0670 Details: (Clk Dis Ct has b, d, pro & ct rec from 1870, m & div rec from 1858)
Washington* www.co.washington.mn.us/	**G9**	**27 Oct 1849**	**St. Croix** Washington County; 14949-62nd St N; Stillwater, MN 55082; Ph. 651.430.6755 Details: (Clk Dis Ct has b & d rec from 1870, m rec from 1845, div & ct rec from 1847 & pro rec from 1850)
Watonwan www3.extension.umn.edu/county/ main/master.asp?county_id=85	**J11**	**6 Nov 1860**	**Brown** Watonwan County; 710 2nd Ave S; PO Box 518; St. James, MN 56081-0518; Ph. 507.375.1216 Details: (Attached to Brown & Blue Earth Cos prior to organization 15 Jun 1871) (Clk Dis Ct has b, m & d rec from 1863, div & ct rec from 1865; Pro Judge has pro rec; Reg of Deeds has land rec)

County Website	Map Index	Date Created	Parent County or Territory From Which Organized Address/Details
Wilkin www.co.wilkin.mn.us/	M6	18 Mar 1858	**Cass, Pembina** Wilkin County; 300 S 5th St; Breckenridge, MN 56520; Ph. 218.643.5112 Details: (Formerly Toombs & Andy Johnson Cos. Name changed to Andy Johnson 8 Mar 1862. Name changed to Wilkin 6 Mar 1868. Attached to Stearns, Crow Wing, Douglas & Otter Tail Cos prior to organization 4 Mar 1872) (Clk Dis Ct has b rec from 1874, m & div rec from 1890, d rec from 1875 & ct rec from 1858; Pro Judge has pro rec)
Winona www.rootsweb.com/~mnwinona/	F11	4 Apr 1854	**Fillmore, Wabasha** Winona County; 171 W 3rd St; Winona, MN 55987; Ph. 507.457.6340 Details: (Clk Dis Ct has b & d rec from 1870, m, div & ct rec from 1854, pro rec from 1871 & school rec 1909-1939)
Wright* www.co.wright.mn.us/	I9	20 Feb 1855	**Cass, Sibley** Wright County; 10 2nd St NW; Buffalo, MN 55313-1165; Ph. 763.682.7357 Details: (License Bur has b & d rec from 1871 & m rec from 1866; Ct Admin has div & ct rec from 1870 & pro rec; Reg of Deeds has land rec)
Yellow Medicine* www.rootsweb.com/~mnyellow/	M10	7 Nov 1871	**Redwood** Yellow Medicine County; 415 9th Ave; Granite Falls, MN 56241-1367; Ph. 320.564.2529 Details: (Organized 25 Feb 1874) (Clk Dis Ct has b, m & nat rec from 1872, d, div, pro & ct rec; Co Rcdr has land rec)

Magnolia

MISSISSIPPI

CAPITAL: JACKSON – TERRITORY 1798 – STATE 1817 (20TH)

Spaniards, including Hernando de Soto, first explored this area between 1539 and 1542. French explorers, led by Marquette and Joliet, toured the area in 1673. They claimed the Mississippi Valley for France in 1682. They established a settlement at Biloxi in 1699 and at Fort Rosalie (now Natchez) in 1716. The British gained control of Mississippi in 1763. Grants of land near Natchez, given to retired English military officers, resulted in migration of Protestants to the formerly Catholic region. During the Revolutionary War, the Natchez District remained loyal to England. Many Tories from the colonies moved into the area at this time. Between 1779 and 1781, Spain took control of the Natchez District. In 1783, Spain gained western Florida, which included part of Mississippi.

The Georgia legislature authorized the Yazoo land sales between 1789 and 1794, bringing hundreds of settlers into the area. Mississippi was made a territory in 1798, with Natchez as the capital. Georgia abandoned claims to the northern portion in 1802 and Spain relinquished the Gulf Coast region during the War of 1812. Thousands of settlers soon entered the area from the eastern and northern states. In 1817, the eastern part of the territory was severed and became the Alabama Territory. Later the same year, Mississippi became the 20th state. Another land boom occurred in 1837 when the last of the Indian lands were opened up to settlement.

In 1861, Mississippi seceded from the Union. Approximately 112,000 men served in the Confederate forces, while just more than 500 fought for the Union. Mississippi was readmitted to the Union in 1870.

Look for vital records in the following locations:

- **Birth and death records:** A few counties kept birth and death records from as early as 1879. State registration of births and deaths began in November 1912. General compliance was reached in 1921. Records are available from Vital Records, State Department of Health, in Jackson, Mississippi.
- **Miscellaneous records:** The Mississippi Department of Archives and History in Jackson has early census records and tax rolls, newspaper files, microfilms of the Federal Censuses, records of Mississippi's Confederate soldiers, and some birth and death records.
- **Wills, deeds and probate records:** Wills, deeds, and probate files are held by the chancery clerks or probate courts in each county.
- **Land records:** Some early land records have been published. Federal land case files are at the National Archives, Atlanta Branch in East Point, Georgia.
- **Census records:** Territorial and state censuses were frequently taken between 1792 and 1866 for various counties. Published indexes are available for many of them.

Vital Records
State Department of Health
2423 North State Street
Jackson, Mississippi 39216
601.960.7988

Mississippi Department of Archives
and History
100 South State Street
PO Box 571
Jackson, Mississippi 39205

National Archives,
Atlanta Branch
1557 St. Joseph Avenue
East Point, Georgia 30334

Societies and Repositories

Aberdeen Genealogical Society; General Delivery; Aberdeen, Mississippi 39730

Alcorn County Genealogical Society; PO Box 1808; Corinth, Mississippi 38835-1808; <www.rootsweb.com/~msacgs/index.html>

Archives & History, Mississippi Dept.; PO Box 57; Jackson, Mississippi 39205

Attala Co. Library; 328 Goodman St.; Kosciusko, Mississippi 39090

Attala Historical Society; Mary Ricks Thornton Cultural Center; PO Box 127; Kosciusko, Mississippi 39090; <www.rootsweb.com/~msahs/>

Batesville Public Library; 106 College St.; Batesville, Mississippi 38606

Biloxi Public Library; PO Box 467; Biloxi, Mississippi 39533

Bolivar County Historical Society; 1615 Terrace Road; Cleveland, Mississippi 38732

Bureau of Land Management, Eastern States Office; 7450 Boston Boulevard; Springfield, Virginia 22153; 703.440.1600; Fax 703.440.1599;

Carnegie Public Library; 114 Delta Ave.; PO Box 280; Clarksdale, Mississippi 38614; 601.624.4461; Fax 601.627.4344

Chickasaw County Historical and Genealogical Society; PO Box 42; Houston, Mississippi 38851; <www.rootsweb.com/~mschchgs/>

Claiborne-Jefferson Genealogical Society; PO Box 1017; Port Gibson, Mississippi 39150

Columbus and Lowndes County Historical Society; 916 College Street; Columbus, Mississippi 39701

Columbus Public Library; 314 N. 7th St.; Columbus, Mississippi 39701

Commission on Archives and History of the United Methodist Church; 36 Madison Avenue, PO Box 127; Madison, New Jersey 07940; 201.408.3590; Fax 201.408.3909

Evans Memorial Library; 105 North Long Street; Aberdeen, Mississippi 39730; 601.369.4601; Fax 601.369.2971

Family Research Association of Mississippi; PO Box 13334; Jackson, Mississippi 39236-3334; 601.372.2959

Family History Library: 35 North West Temple Street: Salt Lake City, Utah 84150: 800.346.6044 or 801.240.2584: <www.familysearch.org>: Find a Family History Center near you: <www.familysearch.org/Eng/Library/FHC/frameset_fhc.asp>

Genealogical Society of Desoto County; PO Box 607; Hernando, Mississippi 38632-0632; <www.rootsweb.com/~msdesoto/gsdcm.htm>

Greenville Public Library; 341 Main St.; Greenville, Mississippi 38701

Greenwood-Leflore Public Library; 408 W. Washington; Greenwood, Mississippi 38930

Gulfport-Harrison Co. Public Library; Box 4018, 14th St. & 21st Ave.; Gulfport, Mississippi 39501

Hancock County Historical Society; 113 Citizen Street; PO Box 1340; Bay Saint Louis, Mississippi 39520

Harriette Person Memorial Library; Port Gibson, Mississippi 39150

Hattiesburg Area Historical Society; 127 W Front St.; Hattiesburg, Mississippi 39401-3461

Historical and Genealogical Society of Panola County; 105 Church St.; Batesville, Mississippi 38606

Homichitto Valley Historical Society; PO Box 337; Crosby, Mississippi 39633

Itawamba County Historical Society; PO Box 7G; Mantachie, Mississippi 38855; <www.rootsweb.com/~msichs/>

Jackson County Genealogical Society; PO Box 994; Pascagoula, Mississippi 39567

Jackson-George Regional Library System, Pascagoula City Library; PO Box 937. 3214; Pascagoula St.; Pascagoula, Mississippi 39567

Jefferson Co. Library; 3033 High Ridge Blvd.; High Ridge, Mississippi 63049; 636.677.8186

Jones County Genealogical and Historical Organization; PO Box 2644; Laurel, Mississippi 39442-2644

L. W. Anderson Genealogical Library; PO Box 1647; Gulfport, Mississippi 39502

Lafayette County-Oxford Public Library; 401 Bramlett Blvd; Oxford, Mississippi 38655

Laurel Jones Co. Lib.; 530 Commerce St., Laurel, Mississippi 39440

Marion County Historical Society; John Ford Home, Sandy Hook Community; PO Box 430; Columbia, Mississippi 39429

Marks-Quitman Co. Library; 315 E. Main; Marks, Mississippi 38646

Marshall County Historical Society; 220 East College Avenue; PO Box 806; Holly Springs, Mississippi 38635

McCain Library & Archives, Univ. of Southern Mississippi; Southern Station, Box 5148; Hattiesburg, Mississippi 39406-5148

Meridian Public Library; 2517 7th St.; Meridian, Mississippi 39301

Methodist, J.B. Cain Archives of Mississippi Methodism, Millsaps-Wilson Library; Millsaps College, 1701 North State Street; Jackson, Mississippi 39210; 601.974.1073; Fax 601.974.1082;

Mississippi Archives and Library; Capers Building; 100 South State Street; PO Box 571; Jackson, Mississippi 39205-0571; 601.359.6964; <www.mdah.state.ms.us/arlib/arlib_index.html>

Mississippi Baptist Historical Commission, Mississippi College Library; PO Box 51; Clinton, Mississippi 39060; 601.925.3434; Fax 601.925.3435

Mississippi Coast Genealogical and Historical Society; PO Box 513; Biloxi, Mississippi 39530

Mississippi Department of Archives and History; 100 South State Street, 100 South State Street; Jackson, Mississippi 39201; 601.359.6850

Mississippi Genealogical Society; PO Box 5301; Jackson, Mississippi 39216

Mississippi Historical Society; PO Box 571; Jackson, Mississippi 39205-0571; <www.mdah.state.ms.us/admin/mhistsoc.html>

Mississippi Society of the Sons of the American Revolution; 12 Avery Circle; Jackson, Mississippi 39211

Mississippi State University-Mitchel Memorial, Special Collections-Genealogical Library; PO Box 5408; Mississippi State, Mississippi 39762; 601.325.7679; Fax 601.325.3560

Mitchell Memorial Library, Acquisitions / Serials Dept; PO Box 5408, Hardy Rd.; Mississippi State, Mississippi 39762

Natchez Historical Society; 307 South Wall Street; PO Box 49; Natchez, Mississippi 39120

National Archives-Southeast Region (Atlanta); 1557 St. Joseph Avenue; East Point, Georgia 30344-2593; 404.763.7477; Fax 404.763.7033

Neshoba Ancestral Group; Route 1, Box 284.D; Philadelphia, Mississippi 39350; 601.656.4787; <www.rootsweb.com/~msneshgg/>

Northeast Mississippi Historical and Genealogical Society; PO Box 434; Tupelo, Mississippi 38802-0434

Northeast Regional Library; 1023 Fillmore; Corinth, Mississippi 38834

Ocean Springs Genealogical Society; PO Box 1765; Ocean Springs, Mississippi 39566-1765; <www.rootsweb.com/~msosgs/>

Pearl River County Genealogy Club, Margaret Reed Crosby Memorial Library; 900 Goodyear Blvd., Picayune, Mississippi 39466

Philadelphia-Neshoba Co. Public Library; 230 Beacon St.; Philadelphia, Mississippi 39350

Prentiss County Historical & Genealogical Society; PO Box 491; Booneville, Mississippi 38829; <www.rootsweb.com/~mspcgs/Index.html>

Rankin County Historical Society; PO Box 841; Brandon, Mississippi 39042

Scott County Genealogical Society; PO Box 737; Forest, Mississippi 39074-0737; 601.469.4799; <www.geocities.com/scottcogensoc>

Skipwith Historical and Genealogical Society, Inc.; PO Box 1392; Oxford, Mississippi 38655

Smith County Mississippi Genealogical Society; Route 1, Box 4B-1; Raleigh, Mississippi 39153

South Mississippi Genealogical Society; Box 15271; Hattiesburg, Mississippi 39404-5271;

Southern Baptist Historical Library and Archives; 901 Commerce Street #400; Nashville, Tennessee 37203-3630; 615.244.0344; Fax 615.782.4821

Sunflower County Historical Society; Sunflower County Library; 201 Cypress Drive; Indianola, Mississippi 38751

Tate Co. Genealogical Library; 102B Robinson St.; Senatobia, Mississippi 38668

Tate County Mississippi Genealogical and Historical Society; PO Box 974; Senatobia, Mississippi 38668

Tippah County Historical and Genealogical Society; Ripley Public Library; 308 North Commerce Street; Ripley, Mississippi 38663

Tishomingo County Historical & Genealogical Society; 204 N Main St; Iuka, Mississippi 38852-2311; 662.423.2543; <www.rootsweb.com/~mstchgs/index.htm>

Union Co., Library; PO Box 846; New Albany, Mississippi 38652-0846

University of Southern Mississippi, McCain Library and Archives; PO Box 5148; Hattiesburg, Mississippi 39406-5148; 601.266.4345; Fax 601.266.4409

Vicksburg Genealogical Society, Inc.; PO Box 1161; Vicksburg, Mississippi 39181-1161; <www.rootsweb.com/~msvgs/index.htm>

Vital Records, State Department of Health; 2423 North State Street; Jackson, Mississippi 39216; 601.960.7981

Wayne County Genealogical Organization, Inc.; 712 Wayne St.; Waynesboro, Mississippi 39367

Webster County Historical Society; Rt. 3, Box 14; Elepora, Mississippi 39744

West Chickasaw County Genealogical and Historical Society; PO Box 42; Houston, Mississippi 38851

Wilkinson Co. Museum; PO Box 1055; Woodville, Mississippi 39669; 601.888.3998

Winston County Historical and Genealogical Society; PO Box 428; Louisville, Mississippi 39339

Woodville Civic Club; Friends of the Museum; PO Box 914; Woodville, Mississippi 39669

Yalobusha County Historical Society; PO Box 258; Coffeeville, Mississippi 38922

Yazoo Historical Society; 332 North Main Street; PO Box 575; Yazoo City, Mississippi 39194; 601.746.2273

Bibliography and Record Sources

General Sources

Adams, Donna Burge. *Women in the Florida Parishes*. 5 vols. Baton Rouge, Louisiana: D.B. Adams, 1985-1991.

Anderson, Hugh George. *Lutheranism In The Southeastern States, 1860-1886: A Social History*. The Hague: Mouton, 1969.

Biographical and Historical Memoirs of Mississippi: Embracing an authentic and Comprehensive Account of the Chief Events in the History of the State, and a Record of the Lives of Many of the Most Worthy and Illustrious Families and Individuals. 2 vols. in 4. Chicago: Goodspeed Publishing Co., 1891.

Cain, Cyril Edward. *Four Centuries on the Pascagoula*, 2 vols. State College, Mississippi: C.E. Cain, 1953-1962.

Church of Jesus Christ of Latter-day Saints. Mississippi District. *Annual Genealogical Report, Form E, 1907-1951; Record Of Members, 1874-1943*. Microfilm of original records in the LDS Church Archives, Salt Lake City. (Salt Lake City: Filmed by the Genealogical Society of Utah, 1953-1954). 3 microfilm.

Claiborne, J.F.H. *Mississippi as a Province, Territory, and State, with Biographical Notices of Eminent Citizens*. (1880) Reprint. Spartanburg, SC: Reprint Company, 1996.

DeRosier, Arthur H. *The Removal of the Choctaw Indians*. Knoxville: University of Tennessee Press, 1989.

Episcopal Diocese of Mississippi (Jackson, Mississippi). *The Episcopal Church in Mississippi.* Jackson, Mississippi: The Diocese, 1992.

First Settlers of the Mississippi Territory. Nacogdoches, Texas: Ericson Books, n.d..

Gillis, Norman E. *Genealogical Abstract of Biographical Section, Alphabetical Arrangement, A Through Z: Biographical and Historical Memoirs of Mississippi.* [S.l.]: Irene S. and Norman E. Gillis, 1962.

Goodspeed Publishing Company. *Biographical and Historical Memoirs of Mississippi, Embracing an Authentic and Comprehensive Account of the Chief Events in the History of the State and a Record of the Lives of Many of the Most Worthy and Illustrious Families and Individuals.* Vols. I and II. (1891) Reprint. Spartanburg, SC: Reprint Company, 1996.

Greenwell, Dale. *Twelve Flags - Triumphs And Tragedies.* 3 vols. Ocean Springs, Mississippi: D. Greenwell, 1968.

Griffin, Benjamin. *History of the Primitive Baptists of Mississippi.* 1853. Reprint, Jonesboro, AR: Sammons Printing, 1958.

Henderson, Thomas W. and Ronald E. Tomlin, comps. *Guide to Official Records in the Mississippi Department of Archives and History.* Jackson, Mississippi: Mississippi Department of Archives and History, 1975.

Jenkins, William L. *Mississippi, United Methodist Churches: Two Hundred Years of Heritage and Hope.* Franklin, Tennessee: Providence House Pub., 1998.

Johnson, Charles Owen, ed. *The Order of the First Families of Mississippi 1699-1817: 1981 Register.* Ann Arbor, MI: Edwards Brothers, Inc., 1981.

Kelly, Thomas E. *Who's Who In Mississippi.*, Mississippi: Tucker Printing House, 1914.

Kidwell, Clara Sue. *Choctaws And Missionaries In Mississippi, 1818-1918.* Norman, Okla.: University of Oklahoma Press, 1995.

Lackey, Richard Stephen. *"Mississippi," Genealogical Research: Methods and Sources, vol. 2: 188-218.* Washington, D.C.: American Society of Genealogists, 1980.

Lindsey, J. Allen. *Methodism in the Mississippi Conference.* Jackson, Mississippi: Hawkins Foundation, Mississippi Conference Historical Society, 1964.

Lipscomb, Anne S., and Kathleen S. Hutchison. *Tracing Your Mississippi Ancestors.* Jackson: University Press of Mississippi, 1994.

Lowry, Robert, and William H. McCardle. *History of Mississippi from the Discovery of the Great River by Hernando Desoto, Including the Earliest Settlement made by The French, Under Iberville, to the Death of Jefferson Davis.* (1891) Reprint. Spartanburg, SC: Reprint Company, 1978.

Menn, Joseph Karl. *The Large Slaveholders of the Deep South, 1860.* Thesis (Ph.D) –University of Texas, 1964.

Mississippi Newspapers, 1805-1940: A Preliminary Union List. Jackson, Mississippi: Mississippi Historical Records Survey, 1942.

Mississippi Research Outline. Series US-States, no. 25. Salt Lake City: Family History Library, 1988.

Mississippi. Department of Archives and History. *Mississippi Provincial Archives [1757-1820] Spanish Dominion.* Jackson, Mississippi: Photoduplication Div., 1969. 9 microfilm.

Mississippi. Department of Archives and History. *Research In The Mississippi Department of Archives And History.* (Salt Lake City: Filmed by the Genealogical Society of Utah, 1972).

Nolan, Charles E. *A Southern Catholic Heritage.* New Orleans: Archdiocese of New Orleans, 1976.

Oakley, Bruce C. *A Postal History of Mississippi, Stampless Period, 1799-1860.* Baldwyn, Mississippi: Magnolia Pub., 1969.

Owens, Harry P. *Steamboats and the Cotton Economy: River Trade in the Yazoo-Mississippi Delta.* Jackson, [Mississippi]: University Press of Mississippi, 1990.

Reorganized Church of Jesus Christ of Latter Day Saints. Mobile District (Alabama & Mississippi). *Church Records, 1868-1911.* Microreproduction of originals housed in the RLDS Library Archives, Independence, Missouri. (Salt Lake City: Filmed by the Genealogical Society of Utah, 1994).

Rowland, Dunbar and A. G. Sanders, ed. *Mississippi Provincial Archives, 1612-1763, French Dominion.* Jackson, Mississippi: Department of Archives and History, 1968.

Rowland, Dunbar. *History of Mississippi, the Heart of the South.* 2 vols. (1925) Reprint. Salem, Massachusetts: Higginson Books, n.d.

Rowland, Dunbar. *Mississippi: Comprising Sketches of Counties, Towns, Events, Institutions, and Persons, Arranged in Cyclopedic Form.* 4 vols. (1907) Reprint. Spartanburg, South Carolina: Reprint Company, 1976.

Rowland, Dunbar. *Mississippi Provincial Archives, 1763-1783; English Dominion: Transcripts of Archives in the Public Record Office, London, England.*

Rowland, Dunbar. *Mississippi.* 4 vols. (1907) Reprint. Spartanburg, South Carolina: The Reprint Co., 1976.

Schilling, T.C. *Abstract History of the Mississippi Baptist Association, 1806-1906.* New Orleans: N.p., 1908.

Strickland, Jean. *Mississippi Biographical Abstracts.* Moss Point, Mississippi: J. Strickland, 1990.

Strickland, Jean. *Residents of the Southeastern Mississippi Territory.* 5 vols. Moss Point, Mississippi: J. Strickland, 1996.

United States. Office of Indian Affairs. Superintendent of Indian Trade. *Records of the Choctaw Trading House, 1803-1824.* Washington: National Archives. Central Plains Region, 1960. 6 microfilm.

Wallace, Jesse Thomas. *A History of the Negroes of Mississippi from 1865 to 1890.* Clinton, Mississippi: [s.n.], 1927.

Willis, John C.. *Forgotten Time: The Yazoo-Mississippi Delta after the Civil War.* Charlottesville, Va.: University Press of Virginia, 2000.

Young, Mary Elizabeth. *Redskins, Ruffleshirts and Rednecks: Indian Allotments in Alabama and Mississippi, 1830-1860.* Norman: University of Oklahoma Press, 1961.

Atlases, Maps and Gazetteers

Brieger, James. *Hometown, Mississippi.* 2nd ed. Jackson, Mississippi: Town Square Books, 1997.

Gallagher, John S. *Mississippi Post Offices.* Lake Grove, Oregon: Depot, 1996.

Long, John H., and Peggy Tuck Sinko, comps. *Mississippi Atlas of Historical County Boundaries.* New York: Simon & Schuster, 1993.

Mississippi Maps, 1816-1873. Jackson, Mississippi: Mississippi Department of Archives and History, 1970.

Oakley, Bruce C. *A Postal History of Mississippi - Stampless Period, 1799-1860.* Baldwyn, Mississippi: Magnolia Publishers, 1969.

Rowland, Dunbar. *Mississippi: Comprising Sketches of Counties, Towns, Events, Institutions, and Persons, Arranged in Cyclopedic Form.* 4 vols. Atlanta: Southern Historical Publishing Association, 1907. Reprint. Spartanburg, SC: Reprint Co., 1976.

United States. Office of Geographic Research. Branch of Geographic Names. *Mississippi Geographic Names: Alphabetical Listing.* Reston, Va.: U.S. Geological Survey, 1985.

Census Records

Available Census Records and Census Substitutes

Federal Census 1820, 1830 (except Pike County), 1840, 1850, 1860 (except Hancock, Washington and Tallahatchie Counties), 1870, 1880, 1900, 1910, 1920, 1930.

Federal Mortality Schedules 1850, 1860, 1870, 1880.

Union Veterans and Widows 1890.

State/Territorial Census 1810, 1816, 1822-1825, 1837, 1841, 1845, 1853, 1866.

Dollarhide, William. *The Census Book: A Genealogist's Guide to Federal Census Facts, Schedules and Indexes.* Bountiful, Utah: Heritage Quest, 1999.

Feldman, Lawrence H. *Anglo-Americans in Spanish Archives: Lists of Anglo-American Settlers in the Spanish Colonies of America; A Finding Aid.* Baltimore: Genealogical Publishing Co., 1991.

Kemp, Thomas Jay. *The American Census Handbook.* Wilmington, Delaware: Scholarly Resources, Inc., 2001.

Lainhart, Anne S.. *State Census Records.* Baltimore: Genealogical Publishing Co., Inc., 1992.

Szucs, Loretto Dennis, and Matthew Wright. *Finding Answers in U.S. Census Records.* Ancestry Publishing, 2001.

Thorndale, William, and William Dollarhide. *Map Guide to the U.S. Federal Censuses, 1790-1920.* Baltimore: Genealogical Publishing Co., 1987.

United States. Bureau of Indian Affairs. *Indian Census Rolls, Choctaw, 1926-1939.* Washington, D.C.: The National Archives, 1965. 2 microfilm.

United States. Bureau of Internal Revenue. *Internal Revenue Lists For Mississippi, 1865-1866.* Washington, D.C.: The National Archives, 1988. 3 microfilm.

Court Records, Probate and Wills

Hendrix, Mary L. *Mississippi Court Records: From the Files of the High Court of Errors and Appeals, 1799-1859.* Jackson, Mississippi: n.d..

King, J. Estelle. *Mississippi Court Records 1799-1835.* (1936) Reprint. Baltimore: Genealogical Publishing Co., 1969.

McBee, May Wilson. *Mississippi County Court Records.* (1858) Reprint. Baltimore: Clearfield Co., 1994.

McBee, May Wilson. *The Natchez Court Records, 1767-1805.*

(1953) Reprint. Baltimore: Clearfield Co., 1994.

Mississippi. State Archives. *Mississippi Territorial Land and Court Records, 1798-1817.* Microfilm of original records at the Mississippi State Archives, Jackson, Mississippi. (Salt Lake City: Filmed by the Genealogical Society of Utah, 1972). 5 microfilm.

Survey of Records in Mississippi Court Houses. Jackson, Mississippi: Mississippi Genealogical Society, 1957.

Wiltshire, Betty Couch, comp. *Mississippi Index of Wills, 1800-1900.* Bowie, Maryland: Heritage Books, 1989.

Emigration, Immigration, Migration and Naturalization

Index to Naturalization Records, Mississippi Courts, 1798-1906. Jacksonville, Mississippi: Old Law Naturalization Records Project, 1942.

Old Law Naturalization Records Project, Division of Community Service Programs, Work Project Administration. *Index to Naturalization Records Mississippi Courts, 1798-1906* Washington DC: Library of Congress Photoduplication Service, 1989.

Land and Property

Ainsworth, Fern. Private Land Claims of Mississippi and Missouri. Natchitoches, Louisiana: Fern Ainsworth, n.d.

DeVille, Winston. *English Land Grants in West Florida: A Register for the States of Alabama, Mississippi, and Parts of Florida and Louisiana, 1766-1776.* Ville Platte, Louisiana: Winston DeVille, 1986.

Guide to Archival Holdings at NARA's Southeast Region (Atlanta). East Point, Georgia: National Archives Records Administration Southeast Region (Atlanta), 2001. Online at - <www.nara.gov/regional/atlanta.html>.

Hone, Wade E. *Land and Property Research in the United States.* Salt Lake City: Ancestry Incorporated, 1997.

Lowrie, Walter. *Early Settlers of Mississippi as Taken from Land Claims in the Mississippi Territory.* (1834) Reprint. Southern Historical Press, 1986.

McMullin, Phillip, ed. *Grassroots of America A Computerized Index to the American State Papers: Land Grants and Claims 1789-1837 with Other Aids to Research (Government Document Serial Set Numbers 28 Through 36).* Salt Lake City: Gendex Corp., 1972.

Mississippi. State Archives. *Mississippi Territorial Land and Court Records, 1798-1817.* Microfilm of original records at the Mississippi State Archives, Jackson, Mississippi. (Salt Lake City: Filmed by the Genealogical Society of Utah, 1972). 5 microfilm.

Smith, Clifford Neal. *Spanish And British Land Grants In Mississippi Territory, 1750-1784.* 3 vols. in 1. McNeal, Arizona: Westland, 1996.

United States. Department of the Interior. Bureau of Land Management. *Mississippi Pre 1908 Patents, Cash, Homestead, Chickasaw Indian Treaty And Choctaw Indian Scrip.* Springfield, Virginia: BLM Eastern States, 1997.

Military

Department of Archives and History. Roster of Mississippi Men Who Served in the War of 1812 and Mexican War. Jackson, Mississippi: Department of Archives and History, n.d..

Master Alphabetical Index, World War Veterans, Army, 1917-1918. (Salt Lake City: Filmed by the Genealogical Society of Utah, 1972).

Mississippi. State Archives. *Master Alphabetical Index, World War Veterans, Army, 1917-1918.* Microreproduction of typescript at the State Archives in Jackson, Mississippi. (Salt Lake City: Filmed by the Genealogical Society of Utah, 1972). 2 microfilm.

Rietti, John C. *Military Annals of Mississippi: Military Organizations Which Entered the Service of the Confederate States of America from the State of Mississippi.* (1976) Reprint. Spartanburg, South Carolina: Reprint Co., 1976.

Rowland, Dunbar. *Military History of Mississippi, 1803-1898.* (1908) Reprint. Spartanburg, South Carolina: Reprint Co., 1996.

Rowland, Dunbar. *Official & Statistical Register of the State of Mississippi, Military History Only.* (1908) Reprint. Salem, Massachusetts: Higginson Co., 1995.

Rowland, Eron Opha. *Mississippi Territory in the War of 1812.* (1921) Reprint. Baltimore: Clearfield Co., 1996.

Strickland, Jean, and Patricia N. Edwards. *Residents of the Mississippi Territory.* 3 vols. Moss Point, Mississippi: Ben Strickland, n.d.

United States. Adjutant General's Office. *Compiled Service Records of Volunteer Soldiers Who Served During the Mexican War in Organizations from the State of Mississippi.* Washington, D.C.: The National Archives, 1971.

United States. Adjutant General's Office. *Compiled Service Records of Volunteer Soldiers Who Served During the War of 1812 in Organizations from the Territory of Mississippi.* Washington, D.C.: The National Archives, 1967.

United States. Record and Pension Office. *Compiled Service Records of Volunteer Union Soldiers Who Served in Organizations from the State of Mississippi.* Washington, D.C.: The National Archives, 1962.

United States. Selective Service System. *Mississippi, World War I Selective Service System Draft Registration Cards, 1917-1918.* National Archives Microfilm Publications, M1509. Washington, D.C.: National Archives, 1987-1988.

Wiltshire, Betty Crouch. *Mississippi Confederate Grave Registrations.* 2 vols. Bowie, Maryland: Heritage Books, 1991.

Wiltshire, Betty Crouch. *Mississippi Confederate Pension Applications.* 3 vols. Carrollton, Mississippi: Pioneer Publishing Co., 1994.

Vital and Cemetery Records

Birth and death records were not kept until 1912 on the state level. It was not until 1921 that the records were kept on a regular basis. Refer to the county section to locate information for individual counties.

Cemetery Index. Jackson: Mississippi Department of Archives & History, 2002. Online database - <www.mdah.state.ms.us/arlib/contents/findaids.html>.

Dodd, Jordan R. *Mississippi Marriages, Early To 1825: A Research Tool Compiled, Extracted & Transcribed By Liahona Research, Inc.* [Bountiful, Utah]: Precision Indexing Publishers, [c1990].

Guide to Vital Statistics in Mississippi: Volume 1, Public Archives. Jackson: Historical Records Survey, 1942.

Ivison, Hazel R. Collins. *These Sacred Places.* [S.l.: s.n.], 1965.

Marriage Records. Orem, Utah: Automated Archives, 1994. CD-ROM.

Mississippi & Florida, 1800-1900. [S.l.]: Broderbund, 1998. CD-ROM.

Mississippi Cemetery and Bible Records. 3 vols. Jackson: Mississippi Genealogical Society, 1954.

Mississippi. State Board of Health. Division of Vital Statistics (Jackson, Mississippi). *Birth Records, 1913-1935; Death Records, 1912-1935.* Microfilm of originals at the Kemper Regional Library, DeKalb, Mississippi. (Salt Lake City: Filmed by Genealogical Society of Utah, 2000).

United States. Census Office. *Mississippi Mortality Schedule For 1850, 1860, 1870, and 1880.* [Washington, D.C.: The National Archives, 198-?]. 3 microfilm.

Wiltshire, Betty Couch. *Early Mississippi Records.* [CD-ROM.] Bowie, Maryland: Heritage Books, 1996.

County Website	Map Index	Date Created	Parent County or Territory From Which Organized Address/Details
Adams www.rootsweb.com/~msadams/	M3	2 Apr 1799	**Natchez District** Adams County; 115 S Wall St; PO Box 1008; Natchez, MS 39120; Ph. 601.446.6684 Details: (Clk Chan Ct has ct, land & pro rec; Clk Cir Ct has m & d rec)
Alcorn www.freedom2000net.com/userpages/ genealogy/alcorn/index.html	B9	15 Apr 1870	**Tippah, Tishomingo** Alcorn County; PO Box 112; Corinth, MS 38834-0112; Ph. 601.286.7702 Details: (Clk Chan Ct has div rec from 1913; Clk Cir Ct has ct rec from 1860)
Amite* www.rootsweb.com/~msamite/	N4	24 Feb 1809	**Wilkinson** Amite County; 243 W Main St; Liberty, MS 39645-0000; Ph. 601.657.8022 Details: (Clk Chan Ct has ct, land & pro rec from 1809; Clk Cir Ct has m rec)
Attala www.rootsweb.com/~msattala/	H7	23 Dec 1833	**Choctaw Cession** Attala County; 230 W Washington St; Kosciusko, MS 39090-0000; Ph. 662.289.2921 Details: (Clk Cir Ct has m rec; Clk Chan Ct has div, pro & land rec & old newspapers)
Bainbridge		17 Jan 1823	**Lawrence, Wayne** Details: (Discontinued 21 Jan 1824 & became Covington Co)
Benton www.rootsweb.com/~msbenton/	B8	21 Jul 1870	**Marshall, Tippah** Benton County; Main St; PO Box 218; Ashland, MS 38603-0000; Ph. 662.224.6300 Details: (Clk Chan Ct has div, pro & land rec from 1871)
Bolivar www.usgw.org/ms/bolivar/	E4	9 Feb 1836	**Choctaw Cession** Bolivar County; 401 S Court St; Cleveland, MS 38732-2696; Ph. 662.843.2071 Details: (Clk Cir Ct, Cleveland Miss has m & ct rec; Clk Chan Ct has div, pro & land rec) (Clk Cir Ct, Rosedale Miss has m rec from 1866 & ct rec from 1870; Clk Chan Ct has div, pro & land rec) (Chan & Cir Clks Office in both Courthouses. Rosedale rec go back about 20 years earlier than Cleveland)
Calhoun www.rootsweb.com/~mscalhou/	E8	8 Mar 1852	**Lafayette, Yalobusha** Calhoun County; PO Box 8; Pittsboro, MS 38951; Ph. 662.983.3122 Details: (Courthouse burned in 1922) (Clk Chan Ct has m, div, pro, ct & land rec from 1922 & land abstracts from 1852)
Carroll www.rootsweb.com/~mscarrol/	G6	23 Dec 1833	**Choctaw Cession** Carroll County; Lexington St; Carrollton, MS 38917; Ph. 662.237.9274 Details: (Co Clk has m, div, pro, ct & land rec from 1870)
Chickasaw www.rootsweb.com/~mschicka/	E9	9 Feb 1836	**Choctaw Cession, 1832** Chickasaw County; 101 N Jefferson; Houston, MS 38851-0000; Ph. 662.456.2531 Details: (Clk Cir Ct, Houston has m, div, pro & ct rec & all land rec for Co) (Clk Cir Ct, Okolona has m rec from 1877 & ct rec; Clk Chan Ct has div & pro rec from 1886)
Choctaw www.rootsweb.com/~mschocta/	G8	23 Dec 1833	**Chickasaw Cession,1832** Choctaw County; 112 Quinn St; PO Box 736; Ackerman, MS 39735-0000; Ph. 662.285.6329 Details: (Clk Cir Ct has m, div, pro, ct & land rec from 1881)
Claiborne www.rootsweb.com/~msclaib2/	K3	27 Jan 1802	**Jefferson** Claiborne County; PO Box 449; Port Gibson, MS 39150; Ph. 601.437.4992 Details: (Clk Chan Ct has m rec from 1816, div rec from 1856, pro & ct rec from 1802)
Clarke www.rootsweb.com/~msclarke/	K9	10 Dec 1812	**Washington** Clarke County; PO Box 689; Quitman, MS 39355; Ph. 662.776.2126 Details: (Clk Chan Ct has div & pro rec from 1875)
Clay www.rootsweb.com/~msclay/	F9	12 May 1871	**Chickasaw, Lowndes, Monroe, Oktibbeha** Clay County; PO Box 815; West Point, MS 39773; Ph. 662.494.3124 Details: (Formerly Colfax Co. Name changed to Clay 10 Apr 1876) (Clk Cir Ct has m & ct rec; Clk Chan Ct has div, pro & land rec from 1872)
Coahoma www.clarksdale.com/county/	D4	9 Feb 1836	**Chickasaw Cession, 1836** Coahoma County; 115 1st St; PO Box 98; Clarksdale, MS 38614; Ph. 662.624.3000 Details: (Clk Cir Ct has m & ct rec from 1848 & voter rec from 1949; Clk Chan Ct has div, pro & land rec)

County Website	Map Index	Date Created	Parent County or Territory From Which Organized Address/Details
Colfax		**12 May 1871**	**Chickasaw, Lowndes, Monroe, Oktibbeha** Details: (see Clay) Name changed to Clay 10 Apr 1876
Copiah www.rootsweb.com/~mscopiah/	L4	**21 Jan 1823**	**Hinds** Copiah County; PO Box 507; Hazlehurst, MS 39083; Ph. 601.894.3021 Details: (Clk Chan Ct has div rec from 1840, pro & land rec from 1825 & confederate veterans rec; Clk Cir Ct has m rec from 1825 & ct rec)
Covington www.rootsweb.com/~mscoving/	L7	**5 Feb 1819**	**Lawrence, Wayne** Covington County; PO Box 1679; Collins, MS 39428; Ph. 601.765.6132 Details: (Clk Chan Ct has m, div & pro rec from 1900, ct & land rec from 1860)
De Soto www.desotonet.com/	B6	**9 Feb 1836**	**Indian Lands** De Soto County; 2535 Hwy 51 S; Courthouse Sq; Hernando, MS 38632; Ph. 662.429.1317 Details: (Clk Chan Ct has div, pro & land rec)
Forrest* www.co.forrest.ms.us/	N8	**19 Apr 1906**	**Perry** Forrest County; 641 Main St; PO Box 951; Hattiesburg, MS 39401; Ph. 601.545.6014 Details: (Clk Cir Ct has m rec from 1893 & ct rec from 1906; Clk Chan Ct has div, land, pro & mil rec)
Franklin www.rootsweb.com/~msfrankl/	M3	**21 Dec 1809**	**Adams** Franklin County; PO Box 297; Meadville, MS 39653; Ph. 601.384.2330 Details: (Clk Chan Ct has ct, land & pro rec; Clk Cir Ct has m rec)
George www.rootsweb.com/~msgeorge/	O10	**16 Mar 1910**	**Greene, Jackson** George County; 355 Cox St; Lucedale, MS 39452-0000; Ph. 601.947.4801 Details: (Clk Cir Ct has m & ct rec from 1911; Clk Chan Ct has div, pro & land rec from 1911)
Greene www.rootsweb.com/~msgreene/	N10	**9 Dec 1811**	**Amite, Franklin, Wayne** Greene County; PO Box 610; Leakesville, MS 39451; Ph. 601.394.2377 Details: (Clk Chan Ct has ct, land & pro rec; Clk Cir Ct has m rec)
Grenada* www.rootsweb.com/~msgrenad/	F7	**9 May 1870**	**Carroll, Yalobusha, Choctaw, Talahatchie** Grenada County; PO Box 1208; Grenada, MS 38902; Ph. 662.226.1821 Details: (Clk Cir Ct has m, div & pro rec from 1870 & land rec from 1835)
Hancock www.rootsweb.com/~mshancoc/	Q7	**18 Dec 1812**	**Mobile District** Hancock County; 150 Main St; Bay St. Louis, MS 39520; Ph. 228.467.5404 Details: (Clk Cir Ct has m & ct rec; Clk Chan Ct has div, pro & land rec)
Harrison co.harrison.ms.us/	P8	**5 Feb 1841**	**Hancock, Jackson** Harrison County; 1801 23rd Ave; PO Box Drawer CC; Gulfport, MS 39502; Ph. 228.865.4118 Details: (Clk Cir Ct has m rec from 1841 & ct rec; Clk Chan Ct has div, pro & land rec)
Hinds www.co.hinds.ms.us/pgs/index.asp	J5	**12 Feb 1821**	**Choctaw Cession, 1820** Hinds County; PO Box 686; Jackson, MS 39205; Ph. 601.968.6237 Details: (Clk Cir Ct has m rec from 1823 & ct rec from 1930; Clk Chan Ct has div, pro & land rec)
Holmes www.rootsweb.com/~msholmes/	H6	**19 Feb 1833**	**Yazoo** Holmes County; PO Box 239; Lexington, MS 39095; Ph. 662.834.2281 Details: (Clk Chan Ct has div rec from 1894, pro & land rec from 1833 & bur rec; Clk Cir Ct has m & ct rec)
Humphreys* www.rootsweb.com/~mshumphr/	H4	**28 Mar 1918**	**Holmes, Washington, Yazoo, Sunflower** Humphreys County; PO Box 547; Belzoni, MS 39038; Ph. 662.247.1740 Details: (Clk Cir Ct has b & m rec; Clk Chan Ct has div, pro & land rec from 1918)
Issaquena www.rootsweb.com/~msissaqu/	I4	**23 Jan 1844**	**Washington** Issaquena County; PO Box 27; Mayersville, MS 39113; Ph. 662.873.2761 Details: (Clk Chan Ct has m rec from 1866, div, pro, ct & land rec from 1850)

County Website	Map Index	Date Created	Parent County or Territory From Which Organized Address/Details
Itawamba www.rootsweb.com/~msitawam/	D10	9 Feb 1836	**Chickasaw Cession, 1832** Itawamba County; 201 W Main St; PO Box 776; Fulton, MS 38843; Ph. 662.862.3421 Details: (Clk Chan Ct has m, div, pro, ct & land rec)
Jackson www.co.jackson.ms.us/	P9	18 Dec 1812	**Mobile District** Jackson County; 3109 Canty St; PO Box 998; Pascagoula, MS 39567; Ph. 228.769.3091 Details: (Clk Chan Ct has div & pro rec, justice of the peace dockets from 1875; Clk Cir Ct has m rec from 1875)
Jasper www.rootsweb.com/~msjasper/	K8	23 Dec 1833	**Choctaw Cession, 1832** Jasper County; Court St; PO Box 1047; Bay Springs, MS 39422-0000; Ph. 601.764.3368 Details: (Co Clk has div, pro & ct rec from 1906; Clk Cir Ct has m rec)
Jefferson www.rootsweb.com/~msjeffer/	L3	2 Apr 1799	**Natchez District** Jefferson County; 307 Main St; PO Box 145; Fayette, MS 39069-0000; Ph. 601.786.3021 Details: (Formerly Pickering Co. Name changed to Jefferson 11 Jan 1802) (Clk Chan Ct has m rec from 1798, div rec from 1860, pro & land rec from 1798)
Jefferson Davis www.rootsweb.com/~msjdavis/	M6	31 Mar 1906	**Covington, Lawrence** Jefferson Davis County; 1025 3rd St; PO Box 1137; Prentiss, MS 39474; Ph. 601.792.4204 Details: (Clk Chan Ct has ct & land rec; Clk Cir Ct has m & pro rec)
Jones www.edajones.com/	M8	24 Jan 1826	**Covington, Wayne** Jones County; PO Box 1468; Laurel, MS 39441; Ph. 601.428.0527 Details: (Clk Cir Ct has m rec from 1882 & ct rec from 1907; Clk Chan Ct at Laurel & Ellisville, Miss has div & land rec)
Kemper www.rootsweb.com/~mskemper/	I9	23 Dec 1833	**Choctaw Cession, 1832** Kemper County; Bell St; PO Box 188; De Kalb, MS 39328; Ph. 601.743.2560 Details: (Clk Cir Ct has m rec from 1912; Clk Chan Ct has div, pro, ct & land rec from 1912)
Lafayette www.rootsweb.com/~mslafaye/	D7	9 Feb 1836	**Chickasaw Cession** Lafayette County; Town Sq; PO Box 1240; Oxford, MS 38655; Ph. 662.234.2131 Details: (Clk Chan Ct has m, div, pro & ct rec)
Lamar* www.lamarcounty.com/	N7	19 Feb 1904	**Marion, Pearl River** Lamar County; 203 Main St; Purvis, MS 39475; Ph. 601.544.4410 Details: (Clk Cir Ct has m rec; Clk Chan Ct has div, pro & land rec from 1900's; JP has ct rec)
Lauderdale www.lauderdalecounty.org/index.htm	J9	23 Dec 1833	**Choctaw Cession** Lauderdale County; 410 Constitution Ave; PO Box 1587; Meridian, MS 39302; Ph. 601.482.9704 Details: (Clk Chan Ct has div, pro & land rec; Clk Cir Ct has m & ct rec; Co Hlth Dept has b & d rec)
Lawrence www.rootsweb.com/~mslawren/	M6	22 Dec 1814	**Marion** Lawrence County; PO Box 40; Monticello, MS 39654; Ph. 601.587.7162 Details: (Clk Cir Ct has m & ct rec; Clk Chan Ct has div, pro & land rec from 1815)
Leake www.rootsweb.com/~msleake/	I7	23 Dec 1833	**Choctaw Cession** Leake County; Court Sq; PO Box 72; Carthage, MS 39051; Ph. 601.267.7371 Details: (Clk Chan Ct has m rec, div rec from 1871, ct rec, land rec from 1833, pro rec from 1840 & mil dis rec from 1918)
Lee www.rootsweb.com/~mslee/	D9	26 Oct 1866	**Itawamba, Pontotoc** Lee County; 200 W Jefferson St; PO Box 7127; Tupelo, MS 38802; Ph. 662.841.9100 Details: (Clk Chan Ct has div, pro & land rec; Clk Cir Ct has m rec; Justice Ct has ct rec)

County Website	Map Index	Date Created	Parent County or Territory From Which Organized Address/Details
Leflore www.rootsweb.com/~msleflor/	F5	15 Mar 1871	**Carroll, Sunflower, Tallahatchie** Leflore County; 317 W Market St; PO Box 250; Greenwood, MS 38935; Ph. 662.453.6203 Details: (Clk Cir Ct has m & ct rec; Clk Chan Ct has div & pro rec from 1871 & land rec from 1834)
Lincoln www.rootsweb.com/~mslincol/	M5	7 Apr 1870	**Franklin, Lawrence, Copiah, Pike, Amite** Lincoln County; 300 S 2nd St; PO Box 555; Brookhaven, MS 39601-3321; Ph. 601.835.3479 Details: (Clk Chan Ct has div, pro & ct rec from 1893; Clk Dis Ct has m rec from 1893)
Lowndes www.rootsweb.com/~mslownde/	G10	30 Jan 1830	**Monroe** Lowndes County; PO Box 684; Columbus, MS 39703; Ph. 662.329.5805 Details: (Dept of Archives & Hist has m, div, pro, ct & land rec 1830-1900 & Bible rec)
Madison www.rootsweb.com/~msmadiso/	I6	29 Jan 1828	**Yazoo** Madison County; PO Box 404; Canton, MS 39046; Ph. 601.859.1177 Details: (Clk Chan Ct has m, div, pro, ct & land rec from 1828)
Marion www.rootsweb.com/~msmarion/	N6	9 Dec 1811	**Amite, Wayne, Franklin** Marion County; 250 Broad St Ste 2; Columbia, MS 39429; Ph. 601.736.2691 Details: (Clk Chan Ct has m, div, pro, ct & land rec)
Marshall www.rootsweb.com/~msmarsha/	C7	9 Feb 1836	**Chickasaw Cession, 1832** Marshall County; PO Box 219; Holly Springs, MS 38635; Ph. 662.252.4431 Details: (Clk Chan Ct has div, pro & land rec from 1836)
Monroe www.rootsweb.com/~msmonroe/ index.htm	E10	9 Feb 1821	**Chickasaw Cession, 1821** Monroe County; PO Box 578; Aberdeen, MS 39730; Ph. 662.369.8143 Details: (Clk Cir Ct has m & ct rec; Clk Chan Ct has div rec, pro & land rec from 1821)
Montgomery www.rootsweb.com/~msmontgo/	G7	13 May 1871	**Carroll, Choctaw** Montgomery County; PO Box 71; Winona, MS 38967; Ph. 662.283.2333 Details: (Clk Chan Ct has div, pro, ct & land rec from 1871; Clk Cir Ct has m rec)
Neshoba www.neshoba.org/	I8	23 Dec 1833	**Chocktaw Cession, 1830** Neshoba County; 401 E Beacon St Ste 107; Philadelphia, MS 39350; Ph. 601.656.3581 Details: (Clk Chan Ct has div & pro rec from 1890; Clk Cir Ct has m rec from 1912)
Newton www.rootsweb.com/~msnewton/	J8	25 Feb 1836	**Neshoba** Newton County; PO Box 68; Decatur, MS 39327; Ph. 601.635.2367 Details: (Clk Chan Ct has div, pro, ct & land rec from 1876; Clk Cir Ct has m rec)
Noxubee www.rootsweb.com/~msnoxube/	H9	23 Dec 1833	**Choctaw Cession, 1830** Noxubee County; PO Box 147; Macon, MS 39341; Ph. 662.726.4243 Details: (Clk Cir Ct has m & ct rec from 1834; Clk Chan Ct has div, pro & land rec from 1834)
Oktibbeha www.eda.co.oktibbeha.ms.us/	G9	23 Dec 1833	**Choctaw Cession, 1830** Oktibbeha County; 101 E Main St; Starkville, MS 39759; Ph. 662.323.5834 Details: (Clk Chan Ct has div, pro & ct rec from 1880 & land rec from 1834; Clk Cir Ct has m rec)
Panola www.geocities.com/Heartland/Plains/ 4399/msgenweb/panola.html	D6	9 Feb 1836	**Chickasaw Cession, 1832** Panola County; 151 Public Sq; Batesville, MS 38606-2220; Ph. 601.563.6205 Details: (Clk Chan Ct has div & pro rec from 1836; Clk Cir Ct has m rec from 1885 & ct rec from 1836)
Pearl River* www.rootsweb.com/~mspearlr/	O7	22 Feb 1890	**Hancock, Marion** Pearl River County; PO Box 431; Poplarville, MS 39470; Ph. 601.795.2237 Details: (Clk Chan Ct has div, pro & ct rec from 1890; Clk Cir Ct has m rec)

County Website	Map Index	Date Created	Parent County or Territory From Which Organized Address/Details
Perry www.usgw.org/ms/perry/	**N9**	**3 Feb 1820**	**Greene** Perry County; PO Box 198; New Augusta, MS 39462; Ph. 601.964.8398 Details: (Clk Chan Ct has div, pro, ct & land rec from 1878; Clk Cir Ct has m rec from 1877)
Pickering		**2 Apr 1799**	**Natchez District** Details: (see Jefferson) Name changed to Jefferson 11 Jan 1802
Pike www.pikeinfo.com/	**N5**	**9 Dec 1815**	**Marion** Pike County; PO Box 309; Magnolia, MS 39652; Ph. 601.783.3362 Details: (Clk Chan Ct has div, pro, ct & land rec from 1882; Clk Cir Ct has m rec)
Pontotoc www.geocities.com/dc031888/msgenweb/ pontotoc/pontotoc.htm	**D8**	**9 Feb 1836**	**Chickasaw Cession, 1832** Pontotoc County; PO Box 209; Pontotoc, MS 38863-0209; Ph. 662.489.3900 Details: (Clk Cir Ct has m rec; Clk Chan Ct has pro, ct & div rec & land rec from 1836)
Prentiss www.rootsweb.com/~msprenti/	**C10**	**15 Apr 1870**	**Tishomingo** Prentiss County; PO Box 477; Booneville, MS 38829-0477; Ph. 662.728.8151 Details: (Clk Chan Ct has div, pro & ct rec from 1870 & land rec from 1836; Clk Cir Ct has m rec)
Quitman www.geocities.com/Heartland/Plains/ 4399/msgenweb/quitman.html	**D5**	**1 Feb 1877**	**Panola, Coahoma, Tunica, Tallahatchie** Quitman County; 230 Chestnut St; PO Box 100; Marks, MS 38646; Ph. 662.326.2661 Details: (Clk Chan Ct has div & pro rec from 1877; Clk Cir Ct has m & ct rec)
Rankin www.rootsweb.com/~msrankin/	**K6**	**4 Feb 1828**	**Hinds** Rankin County; 211 E Government St; Brandon, MS 39042; Ph. 601.825.1469 Details: (Clk Chan Ct has div, pro & land rec from 1829)
Scott www.rootsweb.com/~msscott/	**J7**	**23 Dec 1833**	**Choctaw Cession, 1832** Scott County; PO Box 630; Forest, MS 39074; Ph. 601.469.1922 Details: (Clk Chan Ct has div & ct rec from 1900, pro & land rec from 1835, old church & cem rec; Clk Cir Ct has m rec)
Sharkey www.rootsweb.com/~mssharke/	**H4**	**29 Mar 1876**	**Warren, Washington, Issaquena** Sharkey County; County Courthouse; PO Box 218; Rolling Fork, MS 39159-0000; Ph. 662.873.2755 Details: (Clk Chan Ct has ct, pro & land rec from 1876; Clk Cir Ct has m rec from 1876)
Simpson www.rootsweb.com/~mssimpso/	**L6**	**23 Jan 1824**	**Choctaw Cession, 1820** Simpson County; 109 W Pine Ave; PO Box 367; Mendenhall, MS 39114; Ph. 601.847.2626 Details: (Clk Cir Ct has m & ct rec; Clk Chan Ct has div rec from 1880, some pro & land rec)
Smith www.rootsweb.com/~mssmith/	**K7**	**23 Dec 1833**	**Choctaw Cession, 1820** Smith County; Main St; PO Box 39; Raleigh, MS 39153; Ph. 601.782.9811 Details: (Clk Cir Ct has m rec from 1912 & ct rec; Clk Chan Ct has div, pro, land & mil rec from 1892)
Stone www.stonecounty.com/	**O8**	**3 Apr 1916**	**Harrison** Stone County; PO Box 7; Wiggins, MS 39577; Ph. 601.928.5266 Details: (Clk Chan Ct has div, pro, land & mil dis rec from 1916; Clk Cir Ct has m & ct rec)
Sumner		**6 Apr 1874**	**Montgomery, Chickasaw, Choctaw, Okitbbeha** Details: (see Webster) Name changed to Webster 30 Jan 1882
Sunflower www.rootsweb.com/~mssunflo/	**F4**	**15 Feb 1844**	**Bolivar, Washington** Sunflower County; 200 Main St; PO Box 988; Indianola, MS 38751-0000; Ph. 662.887.4703 Details: (Clk Chan Ct has m, div, pro, ct & land rec from 1871)

County Website	Map Index	Date Created	Parent County or Territory From Which Organized / Address/Details
Tallahatchie www.rootsweb.com/~mstallah/	E6	23 Dec 1833	**Choctaw Cession, 1820** Tallahatchie County; PO Box Drawer 350; Charleston, MS 38921; Ph. 662.647.5551 Details: (Clk Cir Ct has m rec from 1909; Clk Chan Ct has div & pro rec from 1909 & land rec from 1858)
Tate www.rootsweb.com/~mstate/	B6	15 Apr 1873	**Marshall, Tunica, DeSoto** Tate County; 201 Ward St; Senatobia, MS 38668; Ph. 662.562.5661 Details: (Clk Cir Ct has m rec from 1873; Clk Chan Ct has div, pro, ct & land rec from 1873)
Tippah* www.rootsweb.com/~mstippah/	B9	9 Feb 1836	**Chickasaw Cession, 1832** Tippah County; PO Box 99; Ripley, MS 38663; Ph. 662.837.7374 Details: (Clk Chan Ct or Clk Cir Ct has m, div, pro & ct rec from 1856)
Tishomingo www.freedom2000net.com/userpages/ genealogy/Tishom/	B10	9 Feb 1836	**Chickasaw Cession, 1832** Tishomingo County; 1008 Battleground Dr; Iuka, MS 38852-1020; Ph. 662.423.7010 Details: (Clk Chan Ct has div, pro, ct & land rec; Clk Cir Ct has m rec)
Tunica* www.rootsweb.com/~mstunica/	C5	9 Feb 1836	**Chickasaw Cession, 1832** Tunica County; PO Box 217; Tunica, MS 38676; Ph. 662.363.2451 Details: (Clk Chan Ct has div, pro, ct & land rec; Clk Cir Ct has m rec)
Union www.rootsweb.com/~msunion/	C9	7 Jul 1870	**Pontotoc, Tippah** Union County; 109 Main St E; PO Box 847; New Albany, MS 38652-0000; Ph. 662.534.1900 Details: (Clk Chan Ct has div, pro & ct rec; Clk Cir Ct has m rec)
Walthall* www.iocc.com/~swright/walthall/ waltmain.html	N6	16 Mar 1910	**Marion, Pike** Walthall County; PO Box 351; Tylertown, MS 39667; Ph. 601.876.3553 Details: (Clk Cir Ct has m rec from 1914; Clk Chan Ct has div, pro, ct & land rec from 1914)
Warren www.rootsweb.com/~mswarren/	J4	22 Dec 1809	**Natchez District** Warren County; PO Box 351; Vicksburg, MS 39181-0351; Ph. 601.636.4415 Details: (Clk Chan Ct has div, pro, ct & land rec; Clk Cir Ct has m rec)
Washington www.usgw.org/ms/washington/	G4	29 Jan 1827	**Warren, Yazoo** Washington County; PO Box 309; Greenville, MS 38701; Ph. 662.332.1595 Details: (Clk Cir Ct has m rec from 1858 & ct rec from 1890; Clk Chan Ct has div rec from 1856, pro & land rec from 1831)
Washington, old		4 Jun 1800	**Unorganized Territory** Details: (now in Alabama)
Wayne www.wayneco.com/	M9	21 Dec 1809	**Washington, old** Wayne County; 609 Azalea Dr; Waynesboro, MS 39367-0000; Ph. 601.735.2873 Details: (Clk Chan Ct has m, bur, div, pro, ct & land rec)
Webster www.rootsweb.com/~mswebst2/	F8	6 Apr 1874	**Montgomery, Chickasaw, Choctaw, Oktibbeha** Webster County; Hwy 9 N; PO Box 398; Walthall, MS 39771; Ph. 662.258.4131 Details: (Formerly Sumner Co. Name changed to Webster 30 Jan 1882) (Clk Cir Ct has m & ct rec; Clk Chan Ct has div, pro & land rec from 1800's)
Wilkinson www.rootsweb.com/~mswilkin/	N2	30 Jan 1802	**Adams** Wilkinson County; PO Box 516; Woodville, MS 39669-0516; Ph. 601.888.4381 Details: (Clk Chan Ct has m, div, pro, ct & land rec)
Winston www.rootsweb.com/~mswinsto/	H8	23 Dec 1833	**Choctaw Cession, 1830** Winston County; County Courthouse; PO Box Drawer 69; Louisville, MS 39339; Ph. 662.773.3631 Details: (Clk Chan Ct has ct, pro & land rec from 1834; Clk Cir Ct has m rec)
Yalobusha www.rootsweb.com/~msyalobu/	E7	23 Dec 1833	**Choctaw Cession, 1830** Yalobusha County; PO Box 664; Water Valley, MS 38965-0664; Ph. 662.473.2091 Details: (Clk Chan Ct, Water Valley, Miss has div, pro, ct & land rec; Clk Cir Ct, Coffeyville, Miss has m rec; Clk Chan Ct has div, pro, ct & land rec)

County Website	Map Index	Date Created	Parent County or Territory From Which Organized Address/Details
Yazoo genealogyamerica.com/msyazoo/	**15**	**21 Jan 1823**	**Hinds** Yazoo County; PO Box 68; Yazoo City, MS 39194; Ph. 601.746.2213 Details: (Clk Chan Ct has m rec from 1845, div, pro, ct & land rec from 1823 & newspapers)

Notes

Notes

MISSOURI

CAPITAL: JEFFERSON CITY – TERRITORY 1812 – STATE 1821 (24TH)

In 1541, De Soto explored Missouri. The French explorers Marquette and Joliet followed in 1673 and discovered the Missouri River. Robert Cavelier, Sieur de la Salle, claimed the entire Mississippi River Valley for France in 1682. In 1700, the French made the first settlement near the Des Peres River, south of St. Louis. That settlement lasted for only a short time. The first permanent settlement was Ste. Genevieve, which French lead miners established in 1735. France ceded the area to Spain in 1763. Unaware of the cession, the French founded St. Louis the following year.

The first American settlement was in 1787 in Ste. Genevieve County. After 1795, Americans–mainly from Kentucky, Tennessee, Virginia, and the Carolinas–came for the free land Spain was offering. In 1800, Spain returned the region to France. Four years later, the majority of the 10,000 residents were American. The Louisiana Purchase in 1803 made Missouri part of the United States. Two years later Missouri became part of the Territory of Louisiana. Missouri became a territory in 1812. Indian raids continued until about 1815, when treaties were signed and settlement increased. When Missouri became a state in 1821, there were about 57,000 settlers. European immigrants came into the state from Ireland, England, Poland, Switzerland, Bohemia, and Italy to mix with the Americans and descendants of the early French settlers. Members of The Church of Jesus Christ of Latter-day Saints, Mormons, settled in western Missouri in 1831, but were expulsed in 1839. The Platte Purchase of 1837 added six northwestern counties to the state. Missouri was the start of many migrations to the West as both the Santa Fe and Oregon Trails began at Independence, Missouri. Even with all these migrations, Missouri was the fifth most populous state at the end of the Civil War.

In 1861, the legislature considered secession but voted against it. After the start of the Civil War, the governor repudiated Lincoln's call for troops and called up the state militia to fight for the Confederacy. Federal troops defeated the militia, forcing the governor and legislature to flee to the south. A provisional government was installed until the state government was reorganized in 1864. An estimated 40,000 men fought for the Confederacy, while about 109,000 fought for the Union. Numerous battles were fought in the state, which became one of the important battlegrounds of the war.

Look for vital records in the following locations:

- **Birth and death records:** County clerks were required to register births and deaths from 1883 to 1893. Records still extant can be obtained from the county clerk or the Missouri State Archives in Jefferson City. State registration of births and deaths began in 1863, but did not reach full compliance until 1911. The records after 1910 can be obtained from the Bureau of Vital Records.

- **Marriage and divorce records:** Some marriages from 1825 to the present may be obtained at the office of the Recorder of Deeds in each county. Some of the earliest land claims and grants have been published. Divorce proceedings were filed with a court of common pleas, a circuit court, or the state legislature. Most can be obtained from the circuit court clerk. Unfortunately, many of the county courthouses in Missouri, along with their records, have been burned. The State Historical Society of Missouri, in Columbia, has other records that might be of help to researchers.

- **Land records:** Records of the local land offices are in the Missouri State Archives. Tract book, plat maps, and land patents are at the BLM Eastern States Office in Alexandria, Virginia.

- **Census records:** A few Spanish censuses were taken as early as 1772. Portions of Missouri were included in the 1810 census of Louisiana Territory. Missouri Territory took censuses in 1814, 1817,

Genealogy Friends of the Library; PO Box 314; Neosho, Missouri 64850

Graham Historical Society; 417 S. Walnut; Marysville, Missouri 64468

Grundy County Genealogical Society; PO Box 223; Trenton, Missouri 64683; <www.rootsweb.com/~mogrundy/gcgen.html>

Harrison County Genealogical Society; 2243 Central St.; Bethany, Missouri 64424-1335

Heart of America Genealogical Society; c/o Public Library; 311 E. 12th St.; Kansas City, Missouri 64106

Historical Society of Maries County, Missouri; PO Box 289; Vienna, Missouri 65592

Howard County Genealogical Society; 201 S. Main; Fayette, Missouri 65248

Hubbell Family Historical Society; 2051 E. McDaniel St.; PO Box 3813 GS; Springfield, Missouri 65808-3813

Iron County Genealogy Society; PO Box 343; Arcadia, Missouri 63621; <www.angelfire.com/mo3/iron_co_gen/genealogy_society.html>

Jackson County Genealogical Society; Box 2145; Independence, Missouri 64055

Jackson County Historical Society; 129 W. Lexington; Independence, Missouri 64050;

Jefferson County Historical Society; c/o De Soto Public Library; 712 So. Main; De Soto, Missouri 63020-2401; <www.rootsweb.com/~mojeffer/jchs/>

Jefferson County Missouri Genealogical Society; PO Box 1342; High Ridge, Missouri 63049; <www.rootsweb.com/~mojcgs/index.html>

Jewish Genealogical Society of St. Louis; United Hebrew Congregation; 13788 Conway Rd; St. Louis, Missouri 63141; <www.jewishgen.org/jgs.StLouis/>

Joplin Genealogical Society; 300 South Main; Joplin, Missouri 64801

Kansas City Public Library, Heart of America Genealogical Society; 311 East 12th Street; Kansas City, Missouri 64106-2454; 816.221.2685; Fax 816.421.7484

Kimmswick Historical Society; PO Box 41; Kimmswick, Missouri 63053

Laclede County Genealogical Society; PO 350; Lebanon, Missouri 65536

Landon Cheek, Afro-American Historical and Genealogical Society; PO Box 23804-0804; St. Louis, Missouri 63121

Lawrence County Historical Society; PO Box 406; Mt. Vernon, Missouri 65712

Lewis County Historical Society, Inc.; 614 Clark St.; Canton, Missouri 63435

Lincoln County, Missouri Genealogical Society; PO Box 192; Hawk Point, Missouri 63349

Linn County Genealogical Researchers; 708 McGowan; Brookfield, Missouri 64628

Livingston County Genealogical Society; 450 Locust St.; Chillicothe, Missouri 64601

Magic Afro-American Historical & Genealogical Society; 3700 Blue Pkwy.; Kansas City, Missouri 64130

Mercer County Genealogical Society; Princeton, Missouri 64673

Mid-Continent Public Library; 15616 East Highway 24; Independence, Missouri 64050; 816.836.5200; Fax 816.521.7253

Mid-Missouri Genealogical Society, Inc.; PO Box 715; Jefferson, Missouri 65102

Mine Au Breton Historical Society; Rt. 1, Box 3154; Potosi, Missouri 63664; <www.rootsweb.com/~mowashin/mabhs.html>

Mississippi County Genealogical Society; PO Box 5; Charleston, Missouri 63834

Missouri Baptist Historical Commission, William Jewell College; 500 College Hill; Liberty, Missouri 64068; 816.781.7700 Ext.5468; Fax 816.415.5027

Missouri Historical Society Library and Research Center, Jefferson Memorial Building; 255 So. Skinker Blvd.; PO Box 11940; St. Louis, Missouri 63112-0040; 314.746.4599; Fax 314.746.4548

Missouri State Archives; 600 West Main St.; Jefferson City, Missouri 65102; 314.751.3280; Fax 573.526.7333; <mosl.sos.state.mo.us/rec.man/arch.html>

Missouri State Genealogical Association; PO Box 833; Columbia, Missouri 65205-0833; 816.747.9330;

Missouri Territorial Pioneers; 3929 Milton Dr.; Independence, Missouri 64055

Moniteau County, Missouri Historical Society; California, Missouri 65018

Montgomery County Genealogical Society; 112 West Second Street; Montgomery City, Missouri 63361; <www.ktis.net/~nllee/mcgs/index.html>

Morgan County, Missouri Historical Society; PO Box 177; Versailles, Missouri 65084

National Archives-Central Plains Region (Kansas City); 2312 East Bannister Road; Kansas City, Missouri 64131; 816.926.6934; Fax 816.926.6235

Nodaway County Genealogical Society; PO Box 214; Maryville, Missouri 64468

Northeast Missouri Genealogical Society; 614 Clark St.; Canton, Missouri 63435

Northland Genealogical Society; PO Box 14121; Parkville, Missouri 64152; <homepages.rootsweb.com/~kcngs/>

Northwest Missouri Genealogical Society; PO Box 382; St. Joseph, Missouri 64502; <www.rootsweb.com/~monwmgs/index.htm>

Office of the Adjutant General; 1717 Industrial Drive; Jefferson City, Missouri 65101

Old Mines Area Historical Society; Rt. 1, Box 300Z, Cadet; Old Mines, Missouri 63630

Oregon County Genealogical Society; Courthouse; Alton, Missouri 65606

Osage County, Missouri Historical Society; 402 E. Main St.; PO Box 402; Linn, Missouri 65051

Ozark County Genealogical and Historical Society; HCR 2 Box 88; Gainesville, Missouri 65655

Ozark Mountain Chapter, SAR; 1910 N. Lone Pine Ave.; Springfield, Missouri 65803-5117; 417.883.2498; <www.rootsweb.com/~moomcsam/>

Ozarks Genealogical Society; PO Box 3945; Springfield, Missouri 65808-3945; <www.rootsweb.com/~ozarksgs/>

Perry County Historical Society; PO Box 97; Perryville, Missouri 63775

Phelps County Genealogical Society; Box 571; Rolla, Missouri 65402-0571; <www.rollanet.org/~pcgs/>

Phelps County Historical Society; PO Box 1535; Rolla, Missouri 65402-1535; <www.umr.edu/~whmcinfo/pchs/>

Pike County Genealogical Society; PO Box 313; Bowling Green, Missouri 63334

Platte County, Missouri Genealogical Society; PO Box 103; Platte City, Missouri 64079

Polk County Genealogical Society; PO Box 632; Bolivar, Missouri 65613-0632; <www.rootsweb.com/~mopolkgs/>

Randolph County Historical Society; PO Box 116; Moberly, Missouri 65270

Ray County Genealogical Association; 901 W. Royle St.; Richmond, Missouri 64085-1545; <www.rootsweb.org/~morcga/>

Ray County Historical Society; Box 2; Richmond, Missouri 64085

Reynolds County, Missouri Genealogical and Historical Society; PO Box 281; Ellington, Missouri 63638

Ripley County Historical and Genealogical Society; 101 Washington St.; Doniphan, Missouri 63935

Scotland County Historical Society; c/o Downing House &Boyer House Museums; 311 S. Main; Memphis, Missouri 63555

Scott County Historical & Genealogy Society; PO Box 151; Benton, Missouri 63736;

South Vernon Genealogical Society; R.2, Box 280; Sheldon, Missouri 64784

South-Central Missouri Genealogical Society; 1043 W. 5th St.; West Plains, Missouri 65775-2147

Southern Baptist Historical Library and Archives; 901 Commerce St., Suite 400; Nashville, Tennessee 37203-3630; 615.244.0344; Fax 615.782.4821

Spirit of St. Louis Chapter, SAR; 478 Manorcrest; Ballwin, Missouri 63011-3431; 636.227.8883 ;

St. Charles County Genealogical Society; PO Box 715; St. Charles, Missouri 63301

St. Louis Genealogical Society; PO Box 43010; St. Louis, Missouri 63143-0010; 314-647.8548; <www.rootsweb.com/~mostlogs/STINDEX.HTM>

St. Louis Public Library, History and Genealogy Department; 1301 Olive Street; St. Louis, Missouri 63103-2389; 314.241.2288; Fax 314.539.0393

State Historical Society of Missouri; 1020 Lowry Street; Columbia, Missouri 65201-7298; 573.884.4950; <www.system.missouri.edu/shs/>

Stone County Historical Society; PO Box 63; Galena, Missouri 65656

Texas County, Missouri Genealogical & Historical Society; Box 12; Houston, Missouri 65483

Thrailkill Genealogical Society; 2018 Gentry St., North; Kansas City, Missouri 64116

Tri-County Genealogical Society; PO Box B; Nevada, Missouri 64772

Union Cemetery Historical Society; 2727 Main St., Suite 120; Kansas City, Missouri 64108

United Methodist Archives, Central Methodist College Library; 411 Central Methodist Square; Fayette, Missouri 65248; 816.248.3391 Ext. 292; Fax 816.248.3045

Vernon County Historical Society; 231 N. Main St.; Nevada, Missouri 64772;

Warren County Historical Society; PO Box 12; Warrenton, Missouri 63383

Webb City Area Genealogical Society; 101 South Liberty St.; Webb City, Missouri 64870

West Central Missouri Genealogical Society; 705 Broad St.; Warrensburg, Missouri 64093

Westport Historical Society; 4000 Baltimore; Kansas City, Missouri 64111;

White River Valley Historical Society; Box 565; Point Lookout, Missouri 65726

Wright County Historical Society; PO Box 66; Hartville, Missouri 65667

Bibliography and Record Sources

General Sources

A Guide to County Records on Microfilm. Jefferson City, Missouri: Missouri State Archives, 1990.

A Reminiscent History of the Ozark Region: Comprising a Brief Descriptive History of Each County and Numerous Biographical Sketches of Prominent Citizens of Each County. Easley, South Carolina: Southern Historical Press, 1978.

Bibliography of the Ozarks Books. Salt Lake City: Filmed by the Genealogical Society of Utah, 1977.

Bishop, Beverly D., and Janice L. Fox. *A List of Manuscript Collections in the Archives of the Missouri Historical Society*. St. Louis: Missouri Historical Society, 1982.

Blattner, Teresa. *People of Color: Black Genealogical Records And Abstracts From Missouri Sources*. Bowie, Maryland: Heritage Books, 1998.

Bradley, James LeGrand. *Zion's Camp 1834: Prelude to the Civil War*. Logan, Utah: J.L. Bradley, 1990.

Bryan, William S., and Robert Rose. *A History of the Pioneer Families of Missouri, with Numerous Sketches, Anecdotes, Adventures, Etc. Relating to the Early Days in Missouri. Also the Lives of Daniel Boone and the Celebrated Indian Chief Black Hawk*. (1876, 1935, 1992) Reprint. Baltimore: Clearfield Co., 1996.

Burgess, Roy. *Early Missourians and Kin. A Genealogical Compilation of Inter-related Early Missouri Settlers, Their Ancestors, Descendants, and other Kin*. (1984) Reprint. Bowie, Maryland: Heritage Books, 1992.

Campbell, Robert Allen. *Campbell's Gazetteer of Missouri: From Articles Contributed by Prominent Gentlemen in Each County of the State, and Information Collected and Collated From Official and Other Authentic Sources, by a Corps of Experienced Canvassers, Under the Personal Supervision of the Editor.* Rev. ed. St. Louis: Campbell, 1875.

Catholic Church. Archdiocese of Kansas City and St. Joseph (Missouri). *Parish Register Transcripts, Ca. 1830-1900.* Microreproduction of typescript. (Salt Lake City: Filmed by the Genealogical Society of Utah, [19-?]). 13 microfilm.

Church of Jesus Christ of Latter-day Saints. Historical Department. *Index to Journal History.* (Salt Lake City: Filmed by the Historical Dept., 1973). 58 microfilm.

Conrad, Howard Louis. *Encyclopedia of the History of Missouri, a Compendium of History and Biography for Ready Reference.* New York: Southern History Co., 1901.

Davis, Walter Bickford. *An Illustrated History of Missouri: Comprising Its Early Records, and Civil, Political, and Military History From the First Exploration to the Present Time, Including Biographical Sketches of Prominent Citizens.* St. Louis: A. Hall, 1876.

Directory of Local Historical, Museum and Genealogical Agencies in Missouri. Rev. ed. 1996-97. Columbia, Missouri: State Historical Society, 1996-97.

Douglass, Robert Sidney. *Southeast Missouri, A Narrative Account of its Historical Progress, its People and its Principal Interests.* 2 Vols. Chicago: Lewis Pub. Co., 1912.

Duncan, R. S. *A History of the Baptists in Missouri, Embracing an Account of the Organization and Growth of Baptist Churches And Associations.* St. Louis: Scammell, 1882.

Dyer, Alvin R. *The Refiner's Fire: The Significance of Events Transpiring in Missouri.* Salt Lake City: Deseret Book, 1968.

Ellsberry, Elizabeth Prather. *Bible Records of Missouri.* 8 vols. in 3. Chillicothe, Missouri: E. P. Ellsberry, [1963-65].

Gambrill, George. *Genealogical Material and Local Histories in the St. Louis Public Library.* Rev. ed. St. Louis: St. Louis Public Library, 1965.

Gilbert, Joan. *The Trail of Tears Across Missouri.* Columbia, Missouri: University of Missouri Press, 1996.

Goodspeed Publishing Co. *A Reminiscent History of the Ozark Region of Arkansas and Missouri.* (1894) Reprint. Greenville, South Carolina: Southern Historical Press, 1988.

Goodspeed Publishing Co. *General History of Missouri from Earliest Times to the Present.* (1888) Reprint. Greenville, South Carolina: Southern Historical Press, 1992.

Goodspeed Publishing Co., *The History of Southeast Missouri, Embracing an Historical Account of the Counties of St. Genevieve, St. Francois, Perry, Cape Giardeau, Bollinger, Madison, New Madrid, Pemiscot, Dunklin, Scott, Mississippi, Stoddard, Butler, Wayne, and Iron.* (1888) Reprint. Greenville, South Carolina: Southern Historical Press, 1990.

Gray, Marcus Lemon. *1806-1906, The Centennial Volume of Missouri Methodism, Methodist Episcopal Church.* South City, Missouri: Press of Burd & Fletcher, [c1907].

Haley, T. P. *Historical and Biographical Sketches of the Early Churches and Pioneer Preachers of the Christian Church in Missouri.* Kansas City: J.H. Smart, 1888.

Havig, Alan R. *A Centennial History of the State Historical Society of Missouri, 1898-1998.* Columbia, Missouri: University of Missouri Press, 1998.

Hehir, Donald. *Missouri Family Histories and Genealogies, A Bibliography.* Bowie, Maryland: Heritage Books, 1996.

Historical Records Survey (Missouri). *Guide to Public Vital Statistics Records in Missouri.* St. Louis: Historical Records Survey, 1941.

Historical Records Survey (Missouri). *The Organization Of Missouri Counties.* St. Louis: Historical Records Survey, 1941.

History of Franklin, Jefferson, Washington, Crawford & Gasconade Counties, Missouri: From the Earliest Time to the Present, Together With Sundry Personal Business and Professional Sketches and Numerous Family Records, Besides a Valuable Fund of [I.E. Fund Of] Notes, Original Observations, Etc., Etc. Giradeau, Missouri: Ramfre, 1958.

History of Southeast Missouri: Embracing an Historical Account of the Counties of Ste. Genevieve, St. Francois, Perry, Cape Girardeau, Bollinger, Madison, New Madrid, Pemiscot, Dunklin, Scott, Mississippi, Stoddard, Butler, Wayne and Iron, Including a Department Devoted To The Preservation Of Personal, Professional And Private Records. Chicago: Goodspeed Pub., 1888.

Hodges, Nadine, and Audrey L. Woodruff. *Missouri Pioneers: County and Genealogical Records.* 30 vols. Independence: Woodruff, 1967-76.

Houck, Louis. *A History of Missouri from the Earliest Explorations and Settlements until the Admission of the State into the Union.* 3 vols. Chicago: R. R. Donnelley, 1908.

Houck, Louis. *The Spanish Regime in Missouri: A Collection of Papers and Documents Relating to Upper Louisiana Principally Within the Present Limits of Missouri During the Dominion of Spain, From the Archives of the Indies at Seville....* 2 vols. Chicago: R.R. Donnelley & Sons, 1909.

Ingmire, Frances T. *Pioneer Kentuckians with Missouri Cousins.* 2 vols. Signal Mountain, Tennessee: Mountain Press, n.d..

Luebbering, Patsy. *Publications Relating to Missouri Counties.* Jefferson City, Missouri: Records Management and Archives Service, 1980.

McReynolds, Edwin C. *Missouri, a History of the Crossroads State.* Norman, Okla.: University of Oklahoma Press, 1962.

Midwest Pioneers, 1600s-1800s. [S.l.]: Brøderbund, 1999. CD-ROM.

Missouri Newspapers on Microfilm at the State Historical Society of Missouri. Columbia, Missouri: State Historical Society, n.d..

Missouri Research Outline. Series US-States, no. 26. Salt Lake City: Family History Library, 1988.

Parkin, Robert E. *Guide to Tracing Your Family Tree in Missouri.* St. Louis: Genealogical Research and Productions, 1979.

Patrick, Michael D. *Orphan Trains to Missouri.* Columbia, Missouri: University of Missouri Press, 1997.

Seaton, Richard A. *History of the United Methodist Churches of Missouri.* Missouri: Missouri Methodist Historical Society, 1984.

Selby, Paul O. *A Bibliography of Missouri County Histories and Atlases.* 2d ed. Kirksville, Missouri: Northeast Missouri State Teachers College, 1966.

Sources of Genealogical Help in Missouri. Burbank, California: Southern California Genealogical Society, n.d.

State Historical Society of Missouri. *Directory of Local Historical, Museum and Genealogical Agencies in Missouri.* Columbia, Missouri: State Historical Society, 1994.

State Historical Society of Missouri. *Historic Missouri: A Pictorial Narrative.* Columbia, Missouri: State Historical Society, 1988.

State Historical Society of Missouri. *Missouri Newspapers on Microfilm at the State Historical Society.* Columbia, Missouri: State Historical Society, 1993.

Steele, Edward E. *A Guide to Genealogical Research in St. Louis.* St. Louis: St. Louis Genealogical Society, 1992.

Stevens, Walter Barlow. *Missouri, The Center State, 1821-1915.* 2 vols. Chicago: S.J. Clarke, 1915.

The United States Biographical Dictionary and Portrait Gallery of Eminent and Self-Made Men: Missouri Volume. New York: United States Biographical Pub. Co., 1878.

Tucker, Frank C. *The Methodist Church in Missouri: 1798-1939, A Brief History.* [S.l.]: F.C. Tucker, 1966.

United States. Bureau of Marine Inspection and Navigation (Missouri). *Officers License and Related Records, 1905-1942.* Microfilm of originals in the National Archives Branch in Kansas City, Missouri. (Salt Lake City: Filmed by the Genealogical Society of Utah, 1991). 25 microfilm.

Van Nada, M. L. *The Book of Missourians: The Achievements and Personnel of Notable Living Men and Women of Missouri in the Opening Decade of the Twentieth Century.*: Chicago: T.J. Steele, 1906.

Who's What and Why in Missouri: Library of American Lives; A Reference Edition Recording the Biographies of Contemporary Leaders in Missouri With Special Emphasis on Their Achievements in Making the "Show Me" State One osf America's Greatest. Hopkinsville, Kentucky: Historical Record Association, 1959.

Wilcox, Pearl. *Saints of the Reorganization in Missouri.* [S.l.: s.n.], 1974.

Williams, Walter, and Floyd Calvin Shoemaker. *Missouri, Mother of the West.* 5 vols. Chicago: American Historical Society, 1930.

Woodruff, Mrs. Howard W. *Missouri Miscellany: Statewide Missouri Genealogical Records.* 16 vols. Independence: Woodruff, 1976-84.

Atlases, Maps and Gazetteers

Beck, Lewis Caleb. *Gazetteer of the States of Illinois and Missouri.* 1823. Reprint. New York: Arno Press, 1975.

Campbell, Robert Allen *Gazetteer of Missouri: From Articles Contributed by Prominent Gentlemen in Each County of the State, and Information Collected and Collated From Official and Other Authentic Sources, by a Corps Of Experienced Canvassers, Under the Personal Supervision of the Editor:* Rev. ed. St. Louis: Campbell, 1875.

Campbell, Robert Allen. *Campbell's New Atlas of Missouri.* St. Louis: n.p., n.d..

Cohen, Gerald Leonard. *Interesting Missouri Place Names.* Rolla, Missouri: G. Cohen, 1982.

Missouri Atlas [and] Gazetteer. Yarmouth, Massachusetts: DeLorme Mapping Co., 1998.

Ohman, Marian M. "Missouri County Organization 1812-1876." *Missouri Historical Review* 76 (April 1981): 253-81.

Rafferty, Milton D. *Historical Atlas of Missouri.* Norman, Oklahoma: University of Oklahoma Press, 1982.

Ramsay, Robert Lee. *Our Storehouse of Missouri Place Names.* [Columbia]: University of Missouri, 1952.

Selby, P.O. *A Bibliography of Missouri County Histories and Atlases.* 2nd ed. Kirksville, Missouri: Northeast Missouri State Teachers College, 1966.

Selby, Paul D. *Bibliography of Missouri County Histories and Atlases.* 2d ed. Kirksville, Missouri: Northeast Missouri State Teachers College, 1966.

Wetmore, Alphonso. *Gazetteer of the State of Missouri: With a Map of the State…. To Which is Added an Appendix, Containing Frontier Sketches, and Illustrations of Indian Character.* Reprint. New York: Arno Press, 1975.

Census Records

Available Census Records and Census Substitutes

Federal Census 1830, 1840, 1850, 1860, 1870, 1880, 1900, 1910, 1920, 1930.

Federal Mortality Schedules 1850, 1860, 1870, 1880.

Union Veterans and Widows 1890.

State/Territorial Census 1876.

Dollarhide, William. *The Census Book: A Genealogist's Guide to Federal Census Facts, Schedules and Indexes.* Bountiful, Utah: Heritage Quest, 1999.

Eddlemon, Sherida. *Ten Thousand Missouri Taxpayers.* Bowie, Maryland: Heritage Books, 1996.

Feldman, Lawrence H. *Anglo-Americans in Spanish Archives: Lists of Anglo-American Settlers in the Spanish Colonies osf America; A Finding Aid.* Baltimore: Genealogical Publishing Co., 1991.

Kemp, Thomas Jay. *The American Census Handbook.* Wilmington, Delaware: Scholarly Resources, 2001.

Lainhart, Ann S. *State Census Records.* Baltimore: Genealogical Publishing Co., Inc., 1992.

Stanley, Lois. *Missouri Taxpayers, 1819-1826.* Greenville, South Carolina: Southern Historical Press, 1990.

Szucs, Loretto Dennis, and Matthew Wright. *Finding Answers in U.S. Census Records.* Ancestry Publishing, 2001

Thorndale, William, and William Dollarhide. *Map Guide to the U.S. Federal Censuses, 1790-1920.* Baltimore: Genealogical Publishing Co., 1987.

United States. Bureau of Internal Revenue. *Internal Revenue Assessment Lists for the State of Missouri, 1862-1866.* Washington: National Archives and Records Services, 1984. 22 microfilm.

Court Records, Probate and Wills

Casselberry, Evans. *A Digest of all the Decisions of the Supreme Court Of The State Of Missouri, Contained in the First Fifteen Volumes of tshe Missouri Reports.* Saint Louis: Fisher & Bennett, 1853.

Northwest Missouri Genealogical Society. *Gentry County, Missouri Probate Index, 1885-1902*. St. Joseph, Missouri: the Society, n.d.

St. Louis (Missouri). Archival Library. *French and Spanish Archives, 1766-1816*. St. Louis, Missouri: City of St. Louis, 1962. 5 microfilm.

White, William D. *Preliminary Inventory of the Records of the United States Courts for the Western District of Missouri*. Kansas City, Missouri: Federal Records Center, 1969.

Emigration, Immigration, Migration and Naturalization

Brooks, Linda Barber. *Pioneer Kentuckians with Missouri Cousins*. 2 vols. St. Louis: Ingmire Publications, 1985.

Burnett, Robyn. *German Settlement in Missouri: New Land, Old Ways*. Columbia, Missouri: University of Missouri Press, 1996.

Coppage, A. Maxim, and Dorothy Ford Wulfeck. *Virginia Settlers in Missouri*. Owensboro, Ky.: Cook & McDowell Pub., 1979.

Gerlach, Russel L. *Settlement Patterns in Missouri, A Study of Population Origins, With A Wall Map*. Columbia, Missouri: University of Missouri Press, 1986.

Gerlach, Russel L. *Immigrants in the Ozarks: A Study in Ethnic Geography*. Columbia, Missouri: University of Missouri Press, 1976.

Kamphoefner, Walter D. *The Westfalians: From Germany to Missouri*. Princeton: Princeton University Press, 1987.

United States. Circuit Court (Missouri: Eastern Judicial District: Eastern Division: St. Louis). *Declarations of Intention, 1849-1911*. (Salt Lake City: Filmed by the Genealogical Society of Utah, 1991). 5 microfilm.

United States. Circuit Court (Missouri: Western District: Western Division: Kansas City). *Declarations of Intention, 1906-1909*. Microfilm of originals in the National Archives Branch in Kansas City, Missouri. (Salt Lake City: Filmed by the Genealogical Society of Utah, 1991).

United States. Circuit Court (Missouri: Western District: Western Division: Kansas City). *Declarations of Intention, 1910-1911*. Microfilm of originals in the National Archives Branch in Kansas City, Missouri. (Salt Lake City: Filmed by the Genealogical Society of Utah, 1991).

United States. District Court (Missouri: Central Division). *Index to Naturalization Records, 1876-1906*. Microfilm of originals in the National Archives Branch in Kansas City, Missouri. (Salt Lake City: Filmed by the Genealogical Society of Utah, 1991).

United States. District Court (Missouri: Eastern District: Eastern Division: St. Louis). *Naturalization Petitions, Depositions, and Miscellaneous Papers, 1912- 1942; Naturalization Certificate Stubs, 1907-1926*. Microfilm of originals in the National Archives Branch in Kansas City, Missouri. (Salt Lake City: Filmed by the Genealogical Society of Utah, 1991). 19 microfilm.

United States. District Court (Missouri: Northern Division). *Declarations of Intention, 1909-1929*. Microfilm of originals in the National Archives Branch in Kansas City, Missouri. (Salt Lake City: Filmed by the Genealogical Society of Utah, 1991). 5 microfilm.

United States. District Court (Missouri: Northern Division). *Naturalization Petitions, 1907-1929; Naturalization Certificate Stubs, 1907-1929*. Microfilm of originals in the National Archives Branch in Kansas City, Missouri. (Salt Lake City: Filmed by the Genealogical Society of Utah, 1991). 6 microfilm.

United States. District Court (Missouri: Southern Division). *Naturalization Petitions and Record, 1911-1937; Citizenship Petitions, 1930-1936; Naturalization Certificate Stubs, 1916-1927*. Microfilm of originals in the National Archives Branch in Kansas City, Missouri. (Salt Lake City: Filmed by the Genealogical Society of Utah, 1991). 2 microfilm

United States. District Court (Missouri: Southern Division). *Declaration of Intention, 1895-1985*. Microfilm of originals in the National Archives Branch in Kansas City, Missouri. (Salt Lake City: Filmed by the Genealogical Society of Utah, 1991).

United States. District Court (Missouri: Western District: Western Division: Kansas City). *Declarations of Intention, 1892-1936*. Microfilm of originals in the National Archives Branch in Kansas City, Missouri. (Salt Lake City: Filmed by the Genealogical Society of Utah, 1991). 6 microfilm.

United States. District Court (Missouri: Western District: Western Division: Kansas City). *Naturalization Petitions, 1909-1929*. Microfilm of originals in the National Archives Branch in Kansas City, Missouri. (Salt Lake City: Filmed by the Genealogical Society of Utah, 1991). 11 microfilm.

United States. District Court (Missouri: Western District: Western Division: Kansas City). *Naturalization Petitions and Records, 1920-1926*. Microfilm of originals in the National Archives Branch in Kansas City, Missouri. (Salt Lake City: Filmed by the Genealogical Society of Utah, 1991). 8 microfilm.

United States. District Court (Missouri: Western District: Western Division: Kansas City). *Naturalization Petitions, 1929-1935*. Microfilm of originals in the National Archives Branch in Kansas City, Missouri. (Salt Lake City: Filmed by the Genealogical Society of Utah, 1994). 4 microfilm.

Land and Property

Beahan, Gary W. *Missouri's Public Domain: United States Land Sales, 1818-1922*. Jefferson City, Missouri: Records Management and Archives Services, 1980.

Boekman, Laurel, and Pat B. Weiner, comps. *Missouri Plat Books in the State Historical Society of Missouri*. Columbia, Missouri: State Historical Soc., 1992.

Dunaway, Maxine, comp. *Missouri Military Land Warrants, War of 1812*. Springfield, Missouri: Maxine Dunaway, 1985.

Ericson, Carolyn, and Frances Ingmire. *First Settlers of the Missouri Territory*. 2 vols. Nacogdoches, Texas: Ericson Books, ca. 1983.

First Settlers of the Missouri Territory. 2 vols. Nacogdoches, Texas: Ericson Books, 1983.

Hone, Wade E. *Land and Property Research in the United States*. Salt Lake City: Ancestry Incorporated, 1997.

Ingmire, Frances Terry. *Citizens of Missouri*. 3 vols. St. Louis: Frances Ingmire, 1984.

Ingmire, Frances Terry. *Containing Grants in Present States of Missouri, Arkansas and Oklahoma*. St. Louis: the author, 1984.

Louisiana (Territory). Recorder of Land Titles. *Record Books, 1795-1808; Index to French and Spanish Land Grants, 1795-1812.* Jefferson City, Missouri: State of Missouri, 1970.

Lowrie, Walter, ed. *Early Settlers of Missouri as Taken from Land Claims in the Missouri Territory.* Reprint. Easley, South Carolina: Southern Historical Press, 1986.

Lowrie, Walter, ed. *Land Claims in the Missouri Territory.* (1834) Reprint. Greenville, South Carolina: Southern Historical Press, 1986.

McMullin, Phillip, ed. *Grassroots of America.* Salt Lake City: Gendex Co., 1972.

Missouri Land Claims. 1835. Reprint. New Orleans: Polyanthos, 1976.

Missouri Plat Books in the State Historical Society of Missouri. Columbia, Missouri: State Historical Society, n.d.

Missouri. Governor. *Land Patents, 1800's - Early 1900's.* Jefferson City, Missouri: State of Missouri, 1971.

Missouri. Register of Lands. *Tax Deeds, 1847-1878.* Jefferson City, Missouri: State of Missouri, 1970. 7 microfilm.

Missouri. State Archives. *Miscellaneous Records Relating to Missouri Lands, 1700's, 1800's, 1900's.* Jefferson City, Missouri: State of Missouri, 1969-1972.

United States. Bureau of Land Management. *Card Files.* Washington, D.C.: Bureau of Land Management, [19—]. 160 microfilm.

United States. District Court (Missouri). *Land Proceedings, 1824-1884.* Microfilm of originals in the National Archives Branch in Kansas City, Missouri. (Salt Lake City: Filmed by the Genealogical Society of Utah, 1991). 2 microfilm.

United States. General Land Office. *Missouri Land Plats, 1800's.* Jefferson City, Missouri: State of Missouri, 1969.

United States. General Land Office. *Records of Missouri Swamp Lands: Original Selections, New Selections, And Sales, 1800's.* Jefferson City, Missouri: State of Missouri, 1969. 9 microfilm.

United States. General Land Office. *Records of Missouri Swamp Lands: Original Selections, New Selections, and Sales, 1800's.* Jefferson City, Missouri: State of Missouri, 1969.

United States. General Land Office. *United States Land Sales in Missouri, 1827-1903; Index to Land Sales, 1818- 1893.* Jefferson City, Missouri: State of Missouri, 1969.

United States. Veterans Administration. *War of 1812, Military Bounty Land Warrants, 1815-1858.* Washington DC: The National Archives, 1971.

Military

Bartels, Carolyn M. *The Forgotten Men: Missouri State Guards.* Shawnee Mission, Kan.: Two Trails Pub., 1995.

Buss, Karen, comp. *An Every-Name Index to Revolutionary Soldiers and Their Descendants: Missouri Edition.* 1988. Burbank, California: Southern California Genealogical Society, 1988.

Concannon, Marie, and Josiah Parkinson. *Grand Army of the Republic—Missouri Division—Index to Death Rolls, 1882-1940.* Columbia, Missouri: State Historical Society, 1995.

Houp, J. Randall. *The 24th Missouri Volunteer Infantry "Lyon Legion."* Alma, Arkansas: J.R. Houp, 1997.

Houts, Alice Kinyoun. *Revolutionary Soldiers Buried in Missouri.* [Kansas City, Missouri: Houts, 1966].

Langley, Elizabeth B. *Taney County, Missouri Soldiers Who Fought in the Civil War Including Soldiers of Southwest Missouri and Northwest Arkansas: Also the Cherokees Under Stand Watie.* Billings, Missouri: Elizabeth B. Langley, 1963.

Military Records, 1812-1904. Microfilm of original records at the Missouri Department of Records and Archives, Jefferson City, Missouri. (Salt Lake City: Filmed by the Genealogical Society of Utah, 1977-1978). 214 microfilm.

Missouri Confederate Pensions and Confederate Home Applications Index. Hillsboro, Texas: Confederate Research Center, 1996.

Missouri State Archives. *Guide to Military Records.* Jefferson City, Missouri: Missouri State Archives, 2002. Online guide <www.mosl.sos.state.mo.us/rec-man/archives/resources/resources.html>

Missouri. Adjutant General's Office. *Confederate Pension Applications and Soldiers' Home Admission Applications.* Microfilm of original records at the Missouri Department of Records and Archives, Jefferson City, Missouri (Salt Lake City: Filmed by the Genealogical Society of Utah, 1977). 27 microfilm.

Missouri. Adjutant General's Office. *Military Records, 1812-1904.* Microfilm of original records at the Missouri Department of Records and Archives, Jefferson City, Mo. (Salt Lake City: Filmed by the Genealogical Society of Utah, 1977-1978). 214 microfilm.

Missouri. Adjutant General's Office. *Military Records, 1861-1866.* Microfilm of original records at the Missouri Department of Records and Archives, Jefferson City, Mo. (Salt Lake City: Filmed by the Genealogical Society of Utah, 1977). 19 microfilm.

Missouri. Adjutant General's Office. *Military Records, Spanish-American War, 1897-1898.* Microfilm of original records at the Missouri Department of Records and Archives, Jefferson City, Mo. (Salt Lake City: Filmed by the Genealogical Society of Utah, 1977). 2 microfilm.

Sifakis, Stewart. *Compendium of the Confederate Armies: Kentucky, Maryland, Missouri, the Confederate Units and the Indian Units.* Galveston, Texas: Frontier press, 1995.

State Historical Society of Missouri (Columbia, Missouri). *Index of Residents State Federal Soldiers' Home of Missouri, St. James, Missouri, 1899-1946.* Columbia, Missouri: State Historical Society of Missouri, 1998.

United States. Adjutant General's Office. *Index to Compiled Service Records of Volunteer Union Soldiers Who Served in Organizations from the State of Missouri.* Washington, DC: The National Archives, 1962.

United States. Selective Service System. *Missouri, World War I Selective Service System Draft Registration Cards, 1917-1918.* National Archives Microfilm Publications, M1509. Washington, DC: National Archives, 1987-1988.

Vital and Cemetery Records

Blattner, Teresa. *Divorces, Separations and Annulments in Missouri 1769 To 1850.* Bowie, Maryland: Heritage Books, 1993.

Brooks, Linda B. *Missouri Marriages to 1850.* 3 vols. St. Louis: Distributed by Ingmire Publishing, 1983.

Campbell, Kathryn H. *Early Bible and Graveyard Records.* 2 vols. Dallas, Texas: the author, 1972-74.

Carter, Mrs. J.R. *Early Missouri Marriages to 1840.* 3 vols. Sedalia: Mrs. J.R. Carter, n.d.

Cemetary Records of Missouri. 15 vols. Salt Lake City: Genealogical Society of Utah, 1973.

East Central Missouri Cemetery and Bible Records. 3 vols. Afton, Missouri: John Sappington Chapter, Daughters of the American Revolution, 1974.

Eddlemon, Sherida. *Missouri Birth and Death Records.* 3 vols. Bowie, Maryland: Heritage Books, 2001.

Ellsberry, Elizabeth P. *Bible Records of Missouri.* 8 vols. in 3. Chillicothe, Missouri: Elizabeth P. Ellsberry, 1963.

Ellsberry, Elizabeth P. *Cemetery Records of Missouri.* 3 vols. Chillicothe, Missouri: Elizabeth P. Ellsberry, 1965.

Guide to Public Vital Statistics Records in Missouri. St. Louis: Historical Records Survey, 1941.

Hodges, Nadine, Mrs. John Vineyard, and Mrs. Howard W. Woodruff. *Missouri Pioneers, County and Genealogical Records.* 30 vols. Independence, Missouri: the authors, 1967-.

Kot and Thompson. *Missouri Cemetery Inscription Sources: Print & Microform.* Galveston, Texas: Frontier Press, 1995.

Langley, Elizabeth B. *Bible Records of Missouri.* 3 vols. Billings, Missouri: Elizabeth B. Langley, 1968.

Liahona Research. *Missouri Marriages, Early [ca. 1754] to 1825*: a Research Tool. Bountiful, Utah: Precision Indexing, 1990.

Liahona Research. *Missouri Marriages, 1826 to 1850.* Salt Lake City: AGLL, 1993.

Missouri Cemetery Records. Vol. 1. Kansas City, Missouri: Heart of America Genealogical Society & Library, 1981.

Missouri Mortality Schedules, 1850-1880. Columbia, Missouri: State Historical Society of Mo., [19-]. 8 microfilm.

Missouri State Archives. *Guide to Birth and Death Records.* Jefferson City, Missouri: Missouri State Archives, 2002. Online guide - <http://mosl.sos.state.mo.us/rec-man/archives/resources/resources.html>.s

Missouri, 1851-1900. [S.l.]: Brøderbund, 1998. CD-ROM.

Ormesher, Susan. *Missouri Marriages Before 1840.* Baltimore: Genealogical Publishing Co., 1982.

Parker, Ed., comp. *Union Burials—Missouri Units.* 3 vols. Columbia, Missouri: State Historical Society, 1988, 1989, 1993.

Pompey, Sherman L. *List of Missouri Civil War Veteran Burials.* Microfilm. Salt Lake City: Genealogical Society of Utah, 1967.

Stanley, Lois, and George F. Wilson, and Maryhelen Wilson. More *Death Records from Missouri Newspapers, 1810-1857.* (1985) Reprint. Greenville, SC, Southern Historical Press, 1990.

Stanley, Lois, George F. Wilson, and Maryhelen Wilson. *1300 "Missing" Missouri Marriage Records from Newspapers, 1812-1853.* (1979) Reprint. Greenville, South Carolina: Southern Historical Press, 1990.

Stanley, Lois, George F. Wilson, and Maryhelen Wilson. *Death Records from the Missouri Newspapers: The Civil War Years, Jan. 1861-Dec. 1865.* (1983) Reprint, Greenville, South Carolina: Southern Historical Press.

Stanley, Lois, George F. Wilson, and Maryhelen Wilson. *Death Records from Missouri Newspapers, Jan. 1866-Dec. 1870.* (1984) Reprint. Greenville, South Carolina: Southern Historical Press, 1990.

Stanley, Lois, George F. Wilson, and Maryhelen Wilson. *Death Records of Missouri Men, 1808-1854.* (1981) Reprint. Greenville, South Carolina: Southern Historical Press, 1990.

Stanley, Lois, George F. Wilson, and Maryhelen Wilson. *Death Records of Pioneer Missouri Women, 1808-1853.* (1984) Reprint. Greenville, South Carolina: Southern Historical Press, 1990.

Stanley, Lois, George F. Wilson, and Maryhelen Wilson. *Divorces and Separations in Missouri, 1808-1853.* Greenville, South Carolina: Southern Historical Press, 1990.

Stanley, Lois, George F. Wilson, and Maryhelen Wilson. *Early Missouri Ancestors, Vol. I: From Newspapers, 1808-1822.* (1985) Reprint. Greenville, South Carolina: Southern Historical Press, 1990.

Stanley, Lois, George F. Wilson, and Maryhelen Wilson. *Early Missouri Ancestors, Vol. II: From Newspapers, 1823-1832.* (1987) Reprint. Greenville, South Carolina: Southern Historical Press, 1990.

Stanley, Lois, George F. Wilson, and Maryhelen Wilson. *Early Missouri Marriages in the News, 1820-1853.* (1985) Reprint. Greenville, South Carolina: Southern Historical Press, 1990.

Stanley, Lois, George F. Wilson, and Maryhelen Wilson. *Missouri Marriages in the News, 1851-1865.* (1983) Reprint. Greenville, South Carolina: Southern Historical Press, 1990.

Stanley, Lois, George F. Wilson, and Maryhelen Wilson. *Missouri Marriages in the News, Vol. II, 1866-1870.* (1984) Reprint. Greenville, South Carolina: Southern Historical Press, 1990.

Stanley, Lois, George F. Wilson, and Maryhelen Wilson. *Missouri Taxpayers, 1819-1826.* (1979) Reprint. Greenville, South Carolina: Southern Historical Press, 1990.

Stanley, Lois, George F. Wilson, and Maryhelen Wilson. *Death Records from Missouri Newspapers, January 1854-December 1860.* (1982) Reprint. Greenville, South Carolina: Southern Historical Press, 1990.

County Website	Map Index	Date Created	Parent County or Territory From Which Organized Address/Details

Adair   I2   29 Jan 1841   **Macon**
www.rootsweb.com/~moadair/
Adair County; 106 W Washington St; Kirksville, MO 63501; Ph. 660.665.3350
Details: (Co Rcdr has m & land rec from 1840; Clk Cir Ct has div & ct rec; Pro Clk has pro rec; Co Clk has school enumeration rec)

Allen   23 Feb 1843   **Holt**
Details: (see Atchison) Name changed to Atchison 14 Feb 1845

Andrew   N2   29 Jan 1841   **Platte Purchase**
www.rootsweb.com/~moandrew/
index.html
Andrew County; 411 Court St; Savannah, MO 64485-0206; Ph. 816.324.3624
Details: (Co Clk has b & d rec 1883-1893; Clk Cir Ct has m, div & ct rec from 1841, land & mil rec; Pro Judge has pro rec from 1841)

Arkansas   1813   **New Madrid**
Details: (abolished 1819 when Terr. of Arkansas was formed)

Ashley   17 Feb 1843   **Shannon, Wright**
Details: (see Texas) Name changed to Texas 14 Feb 1845

Atchison   O2   23 Feb 1843   **Holt**
www.rootsweb.com/~moatchis/
atchison.html
Atchison County; 400 S Washington St; Rock Port, MO 64482; Ph. 660.744.6214
Details: (Formerly Allen Co. Name changed to Atchison 14 Feb 1845; part of Platte Purchase; attached to Holt Co until 1854; lost 10-mile strip to Iowa in 1848) (Co Rcdr has m & land rec; Clk Cir Ct has d, div & ct rec; Co Clk has b rec 1883-1893; Pro Judge has pro rec)

Audrain   H4   12 Jan 1831   **Ralls**
www.audrain-county.org/
Audrain County; 101 N Jefferson; Mexico, MO 65265; Ph. 573.473.5820
Details: (Created in 1831, but remained attached to Callaway, Monroe & Ralls Cos until 1836. In 1842 gained an additional 31 sq. miles from Monroe Co) (Co Clk has b rec 1883-1886; Rcdr Deeds has m & land rec; Clk Cir Ct has div & ct rec; Pro Judge has pro rec)

Barry   L10   5 Jan 1835   **Greene**
www.rootsweb.com/~mobarry/barry.htm
Barry County; 700 Main St; Cassville, MO 65625; Ph. 417.847.2561
Details: (Fire in 1872 destroyed many rec in Cir Clks office) (Rcdr Deeds has m & land rec; Clk Cir Ct has div & ct rec; Pro Judge has pro rec)

Barton   M8   12 Dec 1855   **Jasper**
www.rootsweb.com/~mobarton/
Barton County; 1004 Gulf St; Lamar, MO 64759; Ph. 417.682.3529
Details: (Courthouse burned in 1860) (Co Clk has b rec 1883-1897 & d rec 1883-1899; Rcdr Deeds has div & land rec; Pro Ct has pro rec; Magistrate Ct, division 2, has ct rec)

Bates   M6   29 Jan 1841   **Cass, Van Buren, Jackson**
www.rootsweb.com/~mobates/index.htm
Bates County; 1 N Delaware St; Butler, MO 64730; Ph. 660.679.3371
Details: (22 Feb 1855 the three southern tiers of townships in Cass Co were added to Bates; Courthouse burned in 1861) (Co Clk has b & d rec 1883-1887; Co Rcdr has m rec from 1860 & land rec from 1840; Clk Cir Ct has div rec from 1860; Pro Judge has pro rec)

Benton   K6   3 Jan 1835   **Pettis, St. Clair**
members.aol.com/hrftx/index.htm
Benton County; PO Box 1238; Warsaw, MO 65355-1238; Ph. 660.438.7326
Details: (Benton remained unorganized until Jan 1837; in 1845, 24 sq. miles of northwest part of Benton became part of Pettis Co & Hickory Co was created, reducing Benton to its present size) (Co Clk has b & d rec from 1883 & m rec from 1839; Clk Cir Ct has div & ct rec; Pro Ct has pro rec; Rcdr Deeds has land rec)

Bollinger   D9   1 Mar 1851   **Cape Girardeau, Stoddard, Wayne**
www.rootsweb.com/~mobollin/
Bollinger County; 204 High St; Marble Hill, MO 63764-0046; Ph. 573.238.2126
Details: (Courthouse burned in 1866; Courthouse burned in 1884 while occupied only by the Co Clks office) (Co Clk has b & d rec 1882-1892; Clk Cir Ct & Rcdr has m, div & land rec; Cir Judge has pro rec)

Boone   I5   16 Nov 1820   **Howard**
www.showmeboone.com/
Boone County; 600 E Broadway; Columbia, MO 65201; Ph. 573.874.7345
Details: (Co Clk has m, div, pro, ct & land rec from 1821)

County Website	Map Index	Date Created	Parent County or Territory From Which Organized Address/Details
Buchanan www.co.buchanan.mo.us/	N3	31 Dec 1838	**Platte Purchase** Buchanan County; 5th & Jules; St. Joseph, MO 64501; Ph. 816.271.1412 Details: (Rcdr Deeds has m rec; Clk Cir Ct has div rec; Pro Judge has pro rec; Mag Ct has ct rec; Co Asr has land rec)
Butler www.rootsweb.com/~mobutle2/ index.html	E11	27 Feb 1849	**Wayne** Butler County; 100 N Main St; Poplar Bluff, MO 63901; Ph. 573.686.8050 Details: (Rcdr Deeds has m & land rec from 1849; Pro Ct has pro rec from 1849; Co Clk has b & d rec 1883-1893)
Caldwell members.aol.com/TerR001/Caldwell/ caldwell.htm	L3	29 Dec 1836	**Ray** Caldwell County; 49 E Main St; PO Box 67; Kingston, MO 64650-0067; Ph. 816.586.2571 Details: (19 April 1860 courthouse destroyed by fire; all rec destroyed except those of the Pro Ct; 28 Nov 1896 courthouse destroyed by fire) (Rcdr Office has m & land rec; Clk Cir Ct has div rec; Cir Ct, division 2, has pro rec; Cir Ct, division 1, has ct rec)
Callaway www.rootsweb.com/~missour/	H6	25 Nov 1820	**Montgomery** Callaway County; 10 E 5th St; Fulton, MO 65251-1700; Ph. 573.642.0730 Details: (Co Clk has b & d rec 1883-1888; Co Rcdr has m & land rec; Clk Cir Ct has div rec; Pro Judge has pro rec)
Camden www.rootsweb.com/~mocamden/ page1.htm	J7	29 Jan 1841	**Benton, Pulaski** Camden County; 1 Court Cir; Camdenton, MO 65020; Ph. 573.346.4440 Details: (Formerly Kinderhook Co. Name changed to Camden 23 Feb 1843; line between Camden & Miller changed 1845; Courthouse burned 1902) (Co Rcdr has m & div rec from 1902; Pro Judge has pro rec from 1902; Clk Cir Ct has ct rec from 1902; Tompkins Abstract Office has land rec)
Cape Girardeau www.showme.net/CapeCounty/	C9	1 Oct 1812	**Original District** Cape Girardeau County; 1 Barton Sq; Jackson, MO 63755; Ph. 573.243.3547 Details: (Present size of county since 5 Mar 1849; Courthouse burned in 1870) (Co Clk has b & d rec 1883-1893 & land rec 1821-1859; Co Rcdr has m rec; Clk Cir Ct has div & ct rec; Pro Judge has pro rec; Riverside Regional Lib has all rec on microfilm)
Carroll us-gen.com/mo/carroll/		2 Jan 1833	**Ray** Carroll County; County Courthouse; Carrollton, MO 64633; Ph. 816.542.0615 Details: (Co Clk has b rec 1883-1895 & d rec 1883-1890; Clk Cir Ct has div & ct rec from 1833 & nat rec 1843-1919; Rcdr Deeds has m rec, land rec from 1833; Pro Office has pro rec)
Carter www.rootsweb.com/~mocarter/	F10	10 Mar 1859	**Ripley, Shannon** Carter County; 105 Main St; Van Buren, MO 63965-0517; Ph. 573.323.4527 Details: (Rcdr of Deeds has m & land rec; Pro Ct has pro rec from 1859)
Cass* www.casscounty.com/	M6	3 Mar 1835	**Jackson** Cass County; 102 E Wall St; Harrisonville, MO 64701; Ph. 816.380.8102 Details: (Formerly Van Buren Co. Name changed to Cass 19 Feb 1849; three southern tiers of townships relinquished to Bates 22 Feb 1855) (Co Clk has b rec 1861-1896 & ct rec from 1843; Rcdr Deeds has m, div & land rec; Associate Division has pro rec)
Cedar www.rootsweb.com/~mocedar/index.htm	L8	14 Feb 1845	**Dade, St Clair** Cedar County; 113 South St; PO Box 158; Stockton, MO 65785-0126; Ph. 417.276.3514 Details: (Co Clk has m, div & land rec from 1845, pro & ct rec)
Chariton www.rootsweb.com/~mocharit/ chariton.htm	K4	16 Nov 1820	**Howard** Chariton County; 306 S Cherry; Keytesville, MO 65261; Ph. 660.288.3273 Details: (Courthouse burned 20 Sept 1864; only a few rec lost) (Co Clk has b & d rec 1883-1887; Cir Ct Clk-Rcdr has m rec from 1821, div & ct rec from 1872, land rec from 1827, nat rec from 1877 & mil dis rec from 1918; Cir Ct-Pro Division has pro srec from 1860)

County Website	Map Index	Date Created	Parent County or Territory From Which Organized Address/Details
Christian www.rootsweb.com/~mochrist/	**K10**	**8 Mar 1859**	**Greene, Taney, Webster** Christian County; 100 W Church; PO Box 549; Ozark, MO 65721-0549; Ph. 417.581.6372 Details: (Courthouse burned 1865) (Clk Cir Ct & Rcdr has m, div, ct & land rec; Pro Office has pro rec)
Clark www.rootsweb.com/~moclark/clark.htm		**16 Dec 1836**	**Lewis** Clark County; 111 E Court St; Kahoka, MO 63445-1268; Ph. 660.727.3283 Details: (Co Clk has m, div, pro, ct & land rec from 1836)
Clark (old)	**H2**	**1818**	**Arkansas** Details: (never organized; abolished in 1819 when terr. of Arkansas was created)
Clay www.claycogov.com/	**N4**	**2 Jan 1822**	**Ray** Clay County; 1 Courthouse Sq; Liberty, MO 64086; Ph. 816.792.7637 Details: (Rcdr Deeds has m & land rec; Clk Cir Ct has div & ct rec from 1822; Pro Ct has pro rec)
Clinton www.rootsweb.com/~moclinto/	**M3**	**2 Jan 1833**	**Clay** Clinton County; 211 N Main St; PO Box 245; Plattsburg, MO 64477-0245; Ph. 816.539.3719 Details: (Co Clk has m, div, ct & land rec from 1833 & mil rec from 1919; Pro Judge has pro rec)
Cole* www.rootsweb.com/~mocole/cole.html	**I6**	**16 Nov 1820**	**Cooper** Cole County; 301 E High St; Jefferson City, MO 65101; Ph. 573.634.9106 Details: (Clk Cir Ct has div & ct rec from 1821; Pro Judge has pro rec from 1821; Rcdr Deeds has m & land rec from 1821)
Cooper www.rootsweb.com/~mocooper/ index.html	**J5**	**17 Dec 1818**	**Howard** Cooper County; 200 Main St; PO Box 123; Boonville, MO 65233-0123; Ph. 660.882.2626 Details: (Co Clk has b & d rec 1883-1893 & bur rec; Cir Clk & Rcdr has m, div, ct & nat rec from 1819 & land rec from 1812; Associate Cir Ct has pro rec from 1828)
Crawford www.rootsweb.com/~mocrawfo/ index.html	**G6**	**23 Jan 1829**	**Gasconade** Crawford County; 302 W Main St; Steelville, MO 65565; Ph. 573.775.2376 Details: (1829-1835 Co Ct rec lost; Courthouse burned 15 Feb 1873; Courthouse burned 5 Jan 1884) (Co Clk has m, div, ct & land rec from 1832; Pro Judge has pro rec from 1889)
Dade www.rootsweb.com/~modade/ modade.htm	**L9**	**29 Jan 1841**	**Greene** Dade County; Main St; Greenfield, MO 65661; Ph. 417.637.2724 Details: (Lost 10-mile strip on northern boundary to Cedar Co & 9-mile strip on southern boundary to Lawrence, reducing it to its present size 28 Mar 1845; Courthouse burned in 1863, but no rec lost) (Co Rcdr has m rec from 1867 & land rec; Clk Cir Ct has div rec from 1867; Pro Judge has pro & ct rec)
Dallas* www.rootsweb.com/~modallas/	**J8**	**29 Jan 1841**	**Polk** Dallas County; 107 Maple St; PO Box 436; Buffalo, MO 65622-0436; Ph. 417.345.2632 Details: (Formerly Niangua Co. Name changed to Dallas 16 Dec 1844; Courthouse burned 18 Oct 1863; second courthouse burned 30 Jul 1864 & rec destroyed; the replaced rec were burned 3 Sep 1867) (Co Rcdr has b, m, d, bur, div, pro, ct & land rec)
Daviess www.rootsweb.com/~modavies/ daviess.htm	**L3**	**29 Dec 1836**	**Ray** Daviess County; 102 N Main St; Gallatin, MO 64640; Ph. 660.663.2641 Details: (Co Lib has b & d rec on microfilm 1883-1893 & local census 1876; Rcdr of Deeds has land rec; Pro Ct has pro rec)
De Kalb www.rootsweb.com/~modekalb/ index.html	**M3**	**25 Feb 1845**	**Clinton** De Kalb County; 109 W Main St; PO Box 248; Maysville, MO 64469-0248; Ph. 816.449.5402 Details: (Courthouse burned in 1878, many rec lost, but rec of Cir Clks Office were preserved along with a few rec from other offices) (Co Rcdr has m & div rec; Co Clk has b rec 1880-1902; Pro Judge has pro rec)

County Website	Map Index	Date Created	Parent County or Territory From Which Organized / Address/Details
Dent www.rootsweb.com/~modent/index.html	G8	10 Feb 1851	**Crawford, Shannon** Dent County; 400 N Main St; Salem, MO 6556; Ph. 573.729.4144 Details: (Courthouse burned in 1864 destroying some rec) (Clk Cir Ct has m, div & ct rec; Clk Mag Ct has pro rec; Co Rcdr has land rec)
Dodge		18 Dec 1846	**Putnam** Details: (Discontinued in 1853; had lost terr when Iowa boundary was established 13 Feb 1849, bringing its area below the constitutional limit of 400 sq miles; its terr was added to Putnam Co 16 Mar 1853)
Douglas www.rootsweb.com/~modougla/doug.htm	I10	29 Oct 1857	**Ozark, Taney** Douglas County; 203 SE 2nd Ave; PO Box 398; Ava, MO 65608; Ph. 417.683.4714 Details: (Terr. increased in 1864 by addition of portions of Taney & Webster Cos) (Clk Cir Ct & Rcdr has m, div & ct rec; Pro & Mag Judge has pro rec)
Dunklin www.rootsweb.com/~modunkl2/ dcgenweb.htm	D12	14 Feb 1845	**Stoddard** Dunklin County; PO Box 188; Kennett, MO 63857-0188; Ph. 573.888.2796 Details: (In 1853 a strip one mile wide was taken from Stoddard & added to northern boundary of Dunklin Co; Courthouse burned in 1872; all rec lost) (Rcdr Deeds has m & land rec; Clk Cir Ct has div & ct rec; Pro Judge has pro rec)
Franklin www.rootsweb.com/~mofrankl/ index.html	G6	11 Dec 1818	**St. Louis** Franklin County; Courthouse Sq; PO Box 311; Union, MO 63084-0311; Ph. 314.583.6355 Details: (Boundaries not accurately defined until 1845) (Co Clk has b rec 1883-1892 & d rec 1883-1887; Rcdr Deeds has m & land rec; Clk Cir Ct has div rec; Pro Judge has pro rec)
Gasconade www.rootsweb.com/~mogascon/x index.html	G6	25 Nov 1820	**Franklin** Gasconade County; 119 E 1st St #2; PO Box 295; Hermann, MO 65041; Ph. 573.486.5427 Details: (In 1869 relinquished 36 sq. miles to Crawford Co) (Co Clk has b rec 1867-1897 & d rec 1883-1901; Rcdr of Deeds has land rec; Pro Judge has pro rec)
Gentry www.rootsweb.com/~mogentry/ index.html	M2	12 Feb 1841	**Clinton** Gentry County; 200 Clay St; Albany, MO 64402-1499; Ph. 660.726.3525 Details: (Organization completed 1843; courthouse burned 1885) (Co Clk has b & d rec 1883-1893 & m rec from 1885; Clk Cir Ct has div, ct & land rec from 1885; Cir Ct, division 2, has pro rec from 1885)
Greene www.greenecountymo.org/	K9	2 Jan 1833	**Crawford** Greene County; 940 Boonville Ave; Springfield, MO 65802; Ph. 417.868.4068 Details: (Courthouse burned 1861; few rec lost) (Co Archives & Rec Center has pro, ct, tax & land rec from 1833, mil dis rec, div rec 1837-1950, b & d rec 1883-1890 & 1876 local cen rec)
Grundy www.rootsweb.com/~mogrundy/ index.html	L2	29 Jan 1841	**Livingston** Grundy County; 700 Main St; Trenton, MO 64683; Ph. 660.359.6305 Details: (Co Clk has b & d rec 1881-1890; Co Rcdr has m, div & land rec; Pro Office has pro rec)
Harrison www.rootsweb.com/~moharris/ index.html	L1	14 Feb 1845	**Daviess** Harrison County; 1500 Central St; Bethany, MO 64424; Ph. 660.425.6424 Details: (Courthouse burned Jan 1874, most rec saved; tax rec destroyed) (Co Clk has some b rec 1883-1893; Clk Cir Ct has m & div rec from 1858 & ct rec from 1845; Pro Judge has pro rec from 1853)
Hempstead		1818	**Arkansas** Details: (abolished 1819 when terr. of Arkansas was created)
Henry* www.rootsweb.com/~mohenry/ henryco.html	L6	13 Dec 1834	**Lafayette** Henry County; Main & Franklin Sts; 100 W Franklin; Clinton, MO 64735-2199; Ph. 660.885.6963 Details: (Formerly Rives Co. Name changed to Henry 15 Feb 1841) (Co Rcdr has m & land rec from 1830 & mil dis rec; Co Clk has div & ct rec; Associate Cir Ct has pro rec; Co Museum has b & bur rec)

County Website	Map Index	Date Created	Parent County or Territory From Which Organized
			Address/Details

Hickory   K7   14 Feb 1845   **Benton, Polk**
www.rootsweb.com/~mohickor/
     index.html

Hickory County; PO Box 3; Hermitage, MO 65668; Ph. 417.745.6450
Details: (Courthouse burned 1852 & 1881; many rec lost) (Co Clk has b rec 1883-1898; Clk Cir Ct has m rec from 1872, div & ct rec from 1858; Pro Judge has pro rec from 1845)

Holt   O2   29 Jan 1841   **Platte Purchase**
www.geocities.com/Heartland/Plains/
     4280/HOLTCTY.html

Holt County; 100 W Nodaway St; Oregon, MO 64473; Ph. 660.446.3303
Details: (Formerly Nodaway Co. Name changed to Holt 15 Feb 1841. Courthouse burned 30 Jan 1965; most rec undamaged) (Co Clk has incomplete b & d rec 1883-1893, m, div & land rec from 1841; Clk Cir Ct has ct rec from 1841; Pro Judge has pro rec from 1849)

Howard   J5   13 Jan 1816   **St. Charles, St. Louis**
www.rootsweb.com/~mohoward/

Howard County; #1 Courthouse Sq; Fayette, MO 65248; Ph. 660.248.2284
Details: (Courthouse burned 1887; few rec lost) (Clk Cir Ct has b rec 1870-1955, m & ct rec from 1870, land & bur rec from 1820, mil & div rec from 1900; Pro Ct has pro rec from 1835; Co Hlth Nurse has d rec from 1870)

Howell   H10   2 Mar 1857   **Oregon, Ozark**
www.rootsweb.com/~mohowell/intro.htm

Howell County; County Courthouse Sq; West Plains, MO 65775; Ph. 417.256.2591
Details: (Courthouse destroyed during Civil War) (Co Clk has b rec 1883-1895 & d rec 1883-1893; Cir Clk & Rcdr Deeds has m, div, ct & land rec; Associate Cir Ct has pro rec)

Iron   F8   17 Feb 1857   **Dent, Madison, Reynolds, St. Francis, Washington, Wayne**
www.rootsweb.com/~moiron2/index.htm

Iron County; 250 S Main St; PO Box 42; Ironton, MO 63650; Ph. 573.546.2912
Details: (Co Clk has b rec 1883-1885, m, div, pro & land rec)

Jackson   M5   15 Dec 1826   **Lafayette**
www.co.jackson.mo.us/

Jackson County; 415 E 12th St; Kansas City, MO 64106-2706; Ph. 816.881.3333
Details: (Nearly all its terr was acquired from Osage & Kansas Indians 2 Jun 1825) (Dept of Rcds has m & land rec; Ct Admin has div & ct rec; Pro Judge has pro rec)

Jasper*   M9   29 Jan 1841   **Newton**
www.rootsweb.com/~mojasper/
     jcpage.htm

Jasper County; 302 S Main St; Carthage, MO 64836-1696; Ph. 417.358.0441
Details: (Courthouse destroyed in 1863; rec had been removed & were returned in 1865; Couthouse burned in 1883; no mention of fate of rec) (Co Clk has b rec 1883-1900 & d rec 1883-1891; Rcdr Deeds has m & land rec; Pro Judge has pro & ct rec)

Jefferson   E6   8 Dec 1818   **Ste. Genevieve, St. Louis**
www.jeffcomo.org/

Jefferson County; 300 2nd St; PO Box 100; Hillsboro, MO 63050-0100; Ph. 636.797.5478
Details: (Rcdr Deeds has m & land rec; Pro Ct has pro rec; Clk Cir Ct has ct rec)

Johnson*   L6   13 Dec 1834   **Lafayette**
www.rootsweb.com/~mojohnso/

Johnson County; 300 N Holden St; Warrensburg, MO 64093; Ph. 660.747.6161
Details: (Co Clk has b & d rec 1883-1893; Rcdr of Deeds has m & land rec from 1835; Clk Cir Ct has div & ct rec from late 1860's; Pro Judge has pro rec from mid-1800's)

Kinderhook   29 Jan 1841   **Benton, Pulaski**
Details: (see Camden) Name changed to Camden 23 Feb 1843

Knox   H2   14 Feb 1845   **Scotland**
www.rootsweb.com/~moknox/index.htm

Knox County; 107 N 4th St; Edina, MO 63537; Ph. 660.397.2184
Details: (Co Rcdr has m, div & land rec; Associate Cir Judge has pro & ct rec; Hist Soc in Courthouse has b & d rec 1883-1890)

Laclede   I8   24 Feb 1849   **Camden, Pulaski, Wright**
laclede.county.missouri.org/

Laclede County; 200 N Adams Ave; Lebanon, MO 65536; Ph. 417.532.5471
Details: (Co Rcdr has m rec; Clk Cir Ct has div & ct rec; Pro Judge has pro rec; Co Asr has land rec)

County Website	Map Index	Date Created	Parent County or Territory From Which Organized Address/Details
Lafayette members.aol.com/TerR001/Lafayette/ lafayette.htm	L5	16 Nov 1820	**Cooper** Lafayette County; 1001 Main St; PO Box 357; Lexington, MO 64067; Ph. 660.259.4315 Details: (Formerly Lillard Co. Name changed to Lafayette 16 Feb 1825) (Co Rcdr has m, div, pro, ct & land rec from 1821)
Lawrence www.rootsweb.com/~molawre2/	L9	14 Feb 1845	**Barry, Dade** Lawrence County; PO Box 309; Mount Vernon, MO 65712; Ph. 417.466.2638 Details: (Rcdr Deeds has m & land rec from 1846; Clk Cir Ct has div & ct rec from 1846; Pro Judge has pro rec from 1846)
Lawrence, old		1 Mar 1815	**New Madrid** Details: (Lost terr. to Wayne 1 Feb 1819. Abolished 16 Feb 1825)
Lewis www.rootsweb.com/~molewis/	H2	2 Jan 1833	**Marion** Lewis County; 100 E Lafayette St; Monticello, MO 63457; Ph. 573.767.5205 Details: (Clk Cir Ct has m, div & land rec; Pro Judge has pro & ct rec)
Lillard		16 Nov 1820	**Cooper** Details: (see Lafayette) Name changed to Lafayette 16 Feb 1825
Lincoln www.rootsweb.com/~molincol/ molincoln.htm	F5	14 Dec 1818	**St. Charles** Lincoln County; 201 Main St; Troy, MO 63379; Ph. 636.528.4415 Details: (Co Rcdr has m rec from 1825, land, d & bur rec; Pro Judge has pro rec from 1823; Clk Cir Ct has div rec)
Linn* www.rootsweb.com/~molinn/linn.html	K3	6 Jan 1837	**Chariton** Linn County; 108 N High; Linneus, MO 64653; Ph. 660.895.5417 Details: (Co Clk has incomplete b & d rec 1883-1888; Co Rcdr has m & land rec from 1842; Clk Cir Ct has div rec from 1837; Pro Office has pro rec from 1840)
Livingston www.greenhills.net/~fwoods/	L3	6 Jan 1837	**Carroll** Livingston County; 700 Webster St; Chillicothe, MO 64601; Ph. 660.646.2293 Details: [Co Clk has b & d rec; Rcdr Deeds has m & land rec; Pro Ct has pro rec; Clk Cir Ct has ct rec)
Macon* www.rootsweb.com/~momacon/	J3	6 Jan 1837	**Randolph** Macon County; 101 E Washington St; Macon, MO 63552-0096; Ph. 660.385.2913 Details: (Co Clk has b & d rec 1883-1893; Co Rcdr has m & land rec; Clk Cir Ct has div rec; Cir Ct, division 2, has pro rec)
Madison www.pastracks.com/states/missouri/ madison.htm	E9	14 Dec 1818	**Cape Girardeau, Ste. Genevieve** Madison County; 1 Courthouse Sq; Fredericktown, MO 63645; Ph. 573.783.2176 Details: (Co Clk has b & d rec 1883-1900 & local cen 1876; Clk Cir Ct has m, div & ct rec from 1821 & mil dis rec from 1943; Co Mag has pro rec from 1820; Co Asr has land rec from 1821)
Maries www.rootsweb.com/~momaries/ maries.htm	H7	2 Mar 1855	**Osage, Pulaski** Maries County; PO Box 205; Vienna, MO 65582; Ph. 573.422.3388 Details: (In 1859 and 1868 small tracts of land were exchanged with Phelps Co; Courthouse burned 6 Nov 1868, nearly all rec destroyed) (Clk Cir Ct has m rec from 1873, div & ct rec from 1866, land rec from 1855 & school rec from 1911; Pro Division has pro rec from 1880)
Marion* www.rootsweb.com/~momarion/ index.htm	H3	14 Dec 1822	**Ralls** Marion County; 100 S Main St; Palmyra, MO 63461; Ph. 573.769.2549 Details: (Clk Cir Ct has m, div, ct & land rec from 1827 & mil dis rec; Pro Ct has pro rec)
McDonald* www.rootsweb.com/~momcdona/ momcdon.htm	M11	3 Mar 1849	**Newton** McDonald County; Hwy W; Pineville, MO 64856-0665; Ph. 417.223.4717 Details: (In 1876 an error in survey was corrected, establishing a new eastern line which annexed a 2 1/2 mile strip previously included in Barry Co; Courthouse & rec burned in 1863) (Rcdr Deeds has m rec; Clk Cir Ct has div, ct & land rec; Pro Judge has pro rec)

County Website	Map Index	Date Created	Parent County or Territory From Which Organized Address/Details

Mercer   L1   14 Feb 1845   **Grundy**
www.rootsweb.com/~momercer/index.html
Mercer County; 802 E Main St; Princeton, MO 64673; Ph. 660.748.3425
Details: (Courthouse burned 24 Mar 1898 & nearly all rec of the Cir Clk & Rcdr, Treas & Sheriff were destroyed or badly damaged; rec in office of Pro Judge & Co Clk were saved but many were badly damaged) (Co Clk has b rec 1883-1894 & d rec 1883-1891; Clk Cir Ct has m, div, ct & land rec; Cir Ct, division 2, has pro rec)

Miller   I7   6 Feb 1837   **Cole**
www.rootsweb.com/~momiller/miller.htm
annexed
Miller County; PO Box 12; Tuscumbia, MO 65082; Ph. 573.369.2731
Details: (Line between Camden & Miller changed 1845; terr. from Morgan Co 1860; minor changes in 1868) (Co Clk has b rec 1883-1891; Co Rcdr has m & div rec; Pro Judge has pro rec; Clk Cir Ct has ct rec)

Mississippi   C10   14 Feb 1845   **Scott**
www.mississippicountymo-online.com/
Mississippi County; PO Box 304; Charleston, MO 63834-0304; Ph. 573.683.2146
Details: (Clk Cir Ct has m, div & ct rec; Pro Judge has pro rec; Co Rcdr has land rec)

Moniteau   J6   14 Feb 1845   **Cole, Morgan**
www.rootsweb.com/~momonite/moniteauhomepage.htm
Moniteau County; 200 E Main St; California, MO 65018; Ph. 573.796.4661
Details: (Rcdr Deeds has m & land rec from 1845; Pro Ct has pro rec from 1845)

Monroe   H4   6 Jan 1831   **Ralls**
www.pastracks.com/states/missouri/monroe/
Monroe County; 300 N Main St; Paris, MO 65275-1399; Ph. 660.327.1019
Details: (Clk Cir Ct has m, div & ct rec; Pro Judge has pro rec; Co Asr has land rec)

Montgomery   G5   14 Dec 1818   **St. Charles**
www.rootsweb.com/~momontgo/index.htm
Montgomery County; 211 E 3rd St; Montgomery City, MO 63361-1956; Ph. 573.564.3357
Details: (Co rec burned 1864) (Clk Cir Ct has m rec from 1864, div & ct rec from 1886; Pro Judge has pro rec from 1890)

Morgan   J6   5 Jan 1833   **Cooper**
www.rootsweb.com/~momorgan/index.htm
Morgan County; 100 E Newton St; Versailles, MO 65084-1298; Ph. 573.378.5436
Details: (Courthouse burned 1887; no rec lost) (Rcdr Deeds has m & land rec; Pro Ct has pro rec from 1834; Clk Cir Ct has ct rec; Co Clk has b & d rec)

New Madrid   D11   1 Oct 1812   **Original district**
www.rootsweb.com/~monewmad/nmgenweb.htm
New Madrid County; PO Box 68; New Madrid, MO 63869; Ph. 573.748.2524
Details: (Rcdr Deeds has m & land rec; Clk Cir Ct has div & ct rec; Pro Ct has pro rec)

Newton   M10   30 Dec 1838   **Barry**
www.rootsweb.com/~monewton/newton.html
Newton County; 101 S Wood St; Neosho, MO 64850; Ph. 417.451.8220
Details: (In 1846 a strip two miles wide was detached from Newton & attached to Jasper; Courthouse burned 1862, no mention of fate of rec) (Co Clk has m, div, pro, ct & land rec)

Niangua   29 Jan 1841   **Polk**
Details: (see Dallas) (Boundaries slightly changed & name changed to Dallas 16 Dec 1844)

Nodaway   N1   2 Jan 1843   **Unorg. Terr.**
www.rootsweb.com/~monodawa/nodaway.html
Nodaway County; 305 N Main St; Maryville, MO 64468-0218; Ph. 660.582.2251
Details: (Attached to Andrew Co until organization 14 Feb 1845) (Clk Cir Ct has m & div rec from 1845; Pro Ct has pro rec)

Oregon   G10   14 Feb 1845   **Ripley**
www.rootsweb.com/~mooregon/
Oregon County; PO Box 324; Alton, MO 65606; Ph. 417.778.7475
Details: (Courthouse burned during Civil War; rec were removed & most of them saved) (Clk Cir Ct has m, div & ct rec; Pro Judge has pro rec; Rcdr Deeds has land rec)

Osage   H7   29 Jan 1841   **Gasconade**
www.osagecountymo.com/
Osage County; 106 E Main St; Linn, MO 65051; Ph. 573.897.2139
Details: (1 Mar 1855 boundaries between Osage & Pulaski defined; Courthouse burned 15 Nov 1880, rec saved) (Rcdr Deeds has m & land rec from 1841; Pro Ct has pro rec from 1841; Co Clk has b & d rec)

County Website	Map Index	Date Created	Parent County or Territory From Which Organized / Address/Details
Ozark www.rootsweb.com/~moozark/oz.htm	I11	29 Jan 1841	**Taney** Ozark County; PO Box 416; Gainesville, MO 65655-0416; Ph. 417.679.3516 Details: (Name changed to Decatur 22 Feb 1843; Name changed back to Ozark 24 Mar 1845) (Clk Cir Ct has m, div & ct rec; Co Clk has Co Comm minutes; Pro Ct has pro rec; Rcdr Deeds has land rec)
Pemiscot www.rootsweb.com/~mopemis2/ pemiscot.htm	D11	19 Feb 1851	**New Madrid** Pemiscot County; 610 Ward Ave; Caruthersville, MO 63830; Ph. 573.333.4203 Details: (Courthouse & rec burned 1883) (Rcdr Deeds has m & land rec from 1883; Clk Cir Ct has div & ct rec from 1890; Pro Judge has pro rec)
Perry www.perrycountymo.com/	D8	16 Nov 1820	**Ste. Genevieve** Perry County; 321 N Main St; Perryville, MO 63775; Ph. 573.547.4242 Details: (Clk Cir Ct has div, land, pro & ct rec; Co Rcdr has m & mil rec; Co Clk has b & d rec 1883-1893 & nat rec from 1821)
Pettis* www.rootsweb.com/~mopettis/pettis.htm	K5	26 Jan 1833	**Cooper, Saline** Pettis County; 415 S Ohio Ave; Sedalia, MO 65301; Ph. 660.826.5395 Details: (Rcdr Deeds has m & land rec from 1833; Pro Ct has pro rec from 1833; Clk Cir Ct has ct rec)
Phelps www.rollanet.org/~phelps/	H8	13 Nov 1857	**Crawford, Pulaski, Maries** Phelps County; 200 N Main St FL 1; Rolla, MO 65401; Ph. 573.364.1891 Details: (Co Clk has m, div, ct & land rec from 1857 & pro rec)
Pike* www.pastracks.com/states/missouri/pike/	G4	14 Dec 1818	**St. Charles** Pike County; 115 W Main St; Bowling Green, MO 63334; Ph. 573.324.2412 Details: (Courthouse burned 1864; no mention of fate of rec) (Rcdr Deeds has land rec from 1819 & m rec from 1825; Pro Ct has pro rec from 1825; Clk Cir Ct has ct rec)
Platte co.platte.mo.us/	N4	31 Dec 1838	**Platte Purchase** Platte County; 415 3rd St; PO Box 30CH; Platte City, MO 64079; Ph. 816.858.2232 Details: (Attached to Clay Co for civil & mil purposes from Dec 1836 to 31 Dec 1838) (Co Clk has b rec 1883-1887 & d rec 1883-1888; Rcdr Deeds has m & land rec; Clk Cir Ct has div rec; Pro Judge has pro & ct rec)
Polk www.rootsweb.com/~mopolk/	K9	5 Jan 1835	**Greene** Polk County; 102 E Broadway St; Bolivar, MO 65613; Ph. 417.326.4031 Details: (Co Rcdr has m rec from 1835 & land rec from 1836; Clk Cir Ct has div & ct rec from 1857; Pro Judge has pro rec from 1947)
Pulaski www.rootsweb.com/~mopulask/ index.htm	I8	19 Jan 1833	**Crawford** Pulaski County; 301 Historic 66 E; Waynesville, MO 65583; Ph. 573.774.4701 Details: (Co Clk has m, div, pro & ct rec from 1903)
Pulaski, old		1818	**Franklin** Details: (Organization not perfected & much of its terr. became Gasconade in 1820; abolished 1819 when terr. of Arkansas was created)
Putnam www.rootsweb.com/~moputnam/	K1	22 Feb 1843	**Linn** Putnam County; Main St #204; Unionville, MO 63565; Ph. 660.947.2674 Details: (When the Iowa boundary was established, the areas of both Putnam & Dodge Cos were below the constitutional limit; Dodge disorganized in 1853 & its terr. was regained by Putnam) (Clk Cir Ct has b rec 1878-1903, m rec from 1854, div & ct rec from 1855 & land rec from 1848; Pro Judge has pro rec from 1848)
Ralls www.pastracks.com/states/missouri/ralls/	G4	16 Nov 1820	**Pike** Ralls County; 311 S Main St; New London, MO 63459; Ph. 573.985.7111 Details: (Co Clk has b & d rec 1883-1886; Clk Cir Ct & Rcdr Deeds has m, div, ct & land rec from 1821; Pro Judge has pro rec)
Randolph www.rootsweb.com/~morandol/	I4	22 Jan 1829	**Chariton** Randolph County; 110 S Main St; Huntsville, MO 65259; Ph. 660.277.4717 Details: (Courthouse burned 1880; a few rec lost) (Co Rcdr has m & land rec; Clk Cir Ct has div rec; Pro Ct has pro rec)

County Website	Map Index	Date Created	Parent County or Territory From Which Organized Address/Details
Ray www.rootsweb.com/~moray/index.htm	L4	16 Nov 1820	**Howard** Ray County; 100 W Main St; PO Box 536; Richmond, MO 64085-0536; Ph. 816.776.4502 Details: (Co Clk has b & d rec 1883-1884; Rcdr Deeds has m & land rec; Clk Cir Ct has div & ct rec; Pro Judge has pro rec) (Rec of interest to genealogists obtainable from Ray Co Hist Soc, Richmond, MO 64085)
Reynolds* www.rootsweb.com/~moreynol/	F9	25 Feb 1845	**Shannon** Reynolds County; Courthouse Sq; Centerville, MO 63633; Ph. 573.648.2494 Details: (Courthouse burned 1872; all rec lost) (Co Clk has b rec from 1883, m, div, pro & ct rec from 1872)
Ripley* www.rootsweb.com/~moripley/	F11	5 Jan 1833	**Wayne** Ripley County; County Courthouse; Doniphan, MO 63935; Ph. 573.996.3215 Details: (Rcdr Deeds has m & land rec from 1833; Pro Ct has pro rec)
Rives		13 Dec 1834	**Lafayette** Details: (see Henry) (Name changed to Henry 15 Feb 1841)
Saline www.rootsweb.com/~mosaline/index.html	K4	25 Nov 1820	**Cooper, Howard** Saline County; 101 E Arrow St; Marshall, MO 65340; Ph. 660.886.3331 Details: (Courthouse burned 1864, but rec were saved) (Co Clk has b & d rec 1883-1885; Marshall Public Lib has cem & genealogy rec)
Schuyler www.rootsweb.com/~moschuy2/index.html	I1	14 Feb 1845	**Adair** Schuyler County; Hwy 136; Lancaster, MO 63548-0187; Ph. 660.457.3842 Details: (Co Clk has b & d rec 1883-1893; Clk Cir Ct has m & div rec; Pro Judge & Mag Cts have pro & ct rec)
Scotland www.rootsweb.com/~moscotla/index.htm	I2	29 Jan 1841	**Lewis** Scotland County; 117 S Market St; Memphis, MO 63555; Ph. 660.465.7027 Details: (Co Clk has b & d rec 1883-1889; Clk Cir Ct has m, div, ct & land rec from 1841; Pro Judge has pro rec from 1841)
Scott www.rootsweb.com/~moscott/ moscott.htm	C10	28 Dec 1821	**New Madrid** Scott County; PO Box 188; Benton, MO 63736-0188; Ph. 573.545.3549 Details: (Rcdr Deeds has m & land rec; Clk Cir Ct has div & ct rec; Pro Judge has pro rec)
Shannon www.rootsweb.com/~moshanno/	G9	29 Jan 1841	**Ripley, Washington** Shannon County; PO Box 187; Eminence, MO 65466; Ph. 573.226.3414 Details: (Courthouse destroyed during Civil War; Courthouse burned 1863, 1871 & 1938; Rcdr Office burned 1893, some land rec in Ironton, MO prior to 1872) (Co Clk has m rec from 1881, div, pro, ct & land rec from 1872)
Shelby* www.rootsweb.com/~moshelby/index.htm	I3	2 Jan 1835	**Marion** Shelby County; PO Box 186; Shelbyville, MO 63469; Ph. 573.633.2181 Details: (Rcdr Deeds has m & land rec; Clk Cir Ct has div rec; Pro Ct has pro rec; Clk Mag Ct has ct rec)
St. Charles www.win.org/county/sccg.htm	F6	1 Oct 1812	**Original district** St. Charles County; 201 N 2nd St; St. Charles, MO 63301; Ph. 636.949.7550 Details: (Rcdr Deeds has m & land rec; Pro Ct has pro rec; Clk Cir Ct has ct rec)
St. Clair www.rootsweb.com/~mostclai/intro.htm	L7	16 Jan 1833	**Lafayette** St. Clair County; PO Box 525; Osceola, MO 64776-0405; Ph. 417.646.2315 Details: (Lost land to Pettis 26 Jan 1833 and attached to Rives until formally organized from Rives Co 29 Jan 1841) (Co Clk has b & d rec 1883-1887; Rcdrs Office has m rec from 1855 & land rec from 1867; Clk Cir Ct has div & pro rec)
St. Francois www.pastracks.com/states/ missouri/stfrancois/	E8	19 Dec 1821	**Jefferson, Ste. Genevieve, Washington** St. Francois County; County Courthouse Sq; Farmington, MO 63640; Ph. 573.756.5411 Details: (Co Rcdr has m & land rec; Clk Cir Ct has div rec; Associate Cir Ct has pro rec)

County Website	Map Index	Date Created	Parent County or Territory From Which Organized / Address/Details
St. Louis www.co.st-louis.mo.us/	E6	1 Oct 1812	**Original district** St. Louis County; 41 S Central Ave; Clayton, MO 63105; Ph. 314.889.2041 Details: (Co Clk has b rec 1877-1910; Rcdr Deeds has m & land rec; Clk Cir Ct has div & ct rec)
St. Louis City stlouis.missouri.org/		5 Mar 1877	**St. Louis** St. Louis City County; 1200 Market St; St. Louis, MO 63103; Ph. 314.622.4000 Details: (City Rcdr has m rec from 1806 & land rec from 1804; Asr has tax rec; Pro Judge has pro rec)
Ste. Genevieve www.geocities.com/Heartland/Estates/ 4882/stegmain.html	E8	1 Oct 1812	**Original District** Ste. Genevieve County; 55 S 3rd St; Ste. Genevieve, MO 63670-1601; Ph. 573.883.5589 Details: (Co Clk has b & d rec 1883-1892; Cir Clk-Rcdr has m, div, ct & land rec; Cir Ct Judge has pro rec)
Stoddard www.rootsweb.com/~mostodd2/ index.html	D10	2 Jan 1835	**Cape Girardeau** Stoddard County; PO Box 110; Bloomfield, MO 63825; Ph. 573.568.3339 Details: (Courthouse burned 1864 but rec had been removed to safety) (Co Clk has b rec 1883-1886 & mil rec; Rcdr Deeds has m & land rec; Clk Cir Ct has div rec; Pro Judge has pro rec; Clk Mag Ct has ct rec)
Stone www.rootsweb.com/~mostone/stone.htm	K10	10 Feb 1851	**Taney** Stone County; PO Box 45; Galena, MO 65656; Ph. 417.357.6127 Details: (Co Clk has m & land rec from 1851, pro & ct rec from 1800's & mil dis rec from 1918)
Sullivan www.rootsweb.com/~mosulliv/index.html	K2	17 Feb 1843	**Linn** Sullivan County; 109 N Main St; Milan, MO 63556; Ph. 660.265.3786 Details: (Rcdr Deeds has incomplete b rec 1867-1895, m & land rec from 1845, d rec 1883-1896; Clk Cir Ct has div & ct rec from 1845; Pro Judge has pro rec from 1845)
Taney www.rootsweb.com/~motaney/taney.htm	J10	6 Jan 1837	**Greene** Taney County; 132 David St; Forsyth, MO 65653-0156; Ph. 417.546.7200 Details: (Courthouse burned 1885) (Clk Cir Ct has m, div, ct & land rec; Pro Judge has pro rec; Co Clk has voter registration rec from 1961)
Texas www.rootsweb.com/~motexas/	H9	17 Feb 1843	**Shannon, Wright** Texas County; 210 N Grand Ave; Houston, MO 65483-1226; Ph. 417.967.2112 Details: (Formerly Ashley Co. Name changed to Texas 14 Feb 1845) (Rcdr Deeds has m rec from 1855 & land rec from 1845; Clk Cir Ct has div & ct rec from 1855; Associate Cir Ct has pro rec from 1850)
Van Buren*		3 Mar 1835	**Jackson** Details: (see Cass) (Name changed to Cass 19 Feb 1849)
Vernon www.rootsweb.com/~movernon/	M8	17 Feb 1851	**Bates** Vernon County; 100 W Cherry St; Nevada, MO 64772; Ph. 417.448.2500 Details: (Vernon created 17 Feb 1851, but act was declared unconstitutional since its territory was exactly that of Bates Co; legally created 27 Feb 1855; reorganized 17 Oct 1865 after total suspension of civil order during Civil War; Courthouse destroyed during that period, but clk had taken the rec with him when he joined the army and all rec were later recovered, except the deed book) (Co Clk has b & d rec 1883-1904; Rcdf Deeds has m & land rec; Clk Cir Ct has div & ct rec; Pro Ct has pro rec; Co Hist Soc has bur rec)
Warren www.rootsweb.com/~mowarren/ index.html	G6	5 Jan 1833	**Montgomery** Warren County; 104 W Market; Warrenton, MO 63383-1903; Ph. 636.456.3331 Details: (Rcdr Deeds has m & land rec from 1833; Pro Ct has pro rec from 1833; Clk Cir Ct has ct rec)
Washington www.rootsweb.com/~mowashin/ index.html	F7	21 Aug 1813	**Ste. Genevieve** Washington County; 102 N Missouri St; Potosi, MO 63664; Ph. 573.438.4901 Details: (Co Clk has b rec 1883-1891 & d rec 1883-1886; Clk Cir Ct has m, div, ct & land rec from 1825; Pro Office has pro rec from 1814)

County Website	Map Index	Date Created	Parent County or Territory From Which Organized Address/Details
Wayne www.rootsweb.com/~mowayne/	**E9**	**11 Dec 1818**	**Cape Girardeau** Wayne County; County Courthouse; Greenville, MO 63944; Ph. 573.224.3011 Details: (Courthouse & all rec burned 1854 & again in 1892) (Co Clk has b & d rec 1914-1940; Clk Cir Ct & Rcdr has m, div & land rec; Associate Cir Ct has pro rec)
Webster www.rootsweb.com/~mowebste/ webster.htm	**J9**	**3 Mar 1855**	**Greene, Wright** Webster County; 100 Crittenden St; Marshfield, MO 65706; Ph. 417.468.2223 Details: (Courthouse burned 1863, but rec were saved, except tax rolls & election returns) (Co Clk has b rec 1883-1893 & d rec 1883-1887; Co Rcdr has m & land rec; Clk Cir Ct has div & ct rec; Pro Judge has pro rec)
Worth www.rootsweb.com/~moworth/worth.html	**M1**	**8 Feb 1861**	**Gentry** Worth County; 4th & Front St; Grant City, MO 64456; Ph. 660.564.2210 Details: (Co Clk has b & d rec 1883-1893, m, div, pro, ct & land rec from 1861)
Wright www.rootsweb.com/~mowright/ wright.htm	**I9**	**29 Jan 1841**	**Pulaski** Wright County; Courthouse Sq; Hartville, MO 65667-0098; Ph. 417.741.6661 Details: (Courthouse burned in 1864, destroying many rec; Courthouse & rec destroyed in 1897) (Clk Cir Ct has m, div & ct rec; Pro Judge has pro rec; Co Rcdr has land rec)

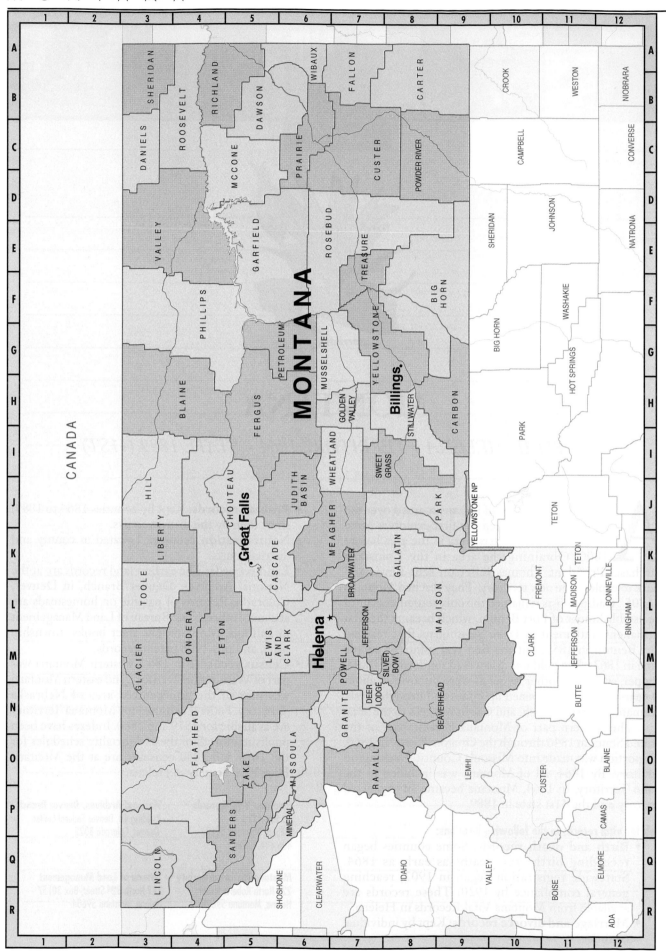

Societies and Repositories

Beaverhead Co. Museum; 15-25 South Montana, PO Box 830; Dillon, Montana 59725

Big Horn County Genealogical Society; Box 51; Hardin, Montana 59034; <www.rootsweb.com/~mtmsgs/soc_bhcgs.htm>

Bitterroot Genealogical Society; 702 S. Fifth Street; Hamilton, Montana 59840; 406.961.3159; <www.rootsweb.com/~mtbgs/>

Broken Mountains Genealogical Society; Box 261; Chester, Montana 59522; <www.rootsweb.com/~mtmsgs/soc_bmgs.htm>

Butte Public Library; 106 W. Broadway St.; Butte, Montana 59701

Carbon County Historical Society; Box 476; Red Lodge, Montana 59068

Cascade Co. Hist. Museum & Archives; 1400 First Ave. North; Great Falls, Montana 59401-3299

Flathead Valley Genealogical Society; 134 Lawrence Lane; Kalispell, Montana 59901

Fort Assiniboine Genealogical Society; c/o Havre Hill County Library; 402 3 St.; Havre, Montana 59501-3644; <www.rootsweb.com/~mtmsgs/soc_fags.htm>

Gallatin Genealogical Society; PO Box 1793; Bozeman, Montana 59715-1783; <www.rootsweb.com/~mtmsgs/soc_ggs.htm>

Glendive Public Library; 200 S. Kendrick Ave.; Glendive, Montana 59330; 406.377.3633

Great Falls Genealogical Society; High Plains Heritage Center; 422 Second Street South; Great Falls, Montana 59405; <www.mt.net/~gfgs/>

Havre-Hill Co. Library; PO Box 1151; Havre, Montana 59501

Historian Archivist, Diocese of Helena; 515 North Ewing, PO Box 1729; Helena, Montana 59624; 406.442.5820; Fax 406.442.5191

Lewis & Clark Co. Gen. Library; 120 S. Last Chance, Goltch; Helena, Montana 59620; 406.447.1690

Lewis and Clark County Genealogical Society; PO Box 5313; Helena, Montana 59604; <www.mth.mtlib.org/Local Information/L&C genealogy.htm>

Lewistown Genealogical Society, Inc.; 701 West Main; Lewistown, Montana 59457;

Liberty Co. Library; PO Box 458; Chester, Montana 59522-0458; 406.759.5445

Mansfield Library; Univ. of Montana; Missoula, Montana 59812

Methodist, Montana Methodist Historical Society; Rocky Mountain College, 1511 Poly Dr.; Billings, Montana 59102; 406.657.1087; Fax 406.657.1085

Miles City Genealogical Society; c/o Miles City Public Library; PO Box 711; Miles City, Montana 59301; <www.geocities.com/Heartland/Fields/6175/>

Miles City Public Library; 1 South 10th; Miles City, Montana 59301

Milk River Genealogical Society; Box 1000; Chinook, Montana 59523; <www.rootsweb.com/~mtmsgs/soc_mrgs.htm>

Mineral County Historical Society; Box 533; Superior, Montana 59872

Missoula Public Library; Pine & Pattee Sts.; Missoula, Montana 59801

Montana Beaverhead-Hunters Genealogical Society; 15 S. Montana; Dillon, Montana 59725; <www.rootsweb.com/~mtbhhgs/>

Montana Historical Society; 225 North Roberts Street; Helena, Montana 59620-1201; Fax 406.444.2696

Montana State Genealogical Society; PO Box 555; Chester, Montana 59522; <www.rootsweb.com/~mtmsgs/>

Montana State Library; 1515 6th Avenue; PO Box 201800; Helena, Montana 59620-1800; 406.444.5612;

Montana State Library; 930 E. Lyndale Ave.; Helena, Montana 59601

Montana State Office of the Bureau of Land Management; 222 North 32nd Street, PO Box 36800; Billings, Montana 59107-6800; 406.255.2885; Fax 406.255.2894

Montana State University, Renne Library; PO Box 173320; Bozeman, Montana 59717-3320; 406.994.3119; Fax 406.994.2851

Montana Vital Records, State Department of Health; PO Box 4210; Helena, Montana 59604-4210; 406.444.2685; Fax 406.444.1803

National Archives Records Administration-Rocky Mountain Region (Denver); Building 48, Denver Federal Center, PO Box 25307; Denver, Colorado 80225; 303.236.0817; Fax 303.236.9297;

Northwest Montana Historical Society; PO Box 2293; Kalispell, Montana 59903; <www.digisys.net/museum/>

Parmly Billings Library; 510 N. Broadway; Billings, Montana 59101

Phillips County Genealogical Society; PO Box 334; Malta, Montana 59538; <www.rootsweb.com/~mtmsgs/soc_phcgs.htm>

Powell County Genealogical Society; 912 Missouri Ave.; Deer Lodge, Montana 59722; <www.rootsweb.com/~mtmsgs/soc_pcgs.htm>

Presbyterian Historical Society, United Presbyterian Church in the U.S.; 425 Lombard Street; Philadelphia, Pennsylvania 19147-1516; 215.627.1852; Fax 215.627.0509

Roman Catholic, Archives of the Diocese of Great Falls-Billings; 121 23rd Street So., PO Box 1399; Great Falls, Montana 59403-1399; 406.727.6683; Fax 406.454.3480

Root Diggers Genealogical Society; PO Box 249; Glasgow, Montana 59230

Sheridan Daybreakers Genealogical Society; 318 N Adams St.; Plentywood, Montana 59254; <www.petersnn.org/daybreakers/scdgsindex.htm>

Sons of the American Revolution, Montana Society; 408 S. Black; Bozeman, Montana 59715

Tangled Roots Genealogical Society; PO Box 1992; Cut Bank, Montana 59427; <www.rootsweb.com/~mtmsgs/soc_trgs.htm>

Tree Branches, Dawson County, Montana; PO Box 1275; Glendive, Montana 59330-1275; <www.cheyenneancestors.com/dawson/dwsgens.html>

University of Montana; Mansfield Library; Missoula, Montana 59812; 406.243.6800; Fax 406.243.2060

Western Montana Genealogical Society; PO Box 2714; Missoula, Montana 59806-2714; <www.rootsweb.com/~mtwmgs/>

Yellowstone Genealogical Forum; c/o Parmly Billings Library; 510 N. Broadway; Billings, Montana 59101; <www.rootsweb.com/~mtygf/>

Yellowstone Valley Chapter, AHSGR; 715 W 5th Street; Laurel, Montana 59044; 406.628.6795

Bibliography and Record Sources

General Sources

A Directory of Churches and Religious Organizations in Montana. Bozeman: Historical Records Survey, 1941.

Borneman, Patricia. *Speaking of Montana: A Guide to The Oral History Collection at the Montana Historical Society, through 1996.* Helena, Montana: Montana Historical Society Press, 1997.

Burlingame, Merrill G. and K. Ross Toole, eds., *A History of Montana, 3 vols.* New York: Lewis Historical Publishing Co., 1957.

Cheney, Roberta Charkeek. *Names on The Face of Montana: The Story of Montana's Place Names.* Missoula, Montana: Mountain Press Pub. Co., 1992, 1983.

Coleman, Julie L. *Golden Opportunities, A Biographical History of Montana's Jewish Communities with Portraits and Maps, vol. 1.* Akron, Ohio: Society of Montana Pioneers, 1899.

Edwards, George. *The Pioneer Work of the Presbyterian Church in Montana.* (Philadelphia: Microfilmed by the Presbyterian Historical Society, 1992).

Flaherty, Cornelia M. *Go With Haste into the Mountains; A History of the Diocese of Helena.* [Helena, Montana]: The Diocese, c[1984?].

Historical Records Survey. *A Directory of Churches and Religious Organizations in Montana, 1941.* Bozeman, Montana: [s.n.], 1941.

Historical Sketch of South-Central Montana. [S.l: s.n., 19-?].

Hyde, C. W. G. *History of The Great Northwest and Its Men of Progress: A Select List of Biographical Sketches and Portraits of The Leaders in Business, Professional and Official Life.* Minneapolis: Minneapolis Journal, 1901.

Johnson, Coburn. *Bibliography of Montana Local Histories.* Montana: Montana Library Association, 1977.

Johnson, Dorothy M. *The Bloody Bozeman: The Perilous Trail to Montana's Gold.* Missoula, Mont.: Mountain Press Pub. Co., 1998, 1983.

Lowe, James A. *The Bridger Trail: A Viable Alternative Route to the Gold Fields of Montana Territory in 1864; With Excerpts from Emigrant Diaries, Letters, and Comparative Material from Oregon and Bozeman Trail Diaries.* Spokane: Arthur H Clark Co, 1999.

Mills, Edward Laird. *Plains, Peaks and Pioneers: Eighty Years of Methodism in Montana.* Portland, Ore.: Binfords & Mort, 1947.

Montana Historical Society, comp. "*List of Early Settlers: A List of All Persons (Except Indians) Who Were in What Is Now Montana During the Winter of 1862-1863,*" *Contributions to the Historical Society of Montana....* 2d ed. Helena: Rocky Mountain Publishing Co., 1902.

Montana Research Outline. Series US-States, NO. 27, Salt Lake City: Family History Library, 1988.

Montana: Inventory of the County Archives: Flathead, Lake, Lincoln, Mineral, Ravalli, Sanders. [S.l.: s.n., 1940?].

Nicklas, Laurie. *The Montana Locator, A Directory of Public Records for Locating People Dead or Alive.* Modesto, California: the author, 1999.

Palladino, Lawrence Benedict. *Indian and White in the Northwest; or, A History of Catholicity in Montana.* Baltimore. John Murphy & Co., 1894.

Parpart, Paulette K., and Donald E. Spritzer, comps. *Montana Data Index: A Reference Guide to Historical and Genealogical Resources.* [Missoula, Mont.?]: Montana Library Association, 1992.

Parpart, Paulette K., and Donald E. Spritzer, comps. *The Montana Historical and Genealogical Data Index.* [Missoula, Mont.?]: Montana Library Association Indexing Special Interest Group, 1987.

Progressive Men of the State of Montana. Chicago: A. W. Bowen and Co., 1901.

Richards, Dennis Lee. *Montana's Genealogical and Local History Records: A Selected List of Books, Manuscripts, and Periodicals.* Detroit: Gale Research Co., 1981.

Richards, Dennis. *Montana's Genealogical and Local History Records. Gale Genealogy*

Sanders, Helen Fitzgerald. *A History of Montana.* 3 vols. Chicago: Lewis Pub. Co., 1913.

Schoenberg, Wilfred P. *A History of the Catholic Church in the Pacific Northwest, 1743-1983.* Washington, D.C.: Pastoral Press, 1987.

Schoenberg, Wilfred P. *Jesuits in Montana, 1840-1960.* Portland, Oregon: Oregon-Jesuit, 1960.

Shirley, Gayle Corbett. *More Than Petticoats: Remarkable Montana Women.* Helena, Mont.: Falcon, 1995.

Southern California Genealogical Society. *Sources of Genealogical Help in Montana.* Burbank, California: SCGS, n.d.

Stoner, Al. *First Families of Montana and Early Settlers.* [Lewistown, Mont.?]: Montana State Genealogical Society, 2000.

Stout, Tom. *Montana, Its Story and Biography: a History of Aboriginal and Territorial Montana and Three Decades of Statehood.* 3 vols. Chicago: American Historical Society, 1921.

Toole, K. Ross. *Twentieth Century Montana: A State of Extremes.* Norman [Okla.]: University of Oklahoma Press, 1972.

United States. Department of State. *Territorial Papers of Montana, 1864-1872.* Washington, D.C.: The National Archives, 1963. 2 microfilm.

United States. Work Projects Administration (Montana). *Inventory of the County Archives of Montana: no. 5 Carbon, no. 16 Gallatin, no. 34 Park, no. 48 Stillwater, no. 49 Sweet Grass.* Bozeman, Mont.: The Survey, 1942.

VanDersal and Conner's Stockgrowers Directory of Marks and Brands for the State of Montana, 1872-1900: Comprising an Alphabetical List of Names of All Livestock Companies and…Sheep and Wool Growers. Glendive, Montana: Review Printing Co., 1974.

Waldron, Ellis. *Montana Legislators, 1864-1979: Profiles and Biographical Directory.* Missoula, Mont.: University of Montana, Bureau of Government Research, 1980.

Weisel, George F. *Men and Trade on the Northwest Frontier as Shown by the Fort Owen Ledger.* Missoula, Montana: Montana State University, 1955

Whithorn, Doris. *Bicentennial Tapestry of the Yellowstone Conference.* [United Methodist Church from 1784- 1984.] [United States: s.n.], 1984 (Livingston, Montana: The Livingston Enterprise.)

Atlases, Maps and Gazetteers

Cheney, Roberta Charkeek. *Names on the Face of Montana: The Story of Montana's Place Names.* Missoula. Montana: Mountain Press Pub. Co., 1992.

Highsmith, Richard M. *Atlas of the Pacific Northwest: Resources and Development.* 4th ed. Corvallis, Oregon: Oregon State University Press, 1968.

Koury, Michael J. *The Military Posts of Montana.* Bellev, Nebraska: Old Army Press, 1970.

Lutz, Dennis, and Meryl Lutz. "Montana Post Offices: 1864-1974." *Montana Postal Cache: Research Journal of the Montana Postal History Society* part 1, A-C, 1 (February 1975) M1-M24; part, D-1, 1(May 1975): M25-M49, part 3, J-P, 1 (August 1975): M50-M74; part 4, Q-Z, 1 (November 1975): M75-M103.

Montana Atlas and Gazetteer. Freeport, Maine: DeLorme Mapping Co., 1995.

Montana Historical Society (Helena, Montana). *Catalog of the Map Collection.* [Helena, Mont.: The Society, 1983?]. 8 microfiche.

Northwestern Gazetteer, Minnesota, North and South Dakota and Montana Gazetteer and Business Directory. St. Paul: R. L. Polk & Company, 1914.

Census Records

Available Census Records and Census Substitutes

Federal Census 1860 (eastern part with Nebraska, western part with Washington), 1870, 1880, 1900, 1910, 1920, 1930.

Federal Mortality Schedules 1870, 1880.

Union Veterans and Widows 1890.

Dollarhide, William. *The Census Book: A Genealogist's Guide to Federal Census Facts, Schedules and Indexes.* Bountiful, Utah: Heritage Quest, 1999.

Kemp, Thomas J. *The American Census Handbook.* Wilmington, Delaware: Scholarly Resources, Inc., 2001.

Lainhart, Ann S. *State Census Records.* Baltimore: Genealogical Publishing Co., Inc, 1992.

Szucs, Loretto Dennis, and Matthew Wright. *Finding Answers in U.S. Census Records.* Ancestry Publishing, 2001.

Thorndale, William, and William Dollarhide. *Map Guide to the U.S. Federal Censuses, 1790-1920.* Baltimore: Genealogical Publishing Co., 1987.

Court Records, Probate and Wills

Note: From 1864 through 1889, probate courts existed in each county. The probate records as well as other court records, are filed in county courthouses. Look for other court records at the National Archives Regional Internet Sites at <www.nara.gov/regional/>.

Emigration, Immigration, Migration and Naturalization

Fuhrman, Diane. *Swedish Immigrants Living in Montana, 1900.* Bozeman, Montana: the author, 1989.

United States. District Court (Montana: Southern District). *Declaration of Intent, 1891-1929; Petition for Naturalization, 1891- 1929; Citizenship Records, 1894-1906; Certificates, 1907-1927.* Microfilm of originals in the Federal Archives, Seattle Branch, Seattle, Washington. (Salt Lake City: Filmed by the Genealogical Society of Utah, 1988). 3 microfilm.

United States. Immigration and Naturalization Service. *Indexes to Naturalization Records of the Montana Territorial and Federal Courts, 1868-1929.* Washington, D.C.: National Archives, 1987.

Land and Property

Note: For land entries, including deeds and land patents, contact individual county clerks. Also contact the Montana Office of The Bureau of Land Management at 405.896.5004. Additional records for land-entry papers prior to 1908 can be found at the National Archives Records Administration, Pacific Alaska Region Branch in Seattle or online at <www.nara.gov/regional/seattle.html>.

Hone, Wade E. *Land and Property Research in the United States.* Salt Lake City: Ancestry Incorporated, 1997.

MacDonald, Marie Peterson. *After Barbed Wire: A Pictorial History of the Homestead Rush into the Northern Great Plains, 1900-1919.* Glendive, Mont.: Frontier Gateway Museum, 1963.

United States. Bureau of Land Management. *Tract Books.* Washington, D.C.: Records Improvement, Bureau of Land Management.

Wollaston, Percy. *Homesteading; A Montana Family Album.* New York: Lyons Press, 1997.

Military

Carroll, John M., and Byron Price. *Roll Call on the Little Big Horn, 28 June 1876.* Fort Collins, Colorado: The Old Army Press, 1974.

Hammer, Kenneth. *Men with Custer: Biographies of the 7th Cavalry, 25 June, 1876.* Fort Collins, Colorado: The Old Army Press, 1972.

Nagles, James C. *U.S. Military Records: A Guide to Federal & State Sources, Colonial America to the Present.* Ancestry Incorporated, 1994.

National Archives Trust Fund Board. *Military Service Records: A Select Catalog of National Archives Microfilm Publications.* Washington, D.C.: National Archives Trust Fund Board, 1985.

United States. Selective Service System. *Montana. World War I Selective Service System Draft Registration Cards, 1917-1918.* National Archives Microfilm Publications, M1509. Washington, D.C.: National Archives, 1987-1988.

Vital and Cemetery Records

Note: Vital records are available at the Montana Department of Public Health and Human Services Vital Statistics Bureau, PO Box 4210, Helena, Montana 59604. For current information on holdings and cost visit the Web site at <www.allvitalrecords.com/>.

Cemetery Records of Montana. 3 vols. Typescript. Salt Lake City: Genealogical Society of Utah, 1947-61.

Historical Records Survey Project, Division of Professional and Service Projects, Work Projects Administration. *Guide to the Public Vital Statistics in Montana....* Bozeman: Historical Records Survey, 1941.

Inventory of the Vital Statistics Records of Church and Religious Organizations in Montana. Bozeman, Montana: Historical Records Survey, 1942.

Jackson, Ronald Vern. *Montana 1870 Mortality Schedule.* Bountiful, Utah: Accelerated Indexing Systems, c1981.

Lewistown Genealogy Society, prep. *Montana Cemetery Records.* Microfilm of original transcript in possession of the Lewistown Genealogy Society, Lewistown, Montana. (Salt Lake City: Filmed by the Genealogical Society of Utah, 1982).

Moog, Una. *Cemetery Inscriptions and Church Records from Hingham, Rudyard, Inverness, Whitlash, Lothair, Joplin and Chester, Montana.* Chester, Montana: Broken Mountains Genealogical Society, 1986.

County Website	Map Index	Date Created	Parent County or Territory From Which Organized Address/Details
Beaverhead*	**N9**	**2 Feb 1865**	**Original county**
www.beaverhead.com/			Beaverhead County; 2 S Pacific Cluster 3; Dillon, MT 59725; Ph. 406.683.2642 Details: (Co Clk has b rec from 1902, d rec from 1901 & land rec from 1864; Clk Dis Ct has div, pro & ct rec)
Big Horn	**F8**	**13 Jan 1913**	**Rosebud, Yellowstone**
www.geocities.com/Heartland/Acres/7759/			Big Horn County; 121 3rd St W; Hardin, MT 59034; Ph. 406.665.1506 Details: (Co Clk has b, d, nat & land rec from 1913; Clk Dis Ct has m, div, pro & ct rec)
Blaine	**H4**	**29 Feb 1912**	**Chouteau**
www.rootsweb.com/~mtblaine/			Blaine County; 400 Ohio St; Chinook, MT 59523; Ph. 406.357.3240 Details: (Co Clk has b, d & land rec from 1912; Clk Dis Ct has m, div, pro & ct rec)
Broadwater	**L7**	**9 Feb 1897**	**Jefferson, Meagher**
www.mtrdp.org/broadwater/			Broadwater County; 515 Broadway; Townsend, MT 59644; Ph. 406.266.3443 Details: (Co Clk-Rcdr has b & d rec from 1900, land & mil rec; Clk Ct has m, div, pro, ct & nat rec)
Carbon*	**H9**	**4 Mar 1895**	**Park, Yellowstone, Custer**
www.rootsweb.com/~mtcarbon/_crb.html			Carbon County; PO Box 948; Red Lodge, MT 59068; Ph. 406.446.1225 Details: (Co Clk has b rec from 1878, d rec from 1903, m, div, pro, ct & land rec from 1895)
Carter	**B8**	**22 Feb 1917**	**Custer**
www.rootsweb.com/~mtcarter/index.html			Carter County; 214 Park St; Ekalaka, MT 59324; Ph. 406.775.8749 Details: (Co Clk has b, d & land rec from 1917; Clk Cts has m, div, pro & ct rec)
Cascade	**K5**	**12 Sep 1887**	**Chouteau, Meagher, Lewis & Clark**
www.rootsweb.com/~mtcascad/			Cascade County; 425 2nd Ave N; Great Falls, MT 59401; Ph. 406.454.6800 Details: (Co Clk & Rcdr has b, d & land rec from 1897 & mil rec from 1918; Clk Cts has m, div, pro & ct rec)
Chouteau	**J4**	**2 Feb 1865**	**Original county**
users.eznet.net/~lynch/chouteau/ chouteau.html			Chouteau County; 1308 Franklin St; Fort Benton, MT 59442; Ph. 406.622.5151 Details: (Co Clk has b & d rec from 1895, bur rec & land rec from 1878; Clk Cts has m rec from 1888, div & ct rec from 1879 & pro rec from 1892)
Custer	**C7**	**2 Feb 1865**	**Original county**
www.rootsweb.com/~mtcuster/			Custer County; 1010 Main St; Miles City, MT 59301-3419; Ph. 406.232.7800 Details: (Formerly Big Horn Co. Name changed to Custer 16 Feb 1877) (Co Clk has b & d rec from 1907 & land rec from 1909; Clk Dis Ct has m, div & pro rec; JP has ct rec)
Daniels	**C3**	**30 Aug 1920**	**Valley, Sheridan**
www.petersnn.org/nemontana/ nemont/index.htm			Daniels County; 213 Main St; PO Box 247; Scobey, MT 59263; Ph. 406.487.5561 Details: (Co Clk-Rcdr has b & d rec from 1920 & land rec; Clk Ct has m, div & pro rec from 1920; Clk Dis Ct has ct rec)
Dawson	**B5**	**15 Jan 1869**	**Original county**
www.cheyenneancestors.com/dawson/			Dawson County; 207 W Bell St; Glendive, MT 59330-1694; Ph. 406.377.3058 Details: (Co Clk has b & d rec from 1895 & land rec from 1882; Clk Cts has m, div & ct rec from 1882 & pro rec from 1889)
Deer Lodge	**N7**	**2 Feb 1865**	**Original county**
www.mtech.edu/silverbow/deerlodge.htm			Deer Lodge County; 800 S Main St; Anaconda, MT 59711-2999; Ph. 406.563.4061 Details: (Co Clk has b, d & land rec; Clk Cts has m, div, ct & pro rec)
Edgerton		**2 Feb 1865**	**Original county**
			Details: (see Lewis & Clark) (Name changed to Lewis & Clark 20 Dec 1867)
Fallon	**B7**	**9 Dec 1913**	**Custer**
www.rootsweb.com/~mtfallon/_fll.html			Fallon County; 10 W Fallon Ave; Baker, MT 59313; Ph. 406.778.7106 Details: (Co Clk-Rcdr has b rec from 1884, d rec from 1919, land & mil dis rec; Clk Cts has m rec from 1913, div, pro & ct rec)
Fergus*	**H5**	**12 Mar 1885**	**Meagher, Chouteau**
www.rootsweb.com/~mtfergus/			Fergus County; 712 W Main St; Lewistown, MT 59457-2562; Ph. 406.538.5119 Details: (Co Clk has b & d rec; Clk Cts has m, div, pro & ct rec; Co Asr has land rec)

County Website	Map Index	Date Created	Parent County or Territory From Which Organized Address/Details
Flathead* www.co.flathead.mt.us/	04	6 Feb 1893	**Missoula** Flathead County; 800 S Main St; Kalispell, MT 59901; Ph. 406.758.5526 Details: (Co Clk & Rcdr has b & d rec from 1882, land rec from 1884 & bur rec from 1893; Clk Dis Ct has m, div, pro & ct rec from 1893)
Gallatin www.rootsweb.com/~mtgallat/ Gallatin.htm	K8	2 Feb 1865	**Original county** Gallatin County; 311 W Main St; Bozeman, MT 59715-4576; Ph. 406.582.3050 Details: (Co Clk-Rcdr has b & d rec from 1890, land rec from 1865 & mil dis rec from 1900; Clk Dis Ct has m, div, pro & ct rec from 1865)
Garfield www.rootsweb.com/~mtgarfie/	E5	7 Feb 1919	**Dawson** Garfield County; Hwy 200; PO Box 7; Jordan, MT 59337-0007; Ph. 406.557.2760 Details: (Co Clk has b rec from 1919, d & land rec; Clk Cts has m, div, pro & ct rec)
Glacier www.rootsweb.com/~mtglacie/	M3	17 Feb 1919	**Teton** Glacier County; 512 E Main St; Cut Bank, MT 59427; Ph. 406.873.5063 Details: (Co Clk has b, d & land rec from 1919; Clk Cts has m, div, pro & ct rec)
Golden Valley www.rootsweb.com/~mtgolden/	H7	4 Oct 1920	**Musselshell, Sweet Grass** Golden Valley County; PO Box 10; Ryegate, MT 59074-0010; Ph. 406.568.2231 Details: (Co Clk-Rcdr has b, m, d, div, land, pro, mil, ct & nat rec from 1920)
Granite www.rootsweb.com/~mtgranit/	N7	2 Mar 1893	**Deer Lodge** Granite County; Courthouse; 107 Kemp; Philipsburg, MT 59858; Ph. 406.859.3771 Details: (Co Clk-Rcdr has b & d rec from 1882, land rec from 1884 & bur rec from 1893; Clk Cts has m, div, pro & ct rec)
Hill co.hill.mt.us/	J3	28 Feb 1912	**Chouteau** Hill County; County Courthouse; 315 4th St; Havre, MT 59501-3999; Ph. 406.265.5481 Details: (Co Clk & Rcdr has b & d rec from 1907 & land rec from 1865; Clk Cts has m, div, pro & ct rec)
Jefferson www.rootsweb.com/~mtjeffer/index.html	L7	2 Feb 1865	**Original county** Jefferson County; 201 Centennial; PO Box H; Boulder, MT 59632; Ph. 406.225.4020 Details: (Co Clk has b & d rec from 1907 & land rec from 1865; Clk Dis Ct has m, div, pro & ct rec)
Judith Basin www.rootsweb.com/~mtjudith/	J6	10 Dec 1920	**Fergus, Cascade** Judith Basin County; 31 1st Ave; PO Box 427; Stanford, MT 59479; Ph. 406.553.2301 Details: (Co Clk & Rcdr has b, d & land rec from 1920; Clk Cts has m, div, pro & ct rec)
Lake* www.rootsweb.com/~mtlake/mtlake.html	O5	11 May 1923	**Flathead, Missoula** Lake County; 106 4th Ave E; Polson, MT 59860-2125; Ph. 406.883.6211 Details: (Co Clk-Rcdr has b, d & land rec from 1923; Clk Cts has m, div, pro & ct rec from 1923 & nat rec 1923-1953)
Lewis & Clark www.co.lewis-clark.mt.us/	M5	2 Feb 1865	**Original county** Lewis & Clark County; 316 N Park Ave; Helena, MT 59624; Ph. 406.447.8335 Details: (Formerly Edgerton Co. Name changed to Lewis & Clark 20 Dec 1867) (Co Clk has b rec from 1907, d rec from 1895 & land rec from 1865; Clk Dis Ct has m, div, pro & ct rec)
Liberty www.rootsweb.com/~mtlibert/	K3	11 Feb 1920	**Chouteau, Hill** Liberty County; 111 1st St E; Chester, MT 59522; Ph. 406.759.5365 Details: (Co Clk has b, d & land rec from 1920; Clk Dis Ct has m rec from 1920, div, pro & ct rec)
Lincoln* www.libby.org/	Q3	9 Mar 1909	**Flathead** Lincoln County; 512 California Ave; Libby, MT 59923; Ph. 406.293.7781 Details: (Co Clk has b, d & land rec from 1909; Clk Dis Ct has m, div, pro & ct rec; Co Clk also has some transcribed b & d rec prior to 1909)

County Website	Map Index	Date Created	Parent County or Territory From Which Organized Address/Details
Madison* www.rootsweb.com/~mtmadiso/ madison.html	L9	2 Feb 1865	**Original county** Madison County; 110 W Wallace St; Virginia City, MT 59755; Ph. 406.843.4270 Details: (Co Clk & Rcdr has b & d rec from 1909 & land rec from 1864; Clk Cts has m rec from 1887, div, pro & ct rec from 1865)
McCone www.rootsweb.com/~mtmccone/	C5	20 Feb 1919	**Dawson, Richland** McCone County; 1004 Ave C; PO Box 199; Circle, MT 59215; Ph. 406.485.3505 Details: (Co Clk & Rcdr has b, d, bur & land rec from 1919; Clk Cts has m, div, pro & ct rec)
Meagher www.rootsweb.com/~mtmeaghe/	K6	16 Nov 1867	**Original county** Meagher County; 15 W Main St; PO Box 309; White Sulphur Springs, MT 59645; Ph. 406.547.3612 Details: (Co Clk & Rcdr has b & d rec from 1896, bur rec from 1884 & land rec from 1866; Clk Cts has m & pro rec from 1866, div, ct & nat rec from 1867)
Mineral* www.rootsweb.com/~mtminera/ mineral.htm	P6	7 Aug 1914	**Missoula** Mineral County; 300 River St; PO Box 550; Superior, MT 59872; Ph. 406.822.4541 Details: (Co Clk & Rcdr has b, d, bur & land rec from 1914; Clk Dis Ct has m, div, pro & ct rec from 1914)
Missoula* www.co.missoula.mt.us/	O6	2 Feb 1865	**Original county** Missoula County; 200 W Broadway St; Missoula, MT 59802-4292; Ph. 406.523.4752 Details: (Co Clk has b & d rec from 1895 & land rec; Clk Cts has m, div, pro & ct rec)
Musselshell www.rootsweb.com/~mtmussel/	G6	11 Feb 1911	**Fergus, Yellowstone** Musselshell County; 506 Main St; Roundup, MT 59072-2498; Ph. 406.323.1104 Details: (Co Clk-Rcdr has b, d & land rec from 1911; Clk of Cts has m, div, pro, mil & ct rec from 1911)
Park* www.parkcounty.org/	J8	23 Feb 1887	**Gallatin** Park County; 414 E Callender St; Livingston, MT 59047-2799; Ph. 406.222.4110 Details: (Co Clk has b, d & land rec from 1907; Clk Dis Ct has m, div, pro & ct rec)
Petroleum www.rootsweb.com/~mtpetrol/	G6	24 Nov 1924	**Fergus, Garfield** Petroleum County; 201 E Main; PO Box 226; Winnett, MT 59087; Ph. 406.429.5311 Details: (Director of Rec has b, m, d, bur, div, pro, ct & land rec from 1925)
Phillips www.rootsweb.com/~mtphilli/	F4	5 Feb 1915	**Valley** Phillips County; 314 S 2nd Ave W; Malta, MT 59538; Ph. 406.654.2423 Details: (Co Clk has b, d & land rec; Clk Cts has m, div, pro & ct rec)
Pondera www.rootsweb.com/~mtponder/	M4	17 Feb 1919	**Chouteau, Teton** Pondera County; 20 4th Ave SW; Conrad, MT 59425-2340; Ph. 406.278.4000 Details: (Co Clk has b, d & land rec from 1919; Clk Cts has m, div, pro & ct rec)
Powder River www.rangeweb.net/~emmov/prc.html/	C9	7 Mar 1919	**Custer** Powder River County; PO Box 270; Broadus, MT 59317; Ph. 406.436.2361 Details: (Co Clk has b, d & election rec from 1919 & land rec from 1890's; Clk Dis Ct has m & div rec from 1919, pro & ct rec)
Powell www.mtech.edu/silverbow/powell.htm	N6	31 Jan 1901	**Missoula, Deer Lodge** Powell County; 409 Missouri Ave; Deer Lodge, MT 59722-1084; Ph. 406.846.3680 Details: (Co Clk has b, d & land rec from 1907; Clk Cts has m, div, pro & ct rec from 1901)
Prairie www.rangeweb.net/~emmov/prairie/ index2.html	C6	5 Feb 1915	**Custer** Prairie County; 217 W Park St; Terry, MT 59349; Ph. 406.635.5575 Details: (Co Clk has b, d & land rec from 1915; Clk Cts has m, div, pro & ct rec from 1915)
Ravalli* www.rootsweb.com/~mtravall/	O7	16 Feb 1893	**Missoula** Ravalli County; 300 W River Rd; Hamilton, MT 59894; Ph. 406.822.3520 Details: (Co Clk & Rcdr has b & d rec from 1911, land rec from 1871 & voter reg from 1937; Clk Cts has m, div & ct rec from 1893 & pro rec from 1888)

County Website	Map Index	Date Created	Parent County or Territory From Which Organized Address/Details
Richland www.midrivers.com/~wyldrose/ index.html	**B4**	**27 May 1914**	**Dawson** Richland County; 201 W Main St; Sidney, MT 59270; Ph. 406.482.1708 Details: (Co Clk has b rec from 1910, d & land rec from 1914; Clk Dis Ct has m, div, pro & ct rec)
Roosevelt www.petersnn.org/nemontana/nemont/ index.htm	**C4**	**18 Feb 1919**	**Valley, Richland, Sheridan** Roosevelt County; 400 2nd Ave S; Wolf Point, MT 59201; Ph. 406.653.6250 Details: (Co Clk & Rcdr has b, d & land rec from 1919; Clk Dis Ct has m, div, pro & ct rec from 1919)
Rosebud www.rosebudcounty.homestead.com/	**E6**	**11 Feb 1901**	**Custer** Rosebud County; 1200 Main St; Forsyth, MT 59327-0047; Ph. 406.356.7318 Details: (Co Clk has b & d rec from 1900 & land rec; Clk Dis Ct has m, div, pro & ct rec)
Sanders* www.rootsweb.com/~mtsander/_snd.html	**Q5**	**7 Feb 1905**	**Missoula** Sanders County; 1111 Main St; Thompson Falls, MT 59873; Ph. 406.827.4392 Details: (Co Clk & Rcdr has b, m, div, pro, ct & land rec from 1906 & d rec from 1907)
Sheridan www.co.sheridan.mt.us/	**B3**	**24 Mar 1913**	**Valley** Sheridan County; 100 W Laurel Ave; Plentywood, MT 59254; Ph. 406.765.2310 Details: (Co Clk has b, d, bur & land rec from 1913; Clk Cts has m, div, pro & ct rec from 1913)
Silver Bow* www.mtech.edu/silverbow/	**M8**	**16 Feb 1881**	**Deer Lodge** Silver Bow County; 155 W Granite St; Butte, MT 59701; Ph. 406.723.8262 Details: (2 May 1977 the city of Butte & co of Silver Bow were unified to form the Butte-Silver Bow government. Co Clk & Rcdr has b & d rec from 1890, land rec from 1881 & mil dis rec from 1932; Clk Cts has m, div, pro & ct rec)
Stillwater* www.rootsweb.com/~mtstillw/	**H8**	**24 Mar 1913**	**Sweet Grass, Yellowstone, Carbon** Stillwater County; PO Box 149; Columbus, MT 59019-0149; Ph. 406.322.8000 Details: (Co Clk-Rcdr has b & d rec from late 1800's, land & mil rec; Clk Cts has m rec from late 1800's, div, pro, ct & nat rec)
Sweet Grass* www.rootsweb.com/~mtsweetg/	**I8**	**5 Mar 1895**	**Meagher, Park, Yellowstone** Sweet Grass County; 200 W 1st Ave; Big Timber, MT 59011-0460; Ph. 406.932.5152 Details: (Co Clk & Rcdr has b rec from 1907, d & bur rec from 1900 & land rec from 1895; Clk Dis Ct has m, div, pro & ct rec from 1895)
Teton www.rootsweb.com/~mtteton/index.htm/	**M4**	**7 Feb 1893**	**Chouteau** Teton County; 915 4th St NW; PO Box 610; Choteau, MT 59422; Ph. 406.466.2693 Details: (Co Clk has b, d & bur rec from 1899 & land rec; Clk Dis Ct has m, div, pro & ct rec)
Toole* www.rootsweb.com/~mttoole/	**L3**	**7 May 1914**	**Teton, Hill** Toole County; 226 1st St S; Shelby, MT 59474-1920; Ph. 406.434.2232 Details: (Co Clk & Rcdr has b, d & bur rec from 1914 & land rec from 1890; Clk Cts has m rec from 1914, div, pro & ct rec)
Treasure www.rootsweb.com/~mttreasu/	**F7**	**7 Feb 1919**	**Rosebud** Treasure County; PO Box 392; Hysham, MT 59038-0392; Ph. 406.342.5547 Details: (Co Clk & Rcdr has b, d & land rec from 1919; Clk Dis Ct has m, div, pro & ct rec)
Valley www.petersnn.org/nemontana/ nemont/index.htm	**E3**	**6 Feb 1893**	**Dawson** Valley County; 501 Court Sq Box 1; Glasgow, MT 59203-0311; Ph. 406.228.8221 Details: (Co Clk & Rcdr has b, d & land rec from early 1900's; Clk Cts has m, div, pro & ct rec)
Wheatland www.rootsweb.com/~mtwheatl/	**I7**	**22 Feb 1917**	**Meagher, Sweet Grass** Wheatland County; 201A Ave NW; PO Box 1903; Harlowton, MT 59036; Ph. 406.632.4891 Details: (Co Clk & Rcdr has b rec from 1917, d, bur & land rec; Clk Cts has m, div, pro & ct rec)

County Website	Map Index	Date Created	Parent County or Territory From Which Organized Address/Details
Wibaux www.rootsweb.com/~mtwibaux/	**A6**	**17 Aug 1914**	**Dawson** Wibaux County; 200 S Wilbaux St; Wibaux, MT 59353; Ph. 406.796.2481 Details: (Co Clk-Rcdr has b & d rec from 1914, bur & land rec from mid-1800's & mil rec from 1917; Clk Dis Ct has m, div, pro, ct & nat rec from 1914)
Yellowstone www.co.yellowstone.mt.us/javadefault.asp	**G7**	**26 Feb 1883**	**Gallatin, Meagher, Custer, Carbon** Yellowstone County; 217 N 27th St; PO Box 35001; Billings, MT 59107-5001; Ph. 406.256.2785 Details: (Co Clk-Rcdr has b, d, land & mil rec from 1883; Clk Dis Ct has m, div, pro & ct rec)

Notes

Goldenrod

NEBRASKA

CAPITAL: LINCOLN – TERRITORY 1854 – STATE 1867 (37TH)

Etienne Veniard de Bourgmond is believed to have been the first European to enter the Nebraska area in 1714 as a French adventurer. His report about the area used the term Nebraska for the first time. Six years later a Spanish soldier, Pedro de Villasur, led an expedition into Nebraska but was massacred by Pawnee Indians. Only fur traders braved the area until after the Louisiana Purchase in 1803. At that time, a number of expeditions explored the area, some of which reported Nebraska to be a vast wasteland. The first permanent settlement was Bellevue, established in 1823. Other forts and trading posts were established, especially along the Oregon and Mormon trails.

In 1834, Nebraska was placed under the supervision of Arkansas, Michigan, and Missouri. It was termed Indian Country from which all others were excluded. Later, Nebraska was made part of the territories of Indiana, Louisiana, and Missouri. Most of the Indian tribes had ceded their land to the United States by 1854 when Nebraska became a territory. It included all territory between 40 and 49 degrees north latitude and between the Missouri River and the crest of the Rocky Mountains. Parts of Colorado, Montana, North Dakota, South Dakota, and Wyoming were then part of Nebraska. In 1861, the Colorado and Dakota Territories were created. In 1863, the formation of the Idaho Territory nearly reduced Nebraska to its present size.

Many early settlers were stragglers from the California Gold Rush and the Oregon migration. Some of the thousands who traveled the Oregon, California, and Mormon Trails either stopped their migration in Nebraska or returned to Nebraska upon seeing the Rocky Mountains. During the 1850's, many Germans settled in Nebraska. Two decades later, a large group of Germans from Russia settled Lancaster and nearby counties. After the passage of the Homestead Act, many Scandinavians came to the area. Today many Nebraskans are of German, Czech, Swedish, or Russian descent.

During the Civil War, Nebraska sided with the Union and supplied more than 3,000 men to its forces. The first railroad to the Pacific Coast began at Omaha in 1865. It was completed four years later. Nebraska was admitted to the Union in 1867 as the 37th state. Many Civil War veterans came to Nebraska to secure cheap land and brought about the state's largest population growth.

Look for vital records in the following locations:

- **Birth and death records:** Bureau of Vital Statistics, State Department of Health in Lincoln, Nebraska. Statewide registration of births and deaths began in 1905 and was generally complied with by 1920. Relationship to the individual and the reason for the request must accompany all applications, along with written permission from the individual if the birth occurred within the last 50 years.
- **Marriage records:** Counties kept marriage records. Relationship to the individual and the reason for the request must accompany all applications, along with written permission from the individual if the marriage occurred within the last 50 years.

1 2 3 4 5 6 7 8 9 10 11 12

A B C D E F G H I J K L M N O P Q R

MURRAY NOBLES OSCEOLA O'BRIEN CHEROKEE IDA CRAWFORD SHELBY POTTAWATTAMIE MILLS FREMONT ATCHISON RICHARDSON BROWN ATCHISON JEFFERSON

PIPESTONE ROCK LYON SIOUX PLYMOUTH WOODBURY MONONA HARRISON WASHINGTON DOUGLAS SARPY CASS OTOE NEMAHA JACKSON

MOODY MINNEHAHA LINCOLN UNION DAKOTA THURSTON BURT Omaha Lincoln Lancaster GAGE JOHNSON PAWNEE NEMAHA POTTAWATOMIE

MINER HANSON TURNER CLAY DIXON WAYNE STANTON COLFAX DODGE SAUNDERS BUTLER SEWARD SALINE JEFFERSON WASHINGTON MARSHALL RILEY GEARY

SANBORN DAVISON HUTCHINSON YANKTON CEDAR PIERCE MADISON PLATTE POLK YORK FILLMORE THAYER REPUBLIC CLAY OTTAWA

BON HOMME KNOX ANTELOPE BOONE NANCE MERRICK HAMILTON CLAY NUCKOLLS CLOUD

DOUGLAS CHARLES MIX WHEELER GREELEY HOWARD HALL ADAMS WEBSTER JEWELL MITCHELL LINCOLN

JERAULD AURORA BOYD HOLT GARFIELD VALLEY SHERMAN BUFFALO KEARNEY FRANKLIN SMITH OSBORNE RUSSELL

BUFFALO BRULE GREGORY ROCK LOUP CUSTER DAWSON PHELPS HARLAN PHILLIPS ROOKS ELLIS

KEYA PAHA BLAINE GOSPER FURNAS

LYMAN TRIPP BROWN THOMAS LOGAN LINCOLN FRONTIER RED WILLOW NORTON GRAHAM

JONES MELLETTE TODD CHERRY HOOKER MCPHERSON KEITH DAWSON HAYES HITCHCOCK DECATUR SHERIDAN

GRANT ARTHUR PERKINS CHASE DUNDY CHEYENNE SHERMAN WALLACE LOGAN

NEBRASKA

SHANNON SHERIDAN GARDEN DEUEL SEDGWICK PHILLIPS YUMA KIT CARSON

JACKSON BENNETT RAWLINS THOMAS LOGAN

PENNINGTON DAWES BOX BUTTE MORRILL CHEYENNE LOGAN WASHINGTON

CUSTER SIOUX SCOTTS BLUFF BANNER KIMBALL MORGAN ADAMS ARAPAHOE ELBERT

FALL RIVER

1 2 3 4 5 6 7 8 9 10 11 12

- **Probate records:** County judges usually keep probate records.
- **Census records:** Territorial and state census records exist for parts of Nebraska for 1854, 1855, 1856, 1860, 1865, and 1869. A detailed census of German immigrants from Russia living in Lincoln was taken from 1913 to 1914. Some of these census records have been transcribed, indexed, and published. Contact the Nebraska State Historical Society, Department of Reference Services.

Bureau of Vital Statistics
State Department of Health
PO Box 95065
Lincoln, Nebraska 68509
402.471.2871

Nebraska State Historical Society
Department of Reference Services
1500 "R" Street; PO Box 82554
Lincoln, Nebraska 68501

Societies and Repositories

Adams County Genealogical Society; PO Box 424; Hastings, Nebraska 68902-0424; <incolor.inetnebr.com/achs/acgs.html>

Adams County Historical Society; PO Box 102; Hastings, Nebraska 68902; <incolor.inetnebr.com/achs/>

Alliance Public Library; 520 PO Box Butte Ave.; Alliance, Nebraska 69301

American Historical Society of Germans from Russia; 631 "D" Street; Lincoln, Nebraska 68502-1199; 402.474.3363; Fax 402.474.7229;

Boone-Nance County Genealogical Society; PO Box 231; Belgrade, Nebraska 68623; <www.rootsweb.com/~nenance/bngensoc.html>

Buffalo County Historical Society; PO Box 523; Kearney, Nebraska 68848-0523; <bchs.kearney.net/index.html>

Bureau of Land Management; 2515 Warren Avenue, PO Box 1828; Cheyenne, Wyoming 82003; 307.775.6001; Fax 307.775.6082

Butler County Historical Society; 1125 3rd St.; David City, Nebraska 68632

Cairo Roots; Rt. 1, PO Box 42; Cairo, Nebraska 68824

Chase County Genealogical Society; PO Box 303; Imperial, Nebraska 69033

Chase County Historical Society; 73989 320th Avenue; Imperial, Nebraska 69033-8616; <freepages.genealogy.rootsweb.com/~chasecountyne/>

Cherry County Genealogical Society; PO Box 380; Valentine, Nebraska 69201

Cheyenne County Genealogical Society; PO Box 802; Sidney, Nebraska 69162

Cozad Genealogical Club; c/o Cozad Public Library; 910 Meridian Ave.; Cozad, Nebraska 69130

Cravath Memorial Library; Hay Spring, Nebraska 69347

Cuming County Historical Society; 130 N. River; West Point, Nebraska 68788

Custer County Historical Society, Inc.; PO Box 334; 445 S. 9th Ave.; Broken Bow, Nebraska 68822-0334; <www.rootsweb.com/~necuster/index.htm>

Dakota County Genealogical Society; PO Box 18; Dakota City, Nebraska 68850

Danish Immigrant Archive; Dana College; Blair, Nebraska 68008-1041

Dawson County Genealogical Society; 514 E. 8th Street; Cozad, Nebraska 69130

Dawson County Historical Society; PO Box 369; Lexington, Nebraska 68850

Denton Community Historical Society; PO Box 405; Denton, Nebraska 68339

Dixon County Historical Society; PO Box 95; Allen, Nebraska 68710

Douglas County Health Department; 1819 Farnam Street Room 401; Omaha, Nebraska 68183-0401; 402.444.7213; Fax 402.444.6267

Eastern Nebraska Genealogical Society; PO Box 541; Fremont, Nebraska 68025; <www.connectfremont.org/CLUB/ENGS.HTM>

Elkhorn Valley Genealogical Society; c/o I.A. Stahl Library, PO Box 259; West Point, Nebraska 68788; <www.rootsweb.com/~necuming/evgs.html>

Family History Library: 35 North West Temple Street: Salt Lake City, Utah 84150: 800.346.6044 or 801.240.2584: <www.familysearch.org>: Find a Family History Center near you: <www.familysearch.org/Eng/Library/FHC/frameset_fhc.asp>

Fillmore Heritage Genealogical Society; Rt. 2, PO Box 28; Exeter, Nebraska 68351

Fort Kearney Genealogical Society; PO Box 22; Kearney, Nebraska 68847; <rootsweb.com/~nebuffal/fkgs.htm>

Frontier County Genealogical Society; PO Box 507; Curtis, Nebraska 69025

Furnas County Genealogical Society; PO Box 391; Beaver City, Nebraska 68926; <www.rootsweb.com/~nefurnas/GenSocResources.html>

Gage County Historical Society; PO Box 793; Beatrice, Nebraska 68310

Genealogical Seekers; 462 East 13th St.; Wahoo, Nebraska 68066-1415

Genealogical Society of Wayne, NE; 1028 Emerald Drive; Wayne, Nebraska 68787-1000

Grand Island Public Library; 211 S. Washington; Grand Island, Nebraska 68801

Greater Omaha Genealogical Society; PO Box 4011; Omaha, Nebraska 68104-0011; <members.aol.com/_ht_a/gromahagensoc/myhomepage/>

Greater York Area Genealogical Society; c/o Kilgore Memorial Library; 6th and Nebraska; York, Nebraska 68467

Holdrege Area Genealogical Club; PO Box 164; Holdrege, Nebraska 68949

Holt County Genealogical Society; PO Box 376; O'Neill, Nebraska 68763

Holt County Historical Society; 402 E Douglas; O'Neill, Nebraska 68763; <www.rootsweb.com/~neholths/>

Hooker County Genealogical Society; PO Box 280; Mullen, Nebraska 69152

Howard County Historical Society; PO Box 304; St. Paul, Nebraska 68873

Howard County Kinquesters; 317 7th Street; St. Paul, Nebraska 68873

J. A. Stahl Library; PO Box 258; West Point, Nebraska 68788; 402.372.3831

Jefferson County Genealogical Society; PO Box 163; Fairbury, Nebraska 68352-0163; <www.rootsweb.com/~nejeffgs/>

Jensen Memorial Library; 443 N. Kearney; Minden, Nebraska 68959

Johnson County Historical Society & Museum; 231 Lincoln Street; Tecumseh, Nebraska 68450; <www.rootsweb.com/~nejohnso/jchstsoc.htm>

Lexington Genealogical Society; PO Box 778; Lexington, Nebraska 68850; <www.rootsweb.com/~nedawson/lexsoc.html>

Lexington Public Library; PO Box 778; Lexington, Nebraska 68850

Lincoln Nebraska Chapter, AHSGR; 3300 Serenity Circle #10; Lincoln, Nebraska 68506; <www.ahsgr.org/nelincol.html>

Lincoln-Lancaster County Genealogical Society; PO Box 30055; Lincoln, Nebraska 68503-0055

Lue R. Spencer DAR Gen. Library, c/o Edith Abbott Memorial Library; 2nd & Washington St.; Grand Island, Nebraska 68801

Lutheran, Archives of the Nebraska Synod; 4980 South 118 Street, Suite D; Omaha, Nebraska 68137; 402.896.5311; Fax 402.896.5354

Madison County Genealogical Society; PO Box 1031; Norfolk, Nebraska 68702-1031

Methodist, Nebraska Wesleyan University, Historical Archives United Methodist Church; 5000 St. Paul Avenue; Lincoln, Nebraska 68504; 402.465.2400; Fax 402.465.2189

Midlands Chapter, AHSGR; 9373 Maplewood Blvd.; Omaha, Nebraska 68134-4663; 402.572.8871

Nancy Fawcett Memorial Library; Lodgepole, Nebraska 69149

Naponee Historical Society; PO Box 128; Naponee, Nebraska 68960; <home.4w.com/pages/psimpson/naponeehist.html>

National Archives-Central Plains Region; 2312 East Bannister Road; Kansas City, Missouri 64131; 816.926.6934; Fax 816.926.6982

Nebraska DAR Library; 202 West 4th St.; Alliance, Nebraska 69301

Nebraska Health and Human Services System, Bureau of Vital Statistics; 301 Centennial Mall So., 3rd Floor, PO Box 95065; Lincoln, Nebraska 68509-5065; 402.471.2871

Nebraska Panhandle Chapter, AHSGR; 2430 Ave. C; Scottsbluff, Nebraska 69361; 308.632.2459

Nebraska State Archives; PO Box 82554; 1500 R Street; Lincoln, Nebraska 68501; <www.nebraskahistory.org/lib.arch/index.htm>

Nebraska State Genealogical Society; PO Box 5608; Lincoln, Nebraska 68505; 402.266.8881; <www.rootsweb.com/~nesgs/>

Nebraska State Historical Society, Department of Reference Services; 1500 "R" Street, PO Box 82554; Lincoln, Nebraska 68501; 402.471.4751; Fax 402.471.3100 <www.rootsweb.com/~negenweb/societies/nshs.html>

Nebraska State Law Library; 3rd Floor, Nebraska State Capitol Bldg., 1445 K; Lincoln, Nebraska 68508

Nebraskans of Irish and Scotch-Irish Ancestry; PO Box 5049; Lincoln, Nebraska 68505-5049

Nemaha Valley Genealogical Society; PO Box 25; Auburn, Nebraska 68305

Nemaha Valley Museum, Inc.; PO Box 25; Auburn, Nebraska 68305

Norfolk Public Library; North 4th St.; Norfolk, Nebraska 68701

North Platte Genealogical Society; PO Box 1452; North Platte, Nebraska 69101

Northeast Nebraska Chapter, AHSGR; 314 S. 13th Place; Norfolk, Nebraska 68701-1214; <www.ahsgr.org/nenorthe.html>

Northeastern Nebraska Genealogical Society (NENGS); PO Box 249; Lyons, Nebraska 68038

Northern Antelope County Genealogical Society; PO Box 267; Orchard, Nebraska 68764

Northern Nebraska Genealogical Society; 401 E. Douglas; O'Neill, Nebraska 68763

Northwest Genealogical Society; 503 Morehead; Chadron, Nebraska 64337

Nuckolls County Genealogical Society; PO Box 441; Superior, Nebraska 68978-0441

Omaha Family History Center; 617 South 153rd Circle; Omaha, Nebraska 68154

Omaha Family History Center; 6601 Lafayette Ave.; Omaha, Nebraska 68132-1147

Omaha Public Library; 215 South 15th St.; Omaha, Nebraska 68102

Pawnee Genealogy Scouters; PO Box 112; Albion, Nebraska 68620

Perkins County Genealogical Society; PO Box 418; Grant, Nebraska 69140

Phelps Co. Museum Library (Holdrege Area); PO Box 164; Holdrege, Nebraska 68949

Plains Genealogical Society; c/o Kimball Public Library; 208 S. Walnut St.; Kimball, Nebraska 69145

Platte Valley Kin Seekers; PO Box 153; Columbus, Nebraska 68601

Potter Public Library; PO Box 317; Potter, Nebraska 69156

Prairie Pioneer Genealogical Society; PO Box 1122; Grand Island, Nebraska 68802

Presbyterian Historical Society, United Presbyterian Church in the U.S.; 425 Lombard Street; Philadelphia, Pennsylvania 19147; 215.627.1852; Fax 215.627.0509

Public Library; 136 S. 14th St.; Lincoln, Nebraska 68508

Quivey Memorial Library; Mitchell, Nebraska 69357

Ravenna Genealogical Society; 105 Alba St.; Ravenna, Nebraska 68869; <www.rootsweb.com/~nebuffal/ravenna.htm>

Rebecca Winter's Genealogical Society; PO Box 323; Scottsbluff, Nebraska 69363-0323

Roman Catholic, Archdiocese of Omaha, Chancery Office; 100 North 62 Street; Omaha, Nebraska 68132-2795; 402.558.3100; Fax 402.558.3026

Saline Co. Pastfinders Library; 730 E. 13th St.; Crete, Nebraska 68333-2308; 402.826.3462;

Saline County Genealogical Society; PO Box 24; Crete, Nebraska 68333

Sarpy County Genealogical Society; 2402 Sac Place; Bellevue, Nebraska 68005-3932

Saunders County Genealogy Seekers; 462 E. 13; Wahoo, Nebraska 68066

Saunders County Historical Society & Museum; 240 N. Walnut; Wahoo, Nebraska 68066; <co.saunders.ne.us/museum.htm>

Schuyler Historical Society and Museum; 1005 B Street; Schuyler, Nebraska 68661

Seward County Genealogical Society; PO Box 72; Seward, Nebraska 68434

Sons of the American Revolution, Nebraska Society; 6731 Sumner St.; Lincoln, Nebraska 68506

South Central Genealogical Society; c/o Jensen Memorial Library; 443 N. Kearney; Minden, Nebraska 68959

Southeast Nebraska Genealogical Society; PO Box 562; Beatrice, Nebraska 68301

Southwest Nebraska Genealogical Society; PO Box 156; McCook, Nebraska 69001-0156; <www.rootsweb.com/~neswngs/>

Textual Reference Branch, National Archives and Records Administration; 7th and Pennsylvania Ave., N.W.; Washington, DC 20408; 202.501.5395; Fax 202.219.6273

Thayer County Genealogical Society; PO Box 398; Belvidere, Nebraska 68315

Thomas County Genealogical Society; PO Box 136; Thedford, Nebraska 69166

Tri-State Comers Genealogical Society; c/o Lydia BruunWoods Memorial Library; 120 E. 18th St.; Falls City, Nebraska 68355

United Methodist Historical Center, Nebraska Conference; PO Box 4553; Lincoln, Nebraska 68504-0553; 402.465.2175

Valley County Genealogical Society; 619 S. 10th; Ord, Nebraska 68862

Wahoo Genealogical Seekers; 871 West 6th; Wahoo, Nebraska 68066

Washington County Genealogical Society; c/o Blair Public Library; Blair, Nebraska 68008

Washington County Historical Association; PO Box 25; Fort Calhoun, Nebraska 68023;

Wayne Public Library; 410 Main St.; Wayne, Nebraska 68787

Wilson Public Library; 910 Meridian St.; Cozad, Nebraska 69130; 308.784.2019

Bibliography and Record Sources

General Sources

A Research Guide to Genealogical Data in Nebraska. Alliance, Nebraska: Nebraska State Genealogical Society, 1980-.

Andreas, A.T. *History of the State of Nebraska.* 2 vols. Chicago: The Western Historical Company, 1882.

Baldwin, Sara Mullin and Robert Morton Mullin. *Nebraskana: Biographical Sketches of Nebraska Men and Women of Achievement.* Hebron, Nebraska: Baldwin Co., 1932.

Bullen, Galen, ed. et. al. *Broken Hoops and Plains People: A Catalogue of Ethnic Resources in the Humanities: Nebraska and Surrounding Area.* Lincoln, Nebraska: Nebraska Curriculum Development Center, 1976.

Casper, Henry Weber. *History of the Catholic Church in Nebraska,* 3 vols. Milwaukee: Catholic Life Pub., 1960-66.

Compendium of History, Reminiscence and Biography of Nebraska. Chicago: Alden Publishing Co., 1912.

Daniels, Sherrill. *An Index to and Bibliography of Reminiscences in the Nebraska State Historical Society Library.* Lincoln, Nebraska: University of Nebraska Dissertation, 1986.

Diffendal, Anne P. *A Guide to the Newspaper Collection of the State Archives, Nebraska State Historical Society* (Lincoln: Nebraska State Historical Society, 1977).

Early Pioneers of Nebraska, With Allied Lines, Vol. 1. Lincoln: Nebraska State Genealogical Society, 1981.

Historical Records Survey (Nebraska). *Preliminary Edition of Guide to Depositories of Manuscript Collections in the United States – Nebraska.* Lincoln, Nebraska: The Survey, 1940.

Index for Biographical and Genealogical History of Southwestern Nebraska 1904. Lincoln: Lincoln-Lancaster County Genealogical Society.

Morton, Julius Sterling et al. *Illustrated History of Nebraska.* 3 vols. Lincoln: Jacob North and Co., 1905-13.

Nebraska Newspaper Abstracts: A Computer Index to Names and Events Abstracted from Selected Nebraska Newspapers. Alliance, Nebraska: Nebraska State Genealogical Society, 1983–.

Nebraska Research Outline, Series US-States, No. 28. Salt Lake City: Family History Library, 1988.

Nebraska State Genealogical Society (Lincoln, Nebraska). *Nebraska Newspaper Abstracts, 1930's.* 6 vols. in 1. Lincoln, Nebraska: Nebraska State Genealogical Society, 2000.

Nebraska State Genealogical Society (Lincoln, Nebraska). *Nebraska Newspaper Abstracts, 1940's.* 6 vols. in 1. Lincoln, Nebraska: Nebraska State Genealogical Society, 1999.

Nebraska State Historical Society (Lincoln, Nebraska). *A Guide to the Newspaper Collection of the State Archives, Nebraska State Historical Society.* Lincoln, Nebraska: Nebraska State Historical Soc., 1977.

Nebraska State Historical Society (Lincoln, Nebraska). *Historical Resources for Genealogists in the Nebraska State Historical Society.* Lincoln, Nebraska: Nebraska State Historical Society, 1986.

Nebraska State Historical Society State Archives. *A Guide to the Manuscript Division of the State Archives, Nebraska State Historical Society.* Lincoln: Nebraska State Historical Society, 1974

Nebraska, a Guide to Genealogical Research. Lincoln: Nebraska State Genealogical Society, 1984.

Nimmo, Sylvia, and Mary Cutler. *Nebraska Local History and Genealogical Reference Guide.* Papillion, Nebraska: S. Nimmo.

Nimmo, Sylvia. *Nebraska Local History and Genealogy Reference Guide: A Bibliography of County Research Materials in Selected Repositories.* Papillion, Nebraska: the author, 1987.

Olson, James C. *History of Nebraska,* 2d ed. Lincoln: University of Nebraska Press, 1966.

Perkey, Elton A. *Perkey's Nebraska Place Names.* Lincoln: Nebraska State Genealogical Society, 1982.

Rife, Janet Warkentin. *Germans and German-Russians in Nebraska: A Research Guide to Nebraska Ethnic Studies.* Lincoln: Center for Great Plains Studies, 1980.

Rosicky, Rose. *A History of Czechs (Bohemians) in Nebraska.* Omaha: Czech Historical Society of Nebraska, 1929.

Sandahl, Charles F. *The Nebraska Conference of the Augustana Synod.* n.p.: Nebraska Conference, 1931.

Sheldon, Addison Erwin. *Nebraska: The Land and the People.* 3 vols. Chicago: Lewis Publishing Co., 1931.

Sittler, Melvin. *Sittler Index of Surnames from the Nebraska State Journal. 5 vols. 1983-85.* Lincoln: Lincoln-Lancaster County Genealogical Society.

Sobotka, Margie. *Nebraska, Kansas Czech Settlers, 1891-1895.* Omaha: the author, 1980.

Source of Genealogical Help in Nebraska. Burbank, CA: Southern California Genealogical Society.

Atlases, Maps and Gazetteers

Fitzpatrick, Lillian Linder. *Nebraska Place Names....* New ed. Lincoln: University of Nebraska Press, 1960.

Nebraska Atlas and Gazetteer. Freeport, Maine: DeLorme Mapping Co., 1997.

Nimmo, Sylvia. *Maps Showing Boundaries, Nebraska, 1854-1925.* Papillion, Nebraska: Sylvia Nimmo, 1978.

Perkey, Elton A. *Perkey's Nebraska Place Names.* Lincoln: Nebraska State Historical Society, 1982.

Rapp, William F. *The Post Offices of Nebraska.* Vol. 1. *Territorial Post Offices.* Crete, Nebraska: J-B Publishing Co., 1971.

Searcy, N.D., and A.R. Longwell. *Nebraska Atlas.* Kearney, Nebraska: Nebraska Atlas Publishing Co., 1964.

The Official State Atlas of Nebraska. 1885. Reprint. Evansville, IN: Unigraphic, 1976.

Census Records

Available Census Records and Census Substitutes

Federal Census 1860, 1870, 1880, 1900, 1910, 1920, 1930.

Federal Mortality Schedules 1860, 1870, 1880.

Union Veterans and Widows 1890.

State/Territorial Census 1854, 1855, 1856, 1865-1884, 1885.

Cox, Eunice Evelyn. *1854, 1855, 1856 Nebraska Territory Censuses.* Ellensburg, Washington: Cox, 1977.

Dollarhide, William. *The Census Book: A Genealogist's Guide to Federal Census Facts, Schedules and Indexes.* Bountiful, Utah: Heritage Quest, 1999.

Kemp, Thomas Jay. *The American Census Handbook.* Wilmington, Delaware: Scholarly Resources, Inc., 2001.

Lainhart, Ann S. *State Census Records.* Baltimore: Genealogical Publishing Co., Inc., 1992.

Szucs, Loretto Dennis, and Matthew Wright. *Finding Answers in U.S. Census Records.* Ancestry Publishing, 2001

Thorndale, William, and William Dollarhide. *Map Guide to the U.S. Federal Censuses, 1790-1920.* Baltimore: Genealogical Publishing Co, 1987.

Court Records, Probate and Wills

Hons, Fred W. and Delbert A. Bishop. *Preliminary Inventory Records of the United States District Court for the District of Nebraska.* Kansas City: Federal Records Center, 1967.

Emigration, Immigration, Migration and Naturalization

Knight, Hal. *111 days to Zion.* [Salt Lake City: Deseret News, 1978].

Sobotka, Margie. *Czech Immigrant Passenger List (for Nebraska) 1879.* [Omaha, Neb.?: Eastern Nebraska Genealogical Society?], 1982.

Land and Property

Homestead Guide of Kansas and Nebraska. Waterville, Kansas: F.G. Adams, 1873.

Hone, Wade E. *Land and Property Research in the United States.* Salt Lake City: Ancestry Incorporated, 1997.

Sheldon, Addison E. *Land Systems and Land Policies in Nebraska: A History of Nebraska Land, Public Domain and Private Property.* Lincoln: Nebraska State Historical Society, 1936.

Military

Dudley, Edgar S. *Roster of Nebraska Volunteers from 1861 to 1869.* Hasting, Nebraska: Wigton & Evans, 1888.

Grand Army of the Republic. Department of Nebraska. *Roster and Indexes of Soldiers, 1911.* Lincoln, Nebraska: Nebraska State Historical Society, 1974. 2 microfilm.

Hartman, Douglas R. *Nebraska's Militia: The History of the Army and Air National Guard, 1854-1991.* Virginia Beach, Virginia: Donning, 1994.

Nebraska Adjutant General. *Roster of Nebraska Volunteers 1861 to 1869.* Hastings, Nebraska: Wigton & Evans, 1888.

Nebraska Secretary of State. *Roster of Soldiers, Sailors, and Marines of the War of 1812, The Mexican War, and The War of the Rebellion Residing in Nebraska, Jun 1, 1891.* Lincoln: State Journal Co., 1892.

Nebraska. Secretary of State. *Roster of Soldiers-Sailors and Marines Who Served in the War of the Rebellion, Spanish-American War and World War.* Omaha: Waters-Barnhart Printing Co., 1925.

Nebraska. Secretary of State. *Roster of Veterans of the Mexican, Civil, and Spanish-American Wars Residing in Nebraska, 1915.* Lincoln: Secretary of State, [1915].

Roster of Nebraska Soldiers. Omaha: Klopp, Bartlett & Co., 1888.

Sherard, Gerald E. *A Nebraska Civil War Ancestor.* Lakewood, Colo.: G.M.E. Sherard, 1994.

Sherard, Gerald E. *Nebraska Born Veterans Buried in Colorado, 1862-1949.* [Lakewood, Colo.: G.E. Sherard, 1997].

United States. Selective Service System. *Nebraska World War I Selective Service System Draft Registration Cards, 1917-1918.* National Archives Microfilm Publications, M1509. Washington, D.C.: National Archives, 1987-1988.

Vital and Cemetery Records

Daughters of the American Revolution (Nebraska). *Miscellaneous Records: 1856-1972*. Microfilm copy of typescript (301 leaves) made in 1972 in possession of DAR Library, Washington, D.C. (Salt Lake City: Filmed by the Genealogical Society of Utah, 1972).

Jackson, Ronald Vern. *Nebraska 1860 Mortality Scheldule*. Bountiful, Utah: Accelerated Indexing Systems, 1980.

Jackson, Ronald Vern. *Nebraska 1870 Mortality* Schedule. Bountiful, Utah: Accelerated Indexing Systems, 1980.

Jackson, Ronald Vern. *Nebraska 1880 Mortality Schedule*. Bountiful, Utah: Accelerated Indexing Systems, 1981.

Nebraska Cemeteries and Burial Sites. 2 parts. Lincoln: Nebraska State Genealogical Society, 1984.

Nebraska Cemeteries and Known Burial Sites. Lincoln: Nebraska State Genealogical Society, 1996.

Sherard, Gerald E. *Nebraska Cemetery Index*. Lakewood, Colo.: G.E. Sherard, [199-?].

Sones, Georgene Morris. *Nebraska Cemeteries and Burial Sites: In Two Parts*. Lincoln, Nebraska: Nebraska State Genealogy Society, 1996.

The Guide to Public Vital Statistics Records In Nebraska. Lincoln: Historical Records Survey, 1941.

United States. Bureau of Indian Affairs. Winnebago Agency. *Vital Statistics: Births, Marriages and Deaths, 1863-1947*. Kansas City, Mo.: Federal Archives and Records Center, 1977.

County Website	Map Index	Date Created	Parent County or Territory From Which Organized
			Address/Details

Adams G9 16 Feb 1867 **Unorganized Territory**
www.rootsweb.com/~neadams/
Adams County; 500 W 5th; Hastings, NE 68901; Ph. 402.461.7107
Details: (Co Judge has m & pro rec; Clk Dis Ct has div & land rec)

Antelope F5 1 Mar 1871 **L'Eau Qui Court, Unorganized Territory**
www.rootsweb.com/~neantelo/
Antelope County; 501 Main St; Neligh, NE 68756; Ph. 402.887.4410
Details: (Co Judge has m & pro rec; Co Clk has land rec)

Arthur M6 31 Mar 1887 **Unorganized Territory**
www.rootsweb.com/~nearthur/
Arthur County; Main St; Arthur, NE 69121; Ph. 308.764.2203
Details: (Arthur County was formed in 1887, but did not become a county until 1913. Before 1913, rec were kept at McPherson Co) (Co Clk has land rec from 1913; Co Ct has m, pro & ct rec from 1913; Clk Dis Ct has div rec from 1913; Co Cem Sexton has bur rec; Co Supt of schools has school cen from 1913)

Banner R7 6 Nov 1888 **Cheyenne**
www.rootsweb.com/~nebanner/
Banner County; State St; PO Box 67; Harrisburg, NE 69345; Ph. 308.436.5265
Details: (Co Clk has b rec from 1920 & land rec from 1890; Co Ct has m, pro & ct rec from 1890; Dept of Hlth has bur & div rec)

Blackbird 7 Mar 1855 **Burt**
Details: (see Thurston) (Name changed to Thurston 28 Mar 1889)

Blaine J6 5 Mar 1885 **Custer**
www.rootsweb.com/~neblaine/
Blaine County; PO Box 136; Brewster, NE 68821; Ph. 308.547.2222
Details: (Co Judge has pro & ct rec; Co Clk has div & land rec from 1887)

Boone F6 1 Mar 1871 **Unorganized Territory**
www.rootsweb.com/~neboone/
Boone County; 222 S 4th St; Albion, NE 68620; Ph. 402.395.2055
Details: (Co Clk has m rec from 1932, div, pro & ct rec; Rcdr Deeds has land rec; State Archives, 1500 "R" St., Lincoln, NE 68508 has m rec to 1932)

Box Butte P5 23 Mar 1887 **Dawes**
www.rootsweb.com/~neboxbut/
Box Butte County; 515 Box Butte Ave #203; Alliance, NE 69301; Ph. 308.762.6565
Details: (Co Clk has m & land rec; Co Judge has pro & ct rec; Clk Dis Ct has div rec)

Boyd H3 20 Mar 1891 **Holt**
www.rootsweb.com/~neboyd/
Boyd County; 401 Thayer St; Butte, NE 68722; Ph. 402.775.2391
Details: (Co Clk has m, div, land, mil & nat rec; Clk Dis Ct has ct rec; Clk Co Ct has pro rec)

Brown J5 19 Feb 1883 **Unorganized Territory**
www.co.brown.ne.us/
Brown County; 148 W 4th St; Ainsworth, NE 69210; Ph. 402.387.2705
Details: (Attached to Holt Co prior to 1883) (Co Clk has m & land rec from 1883, nat rec 1884-1922 & mil dis rec from 1919; Co Judge has pro rec; Clk Dis Ct has div & ct rec; Co Supt of Schools has school cen rec from 1883)

Buffalo H8 14 Mar 1855 **Original county**
www.co.buffalo.ne.us/
Buffalo County; 15th & Central Ave; PO Box 1270; Kearney, NE 68848; Ph. 308.236.1226
Details: (Co Clk has m rec from 1872; Co Judge has pro & ct rec from 1872; Clk Dis Ct has div rec; Reg of Deeds has land rec)

Burt C6 23 Nov 1854 **Original county**
www.rootsweb.com/~neburt/
Burt County; 111 N 13th St; Tekamah, NE 68061; Ph. 402.374.2955
Details: (Co Clk has m & land rec; Co Judge has pro & ct rec; Clk Dis Ct has div rec)

Butler D7 26 Jan 1856 **Greene**
www.rootsweb.com/~nebutler/
Butler County; 451 5th St; David City, NE 68632; Ph. 402.367.7430
Details: (Co Clk has land rec from 1869; Co Ct has m & pro rec; Clk Dis Ct has div & ct rec)

Calhoun 26 Jan 1856 **Lancaster, Douglas**
Details: (see Saunders) (Name changed to Saunders 8 Jan 1862)

Cass B8 23 Nov 1854 **Original county**
www.cassne.org/
Cass County; 346 Main St #202; Plattsmouth, NE 68048; Ph. 402.296.9300
Details: (Co Clk has m rec from 1855; Co Ct has pro & ct rec from 1854; Cem Board has bur rec; Clk Dis Ct has div rec from 1855; Reg of Deeds has land rec)

County Website	Map Index	Date Created	Parent County or Territory From Which Organized Address/Details
Cedar www.rootsweb.com/~necedar/	E4	12 Feb 1857	**Dixon, Pierce** Cedar County; 101 S Broadway Ave; PO Box 47; Hartington, NE 68739; Ph. 402.254.7411 Details: (Co Clk has m & land rec; Co Judge has pro & ct rec; Clk Dis Ct has div rec)
Chase www.chasecounty.com/	M9	27 Feb 1873	**Unorganized Territory** Chase County; 921 Broadway; Imperial, NE 69033; Ph. 308.882.5266 Details: (Co Judge has m, pro & ct rec from 1886; Clk Dis Ct has div rec from 1886; Co Clk has land rec from 1886)
Cherry www.rootsweb.com/~necherry/	L4	23 Feb 1883	**Unorganized Territory** Cherry County; 365 N Main St; PO Box 120; Valentine, NE 69201; Ph. 402.376.2771 Details: (Co Clk has m & land rec; Co Ct has pro & ct rec; Clk Dis Ct has div rec)
Cheyenne www.co.cheyenne.ne.us/	P7	22 Jun 1867	**Unorganized Territory** Cheyenne County; 1000 10th Ave; PO Box 217; Sidney, NE 69162; Ph. 308.254.2141 Details: (Co Clk has m & land rec; Co Ct has pro rec; Clk Dis Ct has div rec)
Clay www.rootsweb.com/~neclay/	F9	16 Feb 1867	**Unorganized Territory** Clay County; 111 W Fairfield St; Clay Center, NE 68933; Ph. 402.762.3463 Details: (Co Clk has b & d rec 1917-1918, m & land rec from 1871 & mil rec from 1921; Clk Dis Ct has div, ct & nat rec; Co Ct has pro rec)
Clay, old		7 Mar 1855	**Original county** Details: (absorbed by Gage Co in 1864)
Colfax www.rootsweb.com/~necolfax/	D6	15 Feb 1869	**Platte** Colfax County; 411 E 11th St; Schuyler, NE 68661; Ph. 402.352.3434 Details: (Co Judge has m rec from 1869, pro rec from 1886 & ct rec from 1885; Clk Dis Ct has div rec from 1881; Co Clk has land rec from 1860)
Cuming www.rootsweb.com/~necuming/	D5	16 Mar 1855	**Burt** Cuming County; 200 S Lincoln St; West Point, NE 68788; Ph. 402.372.6002 Details: (Co Judge has m & pro rec from 1866, ct rec from 1960 & school cen; Clk Dis Ct has div rec from 1869)
Custer www.rootsweb.com/~necuste2/	I7	17 Feb 1877	**Unorganized Territory** Custer County; 431 S 10th Ave; Broken Bow, NE 68822; Ph. 308.872.5701 Details: (Co Clk has b rec from 1910, d rec from 1915, obituaries from 1877 & pioneer biographical data; Co Hist Soc has many other rec; Co Judge has m rec from 1878, pro & ct rec from 1887; Clk Dis Ct has div rec from 1881; Reg of Deeds has and rec from 1880)
Dakota www.sscdc.net/	C4	7 Mar 1855	**Burt** Dakota County; 1601 Broadway St; Dakota City, NE 68731; Ph. 402.987.2126 Details: (Co Clk has m rec from 1856 & mil rec from 1921; Co Ct has pro rec from 1858; Reg of Deeds has land rec from 1856; Clk Dis Ct has div & ct rec from 1862 & nat rec)
Dawes www.homestead.com/DawesCountyNE/ Home.html	P4	19 Feb 1885	**Sioux** Dawes County; 451 Main St; Chadron, NE 69337-2649; Ph. 308.432.0100 Details: (Co Clk has land rec from 1880; Co Judge has m & pro rec; Clk Dis Ct has div rec)
Dawson www.rootsweb.com/~nedawson/	J8	11 Jan 1860	**Unorganized Territory** Dawson County; PO Box 370; Lexington, NE 68850; Ph. 308.324.2127 Details: (Co Clk has m rec from 1873; Co Ct has pro & ct rec; Clk Dis Ct has div & nat rec; Reg of Deeds has land rec; Veterans Service Off has mil rec)
Deuel www.rootsweb.com/~nedeuel/	O7	6 Nov 1888	**Cheyenne** Deuel County; 3rd & Vincent; Chappell, NE 69129; Ph. 308.874.3308 Details: (Co Judge has m & pro rec; Co Clk has bur, div & land rec, ct rec from 1890)

Dixon
www.homestead.com/DixonCoNE
   GenWebProject/DixonCoNE
   GenWebProject.html
	D4	26 Jan 1856	**Blackbird, Izard, Unorganized Territory**
			Dixon County; 302 3rd St; Ponca, NE 68770; Ph. 402.755.2208
			Details: (Co Clk has b, d & bur rec from 1919 & land rec from 1871)

County Website	Map Index	Date Created	Parent County or Territory From Which Organized
			Address/Details

Dodge   C6   23 Nov 1854   **Original county**
www.rootsweb.com/~nedodge/
Dodge County; 435 N Park Ave; Fremont, NE 68025; Ph. 402.727.2767
Details: (Co Clk has m rec; Co Judge has pro rec; Clk Dis Ct has div rec; Reg of Deeds has land rec)

Douglas   C7   23 Nov 1854   **Original county**
www.co.douglas.ne.us/explorer.shtml
Douglas County; 1819 Farman St; Omaha, NE 68102; Ph. 402.444.7143
Details: (Co Judge has m & pro rec; Clk Dis Ct has div rec; Co Clk has mil dis rec)

Dundy   M10   27 Feb 1873   **Unorganized Territory**
www.rootsweb.com/~nedundy/
Dundy County; PO Box 506; Benkelman, NE 69021; Ph. 308.423.2058
Details: (Co Clk has b rec from 1907, d rec from 1904, bur, div & ct rec; Co Judge has pro rec)

Emmet   10 Feb 1857   **Pierce, Unorganized Territory**
Details: (see Knox) (Formerly L'Eau Qui Court Co. Name changed to Emmet 18 Feb 1867. Name changed to Knox 21 Feb 1873)

Fillmore   E9   26 Jan 1856   **Unorganized Territory**
www.fillmorecounty.org/
Fillmore County; 900 G St; Geneva, NE 68361; Ph. 402.759.4931
Details: (Co Clk has m & land rec from 1872 & delayed b rec; Co Ct has pro & ct rec; Clk Dis Ct has div rec; Co Supt of Schools has school cen)

Forney   23 Nov 1854   **Original county**
Details: (see Nemaha) (Name changed to Nemaha 7 Mar 1855)

Franklin   H10   16 Feb 1867   **Kearney**
www.rootsweb.com/~nefrankl/
Franklin County; 405 15th Ave; PO Box 146; Franklin, NE 68939; Ph. 308.425.6202
Details: (Co Clk has m rec from 1872, div & land rec)

Frontier   K9   17 Jan 1872   **Unorganized Territory**
www.rootsweb.com/~nefronti/
Frontier County; 1 Wellington St; PO Box 40; Stockville, NE 69042-0040; Ph. 308.367.8641
Details: (Co Clk has m & mil rec; Co Judge has div, pro, ct & nat rec; Reg of Deeds has land rec; Clk & Treas have cem rec; Supt Schools has school cen)

Furnas   J10   27 Feb 1873   **Unorganized Territory**
www.rootsweb.com/~nefurnas/
Furnas County; 912 R St; PO Box 387; Beaver City, NE 68926-0387; Ph. 308.268.4145
Details: (Co Judge has m, pro & ct rec; Clk Dis Ct has div rec; Co Clk has land rec from 1873)

Gage   C9   16 Mar 1855   **Original county**
www.usgennet.org/usa/ne/county/gage/index.html
Gage County; 612 Grant St; PO Box 429; Beatrice, NE 68310-0429; Ph. 402.223.1300
Details: (Co Judge has m & pro rec from 1860; Clk Dis Ct has div rec)

Garden   O6   2 Nov 1909   **Deuel**
www.rootsweb.com/~negarden/
Garden County; 611 Main St; PO Box 486; Oshkosh, NE 69154; Ph. 308.772.3924
Details: (Co Clk has m & land rec; Co Judge has pro & ct rec; Clk Dis Ct has div rec)

Garfield   H6   8 Nov 1884   **Wheeler**
www.rootsweb.com/~negarfie/
Garfield County; 250 S 8th St; PO Box 218; Burwell, NE 68823-0218; Ph. 308.346.4161
Details: (Co Judge has m, div & pro rec)

Gosper*   J9   26 Nov 1873   **Unorganized Territory, Kearney**
www.rootsweb.com/~negosper/
Gosper County; 507 Smith Ave; PO Box 136; Elwood, NE 68937-0136; Ph. 308.785.2611
Details: (Co Judge has m & pro rec from 1891 & ct rec from 1920; Co Clk has div rec from 1880 & land rec)

Grant   N6   31 Mar 1887   **Unorganized Territory**
www.rootsweb.com/~negrant/
Grant County; PO Box 139; Hyannis, NE 69350-0139; Ph. 308.458.2488
Details: (Co Clk has m & land rec from 1888, ct rec from 1897, nat rec 1891-1912, div rec from 1890 & mil rec from 1921; Co Judge has pro rec)

County Website	Map Index	Date Created	Parent County or Territory From Which Organized / Address/Details
Greeley* www.rootsweb.com/~negreele/	G6	1 Mar 1871	**Unorganized Territory** Greeley County; PO Box 287; Greeley, NE 68842; Ph. 308.428.3625 Details: (Co Clk has m, land, mil & nat rec; Co Ct has pro rec; Clk Dis Ct has div & ct rec)
Greene		6 Mar 1855	**Cass, Pierce, old** Details: (see Seward) (Name changed to Seward 3 Jan 1862)
Hall www.rootsweb.com/~nehall/	G8	4 Nov 1858	**Original county** Hall County; 121 S Pine St; Grand Island, NE 68801; Ph. 308.385.5080 Details: (Co Clk has m rec from 1869; Co Judge has pro rec; Clk Dis Ct has div & ct rec; Reg of Deeds has land rec)
Hamilton www.co.hamilton.ne.us/	F8	16 Feb 1867	**Unorganized Territory** Hamilton County; 1111 13th St Ste 1; Aurora, NE 68818; Ph. 402.694.3443 Details: (Co Clk has m & land rec from 1870; Co Judge has pro & ct rec; Clk Dis Ct has div rec)
Harlan www.rootsweb.com/~neharlan/	I10	3 Jun 1871	**Kearney** Harlan County; 706 W 2nd St; Alma, NE 68920; Ph. 308.928.2173 Details: (Co Clk has m & land rec; Co Judge has pro & ct rec; Clk Dis Ct has div rec; Reg of Deeds has land rec)
Harrison			Details: (Never org co in southwest corner of state. With Lincoln in 1870 cen)
Hayes www.rootsweb.com/~nehayes/	L9	19 Feb 1877	**Unorganized Territory** Hayes County; Troth St; PO Box 370; Hayes Center, NE 69032; Ph. 308.286.3413 Details: (Co Clk has d, bur & land rec)
Hitchcock www.co.hitchcock.ne.us/	L10	27 Feb 1873	**Unorganized Territory** Hitchcock County; 229 E D St; PO Box 248; Trenton, NE 69044; Ph. 308.334.5646 Details: (Co Clk has m, land, div & ct rec; Co Judge has pro rec)
Holt www.rootsweb.com/~neholt/	H4	13 Jan 1860	**Unorganized Territory** Holt County; 204 N 4th St; PO Box 329; O'Neill, NE 68763; Ph. 402.336.1762 Details: (Formerly West Co. Name changed to Holt 9 Jan 1862) (Co Clk has m rec from 1878; Co Judge has pro & ct rec from 1882; Reg of Deeds has land rec from 1879; Clk Dis Ct has div rec from 1879)
Hooker www.rootsweb.com/~nehooker/	L6	29 Mar 1889	**Unorganized Territory** Hooker County; 303 NE 1st St; PO Box 184; Mullen, NE 69152-0184; Ph. 308.546.2244 Details: (Co Clk has b & d rec from 1919 & land rec from 1889; Co Judge has m & pro rec)
Howard* www.rootsweb.com/~nehoward/	G7	1 Mar 1871	**Hall** Howard County; 612 Indian S; PO Box 25; St. Paul, NE 68873; Ph. 308.754.4343 Details: (Co Judge has m, pro, ct, land & nat rec from 1872 & div rec from 1873)
Izard		6 Mar 1855	**Unorganized Territory** Details: (see Stanton) (Name changed to Stanton 10 Jan 1862)
Jackson		1855	**Unorganized Territory** Details: (see Fillmore) (Never organized. Changed to Fillmore 26 Jan 1856)
Jefferson www.rootsweb.com/~nejeffer/	E9	26 Jan 1856	**Unorganized Territory** Jefferson County; 411 4th St; Fairbury, NE 68352; Ph. 402.729.2323 Details: (Formerly Jones Co. Name changed to Jefferson 1864. Boundaries redefined 1867 & 1871) (Co Clk has m rec; Co Judge has pro & ct rec; Clk Dis Ct has div rec; Reg of Deeds has land rec)
Johnson www.rootsweb.com/~nejohnso/	C9	2 Mar 1855	**Nemaha** Johnson County; 4th & Broadway; PO Box 416; Tecumseh, NE 68450-0416; Ph. 402.335.3246 Details: (Co Clk has m & land rec from 1858; Co Judge has pro & ct rec: Clk Dis Ct has div rec from 1858)

County Website	Map Index	Date Created	Parent County or Territory From Which Organized
			Address/Details
Jones		26 Jan 1856	**Unorganized Territory**
			Details: (see Jefferson) (Absorbed by Jefferson, 1867)
Kearney www.rootsweb.com/~nekearne/	H9	10 Jan 1860	**Unorganized Territory** Kearney County; County Courthouse; Minden, NE 68959; Ph. 308.832.2723 Details: (Co Clk has m rec from 1872 & land rec; Co Judge has pro & ct rec; Clk Dis Ct has div rec)
Keith www.rootsweb.com/~nekeith/	M7	27 Feb 1873	**Unorganized Territory** Keith County; 511 N Spruce St; PO Box 149; Ogallala, NE 69153-0149; Ph. 308.284.4726 Details: (Co Clk has b, d & land rec; Co Judge has m rec; Clk Dis Ct has div, pro & ct rec)
Keya Paha www.rootsweb.com/~nekeyapa/	J3	4 Nov 1884	**Brown** Keya Paha County; PO Box 349; Springview, NE 68778-0349; Ph. 402.497.3791 Details: (Co Clk has m, div, pro, ct & land rec from 1886 & school cen)
Kimball www.rootsweb.com/~nekimbal/	Q7	6 Nov 1888	**Cheyenne** Kimball County; 114 E 3rd St; Kimball, NE 69145; Ph. 308.235.2241 Details: (Co Clk has div & pro rec; Co Judge has m & ct rec)
Knox www.rootsweb.com/~neknox/	F4	10 Feb 1857	**Pierce, Unorganized Territory** Knox County; PO Box 166; Center, NE 68724; Ph. 402.288.4282 Details: (Formerly L'Eau Qui Court & Emmet Cos. Created as L'Eau Qui Court Co. Name changed to Emmet 18 Feb 1867. Name changed to Knox 21 Feb 1873) (Co Clk has m rec; Co Judge has pro & ct rec; Clk Dis Ct has div rec; Reg of Deeds has land rec)
Lancaster freepages.genealogy.rootsweb.com/ ~irishrose/lancindex.html	C8	6 Mar 1855	**Cass, Pierce, old** Lancaster County; 555 S 10th St; Lincoln, NE 68508; Ph. 402.441.7484 Details: (Co Judge has m & pro rec; Co Clk has land rec)
L'Eau Qui Court		10 Feb 1857	**Pierce, Unorganized Territory** Details: (see Knox) (Name changed to Emmet 18 Feb 1867. Name changed to Knox 21 Feb 1873)
Lincoln www.wathenadesigns.com/Lincoln/ index_4.html	L8	7 Jan 1860	**Unorganized Territory** Lincoln County; 301 N Jeffers; North Platte, NE 69101; Ph. 308.532.4051 Details: (Formerly Shorter Co. Name changed to Lincoln 11 Dec 1861) (Co Clk has m rec; Clk Dis Ct has div rec; Co Ct has pro & ct rec; Reg of Deeds has land rec)
Logan www.rootsweb.com/~nelogan/	K6	24 Feb 1885	**Unorganized Territory** Logan County; 317 Main St; PO Box 8; Stapleton, NE 69163-0008; Ph. 308.636.2311 Details: (Co Judge has m, div, pro & ct rec from 1885 & partial bur rec; Co Clk has land rec)
Loup* www.rootsweb.com/~neloup/	I6	23 Feb 1883	**Unorganized Territory** Loup County; 4th St; PO Box 187; Taylor, NE 68879; Ph. 308.942.3135 Details: (Co Judge has m & pro rec; Co Clk has div, ct & land rec from 1887)
Loup, old		6 Mar 1855	**Burt** Details: (Disorganized in 1856 & became part of Izard, Madison, Monroe & Platte Cos)
Lyon			Details: (Never org. co in southwest corner of state. With Lincoln in 1870 cen)
Madison www.co.madison.ne.us/		26 Jan 1856	**McNeale, Loup, old** Madison County; 110 Clara Davis Dr; PO Box 290; Madison, NE 68748-0290; Ph. 402.454.3311 Details: (Co Clk has m & land rec from 1868, pro rec from 1863, div & ct rec from 1907)
McNeale		1855	**Burt** Details: (absorbed by Madison & Izard (now Stanton) in 1856)
McPherson www.rootsweb.com/~nemcpher/	L6	31 Mar 1887	**Lincoln, Keith, Logan** McPherson County; 5th & Anderson; PO Box 122; Tryon, NE 69167-0122; Ph. 308.587.2363 Details: (Co Clk has m, div & land rec; Co Judge has pro & ct rec)

County Website	Map Index	Date Created	Parent County or Territory From Which Organized Address/Details
Merrick* www.rootsweb.com/~nemerric/	F7	4 Nov 1858	**Unorganized Territory** Merrick County; 1510 18th St; PO Box 27; Central City, NE 68826-0027; Ph. 308.946.2881 Details: (Co Clk has b & d rec; Co Judge has m, div, pro & ct rec; Reg of Deeds has land rec from 1873)
Monroe		1856	**Loup, old** Details: (Absorbed by Platte Co in 1860)
Morrill www.rootsweb.com/~nemorril/index.html	P6	12 Nov 1908	**Cheyenne** Morrill County; PO Box 610; Bridgeport, NE 69336-0610; Ph. 308.262.0860 Details: (Co Clk has b, d & bur rec from 1917 & land rec from 1909; Co Judge has m & pro rec)
Nance www.rootsweb.com/~nenance/	F7	13 Feb 1879	**Pawnee Indian Reservation** Nance County; 209 Esther St; Fullerton, NE 68638; Ph. 308.536.2331 Details: (Co Clk has m rec from 1890 & land rec from 1879; Co Judge has pro rec; Clk Dis Ct has div & ct rec from 1882)
Nemaha www.rootsweb.com/~nenemaha/	B9	23 Nov 1854	**Original county** Nemaha County; 1824 N St; Auburn, NE 68305; Ph. 402.274.4213 Details: (Formerly Forney Co. Name changed to Nemaha 7 Mar 1855) (Co Clk has m rec from 1856, land & mil rec; Co Judge has pro & ct rec; Clk Dis Ct has div rec)
Nuckolls www.rootsweb.com/~nenuckol/	F9	13 Jan 1860	**Unorganized Territory** Nuckolls County; 150 S Main St; PO Box 366; Nelson, NE 68961; Ph. 409.225.4361 Details: (Co Judge has m & pro rec; Clk Dis Ct has div & ct rec; Co Clk has land rec from 1900)
Otoe www.co.otoe.ne.us/	B9	23 Nov 1854	**Cass, Pierce, old** Otoe County; 1021 Central Ave; PO Box 249; Nebraska City, NE 68410-0249; Ph. 402.873.9505 Details: (Formerly Pierce, old. Name changed to Otoe) (Co Clk has m, div & ct rec; Co Judge has pro rec; Reg of Deeds has land rec)
Pawnee www.rootsweb.com/~nepawnee/	C10	6 Mar 1855	**Richardson** Pawnee County; 625 6th St; PO Box 431; Pawnee City, NE 68420; Ph. 402.852.2962 Details: (Co Clk has m rec from 1858, land, div & ct rec; Co Judge has pro rec)
Perkins www.rootsweb.com/~neperkin/	M8	8 Nov 1887	**Keith** Perkins County; 200 Lincoln Ave; PO Box 156; Grant, NE 69140-0156; Ph. 308.352.4643 Details: (Co Clk has m, div, ct & land rec; Co Judge has pro rec)
Phelps www.rootsweb.com/~nephelps/	I9	11 Feb 1873	**Kearney** Phelps County; PO Box 404; Holdrege, NE 68949; Ph. 308.995.4469 Details: (Co Clk has m & land rec; Co Judge has pro rec; Clk Dis Ct has div rec)
Pierce www.co.pierce.ne.us/	E5	26 Jan 1856	**Izard, Unorganized Territory** Pierce County; 111 W Court St Rm 1; Pierce, NE 68767; Ph. 402.329.4225 Details: (Formerly Otoe Co) (Co Clk has m, land & mil rec; Clk Dis Ct has div & nat rec; Co Ct has pro rec; School Supt has school attendance rec)
Pierce, old		1854	**Original county** Details: (see Otoe) Became part of Otoe Co. 1855
Platte www.rootsweb.com/~neplatte/	E6	26 Jan 1856	**Loup, old** Platte County; 2610 14th St; Columbus, NE 68601; Ph. 402.563.4904 Details: (Co Judge has m & pro rec; Clk Dis Ct has div & ct rec; Co Asr has land rec)
Polk www.wathenadesigns.com/Polk/index.html	E7	26 Jan 1856	**York, Unorganized Territory** Polk County; 400 Hawkeye St; PO Box 276; Osceola, NE 68651; Ph. 402.747.5431 Details: (Co Judge has m & pro rec; Co Clk has land rec)
Red Willow www.rootsweb.com/~neredwil/	K10	27 Feb 1873	**Unorganized Territory** Red Willow County; 502 Norris Ave; McCook, NE 69001-2006; Ph. 308.345.1552 Details: (Co Clk has m rec from 1874 & land rec from 1888; Co Ct has pro rec; Clk Dis Ct has div & ct rec; Veteran Service Off has mil rec; School Supt has school cen)

County Website	Map Index	Date Created	Parent County or Territory From Which Organized Address/Details
Richardson www.rootsweb.com/~nerichar/	**B10**	**23 Nov 1854**	**Original county** Richardson County; 1700 Stone St; Falls City, NE 68355; Ph. 402.245.2911 Details: (Co Clk has b & d rec from 1918; Co Judge has m rec from 1800's, pro & ct rec; Reg of Deeds has land rec; Clk Dis Ct has div rec)
Rock www.co.rock.ne.us/	**I5**	**6 Nov 1888**	**Brown** Rock County; 400 State St; PO Box 367; Bassett, NE 68714; Ph. 402.684.3933 Details: (Co Judge has m rec; Co Clk has div, pro, ct & land rec from 1889)
Saline www.rootsweb.com/~nesaline/	**D9**	**6 Mar 1855**	**Original county** Saline County; 215 S Court St; PO Box 865; Wilber, NE 68465; Ph. 402.821.2374 Details: (Co Clk has b & d rec from 1976 & land rec from 1886; Co Ct has m rec from 1886 & pro rec from 1870; Clk Dis Ct has div & ct rec from 1886)
Sarpy www.sarpy.com/	**B7**	**7 Feb 1857**	**Douglas** Sarpy County; 1210 Golden Gate Dr; Papillion, NE 68046; Ph. 402.593.2100 Details: (Co Judge has m & pro rec; Co Clk has land rec)
Saunders www.co.saunders.ne.us/	**D7**	**26 Jan 1856**	**Lancaster, Douglas** Saunders County; PO Box 61; Wahoo, NE 68066; Ph. 402.443.8101 Details: (Formerly Calhoun Co. Name changed to Saunders 8 Jan 1862) (Co Clk has m, bur, div, pro, ct & land rec)
Scotts Bluff www.scottsbluffcounty.org/	**R6**	**6 Nov 1888**	**Cheyenne** Scotts Bluff County; 1825 10th St; Gering, NE 69341; Ph. 308.436.6600 Details: (Co Clk has m rec; Co Judge has div, pro & ct rec)
Seward* connectseward.org/www/docs/cgov/	**D8**	**6 Mar 1855**	**Cass, Pierce, old** Seward County; 529 Seward St; PO Box 190; Seward, NE 68434; Ph. 402.643.2883 Details: (Formerly Greene Co. Name changed to Seward 3 Jan 1862) (Co Clk has m & land rec from 1866; Co Ct has pro rec from 1869; Clk Dis Ct has div rec from 1868 & ct rec from 1869)
Sheridan www.rootsweb.com/~nesherid/	**O5**	**25 Feb 1885**	**Sioux** Sheridan County; 301 E 2nd St; PO Box 39; Rushville, NE 69360; Ph. 308.327.2633 Details: (Co Judge has m, pro & ct rec; Clk Dis Ct has div rec)
Sherman www.rootsweb.com/~nesherma/	**H7**	**1 Mar 1871**	**Buffalo, Unorganized Territory** Sherman County; 630 O Street; PO Box 456; Loup City, NE 68853; Ph. 308.745.1513 Details: (Co Clk has m rec from 1883, div & ct rec from 1882, land rec from 1873 & nat rec 1882-1920; Co Clk Mag has pro rec)
Shorter		**7 Jan 1860**	**Unorganized Territory** Details: (see Lincoln) (Name changed to Lincoln 11 Dec 1861)
Sioux www.rootsweb.com/~nesioux/	**Q4**	**19 Feb 1877**	**Unorganized Territory** Sioux County; 325 Main St; PO Box 158; Harrison, NE 69346; Ph. 308.668.2443 Details: (Co Clk has land rec; Co Judge has m, pro & ct rec; Clk Dis Ct has div rec)
Stanton www.stanton.net/county.html	**E6**	**6 Mar 1855**	**Unorganized Territory** Stanton County; 804 Ivy St; PO Box 347; Stanton, NE 68779; Ph. 402.439.2222 Details: (Formerly Izard Co. Name changed to Stanton 20 Jan 1862) (Co Clk has m rec from 1869, land rec from 1868, nat & mil rec; Co Ct has pro rec; Clk Dis Ct has div & ct rec from 1875)
Taylor			Details: (Never org. co in southwest corner of state. Became part of Cheyenne Co. With Lincoln in 1870 cen)
Thayer www.rootsweb.com/~nethayer/	**E9**	**26 Jan 1871**	**Jefferson** Thayer County; 225 N 4th St; PO Box 208; Hebron, NE 68370-1549; Ph. 402.768.6126 Details: (Co Judge has m, pro & ct rec; Clk Dis Ct has div rec; Co Clk has land rec)
Thomas www.rootsweb.com/~nethomas/	**K6**	**31 Mar 1887**	**Unorganized Territory** Thomas County; 503 Main St; Thedford, NE 69166; Ph. 308.645.2261 Details: (Co Clk has m rec from 1887 & land rec; Clk Dis Ct has div & ct rec; Co Judge has pro rec)

County Website	Map Index	Date Created	Parent County or Territory From Which Organized Address/Details
Thurston www.rootsweb.com/~nethurst/	**C5**	**28 Mar 1889**	**Burt** Thurston County; 106 S 5th St; PO Box G; Pender, NE 68047; Ph. 402.385.2343 Details: (Thurston Co was originally an Indian reservation & prior to org. was called Blackbird Co, created 7 Mar 1855. From 1884-1889 it was administered by Dakota Co. Name changed to Thurston 28 Mar 1889) (Co Judge has m & pro rec from 1889; Clk Dis Ct has div & ct rec from 1889; Co Clk has land rec from 1885)
Valley www.rootsweb.com/~nevalley/	**H6**	**1 Mar 1871**	**Unorganized Territory** Valley County; 125 S 15th St; Ord, NE 68862; Ph. 308.728.3700 Details: (Co Clk has m & land rec from 1883; Co Judge has pro rec; Clk Dis Ct has div & ct rec)
Washington www.washcone.com/	**C7**	**23 Nov 1854**	**Original county** Washington County; 1555 Colfax St; Blair, NE 68008; Ph. 402.426.6822 Details: (Co Clk has b, d, bur & land rec; Co Judge has m, pro & ct rec; Clk Dis Ct has div rec)
Wayne www.rootsweb.com/~newayne/	**D5**	**4 Mar 1871**	**Unorganized Territory** Wayne County; 510 N Pearl St; PO Box 248; Wayne, NE 68787-1939; Ph. 402.375.2288 Details: (Co Judge has m, pro & ct rec from 1871; Clk Dis Ct has div rec; Co Clk has land rec from 1870)
Webster* www.rootsweb.com/~newebste/	**G9**	**16 Feb 1867**	**Unorganized Territory** Webster County; 621 N Cedar St; Red Cloud, NE 68970; Ph. 402.746.2716 Details: (Co Clk has m, land, div, pro & ct rec from 1871 & nat rec from 1874)
West		**13 Jan 1860**	**Unorganized Territory** Details: (see Holt) (Name changed to Holt 9 Jan 1862)
Wheeler www.rootsweb.com/~newheele/	**G5**	**17 Feb 1877**	**Unorganized Territory** Wheeler County; Main St; PO Box 127; Bartlett, NE 68622; Ph. 308.654.3235 Details: (Co Clk has ct & land rec)
York www.rootsweb.com/~neyork/	**E8**	**13 Mar 1855**	**Cass, Pierce, old** York County; 510 Lincoln Ave; York, NE 68467; Ph. 402.362.7759 Details: (Co Clk has m rec; Co Ct has pro rec; Reg of Deeds has land rec; Clk Dis Ct has div rec; Veteran Service Off has mil rec)

Notes

Nevada
Sagebrush

NEVADA

CAPITAL: CARSON CITY – TERRITORY 1861 – STATE 1864 (36TH)

Explorers began to satisfy their curiosities about the Nevada area in the 1820's. Among those to first visit were Jedediah Smith, Peter Ogden, Kit Carson, and later John C. Fremont. In 1821, Mexico gained its independence from Spain and claimed Nevada as part of its territory. During the 1840's, numerous wagon trains crossed Nevada on their way to California. In 1848, Nevada, along with other western states, became part of the United States.

The first non-Indian settlement was made at Mormon Station (Genoa) in 1849. The following year, most of Nevada became part of the Utah Territory. In 1853 and 1856, residents of the Carson River Valley petitioned to become part of California Territory because Utah was not protecting them. Discovery of gold in 1859 at the Comstock Lode brought thousands to Nevada. People from England, Italy, Scandinavia, Germany, France, and Mexico came to the area to join the migrating Americans in the search for gold and silver. Nevada became a territory in 1861 and achieved statehood just two years later.

During the Civil War, more than 1,000 Nevada men served in the Union forces. After the Civil War, Nevada's borders were enlarged slightly, taking away from both Utah and Arizona. The Comstock Lode declined and with it the population of the state during the 1880s. Discoveries of silver at Tonopah, gold at Goldfield and copper at Ely led to new booms that lasted until World War I. Gambling was legalized in 1931, which brought an additional new boom to Nevada.

Look for vital records in the following locations:

- **Birth, death records:** Birth and death records from 1867 to 30 June 1911 are located in each county recorder's office. Birth and death files from 1 July 1911 are at the Nevada State Department of Health, Division of Vital Statistics in Carson City, Nevada.
- **Marriage records**: Available at each county recorder's office. Record keeping began there in 1864.
- **Land records**: Deeds and other land records available at each county recorder's office. Record keeping began there in 1864.
- **Court records:** Probate actions were recorded in the Utah Territorial Courts beginning in 1861. These records are now at the Nevada State Library and Archives, Division of Archives and Records in Carson City. Probate records after 1864 are in the district courts.
- **Census records:** Federal census records for 1850 and 1860 are with the Utah Territorial Census. Copies of an 1862 territorial census are at the Nevada State Library and Archives.

Nevada State Department of Health
Division of Vital Statistics
505 East King Street, Room 102
Carson City, Nevada 89710
702.687.4481

Nevada State Library and Archives
Division of Archives and Records
101 South Fall Street
Carson City, Nevada 90710

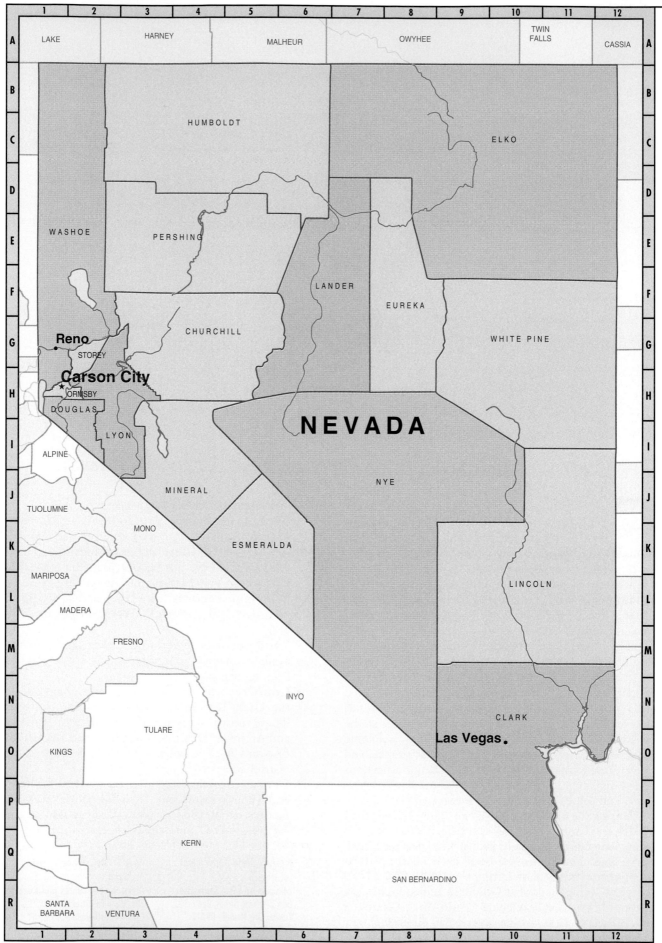

Societies and Repositories

Bureau of Land Management; 850 Harvard Way, PO Box 12000; Reno, Nevada 89520-0006; 702.785.6402; Fax 702.785.6634

Carson Valley Historical Society; 1477 U.S. Highway 395 North; Gardnerville, Nevada 89410; <www.carsonvalleymuseums.com/Pages/staff.html>

Churchill County Historical and Genealogical Society; c/o Churchill County Museum; 1050 S. Main St.; Fallon, Nevada 89406

Clark County Heritage Center; 1830 S Boulder Highway; Henderson, Nevada 89015-8502

Clark County, Nevada Genealogical Society; PO Box 1929; Las Vegas, Nevada 89125.1929; 702.258.4099; <www.rootsweb.com/~nvccngs/>

Elko Genealogical Society; 3001 North Fifth Street; Elko, Nevada 89801

Eureka Historical Society; PO Box 82; Eureka, Nevada 89316

Goldfield Historical Society; PO Box 178; Goldfield, Nevada 89013

Family History Library: 35 North West Temple Street: Salt Lake City, Utah 84150: 800.346.6044 or 801.240.2584: <www.familysearch.org>: Find a Family History Center near you: <www.familysearch.org/Eng/Library/FHC/frameset_fhc.asp>

Humboldt County Genealogical Society; c/o Humboldt County Library; 85 E. 5th St.; Winnemucca, Nevada 89445

Jewish Genealogical Society of Las Vegas, Nevada; PO Box 29342; Las Vegas, Nevada 89126

Las Vegas Family History Center; 509 S. 9th St., PO Box 1360; Las Vegas, Nevada 89125

Las Vegas Public Library; 400 E. Mesquite Ave.; Las Vegas, Nevada 89101

Lincoln County Historical Society; PO Box 515; Pioche, Nevada 89043

National Archives-Pacific Region (Laguna Niguel); 24000 Avila Road, PO Box 6719; Laguna Niguel, California 92677-6719; 714.360.2641; Fax 714.360.2644

National Archives-Pacific Sierra Region (San Bruno); 1000 Commodore Drive; San Bruno, California 94066; 415.876.9009; Fax 415.876.9233

Nevada Historical Society; 1650 North Virginia Street; Reno, Nevada 89503; 702.688.1191; Fax 702.688.2917; <dmla.clan.lib.nv.us/docs/museums/reno/his.soc.htm>

Nevada Office of Vital Statistics; 505 East King Street, Room 102; Carson City, Nevada 89710; 702.687.4481; Fax 702.687.5161

Nevada State Genealogical Society; 2931 Randolph Street, PO Box 20666; Reno, Nevada 89502; 702.826.1130 <www.rootsweb.com/~nvsgs/>

Nevada Historical Society; 1650 North Virginia, Reno, NV 89503

Nevada State Library and Archives; 100 North Stewart Street; Carson City, Nevada 89701-4285; 775.684.3330; <dmla.clan.lib.nv.us/docs/nsla/>

Nevada State Museum and Historical Society; 700 Twin Lakes Drive; Las Vegas, Nevada 89107; 702.486.5205; Fax 702.486.5172; <dmla.clan.lib.nv.us/docs/museums/lv/vegas.htm>

North Las Vegas Library; 2300 Civic Center Dr.; North Las Vegas, Nevada 89030

Northeastern Nevada Genealogical Society; 1515 Idaho St.; Elko, Nevada 89801; <www.rootsweb.com/~nvnengs/index.html>

Pahrump, Nevada Genealogical Society; PO Box 66; Pahrump, Nevada 89048

Protestant Episcopal, The Nevada Historical Society; 1650 N. Virginia Street; Reno, Nevada 89503-1799; 702.688.1191; Fax 702.688.2917

Roman Catholic, Diocese of Reno-Las Vegas, Chancery Office; 336 Cathedral Way; Las Vegas, Nevada 89109; 702.735.7865; Fax 702.735.2996

Roman Catholic, Diocese of Reno-Las Vegas, Chancery Office; PO Box 18316; Reno, Nevada 89504

Sons of the American Revolution, Nevada Society; 309 Duke Circle; Las Vegas, Nevada 89107

Sparks Heritage Society; 814 Victorian Ave.; Sparks, Nevada 89431

Steward Street; Carson City, Nevada 89701-4285; 702.687.8313; Fax 702.687.8330

Town of Round Mountain, Nevada Genealogical Group; PO Box 330; Round Mountain, Nevada 89045

University of Nevada-Reno Library, Special Collections; Mail Stop 332; Reno, Nevada 89557-0044; 702.784.6500 Ext. #327; Fax 702.784.4529

Valley of Fire Chapter, DAR; Las Vegas, Nevada; <www.rootsweb.com/~nvvfcdar/Index.html>

Washoe County Library; Reno, Nevada 89507

Wellington Historical Society; PO Box 36; Wellington, Nevada 89444

White Pine Historical and Archaeological Society; PO Box 1117; Ely, Nevada 89301; <www.webpanda.com/white_pine_county/historical_society/index.html>

Bibliography and Record Sources

General Sources

Angel, Myron. *History of Nevada: With Illustrations and Biographical Sketches of Its Prominent Men and Pioneers.* Oakland, California: Thompson & West, 1881.

Bancroft, Hubert Howe. *History of Nevada, Colorado and Wyoming, 1540-1888.* San Francisco: History Co., 1890.

Dangberg, Grace. *Carson Valley: Historical Sketches of Nevada's First Settlement.* Reno, Nevada: Carson Valley Historical Society, 1979.

Durham, Michael S. *Desert Between the Mountains: Mormons, Miners, Padres, Mountain Men, and The Opening of the Great Basin, 1772-1869.* New York: Henry Holt, 1997.

Edwards, Elbert B. *200 Years in Nevada: A Story of People Who Opened, Explored and Developed the Land; A Bicentennial History.* Salt Lake City: Publishers Press, 1978.

Elliott, Russell R. *History of Nevada, 1973.* Reprint Lincoln, Nebraska: University of Nebraska Press, 1984.

Ellison, Marion. *An Inventory and Index to the Records of Carson County, Utah and Nevada Territories, 1855-1861.* Reno: The Grace Dangberg Foundation, 1984.

County Website	Map Index	Date Created	Parent County or Territory From Which Organized Address/Details
Carson www.rootsweb.com/~nvcarson/index.htm		**17 Jan 1854**	**Original county** Details: (Organized as a co in Utah Terr. Discontinued 2 Mar 1861 when Nevada Terr. was created. Became part of Douglas, Lyon, Ormsby, Storey, Churchill, Pershing, Humboldt & Washoe Cos)
Carson City www.carson-city.nv.us/ccgov.htm	H1	**25 Nov 1861**	**Original county** Carson City County; 885 E Musser St; Carson City, NV 89701; Ph. 775.887.2260 Details: (Organized as Ormsby Co. Consolidated into Carson City 1969 & Ormsby Co discontinued) (Co Clk has div, pro, ct & nat rec from 1864; Co Rcdr has land rec from 1862, mil rec from 1919 & m rec)
Churchill www.governet.net/NV/CO/ CHU/home.cfm	G4	**25 Nov 1861**	**Original county** Churchill County; 155 N Taylor St 110; Fallon, NV 89406; Ph. 775.423.6028 Details: (Co Clk has m, div, pro & ct rec from 1905)
Clark www.co.clark.nv.us/	N10	**5 Feb 1909**	**Lincoln** Clark County; 200 S 3rd St; Las Vegas, NV 89155-1601; Ph. 702.455.3156 Details: (Co Clk has pro, div & ct rec; Co Rcdr has m & land rec; Co Hlth Dept has b & d rec)
Douglas* www.co.douglas.nv.us/	H2	**25 Nov 1861**	**Original county** Douglas County; 1594 Esmeralda Ave Rm 105; Minden, NV 89423-0218; Ph. 775.782.9014 Details: (Co Clk has m, div, pro & ct rec)
Elko* www.governet.net/NV/CO/ ELK/home.cfm	C10	**5 Mar 1869**	**St. Mary's** Elko County; 571 Idaho St #204; Elko, NV 89801-3787; Ph. 775.738.4600 Details: (Co Clk has m applications, div, pro & ct rec from 1876; Co Rcdr has b, d, bur & land rec)
Esmeralda www.governet.net/NV/CO/ESM/ home.cfm	K5	**25 Nov 1861**	**Original county** Esmeralda County; PO Box 547; Goldfield, NV 89013-0547; Ph. 775.485.6367 Details: (Co Clk & Treas Off has m rec from 1898, div & pro rec from 1908, ct rec from 1907 & nat rec from 1904)
Eureka* www.governet.net/NV/CO/ EUR/home.cfm	F8	**1 Mar 1873**	**Lander** Eureka County; 701 S Main St; PO Box 677; Eureka, NV 89316-0677; Ph. 775.237.5262 Details: (Co Rcdr has b, m, d, bur & land rec; Co Clk has div, pro & ct rec from 1874)
Humboldt www.governet.net/NV/CO/HUM/ home.cfm	C4	**25 Nov 1861**	**Original county** Humboldt County; 50 W 5th St; Winnemucca, NV 89445; Ph. 775.623.6343 Details: (Co Clk has m rec from 1881, div & ct rec from 1863, pro rec from 1900 & nat rec from 1864; Co Rcdr has land rec; see 1860 Utah cen)
Lander www.governet.net/NV/CO/LAN/ home.cfm	F6	**19 Dec 1862**	**Original county** Lander County; 315 S Humboldt St; Battle Mountain, NV 89820; Ph. 775.635.5761 Details: (Co Clk has m rec from 1867, div rec, pro & ct rec from 1865; Co Aud has some b rec)
Lincoln www.governet.net/NV/CO/LIN/ home.cfm	L10	**26 Feb 1866**	**Nye** Lincoln County; 1 Main St; Pioche, NV 89043-0000; Ph. 775.962.5390 Details: (Co Clk has m, div, pro, ct & land rec from 1873)
Lyon www.governet.net/NV/CO/LYO/ home.cfm	I2	**25 Nov 1861**	**Original county** Lyon County; 27 S Main St; PO Box 816; Yerington, NV 89447; Ph. 775.577.5043 Details: (Co Rcdr has m & land rec from 1862; Co Clk has div, pro & ct rec from 1890)
Mineral* www.governet.net/NV/CO/MIN/ home.cfm	J4	**10 Feb 1911**	**Esmeralda** Mineral County; PO Box 1450; Hawthorne, NV 89415-1450; Ph. 775.945.2446 Details: (Co Clk has div, pro & ct rec from 1911 with some earlier, nat rec 1911-1956 & bur rec; Co Rcdr has m license applications & mil dis rec from 1911; Co Treas has land rec from 1911)

County Website	Map Index	Date Created	Parent County or Territory From Which Organized Address/Details
Nye* www.governet.net/NV/CO/NYE/ home.cfm	J7	16 Feb 1864	**Esmeralda** Nye County; 101 Radar Rd; PO Box 1031; Tonopah, NV 89049-1031; Ph. 775.482.8127 Details: (Co Clk has m, div, pro & ct rec from 1860; Co Rcdr has land rec)
Ormsby	H1	25 Nov 1861	**Original county** Details: (see Carson City) (Consolidated with Carson City 1969 & discontinued.)
Pahute			Details: (Discontinued)
Pershing www.governet.net/NV/CO/PER/ home.cfm	E4	18 Mar 1919	**Humboldt** Pershing County; 400 Main St; PO Box 820; Lovelock, NV 89419-0820; Ph. 775.273.2208 Details: (Co Clk has m, div, pro & ct rec from 1919)
Roop		1860	Details: (see Washoe) (Discontinued after a boundary dispute with California. Terr. absorbed by Plumas Co, CA & Washoe Co.)
St. Mary's		1856	**Original county** Details: (Organized as a co in Utah Terr. Discontinued 2 Mar 1861 when Nevada Terr. was created)
Storey www.governet.net/NV/CO/STO/ home.cfm	G2	25 Nov 1861	**Original county** Storey County; PO Box D; Virginia City, NV 89440-0139; Ph. 755.847.0969 Details: (Co Rcdr has b, m & d rec from 1875 & land rec; Co Clk has div & ct rec from 1861 & pro rec from 1875)
Washoe* www.co.washoe.nv.us/	E1	25 Nov 1861	**Original county** Washoe County; 75 Court St; PO Box 11130; Reno, NV 89520; Ph. 775.328.3260 Details: (Co Hlth Dept has b, d & bur rec from 1900; Co Clk has div, pro, ct & nat rec from 1862; Co Rcdr has land rec from 1862 & m rec from 1871)
White Pine www.governet.net/NV/CO/WHP/ home.cfm	G10	2 Mar 1869	**Millard, Utah Terr.** White Pine County; 953 Campton St; PO Box 659; Ely, NV 89301-1002; Ph. 775.289.2341 Details: (Co Clk has m rec from 1885, div, pro & ct rec from 1907 & nat rec; Co Rcdr has land rec from 1885)

Notes

Purple Lilac

NEW HAMPSHIRE

CAPITAL: CONCORD – STATE 1788 (9TH)

The first Europeans to see New Hampshire were Martin Pring in 1603, Samuel de Champlain in 1605, and Captain John Smith in 1614. In 1622, the King of England granted all of the land between the Merrimac and Kennebec Rivers to Ferdinando Gorges and John Mason. The first settlement occurred three years later at Little Harbor (present-day Rye). Dover was settled about the same time and Strawberry Bank (later Portsmouth), Exeter, and Hampton were all settled by 1638. In 1629, New Hampshire was separated from Maine and in 1641 was made part of the Massachusetts Colony. It remained so until 1679, when it became a Royal British Province. Seven years later it became part of the Dominion of New England, which lasted three years. Three years of independence followed until a royal government was established in 1692. From 1699 to 1741, the royal governor of Massachusetts governed New Hampshire. Victories over the Indians in 1759 opened New Hampshire to increased settlement. As the population grew, boundary disagreements and land disputes grew more heated. Finally in 1764, the Connecticut River was declared the western boundary.

New Hampshire supported the Revolution, especially following the punitive measures imposed on New England by England. In 1788, New Hampshire was the ninth state to ratify the Constitution. Many settlers heading west from Massachusetts and Connecticut stopped for a time in New Hampshire and Vermont. During the first 200 years of its history, most settlers were English. The next 75 years saw tens of thousands come from Scandinavia, Greece, Italy, and France.

In 1819 the Toleration Act was passed prohibiting taxation to support any church. In 1842, the boundary between New Hampshire and Quebec was settled. During the Civil War, just less than 34,000 men from New Hampshire served in the Union Army. Following the war, industry, transportation, and communications expanded. The textile, leather, and shoe industries brought renewed immigration from French Canadians and others.

Look for vital records in the following locations:

- **Birth and death records:** Check the Bureau of Vital Records, Concord, New Hampshire for records after 1901. Towns kept vital statistics from the time they were organized, but they are not complete. Until 1883, less than half of the vital records were recorded with little information. The records are more complete and informative after 1901. Be sure to state your relationship and reason for requesting records when contacting the bureau.
- **Wills, tax records and probate records:** A provincial Registry of Probate kept probate records until 1771 when probate courts were created. Clerks of probate courts in each county are in charge of wills. Tax records are generally found in the town clerk's office and some might be found in the New Hampshire Division of Records Management and Archives in Concord. Almost all towns have published town histories that contain much genealogical information about early settlers.
- **Census records:** The state office in Concord has charge of the census records.

Bureau of Vital Records
6 Hazen Drive
Concord, New Hampshire 03301
603.271.4651

New Hampshire Division of
Records Management
and Archives
71 South Fruit Street
Concord, New Hampshire 03301

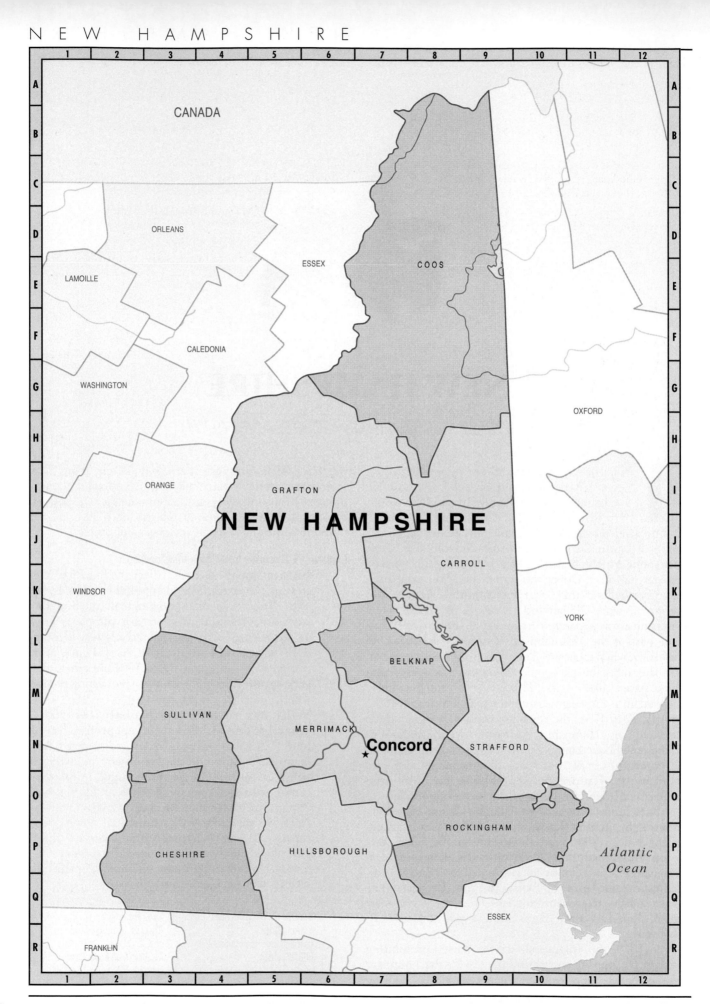

Societies and Repositories

Acadian Genealogical and Historical Association; PO Box 669; Manchester, New Hampshire 03105

American Baptist Churches of Vermont and New Hampshire; 89 North State Street, PO Box 2403; Concord, New Hampshire 03301; 603.225.3316; Fax 603.228.6129

American Baptist-Samuel Colgate Historical Society; 1106 South Goodman Street; Rochester, New York 14620-2532; 716.473-1740; Fax 716.473.1740

American-Canadian Genealogical Society; PO Box 6478; Manchester, New Hampshire 03108-6478; 603.624.8843;

Archive Center of the Historical Society Of Cheshire Co.; 246 Main St.; Keene, New Hampshire 03431; 603.352.1895

Baker Memorial Library; Dartmouth College; Hanover, New Hampshire 03755

Berlin & Coos County Historical Society; PO Box 52; Berlin, New Hampshire 03570

Bureau of Vital Records and Health Statistics, Health and Welfare Building; #6 Hazen Drive; Concord, New Hampshire 03301; 603.271.4650

Carrol County Chapter, NHSOG; PO Box 250; Freedom, New Hampshire 03836

Center Harbor Historical Society; PO Box 74; Center Harbor, New Hampshire 03226

Congregational Library; 14 Beacon Street; Boston, Massachusetts 02108; 617.523.0470; Fax 617.523.0491

Conway Historical Society; PO Box 1949; Conway, New Hampshire 03818; 603.447.1991; <www.conwayhistory.org/index.html>

Dartmouth College; Baker Library; Hanover, New Hampshire 03755

Dover Public Library; 73 Locust St.; Dover, New Hampshire 03820

Exeter Congregational Church; 21 Front Street, PO Box 97; Exeter, New Hampshire 03833; 603.772.4216

Exeter Public Library, Genealogy and local history Rm.; 86 Front St.; Exeter, New Hampshire 03833

Family History Library: 35 North West Temple Street: Salt Lake City, Utah 84150: 800.346.6044 or 801.240.2584: <www.familysearch.org>: Find a Family History Center near you: <www.familysearch.org/Eng/Library/FHC/frameset_fhc.asp>

Hancock Historical Society; PO Box 138; 7 Main Street; Hancock, New Hampshire 03449; <www.mv.com/ipusers/hancocknh/hhs/hhs_home.htm>

Historical Society of Cheshire County, New Hampshire; 246 Main St.; PO Box 803; Keene, New Hampshire 03431

Hollis Historical Society; PO Box 138; Hollis, New Hampshire 03049

Manchester City Library, Carpenter Memorial Bldg; 405 Pine St.; Manchester, New Hampshire 03104

Merrimack Historical Society; 520 Boston Post Road; Merrimack, New Hampshire 03054; <members.aol.com/merrimackhistory/merhis.html>

Merrimack Society Of Genealogists; PO Box 1035; Concord, New Hampshire 03302

N.H. Founders & Patriots; 44 Durham Point Road; Durham, New Hampshire 03824-3126

N.H. Old Graveyard Association; 7 Maple Court; Tilton, New Hampshire 03276

N.H. Society of Colonial Wars; 19 Pearl Street; Concord, New Hampshire 03301-4402

National Archives-Northeast Region (Boston); 380 Trapelo Road; Waltham, Massachusetts 02154; 617.647.8100; Fax 617.647.8460

New Hampshire Division of Records Management and Archives; 71 South Fruit Street; Concord, New Hampshire 03301-2410; 603.271.2236; Fax 603.271.2272

New Hampshire Historical Society Library; 30 Park St.; Concord, New Hampshire 03301; <www.nhhistory.org>; 603.225.3381; Fax 603.224.0463

New Hampshire Society of Genealogists; PO Box 2316; Concord, New Hampshire 03302-2316

New Hampshire Society of Genealogists; RFD 2, Box 668, Wingate Road; Center Barnstead, New Hampshire 03225-9103; <nhsog.org/index.htm>

New Hampshire State Library; 20 Park Street; Concord, New Hampshire 03301; 603.271.6826; Fax 603.271.2205; <www.state.nh.us/nhsl/>

North Country Genealogical Society; PO Box 618; Littleton, New Hampshire 03561

Northwood Historical Society; PO Box 114; Northwood, New Hampshire 03261; <www.rootsweb.com/~nhnhs/>

Piscataqua Pioneers Special Collection, Diamond Library; Univ. of New Hampshire, 3rd Floor; Durham, New Hampshire 03824

Portsmouth Athenaeum; 9 Market St.; Portsmouth, New Hampshire 03801

Rindge Historical Society; Rindge, New Hampshire 03461

Rockingham Society of Genealogists; PO Box 81; 28 Prentiss Way; Exeter, New Hampshire 03833-0081

Roman Catholic, Diocese of Manchester, Chancery Office; 153 Ash Street, PO Box 310; Manchester, New Hampshire 03105; 603.669.3100; Fax 603.669.0377

Strafford County Society Of Genealogists; PO Box 322; Dover, New Hampshire 03821-0322

United Methodist Archives Center, Drew University Library; PO Box 127; Madison, New Jersey 07940; 201.408.3189; Fax 201.408.3909

United Methodist Church; Fountain Square, PO Box 505; Contoocook, New Hampshire 03229; 603.746.4894

Bibliography and Record Sources

General Sources

American Baptist Historical Society. *The Records of American Baptists in New Hampshire and Related Organizations.* Rochester, New York: American Baptist Historical Society, 1981.

Belknap, Jeremy. *The History of New Hampshire.* (1831). Reprint, Bowie, Maryland: Heritage Books, 1992.

Bent, Allen H. *Bent's Bibliography of the White Mountains.* (1911) Reprint. Rockport, ME: Picton Press, 1971.

Biographical Sketches of Representative Citizens of the State of New Hampshire. Boston, Massachusetts: New England Historical Publishing Company, 1902.

Carpenter, Randall C. *Descriptive Inventory of the New Hampshire Collection.* Salt Lake City, Utah: University of Utah Press, 1983.

Carter, Nathan F. *Native Ministry of New Hampshire.* Concord, New Hampshire: Rumford Printing Co., 1906.

Chase, Francis. *Gathered Sketches from the Early History of New Hampshire and Vermont: Containing Vivid and Interesting Accounts of a Great Variety of the Adventures of our Forefathers, and of Other Incidents of Olden Time, Original and Selected.* Clarmont, New Hampshire: Tracy, Kenney & Co., 1856.

Church of Jesus Christ of Latter-day Saints. Vermont District. *Transcript of Record/Record of Members, Early to 1948.* Microfilm of original records in the LDS Church Archives, Salt Lake City. (Salt Lake City: Filmed by the Genealogical Society of Utah, 1953-1954). 2 microfilm.

Committee for a New England Bibliography. *New Hampshire, A Bibliography of its History.* Boston: G.K. Hall, 1979.

Copeley, William N. *Manuscript Church Records at the New Hampshire Historical Society, August 1981.* Salt Lake City: Genealogical Society of Utah, 1985. 1 microfiche.

Copeley, William. *New Hampshire Family Records Vol. I and II.* Bowie, Maryland: Heritage Books, 1994.

Copeley, William. *Index to Genealogies in New Hampshire Town Histories.* Concord, New Hampshire: New Hampshire Historical Society, 1988?

Crandall, Ralph J., ed. *Genealogical Research in New England.* Baltimore: Genealogical Publishing Co., 1984.

Crawford, L. *History of the White Mountains.* (1883) Reprint. Salem, Massachusetts: Higginson Books, 1991.

Daughters of the American Revolution (New Hampshire). *Genealogical Collection.* Microfilm of original records in the D.A.R. Library in Washington, D.C. (Salt Lake City: Genealogical Society of Utah, 1971). 15 microfilm.

Drake, Samuel Adams. *The Heart of the White Mountains: Their Legend and Scenery.* (1881) Reprint. Salem, Massachusetts: Higginson Books, 1995.

Early New England Settlers, 1600s-1800s. [S.l.]: Brøderbund, 1999. CD-ROM.

Fogg, Alonzo J. *The Statistics and Gazetteer of New Hampshire: Containing Descriptions of all the Counties, Towns and Villages, also, Boundaries and Area of the State, and its Natural Resources.* Tucson, Arizona: W.C. Cox & Co., 1972.

Green, Scott E. *Directory of Repositories of Family History in New Hampshire.* Baltimore, Maryland: Clearfield Co., 1993.

Hammond, Otis G. *Hammond's Check List of New Hampshire History.* 1971. Reprint. Somersworth, New Hampshire: New Hampshire Publishing Co., 1971.

Haskell, John D. Jr., and T.D. Seymour Bassett, eds. *New Hampshire: A Bibliography of Its History.* Boston: G.K. Hall, 1979.

Hazen, Henry Allen. *The Pastors of New Hampshire, Congregational and Presbyterian: A Chronological Table of the Beginning And Ending of Their Pastorates.* Bristol, New Hampshire: R.W. Musgrove, 1878.

Historical Records Survey (New Hampshire) *Inventory of the Roman Catholic Church Records in New Hampshire.* Manchester, New Hampshire: Diocese of Manchester, 1938.

Historical Records Survey (New Hampshire). *Guide to Church Vital Statistics Records in New Hampshire.* Manchester, New Hampshire: the Survey, 1942.

Historical Records Survey (New Hampshire). *Guide to Depositories of Manuscript Collections in the United States, New Hampshire.* Manchester, New Hampshire: The Survey, 1940.

Historical Records Survey (New Hampshire). *Inventory of the Church Archives of New Hampshire, Protestant Episcopal Diocese of New Hampshire.* Manchester, New Hampshire: the Survey, 1942.

Hurlin, William, et al. *The Baptists of New Hampshire.* Manchester, New Hampshire: New Hampshire Baptist Convention, 1902.

Kern, Charles W. *God, Grace, and Granite: The History of Methodism in New Hampshire, 1768-1988.* Canaan, New Hampshire: Published for the New Hampshire United Methodist Conference by Phoenix Publishing, 1988.

Lawrence, Robert F. *The New Hampshire Churches: Comprising Histories of the Congregational and Presbyterian Churches in the State, with Notices of Other Denominations; also Containing Many Interesting Incidents Connected with the First Settlement of Towns.* N.p.: S.L. Claremont Manufacturing Co., 1856.

Maine & New Hampshire Settlers, 1600s-1900s. [S.l.]: Brøderbund, 2000. CD-ROM.

Metcalf, Henry Harrison. *New Hampshire Women: A Collection of Portraits and Biographical Sketches of Daughters and Residents of the Granite State, Who are Worthy Representatives of Their Sex in the Various Walks and Conditions of Life.* Concord, N. H.: The New Hampshire Publishing Co., 1895.

Moses, George H. *New Hampshire Men: A Collection of Biographical Sketches, with Portraits, of Sons and Residents of the State Who Have Become Known in Commercial, Professional and Political Life.* Concord, New Hampshire: New Hampshire Publishing, 1893.

New Hampshire Historical Society. *Card Index to Genealogies, Published and Manuscript.* Concord, New Hampshire: New Hampshire Historical Society, 1975.

New Hampshire Historical Society. *New Hampshire Notables Card File, 1600 to the Present.* Microfilm of card file in the New Hampshire Historical Society, Concord, New Hampshire. (Salt Lake City: Filmed by Genealogical Society of Utah, 1988). 8 microfilm.

New Hampshire. *Research Outline.* Series US-States, no. 30. Salt Lake City: Family History Library, 1988.

New Hampshire. Department of State. Division of Records Management and Archives. *Guide to Early Documents (C. 1680-C. 1900) at the New Hampshire Records Management and Archives Center.* Concord, New Hampshire: Division of Records Management and Archives, 1981.

Noyes, Sybil, Charles Thornton Libby, and Walter Goodwin Davis. *Genealogical Dictionary of Maine and New Hampshire. 1928-39.* Reprint. Baltimore: Genealogical Publishing Co., 1983.

Pettengill, Samuel B. *The Yankee Pioneers: A Saga of Courage.* Rutland, Vt.: Charles E. Tuttle, 1971.

Pope, Charles H. *Pioneers of Maine and New Hampshire, 1623 to 1660*. 1908. Reprint. Baltimore: Genealogical Publishing Co., 1965.

Roberts, Richard P. *New Hampshire Name Changes 1768-1923*. Bowie, Maryland: Heritage Books, 1993.

Rollock, Rich. *New Hampshire Family Histories*. 3rd ed. Laconia, New Hampshire: Family Histories Directory, 1993.

Sanborn, Edwin D. *History of New Hampshire, From its First Discovery to the Year 1830: With Dissertations Upon the Rise of Opinions and Institutions, the Growth of Agriculture and Manufactures, and the Influence of Leading Families and Distinguished Men, to the Year 1874*. Manchester, New Hampshire: John B. Clarke, 1875.

Stackpole, Everett S. *History of New Hampshire*. 4 vols. New York: American Historical Society, 1916.

Stearn, Ezra S. *Genealogical and Family History of the State of New Hampshire*. 4 vols. New York: Lewis Publishing Co., 1908.

Tardiff, Olive. *They Paved the Way: A History of N.H. Women*. Exeter, New Hampshire: Women for Women Weekly Publishing, 1980.

The First Laws of the State of New Hampshire. (1780) Reprint. Wilmington, Delaware: Scholarly Resources, 1981.

Towle, Glenn C. *New Hampshire Genealogical Digest, 1623-1900*. Vol. 1. Bowie, Maryland: Heritage Books, 1986.

Towle, Laird C. *New Hampshire Genealogical Research Guide*. Bowie, Md.: Heritage Books, 1983.

Towle, Laird C., and Ann N. Brown. *New Hampshire Genealogical Research Guide*. 2nd ed. Bowie, MD. Heritage Books, 1983.

Whiton, John M. *Sketches of the History of New Hampshire, from its Settlement in 1623 to 1833: Comprising Notices of the Memorable Events and Interesting Incidents of a Period of Two Hundred and Ten Years*. Concord, [N.H.]: Marsh, Capen and Lyon, 1824.

Willey, George F. *State Builders: An Illustrated Historical and Biographical Record of the State of New Hampshire at the Beginning of the Twentieth Century*. Manchester, New Hampshire: New Hampshire Pub. Corp., 1903.

Wilson, Emily S. *Inhabitants of New Hampshire 1776*. (1983) Reprint. Baltimore: Genealogical Publishing Co., 1993.

Atlases, Maps and Gazetteers

Atlas of New Hampshire. Galveston, Texas: Frontier Press, n.d.

Charlton, Edwin A. *New Hampshire As It Is, in Three Parts*. Claremont, New Hampshire: Tracy and Sanford, 1855.

Cobb, David A. *New Hampshire Maps to 1900: An Annotated Checklist*. Hanover, New Hampshire: New Hampshire Historical Society. Distributed by University Press of New England, 1981.

Communities, Settlements and Neighborhood Centers in the State of New Hampshire. Concord: New Hampshire State Planning and Development Commission, 1937. Reprint. 1954.

Farmer, John, and Jacob B. Moore. *A Gazetteer of the State of New Hampshire*. Concord, New Hampshire: Jacob B. Moore, 1823.

Fogg, Alonzo J. *The Statistics and Gazetteer of New Hampshire: Containing Descriptions of all the Counties, Towns and Villages, also, Boundaries and Area of the State, and its Natural Resources*. Tucson, Arizona: W.C. Cox & Co., 1972.

General Highway Maps: County Series. [S.l.]: New Hampshire Department of Public Works and Highways, n.d.

Hayward, John. *A Gazetteer of New Hampshire: Containing Descriptions of all the Counties, Towns, and Districts in the State; also of its Principal Mountains, Rivers, Waterfalls, Harbors, Islands, and Fashionable Resorts, to Which are Added Statistical Accounts of its Agriculture, Commerce and Manufactures*. (1849) Reprint. Bowie, Maryland: Heritage Books, 1993.

Hixon, Robert. *The Place Names of the White Mountains: History and Origins*. Camden, Me.: Down East Books, 1980.

Hunt, Elmer Munson. *New Hampshire Town Names: and Whence They Came*. Peterborough, New Hampshire: Noone House, 1970.

Long, John H., ed. and Gordon DenBoer, comp. *Atlas of Historical County Boundaries: New Hampshire and Vermont*. New York: Simon & Schuster, 1993.

Merrill, Eliphalet. *Gazetteer of the State of New Hampshire*. Bowie, Maryland: Heritage Books, 1987.

New Hampshire Atlas and Gazetteer. 10th ed. Freeport, Maine: DeLorme Mapping Co., 1996.

Simonds, L.W. *New Hampshire Post Offices, 1775-1978*. New London, New Hampshire: Simonds, 1978.

Smith, Chester M. *The Postal History of New Hampshire: the Post Offices and First Postmasters from 1775 to 1985*. Lake Grove, Oregon: The Depot, 1986.

Town and City Atlas of the State of New Hampshire. Boston: D. H. Hurd, Co., 1892.

Census Records

Available Census Records and Census Substitutes

Federal Census 1790, 1800 (except parts of Rockingham and Strafford Counties), 1810, 1820, 1830, 1840, 1850, 1860, 1870, 1880, 1900, 1910, 1920, 1930.

Federal Mortality Schedules 1850, 1860, 1870, 1880.

Union Veterans and Widows 1890.

Residents 1732, 1776.

Census of New Hampshire, for the Years 1767 and 1775. Microfilm of original records in the Records & Archives Center, Concord, New Hampshire. (Salt Lake City: Filmed by the Genealogical Society of Utah, 1975). 1 microfilm.

Dollarhide, William. *The Census Book: A Genealogist's Guide to Federal Census Facts, Schedules and Indexes*. Bountiful, Utah: Heritage Quest, 1999.

Holbrook, Jay Mack. *New Hampshire 1732 Census*. Oxford, Massachusetts: Holbrook Research Institute, 1981.

Holbrook, Jay Mack. *New Hampshire Residents 1633-1699*. Oxford, Massachusetts: Holbrook Research Institute, 1979.

Kemp, Thomas Jay. *The American Census Handbook*. Wilmington, Delaware: Scholarly Resources, Inc., 2001.

Lainhart, Ann S. *State Census Records*. Baltimore: Genealogical Publishing Co., Inc., 1992.

Szucs, Loretto Dennis, and Matthew Wright. *Finding Answers in U.S. Census Records.* Ancestry Publishing, 2001

Thorndale, William, and William Dollarhide. *Map Guide to the U.S. Federal Censuses, 1790-1920.* Baltimore: Genealogical Publishing Co., 1987.

Court Records, Probate and Wills

Batchellor, Albert Stillman. *Probate Records of the Province of New Hampshire.* 9 vols. in 12. Bowie, Maryland: Heritage Books, 1989-1990.

Bell, Charles H. *The Bench and Bar of New Hampshire: Including Biographical Notices of Deceased Judges of the Highest Court, and Lawyers of the Province and State and a List of Names of Those Now Living.* Boston: Houghton, Mifflin and Co., 1894.

New Hampshire (Colony). *Province Deeds and Probate Records– From 1623-1772.* Microfilm of original records at the Historical Society in Concord, New Hampshire. (Salt Lake City: Filmed by the Genealogical Society of Utah, 1975). 118 microfilm.

New Hampshire Provincial and State Papers. 40 vols. Concord, New Hampshire: George E. Jenks, 1867-1943.

New Hampshire. Courts. *Colonial Court Records, 1638-1772 Approx.* Microfilm of original records in Concord, New Hampshire. (Salt Lake City: Filmed by the Genealogical Society of Utah, 1975). 207 microfilm.

Probate Records of the Province of New Hampshire, Vols. 31-39 of *New Hampshire Provincial and State Papers.* 9 vols. Reprint. Bowie, Maryland: Heritage Books, 1989-90.

State of New Hampshire. Division of Records Management and Archives. *General Court Records (1680-Current).* Concord, New Hampshire: State of New Hampshire. Division of Records Management and Archives, 2002. Online guide - <www.state.nh.us/state/archival.html>.

State of New Hampshire. Division of Records Management and Archives. *Provincial Probate Records.* Concord, New Hampshire: State of New Hampshire. Division of Records Management and Archives, 2002. Online guide - <www.state.nh.us/state/archival.html>.

Emigration, Immigration, Migration and Naturalization

Bolton, Ethel Stanwood. *Immigrants to New England, 1700-1775.* Baltimore: Genealogical Publishing, 1966.

Early New England Settlers, 1600s-1800s. [S.l.]: Brøderbund, 1999. CD-ROM.

National Archives Records Administration: Northeastern Region (Boston). *Records of the Immigration and Naturalization Service, RG 85.* Boston, Massachusetts: National Archives Records Administration: Northeastern Region (Boston). Online guide - <www.nara.gov/regional/findaids/bosalrgs.html>.

United States. *Immigration and Naturalization Service. Index to New England Naturalization Petitions, 1791-1906.* Washington: National Archives. Central Plains Region, 1983. 117 microfilm.

Land and Property

Hone, Wade E. *Land and Property Research in the United States.* Salt Lake City: Ancestry Incorporated, 1997.

New Hampshire (Colony). *Province Deeds and Probate Records from 1623-1772.* Microfilm of original records at the Historical Society in Concord, New Hampshire. (Salt Lake City: Filmed by the Genealogical Society of Utah, 1975). 118 microfilm.

New Hampshire. Proprietors. *Proprietors' Records, 1748-1846.* Microfilm of originals in Concord, New Hampshire. (Salt Lake City: Filmed by the Genealogical Society of Utah, 1975).

State of New Hampshire. Division of Records Management and Archives. *Land Surveyors' Records.* Concord, New Hampshire: State of New Hampshire. Division of Records Management and Archives, 2002. Online guide - <www.state.nh.us/state/archival.html>.

State of New Hampshire. Division of Records Management and Archives. *Provincial Land Records.* Concord, New Hampshire: State of New Hampshire. Division of Records Management and Archives, 2002. Online guide - <www.state.nh.us/state/archival.html>.

Military

Draper, Mrs. Amos G. *New Hampshire Pension Records, 1776-1850.* Microfilm of originals at the D.A.R. Library in Washington, D. C. (Salt Lake City: Filmed by the Genealogical Society of Utah, 1971). 25 microfilm.

Hammond, Isaac W., ed. *Rolls of the Soldiers in the Revolutionary War.* Provincial and State Papers of New Hampshire, vols. 14-17. Concord and Manchester, New Hampshire, 1885-89. Reprint. New York: AMS Press, 1973.

New Hampshire. Adjutant General. *Revised Register of New Hampshire Soldiers and Sailors in the War of the Rebellion.* Concord, New Hampshire: adjutant general, 1895.

New Hampshire. *Indian And French Wars And Revolutionary Papers: Collection Of 1880.* Microfilm of originals in Concord, New Hampshire. (Salt Lake City: Filmed by the Genealogical Society of Utah, 1975). 2 microfilm.

New Hampshire's Role in the American Revolution, 1763-1789: A Bibliography. Concord, New Hampshire: New Hampshire American Revolution Bicentennial Commission, 1974.

Potter, Chandler E. *The Military History of the State of New Hampshire from its Settlement, in 1623, to the Rebellion in 1861.* 2 vols. New Hampshire Adjutant General's Report. Concord, NH, 1866-68. Reprint. Baltimore: Genealogical Publishing Co., 1972.

Revised Register of the Soldiers and Sailors of New Hampshire in the War of the Rebellion. Concord, New Hampshire: Ira C. Evans, 1895.

Rolls and Documents Relating to Soldiers in the Revolutionary War. New Hampshire Provincial and State Papers, vols. 14-17. Concord and Manchester, New Hampshire, 1885-89.

State of New Hampshire. Division of Records Management and Archives. *Military Records.* Concord, New Hampshire: State of New Hampshire. Division of Records Management and Archives, 2002. Online guide - <www.state.nh.us/state/archival.html>.

United States. Selective Service System. *New Hampshire, World War I Selective Service System Draft Registration Cards, 1917-1918. National Archives Microfilm Publications, M1509.* Washington, DC: National Archives, 1987-1988.

Waite, Otis F. R. *New Hampshire in the Great Rebellion: Containing Histories of the Several New Hampshire Regiments.* Claremont, New Hampshire: Tracy, Chase & Co., 1870.

Vital and Cemetery Records

Dodge, Nancy L., comp. *Northern New Hampshire Graveyards & Cemeteries.* Salem, Massachusetts: Higginson Books, 1985.

Goss, Winifred L. *Colonial Gravestone Inscriptions in the State of New Hampshire.* Reprint: Baltimore: Clearfield Co., 1997.

Guide to Church Vital Statistics Records in New Hampshire. Manchester, New Hampshire: Historical Records Survey, 1942.

New Hampshire Historical Society. *Card Index to Bible Records.* Microfilm of original records at the New Hampshire Historical Society in Concord, New Hampshire. (Salt Lake City: Genealogical Society of Utah, 1975). 1 microfilm.

New Hampshire Historical Society. *Card File Index to Births, Deaths, and Marriages Found in Published Vital Records of Massachusetts to 1850.* Microfilm of original records in the New Hampshire Historical Society, Concord, New Hampshire. (Salt Lake City: Filmed by the Genealogical Society of Utah, 1975). 7 microfilm.

New Hampshire Historical Society. *Card File Index to Publishments of Marriage Intention Prior to 1900.* Microfilm of originals at the New Hampshire Historical Society in Concord, New Hampshire. (Salt Lake City: Filmed by the Genealogical Society of Utah, 1975).

New Hampshire Registrar of Vital Statistics. *Index of Marriages, Early to 1900.* Salt Lake City: Genealogical Society of Utah, 1975-76. 102 microfilm.

New Hampshire. Division of Vital Statistics. *Bride's Index, 1640-1900.* Microfilm of original records in the New Hampshire State Department of Health. (Salt Lake City: Genealogical Society of Utah, 1975-76). 17 microfilm.

New Hampshire. Registrar of Vital Statistics. *Index of Births, Early to 1900.* Microfilm of original records in Concord, New Hampshire. (Salt Lake City: Genealogical Society of Utah, 1974). 98 microfilm.

New Hampshire. Registrar of Vital Statistics. *Index to Deaths, Early to 1900.* Microfilm of original records in Concord, New Hampshire. (Salt Lake City: Genealogical Society of Utah, 1974). 60 microfilm.

New Hampshire. Registrar of Vital Statistics. *Index to Divorces and Annulments Prior to 1938.* Microfilm of original records at Concord, New Hampshire. (Salt Lake City: Genealogical Society of Utah, 1975). 8 microfilm.

New Hampshire. Secretary of State. *Index to Early Town Records, New Hampshire, Early to 1850.* Microfilm of original records in the Office of Secretary of State, Concord, New Hampshire. (Salt Lake City: Filmed by the Genealogical Society of Utah, 1950). 111 microfilm.

Oesterlin, Pauline Johnson. *New Hampshire Marriage Licenses and Intentions 1709-1961.* Bowie, Maryland: Heritage Books, 1991.

Walterworth, Mrs. E.J. *Location of New Hampshire Revolutionary Soldiers.* n.p., n.d. Copied from the records of the Harold B. Twombly Graves Registration Office by the New Hampshire American Legion.

County Website	Map Index	Date Created	Parent County or Territory From Which Organized Address/Details
Belknap* www.belknapcounty.org/	L7	22 Dec 1840	**Strafford, Merrimac** Belknap County; 64 Court St; Laconia, NH 03246-3679; Ph. 603.524.3570 Details: (Twn or City Clks have b, m & d rec; Clk Sup Ct has div & ct rec; Pro Judge has pro rec from 1841; Reg of Deeds has land rec from 1841) Towns Organized Before 1800: Alton 1796, Barnstead 1727, Centre Harbor 1797, Gilmanton 1727, Meredith 1768, New Hampton 1777, Sanbornton 1770
Carroll* www.rootsweb.com/~nhcarrol/	J8	22 Dec 1840	**Strafford** Carroll County; Rt 171; Ossipee, NH 03864; Ph. 603.539.7751 Details: (Clk Ct has div & ct rec from 1859; Twn Clks have b, m, d & bur rec; Pro Judge has pro rec; Reg of Deeds has land rec) Towns Organized Before 1800: Albany 1766, Brookfield 1794, Chatham 1767, Conway 1765, Eaton 1766, Effingham 1788, Moultonborough 1777, Ossipee 1785, Sandwich 1768, Tamworth 1766, Tuftonborough 1795, Wakefield 1774, Wolfeborough 1770
Cheshire* www.co.cheshire.nh.us/	P3	29 Apr 1769	**Original county** Cheshire County; 33 W St; Keene, NH 03431-3355; Ph. 603.352.6902 Details: (Twn or City Clks have b, m, d & bur rec; Co Clk has div & ct rec; Reg of Pro has pro rec; Reg of Deeds has land rec) Towns Organized Before 1800: Alstead 1763, Chesterfield 1752, Dublin 1771, Fitzwilliam 1773, Gilsum 1763, Hinsdale 1753, Jaffrey 1773, Keene 1753, Marlborough 1776, Marlow 1761, Nelson 1774, Richmond 1752, Rindge 1768, Stoddard 1774, Sullivan 1787, Surry 1769, Swanzey 1753, Walpole 1752, Winchester 1753
Coos* freepages.genealogy.rootsweb.com/ ~dickmarston/Coos.html	E8	24 Dec 1803	**Grafton** Coos County; PO Box 309; Lancaster, NH 03584-0309; Ph. 603.788.4900 Details: (Twn or City Clks have b, m, d & bur rec; Clk Sup Ct has div & ct rec from 1887; Reg of Pro has pro rec; Reg of Deeds has land rec) Towns Organized Before 1800: Bartlett 1790, Cambridge 1773, Colebrook 1790, Columbia 1797, Dalton 1784, Dummer 1773, Jefferson 1796, Kilkenny 1774, Lancaster 1763, Millsfield 1774, Northumberland 1779, Stratford 1773, Stewartstown 1799, Success 1773, Whitefield 1774
Grafton* www.geocities.com/Yosemite/2821/ grafton.htm	I5	29 Apr 1769	**Original county** Grafton County; North Haverhill; RR 1 Box 67; North Haverhill, NH 03774; Ph. 603.787.6941 Details: (Clk Ct has div & ct rec; Pro Judge has pro rec; Reg of Deeds has land rec; Town Clks have b, m & d rec; 1820 census missing?) Towns Organized Before 1800: Alexandria 1782, Bath 1761, Benton 1764, Bethlehem 1799, Bridgewater 1788, Campton 1761, Canaan 1761, Danbury 1795, Dorchester 1761, Enfield 1761, Franconia 1764, Grafton 1778, Groton 1796, Hanover 1761, Haverhill 1763, Hebron 1792, Hill 1778, Holderness 1761, Landaff 1764, Lebanon 1761, Lisbon 1768, Lincoln 1764, Littleton 1784, Lyman 1761, Lyme 1761, Orange 1780, Orford 1761, Plymouth 1763, Rumney 1761, Thornton 1781, Warren 1763, Wentworth 1766, Woodstock 1786
Hillsborough www.hillsboroughcountynh.org/	P6	29 Apr 1769	**Original county** Hillsborough County; 19 Temple St; Nashua, NH 03060-3472; Ph. 603.882.9471 Details: (Co Clk has div & pro rec from 1771; Twn Clks have b, m & d rec; Reg of Deeds has land rec) Towns Organized Before 1800: Amherst 1760, Antrim 1777, Bedford 1780, Brookline 1769, Deering 1774, Francestown 1772, Goffstown 1761, Greenfield 1791, Hancock 1779, Hillsborough 1772, Hollis 1746, Hudson 1746, Litchfield 1749, Lyndeborough 1764, Manchester 1751, Mason 1768, Merrimac 1745, Miford 1794, Nashua 1746, New Ipswich 1762, New Boston 1763, Pelham 1746, Peterborough 1760, Sharon 1791, Temple 1769, Weare 1764, Wilton 1762, Windsor 1798
Merrimack* www.ci.concord.nh.us/	N6	1 Jul 1823	**Rockingham, Hillsboro** Merrimack County; 163 N Main St; Concord, NH 03301; Ph. 603.225.5501 Details: (Co Clk has div rec from 1840 & ct rec from 1823; Twn or City Clks have b, m, d & bur rec; Pro Judge has pro rec from 1823; Reg of Deeds has land rec from 1823)

County Website	Map Index	Date Created	Parent County or Territory From Which Organized Address/Details
			Towns Organized Before 1800: Andover 1779, Bradford 1787, Bow 1727, Boscawen 1760, Canterbury 1727, Chichester 1727, Concord 1765, Dunbarton 1765, Epsom 1727, Henniker 1768, Hopkinton 1765, Loudon 1773, Newbury 1778, New London 1779, Northfield 1780, Pembroke 1759, Pittsfield 1782, Salisbury 1768, Sutton 1784, Warner 1774
Rockingham www.co.rockingham.nh.us/	**P8**	**29 Apr 1769**	**Original county** Rockingham County; 99-119 North Rd; Brentwood, NH 03833; Ph. 603.679.2256 Details: (Clk Cts has div & ct rec from 1769; Twn or City Clks have b, m, d & bur rec; Reg of Pro has pro rec from 1770; Reg of Deeds has land rec from 1643) Towns Organized Before 1800: Atkinson 1767, Brentwood 1742, Candia 1763, Chester 1722, Danville 1760, Deerfield 1766, East Kingston 1738, Epping 1741, Exeter 1638, Gosport 1715, Greenland 1704, Hampstead 1749, Hampton 1638, Hampton Falls 1712, Kensington 1737, Kingston 1694, Londonderry 1722, New Castle 1692, Newington 1764, New Market 1727, Newtown 1749, North Hampton 1742, Northwood 1773, Nottingham 1722, Plaistow 1749, Poplin 1764, Portsmouth 1653, Raymond 1765, Rye 1726, Salem 1750, Sandown 1756, Seabrook 1763, South Hampton 1742, Stratham 1716, Windham 1742
Strafford www.usgennet.org/usa/nh/county/ strafford/	**N9**	**29 Apr 1769**	**Original county** Strafford County; County Farm Rd; PO Box 799; Dover, NH 03820; Ph. 603.742.3065 Details: (Twn or City Clk has b, m, d & bur rec; Clk Sup Ct has div & ct rec; Reg of Pro has pro rec; Reg of Deeds has land rec from 1773) Towns Organized Before 1800: Barrington 1722, Dover 1623, Durham 1732, Farmington 1798, Lee 1766, Madbury 1755, Middleton 1778, New Durham 1762, Rochester 1722, Somersworth 1754
Sullivan www.usgennet.org/usa/nh/county/ sullivan/	**M3**	**5 Jul 1827**	**Cheshire** Sullivan County; 22 Main St; PO Box 45; Newport, NH 03773-0045; Ph. 603.863.3450 Details: (Twn or City Clks have b, m, d & bur rec; Clk Sup Ct has div & ct rec from 1827; Reg of Pro has pro rec; Reg of Deeds has land rec; Richards Library, Newport, NH has other rec of genealogical interest) Towns Organized Before 1800: Acworth 1766, Charlestown 1753, Claremont 1764, Cornish 1763, Croydon 1763, Goshen 1791, Grantham 1761, Langdon 1787, Lempster 1761, Newport 1761, Plainfield 1761, springfield 1794, Unity 1764, Washington 1776, Wendell 1731

Notes

Common Violet

NEW JERSEY

CAPITAL: TRENTON – STATE 1787 (3RD)

In 1524, Verrazano became the first European to stand on New Jersey soil. Henry Hudson laid claim in 1609 to the area for the Dutch, who then set up trading posts at present-day Jersey City and Camden in the 1620's. The Swedes tried to settle the area as well, but were dominated by the Dutch in 1655. Less than a decade later, in 1664, the British captured the entire area. That same year Lord John Berkeley and Sir George Carteret were granted the land between the Delaware and Hudson rivers. They opened the land to settlers who came in large numbers. Among those early settlers were British emigrants; Puritans from Connecticut, who established Newark; Scotch-Irish Presbyterians, who settled the eastern counties; and Quakers, who settled in the Delaware River Valley.

The new settlers were diverse in religion but united in opposition to the tax and monetary policies of the proprietors. In 1682, Carteret's heirs sold East Jersey to William Penn. In 1702, New Jersey was put under a royal governor, which they shared with New York until 1738. In 1738, New Jersey had a governor and a legislature of its own. Many important battles of the Revolutionary War took place in New Jersey. Residents supported both sides in the war. New Jersey was the third state to ratify the Constitution and was one of the major forces behind gaining the rights of small states and equal representation in the Senate. The 1790 census showed New Jersey with a population of 184,139. Most were English, Dutch, or Swedish.

Look for vital records in the following locations:

- **Birth and death records:** Research conditions are not as favorable in New Jersey as in some other states. Since there was no law requiring a record to be kept of births and deaths until 1878, the family Bible is about the only source for this information. The New Jersey Bureau of Vital Statistics in Trenton, New Jersey has birth and death records from 1878. Earlier records are kept in the Bureau of Archives and History, Department of Education, also in Trenton.
- **Marriage and divorce records:** the New Jersey Bureau of Vital Statistics is also a good source for marriage records from 1878. Look for earlier records at the Bureau of Archives and History, Department of Education. Marriage licenses are issued in cities by the registrar of vital statistics or the city clerk. Divorce records are kept in the Superior Court, Chancery Division, at the State House in Trenton.
- **Naturalizations:** Naturalization proceeding records are among those at the federal circuit and district courts and the State Supreme Court.
- **Land records:** Records of deeds from 1664 to 1703 are in the New Jersey Archives Vol. XXI; from 1664 to 1790 in the Secretary of State's Office; and from 1790 to the present in the county clerks' offices.
- **Wills and probate records:** The Secretary of State in Trenton has originals of wills and probate records. Details of early guardianship and orphans' courts proceedings are also available there. Copies of wills and administration of estates beginning in 1804 are at county courthouses. Wills and administrations of estates from 1682 to 1805 have been abstracted and published in the State Archives. An index of New Jersey wills has also been published.
- **Census records:** A 1793 militia enrollment census has been published and helps to make up for the destroyed 1790 Census.

New Jersey Bureau of Vital Statistics
PO Box 370
Trenton, New Jersey 08625
609.292.6260

State Archives
225 West State Street-Level 2
PO Box 307
Trenton, New Jersey 08625-0307

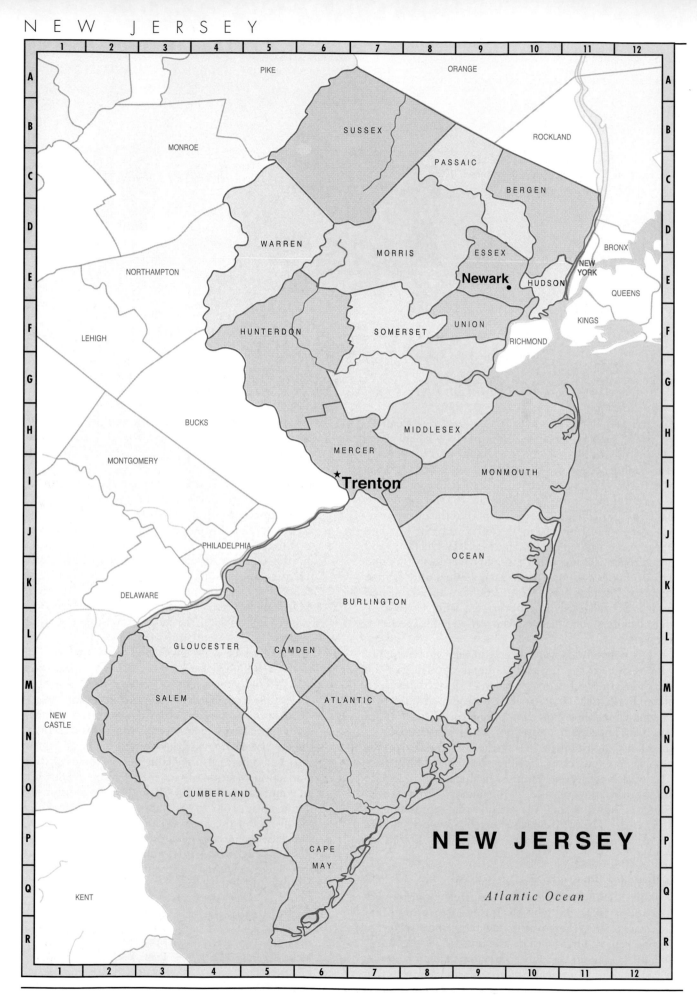

NEW JERSEY

Atlantic Ocean

Societies and Repositories

Afro-American Historical and Genealogical Society, New Jersey; 758 Sterling Dr., East; South Orange, New Jersey 07079-2425

American Baptist-Samuel Colgate Historical Society; 1106 South Goodman Street; Rochester, New Jersey 14620; 716.473.1740; Fax 716.473.1740 (Baptist Church records)

Association of Jewish Genealogical Societies; 155 N. Washington Ave.; Bergenfield, New Jersey 07621

Atlantic County Historical Society; PO Box 301; Somers Point, New Jersey 08244

Atlantic Highlands Historical Society; PO Box 108; Atlantic Highlands, New Jersey 07716; 291.0074; <community.nj.com/cc/historicalsociety>

Bergen County Historical Society; PO Box 55; River Edge, New Jersey 07661; <apollo.carroll.com/bchs/index.html>

Bureau of Vital Statistics; PO Box 370; Trenton, New Jersey 08625; 609.292.4087, 609.633.2860; Fax 609.392.4292

Burlington County Historical Society; Delia Biddle Pug Library; 457 High St.; Burlington, New Jersey 08016

Camden County Historical Society; PO Box 378; Collingswood, New Jersey 08108-0378;

Cape May Historical Society; Courthouse; Cape May, New Jersey 08204

Central Jersey Genealogy Club; PO Box 9903; Hamilton, New Jersey 08650-1903; <www.rootsweb.com/~njcjgc/>

Clerk of the Superior Court, Records Information Center; PO Box 967; Trenton, New Jersey 08625-0967; 609.292.4978; Fax 609.777.0094

Clerk of the Superior Court; R. J. Hughes Justice Complex, CN 971; Trenton, New Jersey 08625-0971

Commission on Archives and History, Southern New Jersey Conference, The Meckler Library, Pennington School; 112 W. Delaware Avenue; Pennington, New Jersey 08534; United Methodist Church

Commission on History, Reformed Church in America, New Brunswick Theological Seminary; Gardner A. Sage Library, 21 Seminary Place; New Brunswick, New Jersey 08901; 732.247.5341; (Dutch Reformed Church records)

Cranford Historical Society; The Hanson House; 38 Springfield Avenue; Cranford, New Jersey 07016; <www.bobdevlin.com/crhissoc.html>

Cumberland County Historical Society; PO Box 16; Greenwich, New Jersey 08323; <www.rootsweb.com/~njcumber/webdoc14.html>

Delaware Valley Finnish Americans; 1752 Dixie Line Road; Newark, New Jersey 19702

Denville, NJ Genealogy Club; Denville, New Jersey; <members.aol.com/DGenealogy/>

Department of Special Collections and Archives, Archibald Stevens Alexander Library, Rutgers University, 169 College Avenue; New Brunswick, New Jersey 08903; 732.932.7509

Descendants of Founders of New Jersey; 950.A Thornhill Court; Lakewood, New Jersey 08701

Division of Archives and Records Management, Bureau of Archives and Records Preservation; 185 West State Street, PO Box 307; Trenton, New Jersey 08625-0307; 609.292.6260

Episcopal, Diocesan House of the Episcopal Church; 808 W. State Street; Trenton, New Jersey 08618; 609.394.5281

Estonian American National Council; 21 Shady Lane Drive; Lakewood, New Jersey 08701; <www.estosite.org/eng/eng_home.htm>

Family History Library: 35 North West Temple Street: Salt Lake City, Utah 84150: 800.346.6044 or 801.240.2584: <www.familysearch.org>: Find a Family History Center near you: <www.familysearch.org/Eng/Library/FHC/frameset_fhc.asp>

Genealogical Club of Metuchen/Edison Regional Historical Society; PO Box 61; Metuchen, New Jersey 08840

Genealogical Society of Bergen County, New Jersey; PO Box 432; Midland Park, New Jersey 07432; <www.rootsweb.com/~njgsbc/>

Genealogical Society of New Jersey; PO Box 1291; New Brunswick, New Jersey 08903-1291; 732.932.7510

Genealogical Society of New Jersey; PO Box 1291; New Brunswick, New Jersey 08903; <www.rootsweb.com/~njgsnj/main.htm>

Genealogical Society of Salem County; PO Box 231; Woodstown, New Jersey 08098; <www.rootsweb.com/~njsalem/gsscnj.html>

Genealogical Society of the West Fields; c/o Westfield Memorial Library; 550 East Broad Street; Westfield, New Jersey 07090-2116; <www.westfieldnj.com/gswf/index.htm>

Genealogical Society of Westfield; c/o Westfield Memorial Library; 425 East Broad St.; Westfield, New Jersey 07090

General Board of Proprietors of the Eastern Division of New Jersey, Registrar; 550 E. Bay Avenue; 550 E. Bay Avenue, PO Box 32; Barnegat, New Jersey 08005

Gloucester County Historical Society Library; 17 Hunter Street, PO Box 409; Woodbury, New Jersey 08096; 609.845.4771, <www.rootsweb.com/~njglouce/gchs/>

Highland Park Historical Society; PO BOX 4255; Highland Park, New Jersey 08904-4255; <www.monmouth.com/~ricekolva/>

Historical Society of Boonton Township; RD 2, Box 152; Boonton, New Jersey 07005

Historical Society of Moorestown; 12 High Street; PO Box 477; Moorestown, New Jersey 08057; <www.moorestown.com/community/history/>

Holland Society of New York Library; 122 E. 58th Street; New York, New York 10022; 212.758.1871

Howell Historical Society; 427 Lakewood-Farmingdale Rd.; Howell, New Jersey 07731-8723; <www.howellnj.com/historic/>

Hunterdon County Historical Society; Hiram E. Deats Memorial Library; 114 Main St.; Flemington, New Jersey 08822; <members.aol.com/njysprez/hchs.htm>

Jewish Genealogical Society of Greater Philadelphia; 109 Society Hill; Cherry Hill, New Jersey 08003; <www.jewishgen.org/jgsp/>

Jewish Genealogical Society of North Jersey; 1 Bedford Rd.; Pompton Lakes, New Jersey 07442

Jewish Historical Society of Central Jersey; 1050 George St, Box 1-L; New Brunswick, New Jersey 08901; 732.249.4894

Jewish Historical Society of Central Jersey; 228 Livingston Ave.; New Brunswick, New Jersey 08901; <www.jewishgen.org/jhscj>

Jewish Historical Society of MetroWest; 901 Route 10 East; Whippany, New Jersey 07981-1156

Methodist, United Methodist Archives Center; Drew University Library, PO Box 127; Madison, New Jersey 07940; 201.408.3189; Fax 201.408.3909

Metuchen-Edison Historical Society; PO Box 61; Metuchen, New Jersey 08840-0061; <www.jhalpin.com/metuchen/met.ed.htm>

Monmouth County Genealogical Society; PO Box 5; Lincroft, New Jersey 07738-0005; <home.infi.net/~kjshelly/mcgs.html>

Monmouth County Historical Association; 70 Court Street; Freehold, New Jersey 07728; 732.462.8346; <www.monmouth.com/~mcha/index.html>

Morris Area Genealogical Society; PO Box 105; Convent Station, New Jersey 07961

National Archives-Northeast Region; 201Varick St., Corner Varick and Houston Sts.; New York, New York 10014; 212.337.1300; Fax 212.337.1306

Navy Lakehurst Historical Society; PO Box 328; Lakehurst, New Jersey 08733; 732.244.8861 732.244.8897;

Neptune Township Historical Society; 25 Neptune Blvd.; Neptune, New Jersey 07753

New Jersey Historical Society Library; 230 Broadway; Newark, New Jersey 07104; 201.483.3939; Fax 201.483.1988

New Jersey Historical Society; 52 Park Place; Newark, New Jersey 07102

New Jersey Reference Division, Newark Public Library; 5 Washington Street, PO Box 630; Newark, New Jersey 07101-0630; 201.733.7800

New Jersey State Archives; 225 West State Street-Level 2, Department of State Building; PO Box 307; Trenton, New Jersey 08625-0307; 609.396.2454; <www.state.nj.us/state/darm/archives.html>

New Jersey State Library, History and Genealogy Unit; 185 West State Street, CN 520; Trenton, New Jersey 08625-0520; 609.292.6200; Fax 609.292.2746

Ocean County Genealogical Society; 135 Nautilus Dr.; Manahawkin, New Jersey 08058-2452

Ocean County Historical Society; 26 Hadley Ave.; Toms River, New Jersey 08754-2191

Old Mill Hill Society; PO Box 1263; Trenton, New Jersey 08607-1263;

Ontario & Western Railway Historical Society, Inc.; 1 Rich Ct; Ho.Ho.Kus, New Jersey 07423; <www.nyow.org/main.html>

Passaic County Historical Society Genealogy Club; Lambert Castle Museum; Valley Road; Paterson, New Jersey 07503; <www.rootsweb.com/~njpchsgc>

Passaic County Historical Society; Lambert Castle, Valley Road; Paterson, New Jersey 07503; 973.357.1070; <www.geocities.com/pchslc/>

Phillipsburg Area Historical Society; 675 Corliss Avenue; Phillipsburg, New Jersey 08865; 908.454.0816; <community.nj.com/cc/pburghistsoc>

Plainsboro Historical Society, Inc.; 641 Plainsboro Rd.; Plainsboro, New Jersey 08536; <www.plainsboro.com/historical/>

Presbyterian Historical Society and Department of History, United Presbyterian Church in the USA; 425 Lombard Street; Philadelphia, Pennsylvania 19147; 215.627.1852

Quaker Collection; Haverford College Library; Haverford, Pennsylvania 19041; 610.896.1161; Fax 610.896.1102

Salem County New Jersey Historical Society; 79-83 Market St.; Salem, New Jersey 08079; <www.salemcounty.com/schs/>

Scandinavian American Heritage Society; 32 Hemlock Terrace; Wayne, New Jersey 07470-4342

Society of Friends, The Friends Historical Library; Swarthmore College; Swarthmore, Pennsylvania 19801; 610.328.8496; Fax 610.328.7329

United Methodist Church Commission on Archives and History, Northern New Jersey Conference; Drew University Library, 36 Madison Avenue, PO Box 127; Madison, New Jersey 07940; 201.822.2787

University Archives, Seton Hall University; South Orange Avenue; South Orange, New Jersey 07079; 201.762.7052

Vineland Historical and Antiquarian Society; PO Box 35; Vineland, New Jersey 08360; <www.vineland.org/history/society/>

West Jersey Orthodox, Haviland Records Room; 15 Rutherford Place; New York, New York 10003; 212.673.6866;

West Jersey Proprietors, Clerk; 230 High Street, PO Box 158; Burlington, New Jersey 08016; 609.386.1636

Westfield Historical Society Museum and Archives; Box 613; Westfield, New Jersey 07091-0613; <www.westfieldnj.com/history/contents.htm>

Bibliography and Record Sources

General Sources

Armstrong, William C. *Pioneer Families of Northwestern New Jersey.* 1979. Reprint. Baltimore: Clearfield Company, 1996.

Bailey, Rosalie Fellows. *Dutch Systems in Family Naming, New York-New Jersey.* Washington, D.C.: National Genealogical Society Bookstore, 1965.

Barber, John W., and Henry Howe. *Historical Collections of New Jersey: Past and Present, Containing a General Collection of the Most Interesting Facts, Traditions, Biographical Sketches, Anecdotes, Etc.* Rev. ed. 1868. Reprint. Baltimore: Clearfield, Co., 1995.

Barker, Bette Marie, Daniel P. Jones, and Karl J. Niederer. *Guide to Family History Sources in the New Jersey State Archives.* 2nd ed. Trenton, New Jersey: Division of Archives and Records Management, 1990.

Burr, Nelson Rollin. *A Narrative and Descriptive Bibliography of New Jersey.* New Jersey Historical Series, vol. 21. Princeton, New Jersey: Van Nostrand, 1964.

Chambers, T. F. *Early Germans of New Jersey, Their History, Churches, and Genealogy.* 1895. Reprint. Baltimore: Genealogical Publishing Co., 1969.

Clark, Patricia L. and Dorothy Huntsman, eds. *American Genealogical Biographical Key Title Index*. Salt Lake City: Genealogical Society of Utah, 1990.

Cohen, David Steven. *New Jersey Ethnic History: A Bibliography*. Trenton: New Jersey Historical Commission, 1986.

Collins, Martha Knowles. *New Jersey Bible Records, 1700's to 1800's, Vols. 3-5, 13*. Salt Lake City: Genealogical Society of Utah, 1971.

Cooley, Eli F., and William S. Cooley. *Genealogy of Early Settlers in Trenton and Ewing*. 1883, reprint ed., Baltimore: Genealogical Publishing, 1977.

Cope, Gilbert. *Collection of Family Data*. Salt Lake City: Genealogical Society of Utah, 1966. Microfilm, 75 rolls.

Cyclopedia of New Jersey Biography: Memorial and Biographical. 5 vols. New York: American Historical Society, 1921-23.

Documents Relating to the Colonial History of the State of New Jersey. [Archives of the State of New Jersey, First Series, Second Series]. 42 vols. Newark, New Jersey: Daily Journal Establishment, 1880-1949.

Dornan, John Pickens. *Collection, Family File*. (Salt Lake City: Filmed by the Genealogical Society of Utah, 1971).

Flynn, Joseph Michael. *The Catholic Church in New Jersey*. Morristown, New Jersey: N.D., 1904.

Gardiner, Charles C. *Collection of New Jersey Families, 1600-1900: Family Records Taken from Civil, Court, Land and Probate Records, Etc.* New Brunswick, New Jersey: Rutgers University Library, 1970.

Gasero, Russell L., ed. *Guide to Local Church Records in the Archives of the Reformed Church in America and to Genealogical Resources in the Gardner Sage Library, New Brunswick Theological Seminary*. New Brunswick, New Jersey: Historical Society of the Reformed Church in America, 1979.

Genealogical Society of New Jersey. *Genealogical Collection*. Salt Lake City: Genealogical Society of Utah, 1971.

Genealogies of New Jersey Families: From the Genealogical Magazine of New Jersey. 2 vols. Baltimore: Genealogical. Publishing Co., 1996.

Gloucester County Historical Society (Woodbury, New Jersey). *Historical and Genealogical Files, 1600's to 1900's*. (Salt Lake City: Filmed by the Genealogical Society of Utah, 1976). Microfilm, 33 rolls.

Heston, Alfred M. *South Jersey, A History, 1664-1924*. 5 vols. New York: Lewis Historical, 1924.

Historical Records Survey (New Jersey). *Guide to Depositories of Manuscript Collections in the United States: New Jersey (preliminary volume)*. Newark, N. J.: Historical Records Survey, 1941.

Historical Records Survey (New Jersey). *Guide to Vital Statistics Records in New Jersey*. New Jersey. Bureau of Archives and History. Trenton: Genealogical Society of New Jersey, 1971.

Historical Records Survey. *Directory of Churches in New Jersey*. 21 vols. Newark, New Jersey: Historical Records Survey, 1940-1941.

Hoelle, Edith. *Genealogical Resources in Southern New Jersey*. Woodbury, New Jersey: Gloucester County Historical Society, 1993.

Honeyman, A. Van Doren, ed. *Northwestern New Jersey, a History of Somerset, Morris, Hunterdon, Warren, and Sussex Counties*. 5 vols. New York: Lewis Historical Publishing, 1927.

Indenture Collection Containing Deeds, Bonds, Commissions, etc. of New Jersey Individuals: and other States, 1600-1900. Salt Lake City: Genealogical Society of Utah, 1970.

Index of Names to Various Records in Various New Jersey Counties, 1600-1800s. Salt Lake City: Genealogical Society of Utah, 1972.

Irwin, Barbara S., and Elizabeth B. Turner. *Guide to the Genealogy Chart Collection in the New Jersey Historical Society*. 1983, revised ed., Newark, New Jersey: New Jersey Historical Society, 1985.

Jackson, Ronald Vern. *New Jersey Tax Lists, 1772-1822*. 4 vols. Bountiful, Utah: Accelerated Indexing Systems, 1981.

Knapp, Fred D. *The Complete Public Records Guide: Central and Northern New Jersey Region*. New Rochelle, New York: REyn, 1993.

Koehler, Albert F. *The Huguenots or Early French in New Jersey*. 1955. Reprint. Baltimore: Clearfield Co., 1996.

Kull, Irving S. *New Jersey A History*. 5 vols. New York City: The American Historical Society, Inc. 1930-1932.

Lee, Francis Bazley. *Genealogical and Memorial History of the State of New Jersey*. 4 vols. New York: Lewis Historical Publishing, 1910.

Littell, John. *Family Records, or Genealogies of the First Settlers of Passaic Valley*. 1852. Reprint. Baltimore: Clearfield Co. 1981.

McCormick. *New Jersey from Colony to State, 1609-1789*. Galveston, Texas: Frontier Press, 1981.

Mellick, Andrew D., Jr. *The Story of an Old Farm, or, Life in New Jersey in the 18th Century*. 1889. Reprint. Salem, Massachusetts: Higginson Book Co., 1992.

Monnette, Orra Eugene. *First Settlers of Ye Plantations of Piscataway and Woodbridge Olde East New Jersey, 1664-1714...* 7 vols. Los Angeles: Leroy Carman Press, 1930-1935.

Murrin, Mary R., comp. *New Jersey Historical Manuscripts: A Guide to Collections in the State*. Trenton, New Jersey: New Jersey Historical Commission, 1987.

Myers, William Starr. *The Story of New Jersey*. 5 vols. New York: Lewis Historical Pub. Co., [1945].

Nelson, William. "Church Records in New Jersey," *Journal of the Presbyterian Historical Society 2:4 (March 1904): 173-88 and 251-66*. Salt Lake City: Genealogical Society of Utah, 1985.

Nelson, William. *Nelson's Biographical Cyclopedia*. 2 vols. New York: Eastern Historical Publishing Society, 1913.

Nelson, William. *New Jersey Biographical and Genealogical Notes*. 1916. Reprint. Baltimore: Clearfield Co., 1997

New Jersey Research Outline. Series US-States, No. 31. Salt Lake City: Family History Library, 1991

New Jersey State Archives. *Guide to Family History Sources in the New Jersey State Archives*. Trenton, New Jersey: New Jersey State Archives.

New Jersey State Archives. *Laws of the Royal Colony of New Jersey 1703-1775, Volumes II-V.* Trenton, New Jersey: New Jersey State Archives.

Nicholson, Anna Lea. *Nicholson Collection: Ca. 1690-1900*. (Salt Lake City: Filmed by the Genealogical Society of Utah, 1987). Microfilm, 22 rolls.

Ogden, Mary Depue. *Memorial Cyclopedia of New Jersey*. 4 vols. Newark, New Jersey: Memorial History, 1915-1921.

Parker, J. Carlyle. *Pennsylvania and Middle Atlantic States Genealogical Manuscripts: A User's Guide to the Manuscript Collections of the Genealogical Society of Pennsylvania as Indexed in Its Manuscript Materials Index.* Turlock, California: Marietta Publishing Co.

Quigley, Mary Alice, Judith A. Fullerton, and Diane E. Kauffman, comps. *Historical Organizations in New Jersey: A Directory.* Rev. ed. Trenton, New Jersey: New Jersey Historical Commission, 1983.

Register of New Jersey County Tax Ratables, Abstracts and Exempt Lists, 1773 to about 1889. Salt Lake City: the Genealogical Society of Utah.

Ricord, Frederick W. *General Index to the Documents Relating to the Colonial History of the State of New Jersey.* Newark, New Jersey: Daily Journal Establishment, 1880.

Rider, Fremont, ed. *American Genealogical Biographical Index.* Vols. 1-186+. Middletown, Connecticut: Godfrey Memorial Library, 1952-.

Rutgers University Library. *A Guide to the Manuscript Collection of the Rutgers University Library.* New Brunswick, New Jersey: Rutgers University Library, 1964.

Shourds, Thomas. *History and Genealogy of Fenwick's Colony.* 1876. Reprint. Baltimore: Clearfield Company, 1991.

Sinclair, Donald A. *A New Jersey Biographical Index Covering Some 100,000 Biographies and Associated Portraits in 237 New Jersey Cyclopedias, Histories, Yearbooks, Periodicals, and Other Collective Biographical Sources Published to about 1980.* Baltimore: Genealogical Publishing, 1993.

Skemer, Don C. and Robert C. Morris. *Guide to the Manuscript Collections of the New Jersey Historical Society.* Newark, New Jersey: New Jersey Historical Society, 1979.

Southern California Genealogical Society. *Sources of Genealogical Help in New Jersey.* Burbank, California: Southern California Genealogical Society.

Stillwell, John E., M.D. *Historical and Genealogical Miscellany: Data Relating to the Settlement & Settlers of New Jersey, Volumes I-V.* 1903-32. Reprint. Baltimore: Genealogical Publishing Co, 1993.

Stockton, Elias Boudinot. *Stockton Collection.* Salt Lake City: Genealogical Society of Utah, 1973. Microfilm, 44 rolls.

Stryker-Rodda, Kenn. *Given Name Index to the Genealogical Magazine of New Jersey, Vol. IV.* Hunterdon House.

Stryker-Rodda, Kenn. *New Jersey: Digging for Ancestors in the Garden State.* Detroit: Detroit Society for Genealogical Research, 1970.

The Biographical Encyclopedia of New Jersey of the Nineteenth Century. Philadelphia, PA: Galaxy Publishing, 1877.

The First Laws of the State of New Jersey. 1783. Reprint. Wilmington, Delaware: Michael Glazier, 1981.

Trinity Church (Newark, New Jersey: Episcopal). *New Jersey Biographical Card Index, 1790-1900.* Microreproduction of documents at New Jersey Historical Society, Newark, New Jersey. (Salt Lake City: Filmed by the Genealogical Society of Utah, 2000). 25 microfilm.

United States. Bureau of Internal Revenue. *Assessment Lists of the Federal Bureau of Internal Revenue, 1862-1866.* Washington, D.C.: National Archives, 1965.

Whitehead, John. *The Judicial and Civil History of New Jersey.* [Boston]: Boston History Co., 1897.

Wilson, Thomas B. *Notices from New Jersey Newspapers, 1781-1790.* Lambertville, New Jersey: Hunterdon House, 1988.

Works Projects Administration. *The WPA Guide to 1930's New Jersey.* 1939. Reprint Galveston, Texas: Frontier Press, 1995.

Wright, William C. and Paul A. Stellhorn, eds. *Directory of New Jersey Newspapers, 1765-1970.* Trenton, New Jersey: New Jersey Historical Commission, 1977.

Year Book of The Holland Society of New York, 1912. New York: The Society, 1912.

Atlases, Maps and Gazetteers

An Alphabetical Listing of Local Places and Incorporated Municipalities in the State of New Jersey. New Jersey Dept. of Transportation, 1967.

Gannett, Henry. *Geographic Dictionary of New Jersey.* 1894. Reprint. Baltimore: Genealogical Publishing Co., 1978.

Gordon, Thomas F. *A Gazetteer of the State of New Jersey.* 1834. Reprint. Westminster, Maryland: Family Line Publications, 1991.

Kay, John L., and Chaester M. Smith, Jr. *New Jersey Postal History: The Post Offices and First Postmasters, 1776-1976.* Lawrence, Massachusetts: Quarterman Publications, 1977.

Long, John H., comp. *Historical Atlas and Chronology of County Boundaries, 1788-1980.* Vol. 1, Delaware, Maryland, New Jersey, Pennsylvania. Boston, Massachusetts: G.K. Hall, 1984.

National Gazetteer of the United States of America—New Jersey 1983. Washington, D.C.: Government Printing Office, 1983.

New Jersey Local Names, Municipalities and Counties. Trenton, New Jersey: State Department of Transportation, 1982.

Origin of New Jersey Place Names. Trenton, New jersey: Public Library Commission, 1945.

Skemer, Don C., comp. *New Jersey Historic Map Portfolio.* Florham Park, New Jersey: Afton Publishing, 1983.

Snyder, John P. *The Story of New Jersey's Civil Boundaries, 1606-1968.* Trenton, New Jersey: Bureau of Geology and Topography, 1969.

Szucs, Loretto Dennis, and Matthew Wright. *Finding Answers in U.S. Census Records.* Ancestry Publishing, 2001.

Census Records

Available Census Records and Census Substitutes

Federal Census 1830, 1840, 1850, 1860, 1870, 1880, 1900, 1910, 1920, 1930.

Federal Mortality Schedules 1850, 1860, 1870, 1880.

Union Veterans and Widows 1890 .

Militia Census 1793.

State/Territorial Census 1885, 1895, 1905, 1915.

Craig, Peter Stebbins. *The 1693 Census of the Swedes on the Delaware: Family Histories of the Swedish Lutheran Church Members Residing in Pennsylvania, Delaware, West New Jersey and Cecil County, Maryland, 1638-1693.* Studies in Swedish American Genealogy 3. Winter Park, Florida: SAG Publications, 1993.

Dollarhide, William. The Census Book: A Genealogist's Guide to Federal Census Facts, Schedules and Indexes. Bountiful, Utah: Heritage Quest, 1999.

George, Shirley J. and Sandra E. Glenn. New Jersey 1850 Mortality Schedule Index. Columbus, New Jersey: G. & G. Genealogical Book, 1982.

Jackson, Ronald Vern. New Jersey 1890. Salt Lake City: Accelerated Indexing Systems, 1990.

Kemp, Thomas Jay. The American Census Handbook. Wilmington, Delaware: Scholarly Resources, Inc., 2001.

Lainhart, Ann S. State Census Records. Baltimore: Genealogical Publishing Co., Inc., 1992.

New Jersey State Archives. New Jersey State Census, 1855-1915. Trenton, New Jersey: New Jersey State Archives.

Stryker-Rodda, Kenn. Revolutionary Census of New Jersey: An Index Based on Ratables, of the Inhabitants of New Jersey During the Period of the American Revolution. Rev. ed. Lambertville, New Jersey: Hunterdon House, 1986.

Thorndale, William, and William Dollarhide. Map Guide to the U.S. Federal Censuses, 1790-1920. Baltimore: Genealogical Publishing Co., 1987.

United States. Census Office. Census of New Jersey, 1850-1880; Third Series (of Persons Who Died During the Years Ending 30 June 1850, 1 June 1860; 1 June 1870; 31 May 1880. Trenton, New Jersey: State Library of Archives and History, Department of Education, 1996.

Court Records, Probate and Wills

Index to Wills, Inventories, Etc. in the Office of the Secretary of State Prior to 1901. 3 vols. 1912. Reprinted as New Jersey Index to Wills. Baltimore: Genealogical Publishing Co., 1969.

Index to Wills, Office of Secretary of State, State of New Jersey, 1804 to 1830. Trenton, New Jersey: John L. Murphy Publishing Co., 1901.

Jamison, Wallace N. Religion in New Jersey: A Brief History. Princeton, New Jersey: D. Van Nostrand, 1964.

Keasbey, Edward Quinton. The Courts and Lawyers of New Jersey, 1661-1912. 3 vols. New York: Lewis Historical Publishing Co., 1912.

Miller, George Julius. The Courts of Chancery in New Jersey, 1684-1696. Washington, D.C.: Library of Congress Photoduplication Service, 1990.

Nelson, William. New Jersey Calendar of Wills, 1670-1780. 1901. Reprint. Arvada, Colorado: Ancestor Publishers.

Nelson, William. The Law and the Practice of New Jersey from the Earliest Times: Concerning the Probate of Wills, the Administration of Estates, the Protection of Orphans and Minors, and the Control of their Estates; The Prerogative Court, the Ordinary, and the Surrogates. Paterson, New Jersey: Paterson History Club, 1909.

New Jersey, Chancery Court. Chancery Court Cases,1743-1845. Salt Lake City: Genealogical Society of Utah, 1978. Microfilm, 86 rolls.

New Jersey, Chancery Court. Enrolled Decrees, 1825-1850; Index to Enrolled Decrees, 1825-1854. Salt Lake City: Genealogical Society of Utah, 1979. Microfilm, 298 rolls.

New Jersey, Supreme Court (Burlington County). Early Index to Supreme Court Minutes, 1681-1842. n.p. Bibliofilm, 1938.

New Jersey, Supreme Court. Index to Supreme Court Cases Before and After the Revolution, 1709 to 1842. Salt Lake City: Genealogical Society of Utah, 1978.

New Jersey. Bureau of Archives and History. Genealogical Research: A Guide to Source Materials in the Archives and History Bureau of the New Jersey State Library. Trenton: Genealogical Society of New Jersey, 1971.

New Jersey. Court of Chancery. Chancery Docket Books, 1824-1900; Index to Chancery Records, 1824-1904. Microfilm of original records at the Mercer County courthouse. (Salt Lake City: Filmed by the Genealogical Society of Utah, 1978). 22 microfilm.

New Jersey. Court of Chancery. Chancery Register, 1781-1894. Salt Lake City: Genealogical Society of Utah, 1977.

New Jersey. Court of Chancery. Court Tickler, 1858-1896. Microfilms of original records in the New Jersey State Library Trenton. (Salt Lake City: Filmed by the Genealogical Society of Utah, 1977). 3 microfilm.

New Jersey. Court of Chancery. Parchment Rolls, 1755-1806. Microfilm made from original records in the New Jersey State Library, Trenton. (Salt Lake City: Filmed by the Genealogical Society of Utah, 1977). 19 microfilm.

Smeal, Lee, and Ronald Vern Jackson. Index to New Jersey Wills, 1689-1890, The Testators. Salt Lake City: Accelerated Indexing Systems, 1979.

Stryker-Rodda, Kenn. New Jersey Index of Wills, Inventories, Etc. 3 vols. 1912-13. Reprint. Baltimore: Clearfield Company, 1994.

United States. District Court (New Jersey). Records of the U. S. District Court of New Jersey and Predecessor Courts: 1789-1950. Washington, D.C.: National Archives, 19-.

Emigration, Immigration, Migration and Naturalization

Boyer, Carl, 3rd. Ship Passenger Lists: New York and New Jersey (1600-1825). Newhall, Calif.: C. Boyer, c1978.

Chambers, Theodore Frelinghuysen. The Early Germans of New Jersey: Their History, Churches, and Genealogies... 1895, reprint ed. Baltimore: Genealogical Publishing, 1982.

Coldham, Peter Wilson. The Complete Book of Emigrants, 1607-1776 and Emigrants in Bondage, 1614-1775. Novato, California: Brøderbund Software, 1996.

Guide to Naturalization Records in New Jersey. Newark, New Jersey: Historical Records Program, 1941.

Howe, Paul Sturtevant. Mayflower Pilgrim Descendants in Cape May County, New Jersey – 1620-1920... 1921, reprint ed. Baltimore: Genealogical Publishing, 1977.

Jones, Henry Z., Jr. More Palatine Families: Some Immigrants to the Middle Colonies 1717-1776 and their European Origins.... Universal City, California: H. Z. Jones, Jr., 1991.

Jones, Henry Z., Jr. The Palatine Families of New York: A Study of the German Immigrants who arrived in Colonial New York in 1710. Universal City, CA: H. Z. Jones, Jr., 1985.

New Jersey. Bureau of Archives and History. Index to Naturalization Records, 1703-1862. Microreproduction of typed index cards at the New Jersey Bureau of Archives and History. (Salt Lake City: Genealogical Society of Utah, 1972.)

New Jersey. Bureau of Archives and History. *Index to Powers of Attorney, Surveyors Reports, Commissions, etc., Referring to Deeds, ca. 1703-1856*. Microreproduction of ms. and typescript at the New Jersey Bureau of Archives and History. (Salt Lake City: Genealogical Society of Utah, 1969.) 2 microfilm.

New Jersey. Supreme Court. *Naturalization Records, 1749-1873; Card Index, 1761-1860*. (Salt Lake City: Filmed by the Genealogical Society of Utah, 1978).

Stevenson, John R. *Persons Naturalized in New Jersey Between 1702 and 1776, The New York Genealogical and Biographical Society Record*, vol.28; April 1897: 86-89.

Winkel, Peter A. "*Naturalizations, Province of New Jersey, 1747-1775," The Genealogical Magazine of New Jersey* 65 (1990): 1-8, 59-66.

Land and Property

Hone, Wade E. *Land and Property Research in the United States.* Salt Lake City: Ancestry Incorporated, 1997.

Index to Powers of Attorney, Surveyor's Reports, Commissions, etc., Referring to Deeds. Salt Lake City: Genealogical Society of Utah, 1972.

Nelson, William. *Patents and Deeds and Other Early Records of New Jersey, 1664-1703*. Baltimore: Genealogical Publishing Co., 1976.

New Jersey State Library (Trenton*). East Jersey Deeds, 1667-1783.* (Salt Lake City: Filmed by the Genealogical Society of Utah, 1967).

New Jersey State Library (Trenton). *Index to Deeds, Grantee and Grantor.* (Salt Lake City: Filmed by the Genealogical Society of Utah, 1967-1968). 7 microfilm.

New Jersey, Surveyor General. *Perth Amboy Surveys, 1678-1814.* Salt Lake City: Genealogical Society of Utah, 1973.

New Jersey. Supreme Court. *Estates and Partitions, 1712-1866.* Microfilm of originals at the State Archives, Trenton. (Salt Lake City: Filmed by the Genealogical Society of Utah, 1993). 2 microfilm.

Stephenson, Richard W. *Land Ownership Maps: A Checklist of Nineteenth Century United States County Maps in the Library of Congress.* Washington, D.C: Library of Congress, 1967.

The Minutes of the Board of Proprietors of the Eastern Division of New Jersey from…1685-1794. 3 vols. Perth Amboy, New Jersey: General Board of Proprietors of the Eastern Division of New Jersey, 1949-60.

Military

Alphabetical Roll of New Jersey Volunteers in the Civil War. (Salt Lake City: Filmed by the Genealogical Society of Utah, 1969).

Bill. *New Jersey and the Revolutionary War.* 1964. Reprint. Galveston, Texas: Frontier Press, 1992.

Campbell, James W.S., comp. *Official Register of the Officers and Men of New Jersey in the Revolutionary War.* 1872. Revised 1911. Reprint, Baltimore: Genealogical Publishing, 1967.

Civil War Pension Claims, New Jersey Soldiers Alphabetical. (Salt Lake City: Filmed by the Genealogical Society of Utah, 1969).

General Society of Colonial Wars (Providence, Rhode Island). *Lineage Records, No. 1-14199, 1607-1967; Supplemental Records, 1-13850, 1607-1967; Register of Members.* (Salt Lake City: Filmed by the Genealogical Society of Utah, 1967).

Jackson, Ronald V. *Index to Military Men of New Jersey, 1775-1815.* Bountiful, Utah: Accelerated Indexing Systems, 1977.

Jones, Edward Alfred. *The Loyalists of New Jersey: Their Memorials, Petitions, Claims, etc. from English Records.* 1927. Reprint. Lambertville, New Jersey: Hunterdon House, 1988.

McNally, Bernard, comp. *Soldiers and Sailors of New Jersey in the Spanish-American War, Embracing a Chronological Account of the Army and Navy.* Newark, New Jersey: Bernard McNally, 1898.

New Jersey Adjutant General. *Register of the Commissioned Officers and Privates of the New Jersey Volunteers in Service of the United States.* 3 vols. Jersey City, New Jersey: John H. Lyon, 1863-1865.

New Jersey Civil War Records, Books 1-829. Trenton, New Jersey: State Library of Archives & History, 1969.

New Jersey Historical Records Survey. *Index to Stryker's Register of New Jersey in the Revolution.* 1941. Reprint. Baltimore: Clearfield Co., 1995.

New Jersey State Archives. *Index to Revolutionary War Manuscripts.* Trenton, New Jersey: New Jersey State Archives.

New Jersey State Library (Trenton). *Index to Records of Spanish American War, Books 1-122.* Salt Lake City: Genealogical Society of Utah, 1969. 2 microfilm.

New Jersey State Library (Trenton). *Military Officers Recorded in the Office of the Secretary of State, Trenton, New Jersey; Colonial Wars, 1668-1774.* Salt Lake City: Genealogical Society of Utah, 1969.

New Jersey State Library (Trenton*). New Jersey in the War of 1812; Books 1-52.* Microreproduction of original at the State Library of Archives and History. (Salt Lake City: Genealogical Society of Utah, 1969.) 16 microfilm.

New Jersey State Library (Trenton). *New Jersey Records; French and Indian War, 1757-1764.* Salt Lake City: Genealogical Society of Utah, 1969.

New Jersey, Adjutant General. *Official Register of the Officers and Men of New Jersey in the Revolutionary War.* Trenton, New Jersey: W. T. Nicholson, 1872.

New Jersey, Adjutant General. *Records of Officers and Men of New Jersey in the Civil War, 1861-1865.* Trenton, New Jersey: J. L. Murphy, 1876-78.

New Jersey, Adjutant General. *Records of Officers and Men of New Jersey in Wars, 1791-1815.* 1909. Reprint. Baltimore: Genealogical Publishing Co., 1970.

Norton, James S. *New Jersey in 1793: An Abstract and Index to the 1793 Militia Census of the State of New Jersey.* Salt Lake City: J. S. Norton, 1973.

Records of Officers and Men of New Jersey in Wars, 1791-1815. 1909. Reprint, Baltimore: Genealogical Publishing, 1970.

Revolutionary War Index: A Compilation of Revolutionary War Slips and Documented Materials from Other Sources. (Salt Lake City: Filmed by the Genealogical Society of Utah, 1968).

Revolutionary War Records of New Jersey. Salt Lake City: Genealogical Society of Utah, 1969.

Revolutionary War Slips, Single Citations of the New Jersey Department of Defense Materials. (Salt Lake City: Filmed by the Genealogical Society of Utah, 1968).

Second Annual Report of the State Historian of the State of New York. Albany, New York: Wynkoop, Hallenbeck, Crawford, 1897.

Sinclair, Donald A. *A Bibliography, the Civil War and New Jersey.* New Brunswick, New Jersey: Friends of the Rutgers University Library, 1968.

Stratford, Dorothy A., and Thomas B. Wilson. *Certificates and Receipts of Revolutionary New Jersey.* Lambertville, New Jersey: Hunterdon House, 1996.

Stryker, William S. *The New Jersey Volunteers (Loyalists) in the Revolutionary War.* Trenton, New Jersey: Narr, Day & Narr, 1887.

Stryker, William S., comp. *Record of Officers and Men of New Jersey in the Civil War, 1861-1865.* 2 vols. Trenton, New Jersey: John L. Murphy, 1876.

United States. Selective Service System. *New Jersey, World War I Selective Service System Draft Registration Cards, 1917-1918.* Washington, D.C.: National Archives, 1987-1988.

Waldenmaier, Inez. *Revolutionary War Pensioners Living in New Jersey before 1834.* Tulsa, Oklahoma: Inez Waldenmaier, 1983.

White, Virgil D. *Genealogical Abstracts of the Revolutionary War Pension Files.* 4 vols. Waynesboro, Tennessee: National Historical Publishing, 1990.

White, Virgil D. *Index to Revolutionary War Service Records.* 4 vols. Waynesboro, Tennessee: National Historical Publishing, 1995.

Vital and Cemetery Records

An Historical Records Survey of a Miscellany of New Jersey Vital Statistics Records, 1753-1870. Microreproduction of manuscript and typescript records at New Jersey Historical Society, Newark, New Jersey. (Salt Lake City: Filmed by the Genealogical Society of Utah, 2000). 2 microfilm.

Card Index to Civil War Soldiers' Graves, 1862. Microreproduction of records at New Jersey Historical Society, Newark, New Jersey. (Salt Lake City: Filmed by Genealogical Society of Utah, 2000). 2 microfilm.

County File of Miscellaneous New Jersey Information. Salt Lake City: Genealogical Society of Utah, 1971.

Dirnberger, Janet Drumm. *New Jersey Catholic Baptismal Records from 1759-1781....* Seabrook, Texas: Brambles, 1981.

Guide to Vital Statistics Records in New Jersey. 2 vols. Newark, New Jersey: New Jersey Historical Records Survey, 1941.

Index to Inquisitions on the Dead, 1700's-1800's. Salt Lake City: Genealogical Society of Utah, 1972.

Nelson, William, ed. *Documents Relating to the Colonial History of the State of New Jersey. Marriage Records, 1665-1800.* [Archives of the State of New Jersey, First Series, vol. 22] 1900, reprinted as *New Jersey Marriage Records.* Baltimore: Genealogical Publishing, 1967.

Nelson, William. *New Jersey Marriage Records, 1665-1800.* Baltimore: Genealogical Publishing Co., 1967.

New Jersey Cemetery Inscriptions. Microrreproduction of records at the New Jersey Historical Society, Newark, New Jersey. (Salt Lake City: Genealogical Society of Utah, 1976.) 3 microfilm.

New Jersey Marriage Bonds, W. P. A. Marriage Records, 1670-1800. (Salt Lake City: Filmed by the Genealogical Society of Utah, 1969).

New Jersey State Archives. *Colonial Marriage Bonds, 1711-1797.* Trenton, New Jersey: New Jersey State Archives. Microfilm, 8 rolls.

New Jersey Tombstone Inscriptions. Salt Lake City: Genealogical Society of Utah, 1969. Microfilm, 7 rolls.

New Jersey W.P.A. Birth and Death Records, Early to 1900. (Salt Lake City: Filmed by the Genealogical Society of Utah, 1969).

New Jersey, 1680-1900. [S.l.]: Brøderbund, c1998. CD-ROM.

New Jersey. Bureau of Archives and History. *Vital Statistics Index from Trenton Newspapers, 1800-1900.* Salt Lake City: Genealogical Society of Utah, 1969.

New Jersey. Department of Education. Division of State Library Archives and History. *New Jersey Marriages, 1711-1878 (Approx.).* (Trenton, New Jersey: Filmed by Microfilm & Record Unit, 1966). 10 microfilm.

New Jersey. Secretary of State. *Marriage Records, 1727-1878.* Trenton, New Jersey: State Library of Archives and History, 1966. 8 microfilm.

Records of Births, Marriages, and Deaths of New Jersey, 1848-1900. Microreproduction of original records at the New Jersey State Library, Trenton. (Salt Lake City: Filmed by the Genealogical Society of Utah, 1969). 290 microfilm.

Source Index of New Jersey Families. Salt Lake City: Genealogical Society of Utah, 1971.

Swapin. *Old Burial Grounds of New Jersey: A Guide.* Galveston, Texas: Frontier Press, 1994.

County Website	Map Index	Date Created	Parent County or Territory From Which Organized Address/Details
Atlantic www.aclink.org/	M6	7 Feb 1837	**Gloucester** Atlantic County; 5901 Main St; Mays Landing, NJ 08330-1800; Ph. 609.625.4011 Details: (Co Clk has div rec from 1949, ct, land & cem rec from 1837; Co Surr has pro rec)
Bergen* www.co.bergen.nj.us/	C10	1 Mar 1683	**Prov. East Jersey** Bergen County; 1 Bergen County Plaza; Hackensack, NJ 07601; Ph. 201.336.7000 Details: (Co Clk has div rec from 1955, ct & land rec; Co Surr has pro rec)
Burlington co.burlington.nj.us/	L7	17 May 1694	**Original county** Burlington County; 49 Rancocas Rd; PO Box 6000; Mount Holly, NJ 8060; Ph. 609.265.5122 Details: (Co Clk has land & mil rec; Co Surr has pro rec; Co Lib has nat rec)
Camden www.co.camden.nj.us/	L5	13 Mar 1844	**Gloucester** Camden County; 520 Market St; Camden, NJ 08102; Ph. 856.225.5300 Details: (Co Clk has ct & land rec; Co Surr has pro rec)
Cape May www.co.cape-may.nj.us/	P6	12 Nov 1692	**West Jersey** Cape May County; 4 Moore Rd; Cape May Court House, NJ 08210; Ph. 609.465.1010 Details: (Co Clk has m rec 1795-1878, land rec from 1692, ct rec 1793-1948, mil rec from 1919 & nat rec 1900-1960; Co Surr has pro rec from 1783)
Cumberland www.co.cumberland.nj.us/	O4	19 Jan 1748	**Salem** Cumberland County; 60 W Broad St; Bridgeton, NJ 08302; Ph. 856.451.8000 Details: (Co Clk has land rec from 1800's & immigration rec 1840-1989; Co Surr has pro rec; Dissolution Off has div rec)
Essex www.co.essex.nj.us/	E9	1 Mar 1683	**Prov. East Jersey** Essex County; 465 Martin Luther King Jr Blvd; Newark, NJ 07102; Ph. 973.621.4920 Details: (Co Clk has m rec 1795-1879, div & ct rec from 1948 & nat rec 1779-1929; City Clks have b & d rec; Co Surr has pro rec; Reg of Deeds has land rec)
Gloucester www.co.gloucester.nj.us/	L4	28 May 1686	**Original county** Gloucester County; 1 N Broad St; Woodbury, NJ 08096-4611; Ph. 856.853.3237 Details: (Courthouse burned 1786) (Co Clk has ct & land rec from 1787; Surr Ct has pro rec; Clk Sup Ct has div rec; early rec preserved at Surveyor General's Office, Burlington & Sec of State Office, Trenton)
Hudson www.hudsoncountynj.org/	E10	22 Feb 1840	**Bergen** Hudson County; 583 Newark Ave; Jersey City, NJ 07306; Ph. 201.795.6112 Details: (Reg of Deeds has land rec; Clk Surr Ct has pro rec)
Hunterdon www.co.hunterdon.nj.us/	F5	13 Mar 1714	**Burlington** Hunterdon County; 71 Main St; PO Box 2900; Flemington, NJ 08822-2900; Ph. 908.788.1221 Details: (Co Clk has m rec 1795-1875, ct rec from 1714 & land rec from 1716; Clk Surr Ct has pro rec; Clk Sup Ct has div rec)
Mercer www.mercercounty.org/	I7	22 Feb 1838	**Somerset, Middlesex, Hunterdon, Burlington** Mercer County; PO Box 8068; Trenton, NJ 08650-0068; Ph. 609.989.6517 Details: (Co Surr has pro rec; Co Clk has ct & land rec from 1838, judgments, tax maps & corporation rec)
Middlesex co.middlesex.nj.us/index.asp	H8	1 Mar 1683	**Prov. East Jersey** Middlesex County; Old Bridge; 235 Ticetown Rd; New Brunswick, NJ 08857; Ph. 732.745.3005 Details: (Co Clk has m, div, ct & land rec; Co Surr has pro rec)
Monmouth shore.co.monmouth.nj.us/	I9	1 Mar 1683	**Prov. East Jersey** Monmouth County; Main St Hall of Records; PO Box 1251; Freehold, NJ 07728; Ph. 732.431.7324 Details: (Co Clk has m rec 1795-1892 & land rec from 1667; Co Surr has pro rec)

County Website	Map Index	Date Created	Parent County or Territory From Which Organized Address/Details
Morris* www.co.morris.nj.us/	E7	15 Mar 1739	**Hunterdon** Morris County; Hall of Rec Admin Bldg; Court St; PO Box 315; Morristown, NJ 07963; Ph. 973.285.6120 Details: (Co Clk has m rec 1795-1881, ct rec 1739-1978, land rec from 1785, slave rec 1804-1820, nat rec from 1816 & mil dis rec from 1945; Co Surr has pro rec; Clk Sup Ct has div rec)
Ocean* www.oceancountygov.com/	J9	15 Feb 1850	**Monmouth** Ocean County; 118 Washington St; PO Box 2191; Toms River, NJ 08754; Ph. 732.929.2018 Details: (Co Clk has pro & ct rec from 1850)
Passaic* www.passaiccountynj.org/	C8	7 Feb 1837	**Bergen, Essex** Passaic County; 401 Grand St #130; Paterson, NJ 07505; Ph. 973.225.3632 Details: (Co Clk has div rec from 1947, ct rec from 1900 & land rec; Co Surr has pro rec)
Salem 216.155.54.158/	M3	17 May 1694	**Original county** Salem County; 92 Market St; Salem, NJ 08079-1913; Ph. 856.935.7510 Details: (Co Clk has m rec 1675-1912, ct rec from 1707, land rec from 1695, nat rec 1808-1958, mil rec from 1715 & newspapers from 1819; Co Surr has pro rec from 1804; City Clks have b & d rec)
Somerset www.co.somerset.nj.us/	F7	May 1688	**Middlesex** Somerset County; 20 Grove St; PO Box 3000; Somerville, NJ 08876; Ph. 908.231.7006 Details: (Co Clk has ct rec from 1777 & land rec from 1785; Co Surr has pro rec)
Sussex* www.rootsweb.com/~njsussex/	B7	16 May 1753	**Morris** Sussex County; 4 Park Pl; Newton, NJ 07860; Ph. 973.579.0900 Details: (Co Clk has slave b rec, m rec 1795-1878, ct rec from 1753, land rec from 1800, nat rec, road returns from 1780; Co Surr has pro rec)
Union www.unioncountynj.org/	F9	19 Mar 1857	**Essex** Union County; 2 Broad St; Elizabeth, NJ 07207-2204; Ph. 908.527.4966 Details: (Co Clk has land rec from 1857 & mil dis rec from 1941; Clk Sup Ct has div rec from 1848 & ct rec; Co Surr has pro rec from 1857; Town Clks have b & d rec)
Warren www.warrennet.org/warrencounty/	D5	20 Nov 1824	**Sussex** Warren County; 165 County Rd; 519 S; Belvidere, NJ 07823; Ph. 908.475.6211 Details: (Municipal Clks have b & d rec; Co Clk has m & land rec from 1825, div & ct rec; Co Surr has pro rec)

Notes

Yucca

NEW MEXICO

CAPITAL: SANTA FE – TERRITORY 1850 – STATE 1912 (47TH)

Although Native Americans had made their home in what we know as New Mexico, Alva Nunez Cabeza de Vaca and his three companions first explored the area representing other cultures in 1536. They had been shipwrecked off the coast of Texas in 1528, and wandered through the Southwest for eight years. During this time, they heard tales of the Seven Cities of Cibola with the gold-studded houses. On returning to Mexico they related these tales and inspired others to explore the area. Among those who followed was Francisco Coronado in 1540. He found only Indian villages, and treated the Indians with hostility.

In 1598, San Juan was founded as the first permanent Spanish settlement in New Mexico. Santa Fe was founded about 1610 and became the capital. Hostilities with the Indians continued for centuries, but became especially fierce around 1680. Pueblo Indians captured Santa Fe and forced the Spaniards to El Paso. The Spanish regained control in 1692-93, but suffered continued raids for the remainder of their control. In 1706, Albuquerque was founded.

Mexico gained its independence from Spain in 1821 and claimed New Mexico as one of its provinces. The same year, the Santa Fe Trail was opened and trade commenced between the United States and Mexico. During the Mexican War, General Stephen Kearny occupied New Mexico and declared it part of the United States. New Mexico officially became part of the United States in 1848. Two years later, the New Mexico Territory was formed. It was comprised of the present state of Arizona and part of Colorado in addition to New Mexico. The Colorado portion was taken away in 1861, and the Arizona section was made into its own territory in 1863. The Gadsden Purchase in 1854 added the Gila Valley in Catron and Grant Counties.

During the Civil War, Confederate forces invaded New Mexico. They were defeated by Union forces in 1862 and forced to withdraw. New Mexico furnished about 6,000 men to the Union forces. The coming of the railroad stimulated settlement in eastern and southern New Mexico

along with economic development. In June 1906, Congress passed a bill providing for the admission of Arizona and New Mexico as one state on the condition that the majority of voters in each state approved it. A majority of New Mexican voters approved statehood, but the Arizona voters did not, so both remained as territories. New Mexico finally became a state in 1912.

Look for vital records in the following locations:

- **Birth and death records:** New Mexico Vital Records and Health Statistics, Santa Fe, New Mexico, has birth and death records from 1880 and delayed birth certificates from 1867. Registration was required after 1920. Copies are available only to the registrant, family members, or by court order.
- **Marriage records, wills, property deeds and administrations:** Check with county clerks.
- **Land records:** County clerks also recorded private land grants. The first land grants were given by Spain and Mexico. These records, along with records of public land distributed while New Mexico was a territory, are located at the BLM, New Mexico State Office in Santa Fe. Many of these records are available on microfilm.
- **Census records:** Spanish and Mexican colonial censuses exist for 1750-1830, 1823, and 1845, although they are not complete. They are available at the New Mexico Records Center and Archives, University of New Mexico Library in Albuquerque, New Mexico. These have been transcribed, indexed, and published.

New Mexico Vital Records and Health Statistics
PO Box 26110
Santa Fe, New Mexico 87502
505.827.2316

BLM, New Mexico State Office
Federal Building
PO Box 1449
Santa Fe, New Mexico 87501

New Mexico Records Center & Archives
University of New Mexico Library
Special Collections
Albuquerque, New Mexico 87131

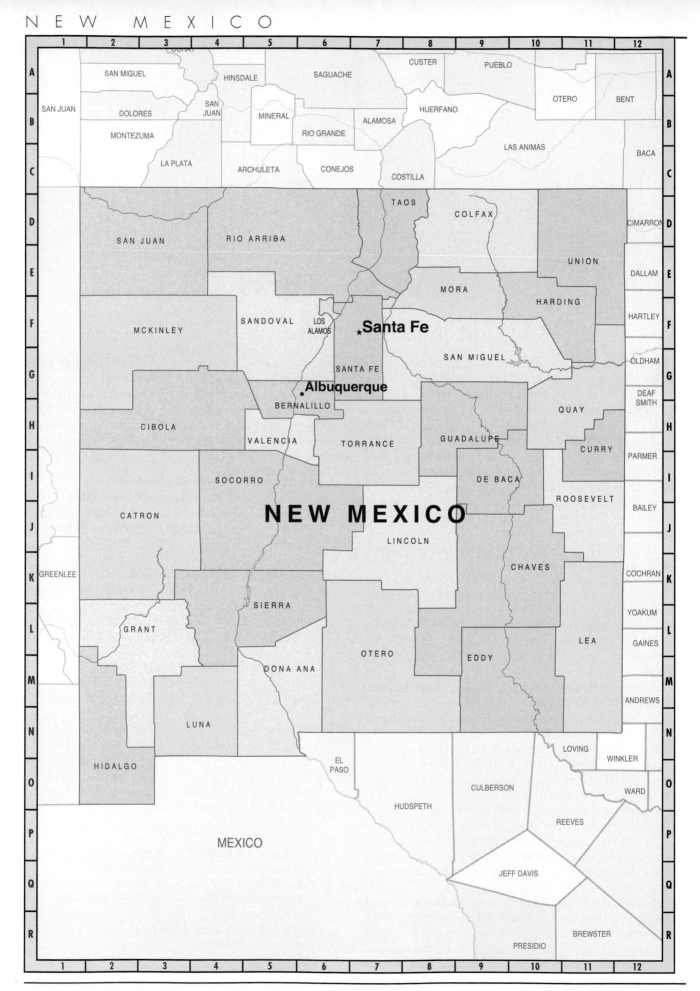

Societies and Repositories

Albuquerque Public Library; 423 East Central Ave.; Albuquerque, New Mexico 87101

Albuquerque Public Library; 501 Copper Ave. N.W.; Albuquerque, New Mexico 87102; 505.768.5100; Fax 505.768.5191

Artesia Genealogical Society; PO Box 803; Artesia, New Mexico 88210

Bureau of Land Management, New Mexico State Office; Federal Building, 1474 Rodeo Rd., PO Box 27115; Santa Fe, New Mexico 87502-0115; 505.438.7450; Fax 505.438.7452

Chaves County Genealogical Society; PO Box 51; Roswell, New Mexico 88201

Eddy County Genealogical Society; PO Box 461; Carlsbad, New Mexico 88220

Genealogical Club of the Albuquerque Public Library; 423 Central Ave. NE; Albuquerque, New Mexico 87102

Genealogy Club of Angel Fire; PO Box 503; Angel Fire, New Mexico 87710

Historical Society of New Mexico; PO Box 1912; Santa Fe, New Mexico 87504; 505.827.7332; Fax 505.827.7331

History Library Museum of New Mexico; Palace of the Governors; Santa Fe, New Mexico 87501

Lea County Genealogical Society; PO Box 1044; Lovington, New Mexico 88260

Los Alamos Family History Society; PO Box 900; Los Alamos, New Mexico 87544

Lovington Public Library; 103 North First St.; Lovington, New Mexico 88260

National Archives-Southwest Region (Fort Worth); 501 West Felix Street - Building 1 Dock, PO Box 6216; Fort Worth, Texas 76115-0216; 817.334.5525

New Mexico Genealogical Society; PO Box 8283; Albuquerque, New Mexico 87198-8283; 505.828.2514; <www.nmgs.org>

New Mexico Records Center and Archives; 404 Montezuma; Santa Fe, New Mexico 87501-2501; 505.827.7332; Fax 505.827.7331

New Mexico State Library Commission; 301 Don Gaspar; Santa Fe, New Mexico 87501

New Mexico State Library; 325 Don Gaspar; Santa Fe, New Mexico 87501-2777; 505.827.3800; Fax 505.827.3888

New Mexico State University Library; Las Cruces, New Mexico 88003

Portales Public Library; 218 S. Ave. B; Portales, New Mexico 88130

Roman Catholic, Archdiocese of Santa Fe; 4000 St. Joseph Place N.W.; Albuquerque, New Mexico 87120; 505.831.8100; Fax 505.831.8345

Roman Catholic, Diocese of Gallup; 711 S. Puerco Dr., PO Box 1338; Gallup, New Mexico 87301; 505.863.4406; Fax 505.722.9131

Roman Catholic, Diocese of Las Cruces; 1280 Med Park, PO Box 16318; Las Cruces, New Mexico 88004; 505.523.7577; Fax 505.524.3874

Roswell Genealogical Society; 807 North Missouri; Roswell, New Mexico 88201

Roswell Public Library; 301 N. Pennsylvania Ave.; Roswell, New Mexico 88201

Salmon Ruins Museum, c/o Totah Tracers Genealogy; 6131 U.S. Hwy. 64, PO Box 125; Bloomfield, New Mexico 87413-0125

Sierra County Genealogical Society; c/o Truth or Consequences Public Library; PO Box 311; Truth or Consequences, New Mexico 87901

Socorro County Genealogical Society; New Mexico; <www.rootsweb.com/~nmscgs/>

Socorro County Historical Society, Inc.; PO Box 923; Socorro, New Mexico 87801-0923; <www.rootsweb.com/~nmschs/>

Sons of the American Revolution, New Mexico Society; 12429 Chelwood Court N.W.; Albuquerque, New Mexico 87112

Southeastern New Mexico Genealogical Society; PO Box 5725; Hobbs, New Mexico 88240

Southern New Mexico Genealogical Society; PO Box 2563; Las Cruces, New Mexico 88004

Thomas Branigan Memorial Library; 200 E. Picacho Ave.; Las Cruces, New Mexico 88001

Totah Tracers Genealogical Society; c/o Salmon Ruins Museum; PO Box 125; Bloomfield, New Mexico 87413-0125

University of New Mexico Library; Special Collections; Albuquerque, New Mexico 87131; 505.277.4241; Fax 505.277.6019

Vital Statistics Bureau, New Mexico Health Services; 1190 St. Francis Drive; Santa Fe, New Mexico 87505; 505.827.2338; Fax 505.984.1048

Wilson-Cobb History and Gen. Research Library; 2212 W. Second, PO Box 2964; Roswell, New Mexico 88202

Bibliography and Record Sources

General Sources

An Illustrated History of New Mexico and Biographical Mention of Many of its Pioneers and Prominent Citizens of Today.... Chicago: The Lewis Publishing Co., 1895.

An Illustrated History of New Mexico: Containing a History of this Important Section of the Great Southwest, from the Earliest Period of its Discovery to the Present Time...Portraits of Some of its Eminent Men, and Biographical Mention of Many of its Pioneers and Prominent Citizens of Today. Chicago: Lewis Pub. Co., 1895.

Athearn, Frederic J. *A Forgotten Kingdom: The Spanish Frontier In Colorado And New Mexico 1540-1821.* Denver: Bureau of Land Management, Colorado State Office, 1989.

Bahti, Tom. *Southwestern Indian Tribes.* Las Vegas, Nevada: KC Publications, 1968.

Beers, Henry P. *Spanish and Mexican Records of the American Southwest: A Bibliographic Guide to Archive and Manuscript Sources.* Tucson, Arizona: University of Arizona Press, 1979.

Bohme, Frederick G. *A History Of The Italians In New Mexico.* New York: Arno Press, 1975.

Bolton, Herbert E. *The Spanish Borderlands: A Chronicle of Old Florida and the Southwest.* Reprint. Galveston, Texas: Frontier Press, 1996.

Brugge, David M. *Navajos in the Catholic Church Records of New Mexico, 1694-1875*. Window Rock, Arizona: Parks and Recreation Dept., 1968.

Chávez, Angélico. *Archives of the Archdiocese of Santa Fe, 1678-1900*. Washington, D.C.: Academy of American Franciscan History, 1957.

Chavez, Fray Angelico. *Origins of New Mexico Families in the Spanish Colonial Period in Two Parts: The Seventeenth (1598-1693) and the Eighteenth (1693-1821) Centuries*. Reprint. Albuquerque: The University of Albuquerque, 1973.

Coan, Charles F. *A History of New Mexico…Historical and Biographical*. 3 vols. Chicago: The American Historical Society, 1925.

Coles, Robert. *The Old Ones of New Mexico*. Rev. ed. Albuquerque, [N.M.]: University of New Mexico Press, 1973.

Delaney, Robert W. *The Ute Mountain Utes*. Albuquerque, New Mexico: University of New Mexico Press, 1989.

Dominquez, Francisco A. *The Missions of New Mexico, 1776*. Albuquerque: University of New Mexico Press, 1956.

Esterly, Robert E. *Genealogical Resources in New Mexico*. Albuquerque, New Mexico: New Mexico Genealogical Society, 1997.

Foote, Cheryl J. *Women of the New Mexico Frontier, 1846-1912*. Niwot, Colo.: University Press of Colorado, 1990.

Foster, H. Mannie. *History of Mormon Settlements in Mexico and New Mexico*. Logan, Utah: Utah State Agricultural College, 1955.

Grant, Blanche Chloe. *The Taos Indians*. Glorieta, New Mexico: Rio Grande Press, 1976.

Griego, Alfonso. *Voices of the Territory of New Mexico: an Oral History of People of Spanish Descent and Early Settlers Born During the Territorial Days*. [S.l.]: Griego, 1985.

Grove, Pearce S. *New Mexico Newspapers: A Comprehensive Guide to Bibliographical Entries and Locations*. Albuquerque: University of New Mexico Press, 1975.

Historical Records Survey (New Mexico). *Directory of Churches and Religious Organizations in New Mexico, 1940*. Albuquerque, New Mexico: New Mexico Historical Records Survey, 1940.

Historical Records Survey (New Mexico). *Inventory of Federal Archives in the States, Series 03, Department of the Treasury, No. 30, New Mexico*. Albuquerque, New Mexico: The Survey, 1941.

History of New Mexico: Its Resources and People. 2 vols. Los Angeles: Pacific States Publishing Co., 1907.

Jefferson, James. *The Southern Utes: A Tribal History*. Ignacio, Colorado: Southern Ute Tribe, [c1972].

New Mexico Research Outline, Series US-States, No. 32. Salt Lake City: Family History Library, 1988.

New Mexico State Records Center and Archives (Santa Fe, New Mexico). *Guide to the Microfilm of the Spanish Archives of New Mexico, 1697-1821*. Santa Fe, New Mexico: New Mexico State Records Center and Archives, 1967. 4 microfilm.

Porter, Lyle K. *A History of the Church of Jesus Christ of Latter-day Saints in New Mexico, 1876-1989*. Albuquerque, New Mexico: [L.K. and W. H. Porter], 2001.

Prince, Le Baron Bradford. *Spanish Mission Churches of New Mexico*. Glorieta, New Mexico: Rio Grande Press, 1977.

Quintana, Frances Leon. Pobladores: *Hispanic Americans of the Ute Frontier*. Notre Dame, Ind.: University of Notre Dame Press, 1991.

Read, Benjamin M. *Illustrated History of New Mexico*: [Santa Fe, New Mexico: New Mexico Print. Co.], 1912.

Reorganized Church of Jesus Christ of Latter Day Saints. Eastern Colorado District (Colorado). *Church Records, 1876-1959*. Microreproduction of originals housed in the RLDS Library Archives, Independence, Missouri. (Salt Lake City: Filmed by the Genealogical Society of Utah, 1994).

Salpointe, Jean Baptiste. *Soldiers of The Cross: Notes on the Ecclesiastical History of New Mexico, Arizona and Colorado*. Banning, Calif.: St. Boniface's Industrial School, 1898.

Simons, Marc. *Coronado's Land: Daily Life in Colonial New Mexico*. Galveston, Texas: Frontier Press, 1996.

Sources of Genealogical Help in New Mexico. Burbank, California: Southern California Genealogical Society.

Spiros, Joyce V. Hawley. *Handy Genealogical Guide to New Mexico*. Gallup, New Mexico: Verlene Publishing, 1981.

Stratton, Porter A. *The Territorial Press of New Mexico, 1834-1912*. Albuquerque: University of New Mexico Press, 1969.

Svenningsen, Robert. *Preliminary Inventory of the Pueblo Records Created by Field Offices of the Bureau of Indian Affairs*. Washington, D.C.: National Archives and Records Service, 1980.

Swadesh, Frances Leon. *20,000 Years of History: A New Mexico Bibliography*. Santa Fe: Sunstone Press, 1973.

Swadesh, Frances Leon. *Los Primeros Pobladores: Antecesores De Los Chicanos En Nuevo México*. México: Fondo de Cultura Económica, 1977.

Terrell, John Upton. *The Navajos: The Past And Present of a Great People*. N.Y.: Weybright and Talley, 1970.

The Historical Encyclopedia of New Mexico. 2 vols. Albuquerque, New Mexico: New Mexico Historical Association, 1945.

Thomas, Alfred Barnaby. *The Plains Indians and New Mexico, 1751-1778: A Collection of Documents Illustrative of the History of the Eastern Frontier of New Mexico*. Ann Arbor, Michigan: University Microfilms International, 1978.

Thrapp, Dan L. *Victorio and the Mimbres Apaches*. Norman, Oklahoma: University of Oklahoma Press, [1974].

Treib, Marc. *Sanctuaries of Spanish New Mexico*. Berkeley, California: University of California Press, 1993.

Twitchell, Ralph Emerson. *Leading Facts of New Mexican History*. 2 vols. Reprint. Salem, MA: Higginson Book Co., 1994.

Twitchell, Ralph Emerson. *The Spanish Archives of New Mexico: Compiled and Chronologically Arranged with Historical, Genealogical, Geographical, and Other Annotations, By Authority of the State of New Mexico*. Cedar Rapids, Iowa: Torch Press, 1914.

Tyler, Daniel. *Sources for New Mexican History, 1821-1848*. Santa Fe, New Mexico: Museum of New Mexico Press, 1984.

United States. National Historical Publications and Records Commission. *Spanish Archives of New Mexico, 1621-1821: A Microfilm Project Sponsored by the National Historical*

Publications Commission. Microfilm of original ms. at New Mexico Records Center, Santa Fe, New Mexico. Santa Fe, New Mexico: State of New Mexico Records Center, 1967. 18 microfilm.

Walker, Randi Jones. *Protestantism in the Sangre De Cristos, 1850-1920.* Albuquerque, New Mexico: University of New Mexico Press, 1991.

Weber, David J. *Foreigners in their Native Land: Historical Roots of the Mexican Americans.* Albuquerque, New Mexico: University of New Mexico Press, 1972.

Wiggins, Marvin E. *Mormons and their Neighbors: An Index to Over 75,000 Biographical Sketches from 1820 to the Present.* 2 vols. [Provo, Utah]: Harold B. Lee Library, Brigham Young University, 1984.

Atlases, Maps and Gazetteers

Beck, Warren A. and Ynez D. Haase. *Historical Atlas of New Mexico.* Norman, Oklahoma: University of Oklahoma Press, 1969.

Coan, Charles F. " The County Boundaries of New Mexico." *Southwestern Political Science Quarterly 3 (December 1922):* 252-86. Reprint. Santa Fe, New Mexico: Legislative Council Service, 1965.

Dike, Sheldon H. "The Territorial Post Offices of New Mexico." *New Mexico Historical Review 33* (October 1958) 322-27; 34 (January-October 1959): 55-69; 145-52, 203-26, 308-09.

Helbock, Richard W. *Post Offices of New Mexico.* Las Cruces, New Mexico: R.W. Helbock, 1981.

Julyan, Robert Hixson. *The Place Names of New Mexico.* Rev., 2nd ed. Albuquerque, New Mexico: University of New Mexico Press, 1998.

New Mexico in Maps. Albuquerque: University of New Mexico Press, 1986.

Pearce, T. M. *New Mexico Place Names: A Geographical Dictionary.* Albuquerque: University of New Mexico Press, 1985.

Census Records

Available Census Records and Census Substitutes

Federal Census 1850, 1860, 1870, 1880, 1900, 1910, 1920, 1930.

Union Veterans and Widows 1890.

Spanish/Mexican Census 1790, 1823, 1845.

State/Territorial Census 1885.

Dollarhide, William. *The Census Book: A Genealogist's Guide to Federal Census Facts, Schedules and Indexes.* Bountiful, Utah: Heritage Quest, 1999.

Kemp, Thomas Jay. *The American Census Handbook.* Wilmington, Delaware: Scholarly Resources, Inc., 2001.

Lainhart, Ann S. *State Census Records.* Baltimore: Genealogical Publishing Co., Inc., 1992.

Olmsted, Virginia L. *Spanish and Mexican Colonial Censuses of New Mexico: 1790, 1823, 1845.* Albuquerque: New Mexico Genealogical Society, 1975.

Olmsted, Virginia L. *Spanish and Mexican Censuses of New Mexico: 1750-1830.* Albuquerque: New Mexico Genealogical Society, 1981.

Platt, Lyman D. *Latin American Census Records.* 2nd. ed. Salt Lake City: Instituto Genealógico e Histórico Latinoamericano, 1992.

Szucs, Loretto Dennis, and Matthew Wright. *Finding Answers in U.S. Census Records.* Ancestry Publishing, 2001.

Thorndale, William, and William Dollarhide. *Map Guide to the U.S. Federal Censuses, 1790-1920.* Baltimore: Genealogical Publishing Co., 1987.

United States. Bureau of Internal Revenue. *Internal Revenue Assessment Lists for the Territory of New Mexico, 1862-1874.* Washington, D.C.: The National Archives, 1988.

Court Records, Probate and Wills

Historical Records Survey (New Mexico). *Inventory of Federal Archives in the States, Series 02, Federal Courts, No. 30, New Mexico.* Albuquerque, New Mexico: The Survey, 1941.

Howard, E. Stuart. *Preliminary Inventory: Records of the United States District Court for the District of New Mexico.* Record group 21. Denver: Federal Archives and Records Center, 1980.

New Mexico Commission of Public Records. State Records Center and Archives. *List of New Mexico County Courthouses.* Santa Fe, NM: State Records Center and Archives, 002. Online guide - <www.nmcpr.state.nm.us/archives/courthouses.htm>.

Emigration, Immigration, Migration and Naturalization

Colligan, John B. *The Juan Páez Hurtado Expedition of 1865: Fraud in Recruiting Colonists for New Mexico.* Albuquerque, New Mexico: University of New Mexico Press, 1995.

Cruz, Gilberto Rafael. *Let There be Towns: Spanish Municipal Origins in the American Southwest, 1610-1810.* College Station, Texas: Texas A & M University Press, 1988.

Gamio, Manuel. *Mexican Immigration to the United States: A Study of Human Migration and Adjustment.* New York: Arno Press and the New York Times, 1969.

Gamio, Manuel. *The Mexican Immigrant: His Life-Story.* New York: Arno Press and the New York Times, 1969.

Over 1400 Naturalization Records for Various Courts of New Mexico: 1882-1917, Denver Federal Archives. Lakewood, Colorado: Foothills Genealogical Society of Colorado, 1998.

Land and Property

Diaz, Albert James. *A Guide to the Microfilm of Papers Relating to New Mexico Land Grants.* Albuquerque, New Mexico: University of New Mexico Press, 1960.

Hone, Wade E. *Land and Property Research in the United States.* Salt Lake City: Ancestry Incorporated, 1997.

Miscellaneous Archives Relating to New Mexico Land Grants, 1695-1842. Albuquerque: University of New Mexico Library, 1955-1957.

New Mexico (Territory). Secretary's office. *Records of Land Titles, 1847-1852.* Albuquerque: University of New Mexico Library, 1955-1957.

New Mexico (Territory). Surveyor-General's Office. *Press Copies of Grant Papers.* Santa Fe: University of New Mexico Library, 1955-57.

New Mexico (Territory). Surveyor-General's Office. *Record of Private Land Claims Adjudicated By the U.S. Surveyor General, 1855-1890.* Albuquerque: University of New Mexico Library, 1955-1957.

New Mexico (Territory). Surveyor-General's Office. *Record of Private Land Claims Adjudicated by the U.S. Surveyor General, 1855-1890.* Microfilm of original records in the U.S. Bureau of Land Management, Santa Fe, New Mexico. Albuquerque, New Mexico: University of New Mexico Library, 1955-1957. 25 microfilm.

New Mexico Commission of Public Records. State Records Center and Archives. *Researching New Mexico Land Grants.* Santa Fe, NM: State Records Center and Archives, 002. Online guide - <www.nmcpr.state.nm.us/archives/courthouses.htm>.

Salazar, J. Richard. *Calendar to the Microfilm Edition of the Land Records of New Mexico: Spanish Archives of New Mexico, Series 1, Surveyor General Records, and, the Records of the Court of Private Land Claims.* [Santa Fe, New Mexico: National Historical Publications and Records Commission?], 1987.

Twitchell, Ralph Emerson. *The Twitchell Archives, 1685-1898.* Albuquerque: Filmed by the University of New Mexico. Library, 1955- 1957.

United States. Court of Private Land Claims. *Private Land Claims Adjudicated by the U.S. Court of Private Land Claims, 1891-1903.*

United States. Surveyor General (New Mexico). *Letters Received, 1854-1892, from the New Mexico Territory.* Albuquerque: University of New Mexico Library, 1955-1957.

United States. Surveyor General (New Mexico). *Pueblo Grants, 1523-1903.* Microfilm of original at the U.S. Bureau of Land Management, Santa Fe, New Mexico. Albuquerque, New Mexico: Filmed by the University of N.M. Library, 1955-1957.

Van Ness, John R., and Christine M. Van Ness, eds. *Spanish & Mexican Land Grants in New Mexico and Colorado.* [S.l.: s.n.], c1980 ([Manhattan, Kan.: AG Press]).

Vigil, Donaciano. *Vigil's Index, 1681-1846.* Albuquerque, New Mexico: University of New Mexico Library, 1955-1957.

Westphall, Victor. *The Public Domain in New Mexico, 1854-1891.* Albuquerque: University of New Mexico, 1965.

Military

Billington, Monroe Lee. *New Mexico's Buffalo Soldiers, 1866-1900.* Niwot, Colorado: University Press of Colorado, 1991.

Haulsee, W. M., F. C. Howe, and A. C. Doyle. *Soldiers of the Great War,* 3 vols. Washington, D.C.: Soldiers Record Publishing Association, 1920.

Historical Records Survey (New Mexico). *Inventory of Federal Archives in the States, Series 07, Department of the Navy, No. 30, New Mexico.* Albuquerque, New Mexico: The Survey, 1940.

Historical Records Survey (New Mexico). *Inventory of Federal Archives in the States, Series 04, Department of War, No. 30, New Mexico.* Albuquerque, New Mexico: The Survey, 1940.

Historical Records Survey (New Mexico). *Inventory of Federal Archives in the States, Series 12, Veterans' Administration, No. 30, New Mexico.* Albuquerque, New Mexico: The Survey, 1940.

Matson, Eva Jane. *It Tolled for New Mexico: New Mexicans Captured by the Japanese, 1941-1945.* Las Cruces, New Mexico: Yucca Tree Press, 1994, 1992.

Miller, Darlis A. *Soldiers and Settlers: Military Supply in the Southwest, 1861-1885.* Albuquerque, New Mexico: University of New Mexico Press, 1989.

Twitchell, Ralph E. *The History of the Military Occupation of the Territory of New Mexico from 1846 to 1851 by the Government of the United States: Together with Biographical Sketches of Men Prominent in the Conduct of the Government During that Period.* Tucson, Arizona: W.C. Cox, 1974.

United States. Selective Service System. *New Mexico, World War I Selective Service System Draft Registration Cards, 1917-1918.* National Archives Microfilm Publications, M1509. Washington, D.C.: National Archives, 1987-1988.

Vital and Cemetery Records

Chavez, Angelico. *New Mexico Roots LTD: A Demographic Perspective from Genealogical, Historical, and Geographical Data Found in the Diligencias Matrimoniales or Pre-nuptial Investigations (1678-1869) of the Archives of the Archdiocese of Santa Fe.* [n.p.]: Angelico Chavez, 1982.

Church of Jesus Christ of Latter-day Saints. Spanish-American Mission. *Family Group Records: Collected and Compiled by the Former Spanish-American Mission.* 11 vols. Original sheets are now interfiled in the "Patron" section of the Family Group Records Archives in the Family History Library, Salt Lake City. (Salt Lake City: Filmed by the Genealogical Society of Utah, 1973, 1980). 8 microfilm.

Guide to Public Vital Statistics Records in New Mexico. Albuquerque: Historical Records Survey, 1942.

Myers, Lee. *Cemetery Records from Southern New Mexico.* The author, 1982.

New Mexico. Department of Health. *Certificates and Records of Death, 1889-1942.* Microfilm of records at Bureau of Vital Records & Health, Department of Health, Santa Fe, New Mexico. (Salt Lake City: Filmed by the Genealogical Society of Utah, 1996). 29 microfilm.

New Mexico. Department of Health. *Delayed Certificates of Birth.* Microfilm of records at New Mexico Department of Public Health, Santa Fe, New Mexico. (Salt Lake City: Filmed by the Genealogical Society of Utah, 1995). 5 microfilm.

New Mexico. Department of Health. *New Mexico Death Certificates, 1927-1945.* Microfilm of records at new Mexico Dept. of Health, Vital Records & Health Statistics, Santa Fe, New Mexico. [Santa Fe, New Mexico: s.n., 1978]. 46 microfilm.

Some Marriages of the State of New Mexico, ca. 1880-1920. 2 vols. New Mexico Chapter, Daughters of the American Revolution, 1971-73.

County Website	Map Index	Date Created	Parent County or Territory From Which Organized Address/Details
Bernalillo* www.bernco.gov/	**G5**	**9 Jan 1852**	**Original county** Bernalillo County; 1 Civic Plaza NW; Albuquerque, NM 87102; Ph. 505.768.4090 Details: (Co Clk has m rec from 1885, pro rec from 1895 & land rec from 1888; Clk Dis Ct has div & ct rec)
Catron bombaci.rootsweb.com/Catron/	**J2**	**25 Feb 1921**	**Socorro** Catron County; 101 Main St; PO Box 507; Reserve, NM 87830-0507; Ph. 505.533.6400 Details: (Co Clk has b, m, pro & land rec from 1921; Clk Dis Ct has div & ct rec)
Chaves www.rootsweb.com/~nmchaves/ index.html	**K10**	**25 Feb 1889**	**Lincoln** Chaves County; 401 N Main St; Roswell, NM 88201-4726; Ph. 505.624.6614 Details: (Co Clk has m, land & mil rec from 1900; Clk Dis Ct has pro rec from 1900, div & ct rec)
Cibola bombaci.rootsweb.com/Cibola/	**H3**	**1981**	**Valencia** Cibola County; 515 W High Ave; Grants, NM 87020-2526; Ph. 505.287.8107 Details: (Co Clk has rec from 1981)
Colfax* nenewmexico.com/counties/colfax/ index.html	**D9**	**25 Jan 1869**	**Mora** Colfax County; 230 N 3rd St; PO Box 1498; Raton, NM 87740-1498; Ph. 505.445.5551 Details: (Co Clk has m rec from 1890, pro rec from 1903 & land rec from 1864; Clk Dis Ct has div & ct rec)
Curry www.currycounty.org/	**H11**	**25 Feb 1909**	**Quay, Roosevelt** Curry County; 700 N Main St Ste 7; PO Box 1168; Clovis, NM 88101; Ph. 505.763.5591 Details: (Co Clk has m rec from 1905, land rec from 1903, pro rec from 1909 & mil dis rec from 1919; Clk Dis Ct has div, nat & ct rec)
De Baca www.rootsweb.com/~nmdebaca/index.htm	**I9**	**28 Feb 1917**	**Chaves, Guadalupe, Roosevelt** De Baca County; 514 Ave C; PO Box 347; Fort Sumner, NM 88119-0347; Ph. 505.355.2601 Details: (Co Clk has m, pro & land rec from 1917; Clk Dis Ct has div rec; Mag Judge has ct rec)
Dona Ana* www.co.dona-ana.nm.us/	**M5**	**9 Jan 1852**	**Original county** Dona Ana County; 180 West Amador; Las Cruces, NM 88001; Ph. 505.647.7285 Details: (Co Clk has m & pro rec from 1870 & land rec from 1801; Clk Dis Ct has div & ct rec)
Eddy* www.caverns.net/ecourt/	**M9**	**25 Feb 1889**	**Lincoln** Eddy County; 101 West Greene; Carlsbad, NM 88220; Ph. 505.885.3383 Details: (Co Clk has m, pro & land rec & newspapers from 1891; Clk Dis Ct has div & ct rec)
Grant* www.rootsweb.com/~nmgrant/index.htm	**L2**	**30 Jan 1868**	**Dona Ana** Grant County; 201 N Cooper St; PO Box 898; Silver City, NM 88062; Ph. 505.538.2979 Details: (Co Clk has m rec from 1872, pro rec from 1884, land rec from 1871 & newspapers from 1900; Clk Dis Ct has div rec; Municipal Ct has ct rec)
Guadalupe www.rootsweb.com/~nmguadal/index.htm	**H8**	**26 Feb 1891**	**Lincoln, San Miguel** Guadalupe County; 420 Parker Ave; Santa Rosa, NM 88435; Ph. 505.472.3791 Details: (Co Clk has m rec from 1895, pro rec from 1894 & land rec from 1893)
Harding nenewmexico.com/counties/harding/ index.html	**F10**	**4 Mar 1921**	**Mora, Union** Harding County; 3rd & Pine; PO Box 1002; Mosquero, NM 87733-1002; Ph. 505.673.2301 Details: (Co Clk has m, div, pro, ct & land rec from 1921)
Hidalgo* www.rootsweb.com/~nmhidalg/	**O2**	**25 Feb 1919**	**Grant** Hidalgo County; 300 S Shakespeare St; Lordsburg, NM 88045-1939; Ph. 505.542.9213 Details: (Co Clk has m, pro & land rec from 1920; Clk Dis Ct has div & ct rec)

County Website	Map Index	Date Created	Parent County or Territory From Which Organized
			Address/Details
Lea www.leacounty-nm.org/	L11	7 Mar 1917	**Chaves, Eddy** Lea County; 100 N Main Ave; PO Box 4C; Lovington, NM 88260; Ph. 505.396.8532 Details: (Co Clk has m & pro rec from 1917 & land rec)
Lincoln www.usgennet.org/usa/nm/county/lincoln/	J8	16 Jan 1869	**Socorro, Dona Ana** Lincoln County; 300 Central Ave; Carrizozo, NM 88301; Ph. 505.648.2331 Details: (Co Clk has m rec from 1882, pro rec from 1880 & newspapers from 1890)
Los Alamos www.lac.losalamos.nm.us/	F6	16 Mar 1949	**Sandoval, Santa Fe** Los Alamos County; PO Box 30 2300 Trinity Dr; Los Alamos, NM 87544-3051; Ph. 505.662.8010 Details: (Co Clk has m rec from 1940, land rec from 1949, pro rec from 1953 & bur rec from 1961; Clk Dis Ct has div & ct rec)
Luna* www.rootsweb.com/~nmluna/	N4	16 Mar 1901	**Dona Ana, Grant** Luna County; PO Box 1838; Deming, NM 88031-1838; Ph. 505.546.0491 Details: (Co Clk has m, d, land, pro & mil rec from 1901, Deming newspapers from 1901)
McKinley bombaci.rootsweb.com/McKinley/	F3	23 Feb 1899	**Bernalillo, Valencia, San Juan, Rio Arriba** McKinley County; 200 W Hill Ave; Gallup, NM 87301-6309; Ph. 505.863.6866 Details: (Co Clk has b rec 1907-1958, m, pro & land rec from 1901 & voter reg; Clk Dis Ct has div rec)
Mora* nenewmexico.com/counties/mora/index.html	E8	1 Feb 1860	**Taos** Mora County; PO Box 360; Mora, NM 87732; Ph. 505.387.2448 Details: (Co Clk has m & pro rec from 1891 & land rec from 1825; Clk Dis Ct has div & ct rec)
Otero* co.otero.nm.us/	L7	30 Jan 1899	**Dona Ana, Lincoln, Socorro** Otero County; 1000 New York Ave #108; Alamogordo, NM 88310; Ph. 505.437.4942 Details: (Co Clk has m, pro & land rec from 1899 & voter reg from 1939; Clk Dis Ct has div & ct rec from 1899)
Quay nenewmexico.com/counties/quay/index.html	H10	28 Feb 1903	**Guadalupe, Union** Quay County; 300 S 3rd St; PO Box 1225; Tucumcari, NM 88401; Ph. 505.461.0510 Details: (Co Clk has m & land rec from 1893, pro rec, mil rec from 1945; Clk Dis Ct has div & ct rec)
Rio Arriba www.usroots.org/~rioarrnm/	D5	9 Jan 1852	**Original county** Rio Arriba County; PO Box 158; Tierra Amarilla, NM 87575; Ph. 505.588.7254 Details: (Co Clk has m & pro rec from 1852)
Roosevelt www.rootsweb.com/~nmroosev/index.html	J11	28 Feb 1903	**Chaves, Guadalupe** Roosevelt County; 101 W 1st St; Portales, NM 88130; Ph. 505.356.8562 Details: (Co Clk has m, pro & land rec from 1903, mil dis rec from 1919 & newspapers; Clk Dis Ct has div & ct rec)
San Juan bombaci.rootsweb.com/SanJuan/	D2	24 Feb 1887	**Rio Arriba** San Juan County; 100 S Oliver Dr; Aztec, NM 87410; Ph. 505.334.9471 Details: (Co Clk has m & land rec from 1887 & pro rec from 1899; Clk Dis Ct has div & ct rec)
San Miguel* www.smcounty.net/	G8	9 Jan 1852	**Original county** San Miguel County; 500 W National St; Las Vegas, NM 87701; Ph. 505.425.9331 Details: (Co Clk has m rec from 1880, pro rec from 1939 & land rec from 1800's; Clk Dis Ct has div & ct rec from 1882)
Sandoval www.rootsweb.com/~nmsandov/	F5	10 Mar 1903	**Bernalillo** Sandoval County; 711 Camino Del Pueblo; PO Box 40; Bernalillo, NM 87004; Ph. 505.867.2209 Details: (Co Clk has m, pro & land rec)
Santa Ana		1850	**Original county** Details: (Became part of Bernalillo Co, 1876)
Santa Fe* www.co.santa-fe.nm.us/	G7	9 Jan 1852	**Original county** Santa Fe County; 102 Grant Ave; Santa Fe, NM 87505; Ph. 505.986.6280 Details: (Co Clk has m rec from 1900, pro rec from 1894 & land rec from 1848)

County Website	Map Index	Date Created	Parent County or Territory From Which Organized Address/Details
Sierra village.globaldrum.com/sierra_newmexico/ county.htm	**K5**	**3 Apr 1884**	**Socorro, Grant, Dona Ana** Sierra County; 311 N Date St; Truth or Consequences, NM 87901-2362; Ph. 505.894.2840 Details: (Co Clk has m & land rec from 1884, pro rec, mil dis rec from 1945; Clk Dis Ct has div & ct rec)
Socorro www.rootsweb.com/~nmsocorr/index.htm	**I4**	**9 Jan 1852**	**Original county** Socorro County; 200 Church St; PO Box 1; Socorro, NM 87801; Ph. 505.835.0589 Details: (Co Clk has m rec from 1885, pro rec from 1912, land rec from 1859, b & d rec 1907-1941)
Taos* www.rootsweb.com/~nmtaos/index.htm	**D7**	**9 Jan 1852**	**Original county** Taos County; 105 Albright St #D; Taos, NM 87571-0676; Ph. 505.751.8654 Details: (Co Clk has b, m, d, bur & pro rec from 1846)
Torrance www.rootsweb.com/~nmtaos/index.htm	**H7**	**16 Mar 1903**	**Lincoln, San Miguel, Socorro, Santa Fe, Valencia, Bernalillo** Torrance County; 9th & Allen; Estancia, NM 87016; Ph. 505.384.2221 Details: (Courthouse burned in 1910) (Co Clk has m, informal pro rec & land rec from 1911; Clk Dis Ct has div & ct rec)
Union* nenewmexico.com/counties/union/ index.html	**E11**	**23 Feb 1893**	**Colfax, Mora, San Miguel** Union County; 200 Court St; PO Box 430; Clayton, NM 88415; Ph. 505.374.9491 Details: (Co Clk has m rec from 1894, pro, ct & land rec; Clk Dis Ct has div rec)
Valencia* www.co.valencia.nm.us/	**H5**	**9 Jan 1852**	**Original county** Valencia County; 444 Luna Ave; PO Box 1119; Los Lunas, NM 87031-1119; Ph. 505.866.2073 Details: (Co Clk has m rec from 1865 & pro rec from 1900; Clk Dis Ct has div & ct rec)

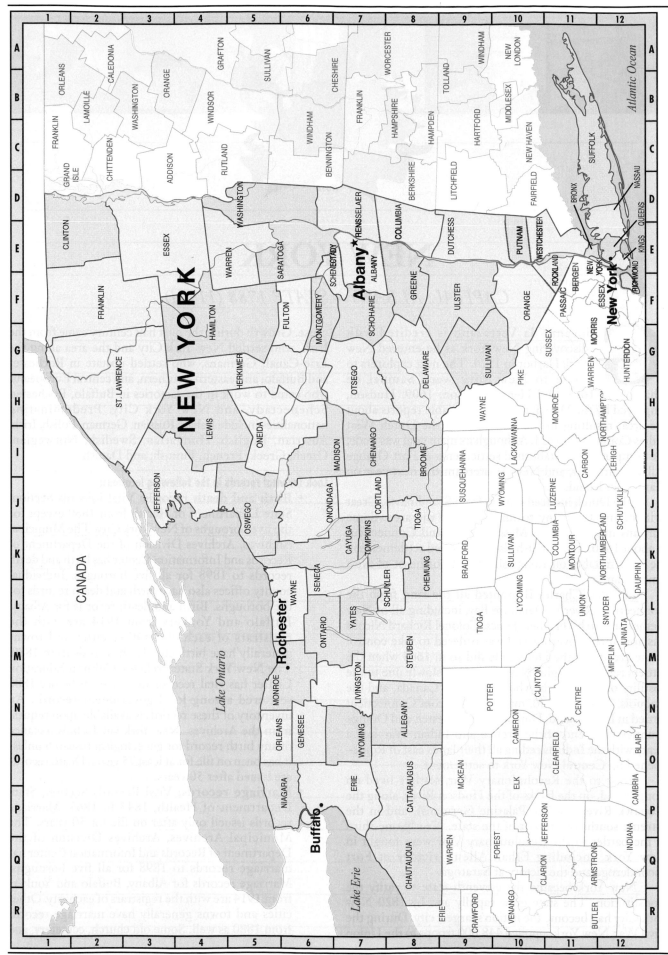

marriage records are in the New York State Library, Department of Education, Manuscripts and History Section. The library also has some published genealogies, and local histories. Marriage bonds, 1753-1783, were extensively damaged in a 1911 fire but have been largely restored. Some of these can be seen at the New York State Archives, Cultural Education Center.

- **Census records:** These censuses show the names and ages of each member of every household and sometimes the county of birth. Most county offices have copies of the returns for their county. The New York State Archives also has the statewide census returns for 1915 and 1925 along with all the earlier state censuses for Albany County.
- **Military records:** Military service, pensions, and land grant records for soldiers who served in the Revolution and the War of 1812 are available through the New York State Archives.

Vital Records Section
State Department of Health
52 Chambers Street
Albany, New York 12237
518.474.3077

The New York State Archives,
Cultural Education Center
Empire State Plaza
Albany, New York 12230

Municipal Archives, Archives Division of the
Department of Records and Information Center
Empire State Plaza
New York, New York 10007
212.619.4530

Societies and Repositories

Adirondack Genealogical Historical Society; 100 Main St.; Saranac Lake, New York 12983

Adriance Memorial Library; 93 Market St.; Poughkeepsie, New York 12601

African-Atlantic Genealogical Society; PO Box 7385; Freeport, New York 11520;

Albany County Hall of Records; 250 South Pearl Street; Albany, New York 12202; 518.447.4500

Albany Jewish Genealogical Society; PO Box 3850; Albany, New York 12208

Allegany Area Historical Association; PO Box 162; Allegany, New York 14706; <bfn.org/~aaha/>

Almond Historical Society; PO Box 187; Almond, New York 14804; <www.rootsweb.com/~nyahs/AlmondHS.html>

American Baptist Samuel Colgate Historical Library; 1106 Goodman Street; Rochester, New York 14620-2532; 716.473.1740; Fax 716.473.1740

American Irish Historical Society; 991 Fifth Ave; New York, New York 10028; 212.628.7927;

American Jewish Historical Society Library; 2 Thornton Road; Waltham, Massachusetts 02154; 617.891.8110; Fax 617.899.9208

American Scandinavian Foundation; 725 Park Avenue; New York, New York 10021

American-Scandinavian Foundation; 58 Park Ave.; New York, New York 10016;

Archdiocese of New York; 1011 First Avenue; New York City, New York 10022; 212.371.1000; Fax 212.319.8265

Archivists Round Table of Metropolitan New York; c/o Amy Surak, Archivist; Covenant House; 346 W. 17th Street; New York, NY 10011-5002; 212.727.4065; <www.nycarchivists.org/board.html>

Bethlehem Historical Association; Clapper Rd.; Selkirk, New York 12158

BIGS Buffalo Irish Genealogical Society; Buffalo Irish Center; 245 Abbott Rd.; Buffalo, New York 14220; <www.buffalonet.org/army/bigs.htm>

Blauvelt Free Library; 86 S. Western Hwy; Blauvelt, New York 10913

Branch of Distribution U.S. Geological Survey; 507 National Center; Reston, Virginia 22092; 703.648.6045

Bridge Line Historical Society; PO Box 13324; Albany, New York 12212; 518.884.9076;

Bronx County Historical Society; 3309 Bainbridge Avenue; Bronx, New York 10467; <www.go.newyorkcity.com/0022index.html>

Brooklyn Genealogical Workshop; c/o The Brooklyn Record 125 Montague St.; Brooklyn, New York 11201

Brooklyn Historical Society; 128 Pierrepont St.; Brooklyn, New York 11201; 718.222.4111;

Buffalo and Erie County Historical Society; 25 Nottingham Court; Buffalo, New York 14216; <intotem.buffnet.net/bechs/>

Bureau of Vital Statistics; City Hall, Room 613; Niagara Square; Buffalo, New York 14202; 716.855.5848

Capital District Genealogical Society; PO Box 2175; Empire State Plaza Station; Albany, New York 12220

Cayuga County Historian; Historic Old Post Office; 157 Genesee St.; Auburn, New York 13021-3423

Cayuga-Owasco Lakes Historical Society; Box 247; Moravia, New York 13118; <www.rootsweb.com/~nycayuga/colhs.htm>

Central New York Genealogical Society; PO Box 104, Colvin Station; Syracuse, New York 13205; <www.rootsweb.com/~nycnygs/>

Chautauqua County, New York Genealogical Society; PO Box 404; Fredonia, New York 14063

Cheektowaga Historical Association; 3329 Broadway; Cheektowaga, New York 14227

Chemung County Historical Society; 415 E. Water St.; Elmira, New York 14901

Chenango County Historical Society; 45 Rexford Street; Norwich, New York 13815; <www.chenangocounty.org/chencohistso/>

Colonial Dames of America; 421 E. 61st St.; New York, New York 10021

Columbia County Historical Society; 5 Albany Ave.; PO Box 311; Kinderhook, New York 12106

Columbia University, Journalism Library; New York, New York 10027

New York Public Library; Jewish Division; Fifth Avenue at 42nd Street; New York, New York 10018; 212.930.0601; Fax; 212.642.0141

New York Public Library; U.S. History, Local History & Genealogy Division; Fifth Avenue and 42nd Street, Room 315S; New York, New York 10018-2788; 212-930-0829

New York State Archives and Records Administration; New York State Education Department, Cultural Education Center; Albany, New York 12230; <http://www.archives.nysed.gov/>

New York State Archives; Cultural Education Center, 11th Floor; Empire State Plaza; Albany, New York 12230; 518.474.8955; Fax 518.473.9985

New York State Council of Genealogical Organizations; PO Box 2593; Syracuse, New York 13220-2593; This council was formed in 1990 for education, publication, communication, and public advocacy in behalf of state genealogical societies and libraries.

New York State Historical Association; PO Box 800; Cooperstown, New York 13326;

New York State Library; Cultural Education Center; Empire State Plaza; Albany, New York 12230; 518.474.5355; Fax 518.474.5786

New York State Museum; 3093 Cultural Education Center; Albany, New York 12230; 518.474.6917

Newburgh Free Library; 124 Grand St.; Newburgh, New York 12550

New-York Historical Society; 170 Central Park West; New York, New York 10024; 212.873.3400; Fax 212-875-1591; The historical society has extensive collections of manuscripts, newspapers, periodicals, histories, city directories, maps, and photographs.

Niagara County Genealogical Society; 215 Niagara Street; Lockport, New York 14094

Northern New York American-Canadian Genealogical Society; PO Box 1256; Plattsburgh, New York 12901; <www.rootsweb.com/~nnyacgs/>

Nyando Roots Genealogical Society; PO Box 175; Massena, New York 13662

Ogdensburg Public Library; 312 Washington St.; Ogdensburg, New York 13669

Olin-Kroch URIS Library; Cornell University; Ithaca, New York 14853-5301; 607.255.5068; 607.255.9346; Cornell University has a large collection of Protestant church records for western New York as well as an excellent collection of histories, maps, newspapers, and New York censuses.

Olive Free Library; PO Box 59; West Shokan, New York 12484; 845.657.2482; <olive.westshokan.lib.ny.us>

Oneida County Historical Society; 1608 Genesee Street; Utica, New York 13502-5425; <www.midyork.org/ochs/>

Oneida Library; 220 Broad St.; Oneida, New York 13421

Onondaga Co. Public Library, Local Hist. & Special Collections; 447 S. Salina St.; Syracuse, New York 13202-2494

Onondaga Historical Association; 311 Montgomery St.; Syracuse, New York 13202

Ontario County Genealogical Society; 55 North Main St; Canandaigua, New York 14424; <www.ochs.org/Genealogy/Ocgs/index.html>

Ontario County Historical Society; 55 N. Main St.; Canandaigua, New York 14424;

Orange Co. Gen. Soc. Research Rm., Historic 1841 Courthouse; 101 Main St.; Goshen, New York 10924 <www.rootsweb.com/~nozell/ocgs/>

Oswego County Genealogical Society; 384 East River Rd.; Oswego, New York 13126

Oyster Bay Historical Society; PO Box 297; Oyster Bay, New York 11771-0297; 516.922.6892; <members.aol.com/OBHistory/>

Palatines to America, New York Chapter; 18 Droms Rd.; Scotia, New York 13202-5304

Patterson Library; 40 S. Portage St.; Westfield, New York 14757

Philadelphia Jewish Archives Centre at the Balch Institute; 18 South 7th Street; Philadelphia, Pennsylvania 19106-1423; 215.925.8090

Plattekill Historical Society; PO Box 357; Clintondale, New York 12515

Polish Genealogical Society of New York State; 12645 Rt. 78; East Aurora, New York 14052;

Port Chester Public Library; 1 Haseco Ave.; Port Chester, New York 10573

Puerto Rican/Hispanic Genealogical Society Inc.; PO Box 260118; Bellerose, New York 11426-0118; <www.rootsweb.com/~prhgs/>

Queens Borough Public Library; 89-11 Merrick Blvd; Jamaica, New York 11432

Queens Genealogical Workshop; 1820 Flushing Ave.; Ridgewood, New York 11385; <home.att.net/~CGohari/index.html>

Queens Historical Society; 143.35 37th Avenue; Flushing, New York 11354; <www.preserve.org/queens/qhs.htm>

Registrar of Vital Statistics; City Hall, Room 107; 24 Eagle Street; Albany, New York 12207

Registrar of Vital Statistics; City Hall; Yonkers, New York 10701; 914.964.3066

Rensselaer County Historical Society; 57 Second Street; Troy, New York;

Richmond Memorial Library; 19 Ross St.; Batavia, New York 14020

Rochester Genealogical Society; PO Box 10501; Rochester, New York 14610

Rochester Public Library, Local History Division; 115 South Ave.; Rochester, New York 14604

Roswell P. Flower Genealogy Library; 229 Washington St.; Watertown, New York 13601

Saint Lawrence County Historical Association; PO Box 8; Canton, New York 13617-0008;

Saint Lawrence Valley Genealogical Society; PO Box 341; Colton, New York 13625-0341

Scarsdale Historical Society; PO Box 431; Scarsdale, New York 10583.0431; 914.723.2185; <www.scarsdalenet.com/historicalsociety/>

Schenectady County Historical Society; 32 Washington Avenue; Schenectady, New York 12305; 208 361.5305;

Schuyler County Historical Society and Library; 108 N. Catherine St., Rt. 14; Montour Falls, New York 14865

Shaker Heritage Society; 875 Watervliet Shaker Rd., Suite 2; Albany, New York 12211; 518.452.7348

Slovak Heritage and Folklore Society International; 151 Colebrook Drive; Rochester, New York 14617-2215; 716.342.0443; <www.iarelative.com/shfsinfo.htm>

Society of Friends - New York Yearly Meeting Archives; Haviland Records Room; 15 Rutherford Place; New York, New York 10003; 212.777.8866

Sons of the American Revolution, Empire State Society; 13 Garden Ave.; Massapequa, New York 11758

Southern Tier Genealogical Club of Broome County; PO Box 690; Vestal, New York 13851-0680; <www.rootsweb.com/~nybroome/stgs/stgs.htm>

Southhold Historical Society; PO Box 1; Southold, New York 11971-0001; <www.longislandlighthouses.com/hortonpoint/>

St. George's Society Of New York; 175 Ninth Avenue; New York, New York 10011-4977; 212.727.1566; <www.stgeorgessociety.org>

Staten Island Historical Society; 441 Clarke Ave.; Staten Island, New York 10306

Steele Memorial Library; One Library Plaza; Elmira, New York 14901

Steuben County Historical Society; PO Box 349; Bath, New York 14810

Suffolk County Historical Society; 300 W. Main St. Riverhead; Long Island, New York 11901

Sullivan County Historical Society; PO Box 247W; Hurleyville, New York 12747;

Three Village Historical Society; PO Box 76; E. Setauket, New York 11733; <members.aol.com/TVHS1/index.html>

Tioga County Historical Society; 110-112 Front St.; Owego, New York 13827

Town of Watertown NY Historical Society; 22867 County Route 67; Watertown, New York 13601; <www.usgennet.org/usa/ny/town/watertown/twhsmain.html>

Troy Public Library; 100 Second St.; Troy, New York 12180

Twin Tiers Genealogical Society; PO Box 763; Elmira, New York 14902

Ulster County Genealogical Society; PO Box 536; Hurley, New York 12443; 845.331.7453; <hurley.lib.ny.us/uc_geneological_society.html>

United Methodist Archives Center; General Commission on Archives and History of the United Methodist Church; Drew University Library; PO Box 127; Madison, New Jersey 07940; 201.408.3189; Fax 201.408.3909

United States/Canadian Map Service; PO Box 249; Neenah, WI 54957-0249; 414.731.0101

Utica Public Library; 303 Genesee St.; Utica, New York 13501

Wayne County Historical Society; 21 Butternut Street; Lyons, New York 14489; <www.cgazette.com/common/standing/WC.historical_society/waynecountyhistorical.htm>

Westchester County Genealogical Society; PO Box 518; White Plains, New York 10603; <www.rootsweb.com/~nywcgs/>

Westchester County Historical Society; 2199 Saw Mill River Road; Elmsford, New York 10523;

Western New York Gen. Soc., Inc., Special Col. Dept., Downtown Buffalo & Erie Co. Public Library; Lafayette Square; Buffalo, New York 14075-0338

Western New York Genealogical Society; PO Box 338; Hamburg, New York 14075; 716.839.1842; <www.pce.net/outram/wny.htm>

Yates County Genealogical and Historical Society; 200 Main St.; Penn Yan, New York 14527;

Yorktown Historical Society; P. O. Box 355; Yorktown Heights, New York 10598;

Bibliography and Record Sources

General Sources

Bailey, Rosalie Fellows. *Guide to Genealogical and Biographical Sources for New York City, Manhattan, 1783-1898*. New York: Bailey, 1954.

Bevier, Louis. *Genealogy of the First Settlers of New Paltz*. 1909. Reprint. Baltimore: Genealogical Publishing Co., 1965.

Breton, Arthur J. *A Guide to the Manuscript Collections of the New-York Historical Society*, 2 vols. (Westport, Conn.; Greenwood Press, Inc., 1972; FHL book 974.7 H23b; computer number 413719).

Brodhead, John Romeyn. *Documents Relative to the Colonial History of the State of New York: Procured in Holland, England, and France*. 15 vols. Albany: Weed, Parsons & Co., printers, 1853-1887.

Burke, Kate. *Searching in New York: A Reference Guide to Public and Private Records*. Costa Mesa, California: ISC Publications, 1987.

Clint, Florence. *New York Area Key: A Guide to the Genealogical Records of the State of New York…*Elizabeth, Colorado: Keyline Publishers, 1979.

Cutter, William Richard. *Families of Western New York: Excerpted from Genealogical and Family History of Western New York: A Record of the Achievements of her People in the Making of A Commonwealth and the Building of a Nation*. 1912. Reprint. Baltimore, Maryland: Clearfield Co., 1996.

Cutter, William Richard. *Genealogical and Family History of Central New York. A Record of the Achievements of Her People in the Making of a Commonwealth and the Building of a Nation*. 3 vols. 1912. Reprint. Baltimore, Maryland: Clearfield Co, 1994.

Documentary History of the State of New York. 4 vols. in 8 parts. Albany: Weed, Parsons and Co., 1849-51.

Epperson, Gwenn F. *New Netherland Roots*. Baltimore: Genealogical Publishing Co., 1994.

Faibisoff, Sylvia G. *A Bibliography of Newspapers in Fourteen New York State Counties*. S.l.: s.n., 197-?].

Falk, Byron A. *Personal Name Index to the New York Times Index, 1851-1993: [with additional supplements to 1996].* Succasunna, New Jersey; Sparks, Nevada: Roxbury Data Interface, 1976-.

Fitch, Charles Elliot. *Encyclopedia of Biography of New York: A Life Record of Men and Women of the Past Whose Sterling Character and Energy and Industry Have Made Them Preeminent in Their Own and Many Other States.* 4 vols. New York: American Historical Society, 1916.

Gehring, Charles T. *New York Historical Manuscripts: Dutch Land Papers, Volumes GG, HH, II.* Baltimore: Genealogical Publishing Co., 1980.

Greene, Nelson, ed. *The History of the Mohawk Valley,* 4 vols. Chicago: S.J. Clarke Publishing Co., 1925.

Greene, Nelson. *History of the Valley of the Hudson: River of Destiny, 1609-1930, Covering the Sixteen New York State Hudson River Counties of New York, Bronx, Westchester, Rockland, Orange, Putnam, Dutchess, Ulster, Greene, Columbia, Albany, Rensselaer, Saratoga, Washington, Warren, Essex.* 5 vols. Chicago: S.J. Clarke Pub. Co., 1931.

Guide to Archival Repositories. Buffalo, NY: Western New York Documentary Heritage Program, 1997.

Guzik, Estelle M., ed. *Genealogical Resources in the New York Metropolitan Area.* New York: Jewish Genealogical Society, 1989.

Hamm, Margherita Arlina. *Famous Families of New York: Historical and Biographical Sketches of Families, which in Successive Generations have been Identified with the Development of the Nation.* New York: Putnam, 1902.

Hoff, Henry Bainbridge. *Genealogies of Long Island Families: from The New York Genealogical and Biographical Record.* 2 vols. Baltimore: Genealogical Publishing Co., Inc., 1987.

Ireland, Norma Olin. *Cutter Index: A Consolidated Index of Cutter's 9 Genealogy Series.* Fallbrook, California: Ireland Indexing Service, [197-?].

Kronman, Barbara. *The Guide to New York City Public Records.* New York: Public Interest Clearinghouse, 1992.

MacWethy, Lou D. *The Book of Names, Especially Relating to the Early Palatines and the First Settlers of the Mohawk Valley.* 1933. Reprint. Baltimore: Genealogical Publishing Co., 1985.

Nestler, Harold. *A Bibliography of New York State Communities, Counties, Town, and Villages.* 3rd ed. Bowie, Maryland: Heritage Books, 1990.

New York Research Outline. Series US-States, No. 33. Salt Lake City: Family History Library, 1988.

New York State Library Surname Index. Albany: State Library of New York, 1979. 33 Microfiche.

New York Times (New York City). *Obituary Index ...* Westport, Conn.: Meckler, 1989.

New York, Commissioners of Indian Affairs. *Proceedings of the Commissioners of Indian Affairs Appointed by Law for the Extinguishment of Indian Titles in the State of New York.* Albany, New York: J. Munsell, 1861.

New York, Secretary of State. *The Balloting Book and Other Documents Relating to Military Bounty Lands, in the State of New York,* Albany, New York, 1825.

New York, State Historian. *Third Annual Report of the State of New York, 1897; Transmitted to the Legislature, March 14, 1898.* New York City and Albany, New York: Wynkoop, Hahlenbeck and Crawford Co., 1898.

Noyes, J.O. and Morrison's Reprint. *Genesee Valley of Western New York.* Reprint. W.E. Morrison & Co., 1972.

O'Callaghan, Edmund B. *Lists of Inhabitants of Colonial New York (1849-51).* Reprint. Baltimore, Maryland: Genealogical Publishing Co., 1989.

O'Callaghan, Edmund B. *The Register of New Netherland, 1626-1674.* 1865. Reprint. Baltimore, Maryland: Clearfield Co., 1996.

O'Callaghan, Edmund B. *Calendar of Dutch (and English) Historical Manuscripts in the Office of Secretary of State, Albany, New York.* 2 vols. 1968-1866. Reprint. Ridgewood, NJ: The Gregg press 1968.

Pearson, Jonathan. *Contributions for the Genealogies of the Descendants of the First Settlers of the Patent and City of Schenectady, from 1662 to 1800.* Baltimore: Reprinted for Clearfield Company Inc. by Genealogical Publishing Co., 1998.

Reynolds, Cuyler. *Genealogical and Family History of Southern New York and the Hudson River Valley.* 1914. Reprint. Baltimore, Maryland: Clearfield Co., 1997.

Reynolds, Helen Wilkinson. *Dutch Houses in the Hudson Valley before 1776.* New York: Payson and Clarke, 1929.

Schweitzer, George K. *New York Genealogical Research.* Knoxville: George K. Schweitzer, 1988.

Scott, Kenneth. *Genealogical Data from Colonial New York Newspapers: A Consolidation of Articles from the New York Genealogical and Biographical Record.* Baltimore: Genealogical Pub. Co., 1977.

Scott, Kenneth. *Genealogical Data From New York Administration Bonds 1753-1799.* New York, New York: New York Genealogical and Biographical Society, 1969.

Scott, Kenneth. *Genealogical Data from the New York Post Boy, 1743-1773.* Arlington, VA: National Genealogical Society, Talcott, Sebastian V. *Genealogical Notes of New York and New England Families.* 1883. Reprint. Baltimore, Maryland: by Clearfield Co., 1994.

Seversmith, Herbert Furman. *Colonial Families of Long Island, New York and Connecticut: Being the Ancestry & Kindred of Herbert Furman Seversmith.* 5 vols. in 7. Washington: H.F. Seversmith, 1939-1958.

Seversmith, Herbert Furman. *Long Island Genealogical Source Material: A Bibliography.* Washington: National Genealogical Society Bookstore, 1962.

Wilson, Thomas B. *Inhabitants of New York, 1774-1776.* Genealogical Publishing Co., 1993.

Worden, Mrs. Jean D., comp. *The New York Genealogical and Biographical Record: 113 Years Master Index, 1870-1892.* Franklin, OH: Jean D. Worden, 1983.

Atlases, Maps and Gazetteers

Catalogue of Maps and Surveys in the Offices of the Secretary of State, State Engineer and Surveyor and Comptroller and the New York State Library. Albany, New York: Charles Van Benthuysen, 1859.

French, John Homer. *Gazetteer of the State of New York. (1860) Reprinted with an Index of Names.* (1860, 1983) Reprint. Baltimore, Maryland: Genealogical Publishing Co., 1995.

Gordon, T.F. *Gazetteer of the State of New York, Comprehending Its Colonial History, General Geography, Geology, Internal Improvements; Its Political State; Minute Description of Its Several Counties, Towns, and Villages; Statistical Tables.* (1836) Reprint. Salem, Massachusetts: Higginson Book Co., 1990.

Hough, Franklin B. *Gazetteer of the State of New York, Embracing a Comprehensive Account of the History and Statistics of the State, with Geographical and Topographical Descriptions of Each County, City, Town & Village.* (1872) Reprint. Salem, Massachusetts: Higginson Book Co., 1993.

Long, John H., ed. *New York Atlas of Historical County Boundaries.* Compiled by Kathryn Ford Thorne. New York, NY: Simon & Schuster, 1993.

New York State County Atlases—Post Civil War—Reprint. 46 vols. Ovid, NY: W.E. Morrison & Co.

Thorne, Kathryn Ford. *New York Atlas of Historical County Boundaries.* New York: Simon & Schuster, 1993.

Wright, Albert H.A. *A Checklist of New York State County Maps Published 1779-1945.* Ithaca, New York: Cornell University, 1965.

Census Records

Available Census Records and Census Substitutes

Federal Census 1790, 1800, 1810, 1820, 1830, 1840, 1850, 1860, 1870, 1880, 1900, 1910, 1920, 1930.

Federal Mortality Schedules 1850, 1860, 1870, 1880.

Union Veterans and Widows 1890.

State/Territorial Census 1663-1772, 1814, 1835, 1845, 1855, 1865, 1875, 1892, 1905, 1915, 1925.

Loyalists 1782.

Dollarhide, William. *The Census Book: A Genealogist's Guide to Federal Census Facts, Schedules and Indexes.* Bountiful, Utah: Heritage Quest, 1999.

Kemp, Thomas Jay. *The American Census Handbook.* Wilmington, Delaware: Scholarly Resources, Inc., 2001.

Kirkham, E. Kay. *A Handy Guide to Record-Searching in the Larger Cities of the United States: Including a Guide to their Vital Records and Some Maps with Street Indexes with Other Information of Genealogical Value.* Logan, Utah: Everton, 1974.

Lainhart, Ann S. *State Census Records.* Baltimore: Genealogical Publishing Co., Inc., 1992.

Meyers, Carol M. *Early New York State Census Records, 1663-1772.* Gardena, California: RAM Publishers, 1965.

Szucs, Loretto Dennis, and Matthew Wright. *Finding Answers in U.S. Census Records.* Ancestry Publishing, 2001.

Thorndale, William, and William Dollarhide. *Map Guide to the U.S. Federal Censuses, 1790-1920.* Genealogical Publishing Co., 1987.

Court Records, Probate and Wills

Barber, Audrey Gertrude. *Index to Letters of Administration of New York County from 1743-1875.* 6 vols. New York: Audrey Gertrude Barber, 1950-51.

Christoph, Peter R. *New York Historical Manuscripts, English.* Baltimore: Genealogical Publishing Company, 1980-.

Christoph, Peter R. *New York Historical Manuscripts, English. Records of the Court of Assizes for the Colony of New York, 1665-1682.* Baltimore: Genealogical Publishing Company, 1983.

Cook, William Burt. *Abstracts of Albany County, NY. Probate and Family Records.* Washington, D.C.: Library of the National Society of the Daughters of the American Revolution, 1930.

Fernow, Berthold, comp. *Calendar of Wills on File and Recorded in the Offices of the Clerk of Appeals, of the County Clerk at Albany and the Secretary of State 1626-1836.* New York: Colonial Dames of the State of New York, 1896. Reprint. Baltimore: Genealogical Publishing Co., 1967.

Fernow, Berthold, ed. *The Records of New Amsterdam from 1653 to 1674 Anon Dominic.* 7 vols. New York: Knickerbockers Press, 1897.

New York State Archives. *List of Pre-1847 Court Records in the State Archives.* Albany, NY: Office of Cultural Education, 1984.

Plateau, William Smith, ed., *Abstracts of Wills on File in the Surrogate's Office, City of New York 1665-1801.* New York: New York Historical Society, 1892-1909.

Sawyer, Ray C., comp. and ed. *Index of Wills for New York County 1662-1875.* 6 vols. New York: Ray C. Sawyer, 1930-51.

Scott, Kenneth and Rosanna Conway. *New York Alien Residents 1825-1848.* Baltimore: Genealogical Publishing Co., 1978.

Scott, Kenneth, and James A. Owre, eds. *Genealogical Data from Further New York Administration Bonds 1791-1798.* vol. 11. New York: New York Genealogical and Biographical Society, 1971.

Scott, Kenneth, and James A. Owre, eds. *Genealogical Data from Inventories of New York Estates, 1666-1825.* New York: New York Genealogical and Biographical Society. 1970.

Scott, Kenneth. *Genealogical Data from New York Administration Bonds, 1753-1799 and Hitherto Unpublished Letters of Administration.* New York: New York Genealogical and Biographical Society, 1969.

Van Lear, Arnold J. F. *Register of the Provincial Secretary; Council minutes.* 4 vols. Baltimore: Genealogical Publishing, 1974.

Emmigration, Immigration, Migration and Naturalization

Bingham, Robert Warwick, ed. *Reports of Joseph Ellicott as Chief of Survey (1797-1800); And As Agent (1800-1821) of the Holland Company's Purchasers in Western New York.* Buffalo, New York: Buffalo Historical Society, 1937-41.

Bowman, Fred Q. *Landholders of Northeastern New York, 1739-1802.* Reprint. Baltimore: Genealogical Publishing Co., 1987.

Boyer, Carl. *Ship Passenger Lists, New York and New Jersey (1600-1825).* 3rd ed. Newhall, California; Carl Boyer, 1987.

Brownell, Elijah Ellsworth. *Lists of Patents of Lands, Etc. to be Sold in January 1822 for Arrears of Quit Rent.* Philadelphia: [s.n.], 1937.

Burleigh, H.C. *New York State—Confiscations of Loyalists.* Toronto, Ontario: United Empire Loyalists Association of Canada, 1970.

Calendar of N.Y. Colonial Manuscripts, Indorsed [sic] Land Papers in the Office of the Secretary of State of New York, 1643-1803. Albany, New York: Weed, Parsons and Co. 1864.

Cayman, Eugene W. *Uprooted from Prussia—Transplanted in America*. Buffalo, NY: Aircraft Printing. 1991.

Dixon, Nancy Waggoner. *Palatine Roots: The 1710 German Settlement in NY as Experienced by Johan Peter Wagner*. Rockport, Maine: Piston Press, 1994.

Gehring, Charles T. *New York Historical Manuscripts: Dutch Land Papers, Volumes GG, HH, II*. Baltimore: Genealogical Publishing Co., 1980

Hewitt, Allen E. and Joyce S. Hewitt. *Naturalization Records, Canadian Extracts*. Hamburg, New York: A.E. Jewitt, Sr.,

Jones, Henry Z. *The Palatine Families of New York: A Study of the German Immigrants Who Arrived in Colonial New York in 1710*. 2 vols. Universal City, California: Henry Z. Jones, 1985.

Kim, Sun Bok. *Landlord and Tenant in Colonial New York: Manorial Society 1664-1775*. Chapel Hill: University of North Carolina Press, 1978.

Land and Property

Livsey, Karen E. *Western New York Land Transactions, 1804-1824: Extracted from the Archives of the Holland Land Company*. 2 vols. Baltimore: Genealogical Publishing Co., 1996.

New York, Secretary of State. *The Balloting Book and Other Documents Relating to Military Bounty Lands, in the State of New York*, Albany, NY, 1825.

New York. Secretary of State. *Patents of the State of New York, 1649-1912*. Microfilm of original records at Office of General Services, B.S.R.P., Albany, New York. (Salt Lake City: Filmed by the Genealogical Society of Utah, 1973). Microfilm, 60 rolls.

O'Callaghan, E.B. *Calendar of New York Colonial Manuscripts 1643-1803*. 1864, Reprint. Rockport, Maine: Picton Press, 1987.

Pieterse, Wilhelmina C. *Inventory of the Archives of the Holland Land Company: Including the Related Amsterdam Companies and Negotiations Dealing with the Purchase of Land and State Funds in the United States of America 1789-1869*. Amsterdam: Municipal Print Office, 1976.

Scott, Kenneth and Rosanne Conway. *New York Alien Residents 1825-1848*. Baltimore: Genealogical Publishing Co., 1978

Scott, Kenneth, and Kenn Stryker-Rodda. *Denizations, Naturalizations, and Oaths of Allegiance in Colonial New York*. Baltimore: Genealogical Publishing co., 1975.

Scott, Kenneth. *Early New York Naturalizations: Abstracts of Naturalization Records from Federal, State, and Local Courts, 1792-1840*. Baltimore: Genealogical Publishing Company, 1981.

Singleton, Esther. *Dutch New York*. 1909, Reprint. Salem, MA: Higginson Books, 1994.

Yoshpe, Harry B. *The Disposition of Loyalist Estates in the Southern District of the State of New York*. New York: Columbia University Press, 1939.

Military

Adjunct General's Office. *Index of Awards on Claims of the Soldiers of the War of 1812*. Baltimore: Genealogical Publishing Co., 1963.

Bielinski, Stefan. *A Guide to the Revolutionary War Manuscripts in the New York State Library*. Albany: New York State American Revolution Bicentennial Commission, 1976.

Cosgrove, Charles H. *A History of the 134th New York Volunteer Infantry Regiment in the American Civil War, 1862-1865, Long Night's Journey into Day*. Lewiston, NY: Mellen, 1997.

Fernow, Bethold, ed., and New York State Archives. *New York in the Revolution. Documents Relating to the Colonial History of the State of New York, Vol. 15*. Albany, NY 1887. Reprint, Baltimore, Maryland: Clearfield Co., 2000.

Hastings, Hugh. State Historian. *Military Minutes of the Council of Appointments of the State of New York*. Albany, New York: State Printer, 1901.

Klein, Milton M. *New York in the American Revolution: A Bibliography*. Albany: New York State American Revolution Bicentennial Commission, 1974.

New York Adjunct General. *Registers in the War of the Rebellion*. Albany, New York: J.B. Lyon, 1894-1906.

New York Adjunct General's Office. *A Record of Commissioned Officers, Non-commissioned Officers and Privates*. Albany, New York: Comstock & Cassidy, 1864-68.

New York Historical Society. *Muster Rolls of New York Provincial Troops 1755-1764*. New York: the society, 1892.

New York, Comptroller's Office. *New York in the Revolution as a Colony and State*. 2 vols. Albany, New York: J.B. Lyon and Co., 1904.

New York, Secretary of State. *The Balloting Book and Other Documents Relating to Military Bounty Lands, in the State of New York*. Provo, Utah: Brigham Young University, 1970.

Roberts, James A. and Frederick G. Mather. *New York in the Revolution as Colony and State [Together With Supplement]*. 2 vols. in 1. (1898, 1901), Reprint. Baltimore, MD: Genealogical Publishing Co., 1996.

Saldana, Richard H., ed. *Index to the New York Spanish-American War Veterans*. 2 vols. Albany, New York: James B. Lyon, 1900.

Sons of the American Revolution. Empire State Society. *Register of the Empire State of the Sons of the American Revolution*. New York: The Society, 1899.

United States. Selective Service System. *New York, World War I Selective Service System Draft Registration Cards, 1917-1918*. Washington, D.C.: National Archives, 1987-1988.

Wilson, Thomas B. *Inhabitants of New York, 1774-1776*. Baltimore: Genealogical Publishing, 1993.

Vital and Cemetery Records

Bowman, Fred Q. *10,000 Vital Records of Eastern New York, 1777-1834*. Baltimore: Genealogical Publishing Co., 1987.

Bowman, Fred Q. *10,000 Vital Records of New York, 1813-1850*. Baltimore: Genealogical Publishing Co., 1986.

Bowman, Fred Q. *10,000 Vital Records of Western New York, 1809-1850*. Baltimore: Genealogical Publishing Co., 1985.

Bowman, Fred Q. *7,000 Hudson-Mohawk Valley (NY) Vital Records, 1808-1850*. Baltimore, Maryland: Genealogical Publishing Co., 1997.

Bowman, Fred Q. *8000 More Vital Records of Eastern New York State, 1804-1850*. Rhinebeck, New York: Kinship, 1991.

Bowman, Fred Q., and Thomas J. Lynch. *Directory to Collections of New York Vital Records, 1726-1989, with Rare Gazetteer*. Bowie, Md.: Heritage Books, 1995.

Bowman, Fred. Q. *8,000 More Vital Records of Eastern New York State, 1804-1850*. Rhinebeck, New York: Kinship, 1991.

Cormack, Marie Noll. *New York State Cemetery Inscriptions: Albany County; Herkimer County; Montgomery County; Saratoga County; Schenectady County*. Federal Writers Project of Works Progress Administration of State of New York. Microfilm. Salt Lake City: Genealogical Society of Utah, 1967.

Dilts, Brain Lee, comp. *1890 New York Veterans Census Index*. 2nd ed. Salt Lake City: Index Publishing, 1984.

Historical Records Survey (New York City). *Guide to Vital Statistics in the City of New York, Borough of Manhattan Churches*. New York: Historical Records Survey, 1942.

Historical Records Survey (New York). *Guide to Vital Statistics Records of Churches in New York State, Exclusive of New York City*. 2 v. Albany: The Survey, 1942.

New York State Cemeteries. 23 vols. Salt Lake City: Genealogical Society of Utah, 1940-69.

New York State Library. *Vital Records Card File*. Microfiche. Albany, NY: New York State Library, Photoduplication Department, 1979.

New York, Secretary of State. *Names of Persons for Whom Marriage Licenses Were Issued by the Secretary of the Province of New York, Prior to 1784*. Albany, NY: Weed, Parsons, and Co., 1860

Robison, Jeannie F.J., and Henrietta C. Bartlett, Eds. *Genealogical Records: Manuscript Entries of Births, Deaths and marriages, Taken from Family Bibles, 1581-1917*. (1917) Reprint. Baltimore, Maryland: Clearfield Co., 1995

Scott, Kenneth. *Marriages and Deaths from the New Yorker (Double Quarto Edition) 1836-1841*. Washington, D.C.: National Genealogical Society Bookstore, 1980.

County Website	Map Index	Date Created	Parent County or Territory From Which Organized Address/Details
Albany* www.albanycounty.com/	E7	1 Nov 1683	**Original county** Albany County; 250 S Pearl St; Albany, NY 12202; Ph. 518.447.4500 Details: (Hall of Rec has land rec from 1630, tax rolls from 1850, nat rec 1827-1991, Albany city directories from 1830 & m rec 1870-1946; Surr Ct has pro rec; Co Clk has div & ct rec)
Allegany www.co.allegany.ny.us/	N8	7 Apr 1806	**Genesee** Allegany County; 7 Court St; Belmont, NY 14813; Ph. 716.268.9222 Details: (Co Clk has m rec 1908-1935, div & ct rec, land rec from 1807; Clk Surr Ct has pro rec)
Bronx www.rootsweb.com/~nybronx/	E11	19 Apr 1912	**New York** Bronx County; 1780 Grand Concourse; Bronx, NY 10451-2937; Ph. 718.590.3644 Details: (Co Clk has m, div & ct rec from 1914)
Broome* www.gobroomecounty.com/index2.php	I8	28 Mar 1806	**Tioga** Broome County; 65 Hawley St; Binghamton, NY 13901-3722; Ph. 607.778.2448 Details: (Co Clk has m rec 1908-1935, mil rolls from 1808, nat rec from 1860, div, ct & land rec & state cen; Surr Ct has pro rec from 1806; Twn & City Clks have b, m, d & bur rec from 1880)
Cattaraugus* www.co.cattaraugus.ny.us/	P8	11 Mar 1808	**Genesee** Cattaraugus County; 303 Court St; Little Valley, NY 14755; Ph. 716.938.9111 Details: (Co Clk has div & land rec from 1808, ct rec from 1850 & nat rec; Surr Ct has pro rec; Twn & City Clks have b, m & d rec)
Cayuga www.co.cayuga.ny.us/	K7	8 Mar 1799	**Onondaga** Cayuga County; 160 Genesee St; Auburn, NY 13021; Ph. 315.253.1271 Details: (Co Clk has pro & ct rec from 1799, land rec from 1794 & DAR co cem rec 1790-1960; Twn & City Clks have b, m & d rec)
Charlotte www.rootsweb.com/~nycharlo/ charlotte.htm		12 Mar 1772	**Albany** Details: (see Washington) (Name changed to Washington 2 Apr 1784)
Chautauqua www.chautauqua-ny.com/	Q8	11 Mar 1808	**Genesee** Chautauqua County; 1 N Erie St; Mayville, NY 14757; Ph. 716.753.4331 Details: (Co Clk has m rec from 1908, div, ct & land rec from 1811; Surr Ct has pro rec; Twn or City Clks have b, m, d & bur rec)
Chemung* www.chemungcounty.com/	K8	29 Mar 1836	**Tioga** Chemung County; 210 Lake St; PO Box 588; Elmira, NY 14901; Ph. 607.737.2920 Details: (Co Clk has m rec 1908-1936, div, ct & land rec; Surr Ct has pro rec; Twn Clks have b, m, & d rec)
Chenango www.chenango.com/	I7	15 Mar 1798	**Herkimer, Tioga** Chenango County; 5 Court St; Norwich, NY 13815; Ph. 607.337.4575 Details: (Co Clk has m, div, ct & land rec; Surr Ct has pro rec; Twn Clks have b, m & d rec)
Clinton www.co.clinton.ny.us/	E1	7 Mar 1788	**Washington** Clinton County; 137 Margaret St; Plattsburgh, NY 12901; Ph. 518.565.4700 Details: (Co Clk has div rec from 1869, land rec from 1778 & state cen; Surr Ct has pro rec; Twn & City Clks have b, m & d rec)
Columbia www.rootsweb.com/~nycolumb/	E8	4 Apr 1786	**Albany** Columbia County; 401 Union St; Hudson, NY 12534; Ph. 518.828.3339 Details: (Co Clk has m rec 1908-1934, ct rec from 1825, land rec from 1790 & nat rec from 1853; Surr Ct has pro rec from 1787; Twn Clks have b, m & d rec)
Cortland www2.cortland-co.org/	J7	8 Apr 1808	**Onondaga** Cortland County; 46 Greenbush St; PO Box 5590; Cortland, NY 13045; Ph. 607.753.5021 Details: (Co Clk has m rec 1910-1935, div rec, ct & land rec from 1808, nat rec 1831-1848 & 1871-1929; Surr Ct has pro rec; Twn & City Clks have b, m & d rec)

County Website	Map Index	Date Created	Parent County or Territory From Which Organized Address/Details
Delaware www.delawarecounty.net/	G8	10 Mar 1797	**Ulster, Otsego** Delaware County; Courthouse Sq; Delhi, NY 13753-1081; Ph. 607.746.2123 Details: (Co Clk has m rec 1908-1931, div, ct & land rec from 1797, nat rec from 1810 & state cen; Surr Ct has pro rec; Twn Clks have b, m, d & bur rec)
Dutchess www.dutchessny.gov/	E9	1 Nov 1683	**Original county** Dutchess County; 22 Market St; Poughkeepsie, NY 12601-3233; Ph. 914.486.2120 Details: (Co Clk has m rec 1908-1935, div & ct rec from 1847, land rec from 1718 & state cen; Surr Ct has pro rec; Twn & City Clks have b, m & d rec; Co Archives has tax rolls 1854-1954 & colonial ct rec 1730-1799)
Erie www.erie.gov/	P7	2 Apr 1821	**Niagara** Erie County; 25 Delaware Ave; Buffalo, NY 14202-3968; Ph. 716.858.8785 Details: (Co Clk has m rec, div & ct rec from 1809 & land rec from 1810; Surr Ct has pro rec)
Essex www.rootsweb.com/~nyessex/	E3	1 Mar 1799	**Clinton** Essex County; 100 Court St; Elizabethtown, NY 12932; Ph. 518.873.3600 Details: (Co Clk has m rec 1908-1936, div rec from 1936, pro, ct & land rec from 1799 & state cen; Twn & City Clks have b, m, d & bur rec)
Franklin www.adirondacklakes.com/	F2	11 Mar 1808	**Clinton** Franklin County; 63 W Main St; Malone, NY 12953-1817; Ph. 518.481.6767 Details: (Co Clk has m rec 1908-1935, some div rec from 1808 & ct rec from 1808; Surr Ct has pro rec; Twn Clks have b, m & d rec)
Fulton www.fulton.ny.us/	F6	18 Apr 1838	**Montgomery** Fulton County; 223 W Main St; Johnstown, NY 12095; Ph. 518.736.5555 Details: (Co Clk has m rec 1900-1926, land & ct rec; Surr Ct has pro rec)
Genesee www.co.genesee.ny.us/	O6	30 Mar 1802	**Ontario** Genesee County; 15 Main St; Batavia, NY 14020; Ph. 716.344.2580 Details: (Co Clk has m rec 1908-1934, div, ct & land rec from 1802 & state cen; Surr Ct has pro rec; Twn & City Clks have b, m, d & bur rec)
Greene www.greene-ny.com/	F8	25 Mar 1800	**Ulster, Albany** Greene County; 320 Main St; Catskill, NY 12414-1396; Ph. 518.943.2050 Details: (Co Clk has m rec 1900-1935, div, ct & land rec from 1800; Surr Ct has pro rec; Twn Clks have b, m & d rec)
Hamilton www.hamiltoncounty.com/	G4	12 Apr 1816	**Montgomery** Hamilton County; RR 8 Box 204; Lake Pleasant, NY 12108; Ph. 518.548.7111 Details: (Co Clk has div, ct & land rec; Surr Ct has pro rec; Twn & City Clks have b, m, d & bur rec)
Herkimer www.rootsweb.com/~nyherkim/	H5	16 Feb 1791	**Montgomery** Herkimer County; 109 Mary St; Herkimer, NY 13350; Ph. 315.867.1002 Details: (Co Clk has m rec 1908-1934, div, ct & land rec; Surr Ct has pro rec)
Jefferson www.sunyjefferson.edu/JC/	J3	28 Mar 1805	**Oneida** Jefferson County; 175 Arsenal St; Watertown, NY 13601-2522; Ph. 315.785.3081 Details: (Co Clk has m rec 1908-1935, land & ct rec from 1805, nat rec from early 1800's-1970, mil dis rec from 1861 & state cen; Surr Ct has pro rec from early 1800's)
Kings community-2.webtv.net/shamrockroots/ kingsny/	E12	1 Nov 1683	**Original county** Kings County; 360 Adams St; Brooklyn, NY 11201-3712; Ph. 718.643.5897 Details: (Dept of Hlth, Brooklyn Borough Office, 295 Flatbush Ave. Extension, Brooklyn, NY 11201 has b, d & bur rec; City Clk, Mun. Bldg, Brooklyn, NY 11201 has m rec; Co Clk, Sup Ct Bldg, 360 Adams St., Brooklyn, NY 11201 has div rec; Surr Ct, Sup Ct Bldg, 360 Adams St., Brooklyn, NY 11201 has pro rec; Clk Civ Ct, 120 Schermerhorn St., Brooklyn NY 11201 has ct rec; Co Reg, Municipal Bldg, Joralemon & Court Sts, Brooklyn, NY 11201 has land rec)
Lewis www.adirondacks.org/lewiscounty/	I4	28 Mar 1805	**Oneida** Lewis County; 7660 N State St; Box 232; Lowville, NY 13367-1328; Ph. 315.376.5333 Details: (Co Clk has incomplete b & d rec 1847-1852, div & ct rec from 1907, land rec from 1805, nat rec 1808-1906, mil rolls 1862-1866 & state cen 1825-1925; Surr Ct has pro rec)

County Website	Map Index	Date Created	Parent County or Territory From Which Organized Address/Details
Livingston www.co.livingston.state.ny.us/	N6	23 Feb 1821	**Genesee, Ontario** Livingston County; 6 Court St, #201; Geneseo, NY 14454; Ph. 716.243.7030 Details: (Co Clk has div, ct & land rec from 1821; Surr Ct has pro rec)
Madison www.madisoncounty.org/	I7	21 Mar 1806	**Chenango** Madison County; N Court St; Wampsville, NY 13163; Ph. 315.366.2261 Details: (Co Clk has m rec 1905-1934, div rec from 1900, ct rec from 1889 & land rec from 1806; Surr Ct has pro rec; Twn Clks have b, m, d & bur rec)
Monroe www.co.monroe.ny.us/	N5	23 Feb 1821	**Genesee, Ontario** Monroe County; 39 Main St W; Rochester, NY 14614-1408; Ph. 716.428.5151 Details: (Co Clk has m rec 1908-1935, div & ct rec from 1860, land rec from 1821 & nat rec from 1822; Surr Ct has pro rec; Twn Clks have m & bur rec; Co Hlth Dept, 111 Westfall Rd., Rochester, NY 14620 has b & d rec; Co Historian, 39 Main St. W., Rochester, NY has state cen)
Montgomery www.montgomeryny.com/	F6	12 Mar 1772	**Albany** Montgomery County; PO Box 1500; Fonda, NY 12068; Ph. 518.853.8111 Details: (Formerly Tryon Co. Name changed to Montgomery 2 Apr 1784) (Co Clk has m rec 1908-1935, div & ct rec from 1795, land rec from 1772, state cen, nat rec from 1850 & survey maps; Surr Ct has pro rec; Twn & City Clks have b, m, d & bur rec)
Nassau www.co.nassau.ny.us/	D12	27 Apr 1898	**Queens** Nassau County; 240 Old Country Rd; Mineola, NY 11501; Ph. 516.571.2663 Details: (Co Clk has m rec 1907-1935, div, ct & land rec from 1899; Surr Ct has pro rec; Twn Clks have b, m & d rec)
New York home.nyc.gov/portal/ index.jsp?pageID=nyc_home	E12	1 Nov 1683	**Original county** New York County; 60 Centre St; New York, NY 10007-1402; Ph. 212.374.8361 Details: (Co Clk has div rec from 1754, nat rec 1794-1924 & state cen; Surr Ct has pro rec)
Niagara www.niagaracounty.com/Insight/ customindex/NCHome.cfm?SID=2	P6	11 Mar 1808	**Genesee** Niagara County; 175 Hawley St; Lockport, NY 14094; Ph. 716.439.7022 Details: (Co Clk has m rec 1908-1935, div rec from 1850, ct & land rec; Surr Ct has pro rec; Twn & City Clks have b, m, d & bur rec)
Oneida www.oneidacounty.org/	I5	15 Mar 1798	**Herkimer** Oneida County; 800 Park Ave; Utica, NY 13501; Ph. 315.798.5775 Details: (Co Clk has div & ct rec, land rec from 1791; Surr Ct has pro rec; Twn Clks have b, m, d & bur rec)
Onondaga www.co.onondaga.ny.us/	J6	5 Mar 1794	**Herkimer** Onondaga County; 200 Courthouse; Syracuse, NY 13202-2984; Ph. 315.435.2226 Details: (Co Clk has land, div & ct rec from 1795, nat rec from 1808, state cen 1850-1925 & mil rec from 1917; Surr Ct has pro rec; Bur of Vit Stat has b, d & bur rec from 1865; Twn & City Clks have m rec)
Ontario www.co.ontario.ny.us/	M6	27 Jan 1789	**Montgomery** Ontario County; 20 Ontario St; Canandaigua, NY 14424; Ph. 716.396.4200 Details: (Rcds Management Officer has m rec 1908-1933, div rec from 1887, pro, ct & land rec from 1789, Revolutionary War service rec 1820-1832, mil rosters 1862-1920, state cen, co maps from 1798 & nat rec 1803-1954; Twn & City Clks have b & d rec)
Orange www.co.orange.ny.us/	F10	1 Nov 1683	**Original county** Orange County; 255-275 Main St; Goshen, NY 10924; Ph. 914.294.5151 Details: (Co Clk has m rec 1908-1933, div & ct rec from 1852, land rec from 1703 & cen rec; Surr Ct has pro rec)
Orleans www.orleansny.com/	O5	12 Nov 1824	**Genesee** Orleans County; Courthouse Sq; Albion, NY 14411; Ph. 716.589.5334 Details: (Co Clk has div & ct rec from 1880, land rec from 1826 & state cen; Surr Ct has pro rec; Twn & City Clks have b, m & d rec)

County Website	Map Index	Date Created	Parent County or Territory From Which Organized Address/Details
Oswego www.co.oswego.ny.us/	J5	1 Mar 1816	**Oneida, Onondaga** Oswego County; 46 E Bridge St; Oswego, NY 13126; Ph. 315.349.8385 Details: (Co Clk has m rec 1907-1934, some div rec, ct rec, land rec from 1791 & mil dis rec; Rec Center has state cen 1850-1925, nat rec 1830's-1950's & some bur rec; Surr Ct has pro rec; City & Twn Clks have b & d rec)
Otsego www.otsegocounty.com/	H7	16 Feb 1791	**Montgomery** Otsego County; 197 Main St; Cooperstown, NY 13326; Ph. 607.547.4276 Details: (Co Clk has m rec 1908-1936, div rec from 1900, ct rec from 1891 & land rec from 1791; Surr Ct has pro rec; Twn & City Clks have b, m & d rec)
Putnam putnamcounty@bestweb.net	E10	12 Jun 1812	**Dutchess** Putnam County; 40 Gleneida Ave; Carmel, NY 10512; Ph. 845.225.3641 Details: (Co Clk has div rec from 1880, pro rec, ct rec from 1820 & land rec from 1814; Twn Clks have b, m, d & bur rec)
Queens www.rootsweb.com/~nyqueens/	E12	1 Nov 1683	**Original county** Queens County; 88-11 Sutphin Blvd; Jamaica, NY 11435-3716; Ph. 718.520.3700 Details: (Co Clk has state cen, div rec, nat rec 1794-1941; Surr Ct has pro rec; NYC Municipal Archives has b, m & d rec; City Reg has land rec; City of NY has ct rec)
Rensselaer www.rensco.com/	D7	7 Feb 1791	**Albany** Rensselaer County; Courthouse; Troy, NY 12180; Ph. 518.270.4080 Details: (Co Clk has m rec 1908-1930's, div, ct & land rec from 1791, nat rec from 1830 & maps; Surr Ct has pro rec)
Richmond www.rootsweb.com/~nyrichmo/	F12	1 Nov 1683	**Original county** Richmond County; 18 Richmond Terr; Staten Island, NY 10301-1935; Ph. 718.390.5386 Details: (Surr Ct has pro rec; Co Clk has land rec; Co Hlth Dept has m & d rec)
Rockland www.co.rockland.ny.us/	F11	23 Feb 1798	**Orange** Rockland County; 27 New Hempstead Rd; New City, NY 10956-3636; Ph. 845.638.5070 Details: (Co Clk has m rec 1908-1935, div, ct & land rec; Surr Ct has pro rec)
Saratoga www.co.saratoga.ny.us/	E6	7 Feb 1791	**Albany** Saratoga County; 40 McMasters St; Ballston Spa, NY 12020-1999; Ph. 518.885.2213 Details: (Co Clk has m rec 1908-1935, div, ct & land rec from 1791; Surr Ct has pro rec)
Schenectady govt.co.schenectady.ny.us/	F7	7 Mar 1809	**Albany** Schenectady County; 620 State St; Schenectady, NY 12305-2113; Ph. 518.388.4220 Details: (Co Clk has m rec 1908-1930, div & ct rec from 1858, land rec & maps from 1630, city directories; Surr Ct has pro rec)
Schoharie www.schopeg.org/schcnet/govt/ cntygovm.html	F7	6 Apr 1795	**Albany, Otsego** Schoharie County; 300 Main St; PO Box 549; Schoharie, NY 12157-0549; Ph. 518.295.8316 Details: (Co Clk has div, ct & land rec; Surr Ct has pro rec; Twn Clks have b, m & d rec)
Schuyler www.lightlink.com/schco/	L8	17 Apr 1854	**Tompkins, Steuben, Chemung** Schuyler County; 105 9th St; Watkins Glen, NY 14891; Ph. 607.535.8133 Details: (Co Clk has div, ct & land rec from 1854 & state cen; Surr Ct has pro rec; Twn Clks have b, m, d & bur rec)
Seneca www.co.seneca.ny.us/	L6	24 Mar 1804	**Cayuga** Seneca County; 1 DiPronio Dr; Waterloo, NY 13165; Ph. 315.539.1770 Details: (Co Seat is Waterloo; ct is held at Waterloo & Ovid; no rec kept at Ovid; Co Clk has div & ct rec from 1900 & land rec from 1804; Surr Ct has pro rec; Twn & City Clks have b, m, d & bur rec)
St. Lawrence www.st-lawrence.ny.us/	H2	3 Mar 1802	**Clinton, Herkimer, Montgomery** St. Lawrence County; 48 Court St; Canton, NY 13617; Ph. 315.379.2237 Details: (Co Clk has div, ct & land rec from 1802; Surr Ct has pro rec; Twn Clks have b, m & d rec)

Notes

Dogwood

NORTH CAROLINA

CAPITAL: RALEIGH – STATE 1789 (12TH)

Sir Walter Raleigh received a grant from Queen Elizabeth in 1584, which he used to colonize North Carolina. Raleigh's first expedition in 1584 produced glowing reports of Roanoke Island. These reports led to attempts to establish a permanent colony in 1585. Internal and external problems led the settlers to return to England the following year with Sir Francis Drake. In 1587, another group was sent, headed by John White. He returned to England later in the year in desperate need of supplies. It took him three years to return, at which time the settlement had vanished with only carvings on trees as evidence of inhabitance.

The first permanent settlement was started in 1653, when groups from Virginia occupied the section north of the Albemarle Sound. North Carolina was first differentiated from South Carolina in 1691, but was ruled by governors from South Carolina until 1711. From 1706 to 1725, French Huguenot, German, and Swiss settlers founded towns near the coast. Between 1730 and 1770, with the heaviest influx around 1746, Scottish Highlanders came to North Carolina. Large groups of Scotch-Irish left Pennsylvania via the Shenandoah Valley to settle in Virginia. Many continued on to North Carolina. They settled mostly in the western section of the state around present-day Iredell County and numbered 20,000 in just a few years. By 1760, Germans in Forsyth and Guilford counties numbered 15,000. A colony of English speaking Quakers from Virginia, Pennsylvania, and Nantucket settled in Rockingham, Guilford, and Chatham Counties.

On achieving statehood, North Carolina ceded Tennessee to the United States. By 1850, a quarter of native North Carolinians had left to live in other states or territories. North Carolina seceded from the Union in 1861. It provided the most troops of any state to the Confederacy, an estimated 125,000. North Carolina also had the most casualties of war; more than 40,000 were killed. Union forces received more than 3,000 soldiers from North Carolina. North Carolina was readmitted to the Union in 1868. Between 1862 and 1907, 24 counties in southern and western North Carolina lost many records to fire or war.

Look for vital records in the following locations:
Note: Most genealogical county records up to about 1910

can be located in the *North Carolina State Archives, Raleigh, North Carolina.*

- **Birth and death records:** Counties where births and deaths occurred kept duplicate copies of information sent to the state. None of the parish registers containing records of births or deaths prior to 1820 have survived. North Carolina Vital Records in Raleigh has birth records from October 1913, and death records from 1 January 1930. Death records from 1913 through 1929 are available from the Archives and Records Section, State Records Center in Raleigh.

- **Marriage records:** After 1741, prior to marriage, one had the choice of publishing banns or buying a license, which required posting of a bond. Surviving marriage bonds, except for Granville and Davie counties, are in the North Carolina State Archives. They contain the names of the groom, the bride, the other bondsman, and the witness. None of the marriage records from before 1820 have survived. North Carolina Vital Records in Raleigh has marriage records from January 1962.

- **Land and census records:** Although many early land grants have been lost, there are still many at the Land Office in Raleigh, North Carolina. They are also on microfilm at the State Archives. Many of these records have been transcribed and indexed by the Alvaretta Kenan Register in the book *State Censuses of North Carolina, 1784-1787*, published by Genealogical Publishing Company, 1973. In 1784, the U.S. Continental Congress demanded a list of inhabitants. The surviving lists have been indexed and published.

North Carolina State Archives
109 East Jones Street
Raleigh, North Carolina 27611

North Carolina Vital Records
PO Box 29537
Raleigh, North Carolina 27626

Land Office, Secretary of State
Administration Building
Raleigh, North Carolina 27603

Archives and Records Section
State Records Center
215 North Blount Street
Raleigh, North Carolina 27602
919.733.3526

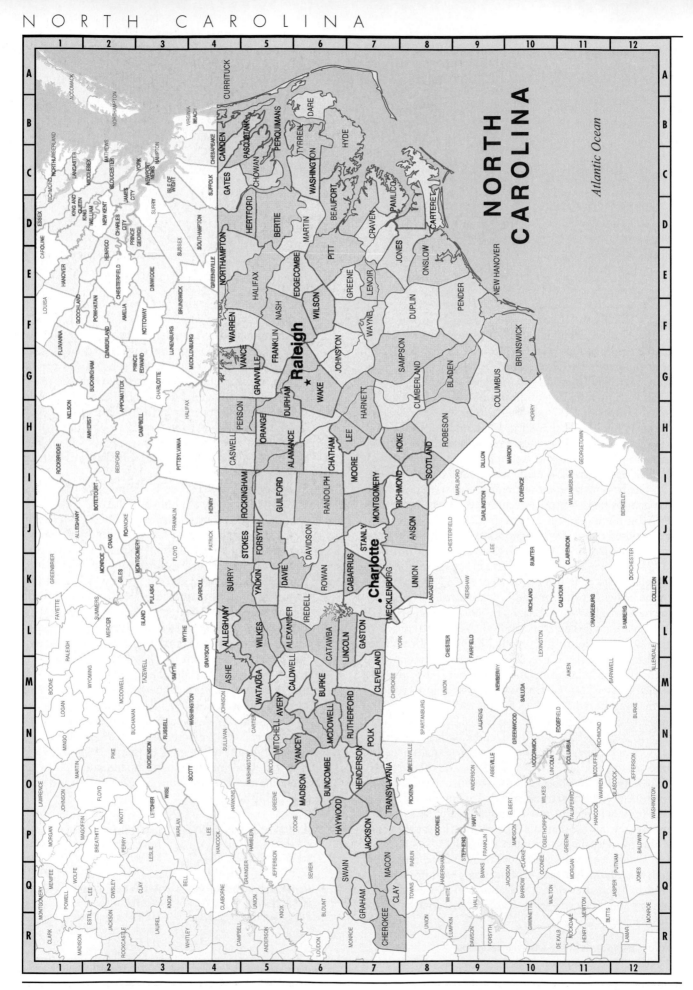

Societies and Repositories

Afro-American Heritage Society of North Carolina; PO Box 26334; Raleigh, North Carolina 27611

Alamance Battleground Chapter; 804 West Davis Street; Burlington, North Carolina 27215; 336.228.0766

Alamance County, North Carolina Genealogical Society; PO Box 3052; Burlington, North Carolina 27215-3052

Albemarle Genealogical Society; PO Box 87; Currituck, North Carolina 27929

Alexander County Ancestry Association; PO Box 241; Hiddenite, North Carolina 28636-0241; <www.Alexnews.com>

Alexander County Genealogical Society, Inc; PO Box 545; Hiddenite, North Carolina 28636

Alleghany Historical-Genealogical Society; PO Box 817; Sparta, North Carolina 28675

Anson County Genealogical Society; 108 Sunset Drive 300 Moores Lake Road; Wadesboro, North Carolina 28170

Archives and Records Section; 109 E. Jones St.; Raleigh, North Carolina 27602; 919.737.3952

Ashe County Historical Society; 148 Library Dr.; West Jefferson, North Carolina 28694

Baptist Historical Collection, Wake Forest University; PO Box 7777; Winston-Salem, North Carolina 27109; 910.759.5472; Fax 910.759.9831

Beaufort County Genealogical Society; PO Box 1089; Washington, North Carolina 27889-1089

Bethabara Chapter; PO Box 5442; Winston-Salem, North Carolina 27104; 336.472.2757

Bladen County Historical Society; PO Box 849; Elizabethtown, North Carolina 28337

Blue Ridge Chapter, SAR; 337 Vanderbilt Road; Asheville, North Carolina 28803; 828.274.3169; 828.274.5429

Broad River Genealogical Society; PO Box 2261; Shelby, North Carolina 28151-2261

Burke Co. Public Library; 204 South King St.; Morganton, North Carolina 28655

Burke County Genealogical Society; PO Box 661; Morganton, North Carolina 28655; <www.rootsweb.com/~ncburke/>

Cabarrus Genealogical Society; PO Box 2981; Concord, North Carolina 28025-2981; <sheilaw@webkorner.com>; <www.rootsweb.com/~nccgs/index.htm>

Caldwell County Genealogical Society; PO Box 2476; Lenior, North Carolina 28645-2476

Carolinas Genealogical Society; PO Box 397; Monroe, North Carolina 28111-0397

Carteret County Historical Society; PO Box 481; 100 Wallace Road; Morehead City, North Carolina 28557.0481; 252.247.7533

Cary Historical Society; PO Box 134; Cary, North Carolina 27511

Caswell County Historical Association; PO Box 278; Yanceyville, North Carolina 27379

Catawba County Genealogical Society; PO Box 2406; Hickory, North Carolina 28603; <www.co.catawba.nc.us/otheragency/ccgs/ccgsmain.htm>

Catawba Valley Chapter, SAR; 165 Lakeshore Lane; Taylorsville, North Carolina 28681; 704.495.4402

Charlotte Jewish Historical Society; 5007 Providence Rd.; Charlotte, North Carolina 28226

Chatham County Historical Association; PO Box 913; Pittsboro, North Carolina 27312-0913

Cumberland County Genealogical Society; PO Box 53299; Fayetteville, North Carolina 28305-3299

Davidson Co. Public Library; 602 S. Main St.; Lexington, North Carolina 27292

Davie County Historical & Genealogical Society; 371 N. Main St.; Mocksville, North Carolina 27038

Dept. of Environment Health, and Natural Resources, Vital Records Section; 225 N. McDowell St., PO Box 29537; Raleigh, North Carolina 27626-0537; 919.733.3526

Descendants of The Knights of The Bath, North Carolina Society; 1404 Shadyside Dr.; Raleigh, North Carolina 27612

Division of Archives & Reports, Office of Archives & Hist.; 109 E. Jones St.; Raleigh, North Carolina 27611

Division of the State Library, Archives and History-State Library Building; 109 East Jones Street; Raleigh, North Carolina 27611; 919.733.2570; Fax 919.733.8748

Duke University, William R. Perkins Library, Manuscript Department; 217 Perkins Library, PO Box 90185; Durham, North Carolina 27706; 919.660.5820; Fax 919.684.2885

Duplin County Historical Society; PO Box 220; Rose Hill, North Carolina 28458-0220; <www.duplinnet.com/historicalsociety/index.htm>

Durham.Orange Genealogical Society; PO Box 4703; Chapel Hill, North Carolina 27515-4703; 919.477.7257; <www.rootsweb.com/~ncdogs>

Eastern North Carolina Genealogical Society; PO Box 395; New Bern, North Carolina 28560

Edgecombe County Genealogical Society; 909 Main St.; Tarboro, North Carolina 27886

Family History Library: 35 North West Temple Street: Salt Lake City, Utah 84150: 800.346.6044 or 801.240.2584: <www.familysearch.org>: Find a Family History Center near you: <www.familysearch.org/Eng/Library/FHC/frameset_fhc.asp>

Family Research Society of Northeastern North Carolina; 106 S. McMorrine St., Suite 6; Elizabeth City, North Carolina 27909-4449; <www.geocities.com/heartland/farm/7890/>

Forsyth County Genealogical Society; PO Box 5715; Winston-Salem, North Carolina 27113-5715; <www.usgennet.org/alhnncus/ahncfors>

Free Will Baptist Collections, Moye Library, Mount Olive College; 634 Henderson St.; Mount Olive, North Carolina 28365; 919.658.7168; Fax 919.658.7180

Gaston/Lincoln Genealogical Society; PO Box 584; Mount Holly, North Carolina 28120

Gates County Historical Society; PO Box 98; Gates, North Carolina 27937

Genealogical Society of Davidson County; PO Box 1665; Lexington, North Carolina 27292.1665

Genealogical Society of Iredell County; PO Box 946; Statesville, North Carolina 28677

Genealogical Society of Old Tryon Co., North Carolina, Inc.; #2 W. Main St., PO Box 938; Forest City, North Carolina 28043-0938

Genealogical Society of Rowan County; PO Box 4305; Salisbury, North Carolina 28145-4305

General Francis Nash Chapter, SAR; 13 Clearwater Drive; Durham, North Carolina 27707; 919.403.1998

Granville County Genealogical Society, Inc.; PO Box 1746; Oxford, North Carolina 27565-1746

Guilford County Genealogical Society; PO Box 9693; Greensboro, North Carolina 27429-0693; <www.greensboro.com/gcgs>

Halifax County Genealogical Society; PO Box 447; Halifax, North Carolina 27839

Harnett County Genealogical Society; PO Box 219; Buies Creek, North Carolina 27506-0219

Haywood County Genealogical Society, Inc.; PO Box 1331; Waynesville, North Carolina 28786-1331; <www.rootsweb.com/~nchcgs>

Henderson County Genealogical & Historical Society; 432 N. Main St.; Hendersonville, North Carolina 28739; <www.brinet.com/~hcgenhis>

Historic Foundation of the Presbyterian and Reformed Churches; Montreat, North Carolina 28757

Hyde County Historical & Genealogical Society; 7820 Piney Woods Rd; Fairfield, North Carolina 27826; <www.rootsweb.com/~nchyde/HCHGS.HTM>

Independent Order of Odd Fellows, Sovereign Grand Lodge; I.O.O.F.; 422 North Trade St.; Winston-Salem, North Carolina 27101-2830

Jackson County Genealogical Society; PO Box 2108; Cullowee, North Carolina 28723; <www.main.nc.us/jcgs>

Jewish Genealogical Society of Raleigh; 8701 Sleepy Creek Dr.; Raleigh, North Carolina 27612

Johnston County Genealogical Society; PO Box 2373; Smithfield, North Carolina 27577-2373

Kinfolk Trackers Genealogical Society; PO Box 1344; New Bern, North Carolina 28563-1344

Kinfolk Trackers; 8375 Hwy 306 South; Arapahoe, North Carolina 28510; <www2.always.online.com/kintracker/>

Lee County Genealogical Society; PO Box 3216; Sanford, North Carolina 27331-3216

Lincoln County Public Library, Lincoln County Room; 306 W. Main St.; Lincolnton, North Carolina 28092; 704.735.8044; Fax 704.732.9042

Lower Cape Fear Chapter, SAR; 900 Seven Oaks Drive; Wilmington, North Carolina 28405; 910.686.9914; 910.686.1768

Lt. Col. Felix Walker Chapter, SAR; 25 Monte Vista Circle; Candler, North Carolina 28715; 828.665.1887

Lt. Col. John Phifer Chapter, SAR; 692 Williamsburg Court; Concord, North Carolina 28025-2538; 704.788.2697

Lutheran, Archives of the North Carolina Synod; 1988 Lutheran Synod Dr.; Salisbury, North Carolina 28144-5700; 704.633.4861; Fax 704.638.0508

Marquis de Lafayette Chapter, SAR; 5360 Amberhill Court; Fayetteville, North Carolina 28311; 910.482.3991

Mecklenburg Chapter, SAR; 9125 B.1 Fishers Pond Drive; Charlotte, North Carolina 28277; 704.541.0881

Mecklenburg, North Carolina Genealogical Society; PO Box 32453; Charlotte, North Carolina 28232; <www.rootsweb.com/~ncomgs/>

Methodist, United Methodist Church Archives, Drew University; 36 Madison Ave.; Madison, New Jersey 07940; 201.408.3590; Fax 201.408.3939

Methodist, Western N.C. Conference Depository; Shamrock Drive, PO Box 12005; Charlotte, North Carolina 28205

Montgomery County Historical Society; PO Box 161; Mount Gilead, North Carolina 27366

Moravian Archives; 4 East Bank Street; Winston-Salem, North Carolina 27101; 910.722.1742

Nathanael Greene Chapter, SAR; 1106 Gretchen Lane; Greensboro, North Carolina 27410; 336.292.4690

National Archives-Southeast Region; 1557 St. Joseph Avenue; East Point, Georgia 30344; 404.763.7477; Fax 404.763.7477

New Bern Chapter, SAR; 812 Plantation Drive; New Bern, North Carolina 28562; 252.633.3450

North Carolina Genealogical Society of Rockingham and Stokes Counties; PO Box 152; Mayodan, North Carolina 27027-0152; <ns.netmcr.com/~lonabec/gsrsinfo.html>

North Carolina Genealogical Society; PO Box 1492, Dept. E; Raleigh, North Carolina 27602; <www.rootsweb.com/~ncgs/>

North Carolina Society of County and Local Historians; 1209 Hill St.; Greensboro, North Carolina 27408

North Carolina State Archives; 109 E. Jones St.; Raleigh, North Carolina 27601; 919.733.1354; <www.ah.dcr.state.nc.us/sections/archives/arch/>

Old Buncombe County Genealogical Society; PO Box 2122; 85 Tunnel Rd.; Innsbruck Mall, Suite 22; Asheville, North Carolina 28802-2122; 828.253.1894;

Old Dobbs County Genealogical Society; PO Box 617; Goldsboro, North Carolina 27530

Old New Hanover County Genealogical Society; PO Box 2536; Wilmington, North Carolina 28402-2536; <www.co.new.hanover.nc.us/lib/oldnew.htm>

Old Tryon County Genealogical Society; PO Box 938; Forest City, North Carolina 28043

Olde Mecklenburg Genealogical Society; PO Box 32453; Charlotte, North Carolina 28232-2453; <www.rootsweb.com/~ncomgs/>

Onslow County Genealogical Society; PO Box 1739; Jacksonville, North Carolina 28541-1739

Pack Memorial Public Library; 67 Haywood St.; Asheville, North Carolina 28801

PAF-Finders Club; 8501 Southampton Dr.; Raleigh, North Carolina 27615

Pitt County Family Researchers; PO Box 20339; Greenville, North Carolina 27858.0339; <www.rootsweb.com/~ncpcfr/>

Polk County North Carolina Genealogical Society; 485 Hunting Country Rd.; Tryon, North Carolina 28782

Presbyterian Church, Department of History; PO Box 849; Montreat, North Carolina 27410; 704.669.7061; Fax 704.669.5369

Presbyterian, Southern Region, Presbyterian Church (USA) Dept. of History; 318 Georgia Terrace, PO Box 849; Montreat, North Carolina 28757; 704.669.7061; Fax 704.669.5369

Public Library of Charlotte and Mecklenburg Co.; 310 N. Tyron St.; Charlotte, North Carolina 28202

Raleigh Chapter, SAR; 2108 Weybridge Dr.; Raleigh, North Carolina 27615; 919.954.9956

Randolph County Genealogical Society; PO Box 4394; Asheboro, North Carolina 27204; <www.rootsweb.com/~ncrcgs/>

Richard H. Thornton, Memorial Library; PO Box 339, Main & Spring Sts.; Oxford, North Carolina 27565

Robeson Co. Public Library; PO Box 1346, 101 N. Chestnut St.; Lumberton, North Carolina 28358

Rockingham County Historical Society; PO Box 84; Wentworth, North Carolina 27375

Rowan Public Library; 201 W. Fisher St., PO Box 1009; Salisbury, North Carolina 28144

Salisbury Chapter, SAR; 114 Ridge Creek Road; Salisbury, North Carolina 28147; 704.639.9845; 704.639.7502

Sandhill Regional Library; PO Box 548, 1104 E. Broad Ave.; Rockingham, North Carolina 28379

Scotland County Genealogical Society, Inc.; PO Box 496; Laurel Hill, North Carolina 28351-0496; <www.txdirect.net/~hpeele/society/scgs.htm>

Silas McDowell Chapter, SAR; 796 Laurel Ridge; Franklin, North Carolina 28744

Society of Friends, Quaker Collections, Guilford College Library; 5800 West Friendly Ave.; Greensboro, North Carolina 27410; 910.316.2450; Fax 910.316.2950

Society of Richmond County Descendants; PO Box 848, Desk 120; Rockingham, North Carolina 28379

Sons of the American Revolution, North Carolina Society; 2221 Oleander Dr.; Wilmington, North Carolina 28403

Southeastern North Carolina Genealogical Society; PO Box 468; Chadbourn, North Carolina 28431.0468; <www.spiritdesign.net/columbus/sencgs.htm>

Southport Historical Society; 501 N. Atlantic Ave.; Southport, North Carolina 28461

Southwestern North Carolina Genealogical Society; 101 Blumenthal; Murphy, North Carolina 28906

Stanley County Genealogical Society; PO Box 31; Albemarle, North Carolina 28001

Surry County Genealogical Society; PO Box 997; Dobson, North Carolina 27017-0997

Swain County, North Carolina Genealogical and Historical Society; PO Box 267; Bryson City, North Carolina 28713

Thomas Hackney Braswell Memorial Library; 334 Falls Rd.; Rocky Mount, North Carolina 27801

Toe Valley Genealogical Society; 491 Beaver Creek Road; Spruce Pine, North Carolina 28777

Union Co. Heritage Rm., 1st Floor Old Courthouse; PO Box 397, 300 N. Main St.; Monroe, North Carolina 28111; 704.289.6737

Union Co. Public Library; 316 E. Windsor; Monroe, North Carolina 28110; 412.437.1165

University of North Carolina at Chapel Hill, Wilson Library, North Carolina Collection; CB 9330; Chapel Hill, North Carolina 27514-8890; 919.962.1172; Fax 919.962.4452

University of North Carolina Library; Drawer 870; Chapel Hill, North Carolina 27514

Wake County Genealogical Society; PO Box 17713; Raleigh, North Carolina 27619-7713; <www.rtpnet.org/wcgs/>

Wayne County Historical Association; PO Box 665; Goldsboro, North Carolina 27530

Wilkes Genealogical Society, Inc.; PO Box 1629; North Wilkesboro, North Carolina 28659; <users.erols.com/fmoran/wilkgen/wilkgen.html>

Wilkes Public Library, Genealogy Research Rm.; C Street; North Wilkesboro, North Carolina 28659

Wilson County Genealogical Society; PO Box 802; Wilson, North Carolina 27894-0802; <www.wcgs.org>

Yadkin County Historical Society; PO Box 1250; Yadkinville, North Carolina 27055

Bibliography and Record Sources

General Sources

Anscombe, Francis Charles. *I Called You Friends: The Story of Quakerism in North Carolina.* Boston: Christopher Pub. House, 1959.

Ashe, Samuel A'Court. *Biographical History of North Carolina from Colonial Times to the Present.* 9 vols. Greensboro, North Carolina: C.L. Van Noppen, 1905-1917.

Ball, Bonnie S. *The Melungeons: Their Origin and Kin.* 6th ed. [Berryville, Virginia: Virginia Book Co.], 1977, 1969.

Bassett, John Spencer. *Slavery in the State of North Carolina.* New York: AMS Press, 1972.

Bernheim, Gotthardt D. *History of the German Settlements and of the Lutheran Church in North and South Carolina.* (1872) Reprint. Baltimore: Clearfield Co., 1996.

Bible, Jean P. *Melungeons–Yesterday and Today.* Signal Mountain, Tennessee: Mountain Press, 1975.

Biographical History of North Carolina from Colonial Times to the Present. Vols. 1-8, 10. Greensboro, North Carolina: Charles L. Van Noppen, 1905-17.

Blosser, Susan Sokol. *The Southern Historical Collection: A Guide to Manuscripts.* Chapel Hill, North Carolina: University of North Carolina Library, 1970.

Broadfoot Publishing. *The Colonial and State Records of North Carolina.* 30 vols. Wilmington, North Carolina: Broadfoot Publishing, 1996.

Bumgarner, George W. *Methodist Episcopal Church in North Carolina, 1865-1939.* Winston-Salem, North Carolina: Hunter Publishing, 1990.

Butler and Watson, eds. *The North Carolina Experience: An Interpretive and Documentary History.* Galveston, Texas: Frontier Press, 1984.

Cain, Barbara T. *Guide to Private Manuscript Collections in the North Carolina State Archives*. 3rd rev. ed. Raleigh: North Carolina Department of Cultural Resources, Division of Archives and History, 1981.

Cain, Barbara T., with Ellen Z. McGrew and Charles E. Morris. *Guide to Private Manuscript Collections in the North Carolina State Archives*. Raleigh, North Carolina: North Carolina Division of Archives and History, 1993.

Cain, Robert J., ed. *Colonial Records of North Carolina [Second Series], Volume IX: Records of the Executive Council, 1755-1775*. Raleigh, North Carolina: North Carolina Division of Archives and History, 1994.

Cain, Robert J., ed. *Colonial Records of North Carolina [Second Series], Volume VI: North Carolina Higher-Court Minutes, 1724-1730*. Raleigh, North Carolina: North Carolina Division of Archives and History, 1981.

Cain, Robert J., ed. *Colonial Records of North Carolina [Second Series], Volume VII: Records of the Executive Council, 1664-1734*. Raleigh, North Carolina: North Carolina Division of Archives and History, 1984.

Cain, Robert J., ed. *Colonial Records of North Carolina [Second Series], Volume VIII: Records of the Executive Council, 1735-1754*. Raleigh, North Carolina. North Carolina Division of Archives and History, 1988.

Chreitzberg, A. M. *Early Methodism in the Carolinas*. Spartanburg, South Carolina: The Reprint Company, 1972.

Colonial Records of North Carolina [Second Series], Volume II: North Carolina Higher-Court Records, 1670-1696. Raleigh, North Carolina: North Carolina Division of Archives and History. Microfilm.

Corbitt, David Leroy. *The Formation of the North Carolina Counties, 1663-1943*. Raleigh, North Carolina: North Carolina Division of Archives and History, 1996.

Crittenden, Charles Christopher. *The Historical Records of North Carolina*. 3 vols. Raleigh, North Carolina: North Carolina Historical Commission, 1938-1939.

Crow, Jeffery J., Paul D. Escott, and Flora J. Hatley. *A History of African Americans in North Carolina*. Raleigh, North Carolina: North Carolina Division of Archives and History, 1994.

Dobson, David. *Directory of Scots in the Carolinas, 1680-1830*. (1986) Reprint. Baltimore: Genealogical Publishing Co., 1994.

Draper, L. C. *King's Mountain and Its Heroes: History of the Battle of King's Mountain, October 7th, 1780*. (1881) Reprint. Baltimore: Genealogical Publishing Co., 1993.

Draughon, Wallace R. *North Carolina Genealogical Reference: A Research Guide for All Genealogists, Both Amateur and Professional*. 2nd ed. Durham, North Carolina: Smith Publishing, 1966.

Early North Carolina settlers, 1700s-1900s. [S.l.]: Brøderbund, 2000. CD-ROM.

Elliott, Wendy L. *Guide To Genealogical Research In North Carolina*. [S.l.]: W.L. Elliott, 1988.

Emory, Frank. *Paths Toward Freedom: A Biographical History of Blacks and Indians in North Carolina*. Raleigh, North Carolina: Center for Urban Affairs, North Carolina State University, 1976.

Family History Library. *Research Outline; North Carolina*. Salt Lake City: Family History Library.

Fisher, P. W. *One Dozen Pre-Revolutionary Families of Eastern North Carolina and Some of Their Descendants*. (1958) Reprint. Salem, Massachusetts: Higginson Book Co., 1995.

Foote, William Henry. *Sketches of North Carolina, Historical and Biographical, Illustrative of the Principles of a Portion of Her Early Settlers*. New York: Robert Carter, 1846.

Guide to Research Materials in the North Carolina State Archives: State Agency Records. Raleigh, North Carolina: North Carolina Division of Archives and History, 1995.

Hamrick, David O. *Index to the North Carolina Historical and Genealogical Register (Hathaway's Register)*, 3 vols. Athens, GA: Iberian Publishing Co., 1983.

Hehir, Donald M. *Carolina Families: A Bibliography of Books About North and South Carolina Families*. Bowie, Maryland: Heritage Books, 1994.

Henry, Linda Simmons *The Heritage of Blacks in North Carolina*. Charlotte, North Carolina: North Carolina African-American Heritage Foundation, 1990.

Hickey, Damon D. *Sojourners No More: The Quakers in the New South, 1865-1920*. Greensboro, North Carolina: North Carolina Friends Historical Society: North Carolina Yearly Meeting of Friends, 1997.

Hinshaw, Seth B. *Quaker Women of Carolina: Freedom – Achievement*. North Carolina: United Society of Friends Women, 1994.

Hinshaw, William Wade. *Index to Encyclopedia of American Quaker Genealogy*. [S.l.]: Genealogical Pub. Co., 1999.

Historical Records Survey (North Carolina). *Guide to the Manuscripts in the Archives of the Moravian Church in America, Southern Province*. Raleigh, North Carolina: Historical Records Survey, 1942.

Historical Records Survey (North Carolina). *Guide to the Manuscripts in the Southern Historical Collection of the University of North Carolina*. Chapel Hill: University of North Carolina Press, 1941.

Hofmann, Margaret M. *An Intermediate Short, Short Course in the Use of Some North Carolina Records in Genealogical Research*. The author, 1992.

Hunter, C.L. *Sketches of Western North Carolina*. (1877) Reprint. Baltimore: Genealogical Publishing, 1992.

Inventory of the State Archives of North Carolina. 4 vols. Raleigh, North Carolina: North Carolina Historical Records Survey Project, 1939-1941.

Jones, H. G., and Julius H. Avant. *Union List of North Carolina Newspapers, 1751-1900*. Raleigh: State Department of Archives and History, 1963.

Jones, Roger C., comp., *Guide to North Carolina Newspapers on Microfilm: Titles Available from the Division of Archives and History*. 6th ed. Rev. Raleigh: Division of Archives and History, 1984.

Kent, Scotti. *More Than Petticoats: Remarkable North Carolina Women*. Helena, Mont.: Falcon, 2000.

Lawson, John. *Lawson's History of North Carolina: Containing the Exact Description and Natural History of that Country, Together with the Present State Thereof and a Journal of a Thousand*

Miles Traveled Through Several Nations of Indians, Giving a Particular Account of Their Customs, Manners, Etc., Etc. Richmond: Garrett and Massie, 1937.

Lawson. *A New Voyage to Carolina.* (1709) Reprint. Galveston, Texas: Frontier Press, 1967.

Leary, Helen F.M., ed. *North Carolina Research.* 2nd ed. Raleigh, North Carolina: North Carolina Genealogical Society, 1996.

Leffer, Hugh Talmage. *History of North Carolina.* 4 Vols., New York: Lewis Historical Pub. Co., [1956].

London, Lawrence Foushee. *The Episcopal Church in North Carolina, 1701-1959.* Raleigh, North Carolina: Episcopal Diocese of North Carolina, 1987.

McCubbin's, Mamie. *McCubbins Collection.* Microfilm of original and typescript in the Rowan County Public Library at Salisbury, North Carolina. (Salt Lake City: Filmed by the Genealogical Society of Utah, 1956). 76 microfilm.

Mooney, Thomas G. *Exploring Your Cherokee Ancestry: A Basic Genealogical Research Guide.* Tahlequah, Oklahoma: Cherokee National Historical Society, Inc., 1990.

Moore, M. H. *Sketches of the Pioneers of Methodism in North Carolina and Virginia.* Nashville, Tenn.: Southern Methodist Publishing House, 1884.

North Carolina Freedmen's Records. North Carolina Genealogical Society. [n.d.]

North Carolina Office of Archives and History. *Guide to Newspapers on Microfilm in the North Carolina State Archives.* Raleigh, North Carolina: North Carolina Office of Archives and History, 2002. Online guide: <statelibrary.dcr.state.nc.us/ncnp/intro.htm>.

North Carolina, Division of Archives and History. *Guide to Research Materials in the North Carolina State Archives. Section B: County Records.* 10th rev. ed. Raleigh: Department of Cultural Resources, Division of Archives and History, 1988.

North Carolina. Division of Archives and History. Archives and Records Section. *Guide to Research Materials in the North Carolina State Archives: State Agency Records.* Raleigh, North Carolina: North Carolina Division of Archives and History, 1995.

North Carolina. Division of Archives and History. Department of Cultural Resources. *Guide to North Carolina Newspapers on Microfilm: Titles Available from the Division of Archives and History.* Raleigh, North Carolina: Division of Archives and History, 1984.

Ormond, Jesse Marvin. *The Country Church in North Carolina: A Study of the Country Churches of North Carolina in Relation to the Material Progress of the State.*: Durham, North Carolina: Duke University Press, 1931.

Paschal, George Washington. *History of the North Carolina Baptists.* 2 vols. Gallatin, Tennessee: Church History Research & Archives, 1990.

Powell, William S. *Dictionary of North Carolina Biography.* 6 vols. Chapel Hill, North Carolina: University of North Carolina Press, 1979-.

Powell, William S. *North Carolina Through Four Centuries.* Galveston, Texas: Frontier Press, 1989.

Powell, William Stevens. *Dictionary of North Carolina Biography.* 6 vols. Chapel Hill, North Carolina: University of North Carolina Press, 1996.

Powell, William Stevens. *North Carolina Lives: The Tar Heel Who's Who: A Reference Edition Recording the Biographies of Contemporary Leaders in North Carolina with Special Emphasis on their Achievements in Making it One of America's Greatest States.* Hopkinsville, Kentucky: Historical Record Association, 1962.

Protestant Episcopal Church (North Carolina). *History of the Protestant Episcopal Church in North Carolina.* Microfilm of original and typescript at the State Archives in Raleigh, North Carolina. Raleigh: North Carolina Dept. of Archives and History, 1961.

Ramsey. *Carolina Cradle: Settlement of the Northwest Carolina Frontier, 1747-1762.* Galveston, Texas: Frontier Press, 1987.

Ray, Worth S. *Lost Tribes of North Carolina, Part I: Index and Digest to Hathaway's North Carolina Historical and Genealogical Register.* (1945) Reprint. Baltimore: Clearfield Co., 1997.

Ray, Worth S. *Lost Tribes of North Carolina, Part II: Colonial Granville County [North Carolina] and Its People.* (1945) Reprint. Baltimore: Clearfield Co., 1996.

Ray, Worth S. *Lost Tribes of North Carolina, Part III: The Mecklenburg Signers and Their Neighbors.* (1946) Reprint. Baltimore: Clearfield Co., 1995.

Ray, Worth S. *Lost Tribes of North Carolina. Part IV: Old Albemarle and Its Absentee Landlords.* (1947) Reprint. Baltimore: Clearfield Co., 1994.

Read, Motte Alston. *Colonial Families of Virginia and North Carolina.* Microfilm of original manuscript at the South Carolina Historical Society, Charleston, S.C. (Salt Lake City: Filmed by the Genealogical Society of Utah, 1952).

Rights, Douglas Le Tell. *The American Indian in North Carolina.* Durham, North Carolina: Duke University Press, 1947.

Roanoke Island Prisoners–Feb. 1862. Signal Mountain, Tennessee: Mountain Press.

Russell, Anne. *North Carolina Portraits of Faith: A Pictorial History of Religions.* Norfolk, Virginia: Donning Co., 1986.

Saunders, William L., ed. *The Colonial Records of North Carolina: Published Under the Supervision of the Trustees of the Public Libraries, by Order of the General Assembly.* 11 vols. Wilmington, North Carolina: Broadfoot Pub., 1993.

Schweitzer, George K. *North Carolina Genealogical Research.* Knoxville, Tennessee: The author, 1996.

Smallwood, Marilu Burch. *Some Colonial and Revolutionary Families of North Carolina.* 3 vols. Washington, North Carolina: M.B. Smallwood, 1964.

Society of North Carolina Archivists. *Archival and Manuscript Repositories in North Carolina: A Directory.* Galveston, Texas: Frontier Press, 1993.

Spence, Wilma C. *North Carolina Bible Records.* Logan, Utah: Unique Printing Services, 1973.

Spindel, Donna. *Introductory Guide to Indian-Related Records (To 1876) in the North Carolina State Archives.* Raleigh, North Carolina: Division of Archives and History, N.C. Dept. of Cultural Resources, 1977.

Starr, Emmet McDonald. *Old Cherokee Families: Old Families and their Genealogy. Reprinted from History of the Cherokee Indians and their Legends and Folklore. With a Comprehensive Index.* Oklahoma City, Okla.: The Warden, 1921, 1922.

Stevenson, George. *North Carolina Local History: A Select Bibliography*. Raleigh, North Carolina: State Department of Cultural Resources, 1975.

The Historical Records of North Carolina. 3 vols. Raleigh: North Carolina Historical Commission, 1938-39.

Thompson, Catherine E. *Selective Guide to Women Related Records in the North Carolina State Archives*. Raleigh, North Carolina: North Carolina Department of Archives and History, 1977.

Thornton, Mary Lindsay. *A Bibliography of North Carolina, 1589-1956*. Westport, Connecticut: Greenwood Press, 1973.

Ware, Charles Crossfield. *North Carolina Disciples of Christ: A History of their Rise and Progress, and of their Contribution to their General Brotherhood*. St. Louis: Christian Board of Publication, 1927.

Watson, Alan D., comp. & ed. *An Index to North Carolina Newspapers, 1784-1789*. Raleigh, North Carolina: North Carolina Department of Archives and History, 1992.

Weeks, Stephen Beauregard. *Index to the Colonial and State Records of North Carolina*. 2 vols. Charlotte, North Carolina: Observer Print. House, 1886.

Weeks, Stephen Beauregard. *The Religious Development in the Province of North Carolina*. New York: Johnson Reprint Corp., 1973.

Wheeler, John Hill. *Historical Sketches of North Carolina from 1584 to 1851*. 2 vols in 1. (1851) Reprint. Baltimore: Clearfield Co., 1993.

Wheeler, John Hill. *Reminiscences and Memoirs of North Carolina and Eminent North Carolinians*. (1884) Reprint. Baltimore: Clearfield Co., 1993.

Woodmason. *The Carolina Backcountry on the Eve of the Revolution*. Galveston, Texas: Frontier Press, 1954.

Atlases, Maps and Gazetteers

Clark, David S. *Index to Maps of North Carolina in Books and Periodicals Illustrating the History of the State from the Voyage of Verrazzano in 1524 to 1975*. Fayetteville, North Carolina: David S. Clark, 1976.

Clay, James W. *North Carolina Atlas*. Chapel Hill, North Carolina: University of North Carolina Press, 1975.

Corbitt, David Leroy. *The Formation Of The North Carolina Counties, 1663-1943*. Raleigh [N.C.]: State Department of Archives and History, 1969.

Cumming, William P. *North Carolina in Maps*. Raleigh, North Carolina: North Carolina Division of Archives and History, 1994.

DeLorme Mapping Company. *North Carolina Atlas and Gazetteer: Topographic Maps of the Entire State, Back Roads and Recreational Places*. Freeport, Maine: DeLorme Mapping, 1993.

DePriest, Virginia Greene. *The National Post Road*. Shelby, North Carolina: V.G. DePriest, 1990.

Edwards, Richard, ed. *Statistical Gazetteer of the States of Virginia and North Carolina*. Richmond, Virginia: published by the proprietor, 1856.

Gioe, Joan Colbert. *North Carolina: Her Counties, Her Townships*

and Her Towns, Indianapolis: The Researchers, 1981.

Powell. *The North Carolina Gazetteer: A Dictionary of Tar Heel Places*. Galveston, Texas: Frontier Press, 1968.

Puetz, C.J., comp. *North Carolina County Maps*. Lyndon Station, Wisconsin: Thomas Publishing Co., 1991.

Stout, Garland P. *North Carolina Counties*. 5 vols. Greensboro, North Carolina: G. P. Stout, 1973.

Census Records

Available Census Records and Census Substitutes

Federal Census 1790 (supplemented by tax lists for Caswell, Granville and Orange Counties), 1800, 1810 (except Craven, Greene, New Hanover, and Wake Counties), 1820 (except Currituck, Franklin, Martin, Montgomery, Randolph, and Wake Counties), 1830, 1840, 1850, 1860, 1870, 1880, 1900, 1910, 1920, 1930.

Federal Mortality Schedules 1850, 1860, 1870, 1880.

Union Veterans and Widows 1890.

State/Territorial Census 1784-1787.

Dollarhide, William. *The Census Book: A Genealogist's Guide to Federal Census Facts, Schedules and Indexes*. Bountiful, Utah: Heritage Quest, 1999.

Kemp, Thomas Jay. *The American Census Handbook*. Wilmington, Delaware: Scholarly Resources, Inc., 2001.

Lainhart, Ann S. *State Census Records*. Baltimore: Genealogical Publishing Co., Inc., 1992.

Ratcliff, Clarence, E. *North Carolina Taxpayers, 1679-1790*. (1987) Reprint. Baltimore: Genealogical Publishing, 1996.

Siler, David W. *Eastern Cherokees: A Census of the Cherokee Nation in North Carolina, Tennessee, Alabama, and Georgia in 1851*. Cottonport, Louisiana: Polyanthos, 1972.

Szucs, Loretto Dennis, and Matthew Wright. *Finding Answers in U.S. Census Records*. Ancestry Publishing, 2001

Thorndale, William, and William Dollarhide. *Map Guide to the U.S. Federal Censuses, 1790-1920*. Baltimore: Genealogical Publishing Co., 1987.

United States. Bureau of Internal Revenue. *Internal Revenue Assessment List for North Carolina, 1864-1866*. Microfilm of originals in the National Archives in Washington, D.C. (Salt Lake City: Filmed by the Genealogical Society of Utah, 1988). 2 microfilm.

Wynne, Frances Holloway. *North Carolina Extant Voter Registrations of 1867*. Bowie, Maryland: Heritage Books, 1992.

Court Records, Probate and Wills

Bennett, William Doub. *Catalogue, North Carolina Federal Court Records [at the] National Archives, Atlanta Branch*. Raleigh: W.D. Bennett, 1987.

Clark, Walter. *The State Records of North Carolina*. Goldsboro, North Carolina: Nash Brothers, 1902.

Grimes, J. Bryan. *Abstract of North Carolina Wills [1663-1760]*. (1910) Reprint. Baltimore: Clearfield Co., Inc., 1997.

Grimes, J. Bryan. *Abstract of North Carolina Wills: Compiled from Original and Recorded Wills in the Office of the Secretary of State*. (1910) Reprint. Greenville, South Carolina: Southern Historical Press, 1985.

Grimes, J. Bryan. *North Carolina Wills and Inventories*. (1912) Reprint. Baltimore; Clearfield Co., 1994.

McCain, Paul M. *The County Court in North Carolina Before 1750*. New York: AMS Press, 1970.

Mitchell, Thornton W. *North Carolina Wills: A Testator Index, 1665-1900*. (1993) Reprint. Baltimore: Genealogical Publishing, 1996.

North Carolina Higher-Court Records. 5 vols. Raleigh, North Carolina: State Department of Archives and History, 1968-1981.

North Carolina Wills and Court Records, 1679-1775. Microfilm of originals at the Secretary of State's Office in Raleigh, North Carolina. (Salt Lake City: Filmed by the Genealogical Society of Utah, 1941). 5 microfilm.

North Carolina. Division of Archives and History (Raleigh, North Carolina). *Colonial Estate Papers, 1669-1759*. Microfilm of original in the North Carolina State Archives in Raleigh, North Carolina. (Salt Lake City: Filmed by the Genealogical Society of Utah, 1996). 4 microfilm.

Olds, Fred A. *An Abstract of North Carolina Wills from About 1760 to About 1800 Supplementing Grimes' Abstract of North Carolina Wills 1663 to 1760*. (1925) Reprint. Baltimore: Clearfield Co., 1996.

The First Laws of the State of North Carolina. 2 vols. (1791) Reprint. Wilmington, Delaware: Scholarly Resources, 1984.

Emigration, Immigration, Migration and Naturalization

Briceland, Alan Vance. *Westward From Virginia: The Exploration Of The Virginia-Carolina Frontier, 1650-1710*. Charlottesville, Virginia: University Press of Virginia, 1987.

Camin, Betty J. *North Carolina Naturalization Index, 1792-1862*. Mt. Airy, North Carolina: B.J. Camin, 1989.

Daughters of the American Revolution, North Carolina. *Roster of Soldiers from North Carolina in the American Revolution: With an Appendix Containing a Collection of Miscellaneous Papers*. (1932) Reprint. Baltimore: Genealogical Publishing Co., 1972.

DeMond, Robert O. *The Loyalists in North Carolina During the Revolution*. (1940) Reprint. Baltimore: Clearfield Co., 1994.

Hakluyt, Richard. *Explorations, Descriptions, And Attempted Settlements Of Carolina, 1584- 1590*. Raleigh: State Department of Archives and History, 1953.

Meyer, Duane. *Highland Scots of North Carolina, 1732-1776*. Chapel Hill, North Carolina: University of North Carolina Press, [1966].

Newsome, A.R., ed. *Record of Emigrants from England and Scotland to North America, 1774-1775*. Raleigh, North Carolina: North Carolina Division of Archives and History, 1989.

Peden, Henry C. *Marylanders to Carolina: Migrations of Marylanders to North and South Carolina Prior to 1800*. Westminster, Maryland: Family Line Publications, 1994.

Reichel, Rev. Levin T. *The Moravians in North Carolina*. (1857) Reprint. Baltimore: Clearfield Co., 1995.

United States. District Court (Alabama: Southern District). *Declarations Of Intentions, Naturalizations, And Petitions, 1855-1960*. Microfilm of originals at the National Archives in East Point, Georgia (Salt Lake City: Filmed by the Genealogical Society of Utah, 1987-1989). 9 microfilm.

Land and Property

Burgner, Goldene Fillers. *North Carolina Land Grants in Tennessee, 1778-1791*. Greenville, South Carolina: Southern Historical Press, 1981.

Cartwright, Betty G. and Lillian J. Gardiner. *North Carolina Land Grants in Tennessee, 1778-1791*. Memphis, Tennessee: Division of Archives, 1958.

Hofmann, Margaret M. *Colony of North Carolina, 1735-1764, 1765-1775; Abstracts of Land Patents*, 2 vols. Weldon, North Carolina: Roanoke New Co., 1982, 1984.

Hofmann, Margaret M. *Province of North Carolina, 1663-1729: Abstracts of Land Patents*. Weldon, North Carolina: Roanoke News Co., 1979.

Hofmann, Margaret M. *The Granville District of North Carolina, 1749-1763: Abstracts of Miscellaneous Land Office Records, Volume 4*. Frontier Press, Galveston, Texas.

Hofmann, Margaret M. *The Granville District of North Carolina, 1748-1763: Abstracts of Land Grants*. 5 vols. Weldon, North Carolina: Roanoke News Co., 1995.

Hone, Wade E. *Land and Property Research in the United States*. Salt Lake City: Ancestry Incorporated, 1997.

North Carolina. Secretary of State. Land Grant Office. *Land Records, 1600 Thru 1957; Land Grant Index, 1693-1959*. Microfilm of originals in the North Carolina State Archives in Raleigh, North Carolina Raleigh, North Carolina: North Carolina State Archives, 1980. 552 microfilm.

North Carolina. Secretary of State. *Land Grants, Land Entries and Warrants and List of Grants for Various Counties of North Carolina, 1764-1853*. Microfilm of originals at the North Carolina Historical Commission in Raleigh, North Carolina. (Salt Lake City: Filmed by the Genealogical Society of Utah, 1941). 3 microfilm.

Powell, William Stevens. *The Proprietors of Carolina*. Raleigh: State Department of Archives and History, 1968.

Pruitt, Albert Bruce. *Colonial Land Entries in North Carolina*. 4 vols. [Whitakers, North Carolina: A.B. Pruitt], c1994, 1995.

Smathers, George Henry. *The History of Land Titles in Western North Carolina: A History of the Cherokee Land Laws Affecting the Title to Land Lying West of the Meigs and Freeman Line, and Laws Affecting the Title of Land Lying East of the Meigs and Freeman Line Back to the Top of the Blue Ridge....* Asheville: Miller Printing Co., 1938.

The Church of Jesus Christ of Latter-day Saints. Genealogical Department. *North Carolina Land and Property Records: A Register of the Several Counties, Alphabetically Arranged, Being a Listing of Deed Records, Mortgages, Trusts, Etc.* (Salt Lake City: Filmed by the Genealogical Society of Utah, 1969).

Military

Bradley, Stephen E., Jr., ed. *North Carolina Confederate Militia Officers Roster, As Contained in the Adjunct-General's Officers Roster*. Wilmington, North Carolina: Broadfoot Publishing, 1996.

Burns, Annie W. *Abstracts of Pension Papers of North Carolina Soldiers of the Revolution, 1812, and Indian Wars*. 15 vols. Washington, DC: 1960-66.

Carter, Mary. *North Carolina Revolutionary Soldiers, Sailors, Patriots and Descendants*. 2 vols. Albany, Georgia: Pioneer Publications, 1978.

Clark, Walter, ed. *Histories of the Several Regiments and Battalions from North Carolina in the Great War 1861-1865.* 5 vols. Wilmington, North Carolina: Broadfoot Publishing.

Crow, Jeffery J. *The Black Experience in Revolutionary North Carolina.* Raleigh, North Carolina: North Carolina Division of Archives and History, 1996.

Jordan, Weymouth T., Jr., ed. *North Carolina Troops, 1861-1865: A Roster.* 14 vols. Raleigh, North Carolina: State Department of Archives and History, 1966-.

Kearney, Timothy. *Abstracts of Letters of Resignation of Militia Officers in North Carolina 1779-1840.* Raleigh, North Carolina: North Carolina Genealogical Society, 1992.

Lemmon, Sarah McCulloh. *North Carolina's Role in the First World War.* Raleigh: North Carolina Department of Cultural Resources, Div. of Arch. and Hist., 1975.

North Carolina Adjunct General's Office. *Muster Rolls of the Soldiers of the War of 1812 Detached From the Militia of North Carolina in 1812 and 1814.* Winston-Salem, North Carolina: Barber Publishing Co., 1969.

North Carolina Adjunct General's Office. *Roster of the North Carolina Volunteers in the Spanish-American War, 1898-1899.* Raleigh, North Carolina: Edwards and Broughton, 1900.

North Carolina Office of Archives and History. *Military Records.* Raleigh, North Carolina: North Carolina Office of Archives and History, 2002. Online guide: <www.ah.dcr.state.nc.us/sections/archives/arch/military.htm>

Pancake. *This Destructive War: The British Campaign in the Carolinas, 1780-1782.* Galveston, Texas: Frontier Press, 1985.

Roster of Soldiers from North Carolina in the American Revolution. (1932) Reprint. Baltimore: Genealogical Publishing Co., 1977.

Roster of the North Carolina Volunteers in the Spanish-American War, 1898-1899. Raleigh, North Carolina: Edwards & Broughton, 1900.

Sifakis, Stewart. *Compendium of the Confederate Armies: North Carolina.* Galveston, Texas: Frontier Press, 1992.

Steelman, Joseph F. *North Carolina's Role In The Spanish-American War.* Raleigh, North Carolina: Department of Cultural Resources, Division of Archives and History, 1975.

Toler, Maurice S. *Muster Rolls of the Soldiers of the War of 1812 Detached from the Militia of North Carolina in 1812 and 1814.* (1851, 1976) Reprint. Baltimore: Clearfield Co., 1996.

United States. Selective Service System. *North Carolina, World War I Selective Service System Draft Registration Cards, 1917-1918.* National Archives Microfilm Publications, M1509. Washington, DC: National Archives, 1987-1988.

Volunteer Soldiers in the Cherokee War–1836-1839. Signal Mountain, Tennessee: Mountain Press.

White, Katherine Keogh. *The King's Mountain Men. The Story of Battle, with Sketches of the American Soldiers Who Took Part.* (1924) Reprint. Baltimore: Clearfield Co., 1996.

Yearns and Barrett, eds. *North Carolina Civil War Documentary.* Galveston, Texas: Frontier Press, 1980.

Vital and Cemetery Records

Broughton, Carrie L. *Marriage and Death Notices from Raleigh Register and North Carolina State Gazette, 1799-1825.* (1942-44) Reprint. Baltimore: Clearfield Co., 1995.

Broughton, Carrie L. *Marriage and Death Notices in Raleigh Register and North Carolina State Gazette, 1826-1845.* (1947) Reprint. Baltimore: Clearfield Co., 1992.

Broughton, Carrie L. *Marriage and Death Notices in Raleigh Register and North Carolina State Gazette, 1846-1867.* 2 vols in one. (1949-50) Reprint. Baltimore: Clearfield Co., 1992.

Cemetery Records of North Carolina. 8 vols. Salt Lake City: Genealogical Society of Utah, 1947-61.

Clemens, William Montgomery. *North and South Carolina Marriage Records, from the Earliest Colonial Days to the Civil War.* (1927) Reprint. Baltimore: Genealogical Publishing Co., 1995.

Dodd, Jordan R. *North Carolina Marriages, 1801 to 1825.* Bountiful, Utah: Precision Indexing, 1993.

Dodd, Jordan R. *North Carolina Marriages, Early to 1800.* Bountiful, Utah: Precision Indexing, 1990.

Historical Records Survey (North Carolina). *Guide To Vital Statistics Records In North Carolina.* Raleigh, North Carolina: The Survey, 1942.

Historical Records Survey (North Carolina). *Post-1914 Cemetery Inscription Card Index* Microfilm of originals in the North Carolina Department of Archives and History in Raleigh, North Carolina. Raleigh, North Carolina: North Carolina Dept. of Archives and History, 1972. 5 microfilm.

Historical Records Survey (North Carolina*). Pre-1914 Cemetery Inscription Card Index.* Microfilm of originals in the North Carolina Department of Archives and History in Raleigh, North Carolina. Raleigh, North Carolina: North Carolina Dept. of Archives and History, 1972. 23 microfilm.

King, Henry. *Tar Heel Tombstones and the Tales They Tell.* Asheboro, North Carolina: Down Home Press, 1990.

Lucas, Silas Emmett Jr. and Brent Holcomb. *Marriage and Death Notices from Raleigh, NC Newspapers: 1796-1826.* (1977) Reprint. Greenville, South Carolina: Southern Historical Press, 1984.

McEachern, Leora H. *North Carolina Gravestone Records.* 10 Vols. Wilmington, North Carolina: The author, 1971-81.

Neal, Lois Smathers. *Abstracts of Vital Records from Raleigh, North Carolina, Newspapers, 1799-1829.* 2 vols. Spartanburg, South Carolina: Reprint Company, 1979-.

North Carolina Division of Archives and History. *An Index to Marriage Bonds Filed in the North Carolina State Archives.* Raleigh, North Carolina: North Carolina Department of Cultural Resources, 1977. 88 Microfiche.

North Carolina. Department of Public Health. Vital Records Section. *Death Certificates, 1906-1994; Still Births, 1914-1953; Fetal Deaths, 1960-1974; Index, 1906-1967.* Microfilm of originals in the North Carolina Department of Archives and History in Raleigh, North Carolina. (Salt Lake City: Filmed by the Genealogical Society of Utah, 1993-1995). 1022 microfilm.

North Carolina. Department of Public Health. Vital Records Section. *Index To Death Certificates, 1968-1994.* Microfilm of originals at the North Carolina Department of Public Health, Vital Records section in Raleigh, North Carolina (Salt Lake City: Filmed by the Genealogical Society of Utah, 1996). 56 microfiche.

North Carolina. Division of Archives and History (Raleigh, North Carolina*). Birth Certificates, 1913-1918.* Microfilm of originals in the North Carolina State Archives in Raleigh, North Carolina. (Salt Lake City: Filmed by the Genealogical Society of Utah, 1998-1999, 2000). 305 microfilm.

Tennessee Valley Authority (Tennessee). *Master File Relocation Card Index for Grave and Cemetery Removal and Relocation, 1934-1954.* Microreproduction of originals housed in the National Archives Record Office, East Point, Georgia. (Salt Lake City: Filmed by the Genealogical Society of Utah, 1996).

Wellborn, Mrs. John Scott. *North Carolina Tombstone Records.* Microfilm. 3 vols in 2 reels. Salt Lake City: Genealogical Society of Utah, 1941.

White, Barnetta McGhee. *Somebody Knows My Name: Marriages of Freed People in North Carolina, County by County.* 3 vols. Athens, Georgia: Iberian Publishing Co., 1995.

Works Progress Administration, Historical Records Survey Services Division. *Pre-1914 Cemetery Inscription Card Index.* 26 vols. Raleigh: North Carolina Department of Archives and History, 1972.

County Website	Map Index	Date Created	Parent County or Territory From Which Organized Address/Details
Alamance* www.alamance-nc.com/	I5	29 Jan 1849	**Orange** Alamance County; 124 W Elm St; Graham, NC 27253-2802; Ph. 336.570.6565 Details: (Clk Sup Ct has div, pro & ct rec from 1849; Reg of Deeds has b, m, d & land rec)
Albemarle www.usgennet.org/usa/nc/county/ albemarle/		1663	**Original county** Details: (1 of 3 original cos. discontinued in 1739)
Alexander www.co.alexander.nc.us/	L6	15 Jan 1847	**Iredell, Caldwell & Wilkes** Alexander County; 201 1st St SW Ste 1; Taylorsville, NC 28681-2592; Ph. 828.632.3152 Details: (Reg of Deeds has b, m, d, bur & land rec; Clk Sup Ct has div, pro & ct rec from 1865)
Alleghany www.sparta-nc.com/	L4	1859	**Ashe** Alleghany County; Main St; PO Box 186; Sparta, NC 28675; Ph. 336.372.4342 Details: (Clk Sup Ct has b & d rec from 1914, m rec from 1868, div rec, pro rec from 1883, ct rec from 1869 & land rec from 1860)
Anson www.co.anson.nc.us/	J8	17 Mar 1749	**Bladen** Anson County; N Green St; PO Box 352; Wadesboro, NC 28170; Ph. 704.694.3212 Details: (Courthouse burned 1868) (Reg of Deeds has b rec from 1913, m rec from 1869, d & land rec; Clk Sup Ct has div rec from 1868, pro rec from 1750 & ct rec from 1770)
Archdale		3 Dec 1705	**Bath** Details: (see Craven) (Name changed to Craven, 1712)
Ashe www.ashechamber.com/	M4	18 Nov 1799	**Wilkes** Ashe County; Court St; PO Box 367; Jefferson, NC 28640; Ph. 336.246.9338 Details: (Clk Sup Ct has b & d rec from 1913, m rec from 1853, div, pro & ct rec from 1800)
Avery www.banner-elk.com/countown.html	N5	23 Feb 1911	**Caldwell, Mitchell, Watauga** Avery County; Main St; Newland, NC 28657; Ph. 828.733.8262 Details: (Clk Sup Ct has div, pro, ct & land rec from 1911)
Bath www.usgennet.org/usa/nc/county/bath/		1696	**Original county** Details: (Divided into Archdale, Pamtecough & Wickham Precincts 3 Dec 1705; Co discontinued in 1739)
Beaufort www.beaufort-county.com/	D6	3 Dec 1705	**Bath** Beaufort County; 112 W 2nd St; Washington, NC 27889; Ph. 252.946.2323 Details: (Reg of Deeds has m & land rec; Clk Sup Ct has pro & ct rec)
Berkeley		1670	**Precinct in Albemarle** Details: (see Perquimans) (Perquimans Co known as Berkeley Precinct from 1671 to 1681)
Bertie www.co.bertie.nc.us/	D5	2 Aug 1722	**Chowan** Bertie County; 108 W Dundee St; Windsor, NC 27983-1208; Ph. 252.794.5309 Details: (Reg of Deeds has b, m, d & land rec; Clk Sup Ct has div & ct rec from 1869 & pro rec from 1763)
Bladen www.rootsweb.com/~ncbladen/ bladen.htm	G9	1734	**New Hanover** Bladen County; Courthouse Dr; PO Box 247; Elizabethtown, NC 28337; Ph. 919.862.6710 Details: (Courthouse burned 1800 & 1893) (Reg of Deeds has b & d rec from 1914, m rec from 1893 & land rec from 1734; Clk Sup Ct has div & ct rec from 1893 & pro rec from 1734)
Brunswick www.brunswick.org/	G10	30 Jan 1764	**New Hanover, Bladen** Brunswick County; PO Box 87; Bolivia, NC 28422-0249; Ph. 910.253.2690 Details: (Reg of Deeds has b, m, d, bur & land rec; Clk Sup Ct has div rec from 1900, pro rec from 1858 & ct rec from 1882)

County Website	Map Index	Date Created	Parent County or Territory From Which Organized Address/Details
Buncombe www.buncombecounty.org/	06	5 Dec 1791	**Burke, Rutherford** Buncombe County; 60 Court Plaza Rm 110; Asheville, NC 28801-3519; Ph. 828.250.4300 Details: (Courthouse burned 1830-1835) (Reg of Deeds has b, m, d, bur & land rec; Clk Sup Ct has div & pro rec from 1832 & ct rec)
Burke www.co.burke.nc.us/	M6	8 Apr 1777	**Rowan** Burke County; 201 S Green St; PO Box 219; Morganton, NC 28680; Ph. 828.438.5450 Details: (Reg of Deeds has b & d rec from 1913, m, land & mil dis rec from 1865; Clk Sup Ct has div, pro & ct rec from 1865)
Bute www.blueridge.net/lds/nc/bute.html		1764	**Granville, Northampton** Details: (Discontinued in 1779)
Cabarrus www.co.cabarrus.nc.us/	K7	15 Nov 1792	**Mecklenburg** Cabarrus County; 65 Church St SE; Concord, NC 28025; Ph. 704.920.2112 Details: (Courthouse burned 1874) (Reg of Deeds has b & d rec from 1913, m & land rec from 1792 & mil dis rec from 1919; Clk Sup Ct has div, pro & ct rec)
Caldwell www.co.caldwell.nc.us/	M5	11 Jan 1841	**Burke, Wilkes** Caldwell County; 905 West Ave NW; Lenoir, NC 28645; Ph. 828.757.1310 Details: (Reg of Deeds has b, m, d & land rec; Clk Sup Ct has div, ct & pro rec from 1841)
Camden www.rootsweb.com/~nccamden/ camden.htm	C4	8 Apr 1777	**Pasquotank** Camden County; Hwy 343; PO Box 190; Camden, NC 27921; Ph. 919.335.4077 Details: (Clk Sup Ct has div & ct rec from 1896 & pro rec from 1912)
Carteret www.mindspring.com/~jsruss/ genweb/NC/carteret.htm	C8	1722	**Craven** Carteret County; Courthouse Sq; Beaufort, NC 28516; Ph. 252.728.8474 Details: (Reg of Deeds has b, m, d & land rec; Clk Sup Ct has div, pro & ct rec)
Caswell www.caswellnc.com/home.htm	I4	8 Apr 1777	**Orange** Caswell County; 139 E Church St; Yanceyville, NC 27379; Ph. 336.694.4197 Details: (Clk Sup Ct has div, pro & ct rec; Reg of Deeds has land rec)
Catawba www.co.catawba.nc.us/	L6	12 Dec 1842	**Lincoln** Catawba County; 100A Southwest Blvd; PO Box 389; Newton, NC 28658-0389; Ph. 828.465.1573 Details: (Clk Sup Ct has div, pro & ct rec from 1843; Reg of Deeds has m & land rec)
Chatham www.rootsweb.com/~ncchatha/ chatham.htm	I6	5 Dec 1770	**Orange** Chatham County; 12 East Rd; Pittsboro, NC 27312; Ph. 919.542.3240 Details: (Reg of Deeds has b & d rec from 1913, m & land rec from 1771; Clk Sup Ct has div rec from 1913, pro rec from 1771 & ct rec from 1869)
Cherokee www.main.nc.us/cherokee/index.html	R7	4 Jan 1839	**Macon** Cherokee County; 53 Peachtree; Murphy, NC 28906; Ph. 282.837.2613 Details: (Clk Sup Ct has div, pro & ct rec; Reg of Deeds has land rec)
Chowan www.co.chowan.nc.us/	C5	1670	**Albemarle** Chowan County; 101 S Broad St; Edenton, NC 27932; Ph. 252.482.3062 Details: (Reg of Deeds has m & land rec; Clk Sup Ct has pro & ct rec)
Clay www.rootsweb.com/~ncclay/	Q7	20 Feb 1861	**Cherokee** Clay County; Town Sq; Hayesville, NC 28904-0118; Ph. 828.389.6301 Details: (Reg of Deeds has b, d & mil rec from 1913, m rec from 1879 & land rec from 1870)
Cleveland www.clevelandcounty.com/nav/index.htm	M7	11 Jan 1841	**Rutherford, Lincoln** Cleveland County; 311 E Marion St; PO Box 1210; Shelby, NC 28150; Ph. 704.484.4834 Details: (Reg of Deeds has b & d rec from 1914, m rec from 1851 & land rec from 1841; Clk Sup Ct has div rec from 1921, pro rec from 1843 & ct rec from 1914)
Columbus* www.columbus.nc.us/	G7	15 Dec 1808	**Bladen, Brunswick** Columbus County; 612 N Madison St; Whiteville, NC 28472; Ph. 910.640.6625 Details: (Reg of Deeds has b & d rec from 1913, m rec from 1867 & land rec; Clk Sup Ct has div & ct rec from 1868 & pro rec from 1817)

County Website	Map Index	Date Created	Parent County or Territory From Which Organized Address/Details
Craven* www.cravencounty.com/	D7	3 Dec 1705	**Archdale Precinct of Bath Co** Craven County; 406 Craven St; New Bern, NC 28560; Ph. 252.636.6617 Details: (Formerly Archdale Co. Name changed to Craven, 1712) (1810 cen missing) (Reg of Deeds has b & d rec from 1914, m & land rec from 1700's & mil dis rec; Clk Sup Ct has div rec from 1915; City Clk has bur rec)
Cumberland www.co.cumberland.nc.us/	G8	19 Feb 1754	**Bladen** Cumberland County; 117 Dick St Rm 114; Fayetteville, NC 28301-5725; Ph. 910.678.7775 Details: (Reg of Deeds has b, m, d, bur & land rec; Clk Sup Ct has div rec from 1930, pro rec from 1850 & ct rec from 1900)
Currituck www.co.currituck.nc.us/	B4	1670	**Albemarle** Currituck County; PO Box 71; Currituck, NC 27929; Ph. 252.232.3297 Details: (1820 cen missing; Courthouse burned 1842) (Reg of Deeds has b, m, d & land rec; Clk Sup Ct has div, pro & ct rec)
Dare www.co.dare.nc.us/	B6	3 Feb 1870	**Currituck, Tyrell, Hyde** Dare County; 400 Budleigh St; PO Box 70; Manteo, NC 27954; Ph. 252.473.3438 Details: (Reg of Deeds has b & d rec from 1913, m rec from 1870 & land rec; Clk Sup Ct has div, pro & ct rec from 1870)
Davidson www.co.davidson.nc.us/	J7	9 Dec 1822	**Rowan** Davidson County; PO Box 464; Lexington, NC 27293; Ph. 336.242.2150 Details: (Reg of Deeds has b, m, d, bur & land rec from 1823; Clk Sup Ct has div, pro & ct rec from 1823)
Davie www.co.davie.nc.us/	K5	20 Dec 1836	**Rowan** Davie County; 123 S Main St; Mocksville, NC 27028; Ph. 336.751.2513 Details: (Reg of Deeds has b, m, d, bur & land rec; Clk Sup Ct has div & ct rec from 1834 & pro rec from 1837)
Dobbs www.rootsweb.com/~ncdobbs/dobbs.htm		1758	**Johnston** Details: (Discontinued & became part of Wayne Co 18 Oct 1779 & Glasgow & Lenoir Cos 5 Dec 1791)
Duplin www.duplincounty.org/	F8	17 Mar 1749	**New Hanover** Duplin County; 118 Duplin St; Kenansville, NC 28349; Ph. 910.296.2108 Details: (Reg of Deeds has b & d rec from 1913, m rec from 1749, maps & land rec from 1749 & business rec from 1899; Clk Sup Ct has pro & ct rec)
Durham www.co.durham.nc.us/	H5	28 Feb 1881	**Orange, Wake** Durham County; 200 E Main St; Durham, NC 27707; Ph. 919.560.0480 Details: (Co Hlth Dept has b, d & bur rec; Reg of Deeds has m & land rec; Clk Sup Ct has div, pro & ct rec from 1881)
Edgecombe www.geocities.com/ncedgecombe/	E6	4 Apr 1741	**Bertie** Edgecombe County; 301 Saint Andrews St; PO Box 386; Tarboro, NC 27886; Ph. 252.641.7924 Details: (Reg of Deeds has b, m & land rec; Clk Sup Ct has pro & ct rec)
Forsyth www.co.forsyth.nc.us/	J5	16 Jan 1849	**Stokes** Forsyth County; 102 W 3rd St; PO Box 20639; Winston-Salem, NC 27101; Ph. 336.727.2903 Details: (Reg of Deeds has b, m, d & land rec; Clk Sup Ct has div, pro & ct rec from 1849)
Franklin www.co.franklin.nc.us/	G5	14 Apr 1778	**Bute** Franklin County; 113 S Main St; PO Box 545; Louisburg, NC 27549; Ph. 919.496.3500 Details: (1820 census missing) (Reg of Deeds has b & d rec from 1913, m rec from 1869, land rec from 1779 & pro rec; Clk Sup Ct has div & ct rec)

County Website	Map Index	Date Created	Parent County or Territory From Which Organized Address/Details
Gaston www.co.gaston.nc.us/	L7	21 Dec 1846	**Lincoln** Gaston County; 325 N Marietta St; PO Box 1578; Gastonia, NC 28053; Ph. 704.868.7684 Details: (Reg of Deeds has b, m & d rec from 1913 & land rec from 1847; Clk Sup Ct has div & ct rec)
Gates albemarle-nc.com/gates/	C4	14 Apr 1778	**Chowan, Hertford, Perquimans** Gates County; PO Box 345; Gatesville, NC 27938; Ph. 252.357.0850 Details: (Reg of Deeds has b, m, d, bur & land rec; Clk Sup Ct has div, pro & ct rec from 1780)
Glasgow www.rootsweb.com/~ncglasgo/glasgow.htm		5 Dec 1791	**Dobbs** Details: (Discontinued & became part of Greene Co 18 Nov 1799)
Graham* www.main.nc.us/graham/index.html	Q7	30 Jan 1872	**Cherokee** Graham County; Main St; PO Box 406; Robbinsville, NC 28771-0575; Ph. 828.479.7971 Details: (Reg of Deeds has b & d rec from 1913, m & land rec from 1873; Clk Sup Ct has div, ct & pro rec from 1872)
Granville www.granvillecounty.org/	G5	28 Jun 1746	**Edgecombe** Granville County; 101 Main St; Oxford, NC 27565-3318; Ph. 919.693.6314 Details: (Clk Sup Ct has div, pro & land rec)
Greene www.co.greene.nc.us/	E6	18 Nov 1799	**Glasgow** Greene County; 2nd & Greene; PO Box 68; Snow Hill, NC 28580; Ph. 252.747.3620 Details: (Courthouse burned in 1876) (Reg of Deeds has b, m, d, bur & land rec from 1876; Clk Sup Ct has div, ct & pro rec from 1876)
Guilford www.co.guilford.nc.us/	I5	5 Dec 1770	**Rowan, Orange** Guilford County; 201 S Eugene St; PO Box 3427; Greensboro, NC 27402; Ph. 336.641.7556 Details: (Courthouse burned 1872; many older rec still available) (Reg of Deeds has b & d rec from 1913, m rec from 1865, land rec from 1771 & mil rec; Clk Cts has div, pro & ct rec)
Halifax www.halifaxnc.com/	E5	12 Dec 1754	**Edgecombe** Halifax County; King St; PO Box 67; Halifax, NC 27839; Ph. 252.583.2101 Details: (Reg of Deeds has b & d rec from 1913, m rec from 1867, div & pro rec from 1868, ct rec from 1893, land rec from 1729 & mil dis rec from 1918)
Harnett www.harnett.org/	H7	7 Feb 1855	**Cumberland** Harnett County; 729 S Main St; PO Box 279; Lillington, NC 27546; Ph. 910.893.7540 Details: (Reg of Deeds has b, m, d & land rec; Clk Sup Ct has div, pro & ct rec from 1920; rec from 1855 to 1920 were destroyed in a fire)
Haywood haywoodnc.org/government/haywoodcountygovt.html	P6	15 Dec 1808	**Buncombe** Haywood County; 215 N Main St; Waynesville, NC 28786; Ph. 828.452.6635 Details: (Reg of Deeds has m & land rec; Clk Sup Ct has pro & ct rec)
Henderson mail.henderson.lib.nc.us/county/	O7	15 Dec 1838	**Buncombe** Henderson County; 200 N Grove St Ste 129; Hendersonville, NC 28792-5053; Ph. 828.697.4901 Details: (Reg of Deeds has b & d rec from 1914, m rec from 1800 & land rec from 1837; Cllk Sup Ct has div, pro & ct rec from 1841)
Hertford www.rootsweb.com/~nchertfo/	D5	12 Dec 1754	**Bertie, Chowan, Northampton** Hertford County; King St; PO Box 36; Winton, NC 27986; Ph. 252.358.7850 Details: (Courthouse burned 1832 & 1862) (Reg of Deeds has b, d & bur rec from 1913, m rec from 1884 & land rec from 1866; Clk Sup Ct has div & ct rec from 1883 & pro rec from 1869)
Hoke www.ncse.org/hoke.html	H7	17 Feb 1911	**Cumberland, Robeson** Hoke County; 304 N Main St; Raeford, NC 28376; Ph. 919.875.2035 Details: (Reg of Deeds has b, m, d & land rec from 1911; Clk Sup Ct has div, pro & ct rec from 1911)

County Website	Map Index	Date Created	Parent County or Territory From Which Organized Address/Details
Hyde albemarle-nc.com/hyde/	B6	3 Dec 1705	**Wickham Precinct of Bath Co** Hyde County; 264 Business Hwy; PO Box 297; Swan Quarter, NC 27885; Ph. 252.926.3011 Details: (Formerly Wickham Co. Name changed to Hyde, 1712) (Reg of Deeds has b, d & bur rec from 1913, m rec from 1850, land rec from 1736, marr bonds 1735-1867 & delayed b rec from late 1800's; Clk Sup Ct has div & ct rec from 1868 & pro rec from 1774)
Iredell www.co.iredell.nc.us/	L6	3 Nov 1788	**Rowan** Iredell County; 221 E Water St; PO Box 904; Statesville, NC 28677; Ph. 704.872.7468 Details: (Courthouse burned in 1854) (Reg of Deeds has b, m, d, bur & land rec; Clk Sup Ct has div rec from 1820, pro & ct rec from 1788)
Jackson main.nc.us/jackson/	P7	29 Jan 1851	**Haywood, Macon** Jackson County; 401 Grind Stass Rd Rm 103; Sylva, NC 28779; Ph. 828.586.7532 Details: (Reg of Deeds has b, m, d, bur & land rec; Clk Sup Ct has div, pro & ct rec from 1851)
Johnston www.co.johnston.nc.us/	F6	28 Jun 1746	**Craven** Johnston County; 207 E Johnston St; PO Box 118; Smithfield, NC 27577-4515; Ph. 919.989.5160 Details: (Reg of Deeds has m & land rec; Clk Sup Ct has pro & ct rec)
Jones www.co.jones.nc.us/	E7	14 Apr 1778	**Craven** Jones County; PO Box 189; Trenton, NC 28585; Ph. 252.448.2551 Details: (Courthouse burned in 1862) (Reg of Deeds has b & d rec from 1913, m rec from 1850, land rec from 1779 & mil dis rec; Clk Cts has pro rec from 1779, ct & div rec)
Lee www.lcedc.com/	H6	6 Mar 1907	**Chatham, Moore** Lee County; 1400 S Horner Blvd; PO Box 2040; Sanford, NC 27330; Ph. 919.774.5063 Details: (Reg of Deeds has b, d & land rec; Clk Sup Ct has m, div, pro & ct rec from 1907)
Lenoir www.co.lenoir.nc.us/	E7	5 Dec 1791	**Dobbs** Lenoir County; PO Box 3289; Kinston, NC 28502; Ph. 252.523.2390 Details: (Courthouse burned 1878) (Clk Sup Ct has div, pro & ct rec from 1880; Reg of Deeds has m & land rec)
Lincoln www.lincolncounty.org/	L6	14 Apr 1778	**Tryon** Lincoln County; 115 W Main St; PO Box 218; Lincolnton, NC 28093; Ph. 704.736.8534 Details: (Reg of Deeds has b, m, d, bur & land rec; Clk Sup Ct has div & ct rec from 1920 & pro rec from 1869)
Macon www.main.nc.us/macon/index.html	Q7	1828	**Haywood** Macon County; Courthouse; Franklin, NC 28734-3005; Ph. 828.349.2095 Details: (Reg of Deeds has m & land rec; Clk Sup Ct has pro & ct rec)
Madison www.main.nc.us/madison/index.html	O6	27 Jan 1851	**Buncombe, Yancey** Madison County; PO Box 66; Marshall, NC 28753; Ph. 828.649.3131 Details: (Reg of Deeds has b, m, d, bur & land rec; Clk Sup Ct has div, pro & ct rec from 1851)
Martin albemarle-nc.com/martin/	D6	2 Mar 1774	**Halifax, Tyrell** Martin County; 305 E Main St; Williamston, NC 27892-0668; Ph. 252.792.1683 Details: (Courthouse burned in 1884; 1820 cen missing) (Reg of Deeds has b, m, d & land rec; Clk Sup Ct has div & ct rec from 1800's & pro rec from 1700's)
McDowell www.main.nc.us/mcdowell/index.html	N6	19 Dec 1842	**Burke, Rutherford** McDowell County; Courthouse Main St; Marion, NC 28752-4041; Ph. 828.652.4727 Details: (Reg of Deeds has b, m, d & land rec; Clk Sup Ct has div, pro & ct rec from 1842)

County Website	Map Index	Date Created	Parent County or Territory From Which Organized
			Address/Details
Mecklenburg www.charmeck.nc.us/	**K7**	**3 Nov 1762**	**Anson** Mecklenburg County; 720 E 4th St; Charlotte, NC 28202-2835; Ph. 704.336.2443 Details: (Reg of Deeds has b & d rec from 1913, m rec from 1850 & land rec from 1763; Clk Sup Ct has div, pro & ct rec from 1930)
Mitchell www.main.nc.us/mitchell/	**N5**	**16 Feb 1861**	**Burke, Caldwell, McDowell, Watauga, Yancey** Mitchell County; Crimson Laurel Way Admin Bldg; PO Box 82; Bakersville, NC 28705; Ph. 828.688.2139 Details: (Clk Sup Ct has div & pro rec from 1861 & ct rec from 1912; Reg of Deeds has m & land rec)
Montgomery www.uwharrie-forest.org/chamber/ main.html	**J7**	**14 Apr 1778**	**Anson** Montgomery County; E Main St; PO Box 695; Troy, NC 27371; Ph. 910.576.4271 Details: (Courthouse burned 1835; 1820 census missing) (Reg of Deeds has b, m, d, bur, pro & land rec; Clk Sup Ct has div & ct rec from 1842)
Moore* www.co.moore.nc.us/	**I7**	**18 Apr 1784**	**Cumberland** Moore County; 100 Downstreet; PO Box 936; Carthage, NC 28327-0936; Ph. 910.947.6370 Details: (Courthouse burned in 1889) (Reg of Deeds has b & d rec from 1913, m & land rec from 1889 & land grants from 1784; Clk Sup Ct has div, pro & ct rec)
Nash* www.co.nash.nc.us/	**F5**	**15 Nov 1777**	**Edgecombe** Nash County; County Courthouse Rm 104; PO Box 974; Nashville, NC 27856; Ph. 252.459.9836 Details: (Reg of Deeds has b & d rec from 1913 & m rec from 1872; Clk Sup Ct has div & ct rec from 1876, pro & land rec from 1869; oldest wills in Dept of Archives, Raleigh, NC)
New Hanover www.co.new-hanover.nc.us/	**F9**	**27 Nov 1729**	**Craven** New Hanover County; 3rd & Princess St Rm 103; Wilmington, NC 28401-4090; Ph. 910.341.7125 Details: (Courthouse burned 1798, 1819 & 1840; 1810 cen missing) (Reg of Deeds has b, m, d & land rec; Clk Sup Ct has div, pro & ct rec)
Northampton www.northamptonnc.com/	**E4**	**1741**	**Bertie** Northampton County; Jefferson St; PO Box 120; Jackson, NC 27845; Ph. 252.534.2511 Details: (Reg of Deeds has b, m, d & land rec; Clk Sup Ct has div rec from 1800, pro & ct rec from 1761)
Onslow co.onslow.nc.us/	**E8**	**1734**	**New Hanover** Onslow County; 109 Old Bridge St Rm 107; Jacksonville, NC 28540; Ph. 910.347.3451 Details: (Reg of Deeds has b & d rec from 1914, m rec from 1893 & land rec from 1734; Clk Sup Ct has div, pro & ct rec from 1915, earlier rec at Dept of Archives, Raleigh NC 27602)
Orange www.co.orange.nc.us/	**H5**	**31 Mar 1752**	**Bladen, Granville, Johnston** Orange County; 200 S Cameron St; Hillsborough, NC 27278; Ph. 919.245.2675 Details: (Courthouse burned 1789) (Reg of Deeds has b & d rec from 1913, m & land rec from 1754, div rec from 1869, pro rec from 1756 & ct rec rec from 1865)
Pamlico www.pamlico.com/	**D7**	**8 Feb 1872**	**Beaufort, Craven** Pamlico County; 202 Main St; PO Box 423; Bayboro, NC 28515; Ph. 252.745.4421 Details: (Reg of Deeds has b rec from 1913, m, d & land rec from 1872; Clk Sup Ct has div, pro & ct rec from 1872)
Pamptecough		**3 Dec 1705**	**Bath** Details: (see Beaufort) (Name changed to Beaufort, 1712)
Pasquotank www.co.pasquotank.nc.us/	**C5**	**1670**	**Precinct in Albemarle** Pasquotank County; 206 E Main; PO Box 154; Elizabeth City, NC 27907-0039; Ph. 252.335.4367 Details: (Courthouse burned 1862) (Clk Sup Ct has div, pro & ct rec; Reg of Deeds has b & d rec from 1913, m rec from 1867 & land rec from 1700's)

County Website	Map Index	Date Created	Parent County or Territory From Which Organized Address/Details
Pender www.pender-county.com/	F9	16 Feb 1875	**New Hanover** Pender County; 300 E Freemont St; PO Box 43; Burgaw, NC 28425; Ph. 910.259.1225 Details: (Reg of Deeds has b, m, d & land rec; Clk Sup Ct has div, pro & ct rec)
Perquimans albemarle-nc.com/hertford/	C5	1670	**Precinct in Albemarle** Perquimans County; PO Box 74; Hertford, NC 27944; Ph. 252.426.5660 Details: (Perquimans Co was known as Berkeley Precinct from 1671 to 1681) (Reg of Deeds has m & land rec; Clk Sup Ct has pro & ct rec)
Person www2.person.net/person/home.htm	H4	5 Dec 1791	**Caswell** Person County; County Courthouse; Roxboro, NC 27573; Ph. 252.597.1733 Details: (Reg of Deeds has b, m, d & land rec; Clk Sup Ct has div, pro & ct rec from 1791)
Pitt www.co.pitt.nc.us/index.asp	E7	24 Apr 1760	**Beaufort** Pitt County; W 3rd St; PO Box 35; Greenville, NC 27835; Ph. 252.830.4128 Details: (Courthouse burned 1857) (Reg of Deeds has b & d rec from 1913, m rec from 1866 & land rec from 1762; Clk Sup Ct has div, pro & ct rec from 1885)
Polk www.polkcounty.org/	N7	18 Jan 1847	**Henderson, Rutherford** Polk County; PO Box 308; Columbus, NC 28722; Ph. 828.894.8450 Details: (Clk Sup Ct has div rec from 1932, pro & ct rec from 1872; Reg of Deeds has m & land rec)
Randolph www.co.randolph.nc.us/	I6	14 Apr 1778	**Guilford** Randolph County; Shaw Bldg; 158 Worth St; Asheboro, NC 27203; Ph. 336.318.6960 Details: (1820 cen missing) (Reg of Deeds has b & d rec from 1913, m rec from 1800 & land rec; Clk Sup Ct has div & ct rec, pro rec from 1786)
Richmond www.co.richmond.nc.us/	I7	14 Apr 1778	**Anson** Richmond County; 114 E Franklin St #101; Rockingham, NC 28379; Ph. 910.997.8250 Details: (Reg of Deeds has b & d rec from 1913, m rec from 1870 & land rec from 1784; Clk Sup Ct has div rec from 1913 & pro rec from 1782)
Robeson www.geocities.com/ncrobeson/	H8	18 Nov 1786	**Bladen** Robeson County; 500 N Elm St; PO Box 22; Lumberton, NC 28358; Ph. 919.671.3044 Details: (Reg of Deeds has b rec from 1913, m rec from 1787, d rec from 1915 & land rec from 1799; Clk Sup Ct has div & ct rec from 1920 & pro rec from 1868)
Rockingham www.co.rockingham.nc.us/	I4	19 Nov 1785	**Guilford** Rockingham County; 371 NC 65 #212; PO Box 56; Wentworth, NC 27375; Ph. 336.342.8820 Details: (Courthouse burned 1906) (Reg of Deeds has m rec from 1868, b & d rec from 1913 & land rec from 1787; Clk Sup Ct has pro rec from 1804; NC Hist Com has m rec 1741-1868)
Rowan www.co.rowan.nc.us/	K6	27 Mar 1753	**Anson** Rowan County; 202 N Main St; PO Box 2568; Salisbury, NC 28144-4346; Ph. 704.636.3102 Details: (Reg of Deeds has b, m, d & land rec; Clk Sup Ct has div rec from 1881, pro & ct rec)
Rutherford www.rutherfordgov.org/	N7	14 Apr 1779	**Tryon** Rutherford County; 229 N Main St; PO Box 551; Rutherfordton, NC 28139-0630; Ph. 828.287.6155 Details: (Courthouse burned in 1857) (Clk Sup Ct has b rec from 1917, d rec from 1913, m, div, pro, ct & land rec from 1779, tax lists & voter registration)
Sampson www.rootsweb.com/~ncsampso/ index.htm	G8	18 Apr 1784	**Duplin** Sampson County; 435 Rowan Rd; PO Box 256; Clinton, NC 28328-4700; Ph. 919.529.8026 Details: (Courthouse burned 1921) (Reg of Deeds has m & land rec; Clk Sup Ct has pro rec)

County Website	Map Index	Date Created	Parent County or Territory From Which Organized / Address/Details
Scotland www.rootsweb.com/~ncscotla/	I8	20 Feb 1899	**Richmond** Scotland County; 212 Biggs St; Laurinburg, NC 28352; Ph. 910.277.2577 Details: (Reg of Deeds has b rec from 1913, m, d & bur rec from 1899 & land rec; Clk Sup Ct has div, pro & ct rec from 1899)
Stanly www.co.stanly.nc.us/	J7	11 Jan 1841	**Montgomery** Stanly County; 201 S 2nd St; Albemarle, NC 28001; Ph. 704.983.3640 Details: (Reg of Deeds has m & land rec; Clk Sup Ct has pro rec)
Stokes www.co.stokes.nc.us/	J5	2 Nov 1789	**Surry** Stokes County; Hwy 89; Danbury, NC 27016; Ph. 336.593.2811 Details: (Reg of Deeds has m & land rec; Clk Sup Ct has pro rec)
Surry www.geocities.com/~surryco/	K4	5 Dec 1770	**Rowan** Surry County; 114 W Atkins St; Dobson, NC 27017-0345; Ph. 336.401.8150 Details: (Reg of Deeds has b, m, d, bur & land rec; Clk Sup Ct has div, ct & pro rec from 1771)
Swain www.rootsweb.com/~ncswain/	Q6	24 Feb 1871	**Jackson, Macon** Swain County; 1 Mitchell St; PO Box 417; Bryson, NC 28713; Ph. 828.488.9273 Details: (Reg of Deeds has b & d rec from 1913, m rec from 1907 & land rec; Clk Sup Ct has div & ct rec from 1900 & pro rec)
Transylvania www.rootsweb.com/~nctransy/	O7	15 Feb 1861	**Henderson, Jackson** Transylvania County; 12 E Main St; PO Box 417; Brevard, NC 28712; Ph. 828.884.3162 Details: (Reg of Deeds has b & d rec from 1913, m & land rec from 1861 & mil dis rec; Clk Sup Ct has div, pro & ct rec)
Tryon www.blueridge.net/lds/nc/tryon.html		1768	**Mecklenburg** Details: (see Lincoln) (Discontinued 1779. Absorbed by Lincoln & Rutherford Cos)
Tyrrell albemarle-nc.com/columbia/	B6	27 Nov 1729	**Chowan, Currituck, Pasquotank** Tyrrell County; 403 Main St; PO Box 449; Columbia, NC 27925; Ph. 252.796.2901 Details: (Reg of Deeds has b & d rec from 1913, m rec from 1862 & land rec; Clk Sup Ct has div rec, pro rec from 1730 & ct rec from 1900)
Union www.co.union.nc.us/	K8	19 Dec 1842	**Anson, Mecklenburg** Union County; PO Box 248; Monroe, NC 28111; Ph. 704.283.3727 Details: (Reg of Deeds has b, m, d & bur rec; Clk Cts has div, pro, mil, ct & nat rec; Co Asr has land rec)
Vance www.vancecounty.org/	G5	5 Mar 1881	**Franklin, Granville, Warren** Vance County; 122 Young St Ste F; Henderson, NC 27536; Ph. 252.438.4155 Details: (Clk Sup Ct has div, pro & ct rec; Reg of Deeds has m & land rec)
Wake www.co.wake.nc.us/	G6	5 Dec 1770	**Cumberland, Johnston, Orange** Wake County; St Garland James Bldg; 300 S Salisbury; PO Box 1897; Raleigh, NC 27602; Ph. 919.856.5460 Details: (1810 & 1820 cen missing) (Reg of Deeds has m & land rec; Clk Sup Ct has pro rec)
Warren www.rootsweb.com/~ncwarren/	F4	14 Apr 1779	**Bute** Warren County; PO Box 506; Warrenton, NC 27589-0709; Ph. 252.257.3265 Details: (Reg of Deeds has b & d rec from 1913, m & land rec from 1764; Clk Sup Ct has div & pro rec from 1764 & ct rec from 1968)
Washington www.washingtoncountygov.com/	C6	15 Nov 1799	**Tyrell** Washington County; 120 Adams St; Plymouth, NC 27962; Ph. 252.793.2325 Details: (Courthouse burned 1862, 1869 & 1873) (Reg of Deeds has b & d rec from 1913, m rec from 1851 & land rec from 1799; Clk Sup Ct has div rec from 1871, pro & ct rec from 1873)
Watauga www.wataugacounty.org/	M5	27 Jan 1849	**Ashe, Caldwell, Wilkes, Yancey** Watauga County; 842 W King St; Boone, NC 28607-3531; Ph. 828.265.8052 Details: (Reg of Deeds has b & d rec from 1914, m rec from 1872 & land rec; Clk Sup Ct has div, pro & ct rec from 1872)

County Website	Map Index	Date Created	Parent County or Territory From Which Organized Address/Details
Wayne www.esn.net/waynecounty/	F7	18 Oct 1779	**Dobbs** Wayne County; 215 S William St; PO Box 267; Goldsboro, NC 27530-4824; Ph. 919.731.1449 Details: (Reg of Deeds has b, m, d, bur & land rec; Clk Sup Ct has div, pro & ct rec)
Wickham		3 Dec 1705	**Precinct of Bath** Details: (see Hyde) (Name changed to Hyde, 1712)
Wilkes www.wilkesnc.org/government/ county.htm	L5	15 Nov 1777	**Surry, Dist. of Washington** Wilkes County; 110 North St; Wilkesboro, NC 28697; Ph. 336.651.7351 Details: (Reg of Deeds has b & d rec from 1913, m & land rec from 1778; Clk Sup Ct has div, pro & ct rec)
Wilson www.wilson-co.com/	F6	13 Feb 1855	**Edgecombe, Johnston, Nash, Wayne** Wilson County; 101 N Goldsboro St; Wilson, NC 27893; Ph. 252.399.2935 Details: (Reg of Deeds has b, m, d & land rec; Clk Sup Ct has div & ct rec from 1868 & pro rec from 1855)
Yadkin www.yadkincounty.gov/	K5	28 Dec 1850	**Surry** Yadkin County; 101 State St; Yadkinville, NC 27055; Ph. 336.679.4225 Details: (Reg of Deeds has b & d rec from 1913, m & land rec from 1850; Clk Sup Ct has div & ct rec, pro rec from 1850)
Yancey* www.main.nc.us/yancey/index.html	N6	1883	**Buncombe, Burke** Yancey County; County Courthouse; Burnsville, NC 28714; Ph. 828.682.2174 Details: (Reg of Deeds has b, m, d & bur rec; Clk Sup Ct has div rec from 1875, pro, ct & land rec from 1870; Dept of Archives & Hist in Raleigh, NC has older rec)

Notes

Notes

Wild Prarie Rose

NORTH DAKOTA

CAPITAL: BISMARCK – TERRITORY 1861 – STATE 1889 (39TH)

Pierre Gaultier de Varennes was the first French explorer in the area. He reached Indian villages on the Missouri River in 1738. The French laid claim to the area in 1682, but permitted British fur trading. The Louisiana Purchase in 1803 gave the southwestern half of North Dakota to the United States. Lewis and Clark explored the area the following year.

The first permanent settlement – besides those of the Native Americans – was made by Scottish pioneers from Canada in 1812 at Pembina. As Indians were driven westward, settlers came into the eastern regions of the state to farm. The Dakota Territory was organized in 1861 and included the two Dakotas, Montana, and Wyoming. The first Homestead Act offered free land to settlers, but the Civil War and Indian wars delayed settlement. During the Civil War, about 200 men fought for the Union forces. In 1864, the Montana Territory was created. It took the Wyoming and Montana areas from the Dakota Territory.

As railroads reached completion, settlement in North Dakota began in earnest. In 1871, railroads reached the Red River from St. Paul and Duluth. Dreams of acres of fertile land drew thousands of northern and middle Europeans to North Dakota. Norwegians led the immigration, but large numbers of Swedes, Danes, Icelanders, Czechs, Poles, and Dutch also came.

French-Canadians came from Canada. Germans settled around Bismarck and the south central counties, which is evident from the names of the cities in the area, such as Leipzig, Strassburg and Danzig. The Dakota Territory was divided into North and South Dakota in about 1873. In 1889, North Dakota became the thirty-ninth state in the Union.

Look for vital records in the following locations:

- **Birth and death records:** Registration of births and deaths was required from 1893 to 1895 and after 1899. General compliance with the law was not reached until about 1923. Copies of these records are available from the Division of Vital Records in Bismarck, North Dakota.
- **Marriage, divorce and probate records:** Marriage certificates and licenses are filed in the office of each county judge. Since 1 July 1925, copies of licenses and marriage certificates have been forwarded to the State Registrar, who can issue certified copies. District Court Clerks have charge of civil court, divorce, and probate records.
- **Census records:** North Dakota was included in the 1836 Wisconsin, 1840 Iowa, 1850 Minnesota, and 1860-1880 Dakota Territorial censuses.
- **Land records:** Original patents and copies of township plats are available from the Bureau of Land Management in Billings, Montana. Records of the local land offices are at the State Historical Society of North Dakota in Bismarck, North Dakota. The county registrars of deeds have deeds and land titles dating from the time land became available for private purchase.

Division of Vital Records
State Capitol
600 East Boulevard Avenue
Bismarck, North Dakota 58505
701.328.2360

Bureau of Land Management
222 North 32nd Street
PO Box 30157
Billings, Montana 59107

State Historical Society of North Dakota
North Dakota Heritage Center
Bismarck, North Dakota 58505

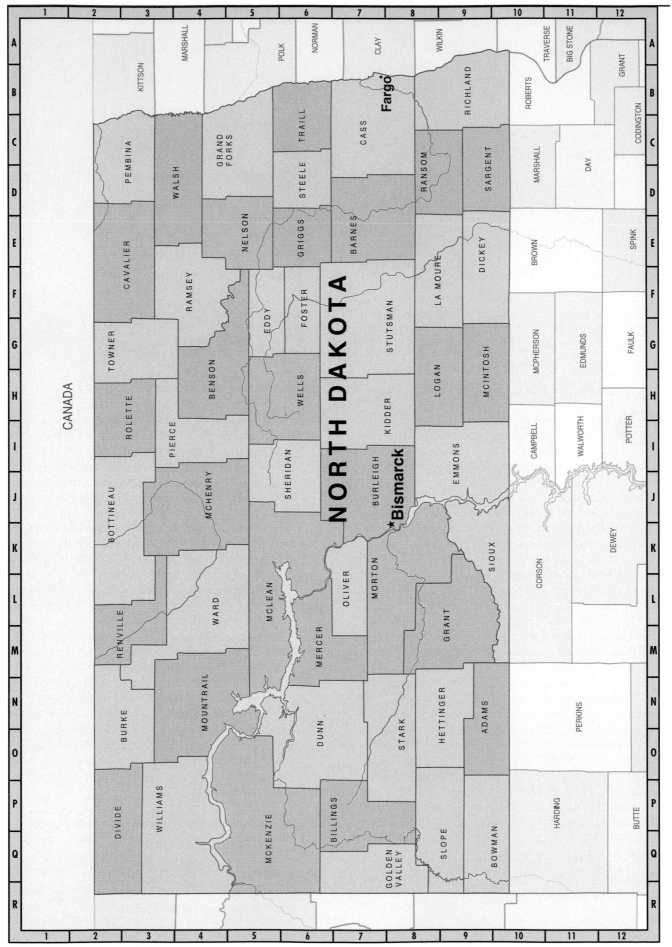

Societies and Repositories

Bottineau County Genealogical Society; 614 W. Pine Circle; Bottineau, North Dakota 58318

Bowman County Genealogical Society; PO PO Box 1044; Bowman, North Dakota 58623

Bureau of Land Management, (ND, tract books, township plats); 222 North 32nd Street, PO Box 36800; Billings, Montana 59101; 406.255.2940

Central North Dakota Genealogical Society; Harvey Public Library; 119 East 10th; Harvey, North Dakota 58341

Department of Special Collections, Chester Fritz Library; PO Box 9000, University of North Dakota; Grand Forks, North Dakota 58202; 701.777.2617; Fax 701.777.3319;

Division of Vital Records, State Capitol; 600 East Boulevard Ave.; Bismarck, North Dakota 58505; 701.224.2350

Family History Library: 35 North West Temple Street: Salt Lake City, Utah 84150: 800.346.6044 or 801.240.2584: <www.familysearch.org>: Find a Family History Center near you: <www.familysearch.org/Eng/Library/FHC/frameset_fhc.asp>

Genealogical Guild of Wilkin County, Minnesota and Richland County, North Dakota; c/o Leach Public Library; Wahpeton, North Dakota 58075

Germans from Russia Heritage Society; 1008 East Central Avenue; Bismarck, North Dakota 58501-1936; 701.223.6167

Griggs County Genealogical Society; PO Box 237, Griggs County Court House; Cooperstown, North Dakota 58425

James River Genealogical Club; 651 4th St. N.; Carrington, North Dakota 58421; <www.rootsweb.com/~ndjrjc/index.htm>

Lutheran, Evangelical Lutheran Church in America; 8765 W. Higgins Rd.; Chicago, Illinois 60631-4198; 773.380.2818; Fax 773.380.2977

McLean County Genealogical Society; PO Box 51; Garrison, North Dakota 58540

Medora Centennial Commission; PO Box 212; Medora, North Dakota 58645

Methodist, Archives and History Library, Dakotas Conference; PO Box 460, 1331 West University Blvd.; Mitchell, North Dakota 57301; 605.996.6552; Fax 605.996.1766

Minot Family History Center, c/o Pat Chalcraft; 62 Western Village; Minot, North Dakota 58701

Minot Public Library; 516 Second Ave., S.W.; Minot, North Dakota 58701

Mouse River Loop Genealogical Society; PO Box 1391; Minot, North Dakota 58702-1391

National Archives-Central Plains Region; National Archives-Central Plains Region; Kansas City, Missouri 64131; 816.926.7271

National Archives-Rocky Mountain Region; PO Box 25307; Denver, Colorado 80225; 303.236.0817; Fax 303.236.9297

North Dakota Bismarck-Mandan Genealogical Society; PO Box 485; Bismarck, North Dakota 58501

North Dakota Institute for Regional Studies, North Dakota State University; PO Box 5599; Fargo, North Dakota 58105-5599; 701.231.8886; Fax 701.237.7138

North Dakota State Archives and Historical Research Library; North Dakota Heritage Center; 612 East Boulevard Avenue; Bismarck, North Dakota 58505-0830; <www.state.nd.us/hist/sal.htm>

North Dakota State Genealogical Society; PO Box 485; Bismarck, North Dakota 58502

North Dakota State University Library; ND Institute for Regional Studies, PO Box 5599; Fargo, North Dakota 58105-5599; 701.231.8886; Fax 701.231.7138

North Dakota Water Commission (Township plats); 900 East Boulevard; Bismarck, North Dakota 58505; 701.328.2750; Fax 701.328.3696

Presbyterian Historical Society, United Presbyterian Church in the U.S.; 425 Lombard St.; Philadelphia, Pennsylvania 19147; 215.627.1852; Fax 215.627.0509

Red River Valley Gen. Soc. Library, Manchester Bld; PO Box 9284, 112 No Univ. Dr., Suite L 116; Fargo, North Dakota 58106-9284

Red River Valley Genealogical Society; PO Box 9284; Fargo, North Dakota 58106; <fargocity.com/~rrvgs/>

Roman Catholic, Diocese of Bismarck, Chancery Office; PO Box 1575; Bismarck, North Dakota 58502-1575; 701.223.1347; Fax 701.223.3693

Roman Catholic, Diocese of Fargo, Chancery Office; Diocese of Fargo; 1310 Broadway, PO Box 1750; Fargo, North Dakota 58107; 701.235.6429; Fax 701.235.0296

Southwestern North Dakota Genealogical Society; HCR 01, PO Box 321; Regent, North Dakota 58650

State Historical Society of North Dakota, North Dakota Heritage Center; 612 E. Boulevard Ave.; Bismarck, North Dakota 58505; 701.328.2668; Fax 701.328.3710; <www.state.nd.us/hist/>

United Methodist Church, North Dakota Conference; 1600 4th Ave. North; Grand Forks, North Dakota 58201

University of North Dakota Library; Grand Forks, North Dakota 58201

Williams County Genealogical Society; 703 W 7th St.; Williston, North Dakota 58801-4908

Bibliography and Record Sources

General Sources

Aberle, George P. *Pioneers and Their Sons: One Hundred Sixty-Five Family Histories.* Bismarck, North Dakota: Tumbleweed Press, 1980.

Albers, Everett C. *Germans from Russia Settlers.* Fessenden, North Dakota: The Grass Roots Press, 1999.

Compendium of History and Biography of North Dakota Containing a History of North Dakota: Embracing an Account of Early Explorations, Early Settlement, Indian Occupancy...and a Concise History of Growth and Development of the State also a Compendium of Biography of North Dakota. (1900) Reprint. Salem Massachusetts: Higginson Books, 1994.

Compendium of History and Biography of North Dakota Containing a History of North Dakota.... Chicago: Geo. A. Ogle & Co., 1900.

Crawford, Lewis Ferandus. *History of North Dakota and North Dakota Biography.* 3 vols. Chicago: American Historical Soc., 1931.

Davenport, John B. and Colleen A. Oihus. *Guide to the Orin G. Libby Manuscript Collection and Related Research Collections*, 2 vols. Grand Forks, North Dakota: Chester Fritz Library, University of North Dakota, 1975, 1983.

History of the Red River Valley, Past and Present. 2 vols. (1909) Reprint. Salem, Maryland: Higginson Books, 1994.

Lareau, Paul J. and Elmer Courteau. *French-Canadian Families of the North Central States: A Genealogical Dictionary.* 8 vols. St. Paul, Minn.: Northwest Territory French and Canadian Heritage Institute, 1980.

Lounsberry, Clement A. *Early History of North Dakota.* Washington, D.C.: Liberty Press, 1919.

Lounsberry, Clement Augustus. *North Dakota History and People, Outlines of American History.* 3 vols. Chicago: S. J. Clarke, 1916.

North Dakota Research Outline. Series US-States, no. 35. Salt lake City: Family History Library. 1988.

Rath, George *The Black Sea Germans in the Dakotas.* Freeman, South Dakota: Pine Hill Press, 1977.

Robinson, Elwyn B. *History of North Dakota.* Lincoln: University of Nebraska Press, 1966.

Rylance, Daniel, and J.F.S. Smeall, *Reference Guide to North Dakota History and North Dakota Literature.* Grand Forks: Chester Fritz Library of the University of North Dakota, 1979.

State Historical Society of North Dakota (Bismarck, North Dakota). *Historical Data Project; Pioneer Biography Files.* Bismarck, North Dakota: State Historical Society of North Dakota, 1988-1989. Microfilm, 34 rolls.

Stupnik, Cynthia Ann. *Steppes to New Odessa: Germans From Russia Who Settled in Odessa Township, Dakota Territory.* 1996. Heritage Books, Bowie, Maryland

The Collections of The State Historical Society of North Dakota 7 vols. (Bismarck, North Dakota: Tribune State Printers, 1906–.

Thorson, Playford V. *Plains Folk: North Dakota's Ethnic History.* Fargo, North Dakota: In cooperation with the North Dakota Humanities Council and the University of North Dakota, 1988.

Vexler, Robert I. *Chronology and Documentary Handbook of the State of North Dakota.* Dobbs Ferry, New York: Oceana Publications, 1978.

Atlases, Maps and Gazetteers

Goodman, Lowell R., and R.J. Eidem. *The Atlas of North Dakota.* Fargo: North Dakota Studies, 1976.

North Dakota County Atlas. Bismark: North Dakota State Highway Dept., Planning Division, 1985.

Patera, Alan H. *North Dakota Post Offices 1850-1982.* Burtonsville, Maryland: The Depot, 1982.

Phillips, George H. *Postoffices and Postmarks of Dakota Territory.* Crete, NB: J-B Publishing Co., 1973.

Wick, Douglas A. *North Dakota Place Names.* Bismark, North Dakota: Hedemarken Collectibles, 1988.

Williams, Mary Ann Barnes. *Origins of North Dakota Place Names.* Washburn, North Dakota: Mary Ann Barnes Williams, 1966.

Census Records

Available Census Records and Census Substitutes

Federal Census 1860, 1870, 1880, 1900, 1910, 1920, 1930.

Federal Mortality Schedules 1870, 1880.

Union Veterans and Widows 1890.

State/Territorial 1836, 1885, 1915, 1925.

Dollarhide, William. *The Census Book: A Genealogist's Guide to Federal Census Facts, Schedules and Indexes.* Bountiful, Utah: Heritage Quest, 1999.

Kemp, Thomas Jay. *The American Census Handbook.* Wilmington, DE: Scholarly Resources, Inc., 2001.

Lainhart, Ann S. *State Census Records.* Baltimore: Genealogical Publishing Co., Inc., 1992.

Szucs, Loretto Dennis, and Matthew Wright. *Finding Answers in U.S. Census Records.* Ancestry Publishing, 2001.

Thorndale, William, and William Dollarhide. *Map Guide to the U.S. Federal Censuses, 1790-1920.* Baltimore: Genealogial Publishing Co., 1987.

Court, Probate and Wills

United States. Bureau of Indian Affairs. *Standing Rock Agency. Heirship Records, Early 1900's.* Kansas City, Missouri: Federal Archives and Records Center, 1977. Microfilm, 3 rolls.

Emmigration, Immigration, Migration and Naturalization

Gilman, Rhonda R. *The Red River Trails: Oxcart Routes Between St. Paul and the Selkirk Settlement 1820-1870.* St. Paul: Minnesota Historical Society, 1979.

Michels, John.M. *North Dakota Pioneers from the Banat.* Bismarck, North Dakota: University of Mary Press, 1992.

Sherman, William C. Prairie Mosaic: *An Ethnic Atlas of Rural North Dakota.* Fargo, North Dakota: North Dakota Institute for Regional Studies, 1983.

United States. Circuit Court (North Dakota: Southeastern Division). *Declarations of Intention, 1890-1924.* Microfilm of original records of Circuit Court held at Fargo. (Salt Lake City: Filmed by the Genealogical Society of Utah, 1991).

United States. District Court (North Dakota: Southeastern District*). Naturalization Records, 1906-1924.* Microfilm of original records of the District Court held at Fargo. (Salt Lake City: Filmed by the Genealogical Society of Utah, 1991).

William C. Sherman, *Prairie Mosaic: An Ethnic Atlas of Rural North Dakota.* Fargo: North Dakota Institute for Regional Studies, 1983.

Writers' Program (North Dakota). *Ethnic Group Files, ca. 1935-1942.* Bismarck, North Dakota: State Historical Society of North Dakota, 1989.

Land and Property

Brown, Ruth. *Sioux Personal Property Claims from the Original Ledger.* Medford Oregon; Rogue Genealogical Society, 1987.

Lindgren, H. Elaine. *Land in Her Own Name: Women as Homesteaders in North Dakota.* Fargo, North Dakota: North Dakota Institute for Regional Studies, 1991.

United States. Bureau of Indian Affairs. Standing Rock Agency. *Land Records, 1906-1921.* Kansas City, Missouri: Federal Archives and Records Center, 1977.

Military

Fraser, G. Angus. *Roster of the Men and Women Who Served in the Army or Naval Service (including the Marine Corps) of the United States or its Allies from the State of North Dakota in the World War, 1917-1918,* 4 vols. (Bismarck: Bismarck Tribune Co., 1931.

Lounsberry, Clement A. *Early History of North Dakota.* Washington, D.C.: Liberty Press, 1919.

Pensioners on the Roll as of January 1, 1883 (Living in Dakota Territory). Park Genealogical Books, 1996.

United States. Adjutant General's Office. *Index to Compiled Service Records of Volunteer Union Soldiers Who Served in Organizations from the Territory of Dakota.* Washington, D.C.: The National Archives, 1964.

United States. Selective Service System. North Dakota, *World War I Selective Service System Draft Registration Cards, 1917-1918.* National Archives Microfilm Publications, M1509. Washington, D.C.: National Archives, 1987-1988.

United States. Veterans Administration. *Pension Index File, Alphabetical; of the Veterans, 1861- 1934.* Washington: Veterans Administration, Publications Service, 1953.

Vital and Cemetery Records

Fargo Genealogical Society. *North Dakota Cemeteries,* 16 vols. Fargo, North Dakota. Fargo Genealogical Society, 1972-77.

Historical Records Survey (North Dakota) *Guide to Public Vital Statistics Records in North Dakota.* Bismarck, North Dakota: The Survey, 1941.

United States. Bureau of Indian Affairs. Standing Rock Agency. *Births, Marriages and Deaths, 1880-1942.* Kansas City, Missouri: Federal Archives and Records Center, 1977.

County Website	Map Index	Date Created	Parent County or Territory From Which Organized Address/Details
Adams www.rootsweb.com/~ndadams/	N9	17 Apr 1907	**Hettinger** Adams County; 602 Adams Ave; Hettinger, ND 58639; Ph. 701.567.2460 Details: (Clk Dis Ct has m, div, pro, ct & land rec from 1907)
Allred		9 Mar 1883	**Howard** Details: (see McKenzie) (Eliminated 16 Mar 1905 & absorbed by McKenzie)
Barnes www.rootsweb.com/~ndbarnes/	E2	4 Jan 1873	**Pembina** Barnes County; 230 4th S NE; Valley City, ND 58072; Ph. 701.845.8512 Details: (Formerly Burbank Co. Name changed to Barnes 14 Jan 1875. Organized 5 Aug 1878) (Clk Dis Ct has b, d, bur & ct rec; Co Judge has m & pro rec)
Benson www.rootsweb.com/~ndbenson/	H4	9 Mar 1883	**DeSmet, Ramsey** Benson County; 311 B Ave S; Minnewaukan, ND 58351; Ph. 701.473.5345 Details: (Clk Dis Ct has b rec from late 1890's, m rec from late 1800's, d, div, pro & ct rec from 1895 & bur rec from 1900; Reg of Deeds has land rec)
Billings www.geocities.com/Athens/Forum/ 2079/BILLINGS.HTM	P6	10 Feb 1879	**Unorganized Territory, Howard** Billings County; 495 4th St; PO Box 138; Medora, ND 58645-0138; Ph. 701.623.4492 Details: (Organized 30 Apr 1886) (Clk Dis Ct has m rec from 1893, bur rec from 1922, div rec, pro rec from 1895, ct rec from 1890 & land rec from 1886)
Bottineau www.geocities.com/Athens/Forum/ 2079/bottine.html	J2	4 Jan 1873	**Buffalo** Bottineau County; 314 W 5th St; Bottineau, ND 58318; Ph. 701.228.3983 Details: (Organized 22 Jul 1884) (Clk Dis Ct has b, d & bur rec from 1943, m rec from 1887, div, pro & ct rec from 1889 & nat rec from 1884; Reg of Deeds has land rec)
Bowman www.rootsweb.com/~ndbowman/	Q9	8 Mar 1883	**Billings** Bowman County; 104 1st St NW; Bowman, ND 58623; Ph. 701.523.3450 Details: (Eliminated 30 Nov 1896. Recreated 24 May 1901. Attached to Stark Co prior to organization 17 Apr 1907) (Clk Dis Ct has m rec from 1907, div rec, pro & ct rec from 1908, land rec from 1896 & bur rec)
Buffalo		6 Jan 1864	**Brugier, Charles Mix & Unorganized Territory, South Dakota** Details: (Now in South Dakota) (see Burleigh, Kidder, Logan, McHenry, Rolette & Sheridan)
Buford		9 Mar 1883	**Wallette** Details: (see Williams) (Eliminated 30 Nov 1892 & added to Williams)
Burbank		4 Jan 1873	**Pembina** Details: (see Barnes) (Name changed to Barnes 14 Jan 1875. Lost to Trail Co 12 Jan 1875 & Griggs Co 18 Feb 1881 & discontinued)
Burke www.rootsweb.com/~ndburke/ burke2.htm	N3	8 Feb 1910	**Ward** Burke County; 103 Main St SW; PO Box 219; Bowbells, ND 58721-0219; Ph. 701.377.2718 Details: (Clk Dis Ct has b rec from 1905, m, d, bur, div, pro & ct rec from 1910, land rec from 1900 & homestead patents from 1903)
Burleigh www.rootsweb.com/~ndburlei/index.htm	J7	4 Jan 1873	**Buffalo** Burleigh County; 514 E Thayer Ave; PO Box 5518; Bismarck, ND 58501-4413; Ph. 701.222.6690 Details: (Clk Dis Ct has m & pro rec from 1898, ct rec from 1876 & bur rec from 1950's)
Cass www.co.cass.nd.us/	C7	4 Jan 1873	**Pembina** Cass County; 211 9th St S; PO Box 2806; Fargo, ND 58103-1833; Ph. 701.241.5646 Details: (Clk Dis Ct has div & ct rec from 1885)
Cavalier www.ccjda.org/	F3	4 Jan 1873	**Pembina** Cavalier County; 901 3rd St; Langdon, ND 58249-2457; Ph. 701.256.2124 Details: (Organized 8 Jul 1884) (Clk Dis Ct has m, pro & ct rec rec from 1881 & div rec from 1888; Reg of Deeds has land rec)

County Website	Map Index	Date Created	Parent County or Territory From Which Organized Address/Details
Chippewa		**24 Apr 1862**	**Unorganized Territory**
			Details: (Eliminated 17 Dec 1863 to Unorganized Territory)
Church		**11 Mar 1887**	**McHenry, Sheridan, old**
			Details: (see Sheridan) (Attached to McHenry. Lost to McHenry, McLean & Pierce Cos. Eliminated 30 Nov 1892 to Sheridan)
De Smet		**4 Jan 1873**	**Buffalo**
			Details: (see Pierce) (Formerly French Co. Name changed to DeSmet 14 Jan 1875. Eliminated 11 Mar 1887 to Pierce)
Dickey www.rootsweb.com/~nddickey/dickey.htm	F9	**5 Mar 1881**	**La Moure, Ransom, Unorganized Territory** Dickey County; 309 N 2nd St; PO Box 215; Ellendale, ND 58436; Ph. 701.349.3560 Details: (Organized 31 Aug 1882) (Clk Dis Ct has m, bur, div, pro, mil & ct rec; Reg of Deeds has land rec; State Hist Soc has nat rec)
Divide www.rootsweb.com/~nddivide/ divide97.htm	P2	**8 Nov 1910**	**Williams** Divide County; 300 N Main St; PO Box 68; Crosby, ND 58730-0068; Ph. 701.965.6831 Details: (Clk Dis Ct has b, m, d, bur, div, pro, ct & mil rec from 1910; Reg of Deeds has land rec from 1910; State Hist Soc has nat rec)
Dunn www.dunnjda.com/	O6	**24 May 1901**	**Stark** Dunn County; 205 Owens St; PO Box 136; Manning, ND 58642; Ph. 701.573.4447 Details: (Organized 17 Jan 1908) (Clk Dis Ct has m, pro, div & ct rec from 1908 & mil dis rec from 1919; Reg of Deeds has land rec from 1900; State Hist Soc has nat rec)
Dunn, old www.rootsweb.com/~nddunn/		**9 Mar 1883**	**Howard** Details: (Discontinued & annexed to Stark 30 Nov 1896)
Eddy www.rootsweb.com/~ndeddy/	G5	**31 Mar 1885**	**Foster** Eddy County; 524 Central Ave; New Rockford, ND 58356; Ph. 701.947.2813 Details: (Clk Dis Ct has m, pro & ct rec; Reg of Deeds has land rec)
Emmons www.rootsweb.com/~ndemmons/ index.htm	I9	**10 Feb 1879**	**Unorganized Territory, Burleigh, Campbell Co, SD** Emmons County; 100 4th St NW; Linton, ND 58552; Ph. 701.254.4812 Details: (Organized 9 Nov 1883) (Clk Dis Ct has b rec from 1889, m rec from 1888, d, bur, div & ct rec from 1890, pro rec from 1884 & nat rec from 1886; Reg of Deeds has land rec)
Flanery		**9 Mar 1883**	**Wallette** Details: (see Williams) (Eliminated 30 Nov 1892 & added to Williams)
Foster www.rootsweb.com/~ndfoster/	F6	**4 Jan 1873**	**Pembina** Foster County; 1000 5th St N; PO Box 257; Carrington, ND 58421; Ph. 701.652.1001 Details: (Organized 11 Oct 1883) (Clk Dis Ct has b & d rec from 1900, m, div, pro & ct rec from 1884, mil & nat rec from 1900 & bur rec from 1950's; Reg of Deeds has land rec)
French		**4 Jan 1873**	**Buffalo** Details: (see Pierce) (Name changed to De Smet 14 Jan 1875. Eliminated 11 Mar 1887 to Pierce)
Garfield		**13 Mar 1885**	**Mountrail, Stevens** Details: (Eliminated 30 Nov 1892 to McLean & Ward)
Gingras		**4 Jan 1873**	**Buffalo** Details: (see Wells) (Name changed to Wells 26 Feb 1881)
Golden Valley* www.rootsweb.com/~ndgolden/	Q8	**19 Nov 1912**	**Billings** Golden Valley County; 150 1st Ave SE; PO Box 9; Beach, ND 58621-0009; Ph. 701.872.4352 Details: (Clk Dis Ct has b, m, d, bur, div, pro & ct rec from 1912; Reg of Deeds has land rec from 1912)

County Website	Map Index	Date Created	Parent County or Territory From Which Organized Address/Details
Grand Forks www.grandforkscountygov.com/ homepage.htm	**C5**	**4 Jan 1873**	**Pembina** Grand Forks County; 151 S 4th St; PO Box 1477; Grand Forks, ND 58201; Ph. 701.780.8238 Details: (Organized 12 Jan 1875) (Clk Dis Ct has b rec from 1903, d rec from 1908, div rec from 1878, bur & ct rec, adoption rec & change of name; Co Judge has m rec from 1887& pro rec from 1880; Reg of Deeds has land rec)
Grant www.rootsweb.com/~ndgrant/	**L9**	**7 Nov 1916**	**Morton** Grant County; 106 2nd Ave NE; Carson, ND 58529; Ph. 701.622.3615 Details: (Clk Dis Ct has b rec from 1945, m, d, bur, div, pro & ct rec from 1916; Reg of Deeds has land rec)
Griggs www.cooperstownnd.com/	**E6**	**18 Feb 1881**	**Foster, Burbank, Traill** Griggs County; 808 Rollin Ave SW; Cooperstown, ND 58425; Ph. 701.797.2772 Details: (Organized 16 Jun 1882) (Clk Dis Ct has b rec from 1901, m & pro rec from 1883, d rec from 1901, div & ct rec from 1887; Reg of Deeds has land rec from 1880)
Hettinger www.hettcnty.com/	**N8**	**24 May 1901**	**Stark** Hettinger County; 336 Pacific Ave; Mott, ND 58646; Ph. 701.824.2645 Details: (Attached to Stark Co prior to organization 17 Apr 1907) (Clk Dis Ct has b, d & bur rec from 1943, m, div, pro & ct rec from 1907; Reg of Deeds has land rec)
Hettinger, old		**9 Mar 1883**	**Stark** Details: (Eliminated 30 Nov 1896 to Stark)
Howard		**8 Jan 1873**	**Unorganized Territory** Details: (Eliminated 9 Mar 1883 to Allred, Dunn, McKenzie, old & Wallace)
Kidder www.rootsweb.com/~ndkidder/	**H7**	**4 Jan 1873**	**Buffalo** Kidder County; 120 E Broadway; PO Box 66; Steele, ND 58482; Ph. 701.475.2651 Details: (Organized 22 Mar 1881) (Clk Dis Ct has b, d & bur rec from 1943, div & ct rec from 1885; Co Judge has m rec from 1887 & pro rec from 1883; Reg of Deeds has land rec from 1881)
Kittson		**24 Apr 1862**	**Unorganized Territory** Details: (Organized 1 Jun 1862. Eliminated 17 Dec 1863 to Unorganized Territory)
La Moure www.rootsweb.com/~ndlamour/	**F8**	**4 Jan 1873**	**Pembina** La Moure County; 202 4th Ave NE; PO Box 128; La Moure, ND 58458; Ph. 701.883.5301 Details: (Organized 27 Oct 1881) (Clk Dis Ct has b, m, d, bur, div, pro & ct rec from 1881; Reg of Deeds has land rec)
Logan www.rootsweb.com/~ndlogan/	**H8**	**4 Jan 1873**	**Buffalo** Logan County; 301 Broadway; Napoleon, ND 58561; Ph. 701.754.2751 Details: (Organized 1 Sep 1884) (Clk Dis Ct has incomplete b & d rec from 1893, m, div & ct rec from 1890, pro rec from 1898, bur rec from 1926 & mil rec from 1920; Reg of Deeds has land rec from 1884)
McHenry www.rootsweb.com/~ndmchenr/	**J4**	**4 Jan 1873**	**Buffalo** McHenry County; 407 Main St; Towner, ND 58788; Ph. 701.537.5729 Details: (Organized 14 May 1885) (Clk Dis Ct has m rec from 1903, div, pro & ct rec from 1900; Reg of Deeds has land rec)
McIntosh www.rootsweb.com/~ndmcinto/	**H9**	**9 Mar 1883**	**Logan, Unorganized Territory, McPherson Co, SD** McIntosh County; 112 NE 1st St; Ashley, ND 58413; Ph. 701.288.3450 Details: (Organized 4 Oct 1884) (Clk Dis Ct has b & d rec from 1899, m rec from 1885, pro rec from 1889, ct & div rec from 1937 & mil dis rec from 1943; Reg of Deeds has land rec; State Hist Soc has nat rec)
McKenzie www.4eyes.net/	**Q5**	**24 May 1901**	**Billings** McKenzie County; 201 5th St NW; PO Box 523; Watford, ND 58854; Ph. 701.444.3452 Details: (Attached to Stark Co prior to organization 16 Mar 1905) (Clk Dis Ct has b & d rec from 1943, m, div, pro & ct rec from 1905 & bur rec; Reg of Deeds has land rec)

County Website	Map Index	Date Created	Parent County or Territory From Which Organized Address/Details
McKenzie, old		**9 Mar 1883**	**Howard**

Details: (Annexed to Billings 30 Nov 1896)

| **McLean** www.visitmcleancounty.com/ | **L5** | **8 Mar 1883** | **Stevens, Burleigh, Sheridan, old** |

McLean County; 712 5th Ave; Washburn, ND 58577; Ph. 701.462.8541
Details: (Clk Dis Ct has m rec from 1887, bur rec from 1920, div & ct rec from 1891 & pro rec from 1900; Reg of Deeds has land rec)

| **Mercer*** www.rootsweb.com/~ndmercer/ | **M6** | **14 Jan 1875** | **Unorganized Territory** |

Mercer County; 1021 Arthur St; Stanton, ND 58571; Ph. 701.745.3262
Details: (Organized 22 Aug 1884) (Clk Dis Ct has b, d & bur rec from 1942, m rec from 1894, div & ct rec from 1906 & pro rec from 1898; Reg of Deeds has land rec; State Archives has nat rec)

| **Morton*** www.rootsweb.com/%7endmorton/ | **L7** | **8 Jan 1873** | **Unorganized Territory** |

Morton County; 210 2nd Ave NW; Mandan, ND 58554; Ph. 701.667.3355
Details: (Organized 28 Feb 1881) (Clk Dis Ct has b rec from 1883, m rec from 1888, d rec from 1873, bur rec from 1943, div & pro rec from 1900's & ct rec from late 1800's; Reg of Deeds has land rec from late 1800's)

| **Mountrail** www.rootsweb.com/~ndmountr/ mountrail.htm | **N4** | **4 Jan 1873** | **Buffalo** |

Mountrail County; PO Box 69; Stanley, ND 58784-0069; Ph. 701.628.2915
Details: (Annexed to Ward in 1891 & eliminated 30 Nov 1892. Recreated 29 Jan 1909 from Ward) (Clk Dis Ct has b, m, d, div, pro, ct & nat rec from 1909, mil dis rec from 1919 & incomplete bur rec; Reg of Deeds has land rec)

| **Nelson** www.rootsweb.com/~ndnelson/ | **E5** | **2 Mar 1883** | **Foster, Grand Forks, Ramsey, Unorganized Territory** |

Nelson County; 210 W B Ave; PO Box 565; Lakota, ND 58344; Ph. 701.247.2462
Details: (Clk Dis Ct has b & d rec from 1903, m, pro & land rec from 1880, div, ct & bur rec)

| **Oliver** www.rootsweb.com/~ndoliver/ | **L7** | **14 Apr 1885** | **Mercer** |

Oliver County; 315 W Main; Center, ND 58530; Ph. 701.794.8777
Details: (Clk Dis Ct has m rec from 1915 & d rec; Co Judge has pro & ct rec; Reg of Deeds has land rec)

| **Pembina** www.rootsweb.com/~ndpembin/ pembina.htm | **D3** | **9 Jan 1867** | **Unorganized Territory** |

Pembina County; 301 Dakota St W #6; Cavalier, ND 58220; Ph. 701.265.4275
Details: (Clk Dis Ct has b & d rec from 1893, m rec from 1882, div, ct & pro rec from 1883, mil rec from 1945 & bur rec from 1943; Reg of Deeds has land rec)

| **Pierce** www.rootsweb.com/~ndpierce/ | **I3** | **11 Mar 1887** | **De Smet, Bottineau, McHenry, Rolette** |

Pierce County; 240 2nd St; Rugby, ND 58368; Ph. 701.776.6161
Details: (Organized 11 Apr 1889) (Clk Dis Ct has b, d & bur rec from 1943, m rec from 1888, div & ct rec from 1900 & pro rec from 1898; Reg of Deeds has land rec)

| **Ramsey** www.rootsweb.com/~ndramsey/ ramsey.htm | **F4** | **4 Jan 1873** | **Pembina** |

Ramsey County; 524 4th Ave #4; Devils Lake, ND 58301; Ph. 701.662.7066
Details: (Organized 25 Jan 1885) (Clk Dis Ct has b, d & bur rec from 1890, div & ct rec; Co Judge has m & pro rec; Reg of Deeds has land rec)

| **Ransom** www.rootsweb.com/~ndransom/ | **D8** | **4 Jan 1873** | **Pembina** |

Ransom County; 204 5th Ave W; Lisbon, ND 58054; Ph. 701.683.5823
Details: (Organized 4 Apr 1881) (Clk Dis Ct has b & d rec from 1943, m rec from 1882, div, pro & ct rec; Reg of Deeds has land rec)

| **Renville** www.upstel.net/~johns/Renville/renv.html | **M2** | **3 Jun 1910** | **Ward** |

Renville County; 205 Main St E; PO Box 68; Mohall, ND 58761; Ph. 701.756.6398
Details: (Clk Dis Ct has incomplete b & d rec from 1910, m, div, pro, mil & ct rec from 1910; Reg of Deeds has land rec from 1910)

| **Renville, old** www.renvillecounty.org/ | | **4 Jan 1873** | **Buffalo** |

Details: (Part taken to form Ward Co 14 Apr 1885. Attached to Ward. Eliminated 30 Nov 1892 to Bottineau & Ward. Recreated 3 Jun 1910)

County Website	Map Index	Date Created	Parent County or Territory From Which Organized Address/Details
Richland www.richlandcounty.org/	B9	4 Jan 1873	**Pembina** Richland County; 418 2nd Ave N; PO Box 966; Wahpeton, ND 58075; Ph. 701.642.7818 Details: (Organized 25 Nov 1875) (Clk Dis Ct has b & d rec from 1900, div & ct rec from 1883 & some bur rec; Co Judge has m rec from 1890 & pro rec from 1876; Reg of Deeds has land rec)
Rolette www.rootsweb.com/~ndrolett/	I3	4 Jan 1873	**Buffalo** Rolette County; 102 2nd St NE; Rolla, ND 58367-0460; Ph. 701.477.3816 Details: (Organized 14 Oct 1884) (Clk Dis Ct has b, d & bur rec from 1943, m, div & ct rec from 1887 & pro rec from 1896; Reg of Deeds has land rec)
Sargent www.rootsweb.com/~ndsargen/index.htm	D9	9 Apr 1883	**Ransom** Sargent County; 355 Main St; PO Box 176; Forman, ND 58032; Ph. 701.724.6241 Details: (Clk Dis Ct has b & d rec from 1943, m rec from 1886, bur rec from 1948, pro rec from 1883, div & ct rec; Reg of Deeds has land rec)
Sheridan www.rootsweb.com/~ndsherid/	J6	24 Dec 1908	**McLean** Sheridan County; 215 E 2nd St; PO Box 668; McClusky, ND 58463; Ph. 701.363.2207 Details: (Clk Dis Ct has b rec from 1943, m, d, div, pro & ct rec from 1909, bur rec from 1910 & mil rec from 1918; Reg of Deeds has land rec from 1909)
Sheridan, old		4 Jan 1873	**Buffalo** Details: (Part taken to form part of Church 11 Mar 1887. Eliminated 30 Nov 1892 to McLean)
Sheyenne		24 Apr 1862	**Unorganized Territory** Details: (Eliminated 17 Dec 1863 to Unorganized Territory)
Sioux www.rootsweb.com/~ndsioux/	K9	3 Sep 1914	**Standing Rock Reservation** Sioux County; 300 2nd Ave; Fort Yates, ND 58538; Ph. 701.854.3853 Details: (Clk Dis Ct has m rec from 1916, bur, div, pro, ct & land rec)
Slope www.rootsweb.com/~ndslope/	Q9	3 Nov 1914	**Billings** Slope County; 206 S Main; Amidon, ND 58620-0449; Ph. 701.879.6260 Details: (Organized 14 Jan 1915) (Clk Dis Ct has m, d, bur, div, pro & ct rec from 1915 & land rec)
Stark www.rootsweb.com/~ndstark/	O8	10 Feb 1879	**Unorganized Territory, Howard, Williams (old)** Stark County; 51 3rd St E; PO Box 130; Dickinson, ND 58602-0130; Ph. 701.264.7639 Details: (Organized 30 May 1883) (Clk Dis Ct has b & d rec from 1898, bur rec, div & ct rec from 1887 & nat rec 1887-1963; Reg of Deeds has land rec)
Steele www.rootsweb.com/~ndsteele/steele.htm	D6	2 Jun 1883	**Griggs, Traill** Steele County; 201 Washington Ave W; PO Box 296; Finley, ND 58230; Ph. 701.524.2152 Details: (Clk Dis Ct has b & d rec 1894-1896 & 1900-1901, div & ct rec from 1886; Co Judge has m rec from 1883 & pro rec from 1886; Reg of Deeds has land rec)
Stevens		4 Jan 1873	**Buffalo** Details: (Eliminated 30 Nov 1892 to McLean & Ward)
Stevens, old		24 Apr 1862	**Unorganized Territory** Details: (Eliminated 17 Dec 1863 to Unorganized Territory)
Stutsman www.rootsweb.com/~ndstutsm/	G7	4 Jan 1873	**Pembina, Buffalo** Stutsman County; 511 2nd Ave SE; Jamestown, ND 58401; Ph. 701.252.9042 Details: (Clk Dis Ct has b, d, bur, div & ct rec; Reg of Deeds has land rec; Co Judge has m & pro rec)
Towner www.rootsweb.com/~ndtowner/	G2	8 Mar 1883	**Rolette, Cavalier** Towner County; 315 2nd St; PO Box 517; Cando, ND 58324-0517; Ph. 701.968.4345 Details: (Organized 24 Jan 1884) (Clk Dis Ct has m rec from 1888, div rec from 1890, pro rec from 1886, ct rec from 1889, land rec from 1884 & bur rec)

County Website	Map Index	Date Created	Parent County or Territory From Which Organized Address/Details
Traill www.rootsweb.com/~ndtraill/	**C6**	**12 Jan 1875**	**Grand Forks, Burbank, Cass** Traill County; 114 W Caledonia; Hillsboro, ND 58045; Ph. 701.436.4454 Details: (Clk Dis Ct has b rec from 1910, m rec from 1887, d rec from 1907, bur rec from 1915, div rec from 1890 & pro rec from 1882; Reg of Deeds has land rec)
Villard		**8 Mar 1883**	**Billings** Details: (Eliminated 10 Mar 1887 to Billings & Stark)
Wallace		**9 Mar 1883**	**Howard** Details: (see McKenzie) (Eliminated 30 Nov 1896 to Billings & Stark. Recreated 24 May 1901 from Billings & Stark & attached to Stark Co. Eliminated 16 Mar 1905 to McKenzie)
Wallette		**4 Jan 1873**	**Buffalo** Details: (Eliminated 9 Mar 1883 to Buford & Flannery)
Walsh www.rootsweb.com/~ndwalsh/walsh.htm	**D4**	**20 May 1881**	**Grand Forks, Pembina** Walsh County; 600 Cooper Ave; Grafton, ND 58237-1542; Ph. 701.352.0350 Details: (Clk Dis Ct has m rec from 1884, div, pro & ct rec from 1881; Reg of Deeds has land rec)
Ward www.geocities.com/Athens/Forum/2079/	**L4**	**14 Apr 1885**	**Stevens, Wynn, Renville, old** Ward County; 315 3rd St SE; Minot, ND 58701-6498; Ph. 701.857.6460 Details: (Clk Dis Ct has b, d, bur & div rec from 1900; Co Judge has m & pro rec; Reg of Deeds has land rec)
Wells www.rootsweb.com/~ndwells/	**H6**	**4 Jan 1873**	**Buffalo** Wells County; 700 Railway St N; PO Box 596; Fessenden, ND 58438; Ph. 701.547.3122 Details: (Formerly Gingras Co. Name changed to Wells 26 Feb 1881. Organized 24 Aug 1884) (Clk Dis Ct has b, m, d, bur, div, pro & ct rec; Reg of Deeds has land rec)
Williams* www.rootsweb.com/~ndwillia/	**P3**	**30 Nov 1892**	**Buford, Flannery** Williams County; Box 2047; Williston, ND 58802; Ph. 701.572.1729 Details: (Organized 10 Mar 1903) (Clk Dis Ct has b, m, d, bur, pro, ct & nat rec; Co Treas-Rcdr has land records; Veterans Service Off has mil rec)
Williams, old		**8 Jan 1873**	**Unorganized Territory** Details: (Eliminated 30 Nov 1892 to Mercer)
Wynn		**9 Mar 1883**	**Bottineau, Renville, old** Details: (Eliminated 11 Mar 1887 to Bottineau, McHenry, Renville, old & Ward)

Notes

Red Carnation

OHIO

CAPITAL: COLUMBUS – TERRITORY 1799 – STATE 1803 (17TH)

French traders settled in the western part of Ohio and the English settled in the eastern part in the early 1700's. English expansion toward the West brought the two into conflict by the 1740's. The French and Indian War finally resolved this and the English won control of the area. However, settlement of the region was discouraged, due in part to the hostile Indians in the area. Americans in their search for space and fertile, inexpensive land came to the area despite British desires to the contrary. Conflicts between the Indians, who sided with the British, and the Americans were the result. The treaty ending the Revolutionary War ceded the area to the United States.

Following acquisition of the new territory, the eastern seaboard states simply extended their borders to include the new area. The establishment of the Northwest Territory put an end to this practice in 1787. The following year, the Ohio Company of New England made the first permanent settlement at Marietta. The company, formed by Puritans from Massachusetts and Connecticut, purchased about a million acres of land in southeast Ohio.

In about 1800, the Virginia Bounty–consisting of more than 4 million acres between the Scioto and Little Miami rivers–was set aside for settlers from Virginia and Kentucky. The Chillicothe section in Ross County attracted many settlers from Kentucky and Tennessee. Mid-state on the eastern border, Germans, Scotch-Irish, and Quakers crossed the Ohio River from Pennsylvania to settle. Another group of settlers from New Jersey traveled down the Ohio River and settled the area between the Little and Big Miami rivers. Here, along with Scotch-Irish and Dutch settlers, they cultivated some 300,000 acres in the southwestern corner of Ohio and established Cincinnati.

Trouble with the Indians continued until 1794, when General Anthony Wayne drove them from the state. The Western Reserve in the northeast corner along Lake Erie was opened to settlers. It included 4 million acres. Connecticut emigrants were the main settlers in this area. In future Erie and Huron counties to the west, Connecticut refugees who had been burned out by the British during the Revolutionary War began to settle. The area became known as the "Fire Lands" for this reason. A "Refugee Tract" (comprising approximately Franklin, Licking, and Perry counties) was set aside east of the Scioto River for Canadians who had aided the Americans in the Revolutionary War and lost their lands in Canada as a punishment.

Ohio became a territory in 1799. The next year, the Indiana Territory was formed, which reduced Ohio to its present size. Ohio was granted statehood in 1803. Steamboat travel brought many settlers up the Ohio River and down Lake Erie. The completion of canals, roads, and railroads opened up the northeastern part of the state after 1815, while the opening of the Erie Canal in 1825 increased settlement from the Northeast. During the Civil War, Ohio had some 313,000 men serving in the Union forces.

Look for vital records in the following locations:

- **Birth and death records:** A few counties have birth and death records from as early as 1840. Individual counties were required to keep these records in 1867. After 1908, birth and death records are at the State Vital Statistics Unit, Ohio Department of Health in Columbus.
- **Marriage and divorce records:** Probate courts have marriage records. A statewide index to marriages since 1949 is at the Division of Vital Statistics. Divorce records were kept by the state Supreme Court until 1852, and then by the Court of Common Pleas in each county.
- **Land records:** The county recorder has land records for each county. Early records of land grants, bounty land, and land purchases are at the Ohio Land Office, Auditor of State in Columbus. Most records of the Western Reserve are at the Connecticut Secretary of State's office. Virginia bounty land warrants are at the Virginia State Library in Richmond Virginia.
- **Census records:** Town or county censuses were taken between 1798 and 1911 in some counties.

State Vital Statistics Unit	**Ohio Land Office**
Ohio Department of Health	**Auditor of State**
PO Box 15098	88 East Broad Street
Columbus, Ohio 43215	Columbus, Ohio 43215
614.466.2531	

Societies and Repositories

Adams County Genealogical Society; PO Box 231; West Union, Ohio 45693

African-American Genealogical Society of Cleveland, Ohio; PO Box 201476; Cleveland, Ohio 44120-8107

African-American Genealogy Group of the Miami Valley; PO Box 485; Yellow Springs, Ohio 45387; 937.767.1949

Akron Public Library; 55 South Main St.; Akron, Ohio 44309

American Jewish Archives; 3101 Clifton Avenue; Cincinnati, Ohio 45220; 513.221.1875; Fax 513.221.7812

American Jewish Archives; Clifton Ave.; Cincinnati, Ohio 45220

Ashtabula County Genealogical Society, Inc.; Geneva Public Library; 860 Sherman Street; Geneva, Ohio 44041.9101;

Athens County Chapter, OGS; Athens County Historical Society & Museum; 65 N. Court Street; Athens, Ohio 45701.2506; 740.698.3551; <www.frognet.net/~achsm/>

Auglaize Co. Genealogical Society; PO Box 2021; Wapakoneta, Ohio 45895-0521; <www.rootsweb.com/~ohaugogs/index.html>

Bedford Historical Society Museum and Library; 30 Squire Place; PO Box 46282; Bedord, Ohio 44146; Ph. 440.232.0796

Belmont County Chapter, OGS; PO Box 285; Barnesville, Ohio 43713; 740.695.3660; <www.rootsweb.com/~ohbelogs/>

Bowling Green State University, Center for Archival Collections; Jerome Library; Bowling Green, Ohio 43403-0175; 419.372.2411; Fax 419.372.0155

Brookville Historical Society Library; PO Box 82; Brookville, Ohio 45309

Brown County Chapter, OGS; PO Box 83; Georgetown, Ohio 45121-0083

Butler County Chapter, PGS; PO Box 2011; Middletown, Ohio 45042-2011; 513.523.3580; <da120757.tripod.com/bcogs/>

Carnegie Library; 520 Sycamore St.; Greensville, Ohio 45331

Carnegie Public Library; 127 S. North St.; Washington Court House, Ohio 43160

Carroll County Genealogical Society; 24 Second St. N.E.; PO Box 36; Carrollton, Ohio 44615-1205; <www.rootsweb.com/~ohcarcgs/>

Champaign Co. Library; 160 W. Market St.; Urbana, Ohio 43078; 513.653.3811;

Champaign County Genealogical Society; PO Box 682; Urbana, Ohio 43078-0680; <www.rootsweb.com/~ohchampa/society.htm>

Chillicothe & Ross Co, Public Library; 140 S. Paint St.; Chillicothe, Ohio 45601

Cincinnati Hist. Soc. Library, The Museum Center at Cincinnati Union Terminal; 1301 Western Ave; Cincinnati, Ohio 45203

Cincinnati Public Library; 800 Vine St.; Cincinnati, Ohio 45202

Clark Co. Chapter of OGS, Library; PO Box 2524; Springfield, Ohio 45501

Clark Co. Friends of the Library Gen. Research Group; 1268 Kenwood Ave.; Springfield, Ohio 45505; 937.323.2905;

Clark Co. Public Library; 201 S. Fountain Ave., PO Box 1080; Springfield, Ohio 45501-1080

Clark County Genealogical Society; PO Box 2524; Springfield, Ohio 45501-2524; 937.323.4728; <www.rootsweb.com/~ohcccogs/>

Clermont County Genealogical Society; PO Box 394; Batavia, Ohio 45103-0394; 513.522.8458; <www.rootsweb.com/~ohclecgs/>

Cleveland Public Library; 325 Superior Ave.; Cleveland, Ohio 44114

Clinton County, Ohio Genealogical Society; PO Box 529; Wilmington, Ohio 45177-0529; 937.382.5209

Columbiana Co. Chapter O.G.S.; PO Box 861 Dept I; Salem, Ohio 44460-0861; 330.223.1447; <www.rootsweb.com/~ohcolumb/>

Columbiana County Historical Society; PO Box 221; Lisbon, Ohio 44432

Columbus Jewish Historical Society; 1175 College Avenue; Columbus, Ohio 43209-2890; <www.gcis.net/cjhs>

Columbus Metropolitan Library, Biography & History; 96 S. Grant Ave.; Columbus, Ohio 43215 <www.cml.lib.oh.us>

Coshocton County Chapter OGS; PO Box 128; Coshocton, Ohio 43812-0128

Coshocton Public Library, Miriam C. Hunter Local History Rm.; 655 Main St.; Coshocton, Ohio 43812-1697; 614.622.0956;

Crawford County Genealogical Society; PO Box 92; Galion, Ohio 44833-0092

Cumberland Trail Genealogical Society; PO Box 576; St. Clairesville, Ohio 43905; 740.676.4132

Cuyahoga Valley Chapter/OGS; PO Box 41414; Brecksville, Ohio 44141-0414

Cuyahoga West Chapter, OGS; PO Box 26196; Fairview Park, Ohio 44126

Cuyahoga-Parma Chapter/OGS; PO Box 29509; Parma, Ohio 44129-0509

Darke County Genealogical Society; PO Box 908; Greenville, Ohio 45331-0908

Dayton & Montgomery Co. Public Library; 215 E. Third St.; Dayton, Ohio 45402-2103; 513.227.9531

Defiance County Chapter, OGS; PO Box 7006; Defiance, Ohio 43512-7006; <www.rootsweb.com/~ohdcgs/>

Delaware County Genealogical Society; PO Box 317; 157 East William Street; Delaware, Ohio 43015-0317; <www.midohio.net/dchsdcgs/>

Division of Vital Statistics, Ohio Department of Health; PO Box 15098; Columbus, Ohio 43215-0098; 614.466.2531;

East Cuyahoga County Genealogical Society; PO Box 24182; Lyndhurst, Ohio 44124-0182

East Liverpool Historical Society; 305 Walnut Street; East Liverpool, Ohio 43920

East Palestine Historical Society; 555 Bacon Avenue; East Palestine, Ohio 44413

Ebenezer Zane Chapter, OHSSAR; 2101 County Road 1; Rayland, Ohio 43943-7866

Erie County Chapter, OGS; PO Box 1301; Sandusky, Ohio 44871-1301

Ethan Allen Chapter, OHSSAR; 1379 Bradford Street; Warren, Ohio 44485-1963; 330.395.0310

Evangelical Friends Church, Eastern Division; 5350 Broadmoor Circle, N.W.; Canton, Ohio 44709; 330.493.1660; Fax 330.493.0852

Ewings Chapter, OHSSAR; 18660 State Route 550; Amesville, Ohio 45711; 740.448.7269; <www.frognet.net/~assar/>

Fairfield Co. District Library; 219 N. Broad St.; Lancaster, Ohio 43130

Fairfield County Chapter, OGS; PO Box 2268; Lancaster, Ohio 43130-5268;

Fayette County Chapter, OGS; PO Box 342; Washington CH, Ohio 43130-0570

Firelands Historical Society Library; 4 Case Ave.; Norwalk, Ohio 44857

Flesh Public Library; 124 W. Greene St.; Piqua, Ohio 45356; 937.773.6753

Franklin and Columbus Cos. Public Library; 96 S. Grant Ave.; Columbus, Ohio 43215

Franklin Co. Gen. Soc. Library; 570 W. Broad St., PO Box 2406; Columbus, Ohio 43216-2406

Franklin County Genealogical & Historical Society; PO Box 44309; Columbus, Ohio 43204-0309

Friends of the Library, Genealogy Research Group; 1268 Kenwood Avenue; Springfield, Ohio 45505

Fulton County Chapter of OGS; PO Box 337; Swanton, Ohio 43558-0337; 419.335.0898; <www.rootsweb.com/~ohfulton/>

Gallia County Historical/Genealogical Society; 410-412 Second Avenue; Gallipolis, Ohio 45631; <www.zoomnet.net/~histsoc>

Garst Museum, Genealogical Library; 205 N. Broadway; Greenville, Ohio 45331

Geauga West Library; 13455 Chillicothe Rd.; Chesterland, Ohio 44026

Geneva Public Library; 860 Sherman St.; Geneva, Ohio 44041

George Rogers Clark Chapter, OHSSAR; Springfield, Ohio; <grccsar.homestead.com/grccsar.html>

Glendover Warren Co. Museum; Lebanon, Ohio 45036

Granville Public Library; 217 E. Broadway; Granville, Ohio 43023

Greene Co. Rm., Greene Co. District Library; 76 E. Market St.; Xenia, Ohio 45385

Greene County Chapter, OGS; PO Box 706; Xenia, Ohio 45385; <www.rootsweb.com/~ohgccogs/main.htm>

Greenville Public Library, Genealogy Dept.; 520 Sycamore St.; Greenville, Ohio 45331

Guernsey Co. District Public Library; 800 Steubenville Ave.; Cambridge, Ohio 43725

Guernsey Co. Gen. Soc; PO Box 661; Cambridge, Ohio 43725-0661; 740.432.9249; <www.usgenet.ogr/usa/oh/county/guernsey/gcgspub.html>

Hamilton Co. and Cincinnati Public Library; Eighth & Vine Sts.; Cincinnati, Ohio 45202-2071

Hamilton County Chapter, OGS; PO Box 15865; Cincinnati, Ohio 45215-0865; <members.aol.com/ogshc/>

Hancock County Chapter, OGS; PO Box 672; Findlay, Ohio 45839-0672; <www.rootsweb.com/~ohhccogs/>

Hanover Township Historical Society; PO Box 381; Hanoverton, Ohio 44423

Hardin Co. Historic Museums; PO Box 521; Kenton, Ohio 43326

Hardin County Ohio Genealogy Society; PO Box 520; Kenton, Ohio 43326-0520; 419.675.6230; <www.kenton.com/users/chuck/soc.htm>

Harrison County Genealogical Society; 45507 Unionvale Road; Cadiz, Ohio 43907-9723; <www.rootsweb.com/~ohharris/>

Hayes Presidential Center Library; 1337 Hayes Ave.; Fremont, Ohio 43420

Historical Society of Columbiana and Fairfield Townships; Dept. I, 10 Park Ave.; Columbiana, Ohio 44408

Hocking County Chapter, OGS; PO Box 115; Rockbridge, Ohio 43149-0115

Holmes County Chapter, OGS; PO Box 136; Millersburg, Ohio 44654-0136

Hudson Genealogical Study Group; Hudson Library and Historical Society, Dept. G.; 22 Aurora Street; Hudson, Ohio 44236-2947; <www.rootsweb.com/~ohhudogs/hudson.htm>

Hudson Library and Historical Society; 22 Aurora St.; Hudson, Ohio 44236; 330.653.6658

Huron County Chapter, OGS; PO Box 923; Norwalk, Ohio 44857-0923; <www.rootsweb.com/~ohhuron/>

Jackson County Chapter, OGS; PO Box 807; Jackson, Ohio 45640-0807; <scioto.org/OGS/Jackson/>

Jefferson County Chapter, OGS; PO Box 4712; Steubenville, Ohio 43952-8712; <www.rootsweb.com/~ohjefogs/>

Jefferson County Historical Society Library; 426 Franklin Ave.; Steubenville, Ohio 43952

John Stark Chapter, OHSSAR; 5220 Woodlynn Drive; East Canton, Ohio 44730-1756; 330.488.2227

Johnson - St. Paris Library; East Main St.; St. Paris, Ohio 43072; 513.663.4349

Knox County Chapter, OGS; PO Box 1098; Mt. Vernon, Ohio 43050-1098

Lafayette Chapter, OHSSAR; 899 Hancock Ave.; Akron, Ohio 44314-1044; 330.745.1532;

Lake County Genealogical Society; 184 Phelps Street; Painesville, Ohio 44077; <131.187.173.99/genealogy_lcgs.htm>

Lakewood Public Library; 15425 Detroit Ave.; Lakewood, Ohio 44107

Lawrence County Chapter, OGS; PO Box 945; Ironton, Ohio 45638-0955

Licking County Genealogical Society; 101 W. Main St.; Newark, Ohio 43055-5054; 740.349.5510; <www.npls.org/lcgs/>

Lisbon Historical Society; 113 E. Washington St.; PO Box 221; Lisbon, Ohio 44432; <countypage.com/lhs/>

Logan County Chapter, OGS; PO Box 36; Bellefontaine, Ohio 43311-0036

Lorain County Chapter, OGS; PO Box 865; Elyria, Ohio 44036-0865; <www.centuryinter.net/lorgen/>

Lorain Public Library; 351 6th St.; Lorain, Ohio 44052

Lucas Co. Public Library; 235 N. Michigan St.; Toledo, Ohio 43624; 419.259.5207; <www.toledolibrary.org>

Lucas County Chapter, OGS; c/o Toledo-Lucas Co. Public Library; Local History and Genealogy Department; 325 N. Michigan Street; Toledo, Ohio 43624-1614; <www.utoledo.edu/~gried/lcogs.htm>

Lucasville Historical Society; PO Box 761; Lucasville, Ohio 45648-0761

Madison County Chapter, OGS; PO Box 102; London, Ohio 43140-0102

Mahoning County Chapter, OGS; PO Box 9333; Boardman, Ohio 44513-0333

Mansfield / Richland Co. Public Library; 43 West Third St.; Mansfield, Ohio 44902

Marion Area Genealogical Society; PO Box 844; Marion, Ohio 43301-0844; <www.genealogy.org/~smoore/marion/>

Medina County Chapter, OGS; PO Box 804; Medina, Ohio 44258-0804

Meigs County Chapter, OGS; PO Box 346; Pomeroy, Ohio 45769-0345

Meigs County Historical Society; PO Box 346; Pomeroy, Ohio 45769

Mennonite Historical Library; Bluffton College; Bluffton, Ohio 45817

Mercer County Chapter, OGS; PO Box 437; Celina, Ohio 45822-0437; <www.calweb.com/~wally/mercer/society.htm>

Methodist Historical Commission; Ohio Wesleyan University; Delaware, Ohio 43015

Miami County Historical & Genealogical Society; PO Box 305; Troy, Ohio 45373-0305; <www.TDS.NET.com/mchgs>

Miami Valley Chapter, OGS; PO Box 1364; Dayton, Ohio 45401-1364

Miamisburg Historical Society; PO Box 774; Miamisburg, Ohio 45343-0774

Middletown Public Library; 1320 1st Ave.; Middletown, Ohio 45042

Milan Public Library; PO Box 1550; Milan, Ohio 44846

Monroe County Genealogical Society; PO Box 641; Woodsfield, Ohio 43793.0641; 740.483.1481; <www.rootsweb.com/~ohmccogs/>

Montgomery County Chapter, OGS; 48 Huffman Avenue; Dayton, Ohio 45403; 937.253.2503

Morgan County Chapter, OGS; PO Box 418; McConnelsville, Ohio 43756-0418

Morley Library; 184 Phelps St.; Painesville, Ohio 44077

Morrow County, Ohio Genealogical Society; PO Box 401; Mt. Gilead, Ohio 43338; <www.rootsweb.com/~ohmorrow/>

Muskingum Co. Gen. Soc., Inc. Library; PO Box 3066, 220 N. 5th St.; Zanesville, Ohio 43702-3066

Muskingum County Chapter, OGS; P O Box 2427; Zanesville, Ohio 43702-2427; <www.rootsweb.com/~ohmuskin/mccogs/>

Nathan Hale Chapter, OHSSAR; 30 Babic Street; Struthers, Ohio 44471-3108; 330.755.8590

National Archives-Great Lakes Region; 7358 S. Pulaski Road; Chicago, Illinois 60629; 312.581.7816; Fax 312.353.1294

Noble County Chapter, OGS; PO Box 174; Caldwell, Ohio 43724-0174

North American Baptist, General Conference; 7308 Madison Street; Forest Park, Illinois 60130

Northeastern Chapter #12, SAR; 1659 Chapel Road; Jefferson, Ohio 44047-8716

Norwalk Public Library; 46 W. Main St.; Norwalk, Ohio 44857

Ohio Genealogical Society; 34 Sturges Avenue, PO Box 2625; Mansfield, Ohio 44906-0625; 419.522.9077; Fax 419.522.0224

Ohio Historical Society Archives/Library; 1982 Velma Avenue; Columbus, Ohio 43211; <www.ohiohistory.org/resource/statearc/>

Ohio Historical Society, Ohio Historical Center; 1982 Velma Avenue; Columbus, Ohio 43211-2497; 614.297.2510; Fax 614.297.2546

Ohio Land Office, Auditor of State; PO Box 1140, 88 East Broad Street; Columbus, Ohio 43266-0040; 614.466.4514; Fax 614.466.6228;

Ohio State Library; 65 S. Front St.; Columbus, Ohio 43215

Ohio University, Archives and Special Collections; Alden Library; Athens, Ohio 45701-2978; 614.593.2710; Fax 614.593.0138

Old Northwest Historical Society; PO Box 62635; Cincinnati, Ohio 45262; 513.530.9546; <home.fuse.net/rrowan/>

Ottawa County Genealogical Society; PO Box 193; Port Clinton, Ohio 43452; 419.734.3895; <www.rootsweb.com/~ohoccgs/>

Palatine Library, Palatines to America, Capital Univ; Box 101; Columbus, Ohio 43209-2394; 614.236.8281; <genealogy.org/~palam/>

Palatines to America; 611 E. Weber Rd.; Columbus, Ohio 43211; 614.267.4888;

Paulding County Carnegie Library; 205 S. Main St.; Paulding, Ohio 45879-1492

Paulding County Chapter, OGS; 205 E. Main St.; Paulding, Ohio 45879-1492

Pemberville Public Library; 375 E. Front St.; Pemberville, Ohio 43450; 419.287.4012; Fax 419.287.4620

Perry County Chapter, OGS; PO Box 275; Junction City, Ohio 43748-0275; <www.perrygenealogy.net/perryogs.htm>

Pickaway County Historical & Genealogical Society; PO Box 85; Circleville, Ohio 43113; <www.rootsweb.com/~ohpickaw/gen.html>

Pike County Genealogy Society; PO Box 224; Waverly, Ohio 45690-0224; <www.rootsweb.com/~ohpcgs/pike.htm>

Polish Genealogical Society of Greater Cleveland, Ohio; 105 Pleasant View Drive; Seville, Ohio 44273

Portage County Chapter, OGS; PO Box 821; Ravenna, Ohio 44266

Portsmouth Public Library; 1220 Gallia St.; Portsmouth, Ohio 45662

Preble Co. District Library, Preble Rm., Eaton Branch; 301 N. Barren St.; Eaton, Ohio 45320

Preble County Genealogical Society; Preble County District Library; 450 S. Barron Street; Eaton, Ohio 45320; <www.pcdl.lib.oh.us/pcgs/>

Preble County Historical Society; 7693 Swartsel Road; Eaton, Ohio 45320; 937.787.9662

Presbyterian Historical Society; 425 Lombard Street; Philadelphia, Pennsylvania 19147-1516; 215.627.1852

Putnam County Chapter, OGS; PO Box 403; Ottawa, Ohio 45875-0403

Randolph Township Historical Society, Inc.; PO Box 355; Clayton, Ohio 45315

Richland County Genealogical Society; PO Box 3823; Mansfield, Ohio 44907-3823; <www.rootsweb.com/~ohrichgs/>

Roman Catholic, Archdiocese of Cincinnati, Chancery; 100 E. Eighth Street; Cincinnati, Ohio 45202; 513.421.3131; Fax 513.421.6225

Roman Catholic, Diocese of Cleveland, Chancery Building; 1027 Superior Ave.; Cleveland, Ohio 44114; 216.696.6525; Fax 216.621.7332

Roman Catholic, Diocese of Columbus, Chancery Office; 198 East Broad Street; Columbus, Ohio 43215; 614.224.2251; Fax 614.224.6306

Roman Catholic, Diocese of Toledo, Chancery; PO Box 985; Toledo, Ohio 43697-0985; 419.244.6711; Fax 419.244.4791

Roman Catholic, Diocese of Youngstown, Chancery Office; 144 West Wood Street; Youngstown, Ohio 44503; 216.744.8451; Fax 216.744.8451/744.2848

Roman Catholic, Diocese of Steubenville; 422 Washington Street, PO Box 969; Steubenville, Ohio 43952; 614.282.3631; Fax 614.282.3327

Ross Co. Gen. Soc. Library; 444 Douglas Ave., PO Box 6325; Chillicothe, Ohio 45601

Ross County Chapter, OGS; PO Box 6352; Chillicothe, Ohio 45601-6352; 740.775.0420; <www.bright.net/~rcgs>

Salem Historical Society; 208 South Broadway Avenue; Salem, Ohio 44460

Samuel Huntington Chapter, OHSSAR; 6366 Indian Point Rd.; Painesville, Ohio 44077-8844; <www.sar.org/ohssar/samuel_huntington_chapter.htm>

Sandusky County Kin Hunters; Spiegle Grove; Fremont, Ohio 43420-2796

Schiappa Branch Library; 4141 Mall Drive; Steubenville, Ohio 43952

Scioto County Chapter, OGS; PO Box 812; Portsmouth, Ohio 45662-0812

Seneca County Genealogical Society; PO Box 157; Tiffin, Ohio 44883-0157; <www.senecasearchers.org/index.html>

Shelby Genealogical Society; PO Box 766; Shelby, Ohio 44875-0766; <www.rootsweb.com/~ohscogs/>

Sidney Public Library; 230 E. North St.; Sidney, Ohio 45365

Society of Friends, Olney Friends School; 61830 Sandy Ridge Road; Barnesville, Ohio 43713; 614.425.3655

Southern Ohio Chapter, OGS; PO Box 414; Hillsboro, Ohio 45133

Southwest Cuyahoga Chapter, OGS; 13305 Pearl Road; Strongsville, Ohio 44136-3403; <members.aol.com/gmtjaden/>

Stark Co. District Library; 715 Market Ave.; North Canton, Ohio 44702

Stark County, Ohio Chapter, OGS; 1950 Market Avenue North, Apt. B2; Canton, Ohio 44714-2242; <www.rootsweb.com/~ohstark/starkogs.htm>

State Library of Ohio Genealogical Section; 65 South Front Street Rm 308; Columbus, Ohio 43215-4163; 614.644.6966; Fax 614.728.2789

Summit County Chapter, OGS; 239 N. Highland Avenue; Akron, Ohio 44303; 330.836.6518; <spot.acorn.net/gen/>

The Greater Cleveland Genealogical Socitey; PO Box 40234; Cleveland, Ohio 44140-0254; <www.rootsweb.com/~ohgcgg/>

The Henry County Genealogical Society; PO Box 231; Deshler, Ohio 43516

Toledo Area Genealogical Society; PO Box 352258; Toledo, Ohio 43635-2258

Toledo Public Library, Local Hist. & Gen. Dept.; 325 Michigan St.; Toledo, Ohio 43624

Tri-County Lineage Research Society (Hancock, Seneca, Wood), Kaubisch Library; Fostoria, Ohio 44830

Trumbull County Chapter, OGS; PO Box 309; Warren, Ohio 44482-0309

Tuscarawas County Genealogical Society; PO Box 141; New Philadelphia, Ohio 44663-0141; <web1.tusco.net/tuscgen/society.htm>

Union County Genealogical Society; PO Box 438; Marysville, Ohio 43040-0438

United Methodist Church; 601 W. Riverview Avenue; Dayton, Ohio 45406

University of Cincinnati Library; Cincinnati, Ohio 45221

University of Cincinnati, Archives Department; Blegen Library; Cincinnati, Ohio 45221-0113; 513.556.1959; Fax 513.556.2113

Van Wert County Chapter, OGS; PO Box 485; Van Wert, Ohio 45891-0485; <www.rootsweb.com/~ohvanwer/vwc_ogs.htm>

Vinton County Historical and Genealogical Society; PO Box 306; Hamden, Ohio 45634-0306; <www.rootsweb.com/~ohvinton/ogschapt.htm>

Warder Public Library; 137 E. High St; Springfield, Ohio 45502

Warren Co. Gen. Resource Center; 300 E. Silver; Lebanon, Ohio 45036

Warren County Chapter, OGS; 406 Justice Drive; Lebanon, Ohio 45036

Warren-Trumbull Co. Public Library; 444 Mahoning Ave., N.W.; Warren, Ohio 44483-4692

Washington Co. Public Library; 418 Washington St.; Marietta, Ohio 45750; 740.373.1057; <www.wcplib.lib.oh.us/lhg.htm>

Washington County Chapter, OGS; PO Box 2174; Marietta, Ohio 45750-2174

Wayne Co. Public Library; 304 N. Market St.; Wooster, Ohio 44691

Wayne County Genealogical Society; PO Box 856; Wooster, Ohio 44691; <www.rootsweb.com/~ohwayne/wcgs.htm>

Wellsville Historical Society; 1003 Riverside Avenue; Wellsville, Ohio 43968

Western Reserve Historical Society Library; 10825 East Blvd.; Cleveland, Ohio 44106

Western Reserve Historical Society; 10825 East Boulevard; Cleveland, Ohio 44106-1788; 216.721.5722; Fax 216.721.0645

Williams County Genealogical Society; PO Box 293; Bryan, Ohio 43506-0293; 636.3751; <www.geocities.com/wmscogen/>

Wood County Chapter of the Ohio Genealogical Society; PO Box 722; Bowling Green, Ohio 43402-0722; <www.rootsweb.com/~ohwood/searchwd.htm#Wood>

Wright State University, Special Collections and Archives; Paul Laurence Dunbar Library; Dayton, Ohio 45435-0001; 937.775.2092; Fax 937.775.4109

Wyandot Tracers OGS; PO Box 414; Upper Sandusky, Ohio 43351-0414; <www.udata.com/users/hsbaker/tracers.htm>

Youngstown & Mahoning Cos. Public Library; 305 Wick Ave.; Youngstown, Ohio 44503

Youngstown Historical Center of Industry and Labor, Archives-Library; PO Box 533, 151 West Wood St.; Youngstown, Ohio 44501; 330.743.5934; Fax 330.743.2999

Bibliography and Record Sources

General Sources

Baldwin, Henry R. *The Henry R. Baldwin Genealogy Records*. 67 Vols. Fort Wayne, Indiana: Allen County Public Library, 1983. (Eastern Ohio and Pennsylvania)

Bell, Carol Willsey. *Ohio Genealogical Guide*. 6th ed. Youngstown, Ohio: Bell Books, 1995.

Bell, Carol Willsey. *Ohio Guide to Genealogical Sources*. Baltimore: Genealogical Publishing Co., Reprint, 1993.

Biographical Encyclopedia of Ohio of the 19th Century. (1876) Reprint. Salem, Massachusetts: Higginson Book Co., 1995.

Bowers, Ruth, and Anita Short. *Gateway to the West*, 2 vols. (1967-1978) Reprint. Baltimore, Maryland: Genealogical Publishing Co., 1989.

Buley, R. Carlyle. *The Old Northwest: Pioneer Period, 1815-1840*. 2 vols. Bloomington: Indiana University Press in association with the Indiana Historical Society, [1983?], 1978.

Cayton. *The Frontier Republic: Ideology and Politics in the Ohio Country, 1780-1825*. Galveston, Texas: Frontier Press, 1986.

Church of Jesus Christ of Latter-day Saints. Historical Department. *Journal History*. (Salt Lake City: Filmed by the Historical Dept., 1968, 1973). 248 microfilm.

Comley, W. J. *Ohio; The Future Great State: Her Manufacturers and a History of Her Commercial Cities, Cincinnati and Cleveland with*

Portraits And Biographies of Some of the Old Settlers, and Many of the Most Prominent Business Men. Cincinnati, Ohio: Comley Brothers Manufacturing and Pub. Co., 1875.

Eltscher, Susan M., comp. *The Records of American Baptists in Ohio, and Related Organizations*. Rochester, NY: American Baptist Historical Society, 1981.

Family History Library. *Research Outline: Ohio*. Salt Lake City, Utah: Family History Library.

Finley, James Bradley. *Sketches of Western Methodism: Biographical, Historical & Miscellaneous, Illustrative Of Pioneer Life*. Cincinnati: Methodist Book Concern, 1856.

Fuller, Sara S. *A Guide to Manuscripts at the Ohio Historical Society*. Columbus, Ohio: The Society, 1972.

Galbreath, Charles Burleigh. *History of Ohio*. 5 vols. Chicago: American Historical Society, 1925.

Gerber, David Allison. *Black Ohio and the Color Line, 1860-1915*. Urbana, Ill.: University of Illinois Press, 1976.

Gilkey, Elliot Howard. *The Ohio Hundred Year Book: A Hand-Book of the Public Men and Public Institutions of Ohio from the Formation of the North-West Territory (1787) to July 1, 1901*. Columbus [Ohio]: F. J. Heer, 1901.

Gill, Charles Otis, and Gifford Pinchot. *Six Thousand Country Churches*. New York, Macmillan, 1919.

Green, Karen Mauer. *Pioneer Ohio Newspapers, 1793-1810 and 1802-1818: Genealogical and Historical Abstracts*. 2 vols. Galveston, Texas: Frontier Press, 1988.

Hall. *The Shane Manuscript Collection: A Genealogical Guide to the Kentucky and Ohio Papers*. Galveston, Texas: Frontier Press, 1990.

Harfst, Linda L. *Local History And Genealogy Resources Guide To Southeastern Ohio*. Wellston, Ohio: Ohio Valley Area Libraries, 1984.

Harter, Frances D. *Guide to the Manuscript Collection of Early Ohio Methodism: United Methodist Church of Ohio*. Delaware, Ohio: United Methodist Archives Center, 1980.

Harter, Stuart. *Ohio Genealogy and Local History Sources Index*. Fort Wayne, Indiana: CompuGen Systems, 1986.

Hatcher. *The Western Reserve: The Story of New Connecticut in Ohio*. Galveston, Texas: Frontier Press, 1991.

Hayden, A. S. *The Disciples Early History in Western Reserve 1875*. (1875) Reprint. Knightstown, Indiana: The Bookmark, 1979.

Hehir, Donald M. *Ohio Families: A Bibliography of Books About Ohio Families*. Bowie, Maryland: Heritage Books, 1993.

Heisey, John W. *Ohio Genealogical Research Guide*. Indianapolis, Indiana: Heritage House, 1987.

Hildreth, S. P. *Memoirs of the Early Pioneer Settlers of Ohio, with Narratives of Incidents and Occurrences in 1775*. (1854). Reprint. Baltimore, Maryland: Clearfield Company, 1995.

Historical Records Survey (Ohio). *Inventory Of The Church Archives Of Ohio Presbyterian Churches*. Microreproduction of xerox copies of the original papers in the Ohio Historical Society. (Salt Lake City: Filmed by the Genealogical Society of Utah, 1972).

Historical Records Survey (Ohio). *Inventory of the State Archives of Ohio*. Columbus, Ohio: Ohio Historical Records Survey Project, 1940.

Hover, John Calvin. *Memoirs of the Miami Valley*. 3 vols. Chicago: R. O. Law Co., 1919.

Howe, Henry. *Historical Collections of Ohio.* 2 vols. Rev. ed. (1888-1908) Reprint. Salem, Massachusetts: Higginson Book Co., 1994.

Hulbert, Archer Butler. *The Ohio River: A Course of Empire.* (1906) Reprint. Salem, Massachusetts: Higginson Book Co., 1996.

Hutslar. *Log Construction in the Ohio Country, 1750-1850.* Galveston, Texas: Frontier Press, 1992.

Kern, Richard. *A History of the Ohio Conference of the Churches of God, General Conference, 1836-1986.* [Findlay, Ohio]: Richard Kern, 1986.

Larson, David R., ed. *Guide to Manuscript Collections and Institutional Records in Ohio.* N.p.: Society of Ohio Archivists, 1974.

Lentz, Andrea D., ed. *A Guide to Manuscripts at the Ohio Historical Society.* Columbus: The Ohio Historical Society, 1972.

Memoirs of the Lower Ohio Valley: Personal and Genealogical with Portraits. 2 vols. Madison, Wis.: Federal Publishing, 1905.

Ohio Genealogical Society. *First Families of Ohio, Official Roster, Vol. 2.* Mansfield, Ohio: Ohio Genealogical Society, 1988.

Ohio Genealogical Society. *Ohio Source Records from The Ohio Genealogical Quarterly.* (1937-1944, 1986) Reprint. Baltimore, Maryland: Genealogical Publishing Co., 1993.

Ohio Historical Society (Columbus, Ohio*). Newspapers: Microfilm Available from The Ohio Historical Society.* Columbus, Ohio: The Society, 1987.

Ohio Historical Society. Archives-Libraries Division. *Ohio County Records Manual.* Rev. ed. [Columbus, Ohio]: Archives-Library Division, Ohio Historical Society, 1983.

Ohio Historical Society. *Ohio Newspaper Index* Columbus, Ohio: Ohio Historical Society, 1996-2001. Online guide - <www.ohiohistory.org/dindex/>.

Ohio Research Outline. Series US-States, no. 36. Salt Lake City: Family History Library, 1988.

Ohio, 1780-1970. [S.l.]: Brøderbund, 1998. CD-ROM.

Ohio's Progressive Sons, A History of the State: Sketches of Those Who Have Helped to Build Up the Commonwealth. Cincinnati: Queen City Publishing, 1905.

Pike, Kermit J. *A Guide to Shaker Manuscripts in the Library of the Western Reserve Historical Society, with an Inventory of its Shaker Photographs.* Cleveland: Western Reserve Historical Society, 1974.

Pike, Kermit J. *A Guide to the Manuscripts and Archives of the Western Reserve Historical Society.* Cleveland: Western Reserve Historical Society, 1972.

Powell, Esther Weygandt. *Early Ohio Tax Records.* 2 vols. in 1. Reprint. Baltimore, Maryland: Genealogical Publishing Co., 1993.

Progressive Men Of Northern Ohio. Cleveland: Plain Dealer Pub. Co., 1906.

Reed, George Irving. *Bench and Bar of Ohio: A Compendium of History and Biography.* 2 vols. Chicago: Century Pub. and Engraving Co., 1897.

Rerick, Rowland H. *State Centennial History of Ohio, Covering the Periods of Indian, French and British Dominion, the Territory Northwest, and the Hundred Years of Statehood.* (1902) Reprint. Salem, Massachusetts: Higginson Book Co., 1995.

Robson, Charles. *The Biographical Encyclopedia of Ohio of the Nineteenth Century.* Cincinnati: Galaxy Pub. Co., 1876.

Rust, Orton G. *History of West Central Ohio.* 3 vols.: Indianapolis, Ind.: Historical Pub. Co., 1934.

Sargent, M.P. *Pioneer Sketches: Scenes and Incidents of Former Days.* (1891) Reprint. Salem, Massachusetts: Higginson Book Co., 1993.

Schweitzer, George K. *Ohio Genealogical Research.* Knoxville, Tennessee: George K. Schweitzer, 1995.

Shane, John Dabney. *Shane Manuscript Collection.* Microfilm of the original records in the Presbyterian Historical Society in Philadelphia, Pennsylvania. (Salt Lake City: Filmed by the Genealogical Society of Utah, 1966-1967). 36 microfilm.

Short, Mrs. Don R. and Mrs. Denver Eller. *Ohio Bible Records.* 2 vols. 1971. Reprint. Fort Wayne, Indiana: Allen County Public Library, 1983.

Smythe, George Franklin. *A History of the Diocese of Ohio Until the Year 1918.* [n.d.]

Southern Ohio And Its Builders: A Biographical Record of Those Personalities, Who by Reason of Their Achievements Have Merited a Permanent Place in the Story of Twentieth Century Southern Ohio. [S.l.]: Southern Ohio Biographical Association, 1927.

Sperry, Kip. *Genealogical Research in Ohio.* Baltimore: Genealogical Publishing Co., 1997.

The Encyclopedia Of Quaker Genealogy, 1750-1930. [S.l.]: Brøderbund, 1998. CD-ROM.

Thomson, Peter G. *Bibliography of the State of Ohio, Being a Catalog of the Books and Pamphlets Relating to the History of the State, the West and Northwest.* (1880) Reprint. Salem, Massachusetts: Higginson Book Co., 1993.

Tolzman, Don Heinrich. *Ohio Valley German Biographical Index.* Bowie, Maryland: Heritage Books, 1992.

United Methodist Archives (Ohio). *Methodist Ministers Card Index: All Ohio Conferences, 1797-1981.* Columbus, Ohio: Ohio Historical Society, 1982.

Upton, Harriet T. *History of the Western Reserve.* 3 vols. Reprint. Salem, Massachusetts: Higginson Book Co., 1995.

Western Reserve Historical Society. History Library. *Card Catalog to the Manuscripts Collection in the Library of the Western Reserve Historical Society.* Microfilm of the original records from the Western Reserve Historical Society. (Salt Lake City: Filmed by the Genealogical Society of Utah, 1974). 6 microfilm.

Wittke, Carl F., ed. *The History of the State of Ohio.* 6 vols. Columbus, Ohio: The Society, 1941-1944.

Women's Department, Cleveland Centennial Commission, comp. *Genealogical Data Relating to Women in the Western Reserve Before 1840* (1850). Columbus, Ohio: Ohio Historical Society, 1973.

Yon, Paul D. *Guide to Ohio County and Municipal Records for Urban Research.* Columbus: Ohio Historical Society, 1973.

Atlases, Maps and Gazetteers

Atlas of Ohio. Madison, Wisconsin: American Publishing Co., 1975.

Brown, Lloyd Arnold. *Early Maps of the Ohio Valley.* Pittsburgh: University of Pittsburgh Press, 1959.

Burk, Thomas A. *Ohio Lands: A Short History.* 3rd ed. Columbus, Ohio: Auditor of the State, 1991.

Gallagher, John S. *The Post Offices Of Ohio.* Burtonsville, Maryland: The Depot, 1979.

Jenkins, Warren. *The Ohio Gazetteer And Traveler's Guide: Containing A Description Of The Several Towns, Townships And Counties, With Their Water Courses, Roads, Improvements, Mineral Productions....* Columbus, Ohio: Isaac N. Whiting, 1837.

Kilbourne, John. *1833 Ohio Gazetteer.* (1833) Reprint. Knightstown, Indiana: The Bookmark, 1981.

Long, John H., ed. *Historical Atlas and Chronology of County Boundaries, 1788-1980, Illinois, Indiana, Ohio.* Boston, Massachusetts: G.K. Hall, 1984.

Marzulli, Lawrence J. *The Development Of Ohio's Counties And Their Historic Courthouses.* Columbus, Ohio: County Commissioners Assn. of Ohio, [1980?].

Miller, Larry L. *Ohio Place Names.* Bloomington, Indiana: Indiana University Press, 1996.

Ohio Atlas and Gazetteer. 4th ed. Freeport, Maine: DeLorme Mapping Co., 1996.

Overman, William D. *Ohio Town Names.* Akron, Ohio: Atlantic Press, 1958.

Phillips, W. Louis. *Jurisdictional Histories For Ohio's Eighty-Eight Counties, 1788- 1985.* Bowie, Md.: Heritage Books, 1986.

Puerta, C.J., comp. *Ohio County Maps.* Lyndon Station, Wisconsin: Thomas Publishing Co., 1992.

W. L. Howison & Associates. *Maps Of Ohio Showing The Development Of Its Counties.* [Columbus, Ohio: W.L. Howison & Assoc., 198-?].

Walling, H. F. *1868 Ohio Atlas.* (1868) Reprint. Knightstown, Indiana: The Bookmark, 1995.

Census Records
Available Census Records and Census Substitutes
Federal Census 1820, 1830, 1840, 1850, 1860, 1870, 1880, 1900, 1910, 1920, 1930.

Federal Mortality Schedules 1850, 1860, 1870.

Union Veterans and Widows 1890.

Dollarhide, William. *The Census Book: A Genealogist's Guide to Federal Census Facts, Schedules and Indexes.* Bountiful, Utah: Heritage Quest, 1999.

Kemp, Thomas Jay. *The American Census Handbook.* Wilmington, Delaware: Scholarly Resources, Inc., 2001.

Lainhart, Ann S. *State Census Records.* Baltimore: Genealogical Publishing Co., Inc., 1992.

Szucs, Loretto Dennis, and Matthew Wright. *Finding Answers in U.S. Censuses Records.* Ancestry Publishing, 2001

Thorndale, William, and William Dollarhide. *Map Guide to the U.S. Federal Censuses, 1790-1920.* Baltimore: Genealogical Publishing Co., 1987.

United States. National Archives and Records Administration. *Federal Non-Population Census Schedules, Ohio, 1850-1880, in the Custody of the State Library of Ohio: Products of Agriculture, and Products of Industry.* Washington, D.C.: National Archives & Records Admin., 1988. 104 microfilm.

Court Records, Probate and Wills

Bell, Carol Willsey. *Ohio Wills and Estates to 1850: An Index.* Youngstown, Ohio: Bell Books, 1981.

Bowman, Mary L. *Abstracts and Extracts of the Legislative Acts and Resolutions of the State of Ohio: 1803-1821.* Mansfield, Ohio: Ohio Genealogical Society, 1994.

Daughters of the American Revolution. Independence Pioneers Chapter (Missouri). *Wills, 1655-1871, 1917.* Independence, Missouri: The D.A.R. chapter, 1970-1971.

Historical Records Survey (Ohio). *Inventory Of The State Archives Of Ohio.* Columbus, Ohio: Ohio Historical Records Survey Project, 1940.

Marshall, Carrington Tanner, ed. *A History of the Courts and Lawyers of Ohio.* 4 vols. New York: American Historical Society, 1934.

Nathan, Jean. *Ohio Marriages Recorded in County Courts Through 1820: An Index.* [Mansfield, Ohio]: The Society, 1996.

National Archives Records Administration. Great Lakes Region (Dayton). *Ohio Circuit Court Records.* Dayton, Ohio: National Archives Records Administration. Online guide - <www.nara.gov/regional/dayton.html>.

Ohio Federal Court Orders, 1803-1807. Miami Beach, Florida: TLC Genealogy, 1998.

Ohio Historical Society (Columbus, Ohio). *Ohio County Government Microfilm: Microfilm Available from the Ohio Historical Society.* Columbus, Ohio: Ohio Historical Society, 1987.

Ohio Historical Society. Local Government Records Program. *Guide to Local Government Records at the Ohio University Library.* Athens, Ohio: Ohio University Library, 1986.

Emigration, Immigration, Migration and Naturalization

Aughenbaugh, Gloria L. *Gone to Ohio: Ashland, Brown, Columbiana, Harrison, Jefferson, Richland, Champaign, Crawford, Wood, Logan, Mahoning, Stark and Trumbull Counties, from the Pennsylvania Counties: Adams, Cumberland, Dauphin, Franklin, Lancaster, and York.* 3 vols. York, Pennsylvania: South Central Pennsylvania Genealogical Society, 1990-1996.

Feather, Carl E. *Mountain People in a Flat Land: A Popular History of Appalachian Migration to Northeast Ohio, 1940-1965.* Athens, Ohio: Ohio University Press, 1998.

Ohio Historical Society. *County Naturalizations Held by the Ohio Historical Society.* Columbus, Ohio: Ohio Historical Society, 1996-2001. Online guide - <www.ohiohistory.org/resource/archlib/natural.html>.

Ohio, Trailways to Highways 1776-1976. Salt Lake City, Utah: Genealogical Society of Utah, 1977.

United States. District Court (Ohio: Southern District). *Naturalization Index, 1852-1991.* Microfilm of original records located at U.S. District Court, Southern District of Ohio, Cincinnati. (Salt Lake City: Filmed by the Genealogical Society of Utah, 1992). 16 microfilm.

Wilhelm, Hubert G. H. *The Origin and Distribution of Settlement Groups.* Athens, Ohio: Ohio University, 1982.

Winkle, Kenneth J. *The Politics of Community: Migration and Politics in Antebellum Ohio.* New York: Press Syndicate of the University of Cambridge, 1988.

Land and Property

Berry, Ellen, and David Berry. *Early Ohio Settlers Purchasers of Land in Southwestern Ohio, 1800-1840*. (1986). Reprint. Baltimore, Maryland: Genealogical Publishing, 1993.

Clark, Marie Taylor. *Ohio Lands South of the Indian Boundary Line*. Chillicothe, Ohio: Marie Taylor Clark, 1984.

Clark, Marie Taylor. *Ohio Lands-Chillicothe Land Office: Entries Encompassing the lands of Congress Lands, Refuge Tract, United States Military District, and French Grants; Contains Maps and Histories of Land Areas, 1800-1829*. [S.l.: Clark], 1984.

Dyer, Albion Morris. *First Ownership of Ohio Lands*. Baltimore: Genealogical Publishing Co., 1982.

Ferguson, Thomas E. *Ohio Lands: A Short History*, 6th ed. Columbus, Ohio: Auditor's Office, State of Ohio, 1995.

Hone, Wade E. *Land and Property Research in the United States*. Salt Lake City: Ancestry Incorporated, 1997.

Hutchinson, William Thomas. *The Bounty Lands of the American Revolution in Ohio*. New York: Arno Press, 1979.

Ohio, 1787-1840. [S.l.]: Brøderbund, 1999. CD-ROM.

Ohio. Auditor of State. *Canal Lands*. Microfilm of records at the Ohio Historical Society in Columbus. (Salt Lake City, Utah: Genealogical Society of Utah, 1959). Microfilm, 50 rolls.

Ohio. Auditor of State. *Governor's Deeds Card Index, 1833-1994*. Microfilm of original records at the Ohio Historical Society, Columbus, Ohio. (Salt Lake City: Filmed by the Genealogical Society of Utah, 1995). 4 microfilm.

Ohio. Auditor of State. *Miscellaneous Lands*. Columbus, Ohio: Columbus Microfilm, Inc., 1954-1958, 1995. 23 microfilm.

Ohio. Auditor of State. *Virginia Military District Lands of Ohio; Indexes*. Microfilm of index and original records at the State Auditor's Office in Columbus, Ohio. (Salt Lake City: Filmed by the Genealogical Society of Utah, 1995, 1958). 33 microfilm.

Peters, William Edwards. *Ohio Lands and Their History*. Athens, Ohio: W.E. Peters, 1930.

Peters, William Edwards. *Ohio Lands and Their Subdivision*. 2nd ed. Athens, Ohio: William Edwards Peters, 1918.

Petro, Jim. *Ohio Lands: A Short History*. Ohio: The Ohio Auditor of State, 1994.

Riegel, Mayburt Stephenson. *Early Ohioans' Residences from the Land Grant Records*. Mansfield, Ohio: Ohio Genealogical Society, 1976.

Sherman, C. E. *Original Ohio Land Subdivision Being Volume III: Final Report Ohio Cooperative Topographic Survey*. Columbus: State Reformatory Press, 1925.

United States. Bureau of Land Management. *Card Files*. Microfilm of original card files located at the Bureau of Land Management's Eastern States Office in Alexandria, Virginia. Washington, D.C.: Bureau of Land Management, [19–]. 160 microfilm.

United States. General Land Office. *U.S. Revolutionary War Bounty Land Warrants Used in the U.S. Military District of Ohio and Related Papers, Acts of 1788, 1803, 1806*. Washington, D.C.: National Archives, 1971.

Military

Broglin, Jana Sloan. *Index to the Official Roster of Ohio Soldiers in the War with Spain*. Mansfield, Ohio: Ohio Genealogical Society, 1990.

Broglin, Jana Sloan. *Roster of the Soldiers of Ohio in the War with Mexico*. (1897) Reprint. Mansfield, Ohio: Ohio Genealogical Society, 1991.

Canfield, Capt. S. S. *History of the 21st Regiment, Ohio Volunteer Infantry, in the War of the Rebellion*. (1893) Reprint. Salem, Massachusetts: Higginson Book Co., 1995.

Dailey, Mrs. Orville D. *The Official Roster of the Soldiers of the American Revolution Who Lived in the State of Ohio: Vol. 2, A-Z*. Columbus, Ohio: State Society DAR, State of Ohio, 1938?.

Garner, Grace. *Index to Roster of Ohio Soldiers, War of 1812*. Spokane, Washington: Eastern Washington Genealogical Society, 1974.

Hardesty's Historical and Geographical Encyclopedia, Illustrated… Containing… Maps of Each State and Territory of the United States, and the Provinces of Canada...History of the United States, History of Each State and Territory of the United States...Special Military History of Ohio...Ohio's Rank and File in the War of the Rebellion…. New York: [s.n.], 1885.

Maxwell, Fay. *Ohio Indian, Revolutionary War, and War of 1812 Trails*. St. Peter, Minnesota: Ohio Genealogy Center, 1974.

Maxwell, Fay. *Ohio Revolutionary War Soldiers 1840 Census and Grave Locations*. St. Peter, Minnesota: Ohio Genealogy Center, 1985.

Maxwell, Fay. *Ohio's Virginia Military Tract Settlers, Also 1801 Tax List*. St. Peter, Minnesota: Ohio Genealogy Center, 1991.

Middle Western Section Records. Colonial and Genealogical Records Committee, Daughters of the American Revolution, Ohio. Fort Wayne, Indiana: Allen County Public Library, 1983.

Ohio Adjutant General's Department. *Roster of Ohio Soldiers in the War of 1812*. (1968) Reprint. Baltimore, Maryland: Clearfield Company, 1989.

Ohio Adjutant General's Office. *The Official Roster of Ohio Soldiers in the War with Spain 1898-1899*. Columbus, Ohio: Edward T. Miller Co., 1916.

Ohio Historical Society. *Civil War Documents*. Columbus, Ohio: Ohio Historical Society, 1996-2001. Online guide - <www.ohiohistory.org/dindex/>.

Ohio Historical Society. *War of 1812, Roster of Ohio Soldiers*. Columbus, Ohio: Ohio Historical Society, 1996-2001. Online database - <www.ohiohistory.org/dindex/>.

Ohio Roster Commission. *Official Roster of the Soldiers of the State of Ohio in the War of the Rebellion, 1861-1866*. Akron, Ohio: Werner Co., 1886-1895.

Ohio, Adjutant General's Office. *The Official Roster of the Soldiers of the American Revolution Buried in the State of Ohio*. Columbus, Ohio: F. J. Heer Printing Co., 1929-1959.

Ohio. Adjutant General's Office. *The Official Roster of Ohio Soldiers, Sailors, and Marines in the World War, 1917-1918*. Microfilm of original published: Columbus, Ohio: F.J. Heer Printing Co., 1926-1929. 22 volumes.. (Salt Lake City: Filmed by the Genealogical Society of Utah, 1959). 23 microfilm.

Phillips, William Louis. *Annotated Bibliography of Ohio Patriots: Revolutionary War & War of 1812*. Bowie, Maryland: Heritage Books, 1985.

Two Hundred Years the Military History of Ohio: Its Border Annals, its Part in the Indian Wars, in the War of 1812, in the Mexican War, and in the War of the Rebellion, with a Prefix, Giving a Compendium of the History of the United States, History of the Declaration of Independence, Sketches of its Signers, and of the Presidents, with Portraits and Autographs. New York: H. H. Hardesty, 1886.

United States, Selective Service System. *Ohio, World War I Selective Service System Draft Registration Cards, 1917-1918*. Washington, D.C.: National Archives, 1987-1988.

United States. Navy Department. *State Summary of War Casualties (Ohio), U.S. Navy, 1946: (Includes Navy, Marine, and Coast Guard)*. (Salt Lake City: Filmed by the Genealogical Society of Utah, 1960).

United States. Veterans Administration. *Revolutionary War Pension and Bounty-Land- Warrant Application Files*. Washington, D.C.: National Archives, 1969.

United States. War Department. *World War II Honor List of Dead and Missing - State Of Ohio, June 1946*. (Salt Lake City: Filmed by the Genealogical Society of Utah, 1960.)

White, Virgil D. *Genealogical Abstracts of the Revolutionary War Pension Files*. 4 vols. Waynesboro, Tennessee: National Historical Publishing, 1990.

Young American Patriots: The Youth of Ohio in World War II.: Richmond, Virginia: National Publishing Co., 1947.

Vital and Cemetery Records

Bell, Carol Willsey. *Ohio Divorces: The Early Years*. Boardman, Ohio: Bell Books, 1994.

Caccamo, James F. *Marriage Notices from the Ohio Observer Series*. Apollo, Pennsylvania: Closson Press, 1994.

Daughters of the American Revolution (Ohio). *Early Vital Records of Ohio, 1750-1970*. Microfilm of manuscripts from the DAR Library, Washington, D.C. (Salt Lake City: Genealogical Society of Utah, 1972).

Diefenbach, Mrs. H. B., and Mrs. C. O. Ross. *Index to the Grave Records of Soldiers in the War of 1812 Buried in Ohio*. [S.l.: s.n., 1945].

Herbert, Jeffrey G. *Index of Death and Other Notices Appearing in the Cincinnati Free Press 1874-1920*. Bowie, Maryland: Heritage Books, 1993.

Index to Grave Records of Servicemen in the War of 1812. State of Ohio. Lancaster, Ohio: Society of the United States Daughters of 1812, 1969.

Marriage Records. Orem, Utah: Automated Archives, 1994. CD-ROM.

Official Roster of the Soldiers of the American Revolution Buried in the State of Ohio. 3 vols. Columbus, Ohio: F.J. Heer Printing, 1929-59.

Ohio Cemetery Records. (Salt Lake City: Filmed by the Genealogical Society of Utah, 1972). 2 microfilm.

Ohio Cemetery Records: Extracted from the "Old Northwest" Genealogical Quarterly. Reprint. Baltimore, Maryland: Genealogical Publishing Co., 1989.

Ohio Historical Society. *Death Certificate Index, 1913-1937*. Columbus, Ohio: Ohio Historical Society, 1992. Online database - <www.ohiohistory.org/dindex/>.

Ohio. Department of Health. *Certificates of Death, 1908-1944; Index, 1908-1911*. Microfilm of original records at Ohio Historical Society, Columbus, Ohio. Columbus, Ohio: Ohio Historical Society, 1983, 1994-1995. 962 microfilm.

Ohio. Department of Health. *Veteran's Records, 1941-1964*. Microfilm of original records located in the Licking County Courthouse in Newark, Ohio. (Salt Lake City: Filmed by the Genealogical Society of Utah, 1974). 7 microfilm.

Smith, Marjorie, ed. *Ohio Marriages: Extracted from the Old Northwest Genealogical Quarterly*. Baltimore: Genealogical Publishing Co., 1980.

Smith, Maxine Hartmann, ed. *Ohio Cemeteries*. Mansfield: Ohio Genealogical Society, 1978. (Addendum, 1990).

State Library of Ohio. *Ohio Birth and Death Records by County*. Columbus, Ohio: State Library of Ohio, 2001. Online guide - <winslo.state.oh.us/services/genealogy/slogenebir.html>.

County Website	Map Index	Date Created	Parent County or Territory From Which Organized Address/Details
Adams* www.rootsweb.com/~ohadams/	**N4**	**10 Jul 1797**	**Hamilton** Adams County; 110 W Main St; West Union, OH 45693-1347; Ph. 937.544.5547 Details: (Courthouse burned in 1910, some rec saved, some as early as 1796; rec of several adjacent cos prior to their formation included) (Pro Ct has b & d rec 1888-1893, m rec 1803-1853 & from 1910, pro rec 1849-1860 & from 1910; Board of Hlth has b & d rec from 1908; Clk Ct has div & ct rec from 1910; Co Rcdr has land rec from 1797)
Allen* www.co.allen.oh.us/	**H3**	**12 Feb 1820**	**Shelby** Allen County; 301 N Main St; Lima, OH 45801-4456; Ph. 419.223.8513 Details: (Pro Ct has b & d rec from 1867, m rec from 1831 & pro rec; Clk Cts has div & ct rec from 1831; Co Museum has nat rec 1851-1929)
Ashland* www.ashlandcounty.org/	**H8**	**24 Feb 1846**	**Wayne, Richland, Huron, Lorain** Ashland County; 110 W 2nd St; Ashland, OH 44805; Ph. 419.289.0000 Details: (Clk Cts has div & ct rec; Pro Ct has m & pro rec; Co Rcdr has land rec)
Ashtabula www.co.ashtabula.oh.us/	**E11**	**10 Feb 1807**	**Trumbull, Geauga** Ashtabula County; 25 W Jefferson St; Jefferson, OH 44047; Ph. 440.576.3637 Details: (Pro Ct has b & d rec 1867-1908, m rec from 1811 & pro rec from 1800's; Co Hlth Dept has b & d rec from 1909; Clk Cts has div rec from 1811 & ct rec from 1800's; Co Rcdr has land rec from 1800)
Athens* www.seorf.ohiou.edu/athens_county.html	**L8**	**20 Feb 1805**	**Washington** Athens County; Court & Washington Sts; PO Box 290; Athens, OH 45701-0000; Ph. 740.592.3242 Details: (Pro Judge has b, m & pro rec; Clk Cts has div & ct rec from 1800; Co Rcdr has land rec)
Auglaize www.genweb.brightusa.net/index.html	**I3**	**14 Feb 1848**	**Allen, Mercer, Darke, Hardin, Logan, Shelby, Van Wert** Auglaize County; 214 S Wagner St; Wapakoneta, OH 45895; Ph. 419.738.3410 Details: (Pro Judge has b, m, d & pro rec; Clk Cts has div & ct rec from 1848; Co Rcdr has land rec)
Belmont* www.belmontcountyohio.org/	**K11**	**7 Sep 1801**	**Jefferson, Washington** Belmont County; 100 W Main St; St. Clairsville, OH 43950-1225; Ph. 740.699.2139 Details: (Clk Cts has div & ct rec from 1820; Pro Ct has b, m, d & pro rec; Co Hlth Dept has bur rec)
Brown* www.rootsweb.com/~ohbrown/index.htm	**N3**	**27 Dec 1817**	**Adams, Clermont** Brown County; 101 S Main St; Georgetown, OH 45121-0000; Ph. 937.378.3100 Details: (Pro Judge has b, m & pro rec from 1800's; Co Hlth Dept has d rec from 1800's; Clk Cts has div & ct rec from 1800's; Co Rcdr has land rec)
Butler www.butlercountyohio.org/	**L2**	**24 Mar 1803**	**Hamilton** Butler County; 315 High St; Hamilton, OH 45011-2756; Ph. 513.887.3278 Details: (Co Hlth Dept has b & d rec; Pro Judge has m & pro rec; Clk Cts has div & ct rec; Co Aud has land rec)
Carroll pages.eohio.net/carrcomm/	**I11**	**25 Dec 1832**	**Columbiana, Stark, Harrison, Jefferson, Tuscarawas** Carroll County; 119 Public Sq; Carrollton, OH 44615-1448; Ph. 330.627.4886 Details: (Clk Cts has div & ct rec from 1833; Pro Ct has b & d rec 1867-1909, m & pro rec from 1833; Co Rcdr has land rec from 1833; Board of Hlth has b & d rec from 1909)
Champaign www.rootsweb.com/~ohchampa/	**J3**	**20 Feb 1805**	**Greene, Franklin** Champaign County; 200 N Main St; Urbana, OH 43078-0000; Ph. 937.653.2746 Details: (Pro Judge has b, m & pro rec; Co Hlth Dept has d rec; Co Aud has bur rec; Co Rcdr has land rec; Clk Cts has div & ct rec)
Clark www.rootsweb.com/~ohclark/	**K3**	**26 Dec 1817**	**Champaign, Madison, Greene** Clark County; Ab Graham Bldg; Springfield, OH 45502; Ph. 937.328.2458 Details: (Clark Co Hist Soc, Memorial Hall, Springfield, OH 45502 may assist you in your work, also Warder Public Lib, Springfield) (Pro Judge has b, m, d, pro & nat rec; Clk Cts has div & ct rec; Co Rcdr has land rec)

County Website	Map Index	Date Created	Parent County or Territory From Which Organized Address/Details
Clermont www.co.clermont.oh.us/	N3	6 Dec 1800	**Hamilton** Clermont County; 212 E Main St; Batavia, OH 45103; Ph. 513.732.7308 Details: (Pro Ct has b & d rec 1867-1950, m & pro rec from 1800 & nat rec from 1860's; Clk Cts has div rec from 1861 & ct rec from 1803)
Clinton www.rootsweb.com/~ohclinto/	L4	19 Feb 1810	**Highland, Warren** Clinton County; 46 S South St; Wilmington, OH 45177-2214; Ph. 937.382.2103 Details: (Pro Judge has b & d rec 1867-1908, m & pro rec from 1810; Co Hlth Office has b & d rec from 1908; Co Rcdr has land rec from 1810; Clk Cts has div & ct rec from 1810)
Columbiana* www.rootsweb.com/~ohcolumb/index.htm	H11	25 Mar 1803	**Jefferson, Washington** Columbiana County; 105 S Market St; Lisbon, OH 44432-1255; Ph. 440.424.9511 Details: (Clk Cts has div & ct rec; Pro Judge has m & pro rec; Co Rcdr has land rec)
Coshocton www.co.coshocton.oh.us/	I8	31 Jan 1810	**Tuscarawas, Muskingum** Coshocton County; 318 Main St; Coshocton, OH 43812; Ph. 740.622.1456 Details: (Pro Ct has m & pro rec from 1811 & some nat rec from 1862; Co Hlth Dept has b & d rec 1867-1909; Com Pleas Ct has div & ct rec; Co Aud has land rec)
Crawford www.rootsweb.com/~ohcrawfo/index.htm	H6	12 Feb 1820	**Delaware** Crawford County; 112 E Mansfield St; Bucyrus, OH 44820; Ph. 419.562.2766 Details: (City & Co Hlth Depts have b & d rec from 1908; Pro Judge has b & d rec 1867-1908, m & pro rec from 1831; Co Rcdr has land rec; Clk Cts has div & ct rec from 1834)
Cuyahoga* www.cuyahoga.oh.us/home/default.asp	F9	10 Feb 1808	**Geauga** Cuyahoga County; 1200 Ontario St; Cleveland, OH 44113; Ph. 216.443.7950 Details: (Pro Ct has b rec 1859-1901 & d rec 1868-1908; Western Reserve Hist Soc has m rec 1810-1941 & tax rec 1819-1869; M Lic Bureau has m rec from 1810; Co Courthouse has nat rec 1818-1906 & pro rec from 1810; Clk Cts has div rec 1837-1925; Co Admin Bldg has land rec from 1810)
Darke www.calweb.com/~wally/ohdarke/index.htm	J2	3 Jan 1809	**Miami** Darke County; 504 S Broadway St; Greenville, OH 45331-0000; Ph. 937.547.7335 Details: (Pro Judge has b & d rec 1867-1908, m rec from 1817 & pro rec; Clk Cts has div & ct rec from 1820; Co Rcdr has land rec from 1816 & bur rec (veterans graves) from 1832)
Defiance www.rootsweb.com/~ohdefian/index.html	F2	4 Mar 1845	**Williams, Henry, Paulding** Defiance County; 510 Court St; Defiance, OH 43512-2157; Ph. 419.782.4761 Details: (Co Rec Center has b & d rec 1867-1908, m rec from 1845, land rec from 1843, pro rec from 1845, div & ct rec from 1800's, nat rec 1872-1903 & mil dis rec 1865-1973; Co Hlth Dept has b & d rec from 1908)
Delaware www.co.delaware.oh.us/	J6	10 Feb 1808	**Franklin** Delaware County; 91 N Sandusky St; Delaware, OH 43015; Ph. 740.369.8761 Details: (Clk Chan Ct has div & ct rec from 1825; Pro Ct has b, m, d & pro rec; Co Rcdr has land rec)
Erie www.erie-county-ohio.net/	F7	15 Mar 1838	**Huron, Sandusky** Erie County; 323 Columbus Ave; Sandusky, OH 44870; Ph. 419.627.7705 Details: (Co Hlth Dept has b rec from 1908, d & bur rec; Pro Judge has m & pro rec; Clk Cts has div & ct rec from 1870; Co Rcdr has land rec)
Fairfield www.co.fairfield.oh.us/	K7	9 Dec 1800	**Ross, Washington** Fairfield County; 224 E Main St; PO Box 370; Lancaster, OH 43130-3842; Ph. 740.687.7030 Details: (Pro Judge has b rec 1803-1907, m, d & pro rec; Clk Cts has div rec from 1860 & ct rec from 1800; Co Rcdr has land rec from 1803)
Fayette* www.fayette-co-oh.com/	L4	19 Feb 1810	**Ross, Highland** Fayette County; 110 E Court St; Washington Court House, OH 43160-1355; Ph. 614.335.5910 Details: (Clk Cts has div rec from 1853 & ct rec from 1828; Pro Judge has pro rec; Co Rcdr has land rec)

County Website	Map Index	Date Created	Parent County or Territory From Which Organized Address/Details
Franklin* www.co.franklin.oh.us/	K6	30 Mar 1803	**Ross** Franklin County; 3695 High St; Columbus, OH 43215; Ph. 614.645.3600 Details: (Pro Ct has b & d rec before 1908, m & pro rec; Clk Cts has div & ct rec from 1803; Co Aud has land rec)
Fulton www.fultoncountyoh.com/	E3	28 Feb 1850	**Lucas, Henry, Williams** Fulton County; 210 S Fulton St; Wauseon, OH 43567-1355; Ph. 419.337.9230 Details: (Pro Ct has b & d rec 1867-1908, m, pro & nat rec; Clk Cts has div & ct rec; Co Rcdr has mil & bur rec; Co Aud has land rec)
Gallia www.rootsweb.com/~ohgallia/gallia.htm	N7	25 Mar 1803	**Washington, Adams** Gallia County; 18 Locust St; Gallipolis, OH 45631-1251; Ph. 740.446.4374 Details: (Pro Judge has b, m, d & pro rec; Co Hlth Dept has bur rec; Clk Cts has div & ct rec from 1850; Co Rcdr has land rec)
Geauga* www.co.geauga.oh.us/	F10	31 Dec 1805	**Trumbull** Geauga County; 231 Main St; Chardon, OH 44024-1243; Ph. 216.285.2222 Details: (Pro Judge has b, m, d & pro rec; Co Hlth Dept has bur rec; Clk Cts has div & ct rec from 1806; Co Rcdr has land rec)
Greene www.co.greene.oh.us/	K3	24 Mar 1803	**Hamilton, Ross** Greene County; 45 N Detroit St; Xenia, OH 45385; Ph. 937.376.5290 Details: (Pro Judge has b rec 1869-1908, m & pro rec from 1803; Clk Cts has div & ct rec from 1802; Co Rcdr has land rec from 1803; Co Aud has tax rec from 1803; Co Hlth Dept has b rec from 1908)
Guernsey www.usgennet.org/usa/oh/county/ guernsey/	K10	31 Jan 1810	**Belmont, Muskingum** Guernsey County; 801 Wheeling Ave; Cambridge, OH 43725-2335; Ph. 740.432.9230 Details: (Clk Cts has div rec from 1850 & ct rec from 1810; Pro Judge has b, m & pro rec; Co Rcdr has land rec; City-Co Hlth Dept has d rec)
Hamilton* www.hamilton-co.org/	M1	2 Jan 1790	**Original county** Hamilton County; 1000 Main St; Cincinnati, OH 45202; Ph. 513.632.5656 Details: (Pro Judge has m, bur & pro rec; Co Hlth Dept has d rec; Clk Cts has div & ct rec from 1900; Co Rcdr has land rec)
Hancock* www.co.hancock.oh.us/	G4	12 Feb 1820	**Logan** Hancock County; 300 S Main St; Findlay, OH 45840-3345; Ph. 419.424.3911 Details: (Co Rcdr has land rec; Pro Judge has b, m, d & pro rec)
Hardin www.kenton.com/users/chuck/index.htm	I4	12 Feb 1820	**Logan** Hardin County; Public Sq; Kenton, OH 43326; Ph. 419.673.6283 Details: (Clk Cts has div & ct rec from 1864; Co Hlth Dept has b & d rec; Pro Ct has m, d & pro rec; Co Rcdr has land rec)
Harrison Future website at scioto.org/ OHGenWeb/ohiomap.html	J10	2 Jan 1813	**Jefferson, Tuscarawas** Harrison County; 100 W Market St; Cadiz, OH 43907-1132; Ph. 740.942.4623 Details: (Clk Cts has div & ct rec from 1813; Pro Judge has b rec to 1917, m & pro rec; Co Hlth Office has b rec from 1917, d & bur rec; Co Rcdr has land rec)
Henry www.rootsweb.com/~ohhenry/	F3	12 Feb 1820	**Shelby** Henry County; 660 N Perry St; Napoleon, OH 43545-0546; Ph. 419.592.4876 Details: (Pro Judge has b & d rec 1867-1908, m & pro rec from 1847; Clk Cts has div & ct rec from 1880; Co Rcdr has land rec from 1835)
Highland www.usgennet.org/usa/oh/ county/highland/	M4	18 Feb 1805	**Ross, Adams, Clermont** Highland County; 114 Governor Foraker Pl; Hillsboro, OH 45133; Ph. 937.393.1981 Details: (Pro Ct has m & d rec 1867-1909, b rec to 1905 & pro rec; Co Hlth Dept has b, m & d rec from 1909; Clk Cts has div & ct rec from 1832, some nat & adoption rec; Co Rcdr has land rec)
Hocking www.co.hocking.oh.us/	L7	3 Jan 1818	**Athens, Ross, Fairfield** Hocking County; 1 E Main St; Logan, OH 43138-1207; Ph. 740.385.3022 Details: (Pro Judge has b, m & pro rec; Co Hlth Dept has d rec; Clk Cts has div & ct rec from 1873; Co Rcdr has land rec)

County Website	Map Index	Date Created	Parent County or Territory From Which Organized / Address/Details
Holmes www.holmescounty.com/gov/	I8	20 Jan 1824	**Coshocton, Wayne, Tuscarawas** Holmes County; 1 E Jackson St; Millersburg, OH 44654; Ph. 330.674.0286 Details: (Pro Ct has b & d rec 1867-1982, m & pro rec from 1825 & nat rec; Clk Cts has div & ct rec; Co Rcdr has land & mil rec; Co Lib has bur & cen rec)
Huron www.hccommissioners.com/ homepage.htm	G7	7 Feb 1809	**Portage, Cuyahoga** Huron County; 2 E Main St; Norwalk, OH 44857; Ph. 419.668.5113 Details: (Pro Judge has b & d rec 1867-1908, m & pro rec from 1815 & nat rec from 1859; City & Co Hlth Dept have b & d rec from 1908; Co Clk has ct rec from 1815, div & nat rec to 1859; Co Rcdr has land rec from 1808, Connecticut Fire Sufferers rec 1792-1808 & mil dis rec from 1865; Co Aud has tax rec from 1820; Co Hist Lib has infirmary rec 1848-1900, tax rec 1815-1825, Co Comm journals from 1815, land partition rec 1815-1920, co militia lists 1864-1865 & indigent soldier bur rec 1880-1920)
Jackson* www.rootsweb.com/~ohjackso/ jackson.htm	M7	12 Jan 1816	**Scioto, Gallia, Athens, Ross** Jackson County; 226 E Main St; Jackson, OH 45640-0000; Ph. 740.286.2006 Details: (Pro Judge has b, m & pro rec; Co Hlth Dept has d & bur rec; Clk Cts has div & ct rec; Co Rcdr has land rec)
Jefferson www.rootsweb.com/~ohjeffer/	I11	27 Jul 1797	**Washington** Jefferson County; 301 Market St; Steubenville, OH 43952; Ph. 740.283.8583 Details: (Pro Judge has m, pro & nat rec; Clk Cts has div & ct rec from 1797; Co Rcdr has land rec from 1797; Board of Hlth has b & d rec)
Knox* www.knoxcountyohio.org/	I7	30 Jan 1808	**Fairfield** Knox County; 111 E High St; Mount Vernon, OH 43050-3453; Ph. 740.393.6788 Details: (Co Hlth Dept has b rec from 1908, d & bur rec; Pro Judge has m rec from 1803 & pro rec; Clk Cts has div & ct rec from 1810; Co Rcdr has land rec)
Lake* www.rootsweb.com/~ohlake/	E10	6 Mar 1840	**Geauga, Cuyahoga** Lake County; 47 N Park Pl; Painesville, OH 44077-3414; Ph. 440.350.2657 Details: (Clk Cts has ct rec from 1840; Pro Judge has m & pro rec; Co Rcdr has land rec)
Lawrence www.db.k12.oh.us/community/lcc_1.htm	O7	21 Dec 1815	**Gallia, Scioto** Lawrence County; 111 N 4th St; Ironton, OH 45638; Ph. 740.533.4300 Details: (Pro Ct has b rec 1864-1908, m rec from 1900, d rec 1868-1933 & pro rec from 1817; Co Hlth Dept has b & d rec from 1908; Clk Cts has ct rec from 1817 & div rec from 1819; Co Rcdr has land rec from 1817)
Licking www.lcounty.com/	J7	30 Jan 1808	**Fairfield** Licking County; 20 S 2nd St; Newark, OH 43058; Ph. 740.349.6062 Details: (Pro Judge has b, m & pro rec; Co Hlth Dept has d rec; Clk Cts has div rec from 1876 & ct rec from 1872; Co Rcdr has land rec)
Logan www.co.logan.oh.us/	I4	30 Dec 1817	**Champaign** Logan County; 101 S Main St Courthouse; Bellefontaine, OH 43311; Ph. 937.599.7275 Details: (Pro Ct has b & d rec 1867-1909, m rec from 1818 & pro rec from 1820; Co Rcdr has land, mil & bur rec; Com Pleas Ct has div & ct rec)
Lorain* www.centurytel.net/lorgen/	G8	26 Dec 1822	**Huron, Cuyahoga, Medina** Lorain County; 226 Middle Ave; Elyria, OH 44035; Ph. 440.329.5428 Details: (Pro Judge has b, m & pro rec; Clk Cts has div rec from 1850 & ct rec from 1824; Co Rcdr has land rec; Elyria Public Lib & Lorain Co Hist Soc have books of genealogical interest)
Lucas* co.lucas.oh.us/	E4	20 Jun 1835	**Wood, Sandusky, Henry** Lucas County; 700 Adams St; Toledo, OH 43624; Ph. 419.245.4000 Details: (Clk Cts has div & ct rec from 1850; Pro Judge has b rec 1865-1908, d rec from 1935, m & pro rec; Co Rcdr has land rec)
Madison* www.co.madison.oh.us/	K5	16 Feb 1810	**Franklin** Madison County; 1 N Main St; London, OH 43140; Ph. 740.852.9776 Details: (Pro Ct has b & d rec 1867-1908, m & pro rec from 1810 & nat rec; Co Hlth Dept has b rec from 1908; Co Rcdr has land & mil dis rec; Clk Cts has div & ct rec)

County Website	Map Index	Date Created	Parent County or Territory From Which Organized Address/Details
Mahoning mahoningcountygov.com/	G11	16 Feb 1846	**Columbiana, Trumbull** Mahoning County; 120 Market St; Youngstown, OH 44503; Ph. 330.740.2104 Details: (Co Hlth Dept has b & d rec; Pro Judge has m & pro rec; Clk Cts has div & ct rec; Co Aud has land rec)
Marion www.mariononline.com/county/	I5	12 Feb 1820	**Delaware** Marion County; 100 N Main St; Marion, OH 43302; Ph. 740.387.8128 Details: (Pro Ct has m & pro rec; City Hlth Dept has b & d rec from 1908; Pub Lib has b & d rec 1867-1908; Clk Cts has div & ct rec; Co Rcdr has land rec)
Medina www.co.medina.oh.us/	G8	18 Feb 1812	**Portage** Medina County; 93 Public Sq; Medina, OH 44256; Ph. 330.723.3641 Details: (Pro Ct has b & d rec to 1909, m & pro rec; Co Hlth Dept has b & d rec from 1909; Clk Cts has div & ct rec from 1818; Co Rcdr has land rec)
Meigs genealogy.rootsweb.com/~baf/meigs.html	M8	21 Jan 1819	**Gallia, Athens** Meigs County; 100 E 2nd St; Pomeroy, OH 45769-0000; Ph. 740.992.5290 Details: (Pro Judge has b, m, d & pro rec; Clk Cts has div & ct rec from 1819; Co Rcdr has land rec)
Mercer www.mercercountyohio.org/	I2	12 Feb 1820	**Darke** Mercer County; 101 N Main St; PO Box 28; Celina, OH 45822; Ph. 419.586.6461 Details: (Pro Judge has b & d rec 1867-1908, m rec from 1830 & pro rec from 1829; Clk Cts has div & ct rec from 1824; Co Rcdr has land rec)
Miami www.co.miami.oh.us/	J2	16 Jan 1807	**Montgomery** Miami County; 201 W Main St; Troy, OH 45373-3263; Ph. 937.332.6855 Details: (Clk Cts has div & ct rec from 1807; Pro Judge has m, d & pro rec; Co Hlth Dept has b rec; Co Rcdr has land rec)
Monroe www.rootsweb.com/~ohmonroe/	K11	29 Jan 1813	**Belmont, Washington, Guernsey** Monroe County; 101 N Main St; Woodsfield, OH 43793; Ph. 740.472.0761 Details: (Clk Cts has div & ct rec from early 1800's; Pro Judge has m & pro rec; Co Rcdr has land rec)
Montgomery* www.co.montgomery.oh.us/	K2	24 Mar 1803	**Hamilton, Wayne, old** Montgomery County; 41 N Perry; Dayton, OH 45422-0002; Ph. 937.225.6118 Details: (Clk Cts has div & ct rec; Pro Judge has b, m, d & pro rec; Co Rcdr has land rec)
Morgan www.rootsweb.com/~ohmorgan/ index.htm	L9	29 Dec 1817	**Washington, Guernsey, Muskingum** Morgan County; 19 E Main St; McConnelsville, OH 43756-1198; Ph. 740.962.4752 Details: (Co Rcdr has land rec; Pro Judge has b, m, d, pro & nat rec)
Morrow www.rootsweb.com/~ohmorrow/	I6	24 Feb 1848	**Knox, Marion, Delaware, Richland** Morrow County; 48 E High St; Mount Gilead, OH 43338; Ph. 419.947.2085 Details: (Pro Ct has b & d rec 1856-1857 & 1867-1908, m & pro rec from 1848 & nat rec 1848-1894; Co Hlth Dept has b & d rec from 1908; Co Rcdr has land rec from 1848 & mil rec; Com Pleas Ct has div & ct rec)
Muskingum www.rootsweb.com/~ohmuskin/	K8	7 Jan 1804	**Washington, Fairfield** Muskingum County; 401 Main St; Zanesville, OH 43701; Ph. 740.455.7104 Details: (Pro Ct has b & d rec 1867-1908, m & pro rec from 1804 & nat rec; Co Rcdr has land rec from 1803 & mil rec from 1865; Clk Cts has div & ct rec from 1804)
Noble www.rootsweb.com/~ohnoble/index.htm	K10	11 Mar 1851	**Monroe, Washington, Morgan, Guernsey** Noble County; County Courthouse; Caldwell, OH 43724-0000; Ph. 740.732.4408 Details: (Clk Cts has div & ct rec from 1851; Pro Judge has m & pro rec; Co Rcdr has land rec)
Ottawa www.co.ottawa.oh.us/OCHome/ OCFrameset.htm	F5	6 Mar 1840	**Erie, Sandusky, Lucas** Ottawa County; 315 Madison St Rm 103; Port Clinton, OH 43452-1936; Ph. 419.734.6752 Details: (Co Hlth Dept has b, d & bur rec; Pro Judge has m & pro rec; Clk Cts has div & ct rec from 1840 & nat rec 1905-1929; Co Rcdr has land rec)

County Website	Map Index	Date Created	Parent County or Territory From Which Organized Address/Details
Paulding Future website at scioto.org/ OHGenWeb/ohiomap.html	G2	12 Feb 1820	**Darke** Paulding County; Perry & N Williams; Paulding, OH 45879-0000; Ph. 419.399.8210 Details: (Co Hlth Dept has b & d rec; Pro Judge has m & pro rec; Clk Cts has div rec; Co Judge has ct rec; Co Rcdr has land rec)
Perry www.perrygenealogy.net/	K8	26 Dec 1817	**Washington, Fairfield, Muskingum** Perry County; 105 N Main St; New Lexington, OH 43764-1241; Ph. 740.342.1022 Details: (Pro Ct has b & d rec from 1867, m rec from 1818 & pro rec; Co Rcdr has land rec)
Pickaway www.rootsweb.com/~ohpickaw/ index.html	L5	12 Jan 1810	**Ross, Fairfield, Franklin** Pickaway County; 207 S Court St; Circleville, OH 43113; Ph. 740.474.5231 Details: (Co Rcdr has land rec from 1810; Pro Ct has b, m, d & pro rec)
Pike* www.scioto.org/Pike/	M5	4 Jan 1815	**Ross, Scioto, Adams** Pike County; 100 E 2nd St; Waverly, OH 45690; Ph. 740.947.2715 Details: (Pro Judge has b, m & pro rec; Clk Cts has div & ct rec from 1815; Co Rcdr has land rec)
Portage www.portageworkforce.org/ portagecountydirectory/	G10	10 Feb 1807	**Trumbull** Portage County; 449 S Meridian St; PO Box 1035; Ravenna, OH 44266; Ph. 330.297.3450 Details: (Mayor's Office has b, d & bur rec; Pro Judge has m & pro rec; Clk Cts has div & ct rec from 1820; Co Treas has land rec)
Preble www.calweb.com/~wally/preble/ index.htm	K2	15 Feb 1808	**Montgomery, Butler** Preble County; 100 Main St; Eaton, OH 45320-0000; Ph. 937.456.8160 Details: (Pro Judge has b & d rec from 1867, pro rec from 1800 & m rec from 1808; Clk Cts has div & ct rec from 1850; Co Rcdr has land rec from 1804)
Putnam www.rootsweb.com/~ohputnam/	G3	12 Feb 1820	**Shelby** Putnam County; 245 E Main St; Ottawa, OH 45875-1968; Ph. 419.523.3110 Details: (Clk Cts has div & ct rec from 1834; Pro Judge has m & pro rec; Co Rcdr has land rec)
Richland www.rootsweb.com/~ohrichla/	H7	30 Jan 1808	**Fairfield** Richland County; 50 Park Ave E; Mansfield, OH 44902; Ph. 419.884.0278 Details: (Clk Cts has div & ct rec from 1815; Pro Judge has m & pro rec; Co Rcdr has land rec)
Ross* www.co.ross.oh.us/	L5	20 Aug 1798	**Adams, Washington** Ross County; 2 N Paint St; Chillicothe, OH 45601-0000; Ph. 740.702.3085 Details: (Pro Judge has b, m, d & pro rec; Clk Cts has div rec from late 1800's & ct rec; Co Rcdr has land rec)
Sandusky www.sandusky-county.org/	F5	12 Feb 1820	**Huron** Sandusky County; 100 N Park Ave; Fremont, OH 43420-2473; Ph. 419.334.6100 Details: (Co Hlth Dept has b, d & bur rec; Pro Judge has m & pro rec; Clk Cts has div rec from 1820 & ct rec; Co Rcdr has land rec from 1822)
Scioto* www.sciotocountyohio.com/	N5	24 Mar 1803	**Adams** Scioto County; 602 7th St; Portsmouth, OH 45662-3948; Ph. 740.355.8313 Details: (Clk Cts has div & ct rec from 1817; Pro Judge has m & pro rec; Co Rcdr has land rec)
Seneca* www.rootsweb.com/~ohseneca/ seneca.html	G5	12 Feb 1820	**Huron** Seneca County; 103 S Washington St; Tiffin, OH 44883-2354; Ph. 419.447.0671 Details: (Pro Judge has b, m & pro rec; Co Hlth Dept has d rec; Clk Cts has div & ct rec from 1826; Co Rcdr has land rec)
Shelby www.co.shelby.oh.us/	J2	7 Jan 1819	**Miami** Shelby County; 129 E Court St; PO Box 809; Sidney, OH 45365; Ph. 937.498.7221 Details: (Clk Cts has ct rec from 1819; Pro Judge has b, m, d & pro rec from 1825; Co Rcdr has land rec from 1819)

County Website	Map Index	Date Created	Parent County or Territory From Which Organized Address/Details
Stark* www.co.stark.oh.us/	H10	13 Feb 1808	**Columbiana** Stark County; 110 Central Plaza S; Canton, OH 44702-2219; Ph. 330.438.0796 Details: (Co Hlth Dept has b rec; Pro Ct has m & pro rec; Clk Cts has ct rec; Family Ct has div rec; Co Rcdr has land rec)
Summit* www.co.summit.oh.us/	G9	3 Mar 1840	**Portage, Medina, Stark** Summit County; 53 University Ave; Akron, OH 44301; Ph. 330.643.2900 Details: (Co Rcdr has land rec from 1840; Pro Ct has b, m, d & pro rec)
Trumbull* www.co.trumbull.oh.us/	F11	10 Jul 1800	**Jefferson, Wayne, old** Trumbull County; 160 High St NW; Warren, OH 44481; Ph. 330.675.2557 Details: (Clk Cts has div, ct & nat rec from 1800; Pro Judge has m & pro rec; Co Rcdr has land rec)
Tuscarawas web1.tusco.net/tuscgen/	I10	13 Feb 1808	**Muskingum** Tuscarawas County; Public Sq; New Philadelphia, OH 44663; Ph. 330.365.3243 Details: (Pro Judge has b, m, d & pro rec; Clk Cts has div & ct rec from 1808 & nat rec from 1907; Co Rcdr has land rec)
Union www.co.union.oh.us/	I5	10 Jan 1820	**Franklin, Madison, Logan, Delaware** Union County; 215 W 5th St; Marysville, OH 43040-0000; Ph. 937.645.3006 Details: (Co Rcdr has land rec from 1819; Pro Ct has b, m, d & pro rec)
Van Wert www.rootsweb.com/~ohvanwer/	H2	12 Feb 1820	**Darke** Van Wert County; 121 E Main St 2nd Fl; Van Wert, OH 45891; Ph. 419.238.1022 Details: (Clk Cts has div & ct rec; Pro Judge has b & d rec 1867-1908, m rec from 1840 & pro rec from 1837; Board of Hlth has b & d rec from 1908; Co Rcdr has land rec from 1823)
Vinton www.rootsweb.com/~ohvinton/ vinton.htm	M7	23 Mar 1850	**Gallia, Athens, Ross, Jackson, Hocking** Vinton County; County Courthouse; McArthur, OH 45651-1296; Ph. 740.596.4571 Details: (Pro Judge has b & d rec 1867-1950, m rec from 1850 & pro rec from 1867; Co Hlth Dept has b rec from 1950; Clk Cts has div, ct & land rec from 1850)
Warren www.co.warren.oh.us/geninfo/index.htm	M3	24 Mar 1803	**Hamilton** Warren County; 500 Justice Dr; PO Box 238; Lebanon, OH 45036; Ph. 513.695.1120 Details: (Pro Judge has b & d rec from 1867, m & pro rec from 1803; Clk Cts has div & ct rec; Co Rcdr has land rec)
Washington* www.washingtongov.org/	L10	27 Jul 1788	**Original county** Washington County; 205 Putnam St; Marietta, OH 45740; Ph. 740.373.6623 Details: (Pro Judge has b & d rec from 1867, m & pro rec from 1789; Clk Cts has div & ct rec from 1795; Co Rcdr has land rec)
Wayne www.wooster-wayne.com/county/	H8	13 Feb 1808	**Columbiana** Wayne County; 107 W Liberty St; PO Box 407; Wooster, OH 44691-4850; Ph. 330.287.5590 Details: (Pro Ct has b & d rec 1867-1908, m rec from 1813 & pro rec from 1812; Board of Hlth has b & d rec from 1908; Clk Common Pleas Ct has div & ct rec from 1812; Co Rcdr has land rec from 1812)
Wayne, old		15 Aug 1786	**Original county** Details: (This county disappeared from Ohio in 1803 when Ohio became a state. It ultimately became Wayne Co, Michigan)
Williams www.co.williams.oh.us/	F2	12 Feb 1820	**Darke** Williams County; 107 W Butler St; Bryan, OH 43506; Ph. 419.636.8253 Details: (Co Rec Center has b & d rec 1867-1908, m & pro rec 1824-1984, div & ct rec 1824-1977 & nat rec 1860-1926; Co Hlth Dept has b & d rec from 1909)
Wood www.wcnet.org/wcgovt/	F4	12 Feb 1820	**Logan** Wood County; 1 Courthouse Sq; Bowling Green, OH 43402-2473; Ph. 419.354.9230 Details: (Clk Cts has div rec from 1851 & ct rec; Pro Judge has b rec to 1908, m, d & pro rec; Co Hlth Dept has b rec from 1908; Co Rcdr has land rec)

County Website	Map Index	Date Created	Parent County or Territory From Which Organized Address/Details
Wyandot www.co.wyandot.oh.us/	H5	3 Feb 1845	Marion, Crawford, Hardin, Hancock Wyandot County; County Courthouse; Upper Sandusky, OH 43351-0000; Ph. 419.294.1432 Details: (Co Hlth Dept has b rec 1845-1908; Pro Judge has m & pro rec from 1845, d & bur rec 1845-1908; Clk Cts has div & ct rec from 1845; Co Rcdr has land rec from 1845)

Notes

Mistletoe

OKLAHOMA

CAPITAL: OKLAHOMA CITY – TERRITORY 1890 – STATE 1907 (46TH)

In 1541, Coronado became the first non-Native American explorer to enter Oklahoma. French traders passed through the area in the 16th and 17th centuries, but no settlements were made. The United States acquired the area in the Louisiana Purchase in 1803. Oklahoma then became part of the Indiana Territory, except for the Panhandle, which remained under Spanish control. Oklahoma became part of the Missouri Territory in 1812. In 1817, the federal government began sending Indians to the area from Alabama, Georgia, Florida, and Mississippi. The state was divided among five Indian nations: Creek, Cherokee, Chickasaw, Choctaw, and Seminole. Most of Oklahoma became part of the Arkansas Territory in 1819. The Panhandle became part of Mexico following its independence from Spain in 1821.

The western part of the Louisiana Purchase, including the Arkansas Territory, was designated as Indian Territory in 1830. When the United States annexed the Republic of Texas, the Panhandle of Oklahoma (which became "No Man's Land") was included because it was unattached to any territory. During the Civil War, the five Indian nations sided with the Confederacy. About 3,500 Indians helped the Confederates, mostly through the Confederate Indian Brigade and the Indian Home Guard. The Indians suffered horribly during the war as both life and property were wantonly destroyed. The peace treaties forced them to surrender land in western Oklahoma and grant rights-of-way to the railroads. The central part of the state was designated as "Unassigned Lands." By 1872, railroads crossed the area and hordes of settlers arrived. Soldiers drove them away, but these settlers, along with the railroad companies, petitioned Congress to open up these areas. As a result, the government purchased the "Unassigned Lands" and "No Man's Land" from the Indians in 1889.

Oklahoma was unique in its use of land runs. During a land run, an entire district would be opened to settlement on a given day on a first-come basis. The first run in 1889 attracted about 50,000 people. Farmers from Illinois, Iowa, and Kansas chose the western and northwestern sections of the state, while those from Arkansas, Missouri, and Texas chose the southern and eastern parts of the state. The territorial government was established in 1890, with Guthrie as its capital. Absorption of reservations opened more territory for settlement in the years that followed. The 1893 land run in the northwest section of the state attracted nearly 100,000 new settlers. The first oil boom occurred in 1897 at Bartlesville, bringing thousands more new settlers. More absorption of reservations occurred until only the eastern part of the state remained as Indian Territory. In 1906, the Oklahoma and Indian territories were combined, allowing Oklahoma to be admitted to the Union the following year. The capital was moved to Oklahoma City in 1910.

Look for vital records in the following locations:

- **Birth and death records:** Some early birth and death records from 1891 are scattered among county clerk records. Statewide registration began in 1908, with general compliance by 1930. These records are available from the Registrar of Vital Statistics, State Department of Health in Oklahoma City, Oklahoma.
- **Marriage, court and land records:** County clerks have all marriage, court, and land records. Local land office records are at the Oklahoma Department of Libraries, State Archives Division in Oklahoma City, Oklahoma. The National Archives, Kansas City Branch, in Kansas, and Fort Worth Branch in Texas, have the land entry case files, the original tract books

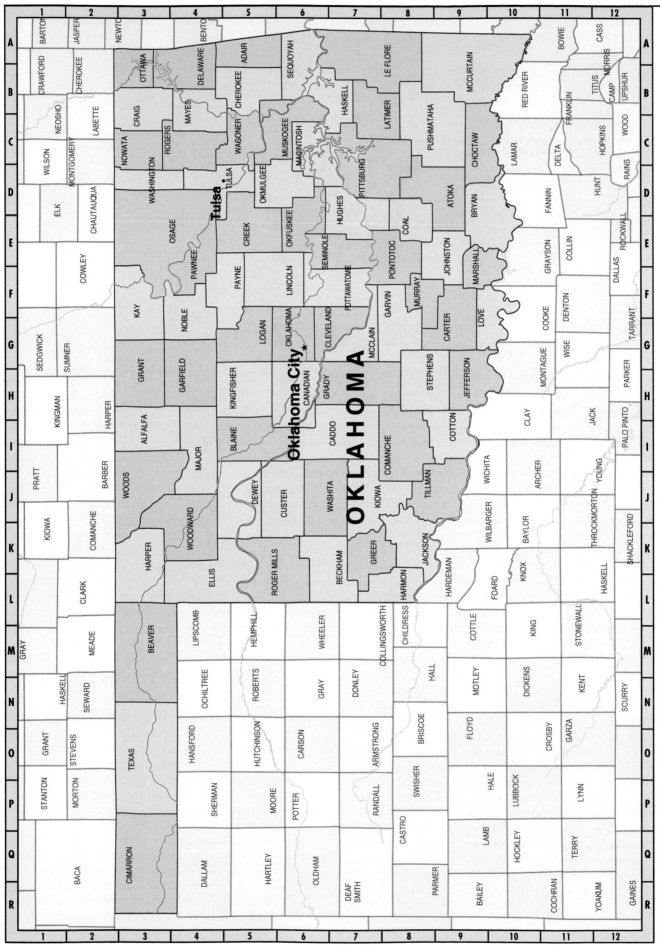

and the township plats of the general land office. The patents and copies of the tract books and township plats are at the Bureau of Land Management, New Mexico State Office in Santa Fe, New Mexico.

Registrar of Vital Statistics State Department of Health
1000 Northeast Tenth Street, Room
Oklahoma City, Oklahoma 73117
405.271.4040

Oklahoma Department of Libraries,
117State Archives Division
200 N.E. 18th Street
Oklahoma City, Oklahoma 73105

The National Archives Kansas City Branch
2306 East Bannister Road
Kansas City, Kansas 64131

The National Archives Fort Worth Branch
501 West Felix Street; PO Box 6216
Fort Worth, Texas 76115

Societies and Repositories

Abraham Coryelle Chapter D.A.R; RR 3; Vinita, Oklahoma 74301

American Heritage Library; PO Box 176; Davis, Oklahoma 73030

American Indian Institute; The University of Oklahoma; 555 East Constitution St., Suite 237; Norman, Oklahoma 73072-7920

Arbuckle Historical Society; 201 S. 4th; Davis, Oklahoma 73030

Atoka Co. Library; 205 East 1st; Atoka, Oklahoma 74525

Atoka County Genealogical Society; PO Box 93; Atoka, Oklahoma 74525

Baptist, Southern Baptist Convention; 901 Commerce Street #750; Nashville, Tennessee 37203; 615.224.2355; Fax 615.742.8919

Bartlesville Genealogical Society; c/o Bartlesville Public Library; 600 S. Johnstone Ave.; Bartlesville, Oklahoma 74003

Bartlesville Public Library; 600 S. Johnstone; Bartlesville, Oklahoma 74003

Beaver River Genealogical and Historical Society; Rt. 1, PO Box 79; Hooker, Oklahoma 73945

Broken Arrow Genealogical Society Library; PO Box 1244; Broken Arrow, Oklahoma 74013-1244

Bryan County Heritage Society; PO Box 153; Calera, Oklahoma 74730

Bureau of Land Management, New Mexico State Office, Federal Building; 1474 Rodeo, PO Box 27115; Santa Fe, New Mexico 87502-0115; 505.438.7400

Canadian County Genealogical Society; PO Box 866; El Reno, Oklahoma 73036-0866

Carter County Genealogical Society; PO Box 1014; Ardmore, Oklahoma 73402

Central Oklahoma Chapter, AHSGR; 1106 W Brooks St.; Norman, Oklahoma 73069-4539; 405.321.7835; <www.ahsgr.org/okcentra.html>

Cherokee City-County Public Library; 602 S. Grand Ave.; Cherokee, Oklahoma 73728

Chickasha Public Library; 527 Iowa Ave.; Chickasha, Oklahoma 73018

Choctaw County Genealogical Society; PO Box 1056; Hugo, Oklahoma 74743

Cleveland County Genealogical Society; PO Box 6176; Norman, Oklahoma 73070-6176

Coal County Historical and Genealogical Society; 111 West Ohio; Coalgate, Oklahoma 74538

Craig County Oklahoma Genealogical Society; PO Box 484; Vinita, Oklahoma 74301

Cushing Genealogical Society; c/o Cushing Public Library

Cushing Public Library; PO Box 551, 215 N. Steele; Cushing, Oklahoma 74203

DAR State Library; Historical Bldg.; Oklahoma City, Oklahoma 73105

Delaware County Genealogical Society; c/o Grove Public Library; 206 S. Elk St.; Grove, Oklahoma 74344

Delaware County Oklahoma Historical Society; PO Box 855; Jay, Oklahoma 74346

Disciples of Christ Historical Society; 1101 Nineteenth Avenue, South; Nashville, Tennessee 37212; 615.327.1444; Fax 615.327.1445

Edmond Genealogical Society; PO Box 1984; Edmond, Oklahoma 73093; <www.rootsweb.com/~okegs>

Federation of Oklahoma Genealogical Societies; PO Box 26151; Oklahoma City, Oklahoma 73126

Five Civilized Tribes Museum; Federal Building, Agency Hill, Honor Heights Drive; Muskogee, Oklahoma 74401; 918.683.1701; Fax 918.683.3171

Fort Gibson Genealogical and Historical Society; PO Box 416; Fort Gibson, Oklahoma 74434

Garfield County Genealogists, Inc.; PO Box 1106; Enid, Oklahoma 73702-1106

Genealogical Group of Oklahoma City LDS Stake; 3108 Windsor Terrace; Oklahoma City, Oklahoma 73122

Golden Spread Chapter, AHSGR; RR 2 Box 88; Shattuck, Oklahoma 73858

Grady County Genealogical Society; PO Box 792; Chickasha, Oklahoma 73023

Grant County Historical Society; PO Box 127; Medford, Oklahoma 73759

Greer County Genealogical & Historical Society; 201 W. Lincoln; Mangum, Oklahoma 73554

Haskell County Genealogical Society; 408 N.E. 6th St.; Stigler, Oklahoma 74462

Kiowa County Genealogical Society; PO Box 191; Hobart, Oklahoma 73651-0191

Lawton Public Library; 110 S.W. Fourth St.; Lawton, Oklahoma 73501

Logan Co. Genealogical Soc., Inc. Library; PO Box 1419; Guthrie, Oklahoma 73044; 405.282.8492; <www.rootsweb.com/~oklcgs>

Love County Historical Society; PO Box 134; Marietta, Oklahoma 73448

Major Co. Genealogical Research Library; PO Box 74; Fairview, Oklahoma 73737

Major County Genealogical Society; PO Box 74; Fairview, Oklahoma 73737

Mayes County Genealogical Society; PO Box 924; Chouteau, Oklahoma 74337

McClain County Oklahoma Historical and Genealogical Society; 203 Washington St.; Purcell, Oklahoma 73090

McCurtian County Genealogical Society; PO Box 1832; Idabel, Oklahoma 74745

Methodist, United Methodist; PO Box 1138; Bristow, Oklahoma 74010; 918.367.3227

Metropolitan Library System; 131 Dean McGee Ave.; Oklahoma City, Oklahoma 73102

Muldrow Genealogical Society; PO Box 1253; Muldrow, Oklahoma 74949

Muldrow Public Library; City Hall Bldg., Main Street; Muldrow, Oklahoma 74948

Museum of the Great Plains; 601 Ferris, PO Box 68; Lawton, Oklahoma 73502; 405.581.3460; Fax 405.581.3458

Muskogee County Genealogical Society; 801 W. Okmulgee; Muskogee, Oklahoma 74401

National Archives-Central Plains Region; 2312 East Bannister Road; Kansas City, Missouri 64131; 816.926.6272; Fax 816.926.6982

Noble County Genealogical Society; PO Box 785; Perry, Oklahoma 73077

Northwest Oklahoma Genealogical Society; RO. Box 834; Woodward, Oklahoma 73901

Oklahoma Department of Libraries; 200 N.E. 18th Street; Oklahoma City, Oklahoma 73105-3298; 405.521.2502, 800.522.8116; Fax 405.525.7804

Oklahoma Dept. of Libraries, Legislative Reference Division; 109 Capitol; Oklahoma City, Oklahoma 73105

Oklahoma Genealogical Society; PO Box 12986; Oklahoma City, Oklahoma 73101

Oklahoma Historical Society, Wiley Post Historical Building Library Center; 2100 North Lincoln Boulevard; Oklahoma City, Oklahoma 73105-4997; 405.521.2491; Fax 405.525.3272;

Oklahoma State Archives; 200 NE 18th St.; Oklahoma City, Oklahoma 73105; 405.522.3583; <www.odl.state.ok.us/oar/index2.htm>

Okmulgee County Genealogical Society; PO Box 905; Okmulgee, Oklahoma 74447

Ottawa County Genealogical Society; PO Box 1383; Miami, Oklahoma 74355-1383

Pawhuska Oklahoma Genealogical Society; PO Box 907; Pawhuska, Oklahoma 74056

Payne County Genealogical Society; PO Box 2708; Stillwater, Oklahoma 74076

Pioneer Genealogical Society; PO Box 1965; Ponca City, Oklahoma 74602

Pioneer Sons and Daughters of the Cherokee Strip; PO Box 465; Enid, Oklahoma 73702

Pittsburg County Genealogical and Historical Society, Inc.; 113 E. Carl Albert Parkway; McAlester, Oklahoma 74501

Pocahontas Trails Genealogical Society (Oklahoma-Texas Regional Chapter); Rt. 2, Box 40; Mangum, Oklahoma 73554

Ponca City Library; 515 East Grand; Ponca, Oklahoma 74601

Pontotoc County Historical and Genealogical Society; 221 W. 16th St.; Ada, Oklahoma 74920

Poteau Valley Genealogical Society; PO Box 1031; Poteau, Oklahoma 74953

Pushmataha County Historical Society; PO Box 285; Antler, Oklahoma 74523

Ralph Ellison Library; 2000 North East 23rd; Oklahoma City, Oklahoma 73111; 405.424.1437

Roger Mills County Genealogical Society; PO Box 205; Cheyenne, Oklahoma 73629

Rogers County Genealogical Society; PO Box 2493; Claremore, Oklahoma 74018

Roman Catholic, Chancery Office; 7501 N.W. Expressway; Oklahoma City, Oklahoma 73123; 405.721.5651

Rudisill North Regional Library; 1520 N. Hartford; Tulsa, Oklahoma 74106; 918.596.7280

Sapulpa Public Library; 27 W. Dewey; Sapulpa, Oklahoma 74066

Seminole Public Library; 424 N. Main; Seminole, Oklahoma 74868

Sons of Confederate Veterans; PO Box 57312; Oklahoma City, Oklahoma 73157;

Sons of the American Revolution, Oklahoma Society; 9211 39th St.; Tulsa, Oklahoma 74145

Southwest Oklahoma Genealogical Society; PO Box 148; Lawton, Oklahoma 73502-0148; <www.sirinet.net/~lgarris/swogs>

Stanley Tubbs Memorial Library; 101 E. Cherokee; Sallisaw, Oklahoma 74955

Stephens County Oklahoma Genealogical Society; 301 N. 8th St.; Duncan, Oklahoma 73534; 405.255.8718

Swink Historical Preservation Association; PO Box 165; Swink, Oklahoma 74761; 580.873.2049

Talbot Library & Museum; 406 S. Colcord Ave., PO Box 349; Colcord, Oklahoma 74338-0349

Thomas Gilcrease Institute of American History and Art; 1400 Gilcrease Museum Road; Tulsa, Oklahoma 74127; 918.596.2700; Fax 918.596.2700

Three Forks Genealogical Society; 102-1/2 South State St.; Wagoner, Oklahoma 74467

Tulsa Co. Public Library, Schusterman-Benson Branch; 3333 E. 32nd Pl.; Tulsa, Oklahoma 74135

Tulsa Gen. Soc. Library; 9072 E. 31st St.; Tulsa, Oklahoma 74105; 918.627.4224

Tulsa Genealogical Society; PO Box 585; Tulsa, Oklahoma 74101-0585; <www.tulsagenealogy.org>

Tulsa Public Library; 220 So. Cheyenne; Tulsa, Oklahoma 74103

University of Oklahoma, Western History Collection; 630 Parrington Oval, Room 452; Norman, Oklahoma 73019; 405.325.2904; Fax 405.325.2943

Vinita Public Library, Maurice Haynes Memorial Bldg.; 211 W. Illinois; Vinita, Oklahoma 74301

Vital Records Section, State Department of Health; 1000 Northeast Tenth Street, PO Box 53551; Oklahoma City, Oklahoma 73152; 405.271.4040

Weatherford Public Library; 219 E. Franklin; Weatherford, Oklahoma 73096

Western Plains Weatherford Genealogical Society; PO Box 1672; Weatherford, Oklahoma 73096

Western Trails Genealogical Society; PO Box 70; Altus, Oklahoma 73521

Western Trails Genealogy Library, c/o Southern Prairie Library; 421 Hudson St., PO Box 70; Altus, Oklahoma 73521

Woods County Genealogists; PO Box 234; Alva, Oklahoma 73717

Bibliography and Record Sources

General Sources

Ashton, Sharron Standifer. *Guide to Cherokee Indian Records Microfilm Collection: Archives and Manuscripts Division, Oklahoma Historical Society*. Norman, Oklahoma: Ashton Books, 1996.

Babcock, Sidney H., and John Y. Bryce. *History of Methodism in Oklahoma: Story of the Indian Mission Annual Conference of The Methodist Episcopal Church, South*. N.p.: 1935.

Baird, W. David. *The Story of Oklahoma*. Norman, Oklahoma: University of Oklahoma Press, 1994.

Bell, George. *Genealogy of Old and New Cherokee Indian Families*. Bartlesville, Oklahoma: George Bell, 1972.

Bernard, Richard M. *The Poles in Oklahoma*. Norman: University of Oklahoma Press, 1980.

Bicha, Karel D. *The Czechs in Oklahoma*. Norman, Oklahoma: University of Oklahoma Press, 1980.

Bingham, Lynetta K. *A History of the Church of Jesus Christ of Latter-day Saints in Eastern Oklahoma: From Oklahoma and Indian Territories to 1980: A History Prepared for the Sesquicentennial of the Organization of the Church*. Tulsa: Tulsa Oklahoma Stake, [1980?].

Bivins, Willie Reeves Hardin, et al. *Southwest Oklahoma Keys*. Oklahoma City: Southwest Oklahoma Genealogical Society, 1982.

Blessing, Patrick J. *Oklahoma: Records and Archives*. Tulsa, Oklahoma: University of Tulsa Publications, 1978.

Brown, Jean C. *Oklahoma Research: The Twin Territories*. Sapulpa, Oklahoma: [J. C. Brown], 1975.

Brown, Thomas E. *Bible Belt Catholicism: A History of The Roman Catholic Church in Oklahoma, 1905-1945*. New York: United States Catholic Historical Society, 1977.

Burke, Bob. *Like A Prairie Fire: A History of the Assemblies of God in Oklahoma*. Oklahoma City: Oklahoma District Council of the Assemblies of God, 1994.

Carselowey, James Manford. *Cherokee Notes*. Tulsa, Oklahoma: Yesterdays Publications, [1980].

Carselowey, James Manford. *Cherokee Pioneers*. Adair, Oklahoma: J.M. Carselowey, 1961.

Cook, Mrs. John P. *Collection of Oklahoma Bible and Family Records*. N.p., 1954.

Corwin, Hugh D. *The Kiowa Indians: Their History & Life Stories*. Lawton, Oklahoma: H.D. Corwin, 1958.

Dewitt, Donald L. *American Indian Resource Materials in the Western History Collections, University Of Oklahoma*. Norman, Oklahoma: University of Oklahoma Press, 1990.

Dewitt, Donald L. *Guide to Manuscript Collections Western History Collections University of Oklahoma*. Bowie, Maryland: Heritage Books, 1994.

England, Stephen J. *Oklahoma Christians: A History of Christian Churches and of the Start of the Christian Church (Disciples of Christ) in Oklahoma*. [S.l.: s.n.], 1975 ([S.l.]: Bethany Press.

Federation of Oklahoma Genealogical Societies (Oklahoma City, Oklahoma). *Directory of Oklahoma Sources*. Oklahoma City: Federation of Oklahoma Genealogical Societies, 1993.

Ferguson, Mrs. Tom B. *They Carried the Torch: The Story of Oklahoma's Pioneer Newspapers*. Norman, Oklahoma: Levite of Apache, 1989.

First Families of the Twin Territories: Our Ancestors in Oklahoma before Statehood. Oklahoma Genealogical Society, Special Publication, no. 13. Oklahoma City, Oklahoma: The Society, 1997.

Franklin, Jimmie L. *Journey Toward Hope: A History Of Blacks In Oklahoma*. Norman, Oklahoma: University of Oklahoma Press, 1982.

Gard, Wayne. *The Chisholm Trail*. Norman [Okla.]: University of Oklahoma Press, 1976.

Garrett, Sandi. *Where Are My Cherokees*. Spavinaw, Oklahoma: Cherokee Woman Pub., 1997.

Gaskin, J. M. *Baptist Milestones In Oklahoma*. [S.l.: s.n.], 1966.

Gibson, Arrell M. *Oklahoma: A Student's Guide to Localized History*. New York: Columbia University, 1965.

Gibson, Arrell Morgan. *A Guide to Regional Manuscript Collections in the Division of Manuscripts, University of Oklahoma Library*. Norman, Oklahoma: University of Oklahoma Press, 1960.

Gray, Robert N. *The Cherokee Strip of Oklahoma: A Hundred Yesteryears*. Enid, Oklahoma: Sons and Daughters of the Cherokee Strip Pioneers Museum, 1992.

Hale, Duane Kendall. *Tracing Indian Family Histories*. Norman, Oklahoma: OCCE Copy Service, University of Oklahoma, 1983.

Hill, Edward E., comp., *Guide to Records in the National Archives Relating to American Indians*. Washington, DC: National Archives, 1981.

Hill, Luther B. *A History of the State of Oklahoma*. 2 vols. Chicago: Lewis Publishing Co., 1908.

Historical Records Survey (Oklahoma). *A List of the Records of the State of Oklahoma*. Oklahoma City: Historical Records Survey, 1938.

Huffman, Mary. *Family History: A Bibliography of the Collection in the Oklahoma Historical Society*. Oklahoma City: The Society, 1992.

Huffman, Mary. *The Five Civilized Tribes: A Bibliography*. Oklahoma City: Oklahoma Historical Society, Library Resources Division, 1991.

Jordan, H. Glenn. *Indian Leaders: Oklahoma's First Statesmen*. Oklahoma City: Oklahoma Historical Society, 1979.

Koplowitz, Bradford. *Guide to the Historical Records of Oklahoma.* Rev. ed. Bowie, Maryland: Heritage Books, c1997.

Lemons, Nova A. *Pioneers of Chickasaw Nation, Indian Territory.* 2 vols. Miami, Oklahoma: Timbercreek Ltd., 1997.

Littlefield, Daniel F. *The Chickasaw Freedmen: A People Without a Country.* Westport, Connecticut: Greenwood Press, 1980.

Litton, Gaston. *History of Oklahoma.* 4 vols. New York: Lewis Historical Publishing Co., 1957.

Martin, Laura. *Oklahoma Marriages: A Bibliography.* Oklahoma City, Oklahoma: Library Resources Division, 1996.

McKee, Wilma. *Growing Faith: General Conference Mennonites In Oklahoma.* Newton, Kansas: Faith and Life Press, 1988.

Mooney, Thomas G. *Exploring Your Cherokee Ancestry: A Basic Genealogical Research Guide.* Tahlequah, Oklahoma: Cherokee National Historical Society, 1990.

O'Beirne, Harry F. and Edward S., *The Indian Territory: Its Chiefs, Legislators and Leading Men.* St. Louis: C.B. Woodward Co., 1892.

O'Beirne, Harry F. *Leaders and Leading Men of the Indian Territory with Interesting Biographical Sketches: Choctaws and Chickasaws.* Chicago: American Publishers Association, 1891.

O'Brien, Mary Metzger. *Oklahoma Genealogical Research.* Sand Springs, Oklahoma: M. O'Brien Bookshop, 1986.

Oklahoma Historical Society. *Index to Oklahoma Newspapers.* Oklahoma City, Oklahoma: Oklahoma Historical Society, 2002. Online guide – <www.ok-history.mus.ok.us/news/newsindex.htm>

Oklahoma Historical Society. Indian Archives Division. *Catalog Of Microfilm Holdings in the Archives & Manuscripts Division Oklahoma Historical Society 1976-1989:* Native American tribal records and special collections. Oklahoma City: The Society, 1976-1989.

Oklahoma Historical Society. Indian Archives Division. *Establishing of Churches in the Cherokee Nation, 1866-1908.* Oklahoma City: The Society, 1976-.

Oklahoma Historical Society. *Oklahoma State, County and Town Records.* Oklahoma City, Oklahoma: Oklahoma Historical Society, 2002. Online guide – <www.ok-history.mus.ok.us/lib/staterec.htm>

Oklahoma Research Outline. Series US-Sates, no 37. Salt Lake City: Family History Library, 1988.

Parker, James W. *All Along the Chisholm Trail.* 2 vols. Yukon, Oklahoma: J.W. Parker, 1988.

Portrait and Biographical Record of Oklahoma: Commemorating the Achievements of Citizens Who Have Contributed to the Progress of Oklahoma and the Development of its Resources. Chicago: Chapman Publishing Co., 1901.

Preliminary List of Churches and Religious Organizations in Oklahoma. Oklahoma City, Oklahoma: Historical Records Survey, 1942.

Reese, Linda Williams. *Women of Oklahoma, 1890-1920.* Norman, Oklahoma: University of Okla., 1997.

Routh, E. C. *The Story of Oklahoma Baptists.* Oklahoma City: Baptist General Convention, 1932.

Smith's First Directory of Oklahoma Territory, for the Year Commencing August 1st, 1890. Oklahoma City, Oklahoma: Oklahoma Historical Society, Research Library, [1986].

Stewart, John and Kenny A. Franks. *State Records, Manuscripts, and Newspapers at the Oklahoma State Archives and Oklahoma Historical Society.* Oklahoma City, Oklahoma: State Department of Libraries and Oklahoma Historical Society, 1975.

Sturtevant, William C. *A Seminole Sourcebook.* New York: Garland Pub., 1987.

Thoburn, Joseph Bradfield. *A Standard History of Oklahoma: An Authentic Narrative of its Development from the Date of the First European Exploration Down to the Present Time, Including Accounts of the Indian Tribes, Both Civilized and Wild, of the Cattle Range, of the Land Openings and the Achievements of the Most Recent Period.* 5 vols. Chicago: American Historical Society, 1916.

Thoburn, Joseph Bradfield. *Oklahoma, A History of the State and its People.* 4 vols. New York: Lewis Historical Pub. Co., 1929.

Tobias, Henry J. *The Jews in Oklahoma.* Norman, Oklahoma: University of Oklahoma Press, 1980.

United States. Commission to the Five Civilized Tribes. *Applications for Enrollment of the Commission to the Five Civilized Tribes, 1898-1914.* Washington, DC: National Archives and Records Service, 1983.

Walton-Raji, Angela Y. *Black Indian Genealogy Research: African-American Ancestors Among the Five Civilized Tribes.* Bowie, Maryland: Heritage Books, 1993.

Welch, W. E. *The Oklahoma Spirit of '17: Biographical Volume.* Oklahoma City, Oklahoma: Historical Pub., 1920.

Welsh, Carol. *An Annotated Guide to the Chronicles of Oklahoma, 1921-1994.* Oklahoma City: Oklahoma Historical Society, 1996.

West, C. W. *Missions and Missionaries of Indian Territory.* Muskogee, Oklahoma: Muscogee Pub., 1990.

Western Oklahoma Historical Society. *Prairie Fire: A Pioneer History of Western Oklahoma.* [S.l.]: The Society, 1978.

White, James D. *The Souls of the Just: A Necrology of the Catholic Church in Oklahoma.* Tulsa, Oklahoma: Sarto Press, 1983.

Wright, Muriel Hazel. *A Guide to the Indian Tribes of Oklahoma.* Norman, Oklahoma: University of Oklahoma Press, 1951. Reprint. 1986.

Atlases, Maps and Gazetteers

Gannett, Henry A. *A Gazetteer of Indian Territory.* Washington, D.C.: U.S. Government Printing Office, 1905. Reprint. Tulsa, Oklahoma: Oklahoma Yesterday Pub., 1980.

Morris, John W. *Boundaries of Oklahoma.* Oklahoma City: Oklahoma Historical Society, 1980.

Morris, John W. *Ghost Towns of Oklahoma.* Norman, Oklahoma: University of Oklahoma Press, 1977.

Morris, John Wesley, and Edwin C. McReynolds, *Historical Atlas of Oklahoma.* Rev. ed. Norman, Oklahoma: University of Oklahoma Press, 1976.

Oklahoma Historical Society (Oklahoma City, Oklahoma*). Boundaries of Oklahoma.* Oklahoma City: Oklahoma Historical Society, 1980.

Oklahoma. Department of Transportation. *Town and Place Locations.* Oklahoma City: Oklahoma Department of Transportation, 1991.

Shirk, George H. *Oklahoma Place Names.* 2nd ed. Norman, Oklahoma: University of Oklahoma Press, 1974.

Census Records

Available Census Records and Census Substitutes

Federal Census 1860 (with Arkansas), 1900, 1910, 1920, 1930.

Union Veterans and Widows 1890.

Dollarhide, William. *The Census Book: A Genealogist's Guide to Federal Census Facts, Schedules and Indexes.* Bountiful, Utah: Heritage Quest, 1999.

Kemp, Thomas Jay. *The American Census Handbook.* Wilmington, Delaware: Scholarly Resources, Inc., 2001.

Lainhart, Ann S. *State Census Records.* Baltimore: Genealogical Publishing Co., Inc., 1992.

Oklahoma Territory. *First Territorial Census of Oklahoma, 1890.* [Oklahoma City: Oklahoma Historical Society, 1961?].

Szucs, Loretto Dennis, and Matthew Wright. *Finding Answers in U.S. Census Records.* Ancestry Publishing, 2001.

Thorndale, William, and William Dollarhide. *Map Guide to the U.S. Federal Censuses, 1790-1920.* Baltimore: Genealogical Publishing Co., 1987.

United States. Census Office. 11th census, 1890. *Schedules Enumerating Union Veterans and Widows of Union Veterans of the Civil War.* Washington, DC: The National Archives, 1948.

Court Records, Probate and Wills

Cook, Mrs. John P. *Collection of Old Wills Assembled by D.A.R. Chapters of Oklahoma.* (Salt Lake City: Filmed by the Genealogical Society of Utah, 1970).

Daughters of the American Revolution. Black Beaver Chapter (Norman, Oklahoma). *Abstracts of Wills from Oklahoma Chapters N.S.D.A.R.* Microfilm of original records in the D.A.R. Library in Washington, D.C. (Salt Lake City: Filmed by the Genealogical Society of Utah, 1970).

Daughters of the American Revolution. Enid Chapter (Enid, Oklahoma*). Abstracts of Wills of Our Forefathers.* (Salt Lake City: Filmed by the Genealogical Society of Utah, 1972).

Louisiana (Territory). Probate Court. *Probate Records, 1808-1812.* (Salt Lake City: Filmed by the Genealogical Society of Utah, 1975).

Wever, Orpha Jewell. *Probate Records, 1892-1908. Northern District Cherokee Nation.* 3 vols. Vinita, Oklahoma: Northeast Oklahoma Genealogical Society, 1982-83.

Emigration, Immigration, Migration and Naturalization

American Historical Society of Germans from Russia. Oklahoma Harvester Chapter (Oklahoma). *German-Russian Heritage, Steppes to America.* [Oklahoma]: AHSGR, 1991.

Olsen, Monty. *Choctaw Emigration Records.* 2 vols. Calera, Oklahoma: Bryan County Heritage Association, 1990.

Land and Property

Hinton, Julie Peterson, and Louise F. Wilcox. *El Reno District 1901 Land Lottery: Index to Names of Homesteaders Filings.* [El Reno, Oklahoma]: J. P. Hinton, 1985.

Hoig, Stan. *The Oklahoma Land Rush of 1889.* Oklahoma City: Oklahoma Historical Society, 1984.

Hone, Wade E. *Land and Property Research in the United States.* Salt Lake City: Ancestry Incorporated, 1997.

Ingmire, Frances Terry. *Containing Grants in Present States of Missouri, Arkansas and Oklahoma.* St. Louis: the author, 1984.

Morris, John W. ed., *Boundaries of Oklahoma.* Oklahoma City: Oklahoma Historical Society, 1980.

Oklahoma Historical Society. *Oklahoma Land Records.* Oklahoma City, Oklahoma: Oklahoma Historical Society, 2002. Online guide – <www.ok-history.mus.ok.us/lib/landrecords.htm>

Sober, Nancy Hope. *The Intruders: The Illegal Residents of the Cherokee Nation, 1866-1907.* Ponca City, Oklahoma: Cherokee Books, 1991.

Military

A History of the Second World War: A Remembrance, An Appreciation, A Memorial. Oklahoma City: Victory Publishing Co., 1946.

Burton, Arthur T. *Black, Buckskin And Blue: African American Scouts And Soldiers On The Western Frontier.* Austin Tex.: Eaton Press, 1999.

Faulk, Odie B., Kenny A. Franks, and Paul F. Lambert, eds. *Early Military Forts and Posts in Oklahoma.* Oklahoma City: Oklahoma Historical Society, 1978.

Haulsee, W. M., et al, *Soldiers of the Great War.* 3 vols. Washington, DC: Soldiers Record Publishing Association, 1920.

Hoffmann, Roy. *Oklahoma Honor Roll, World War I, 1917-1918.* [Oklahoma]: R. Hoffman, [19–].

Index to Applications for Pensions From the State of Oklahoma Submitted by Confederate Soldiers, Sailors and their Widows. Oklahoma City: Oklahoma Genealogical Society, 1969.

Military Information. [n.p.]: USGenWeb Project, Oklahoma Archives, 2002. Online database – <www.rootsweb.com/~usgenweb/ok/military/military.html>

Newman, Stanley. *Oklahoma Air National Guard Pilots in the Korean War.* [Oklahoma City: 45th Infantry Division Museum], 1990.

Oklahoma Historical Society. *Oklahoma Military Records.* Oklahoma City, Oklahoma: Oklahoma Historical Society, 2002. Online guide – <www.ok-history.mus.ok.us/lib/military.htm>

Pompey, Sherman Lee. *Master Lists of the Cherokee Confederate Indians.* Independence, California: Historical and Genealogical Publishing Co., 1965.

Pompey, Sherman Lee. *Muster Lists of the Creek and Other Confederate Indians.* Independence, California: Historical and Genealogical Publishing Co., 1966.

United States. Adjutant General's Office. *Confederate States Army Casualties: Lists and Narrative Reports.* Washington, DC: The National Archives, 1970.

United States. Selective Service System. *Oklahoma, World War I Selective Service System Draft Registration Cards, 1917-1918.* National Archives Microfilm Publications, *M1509.* Washington, DC: National Archives, 1987-1988.

Vital and Cemetery Records

Bode, Frances M. *Oklahoma Territory Weddings.* Geary, Oklahoma: Pioneer Book Committee, 1983.

Bogle, Dixie. *Cherokee Nation Births and Deaths, 1884-1901.* Utica, Kentucky: Cook and McDowell Publishers, 1980.

Bogle, Dixie. *Cherokee Nation Marriages, 1884-1901.* Utica, Kentucky: Cook and McDowell Publishers, 1980.

Cemetery Records of Oklahoma. 9 vols. Typescript. Salt Lake City: Genealogical Society of Utah, 1959-62.

Guide to Public Vital Statistics Records in Oklahoma. Oklahoma City: Historical Records Survey, 1941.

Index to the Oklahoma County Vital Records Offices. [N.p]: USGenWeb Project, Oklahoma Archives, 2002. Online Guide – <www.vitalrec.com/ok.html>

Mills, Madeline S., and Helen R. Mullenax. *Relocated Cemeteries in Oklahoma and Parts of Arkansas, Kansas, Texas.* Tulsa: Mills and Mullenax, 1974.

Pierce, Barbara and Brian Basore. *Oklahoma Cemeteries: A Bibliography of the Collections in the Oklahoma Historical Society.* Oklahoma City, Oklahoma: Library Resources Division, The Society, 1993.

Talkington, N. Dale. *Birth And Death Notices In Oklahoma And Indian Territories From 1871.* Houston, Texas: N.D. Talkington, 1999.

Tiffee, Ellen, and Gloryann Hankins Young. *Oklahoma Marriage Records, Choctaw Nation, Indian Territory.* 10 vols. Norman, Oklahoma: University of Oklahoma, 1969-78.

Tyner, James W., and Alice Tyner Timmons. *Our People and Where They Rest.* 12 vols. Norman, Oklahoma: University of Oklahoma, 1969-78.

Union List of Oklahoma Cemeteries. Oklahoma City, Oklahoma: Oklahoma Genealogical Society, 1969.

County Website	Map Index	Date Created	Parent County or Territory From Which Organized Address/Details
A		1891	**Iowa-Sac-Fox & Pottawatomie-Shawnee Lands** Details: (see Lincoln) (Name changed to Lincoln)
Adair www.rootsweb.com/~okadair/adaircty.htm	A5	16 Jul 1907	**Cherokee Lands** Adair County; 2nd & Division Sts; PO Box 169; Stilwell, OK 74960-0169; Ph. 918.696-7198 Details: (Clk Cts has m, div, pro & ct rec from 1907; Co Asr has land rec)
Alfalfa www.rootsweb.com/~okalfalf/ main-alfalfa.htm	I3	16 Jul 1907	**Woods** Alfalfa County; County Courthouse; 300 S Grand St; Cherokee, OK 73728-8000; Ph. 580.596-3158 Details: (Clk Cts has m, div, pro, ct & land rec)
Atoka* www.rootsweb.com/~okatoka/atoka.htm	D9	16 Jul 1907	**Choctaw Lands** Atoka County; 200 E Court St; Atoka, OK 74525; Ph. 580.889-5157 Details: (Clk Cts has m rec from 1897, div, pro & ct rec from 1913; Co Clk has land rec)
B		1891	**Original county (Pottawatomie-Shawnee Lands)** Details: (see Pottawatomie) (Name changed to Pottawatomie)
Beaver www.rootsweb.com/~okbeaver/beav.htm	M3	1890	**Original county (Public Lands)** Beaver County; 111 W 2nd St; Beaver, OK 73932-0000; Ph. 580.625-3418 Details: (Clk Cts has m, div & ct rec from 1890 & pro rec from 1891)
Beckham* www.rootsweb.com/~okbeckha/	K7	16 Jul 1907	**Roger Mills, Greer Territory** Beckham County; 302 E Main St; Sayre, OK 73662; Ph. 580.928-3383 Details: (Clk Cts has m, pro, land & ct rec)
Blaine www.rootsweb.com/~okblaine/blaine.html	I5	1892	**Original county** Blaine County; 212 N Weigle Ave; Watonga, OK 73772; Ph. 580.623-5890 Details: (Formerly C Co. Name changed to Blaine) (Clk Cts has m, div, pro & ct rec from 1892; Co Clk has land rec from 1892)
Bryan www.rootsweb.com/~okbryan/	D9	16 Jul 1907	**Choctaw Lands** Bryan County; 402 W Evergreen St; PO Box 1789; Durant, OK 74701-4703; Ph. 580.924-1446 Details: (Co Clk has m, div & land rec from 1907, pro & ct rec)
C		1892	**Original county** Details: (see Blaine) (Name changed to Blaine)
Caddo www.rootsweb.com/~okcaddo/ccpage.htm	I7	1901	**Original Lands** Caddo County; SW 2nd St & Oklahoma Ave; Anadarko, OK 73005-1427; Ph. 405.247-6609 Details: (Formerly I Co. Name changed to Caddo 8 Nov 1902) (Clk Cts has m, div, pro & ct rec from 1902)
Canadian www.canadiancounty.org/	H6	1889	**Original county** Canadian County; 201 N Choctaw Ave; PO Box 458; El Reno, OK 73036; Ph. 405.262-1070 Details: (Clk Ct has land, m, div, pro & ct rec)
Carter www.brightok.net/chickasaw// ardmore/county	G9	16 Jul 1907	**Chickasaw Lands** Carter County; 1st & B St SW; PO Box 1236; Ardmore, OK 73401-0000; Ph. 580.223-8162 Details: (Clk Cts has pro, ct & land rec; Co Clk has m rec)
Cherokee* www.rootsweb.com/~okchero2/	B5	16 Jul 1907	**Cherokee Lands** Cherokee County; 213 W Delaware St; Tahlequah, OK 74464; Ph. 918.456-3171 Details: (Clk Ct has m, div, pro & ct rec from 1907; Co Clk has land rec from 1907 & mil dis rec from 1917)
Choctaw www.rootsweb.com/~okchocta/	C9	16 Jul 1907	**Choctaw Lands** Choctaw County; 300 E Duke St; Hugo, OK 74743-0000; Ph. 580.326-3778 Details: (Clk Ct has m, div, pro & ct rec from 1907; Co Clk has land rec)

County Website	Map Index	Date Created	Parent County or Territory From Which Organized Address/Details
K		1893	**Original county** Details: (see Kay) (Name changed to Kay)
Kay www.courthouse.kay.ok.us/home.html	F3	1893	**Original county (Cherokee Outlet)** Kay County; 201 S Main; PO Box 450; Newkirk, OK 74647-0450; Ph. 580.362-2537 Details: (Formerly K Co. Name changed to Kay) (Clk Ct has m, div, pro & ct rec from 1893; Co Clk has land rec from 1893)
Kingfisher www.pldi.net/~kgfcounty/	H5	1890	**Original county** Kingfisher County; 101 S Main St; Kingfisher, OK 73750; Ph. 405.375-3887 Details: (Co Clk has m rec from 1900, div, pro & ct rec from 1896 & land rec from 1898)
Kiowa rebelcherokee.tripod.com/okkiowa.html	J7	1901	**Kiowa-Comanche-Apache & Caddo-Wichita Lands** Kiowa County; 316 S Main; PO Box 73; Hobart, OK 73651; Ph. 580.726-5286 Details: (Clk Ct has m, div, pro & ct rec from 1905; Co Clk has bur, land & mil rec from 1905)
L		1893	**Chickasaw Lands** Details: (see Grant) (Name changed to Grant 6 Nov 1894)
Latimer www.rootsweb.com/~oklatime/	C8	1902	**Choctaw Lands** Latimer County; 109 N Central St; Wilburton, OK 74578; Ph. 918.465-3543 Details: (Clk Ct has m rec from 1906, div, pro & ct rec)
Le Flore www.rootsweb.com/~okleflor/	A8	16 Jul 1907	**Choctaw Lands** Le Flore County; 100 S Broadway St; Poteau, OK 74953-0607; Ph. 918.647-5738 Details: (Clk Ct has m rec from 1898, div, pro & ct rec from 1907; Co Clk has land rec)
Lincoln* www.rootsweb.com/~oklincol/	F6	1891	**Iowa-Sac-Fox & Pottawatomie-Shawnee Lands** Lincoln County; 800 Manvel Ave; Chandler, OK 74834-0126; Ph. 405.258-1264 Details: (Formerly A Co. Name changed to Lincoln) (Clk Dis Ct has m, div, pro & ct rec from 1900; Co Clk has land rec)
Logan www.rootsweb.com/~oklogan/ oklogan.htm	G5	1890	**Original county** Logan County; 301 E Harrison Ave; Guthrie, OK 73044; Ph. 405.282-0266 Details: (Clk Ct has m rec from 1889, div, pro & ct rec; Co Clk has land rec from 1889)
Love www.rootsweb.com/~oklove/love.htm	G9	16 Jul 1907	**Chickasaw Lands** Love County; 405 W Main St; Marietta, OK 73448; Ph. 580.276-3059 Details: (Co Clk has b & d rec from 1958 & land rec from 1904; Clk Ct has m, div, pro & ct rec)
M		1893	**Cherokee Outlet** Details: (see Woods) (Name changed to Woods 6 Nov 1894)
Major www.rootsweb.com/~okmajor/major.htm	I4	16 Jul 1907	**Woods** Major County; 500 E Broadway St; Fairview, OK 73737; Ph. 580.227-4712 Details: (Clk Ct has m rec from late 1800's, div, pro & ct rec from 1908; Co Clk has land rec)
Marshall www.rootsweb.com/~okmarsha/ index.html	F9	16 Jul 1907	**Chickasaw Lands** Marshall County; 1 Courthouse Sq; Madill, OK 73446; Ph. 580.795-3220 Details: (Clk Ct has m, div, pro & ct rec from 1907; Co Clk has land rec from 1907 & mil dis rec; Co Supt has school rec)
Mayes* www.rootsweb.com/~okmayes/	B4	16 Jul 1907	**Cherokee Lands** Mayes County; NE 1st Adair; Pryor, OK 74361; Ph. 918.825-2426 Details: (Clk Ct has m, div, pro & ct rec from 1907; Co Clk has land rec from 1907; Co Treas has tax rec)
McClain www.rootsweb.com/~okmcclai/ okmcclain.html	G7	16 Jul 1907	**Chickasaw Lands** McClain County; PO Box 629; Purcell, OK 73080; Ph. 405.527-3360 Details: (Co Clk has land rec, mil rec from 1918 & school rec 1912-1968)

County Website	Map Index	Date Created	Parent County or Territory From Which Organized Address/Details
McCurtain www.rootsweb.com/~okmccurt/ mccurt.htm	B9	16 Jul 1907	**Choctaw Lands** McCurtain County; 108 N Central Ave; Idabel, OK 74745; Ph. 580.286-2370 Details: (Clk Ct has m, div, pro & ct rec from 1907)
McIntosh* www.rootsweb.com/~okmccurt/ mccurt.htm	C6	16 Jul 1907	**Creek Lands** McIntosh County; 110 N 1st St; Eufaula, OK 74432; Ph. 918.689-2741 Details: (Co Clk has b & d rec 1911-1918 & land rec; Clk Ct has m, div, pro & ct rec from 1907)
Murray www.rootsweb.com/~okmurray/	F8	16 Jul 1907	**Chickasaw Lands** Murray County; 10th St & Wyandotte St; Sulphur, OK 73086; Ph. 580.622-3920 Details: (Co Clk has land rec; Clk Ct has m, div, pro & ct rec)
Muskogee* www.rootsweb.com/~okmuskog/ index.htm	C6	1898	**Creek Lands** Muskogee County; 400 W Broadway St; Muskogee, OK 74401; Ph. 918.682-7781 Details: (Clk Ct has m rec from 1890, div, pro & ct rec from 1907; Co Clk has land rec)
N		1893	**Cherkoee Outlet** Details: (see Woodward) (Name changed to Woodward 6 Nov 1894)
Noble www.rootsweb.com/~oknoble/	G4	1893	**Cherokee Outlet** Noble County; 300 Courthouse Dr; Perry, OK 73077; Ph. 580.336-2141 Details: (Formerly P Co. Name changed to Noble 6 Nov 1894) (Clk Ct has m, div, pro & ct rec from 1893; Co Clk has land rec from 1893)
Nowata www.rootsweb.com/~oknowata/ NowCty.htm	C3	16 Jul 1907	**Cherokee Lands** Nowata County; 229 N Maple St; Nowata, OK 74048-2654; Ph. 918.273-2480 Details: (Clk Dis Ct has m, div, pro & ct rec from 1907; Co Clk has land rec from 1911)
O		1893	**Cherokee Outlet** Details: (see Garfield) (Name changed to Garfield 6 Nov 1894)
Okfuskee www.rootsweb.com/~okokfusk/	E6	16 Jul 1907	**Creek Lands** Okfuskee County; 3rd & Atlanta Sts; Okemah, OK 74859-0026; Ph. 918.623-1724 Details: (Clk Ct has m, div, pro & ct rec; Co Clk has land rec)
Oklahoma www.oklahomacounty.org/	G6	1890	**Original county** Oklahoma County; 320 Robert S Kerr Ave; Office 409; Oklahoma City, OK 73102; Ph. 405.713-1721 Details: (Co Clk has m, div, pro & ct rec from 1890)
Okmulgee www.rootsweb.com/~okokmulg/ index.html	D5	16 Jul 1907	**Creek Lands** Okmulgee County; 314 W 7th St; Okmulgee, OK 74447-5028; Ph. 918.756-0788 Details: (Clk Ct has m, div, pro & ct rec; Co Clk has land & mil rec)
Osage www.rootsweb.com/~okosage2/osage.htm	E4	16 Jul 1907	**Osage Indian Lands** Osage County; 600 Grandview Ave; Pawhuska, OK 74056; Ph. 918.287-3136 Details: (Co Clk has land rec from 1907; Clk Ct has m, div, pro & ct rec)
Ottawa www.rootsweb.com/~okottawa/	B3	16 Jul 1907	**Indian Territory** Ottawa County; 102 E Central; Miami, OK 74354-0000; Ph. 918.542-3332 Details: (Clk Ct has m, div, pro & ct rec; Co Clk has land rec from 1890)
P		1893	**Cherokee Outlet** Details: (see Noble) (Name changed to Noble 6 Nov 1894)
Pawnee www.rootsweb.com/~okpawnee/ pawnee.htm	E4	1893	**Pawnee Lands** Pawnee County; 500 Harrison St Rm 202; Pawnee, OK 74058; Ph. 918.762-2732 Details: (Formerly Q Co. Name changed to Pawnee) (Co Clk has land & mil rec; Clk Ct has m, div, pro & ct rec)
Payne www.paynecounty.org/	F5	1890	**Original county** Payne County; 606 S Husband St; Stillwater, OK 74074; Ph. 405.747-8310 Details: (Clk Ct has m, div, pro & ct rec from 1894; Co Clk has land rec)

County Website	Map Index	Date Created	Parent County or Territory From Which Organized Address/Details
Pittsburgh* www.rootsweb.com/~okpitts2/	D7	16 Jul 1907	**Choctaw Lands** Pittsburgh County; 115 E Carl Albert Pkwy; McAlester, OK 74501; Ph. 918.423-6865 Details: (Co Hlth Dept has b, d & bur rec; Clk Ct has m, div, pro & ct rec from 1890; Co Clk has land rec from 1890)
Pontotoc www.rootsweb.com/~itponca/	E8	16 Jul 1907	**Chickasaw Lands** Pontotoc County; 100 W 13th St; PO Box 1425; Ada, OK 74820; Ph. 580.332-1425 Details: (Clk Ct has m, div, pro & ct rec from 1907)
Pottawatomie www.rootsweb.com/~okpottaw/ pottawatomie.html	F7	1891	**Original county (Pottawatomie-Shawnee Lands)** Pottawatomie County; 325 N Broadway St; Shawnee, OK 74801; Ph. 405.273-8222 Details: (Formerly B Co. Name changed to Pottawatomie) (Clk Ct has m, div, pro & ct rec; Co Clk has land rec from 1892)
Pushmataha* www.rootsweb.com/~okpushma/	C8	16 Jul 1907	**Choctaw Lands** Pushmataha County; 203 SW 3rd; Antlers, OK 74523-3899; Ph. 580.298-3626 Details: (Clk Ct has m & pro rec; Co Clk has land rec)
Q		1893	**Pawnee Lands** Details: (see Pawnee) (Name changed to Pawnee)
Roger Mills www.rootsweb.com/~okrogerm/	L5	1892	**Cheyenne-Arapaho Lands** Roger Mills County; 506 E Broadway; Cheyenne, OK 73628-0000; Ph. 580.497-3395 Details: (Formerly F Co. Name changed to Roger Mills 8 Nov 1892) (Clk Ct has m, pro & ct rec from 1800's & div rec from 1900; Co Clk has land rec from 1800's)
Rogers users.rootsweb.com/~okrogers/	C3	16 Jul 1907	**Cherokee Nation** Rogers County; 219 S Missouri Ave; Claremore, OK 74017; Ph. 918.341-2518 Details: (Clk Ct has m, div, pro & ct rec from 1907)
Seminole www.rootsweb.com/~oksemino/index.htm	E6	16 Jul 1907	**Seminole Indian Lands** Seminole County; 110 N Wewoka Ave; Wewoka, OK 74884; Ph. 405.257-2501 Details: (Clk Ct has m, div, pro & ct rec from 1907)
Sequoyah www.rootsweb.com/~oksequo2/	A6	16 Jul 1907	**Cherokee Indian Lands** Sequoyah County; 120 E Chickasaw Ave Box 8; Sallisaw, OK 74955; Ph. 918.775-4517 Details: (Clk Ct has m, div, pro & ct rec from 1907)
Stephens www.rootsweb.com/~okstephe/ stephens.htm	H8	16 Jul 1907	**Comanche, Chickasaw Lands** Stephens County; 101 S 11th St #203; Duncan, OK 73533-0000; Ph. 580.255-0977 Details: (Clk Ct has m & pro rec; Co Clk has land rec)
Texas www.texascounty.org/	O3	16 Jul 1907	**Beaver** Texas County; PO Box 197; Guymon, OK 73942; Ph. 580.335-3141 Details: (Clk Ct has m, div, pro & ct rec from 1907 & nat rec 1864-1929; Co Clk has cem rec, land rec from 1889 & mil rec from 1917)
Tillman www.rootsweb.com/~oktillma/	J8	16 Jul 1907	**Comanche, Kiowa** Tillman County; 201 N 10th St; Frederick, OK 73542; Ph. 580.335-3421 Details: (Clk Ct has m, div, pro & ct rec from 1907; Co Clk has land rec from 1907)
Tobucksy			**Choctaw Lands** Details: (see Pittsburg)
Tulsa www.tulsacounty.org/	D5	1905	**Creek Lands, Cherokee Lands** Tulsa County; 500 S Denver Ave; Tulsa, OK 74103-3835; Ph. 918.596-5000 Details: (Clk Ct has m, div, pro & ct rec from 1907)
Wagoner www.rootsweb.com/~okwagone/	C5	16 Jul 1907	**Cherokee Lands** Wagoner County; 307 E Cherokee St; Wagoner, OK 74467-0000; Ph. 918.485-2216 Details: (Clk Ct has m, div, pro & ct rec from 1908)
Washington www.co.washington.ok.us/	D3	1897	**Cherokee Lands** Washington County; 420 S Johnstone Ave; Bartlesville, OK 74003-6602; Ph. 918.337-2840 Details: (Clk Ct has m, div, pro & ct rec from 1907)

County Website	Map Index	Date Created	Parent County or Territory From Which Organized Address/Details
Washita www.rootsweb.com/~okwashit/	J6	1892	**Cheyenne-Arapaho Lands** Washita County; PO Box 380; Cordell, OK 73632-0380; Ph. 580.832-3548 Details: (Formerly H Co. Name changed to Washita) (Clk Ct has m, div, pro & ct rec from 1900)
Woods www.rootsweb.com/~okwoods/ main-woods.html	J3	1893	**Cherokee Outlet** Woods County; 407 Government St; Alva, OK 73717-0000; Ph. 580.327-0942 Details: (Formerly M Co. Name changed to Woods 6 Nov 1894) (Co Clk has m rec from 1894, div, ct & land rec from 1893, pro rec from 1901 & school rec)
Woodward www.rootsweb.com/~okwoodwa/ woodward.htm	J4	1893	**Cherokee Outlet** Woodward County; 1600 Main St; Woodward, OK 73801; Ph. 580.256-8097 Details: (Formerly N Co. Name changed to Woodward 6 Nov 1894) (Clk Ct has m & pro rec; Co Clk has land rec)

Notes

Grape

OREGON

CAPITAL: SALEM – TERRITORY 1848 – STATE 1859 (33RD)

In 1543, Spanish explorers sighted the Oregon coast. Captain James Cook sighted Oregon in 1778. But, it was Americans–under Captain Robert Gray–who sailed up the Columbia River in 1792 and made the first landing. A few days later, the British sailed further inland and claimed the Columbia and its drainage basin for the British, thereby establishing a rivalry for control of Oregon that lasted until 1846.

Sea otter trade was the basic impetus for settlement in the early years. John Astor's American Fur Company established Fort Astoria on the coast, but due to the War of 1812 sold out to the Northwest Company in 1813. Hudson's Bay Company absorbed the Northwest Company in 1821 and dominated the fur trade for the next two decades. The early fur traders were mainly Canadian, British, and American and they often married Indian women.

Missionaries entered the area in the 1830's, leading to the first substantial migration along the Oregon Trail in 1842. By 1843, Willamette Valley settlers had set up their own government and were demanding that the British leave the area. Most of these early settlers were from Missouri, Ohio, Illinois, Tennessee, Kentucky, and New England.

In 1846, the British signed the Treaty of Washington, which established the 49th parallel as the international boundary between Canada and the United States.

The Oregon Territory was organized in 1848, comprising present-day Oregon, Washington, Idaho, western Montana, and a corner of Wyoming. Two years later, the Territorial Legislature passed the Donation Land Act of 1850. This act gave 320 acres to every male American over age 18 already in Oregon. If he were to marry by 1 December 1851, his wife would receive an equal amount of land. Men settling in the area by the end of 1853 were granted 160 acres of land and, if married, an equal amount was allotted to their wives. The act encouraged migration to Oregon. Over the next decade, the population quadrupled due to settlers from the United States, Germany, Sweden, England, Norway, Russia, Finland,

Italy, Denmark, Ireland, Austria, Greece, and Czechoslovakia. Statehood was granted in 1859. During the Civil War, the Union received nearly 2,000 soldiers from Oregon. After the war, Indian uprisings resulted in many battles and eventual relegation of the Indians to reservations. The Union Pacific Railroad was completed in 1869, beginning a 30-year expansion in population, which quadrupled Oregon's population.

Look for vital records in the following locations:

- **Birth and death records:** Available from 1903 at the Oregon State Health Division, Center of Health Statistics in Portland. State relationship and Reason for the request when writing. Only immediate family members can obtain copies of records. An index to births and deaths from 1903 to 1984 is available from the Oregon State Archives in Salem.
- **Marriage and divorce records:** County clerks have marriage records from the date of organization. Records after 1906 can be obtained from the county or the state. Divorces were granted by the territorial legislature prior to 1853. These records are available at the Oregon State Archives. After 1853, they were recorded in the circuit court of each county. Since 1925, divorces are also stored at the Oregon State Health Division.
- **Probate records:** A probate court handled probate matters in the territorial era. A few early records are at the Oregon State Archives. Since 1859, the probate judge in each county has had jurisdiction over wills. Some records are in the circuit court but county court clerks keep most records.
- **Census records:** The 1850 census for the Oregon Territory indexed and available. Territorial and state censuses also exist for a few counties for many years between 1842 and 1905.

Oregon State Health Division
Center of Health Statistics
800 N.E. Oregon Street, Suite 205
Portland, Oregon 97232

Oregon State Archives
1005 Broadway N.E.
Salem, Oregon 97310
503.731.4108

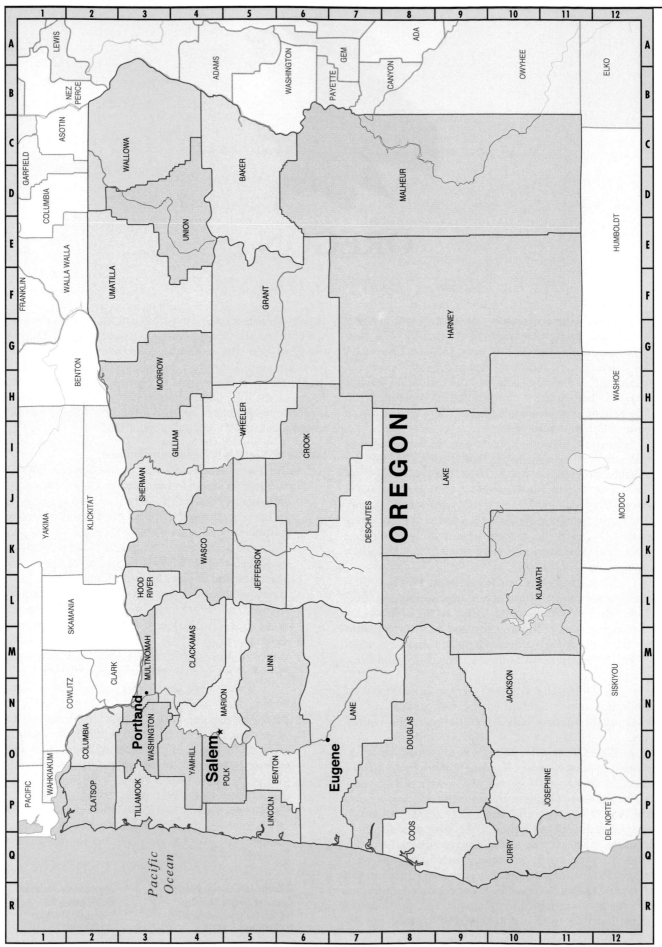

Societies and Repositories

ALSI Historical and Genealogical Society, Inc.; PO Box 922; Waldport, Oregon 97394

Astoria Public Library; 450 10th St.; Astoria, Oregon 97103

Baker County Genealogical Group; c/o Baker County Public Library; 2400 Resort St.; Baker City, Oregon 97814

Baptist, American Baptist-Samuel Colgate Historical Society; 1106 S. Goodman St.; Rochester, New York 14620-2532; 716.473.1740; Fax 716.473.1740

Bend Genealogical Society; PO Box 8254; Bend, Oregon 97708-8254; <www.rootsweb.com/~ordeschu/BGS/bgsindex.htm>

Benton County Genealogical Society; PO Box 1646; Philomath, Oregon 97370-1646; 541.752.6425

Blue Mountain Genealogical Society; PO Box 1801; Pendleton, Oregon 97801

Clackamas County Family History Society; PO Box 995; 211 Tumwater Dr.; Oregon City, Oregon 97045; <www.rootsweb.com/~genepool/ccfhs.htm>

Clatsop County Genealogical Society; c/o Astoria Public Library; 450 10th St.; Astoria, Oregon 97103

Clatsop County Historical Society; 1618 Exchange St.; Astoria, Oregon 97103

Columbia Gorge Genealogical Society; c/o The Dallas Public Library; 722 Court St.; The Dallas, Oregon 97058; 541.296.2815

Cottage Grove Genealogical Society; PO Box 399; Cottage Grove, Oregon 97424; <www.rootsweb.com/~orlane/links/cggs.htm>

Crook County Genealogical Society; 246 N. Main St.; Prineville, Oregon 97754-1852

Curry County Historical Society; 29410 Ellensburg Ave.; Gold Beach, Oregon 97444

Dalles-Wasco Co. Public Library; 722 Court St.; The Dalles, Oregon 97058; 541.296.2815

Deschutes County Historical Society; PO Box 5252; Bend, Oregon 97708

Disciples of Christ Historical Society; 1101 19th Avenue South; Nashville, Tennessee 37212; 615.327.1444; Fax 615.327.1445

Eugene City Library; 100 West 13th Ave.; Eugene, Oregon 97401

Family History Library: 35 North West Temple Street: Salt Lake City, Utah 84150: 800.346.6044 or 801.240.2584: <www.familysearch.org>: Find a Family History Center near you: <www.familysearch.org/Eng/Library/FHC/frameset_fhc.asp>

Genealogical Forum of Oregon Library; 1 S.W. Morrison #812; Portland, Oregon 97201

Genealogical Forum of Oregon, Inc.; 2130 S.W. Fifth Ave. Suite 220; Portland, Oregon 97201-4934; 503.227.2398

Grant Co. Museum; PO Box 416; Canyon City, Oregon 97820

Grant County Genealogical Society; PO Box 419; Canyon City, Oregon 97820

Grants Pass Genealogical Society; PO Box 1934; Grants Pass, Oregon 97526

Harney County Genealogical Society; c/o 426 E. Jefferson; Burns, Oregon 97720

Jewish Genealogical Society of Oregon; c/o Mittleman Jewish Community Center; 6651 SW Capitol Highway; Portland, Oregon 97219; <www.rootsweb.com/~orjgs/>

Juniper Branch of the Family Finders; PO Box 652; Madras, Oregon 97741

Klamath Basin Genealogical Society; 126 S. 3rd St.; Klamath Falls, Oregon 97601

Klamath Co. Library; 126 S. Third St.; Klamath Falls, Oregon 97601

Lake County Historical Society; PO Box 49; Lakeview, Oregon 97630

LaPine Genealogical Society; PO Box 1081; LaPine, Oregon 97739

Lebanon Genealogical Society; c/o Lebanon Public Library; 626 2nd St.; Lebanon, Oregon 97355

Linn Genealogical Society; PO Box 1222; Albany, Oregon 97321; <www.rootsweb.com/~orlinngs/>

Madras Genealogical Society; 671 SW Fairgrounds; Madras, Oregon 97741

Mennonite Historical and Genealogical Society of Oregon; 675 Elma Ave. SE; Salem, Oregon 97301

Milton-Freewater Genealogical Club; 127 S.E. 6th St.; Milton-Freewater, Oregon 97962

Mt. Hood Genealogical Forum; 950 South End Rd.; Oregon City, Oregon 97045

Multnomah County Library, Humanities Division; 801 S.W. Tenth Avenue; Portland, Oregon 97205; 503.248.5234

National Archives-Pacific Northwest Region (Seattle); 6125 Sand Point Way, N.E.; Seattle, Washington 98115; 206.526.6507; Fax 206.526.6545

Northrup Library, Linfield College; 900 S. Baker; McMinnville, Oregon 97128-9989; 503.434.2262; Fax 503.434.2566

Oregon Chapter, AHSGR; 8618 S.E. 36th Ave.; Portland, Oregon 97222-5522; 503.659.8248; <www.ahsgr.org/orportla.html>

Oregon Genealogical Society, Inc.; PO Box 10306; Eugene, Oregon 97449-2306; <www.rootsweb.com/~orlncogs/ogsinfo.htm>; 541.345.0399

Oregon Genealogical Society; 223 North A Street-Suite F; Springfield, Oregon 97477; 541.746.7924

Oregon Genealogical Society; PO Box 10306; Eugene, Oregon 97440-2306

Oregon Historical Society Library; 1230 S.W. Park Avenue; Portland, Oregon 97205-2483; 503.306.5240; Fax 503.219.2040

Oregon State Archives; 800 Summer St. NE; Salem, Oregon 97310; 503.373.0701; Fax 503.373.0953;

Oregon State Health Division, Center for Health Statistics; PO Box 14050; Portland, Oregon 97293-0050; 503.731.4095; Fax 503.731.4084

Oregon State Library; 250 Winter St. NE; Salem, Oregon 97310-3950; 503.378.4243 x221; Fax 503.588.7119; <www.osl.state.or.us/home/>

Oregon State Office of the Bureau of Land Management; 1515 S.W. 5th Ave., PO Box 2965; Portland, Oregon 97208-2965; 503.952.6287; Fax 503.952.6333

Polk County Genealogical Society; 535S.E. Ash St.; Dallas, Oregon 97338

Port Orford Genealogical Society; c/o Port Orford Public Library; 555 W. 20th St.; Port Orford, Oregon 97465

Portland Library Association; 801 S.W. Tenth Ave.; Portland, Oregon 97205

Presbyterian, Presbyterian Historical Society, Presbyterian Church (U.S.A.); 425 Lombard St.; Philadelphia, Pennsylvania 19147-1516; 215.627.1852; Fax 215.627.0509

Rogue Valley Gen. Society and Library; PO Box 1468, 95 Houston Rd.; Phoenix, Oregon 97535; 541.512.2340

Roman Catholic, Archdiocese of Portland in Oregon, Chancery Office; 2838 E. Burnside St., PO Box 351; Portland, Oregon 97214-1895; 503.234.5334; Fax 503.234.2545

Scandinavian Genealogical Society; 9143 Olney St. S.E.; Salem, Oregon 97301

Sherman County Historical Society; PO Box 173; Moro, Oregon 97039

Siuslaw Genealogical Society; c/o Siuslaw Public Library; PO Box 1540; Florence, Oregon 97439

Sons of the American Revolution, Oregon Society; 5190 S.W. Chestnut Ave.; Beaverton, Oregon 97005

Sweet Home Genealogical Society; c/o Sweet Home Library; PO Box 279; Sweet Home, Oregon 97386

Tillamook County Historical Society Genealogical Study Group; PO Box 123; Tillamook, Oregon 97141

Umatilla County Historical Society; PO Box 253; Pendleton, Oregon 97801

University of Oregon; Knight Library; Eugene, Oregon 97403-1299; 541.346.1818; Fax 541.346.3485

Waldport Heritage Museum; PO Box 882; Waldport, Oregon 97394; 541.563.7092

Willamette Valley Genealogical Society; PO Box 2093; Salem, Oregon 97308

Yamhill County Genealogical Society; P. 0. Box 569; McMinnville, Oregon 97128

Yaquina Chapter, NSDAR, Oregon; <www.rootsweb.com/~oryaqdar/Yaquina.htm>

Yaquina Genealogical Society; c/o Toledo Public Library; 173 NW Seventh St.; Toledo, Oregon 97391; <www.rootsweb.com/~orygs/>

Bibliography and Record Sources

General Sources

Armstrong, A. N. *Oregon: Comprising a Brief History and Full Description of the Territories of Oregon and Washington... Together with Remarks Upon the Social Position, Productions, Resources and Prospects of the Country, a Dissertation Upon the Climate, and a Full Description of the Indian Tribes of the Pacific Slope...Interspersed with Incidents of Travel and Adventure.* Washington, D.C.: Library of Congress, 1989.

Bancroft, Hubert Howe. *History of Oregon.* 2 vols. San Francisco: The History Co., 1886-1888.

Beebe, Ralph K. *A Garden of The Lord: A History of Oregon Yearly Meeting of Friends Church.* S.l.: s.n.], 1968.

Book, Betty. *Indians of Oregon Bibliography, 1966-1983.* Portland, Oregon: Genealogical Council of Oregon, 1991.

Brandt, Patricia and Nancy Guilford, eds. *Oregon Biography Index. Oregon State University Bibliographic Series, no. 11.* Corvallis, Oregon: Oregon State University, 1976.

Capitol's Who's Who for Oregon, 1936-1944. 2 vols. Portland, Oregon: Capitol Pub. Co., 1936-1942.

Carey, Charles Henry. *History of Oregon.* 3 vols. Chicago: Pioneer History Publishing Co., 1922.

Clark, Keith. *Terrible Trail: The Meek Cutoff, 1845.* Caldwell, Idaho: Caxton Printers, 1966.

Cogswell, Philip. *Capitol Names: Individuals Woven into Oregon's History.* Portland, Oregon: Oregon Historical Society, 1977.

Directory of Churches and Religious Organizations, State of Oregon. Portland: Historical Records Survey, 1940.

Dryden, Cecil Pearl. *Give all to Oregon: Missionary Pioneers of the Far West.* New York: Hastings House, [1968].

Evans, Elwood. *History Of The Pacific Northwest: Oregon and Washington; Embracing an Account of the Original Discoveries on the Pacific Coast of North America, and a Description of the Conquest, Settlement and Subjugation of the...Original Territory of Oregon; Also Interesting Biographies of the Earliest Settlers...* 2 vols. Portland, Oregon: North Pacific History Co., [1889].

Gaston, Joseph. *The Centennial History of Oregon, 1811-1912,* 4 vols. Chicago: S.J. Clarke Publishing Co., 1912.

Gregg, Jacob Ray. *A History of the Oregon Trail, Santa Fe Trail, and Other Trails.* Portland, Oregon: Binfords & Mort, 1955.

Guide to Depositories of Manuscript Collections in the United States: Oregon-Washington. Portland: Oregon Historical Records Survey, 1940.

Guide to the Manuscript Collections of the Oregon Historical Society. Portland, Oregon: Historical Records Survey, 1940.

Hawthorne, Julian. *The Story of Oregon: A History With Portraits and Biographies.* 2 vols. New York: American Historical Pub. Co., 1892.

Herzberg, Alice Stansfield. *Index to Oregon Newspaper Clippings, 1895-1952.* [Medford, Oregon: Rogue Valley Genealogical Society], 1995.

Hines, Harvey K. *An Illustrated History of the State of Oregon: Containing a History of Oregon from the Earliest Period of its Discovery to the Present Time, Together with Glimpses of its Auspicious Future; Illustrations and Full-Page Portraits of Some of its Eminent Men and Biographical Mention of Many of its Pioneers and Prominent Citizens of Today.* Chicago: Lewis Pub. Co., 1893.

Holmes, Kenneth L. *Covered Wagon Women: Diaries & Letters from the Western Trails, 1840-1890.* 11 vols. Glendale, Calif.: Arthur H. Clark Co., 1983-1991.

Horner, John B. *Oregon History and Early Literature: A Pictorial Narrative of the Pacific Northwest.* Portland, Oregon: The J. K. Gill Company, 1931.

Inventory of Church Archives of Oregon Presbyterian Churches: Microreproductions of original records at the Presbyterian Historical Society, in Philadelphia, Pennsylvania. (Salt Lake City: Filmed by the Genealogical Society of Utah, 1967).

Kullberg, Lois G. Gassaway. *Saints to the Columbia: A History of the Church of Jesus Christ of Latter-day Saints in Oregon and Southwestern Washington, 1850-1990*. Vancouver, Wash.: L-K Publications, 1991.

Lenzen, Connie Miller. *Research in Oregon*. Arlington, Virginia: National Genealogical Society, 1992.

Lenzen, Connie. *Guide to Genealogical Sources*. Rev. ed. Portland: Genealogical Forum of Oregon, 1994.

Lind, Hope Kauffman. *Apart and Together, Mennonites in Oregon and Neighboring States, 1876-1976*. Scottdale, Pennsylvania: Herald Press, 1990.

Lockley, Fred. *History of the Columbia River Valley from The Dalles to the Sea*. 3 vols. Chicago: S.J. Clarke Publishing Co., 1928.

Lyman, Horace Sumner. *History of Oregon: The Growth of an American State*. New York: North Pacific Pub. Society, 1903.

Mattoon, Charles Hiram. *Baptist Annals of Oregon, 1844-1900*. 2 vols. McMinnville, Oregon: Telephone Register Pub. Co., 1913.

McChesney, Charles E. *Rolls of Certain Indian Tribes in Oregon and Washington*. Fairfield, Washington: Ye Galleon Press, l969.

Mitchelmore, Lawrence H. *Presbyterianism in Southern Oregon: A History of The Presbytery of Southwest Oregon and its Forebears 1851-1949*. North Bend, Oregon: L.H. Mitchelmore, 1949.

Munnick, Harriet Duncan. *Catholic Church Records of the Pacific Northwest: Missions of St. Ann and St. Rose of the Cayuse, 1847-1888; Walla Walla and Frenchtown, 1858-1872; Frenchtown, 1872-1888*. Portland, Oregon: Binford & Mort, 1989.

Munnick, Harriet Duncan. *Catholic Church Records of the Pacific Northwest: Grand Ronde Register I (1860-1885), Grand Ronde Register II (1886-1898): St. Michael the Archangel Parish, Grand Ronde Indian Reservation, Grand Ronder, Oregon; St. Patrick's Parish, Muddy Valley, Oregon*. Portland, Oregon: Binford & Mort, 1987.

Nichols, M. Leona. *Mantle of Elias, The Story of Fathers Blanchet and Demers in Early Oregon*. Portland: Binfords and Mort, 1941.

Oregon Genealogical Society (Eugene, Oregon). *Oregon Pioneers*. Eugene, Oregon: The Society, c [198-?].

Oregon Research Outline. Series US-States, No. 38. Salt Lake City: Family History Library, 1988.

Portrait and Biographical Record of the Willamette Valley, Oregon. Chicago: Chapman Publishing Co., 1903.

Portrait and Biographical Record of Western Oregon: Containing Original Sketches of Many Well Known Citizens of the Past and Present…. Chicago: Chapman Publishing Co., 1904.

Rushford, Jerry. *Christians on the Oregon Trail: Churches of Christ and Christian Churches in Early Oregon, 1842-1882*. Joplin, Mo.: College Press Pub. Co., 1997.

Schoenberg, Wilfred P. *Paths to the Northwest: A Jesuit History of the Oregon Province*. Chicago: Loyola University Press, 1982.

Schoenberg, Wilfred P. *These Valiant Women: History of the Sisters of St. Mary of Oregon, 1886-1986*. Beaverton, Oregon: Sisters of St. Mary of Oregon, 1986.

Shacer, F. A. Shaver, Arthur P. Rose, R. F. Steele, and A. E. Adams, comps. *An Illustrated History of Central Oregon: Embracing Wasco, Sherman, Gilliam, Wheeler, Crook, Lake, and Klamath Counties*. Spokane, Wash.: Western Historical Pub. Co., 1905.

Southern Oregon Library Federation. *A Guide to the State of Jefferson: A Union List of Historical Materials Relating to Northern California and Southern Oregon*. Portland, Oregon: Filmed by the Oregon Historical Society, [197-?].

Steber, Rick. Oregon Trail: *Last of the Pioneers*. Prineville, Oregon: Bonanza Publishing, 1993.

The Oregonian's Handbook of the Pacific Northwest: Portland: Oregonian, 1894.

United States. Bureau of Indian Affairs. Klamath Agency. *Family History and Medical Data, 1904-1937*. Microfilm of originals at the Federal Record Center, Seattle, Washington. (Salt Lake City: Filmed by the Genealogical Society of Utah, 1978). 2 microfilm.

United States. Bureau of Indian Affairs. Portland Area Office. *Family Index Cards, 1938-1950*. Microfilm of originals at the Federal Record Center, Seattle, Washington. (Salt Lake City: Filmed by the Genealogical Society of Utah, 1978). 2 microfilm.

Vaughn, Thomas. *A Bibliography of Pacific Northwest History*. Oregon Historical Society, n.d.

Who's Who for Idaho, Combined With Who's Who for Oregon and Who's Who for the Western States. Portland, Oregon: Capitol Publishing Co., 1970.

Yarnes, Thomas D. *A History of Oregon Methodism*. Portland: Oregon Methodist Conference Historical Society, 1957.

Atlases, Maps and Gazetteers

Brown, Erma Skyles. *Oregon County Boundary Change Maps, 1843-1916*. Lebanon, Oregon: End of Trail Researchers, 1970.

Loy, William G. *A Preliminary Atlas of Oregon*. Eugene: Geography Dept., University of Oregon, 1972.

McArthur, Lewis A. *Oregon Geographic Names*. 6th ed. Portland: Oregon Historical Society, 1992.

Middleton, Lynn. *Places Names of the Pacific Northwest Coast: Origins, Histories and Anecdotes in Bibliographic Form About the Coast of British Columbia, Washington and Oregon*. Seattle, Wash.: Superior Pub. Co, 1969.

Oregon Atlas and Gazetteer. 2nd ed. Freeport, Maine: DeLorme Mapping Co., 1995.

Payne, Edwin R. *Oregon Post Offices*. 2nd ed. Rev. to January 1955. Salem, Oregon, 1955.

Preston, Ralph N. *Historical Maps of Oregon: Overland Stage Routes, Old Military Roads, Indian Battle Grounds, Old Forts, and Old Gold Mines*. Corvallis, Oregon: Western Guide Publishers, 1972.

R. L. Polk & Co. Oregon and Washington Gazetteer and Business Directory, 1909-1910. Seattle: R.L. Polk, 1909.

Census Records

Available Census Records and Census Substitutes

Federal Census 1850, 1860, 1870, 1880, 1900, 1910, 1920, 1930.

Federal Mortality Schedules 1850, 1860, 1870, 1880.

Union Veterans and Widows 1890.

State/Territorial Census 1845-1857.

Dollarhide, William. *The Census Book: A Genealogist's Guide to Federal Census Facts, Schedules and Indexes.* Bountiful, Utah: Heritage Quest, 1999.

Kemp, Thomas Jay. *The American Census Handbook.* Wilmington, Delaware: Scholarly Resources, Inc., 2001.

Lainhart, Ann S. *State Census Records.* Baltimore: Genealogical Publishing Co., Inc., 1992.

Oregon Memorial of Citizens of the U. S. and Miscellaneous Information: Census Records for 1843, Tax Rolls, Newspaper Clippings of Oregon Pioneers, Government Document on the Boundary Line Between the British and United States Territories in Northwestern America. (Salt Lake City: Filmed by the Genealogical Society of Utah, 1966).

Szucs, Loretto Dennis, and Matthew Wright. *Finding Answers in U.S. Census Records.* Ancestry Publishing, 2001

Thorndale, William, and William Dollarhide. *Map Guide to the U.S. Federal Censuses, 1790-1920.* Baltimore: Genealogical Publishing Co., 1987.

United States. Bureau of Internal Revenue. *Oregon Internal Revenue Assessment Lists, 1867-1873.* Microfilm of originals in the National Archives Branch in Seattle, Washington. (Salt Lake City: Filmed by the Genealogical Society of Utah, 1989). 2 microfilm.

Court Records, Probate and Wills

Note: Court, probate and will records are held in individual courthouses. Additional court records can be found at the Oregon State Archives. For a preview of the collections see their online database at -

Reiner, Mary Hedges. *Early Oregon Wills, Multnomah County, 1884-1887.* Vol. 3. N.p., 1953.

Reiner, Mary Hedges. *Probated Intestate Estates: Early Oregon, Multnomah County, 1884-1887, with a Few as Early as 1852.* N.p., 1953.

Emigration, Immigration, Migration and Naturalization

Bowen, William Adrian. *The Willamette Valley: Migration and Settlement on the Oregon Frontier.* Seattle: University of Washington Press, 1978.

Lenzen, Connie. *How to Find Oregon Naturalization Records.* [S.l.: C. Lenzen], 1991.

Oregon Pioneer Association (Salem, Oregon). *Pioneer Registers, 1818-1859.* Microfilm of originals at the Oregon Historical Society in Portland, Oregon. (Salt Lake City: Filmed by the Genealogical Society of Utah, 1999).

Oregon Trail Links. Oregon GenWeb Project, 2002. Online database - <www.rootsweb.com/~orgenweb/otlinks.html>.

Oregon-California Trails Association Online Database. Independence, Missouri: Oregon-California Trails Association, 2001. Online database - <www.octa-trails.org/>.

Samuelsen, W. David. *Oregon Naturalization Records Index: Declaration of Intention.* 2 vols. Salt Lake City: Sampubco, 1995.

United States. Circuit Court (Oregon). *Indexes to Naturalization Records in the U. S. Circuit and District Courts.* Washington, DC: National Archives, [198-?]. 3 microfilm.

United States. District Court (Oregon). *Declaration of Intentions, 1859-1941; Petitions for Naturalization, 1906-1941; Indexes, 1863-1956; Military Petitions for*

Naturalization, 1917- 1918. Microfilm of originals at the National Archives, Seattle Branch, Seattle, Washington. (Salt Lake City: Filmed by the Genealogical Society of Utah, 1988). 60 microfilm.

United States. Immigration and Naturalization Service. *Chinese and Japanese Emigrants into Portland, Oregon.* Microfilm of originals in the National Archives Branch in Seattle, Washington. (Salt Lake City: Filmed by the Genealogical Society of Utah, 1990). 15 microfilm.

White, Kris. Overland Passages: *A Guide to Overland Documents in the Oregon Historical Society.* Portland, Oregon: Oregon Historical Society Press, 1993.

Land and Property

Genealogical Material in Oregon Donation Land Claims, 5 vols. Portland: Genealogical Forum of Portland, 1957-1975.

Gibson, James R. Farming *The Frontier: The Agricultural Opening of the Oregon Country, 1786-1846.* Vancouver: University of British Columbia Press, 1985.

Harry P. Yoshpe and Philip P. Brower, comps., *Preliminary Inventory of the Land-Entry Papers of the General Land Office.* Seattle: National Archives Pacific Alaska Region, 1949.

Hone, Wade E. *Land and Property Research in the United States.* Salt Lake City: Ancestry Incorporated, 1997.

National Archives Records Administration. Pacific Alaska Region. *Records of the District Land Offices for Oregon.* Seattle: National Archives Records Administration. Pacific Alaska Region, 2001. Online database - <www.nara.gov/regional/seattle.html>.

National Archives Records Administration. Pacific Alaska Region. *Records of Land Offices in Roseburg and Oregon City, Oregon.* Seattle: National Archives Records Administration. Pacific Alaska Region, 2001. online database - <www.nara.gov/regional/seattle.html>.

Oregon State Archives, comp. *Index of Oregon Donation Land Claims.* 2nd ed. Portland: Genealogical Forum of Portland, 1987.

United States. General Land Office (Oregon). *Abstracts of Oregon Donation Land Claims, 1852-1903.* Microfilm of original records at the National Archives. (Salt Lake City: Filmed by the Genealogical Society of Utah, 1949). 7 microfilm.

United States. General Land Office. *Oregon and Washington Donation Land Files, 1851-1903.* Washington, D.C.: The National Archives, 1970.

Military

Drew, Charles S. *An Account of the Origin and Early Prosecution of the Indian War in Oregon.* Fairfield, Washington: Ye Galleon Press, 1972.

Gantenbein, C. U. *The Official Records of the Oregon Volunteers in the Spanish War and Philippine Insurrection.* 2nd ed. Salem, Oregon: J.R. Whitney, 1903.

Indian War Pensions [Index, Oregon]. [S.l.: s.n.], 1998.

Leonard, Spencer. *A Partial List of Military Casualties and MIA's from the State of Oregon During World War II.* Portland, Oregon: Genealogical Forum of Oregon, Inc., 1993.

Myers, Jane. *Honor Roll of Oregon Grand Army of the Republic, 1881-1935.* Cottage Grove, Oregon: Cottage Grove Genealogical Society, 1980.

Oregon Military Department. Oregon Soldiers Home Applications, 1894-1933. Microfilm of original records at the Oregon State Archives in Salem, Oregon. (Salt Lake City: Filmed by the Genealogical Society of Utah, 2000). 16 microfilm.

Oregon State Defense Council. Oregon War Records - Personal Military Service, 1919-1920. Salt Lake City: Filmed by the Genealogical Society of Utah, 2000. 17 microfilm.

Oregon. Division of State Archives. *Oregon Combined Military Alphabetical Index, 1837-1933*. Microfilm of original index at the Oregon State Archives in Salem, Oregon. (Salt Lake City: Filmed by the Genealogical Society of Utah, 2000). 37 microfilm.

Oregon. Division of State Archives. *Oregon Combined Military Service Records Index, 1852-1954*. Microfilm of original records at the Oregon State Archives in Salem, Oregon. (Salt Lake City: Filmed by the Genealogical Society of Utah, 2000). 44 microfilm.

Pekar, M. A. *Soldiers Who Served in the Oregon Volunteers: Civil War Period, Infantry and Cavalry*. Portland, Oregon: Genealogical Forum of Portland, 1961.

United States. Department of the Interior. *Bureau of Pensions. Indian War Pension Papers, 1897-1902*. Microfilm of original records at the Oregon Historical Society in Portland, Oregon. (Salt Lake City: Filmed by the Genealogical Society of Utah, 1998-1999). 14 microfilm.

United States. Selective Service System. *Oregon, World War I Selective Service System Draft Registration Cards, 1917-1918*. National Archives Microfilm Publications, M1509. Washington, D.C.: National Archives, 1987-1988.

Vital and Cemetery Records

Eakley, Barbara Brown. *Episcopal Marriages of the Southern Oregon Coast, 1884-1940*. Coos Bay, Oregon: Bayview Publishers, 1997.

Guide to Public Vital Statistics Records in Oregon. Portland, Oregon: Historical Records Survey, 1942.

Oregon Cemetery Directory. Salem, Oregon: Oregon Heritage Council, 1976.

Oregon Cemetery Records. 2 vols. Salt Lake City: Genealogical Society of Utah, 1956-61.

Oregon Death Records Index, 1903-1970. Salem, Oregon: Filmed by the Oregon State Archives and Records Center, [197-?]. 12 microfilm.

Oregon State Archives. Genealogical Information Locator. Salem, Oregon: Oregon State Archives, 2002. online database - <159.121.172.88/genealogy/search.lasso>.

Oregon. Board of Health. Division of Vital Statistics. *Statewide Delayed Filings of Births, 1842-1893*. Microfilm of original records at the Oregon State Archives in Salem, Oregon. (Salt Lake City: Filmed by the Genealogical Society of Utah, 2001). 64 microfilm.

Osborn-Ryan, Sharon E. *Cumulative Baptism Index to the Catholic Church Records of the Pacific Northwest*. [S.l.]: Oregon Heritage Press, 1999.

Osborn-Ryan, Sharon E. *Cumulative Death Index to the Catholic Church Records of the Pacific Northwest*. [Portland, Oregon: S. Osborn-Ryan, 1998].

Osborn Ryan, Sharon E. *Cumulative Marriage Index to the Catholic Church Records of the Pacific Northwest*. [S.l.]: Oregon Heritage Press, 1998.

County Website	Map Index	Date Created	Parent County or Territory From Which Organized Address/Details
Sherman www.rootsweb.com/~orsherma/	J3	25 Feb 1889	**Wasco** Sherman County; 500 Court St; Moro, OR 97039; Ph. 541.565.3606 Details: (Co Clk has m & pro rec from 1889, b rec 1904-1939, d rec 1905-1952 & ct rec from 1894)
Tillamook* www.rootsweb.com/~ortillam/	P3	15 Dec 1853	**Clatsop, Polk, Yamhill** Tillamook County; 201 Laurel Ave; Tillamook, OR 97141; Ph. 503.842.3402 Details: (Co Clk has m rec from 1862, div, pro & ct rec from 1860)
Twality		5 Jul 1843	**Original county** Details: (see Washington) (Name changed to Washington 3 Sep 1849)
Umatilla* www.co.umatilla.or.us/	F3	27 Sep 1862	**Wasco** Umatilla County; 216 SE 4th St; Pendleton, OR 97801-2590; Ph. 541.276.7111 Details: (Co Clk has m, div, pro, ct & land rec from 1862)
Umpqua		1851	**Benton, Linn** Details: (Absorbed by Douglas Co 1863)
Union www.usgennet.org/usa/or/county/ union1/union.htm	E4	14 Oct 1864	**Baker** Union County; 1106 K Ave; LaGrande, OR 97850; Ph. 541.963.1006 Details: (Co Clk has m & land rec from 1875 & nat rec 1900-1975; Clk Cir Ct has div, pro & ct rec from 1854)
Wallowa www.co.wallowa.or.us/	C3	11 Feb 1887	**Union** Wallowa County; 101 S River St; Enterprise, OR 97828-1300; Ph. 541.426.4543 Details: (Co Clk has b rec 1907-1943, m, land & mil rec from 1897, div, pro & ct rec from 1897-1970 & nat rec 1897-1920; Cir Ct has div, pro & ct rec from 1971)
Wasco* www.historysavers.com/orwasco/	K4	11 Jan 1854	**Clackamas, Marion, Linn** Wasco County; 511 Washington St; The Dalles, OR 97058-0000; Ph. 541.296.6159 Details: (Co Clk has m & land rec from 1854; Clk Cir Ct has div, pro & ct rec from 1854)
Washington* www.co.washington.or.us/cgi/home/ washco.pl	03	5 July 1843	**Original county** Washington County; 155 N 1st Ave Ste 130; Hillsboro, OR 97124-3072; Ph. 503.864.8741 Details: (Formerly Twality [or Falatine Co]. Name changed to Washington 3 Sep 1849) (Rec Section, Assessment & Taxation has m, land & mil rec from 1850; Clk Cir Ct has div & ct rec from 1896, pro rec from 1871 & nat rec from 1906)
Wheeler Future website at www.rootsweb.com/ ~orgenweb/counties.html	I5	17 Feb 1899	**Crook, Gilliam, Grant** Wheeler County; 701 Adams St; PO Box 327; Fossil, OR 97830; Ph. 541.763.2400 Details: (Co Clk has pro rec from 1899 & land rec; Clk Cir Ct has div & ct rec)
Yamhill www.co.yamhill.or.us/	04	5 Jul 1843	**Original county** Yamhill County; 535 NE 5th St; McMinnville, OR 97128; Ph. 503.434.7518 Details: (Co Clk has m rec from 1881 & land rec from 1853)

Mountain Laurel

PENNSYLVANIA

CAPITAL: HARRISBURG – STATE 1787 (2ND)

The Swedes made the first permanent settlement in Pennsylvania in 1643 and built the first log cabins in America. These settlers became the nucleus for William Penn's colony despite being conquered by the Dutch and the English. In 1681, King Charles II granted William Penn a charter, which made Penn proprietor and governor of Pennsylvania. He first visited the colony in 1682 and set up a General Assembly at Chester. Penn named his capital Philadelphia, and before allowing settlers into any area, bought the land from the Indians. On Penn's second visit (1699-1701), he granted the Charter of Privileges, which made the legislature independent of the executive and virtually in control of the colony.

Penn established the colony as a refuge for those who were persecuted for their religious beliefs. The persecuted from throughout Europe came, including Quakers from England, Scotland, Ireland, and Wales; Palatines from the Rhine Valley; Anabaptists (Mennonites) from Germany and Switzerland; Dunkards (members of the Church of the Brethren) from Germany in 1721; Roman Catholics from England in 1732; Moravians via Georgia in 1740; Welsh, Swiss, and Scotch-Irish between 1700 and 1728; and the Pennsylvania Dutch (who were Germans) around 1740. Indian relations remained peaceable until the French arrived in 1753. Their arrival lead to the French and Indian War and Pontiac's War.

Philadelphia played an important role during the Revolution and in the drafting of the Constitution. Pennsylvania was among the greatest contributors of men, money, and supplies to the Revolutionary War and was the site of many important battles, such as Washington's crossing of the Delaware, the battles of Brandywine and Germantown, and the winter camp at Valley Forge. In 1787, Pennsylvania was the second state to ratify the Constitution. Philadelphia served as the capital of the United States from 1790 to 1800.

Boundary disputes were nearly constant until 1800.

The boundary with Maryland was settled by the Mason and Dixon survey, 1763-1767. The Pennamite War between 1769 and 1775 was fought between settlers from Connecticut and Pennsylvania over the Wyoming Valley. This was finally settled in 1782 by the Decree of Trenton, which gave the land to Pennsylvania. Connecticut finally yielded in 1784. Southwestern Pennsylvania was also claimed by Virginia, but this dispute was settled in 1785. In 1792, Pennsylvania bought the Erie triangle to gain a port on Lake Erie.

Tens of thousands of settlers came in the early 1800's to work in mines and industry. These came from Italy, Poland, Russia, Austria, Germany, Czechoslovakia, England, Ireland, Hungary, Sweden, Greece, France, Norway, Denmark, and Finland. By 1811, steamboats began traveling from Pittsburgh to New Orleans. The railroad canal line extended from Philadelphia to Pittsburgh by 1834. With these improvements came more immigrants, so that by 1840 there was no longer a frontier in Pennsylvania. Pennsylvania had the first anti-slavery society in 1775. It is no wonder that the state was so pro-Union. Nearly 400,000 men served for the Union, and the battle of Gettysburg was fought on Pennsylvania soil.

Look for vital records in the following locations:

- **Birth and death records:** Statewide registration of births and deaths began in January 1906. Copies are available from the Division of Vital Statistics, State Department of Health in Newcastle, Pennsylvania. Records prior to 1906 were kept (by the registrar of wills) in individual counties or cities, some as early as 1852.
- **Marriage records:** Individual counties or cities also kept marriage records, some from the early 1800's, through most of 1885.
- **Naturalizations:** Original Oaths of Allegiance, 1727 to 1794, are at the Bureau of Archives and History, Harrisburg, Pennsylvania. Most later immigrants

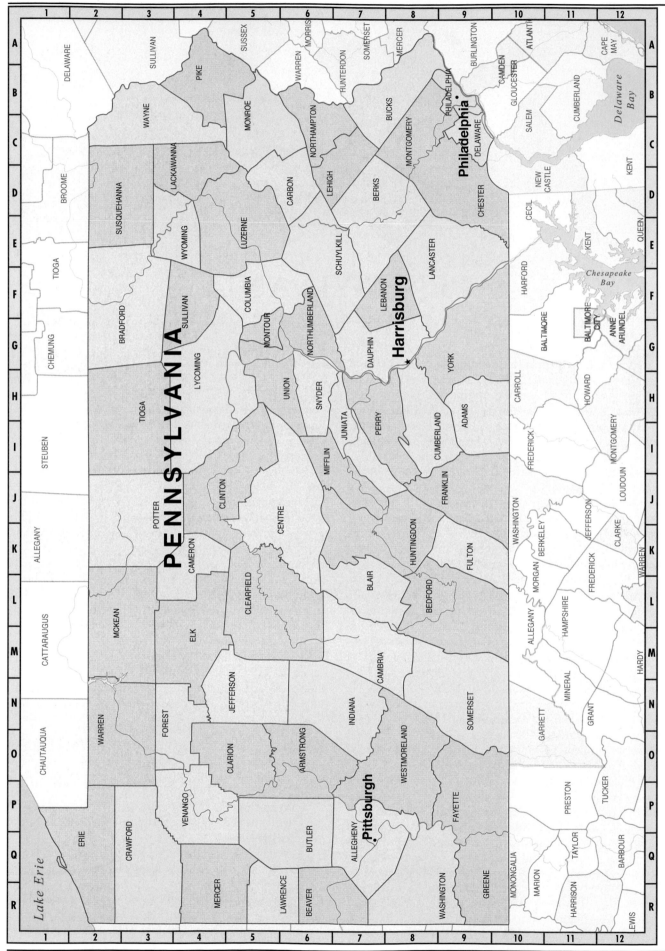

filed for naturalization in a county court.

- **Land records:** The state land office, established in 1682, is now the Bureau of Land Records. The Bureau of Archives and History in Harrisburg, Pennsylvania sells warrantee township maps which show the original land grants within present township boundaries, as well as names and other information for the original warrantee and patentee. Records about the Wyoming Valley prior to 1782 are kept in Hartford, Connecticut.

Division of Vital Statistics
State Department of Health
101 South Mercer Street / PO Box 1528
New Castle, Pennsylvania 16101
724.652.8951

Bureau of Archives and
History
PO Box 1026
Harrisburg, Pennsylvania 17108

Societies and Repositories

Adams County Pennsylvania Historical Society; PO Box 4325; Gettysburg, Pennsylvania 17325

African-American Genealogical Group; PO Box 1798; Philadelphia, Pennsylvania 19105-1798

African-American Historical & Genealogical Society, Western Pennsylvania; 1307 Pointview St.; Pittsburgh, Pennsylvania 15206

Allegheny Foothills Historical Society; Boyce Park Adm. Bldg.; 675 Old Franklin Rd.; Pittsburgh, Pennsylvania 15239

Allegheny Valley Community Library; 315 E. 6th Avenue; Tarentum, Pennsylvania 15084; 724.226.0770; <www.einpgh.org/ein/alvalley>

Altoona Public Library; 1600 Fifth Ave.; Altoona, Pennsylvania 16602-3693

American Swedish Historical Foundation; 1900 Pattison Ave.; Philadelphia, Pennsylvania 19145;

Ancient Order of Hiberians; McKeesport Heritage Center; 190 W. Schwab Ave.; Munhall, Pennsylvania 15120

Annie Halenbake Ross Library; 232 W. Main St.; Lock Haven, Pennsylvania 17745; 717.748.3321

Armstrong County Genealogical Society; 300 North McKean Street; PO Box 735; Kittanning, Pennsylvania 16201-1345; <www.angelfire.com/pa2/acgs/>

Beaver County Genealogical Society; 3225 Dutch Ridge Road; Beaver, Pennsylvania 15009; <www.rootsweb.com/~pabecgs/>

Bedford County, Pioneer Historical Society, Inc.; 242 E. John St.; Bedford, Pennsylvania 15522

Berks County Genealogical Society; 3618 Kutztown Road; Laureldale, Pennsylvania 19605;

Berks County Genealogical Society; PO Box 305; Kutztown, Pennsylvania 19530-0305

Berks County Historical Society; 940 Centre Ave.; Reading, Pennsylvania 19605

Berwick Historical Society; 102 Fast Second St.; Berwick, Pennsylvania 18603-4827; <www.berwickhistoricalsociety.org>

Blair County Genealogical Society; 431 Scotch Valley Rd.; Hollidaysburg, Pennsylvania 16648; <www.rootsweb.com/~pabcgs/>

Blair County Historical Society; PO Box 1083; Altoona, Pennsylvania 16603

Bloomsburg Public Library; 225 Market St.; Bloomsburg, Pennsylvania 17815

Bradford Landmark Society; 45 E. Corydon; Bradford, Pennsylvania 16701

Brownsville Historical Society; PO Box 24; Brownsville, Pennsylvania 15417

Bucks Co. Historical Society Library; 84 South Pine St.; Doylestown, Pennsylvania 18901

Bucks County Genealogical Society; PO Box 1092; Doylestown, Pennsylvania 18901

Bucks County Historical Society; 94 S. Pine St.; Doylestown, Pennsylvania 18901

Buhl-Henderson Community Library; 11 Sharpsville Ave.; Sharon, Pennsylvania 16146

Cambria County Historical Society; PO Box 274 West High St.; Ebensburg, Pennsylvania 15931

Cameron County Historical Society; 139 E. Fourth St.; Emporium, Pennsylvania 15834

Capital Area Genealogical Society; PO Box 4502; Harrisburg, Pennsylvania 17111-0502; <www.maley.net/cags/>

Carnegie Free Library; 1301 7th Ave.; Beaver Falls, Pennsylvania 15010

Carnegie Library of Pittsburgh; 4400 Forbes Avenue; Pittsburgh, Pennsylvania 15213-4080; 412.622.3100; Fax 412.621.1267

Carnegie Library of Pittsburgh; Penn. Dept., 4400 Forbes Ave.; Pittsburgh, Pennsylvania 15213-4080

Central Pennsylvania Genealogical Pioneers; Northumberland, Pennsylvania 17857

Centre Co. Library & Historical Museum; 203 N. Allegheny St.; Bellefonte, Pennsylvania 16823

Centre County Genealogical Society; PO Box 1135; State College, Pennsylvania 16804-1135; <www.rootsweb.com/~paccgs/>

Centre County Historical Society; 1001 E. College Ave.; State College, Pennsylvania 16801

Chester Co. Archives & Records Service; 117 W. Gay St.; West Chester, Pennsylvania 19380

Chester County Historical Society; 225 N. High St.; West Chester, Pennsylvania 19380-2691; 610.692.4800; Fax 610.692.4357

Citizens Library; 55 S. College St.; Washington, Pennsylvania 15301

City Archives of Philadelphia, Dept. of Records; 401 N. Broad Street, Suite 942; Philadelphia, Pennsylvania 19108-1099; 215.686.1580; Fax 215.686.2283

Clarion County Historical and Genealogical Society; Courthouse Square; Clarion, Pennsylvania 16214

Clearfield County Historical Society; 104 E. Pine St.; Clearfield, Pennsylvania 16830

Clinton County Genealogical Society; PO Box 193; Castanea, Pennsylvania 17726

Clinton County Historical Society; 362 E. Water St.; Lock Haven, Pennsylvania 17740

Cocalico Valley Historical Society; 249 W. Main St.; Ephrata, Pennsylvania 17522

Columbia County Historical and Genealogical Society; 225 Market Street; PO Box 360; Bloomsburg, Pennsylvania 17815-0360 <www.colcohist.gensoc.org/CCHGShome.html>

Connellsville Area Historical Society; Connellsville, Pennsylvania 15425

Cornerstone Genealogical Society; PO Box 547; Waynesburg, Pennsylvania 15370; <www.vicoa.com/cornerstone/>

Coyle Free Library; 102 N. Main St.; Chambersburg, Pennsylvania 17201

Crawford County Genealogical Society; 848 N. Main St.; Meadville, Pennsylvania 16335

Cumberland County Historical Society; PO Box 626; Carlisle, Pennsylvania 17013

Delaware County Historical Society; 85 N. Malin Rd.; Broomall, Pennsylvania 19008-1928

Division of Vital Statistics State Department of Health; 101 South Mercer St., PO Box 1528; New Castle, Pennsylvania 16103

Easton Area Public Library; 6th & Church Sts.; Easton, Pennsylvania 18042

Elizabeth Township Historical Society; 5811 Smithfield St.; Boston, Pennsylvania 15135

Elk County Historical Society; County Courthouse; Ridgway, Pennsylvania 15853

Episcopal, Diocese of Pennsylvania, The History Committee; 240 S. 4th Street; Philadelphia, Pennsylvania 19106; 215.627.0615; Fax 215.627.7550

Erie County Library System; 160 E. Front St.; Erie, Pennsylvania 16507

Erie County Historical Society; 419 State St.; Erie, Pennsylvania 16501

Erie Society for Genealogical Research; PO Box 1403; Erie, Pennsylvania 16512

Evangelical and Reformed Historical Library; 555 W. James Street; Lancaster, Pennsylvania 17603; 717.290.8711; Fax 717.393.4254

Fackenthal Library; Franklin & Marshall College; Lancaster, Pennsylvania 17602

Family History Library: 35 North West Temple Street: Salt Lake City, Utah 84150: 800.346.6044 or 801.240.2584: <www.familysearch.org>: Find a Family History Center near you: <www.familysearch.org/Eng/Library/FHC/frameset_fhc.asp>

Fayette County Genealogical Society; 24 Jefferson Street; Uniontown, Pennsylvania 15401; <www.fforward.com/gene/fcgene.htm>

Ford City Public Library; 1136 4th Ave.; Ford City, Pennsylvania 16226

Forest County Historical Society; c/o Courthouse; Tionesta, Pennsylvania 16353

Frackville Area Historical Society; 104 Broad Mountain Avenue; Frackville, Pennsylvania 17931; <www.geocities.com/Heartland/Acres/5200/>

Franklin Public Library; 421 12th St.; Franklin, Pennsylvania 16323

Friends Historical Association; Haverford College; Haverford, Pennsylvania 19041

Fulton County Historical Society; PO Box 115; McConnellsburg, Pennsylvania 17233

Genealogical Research Society; of Northeastern Pennsylvania; PO Box 1; Olyphant, Pennsylvania 18447-0001; 570.383.7466; <www.cfrobbins.com/grsnp/>

Genealogical Society of Pennsylvania; 1305 Locust Street; Philadelphia, Pennsylvania 19107-5699; 215.545.0391; Fax 215.545.0936

Genealogical Society of Pennsylvania; 215 S. Broad St., 7th Floor; Philadelphia, Pennsylvania 19107-5325; 215.545.0936; <www.libertynet.org/gspa/>

Genealogical Society of Southwestern Pennsylvania; PO Box 894; Washington, Pennsylvania 15301-0894

German Society, Pennsylvania; PO Box 397; Birdsboro, Pennsylvania 19508

Green Free Library; 134 Main St.; Wellsboro, Pennsylvania 16901

Greene County Historical Society; Rd #2; Waynesburg, Pennsylvania 15370

Heritage Society of Pennsylvania; PO Box 146; Laughlintown, Pennsylvania 15655

Hicksite Records, Friends Historical Library, Swarthmore College; 500 College Ave.; Swarthmore, Pennsylvania 19081; 610.328.8496

Historic Schaefferstown, Inc.; PO Box 1776; Schaefferstown, Pennsylvania 17088

Historical & Genealogical Society of Indiana County, Pennsylvania; 200 S. Sixth Street; Indiana, Pennsylvania 15701; <www.rootsweb.com/~paicgs/>

Historical and Genealogical Society of Jefferson County; PO Box 51; Brookville, Pennsylvania 15825

Historical and Genealogical Society of Somerset County, Inc.; PO Box 533; Somerset, Pennsylvania 15501

Historical Soc. of Evangelical & Reformed Church Archives & Libraries; College Ave. & James St.; Lancaster, Pennsylvania 17604

Historical Society of Dauphin County; 219 S. Front St.; Harrisburg, Pennsylvania 17104

Historical Society of Green Tree; 10 W. Manilla Ave.; Pittsburgh, Pennsylvania 15220

Historical Society of Pennsylvania Library; 1300 Locust St.; Philadelphia, Pennsylvania 19107; 215.732.6201; Fax 215.732.2680

Historical Society of Perry County, Headquarters and Museum; 129 N. Second St.; Newport, Pennsylvania 17074

Historical Society of Schuylkill County; 14 N. 3rd St.; Pottsville, Pennsylvania 17901

Historical Society of Western Pennsylvania/Western Pennsylvania Genealogical Society; 1212 Smallman Street; Pittsburgh, Pennsylvania 15222; 412.454.6000; Fax 412.454.6028

Historical Society of Westmoreland; 151 Old Salem Rd.; Greensburg, Pennsylvania 15601

Homestead Historical Society; 1110 Silvan Ave.; Homestead, Pennsylvania 15120

Huntingdon County Historical Society; PO Box 305; Huntingdon, Pennsylvania 16652

Indiana County Historical & Genealogical Society; So. 6th & Wayne Ave.; Indiana, Pennsylvania 15701

Indiana LDS Family Hist. Center; 366 N. 6th. St.; Indiana, Pennsylvania 15701; 724.349.1337; <www.rootsweb.com/~paifhc>

James V. Brown Library; 19 East 4th St.; Williamsport, Pennsylvania 17701

Jewish Genealogical Society of Philadelphia; 332 Harrison Ave.; Elkins Park, Pennsylvania 19117-2662

Jewish Genealogical Society of Pittsburgh; 2131 Fifth Ave.; Pittsburgh, Pennsylvania 15219

Johnstown Genealogical Society; No. 1 Mine 30; Windber, Pennsylvania 15963

Juniata County Historical Society; 498 Jefferson St., Suite B; Mifflintown, Pennsylvania 17059-1424

Kittochtinny Historical Society, Inc.; 175 E. King St.; Chambersburg, Pennsylvania 17201

Lackawanna County Historical Society; 232 Monroe Ave.; Scranton, Pennsylvania 18510

Lackawanna Hist. Soc. Library; George H. Catlin House, 232 Monroe Ave.; Scranton, Pennsylvania 18510

Lancaster County Historical Society; 230 N. President Ave.; Lancaster, Pennsylvania 17603

Lancaster Mennonite Historical Society; 2215 Millstream Road; Lancaster, Pennsylvania 17602-1499

Lawrence County Historical Society; 2nd Floor, PO Box 1745; Public library; New Castle, Pennsylvania 16103

Lebanon County Historical Society; 924 Cumberland St.; Lebanon, Pennsylvania 17042

Lehigh County Historical Society; PO Box 1548; Allentown, Pennsylvania 18105

Ligonier Valley Historical Society; Star Route East; Ligonier, Pennsylvania 15658

Lutheran Historical Society Library; Gettysburg, Pennsylvania 17325

Lutheran Theological Seminary Library; Mt. Airy, Pennsylvania 19119

Lutheran, A. R. Wentz Library, Lutheran Theological Seminary; 66 W. Confederate Ave.; Gettysburg, Pennsylvania 17325-1795; 717.334.6286; Fax 717.334.3469

Lycoming County Genealogical Society; PO Box 3625; Williamsport, Pennsylvania 17701; <members.aol.com/LCGSgen/lcgs.htm>

Lycoming County Genealogical Society; PO Box 3625; Williamsport, Pennsylvania 17701

Lycoming County Historical Society and Museum; 958 W. 4th St.; Williamsport, Pennsylvania 17701

Mahanoy and Mahantongo Historical & Preservation Society; PO Box 143; Dalmatia, Pennsylvania 17017;

Martinsburg Public Library (Blair Co.); 201 S. Walnut; Martinsburg, Pennsylvania 16662

Masontown Historical Society; PO Box 769; Masontown, Pennsylvania 15461

McKean County Genealogical Society; PO Box 207A; Derrick City, Pennsylvania 16727

McKean County Historical Society; Courthouse; Smethport, Pennsylvania 16749

Mennonite Historical Library; 565 Yoder Rd., Box 82; Harleysville, Pennsylvania 19438; 215.256.3020

Mennonite Historical Society; 2215 Millstream Road; Lancaster, Pennsylvania 17602

Mercer County Genealogical Society; PO Box 812; Sharon, Pennsylvania 16146

Mercer County Historical Society; 119 S. Pitt St.; Mercer, Pennsylvania 16137

Methodist Historical Center; 326 New St.; Philadelphia, Pennsylvania 19106

Mifflin County Historical Society; 1 W. Market St., Ste. 1; Lewistown, Pennsylvania 17044-2128

Monroe County Historical Society; 9th and Main St.; Stroudsburg, Pennsylvania 18360

Montgomery County Historical Society; 1654 Dekalb St.; Norristown, Pennsylvania 19401

Montour County Historical Society; PO Box 8, 1 Bloom St.; Danville, Pennsylvania 17821

Mt. Lebanon Public Library; 16 Castle Shannon Blvd.; Pittsburgh, Pennsylvania 15228

Muncy Historical Society and Museum of History; 131 So. Main St.; Muncy, Pennsylvania 17756

Myerstown Community Library; PO Box 242, 199 N. College St.; Myerstown, Pennsylvania 17067

National Archives-Philadelphia Branch; 9th and Market Streets; Philadelphia, Pennsylvania 19107; 215.597.3000; Fax 215.597.2303

New Castle Public Libra; 207 E. North St.; New Castle, Pennsylvania 16101

Northampton County Historical and Genealogical Society; 101 So. 4th St.; Easton, Pennsylvania 18042

Northeast Pennsylvania Genealogical Society, Inc.; PO Box 1776; Shavertown, Pennsylvania 18708-0776; <www.rootsweb.com/~panepgs/>

Northeast Regional Archives of the Evangelical Lutheran Church in America; Krauth Memorial Library, 7301 Germantown Avenue; Philadelphia, Pennsylvania 19119; 215.248.6383; Fax 215.248.4577

Northeastern Pennsylvania, Genealogical Research Society, Inc.; 210 Grant St.; Olyphant, Pennsylvania 18447

Northumberland County Historical Society; 1150 N. Front St.; Sunbury, Pennsylvania 17801

Oil City Heritage Society; PO Box 962, Oil Creek Station; Oil City, Pennsylvania 16301

Oil City Library; 2 Central Ave.; Oil City, Pennsylvania 16301

Old York Road Genealogical Society; 1030 Old York Road; Abington, Pennsylvania 19001

Orthodox, Quaker Collection, Haverford College; James P. Magill Library; Haverford, Pennsylvania 19041; 215.896.1175; Fax 215.896.1224

Osterhout Free Public Library; 71 So. Franklin St.; Wilkes-Barre, Pennsylvania 18701

Palatines to America, Pennsylvania Chapter; PO Box 280; Strasburg, Pennsylvania 17579-0280

Palmyra Area Genealogical Society; PO Box 544; Palmyra, Pennsylvania 17078

Paul Miller Ruff Library; Baltzer Meyer Hist. Soc.; RD 11, Box 211; Greensburg, Pennsylvania 15601-9711; 724.836.6915; <pa-roots.com/baltzer/index.html>

Penn. Hist. & Museum Comm., Div. of Archives & Manuscripts; PO Box 1026; Harrisburg, Pennsylvania 17108

Pennsylvania German Society; PO Box 244; Kutztown, Pennsylvania 19530-0244; (610) 894.9808;

Pennsylvania State Archives; 350 North Street; Harrisburg, Pennsylvania 17120-0090;

Pennsylvania State Archives; PO Box 1026; Harrisburg, Pennsylvania 17108-1026; 717.783.3281

Pennsylvania State Library; PO Box 1601; Harrisburg, Pennsylvania 17105-1601

Perry Historian Genealogical Society; PO Box 73; Newport, Pennsylvania 17074

Philadelphia Branch National Archives; 9th & Chestnut Sts.; Philadelphia, Pennsylvania 19107

Philadelphia Free Library; Logan Square; Philadelphia, Pennsylvania 19141

Pike County Historical Society; c/o Milford Comm. House; Milford, Pennsylvania 18337

Pinegrove Historical Society; PO Box 65; Pine Grove, Pennsylvania 17963; <www.rootsweb.com/~papghs/index.htm>

Pioneer Historical Society of Bedford County; PO Box 421; Bedford, Pennsylvania 15522

Pittsburgh, North Hills Genealogists; c/o Northland Public Library; 300 Cumberland Rd.; Pittsburgh, Pennsylvania 15237-5455

Potter County Historical Society; 308 N. Main St.; Coudersport, Pennsylvania 16915

Presbyterian Historical Society, Northern Region; 425 Lombard Street; Philadelphia, Pennsylvania 19147-1516; 215.627.1852; Fax 215.627.0509

Punxsutawney Area Historical and Genealogical Society; 401 W. Mahoning Street; Punxsutawney, Pennsylvania 15767; <users.penn.com/~mweimer/historcl.html>

Quakers, Friends Historical Library of Swarthmore College, Swarthmore College; 500 College Ave.; Swarthmore, Pennsylvania 19081; 610.328.8496; Fax 610.328.7329

Reading Public Library; Fifth & Franklin Sts.; Reading, Pennsylvania 19607

Resource & Research Center for Beaver Co. & Local History; Carnegie Free Library, 1301 Seventh Ave.; Beaver Falls, Pennsylvania 15010

Roman Catholic, Archives of the American Catholic Historical Society of Philadelphia, St. Charles Borromeo Seminary; 100 E. Wynnewood Road; Wynnewood, Pennsylvania 19096; 610.667.2125; Fax 610.664.7913

Schlow-Memorial Library; 100 E. Beaver Ave.; State College, Pennsylvania 16801

Scottish Historic and Research Society of the Delaware Valley, Inc.; 102 St. Paul's Rd.; Ardmore, Pennsylvania 19003

Sewickley Valley Historical Society; 200 Broad; Sewickley, Pennsylvania 15143

Slovenian Genealogical Society; 609 Gale Rd.; Camp Hill, Pennsylvania 17011

Snyder County Historical Society; 30 E. Market St.; PO Box 276; Middleburg, Pennsylvania 17842

Society of Friends (Quakers), Orthodox Records, Magill Historical Library; Haverford College; Haverford, Pennsylvania 19041; 610.896.1175; Fax 610.896.1102

Sons of the American Revolution, Pennsylvania Society; 510 Vine St.; Perkasie, Pennsylvania 18944

Sons of Union Veterans of the Civil War; PO Box 1865; Harrisburg, Pennsylvania 17105;

South Central Pennsylvania Genealogical Society, Inc.; PO Box 1824; York, Pennsylvania 17405; <www.innernet.net/hively/SouthCentralPAGenealogicalSociety.htm>

Spruance Library, Bucks Co. Hist. Soc.; 84 S. Pine St.; Doylestown, Pennsylvania 18901-4999; 215.345.0210

St. Marys and Benzinger Township Historical Society, Genealogical Dept.; 319 Eric Ave.; St. Marys, Pennsylvania 15857

State Library of Pennsylvania, Commonwealth Libraries; Walnut St. and Commonwealth Ave., PO Box 1601; Harrisburg, Pennsylvania 17105; 717.787.4440; Fax 717.783.5420

Sullivan County Historical Society; Courthouse Square; LaPorte, Pennsylvania 18626

Susquehanna Co. Free Library; Monument Square; Montrose, Pennsylvania 18801

Susquehanna County Historical Society; Montrose, Pennsylvania 18801

Susquehanna Depot Historical Society, Inc.; PO Box 161; Susquehanna, Pennsylvania 18847

Tarentum Genealogical Society; PO Box 66; Tarentum, Pennsylvania 15084; <www.targensoc.homestead.com/home.html>

The Eastern Baptist Theological Seminary; City Avenue at Lancaster Avenue; Philadelphia, Pennsylvania 19104; 610.642.9692

Tioga County Historical Society; 120 Main St., PO Box 724; Wellsboro, Pennsylvania 16901

Tri-County Heritage Society; PO Box 352; Morgantown, Pennsylvania 19543

Tulpehocken Settlement Historical Society; 116 N. Front St.; PO Box 53; Womelsdorf, Pennsylvania 19567

Tuscarora Township Historical Society, Bradford County; R.D. #2, Box 105-C; Laceyville, Pennsylvania 18623

Union County Historical Society; Courthouse; Lewisburg, Pennsylvania 17837

Uniontown Library; 24 Jefferson St., Pennsylvania Rm., 2nd Floor; Uniontown, Pennsylvania 15401-3699

Univ. of Pennsylvania Library; Central Bldg., 34th St.; Philadelphia, Pennsylvania 19104

University Library; Pennsylvania State Univ.; University Park, Pennsylvania 16802

Venango County Genealogy Club; 2 Central Ave.; Oil City, Pennsylvania 16301

Venango County Historical Society; PO Box 101; 301 S. Park St.; Franklin, Pennsylvania 16323

Warren County Genealogical Society; 6 Main St.; Warren, Pennsylvania 16365

Warren County Historical Society; PO Box 427; Warren, Pennsylvania 16365

Warren Public Library; PO Box 489, 205 Market St.; Warren, Pennsylvania 16365

Washington County Historical Society and Library; LeMoyne House, 49 E. Maiden St.; Washington, Pennsylvania 15301

Wattsburg Area Historical Society; PO Box 240; Wattsburg, Pennsylvania 16442-0240

Wayne Co. Hist. Soc.; 810 Main St.; Honesdale, Pennsylvania 18431; 570.253.5468; <www.waynehistorypa.or>

Wayne County Historical Society; 910 Main St, PO Box 44; Honesdale, Pennsylvania 18431

Western Pennsylvania Afro-American Historical & Genealogical Society; 1307 Point View St.; Pittsburgh, Pennsylvania 15206

Western Pennsylvania Genealogical Society; c/o Carnegie Library; 4400 Forbes Ave.; Pittsburgh, Pennsylvania 15213.4080

Windber-Johnstown Area Genealogical Society; PO Box 5048; Johnstown, Pennsylvania 15904-5048; <www.ccacc.cc.pa.us/library/genealogy.htm>

Wyoming County Historical Society; PO Box 309; Tunkhannock, Pennsylvania 18657-9998;

York Co. Archives; 150 Pleasant Acres Rd.; York, Pennsylvania 17402; 717.840.7222; Fax 717.840.7224

York County Historical Society; 250 E. Market St.; York, Pennsylvania 17403

Bibliography and Record Sources

General Sources

Baumann, Roland M. *Guide to the Microfilm of the Records of Pennsylvania's Revolutionary Governments, 1775-1790: (Record Group 27) in the Pennsylvania State Archives.* Harrisburg: Pennsylvania Historical and Museum Commission, 1978, 1979.

Bining, Arthur C., et al. *Writing on Pennsylvania History: A Bibliography.* Harrisburg, Pennsylvania: Pennsylvania Historical and Museum Commission, 1946.

Blockson, Charles L. *African Americans in Pennsylvania: A History and Guide.* Baltimore, Maryland: A DuForcelf book published by Black Classic Press, 1994.

Brecht, Samuel Kriebel. *The Genealogical Record of the Schwenkfelder Families: Seekers of Religious Liberty Who Fled from Silesia to Saxony and Thence to Pennsylvania in the Years 1731 to 1737.* New York: Rand McNally, printed for the Board of Publication of the Schwenkfelder Church, Pennsburg, Pennsylvania, 1923.

Bricker, Florence M., comp. and ed. *Church and Pastoral Records in the Archives of the United Church of Christ and the Evangelical and Reformed Historical Society, Lancaster, Pennsylvania* Lancaster, Pennsylvania: The Society, 1982.

Browing, Charles Henry. *Welsh Settlement of Pennsylvania.* Philadelphia, Pennsylvania: William J. Campbell, 1912.

Card Index to Pennsylvania Germans in the Magazines: Proceedings and Addresses (Pennsylvania German Society); Pennsylvania Dutchman; PGFS or Pennsylvania German Folklore Society; Penn-Germania; the Pennsylvania-German; Historical Review of Berks County. Salt Lake City: Genealogical Society of Utah, 1978. Microfilm, 38 rolls.

Chester County Historical Society (West Chester, Pennsylvania). *Genealogical Clippings File, Up to 1968.* Microfilm, 151 rolls.

Chester County Historical Society (West Chester, Pennsylvania). *Genealogical Manuscripts Up to 1968.* (Salt Lake City: Filmed by the Genealogical Society of Utah, 1968). Microfilm, 104 rolls.

Clint, Florence. *Pennsylvania Area Key: A Guide to the Genealogical Records of the State of Pennsylvania; Including Maps, Histories, Charts and Other Helpful Materials.* 2nd ed. Denver: Area Keys, 1976.

Colonial Society of Pennsylvania (Philadelphia, Pennsylvania). *Applications for Membership in Alphabetical Order by Member With a Complete Genealogy Back to Original Ancestor.* Salt Lake City: Genealogical Society of Utah, 1968

Crist, Robert Grant. *Penn's Example to the Nations: 300 Years of the Holy Experiment.* Harrisburg, Pennsylvania: Pennsylvania Council of Churches, Inc. for the Pennsylvania Religious Tercentenary Committee, 1987.

Cutler, Jean H. *Directory of Museums and Historical Organizations in Pennsylvania.* Harrisburg, Pennsylvania: The Federation, 1991.

Donehoo, George P. *Pennsylvania; A History.* 9 vols. New York: Lewis Historical Pub. Co., 1926-1931.

Downey, Dennis B. and Francis J. Bremer, *A Guide to the History of Pennsylvania.* Westport, Connecticut: Greenwood Press, 1993.

Dunaway, Wayland Fuller. *The Scotch-Irish of Colonial Pennsylvania.* Chapel Hill, North Carolina: The University of North Carolina Press, 1944.

Egle, William Henry, ed. *Notes and Queries: Historical, Biographical, and Genealogical, Relating Chiefly to Interior Pennsylvania. 1894-1904.* Reprint, Baltimore: Genealogical Publishing, 1971.

Egle, William Henry. *An Illustrated History of the Commonwealth of Pennsylvania: Civil, Political, and Military from its Earliest Settlement to the Present Time, Including Historical Descriptions of Each County in the State, Their Towns, and Industrial Resources.* Philadelphia: E. M. Gardner, 1880.

Egle, William Henry. *Pennsylvania Genealogies, Chiefly Scotch-Irish and German.* Reprint. Baltimore: Genealogical Publishing, 1969.

Elliot, Margaret Sherburne. *Guide to Depositories of Manuscript Collections in Pennsylvania.* Harrisburg, Pennsylvania: Pennsylvania Historical Commission, 1939.

Ely, Warren S. *Warren S. Ely Collection, Genealogical Data, Letters.* (Salt Lake City: Filmed by the Genealogical Society of Utah, 1967). Microfilm, 46 rolls.

Eshleman, Frank. *Historic Background and Annals of the Swiss and German Pioneer Settlers of Southeastern Pennsylvania and of their Remote Ancestors from the Middle of the Dark Ages, Down* to the Time of the Revolutionary War…With Particular Reference to the German-Swiss Mennonites or Anabaptists, the Amish and Other Non-resistant Sects. 1917. Reprint. Baltimore: Genealogical Publishing Co., 1969.

Evans, Frank B. and Martha L. Simonetti, eds. *Summary Guide to the Pennsylvania State Archives*, Harrisburg, Pennsylvania: Pennsylvania Historical and Museum Commission, 1970.

Genealogical and Biographical Records File, Up to 1968. (Salt Lake City: Filmed by the Genealogical Society of Utah, 1968). Microfilm, 41 rolls.

Genealogies of Pennsylvania Families: From the Pennsylvania Genealogical Magazine. 3 vols. Baltimore, Maryland: Genealogical Publishing, 1982.

Genealogies of Pennsylvania Families: From the Pennsylvania Magazine of History and Biography. Baltimore: Genealogical Publishing, 1981

Gerberich, Albert Henry. *Pennsylvania German Families.* (Salt Lake City: Filmed by the Genealogical Society of Utah, 1967). Microfilm, 16 rolls.

Gibson, Gail M. *Pennsylvania Directory of Historical Organizations, 1970.* Harrisburg, Pennsylvania: Pennsylvania Historical and Museum Commission, 1970.

Glenn, Thomas Allen. *Merion in the Welsh Tract: With Sketches of the Townships of Haverford and Radnor, Historical and Genealogical Collections Concerning the Welsh Barony in the Province of Pennsylvania, Settled by the Cymric Quaker in 1682.* Norristown, Pennsylvania: Herald Press, 1896.

Glenn, Thomas Allen. *Welsh Founders of Pennsylvania.* 2 vols. Oxford: Fox, Jones and Co., 1911-1913.

Godcharles, Frederic Antes. *Index to the Encyclopedia of Pennsylvania Biography.* [Philadelphia]: W.D. Stock, 1996 (Baltimore, Md.: Printed for Clearfield Co. by Genealogical Pub. Co.).

Grand Army of the Republic, Department of Pennsylvania. *Record of Eligibility of Ladies of the Grand Army of the Republic, Department of Pennsylvania 1883-1992.* Salt Lake City: Genealogical Society of Utah, 1993.

Heisey, John W. *Handbook for Genealogical Research in Pennsylvania.* Indianapolis: Heritage House, 1985.

Hinshaw, William Wade. *The William Wade Hinshaw Index to Quaker Meeting Records in the Friends Library in Swarthmore College, Pennsylvania.* (Salt Lake City: Filmed by the Genealogical Society of Utah, 1957). Microfilm, 73 rolls.

Historical Records Survey (Pennsylvania). *Inventory of Church Archives in Pennsylvania.* Microfilm of original records in the State Archives in Harrisburg. (Salt Lake City: Filmed by the Genealogical Society of Utah, 1977). 72 microfilm.

Historical Records Survey (Pennsylvania). *Inventory of Church Archives, Society of Friends in Pennsylvania.* Philadelphia: Friends' Historical Association, 1941.

Historical Records Survey (Pennsylvania). *Inventory of the Church Archives of Pennsylvania Presbyterian Churches.* Microreproductions of original records at the Presbyterian Historical Society, in Philadelphia, Pennsylvania. (Salt Lake City: Filmed by the Genealogical Society of Utah, 1967, 1972). 24 microfilm.

Historical Records Survey (Pennsylvania). *Inventory of the County Archives of Pennsylvania: Records of the Works Project Administration, Pennsylvania Historical Writer's Project.*

Microfilms of original records in the Pennsylvania State Archives. (Salt Lake City: Filmed by the Genealogical Society of Utah, 1977). 5 microfilm.

Historical Society of Pennsylvania. *Guide to the Manuscript Collections of the Historical Society of Pennsylvania.* Philadelphia: The Society, 1991.

Hocker, Edward W. *Genealogical Data Relating to the German Settlers of Pennsylvania….* 1743-1800. 1935.

Hoenstine, Floyd G. *Guide to Genealogical and Historical Research in Pennsylvania.* Hollidaysburg, Pennsylvania: the author, 1978. Supplements 1985, 1990.

Huguenot Society of Pennsylvania. *Application Papers; Ancestor Index.* (Salt Lake City: Filmed by the Genealogical Society of Utah, 1967). Microfilm, 12 rolls.

Iscrupe, William L., and Shirley G. M. Iscrupe, comps. *Pennsylvania Line: A Research Guide to Pennsylvania Genealogy and Local History.* 4th ed. Laughlintown, Pennsylvania: Southwest Pennsylvania Genealogical Services, 1990.

Jordan, John W. *Genealogical and Personal History of the Allegheny Valley, Pennsylvania.* 3 vols. New York: Lewis Historical Publishing, 1913.

Jordan, John W., ed. *Genealogical and Personal History of Northern Pennsylvania.* 3 vols. New York: Lewis Historical Publishing, 1913.

Jordan, John W., et al. *Encyclopedia of Pennsylvania Biography.* 32 vols. New York: Lewis Historical Publishing Co, 1914-67.

Jordan, John W., et.al. *Colonial and Revolutionary Families of Pennsylvania.* 11 vols. New York: Lewis Publishing, 1911-65.

Manning, Barbara. *Genealogical Abstracts from Newspapers of the German Reformed Church, 1830-1839.* Bowie, Maryland: Heritage Books, 1992.

Manning, Barbara. *Genealogical Abstracts from Newspapers of the German Reformed Church 1840-1843.* Bowie, Md.: Heritage Books, Inc., 1995.

Manuscript Card Catalog of the Genealogical Society of Pennsylvania. Salt Lake City: Genealogical Society of Utah, 1964.

McConnell, Michael N. *A Country Between: The Upper Ohio Valley and Its Peoples, 1724-1774.* Lincoln, NE: University of Nebraska Press, 1992.

Meyen, Emil. *Bibliography on the Colonial Germans of North America: Especially the Pennsylvania Germans and their Descendants.* Reprint. Baltimore, Maryland: Genealogical Publishing, 1982.

Parker, J. Carlyle. *Pennsylvania and Middle Atlantic States Genealogical Manuscripts: A User's Guide to the Manuscript Collections of the Genealogical Society of Pennsylvania* (Turlock, CA: Marietta Publishing, 1986.

Parsons, William T. *The Pennsylvania Dutch: A Persistent Minority.* Boston: Twayne Publishers, 1976.

Pennsylvania Archives. Philadelphia: J. Severns, 1852-1856, 1874-1935.

Pennsylvania Biographical Dictionary: People of All Times and Places Who Have Been Important to the History and Life of the State. Wilmington, Delaware: American Historical Publications, 1989.

Pennsylvania Historical Society. *Genealogical Collections; Families of Pennsylvania, New Jersey, Etc., 1700- 1950.* Salt Lake City: Genealogical Society of Utah, 1966.

Pennsylvania Historical Survey, Division of Community Service Programs, Work Projects Administration. *A Checklist of Pennsylvania Newspapers, Philadelphia County*. Harrisburg, Pennsylvania: Pennsylvania Historical Commission, 1944.

Pennsylvania Historical Survey. *County Government and Archives in Pennsylvania*. Harrisburg, Pennsylvania: Pennsylvania Historical and Museum Commission, 1947.

Presbyterian Historical Society (Philadelphia, Pennsylvania). *Miscellaneous Biographical Collection*. (Salt Lake City: Filmed by the Genealogical Society of Utah, 1967).

Rauco, Louis F. *Pennsylvania Newspapers and Selected Out-of-State Newspapers* [S. l.: s. n.], 1984.

Richman, Irwin. *Historical Manuscript Depositories in Pennsylvania*. Harrisburg: The Pennsylvania Historical and Museum Commission, 1965.

Rider, Fremont, ed. *American Genealogical- Biographical Index*. Vols. 1-186+. Middletown, Connecticut: Godfrey Memorial Library, 1952-.

Robson, Charles, ed. *The Biographical Encyclopedia of Pennsylvania of the Nineteenth Century*. Philadelphia, Pennsylvania: Galaxy, 1874.

Rosenberger, Homer Tope. *The Pennsylvania Germans, 1891-1965, Frequently Known as the "Pennsylvania Dutch"* [S.l.]: H. T. Rosenberger, 1966, Lancaster, Pennsylvania: Printed for the Pennsylvania German Society.

Salisbury, Ruth, ed. *Pennsylvania Newspapers, a Bibliography and Union List*. Pittsburgh: Pennsylvania Library Association, 1969

Schory, Eva Draegert. *Every Name Index to Egle's Notes and Queries*. 2 vols. Decatur, Illinois: Decatur Genealogical Society, 1982-1986.

Schweitzer, George K. *Pennsylvania Genealogical Research*. Knoxville, Tennessee: G. Schweitzer, 1986.

Stapleton, Ammon. *Memorials of the Huguenots in America, With Special Reference to Their Emigration [sic] to Pennsylvania*. 1901. Reprint: Baltimore: Genealogical Publishing, 1969.

State Library of Pennsylvania (Harrisburg). *Genealogical Surname Card Index*. Microfilm of records in the Pennsylvania State Library. (Salt Lake City: Filmed by the Genealogical Society of Utah, 1977). Microfilm, 42 rolls.

State Library of Pennsylvania (Harrisburg, Pennsylvania). *County Records Card File, 1651-1977*. Microfilm of original records in the Pennsylvania State Library. (Salt Lake City: Filmed by the Genealogical Society of Utah, 1977).

Stevens, Sylvester Kirby, and Donald H. Kent, ed. *Bibliography of Pennsylvania History*. 2nd ed. Harrisburg, Pennsylvania: Pennsylvania Historical and Museum Commission, 1957.

Stevens, Sylvester Kirby. *Pennsylvania: The Heritage of a Commonwealth*. 4 vol. West Palm Beach, Florida: The American Historical Company, 1968.

Suran, Frank M. *Guide to the Record Groups in the Pennsylvania State Archives*. Harrisburg, Pennsylvania: Pennsylvania Historical and Museum Commission, 1980.

Trussell, John B. B. Jr. *Pennsylvania Historical Bibliography*. Vols. 1-6. Harrisburg, Pennsylvania: Pennsylvania Historical and Museum Commission, 1979-1989.

Turner, Edward Raymond. *The Negro in Pennsylvania: Slavery-Servitude-Freedom, 1639-1861*. New York: Negro Universities Press, 1969.

United States. Commissioner of Internal Revenue. *Internal Revenue Assessment Lists for Pennsylvania, 1862-1865*. Washington D.C.: National Archives and Record Service, 1975. Microfilm, 106 rolls.

United States. Secretary of the Treasury. *United States Direct Tax of 1798: Tax Lists for the State of Pennsylvania*. Salt Lake City: Genealogical Society of Utah, 1962. Microfilm, 23 rolls.

Virdin, Donald Odell. *Pennsylvania Family Histories and Genealogies*. Bowie, Maryland: Heritage Books, 1992.

Wall, Carol, ed. *Bibliography of Pennsylvania History: A Supplement*. Harrisburg, Pennsylvania: Pennsylvania Historical and Museum Commission, 1976.

Whipkey, Harry E. *Guide to the Manuscript Groups in the Pennsylvania State Archives*. Harrisburg, Pennsylvania: Pennsylvania Historical and Museum Commission, 1976.

Wilkinson, Norman B. *Bibliography of Pennsylvania History*. 2nd ed. Harrisburg, Pennsylvania: Pennsylvania Historical and Museum Commission, 1957.

Woodroofe, Helen Hutchison, comp. *A Genealogist's Guide to Pennsylvania Records*. Reprinted from the Pennsylvania Genealogical Magazine. Philadelphia: Genealogical Society of Pennsylvania, 1995.

Works Progress Administration. *Inventory of the Church Archives of Pennsylvania Presbyterian Churches*. (Salt Lake City: Filmed by the Genealogical Society of Utah, 1967, 1972).

Atlases, Maps and Gazetteers

Atlas of Pennsylvania. Philadelphia: Temple University, 1989.

Bien, Joseph R. *Atlas of the State of Pennsylvania: Grom Original Surveys and Various Loval Surveys Revised and Corrected*. New York: Julius Bein & co., 1900.

County Historical Maps. Harrisburg, Pennsylvania: Archives Publishing of Pennsylvania, [19–].

Espenschade, Abraham H. *Pennsylvania Place Names*. 1925. Reprint, Baltimore, Maryland: Genealogical Publishing, 1970.

Gordon, Thomas F. *A Gazetteer of the State of Pennsylvania*. Philadelphia: T. Belknap, 1832.

Historical Collections of the State of Pennsylvania: Containing a Copious Selection of the Most Interesting Facts, Traditions, Biographical Sketches, Anecdotes, etc., Relating to its History and Antiquities, Both General and Local, with Topographical Descriptions of Every County and all the Larger Towns in the State. Philadelphia: G. W. Gorton, [1843?] (New Haven, Connecticut: Durrie and Peck [1843]).

Kay, John L., and Chester M. Smith, Jr. *Pennsylvania Postal History*. Lawrence, Massachusetts: Quarterman Publications, 1976.

Long, John H., ed. *Historical Atlas and Chronology of County Boundaries, 1788-1980*. Vol. 1, Delaware, Maryland, New Jersey, Pennsylvania. Boston: G.K. Hall, 1984.

Long, John H., ed. *Pennsylvania: Atlas of Historical County Boundaries*. New York: Charles Scribner's Sons, Simon and Schuster Macmillan, 1996.

Pennsylvania Gazetteer. Wilmington, DE: American Historical Publications, 1989.

Russ, William A., Jr. *How Pennsylvania County Maps*. Lyndon Station, University Park: Pennsylvania Historical Association, 1966.

Scott, Joseph. *A Geographical Description of Pennsylvania: Also of the Counties Respectively, in the Order in Which They Were Established by the Legislature: With an Alphabetical List of the Townships in Each County; and Their Population in 1800.* Philadelphia: Robert Cochran, 1806. Reprint, Microfiche, Early American Imprints, Second Series, no. 11331.

Simonetti, Martha L. comp., Donald H. Kent and Harry E. Whipkey, eds., *Descriptive List of the Map Collection in the Pennsylvania State Archives.* Harrisburg, Pennsylvania; Pennsylvania Historical and Museum Commission, 1976

United States, Geological Survey, *Pennsylvania: Index to Topographic and Other Map Coverage.* Reston, Virginia: The Survey, [1983?]

Walling, H. F., and O.W. Gray. *Historical Topographical Atlas of the State of Pennsylvania.* 1872; reprint, Knightstown, Indiana: Bookmark, 1977.

Census Records

Available Census Records and Census Substitutes

Federal Census 1790, 1800, 1810, 1820, 1830, 1840, 1850, 1860, 1870, 1880, 1900, 1910, 1920, 1930.

Federal Mortality Schedules 1850, 1860, 1870, 1880.

Union Veterans and Widows 1890.

U.S. Direct Tax 1798.

Dollarhide, William. *The Census Book: A Genealogist's Guide to Federal Census Facts, Schedules and Indexes.* Bountiful, Utah: Heritage Quest, 1999.

Kemp, Thomas Jay. *The American Census Handbook.* Wilmington, Delaware: Scholarly Resources, Inc., 2001.

Szucs, Loretto Dennis, and Matthew Wright. *Finding Answers in U.S. Census Records.* Ancestry Publishing, 2001

Thorndale, William, and William Dollarhide. *Map Guide to the U.S. Federal Censuses, 1790-1920.* Baltimore: Genealogical Publishing Co., 1987.

United States, Census Office, *Non-population Census Schedules for Pennsylvania; Agricultural Schedules, 1850-1880.* Washington: National Archives, 1970. Microfilm, 61 rolls.

United States, Census Office, *Non-population Census Schedules for Pennsylvania; Manufacturers Schedules 1850-1880.* Washington, D.C.: National Archives, 1971 and [19–?]; [Wooster, OH]: Microfilmed by Micro Photo Division of Bell & Howell. Microfilm, 21 rolls.

Court Records, Probate and Wills

Armstrong, Edward, ed. *Record of Upland Court from the 14th of November, 1676, the 14th of June, 1681.* (Salt Lake City: Filmed by the Genealogical Society of Utah, 1969).

Beers, Donna. *Pennsylvania in the 1700's: An Index to Who Was There and Where.* Warrensburg, Missouri: D. Beers, 1998.

Brodhead, John Romeyn, agent; and E. B. O'Callaghan, ed. *Documents Relative to the Colonial History of the State of New York: Procured in Holland, England, and France.* Albany, New York: Weed, Parsons & Co., Print, 1853-1887.

Catanese, Lynn Ann. *Guide to Records of the Court of Common Pleas, Chester County, Pennsylvania, 1681-1900: Records of the Prothonotary, Civil Records of the Sheriff, Select Civil Records of the Circuit Court of Chester County and the Supreme Court of Pennsylvania.* West Chester, Pennsylvania: Chester County Historical Society, 1987.

Catanese, Lynn Ann. *Guide to Records of the Court of Quarter Sessions, Chester County, Pennsylvania, 1681-1969: Records of the Clerk of Courts, Records of the Court of Oyer and Terminer and General Jail Delivery, Criminal Records of the Sheriff.* West Chester, Pennsylvania: Chester County Historical Society, 1988.

Pennsylvania. Court of Quarter Sessions (Philadelphia County). *Court Docket, 1753-1879.* (Salt Lake City: Filmed by the Genealogical Society of Utah, 1974).

Pennsylvania. Orphans' Court (Philadelphia County). *Orphans' Court Records, 1719-1880: Orphans' Court Index, 1719-1938.* Salt Lake City: Genealogical Society of Utah, 1947, 1980-81. Microfilm, 417 rolls.

Philadelphia County (Pennsylvania). *Register of Wills.* Wills, 1682-1916; Indexes to Wills, 1682-1924. Salt Lake City: Genealogical Society of Utah, 1947, 1981-82. Microfilm, 327 rolls.

Registrar's Book of Governor Keith's Court of Chancery of the Province of Pennsylvania, 1720-1735. Reprint. Harrisburg, Pennsylvania: Pennsylvania Bar Association, 1941.

United States. District Court (Pennsylvania: Eastern District). *Law Records, 1789-1844.* Washington, D.C.: National Archives. Central Plains Region, 1977. 32 microfilm.

Emigration, Immigration, Migration and Naturalization

Bentley, Elizabeth P., and Michael H. Tepper. *Passenger Arrivals at the Port of Philadelphia, 1800-1819.* Baltimore, Maryland: Genealogical Publishing, 1986.

Boyer, Carl. *Ship Passenger Lists, Pennsylvania and Delaware, 1641-1825.* Newhall, California: C. Boyer, 1980.

Egle, William Henry. *Names of Foreigners Who Took the Oath of Allegiance to the Province and State of Pennsylvania, 1727-1775, with Foreign Arrivals, 1786-1808.* Reprint. Baltimore: Genealogical Publishing Co., 1967.

Emigrants to Pennsylvania, 1641-1819: A Consolidation of Ship Passenger Lists from the Pennsylvania Magazine of History and Biography. Baltimore, Maryland: Genealogical Publishing, 1975.

Filby, P. William, and Mary K. Meyer. *Philadelphia Naturalization Records, an Index to Records of Aliens' Declarations of Intentions and/or Oaths of Allegiance, 1789-1880....* Detroit, MI: Gale Research, 1982.

Filby, P. William. *Passenger and Immigration Lists Index.* 15 vols. Detroit: Gale Research, 1981-.

Giuseppi, M. S., ed. *Naturalizations of Foreign Protestants in the American And West Indian Colonies (Pursuant to Statute 13 George II, c. 7).* (Originally published as *Publications of the Huguenot Society of London*, volume XXIV, London, 1921). Reprint, Baltimore: Genealogical Pub. Co., 1969.

Immigrants to Pennsylvania, 1600's-1800's. [S.l.]: Brøderbund, 1999. CD-ROM.

Koger, M.V. *Index to the Names of 30,000 Immigrants - German, Swiss, Dutch and French - into Pennsylvania, 1727-1776.* (Salt Lake City: Filmed by Genealogical Society of Utah, 1972).

Myers, Albert C., comp. *Notes on Immigrants to Pennsylvania, 1681-1737.* Microfilm of manuscripts (54 vols.) at the Chester County Historical Society, West Chester, Pennsylvania. (Salt Lake City: Filmed by the Genealogical Society of Utah, 1968). Microfilm, 14 rolls.

Pennsylvania. Court of Common Pleas (Philadelphia County). *Declarations of Intention, 1821-1911.* Microfilm of original records at the Philadelphia City Archives. (Salt Lake City: Genealogical Society of Utah, 1974). Microfilm, 38 rolls.

Pennsylvania. Court of Common Pleas (Philadelphia County). *Petitions for Naturalization 1793-1906; Indexes 1793-1930.* Microfilm of original records at the Philadelphia City Archives. (Salt Lake City: Genealogical Society of Utah, 1974). Microfilm, 176 rolls.

Pennsylvania. Court of Quarter Sessions (Philadelphia County). *Declarations of Intentions, 1810-1932; Index, 1810-1887.* Microfilm of original records at the Philadelphia city archives. (Salt Lake City: Genealogical Society of Utah, 1974, 1991). Microfilm, 48 rolls.

Pennsylvania. Court of Quarter Sessions (Philadelphia County). *Petitions for Naturalization 1800-1929; Indexes 1802-1930.* Microfilm of original records at the Philadelphia city archives. (Salt Lake City: Genealogical Society of Utah, 1974). Microfilm, 185 rolls.

Pennsylvania. Supreme Executive Council. *Application for Passes, 1775-1790.* Harrisburg, Pennsylvania: Pennsylvania Historical & Museum Commission, [1978?]

Reaman, George Elmore. *The Trail of the Black Walnut.* Reprint. Baltimore, Md.: Genealogical Pub. Co., Inc., (1993.

Strassburger, Ralph Beaver, and William John Hinke. *Pennsylvania German Pioneers: A Publication of the Original Lists of Arrivals in the Port of Philadelphia from 1727 to 1808.* Norristown, Pennsylvania: Pennsylvania German Society, 1934.

United States. Circuit Court (Pennsylvania: Eastern District). *Naturalization Petitions and Records, 1795-1911.* Microfilm of original records at the National Archives, Philadelphia Branch, Philadelphia, Pennsylvania. (Salt Lake City: Genealogical Society of Utah, 1987, 1990-91). Microfilm, 53 rolls.

Westcott, Thompson. *Names of Persons Who Took the Oath of Allegiance to the State of Pennsylvania Between the Years 1777 and 1789: With a History of the "Test Laws" of Pennsylvania.* 1865. Reprint, Baltimore: Genealogical Pub. Co., 1965.

Land and Property

Boyd, Julian P., and Robert J. Taylor. *Susquehanna Company Papers.* 11 vols. Ithaca, New York: Cornell University Press, 1962-71.

Egle, William Henry, ed. *Early Pennsylvania Land Records: Minutes of The Board of Property.* Baltimore: Genealogical Publishing, 1976.

Egle, William Henry. *Warrantees of Land in the Several Counties of the State of Pennsylvania, 1730-1898.* 3 vols. Harrisburg, Pennsylvania: W.S. Ray, State Printer, 1897.

Hone, Wade E. *Land and Property Research in the United States.* Salt Lake City: Ancestry Incorporated, 1997.

Munger, Donna Bingham. *Pennsylvania Land Records: A History and Guide for Research.* Wilmington, DE: Scholarly Resources, 1991.

Pennsylvania, Bureau of Land Records, *Patent Books, 1676-1960.* Harrisburg, Pennsylvania: Bureau of Land Records, 1957?-1972.

Pennsylvania, Bureau of Land Records, *Warrant Register, 1682-1950.* Microfilm of original records found in the Bureau of Land Records in Harrisburg, Pennsylvania (Salt Lake City: Genealogical Society of Utah, 1976). 6 microfilm.

Pennsylvania, Land Office, *Caveats, 1699-1890.* Salt Lake City: Genealogical Society of Utah, 1976. Microfilm, 19 rolls.

Pennsylvania, Land Office, *Depositions, 1683-1881.* Microfilm of original records in the Pennsylvania Bureau of Land Records, Harrisburg, Pennsylvania. (Salt Lake City: Genealogical Society of Utah, 1976).

Pennsylvania, Land Office, *Original Warrants of Depreciation Lands, 1780-1800.* Microfilm of original records in the Pennsylvania Bureau of Land Records, Harrisburg, Pennsylvania. (Salt Lake City: Genealogical Society of Utah, 1976).

Pennsylvania, Land Office, *Proof of Settlement Records, 1797-1869.* Salt Lake City: Genealogical Society of Utah, 1976. Microfilm, 15 rolls.

Pennsylvania, Surveyor General. *Original Surveys, 1682-1920.* Microfilm of original records in the Bureau of Land Records in Harrisburg, Pennsylvania (Salt Lake City: Genealogical Society of Utah, 1976). Microfilm, 499 rolls.

Pennsylvania, Surveyor General's Office, *Donation Lands Records, 1780-1800.* Microfilm of original records in the Pennsylvania Bureau of Land Records, Harrisburg, Pennsylvania. (Salt Lake City: Genealogical Society of Utah, 1976).

Pennsylvania. Board of Property. *Board of Property Papers, 1682-1850.* Microfilm of original records in the Pennsylvania Bureau of Land Records, Harrisburg, Pennsylvania. (Salt Lake City: Genealogical Society of Utah, 1976). Microfilm, 19 rolls.

Pennsylvania. Secretary of the Land Office. *Rent Rolls, 1703-1744.* Microfilm of original records in the State Archives in Harrisburg. (Salt Lake City: Genealogical Society of Utah, 1979).

Pennsylvania. Supreme Court. *Sheriff's Deed Book for the Eastern District, 1796-1876.* Microfilms of original records in the Pennsylvania State Archives. (Salt Lake City: Filmed by the Genealogical Society of Utah, 1977). 4 microfilm.

Weinberg, Allen, and Thomas E. Slatterly. *Warrants and Surveys of the Province of Pennsylvania Including the Three Lower Counties, 1759.* Philadelphia: City of Philadelphia, Department of Records, 1965.

Military

Bates, Samuel P. *History of Pennsylvania Volunteers.* Harrisburg, Pennsylvania: state printer, 1869-71.

Cope, Harry E. *Soldiers and Widows of Soldiers of the Revolutionary War Granted Pensions by the Commonwealth of Pennsylvania.* [n.d.]

Hackenburg, Randy W. *Pennsylvania in the War with Mexico.* Shippensburg, Pennsylvania: White Mane Pub. Co., 1992.

Historical Society of Pennsylvania. *Index to Pennsylvania in the War of the Revolution: Battalions and Line, 1775-1783; Associated Battalions and Militia, 1775-1783.* Microfilm of the original records at the Historical Society of Pennsylvania in Philadelphia, Pennsylvania. (Salt Lake City: Genealogical Society of Utah, 1966.) 10 microfilm.

Linn, John Blair, *Pennsylvania in the War of the Revolution, Battalions and Line 1775-1783.* Harrisburg, Pennsylvania: state printer, 1880.

Military Abstract Card File for the Revolutionary War, 1775-1783. (Salt Lake City: Filmed by the Genealogical Society of Utah, 1978). Microfilm, 48 rolls.

County Website	Map Index	Date Created	Parent County or Territory From Which Organized Address/Details
Adams* www.rootsweb.com/~paadams/adams.htm	H9	22 Jan 1800	**York** Adams County; 111 Baltimore St; Gettysburg, PA 17325-2312; Ph. 717.334.6781 Details: (Clk Ct has b & d rec 1852-1855 & 1893-1905, m rec 1852-1855 & from 1856; Prothonotary Office has div & ct rec from 1800; Co Rcdr has pro & land rec from 1800)
Allegheny www.county.allegheny.pa.us/	Q7	24 Sep 1788	**Westmoreland, Washington** Allegheny County; 436 Grant St; Pittsburgh, PA 15219-2403; Ph. 412.355.5322 Details: (Reg of Wills has m rec; Prothonotary Office, 1st Floor, City Co Bldg. has div rec; Clk Ct has pro & ct rec; Rcdr Deeds has land rec)
Armstrong www.armstrongcounty.com/	O6	12 Mar 1800	**Allegheny, Lycoming, Westmoreland** Armstrong County; 450 Market St; Kittanning, PA 16201; Ph. 724.548.3256 Details: (Co Reg & Rcdr has b, d & bur rec 1893-1905, m rec from 1895, pro & land rec from 1805)
Beaver* www.co.beaver.pa.us/	R6	12 Mar 1800	**Allegheny, Washington** Beaver County; 810 3rd St; Beaver, PA 15009-2187; Ph. 724.728.3934 Details: (Reg of Wills has b rec 1893-1906, d rec 1852-1854 & 1893-1906, m rec 1852-1854 & from 1886 & pro rec from 1800; Rcdr Deeds has land rec from 1800; Prothonotary has div, ct & nat rec; Veterans Off has mil rec)
Bedford www.rootsweb.com/~pabedfor/l bedford.htm	L8	9 Mar 1771	**Cumberland** Bedford County; 230 S Juliana St; Bedford, PA 15522; Ph. 814.623.4833 Details: (Prothonotary has b & d rec 1852-1854 & 1893-1906, m rec 1852-1854 & from 1885, div rec from 1804, pro & ct rec from 1771)
Berks* www.rootsweb.com/~paberks/	D7	14 Oct 1751	**Lancaster, Philadelphia, Chester** Berks County; 633 Court St; Reading, PA 19601; Ph. 610.478.6600 Details: (Co Clk has b & d rec 1894-1905, m rec from 1885 & pro rec from 1752; Prothonotary Office has div & ct rec; Rcdr Deeds has land rec)
Blair* www.rootsweb.com/~pablair/	L7	26 Feb 1846	**Huntingdon, Bedford** Blair County; 423 Allegheny St; Hollidaysburg, PA 16648-2022; Ph. 814.693.3000 Details: (Prothonotary Office has div, pro & ct rec from 1846, nat rec from 1848, m rec from 1885 & b & d rec 1893-1905)
Bradford* www.rootsweb.com/~pabradfo/ bradweb.htm	G2	21 Feb 1810	**Luzerne, Lycoming** Bradford County; 301 Main St; Towanda, PA 18848-1884; Ph. 570.265.1727 Details: (Formerly Ontario Co. Name changed to Bradford 24 Mar 1812) (Prothonotary & Clk Cts has div rec from 1878, ct rec from 1813 & nat rec 1832-1960; Reg & Rcdr Off has b & d rec 1895-1905, m rec from 1885, pro & land rec from 1812 & mil rec from 1940)
Bucks www.buckscounty.org/	B8	10 Mar 1682	**Original county** Bucks County; Main & Court Sts; Doylestown, PA 18901; Ph. 215.348.6265 Details: (Orph Ct has b & d rec 1893-1906 & m rec from 1885; Prothonotary Office has div rec from 1878 & ct rec from 1682; Reg of Wills has pro rec from 1684)
Butler www.co.butler.pa.us/	Q6	12 Mar 1800	**Allegheny** Butler County; 124 W Diamond St; PO Box 1208; Butler, PA 16001; Ph. 724.284.5348 Details: (Co Clk has b & d rec 1893-1906, m rec from 1885, div rec from 1805 & nat rec from 1804; Orph Ct has pro rec from 1804; Prothonotary Office has ct & land rec from 1804)
Cambria* www.co.cambria.pa.us/	M7	26 Mar 1804	**Somerset, Bedford, Huntingdon** Cambria County; 200 S Center St; Edensburg, PA 15931-1936; Ph. 814.472.5440 Details: (Co Clk has b & d rec 1893-1906, m rec from 1885, div rec from 1866, pro rec from 1819, ct rec from 1849 & land rec from 1846)
Cameron www.rootsweb.com/~pacamero/	K4	29 Mar 1860	**Clinton, Elk, McKean, Potter** Cameron County; 20 E 5th St; Emporium, PA 15834; Ph. 814.486.2315 Details: (Co Clk has b & d rec 1860-1905, m, div, pro, ct & land rec from 1860)

County Website	Map Index	Date Created	Parent County or Territory From Which Organized / Address/Details
Carbon www.rootsweb.com/~pacarbon/	D6	13 Mar 1843	**Northampton, Monroe** Carbon County; Broadway Lock Box 129; Jim Thorpe, PA 18229-0129; Ph. 570.325.3611 Details: (Co Clk has b rec 1894-1905, d rec 1890-1904, m rec from 1885 & pro rec from 1843; Prothonotary Office has div rec; Clk Cts has ct rec; Rcdr Deeds has l and rec)
Centre county.centreconnect.org/index.htm	J5	13 Feb 1800	**Lycoming, Mifflin, Northumberland** Centre County; Willowbank County Bldg; 414 Holmes St; Bellefonte, PA 16823; Ph. 814.355.6724 Details: (Co Clk has b & d rec 1893-1905 & m rec from 1885; Prothonotary Office has div rec from 1890, ct & nat rec from 1800; Reg of Wills has pro rec from 1800; Rcdr Deeds has land rec from 1801)
Chester www.chesco.org/	D9	10 Mar 1682	**Original county** Chester County; 601 W Town Rd; PO Box 2747; West Chester, PA 19380; Ph. 610.344.6760 Details: (Co Archives has b & d rec 1852-1855 & 1893-1906, m rec 1852-1855 & 1885-1930, div rec 1804-1828, pro rec 1714-1923, ct rec 1681-1900, land rec 1716-1905, tax rec 1715-1939 & poorhouse rec 1798-1937)
Clarion www.co.clarion.pa.us/	O5	11 Mar 1839	**Venango, Armstrong** Clarion County; 421 Main St; Clarion, PA 16214-1028; Ph. 814.226.4000 Details: (Reg and Rcdr has b & d rec 1893-1906, m rec from 1885, pro & land rec from 1840; Prothonotary Clk has div rec from 1880 & ct rec from 1874)
Clearfield www.clearfieldco.org/	L5	26 Mar 1804	**Huntingdon, Lycoming** Clearfield County; 230 Market St; Clearfield, PA 16830; Ph. 814.765.2641 Details: (Co Reg & Rcdr has b & d rec 1893-1905 & m rec from 1885; Prothonotary Office has div & ct rec from 1828; Co Rcdr has pro rec from 1875; Co Comm has land rec)
Clinton www.clintoncountypa.com/	J4	21 Jun 1839	**Lycoming, Centre** Clinton County; County Courthouse; Lock Haven, PA 17745; Ph. 717.893.4000 Details: (Co Clk has b, m, d, div, pro, ct & land rec)
Columbia www.columbiapa.org/	F5	22 Mar 1813	**Northumberland** Columbia County; PO Box 380; Bloomsburg, PA 17815; Ph. 570.389.5632 Details: (Co Clk has b & d rec 1893-1905, m rec from 1888, ct rec from 1814 & div rec)
Crawford www.co.crawford.pa.us/	Q3	12 Mar 1800	**Allegheny** Crawford County; 903 Diamond Park; Meadville, PA 16335; Ph. 814.336.1151 Details: (Co Clk has b, d & bur rec 1893-1905, m rec from 1885, div rec, pro, ct & land rec from 1800)
Cumberland www.co.cumberland.pa.us/	I8	27 Jan 1750	**Lancaster** Cumberland County; 1 Courthouse Sq; Carlisle, PA 17013; Ph. 717.240.6370 Details: (Reg of Wills has b & d rec 1894-1905, m rec from 1885 & pro rec from 1750; Prothonotary Office has div & ct rec from 1751; Rcdr Deeds has land rec from 1751)
Dauphin www.dauphinc.org/	G7	4 Mar 1785	**Lancaster** Dauphin County; Front & Market Sts; Harrisburg, PA 17101-2012; Ph. 717.255.2692 Details: (Co Clk has b & d rec 1893-1906, m rec from 1885 & pro rec from 1795; Prothonotary Office has div & ct rec; Rcdr Deeds has land rec)
Delaware* www.co.delaware.pa.us/	C9	26 Sep 1789	**Chester** Delaware County; 201 W Front St; Media, PA 19063; Ph. 610.891.4260 Details: (Co Clk has b & d rec 1893-1906, m rec from 1885, div rec from 1927, pro rec from 1790, ct rec from 1897, land rec from 1789, orph ct rec from 1865 & delayed b rec 1875-1900)
Elk www.co.elk.pa.us/	M4	18 Apr 1843	**Jefferson, McKean, Clearfield** Elk County; Main St; Ridgway, PA 15853; Ph. 814.776.1161 Details: (Reg & Rcdr has b & d rec 1893-1906, m rec from 1895, pro rec from 1847 & land rec from 1861; Prothonotary Office has div & ct rec from 1843)

County Website	Map Index	Date Created	Parent County or Territory From Which Organized Address/Details
Erie* www.eriecountygov.org/	Q2	12 Mar 1800	**Allegheny** Erie County; 140 W 6th St; Erie, PA 16501; Ph. 814.451.6080 Details: (Courthouse burned 1823; all rec destroyed) (Co Clk has b & d rec 1893-1906 & m rec from 1885; Prothonotary Office has div & ct rec from 1823; Reg of Wills has pro rec from 1823; Co Rcdr has land rec from 1823)
Fayette* www.fforward.com/	P9	26 Sep 1783	**Westmoreland** Fayette County; 61 E Main St; Uniontown, PA 15401-3514; Ph. 724.430.1206 Details: (Clk Orph Ct has b & d rec 1893-1905, m rec from 1885 & pro rec from 1784; Prothonotary Office has div rec & ct rec from 1784; Rcdr Deeds has land rec from 1784)
Forest* forestcounty.com/	N3	11 Apr 1848	**Jefferson** Forest County; 526 Elm St; PO Box 423; Tionesta, PA 16353; Ph. 814.755.3526 Details: (Co Reg & Rcdr has b rec 1893-1906, m, div & land rec)
Franklin www.franklinco.pa.net/	J9	9 Sep 1784	**Cumberland** Franklin County; 157 Lincoln Way E; Chambersburg, PA 17201-2211; Ph. 717.261.3805 Details: (Co Clk has b & d rec 1894-1906, m rec from 1885, div rec from 1884, pro & land rec from 1785)
Fulton www.rootsweb.com/~pafulton/index.htm	K9	19 Apr 1850	**Bedford** Fulton County; 201 N 2nd St; McConnellsburg, PA 17233; Ph. 717.485.4212 Details: (Clk Orph Ct has b & d rec 1895-1905, m rec from 1885 & orph ct rec from 1850; Prothonotary Office has div & ct rec from 1850; Reg of Wills has pro rec from 1850; Rcdr Deeds has land rec from 1850)
Greene* county.greenepa.net/	R9	9 Feb 1796	**Washington** Greene County; 93 E High St; County Office Bldg; Waynesburg, PA 15370; Ph. 724.852.5281 Details: (Co Clk has b & d rec 1893-1915 & m rec from 1885; Prothonotary Office has div rec from 1816 & ct rec from 1797; Co Reg has pro rec from 1796; Rcdr Deeds has land rec from 1796)
Huntingdon www.huntingdoncounty.net/	K8	20 Sep 1787	**Bedford** Huntingdon County; 223 Penn St; PO Box 39; Huntingdon, PA 16652; Ph. 814.643.2740 Details: (Co Clk has b rec 1894-1906, d rec 1894-1905, m rec from 1885, div, pro & ct rec from 1787)
Indiana www.rootsweb.com/~paindian/	N7	30 Mar 1803	**Westmoreland, Lycoming** Indiana County; 825 Philadelphia St; Indiana, PA 15701-3934; Ph. 724.465.3860 Details: (Prothonotary & Clk Cts has div, land & ct rec from 1807 & nat rec 1806-1958; Reg of Wills has pro rec)
Jefferson www.pa-roots.com/~jefferson/	N5	26 Mar 1804	**Lycoming** Jefferson County; 155 Jefferson Pl; Brookville, PA 15825-1236; Ph. 814.849.1610 Details: (Clk Orph Ct has b & d rec 1893-1906 & m rec from 1885; Reg of Wills has pro rec from 1830; Rcdr Deeds has land rec from 1828; Prothonotary & Clk Cts has div & ct rec)
Juniata www.co.juniata.pa.us/	I7	2 Mar 1831	**Mifflin** Juniata County; Bridge St; PO Box 68; Mifflintown, PA 17059-0068; Ph. 717.436.8991 Details: (Co Clk has b & d rec 1893-1907, m rec from 1885, div rec from 1900, pro, ct & land rec from 1831 & nat rec from early 1800's to 1930)
Lackawanna www.rootsweb.com/~palackaw/	D3	21 Aug 1878	**Luzerne** Lackawanna County; 200 Adams Ave; Scranton, PA 18503; Ph. 570.963.6723 Details: (Co Comm Office has m, div, pro & ct rec from 1878)
Lancaster* www.co.lancaster.pa.us/lanco/site/default.asp	E8	14 Oct 1728	**Chester** Lancaster County; 50 N Duke St; PO Box 3480; Lancaster, PA 17602-2805; Ph. 717.299.8319 Details: (Reg of Wills has b rec 1893-1905, m rec from 1885, pro & ct rec from 1729; Prothonotary Ct has rec of Common Pleas ct & div rec; Clk Orph Ct has orph ct rec; Rcdr Deeds has land rec from 1729; Ct Common Pleas has d rec 1894-1927)

County Website	Map Index	Date Created	Parent County or Territory From Which Organized Address/Details
Lawrence* www.lawrencecounty.com/	R6	20 Mar 1849	Beaver, Mercer Lawrence County; 433 Court St; New Castle, PA 16101-3599; Ph. 724.656.2127 Details: (Co Clk has b, d & bur rec 1893-1905, m rec from 1893, div & ct rec from 1855; Reg & Rcdr has pro & land rec)
Lebanon www.chm.davidson.edu/PAGenWeb/	F7	16 Feb 1813	Dauphin, Lancaster Lebanon County; 400 S 8th St; Lebanon, PA 17042-6794; Ph. 717.274.2801 Details: (Clk Orph Ct has b rec 1893-1906 & m rec from 1885; Prothonotary Office has div rec from 1888; Reg of Wills has pro rec from 1813)
Lehigh* www.lehighcounty.org/	D6	6 Mar 1812	Northampton Lehigh County; 455 W Hamilton St; Allentown, PA 18105; Ph. 610.782.3148 Details: (Clk Orph Ct has b rec 1895-1905, d rec 1893-1904 & m rec from 1885; Prothonotary Ct has div & ct rec from 1812; Reg of Wills has pro rec from 1812; Rcdr Deeds has land rec from 1812)
Luzerne* www.rootsweb.com/~paluzern/	E5	25 Sep 1786	Northumberland Luzerne County; 200 N River St; Wilkes-Barre, PA 18711; Ph. 570.825.1585 Details: (Reg of Wills has b, d & bur rec 1893-1906, m rec from 1885 & pro rec from 1786; Prothonotary Office has div & ct rec; Rcdr Deeds has land rec)
Lycoming www.lyco.org/	H4	13 Apr 1795	Northumberland Lycoming County; 48 W 3rd St; Williamsport, PA 17701; Ph. 570.327.2251 Details: (Co Clk has b rec 1893-1905, d rec 1893-1898, m rec from 1885, pro rec from 1850 & land rec from 1795; Prothonotary Ct has div & ct rec from 1795; The James V. Brown Lib, 19 E. Fourth St., Williamsport, PA is the major source of Lycoming Co genealogical info)
McKean www.rootsweb.com/~pamckean/	L2	26 Mar 1804	Lycoming McKean County; 500 W Main St; Smethport, PA 16749; Ph. 814.887.3260 Details: (Reg of Wills has pro rec; Rcdr Deeds has land rec from 1806)
Mercer www.mcc.co.mercer.pa.us/	R4	12 Mar 1800	Allegheny Mercer County; 138 S Diamond St; Mercer, PA 16137; Ph. 724.662.3800 Details: (Co Clk has b & d rec 1893-1905, m rec from 1885 & pro rec from 1800; Prothonotary Office has div & ct rec; Rcdr Deeds has land rec)
Mifflin mifflincounty.lcworkshop.com/	I6	19 Sep 1789	Cumberland, Northumberland Mifflin County; 20 N Wayne St; Lewistown, PA 17044; Ph. 717.248.6733 Details: (Co Clk has b rec 1893-1905, m rec from 1885, pro & land rec from 1789; Prothonotary Office has div & ct rec)
Monroe www.co.monroe.pa.us/	C5	1 Apr 1836	Pike, Northampton Monroe County; 7 Monroe St; Stroudsburg, PA 18360; Ph. 570.420.3710 Details: (Co Clk has b rec 1892-1905, m rec from 1885, ct rec from 1845 & div rec from 1900; Reg of Wills has pro rec; Rcdr Deeds has land rec)
Montgomery www.montcopa.org/	C8	10 Sep 1784	Philadelphia Montgomery County; Airy & Swede St; Norristown, PA 19404; Ph. 610.278.3020 Details: (Clk Orph Ct has b & d rec 1893-1913 & m rec from 1885; Reg of WIlls has pro rec from 1784; Rcdr Deeds has land rec from 1784; Prothonotary Office has div & ct rec from 1784)
Montour www.montourco.org/	G5	3 May 1850	Columbia Montour County; 29 Mill St; Danville, PA 17821-1945; Ph. 570.271.3012 Details: (Prothonotary & Clk Cts has b & d rec 1893-1905, m rec from 1885, div & ct rec from 1850; Reg of Wills has pro rec; Rcdr Deeds has land rec)
Northampton www.northamptoncounty.org/	C6	14 Oct 1751	Bucks Northampton County; 7th & Washington St; Easton, PA 18042-7411; Ph. 610.559.3000 Details: (Clk Orphan Ct has b rec 1893-1936 & m rec from 1885; Prothonotary Office has div & ct rec; Reg of Wills has pro rec; Rcdr Deeds has land rec)

County Website	Map Index	Date Created	Parent County or Territory From Which Organized Address/Details
Northumberland www.northumberlandco.org/	G6	21 Mar 1772	**Lancaster, Berks, Cumberland, Bedford, Northampton** Northumberland County; 2nd & Market St; Sunbury, PA 17801; Ph. 570.988.4100 Details: (Reg and Rcdr has b & d rec 1893-1905, m rec from 1885, pro & land rec from 1772; Prothonotary Office has div & ct rec)
Ontario		21 Feb 1810	**Luzerne, Lycoming** Details: (see Bradford) (Name changed to Bradford 24 Mar 1812)
Perry www.perryco.org/	I7	22 Mar 1820	**Cumberland** Perry County; PO Box 37; New Bloomfield, PA 17068; Ph. 717.582.2131 Details: (Co Clk has b rec 1893-1918, m rec from 1870 & land rec from 1820; Reg of Wills has pro rec)
Philadelphia www.phila.gov/	B9	10 Mar 1682	**Original county** Philadelphia County; Broad & Market St; Philadelphia, PA 19107; Ph. 215.686.1776 Details: (Clk Orph Ct has m rec; Prothonotary Office has div & ct rec from 1874; Reg of Wills has pro rec; Dept Rec has land rec)
Pike www.pa-roots.com/~pike/	B4	26 Mar 1814	**Wayne** Pike County; 506 Broad St; Milford, PA 18337-1511; Ph. 570.296.7231 Details: (Clk Comm has b & d rec 1893-1905, m rec from 1885, div, pro, ct & land rec from 1814)
Potter www.pottercountypa.net/	J3	26 Mar 1804	**Lycoming** Potter County; 1 E 2nd St; Coudersport, PA 16915; Ph. 814.274.8290 Details: (Prothonotary has b, d & bur rec 1893-1905, m & div rec from 1885; Reg of Wills has pro rec; Rcdr Deeds has land rec)
Schuylkill www.co.schuylkill.pa.us/	E7	1 Mar 1811	**Berks, Northampton** Schuylkill County; N 2nd St & Laurel Blvd; Pottsville, PA 17901; Ph. 570.622.5570 Details: (Clk Comm has b & d rec 1893-1905, m rec from 1885, div rec from 1878, pro, ct & land rec from 1811)
Snyder www.rootsweb.com/~pasnyder/	H6	2 Mar 1855	**Union** Snyder County; 11 W Market St; Middleburg, PA 17842; Ph. 570.837.4207 Details: (Clk Cts has b, d & bur rec 1893-1905, m rec from 1885, div & ct rec from 1855; Co Reg & Rcdr has pro & land rec; Susquehanna Univ Lib in Selinsgrove has local cen rec)
Somerset www.rootsweb.com/~pasomers/	N9	17 Apr 1795	**Bedford** Somerset County; 111 E Union St; Somerset, PA 15501; Ph. 814.445.5154 Details: (Reg of Wills has b & d rec 1893-1906, m rec from 1885 & pro rec from 1795; Rcdr Deeds has land rec from 1795 & mil dis rec from 1865; Prothonotary Office has div & ct rec from 1795 & nat rec 1795-1955)
Sullivan www.sullivancountypa.org/	F4	15 Mar 1847	**Lycoming** Sullivan County; Main & Muncy; Laporte, PA 18626; Ph. 570.946.5201 Details: (Clk Orph Ct has b & d rec 1893-1905 & m rec from 1885; Prothonotary Office has div & ct rec from 1847; Reg of Wills has pro rec from 1847; Rcdr Deeds has land rec)
Susquehanna www.susquehanna.pa.us/	D2	21 Feb 1810	**Luzerne** Susquehanna County; County Courthouse; Montrose, PA 18801; Ph. 570.278.4600 Details: (Reg & Rcdr has b & d rec 1893-1906, m rec from 1885, pro rec from 1810 & mil rec from 1918; Prothonotary & Clk Cts has div rec from 1877, ct rec from 1812 & nat rec 1844-1956)
Tioga www.rootsweb.com/~patioga/ tiogaweb.htm	H3	26 Mar 1804	**Lycoming** Tioga County; 116 Main St; Wellsboro, PA 16901; Ph. 717.724.1906 Details: (Reg & Rcdr has b & d rec 1893-1905, m rec from 1885, pro rec from 1806, land rec from 1807 & mil rec from 1868; Prothonotary & Clk Cts has div & ct rec from 1813 & nat rec from 1818)
Union www.unionco.org/	H6	22 Mar 1813	**Northumberland** Union County; 103 S 2nd St; Lewisburg, PA 17837; Ph. 717.524.4461 Details: (Prothonotary Office has b rec 1893-1905, m rec from 1885, d rec from 1898, div & ct rec from 1813; Reg & Rcdr has pro & land rec from 1813)

County Website	Map Index	Date Created	Parent County or Territory From Which Organized Address/Details
Venango www.co.venango.pa.us/	P4	12 Mar 1800	**Allegheny, Lycoming** Venango County; 1168 Liberty St; Franklin, PA 16323-1295; Ph. 814.432.9577 Details: (Clk Cts & Rcdr Deeds has b & d rec 1893-1905, m rec from 1885, pro & land rec from 1806, div & ct rec)
Warren* www.warren-county.net/	O2	12 Mar 1800	**Allegheny, Lycoming** Warren County; 204 4th Ave; Warren, PA 16365-2399; Ph. 814.723.7550 Details: (Reg and Rcdr has b & d rec 1893-1906, m rec from 1885, pro & land rec from 1819; Prothonotary Office has div & ct rec)
Washington* www.co.washington.pa.us/	R9	28 Mar 1781	**Westmoreland** Washington County; 100 W Beau St; Washington, PA 15301; Ph. 724.228.6723 Details: (Reg of Wills has b & d rec 1893-1906, m rec from 1885 & pro rec from 1781; Rcdr Deeds has land & mil rec from 1781; Prothonotary & Clk Cts has div & ct rec from 1781 & nat rec 1802-1964)
Wayne* www.co-wayne-pa-us.org/	C3	21 Mar 1798	**Northampton** Wayne County; 925 Court St; Honesdale, PA 18431-1922; Ph. 570.253.5970 Details: (Prothonotary Office has b & d rec 1893-1906, m rec from 1885, div rec from 1900 & ct rec from 1798; Co Reg & Rcdr has pro & land rec from 1798)
Westmoreland* www.co.westmoreland.pa.us/index.shtml	O8	26 Feb 1773	**Bedford** Westmoreland County; 2 N Main St; Greensburg, PA 15601-2405; Ph. 724.830.3000 Details: (Co Clk has b rec 1893-1905, m rec from 1893 & pro rec from 1800; Prothonotary Office has div rec; Clk Cts has ct rec; Reg of Deeds has land rec)
Wyoming www.wycopa.com/	E4	4 Apr 1842	**Luzerne** Wyoming County; 1 Courthouse Sq; Tunkhannock, PA 18657; Ph. 570.836.3200 Details: (Clk Cts has b & d rec 1893-1905, m rec from 1885, div, pro, ct & land rec from 1842)
York www.york-county.org/	G9	14 Oct 1748	**Lancaster** York County; 28 E Market St; York, PA 17401; Ph. 717.771.9675 Details: (Co Clk has b & d rec 1893-1907, m rec from 1885, div, ct & land rec from 1749; Reg of Wills has pro rec)

Notes

Violet

RHODE ISLAND

CAPITAL: PROVIDENCE – STATE 1790 (13TH)

Giovanni da Verrazano was the first proven explorer to visit Rhode Island. In 1524, he visited Block Island, the site of present-day Newport. The first non-Native American settler was the Reverend William Blackstone. He came from Boston to Cumberland in 1634. Two years later, Roger Williams established the first permanent settlement at Providence and bought land from the Indians to settle. Banned from the Massachusetts Bay Colony because of his religious and political views, Williams helped other refugees from the colony to settle in Rhode Island. Among these were Anne Hutchinson, John Clarke, and William Coddington. With Williams' help, Coddington bought the island of Aquidneck and founded Portsmouth. The next year, internal dissension led to the founding of Newport at the other end of the island. In 1642, Samuel Gorton settled Warwick. These four settlements united and sent Roger Williams to England to obtain a charter. The grant he obtained from Parliament in 1644 permitted them to choose their own form of government. In 1647, the four settlements created a government under the name of Providence Plantations. In 1663, King Charles II granted "Rhode Island and Providence Plantations" a new charter, which guaranteed religious freedom and democratic government.

Early settlers included Quakers and refugees from Massachusetts. The towns of Bristol, Little Compton, Tiverton, and Warren from Massachusetts became part of Rhode Island in 1747. Newport became a shipping center due to the triangular trade between the West Indies and Africa. Rum was taken to Africa in exchange for slaves. These slaves were taken to the West Indies in exchange for molasses, which was taken to Newport to be made into rum.

Border disputes arose between Rhode Island, Massachusetts, and Connecticut. Rhode Island was the first colony to declare independence from England in May 1776. The British occupied Newport for nearly three years during the Revolutionary War. Rhode Island was the last to accept the Constitution, fearful of a strong central government and high taxes.

Slavery was gradually abolished, starting in 1784. The decline in trade, agriculture (due to more fertile lands opening in the west), and whaling led to the growth of factories in the state. Thousands of foreign laborers entered the state to fill the new jobs. They were of all nationalities, but especially Italian, English, Irish, Polish, Russian, Swedish, German, and Austrian.

In 1843, the Freeman's Constitution was adopted, which entitled anyone born in the United States instead of just landowners to vote. During the Civil War, about 23,000 men served in the Union armed forces. In 1862, Rhode Island gained the town of East Providence and part of the town of Pawtucket from Massachusetts and gave Fall River to Massachusetts.

Look for vital records in the following locations:

- **Birth, death and marriage records:** Contact Rhode Island Department of Health, Division of Vital Statistics in Providence, Rhode Island. Town clerks have kept records of births, marriages, and deaths since the 1630's. The records are more complete after 1700. Statewide registration began in January 1853 with general compliance by 1915.
- **Divorce records:** The Supreme Court kept early divorce records. Those made before 1962 are at the Providence Archives, Phillips Memorial Library in Providence.
- **Census records:** Colonial censuses and lists exist for 1747 to 1754, 1774, and 1782. State censuses were taken at 10-year intervals from 1865 to 1935, but the 1895 census is missing. Originals are at the Rhode Island State Archives, State House in Providence. The Rhode Island Historical Society Library in Providence has one of the largest collections of early records in New England.

Rhode Island Department of Health
Division of Vital Statistics
3 Capitol Hill, Room 101
Providence, Rhode Island 02908
401.222.2811

Providence Archives
Phillips Memorial Library
River Avenue and Eaton Street
Providence, Rhode Island 02918

Rhode Island State Archives
State House, Room 43
Providence, Rhode Island 02903

Rhode Island Historical
Society Library
121 Hope Street
Providence, Rhode Island 02903

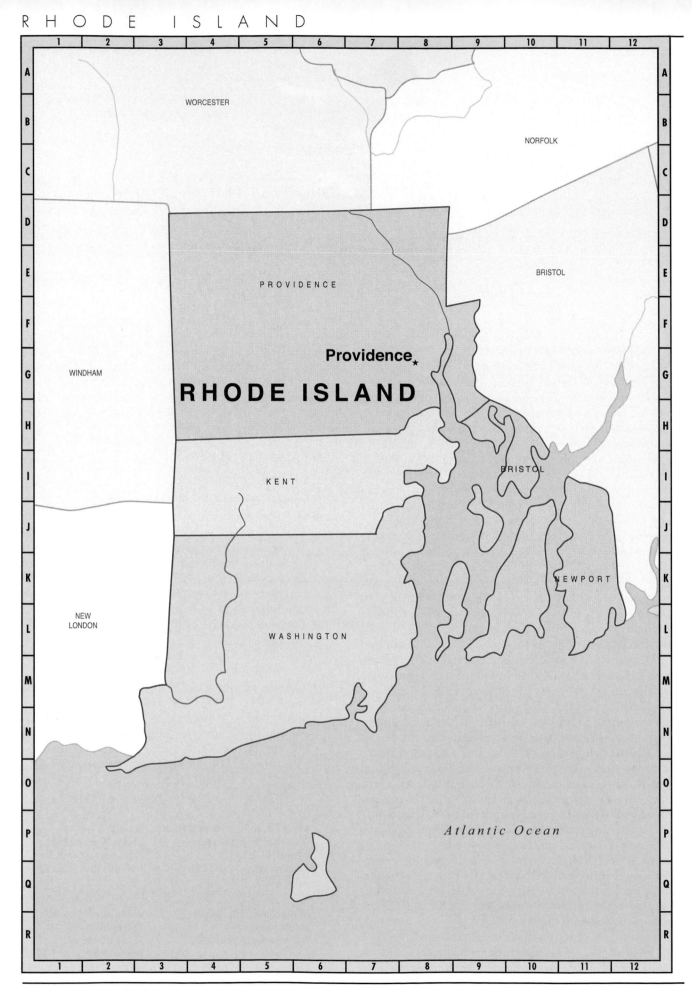

Societies and Repositories

American Baptist-Samuel Colgate Historical Society; 1106 S. Goodman Street; Rochester, New York 14620-2532; 716.473.1740; Fax 716.473.1740

American-French Genealogical Society; PO Box 830; Woonsocket, Rhode Island 02895-0870;

American-French Genealogical Society; 78 Earle Street, PO Box 2010; Woonsocket, Rhode Island 02895; 401.765.6141; Fax 401.765.6141

Black Heritage Society of Rhode Island; 46 Aborn St.; Providence, Rhode Island 02903

Boston University Theological School Library; 745 Commonwealth Avenue; Boston, Massachusetts 02215; 617.353.3034; Fax 617.353.3061; Methodist church records

Clerk of Family Court; 1 Dorrance Plaza; Providence, Rhode Island 02903; 401.277.3340

Congregational Library; 14 Beacon Street; Boston, Massachusetts 02108-3704; 617.523.0470

Diocese of Connecticut; 135 Asylum Ave.; Hartford, Connecticut 06105-2295; 860.233.4481; Fax 860.523.1410; (Episcopal Church records)

Diocese of Providence, The Chancery Office; 34 Fenner Street; Providence, Rhode Island 02903-3695; 401.278.4500; Fax 401.278.4548; (Roman Catholic church records)

East Greenwich Free Library; 82 Pierce St.; East Greenwich, Rhode Island 02818

Family History Library: 35 North West Temple Street: Salt Lake City, Utah 84150: 800.346.6044 or 801.240.2584: <www.familysearch.org>: Find a Family History Center near you: <www.familysearch.org/Eng/Library/FHC/frameset_fhc.asp>

John Hay Library; Brown University; Providence, Rhode Island 02912

Knight Memorial Library; 275 Elmwood Avenue; Providence, Rhode Island 02907

Mayflower Descendants of Rhode Island; 128 Massasoit; Warwick, Rhode Island

National Archives-New England Region; 380 Trapelo Road; Waltham, Massachusetts 02154; 617.647.8100; Fax 617.647.8460

New England Historic Genealogical Society; 101 Newbury Street; Boston, Massachusetts 02116-3007; 617.536.5740; Fax 617.536.7307

Newport Historical Society; 82 Touro St.; Newport, Rhode Island 02840

Providence College Archives, Phillips Memorial Library; River Avenue and Eaton Street; Providence, Rhode Island 02918

Providence Public Library; 229 Washington St.; Providence, Rhode Island 02903

Rhode Island American-French Genealogical Society; PO Box 2113; Pawtucket, Rhode Island 02861

Rhode Island Department of Health, Vital Records; #3 Capitol Hill, Rm 101; Providence, Rhode Island 02908-5097; 401.277.2812

Rhode Island Genealogical Society; PO Box 433; Greenville, Rhode Island 02828; <users.ids.net/~ricon/rigs.html>

Rhode Island Historical Society; 121 Hope St.; Providence, Rhode Island 02906; 401.331.8575; Fax 401.351.0127; <www.rihs.org>

Rhode Island Jewish Historical Association; 130 Sessions St.; Providence, Rhode Island 02906; 401.272.6729; <www.dowtech.com/rijha>

Rhode Island State Archives; 314 State House; Providence, Rhode Island 02900

Rhode Island State Archives; 337 Westminster St.; Providence, Rhode Island 02903-3302; 401.277.2353; Fax 401.277.3199

Rhode Island State Historical Society; 52 Power St.; Providence, Rhode Island 02906;

Rhode Island State Library; 82 Smith, State House; Providence, Rhode Island 02903

Sons of the American Revolution, Rhode Island Society; PO Box 137; East Greenwich, Rhode Island 02818

State Archives and Public Records Administration; 337 Westminster St.; Providence, Rhode Island 02903; 401.222.3199; <www.state.ri.us/archives/>

United Methodist Archives Center; Drew University Library, PO Box 127; Madison, New Jersey 07940; 201.408.3189; Fax 201.408.3909

Westerly Public Library; PO Box 356, Broad St.; Westerly, Rhode Island 02891

Bibliography and Record Sources

General Sources

A Guide to Newspaper Indexes in New England. Holden, Massachusetts: New England Library Association, 1978.

American Baptist Historical Society. *The Records of American Baptists in Rhode Island and Related Organizations.* Rochester, New York: American Baptist Historical Society, 1981.

Arnold, Samuel Greene. *History of the State of Rhode Island and Providence Plantations: 1636-1790.* 2 vols. Spartanburg, South Carolina: The Reprint Co., 1970.

Austin, John Osborne. *The Genealogical Dictionary of Rhode Island: Comprising Three Generations of Settlers Who Came Before 1690 (with Many Families Carried to the Fourth Generation).* Reprint with additions and corrections. Baltimore: Genealogical Publishing Co., 1978.

Bartlett, John Russell. *Bibliography of Rhode Island: A Catalogue of Books and Other Publications Relating to the State of Rhode Island, With Notes, Historical, Biographical and Critical.* Ann Arbor, Michigan: University Microfilms Inc., 1987. 3 microfiche.

Bates, Louise Prosser. *Bates Collection of Genealogical Data of Rhode Island Families: with General Index to Surnames, A-Z.* (Salt Lake City: Filmed by the Genealogical Society of Utah, 1950). Microfilm, 23 rolls.

Benns, Martha A. (Martha Adela Halton). *Rhode Island Family Records: Vol. 1-3.* (Salt Lake City: Filmed by the Genealogical Society of Utah, 1950).

Bicknell, Thomas Williams. *The History of the State of Rhode Island and Providence Plantations.* Tucson, Arizona: Filmed by W.C. Cox, 1974.

Biographical Cyclopedia of Representative Men of Rhode Island. 2 vols. Providence: National Biographical Publishing Co., 1881.

Briggs, Anthony Tarbox. *Briggs Collection of Cemetery Records, Wills, Record Books of Genealogy and Scrapbooks of Vital Records and Historical Events: with General Index to Surnames, A-Z.* (Salt Lake City: Filmed by the Genealogical Society of Utah, 1950). Microfilm, 24 rolls.

Brigham, Clarence Saunders. *Bibliography of Rhode Island History.* Ann Arbor, Mich.: University Microfilms Inc., 1987.

Brigham, Clarence Saunders. *Report on the Archives of Rhode Island.* Ann Arbor, Michigan: University Microfilms Inc., 1989.

Calef, Frank T. *Genealogical Index Rhode Island Records.* (Salt Lake City: Filmed by the Genealogical Society of Utah, 1950). Microfilm, 41 rolls.

Chapin, Howard Millar. *Documentary History of Rhode Island.* 2 vols. Providence: Preston and Rounds, 1916, 1919.

Conley, Patrick T. *An Album of Rhode Island History, 1636 – 1986.* Norfolk, Virginia: Donning, 1986. Cox, Lynn T. *Rhode Island Register.* [S.l.: s.n., 19–].

Cullen, Thomas F. *The Catholic Church in Rhode Island.* North Providence, Rhode Island: Franciscan Missionaries of Mary, 1936.

Cutter, William Richard. *New England Families: Genealogical and Memorial.* 4 vols. 1913. Reprint. New York: Lewis Historical Publishing Co., 1914.

Farnham, Charles W. *Rhode Island Colonial Records.* Salt Lake City: Genealogical Society, 1969.

Field, Edward, ed., *State of Rhode Island and Providence Plantations at the End of the Century,* 3 vols. Boston: Mason Publishing Co, 1902.

Genealogies of Rhode Island Families: From Rhode Island Periodicals. 2 vols. Baltimore: Genealogical Publishing Co., 1983.

Greenlaw, William Prescott. *The Greenlaw Index of the New England Historic Genealogical Society.* 2 vols. Boston: G. K. Hall, 1979.

Hall, Lu Verne V. *New England Family Histories: States of Maine and Rhode Island.* Bowie, Maryland: Heritage Books, 2000.

Herndon, Richard. *Men of Progress: Biographical Sketches and Portraits of Leaders in Business and Professional Life in the State of Rhode Island and Providence Plantations.* Boston: New England Magazine, 1896.

Historical Records Survey (Rhode Island). *Inventory of the Church Archives of Rhode Island; Society of Friends.* Providence: The Survey, 1939.

Kirkham, E. Kay. *An Index to Some of the Bibles and Family Records of the United States,* vol. 2. Logan, Utah: Everton Publishers, 1984.

Munro, Wilfred H. *Memorial Encyclopedia of the State of Rhode Island.* Boston: American Historical Society, 1916.

New England Historic Genealogical Society. *English Origins of New England Families: From the New England Historical and Genealogical Register.* First Series, 3 vols., 1984. Second Series, 3 vols., 1985. Baltimore: Genealogical Publishing Co.

Parker, J. Carlyle. *Rhode Island Biographical and Genealogical Sketch Index.* Turlock, California: Marietta Pub. Co., 1991.

Parks, Roger, ed. *Rhode Island: A Bibliography of Its History.* Hanover, New Hampshire: University Press of New England, 1983.

Pierce, Ebenezer Weaver. *Civil, Military and Professional Lists of Plymouth and Rhode Island Colonies: Comprising Colonial, County, and Town Officers, Clergymen, Physicians and Lawyers…1881.* Reprint. Baltimore: Genealogical Publishing Co., 1968.

Representative Men and Old Families of Rhode Island: Genealogical and Historical Sketches of Prominent and Representative Citizens of Many of the Old Families, 3 vols. Chicago: J. H. Beers & Co., 1908.

Rhode Island Baptist State Convention. *Inventory of the Church Archives of Rhode Island (Baptist).* Providence: The Survey, 1941.

Rhode Island Conference of Business Associations. *The Book of Rhode Island: An Illustrated Description of the Advantages and Opportunities of the State of Rhode Island and the Progress That Has Been Achieved, With Historical Sketches of Many Leading Industries and a Biographical Record of Citizens Who Have Helped to Produce the Superb Structure- Historical, Commercial, Industrial, Agricultural and Recreational- Which Comprises the Strength of this Charming State.* [Providence?]: Rhode Island Conference of Business Associations, 1930.

Rhode Island Genealogies. [S.l.]: Brøderbund, 1996. CD-ROM.

Rhode Island Research Outline. Series US-States, No. 40. Salt Lake City: Family History Library, 1988.

Rhode Island Society of Colonial Dames. *Genealogical Chart about Many Rhode Island families. Microfilm of Manuscripts in the Rhode Island Historical Society.* Salt Lake City: Filmed by the Genealogical Society of Utah, 1950. 3 microfilm.

Rhode Island State Archives, coll. *Certificates for Deputies and Freemen of Rhode Island Towns, 1663-1778.* [n.d.]

Rider, Fremont, ed. *American Genealogical-Biographical Index.* Vols. 1-186+. Middletown, CT: Godfrey Memorial Library, 1952-. (Salt Lake City: Filmed by the Genealogical Society of Utah, 1974).

Savage, James. *A Genealogical Dictionary of the First Settlers of New England…..* 4 vols. 1860-62. Reprint. Baltimore: Genealogical Publishing Co., 1965.

Short, Josephine Keefer, and Mrs. Bentley W. Morse. *Rhode Island Bible Records.* (Salt Lake City: Filmed by the Genealogical Society of Utah, 1950).

Sperry, Kip. *Rhode Island Sources for Family Historians and Genealogists.* Logan, Utah: Everton Publishers, 1986.

The Early Records of the Town of Providence, 21 vols. Providence: Snow and Farnham, City Printers, 1892-1915.

Works Projects Administration. *Inventory of Church Archives in Rhode Island: Baptist Bodies.* Providence: Historical Records Survey, 1939.

Atlases, Maps and Gazetteers

Cady, John H. *Rhode Island Boundaries, 1636-1936.* Providence: State of Rhode Island and Prividence Plantations, 1936.

Gallagher, John S. *The Post Offices of Rhode Island.* Burtonsville, Maryland: The Depot, 1977.

Gannett, Henry. *A Geographic Dictionary of Connecticut and Rhode Island.* 1894. Reprint. Baltimore: Genealogical Publishing Co., 1978.

Long, John H. *Connecticut, Maine, Massachusetts, Rhode Island, Atlas of Historical County Boundaries.* New York: Simon & Schuster, 1994.

Merolla, Lawrence M., Arthur B. Jackson, and Frank M. Crowther. *Rhode Island Postal History: The Post Offices.* Providence: Rhode Island Postal History Society, 1977.

Pease, John Chauncey, and john M. Niles. *A Gazetteer of the State of Connecticut and Rhode Island.* Hartford, CN: Heritage Books, 1991.

Rhode Island—A Guide to the Smallest State. Boston: Houghton Mifflin Co., 1937.

Wright, Marion I., and Robert J. Sullivan. *Rhode Island Atlas.* Providence: Rhode Island Publications Society, 1982.

Census Records

Available Census Records and Census Substitutes

Federal Census, 1790, 1800, 1810, 1820, 1830, 1840, 1850, 1860, 1870, 1880, 1900, 1910, 1920, 1930.

Union Veteran and Widows 1890.

State/Territorial Census 1747, 1770, 1774, 1777, 1779, 1782, 1865, 1875, 1885, 1905, 1915, 1925, 1935.

Bartlett, John R., comp. *Census of the Inhabitants of the Colony of Rhode Island and Providence Plantations, 1774.* Baltimore: Genealogical Publishing Co., 1969.

Beers, Daniel G. *Atlas of the State of Rhode and Providence Plantations.* Philadelphia: Pomeroy & Beers, 1870.

Chamberlain, Mildred M. *The Rhode Island 1777 Military Census.* Baltimore: Genealogical Publishing Co., 1985.

Dollarhide, William. The Census Book: *A Genealogist's Guide to Federal Census Facts, Schedules and Indexes.* Bountiful, Utah: Heritage Quest, 1999.

Kemp, Thomas Jay. *The American Census Handbook.* Wilmington, Delaware: Scholarly Resources, Inc., 2001.

Lainhart, Ann S. *State Census Records.* Baltimore: Genealogical Publishing Co., Inc., 1992.

Szucs, Loretto Dennis, and Matthew Wright. *Finding Answers in U.S. Census Records.* Ancestry Publishing, 2001

Thorndale, William, and William Dollarhide. *Map Guide to the U.S. Federal Censuses, 1790-1920.* Baltimore: Genealogical Publishing Co., 1987.

United States. Census Office. *Rhode Island, 1790 thru 1840 Federal Census: Population Schedules.* Washington, D.C.: The National Archives, 1938, 1949, 1950, 1958-1961, 1969. 12 microfilm.

Court Records, Probate and Wills

Bartlett, John R. *Records of the Colony of Rhode Island and Providence Plantations in New England.*10 vols. Providence: A. C. Green, 1856-1865.

Beaman, Nellie M. C. *Index of Wills, 1636-1850.* Vol. 16 in *Rhode Island Genealogical Register.* New Series. Princeton, Massachusetts: Rhode Island Families Association, 1992.

Calef, Frank T. *The Providence Probate Records to 1775 with Index.* (Salt Lake City: Filmed by the Genealogical Society of Utah, 1950).

Field, Edward, ed. *Index to the Probate Records of the Municipal Court of the City of Providence, Rhode Island: From 1646 to and Including the Year 1899.* Providence, Rhode Island: Providence Press, 1902.

Records of the Vice - Admiralty Court of Rhode Island: 1716-1752. Millwood, New York: Kraus Reprint, 1975.

Rhode Island Court Records: Records of the Court of Trials of the Colony of Providence Plantations, 1647-1670. 2 vols. Providence: Rhode Island Historical Society, 1920-1922.

Rhode Island General Court of Trials, 1671-1704. Boxford, Mass.: J.F. Fiske, 1998, 1998.

Rhode Island. General Council. *General Council Meeting Minutes and Documents.* (Salt Lake City: Filmed by the Genealogical Society of Utah, 1974).

Rhode Island. Supreme Court. Court Records, 1671-1879. Microfilm of records in Newport, Rhode Island. (Salt Lake City: Filmed by the Genealogical Society of Utah, 1973). 9 microfilm.

Wakefield, Robert S. *Index to Wills in Rhode Island Genealogical Register, Vol. 1-4.* Warwick, Rhode Island: Plymouth Colony Research Group, 1982.

Emigration, Immigration, Migration and Naturalization

Bolton, Ethel Stanwood. *Immigrants to New England, 1700-1775.* Salem, Massachusetts: The Essex Institute, 1931.

Deputies & Freemen Index, 1664-1778 [i.e. 1806]. Microfilm of typed index cards at the Rhode Island State Archives in Providence at the statehouse. (Salt Lake City: Filmed by the Genealogical Society of Utah, 1974). 3 microfilm.

Filby, P. William. *Passenger and Immigration Lists Index.* 15 vols. Detroit: Gale Research, 1981-.

List of American Seamen of Providence District Pursuant to the Act for the Relief and Protection of American Seamen: Found At U.S. Customs House, Providence, Rhode Island. (Salt Lake City: Filmed by the Genealogical Society of Utah, 1950).

Taylor, Maureen. *Rhode Island Passenger Lists: Port of Providence 1798-1808: 1820-1872 and Port of Bristol and Warren 1820-1871.* Baltimore: Genealogical Publishing Co., 1993.

United States. Bureau of Customs. *Copies of Lists of Passengers Arriving At Miscellaneous Ports on the Atlantic and Gulf Coasts and At Ports on the Great Lakes, 1820-1873.* Washington, D.C.: The National Archives, 1964.

United States. Bureau of Customs. *Passenger Lists of Vessels Arriving At Boston, 1820-1891: with Index 1848-1891.* Washington, DC: National Archives Record Service, 1959-1960.

United States. *Immigration and Naturalization Service. Passenger Lists, Providence, Rhode Island, 1911-1916; Book Indexes, 1911-1934; Card Indexes, 1911-1954.* Washington, D.C.: National Archives and Records Service, 1944-1945.

United States. Immigration and Naturalization Service. *Index to New England Naturalization Petitions, 1791-1906.* Washington: National Archives. Central Plains Region, 1983. 117 microfilm.

United States. Immigration and Naturalization Service. *St. Albans District Manifest Records of Aliens Arriving from Foreign Contiguous Territory: Arrivals At Canadian Border Ports from January 1895 to June 30, 1954: Indexes (Soundex), 1895-1924.* Washington, D.C.: National Archives Records Service, 1986. Microfilm, 400 rolls.

Land and Property

Arnold, James N. *The Records of the Proprietors of the Narragansett, Otherwise Called the Fones Record.* Providence, Rhode Island: Narragansett Historical Publishing, 1894.

Dougine, Genevieve N. *Index to Rhode Island Land Evidences, 1648-1696: Also Record of Marriages, 1800.* Microfilm of manuscripts at the New York Genealogical and Biographical Society in New York. (Salt Lake City: Filmed by the Genealogical Society of Utah, 1941).

Field, Edward. *Revolutionary Defenses in Rhode Island: An Historical Account of the Fortifications and Beacons Erected During the American Revolution, With Muster Rolls of the Companies Stationed Along the Shores of Narragansett Bay: Preston and Rounds, 1896.* (Salt Lake City: Filmed by the Genealogical Society of Utah, 1992).

Hone, Wade E. *Land and Property Research in the United States.* Salt Lake City: Ancestry Incorporated, 1997.

Land and Public Notary Records of Rhode Island, 1648-1795. Microfilm of manuscripts from the Rhode Island State Archives, Providence, Rhode Island. (Salt Lake City: Filmed by the Genealogical Society of Utah, 1973). 4 microfilm.

Records of Rhode Island, 1638-1644. Microfilm of manuscripts in the Rhode Island State Archives in Providence, Rhode Island. (Salt Lake City: Filmed by the Genealogical Society of Utah, 1974).

Rhode Island Miscellaneous Records, ca. 1600-1900. (Salt Lake City: Filmed by the Genealogical Society of Utah, 1992).

Rhode Island. General Assembly. *Proceedings of the General Assembly: 1646-1851.* Microfilm of manuscripts in the Rhode Island State Archives in Providence. (Salt Lake City: Filmed by the Genealogical Society of Utah, 1974). 18 microfilm.

Rhode Island. State Archives. *Rhode Island Militia and National Guard Enlistment Papers, 1890-1919.* Microreproduction of documents in State Archives, Providence, Rhode Island. (Salt Lake City: Filmed by the Genealogical Society of Utah, 1993). 41 microfilm.

Worthington, Dorothy, comp. *Rhode Island Land Evidences, Vol. 1, 1648-96.* Providence, Rhode Island: Rhode Island Historical Society, 1921. Reprinted with a preface by Albert T. Klyberg. Baltimore: Genealogical Publishing Co., 1970.

Military

Chapin, Howard Miller. *Rhode Island in the Colonial Wars: A List of Rhode Island Soldiers and Sailors in King George's War, 1740-1748.* Providence, Rhode Island: Rhode Island Historical Society, 1920.

Chapin, Howard Miller. *Rhode Island in the Colonial Wars: A List of Rhode Island Soldiers and Sailors in the Old French and Indian Wars, 1755-1762.* Providence, Rhode Island: Rhode Island Historical Society, 1918.

Cowell, Benjamin. *Spirit of '76 in Rhode Island.* Boston: A. J. Wright, 1850.

Index to Register of Seamen's Protection, 1796-1868. Microfilm of manuscripts at the Rhode Island Historical Society in Providence. (Salt Lake City: Filmed by the Genealogical Society of Utah, 1974). 3 microfilm.

Military papers- War of 1812: 1792-1794, 1812-1815. Microfilm of manuscripts filmed at the Rhode Island State Archives in Providence. (Salt Lake City: Filmed by the Genealogical Society of Utah, 1974). 2 microfilm.

Rhode Island. Adjutant General's Office. *Military Records, 1847-1900.* Microreproduction of documents at Rhode Island State Archives, Providence, Rhode Island. (Salt Lake City: Filmed by the Genealogical Society of Utah, 1994). 7 microfilm.

Rhode Island. State Archives. *Card Index to Military and Naval Records, 1774-1805.* Microfilm of original records in the State Archives, Providence, Rhode Island. (Salt Lake City: Filmed by the Genealogical Society of Utah, 1974, 1980). 19 microfilm.

Smith, Joseph J. *Civil and Military List of Rhode Island, 1647-1800.* 3 vols. Providence, Rhode Island: Preston and Rounds, 1901.

United States. Selective Service System. *Rhode Island, World War I Selective Service System Draft Registration Cards, 1917-1918.* National Archives Microfilm Publications, M1509. Washington, D.C.: National Archives, 1987-1988.

Walker, Anthony. *So Few the Brave: Rhode Island Continentals, 1775-1783.* Newport, Rhode Island: Seafield, 1981.

Vital and Cemetery Records

Index to Arnold's Rhode Island Vital Records: Rhode Island Cemetery Records. Salt Lake City: Genealogical Society of Utah, 1950. Microfilm, 11 rolls.

Arnold, James N. *Coventry R.I. Headstone Inscriptions.* (Salt Lake City: Filmed by the Genealogical Society of Utah, 1950).

Arnold, James N. *Vital Records of Rhode Island, 1636-1850: A Family Register for the People.* 20 vols. Providence, Rhode Island: Narragansett Historical Publishing Co., 1891-1912.

Beaman, Alden G. *Vital Records of Rhode Island, New Series.* 13 vols. Princeton, Massachusetts: the compiler, 1975-87.

Benns, Charles P. and Martha A. Benns. *Rhode Island Cemetery Records, 1931-1941.* 6 vols. N.p., n.d. Salt Lake City: Genealogical Society of Utah, 1950. Microfilm.

Briggs, Anthony T. *Briggs Collection of Cemetery Records, Wills, Record Books of Genealogy and Scrapbooks of Vital Records and Historical Events.* Salt Lake City: Genealogical Society of Utah, 1950. Microfilm.

Brown, Clarence I. *Rhode Island Cemetery and Genealogical Records.* Salt Lake City: Genealogical Society of Utah, 1950. Microfilm.

Calef, Frank T. *Genealogical Index Rhode Island Records.* (Salt Lake City: Filmed by the Genealogical Society of Utah, 1950). 42 microfilm.

Calef, Frank T. *Rehoboth Cemetery Records.* (Salt Lake City: Filmed by the Genealogical Society of Utah, 1950).

Guide to the Public Vital Statistics Records: Births, Marriages, Deaths, in the State of Rhode Island and Providence Plantations. Providence: Historical Records Survey, 1941.

Miscellaneous Vital Records, 1700-1850. Microfilm of records in James Arnold's family notes - town note's collection at the Knight Memorial Library, Providence, Rhode Island. (Salt Lake City: Filmed by the Genealogical Society of Utah, 1992).

Potter, Nellie Brownell. *Rhode Island Burial Grounds.* (Salt Lake City: Filmed by the Genealogical Society of Utah, 1950).

Rhode Island Returns of Birth (1893-1898), Certificates of Death (1946-1948), Out of State Deaths (1946-1947), and out of State Death Index (1900-1948). Microreproduction of records at Rhode Island State Archives, Providence. (Salt Lake City: The Genealogical Society of Utah, 1999.) 24 microfilm.

Rhode Island. Department of State. Record Commissioner. *Guide to the Public Vital Statistics Records (Births, Marriages, Deaths) in the State of Rhode Island and Providence Plantations: Containing Chronologies of the Legislation Relating to or Affecting the Records Together with an Outline of the Civic Division of the State.* Providence: [The Survey?], 1941.

Rhode Island. Division of Vital Records. *Vital records & Indexes for Births, Deaths, and Marriages: 1853 through 1900.* Microreproduction of computer printout at the Rhode Island Department of Health, Division of Vital Records, Providence. (Salt Lake City: Filmed by the Genealogical Society of Utah, 1991). 72 microfilm.

Rhode Island. State Archives. *Deaths (1901-1943) and Index of Deaths (1901-1920).* Microreproduction of documents at Rhode Island State Archives, Providence, Rhode Island. (Salt Lake City: Filmed by the Genealogical Society of Utah, 1993-1994). 158 microfilm.

Rhode Island. State Archives. *Delayed Births, 1846-1892, 1896-1898; Index 1846-1898.* Microreproduction of documents at Rhode Island State Archives, Providence, Rhode Island. (Salt Lake City: Filmed by the Genealogical Society of Utah, 1994). 5 microfilm.

Snow, Edwin M., Charles V. Chapin, Dennett L. Richardson, and Michael J. Nestor. *Alphabetical Index of the Births, Marriages and Deaths Recorded in Providence.* 32 vols. Providence, Rhode Island, 1879-[1946].

Torrey, Clarence Almon. *New England Marriages Prior to 1700.* Baltimore: Genealogical Publishing Co., 1985.

Turner, H. E. *Cemetery Records of Rhode Island.* (Salt Lake City: Filmed by the Genealogical Society of Utah, 1950).

County Website	Map Index	Date Created	Parent County or Territory From Which Organized Address/Details
Bristol www.rootsweb.com/~ribristo/	I10	17 Feb 1747	**Newport** Bristol County; 1 Dorrance Plaza; Warren, RI 02885-4369; Ph. 508.823.6588 Details: (There is no Co Clk in Bristol Co; Twn & City Clks have b, m, d, bur & pro rec; Clk Dis Ct has ct rec) (Four twns in Bristol Co) Towns Organized Before 1800: Barrington 1717, Bristol 1681, Warren 1746-7
Kent www.rootsweb.com/~rikent/kent.html	I5	11 Jun 1750	**Providence** Kent County; 222 Quaker Ln; West Warwick, RI 02893; Ph. 401.841.835 Details: (Twn & City Clks have b, m, d, bur, pro & land rec) (Five twns in Kent Co) Towns Organized Before 1800: Coventry 1741, East Greenwich 1677, Warwick 1642-3, West Greenwich 1741
King's		3 Jun 1729	**Newport** Details: (see Washington) (Name changed to Washington 29 Oct 1781)
Newport www.rootsweb.com/~rinewpor/	K10	22 Jun 1703	**Original county** Newport County; 8 Washington Sq; Newport, RI 02840-7199; Ph. 401841.835 Details: (Formerly Rhode Island Co. Name changed to Newport 16 Jun 1729. 1746-7 eastern boundary adjusted under decree of the King of England) (City & Twn Clks have b, m, d & bur rec; Family & Sup Cts have div rec; Pro Ct has pro rec from 1784, Dis Ct has ct rec; Rcdr Deeds has land rec from 1780; Newport Hist Soc, 82 Truro St., newport, RI has early church , land & pro rec) (Five twns & one city in Newport Co) Towns Organized Before 1800: Jamestown 1678, Little Compton 1746-7, Middletown 1743, New Shoreham 1672, Portsmouth 1638, Tiverton 1746-7
Providence www.rootsweb.com/~riprovid/	E5	22 Jun 1703	**Original county** Providence County; 250 Benefit St; Providence, RI 02903; Ph. 401.277.671 Details: (Formerly Providence Plantations. Name changed to Providence Co 16 Jun 1729) (Pro Judge has pro rec; Family Ct has div rec; Municipal Ct has ct rec; Rcdr Deeds has land rec; Twn & City Clks have b, m & d rec) (22 twns in Providence Co) Towns Organized Before 1800; Cranston 1754, Cumberland 1746-7, Foster 1781, Gloucester 1730-1, Johnston 1759, North Providence 1765, Providence 1636, Scituate 1730-1, Smithfield 1730-1
Providence Plantations		22 Jun 1703	**Original county** Details: (see Providence) (Name changed to Providence Co 16 Jun 1729)
Rhode Island		22 Jun 1703	**Original county** Details: (see Newport) (Name changed to Newport 16 Jun 1729)
Washington www.rootsweb.com/~riwashin/ riwash.html	L5	3 Jun 1729	**Newport** Washington County; 4800 Tower Hill Rd; Wakefield, RI 02879-2239; Ph. 401.841.835 Details: (Formerly King's Co. Name changed to Washington 29 Oct 1781) (Twn & City Clks have b, m, d, pro & land rec) (Twenty twns in Washington Co) Towns Organized Before 1800: Charlestown 1738, Exeter 1742-3, Hopkinton 1757, North Kingstown 1641, Richmond 1747, South Kingstown (Pettaquamscutt) 1656-7, Westerly 1669

Yellow Jasmine

SOUTH CAROLINA

CAPITAL: COLUMBIA – STATE 1788 (8TH)

The Spanish and French attempted to settle South Carolina from its discovery in 1521 until 1663, but they failed. In 1663, King Charles II granted the territory between the 31st and 36th parallels from ocean to ocean to eight noblemen. The first permanent settlement, called Charles Town, was situated on the Ashley River. It was settled by a group from England and Barbados. A group of Dutch settlers came from New York after a few months, and were later joined by others direct from Holland. Ten years later, the town was moved to the present site of Charleston.

Other early settlers include Quakers in 1675; Huguenots in 1680; dissenters from the Episcopal Church in Somerset in 1683; Irish in 1675; and Scotch Presbyterians in 1684 who settled at Port Royal. In 1729, Carolina was divided into North and South Carolina. In 1732, part of South Carolina became Georgia. In 1730, the colonial government provided incentives for landowners in new townships, so settlers gathered along the banks of the Santee and the Edisto Rivers. From 1732 to 1763, a number of families came from England, Scotland, Ireland, Wales, Switzerland, and Germany into the central section of South Carolina. The "Up Country," or western half of the state, was first settled between 1745 and 1760 by immigrants from the Rhine area of Germany, the Northern American colonies, and the Ulster section of Ireland.

Battles with Spanish, French, Indians, and pirates occupied the settlers prior to the Revolutionary War. A treaty in 1760 ended the Cherokee War and opened up more land for settlement. With the offer of tax-free land for a decade, Scotch-Irish immigrants and settlers from other colonies swelled the western lands. South Carolina entered the Union in 1788 as the eighth state. Overseas immigration dwindled about 1815 and virtually ceased between 1830 and 1840. Political refugees from Germany immigrated to South Carolina in 1848.

South Carolina was the first state to secede from the Union in 1860. The first shots were fired by South Carolina troops on Fort Sumter on 12 April 1861. The state was devastated by General William Tecumseh Sherman during the war. An estimated 63,000 men served in the Confederate forces from South Carolina. Readmission to the Union came in 1868. After the Civil War, agriculture declined and employment shifted to the textile industry.

In 1769, nine judicial districts were established – Charleston, Georgetown, Beaufort, Orangeburg, Ninety-Six, Camden, and Cheraws. Records were kept at Charleston until 1780. In 1790, the capital was moved from Charleston to Columbia, although some functions remained at Charleston until after the Civil War. In 1795, Pinckney and Washington districts were created. Three years later the nine districts were divided into several more including the following:

- Ninety-Sixth District: Abbeville, Edgefield, Newberry, Laurens, and Spartanburg (all formed in 1795)
- Washington District: Pendleton and Greenville
- Pinckney District: Union and York
- Camden District: Chester, Lancaster, Fairfield, Kershaw, and Sumter
- Cheraws District: Chesterfield, Darlington, and Marlborough
- Georgetown District: Georgetown and Marion
- Charleston District: Charleston and Colleton
- Orangeburg District: Orangeburg and Barnwell Districts were changed to counties in 1868.

Look for vital records in the following locations:

- **Birth and death records:** Contact the Office of Vital Records in Columbia, South Carolina and with individual county clerks for birth and death records from 1915 to present. City of Charleston birth records, beginning in 1877, are at the City Health Department. Death records for the city are also available from 1821.
- **Marriage and divorce records:** Contact the Office of Vital Records in Columbia for marriage records beginning with 1 July 1850. Marriage records from about July 1910, plus some in the early 1800's, are at the offices of Probate Judges in each county. Before statewide registration, the Ordinary of the Province could issue a marriage license or banns could be published in a church. Some marriage settlements from the 1760's to the 1800's are at the South Carolina Department of Archives and History

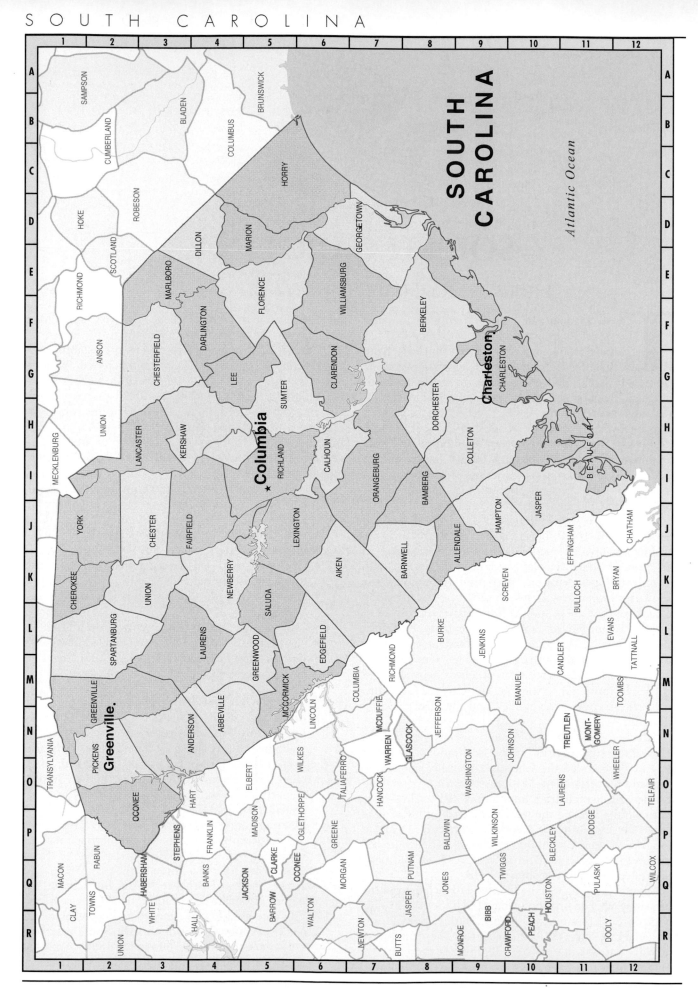

SOUTH CAROLINA

Atlantic Ocean

in Capitol Station, Columbia, South Carolina. Divorce was illegal in South Carolina until 1949. Proceedings are kept by the county court, but there are restrictions on availability.

- **Probate and court records**: Before 1732, the secretary of the province kept probate records. After that, they were kept by the clerks of ordinary and probate courts in each county.
- **Census records**: No colonial censuses remain. State censuses exist for 1829 (Fairfield and Laurens districts) and 1839 (Kershaw District) along with the 1869 population returns and 1875 agricultural and population returns. These are all kept at the South Carolina Department of Archives and History.

Office of Vital Records
2600 Bull Street, Columbia
South Carolina 29201
803.734.4830

South Carolina Department of Archives and History
1430 Senate Street
PO Box 11669
Capitol Station, Columbia,
South Carolina 29211

Societies and Repositories

Abbeville-Greenwood Regional Library; N. Main St.; Greenwood, South Carolina 29646

Aiken-Barnwell Genealogical Society; PO Box 415; Aiken, South Carolina 29802; <http://www.ifx.net/~lhutto/page2.html>

Allendale County Historical Society; PO Box 523; Allendale, South Carolina 29810

Anderson County Chapter of SCGS; PO Box 74; Anderson, South Carolina 29622.0074; <http://www.rootsweb.com/~scanders/andgensoc.html>

Bluffton Historical Preservation Society, Inc.; PO Box 742; Bluffton, South Carolina 29910; <www.heywardhouse.org>

Calhoun County Museum, Archives Library; 303 Butler Street; St. Matthews, South Carolina 29135

Camden Archives & Museum; 1314 Broad St.; Camden, South Carolina 29020

Catawba Wateree Genealogical Society; Camden Archives and Museum; 1314 Broad Street; Camden, South Carolina 29020; <http://www.mindspring.com/~graysky1/page3.html>

Charleston Chapter, South Carolina Genealogical Society; PO Box 20266; Charleston, South Carolina 29413-0266

Charleston Diocesan Archives; 119 Broad Street, PO Box 818; Charleston, South Carolina 29402; 803.723.3488; Fax 803.724.6387 (Roman Catholic Church records)

Charleston Library Society; 164 King Street; Charleston, South Carolina 29401; 803.723.9912

Chester County Genealogical Society; PO Box 336; Richburg, South Carolina 29729

Clarendon County Genealogical Society; Clarendon Co. Archives; 211 N. Brooks Street; Manning, South Carolina 29102; <http://www.rootsweb.com/~scclaren/archives.html>

Columbia Chapter, SCGS; PO Box 11353; Columbia, South Carolina 29211

Darlington County Historical Commission; 204 Hewitt St.; Darlington, South Carolina 29532

Department of History-Montreat Presbyterian Church; 318 Georgia Terr.; PO Box 849; Montreat, South Carolina 28757; 704.669.7061; Fax 704.669.5369

Faith Clayton Research Center, Rickman Library; Southern Wesleyan Univ.; Central, South Carolina 29630

Family History Library: 35 North West Temple Street: Salt Lake City, Utah 84150: 800.346.6044 or 801.240.2584: <http://www.familysearch.org>: Find a Family History Center near you: <http://www.familysearch.org/Eng/Library/FHC/frameset_fhc.asp>

Free Library; 404 King St.; Charleston, South Carolina 29407

General Thomas Sumter Chapter, SAR; Camden, South Carolina; <http://www.rocsoft.net/~mreich/>

Greenville Co. Library; 300 College St.; Greenville, South Carolina 29601

Greenville County Historical Society; PO Box 10472; Greenville, South Carolina 29603-0472; <http://www.greenvillehistory.org/>

Hilton Head Island Genealogical Society; 32 Office Park Rd Ste. 300; Hilton Head Island, South Carolina 29928-4640; 843.785-6834; 843.341.6493; <http://ourtown.islandpacket.com/32/>

Horry County Historical Society; 606 Main Street; Conway, South Carolina 29526-4340; <http://www.hchsonline.org/>

Huguenot Society of South Carolina; 138 Logan St.; Charleston, South Carolina 29401; 843.853.8476; <http://www.huguenotsociety.org/>

Jasper County Historical Society; PO Box 2111; Ridgeland, South Carolina 29936

Kershaw County Historical Society; 811 Fair Street; PO Box 501; Camden, South Carolina 29020; <http://www.mindspring.com/~ekchistory/>

Laurens Co. Library; 1017 W. Main St.; Laurens, South Carolina 29360-2647

Laurens District Chapter, SCGS; PO Box 1217; Laurens, South Carolina 29360-1217

Lexington County, South Carolina Genealogical Association; PO Box 1442; Lexington, South Carolina 29072

National Archives-Southeast Region (Atlanta); 1557 St. Joseph Avenue; East Point, Georgia 30344; 404.763.7477; Fax 404.763.7033

Office of Vital Records and Public Health Statistics; 2600 Bull Street; Columbia, South Carolina 29201; 803.734.4830; Fax 803.799.0301

Old Darlington District Chapter, SCGS; 307 Kings Place; Hartsville, South Carolina 29550; <http://www.geocities.com/Heartland/Estates/7212/>

Old Edgefield Dist. Archives Chapter, South Carolina Gen. Soc.; PO Box 468; Edgefield, South Carolina 29824

Old Edgefield District Genealogical Society; PO Box 546; Edgefield, South Carolina 29824.0546; <http://www.rootsweb.com/~scedgefi/oedgs.html>

Old Pendleton District Chapter, SCGS; 228 Ivydale Drive; Greenville, South Carolina 29609; <http://oldpendleton.homestead.com/>

Old St. Bartholomew Chapter, SCGS; 104 Wade Hampton Avenue; Walterboro, South Carolina 29488

Orangeburg German-Swiss Genealogical Society; PO Box 20266; Charleston, South Carolina 29413

Orangeburg German-Swiss Genealogical Society; PO Box 974; Orangeburg, South Carolina 29119-0974; <http://www.netside.com/~genealogy/orangeburgh.htm>

Parris Island Historical and Museum Society; PO Box 5202; Parris Island, South Carolina 29905.5202; <http://www.parrisisland.com/historic.htm>

Pee Dee Chapter, South Carolina Genealogical Society; PO Box 236; Latta, South Carolina 29565

Piedmont Historical Society; PO Box 8096; Spartanburg, South Carolina 29305; <http://www.angelfire.com/sc/piedmonths/info.html>

Pinckney District Chapter, SCIGS; PO Box 5281; Spartanburg, South Carolina 29304

Public Library; So. Pine St.; Spartanburg, South Carolina 29302

Richland Co. Public Library; 1431 Assembly St.; Columbia, South Carolina 29201-3101; 803.799.9084

Rock Hill Public Library; Box 32, 325 S. Oakland Ave.; Rock Hill, South Carolina 29730

Saluda County Historical Society; PO Box 22; Saluda, South Carolina 29138; <http://www.saludaschistorical.org/>

SCGS, Chesterfield District Chapter; PO Box 167; Chesterfield, South Carolina 29709-0167

Sons of the American Revolution, South Carolina Society; 2805 Highway 414; Taylors, South Carolina 29687

South Carolina Archives Dept.; 1430 Senate St.; Columbia, South Carolina 29201

South Carolina Baptist Historical Collection, James B. Duke Library; Furman University, 3300 Poinsett Highway; Greenville, South Carolina 29613-0600; 864.294.2194; Fax 864.294.2194

South Carolina Department of Archives and History; 1430 Senate Street, PO Box 11669, Capitol Station; Columbia, South Carolina 29211-1669; 803.734.8577; Fax 803.734.8820

South Carolina Department of Archives and History; Archives & History Center; 8301 Parklane Road; Columbia, South Carolina 29223; 803.896.6198; <http://www.state.sc.us/scdah/homepage.htm>

South Carolina Division Sons of Confederate Veterans; 1309 Fairlawn Drive; Sumter, South Carolina 29154; 803.481.3223; 803.691.4751; <http://www.scscv.org/>

South Carolina Genealogical Society; 2910 Duncan St.; Columbia, South Carolina 29205; <http://www.geocities.com/Heartland/Woods/2548/>

South Carolina Historical Society; 100 Meeting Street; Charleston, South Carolina 29401-2299; 803.723.3225; Fax 803.723.8584

South Carolina Methodist Conference Archives, Sandor Teszler Library; Wofford College, 429 N. Church Street; Spartanburg, South Carolina 29301-3663; 864.597.4300; Fax 864.597.4329

South Carolina State Library; 1500 Senate St.; Columbia, South Carolina 29201

Spartanburg County Historical Association; PO Box 887; Spartanburg, South Carolina 29304; <http://www.spartanarts.org/history/>

Thomas Cooper Library; University of South Carolina; Columbia, South Carolina 29208-0103; 803.777.3142; Fax 803.777.4661

Three Rivers Historical Society; 414 N. Main St.; Hemingway, South Carolina 29554; <http://www.threerivershistsoc.org/index.htm>

Bibliography and Record Sources

General Sources

Andrea, Leonardo. *Genealogical Correspondence: Collection of the Late Leonardo Andrea*. Microfilm of ms. and typescript collection in possession of Connie Andrea, Columbia, South Carolina. (Salt Lake City: Filmed by the Genealogical Society of Utah, 1974). 21 microfilm.

Andrea, Leonardo. *Genealogical Folders in the Leonardo Andrea Collection: Collection of the Late Leonardo Andrea*. Microfilm of ms., typescript, and printed materials collection in possession of Connie Andrea, Columbia, South Carolina. (Salt Lake City: Filmed by the Genealogical Society of Utah, 1974). 51 microfilm.

Austin, Jeannette H. *North Carolina - South Carolina Bible Records*. Riverdale, Georgia: J. H. Austin, 1987.

Bodie, Idella. *South Carolina Women*. 2nd ed. Orangeburg, South Carolina: Sandlapper Pub., 1991.

Carson, Helen C. *Records in the British Public Records Office Relating to South Carolina, 1663-1782*. Columbia, South Carolina: South Carolina Department of Archives and History, 1973.

Chandler, Marion C. *The South Carolina Archives: A Temporary Summary Guide*. 2nd ed. Columbia: South Carolina Department of Archives and History, 1976.

Cote, Richard N. *Local and Family History in South Carolina: A Bibliography*. Easley, South Carolina: Southern Historical Press, 1981.

Cote, Richard N.; and Patricia H. Williams, *Dictionary of South Carolina Biography, Vol. 1*. Easley, South Carolina: Southern Historical Press, 1985.

Cyclopedia of Eminent and Representative Men of the Carolinas of the Nineteenth Century. Madison, Wisconsin: Brant & Fuller, 1892.

Easterby, James H. *Guide to the Study and Reading of South Carolina History*. 2 vols. Columbia, South Carolina: Historical Commission of South Carolina, 1949-1950.

Hehir, Donald M. *Carolina Families: A Bibliography of Books about North and South Carolina Families*. Bowie, Maryland: Heritage Books, 1994.

Hemphill, James C. *Men of Mark in South Carolina…A Collection of Biographies of Leading Men of the State*. 4 vols. Washington, D.C.: Men of Mark Publishing Co., 1907-9.

Hendrix, Ge Lee Corley. *Research in South Carolina*. Arlington, Virginia: National Genealogical Society, 1992.

Hicks, Theresa. *South Carolina: A Guide for Genealogists*. Rev. ed. Columbia, South Carolina: Columbian Chapter, South Carolina Genealogical Society, 1996.

Holcomb, Brent Howard. *A Guide to South Carolina Genealogical Research and Records*. Rev. ed. Columbia, South Carolina: Brent Howard Holcomb, 1991.

Jones, Lewis P. *Books and Articles on South Carolina History*. 2nd ed. Columbia, South Carolina: University of South Carolina Press, 1991.

Journal of the Commons House of Assembly, 1736-1754. Columbia: Historical Commission of South Carolina, 1951-.

Kirkham, E. Kay. *An Index to Some of the Family Records of the Southern States*. Logan, Utah: Everton Publishers, 1979.

Lester, Memory Aldridge. *Bible Records from the Southern States*, 7 vols. in 6. Chapel Hill, North Carolina: Memory Aldridge Lester, 1956-62.

Lineage Charts South Carolina Genealogical Society Chapters. 4 vols. Greenville, South Carolina: Greenville Chapter, The South Carolina Genealogical Society, 1976-87?

Mizell, M. Hayes. *A Checklist of South Carolina State Publications*. 3 v. in 1. Columbia, South Carolina: Archives Department of South Carolina, 1962.

Moore, John Hammond. *Research Materials in South Carolina: A Guide Compiled and Edited for the South Carolina State Library Board with the Cooperation of the South Carolina Library Association*. Columbia, South Carolina: University of South Carolina Press, 1967.

Moore, John Hammond. *South Carolina Newspapers*. Columbia, South Carolina: University of South Carolina Press, 1988.

Neuffer, Claude. *Correct Mispronunciations of Some South Carolina Names*. Columbia, South Carolina: University of South Carolina Press, 1983.

Petty, Julian J. *The Growth and Distribution of Population in South Carolina*. Spartanburg, South Carolina: The Reprint Co., 1975.

Read, Motte Alston, comp. *Colonial Families of South Carolina* (Salt Lake City: Filmed by the Genealogical Society of Utah, 1952).

Rivers, William James. *A Sketch of the History of South Carolina to the Close of the Proprietary Government by the Revolution of 1719: With an Appendix Containing Many Valuable Records Hitherto Unpublished*. Charleston, South Carolina: McCarter & Co., 1856.

Sass, Herbert Ravenel. *The Story of the South Carolina Lowcountry*. 3 vols. West Columbia, South Carolina: J. F. Hyer Pub., [1956?].

Schweitzer, George K. *South Carolina Genealogical Research*. Knoxville: the author, 1985.

Snowden, Yates, and Harry G. Cutler. *History of South Carolina*. 5 vols. Chicago: Lewis Publishing Co., 1920.

South Carolina Genealogies: Articles from the South Carolina Historical and Genealogical Magazine. 5 vols. Spartanburg, South Carolina: The Reprint Co., 1983.

South Carolina Research Outline. Series US-States, No. 41. Salt Lake City: Family History Library, 1988.

South Carolina. Department of Archives and History. *A Guide to Local Government Records in the South Carolina Archives*. [South Carolina]: University of South Carolina Press, 1988.

South Carolina. Department of Archives and History. *Combined Alphabetical Index, 1695-1925: Consolidated Index & Spandex*. Microreproduction of original manuscript at the South Carolina Department of Archives and History, Columbia, South Carolina. c1992. [S.l.: s.n., 199-]. 19 microfilm.

Stampp, Kenneth M. *Records of Ante-Bellum Southern Plantations from the Revolution through the Civil War: Series A, Selections from the South Caroliniana Library, University of South Carolina*. Microfilm of original records in the South Caroliniana Library, University of South Carolina, Columbia, South Carolina. Frederick, Maryland: University Publications of America, 1985. 41 microfilm

Stampp, Kenneth M. *Records of Ante-Bellum Southern Plantations from the Revolution through the Civil War: Series B, Selections from the South Carolina Historical Society*. Microfilm of original records in the South Carolina Historical Society. Frederick, Maryland: University Publications of America, 1985. 10 microfilm.

Stokes, Allen H. *A Guide to the Manuscript Collection of the South Caroliniana Library*. Columbia, South Carolina: The Library, 1982.

The Huguenots of South Carolina and their Descendants. Microfilm of originals in Charleston, South Carolina. (Salt Lake City: Filmed by the Genealogical Society of Utah, 1952).

Wallace, David Duncan. *South Carolina: A Short History 1520-1948*. Columbia, South Carolina: University of South Carolina Press, 1951.

Weston, Plowden Charles Jennett. *Documents Connected with the History of South Carolina*. Woodbridge, Connecticut: Research Publications, [197-?].

Wooley, James E., ed. *A Collection of Upper South Carolina Genealogical and Family Records*. 3 vols. Easley, South Carolina: Southern Historical Press, 1979-82.

Atlases, Maps and Gazetteers

Black, James. "The Counties and Districts of South Carolina," in *Genealogical Journal*, vol. 5, no. 3, pp. 100-113. Salt Lake City: Utah Genealogical Association, 1976.

Cropper, Mariam D. *South Carolina Waterways As They Appear in Mill's Atlas…*. Salt Lake City: Accelerated Indexing Systems, 1977.

Mills, Robert. *Atlas of the State of South Carolina*. Reprinted as *Atlas of the States of South Carolina, 1825*. Easley, South Carolina: Southern Historical Press, 1980.

Names in South Carolina, 1954-. Columbia: University of South Carolina, 1954-1983.

Neuffer, Claude H., ed. *Names of South Carolina*. Vols. 1-12, 1954-1965. Columbia: Department of English, University of South Carolina, 1967. Reprint. Spartanburg, South Carolina: Reprint Co., 1976.

Puetz, C.J., comp. *South Carolina County Maps*. Lyndon Station, Wisconsin: Thomas Publishing Co., 1989.

Salley, Olin J. *Post Offices of Yesteryear, Interesting Old Lists Reveals Many Unusual Place Names and Changes Wrought by a Century of Progress*. (Salt Lake City: Filmed by the Genealogical Society of Utah, 1974).

Sheriff, G. Anne Campbell. *Pickens and Oconee Counties Post Offices, 1797-1971: Including South Carolina Post Offices, 1793-1832*. [S.l.]: Oconee County Historical Society, 1995.

Work Projects Administration. *Palmetto Place Names*. 1941. Reprint. Spartanburg, South Carolina: The Reprint Co., 1975.

Census Records

Available Census Records and Census Substitutes

Federal Census 1790, 1800, 1810, 1830, 1840, 1850, 1860, 1870, 1880, 1900, 1910, 1920, 1930.

Federal Mortality Schedules 1850, 1860, 1870, 1880.

Union Veterans and Widows 1890.

Dollarhide, William. *The Census Book: A Genealogist's Guide to Federal Census Facts, Schedules and Indexes*. Bountiful, Utah: Heritage Quest, 1999.

Kemp, Thomas Jay. *The American Census Handbook*. Wilmington, Delaware: Scholarly Resources, Inc., 2001.

Lainhart, Ann S. *State Census Records*. Baltimore: Genealogical Publishing Co., Inc., 1992.

Szucs, Loretto Dennis, and Matthew Wright. *Finding Answers in U.S. Census Records*. Ancestry Publishing, 2001

Thorndale, William, and William Dollarhide. *Map Guide to the U.S. Federal Censuses, 1790-1920*. Baltimore: Genealogical Publishing Co., 1987.

United States. Bureau of Internal Revenue. *Internal Revenue Assessment Lists for South Carolina, 1864-1866*. Washington, D.C.: The National Archives, 1972.

Court Records, Probate and Wills

Esker, Katie-Prince Ward. *South Carolina Wills and Other Court Records*. (Salt Lake City: Filmed by the Genealogical Society of Utah, 1998).

Gregorie, Anne King. *Records of the Court of Chancery of South Carolina, 1671-1779*. Washington, D.C.: American Historical Association, 1950.

Holcomb, Brent H. *Probate Records of South Carolina*. 3 vols. Easley, South Carolina: Southern Historical Press, 1977.

Houston, Martha Lou, comp. *Indexes to the County Wills of South Carolina*. 1939. Reprint. Baltimore: Genealogical Publishing Co., 1964.

Lesser, Charles H. *South Carolina Begins: The Records of a Proprietary Colony, 1663-1721*. Columbia, South Carolina: South Carolina Dept. of Archives and History, 1995.

Moore, Carolina T., and Agatha Aimar Simmons. *Abstracts of the Wills of the State of South Carolina*. 3 vols. Columbia, South Carolina: the compilers, 1960-69.

Moore, Caroline T. *Records of the Secretary of the Province of South Carolina, 1692-1721*. Columbia, South Carolina: R. L. Bryan Co, 1978.

South Carolina Will Transcripts, 1782-1868. Columbia, South Carolina: South Carolina Department of Archives and History, 1978. 31 microfilm.

South Carolina. Court of Vice-Admiralty. *Pre-federal Admiralty Court Records, Province and State of South Carolina, 1716-1789*. Washington, D.C.: The National Archives, [1981?]. 3 microfilm.

Warren, Mary B. *South Carolina Jury Lists, 1718 through 1783*. Danielsville, GA: Heritage Papers, 1977.

Warren, Mary B. *South Carolina Wills, 1670-1853, or Later:*

Compiled from C.W.A., W.P.A. Microfilms, and Original Volumes. Danielsville, Georgia: Heritage Papers, 1981.

Young, Willie Pauline. *A Genealogical Collection of South Carolina Wills and Records*. 2 vols. 1955. Reprint, Easley, South Carolina: Southern Historical Press, 1981.

Emigration, Immigration, Migration and Naturalization

Baldwin, Agnes Lelans. *First Settlers of South Carolina 1670-1700*. Easley, South Carolina: Southern Historical Press, 1985.

Filby, P. William. *Passenger and Immigration Lists Index*. Detroit: Gale Research Co., 1981, 1985, 1986.

Holcomb, Brent H. *South Carolina Naturalizations, 1783-1850*. Baltimore: Genealogical Publishing Co., 1985.

Jones, Jack Moreland, and Mary Bondurant Warren. *South Carolina Immigrants, 1760 to 1770*. Danielsville, Georgia: Heritage Papers, 1988.

Revill, Janie. *A Compilation of the Original Lists of Protestant Immigrants to South Carolina, 1763-1773*. 1939. Reprint. Baltimore: Genealogical Publishing Co., 1968.

Stephenson, Jean. *Scotch-Irish Migration to South Carolina, 1772*. Strasburg, Virginia Shenandoah Publishing House, 1971.

United States. District Court (Alabama: Southern District). *Declarations of Intentions, Naturalizations, and Petitions, 1855-1960*. Microfilm of originals at the National Archives in East Point, Georgia. (Salt Lake City: Filmed by the Genealogical Society of Utah, 1987-1989). 9 microfilm.

United States. District Court (South Carolina). *Record of Admissions to Citizenship, District of South Carolina, 1790-1906*. Microfilm of original records in the Federal Archives and Records Center, Atlanta, Georgia. Washington, D.C.: National Archives and Records Service, 1981.

United States. District Court. *Naturalization Records, South Carolina, 1790-1906*. Microfilm of originals at the National Archives in East Point, Georgia. (Salt Lake City: Filmed by the Genealogical Society of Utah, 1987-1989).

United States. Immigration and Naturalization Service. *Index to Passenger Lists of Vessels Arriving at Miscellaneous Ports in Alabama, Florida, Georgia, and South Carolina, 1890-1924*. Microreproduction of original records at the National Archives. [Washington, D.C.]: Microphotographed by Immigration and Naturalization Service, 1957. 26 microfilm.

Warren, Mary Bondurant. *Citizens and Immigrants–South Carolina, 1768*. Danielsville, Georgia: Heritage Papers, ca. 1980.

Land and Property

Bleser, Carol K. Rothrock. *The Promised Land: The History of the South Carolina Land Commission 1869-1890*. Columbia, South Carolina: University of South Carolina Press, 1969.

Bratcher, R. Wayne. *Index to Commissioner of Locations, Plat Books A and B, 1784-1788: In Addition to Families Naming Swamps, Branches, Creeks, Ponds, Rivers, Roads, and Counties of the Lower Ninety-Six District from the Coast of South Carolina as Far Inland as There Were Settlements*. Greenville, South Carolina: A Press, 1986.

Charleston County (South Carolina), Register of Mesne Conveyance. *An Index to Deeds of the Province State of South Carolina, 1719-1785, and Charlestown District, 1785-1800.* Easley, South Carolina: Southern Historical Press, 1977.

Early South Carolina Settlers, 1600's-1800's. [S.l.]: Brøderbund, 2000. CD-ROM.

Esker, Katie-Prince Ward. *South Carolina Memorials, 1731-1776: Abstracts of Selected Land Records from a Collection in the Department of Archives and History....* 2 vols. New Orleans: Polyanthos, 1973-1977.

Holcomb, Brent H. *North Carolina Land Grants in South Carolina,* 2 vols. Clinton, South Carolina: the author, 1975, 1976.

Holcomb, Brent H. *Petitions for Land from the South Carolina Council Journals.* Columbia, South Carolina: SCMAR, c1996-c1999.

Holcomb, Brent H. *South Carolina Deed Abstracts.* 3 vols. Columbia, South Carolina: SCMAR, 1996.

Hone, Wade E. *Land and Property Research in the United States.* Salt Lake City: Ancestry Incorporated, 1997.

Jackson, Ronald Vern. *Index to South Carolina Land Grants, 1784-1800.* Bountiful, Utah: Accelerated Indexing Systems, 1977.

Langley, Clara A. *South Carolina Deed Abstracts, 1719-1772.* 4 vols. Easley, South Carolina: Southern Historical Press, 1983-1984.

Lucas, Silas Emmett, Jr. *An Index to Deeds of the Province and State of South Carolina 1719-1785 and Charleston District 1785-1800.* Easley, South Carolina: Southern Historical Press, 1977.

Motes, Jesse Hogan. *South Carolina Memorials, Abstracts of Land Titles.* Greenville, South Carolina: Southern Historical Press, 1996.

Salley, A. S., Jr., and R. N. Olsberg, eds. *Warrants for Land in South Carolina 1672-1711.* Rev. ed. Columbia, South Carolina: University of South Carolina Press, 1973.

Salley, Alexander S. *Records of the Secretary of the Province and the Register of the Province of South Carolina, 1671-1675.* Columbia, South Carolina: Historical Commission of South Carolina, 1944.

Smith, William Roy. *South Carolina as a Royal Province, 1719-1776.* New York: Macmillan, 1903.

South Carolina Memorials; Registration of Land Grants, 1704-1776 and Index. Salt Lake City: Genealogical Society of Utah, 1950. 9 microfilm.

South Carolina. Secretary of State. *Miscellaneous Records, 1771-1868.* Microfilm of original records filmed at the Historical Commission of South Carolina located in Columbia, South Carolina (Salt Lake City: Filmed by the Genealogical Society of Utah, 1950-1951). 56 microfilm.

South Carolina. Secretary of State. *Mortgage Records, 1734-1860; Index, 1709-1840.* Microfilm of original records filmed at the Historical Commission in Columbia, South Carolina. (Salt Lake City: Filmed by the Genealogical Society of Utah, 1951). 27 microfilm.

South Carolina. Secretary of State. *Royal Land Grants, 1731-1775; Index, 1695-1775.* Microfilm of original records filmed at the Secretary of State's Office in Columbia, South Carolina. (Salt Lake City: Filmed by the Genealogical Society of Utah, 1951). 17 microfilm.

South Carolina. Surveyor General. *Land Grants, 1784-1882.* Microfilm of original records filmed in the Secretary of State's Office at Columbia, South Carolina. (Salt Lake City: Filmed by the Genealogical Society of Utah, 1950-1951). 50 microfilm.

South Carolina. Surveyor General. *South Carolina Land Plats, 1731-1861; Indexes, 1688-1872.* Microfilm of original records filmed at the Secretary of State's Office in Columbia, South Carolina. (Salt Lake City: Filmed by the Genealogical Society of Utah, 1950). 28 microfilm.

Military

Andrea, Leonardo. *South Carolina Colonial Soldiers and Patriots.* Columbia, South Carolina: N.p., 1952.

Clark, Murtie June, comp. *Colonial Soldiers of the South, 1732-1774.* Baltimore: Genealogical Publishing Co., 1983.

Ervin, Sara A., ed. *South Carolinians in the Revolution, with Service Records and Miscellaneous Data...1775-1855.* Ypsilanti, MI. 1959. Reprint. Baltimore: Genealogical Publishing Co., 1971.

Ervin, Sara Sullivan. *South Carolinians in the Revolution.* 1949. Reprint. Baltimore: Genealogical Publishing Co., 1965.

Flynn, Jean Martin. *The Militia in Antebellum South Carolina Society.* Spartanburg, South Carolina: The Reprint Co., c1991.

Haulsee, W. M., F.C. Howe, and Alfred C. Doyle. *Soldiers of the Great War,* 3 vols. Washington, D.C.: Soldiers Record Publishing Association, 1920.

Meyer, Jack Allen. *South Carolina in the Mexican War: A Regiment of Volunteers, 1846-1917.* [Columbia, South Carolina]: South Carolina Dept. of Archives and History, 1996.

Moss, Bobby Gilmer. *Roster of South Carolina Patriots in the American Revolution.* Baltimore: Genealogical Publishing Co., 1983.

Pierce, Alycon Trubey. *South Carolina Revolutionary Records, Selected Final Pension Payment Vouchers, 1818-1864: South Carolina: Charleston.* Athens, Georgia: Iberian Pub. Co., 1996.

Pruitt, Janye C. G. *Revolutionary War Pension Applicants Who Served from South Carolina.* N.p.: 1946.

Revill, Janie. *Copy of the Original Index Book Showing the Revolutionary Claims Filed in South Carolina Between August 20, 1783 and August 31, 1786, 1941.* Reprint. Baltimore: Genealogical Publishing Co., 1969.

Salley, A. S., Jr. *South Carolina Troops in Confederate Service.* Columbia, South Carolina: R. L. Bryan, 1913-30.

Salley, Alexander S., comp. *Records of the Regiments of the South Carolina Line.* Baltimore: Genealogical Publishing Co., 1977.

South Carolina, Department of Archives and History. *Stub Entries to Indents Issues in Payment of Claims Against South Carolina Growing Out of the Revolution.* 12 vols. Columbia, SC. 1919-57.

United Daughters of the Confederacy. *South Carolina Division. Recollections and Reminiscences, 1861-1865 through World War.* [S.l.]: The Society, c1990-.

United States. Adjutant General's Office. *Index to Compiled Service Records of Confederate Soldiers Who Served in Organizations from the State of South Carolina.* Washington, D.C.: The National Archives, 1962. 35 microfilm.

United States. Adjutant General's Office. *Index to Compiled Service Records of Volunteer Soldiers Who Served During the War of 1812 in Organizations from the State of South Carolina.* Washington, D.C.: The National Archives, 1966. 7 microfilm.

United States. Selective Service System. *South Carolina, World War I Selective Service System Draft Registration Cards, 1917-1918.* National Archives Microfilm Publications, M1509. Washington, D.C.: National Archives, 1987-1988.

Vital and Cemetery Records

Cemetery Records of Confederate Soldiers Buried in South Carolina. Typescript. Salt Lake City: Genealogical Society of Utah, 1947.

Clemens, William M. *North and South Carolina Marriage Records: From the Earliest Colonial Days to the Civil War.* Baltimore, Maryland: Genealogical Publishing Company, 1981.

Holcomb, Brent H. *South Carolina Marriages: 1688-1799.* 3 vols. Baltimore: Genealogical Publishing Co., 1980-81, 1984.

Holcomb, Brent H. *Supplement to South Carolina Marriages, 1688-1820.* Baltimore: Genealogical Publishing Co., 1984.

Huey, Olga Crosland. *South Carolina Cemetery Epitaphs.* Microfilm. Salt Lake City: Genealogical Society of Utah, 1974.

South Carolina Cemetery Records, 3 vols. Salt Lake City: Genealogical Society of Utah, 1941-54.

South Carolina Marriage Settlements, 1785-1889. Microfilm of originals in Columbia, South Carolina. (Salt Lake City: Filmed by the Genealogical Society of Utah, 1950). 9 microfilm.

South Carolina. State Board of Health. *Death Certificate Indexes, 1915-1944.* Columbia, South Carolina. [Columbia, South Carolina: State Records Center, 19–]. 53 microfiche.

South Carolina. State Board of Health. *South Carolina Death Certificates, 1915-1944.* Columbia, South Carolina. [Columbia, South Carolina: State Records Center, 19–]. 418 microfilm.

Works Progress Administration, South Carolina Historical Records Survey. *Index to Tombstone Inscriptions, 1930s.* Spartanburg, North Carolina: Historical Records Survey, n.d.

County Website	Map Index	Date Created	Parent County or Territory From Which Organized / Address/Details
Abbeville* www.sccounties.org/counties/ abbeville.htm	**N4**	**12 Mar 1785**	**District 96** Abbeville County; 102 Court Sq; PO Box 99; Abbeville, SC 29620-0099; Ph. 864.459.5074 Details: (Clk Ct has land rec from 1873, div & ct rec; Pro Judge has m & pro rec)
Aiken* www.aikencounty.net/	**K6**	**10 Mar 1871**	**Edgefield, Orangeburg, Barnwell, Lexington** Aiken County; 828 Richland Ave W; Aiken, SC 29801-3834; Ph. 803.642.1715 Details: (Co Hlth Dept has b & d rec; Pro Judge has m rec from 1911 & pro rec from 1875; Clk Ct has div, ct & land rec)
Allendale* www.allendalecounty.com/	**J9**	**6 Feb 1919**	**Barnwell, Hampton** Allendale County; 526 Memorial Ave; PO Box 126; Allendale, SC 29810-0126; Ph. 803.584.2737 Details: (Pro Judge has m & pro rec; Clk Cts has ct & land rec)
Anderson* www.andersoncountysc.org/	**N4**	**20 Dec 1826**	**Pendleton District** Anderson County; 100 S Main St; PO Box 8002; Anderson, SC 29624; Ph. 864.260.4053 Details: (Co Hlth Dept has b, d & bur rec; Pro Judge has m & pro rec; Clk Ct has div rec from 1949, land rec from 1788 & ct rec)
Bamberg www.sccounties.org/counties/ Bamberg.htm	**I8**	**25 Feb 1897**	**Barnwell** Bamberg County; 110 N Main St; PO Box 150; Bamberg, SC 29003-0150; Ph. 803.245.3025 Details: (Clk Ct has div, ct & land rec; Pro Judge has m & pro rec; Co Hlth Dept has b & d rec)
Barnwell www.sccounties.org/counties/ Barnwell.htm	**K8**	**1798**	**Orangeburg District** Barnwell County; Main St; PO Box 723; Barnwell, SC 29812-0723; Ph. 803.541.1020 Details: (Co Clk has ct & land rec from mid-1700's & div rec; Pro Judge has m & pro rec)
Beaufort www.co.beaufort.sc.us/	**I11**	**1769**	**Granville** Beaufort County; 100 Ribaut Rd; Beaufort, SC 29902; Ph. 843.470.5227 Details: (Created 1769 from Granville Co as an original judicial district) (Co Clk has b & d rec from 1915; Pro Judge has m & pro rec; rec prior to 1785 are filed in Charleston)
Berkeley www.berkeley.lib.sc.us/gov.html	**F8**	**31 Jan 1882**	**Charleston** Berkeley County; 223 N Live Oak Dr; Moncks Corner, SC 29461-3707; Ph. 843.761.6900 Details: (Clk Ct has div, ct & land rec; Pro Judge has m & pro rec; Co Hlth Dept has b, d & bur rec)
Berkeley, old		**1683**	**Original county (not present Berkeley Co.)** Details: (One of 4 original counties. Discontinued, 1769)
Calhoun www.inls.com/calhoun/index.asp	**I6**	**14 Feb 1908**	**Lexington, Orangeburg** Calhoun County; 302 S Railroad Ave; St. Matthews, SC 29135-1452; Ph. 803.874.3524 Details: (Co Hlth Dept has b & d rec from 1915; Pro Judge has m rec from 1911 & pro rec from 1908; Clk Ct has ct rec from 1908 & div rec 1949; Hist Commission has land, Bible, cem & other genealogical rec from 1735)
Camden District		**1769**	**Craven, Berkeley, old** Details: (Created from portions of Berkeley, old & Craven Cos as one of 7 original judicial districts. Discontinued in 1798 to form Chester, Lancaster, Fairfield, Kershaw & Sumter Counties)
Carteret District			Details: (Name changed to Granville 1700)
Charleston www.charlestoncounty.org/	**G9**	**1769**	**Colleton, Berkeley, old** Charleston County; 2144 Melbourne Ave; Charleston, SC 29405; Ph. 843.740.5700 Details: (Created in 1769 from portions of Colleton & Berkeley, old, as one of 7 original judicial districts; Split in 1798 to form Charleston & Colleton Cos) (Co Hlth Dept has b & d rec; Pro Judge has m, pro & ct rec; Clk Ct has div rec; Co Reg has land rec)

County Website	Map Index	Date Created	Parent County or Territory From Which Organized Address/Details
Cheraws District		1769	**Craven** Details: (Created in 1769 from Craven Co as one of 7 original judicial districts. Discontinued in 1798 to form Chesterfield, Darlington & Marlboro Cos)
Cherokee* www.sccounties.org/counties/ Cherokee.htm	L1	25 Feb 1897	**Union, York, Spartanburg** Cherokee County; 125 E Floyd Baker Blvd; PO Box Drawer 2289; Gaffney, SC 29340; Ph. 864.487.2574 Details: (Co Hlth Dept has b & d rec; Pro Judge has m & pro rec; Clk Ct has div, ct & land rec)
Chester www.sccounties.org/counties/Chester.htm	J3	1798	**Camden District** Chester County; 140 Main St; PO Box Drawer 580; Chester, SC 29706; Ph. 803.385.2605 Details: (Pro Judge has pro rec from 1789 & m rec from 1911; Clk Ct has land rec from 1785, div & ct rec)
Chesterfield www.sccounties.org/counties/ Chesterfield.htm	G3	1798	**Cheraws District** Chesterfield County; 200 W Main St; PO Box 529; Chesterfield, SC 29709; Ph. 843.623.2574 Details: (Clk Ct has b, d, bur, div, land & ct rec; Pro Judge has m & pro rec)
Claremont			Details: (see Sumter)
Clarendon www.clarendoncounty.com/	G6	1855	**Sumter District** Clarendon County; W Boyce St; PO Box E; Manning, SC 29102-0136; Ph. 803.435.4443 Details: (Cen schedules missing for 1820, 1830, 1840 & 1850) (Co Hlth Dept has b, d & bur rec from 1915; Pro Judge has m rec from 1911 & pro rec from 1856; Clk Ct has div rec from 1947, ct & land rec from 1856)
Colleton www.sccounties.org/counties/ Colleton.htm	H9	1798	**Charleston District** Colleton County; PO Box 620; Walterboro, SC 29488; Ph. 843.549.5791 Details: (Pro Ct has m rec from 1911 & pro rec from 1865; Co Hlth Dept has b & d rec from 1915; Clk Ct has div rec from 1949, land & ct rec from 1865; Veterans Affairs Off has mil rec from 1865; Co Lib has cem & other genealogical rec; rec prior to 1785 are filed
Colleton, old		1683	**Original county** Details: (One of 4 original counties. Discontinued, 1769)
Craven, old		1683	**Original county** Details: (One of 4 original counties. Discontinued, 1769)
Darlington www.sccounties.org/counties/ Darlington.htm	F4	1798	**Cheraws District** Darlington County; 1 Public Sq; Darlington, SC 29532; Ph. 843.398.4330 Details: (Co Clk has m rec from 1912, div rec from 1950, land rec from 1806 & ct rec; Pro Judge has m & pro rec)
Dillon* www.sccounties.org/counties/Dillon.htm	E4	5 Feb 1910	**Marion** Dillon County; PO Drawer 1220; Dillon, SC 29536-0449; Ph. 843.774.1425 Details: (Clk Cts has ct & land rec from 1910; Pro Judge has m & pro rec)
Dorchester www.sccounties.org/counties/ Dorchester.htm	H8	25 Feb 1897	**Berkeley, Colleton** Dorchester County; PO Box 158; St. George, SC 29477; Ph. 843.563.0120 Details: (Co Clk has b rec from 1915; Pro Judge has m & pro rec)
Edgefield www.edgefieldcounty.org/	L6	1795	**District 96** Edgefield County; 129 Courthouse Sq; Edgefield, SC 29824-0663; Ph. 803.637.4080 Details: (small portion of Aiken Co added to Edgefield in 1966) (Co Hlth Dept has b, d & bur rec; Pro Judge has m & pro rec; Co Clk has land, div & ct rec)
Fairfield www.sccounties.org/counties/ Fairfield.htm	J3	1798	**Camden District** Fairfield County; PO Drawer 299; Winnsboro, SC 29180; Ph. 803.712.6526 Details: (Clk Ct has div, land & ct rec; Co Hlth Dept has b & d rec; Pro Judge has m & pro rec)

County Website	Map Index	Date Created	Parent County or Territory From Which Organized Address/Details
Florence* www.florenceco.org/index.html	E5	22 Dec 1888	**Marion, Darlington, Clarendon, Williamsburg** Florence County; 180 N Irby St; Florence, SC 29501-3456; Ph. 843.665.3031 Details: (Co Hlth Dept has b & d rec; Pro Judge has m & pro rec; Clk Ct has div, ct & land rec)
Georgetown www.co.georgetown.sc.us/	D7	1769	**Craven** Georgetown County; 715 Prince St; Georgetown, SC 29440-3631; Ph. 843.546.5011 Details: (Created in 1769 from Craven Co as one of 7 original judicial districts; Split in 1798 to form Georgetown & Marion Cos) (Co Hlth Dept has b & d rec; Pro Judge has m rec from 1911 & pro rec; Clk Ct has div rec from 1949, land rec from 1866 & ct rec; rec prior to 1785 are filed in Charleston)
Granville www.co.greenville.sc.us/		1683	**Original county** Details: (One of 4 original counties. Discontinued, 1769)
Greenville www.co.greenville.sc.us/	M2	1798	**Washington District** Greenville County; 301 University Ridge Ste 100; Greenville, SC 29601-3665; Ph. 864.467.8551 Details: (Clk Ct has b & d rec from 1915, m rec from 1911, div & pro rec)
Greenwood www.co.greenwood.sc.us/	M5	2 Mar 1897	**Abbeville, Edgefield** Greenwood County; 528 Monument St; Greenwood, SC 29646; Ph. 864.942.8546 Details: (Co Hlth Dept has b & d rec; Pro Judge has m & pro rec; Clk Ct has div rec from 1937, ct & land rec from 1897)
Hampton www.sccounties.org/counties/ Hampton.htm	J9	18 Feb 1878	**Beaufort** Hampton County; 1 Elm St; PO Box 7; Hampton, SC 29924-0007; Ph. 803.943.7510 Details: (Co Hlth Dept has b & d rec; Clk Ct has ct & land rec; Pro Judge has m & pro rec)
Horry www.horrycounty.org/	C5	19 Dec 1801	**Georgetown District** Horry County; 1201 3rd Ave; Conway, SC 29526; Ph. 803.248.1885 Details: (Co Hlth Dept has b, d & bur rec; Clk Ct has div rec from 1947, ct & land rec; Pro Judge has m & pro rec)
Jasper* www.sccounties.org/counties/Jasper.htm	J10	30 Jan 1912	**Beaufort, Hampton** Jasper County; 305 Russell St; PO Box 248; Ridgeland, SC 29936-0248; Ph. 843.726.7781 Details: (Co Hlth Dept has b & d rec; Pro Judge has m & pro rec; Clk Ct has div, ct & land rec)
Kershaw www.camden-sc.org/	H3	1798	**Camden District** Kershaw County; 1121 Broad St; Camden, SC 29020-3638; Ph. 803.425.1527 Details: (Clk Ct has div rec from 1949, ct & land rec from 1791; Pro Judge has m & pro rec)
Lancaster www.sccounties.org/counties/ Lancaster.htm	H2	1798	**Camden District** Lancaster County; PO Box 1809; Lancaster, SC 29720-1585; Ph. 803.285.1585 Details: (Co Hlth Dept has b & d rec; Pro Judge has m & pro rec; Clk Ct has div rec from 1958, ct rec from 1800 & land rec from 1762)
Laurens www.geocities.com/BourbonStreet/4492/	L4	1795	**District 96** Laurens County; PO Box 445; Laurens, SC 29360-0445; Ph. 864.984.3538 Details: (Co Hlth Dept has b & d rec; Pro Judge has m & pro rec; Clk Ct has div rec, ct rec from 1900 & land rec from 1790)
Lee www.rootsweb.com/~sclee/index.html	G4	25 Feb 1902	**Darlington, Sumter, Kershaw** Lee County; 11 Courthouse Sq; PO Box 281; Bishopville, SC 29010; Ph. 803.484.5341 Details: (Co Hlth Dept has b rec from 1915, d rec from 1902, div & bur rec; Pro Judge has m & pro rec from 1902; Clk Ct has ct & land rec from 1902)
Lexington www.lex-co.com/my_lex.html	J5	1804	**Orangeburg District** Lexington County; 139 E Main St; Lexington, SC 29072; Ph. 803.359.8235 Details: (Co Hlth Dept has b & d rec; Pro Judge has m & pro rec; Clk Ct has div rec from 1949, land rec from 1839 & ct rec)

County Website	Map Index	Date Created	Parent County or Territory From Which Organized Address/Details
Liberty			Details: (see Marion) (used briefly as a subdivision of Marion Co)
Marion www.geocities.com/BourbonStreet/ 1786/marion.html	D5	1798	**Georgetown District** Marion County; PO Box 295; Marion, SC 29571-0183; Ph. 843.423.8240 Details: (Co Hlth Dept has b, d & bur rec; Pro Judge has m & pro rec; Clk Ct has div rec from 1948, ct & land rec from 1800)
Marlboro www.rootsweb.com/~scmarlbo/	E3	1798	**Cheraws District** Marlboro County; 205 Usher St; Bennetsville, SC 29512-0996; Ph. 843.479.5613 Details: (Co Clk has b, d, bur, div & ct rec; Pro Judge has m & pro rec)
McCormick* www.geocities.com/BourbonStreet/6420/	M5	19 Feb 1916	**Greenwood, Abbeville** McCormick County; 133 S Mine St; McCormick, SC 29835; Ph. 864.465.2195 Details: (Clk Ct has div, land & ct rec from 1916; Pro Judge has m & pro rec from 1916; Co Hlth Dept has b & d rec from 1916)
Newberry www.rootsweb.com/~scnewbe2/	K4	1795	**District 96** Newberry County; 1226 College St; PO Box 278; Newberry, SC 29108-0278; Ph. 803.321.2110 Details: (Clk Ct has b & d rec from 1915, m rec from 1911, div rec from 1949, pro, ct & land rec from 1776)
Ninety-Six District		1769	**Granville, Colleton, old** Details: (Created in 1769 from Colleton, old & Granville as one of 7 original judicial districts. Discontinued in 1798 to form Abbeville, Edgefield, Newberry, Laurens & Spartanburg Cos)
Oconee* www.rootsweb.com/~scoconee/ oconee.html	P2	29 Jan 1868	**Pickens** Oconee County; W Main St; PO Box 678; Walhalla, SC 29691; Ph. 864.638.4280 Details: (Co Hlth Dept has b & d rec from 1915; Pro Judge has m rec from 1911 & pro rec from 1868; Clk Ct has div rec from 1949, ct & land rec from 1868)
Orange		1800	**Orangeburg District** Details: (Former county in Orangeburg District abt 1800, mostly in present-day Orangeburg Co., with parts in present-day cos of Bamberg, Calhoun & Lexington)
Orangeburg www.orangeburgsc.net/	I7	1769	**Colleton, old, Berkeley, old** Orangeburg County; 190 Gibson St; Orangeburg, SC 29115-5463; Ph. 803.533.6260 Details: (Created in 1769 from Colleton, old & Berkeley, old as one of 7 original judicial districts; Split in 1798 to form Orangeburg & Barnwell Cos) (Clk Ct has div rec from 1949, ct & land rec from 1865; Co Hlth Dept has b, d & bur rec; Pro Judge has m & pro re
Pendleton		1798	**Washington District** Details: (see Pickens & Anderson) (Discontinued in 1826 to form Pickens & Anderson Cos)
Pickens* www.rootsweb.com/~scpicke2/	O2	20 Dec 1826	**Pendleton District** Pickens County; 214 E Main St; Pickens, SC 29671-0215; Ph. 864.898.5862 Details: (Clk Ct has b & d rec from 1915, div rec from 1949, ct rec from 1868 & land rec; Pro Judge has m & pro rec)
Pickney District		1795	**Original District** Details: (Discontinued in 1798 to form Union & York Cos)
Richland* www.geocities.com/frankoclark/richland/	I5	1799	**Kershaw District** Richland County; 1701 Main St #205; Columbia, SC 29202; Ph. 803.748.4684 Details: (1800 cen schedules missing) (Pro Judge has m, pro & ct rec; Co Aud has land rec)
Salem		1800	**Sumter District** Details: (see Sumter) (Former county in Sumter District abt 1800; part of Sumter Co abt 1810. Parts lay in the present-day cos of Lee, Sumter, Clarendon & Florence)
Saluda* www.rootsweb.com/~scsaluda/index.htm	L5	25 Feb 1896	**Edgefield** Saluda County; 100 E Church St; Saluda, SC 29138; Ph. 864.445.3303 Details: (Clk Ct has div, ct & land rec; Pro Judge has m & pro rec)

County Website	Map Index	Date Created	Parent County or Territory From Which Organized Address/Details
Spartanburg www.rootsweb.com/~scsparta/	L2	1795	**96 District** Spartanburg County; 180 Magnolia St; Spartanburg, SC 29306; Ph. 864.596.2591 Details: (Co Hlth Dept has b & d rec; Pro Judge has m rec from 1911 & pro rec from 1700; Clk Ct has div rec & ct rec from 1785; RMC Office has land rec)
Sumter www.rootsweb.com/~scsumter/index.html	G5	1798	**Camden District** Sumter County; 141 N Main St; Sumter, SC 29150-4965; Ph. 803.773.1581 Details: (Co Hlth Dept has b & d rec; Pro Judge has m rec from 1910 & pro rec from 1900; Clk Ct has div, ct & land rec)
Union www.rootsweb.com/~scunion/union.html	K3	1798	**Pinckney District** Union County; 210 W Main St; PO Box 200; Union, SC 29379-0200; Ph. 864.429.1630 Details: (Clk Ct has ct rec from 1785, div & land rec; Pro Judge has m & pro rec)
Washington		1795	**Original District** Details: (Discontinued in 1798 to form Pendleton & Greenville Cos)
Williamsburg www.rootsweb.com/~scwillia/html.htm	E6	1802	**Georgetown District** Williamsburg County; 125 W Main St; Kingstree, SC 29556-3347; Ph. 843.354.9321 Details: (Clk Ct has div rec from 1948, ct & land rec from 1806; Pro Judge has m rec from 1911 & pro rec)
Winyaw			Details: (Formerly a county in Georgetown District, later became Georgetown Co)
York www.rootsweb.com/~scyork/	J1	1798	**Pickney District** York County; S Congress; PO Box 649; York, SC 29745; Ph. 803.684.8505 Details: (Co Hlth Dept has b rec from 1915, d & bur rec; Pro Judge has m & pro rec; Clk Ct has div rec from 1942, ct & land rec from 1786)

Notes

Pasque

SOUTH DAKOTA

CAPITAL: PIERRE – TERRITORY 1861 – STATE 1889 (40TH)

French explorers entered South Dakota in 1742, but French interest waned after the French and Indian War. The United States gained the region with the Louisiana Purchase in 1803. Lewis and Clark made their exploration of the area between 1804 and 1806. Only hardy fur traders ventured into the area before 1858. In that year, the Yankton Sioux Indians ceded their claim to southeastern Dakota to the United States. Settlements sprang up at Yankton, Vermillion, and other sites between the Big Sioux and Missouri rivers. In 1861, the Dakotas were made into one territory, after years in the Missouri, Minnesota, Iowa, Wisconsin, Michigan and Nebraska territories. The Dakota Territory covered all of North and South Dakota, Montana, and northern Wyoming. Montana was taken away in 1864, Wyoming in 1868, and the territory divided into North and South Dakota in 1867.

About 200 men from the Dakota Territory served with the Union during the Civil War. Discovery of gold in the Black Hills in 1875 led to an upswing in settlement. Railroads came into the area between 1878 and 1888 and stimulated the Dakota land boom. South Dakota entered the Union in 1889 and all but three of its 68 counties were formed. Railroads reached the western part of the state during the first decade of the 20th century, bringing thousands of homesteaders to the area. The predominating nationalities in South Dakota are Norwegian, German, Russian, Swedish, Danish, Czech, English, Austrian, Irish, Finnish, Polish, Greek, and Italian.

Look for vital records in the following locations:

- **Birth and death records:** Contact Registrar of Deeds for some records created before 1905. Records of births, marriages, divorces, and deaths from 1905 on file with the State Department of Health, Vital Records in Pierre, South Dakota.
- **Wills and probate matters:** Kept by district court clerks. Probate records prior to statehood were kept by the Territorial Probate Court and are available from the Archives Division of the South Dakota State Historical Society in Pierre.
- **Census records:** South Dakota was included in the 1836 Wisconsin, 1840 Iowa, 1850 Minnesota (Pembina District), and 1860 to 1880 Dakota territorial censuses. Indexes have been published for some of these censuses. State and territorial censuses for 1885, 1895, 1905, 1915, 1925, 1935, and 1945 are available at the State Historical Society.

State Department of Health Vital Records	South Dakota State Historical Society
600 East Capitol	Archives Division
Pierre, South Dakota 57501	800 Governors Drive
605.773.4961	Pierre, South Dakota 57501

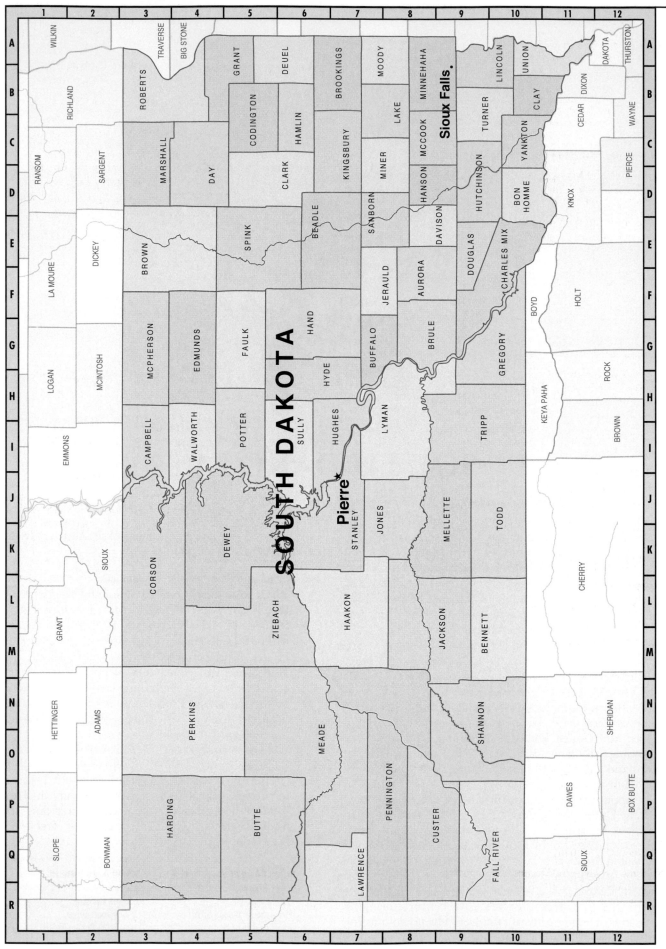

Societies and Repositories

Aberdeen Area Genealogical Society; PO Box 493; Aberdeen, South Dakota 57402-0493

Alexander Mitchell Public Library; 519 S. Kline St.; Aberdeen, South Dakota 57401

Bennett County Genealogical Society; PO Box 483; Allen, South Dakota 57714

Brookings Area Genealogical Society; 524 Fourth St.; Brookings, South Dakota 57006

Bureau of Land Management (BLM); 222 North 32nd Street, PO Box 36800; Billings, Montana 59101; 406.255.2940; Fax 406.255.2894

Center for Western Studies; PO Box 727, Augustana College; Sioux Falls, South Dakota 57197; 605.336.4921; Fax 605.336.5447

Center of the Nation, AHSGR; 7 Swan Lane; Spearfish, South Dakota 57783; 605.642.1149

Congregational Library; 14 Beacon Street; Boston, Massachusetts 02108; 617.523.0470; Fax 617.523.0470;

East River Genealogical Forum; R.R. 2, PO Box 148; Wolsey, South Dakota 57394

Evangelical Lutheran Church of America (ELCA Archives); 8765 West Higgins Road; Chicago, Illinois 60631-4198; 773.380.2818

Family Tree Genealogical Society; PO Box 202; Winner, South Dakota 57580-0202

Heritage Club-Platte; Rt. 2, PO Box 128; Platte, South Dakota 57369-0128

Homestead Chapter, AHSGR; PO Box 98; Freeman, South Dakota 57029-0098; 605.925.7834

Hyde County Historical & Genealogical Society; PO Box 392; Highmore, South Dakota 57345-0392

I.D. Weeks Library, University of South Dakota; 414 E. Clark Street; Vermillion, South Dakota 57069; 605.677.5371; Fax 605.677.5488

Kingsbury Genealogical Society; PO Box 330; DeSmet, South Dakota 57231-0330

Lake County Genealogical Society; c/o Karl Mundt Library; Dakota State College; Madison, South Dakota 57042

Lyman-Brule Genealogical Society; 110 E. Lawler; Chamdberlain, South Dakota 57325

Methodist, Archives and History Library, Dakotas Conference, United Methodist Church; 1331 West University Boulevard, PO Box 460; Mitchell, South Dakota 57301; 605.996.6552; Fax 605.996.1766

Mitchell Area Genealogical Society; 620 N. Edmunds; Mitchell, South Dakota 57301

Moody County Genealogical Society; 501 W. First Ave.; Flandreau, South Dakota 57028-1003

Murdo Genealogical Society; PO Box 441; Murdo, South Dakota 57559-0441

National Archives and Records Administration-Rocky Mountain Region; PO Box 25307, Denver Federal Center; South Dakota; Denver, Colorado 80225; 303.236.0817; Fax 303.236.9297;

National Archives-Central Plains Region; 2312 East Bannister Road; Kansas City, Missouri 64131-3011; 816.926.6272; Fax 816.926.6982

North Central South Dakota Genealogical Society; 178 Southshore Drive; Mina, South Dakota 57462-3000

Pierre-Ft. Pierre Genealogical Society; PO Box 925; Pierre, South Dakota 57501-0925

Platte Heritage Club; Rt. 2, PO Box 128; Platte, South Dakota 57369

Rapid City Society for Genealogical Research; PO Box 1495; PO Box 1495; Rapid City, South Dakota 57709-1495

Roman Catholic, Diocese of Rapid City, Chancery Office; 606 Cathedral Drive, PO Box 678; Rapid City, South Dakota 57709; 605.343.3541; Fax 605.348.7985

Roman Catholic, Diocese of Sioux Falls, Chancery Office; 3100 West 41st Street; Sioux Falls, South Dakota 57105; 605.334.9861; Fax 605.333.3346

Sioux Valley Genealogical Society; 200 W. 6th St.; Sioux Falls, South Dakota 57104-6001

South Dakota Genealogical Society; PO Box 1101; Pierre, South Dakota 57501-1101; <www.rootsweb.com/ ~sdgenweb/gensoc/sdgensoc.html>

South Dakota State Historical Society; 900 Governors Drive; Pierre, South Dakota 57501-2217; 605.773.3458; Fax 605.773.6041;

State Department of Health, Vital Records, Department of Health; 445 East Capitol; Pierre, South Dakota 57501-3185; 605.773.3355

State Historical Society Library; Memorial Bldg.; Pierre, South Dakota 57501

Tri-State Genealogical Society; c/o Public Library; 905 5th St.; Belle Fourche, South Dakota 57717-1705; <scream.iw.net/ ~shepherd/>

Union County Historical Society; PO Box 552; Elk Point, South Dakota 57025

University of South Dakota Library; Vermillion, South Dakota 57069

Watertown Genealogical Society; 611 N.E. B Ave.; Watertown, South Dakota 57201

Yankton Genealogical Society; PO Box 71; Missions Hills, South Dakota 57406

Bibliography and Record Sources

General Sources

Alexander, Ruth A., et al., comps. *South Dakota: Changing, Changeless, 1889-1989 [sic]*. South Dakota Library Association, 1985.

Fox's Who's Who Among South Dakotans: A Biographical Directory of Citizens Who Are Prominent in Professional, Political, Business and Civic Affairs of the State. 2 vols. Pierre, South Dakota: Fox Kindley, 1929.

Holley, Frances Chamberlain. *Once Their Home: or Our Legacy From the Dahkotahs*. Chicago: Donohue & Henneberry, 1892.

Kingsbury, George Washington. *History of Dakota Territory and South Dakota: Its History and Its People By George Martin Smith*. 5 vols. Chicago: S.J. Clarke Co., 1915.

Memorial and Biographical Record and Illustrated Compendium of Biography [Central South Dakota]: Containing a Compendium of Local Biography...of Central South Dakota...also a Compendium of the National Biography, Containing Biographical Sketches of Hundreds of the Greatest Men and Celebrities America has Produced. Chicago: George A. Ogle, 1899. Salt Lake City: Genealogical Society of Utah, 1963. Microfilm.

Memorial and Biographical Record, the Black Hills Region: an Illustrated Compendium of Biography Containing a Compendium of Local Biography, Including Biographical Sketches of Prominent Old Settlers and Representative Citizens of the Black Hills Region...also a Compendium of National Biography. Chicago: Geo. A. Ogle & co., 1898. Salt Lake City: Genealogical Society of Utah, 1976. Microfilm.

Memorial and Biographical Record: An Illustrated Compendium of Biography Containing a Compendium of Local Biography. Chicago: George A. Ogle Co., 1897. Tucson, Arizona: W.C. Cox Co., 1974. Microfilm.

Prairie Progress in West Central South Dakota. Sioux Falls, South Dakota: Historical Society of Old Stanley County, South Dakota, 1968

Schell, Herbert S. *History of South Dakota.* 2nd ed. Lincoln, Nebraska: University of Nebraska Press, 1968.

Sioux Valley Genealogical Society. *Pioneer certificates.* (Salt Lake City: Filmed by the Genealogical Society of Utah, 1990). 20 Microfilm.

South Dakota Research Outline. Series US-States, no. 41. Salt Lake City: Family History Library, 1988.

State Historical Society of North Dakota. *Historical Data Project; Pioneer Biography Files.* Bismarck, North Dakota: State Historical Society of North Dakota, 1988-1989. 34 Microfilm.

Wagner, Sally Roesch. *Daughters of Dakota.* 6 vols. Yankton, South Dakota: Daughters of Dakota, c1989.

Atlases, Maps and Gazetteers

Federal Writer's Project. *South Dakota Place Names.* Vermillion: University of South Dakota. 1940.

Phillips, George H. *Postoffices and Postmarks of Dakota Territory.* Crete, Nebraska: J-B Publishing, 1973.

Phillips, George H. *The Postoffices of South Dakota, 1861-1930.* Crete, Nebraska: J-B Publishing, 1975.

R. L. Polk & Company. *Northwestern Gazetteer: Minnesota, North and South Dakota and Montana Gazetteer and Business Directory.* St. Paul, Minnesota: R. L. Polk & Company, 1914.

Sneve, Virginia D. H. *South Dakota Geographic Names.* Vermillion: University of South Dakota, 1941. Reprint. Sioux Falls, South Dakota: Brevet Press, 1973.

Census Records

Available Census Records and Census Substitutes

Federal Census 1860, 1870, 1880, 1900, 1910, 1920, 1930.

Federal Mortality Schedules 1860, 1870, 1880.

Union Veterans and Widows 1890.

State/Territorial Census 1836, 1885, 1895, 1905, 1915, 1925, 1935, 1945.

Dollarhide, William. *The Census Book: A Genealogist's Guide to Federal Census Facts, Schedules and Indexes.* Bountiful, Utah: Heritage Quest, 1999.

Kemp, Thomas Jay. *The American Census Handbook.* Wilmington, Delaware: Scholarly Resources, Inc., 2001.

Lainhart, Ann S. *State Census Records.* Baltimore: Genealogical Publishing Co., Inc., 1992.

Szucs, Loretto Dennis, and Matthew Wright. *Finding Answers in U.S. Census Records.* Ancestry Publishing, 2001.

Thorndale, William, and William Dollarhide. *Map Guide to the U.S. Federal Censuses, 1790-1920.* Baltimore: Genealogical Publishing Co., 1987.

Court Records, Probate and Wills

Note: For these records search the individual counties.

Emigration, Immigration, Migration and Naturalization

Lareau, Paul J. and Elmer Courteau. *French-Canadian Families of the North Central States: A Genealogical Dictionary.* 8 vols. St. Paul, Minnesota: Northwest Territory French and Canadian Heritage Institute, 1980.

University of Minnes. *The Immigration History Research Center: A Guide to Collections.* New York: Greenwood Press, 1991.

Land and Property

Bureau of Land Management. *South Dakota BLM Database.* South Dakota: SDGENWEB, 2002. Online database - <www.rootsweb.com/~usgenweb/sd/land/sdland.htm>

Gates, Paul Wallace. *Fifty Million Acres: Conflicts Over Kansas Land Policy, 1854-1890.* Norman, Oklahoma: University of Oklahoma Press, 1997.

Green, Charles L. *The Administration of the Public Domain in South Dakota.* Pierre, South Dakota: Hipple Printing, 1939.

Hibbard, Benjamin Horace. *A History of the Public Land Policies.* Madison: University of Wisconsin Press, 1965.

Hone, Wade E. *Land and Property Research in the United States.* Salt Lake City: Ancestry Incorporated, 1997.

Skogen, Larry C. *Indian Depredation Claims, 1796-1920.* Norman: University of Oklahoma Press, c1996.

Military

Haulsee, W. M., F.G. Howe, A. C. Doyle, *Soldiers of the Great War.* 3 vols. Washington, DC: Soldiers Record Publishing Association, 1920.

United States Selective Service System. *South Dakota, World War I Selective Service System Draft Registration Cards, 1917-1918.* National Archives Microfilm Publications, M1509. Washington, DC: National Archives, 1987-1988.

United States. Adjutant General's Office. *Index to Compiled Service Records of Volunteer Union Soldiers Who Served in Organizations from the Territory of Dakota.* Washington, DC: The National Archives, 1964.

United States. Army. *Registers of Enlistments in the United States Army, 1798-1914.* Washington, DC: National Archives, 1956.

United States. Veterans Administration. *Pension Index File, Alphabetical; of the Veterans Administrative Contact and Administrative Services, Administrative Operations Services, 1861-1934.* Washington, DC: Veterans Administration, Publications Service, 1953.

United States. Veterans Administration. *Pension Index Files, Indian Wars, 1892-1926.* Washington, DC: Veterans Administration, 1959.

Vital and Cemetery Records

Krueger, Maurice, and Florence Krueger. *South Dakota Cemeteries, 1990.* Mina, South Dakota: the authors, 1990.

Rapid City Society for Genealogical Research. *Some Black Hills Area Cemeteries, South Dakota.* 6 vols. Rapid City, South Dakota: Rapid City Society for Genealogical Research, 1993.

United States. Bureau of Indian Affairs. Cheyenne River Agency. *Agency Records, 1869-1951.* (Kansas City, Missouri: Filmed by the National Archives, 1978). 14 Microfilm.

United States. Bureau of Indian Affairs. Crow Creek Agency. *Birth and Death Records, 1919-1939.* Kansas City, Missouri: Federal Archives and Records Center, 1976. Microfilm.

United States. Bureau of Indian Affairs. Pine Ridge Agency. *Birth and Death Records, 1895-1950.* Kansas City, Missouri: Federal Archives and Records Center, 1976. 2 Microfilm.

United States. Bureau of Indian Affairs. Rosebud Agency. *Birth and Death Records, 1900-1946.* (Salt Lake City: Filmed by the Genealogical Society of Utah, 1976). 2 Microfilm.

United States. Bureau of Indian Affairs. Sisseton Agency. *Birth and Death Records, 1928-1945.* Kansas City, Missouri: Federal Archives and Records Center, 1977. Microfilm.

United States. Bureau of Indian Affairs. Standing Rock Agency. *Births, Marriages and Deaths, 1880-1942.* Kansas City, Missouri: Federal Archives and Records Center, 1977. 2 Microfilm.

United States. Work Projects Administration (South Dakota). *South Dakota Grave Registration Project; Cemetery Information.* Salt Lake City: Genealogical Society of Utah. 1980. 17 Microfilm.

United States. Work Projects Administration (South Dakota). *South Dakota Graves Registration Service; Field Data— Veterans.* Salt Lake City: Genealogical Society of Utah, 1980. 12 Microfilm.

County Website	Map Index	Date Created	Parent County or Territory From Which Organized Address/Details
Armstrong		8 Mar 1883	**Cheyenne, Rusk, Stanley** Details: (see Dewey) (Formerly Pyatt Co. Name changed to Armstrong 6 Jan 1895. Eliminated 4 Nov 1952 to Dewey)
Armstrong, old		8 Jan 1873	**Charles Mix, Hutchinson** Details: (see Hutchinson) (Eliminated 1 Oct 1879 to Hutchinson)
Ashmore		8 Jan 1873	**Buffalo** Details: (see Potter) (Name changed to Potter 14 Jan 1875)
Aurora www.rootsweb.com/~sdaurora/	F8	1 Oct 1879	**Cragin, Wetmore** Aurora County; 401 S Main St; PO Box 366; Plankinton, SD 57368; Ph. 605.942.7165 Details: (Organized 29 Aug 1881) (Clk Ct has div, pro & ct rec from 1879; Reg of Deeds has b, m, d & bur rec; Co Asr has land rec)
Beadle www.rootsweb.com/~sdbeadle/	E6	1 Oct 1879	**Spink, Clark, Burchard, Kingsbury** Beadle County; 450 3rd St SW; Huron, SD 57350; Ph. 605.353.7165 Details: (Organized 9 Jul 1880) (Clk Cts has div rec from 1884, pro & ct rec from 1893 & land rec; Reg of Deeds has b, m, d & bur rec)
Beadle, old		8 Jan 1873	**Hanson** Details: (see Brown) (Eliminated 1 Oct 1879 to Brown & Unorganized Territory)
Bennett* www.rootsweb.com/~sdbennet/	M9	3 Jun 1909	**Lugenbeel, Shannon, Washington, Washabaugh** Bennett County; 202 Main St; Martin, SD 57551; Ph. 605.685.6969 Details: (Attached to Fall River Co prior to organization 27 Apr 1912) (Reg of Deeds has land rec from 1907, m rec from 1912, b & d rec from 1913 & bur rec from 1943; Clk Cts has div, pro & ct rec)
Big Sioux		23 May 1857	**Brown County, Minnesota** Details: (Attached to Pipestone County, Minnesota. Eliminated 11 May 1858 when Minnesota state was created)
Bon Homme www.rootsweb.com/~sdbonhom/	D10	5 Apr 1862	**Unorganized Territory** Bon Homme County; PO Box 6; Tyndall, SD 57066; Ph. 605.589.4215 Details: (Clk Ct has pro rec from 1900, ct rec from 1878 & div rec; Reg of Deeds has b, m, d & mil rec)
Boreman		8 Jan 1873	**Unorganized Territory** Details: (see Corson) (Attached to Campbell Co. Eliminated 2 Mar 1909 to Corson)
Bramble		8 Jan 1873	**Hanson** Details: (Eliminated 1 Oct 1879 to Miner)
Brookings www.rootsweb.com/~sdbrooki/	B7	5 Apr 1862	**Unorganized Territory** Brookings County; 314 6th Ave; Brookings, SD 57006; Ph. 605.692.6284 Details: (Organized 13 Jan 1871) (Clk Ct has div, pro & ct rec; Reg of Deeds has b, m & d rec from 1905, bur rec from 1940, land & mil rec)
Brown www.brown.sd.us/	E3	1 Oct 1879	**Mills, Stone, Beadle, old** Brown County; 101 1st Ave SE; Aberdeen, SD 57401-4203; Ph. 605.622.2266 Details: (Organized 14 Sep 1880) (Clk Cts has b, m, d, bur, div, pro & ct rec; Reg of Deeds has land rec)
Bruguier		8 May 1862	**Unorganized Territory** Details: (Attached to Charles Mix. Eliminated 6 Jan 1864 to Buffalo & Charles Mix)
Brule www.rootsweb.com/~sdbrule/	G8	14 Jan 1875	**Charles Mix** Brule County; 300 S Courtland St; Chamberlain, SD 57325; Ph. 605.734.5443 Details: (Reg of Deeds has b & d rec from 1905, bur rec from 1941 & land rec from 1880; Co Treas has m rec from 1882; Co Clk has div rec from 1885, pro & nat rec from 1880 & ct rec from 1882)
Buffalo* www.geocities.com/lynettet.geo/ buffalo/buffalo.html	G7	6 Jan 1864	**Brugier, Charles Mix, Unorganized Territory** Buffalo County; PO Box 148; Gann Valley, SD 57341-0148; Ph. 605.293.3234 Details: (Attached to Bon Homme Co prior to organization 13 Jan 1871) (Reg of Deeds has b & d rec from 1905, bur rec from 1941 & land rec; Co Treas has m rec from 1887; Co Clk has div rec from 1915, pro & ct rec from 1885)

County Website	Map Index	Date Created	Parent County or Territory From Which Organized Address/Details
Burchard		8 Jan 1873	**Hanson** Details: (Eliminated 1 Oct 1879 to Beadle & Hand)
Burdick		8 Mar 1883	**Harding** Details: (Eliminated 28 Feb 1889 to Harding)
Butte www.rootsweb.com/~sdbutte/	P5	6 May 1883	**Lawrence, Mandan** Butte County; 839 5th Ave; Belle Fourche, SD 57717; Ph. 605.892.2516 Details: (Reg of Deeds has b & d rec from 1905, bur rec from 1930 & land rec; Co Treas has m rec from 1890; Clk Ct has div rec from 1890, pro rec from 1884 & ct rec from 1892)
Campbell www.ehrman.net/campbell/index.html	I3	8 Jan 1873	**Buffalo** Campbell County; PO Box 146; Mound City, SD 57646; Ph. 605.955.3536 Details: (Organized 17 Apr 1884) (Reg of Deeds has b, m & cem rec from late 1800's, d rec from 1905, land rec from 1884 & mil dis rec from 1921; Clk Ct has div & ct rec from 1890, pro rec from 1891 & nat rec from 1884; Co Aud has school cen rec from early 1900's)
Charles Mix www.rootsweb.com/~sdcharle/	E10	8 May 1862	**Unorganized Territory** Charles Mix County; 400 Main St E; PO Box 490; Lake Andes, SD 57356; Ph. 605.487.7511 Details: (Clk Cts has b, m & d rec from 1905, bur rec, div, pro & ct rec from 1890)
Cheyenne		11 Jan 1875	**Pratt, Rusk, Stanley, Unorganized Territory** Details: (Eliminated 8 Mar 1883 to Jackson, Nowlin, Pyatt & Sterling)
Choteau		9 Mar 1883	**Martin** Details: (Attached to Lawrence & Butte Cos. Eliminated 8 Nov 1898 to Butte & Meade)
Clark* www.rootsweb.com/~sdclark/index.htm	D6	8 Jan 1873	**Hanson** Clark County; PO Box 294; Clark, SD 57225; Ph. 605.532.5363 Details: (Organized 23 May 1881) (Reg of Deeds has m rec from 1884, b & d rec from 1905, bur rec from 1941, mil dis rec from 1919 & land rec; Clk Cts has div, pro & ct rec)
Clay www.rootsweb.com/~sdclay/	B10	10 Apr 1862	**Unorganized Territory** Clay County; 211 W Main St; PO Box 403; Vermillion, SD 57069; Ph. 605.677.2871 Details: (Reg of Deeds has b & d rec from 1905, m rec from 1880, land rec from 1863 & bur rec from 1962; Clk Ct has pro rec from 1875, ct rec from 1866 & div rec from 1889)
Codington www.rootsweb.com/~sdcoding/	C5	15 Feb 1877	**Clark, Grant, Hamlin, Unorganized Territory** Codington County; 14 1st Ave SW; Watertown, SD 57201; Ph. 605.882.4850 Details: (Organized 7 Aug 1878) (Clk Cts has b, d, bur & div rec from 1905, m rec from 1900, pro rec from 1893 & ct rec from 1883)
Cole		10 Apr 1862	**Unorganized Territory** Details: (see Union) (Name changed to Union 7 Jan 1864)
Corson www.rootsweb.com/~sdcorson/	L3	2 Mar 1909	**Boreman, Dewey, Schnasse** Corson County; 200 1st St E; McIntosh, SD 57641; Ph. 605.273.4201 Details: (Reg of Deeds has b, d & land rec from 1909; Co Treas has m rec; Clk Ct has div, pro & ct rec)
Cragin		8 Jan 1873	**Hanson** Details: (Eliminated 1 Oct 1879 to Aurora & Unorganized Territory)
Custer www.rapidnet.com/~saj/custer/	P8	11 Jan 1875	**Unorganized Territory** Custer County; 420 Mt Rushmore Rd; Custer, SD 57730; Ph. 605.673.4816 Details: (Organized 26 Apr 1877) (Clk Cts has b & d rec from 1905, m rec from 1887, div, pro & ct rec from 1890)
Davison www.davisoncounty.org/	E9	8 Jan 1873	**Hanson** Davison County; 200 E 4th Ave; Mitchell, SD 57301; Ph. 605.995.8616 Details: (Organized 31 Jul 1874) (Reg of Deeds has b & d rec from 1905, m, bur & land rec; Clk Ct has div, pro & ct rec from 1880)

County Website	Map Index	Date Created	Parent County or Territory From Which Organized Address/Details
Day curie.bcc.louisville.edu/~cps/dayco/	D4	1 Oct 1879	**Greeley, Stone** Day County; 710 W 1st St; Webster, SD 57274-1391; Ph. 605.345.3771 Details: (Organized 2 Jan 1882) (Reg of Deeds has b & d rec from 1905, land rec from 1879 & bur rec from 1930; Co Treas has m rec from 1880; Clk Ct has div & ct rec from 1885 & pro rec from 1898)
Delano		11 Jan 1875	**Unorganized Territory** Details: (Attached to Lawrence & Butte Cos. Eliminated 8 Nov 1898 to Meade)
Deuel www.rootsweb.com/~sddeuel/index.html	A6	5 Apr 1862	**Unorganized Territory** Deuel County; PO Box 125; Clear Lake, SD 57226; Ph. 605.874.2120 Details: (Organized 20 May 1878) (Reg of Deeds has b rec from 1876, d rec from 1905 & bur rec from 1941; Co Treas has m rec from 1887; Clk Ct has div & pro rec from 1889 & ct rec from 1880)
Dewey www.rootsweb.com/~sddewey/	K5	8 Jan 1873	**Unorganized Territory** Dewey County; 710 C St; PO Box 117; Timber Lake, SD 57656; Ph. 605.865.3661 Details: (Formerly Rusk Co. Name changed to Dewey 9 Mar 1883. Attached to Walworth Co prior to organization 3 Dec 1910) (Reg of Deeds has b, m & land rec from 1910, d rec from 1911, cem rec from 1941 & mil rec from 1919; Clk Ct has div & pro rec from 1911 & ct rec from 1910; Co Aud has school cen rec 1911-1972)
Douglas www.rootsweb.com/~sddougla/	E9	10 Jan 1873	**Charles Mix** Douglas County; 706 Braddock St; Armour, SD 57313; Ph. 605.724.2585 Details: (Organized 7 Jun 1882) (Reg of Deeds has b & d rec from 1905 & land rec; Co Treas has m rec from 1884; Clk Cts has ct rec from 1884, div & pro rec from 1887)
Edmunds www.rootsweb.com/~sdedmund/	G4	8 Jan 1873	**Buffalo** Edmunds County; 2nd St; Ipswich, SD 57451; Ph. 605.426.6671 Details: (Organized 27 Jul 1883) (Reg of Deeds has b rec from 1905, d rec from 1887, land rec from 1883, bur rec from 1941 & m rec from 1887; Clk Ct has div rec from 1887, ct & pro rec from 1884)
Ewing		8 Mar 1883	**Harding** Details: (Attached to Butte Co. Eliminated 6 Nov 1894 to Harding)
Fall River www.rootsweb.com/~sdfallsr/	Q10	3 Apr 1883	**Custer** Fall River County; 906 N River St; Hot Springs, SD 57747-1387; Ph. 605.745.5132 Details: (Reg of Deeds has land rec from 1883, b & d rec from 1905 & m rec; Clk Cts has div, pro & ct rec from 1890)
Faulk* www.rootsweb.com/~sdfaulk/findex.htm	G5	8 Jan 1873	**Buffalo** Faulk County; PO Box 309; Faulkton, SD 57438-0309; Ph. 605.598.6223 Details: (Organized 5 Nov 1883) (Reg of Deeds has b, m, d, bur & land rec from 1888 & mil rec; Clk Ct has div & ct rec from 1900 & pro rec from 1888)
Forsythe		11 Jan 1875	**Unorganized Territory** Details: (Eliminated 19 Feb 1881 to Custer)
Grant www.rootsweb.com/~sdgrant/	B5	8 Jan 1873	**Deuel, Hanson** Grant County; 210 E 5th Ave; PO Box 509; Milbank, SD 57252-2433; Ph. 605.432.5482 Details: (Organized 17 Jun 1878) (Clk Cts has b & d rec from 1905, m rec from 1890, div, pro & ct rec from 1897 & newspapers from 1880; Reg of Deeds has land rec)
Greely		8 Jan 1873	**Hanson** Details: (Eliminated 1 Oct 1879 to Day)
Gregory www.rootsweb.com/~sdgregor/ Gregory_websit/Page_1x.html	G10	8 May 1862	**Unorganized Territory** Gregory County; PO Box 413; Burke, SD 57523; Ph. 605.775.2664 Details: (Attached to Todd & Charles Mix Cos prior to organization 5 Sep 1898) (Reg of Deeds has m rec from 1898, b, d, land & mil dis rec from 1905 & bur rec from 1941; Clk Ct has div, pro & ct rec from 1899)
Haakon* www.rootsweb.com/~sdhaakon/	L7	3 Nov 1914	**Stanley** Haakon County; 140 S Howard; Philip, SD 57567; Ph. 605.859.2627 Details: (Organized 8 Feb 1915) (Clk Cts has b, m, d, bur, div, pro, ct & adoption rec from 1915)

County Website	Map Index	Date Created	Parent County or Territory From Which Organized
			Address/Details

Hamlin   **C6**   **8 Jan 1873**
www.rootsweb.com/~sdhamlin/

Deuel, Hanson
Hamlin County; PO Box 237; Hayti, SD 57241; Ph. 605.783.3201
Details: (Organized 10 Sep 1878) (Reg of Deeds has b, d & bur rec from 1905, land rec, m rec from 1879; Clk Ct has div & ct rec from 1885, pro rec from 1890, nat rec from 1880, school cen rec from 1903 & school rec from 1890)

Hand   **G6**   **8 Jan 1873**
www.geocities.com/lynettet.geo/
hand/hand.html

Buffalo
Hand County; 415 W 1st Ave; Miller, SD 57362-1346; Ph. 605.853.3512
Details: (Organized 1 Sep 1882) (Reg of Deeds has b & d rec from 1905, bur & land rec; Co Treas has m rec from 1883; Clk Ct has div rec from late 1800's, pro rec from 1880's & ct rec from 1889)

Hanson   **D8**   **13 Jan 1871**
www.rootsweb.com/~sdhanson/
index.html

Buffalo, Deuel, Brookings, Charles Mix, Hutchinson, Jayne, Minnehaha
Hanson County; 720 5th St; Alexandria, SD 57311; Ph. 605.239.4446
Details: (Organized 16 Aug 1873) (Clk Cts has b, m, d, bur, div, pro & ct rec from 1905)

Harding   **P3**   **5 Mar 1881**
www.rootsweb.com/~sdhardin/

Unorganized Territory
Harding County; 901 Ramsland St; Buffalo, SD 57720; Ph. 605.375.3351
Details: (Attached to Butte Co. Eliminated 8 Nov 1898 to Butte. Recreated 3 Nov 1908 from Butte. Organized 30 Jan 1911) (Reg of Deeds has b, d, bur & land rec from 1909; Co Treas has m rec from 1909; Clk Ct has div, pro, ct & school cen rec from 1909)

Hughes   **I7**   **8 Jan 1873**
www.rootsweb.com/~sdhughes/

Buffalo
Hughes County; 104 E Capitol Ave; Pierre, SD 57501-2563; Ph. 605.773.3713
Details: (Organized 26 Nov 1880) (Clk Cts has div & ct rec from 1880 & pro rec from 1890; Reg of Deeds has b, m, d, bur & land rec)

Hutchinson   **D9**   **8 May 1862**
www.rootsweb.com/~sdhutchi/

Unorganized Territory
Hutchinson County; 140 Euclid St; Olivet, SD 57052; Ph. 605.387.2838
Details: (Organized 13 Jan 1871) (Reg of Deeds has land rec from 1876, m rec from 1887, b & d rec from 1905 & bur rec from 1914; Clk Cts has div & ct rec from 1883 & pro rec from 1899; Co Aud has school rec from 1924)

Hyde   **H6**   **8 Jan 1873**
www.rootsweb.com/~sdhyde/

Buffalo
Hyde County; PO Box 306; Highmore, SD 57345-0306; Ph. 605.852.2512
Details: (Organized 1 Oct 1883) (Clk Ct has b & d rec from 1905, m rec from 1887, bur rec from 1936, div & ct rec from 1884 & pro rec from 1892; Reg of Deeds has land rec from 1880's)

Jackson*   **M9**   **8 Mar 1883**
www.rootsweb.com/~sdjackso/

Cheyenne, Lugenbeel, White River
Jackson County; 1 S Main St; Kadoka, SD 57543; Ph. 605.837.2420
Details: (Attached to Stanley & Pennington Cos. Eliminated 3 Jun 1909 to Mellette & Washabaugh. Recreated 3 Nov 1914 from Stanley. Organized 9 Feb 1915) (Reg of Deeds has b, m, d, bur, div, pro, ct & land rec)

Jayne   **8 May 1862**

Unorganized Territory
Details: (Attached to Yankton Co. Eliminated 13 Jan 1871 to Hanson, Hutchinson & Turner Cos)

Jerauld   **F8**   **17 Apr 1883**
www.rootsweb.com/~sdjeraul/jindex.htm

Aurora, Buffalo
Jerauld County; 205 S Wallace St; Wessington Springs, SD 57382; Ph. 605.539.1221
Details: (Reg of Deeds has b, d & bur rec from 1905, m rec from 1890 & land rec; Clk Cts has pro rec from 1890, ct rec from 1889 & div rec from 1900; Co Aud has school cen rec)

Jones   **K7**   **15 Jan 1917**
www.rootsweb.com/~sdjones/

Lyman
Jones County; 310 Main; Murdo, SD 57559; Ph. 605.669.2361
Details: (Reg of Deeds has b, m, d & land rec; Clk Ct has div, pro & ct rec from 1917)

Kingsbury   **C7**   **8 Jan 1873**
www.rootsweb.com/~sdkingsb/

Hanson
Kingsbury County; 102 2nd St SE; De Smet, SD 57231; Ph. 605.854.3832
Details: (Organized 18 Feb 1880) (Clk Cts has b, d & bur rec from 1905, m rec from 1890, div & ct rec from 1920, pro & nat rec)

County Website	Map Index	Date Created	Parent County or Territory From Which Organized Address/Details
Lake www.rootsweb.com/~sdlake/	B8	8 Jan 1873	**Brookings, Hanson, Minnehaha** Lake County; County Courthouse; 200 E Center; Madison, SD 57042; Ph. 605.256.4876 Details: (Clk Cts has b & d rec from 1905, m rec from 1874, bur rec from 1941, div & ct rec from 1881 & pro rec from 1884)
Lawrence www.lawrence.sd.us/	Q7	11 Jan 1875	**Unorganized Territory** Lawrence County; 644 Main St; Deadwood, SD 57732; Ph. 605.578.2040 Details: (Organized 5 Mar 1877) (Reg of Deeds has b rec from 1905 & d rec from 1906; Co Treas has m rec from 1887; Clk Ct has div, pro, ct & land rec from 1895; City Aud has bur rec)
Lincoln www.rootsweb.com/~sdlincol/	B10	5 Apr 1862	**Unorganized Territory** Lincoln County; 100 E 5th St; Carton, SD 57013-1732; Ph. 605.987.5661 Details: (Organized 30 Dec 1867) (Reg of Deeds has b & d rec from 1905, land & bur rec; Co Treas has m rec from 1890; Clk Ct has pro rec from 1890, ct & div rec from 1872)
Lugenbeel		11 Jan 1875	**Meyer, Pratt** Details: (see Washabaugh) (Attached to Fall River. Eliminated 3 Jun 1909 to Bennett & Todd)
Lyman www.rootsweb.com/~sdlyman/	I8	8 Jan 1873	**Gregory, Unorganized Territory** Lyman County; PO Box 235; Kennebec, SD 57544; Ph. 605.869.2277 Details: (Attached to Brule Co prior to organization 21 May 1893) (Reg of Deeds has b rec from 1905, d rec from 1920, bur & land rec; Co Treas has m rec from 1905; Clk Ct has div, pro & ct rec from 1880)
Mandan		11 Jan 1875	**Unorganized Territory** Details: (Eliminated 10 Mar 1887 to Lawrence)
Marshall www.rootsweb.com/~sdmarsha/ mindex.htm	D3	2 May 1885	**Day** Marshall County; County Courthouse; Britton, SD 57430; Ph. 605.448.5213 Details: (Reg of Deeds has b & d rec from 1905, m rec from 1887, bur & land rec; Clk Ct has div rec from 1888, pro rec from 1889 & ct rec)
Martin		5 Mar 1881	**Unorganized Territory** Details: (Attached to Butte Co. Eliminated 8 Nov 1898 to Butte)
McCook www.rootsweb.com/~sdmccook/ index.htm	C8	8 Jan 1873	**Hanson** McCook County; 130 W Essex Ave; Salem, SD 57058; Ph. 605.425.2781 Details: (Organized 15 Jun 1878) (Reg of Deeds has m rec from 1882, bur rec from 1895, b & d rec from 1905 & land rec; Clk Cts has ct & nat rec from 1880, pro rec from 1881 & some school cen rec from 1900)
McPherson www.rootsweb.com/~sdmcpher/	G3	8 Jan 1873	**Buffalo** McPherson County; County Courthouse; PO Box L; Leola, SD 57456; Ph. 605.439.3351 Details: (Organized 6 Mar 1884) (Clk Ct has pro rec from 1893, ct rec from 1889, nat rec from 1884 & div rec; Reg of Deeds has b & d rec from 1905, bur rec from 1941, m & land rec)
Meade www.rootsweb.com/~sdmeade/ Meade Co/	O6	7 Feb 1889	**Lawrence** Meade County; 1425 Sherman St; PO Box 939; Sturgis, SD 57785; Ph. 605.347.2356 Details: (Reg of Deeds has m & land rec; Clk Cts has pro & ct rec)
Mellette* www.rootsweb.com/~sdmellet/	K9	3 Jun 1909	**Jackson, Meyer, Pratt, Washabaugh, Unorganized Territory** Mellette County; S 1st St; PO Box C; White River, SD 57579; Ph. 605.259.3230 Details: (Organized 31 May 1911) (Reg of Deeds has b & d rec from 1912, bur rec from 1913 & land rec; Co Treas has m rec from 1912; Clk Ct has div, pro & ct rec from 1911)
Meyer		8 Jan 1873	**Unorganized Territory** Details: (Attached to Lyman. Eliminated 3 Jun 1909 to Mellette & Todd)
Midway		23 May 1857	**Brown County, Minnesota** Details: (Eliminated 11 May 1858 when Minnesota became a state)

County Website	Map Index	Date Created	Parent County or Territory From Which Organized Address/Details
Mills		8 Jan 1873	**Hanson** Details: (Eliminated 1 Oct 1879 to Brown & Unorganized Territory)
Miner* www.geocities.com/lynettet.geo/miner/ miner.html	D8	8 Jan 1873	**Hanson** Miner County; 401 N Main St; PO Box 265; Howard, SD 57349; Ph. 605.772.4612 Details: (Organized 2 Dec 1880) (Reg of Deeds has b & d rec from 1905, m rec from 1886, bur & land rec; Clk Ct has pro & ct rec from 1886 & div rec)
Minnehaha www.minnehahacounty.org/	B8	5 Apr 1862	**Unorganized Territory** Minnehaha County; 415 N Dakota Ave; Sioux Falls, SD 57102; Ph. 605.367.4223 Details: (Attached to Union Co prior to organization 4 Jan 1868) (Clk Cts has div, pro & ct rec from 1876; Reg of Deeds has m rec from 1876, b & d rec from 1905 & land rec)
Moody www.rootsweb.com/~sdmoody/	B7	8 Jan 1873	**Brookings, Minnehaha** Moody County; 101 E Pipestone Ave; PO Box 152; Flandreau, SD 57028; Ph. 605.997.3181 Details: (Reg of Deeds has b & d rec from 1905, bur & land rec; Co Treas has m rec from 1873; Clk Ct has pro rec from 1890, ct rec from 1905, div rec, newspapers from 1880's)
Nowlin		8 Mar 1883	**Cheyenne, White River** Details: (Attached to Pennington, Hughes, Meade & Stanley Cos. Eliminated 8 Nov 1898 to Lyman & Stanley)
Pennington www.co.pennington.sd.us/	P8	11 Jan 1875	**Unorganized Territory** Pennington County; 315 St Joseph St; Rapid City, SD 57709-0230; Ph. 605.394.2575 Details: (Organized 19 Apr 1877) (Reg of Deeds has b & d rec from 1905 & land rec; Co Treas has m rec from 1887; Clk Ct has div & ct rec from 1877 & pro rec from 1884)
Perkins www.rootsweb.com/~sdperkin/	N4	3 Nov 1908	**Butte** Perkins County; PO Box 27; Bison, SD 57620; Ph. 605.244.5626 Details: (Organized 9 Feb 1909) (Reg of Deeds has b, d & bur rec from 1909 & land rec; Co Treas has m rec from 1909; Clk Ct has pro, ct, div & nat rec from 1909)
Potter www.rootsweb.com/~sdpotter/ potterindex.htm	I5	8 Jan 1873	**Buffalo** Potter County; 201 S Exene St; Gettysburg, SD 57442; Ph. 605.765.9472 Details: (Formerly Ashmore Co. Name changed to Potter 14 Jan 1875. Organized 27 Dec 1883) (Clk Cts has b & d from 1885, ct rec from 1884 & adoption rec from 1941; Reg of Deeds has land rec)
Pratt		8 Jan 1873	**Unorganized Territory** Details: (Attached to Brule & Lyman Cos. Eliminated 3 Jun 1909 to Mellette)
Presho		8 Jan 1873	**Unorganized Territory** Details: (Attached to Brule & Lyman Cos. Eliminated 6 June 1907 to Tripp)
Pyatt		8 Mar 1883	**Cheyenne, Rusk, Stanley** Details: (see Dewey) (Name changed to Armstrong 6 Jan 1895. Armstrong eliminated 4 Nov 1952 to Dewey)
Rinehart		9 Mar 1883	**Martin** Details: (Attached to Lawrence & Butte Cos. Eliminated 8 Nov 1898 to Butte & Meade)
Roberts www.rootsweb.com/~sdrobert/	B3	8 Mar 1883	**Grant, Sisseton/Wahpeton Indian Reserve** Roberts County; 411 2nd Ave E; Sisseton, SD 57262; Ph. 605.698.7152 Details: (Clk Cts has b, d & bur rec from 1905, m & div rec from 1890, pro & ct rec from 1889; Reg of Deeds has land rec)
Rusk		8 Jan 1873	**Unorganized Territory** Details: (see Dewey) (Name changed to Dewey 9 Mar 1883)
Sanborn www.rootsweb.com/~sdsanbor/	E7	1 May 1883	**Miner** Sanborn County; 604 W 6th St; PO Box 7; Woonsocket, SD 57385; Ph. 605.796.4515 Details: (Clk Cts has div, pro & ct rec from 1905; Reg of Deeds has b, m, d, bur & land rec)

County Website	Map Index	Date Created	Parent County or Territory From Which Organized Address/Details
Schnasse		**9 Mar 1883**	**Boreman, Unorganized Territory**
			Details: (Attached to Walworth Co. Eliminated 1 Feb 1911 to Ziebach)
Scobey		**8 Mar 1883**	**Delano**
			Details: (Attached to Lawrence & Meade Cos. Eliminated 8 Nov 1898 to Meade)
Shannon www.rootsweb.com/~sdshanno/index.htm	N9	**11 Jan 1875**	**Unorganized Territory** Shannon County; 906 N River St; Hot Springs, SD 57747-1387; Ph. 605.745.5131 Details: (Attached to Fall River Co) (Reg of Deeds has m & land rec; Clk Cts has pro & ct rec)
Spink www.rootsweb.com/~sdspink/sindex.htm	E5	**8 Jan 1873**	**Hanson** Spink County; 210 E 7th Ave; Redfield, SD 57469; Ph. 605.472.1825 Details: (Organized 1 Aug 1879) (Clk Cts has b & d rec from 1905, m rec from 1887, bur rec from 1941, div & ct rec from 1882 & pro rec from 1880; Reg of Deeds has l and rec)
Stanley www.rootsweb.com/~sdstanle/	K7	**8 Jan 1873**	**Unorganized Territory** Stanley County; 40 E 2nd Ave; Fort Pierre, SD 57532; Ph. 605.223.2673 Details: (Attached to Hughes Co prior to organization 23 Apr 1890) (Reg of Deeds has m rec from 1890, bur rec from 1892, b & d rec from 1905 & land rec; Clk Cts has div, pro & ct rec from 1890)
Sterling		**8 Mar 1883**	**Cheyenne** Details: (Attached to Lawrence, Hughes, Meade & Stanley Cos. Eliminated 1 Feb 1911 to Ziebach)
Stone		**8 Jan 1873**	**Hanson** Details: (Eliminated 1 Oct 1879 to Brown, Day & Unorganized Territory)
Sully www.sdcounties.org/sully/	I6	**8 Jan 1873**	**Buffalo** Sully County; 700 Ash Ave; Onida, SD 57564; Ph. 605.258.2535 Details: (Organized 19 Apr 1883) (Reg of Deeds has b, m, d, bur & land rec; Clk Cts has pro & ct rec)
Thompson		**8 Jan 1873**	**Hanson** Details: (Eliminated 1 Oct 1879 to Spink & Unorganized Territory)
Todd www.rootsweb.com/~sdtodd/	K10	**9 Mar 1909**	**Lugenbeel, Meyer, Washabaugh, Unorganized Territory** Todd County; 200 E 3rd St; Winner, SD 57580; Ph. 605.842.2266 Details: (Though created by legislative act 9 Mar 1909, Todd has never been fully organized. Part of the unorg. co of Bennett, comprising part of Rosebud Indian Reservation, annexed in 1911; within the limits of Rosebud Indian Reservation. Attached to Lyman & Trip Cos) (Reg of Deeds has m & land rec; Clk Cts has pro & ct rec)
Todd, old		**8 May 1862**	**Unorganized Territory** Details: (Disorganized 7 Mar 1890 & attached to Charles Mix Co. Eliminated 3 Jun 1897 to Gregory)
Tripp www.rootsweb.com/~sdtripp/	I9	**8 Jan 1873**	**Unorganized Territory, Gregory, Todd, old** Tripp County; 200 E 3rd St; Winner, SD 57580; Ph. 605.842.2266 Details: (Organized 15 Jun 1909) (Reg of Deeds has b rec from 1909, bur rec from 1941 & land rec; Co Treas has m rec from 1909; Clk Ct has div, pro & ct rec from 1912)
Turner www.rootsweb.com/~sdturner/	C9	**13 Jan 1871**	**Lincoln, Jayne** Turner County; 400 S Main St; Parker, SD 57053-0446; Ph. 605.297.3115 Details: (Clk Cts has b & d rec from 1905, m rec from 1872, div rec from 1907, pro rec from 1886 & ct rec from 1900; Reg of Deeds has land rec)
Union www.rootsweb.com/~sdunion/	A10	**10 Apr 1862**	**Unorganized Territory** Union County; PO Box 757; Elk Point, SD 57025-0757; Ph. 605.356.2132 Details: (Formerly Cole Co. Name changed to Union 7 Jan 1864) (Reg of Deeds has b rec from 1866, m rec from 1886, d rec from 1905, bur rec from 1961, land rec from 1863 & mil dis rec from 1919; Clk Ct has pro rec from 1875, ct rec from 1890 & div rec)

County Website	Map Index	Date Created	Parent County or Territory From Which Organized Address/Details
Wagner		9 Mar 1883	**Martin** Details: (Attached to Lawrence & Butte Cos. Eliminated 8 Nov 1898 to Butte)
Walworth www.rootsweb.com/~sdwalwor/	I4	8 Jan 1873	**Buffalo** Walworth County; PO Box 199; Selby, SD 57472-0199; Ph. 605.649.7878 Details: (Organized 28 Mar 1883) (Reg of Deeds has b, d & bur rec from 1905 & land rec; Co Treas has m rec from 1889; Clk Ct has div rec from 1889, pro & ct rec from 1892)
Washabaugh*		9 Mar 1883	**Lugenbeel, Shannon** Details: (Unorg; Attached to Custer Co; within limits of Pine Ridge Indian Reservation; part taken to form parts of Bennet, Mellette & Todd 3 Jun 1909 & part comprising part of Rosebud Indian Reservation; annexed to Mellette in 2 Mar 1911. Attached to Jackson 3 Jun 1915)
Washington		9 Mar 1883	**Shannon, Lugenbeel** Details: (Unorg; Attached to Custer & Pennington Cos; within limits of Pine Ridge Indian Reservation; part taken to form part of Bennet 3 Jun 1909; Eliminated 2 Nov 1943 to Shannon)
Wetmore		8 Jan 1873	**Hanson** Details: (Eliminated 1 Oct 1879 to Aurora & Miner)
White River		11 Jan 1875	**Pratt, Unorganized Territory** Details: (Eliminated 8 Mar 1883 to Jackson & Nowlin)
Wood		8 Jan 1883	**Hanson** Details: (Eliminated 1 Oct 1879 to Kingsbury)
Yankton www.rootsweb.com/~sdyankto/index.html	C10	10 Apr 1862	**Unorganized Territory** Yankton County; 410 Walnut St; PO Box 155; Yankton, SD 57078; Ph. 605.668.3438 Details: (Reg of Deeds has b & d rec from 1905 & bur rec; Co Treas has m rec from 1900; Clk Ct has div, pro & ct rec from 1900; Director Assessments has land rec)
Ziebach www.rootsweb.com/~sdziebac/index.html	L5	1 Feb 1911	**Schnasse, Sterling, Armstrong, Unorganized Territory** Ziebach County; PO Box 68; Dupree, SD 57623; Ph. 605.365.5159 Details: (Within limits of Cheyenne River Indian Reservation) (Reg of Deeds has b, m, d, bur & land rec from 1911; Clk Cts has div, pro & ct rec from 1911)
Ziebach, old		10 Feb 1877	**Pennington** Details: (Attached to Pennington Co. Eliminated 8 Nov 1898 to Pennington)

Societies and Repositories

Art Circle Public Library; Old Stage Road; Crossville, Tennessee 38555

Bedford County Historical Society; 624 S. Brittain St.; Shelbyville, Tennessee 37160

Blount Co. Library; 300 E. Church St.; Maryville, Tennessee 37801

Blount County Genealogical and Historical Society; PO Box 4986; Maryville, Tennessee 37902-4986

Bradley County Genealogical Society; PO Box 1384; Cleveland, Tennessee 37364-1384

Campbell County Historical Society; 101 Sixth St.; LaFollette, Tennessee 37766

Carroll Co. Library; 159 E. Main St.; Huntingdon, Tennessee 38344

Central of Georgia Railway Historical Society; 4403 Sunnybrook Dr.; Nashville, Tennessee 37205; <www.cofg.org.>

Chattanooga-Hamilton Co. Bicentennial Library, Gen. / Local Hist. Dept.; 1001 Broad St.; Chattanooga, Tennessee 37402

Chattanooga-Hamilton County Bicentennial Library; 1001 Broad Street; Chattanooga, Tennessee 37402; 423.757.5310; Fax 423.757.5090

Civil War Plymouth Pilgrims Descendants Society; c/o Scott Holmes, Treasurer; 10106 Champions Circle; Franklin, Tennessee 37064; <home.att.net/~cwppds/homepage.htm>

Claiborne County Historical Society; PO Box 32; Tazewell, Tennessee 37879

Cleveland Public Library-History Branch; 833 N. Ocoee St.; Cleveland, Tennessee 37311

Clyde W. Roddy Library; 371 First Ave.; Dayton, Tennessee 37321; 423.775.8406

Coffee County Historical Society; PO Box 524; Manchester, Tennessee 37355

Cossitt-Goodwyn Library; 33 So. Front St.; Memphis, Tennessee 38103

Dandridge Memorial Library; PO Box 339; Dandridge, Tennessee 37725; 615.397.9758

Disciples of Christ Historical Society; 1101 Nineteenth Avenue, South; Nashville, Tennessee 37212; 615.327.1444; Fax 615.327.1445

East Tennessee Historical Society; 500 W. Church Ave.; Knoxville, Tennessee 37902-2505

Fayetteville-Lincoln Co. Public Library; 400 Rocky Knob Ln.; Fayetteville, Tennessee 37334

Fentress County Genealogical Society; PO Box 178; Jamestown, Tennessee 38556

Franklin County Historical Society; PO Box 130; Winchester, Tennessee 37398

Genealogy Friends; PO Box 863; Hendersonville, Tennessee 37077

Giles County Historical Society; PO Box 693; Pulaski, Tennessee 38478

Greene County Genealogical Society; PO Box 1903; Greeneville, Tennessee 37744

H. B. Stamps Memorial Library; 415 W. Main St.; Rogersville, Tennessee 37857

Hamblen County Genealogical Society; PO Box 1213; Morristown, Tennessee 37816-1213

Hancock County Historical & Genealogical Society; PO Box 307; Sneedville, Tennessee 37869; <www.korrnet.org/overhome/page3.html>

Hawkins County Genealogical and Historical Society; PO Box 429; Rogersville, Tennessee 37857-3424

Henry County Genealogical Society of Tennessee; PO Box 1411; Paris, Tennessee 38242

Highland Rim Regional Library Center; 2102 Mercury Blvd.; Murfreesboro, Tennessee 37130

Isaac Shelby Chapter, SAR; 48 Redthorn Cove; Cordova, Tennessee 38018-7244; <members.aol.com/memphisar/htmls/memsarww.htm>

Jackson-Madison Co. Library; 433 E. Lafayette; Jackson, Tennessee 38301

Jefferson County Genealogical Society; PO Box 267; Jefferson City, Tennessee 37760

John Sevier Chapter, SAR; 7825 Hixson Pike; Hixson, Tennessee 37343; 423.842.1810; <www.sar.org/tnssar/js.tn.htm>

Jonesborough Genealogical Society; c/o Washington County-Jonesborough Library; 200 Sabine Dr.; Jonesborough, Tennessee 37659

Kings Mountain Chapter, SAR; 1314 Woodland Dr.; Johnson City, Tennessee 37601; 423.928.1341; <www.sar.org/tnssar/km.tn.htm>

Kingsport Public Library & Archives, J. Fred Johnson Memorial Library; 400 Broad St.; Kingsport, Tennessee 37660-4208; 423.224.2539; Fax 423.224.2558; <www.kingsportlibrary.or>

Lawrence County Genealogical Society; 218 N. Military Ave., Suite B.1; Lawrenceburg, Tennessee 38464

Lawson McGhee Library, East Tennessee Historical Center; 500 West Church Avenue; Knoxville, Tennessee 37902-2505; 423.544.4304; Fax 423.544.5708

Lincoln County Genealogical Society; 1508 West Washington St.; Fayetteville, Tennessee 37334

Louisville Presbyterian Seminary; 1044 Alta Vista Rd.; Louisville, Kentucky 40205-1798; 502.895.3411

Macon County Historical Society; 4233 Green Grove Rd.; Hartsville, Tennessee 37074

Magness Memorial Library; McMinnville, Tennessee 37110

Marion County Genealogical Group; 6611 Old Dunlap Rd.; Whitwell, Tennessee 37397

Marshall County, Tennessee Historical Society; 2243rd Ave. North; Lewisburg, Tennessee 37091

Maury Co. Public Library; 211 West 8th St.; Columbia, Tennessee 38402

Maury County, Tennessee Historical Society; PO Box 147; Columbia, Tennessee 38401

McClung Hist. Collection, East Tennessee Hist. Center; 314 W. Clinch Ave.; Knoxville, Tennessee 37902-2203

Memphis Conference United Methodist Archives, Luther L. Gobbel Library; Lambuth College, 705 Lambuth Boulevard; Jackson, Tennessee 38301; 901.425.2500; Fax 901.425.3200

Memphis Public Library & Information Center; 1850 Peabody; Memphis, Tennessee 38104

Memphis State Univ. Library; Mississippi Valley Collection; Memphis, Tennessee 38104

Memphis/Shelby County Public Library and Information Center; 1850 Peabody Avenue; Memphis, Tennessee 38104; 901.725.8895; Fax 901.725.8814

Middle Tennessee Genealogical Society; PO Box 190625; Nashville, Tennessee 37219-0625

Mid-West Tennessee Genealogical Society; PO Box 3343; Jackson, Tennessee 38301

Morgan County Genealogical and Historical Society; Rt. 2, Box 992; Wartburg, Tennessee 37887

Morristown-Hamblen Library; 417 W. Main St.; Morristown, Tennessee 37814

Mt. Juliet Public Library; PO Box 319, 2765 N. Mt. Juliet Rd.; Mt. Juliet, Tennessee 37122; 615. 758.7051

Mt. Pleasant Public Library; Hay Long Ave.; Mt. Pleasant, Tennessee 38474

Nashville & Davidson Co. Public Library; 222 8th Ave. No.; Nashville, Tennessee 37203

National Archives and Federal Record Center Southeast Region(Atlanta); 1557 St. Joseph Avenue; East Point, Georgia 30344; 404.763.7477; Fax 404.763.7477

Obion County Genealogical Society; PO Box 241; Union City, Tennessee 38261

Old James County Historical Society; PO Box 203; Ooltewah, Tennessee 37363

Pellissippi Genealogical and Historical Society; c/o Clinton Public Library; Anderson County; 118 South Hicks; Clinton, Tennessee 37716

Polk Co. Hist. & Gen. Soc. Library; PO Box 636; Benton, Tennessee 37307-0636; 423.338.1005

Public Library of Nashville and Davidson County; 225 Polk Ave.; Nashville, Tennessee 37203; 615.862.5800; Fax 615.862.5771

Roane County Genealogical Society; PO Box 297; Kingston, Tennessee 37763-0297

Shelby County Health Department, Division of Vital Records; 814 Jefferson Street; Memphis, Tennessee 38105

Signal Mountain Genealogical Society, Inc.; 103 Florida Ave.; Signal Mountain, Tennessee 37377

Sons of the American Revolution, Society of Tennessee; 1712 Natchez Trace; Nashville, Tennessee 37212

Southern Baptist Historical Library and Archives; 901 Commerce, Suite 200; Nashville, Tennessee 37203; 815.224.0344

Stephen Holston Chapter, SAR; 102 Case Ln.; Oak Ridge, Tennessee 37830; 865.483.3337 865.483.7414; <www.sar.org/tnssar/sh.tn.htm>

Stones River Chapter, SAR; 2808 Clearview Ct.; Murfreesboro, Tennessee 37129; <www.sar.org/tnssar/sr.tn.htm>

Sumner Co. Archives; 155 East Main St.; Gallatin, Tennessee 37066; 615.452.0037

Tennessee Genealogical Society; 9114 Davies Plantation Rd.; Memphis, Tennessee 38133; 901.381.1447

Tennessee Genealogical Society; PO Box 247; Brunswick, Tennessee 38014-0247

Tennessee State Library & Archives; 403 Seventh Avenue North; Nashville, Tennessee 37243-0312; 615.741.6471; Fax 615.532.2472; <www.state.tn.us/sos/statelib/tslahome.htm>

Tennessee Vital Records, Department of Health; Cordell Hull Building; Nashville, Tennessee 37247-0350; 615.741.1763

The Andrew Jackson Chapter, SAR; 1605 Craggie Hope Rd.; Kingston Springs, Tennessee 37082; 615.952.9552; <www.sar.org/tnssar/aj.tn.htm>

Tombigbee Chapter, SAR; 117 Seventh Avenue; Columbia, Tennessee 38401; 931.381.5150; <www.sar.org/tnssar/t.tn.htm>

Trousdale County Historical Society; 4233 Green Grove Rd.; Hartsville, Tennessee 37074

Union County Historical Society, Inc.; PO Box 95; Maynardville, Tennessee 37807

University of Memphis Library, Special Collections Dept.; Campus Box 526500; Memphis, Tennessee 38152-6500; 901.678.2205; Fax 901.678.8218

University of Tennessee, Knoxville; Hoskins Library, 1015 Volunteer; Knoxville, Tennessee 37996-1000; 423.974.4351; Fax 423.974.0555

Upper Cumberland Genealogical Association; Putnam Library; 48 E. Broad St.; Cookeville, Tennessee 38501

Upper Cumberland Genealogical Support Group; Art Circle Public Library; 306 E. First St.; Crossville, Tennessee 38555

Valentine Sevier Chapter, SAR; 331 Grassland Dr.; Clarksville, Tennessee 37043; 931.647.0954; <www.sar.org/tnssar/vs.tn.htm>

Van Buren County Historical Society; PO Box 126; Spencer, Tennessee 38585

Vardy Community Historical Society; PO Box 554; Sneedville, Tennessee 37869; <hometown.aol.com/vardyvalley/index.html>

Watauga Association of Genealogists, Upper East Tennessee; PO Box 117; Johnson City, Tennessee 37605-0117

Weakley County Genealogical Society; PO Box 92; Martin, Tennessee 38237

White County Genealogical-Historical Society; PO Box 721; Sparta, Tennessee 38583-0721

Williamson County Public Library; 611 West Main St.; Franklin, Tennessee 37064-2723; 615.794.3105; Fax 615.591.8684

Bibliography and Record Sources

General Sources

Allison, John Roy V. *Notable Men of Tennessee: Personal and Genealogical With Portraits.* 2 vols. Atlanta: Southern Historical Association, 1905.

Bamman, Gale Williams, *Research in Tennessee*. Arlington, Virginia: National Genealogical Society, 1993.

Bible Records of Families in East Tennessee and Their Connections in Other Areas. 3 vols. Genealogical Record Committee, Daughters of the American Revolution, 1959-60.

Carr, John. *Early Times in Middle Tennessee*. Nashville, Tennessee: R.H. Horsley and Associates, 1958.

Crutchfield, James A. *Timeless Tennesseans*. Huntsville, Alabama: Strode Publishers, 1984.

Folmsbee, Stanley John. *History of Tennessee*. 4 vols. New York: Lewis Historical Publishing Co., 1960.

Fulcher, Richard Carlton. *Guide to County Records and Genealogical Resources in Tennessee*. Baltimore: Genealogical Publishing Co, 1987.

Guide to Microfilmed Manuscript Holdings of the Tennessee State Library and Archives. 3rd ed. Nashville: Tennessee State Library and Archives, 1983.

Hale, William T., and Dixon L. Merritt. *A History of Tennessee and Tennesseans*. 8 vols. Chicago: Lewis Publishing Co., 1913.

Hathaway, Beverly W. *Genealogy Research Sources in Tennessee*. West Jordan, Utah: Allstates Research Co., 1972.

Historical Records Survey (Tennessee). *Check List of Tennessee Imprints, 1841-1850*. Nashville, Tennessee: Tennessee Historical Records Survey, 1941.

Historical Records Survey (Tennessee). *List of Tennessee Imprints, 1793-1840, in Tennessee Libraries*. Nashville, Tennessee: Tennessee Historical Records Survey, 1941.

Inventory of the Church Archives of Tennessee: Nashville Baptist Association. Nashville: Historical Records Survey, WPA, 1939.

Inventory of the Church Archives of Tennessee: Tennessee Baptist Convention, Ocoee Baptist Association. Nashville: Historical Records Survey, WPA, 1942.

Moore, John Trotwood, and Austin P. Foster. *Tennessee, the Volunteer State, 1760-1923*. 4 vols. Chicago: S.J. Clark Publishing Co., 1923.

Ray, Worth Stickley. *Tennessee Cousins: A History of Tennessee People*. 1950. Reprint. Baltimore: Genealogical Publishing Co., 1968.

Schweitzer, George K. *Tennessee Genealogical Research*. Knoxville: George K. Schweitzer, 1986.

Sistler, Byron, and Barbara Sistler, *Vital Statistics from Nineteenth Century Tennessee Church Records*. Nashville: B. Sistler and Assoc., 1979.

Smith, Sam B., and Luke H. Banker, ed. and comp. *Tennessee History: A Bibliography*. Knoxville: University of Tennessee Press, [1974].

Sneed, Adele Weiss. *Bible Records of Families of East Tennessee and Their Connections From Other Areas*. 3 vols. Tennessee: Knoxville Chapter of the Daughters of the American Colonists and James White Chapter of the Daughters of the American Revolution, 1959-60.

Speer, William S. *Sketches of Prominent Tennesseans*. Nashville: A.B. Tavel, 1888.

Stanley J. Folmsbee, et al. *History of Tennessee*. 4 vols. (New York: Lewis Historical Publishing Co., 1960.

Tennessee County Records Manual. Nashville: Tennessee State Library and Archives, 1968?

Tennessee Newspapers: A Cumulative List of Microfilmed Tennessee Newspapers in the Tennessee State Library. Nashville: Tennessee State Library and Archives, 1978.

Tennessee Research Outline. Series US-States, no. 42. Salt Lake City: Family History Library. 1988.

United States. Court of Claims. *Eastern Cherokee Applications, August 29, 1906 - May 26, 1909*. Washington, D.C.: National Archives, 1981.

Whitley, Edythe Rucker. *Tennessee Genealogical Records: Records of Early Settlers from State and County Archives*. Baltimore: Genealogical Publishing Co., 1981.

Atlases, Maps and Gazetteers

Foster, Austin P. *Counties of Tennessee*. Nashville: Department of Education, Division of history, State of Tennessee, 1923.

Fullerton, Ralph O. *Place Names of Tennessee*. Nashville: Tennessee Department of Conservation, Division of Geology, 1974.

McBride, Robert M. and Owen Meredith, ed. *Eastin Morris' Tennessee Gazetteer 1834 and Matthew Rhea's Map of the State of Tennessee, 1832*. Nashville: The Gazetteer Press, 1971.

Puetz, C.J., comp. *Tennessee County Maps*. Lyndon Station, Wisconsin: Thomas Publishing Co., 1992.

Tennessee Atlas and Gazetteer. 3rd ed. Freeport, Maine: DeLorme Mapping Co., 1995.

Census Records

Available Census Records and Census Substitutes

Federal Census 1810 (Rutherford and Grainger Counties only), 1820, 1830, 1840, 1850, 1860, 1870, 1880, 1900, 1910, 1920, 1930.

Federal Mortality Schedules 1850, 1860, 1880.

Union Veterans and Widows 1890.

Allen, Maud Bliss. *Census Records and Cherokee Muster Rolls*. Washington: [N.p.], 1935.

Dollarhide, William. *The Census Book: A Genealogist's Guide to Federal Census Facts, Schedules and Indexes*. Bountiful, Utah: Heritage Quest, 1999.

Early Tennessee Tax Lists. Evanston, Illinois: Byron Sistler and Assoc., 1977.

East Tennessee Tax Lists. Fort Worth, Texas: Arrow Printing Co., 1964.

Kemp, Thomas Jay. *The American Census Handbook*. Wilmington, Delaware: Scholarly Resources, Inc., 2001.

Lainhart, Ann S. *State Census Records*. Baltimore: Genealogical Publishing Co., Inc., 1992.

McGhee, Lucy Kate. *Partial Census of 1787 to 1791 of Tennessee as taken from the North Carolina Land Grants*. (Salt Lake City: Filmed by the Genealogical Society of Utah, 1990). Microfilm, 2 rolls.

Siler, David W. *Eastern Cherokees: A Census of the Cherokee Nation, 1851*. Cottonport, La: Polyanthos, 1972.

Thorndale, William, and William Dollarhide. *Map Guide to the U.S. Federal Censuses, 1790-1920*. Baltimore: Genealogical Publishing Co., 1987.

Court, Probate and Wills

Fischer, Marjorie Hood. Ruth Blake Burns. *Tennessee Tidbits, 1778-1914*. Vol. 2. Vista, California: Ram Press, 1988.

Fischer, Marjorie Hood. *Tennessee Tidbits, 1778-1914*. Vol. 1. Easley, South Carolina: Southern Historical Press, 1986.

Fischer, Marjorie Hood. *Tennessee Tidbits, 1778-1914*. Vol. 3. Vista, California: RAM Press, 1989.

Historical Records Survey (Tennessee). *Survey to Tennessee County Court Records, Prior to 1860, in the Second, Third and Fourth Districts*. Microfilm of typescript in Nashville, Tennessee. (Salt Lake City: Filmed by the Genealogical Society of Utah, 1943). Microfilm.

Sistler, Byron, and Barbara Sistler. *Index to Tennessee Wills and Administrations, 1779-1861*. Nashville, Tennessee: Byron Sistler & Associates, 1990.

Survey to Tennessee County Court Records, Prior to 1860, in the Second, Third and Fourth Districts. Nashville: Historical Records Survey, 1943.

Emigration, Immigration, Migration and Naturalization

Naturalization Index Cards for Chattanooga, Tennessee. Microfilm of originals in the National Archives Branch in East Point, Georgia. (Salt Lake City: Filmed by the Genealogical Society of Utah, 1989). Microfilm.

United States. District Court (Alabama: Southern District*). Declarations of Intentions, Naturalizations, and Petitions, 1855-1960*. Microfilm of originals at the National Archives in East Point, Georgia. (Salt Lake City: Filmed by the Genealogical Society of Utah, 1987-1989). Microfilm, 9 rolls.

Land and Property

Goldene F. Burgner, *North Carolina Land Grants in Tennessee, 1778-1791*. (N.p.: Southern Historical Press, 1981.

Griffey, Irene M. *Earliest Tennessee Land Records & Earliest Tennessee Land History*. Baltimore: Clearfield Co., 2000.

Land Grants, 1775-1905, 1911. Nashville, Tennessee: Tennessee State Library and Archives, 1976. Microfilm, multiple rolls.

McNamara, Billie R. *Tennessee Land: Its Early History and Laws*. Knoxville, Tennessee: B.R. McNamara, 1997.

North Carolina. Secretary of State. Land Grant Office. *Land Records, 1600 thru 1957; Land Grant Index, 1693-1959*. Raleigh, N.C.: North Carolina State Archives, 1980. Microfilm, 552 rolls.

Pruitt, Albert Bruce. *Tennessee Land Entries Military Bounty Land (1783-1841)*. 7 vols. Whitakers, NC: Pruitt, A. Bruce, 1997.

Pruitt, Albert Bruce. *Tennessee Land Entries: John Armstrong's Office*. 2 vols. [S.l.: A.B. Pruitt], 1995.

Pruitt, Albert Bruce. *Tennessee Land Warrants*. Whitakers, N.C.: A.B. Pruitt, 1999.

Rice, Shirley Hollis. *The Hidden Revolutionary War Land Grants in the Tennessee Military Reservation*. Lawrenceburg, Tennessee: Family Tree Press, 1992.

Sistler, Byron. *Tennessee Land Grants, Surnames*. 17 vols. Nashville, Tennessee: Byron Sistler, 1997.

Tennessee Valley Authority (Tennessee). *Tennessee Population Relocation Files, 1934-1954*. Microreproduction of originals housed in the National Archives Record Office, East Point, Georgia. (Salt Lake City: Filmed by the Genealogical Society of Utah, 1996). Microfilm, 41 rolls.

United States. District Court (Tennessee). *Final Record Books, 1803-1850; Land Claim Records, 1807-1820*. Washington, D.C.: National Archives. Central Plains Region, 1982.

Military

Allen, Penelope J. *Tennessee Soldiers in the Revolution*. Baltimore: Genealogical Publishing Co., 1975.

Armstrong, Zella, comp. *Some Tennessee Heroes of the Revolution Compiled from Pension of the Republic of Texas. Muster Rolls of the Texas Revolution*. Austin, TX: Daughters of the Republic of Texas, 1986.

Armstrong, Zella, comp. *Twenty-four Hundred Tennessee Pensioners of the Revolution, War of 1812*. Chattanooga, Tennessee: Lookout Publishing Co., 1937.

Barron, John C., et al. *Republic of Texas Pension Application Abstracts*. Austin, Texas: Austin Genealogical Society, 1987.

Barton, Henry W. *Texas Volunteers in the Mexican War*. Wichita Falls, Texas: Texan Press, 1970.

Bates, Lucy W. *Roster of Soldiers and Patriots of the American Revolution Buried in Tennessee*. 1974.

Brock, Reid. *Volunteers: Tennesseeans in the War with Mexico*. 2 vols. Salt Lake City: Kitchen Table Press, 1986.

Confederate Patriot Index (1894-1978) 2 vols., S.p.: Tennessee Division, United Daughters of the Confederacy, 1976, 1978.

Dyer, Gustavus. *The Tennessee Civil War Veterans Questionnaires*. 5 Vols. Easley, SC: Southern Historical Press, 1985.

Haywood, John. "List of North Carolina Revolutionary Soldiers Given Land in Tennessee, by the Act of 1782-83." In *The History of Tennessee*. Reprint. New York: Arno Press, 1971.

McCown, M. H., and I. E. Burns. *Soldiers of the War of 1812 Buried in Tennessee*. Johnson City, Tennessee: Society of U.S. Daughters of 1812, 1959.

Moore, Mrs. J. T. *Record of Commissions of Officers in the 1796-1815 Tennessee Militia*. Baltimore: Genealogical Publishing Co., 1977.

Rosenthal, Phil, and Bill Groneman. *Roll Call at the Alamo*. Fort Collins, Colorado: Old Army Press, 1985.

Sistler, Samuel. *Index to Tennessee Confederate Pension Applications*. Nashville: Byron Sistler, 1995.

Spurlin, Charles D. *Texas Veterans in the Mexican War*. St. Louis: Ingmire Pub., 1984.

Tennesseans in the Civil War. Nashville: Civil War Commission, 1965.

United States Selective Service System. *Tennessee World War I Selective Service System Draft Registration Cards, 1917-1918*. National Archives Microfilm Publications, M1509. Washington, D.C.: National Archives, 1987-1988.

United States. Adjutant General's Office. *Compiled Service Records of Volunteer Soldiers Who Served During the Mexican War in Organizations from the State of Tennessee.* Washington, D.C.: The National Archives, 1965. Microfilm, multiple rolls.

Wiefering, Edna. *Tennessee Confederate Widows and Their Families: Abstracts of 11,190 Confederate Widows' Applications.* Cleveland, Tennessee: Cleveland Public Library, 1992.

Vital and Cemetery Records

Acklen, Jeannette T. *Tennessee Records: Bible Records and Marriages Bonds.* Reprint. Baltimore, Maryland: Clearfield Co., 1997.

Acklen, Jeannette T. *Tennessee Records: Tombstone Inscriptions and Manuscripts, Historical and Biographical.* Nashville, Tennessee: Cullom and Ghertner, 1976.

Acklen, Jeannette Tillotson. *Tennessee Records: Bible Records and Marriage Bonds.* Baltimore: Genealogical Publishing Co., 1967.

Baker, Russell Pierce. *Obituaries and Marriage Notices From the Tennessee Baptist: 1844-1862.* Easley, South Carolina: Southern Historical Press, 1979.

Cemetery Records of Tennessee. 2 vols. Salt Lake City: Genealogical Society, 1951-62.

Gale W. Bamman, *Tennessee Divorces, 1797-1858.* Nashville: G. Bamman, 1985.

Garrett, Jill L. *Obituaries from Tennessee Newspapers.* Easley, South Carolina: Southern Historical Press, 1980.

Guide to Church Vital Statistics in Tennessee. Nashville: War Services Section, WPA, 1942;

Historical Records Project and Historical Records Survey. *Church, Cemetery, Bible, and Family Records from Tennessee.* (Salt Lake City: Filmed by the Genealogical Society of Utah, 1943).

Lucas, Silas E., and Ella L. Sheffield, *35,000 Tennessee Marriage Records and Bonds, 1783-1870.* 3 vols. Easley, S.C.: Southern Historical Press, 1981.

Lucas, Silas Emmett. *Marriages from Early Tennessee Newspapers, 1794-1851.* Easley, SC: Southern Historical Press, 1978.

Meier, Oveda. *Tennessee Ancestors: The Brave and the Dead, Probate and Death Records of Early Middle Tennessee, 1780-1805.* Salt Lake City: O. Meier, 1990.

Sistler, Byron, and Barbara Sistler. *Early East Tennessee Marriages.* 2 vols. Nashville: Byron Sistler & Assoc., 1987.

Sistler, Byron, and Barbara Sistler. *Early Middle Tennessee Marriages.* 2 vols. Nashville: Byron Sistler and Assoc., 1988.

Sistler, Byron, and Barbara Sistler. *Early West Tennessee Marriages.* 2 vols. Nashville: B. Sistler & Associates, 1989.

Tennessee. Division of Vital Records. *Births (Enumerator Record Series), 1908-1912.* Nashville, Tennessee: Tennessee State Library and Archives, 1980. Microfilm, 85 rolls.

Tennessee. State Library and Archives *Marriages, 1919-1974; Marriage Indexes for Several Counties, 1837-1987, 1837-1987.* Nashville, Tennessee: Tennessee State Library and Archives, 1988. Microfilm, 262 rolls.

Tennessee. State Library and Archives. *Births & Deaths, 1925-1940; Wills, 1889-Sept. 1958.* Nashville, Tennessee: Tennessee State Library and Archives, 1988.

Tennessee. State Library and Archives. *Record of Deaths, 1920-1939.* Tennessee. Nashville, Tennessee: Tennessee State Library and Archives, 1988. Microfilm, 277 rolls.

County Website	Map Index	Date Created	Parent County or Territory From Which Organized Address/Details
Anderson*	F6	6 Nov 1801	**Knox, Grainger**
www.korrnet.org/anderson/			Anderson County; 100 N Main St; Clinton, TN 37716-3615; Ph. 865.457.6232 Details: (Co Clk has m & pro rec)
Bedford*	K8	3 Dec 1807	**Rutherford**
www.tngenweb.org/bedford/			Bedford County; 100 N Side Sq; Shelbyville, TN 37160; Ph. 931.684.1921 Details: (Courthouse destroyed by fire & by a tornado in the past) (Co Clk has m rec from 1863 & pro rec; Clk Cir Ct has div rec)
Benton	N6	19 Dec 1835	**Henry, Humphreys**
www.rootsweb.com/~tnbenton/index.htm			Benton County; Court Sq; Camden, TN 38320; Ph. 901.584.6053 Details: (Co Clk has m rec from 1836 & pro rec from 1840; Clk Cir Ct has div & ct rec; Reg of Deeds has land rec)
Bledsoe	H7	30 Nov 1807	**Roane**
www.tngenweb.org/bledsoe/			Bledsoe County; Main St; PO Box 149; Pikeville, TN 37367-0212; Ph. 423.447.2137 Details: (Courthouse burned in 1908) (Co Clk has m & pro rec from 1908; Reg of Deeds has land rec)
Blount*	F7	11 Jul 1795	**Knox**
www.korrnet.org/blountco/			Blount County; 345 Court St; Maryville, TN 37804; Ph. 865.273.5800 Details: (Co Clk has m & pro rec from 1795; Clk Cir Ct has div rec; Reg of Deeds has land rec)
Bradley*	H8	10 Feb 1836	**Cherokee Indian Lands**
www.bradleyco.net/			Bradley County; PO Box 46; Cleveland, TN 37364-0046; Ph. 423.476.0520 Details: (Courthouse rec destroyed by fire in Nov 1864) (Co Clk has m rec from 1864; Clk & Master has pro rec from 1864; Reg of Deeds has land & mil dis rec from 1864; Cir & Session Ct has div & ct rec from 1864; Cleveland Pub Lib has early ct rec, cen, pro, m & d rec)
Campbell	F6	11 Sep 1806	**Anderson, Claiborne**
www.rootsweb.com/~tncampbe/			Campbell County; Main St; Jacksboro, TN 37757; Ph. 423.562.3496 Details: (Co Clk has m rec from 1838; Reg of Deeds has land rec)
Cannon	J6	31 Jan 1836	**Coffee, Warren, Wilson, Rutherford**
www.cafes.net/jlewis/cannon.htm			Cannon County; County Courthouse; Woodbury, TN 37190; Ph. 615.563.5936 Details: (Co Clk has m rec from 1838; Reg of Deeds has land rec)
Carroll	O7	7 Nov 1821	**Chickasaw Indian Lands**
www.rootsweb.com/~tncarrol/			Carroll County; 625 High St; PO Box 110; Huntingdon, TN 38344; Ph. 731.986.1960 Details: (Co Clk has m rec from 1838; Reg of Deeds has land rec)
Carter	B6	9 Apr 1796	**Washington**
www.tngenweb.org/carter/			Carter County; 801 E Elk Ave; Elizabethton, TN 37643; Ph. 423.542.1814 Details: (Co Clk has pro rec from 1800; Chan & Cir Ct has div & ct rec; Reg of Deeds has land rec)
Cheatham*	L6	28 Feb 1856	**Davidson, Dickson, Montgomery, Robertson**
www.cheathamcounty.net/			Cheatham County; 100 Public Sq; Ashland City, TN 37015; Ph. 615.792.5179 Details: (Co Clk has m & pro rec from 1865; Clk Cir Ct has div & ct rec; Reg of Deeds has land rec)
Chester	O8	4 Mar 1875	**Hardeman, Madison, Henderson, McNairy**
www.rootsweb.com/~tncheste/chester.htm			Chester County; 126 Crook Ave; Henderson, TN 38340; Ph. 731.989.7171 Details: (Co Clk has m & pro rec from 1890; Clk Cir Ct has div & ct rec; Reg of Deeds has land rec)
Claiborne	E5	29 Oct 1801	**Grainger, Hawkins**
www.tngenweb.org/claiborne/			Claiborne County; PO Box 173; Tazewell, TN 37879; Ph. 423.626.3284 Details: (Co Clk has m rec; Clk Cir Ct has div & ct rec; Reg of Deeds has land rec)
Clay	I5	24 Jun 1870	**Jackson, Overton**
www.tngenweb.org/clay/			Clay County; 100 Courthouse Sq; Celina, TN 38551; Ph. 931.243.3145 Details: (Co Clk has m rec from 1870; Clk & Master has pro rec from 1870; Co Asr has land rec; Clk Cir Ct has div & ct rec from 1870)

County Website	Map Index	Date Created	Parent County or Territory From Which Organized Address/Details
Cocke www.rootsweb.com/~tncocke/Index.html	D7	9 Oct 1797	**Jefferson** Cocke County; 111 Court Ave; Newport, TN 37821; Ph. 423.623.6176 Details: (Co Clk has b & d rec 1909-1911 & 1928-1930 & m rec; Clk & Master has div & pro rec from 1877; Clk Cir Ct has ct rec; Reg of Deeds has land rec; Stokely Memorial Lib has a genealogical section)
Coffee www.cafes.net/jlewis/	J7	8 Jan 1836	**Franklin, Warren, Bedford** Coffee County; 300 Hillsboro Blvd; PO Box 8; Manchester, TN 37355; Ph. 931.723.5106 Details: (Co Clk has m rec from 1854 & pro rec from 1836; Clk Cir Ct has div & ct rec; Reg of Deeds has land rec)
Crockett* www.rootsweb.com/~tncrocke/	P7	20 Dec 1845	**Dyer, Madison, Gibson, Haywood** Crockett County; 1 S Bells St; Alamo, TN 38001; Ph. 731.696.5452 Details: (Many early cen rec of residents of Crockett Co can be found in surrounding cos; Co Clk has m, div, pro, ct & land rec from 1872, b & d rec from 1925)
Cumberland www.upper-cumberland.net/ users/mboniol/	H7	16 Nov 1855	**Bledsoe, Morgan, Roane, White, Rhea, Van Buren, Putnam** Cumberland County; 2 N Main St; #206; Crossville, TN 38555; Ph. 931.484.6442 Details: (Co Clk has m & pro rec from 1905; Clk & Master & Clk Cir Ct have div rec; Reg of Deeds has land rec)
Davidson www.rootsweb.com/~tndavids/x users/mboniol/	K6	18 Apr 1783	**Washington** Davidson County; 700 2nd Ave S; Nashville, TN 37210; Ph. 615.862.5710 Details: (Co Clk has m rec from 1789 & pro rec from 1783; Clk Cir Ct has div & ct rec; Reg of Deeds has land rec)
De Kalb www.tngenweb.org/dekalb/	I7	11 Dec 1837	**Cannon, Warren, White, Wilson, Jackson** De Kalb County; County Courthouse; Rm 205; Smithville, TN 37166; Ph. 615.597.5159 Details: (Co Clk has m rec from 1848 & pro rec from 1854; Clk Chan Ct has div rec; Reg of Deeds has land rec)
Decatur www.netease.net/decatur/	N8	Nov 1845	**Perry** Decatur County; PO Box 488; Decaturville, TN 38329-0488; Ph. 731.852.3417 Details: (Co Clk has m rec from 1869; Reg of Deeds has land rec)
Dickson www.rootsweb.com/~tndickso/	M6	25 Oct 1803	**Montgomery, Robertson** Dickson County; 4 Court Sq; Charlotte, TN 37036; Ph. 615.789.4171 Details: (Courthouse was destroyed by tornado about 1835; many rec were destroyed) (Co Clk has b & d rec 1908-1912 & 1925-1939, m rec from 1817 & pro rec from 1977; Reg Off has land rec from 1804 & mil dis rec from 1946)
Dyer www.rootsweb.com/~tndyer/	Q6	16 Oct 1823	**Chickasaw Indian Lands** Dyer County; PO Box 1360; Dyersburg, TN 38025-1360; Ph. 731.286.7814 Details: (Co Clk has m & pro rec from 1850, div & ct rec from 1927 & funeral rec 1914-1956; Reg of Deeds has land rec)
Fayette www.wdbj.net/~wdbj/fayette/index.html	Q9	29 Sep 1824	**Shelby, Hardeman** Fayette County; 1 Court Sq; County Courthouse; Somerville, TN 38068; Ph. 901.465.2871 Details: (Co Clk has b & d rec 1925-1929, m rec from 1838 except m rec 1918-1925 lost in fire; Clk & Master has pro rec; Reg of Deeds has land rec)
Fentress www.rootsweb.com/~tnfentre/fent.htm	H6	28 Nov 1823	**Morgan, Overton** Fentress County; 101 S Main St; Jamestown, TN 38556; Ph. 931.879.8615 Details: (Co Clk has m rec from 1905; Reg of Deeds has land rec)
Franklin www.tngenweb.org/franklin/	J8	3 Dec 1807	**Bedford, Warren** Franklin County; 1 So Jefferson St; Winchester, TN 37398; Ph. 931.967.2541 Details: (Co Clk has m rec from 1838 & pro rec from 1808; Reg of Deeds has land rec)
Gibson www.rootsweb.com/~tngibson/	P6	21 Oct 1823	**Chickasaw Indian Lands** Gibson County; County Courthouse; PO Box 228; Trenton, TN 38382; Ph. 731.855.7639 Details: (Co Clk has m rec from 1824 & pro rec 1824-1981; Reg of Deeds has land rec)

County Website	Map Index	Date Created	Parent County or Territory From Which Organized Address/Details
Giles www.tngenweb.org/giles/	L8	14 Nov 1809	**Maury** Giles County; PO Box 678; Pulaski, TN 38478-0678; Ph. 931.363.1509 Details: (Courthouse burned during Civil War) (Co Clk has m rec from 1865 & pro rec; Clk & Master has div rec; Clk Cir Ct has ct rec; Reg of Deeds has land rec)
Grainger www.rootsweb.com/~tngraing/	E6	22 Apr 1796	**Hawkins, Knox** Grainger County; County Courthouse; PO Box 116; Rutledge, TN 37861; Ph. 865.828.3511 Details: (Co Clk has m rec from 1796; Reg of Deeds has land rec)
Greene www.rootsweb.com/~tngreene/	D6	18 Apr 1783	**Washington** Greene County; 101 S Main St; Greenville, TN 37743; Ph. 423.798.1708 Details: (Co Clk has m & pro rec; Reg of Deeds has land rec)
Grundy www.tngenweb.org/grundy/	I8	29 Jan 1844	**Coffee, Warren** Grundy County; Hwy 56 & 108; Altamont, TN 37301; Ph. 931.692.3455 Details: (Co Clk has m & pro rec from 1850; Reg of Deeds has land rec)
Hamblen www.tngenweb.org/hamblen/	D6	8 Jun 1870	**Grainger, Hawkins, Jefferson** Hamblen County; 511 W 2nd N St; Morristown, TN 37814; Ph. 423.586.9112 Details: (Co Clk has m & pro rec from 1870; Clk & Master has div rec; Clk Cir Ct has ct rec; Reg of Deeds has land rec)
Hamilton* www.hamiltontn.gov/	H8	25 Oct 1819	**Cherokee Indian Lands** Hamilton County; County Courthouse; Rm 201; Chattanooga, TN 37402; Ph. 423.209.6500 Details: (Co Clk has m rec from 1857; Co Hlth Dept has b rec from 1949 & d rec from 1972; Cir Ct & Clk & Masters has div rec; Clk & Masters has pro rec from 1865; Clk & Masters & Reg of Deeds has land rec; Reg of Deeds has mil dis rec; Clk Cir Ct has ct rec)
Hancock www.rootsweb.com/~tnhancoc/	D5	7 Jan 1844	**Claiborne, Hawkins** Hancock County; PO Box 347; Sneedville, TN 37869; Ph. 423.733.4341 Details: (Co Clk has m, div, pro & ct rec from 1930, land rec from 1875 & mil rec from 1917)
Hardeman www.tngenweb.org/hardeman/	P8	16 Oct 1823	**Chickasaw Indian Lands** Hardeman County; 100 N Main St; Bolivar, TN 38008-2322; Ph. 901.658.3541 Details: (Co Clk has m & pro rec from 1823; Reg of Deeds has land rec)
Hardin www.hardinhistory.com/history/ genealog.htm	N8	13 Nov 1819	**Chickasaw Indian Lands** Hardin County; 601 Main St; Savannah, TN 38372; Ph. 901.925.8166 Details: (Co Clk has m rec from 1864, div, land, pro & ct rec)
Hawkins www.rootsweb.com/~tnhawkin/ index.html	D6	18 Nov 1786	**Sullivan** Hawkins County; 100 E Main St; Rogersville, TN 37857-3390; Ph. 423.272.8150 Details: (Co Clk has m rec from 1789 & pro rec; Clk Cir Ct has div & ct rec; Reg of Deeds has land rec)
Haywood* www.rootsweb.com/~tnhaywoo/	P7	3 Nov 1823	**Chickasaw Indian Lands** Haywood County; 1 N Washington St; Brownsville, TN 38012; Ph. 731.772.2362 Details: (Co Clk has m rec from 1859, div rec 1941-1965 & pro rec from 1826; Reg of Deeds has land rec)
Henderson www.tngenweb.org/henderson/	O7	7 Nov 1821	**Chickasaw Indian Lands** Henderson County; 17 Monroe St; Lexington, TN 38351; Ph. 731.968.2801 Details: (Courthouse burned 1863 & 1895; some rec saved) (Clk Chan Ct has b rec; Co Clk has m rec from 1893; Clk Cir Ct has div & ct rec; Reg of Deeds has land rec)
Henry www.rootsweb.com/~tnhenry/	N6	7 Nov 1821	**Chickasaw Indian Lands** Henry County; 100 W Washington St; Paris, TN 38242-0024; Ph. 731.642.2412 Details: (Reg of Deeds has land rec; Co Clk has b, m, d & pro rec; Clk Cir Ct has ct rec)
Hickman www.rootsweb.com/~tnhickma/	M7	3 Dec 1807	**Dickson** Hickman County; Public Square; Centerville, TN 37033; Ph. 931.729.2621 Details: (Courthouse burned 1865; all rec lost) (Co Clk has m & pro rec from 1867; Clk Cir Ct has div & ct rec; Reg of Deeds has land rec from 1807)

County Website	Map Index	Date Created	Parent County or Territory From Which Organized / Address/Details
Houston www.rootsweb.com/~tnhousto/	M6	23 Jan 1871	**Dickson, Stewart, Humphreys** Houston County; PO Box 388; Erin, TN 37061-0388; Ph. 931.289.3870 Details: (Co Clk has m rec; Clk Cir Ct has div & ct rec; Co Ct has pro rec; Reg of Deeds has land rec)
Humphreys www.tngenweb.org/humphreys/	M6	19 Oct 1809	**Stewart** Humphreys County; 102 Thompson St; Waverly, TN 37185; Ph. 931.296.7671 Details: (Courthouse burned in 1876 & 1898; many rec lost; only land rec are complete) (Co Clk has land rec from 1809, m rec from 1861 & pro rec from 1838)
Jackson www.tngenweb.org/jackson/	I6	6 Nov 1801	**Smith** Jackson County; 101 E Hill Rd; PO Box 346; Gainesboro, TN 38562-0346; Ph. 931.268.9516 Details: (Co Clk has m & pro rec from 1870; Reg of Deeds has land rec)
Jefferson www.tngenweb.org/jefferson/	E6	11 Jun 1792	**Green, Hawkins** Jefferson County; 214 W Main St; Dandridge, TN 37725-0710; Ph. 865.397.2935 Details: (Co Clk has m & pro rec from 1792; Clk & Master has div rec; Clk Cir Ct has ct rec; Reg of Deeds has land rec)
Johnson www.jacksonco.com/	B5	2 Jan 1836	**Carter** Johnson County; 210 College St; Mountain City, TN 37683; Ph. 423.727.7853 Details: (Co Clk has m & pro rec from 1836; Clk Chan Ct has div & ct rec; Reg of Deeds has land rec)
Knox www.korrnet.org/knox/	F6	11 Jun 1792	**Greene, Hawkins** Knox County; Old Knox County Courthouse; Knoxville, TN 37902-1805; Ph. 865.215.2390 Details: (Co Archives has pro rec from 1789, m, div & ct rec from 1792 & tax rec from 1806; Reg of Deeds has land rec)
Lake www.ecsis.net/lakecounty/history/	Q6	24 Jun 1870	**Obion** Lake County; 229 Church St; Tiptonville, TN 38079-1162; Ph. 731.253.8926 Details: (Co Clk has pro rec from 1870 & m rec from 1883; Clk Chan & Cir Ct have div rec; Reg & Tax Asr have land rec)
Lauderdale www.rootsweb.com/~tnlauder/	Q7	24 Nov 1835	**Dyer, Tipton, Haywood** Lauderdale County; County Courthouse; Ripley, TN 38063; Ph. 731.635.2561 Details: (Co Clk has m rec from 1838 & pro rec; Clk Chan Ct has div rec; General Sessions Ct has ct rec; Reg of Deeds has land rec)
Lawrence www.tngenweb.org/lawrence/	M9	21 Oct 1817	**Hickman, Maury** Lawrence County; 240 W Gaines St; Lawrenceburg, TN 38464; Ph. 931.762.7700 Details: (Co Hlth Dept has b rec; Co Clk has m rec from 1818 & pro rec from 1829; Clk Cir Ct has div rec; Reg of Deeds has land rec)
Lewis www.tngenweb.org/lewis/	M8	21 Dec 1843	**Hickman, Maury, Wayne, Lawrence** Lewis County; 110 N Park St; Hohenwald, TN 38462; Ph. 931.796.3734 Details: (Co completely abolished for one year following the Civil War; for that year rec will be found in Maury, Lawrence, Hickman & Wayne Cos) (Co Clk has m rec from 1881, pro & ct rec; Clk Cir Ct has div rec; Reg of Deeds has land rec)
Lincoln www.rootsweb.com/~tnlincol/	K9	14 Nov 1809	**Bedford** Lincoln County; 112 Main Ave S; PO Box 577; Fayetteville, TN 37334-0577; Ph. 931.433.2454 Details: (Co Clk has m & pro rec; Clk Cir Ct has div rec; Clk & Master has ct rec; Reg of Deeds has land rec)
Loudon* www.rootsweb.com/~tnloudon/	F7	2 Jun 1870	**Blount, Monroe, Roane** Loudon County; 601 Grove St; Loudon, TN 37774; Ph. 423.458.2630 Details: (Co Clk has m rec from 1870; Clk Cir Ct has div & ct rec from 1870; Reg of Deeds has land rec from 1870)
Macon maconcountytennessee.com/	J5	18 Jan 1842	**Smith, Sumner** Macon County; 106 County Courthouse; Lafayette, TN 37083; Ph. 615.666.2000 Details: (Co Clk has b rec 1908-1912, m rec from 1901 & pro rec from 1900; Clk Cir Ct has div & ct rec; Reg of Deeds has land rec)

Census Records

Available Census Records and Census Substitutes

Federal Census 1850, 1860, 1870, 1880, 1900, 1910, 1920, 1930.

Federal Mortality Schedules 1850, 1860, 1870, 1880.

Union Veterans and Widows 1890.

State/Territorial Census 1829-1836.

School Census 1854-1855.

Dollarhide, William. *The Census Book: A Genealogist's Guide to Federal Census Facts, Schedules and Indexes.* Bountiful, Utah: Heritage Quest, 1999

Jackson, Ronald Vern, et al. *Texas, 1840-49.* North Salt Lake, Utah: Accelerated Indexing Systems International, 1981.

Jackson, Ronald Vern. *Texas, 1830-1839, Census Index.* North Salt Lake, Utah: Accelerated Indexing Systems International, 1981.

Kemp, Thomas Jay. *The American Census Handbook.* Wilmington, Delaware: Scholarly Resources, Inc., 2001.

Lainhart, Ann S. *State Census Records.* Baltimore: Genealogical Publishing Co., Inc., 1992

Mullins, Marion D. *The First Census of Texas, 1829-1836: To Which are Added Texas Citizenship Lists, 1821-1845, and Other Early Records of the Republic of Texas.* Washington, D.C.: National Genealogical Society, 1962.

Thorndale, William, and William Dollarhide. *Map Guide to the U.S. Federal Censuses, 1790-1920.* Baltimore: Genealogical Publishing Co., 1987.

White, Gifford E. *1830 Citizens of Texas.* Austin, Texas: Eakin Press, 1983.

Court, Probate and Wills

Daughters of the American Revolution *Texas Records from Bibles, Probate Records, Wills, Cemeteries, 1639-1954.* Dallas, Texas: Filmed by Microfilm Sales & Service, 1961. Microfilm.

Index to Probate Cases of Texas. 1940. Reprint. San Antonio: Bureau of Research in the Social Sciences, University of Texas, 1980. Compiled by the Work Projects Administration for 31 counties.

Emigration, Immigration, Migration and Naturalization

Blaha, Albert J. *Passenger Lists for Galveston, 1850-1855.* [Houston, Texas: A.J. Blaha], 1985.

Geue, Chester W., and Ethel H. Geue. *A New Land Beckoned: German Immigration to Texas, 1844-7.* Enlarged ed. Waco: Texian Press, 1972.

Hejl, Edmond H. *Czech Footprints Across the Bluebonnet Fields of Texas: Villages of Origin.* N.p., 1983.

Marsh, Helen and Timothy. *Tennesseans in Texas.* Easley, South Carolina: Southern Historical Press, 1986.

McManus, J. *Comal County, Texas, and New Braunfels, Texas, German Immigrant Ships, 1845-1846.* St. Louis, Missouri: F.T. Ingmire, 1985.

Ships Passenger Lists, Port of Galveston, Texas, 1846-1871. Easley, South Carolina: Southern Historical Press, 1984.

Williams, Villamae, ed. *Stephen F. Austin's Register of Families.* Baltimore: Genealogical Publishing Co., 1989.

Land and Property

Abstract of Land Claims, Compiled From the Records of the General Land Office. Galveston: Civilian Book Office, 1852.

Abstract *of Land Titles of Texas Comprising the Titled, Patented, and Located Lands in the State.* Galveston: Shaw and Blaylock, 1878.

An Abstract of the Original Titles of Records in the General Land Office. 1838. Reprint. Austin, Texas: Pemberton Press, 1964.

Bowden, J. J. *Spanish and Mexican Land Grants in the Chihuahuan Acquisition.* El Paso, Texas: Texas Western Press, 1971.

Early Texas Settlers, 1700's-1800's. [S.l.]: Brøderbund, 2000. CD-ROM.

Ericson, Carolyn Reeves. *First Settlers of the Republic of Texas: Headright Land Grants Which Were Reported as Genuine and Legal by the Traveling Commissioners, January 1840.* 2 vols. Reprint. Nacogdoches, Texas: Carolyn Reeves Ericson, 1982.

First Settlers of the Republic of Texas: Headright Land Grants, 1840. 2 vols., 1841, Reprint. Nacogdoches, Texas: Carolyn R. Ericson, 1982—.

Gould, Florence C. *Claiming Their Land: Women Homesteaders in Texas.* El Paso, Texas: Texas Western Press, 1991.

Mauro, Garry. *The Land Commissioners of Texas: 150 Years of the General Land Office.* Austin: Texas General Land Office, 1986.

Miller, Thomas Lloyd. *Bounty and Donation Land Grants of Texas 1835-1888.* Austin: University of Texas Press, 1967.

Miller, Thomas Lloyd. *Texas Confederate Scrip Grantees.* N.p., 1985.

Miller, Thomas Lloyd. *The Public Lands of Texas 1519-1970.* Norman, Oklahoma: University of Oklahoma Press, [1972].

Miller, Thomas Lloyd. *The Public Lands of Texas, 1519-1970.* Norman: University of Oklahoma Press, 1971.

Taylor, Virginia H. *Index to Spanish and Mexican Land Grants in Texas.* Austin, Texas: Lone Star Press, 1974.

University of Texas (San Antonio). Institute of Texan Cultures. *Residents of Texas, 1782-1836.* 3 v. [San Antonio, Texas: The Institute, 1984].

White, Gifford. *Character Certificates in the General Land Office of Texas.* [Austin: G. White, 1985.]

Military

Barron, John C., et al. *Republic of Texas Pension Application Abstracts.* Austin, Texas: Austin Genealogical Society, 1987.

Barton, Henry W. Texas *Volunteers in the Mexican War.* Wichita Falls, Texas: [Texican Press, 1970].

Dixon, Sam Houston, and Louis Wiltz Kemp. *The Heroes of San Jacinto.* Houston: The Anson Jones Press, 1932.

Fay, Mary Smith. *War of 1812 Veterans in Texas.* New Orleans: Polyanthos, 1979.

Ingmire, Frances Terry. *Texas Frontiersmen, 1839-1860: Minute Men, Militia, Home Guard, Indian Fighters.* St. Louis: F.T. Ingmire, 1982.

Ingmire, Frances Terry. *Texas Rangers: Frontier Battalion, Minute Men, Commanding Officers, 1847-1900.* 6 vols. St. Louis: Ingmire Publications, 1982.

Kinney, John M. *Index to Applications for Texas Confederate Pensions.* Austin, Texas: Archives Division, Texas State Library, 1977.

Muster Rolls of the Texas Revolution. Austin, Texas: Daughters of the Republic of Texas, Inc., 1986.

Pompey, Sherman L. *Muster Lists of the Texas Confederate Troops.* Independence, CA: Historical and Genealogical Publishing Co., 1966.

Roll Call at the Alamo. Ft. Collins, Colo.: The Old Army Press, 1985.

Sibley, Marilyn McAdams. *Lone Stars and State Gazettes: Texas Newspapers Before the Civil War.* College Station, Texas: Texas A&M University Press, 1983.

Stephens, Robert W. *Texas Ranger Indian War Pensions.* Quanah, Texas: Nortex Press, 1975.

Texas Confederate Index: Confederate Soldiers of the State of Texas. Dallas, Texas: Presidial Press, 1978.Microfiche.

Texas Newspapers, 1813-1939: A Union List. Houston: [N.p.]: San Jacinto Museum of History Association, 1951

United States. Record and Pension Office. *Compiled Service Records of Volunteer Soldiers Who Served During the Mexican War in Organizations from the State of Texas.* Washington, D.C.: The National Archives, 1959. Microfilm, multiple rolls.

United States. Selective Service System. *Texas, World War I Selective Service System Draft Registration Cards, 1917-1918.* National Archives Microfilm Publications, M1509. Washington, D.C.: National Archives, 1987-1988.

White, Virgil D. *Index to Texas CSA Pension Files.* Waynesboro, Tennessee: National Historical Publishing Co., 1989.

Vital and Cemetery Records

An Index to Texas Probate Birth Records, ca. 1900-1945, ca. 1900-1945. Austin: Texas State Library, 1988. Microfilm, 11 rolls.

Biggerstaff, Mrs. Malcolm B. *4000 Tombstone Inscriptions from Texas. 1745-1870: Along the Old San Antonio Road and the Trail of Austin's Colonists.* Oklahoma City, OK: Oklahoma Historical Society, 1952.

Cemetery Records of Texas. 6 vols. Typescript. Salt Lake City: Genealogical Society of Utah, 1956-63.

Daughters of the American Revolution. Alamo Chapter (San Antonio, Texas). *Texas Cemetery Records, Miscellaneous Bible Records, 1782-1955.* San Antonio, Texas: Microfilm Center, 1973.

Dodd, Jordan R. *Texas Marriages, Early to 1850: A Research Tool.* Bountiful, Utah: Precision Indexing, 1990.

Frazier, John P. *Northeast Texas Cemeteries.* Shreveport, California: S. and W. Enterprises, 1984.

Gracy, Alice D., Emma G. S. Gentry, and Jane Sumner. *Early Texas Birth Records, 1838-1878.* 2 vols. Austin, Texas: the authors, 1969, 1971.

Grammer, Norma R. *Marriage Records of Early Texas, 1826-1846.* Fort Worth, Texas: Fort Worth Genealogical Society, 1971.

Guide to Public Vital Statistics Records in Texas [N.p.]: Historical Records Survey, 1941.

Inscriptions from Texas, 1745-1870: Along the Old San Antonio Road and the Trail of Austin's Colonists. Oklahoma City: Oklahoma Historical Society, 1952.

Parsons, Kim. *A Reference to Texas Cemetery Records.* Humble, Texas: the author, 1988.

Sharry Crofford-Gould, *Texas Cemetery Inscriptions: A Source Index* San Antonio: Limited Editions, 1977.

Swenson, Helen S. *8,800 Texas Marriages, 1824-1850.* 2 vols. Round Rock, Texas: Helen S. Swanson, 1981.

County Website	Map Index	Date Created	Parent County or Territory From Which Organized Address/Details
Anderson www.wwits.net/counties/anderson.phtml	H10	24 Mar 1846	**Houston** Anderson County; 500 N Church St; Palestine, TX 75801-3024; Ph. 903.723.7432 Details: (Dis Clk has div rec; Co Clk has b & d rec from 1903, m, pro & land rec from 1846 & ct rec; cities have b & d rec from 1953)
Andrews www.rootsweb.com/~txandrew/	H4	21 Aug 1876	**Bexar Land District** Andrews County; 215 NW 1st St; Andrews, TX 79714; Ph. 915.524.1426 Details: (Co Clk has b, m & ct rec from 1910, pro rec from 1911 & land rec from 1884; Dis Clk has div rec)
Angelina www.rootsweb.com/~txangeli/	I11	22 Apr 1846	**Nacogdoches** Angelina County; PO Box 908; Lufkin, TX 75902-0908; Ph. 936.634.8339 Details: (Co Clk has some b rec from 1875, d rec from 1903, m, pro & land rec from 1846; Dis Clk has div rec; Co Clk & Dis Ct have ct rec from 1920)
Aransas www.rootsweb.com/~txaransa/	M9	18 Sep 1871	**Refugio** Aransas County; 301 N Liveoak St; Rockport, TX 78382-2744; Ph. 361.790.0122 Details: (Co Clk has b & d rec from 1901, m, pro, ct & land rec from 1871)
Archer www.rootsweb.com/~txarcher/archer.htm	F8	22 Jan 1858	**Fannin Land District** Archer County; 112 E Walnut; PO Box 458; Archer City, TX 76351; Ph. 940.574.4615 Details: (Co Clk has b rec from 1880, m, d, bur, div, pro, ct & land rec)
Armstrong www.rootsweb.com/~txarmstr/	E5	21 Aug 1876	**Bexar Land District** Armstrong County; PO Box 309; Claude, TX 79019; Ph. 806.226.2081 Details: (Co Clk has b & d rec from 1903, m & pro rec from 1890, ct rec from 1898 & land rec from 1883; Clk Cir Ct has div rec)
Atascosa bsd.pastracks.com/states/texas/atascosa/	L8	25 Jan 1856	**Bexar Land District** Atascosa County; 5 Courthouse Cir Dr; Jourdanton, TX 78026; Ph. 830.769.2511 Details: (Co Clk has b rec from 1890, d rec from 1903, m, pro & land rec from 1856 & ct rec from 1860; Dis Clk has div rec)
Austin www.austincounty.com/	J10	17 Mar 1836	**Old Mexican Municipality** Austin County; 1 E Main St; Bellville, TX 77418; Ph. 979.865.5911 Details: (Co Clk has b & d rec from 1903, m, land & pro rec from early 1800's, cem, ct, mil dis & nat rec; Dis Ct has div rec)
Bailey www.rootsweb.com/~txbailey/index.htm	F4	21 Aug 1876	**Bexar Land District** Bailey County; 300 S 1st St; Muleshoe, TX 79347-3621; Ph. 806.272.3044 Details: (Co Clk has b, m, pro & ct rec from 1918 & land rec from 1882; Dis Clk has div rec)
Bandera* www.rootsweb.com/~txbander/	K7	26 Jan 1856	**Bexar Land District** Bandera County; County Courthouse; Bandera, TX 78003; Ph. 830.796.3332 Details: (Co/Dis Clk has b & d rec from 1904, m, div, land, pro, ct & nat rec from 1856 & mil dis rec from 1900)
Bastrop* www.rootsweb.com/~txbastro/ bastrop.htm	J9	17 Mar 1836	**Old Mexican Municipality** Bastrop County; 804 Pecan St; PO Box 577; Bastrop, TX 78602; Ph. 512.332.7234 Details: (Co Clk has b & d rec from 1903, m rec from 1860, pro rec from 1850, ct rec from 1890, land rec from 1837, mil dis rec from 1919 & nat rec from 1855; Dis Clk has div rec)
Baylor www.rootsweb.com/~txbaylor/baylor.htm	F7	1 Feb 1858	**Fannin Land District** Baylor County; 101 S Washington; PO Box 689; Seymour, TX 76380-0689; Ph. 940.888.3322 Details: (Co Clk has b & d rec from 1903, m rec from 1879, div rec from 1881, pro & ct rec from 1880)
Bee bsd.pastracks.com/states/texas/bee/	G5	8 Dec 1857	**Goliad, Refugio, Live Oak, San Patricio, Karnes** Bee County; 105 W Corpus Christi St; Beeville, TX 78102-5684; Ph. 361.362.3245 Details: (Co Clk has b & d rec from 1903, m, pro & land rec from 1858 & ct rec from 1876; Dis Clk has div rec)

County Website	Map Index	Date Created	Parent County or Territory From Which Organized Address/Details
Bell www.bellcountytx.com/	19	22 Jan 1850	**Milam** Bell County; 550 E 2nd St; PO Box 480; Belton, TX 76513; Ph. 254.933.5174 Details: (Co Clk has b & d rec from 1903, m, pro & land rec from 1850, mil rec & school cen; Clk Dis Ct has div rec from 1850, ct & nat rec)
Bexar www.co.bexar.tx.us/	K8	1836	**Old Mexican Municipality (established 1731)** Bexar County; 100 Dolorosa St Ste 108; San Antonio, TX 78205-3083; Ph. 210.335.2585 Details: (Co Clk has b rec from 1838, m rec from 1837, d rec from 1903, pro rec from 1843, land rec from 1700's, Spanish church rec 1737-1859 & Spanish City Council minutes 1815-1820)
Blanco www.moment.net/~blancoco/	J8	12 Feb 1858	**Gillespie, Comal, Burnet, Hays** Blanco County; PO Box 65; Johnson City, TX 78636-0117; Ph. 830.868.7357 Details: (Co Clk has b & d rec from 1903, m, div, pro, ct & land rec from 1876)
Borden www.pastracks.com/states/texas/borden/	G5	21 Aug 1876	**Bexar Land District** Borden County; 117 E Wasson; PO Box 124; Gail, TX 79738; Ph. 806.756.4312 Details: (Co Clk has b & d rec from 1903, div & ct rec from 1891, land rec from 1880 & pro rec from 1894)
Bosque users.htcomp.net/bosque/	H9	4 Feb 1854	**McLennan, Milam** Bosque County; PO Box 617; Meridian, TX 76665; Ph. 254.435.2201 Details: (Co Clk has b & d rec from 1902, m, pro & land rec from 1854 & ct rec; Dis Clk has div rec)
Bowie www.usroots.com/~jmautrey/	G12	17 Dec 1840	**Red River** Bowie County; PO Box 248; New Boston, TX 75570; Ph. 903.628.2571 Details: (Co Clk has b, m, d, pro, land & mil rec, school cen; Clk Dis Ct has div & ct rec)
Brazoria www.brazoria-county.com/	K10	17 Mar 1836	**Old Mexican Municipality** Brazoria County; 111 E Locust St Ste 200; Angleton, TX 77515; Ph. 979.864.1357 Details: (Co Clk has b rec from 1901, d rec from 1903, m rec from 1829, pro rec from 1837, ct rec from 1896, land rec from 1826, mil rec from 1919, delayed b rec & election rec from 1800's)
Brazos www.co.brazos.tx.us/	J10	30 Jan 1841	**Washington, Robertson** Brazos County; 300 E 26th St Ste 120; Bryan, TX 77803; Ph. 979.361.4528 Details: (Formerly Navasota Co. Name changed to Brazos 28 Jan 1842) (Co Clk has m rec from 1841, b & d rec from 1900, pro rec from 1844 & ct rec from 1959 with some earlier)
Brewster www.rootsweb.com/~txbrewst/	K4	2 Feb 1887	**Presidio** Brewster County; 201 W Ave E; Alpine, TX 79830; Ph. 915.837.3366 Details: (Co Clk has b, pro, mil & ct rec from 1900, m rec from 1887, d rec from 1903 & land rec from 1800; Dis Ct has div rec)
Briscoe www.rootsweb.com/~txbrisco/	E5	21 Aug 1876	**Bexar Land District** Briscoe County; 415 Main; PO Box 375; Silverton, TX 79257; Ph. 806.823.2134 Details: (Co Clk has b & land rec from 1887, m, d, pro & mil rec from 1900 & ct rec from 1945; Dis Ct has div rec)
Brooks bsd.pastracks.com/states/texas/brooks/	N8	11 Mar 1911	**Starr, Zapata, Hidalgo** Brooks County; PO Box 427; Falfurrias, TX 78355; Ph. 361.325.3053 Details: (Co Clk has b, m, d, pro & ct rec from 1911)
Brown* www.rootsweb.com/~txbrown/	17	27 Aug 1856	**Travis, Comanche** Brown County; 200 S Broadway St; Brownwood, TX 76801; Ph. 915.643.2594 Details: (Co Clk has b rec from 1900, d rec from 1903, m, land, pro, ct & mil rec from 1880; Dis Ct has div rec from 1880)
Buchanan		22 Jan 1858	**Bosque** Details: (see Stephens) (Name changed to Stephens 17 Dec 1861)

County Website	Map Index	Date Created	Parent County or Territory From Which Organized Address/Details
Burleson www.rootsweb.com/~txburles/burles.htm	J9	15 Jan 1846	**Milam, Washington** Burleson County; PO Box 57; Caldwell, TX 77836; Ph. 409.567.2329 Details: (Co Clk has b & d rec from 1903, m, pro, ct & land rec from 1845; Dis Clk has div rec from 1845)
Burnet www.rootsweb.com/~txburnet/	I8	5 Feb 1852	**Travis, Bell, Williamson** Burnet County; 220 S Pierce St; Burnet, TX 78611-3136; Ph. 512.756.5420 Details: (Co Clk has b & d rec from 1903, m, bur, pro & land rec from 1852 & ct rec from 1876; Dis Clk has div rec)
Caldwell* www.rootsweb.com/~txcaldwe/index.htm	K9	6 Mar 1848	**Gonzales, Bastrop** Caldwell County; 110 S Main St; Lockhart, TX 78644; Ph. 512.398.1804 Details: (Co Clk has b & d rec from 1903, m & land rec from 1848 & ct rec; Dis Clk has div rec)
Calhoun* www.tisd.net/~calhoun/	L10	4 Apr 1846	**Victoria, Matagorda, Jackson** Calhoun County; 211 S Ann St; Port Lavaca, TX 77979-4249; Ph. 361.553.4411 Details: (Co Clk has b & d rec from 1903, probated b rec from 1863, m & land rec from 1846, pro rec from 1849, ct rec from 1850 & mil dis rec from 1919)
Callahan www.rootsweb.com/~txcallah/	H7	1 Feb 1858	**Bexar, Travis, Bosque** Callahan County; 400 Market St; Baird, TX 79504-5305; Ph. 915.854.1217 Details: (Co Clk has b & d rec from 1903, m, pro & land rec from 1877; Dis Clk has div & ct rec)
Cameron bsd.pastracks.com/states/texas/cameron/	O9	12 Feb 1848	**Nueces** Cameron County; PO Box 2178; Brownsville, TX 78522-2178; Ph. 956.544.0817 Details: (Co Clk has b, d & mil rec from 1848, m rec from 1800, land rec from 1845, pro rec from 1850 & ct rec from 1964)
Camp www.rootsweb.com/~txcamp/	G11	6 Apr 1874	**Upshur** Camp County; 126 Church St; Pittsburg, TX 75686; Ph. 903.856.2731 Details: (Co Clk has b & d rec from 1903, m, pro & ct rec from 1874 & land rec from 1854)
Carson www.rootsweb.com/~txcarson/	D5	21 Aug 1876	**Bexar Land District** Carson County; PO Box 487; Panhandle, TX 79068; Ph. 806.537.3873 Details: (Co Clk has b & d rec from 1903, m rec from 1888, div rec from 1902, pro rec from 1907 & land rec from 1883)
Cass www.rootsweb.com/~txcass/	G12	25 Apr 1846	**Bowie** Cass County; PO Box 468; Linden, TX 75563; Ph. 903.756.5071 Details: (Name changed to Davis 17 Dec 1861; Name changed back to Cass 16 May 1871) (Co Clk has some delayed b rec from 1873, d rec 1903-1933, m, pro & land rec from 1846, school cen 1932-1971 & mil dis rec from 1917; Dis Ct has div & ct rec)
Castro www.rootsweb.com/~txcastro/ castro/index.htm	F4	21 Aug 1876	**Bexar Land District** Castro County; 100 E Bedford St; Dimmitt, TX 79027-2643; Ph. 806.647.3338 Details: (Co Clk has b & d rec from 1903, m, div & ct rec from 1892, land rec from 1911, pro rec from 1948 & mil rec from 1917)
Chambers co.chambers.tx.us/	K11	12 Feb 1858	**Jefferson, Liberty** Chambers County; 404 Washington; Anahuac, TX 77514; Ph. 409.267.8309 Details: (Co Clk has b rec from 1903, d rec from 1908, m, pro, ct & land rec from 1875 & div rec from 1910)
Cherokee www.tyler.net/ccgs/default.html	H11	11 Apr 1846	**Nacogdoches** Cherokee County; 520 N Main St; PO Drawer 420; Rusk, TX 75785; Ph. 903.683.2350 Details: (Co Clk has b & d rec from 1903, m, pro & land rec from 1846, ct & div rec)
Childress www.rootsweb.com/~txchildr/	E6	21 Aug 1876	**Bexar Land District** Childress County; Courthouse Box 4; Childress, TX 79201-3755; Ph. 940.937.6143 Details: (Co Clk has b & d rec from 1903, m rec from 1893, div & ct rec from 1900, pro rec from 1894 & land rec from 1895)

County Website	Map Index	Date Created	Parent County or Territory From Which Organized Address/Details
Clay www.co.clay.tx.us/	F8	24 Dec 1857	**Cooke** Clay County; 100 N Bridge St; PO Box 548; Henrietta, TX 76365-2858; Ph. 940.538.4631 Details: (Co Clk has b & d rec from 1903, m rec from 1874, pro & land rec from 1873 & ct rec from 1876)
Cochran www.rootsweb.com/~txcochra/index.htm	G4	21 Aug 1876	**Bexar Land District** Cochran County; Courthouse; Morton, TX 79346; Ph. 806.266.5450 Details: (Co Clk has b, d, div, pro & ct rec from 1926, m rec from 1924 & land rec from 1884)
Coke www.cvcog.org/coke/coke.htm	H6	13 Mar 1889	**Tom Green** Coke County; PO Box 150; Robert Lee, TX 76945; Ph. 915.453.2631 Details: (Co Clk has b & d rec from 1903, m, div, pro & ct rec from 1891 & land rec from 1875)
Coleman www.rootsweb.com/~txcolema/	H7	1 Feb 1858	**Travis, Brown** Coleman County; PO Box 591; Coleman, TX 76834-0591; Ph. 915.625.2889 Details: (Co Clk has b & d rec from 1900, m rec from 1878, land rec from 1849, pro rec from 1876, mil rec from 1918 & ct rec from 1977; Dis Ct has div rec)
Collin www.starbase21.com/PSGenealogy/ Collin.html	G9	3 Apr 1846	**Fannin** Collin County; 210 S McDonald St Ste 124; McKinney, TX 75069-5655; Ph. 972.548.4134 Details: (Co Clk has b & d rec from 1903, ct rec to 1970, m & pro rec; Dis Clk has div & land rec)
Collingsworth www.rootsweb.com/~txcollin/	E6	21 Aug 1876	**Bexar Land District** Collingsworth County; County Courthouse Rm 3; Wellington, TX 79095; Ph. 806.447.2408 Details: (Co Clk has b rec from 1891, m rec from 1890, d rec from 1892, div & ct rec from 1903 & land rec)
Colorado www.rtis.com/reg/colorado-cty/gov.htm	K10	17 Mar 1836	**Old Mexican Municipality** Colorado County; PO Box 68; Columbus, TX 78934; Ph. 979.732.2155 Details: (Co Clk has b & d rec from 1903, m & pro rec from 1837 & land rec; Dis Clk has div & ct rec)
Comal www.co.comal.tx.us/	K8	24 Mar 1846	**Bexar, Gonzales, Travis** Comal County; 150 N Seguin Ste 101; New Braunfels, TX 78130; Ph. 830.620.5513 Details: (Co Clk has b rec 1903-1910 & 1930-1950, m rec from 1846, d rec from 1903, pro, land, nat & ct rec from 1846 & mil dis rec from 1919)
Comanche www.rootsweb.com/~txcomanc/ comanche.htm	H8	25 Jan 1856	**Bosque, Coryell** Comanche County; County Courthouse; Comanche, TX 76442; Ph. 915.356.2655 Details: (Co Clk has b, d & bur rec from 1903, m rec from 1856, pro rec from 1897, ct rec from 1934 & land rec from 1859)
Concho www.rootsweb.com/~txconcho/	I7	1 Feb 1858	**Bexar** Concho County; PO Box 98; Paint Rock, TX 76866-0098; Ph. 915.732.4322 Details: (Co Clk has b rec from 1800, m, pro & land rec from 1879, bur rec from 1883, d rec from 1903, div & ct rec from 1907)
Cooke www.rootsweb.com/~txcooke/index.html	F9	20 Mar 1848	**Fannin** Cooke County; 100 Dixon St; Gainesville, TX 76240; Ph. 940.668.5420 Details: (Co Clk has b & d rec from 1903, m, pro, ct & land rec from 1850; Dis Clk has div rec)
Coryell www.rootsweb.com/~txcoryel/	I8	4 Feb 1854	**Bell, McLennan** Coryell County; PO Box 237; Gatesville, TX 76528; Ph. 254.865.5016 Details: (Co Clk has b & d rec from 1903, m, pro, ct & land rec from 1854)
Cottle www.rootsweb.com/~txcottle/	F6	21 Aug 1876	**Fannin Land District** Cottle County; PO Box 717; Paducah, TX 78248; Ph. 806.492.3823 Details: (Co Clk has b, m, d, bur, div, pro, ct & land rec from 1892)

County Website	Map Index	Date Created	Parent County or Territory From Which Organized / Address/Details
Crane www.rootsweb.com/~txcrane/	I4	26 Feb 1887	**Tom Green** Crane County; PO Box 578; Crane, TX 79731; Ph. 915.558.3581 Details: (Co Clk has b rec from 1928, m, d, div, pro, ct & land rec from 1927 & bur rec from 1953)
Crockett www.rootsweb.com/~txcrocke/	J5	22 Jan 1875	**Bexar Land District** Crockett County; PO Drawer C; Ozona, TX 76943; Ph. 915.392.2022 Details: (Co Clk has b & d rec from 1903, div, pro & ct rec from 1892 & bur rec after 1980)
Crosby www.rootsweb.com/~txcrosby/	G5	21 Aug 1876	**Bexar Land District** Crosby County; PO Box 218; Crosbyton, TX 79322; Ph. 806.675.2334 Details: (Co Clk has b & d rec from 1903, m, pro & ct rec from 1887 & land rec from 1886; Dis Clk has div rec)
Culberson www.rootsweb.com/~txculber/	I3	10 Mar 1911	**El Paso** Culberson County; PO Box 158; Van Horn, TX 79855-0158; Ph. 915.283.2058 Details: (Co Clk has b, m, d, bur, div, land, pro, mil & ct rec from 1911)
Dallam www.dallam.org/county/	D4	21 Aug 1876	**Bexar Land District** Dallam County; PO Box 1352; Dalhart, TX 79022; Ph. 806.249.4751 Details: (Co Clk has b & d rec from 1903, m & ct rec from 1891, div rec from 1892, pro rec from 1900 & land rec from 1876)
Dallas www.dallascounty.org/	G9	30 Mar 1846	**Nacogdoches, Robertson** Dallas County; 500 Main St; Dallas, TX 75202; Ph. 214.653.7131 Details: (Co Clk has b & d rec from 1903, m rec from 1846, pro, ct & land rec; Dis Ct has div rec)
Davis		25 Apr 1846	**Bowie** Details: (Formerly Cass Co. Name changed to Davis 17 Dec 1861. Name changed back to Cass 16 May 1871)
Dawson www.abq.com/counties/txdawson/	G5	1 Feb 1858	**Bexar Land District** Dawson County; PO Drawer 1268; Lamesa, TX 79331; Ph. 806.872.3778 Details: (Co Clk has b, m, d, bur, pro & land rec from 1905 & ct rec from 1920; Dis Clk has div rec)
De Witt* www.rootsweb.com/~txdewitt/	K9	24 Mar 1846	**Goliad, Gonzales, Victoria** De Witt County; 307 N Gonzales St; Cuero, TX 77954-2870; Ph. 512.275.3724 Details: (Co Clk has b & d rec from 1903, m, pro, ct & land rec from 1846; Civil War muster rolls from 1861)
Deaf Smith www.rootsweb.com/~txdeafsm/	E4	21 Aug 1876	**Bexar Land District** Deaf Smith County; 235 E 3rd Rm 203; Hereford, TX 79045; Ph. 806.364.1746 Details: (Co Clk has b & d rec from 1903, m, pro & ct rec from 1891, land rec from 1882 & mil dis rec from 1919; Dis Clk has div rec & doctor rec from 1903)
Delta gen.1starnet.com/delta/	G10	29 Jul 1870	**Hopkins, Lamar** Delta County; 200 W Dallas Ave; Cooper, TX 75432; Ph. 903.395.4110 Details: (Co Clk has b, pro & ct rec from 1903, m rec from 1870, d rec from 1916 & land rec)
Denton* dentoncounty.com/default1001.htm	G9	11 Apr 1846	**Fannin** Denton County; PO Box 2187; Denton, TX 76202; Ph. 940.349.2021 Details: (Courthouse burned 1875; a few rec saved) (Co Clk has b, d & bur rec from 1903, m, pro, ct & land rec from 1876; Dis Clk has div rec from 1876)
Dickens www.rootsweb.com/~txdicken/	F6	21 Aug 1876	**Bexar Land District** Dickens County; PO Box 179; Dickens, TX 79229; Ph. 806.623.5531 Details: (Co Clk has b, m, d, bur, div, pro, ct & land rec from 1891)
Dimmit www.historicdistrict.com/Genealogy/ dimmit/dimmit.htm	L7	1 Feb 1858	**Uvalde, Bexar, Maverick, Webb** Dimmit County; 103 N 5th St; Carrizo Springs, TX 78834; Ph. 830.876.3569 Details: (Co Clk has b & d rec from 1903, m & ct rec from 1881, pro rec from 1882 & land rec; Dis Clk has div rec)

County Website	Map Index	Date Created	Parent County or Territory From Which Organized Address/Details
Donley www.rootsweb.com/~txdonley/	F6	21 Aug 1876	**Bexar Land District** Donley County; 300 S Sally; Clarendon, TX 79226; Ph. 806.874.3436 Details: (Co Clk has b rec from 1877, m & land rec from 1882, d rec from 1903, pro rec from 1923 & mil dis rec from 1919)
Duval www.vsta.com/~rlblack/duvalpage.html	M8	1 Feb 1858	**Live Oak, Starr, Neuces** Duval County; PO Box 248; San Diego, TX 78384-1816; Ph. 512.279.3322 Details: (Co Clk has b & d rec from 1903, m, pro & land rec from 1877 & ct rec)
Eastland www.rootsweb.com/~txeastla/	H8	1 Feb 1858	**Bosque, Coryell, Travis** Eastland County; PO Box 110; Eastland, TX 76448; Ph. 254.629.1583 Details: (Co Clk has b & d rec 1903-1930 & 1940-1950, m rec from 1874, land rec from 1870, pro rec from 1882 & mil dis rec from 1919; Dis Ct has div rec from 1903)
Ector www.rootsweb.com/~txector/index.htm	H4	26 Feb 1887	**Tom Green** Ector County; 300 N Grant Ave; Odessa, TX 79761; Ph. 915.335.3030 Details: (Co Clk has b, m, d, bur, pro, ct & land rec from 1896; Dis Clk has div rec)
Edwards www.rootsweb.com/~txedward/	J6	1 Feb 1858	**Bexar Land District** Edwards County; PO Box 184; Rocksprings, TX 78880-0184; Ph. 830.683.2235 Details: (Co Clk has b & d rec from 1903, m, div, pro, ct & land rec from 1884)
El Paso www.co.el-paso.tx.us/	I1	3 Jan 1850	**Bexar Land District** El Paso County; 500 E San Antonio St; El Paso, TX 79901-2421; Ph. 915.546.2071 Details: (Co Clk has b, d & bur rec from 1903, m rec from 1880, mil dis rec from 1919, pro, ct & land rec)
Ellis www.rootsweb.com/~txellis/	H9	20 Dec 1849	**Navarro** Ellis County; 115 W Franklin; Waxahachie, TX 75165; Ph. 972.923.5070 Details: (Co Clk has b, m, d, land, pro, mil & ct rec)
Encinal		1 Feb 1858	**Webb** Details: (see Webb) (Never organized. Discontinued 12 Mar 1899 & returned to Webb Co.)
Erath www.rootsweb.com/~txerath/erath.htm	H8	25 Jan 1856	**Bosque, Coryell** Erath County; 100 W Washington St; Stephenville, TX 76401; Ph. 254.965.1482 Details: (Co Clk has b & d rec from 1903, m rec from 1869, pro rec from 1876 & land rec from 1867)
Falls www.rootsweb.com/~txfalls/	I9	28 Jan 1850	**Limestone, Milam** Falls County; PO Box 458; Marlin, TX 76661-0458; Ph. 254.883.1408 Details: (Co Clk has b & d rec from 1903, m rec from 1854, land rec from 1835 & pro rec from 1870)
Fannin www.rootsweb.com/~txfannin/	G10	14 Dec 1837	**Red River** Fannin County; 101 Sam Rayburn Dr; Bonham, TX 75418; Ph. 903.583.7486 Details: (Co Clk has b rec from 1903 with a few 1874-1876, d rec from 1903, m rec from 1852, pro, land & ct rec from 1838)
Fayette* www.co.fayette.tx.us/	K9	14 Dec 1837	**Bastrop, Colorado** Fayette County; PO Box 59; La Grange, TX 78945-2657; Ph. 979.968.3251 Details: (Co Clk has b & d rec from 1903, m, pro & land rec from 1838; Dis Clk has div rec from 1838)
Fisher www.rootsweb.com/~txfisher/	G6	21 Aug 1876	**Bexar Land District** Fisher County; PO Box 368; Roby, TX 79543; Ph. 915.776.2401 Details: (Co Clk has b, d & m rec from 1903, land rec from 1886, pro & ct rec from 1920)
Floyd www.rootsweb.com/~txfloyd/	F5	21 Aug 1876	**Bexar Land District** Floyd County; 100 S Main St; PO Box 476; Floydada, TX 79235; Ph. 806.983.4900 Details: (Co Clk has b, m, d, pro & ct rec from 1903 & land rec from 1876; Dis Clk has div rec)
Foard www.foardcounty.org/	F7	3 Mar 1891	**Hardeman, Knox, King, Cottle** Foard County; PO Box 539; Crowell, TX 79227; Ph. 940.684.1365 Details: (Co Clk has b & d rec from 1903, m, div, pro, ct & land rec from 1891)

County Website	Map Index	Date Created	Parent County or Territory From Which Organized Address/Details
Fort Bend www.co.fort-bend.tx.us/	K10	29 Dec 1837	**Austin** Fort Bend County; 301 Jackson St; PO Box 520; Richmond, TX 77469; Ph. 281.341.8685 Details: (Co Clk has b & d rec from 1903, m & land rec from 1838, pro rec from 1836 & ct rec from 1876)
Franklin www.mt-vernon.com/~skelly/	G11	6 Mar 1875	**Titus** Franklin County; PO Box 68; Mount Vernon, TX 75457; Ph. 903.537.4252 Details: (Co Clk has div rec from 1884, b & d rec from 1903, m & pro rec from 1875 & land rec from 1846)
Freestone www.rootsweb.com/~txfreest/	I10	6 Sep 1850	**Limestone** Freestone County; PO Box 307; Fairfield, TX 75840; Ph. 903.389.2635 Details: (Co Clk has b & d rec from 1903, m rec from 1853, land, pro, mil dis & ct rec from 1851)
Frio www.rootsweb.com/~txfrio/	L7	1 Feb 1858	**Atascosa, Bexar, Uvalde** Frio County; PO Box 847; Pearsall, TX 79360; Ph. 830.334.2214 Details: (Co Clk has b & d rec from 1903, m rec from 1876, pro rec from 1874, ct rec from 1907 & land rec from 1871)
Gaines www.gainescounty.org/	G4	21 Aug 1876	**Bexar Land District** Gaines County; 100 S Main St; PO Box 847; Seminole, TX 79360-4342; Ph. 915.758.4003 Details: (Co Clk has b, m, d, bur, pro & ct rec from 1905 & land rec)
Galveston www.co.galveston.tx.us/	K11	15 May 1838	**Brazoria, Liberty** Galveston County; 722 Moody; Galveston, TX 77550; Ph. 409.766.2210 Details: (Co Clk has b & d rec 1903-1910 & 1941-1951, m, pro & land rec from 1838 & ct rec from 1875)
Garza www.angelfire.com/tx/gcounty/ index.html	G5	21 Aug 1876	**Bexar Land District** Garza County; 300 W Main St; Post, TX 79356; Ph. 806.495.4430 Details: (Co Clk has b, m, d, div, pro & ct rec from 1907 & land rec)
Gillespie* www.rootsweb.com/~txgilles/	J7	23 Feb 1848	**Bexar, Travis** Gillespie County; 101 W Main St; PO Box 551; Fredericksburg, TX 78624; Ph. 830.997.6515 Details: (Co Clk has b, m & pro rec from 1850, d rec from 1902, land rec from 1848 & ct rec from 1954; Dis Clk has div rec)
Glasscock www.rootsweb.com/~txglassc/	H5	4 Apr 1887	**Tom Green** Glasscock County; PO Box 190; Garden City, TX 79739-0190; Ph. 915.354.2371 Details: (Co Clk has b & d rec from 1903, m & ct rec from 1893, pro rec from 1895 & land rec from 1883; Dis Clk has div rec; Co Judge has recent bur rec)
Goliad www.goliad.org/goliad.html	L9	17 Mar 1836	**Old Mexican Municipality** Goliad County; 127 S Courthouse Square; PO Box 5; Goliad, TX 77963-0005; Ph. 361.645.3294 Details: (Co Clk has b & d rec from 1903, m, pro, ct & land rec from 1870 & div rec)
Gonzales www.rootsweb.com/~txgonzal/	K9	17 Mar 1836	**Old Mexican Municipality** Gonzales County; 1709 Dewitt Dr; PO Box 77; Gonzales, TX 78629-0077; Ph. 830.672.2801 Details: (Co Clk has b & d rec from 1903, m, pro & land rec from 1829; Dis Clk has div rec; Archives & Rec Center has all older rec from Co & Dis Clks, cem rec & school cen)
Gray www.rootsweb.com/~txgray/	E6	21 Aug 1876	**Bexar Land District** Gray County; 200 N Russell St; PO Box 1902; Pampa, TX 79066; Ph. 806.669.8004 Details: (Co Clk has b rec from 1903, m, d, pro & ct rec from 1902, bur rec from 1930, land rec from 1887 & mil dis rec from 1919; Dis Clk has div rec)
Grayson www.co.grayson.tx.us/	G9	17 Mar 1846	**Fannin Land District** Grayson County; 100 W Houston St; Sherman, TX 75090; Ph. 903.813.4243 Details: (Co Clk has b & d rec from 1900, m, pro, ct & land rec from 1846; Dis Clk has div rec)

County Website	Map Index	Date Created	Parent County or Territory From Which Organized Address/Details
Gregg*	**H11**	**12 Apr 1873**	**Rusk, Upshur**

www.co.gregg.tx.us/

Gregg County; 101 E Methvin St; PO Box 3049; Longview, TX 75606-3049;
Ph. 903.236.8430
Details: (Co Clk has b, m, ct & land rec from 1873, d rec from 1900 & pro rec)

Grimes	**J10**	**6 Apr 1846**	**Montgomery**

www.rootsweb.com/~txgrimes/

Grimes County; PO Box 209; Anderson, TX 77830; Ph. 409.873.2111
Details: (Co Clk has b, d & ct rec from 1903, m & pro rec from 1848 & land rec
rom 1843)

Guadalupe*	**K8**	**30 Mar 1846**	**Bexar, Gonzales**

www.co.guadalupe.tx.us/

Guadalupe County; PO Box 951; Seguin, TX 78155-0951; Ph. 830.379.4188
Details: (Co Clk has b, d & bur rec from 1935, m & pro rec from 1838, ct & land rec;
Dis Clk has div rec)

Hale	**F5**	**21 Aug 1876**	**Bexar Land District**

www.texasonline.net/halecounty/

Hale County; 500 Broadway; Plainview, TX 79072-8050; Ph. 806.291.5261
Details: (Co Clk has m & land rec from 1888 & pro rec from 1889; Dis Clk has div &
ct rec)

Hall	**F6**	**21 Aug 1876**	**Bexar Land District**

www.rootsweb.com/~txhall/

Hall County; County Courthouse Box 8; Memphis, TX 79245; Ph. 806.259.2627
Details: (Co Clk has b, m, d, div, pro, ct & land rec from 1890)

Hamilton	**I8**	**22 Jun 1858**	**Bosque, Comanche, Lampasas, Coryell**

www.rootsweb.com/~txhamilt/main.htm

Hamilton County; County Courthouse; Hamilton, TX 76531-1859; Ph. 254.386.3518
Details: (Created 2 Feb 1842, but not organized until 1858) (Co Clk has incomplete b
& d rec from 1903, m rec from 1885, div rec from 1875, pro rec from 1870 & land rec)

Hansford	**D5**	**21 Aug 1876**	**Bexar Land District**

www.rootsweb.com/~txhansfo/

Hansford County; PO Box 397; Spearman, TX 79081-3499; Ph. 806.659.4110
Details: (Co Clk has land rec from 1875, b, m, d, div, pro & ct rec from 1900)

Hardeman	**F7**	**1 Feb 1858**	**Fannin Land District**

www.rootsweb.com/~txhardem/

Hardeman County; PO Box 30; Quanah, TX 79252-0030; Ph. 940.663.2901
Details: (Co Clk has b & d rec from 1903, m rec from 1885, pro & ct rec from 1886 &
land rec from 1871; Dis Clk has div rec)

Hardin	**J11**	**22 Jan 1858**	**Jefferson, Liberty**

www.rootsweb.com/~txhardin/index.htm

Hardin County; PO Box 38; Kountze, TX 77625; Ph. 409.246.5185
Details: (Co Clk has b rec from 1892, m, d & land rec from 1859 & pro rec from 1888;
Dis Clk has div rec)

Harris	**J10**	**17 Mar 1836**	**Old Mexican Municipality**

www.co.harris.tx.us/

Harris County; 1001 Preston 4th Floor; Houston, TX 77251-1525; Ph. 713.755.6405
Details: (Formerly Harrisburg Co. Name changed to Harris 28 Dec 1839) (Co Clk has
b & d rec from 1903, m & land rec from 1836, pro rec from late 1800's, ct rec from
1920's & immigration rec 1880-1890; Dis Clk has div rec)

Harrisburg		**17 Mar 1836**	**Old Mexican Municipality**

Details: (see Harris) (Name changed to Harris 28 Dec 1839)

Harrison	**H12**	**28 Jan 1839**	**Shelby**

www.rootsweb.com/~txharris/

Harrison County; PO Box 1365; Marshall, TX 75671; Ph. 903.935.4858
Details: (Co Clk has b & d rec from 1903, m, land & pro rec from 1800)

Hartley	**D4**	**21 Aug 1876**	**Bexar Land District**

www.rootsweb.com/~txhartle/

Hartley County; PO Box 147; Channing, TX 79018-0147; Ph. 806.235.3582
Details: (Co Clk has b rec from 1898, m & pro rec from 1891, d rec from 1903, land
rec from 1888 & mil dis rec from 1919; Dis Ct has div rec from 1891 & ct rec
from 1892)

Haskell	**G7**	**1 Feb 1858**	**Fannin, Milam**

www.rootsweb.com/~txhaskel/
  haskell.htm

Haskell County; PO Box 725; Haskell, TX 79521-0905; Ph. 940.864.2451
Details: (Co Clk has b rec from late 1800's, m & pro rec from 1885, d rec from 1903,
mil rec from 1917, land & ct rec; Dis Ct has div rec)

County Website	Map Index	Date Created	Parent County or Territory From Which Organized Address/Details
Hays* www.co.hays.tx.us/	J8	1 Mar 1848	**Travis** Hays County; 137 N Guadalupe St; San Marcos, TX 78666; Ph. 512.393.7330 Details: (Co Clk has pro rec from 1839, b rec from 1865, m, ct & land rec from 1848 & mil rec from 1919; Dis Clk has div rec from 1897)
Hemphill www.rootsweb.com/~txhemphi/	D6	21 Aug 1876	**Bexar Land District** Hemphill County; PO Box 867; Canadian, TX 79014-0867; Ph. 806.323.6212 Details: (Co Clk has b rec from 1876, d rec from 1910, m, div, pro, ct & land rec from 1887)
Henderson www.hendersoncotx.com/	H10	27 Apr 1846	**Houston, Nacogdoches** Henderson County; 100 E Tyler St Ste 107; Athens, TX 75751; Ph. 903.675.6140 Details: (Co Clk has b & d rec from 1903, m rec from 1880, pro rec from 1860, ct rec from 1910 & land rec from 1846)
Hidalgo www.co.hidalgo.tx.us/	N8	24 Jan 1852	**Cameron, Starr** Hidalgo County; PO Box 58; Edinburg, TX 78540; Ph. 956.318.2100 Details: (Co Clk has b, m, d, pro, ct & land rec; Dis Clk has div rec)
Hill www.rootsweb.com/~txhill/index.html	H9	7 Feb 1853	**Navarro** Hill County; PO Box 398; Hillsboro, TX 76645-0398; Ph. 254.582.4030 Details: (Courthouse burned between 1874 & 1878) (Co Clk has b & m rec from 1876, pro rec from 1879 & land rec from 1853; Dis Clk has div rec)
Hockley www.rootsweb.com/~txhockle/index.htm	F4	21 Aug 1876	**Bexar Land District** Hockley County; County Courthouse Box 1; Levelland, TX 79336; Ph. 806.894.3185 Details: (Attached to Lubbock Co from 1891 to 1921) (Co Clk has b, m, d, pro, ct & land rec from 1921)
Hood* www.granburydepot.org/	H8	3 Nov 1865	**Johnson** Hood County; 100 E Pearl St; PO Box 339; Granbury, TX 76048-0339; Ph. 817.579.3222 Details: (Co Clk has b & d rec from 1903, m, div, pro, ct & land rec from 1875; Hood Public Lib in Granbury has many rec of the late Judge Henry Davis)
Hopkins gen.1starnet.com/hopkins/	G10	25 Mar 1846	**Lamar, Nacogdoches** Hopkins County; PO Box 288; Sulphur Springs, TX 75482; Ph. 903.885.3929 Details: (Co Clk has b & d rec from 1903, m, pro, ct & land rec from 1846; Dis Clk has div rec)
Houston www.io.com/~dwhite/more.html	I10	12 Jun 1837	**Nacogdoches** Houston County; PO Box 370; Crockett, TX 75835; Ph. 936.544.3255 Details: (Co Clk has b, m & d rec from 1903, pro, ct & land rec from 1882; Dis Clk has div rec from 1920; Co Hist Commission has bur rec, family & local histories)
Howard www.rootsweb.com/~txhoward/	H5	21 Aug 1876	**Bexar Land District** Howard County; 300 Main St; PO Box 1468; Big Spring, TX 79721; Ph. 915.264.2213 Details: (Co Clk has b & d rec from 1903, m rec from 1882, pro rec from 1884 & land rec; Dis Clk has div & ct rec from 1883)
Hudspeth www.rootsweb.com/~txhudspe/	I2	16 Feb 1917	**El Paso** Hudspeth County; PO Drawer A; Sierra Blanca, TX 79851; Ph. 915.369.2301 Details: (Co Clk has b, m, d, div, pro & ct rec from 1917 & land rec from 1836)
Hunt www.rootsweb.com/~txhunt/	G10	11 Apr 1846	**Fannin, Nacogdoches** Hunt County; PO Box 1316; Greenville, TX 75401; Ph. 903.408.4130 Details: (Co Clk has b, d & bur rec from 1903, m & land rec from 1846, pro rec from 1800's, mil rec from early 1900's & ct rec from 1967; Dis Clk has div rec)
Hutchinson www.usroots.org/~hutchitx/	D5	21 Aug 1876	**Bexar Land District** Hutchinson County; PO Box 1186; Stinnett, TX 79083-0580; Ph. 806.878.4002 Details: (Co Clk has m, pro, ct & land rec from 1901, b rec from 1876 & d rec; Dis Clk has div rec)
Irion www.rootsweb.com/~txirion/	I6	7 Mar 1889	**Tom Green** Irion County; PO Box 736; Mertzon, TX 76941-0736; Ph. 915.835.2421 Details: (Co Clk has b, m, d, div, land, pro, mil & ct rec from 1889; Tax Asr has poll tax rec)

County Website	Map Index	Date Created	Parent County or Territory From Which Organized Address/Details
Jack www.rootsweb.com/~txjack/	G8	27 Aug 1856	**Cooke** Jack County; 100 N Main St; Jacksboro, TX 76458; Ph. 940.567.2111 Details: (Co Clk has b & d rec from 1903, pro rec from 1857, land rec from 1860, m & ct rec; Dis Clk has div rec)
Jackson* www.rootsweb.com/~txjackso/index.htm	L10	17 Mar 1836	**Old Mexican Municipality** Jackson County; 115 W Main St; Edna, TX 77957-2733; Ph. 361.782.3563 Details: (Co Clk has b & d rec from 1903, m, pro & land rec from 1836 & ct rec from 1910; Dis Clk has div rec)
Jasper www.rootsweb.com/~txjasper/index.htm	I12	17 Mar 1836	**Old Mexican Municipality** Jasper County; PO Box 2070; Jasper, TX 75951; Ph. 409.384.2632 Details: (Co Clk has m, pro & land rec from 1849, b rec from 1874, d rec from 1903, ct rec from 1911 & cem rec; Dis Clk has div rec)
Jeff Davis www.rootsweb.com/~txjeffda/	J3	15 Mar 1887	**Presidio** Jeff Davis County; PO Box 398; Fort Davis, TX 79734-0398; Ph. 915.426.3251 Details: (Co Clk has d rec from 1904, b rec from 1883, div rec from 1946, m, pro, ct & land rec from 1887)
Jefferson www.co.jefferson.tx.us/	K12	17 Mar 1836	**Old Mexican Municipality** Jefferson County; PO Box 1151; Beaumont, TX 77704; Ph. 409.835.8475 Details: (Co Clk has b & d rec 1903-1966, m, land, pro, ct & mil dis rec from 1836; Dis Clk has div rec)
Jim Hogg www.vsta.com/~rlblack/jimhogg.html	N8	31 Mar 1913	**Brooks, Duval** Jim Hogg County; PO Box 878; Hebbronville, TX 78361; Ph. 361.527.4031 Details: (Co Clk has b, m, d, div, land, pro, mil & ct rec from 1913)
Jim Wells bsd.pastracks.com/states/texas/jimwells/	M8	25 Mar 1911	**Nueces** Jim Wells County; 200 N Almond St; Alice, TX 78332; Ph. 361.668.5702 Details: (Co Clk has b, d, m, pro & ct rec from 1911 & land rec from 1848; Dis Clk has div rec)
Johnson www.htcomp.net/jcgs/	H9	13 Feb 1854	**Ellis, Hill, Navarro, McLennan** Johnson County; PO Box 662; Cleburne, TX 76031; Ph. 817.556.6311 Details: (Co Clk has m, land & pro rec from 1854, b & d rec from 1903; Dis Clk has div rec)
Jones www.rootsweb.com/~txjones/	G7	1 Feb 1858	**Bexar Land District, Bosque** Jones County; PO Box 552; Anson, TX 79501; Ph. 915.823.3762 Details: (Co Clk has b & d rec from 1903, m & land rec from 1881 & pro rec from 1882; Dis Clk has div & ct rec)
Karnes www.rootsweb.com/~txkarnes/	L8	4 Feb 1854	**Bexar, DeWitt, Goliad, San Patricio** Karnes County; 101 N Panna Maria St; Karnes City, TX 78118; Ph. 830.780.3938 Details: (Co Clk has b, d & ct rec from 1900, m rec from 1875, pro rec from 1870 & land rec from 1854; Dis Clk has div rec from 1858)
Kaufman www.kaufmancounty.net/	H10	26 Feb 1848	**Henderson** Kaufman County; County Courthouse; Kaufman, TX 75142; Ph. 972.932.4331 Details: (Co Clk has b & d rec from 1903, m & pro rec from 1850 & land rec)
Kendall www.rootsweb.com/~txkendal/index.htm	J8	10 Jan 1862	**Kerr, Blanco** Kendall County; 204 E San Antonio St; Boerne, TX 78006; Ph. 830.249.9343 Details: (Co Clk has m, pro & land rec)
Kenedy bsd.pastracks.com/states/texas/kenedy/	N9	2 Apr 1921	**Willacy, Hidalgo, Cameron** Kenedy County; PO Box 37; Sarita, TX 78385; Ph. 361.294.5220 Details: (Co Clk has b rec from 1926, m rec from 1923, d rec from 1929, div & ct rec from 1914, pro & land rec)
Kent www.rootsweb.com/~txkent/	G6	21 Aug 1876	**Bexar Land District** Kent County; PO Box 9; Jayton, TX 79528; Ph. 806.237.3881 Details: (Co Clk has b, m, d, div, land, pro, mil & ct rec from 1876)

TEXAS...

County Website	Map Index	Date Created	Parent County or Territory From Which Organized / Address/Details
Kerr www.ktc.net/kgs/	J7	26 Jan 1856	**Bexar** Kerr County; 700 Main St; Kerrville, TX 78028-5323; Ph. 830.792.2255 Details: (Co Clk has b & d rec from 1903, m, pro, land & ct rec from 1856; Dis Clk has div rec)
Kimble www.rootsweb.com/~txkimble/	J7	22 Jan 1858	**Bexar Land District** Kimble County; 501 Main St Courthouse; Junction, TX 76849-4763; Ph. 915.446.3353 Details: (Co Clk has b & d rec from 1900, m, div, land & ct rec from 1884, pro rec from early 1900's & mil rec from 1915)
King www.rootsweb.com/~txking/	F6	21 Aug 1876	**Bexar Land District** King County; PO Box 135; Guthrie, TX 79236; Ph. 806.596.4412 Details: (Co Clk has b, div & ct rec from 1914, m rec from 1891, d rec from 1925, pro rec from 1915 & land rec from 1878)
Kinney www.rootsweb.com/~txkinney/	K6	28 Jan 1850	**Bexar Land District** Kinney County; PO Drawer 9; Brackettville, TX 78832; Ph. 830.563.2521 Details: (Co Clk has b & d rec from 1903, m rec from 1872, div, pro, ct & land rec from 1873; St. Mary's Catholic Church, Brackettville, TX has bur rec)
Kleberg bsd.pastracks.com/states/texas/kleberg/	M9	27 Feb 1913	**Nueces** Kleberg County; PO Box 1327; Kingsville, TX 78364-1327; Ph. 361.595.8548 Details: (Co Clk has b, m, d, pro, ct & land rec from 1913; Dis Clk has div rec)
Knox www.knoxcountytexas.com/	F7	1 Feb 1858	**Fannin Land District** Knox County; PO Box 196; Benjamin, TX 79505; Ph. 940.454.2441 Details: (Co Clk has b rec from 1905, m rec from 1886, d rec from 1917, div rec from 1900's, pro, ct & land rec from 1887)
Lamar gen.1starnet.com/	F10	17 Dec 1840	**Red River** Lamar County; 119 N Main St; Paris, TX 75460-4265; Ph. 903.737.2420 Details: (Co Clk has b & d rec from 1903, m, pro, ct & land rec from 1843; Dis Clk has div rec)
Lamb www.rootsweb.com/~txlamb/index.htm	F4	21 Aug 1876	**Bexar Land District** Lamb County; 100 6th St; Littlefield, TX 79339-3366; Ph. 806.385.5173 Details: (Co Clk has b, m, d & pro rec from 1920, land rec from 1915 & ct rec)
Lampasas www.rootsweb.com/~txlampas/ lampasas.html	I8	1 Feb 1856	**Bell, Travis** Lampasas County; PO Box 231; Lampasas, TX 76550-0231; Ph. 512.556.8271 Details: (Co Clk has b rec from 1895, d rec from 1910, m rec from 1879, pro rec from 1876, ct rec from 1899 & land rec from 1872)
LaSalle www.historicdistrict.com/Genealogy/ lasalle/lasalle.htm	L7	1 Feb 1858	**Bexar, Webb** LaSalle County; PO Box 340; Cotulla, TX 78014-0340; Ph. 210.879.2117 Details: (Co & Dis Clk has m, d, div, land, pro, mil & ct rec from 1881)
Lavaca www.rootsweb.com/~txlavaca/index.htm	K9	6 Apr 1846	**Colorado, Victoria, Jackson, Gonzales, Fayette** Lavaca County; PO Box 326; Hallettsville, TX 77964; Ph. 361.798.3612 Details: (Co Clk has b & d rec from 1903, m & pro rec from 1847, land rec from 1846, mil rec from 1918, ct & nat rec)
Lee www.jamesdavidwalker.com/lee/	J9	14 Apr 1874	**Bastrop, Burleson, Washington, Fayette** Lee County; PO Box 419; Giddings, TX 78942; Ph. 409.542.3684 Details: (Co Clk has b & d rec from 1903, m, pro, ct & land rec from 1874; Dis Clk has div rec)
Leon www.rootsweb.com/~txleon/	I10	17 Mar 1846	**Robertson** Leon County; PO Box 98; Centerville, TX 75833-0098; Ph. 903.536.2352 Details: (Co Clk has b & d rec from 1903, m rec from 1885, pro rec from 1846, ct & land rec)
Liberty www.rootsweb.com/~txlibert/	J11	17 Mar 1836	**Old Mexican Municipality** Liberty County; 1923 Sam Houston St; Liberty, TX 77575; Ph. 409.336.4670 Details: (Courthouse burned 11 Dec 1874; rec destroyed) (Co Clk has b & d rec from 1903, m rec from 1875, pro, ct & land rec from 1874; Dis Clk has div rec)

County Website	Map Index	Date Created	Parent County or Territory From Which Organized Address/Details

Limestone   I9   11 Apr 1846   **Robertson**
www.rootsweb.com/~txlimest/index.html Limestone County; 200 W State St; PO Box 350; Groesbeck, TX 76642;
Ph. 254.729.5504
Details: (Co Clk has b & d rec from 1903, m rec from 1873, pro rec from 1880's, land rec from late 1800's, ct rec from 1900's & mil rec from 1920's; Dis Clk has div rec)

Lipscomb   D6   21 Aug 1876   **Bexar Land District**
www.rootsweb.com/~txlipsco/ Lipscomb County; PO Box 70; Lipscomb, TX 79056; Ph. 806.862.3091
Details: (Co Clk has b, m, d, div, pro, ct & land rec from 1887, mil dis rec from 1919 & nat rec 1926-1927)

Live Oak   L8   2 Feb 1856   **Nueces, San Patricio**
www.rootsweb.com/~txliveoa/ Live Oak County; PO Box 280; George West, TX 78022; Ph. 512.449.2733
Details: (Co Clk has b & d rec from 1903, m & land rec from 1856, pro rec from 1857 & ct rec; Dis Clk has div rec)

Llano   J8   1 Feb 1856   **Bexar, Gillespie**
www.rootsweb.com/~txllano/ Llano County; 801 Ford; Llano, TX 78643; Ph. 915.247.4455
Details: (Co Clk has b & d rec from 1903, m, land, pro & ct rec from 1880 & mil rec from 1919; Dis Clk has div & nat rec)

Loving   H3   26 Feb 1887   **Tom Green**
www.rootsweb.com/~txloving/ Loving County; PO Box 194; Mentone, TX 79754-9999; Ph. 915.377.2441
Details: (Attached to Reeves Co. Reorganized 1931) (Co Clk has b, m, d, div, pro & ct rec from 1931 & land rec from 1920)

Lubbock   F5   21 Aug 1876   **Bexar Land District**
www.co.lubbock.tx.us/ Lubbock County; PO Box 10536; Lubbock, TX 79408; Ph. 806.775.1054
Details: (Attached to Crosby Co at one time) (Co Clk has b & d rec from 1903, m rec from 1891, pro & ct rec from 1904 & land rec)

Lynn   G5   21 Aug 1876   **Bexar Land District**
www.rootsweb.com/~txlynn/index.htm Lynn County; PO Box 1256; Tahoka, TX 79373; Ph. 806.998.4750
Details: (Co Clk has b, m & d rec from 1910, land, pro, mil & ct rec; Dis Clk has div rec)

Madison   I10   27 Jan 1853   **Leon, Grimes, Walker**
www.rootsweb.com/~txmadiso/ Madison County; 101 W Main St; Madisonville, TX 77864; Ph. 936.348.2638
Details: (Co Clk has b & d rec from 1903, m, pro, land, mil & ct rec from 1873)

Marion*   G12   8 Feb 1860   **Cass, Harrison**
www.rootsweb.com/~txmarion/ Marion County; 102 W Austin St Rm 206; PO Box F; Jefferson, TX 75657-0420;
Ph. 903.665.3971
Details: (Co Clk has b & d rec from 1903, m, pro & land rec from 1860)

Martin   H5   21 Aug 1876   **Bexar Land District**
www.rootsweb.com/~txmartin/ Martin County; PO Box 906; Stanton, TX 79782; Ph. 915.756.3412
Details: (Co Clk has b & d rec from 1910, m, ct, div & pro rec from 1885 & land rec)

Mason   J7   22 Jan 1858   **Gillespie, Bexar Land District**
www.rootsweb.com/~txmason/ Mason County; PO Box 702; Mason, TX 76856; Ph. 915.347.5253
Details: (Co Clk has b, d & bur rec from 1903, m, div, pro & ct rec from 1877 & land rec from 1850)

Matagorda   L10   17 Mar 1836   **Old Mexican Municipality**
www.rootsweb.com/~txmatago/ Matagorda County; 1700 7th St; Bay City, TX 77414; Ph. 979.244.7680
Details: (Co Clk has b rec from 1903, m rec from 1838, d rec from 1917, land rec from 1827, pro rec from late 1800's, mil rec from 1919 & ct rec from 1981)

Maverick   L6   2 Feb 1856   **Kinney**
www.geocities.com/maverickcotx/ Maverick County; 500 Quarry St; PO Box 4050; Eagle Pass, TX 78853;
Ph. 830.773.2829
Details: (Co Clk has b & d rec from 1903, m rec from 1871, pro, ct & land rec)

McCulloch   I7   27 Aug 1856   **Bexar**
www.rootsweb.com/~txmccull/ McCulloch County; County Courthouse; Brady, TX 76825; Ph. 915.597.0733
Details: (Co Clk has b & d rec from 1903, m rec from 1878, land rec from 1860, ct rec from 1876 & mil rec from 1918)

County Website	Map Index	Date Created	Parent County or Territory From Which Organized Address/Details
McLennan www.co.mclennan.tx.us/	I9	22 Jan 1850	**Milam, Limestone, Navarro** McLennan County; PO Box 1727; Waco, TX 76703; Ph. 254.757.5078 Details: (Co Clk has b & d rec from 1929, m, pro, ct & land rec from 1850; Dis Clk has div rec)
McMullen www.rootsweb.com/~txmcmull/	L8	1 Feb 1858	**Bexar, Live Oak, Atascosa** McMullen County; PO Box 235; Tilden, TX 78072; Ph. 512.274.3215 Details: (Co Clk has b & d rec from 1903, m, pro, ct & land rec from 1850)
Medina www.summitsoftware.com/medina/	K7	12 Feb 1848	**Bexar Land District** Medina County; County Courthouse; 2516 McHaughten; Hondo, TX 78861; Ph. 830.741.6041 Details: (Co Clk has b & d rec from 1903, m, pro & land rec from 1848 & ct rec from 1876)
Menard www.menardtexas.com/	I7	22 Jan 1858	**Bexar Land District** Menard County; PO Box 1028; Menard, TX 76859; Ph. 915.396.4682 Details: (Co Clk has b & ct rec from 1900, m rec from 1878, d rec from 1917, div rec from 1889, pro & land rec from 1880)
Midland www.co.midland.tx.us/	H5	4 Mar 1885	**Tom Green** Midland County; PO Box 211; Midland, TX 79702; Ph. 915.688.1059 Details: (Co Clk has b & d rec from 1917, m & land rec from 1885 & pro rec from 1911; Dis Clk has div & ct rec)
Milam* www.milamcounty.org/	J9	17 Mar 1836	**Old Mexican Municipality** Milam County; PO Box 191; Cameron, TX 76520-4216; Ph. 254.697.6596 Details: (Co Clk has b & d rec from 1903, m rec from 1873, pro, ct & land rec, school cen rec 1909-1970 & mil dis rec from 1919)
Mills* www.rootsweb.com/~txmills/mills.html	I8	15 Mar 1887	**Comanche, Brown, Hamilton, Lampasas** Mills County; PO Box 646; Goldthwaite, TX 76844-0646; Ph. 915.648.2711 Details: (Co Clk has b & d rec from 1903, m, div, pro, ct & land rec from 1887)
Mitchell www.rootsweb.com/~txmitche/	H6	21 Aug 1876	**Bexar Land District** Mitchell County; PO Box 1166; Colorado City, TX 79512; Ph. 915.728.3481 Details: (Co Clk has b, m, d, pro, ct & land rec)
Montague www.rootsweb.com/~txmontag/ index.html	G9	24 Dec 1857	**Cooke** Montague County; PO Box 77; Montague, TX 76251-0077; Ph. 940.894.2461 Details: (Co Clk has b & d rec from 1903, m, pro & ct rec from 1873 & land rec)
Montgomery www.co.montgomery.tx.us/	J10	14 Dec 1837	**Washington** Montgomery County; 301 N Main; PO Box 959; Conroe, TX 77305-0959; Ph. 936.539.7885 Details: (Co Clk has b, d & bur rec from 1903, m, pro & land rec from 1838 & ct rec from 1929; Dis Clk has div rec from 1914)
Moore www.rootsweb.com/~txmoore/ moore.htm	D5	21 Aug 1876	**Bexar Land District** Moore County; 715 Dumas Ave; Dumas, TX 79029-0396; Ph. 806.935.6164 Details: (Co Clk has b, d, bur, pro & ct rec from 1901, m rec from 1894 & land rec from 1877; Dis Clk has div rec)
Morris www.rootsweb.com/~txmorris/ morris.htm	G11	6 Mar 1875	**Titus** Morris County; 500 Broadnax St; Daingerfield, TX 75638-1315; Ph. 903.645.3911 Details: (Co Clk has b & d rec from 1903, m & pro rec from 1875, land rec from 1849 & some delayed b rec; Dis Clk has div & ct rec)
Motley www.rootsweb.com/~txmotley/	F6	21 Aug 1876	**Bexar Land District** Motley County; PO Box 66; Matador, TX 79244; Ph. 806.347.2621 Details: (Co Clk has b & d rec from 1903, m, div, pro & ct rec from 1891 & land rec from 1891 with some earlier)
Nacogdoches www.rootsweb.com/~txnacogd/	I11	17 Mar 1836	**Old Mexican Municipality** Nacogdoches County; 101 W Main St; Nacogdoches, TX 75961-5119; Ph. 936.560.7733 Details: (Co Clk has b & d rec from 1903, m rec from 1793, land rec from 1833, pro rec from 1837, ct rec from late 1800's & mil rec from 1918; Dis Clk has div rec)

County Website	Map Index	Date Created	Parent County or Territory From Which Organized Address/Details
Navarro www.rootsweb.com/~txnavarr/	H10	25 Apr 1846	**Robertson** Navarro County; 300 W 3rd Ave; PO Box 423; Corsicana, TX 75151; Ph. 903.654.3035 Details: (Co Clk has b & d rec from 1903, m rec from 1846, pro & land rec from 1850 & ct rec; Dis Clk has div rec)
Navasota		30 Jan 1841	**Washington, Robertson** Details: (see Brazos) (Name changed to Brazos in 28 Jan 1842)
Newton www.jas.net/~newton/	I12	22 Apr 1846	**Jasper** Newton County; PO Box 484; Newton, TX 75966; Ph. 409.379.5341 Details: (Co Clk has b & d rec from 1903, m rec from 1846, pro rec from 1870, ct & land rec)
Nolan www.rootsweb.com/~txnolan/	H6	21 Aug 1876	**Bexar Land District** Nolan County; 100 E 3rd St; PO Box 98; Sweetwater, TX 79556-4511; Ph. 915.235.2462 Details: (Co Clk has b, d & ct rec from 1900, m rec from 1881, pro rec from 1884 & land rec from 1889; Dis Clk has div rec; Co JP has bur rec)
Nueces www.co.nueces.tx.us/	M9	18 Apr 1846	**San Patricio** Nueces County; 901 Leopard St; Corpus Christi, TX 78401; Ph. 361.888.0580 Details: (Co Clk has m, pro, ct & land rec)
Ochiltree www.rootsweb.com/~txochilt/	D6	21 Aug 1876	**Bexar Land District** Ochiltree County; 511 S Main St; Perryton, TX 79070-3154; Ph. 806.435.8039 Details: (Co Clk has b rec from 1903, d & bur rec from 1904, m rec from 1889, pro rec from 1906, land rec from 1890, ct rec from 1909 & mil rec from 1918; Dis Clk has div rec from 1891)
Oldham www.rootsweb.com/~txoldham/	E4	21 Aug 1876	**Bexar Land District** Oldham County; PO Box 469; Vega, TX 79092-0469; Ph. 806.267.2667 Details: (Co Clk has b rec from 1917, d rec from 1918, m & div rec from 1881, bur & pro rec from 1887, ct rec from 1911 & land rec from 1878)
Orange* www.co.orange.tx.us/	J12	5 Feb 1852	**Jefferson** Orange County; 801 W Division St; PO Box 1536; Orange, TX 77631; Ph. 409.882.7055 Details: (Co Clk has b rec from 1878, d rec from 1903, m, land & pro rec from 1852, mil rec from 1898 & ct rec from 1896; Dis Clk has div rec)
Palo Pinto www.rootsweb.com/~txpalopi/	G8	27 Aug 1856	**Navarro, Bosque** Palo Pinto County; PO Box 219; Palo Pinto, TX 76484; Ph. 940.659.1277 Details: (Co Clk has b & d rec from 1903, m & land rec from 1857, pro rec from 1860; Dis Clk has div rec from 1900)
Panola www.carthagetexas.com/county.htm	H12	30 Mar 1846	**Harrison, Shelby** Panola County; 110 S Sycamore St; Carthage, TX 75633; Ph. 903.693.0302 Details: (Co Clk has b & d rec from 1903, m rec from 1846, pro, ct & land rec)
Parker www.rootsweb.com/~txparker/	G8	12 Dec 1855	**Bosque, Navarro** Parker County; 1112 Santa Fe; PO Box 819; Weatherford, TX 76086-0819; Ph. 817.594.7461 Details: (Co Clk has b, m & d rec from 1903, land rec from 1874, pro, mil & ct rec; Dis Clk has div rec)
Parmer www.rootsweb.com/~txparmer/	E4	21 Aug 1876	**Bexar Land District** Parmer County; 401 3rd St; PO Box 356; Farwell, TX 79325; Ph. 806.481.3691 Details: (Co Clk has b, m, d, pro, ct & land rec from 1908; Dis Clk has div rec from 1908)
Pecos www.co.pecos.tx.us/	J4	3 May 1871	**Presidio** Pecos County; 103 W Callaghan St; Fort Stockton, TX 79735-7101; Ph. 915.336.7555 Details: (Co Clk has b, m, d, pro & land rec)

County Website	Map Index	Date Created	Parent County or Territory From Which Organized Address/Details
Polk www.polkcountytexas.com/	I11	30 Mar 1846	**Liberty** Polk County; 101 Church St W; PO Box 2119; Livingston, TX 77351; Ph. 936.327.6804 Details: (Co Clk has b & d rec from 1903, cem rec, m, land, pro & ct rec from 1846, mil dis rec from 1940 & school rec 1905-1970; Dis Clk has div rec)
Potter www.co.potter.tx.us/home.html	E5	21 Aug 1876	**Bexar Land District** Potter County; PO Box 9638; Amarillo, TX 79105; Ph. 806.379.2275 Details: (Co Clk has b & d rec 1903-1910 & 1941-1951, m rec from 1888, pro rec from 1896, ct rec from 1889 & land rec from 1878; Dis Clk has div rec)
Presidio www.rootsweb.com/~txpresid/	J3	3 Jan 1850	**Bexar Land District** Presidio County; PO Box 789; Marfa, TX 79843; Ph. 915.729.4812 Details: (Co & Dis Clk has b & d rec from 1903, m & land rec from 1875, div & ct rec from 1886, pro rec from 1884 & mil rec from 1944)
Rains www.rootsweb.com/~txrains/rains.htm	G10	9 Jun 1870	**Hopkins, Hunt, Wood** Rains County; PO Box 187; Emory, TX 75440-0187; Ph. 903.473.2461 Details: (Co Clk has b rec from 1902, d rec from 1903, m, div & land rec from 1880 & pro rec from 1894)
Randall www.randallcounty.org/	E5	21 Aug 1876	**Bexar Land District** Randall County; PO Box 660; Canyon, TX 79015-0660; Ph. 806.655.6330 Details: (Co Clk has m, pro, ct & land rec; Dis Clk has div rec)
Reagan www.cvcog.org/reagan/reagan.htm	I5	7 Mar 1903	**Tom Green** Reagan County; PO Box 100; Big Lake, TX 76932-0100; Ph. 915.884.2442 Details: (Co Clk has b, m, d, div, pro, ct & land rec from 1903, some rec from 1883 transferred from Tom Green Co)
Real www.rootsweb.com/~txreal/	K7	3 Apr 1913	**Bandera, Kerr, Edwards** Real County; PO Box 656; Leakey, TX 78873-0656; Ph. 830.232.6888 Details: (Co Clk has b, m, d, div, pro, ct & land rec from 1913)
Red River www.rootsweb.com/~txredriv/	F11	7 Mar 1836	**Old Mexican Municipality** Red River County; 200 N Walnut St; Clarksville, TX 75426; Ph. 903.427.2401 Details: (Co Clk has b & d rec from 1903, m rec from 1845, pro & land rec from 1835; Dis Clk has div & ct rec)
Reeves www.rootsweb.com/~txreeves/	I3	14 Apr 1883	**Pecos** Reeves County; PO Box 867; Pecos, TX 79772-0867; Ph. 915.445.5467 Details: (Co Clk has b & d rec from 1903, m, pro, ct & land rec from 1885 & some deferred b rec from the 1800's)
Refugio bsd.pastracks.com/states/texas/refugio/	L9	17 Mar 1836	**Old Mexican Municipality** Refugio County; 808 Commerce St; Refugio, TX 78377-0704; Ph. 361.526.2727 Details: (Co Clk has b & d rec from 1903, m rec from 1851, pro rec from 1840, ct rec from 1881 & land rec from 1835)
Roberts www.rootsweb.com/~txrobert/	D6	21 Aug 1876	**Bexar Land District** Roberts County; PO Box 477; Miami, TX 79059; Ph. 806.868.2341 Details: (Co Clk has b & d rec from 1903, m, div, pro, ct & land rec from 1889 & bur rec from 1900)
Robertson* www.rootsweb.com/~txrober2/	I10	14 Dec 1837	**Milam** Robertson County; PO Box 1029; Franklin, TX 77856; Ph. 979.828.4130 Details: (Co Clk has b & d rec from 1903, m & pro rec from 1837 & land rec; Dis Clk has div & ct rec)
Rockwall* www.rockwall.net/	G10	1 Mar 1873	**Kaufman** Rockwall County; 1101 Ridge Rd Ste 101; Rockwall, TX 75087; Ph. 972.882.0240 Details: (Co Clk has b, m & d rec from 1875, land rec from 1890, pro rec from 1877 & ct rec)
Runnels www.rootsweb.com/~txrunnel/	H7	1 Feb 1858	**Bexar Land District, Travis** Runnels County; PO Box 189; Ballinger, TX 76821; Ph. 915.365.2720 Details: (Co Clk has b, d & ct rec from 1903, m, pro & land rec from 1880, mil dis rec from 1918 & school cen rec 1925-1970; Dis Clk has div rec)

County Website	Map Index	Date Created	Parent County or Territory From Which Organized / Address/Details
Rusk www.rootsweb.com/~txrusk/index.htm	H11	16 Jan 1843	**Nacogdoches** Rusk County; PO Box 758; Henderson, TX 75653; Ph. 903.657.0330 Details: (Courthouse fire in 1878 destroyed some rec) (Co Clk has b & d rec from 1903, m, land & pro rec from 1843, ct rec from 1844 & mil dis rec from 1917; Dis Ct has div rec from 1844)
Sabine* www.rootsweb.com/~txsabine/index.htm	I12	17 Mar 1836	**Old Mexican Municipality** Sabine County; PO Drawer 580; Hemphill, TX 75948; Ph. 409.787.3786 Details: (Co Clk has b & d rec from 1903, m rec from 1880, land rec from 1875 & pro rec; Dis Clk has div & ct rec)
San Augustine www.rootsweb.com/~txsanaug/ index_1.htm	I12	17 Mar 1836	**Old Mexican Municipality** San Augustine County; 106 Courthouse; San Augustine, TX 75972; Ph. 936.275.2452 Details: (Co Clk has b rec from 1905, d rec from 1903, m rec from 1837, pro rec from 1828 & land rec from 1833; Dis Clk has div & ct rec from 1837)
San Jacinto www.co.san-jacinto.tx.us/	J11	13 Aug 1870	**Liberty, Polk, Montgomery, Walker** San Jacinto County; PO Box 669; Cold Spring, TX 77331; Ph. 936.653.2324 Details: (Co Clk has b, m & d rec from 1888, land & pro rec from 1800's, mil dis rec from 1919 & ct rec from 1907; Dis Clk has div rec)
San Patricio bsd.pastracks.com/states/texas/ sanpatricio/	M9	17 Mar 1836	**Old Mexican Municipality** San Patricio County; 400 W Sinton Rm 105; Sinton, TX 78387-0578; Ph. 361.364.6290 Details: (Co Clk has b rec from 1893, d rec from 1903, m rec from 1858, pro rec from 1847, ct rec from 1876 & land rec from 1848)
San Saba www.rootsweb.com/~txssaba/	I8	1 Feb 1856	**Bexar Land District** San Saba County; County Courthouse; San Saba, TX 76877; Ph. 915.372.3301 Details: (Co Clk has b & d rec from 1903, m, div, ct & land rec from 1856 & pro rec from 1890)
Schleicher www.cvcog.org/schlcher/eldorado.htm	I6	1 Apr 1887	**Crockett** Schleicher County; PO Drawer 580; Eldorado, TX 76936; Ph. 915.853.2833 Details: (Co Clk has b & d rec from 1903, m, div, pro & ct rec from 1901 & land rec from 1889)
Scurry www.rootsweb.com/~txscurry/	G6	21 Aug 1876	**Bexar Land District** Scurry County; 1806 25th St Ste 300; Snyder, TX 79549; Ph. 915.573.5332 Details: (Co Clk has b & d rec from 1903, m, land & pro rec from 1884, ct rec from 1909 & mil rec from 1918; Dis Clk has div rec)
Shackelford www.albanytexas.com/	G7	1 Feb 1858	**Bosque** Shackelford County; PO Box 247; Albany, TX 76430-0247; Ph. 915.762.2232 Details: (Co Clk has b rec from 1903, m & land rec from 1874, d & pro rec from 1875, ct rec from 1899 & div rec)
Shelby www.rootsweb.com/~txshelby/	H12	17 Mar 1836	**Old Mexican Municipality** Shelby County; 200 San Augustine St; PO Box 1987; Center, TX 75935-3945; Ph. 936.598.6361 Details: (Co Clk has b, m, pro, ct & land rec from 1882, d & bur rec from 1903; Dis Clk has div rec)
Sherman www.rootsweb.com/~txshelby/	D5	21 Aug 1876	**Bexar Land District** Sherman County; 701 N 3rd; PO Box 270; Stratford, TX 79084; Ph. 806.396.2371 Details: (Co Clk has b, d, pro & ct rec from 1903, m & land rec from 1901, bur rec from 1895, div rec from 1914 & commission ct minutes from 1889)
Smith www.smith-county.com/	H11	11 Apr 1846	**Nacogdoches** Smith County; 100 N Broadway Ave; Tyler, TX 75702-1018; Ph. 903.535.0630 Details: (Co Clk has b & d rec from 1903, m rec from 1848, pro rec from 1847, ct & land rec from 1846)
Somervell* vip.hpnc.com/~clerk/	H8	13 Mar 1875	**Hood, Johnson** Somervell County; PO Box 1098; Glen Rose, TX 76043-1098; Ph. 254.897.4427 Details: (Co Clk has b & d rec from 1903, m rec from 1885, div & ct rec from 1898, pro & land rec from 1875)

County Website	Map Index	Date Created	Parent County or Territory From Which Organized Address/Details
Starr www.rootsweb.com/~txstarr/	N8	10 Feb 1848	**Nueces** Starr County; County Courthouse Rm 201; Rio Grande City, TX 78582; Ph. 956.487.2101 Details: (Co Clk has b rec from 1880, d rec from 1903, m rec from 1858, pro rec from 1853, land rec from 1848, ct rec from 1932, nat rec 1883-1898 & mil dis rec from 1919)
Stephens www.rootsweb.com/~txstephe/	H7	22 Jan 1858	**Bosque** Stephens County; County Courthouse; 200 W Walker; Breckenridge, TX 76424; Ph. 254.559.3700 Details: (Formerly Buchanan Co. Name changed to Stephens 17 Dec 1861) (Co Clk has b & d rec from 1903, m rec from 1876, pro rec from 1886 & land rec from 1858; Dis Clk has div & ct rec)
Sterling www.rootsweb.com/~txsterli/	H6	4 Mar 1891	**Tom Green** Sterling County; 615 4th; PO Box 55; Sterling City, TX 76951-0055; Ph. 915.378.5191 Details: (Co Clk has b & d rec from 1903, m rec from 1913, div, pro, ct & land rec from 1891)
Stonewall www.rootsweb.com/~txstonew/	G6	21 Aug 1876	**Bexar Land District** Stonewall County; PO Drawer P; Aspermont, TX 79502-0914; Ph. 940.989.2272 Details: (Co Clk has b, m, d, div, pro, ct & land rec from 1900's)
Sutton www.rootsweb.com/~txsutton/	J6	1 Apr 1887	**Crockett** Sutton County; 300 E Oak St Ste 3; Sonora, TX 76950; Ph. 915.387.3815 Details: (Co Clk has b & d rec from 1903, m, div, pro, ct & land rec from 1891)
Swisher www.rootsweb.com/~txswishe/ Swisher.html	E5	21 Aug 1876	**Bexar Land District** Swisher County; County Courthouse; Tulia, TX 79088; Ph. 806.995.3294 Details: (Co Clk has b rec from 1904, m, d & bur rec from 1900, div rec from 1905, pro & ct rec from 1890 & land rec from 1888)
Tarrant www.co.tarrant.tx.us/tarrantco/site/ default.asp	G9	20 Dec 1849	**Navarro** Tarrant County; 100 W Weatherford Rm 130; Fort Worth, TX 76196; Ph. 817.884.1195 Details: (Co Clk has b, m, land & pro rec from 1876 & d rec from 1903; Dis Clk has div & ct rec; 1860 cen missing)
Taylor www.rootsweb.com/~txtaylor/	H7	1 Feb 1858	**Bexar, Travis** Taylor County; 300 Oak St; Abilene, TX 79602; Ph. 915.674.1202 Details: (Co Clk has m, pro & land rec)
Terrell www.rootsweb.com/~txterrel/	J5	8 Apr 1905	**Pecos** Terrell County; PO Drawer 410; Sanderson, TX 79848-0410; Ph. 915.345.2391 Details: (Co Clk has m, pro & land rec)
Terry www.rootsweb.com/~txterry/index.htm	G4	21 Aug 1876	**Bexar Land District** Terry County; 500 W Main Rm 105; Brownfield, TX 79316; Ph. 806.637.8551 Details: (Attached to Martin Co from 1889 to 1904) (Co Clk has b, m, d, land, pro, mil & ct rec from 1904)
Throckmorton www.rootsweb.com/~txthrock/ throck.htm	G7	13 Jan 1858	**Fannin Land District, Bosque** Throckmorton County; PO Box 309; Throckmorton, TX 76483-0309; Ph. 940.849.2501 Details: (Co Clk has b rec from 1903, m, d, div & pro rec from 1879, ct & land rec; 1870 cen missing)
Titus www.rootsweb.com/~txtitus/	G11	11 May 1846	**Red River, Bowie** Titus County; 100 W 1st St Ste 204; Mt. Pleasant, TX 75455; Ph. 903.577.6796 Details: (Co Clk has b, m, d, land, pro, ct & mil rec from 1895; Dis Clk has div rec from 1895)
Tom Green www.co.tom-green.tx.us/	I6	13 Mar 1874	**Bexar Land District** Tom Green County; 124 W Beauregard Ave; San Angelo, TX 76903-5850; Ph. 915.659.6553 Details: (Co Clk has b & d rec from 1903, m, pro & ct rec from 1875 & land rec from 1860)

County Website	Map Index	Date Created	Parent County or Territory From Which Organized Address/Details
Travis www.co.travis.tx.us/	J8	25 Jan 1840	**Bastrop** Travis County; 100 Guadalupe St #222; PO Box 1748; Austin, TX 78767; Ph. 512.473.9188 Details: (Co Clk has b & d rec from 1903, m, pro, ct & land rec from 1840)
Trinity people.txucom.net/dford/tcp.html	I11	11 Feb 1850	**Houston** Trinity County; PO Box 456; Groveton, TX 75845; Ph. 936.642.1208 Details: (Courthouse burned 1876; some deeds refiled) (Co Clk has b rec from 1911, d rec from 1919, m & land rec from 1876, div rec from 1920, pro & ct rec; Co Judge has school rec)
Tyler www.rootsweb.com/~txtyler/index_1.htm	J11	3 Apr 1846	**Liberty** Tyler County; 100 W Bluff St; Woodville, TX 75979; Ph. 409.283.2281 Details: (Co Clk has b rec from 1838, m rec from 1849, d & bur rec from 1903, pro rec from 1845 & land rec from 1846; Dis Clk has div & ct rec)
Upshur www.upshurcounty.com/	G11	27 Apr 1846	**Harrison, Nacogdoches** Upshur County; 100 W Tyler St; PO Box 730; Gilmer, TX 75644-2198; Ph. 903.843.4015 Details: (Co Clk has b & d rec from 1903, m rec from 1873, land rec from 1845, pro rec from 1853 & mil rec from 1919; Dis Clk has div rec)
Upton www.rootsweb.com/~txupton/	I5	26 Feb 1887	**Tom Green** Upton County; 205 E 10; PO Box 465; Rankin, TX 79778-0465; Ph. 915.693.2861 Details: (Co Clk has b, m, div, land, pro & mil rec from 1910; Dis Clk has ct rec)
Uvalde* www.uvaldecounty.com/	K7	8 Feb 1850	**Bexar** Uvalde County; PO Box 284; Uvalde, TX 78802; Ph. 830.278.6614 Details: (Co Clk has b, m, d, pro, ct & land rec from 1856; Dis Clk has div rec)
Val Verde www.rootsweb.com/~txvalver/	J5	20 Feb 1885	**Crockett, Kinney, Pecos** Val Verde County; PO Box 1267; Del Rio, TX 78841-1267; Ph. 830.774.7564 Details: (Co Clk has m, land, pro, mil & ct rec from 1885; Dis Clk has div rec)
Van Zandt www.rootsweb.com/~txvanzan/ vzcpage.htm	H10	20 Mar 1848	**Henderson** Van Zandt County; 121 E Dallas St Rm 202; Canton, TX 75103; Ph. 903.567.6503 Details: (Co Clk has b & d rec from 1903, m, land, pro & ct rec from 1848 & mil dis rec from 1918; Dis Clk has div rec from 1848)
Victoria www.viptx.net/vcgs/	L9	17 Mar 1836	**Old Mexican Municipality** Victoria County; 115 N Bridge; Victoria, TX 77901; Ph. 361.575.1478 Details: (Co Clk has b & d rec from 1903, m, pro & land rec from 1838 & ct rec from 1867; Dis Clk has div rec)
Walker www.rootsweb.com/~txwalker/index.htm	J10	6 Apr 1846	**Montgomery** Walker County; 1100 University Ave; PO Box 210; Huntsville, TX 77340; Ph. 936.436.4922 Details: (Co Clk has m, land & ct rec from 1846, b, d & pro rec; Dis Clk has div rec)
Waller www.rootsweb.com/~txwaller/	J10	28 Apr 1873	**Austin, Grimes** Waller County; 836 Austin St #217; Hempstead, TX 77445-4667; Ph. 979.826.7711 Details: (Co Clk has b & d rec from 1903, m, pro, ct & land rec from 1873)
Ward www.rootsweb.com/~txward/	I4	26 Feb 1887	**Tom Green** Ward County; 400 S Allen St; Monahans, TX 79756; Ph. 915.943.3294 Details: (Co Clk has b, m, d, pro, ct & land rec from 1892 & mil rec; Dis Clk has div rec)
Washington www.startel.net/users/awhart/ wgenweb/washiton.htm	J10	17 Mar 1836	**Texas Municipality** Washington County; 100 E Main St; Brenham, TX 77834; Ph. 409.277.6200 Details: (Co Clk has b & d rec from 1903, m rec from 1837, pro & land rec; Dis Clk has div rec)
Webb webbcounty.com/	M7	28 Jan 1848	**Bexar, Nueces** Webb County; 1110 Victoria St; PO Box 29; Laredo, TX 78042; Ph. 956.721.2645 Details: (Co Clk has b & d rec from 1856, m rec from 1850, pro rec from 1870 & l and rec)

County Website	Map Index	Date Created	Parent County or Territory From Which Organized Address/Details
Wharton www.rootsweb.com/~txwharto/	**K10**	**3 Apr 1846**	**Matagorda, Jackson, Colorado,** Wharton County; 100 E Milam St; PO Box 69; Wharton, TX 77488; Ph. 979.532.2381 Details: (Co Clk has b & d rec from 1903, m rec from 1857, land rec from 1846, pro rec from 1849, ct rec from 1909 & mil rec from 1919)
Wheeler www.rootsweb.com/~txwheele/	**E6**	**21 Aug 1876**	**Bexar Land District** Wheeler County; PO Box 465; Wheeler, TX 79096-0465; Ph. 806.826.5544 Details: (Co Clk has b & d rec from 1906, m, pro, ct & land rec from 1879; Dis Clk has div rec)
Wichita www.rootsweb.com/~txwichit/	**F8**	**1 Feb 1858**	**Fannin Land District** Wichita County; 900 7th St; PO Box 1679; Wichita Falls, TX 76307-1679; Ph. 940.766.8144 Details: (Co Clk has incomplete b rec from 1890, incomplete d rec from 1900, m, pro & land rec from 1882; Dis Clk has div & ct rec)
Wilbarger www.co.wilbarger.tx.us/	**F7**	**1 Feb 1858**	**Bexar Land District** Wilbarger County; 1700 Wilbarger St; Vernon, TX 76384-4742; Ph. 940.552.5486 Details: (Co Clk has b, m, d, pro, ct & land rec from 1900; Dis Clk has div rec; City Sec has bur rec)
Willacy www.pastracks.com/states/texas/willacy/	**N9**	**11 Mar 1911**	**Hidalgo, Cameron** Willacy County; Courthouse Annex Bldg; 190 N 3rd St; Raymondville, TX 78580; Ph. 956.689.2710 Details: (Co Clk had b, m, d, pro & ct rec from 1921 & land rec from 1891)
Williamson www.wilco.org/	**J9**	**13 Mar 1848**	**Milam** Williamson County; PO Box 18; Georgetown, TX 78627; Ph. 512.943.1515 Details: (Co Clk has b & d rec from 1903, m, land, pro & ct rec from 1848 & mil dis rec from 1917; Dis Clk has div rec)
Wilson* www.pastracks.com/states/texas/wilson/	**K8**	**13 Feb 1860**	**Bexar, Karnes** Wilson County; PO Box 27; Floresville, TX 78114; Ph. 830.393.7308 Details: (Co Clk has b & d rec from 1903, m rec from 1860, pro rec from 1862, ct rec from 1876 & land rec)
Winkler www.rootsweb.com/~txwinkle/	**H4**	**26 Feb 1887**	**Tom Green** Winkler County; PO Box 1007; Kermit, TX 79745-4236; Ph. 915.586.3401 Details: (Co Clk has b rec from 1919, d & pro rec from 1912, m & ct rec from 1911 & land rec from 1887; Dis Clk has div rec)
Wise www.wisecounty.com/	**G9**	**23 Jan 1856**	**Cooke** Wise County; 200 N Trinity St; PO Box 359; Decatur, TX 76234-0359; Ph. 940.627.3351 Details: (Co Clk has b & d rec from 1903, m rec from 1881, pro rec from 1882, land rec from 1852 & ct rec)
Wood www.rootsweb.com/~txwood/index.htm	**G11**	**5 Feb 1850**	**Van Zandt** Wood County; PO Box 338; Quitman, TX 75783-0338; Ph. 903.763.2711 Details: (Co Clk has b & d rec from 1903, m, land & pro rec from 1879, cem & ct rec, mil rec from 1918; Dis Clk has div rec)
Yoakum www.pastracks.com/states/texas/yoakum/	**G4**	**21 Aug 1876**	**Bexar Land District** Yoakum County; PO Box 309; Plains, TX 79355; Ph. 806.456.2721 Details: (Attached to Martin Co from 1904 to 1907) (Co Clk has b rec from 1878, m & d rec from 1908, pro rec from 1907, ct rec from 1930 & land rec from 1898; Dis Clk has div rec)
Young www.rootsweb.com/~txyoung/young.htm	**G8**	**2 Feb 1856**	**Bosque, Fannin** Young County; 516 4th St Rm 104; Graham, TX 76450; Ph. 940.549.8432 Details: (Co Clk has b & d rec from 1903, m, pro, ct & land rec from 1856; Dis Clk has div rec)
Zapata www.vsta.com/~rlblack/zapata.html	**N7**	**22 Jan 1858**	**Starr, Webb** Zapata County; PO Box 789; Zapata, TX 78076; Ph. 956.765.9915 Details: (Co Clk has b rec 1870's-1930's, m & land rec from 1800's, pro & ct rec from 1900's; Dis Clk has div rec; JP Off has b rec from 1930's & d rec)

County Website	Map Index	Date Created	Parent County or Territory From Which Organized Address/Details
Zavala www.historicdistrict.com/Genealogy/ zavala/zavala.htm	**L7**	**1 Feb 1858**	**Uvalde, Maverick** Zavala County; County Courthouse; Crystal City, TX 78839; Ph. 830.374.2331 Details: (Co Clk has b, m, d, pro & ct rec from 1884, land & mil rec; Dis Clk has div rec)

Notes

Sego Lily

UTAH

CAPITAL: SALT LAKE CITY – TERRITORY 1850 – STATE 1896 (45TH)

The first documented explorers in Utah were Father Silvestre Escalante and Father Francisco Dominguez in 1776. Between 1811 and 1840, fur trappers entered Utah and prepared the way for future settlers. The first permanent settlers were members of The Church of Jesus Christ of Latter-day Saints, also known as Mormons. They entered the Salt Lake Valley on 24 July1847, led by their church president Brigham Young. They had been forced out of their homes in Nauvoo, Illinois and crossed the plains to the desert. New groups arrived several times each month, so that by 1850, there were 11,380 residents. Most of the early settlers came from New England, Ohio, Illinois, Missouri, and Canada. Most of the Europeans were English, Germans, Danes, Swedes, Norwegians, Swiss, Hollanders, Welsh, and Scottish. Despite warnings from Jim Bridger that corn could never grow in Utah, the Mormons were able to irrigate the land and develop a healthy agriculture.

With the end of the Mexican War, Utah became a part of the United States. The Mormons created the State of Deseret in 1849 and petitioned Congress for admission to the Union. Deseret included parts of present-day California, Oregon, Idaho, Wyoming, Nevada, Arizona, New Mexico, and Utah. Congress denied the petition, but did create the Territory of Utah in 1850, which included parts of Nevada, Wyoming, Colorado, and Utah. With the creation of the territories of Nevada and Colorado in 1861 and Wyoming in 1868, Utah reached it present size.

In the decade following their arrival in Utah, the Mormon settlers founded some 100 towns in Utah, Nevada, Idaho, California, and Wyoming. Between 1856 and 1860, another 8,000 immigrants came to Utah in handcart companies. The Utah War of 1857-58, which occurred when United States troops were sent to suppress a rebellion that never existed, was peaceably settled. Federal troops, however, remained in Utah after the war until 1861. Another wave of Mormon settlement occurred between 1858 and 1868, which established communities in southern Utah, southern Idaho, southeastern Nevada and northern Arizona. The first transcontinental railroad was completed at Promontory in Utah in 1869.

A series of acts passed by Congress were aimed at the Mormons and their practice of polygamy. Additionally, these acts abolished women's suffrage and certain civil rights so that prosecution of polygamists would be easier. As a result of these laws, many Mormons fled the area to Sonora and Chihuahua, Mexico and to Alberta, Canada. Mormon Church President Wilford Woodruff made a proclamation known as the Manifesto in 1890, which discontinued the practice of polygamy. With this roadblock to statehood removed, Utah became a state in 1896.

Look for vital records in the following locations:

- **Birth and death records:** Bureau of Vital Records, Utah State Department of Health. Registration began in 1905. Most counties began keeping ledger entries of births and deaths in 1898. Salt Lake City, Ogden, and Logan also have some birth and death records.
- **Marriage records:** Most marriage records since 1887 are at the county clerk's office or the Utah State Archives.
- **Census records:** An 1856 territorial census is at the Historical Department of the LDS Church. The Family History Library of The Church of Jesus Christ of Latter-day Saints has one of the largest collections of genealogical resources, records, books, microfilm, and microfiche in the world. These resources are also available through Family History Centers (branches) located throughout the world.

Bureau of Vital Records **Utah State Department of Health** PO Box 141012 Salt Lake City, Utah 84114 801.538.6380	**Utah State Archives, Archives** **Building** State Capitol Salt Lake City Utah 84114
Historical Department of **the LDS Church** 50 East North Temple Salt Lake City, Utah 84150	**Family History Library of** **The Church of Jesus Christ of** **Latter-day Saints** 35 North West Temple Salt Lake City, Utah 84150

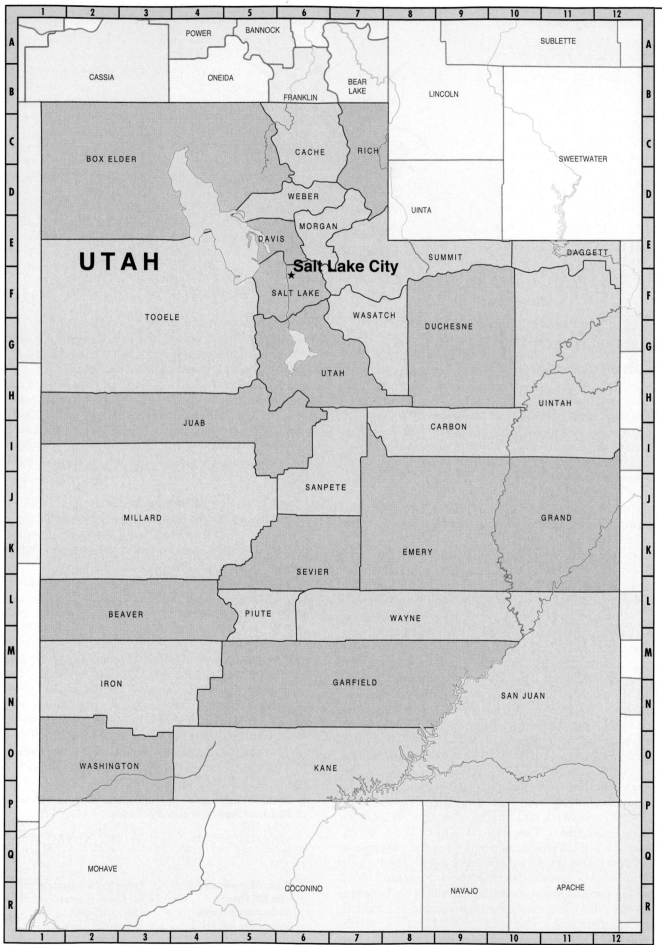

UTAH

★ **Salt Lake City**

Societies and Repositories

Bear River District Health Department; 655 East 1300 North Street; Logan, Utah 84341; 801.752.3730

Brigham Carnegie Library; 26 E. Forest; Brigham City, Utah 84302

Bureau of Land Management; 7450 Boston Blvd.; Springfield, Virginia 22153; 703.440.1600; Fax 703.440.1609; Has patents for Utah since 1908.

Bureau of Land Management; Utah State Office; 324 South State Street Suite 400; Salt Lake City, Utah 84111-2303; 801.539.4001; Fax 801.539.4260; This office has copies of patents and tractbooks from 1869 to the present, survey plats and notes beginning in the 1850s, and township plats showing who the land was sold to.

Bureau of Vital Records; Utah State Department of Health; 288 North 1460 West Street; Salt Lake City, Utah 84114; 801.538.6105

BYU-LDS Branch Library; 4385 Harold B. Lee Library, BYU; Provo, Utah 84602

Cuban Genealogical Society; PO Box 2650; Salt Lake City, Utah 84110-2650; <http://www.rootsweb.com/~utcubangs/>

Daughters of the American Revolution, Utah Society; 6855 So. Willow Way; Salt Lake City, Utah 84121

Daughters of the Utah Pioneers; 300 North Main Street; Salt Lake City, Utah 84103; 801.538.1050

Division of Indian Affairs; State Office Building; Salt Lake City, Utah 84114

Dixie Gen. Library; St. George, Utah 84770

Episcopal Diocese of Utah; 80 South 300 East Street; Salt Lake City, Utah 84111; 801.322.4131; Each parish maintains its own records. The diocese has records for some discontinued parishes.

Everton's Genealogical Library; 3223 S. Main St. Nibley, Utah 84321

Family History Library; 35 North West Temple Street; Salt Lake City, Utah 84150; 800.346.6044 or 801.240.2584; <http://www.familysearch.org>; Find a Family History Center near you; <http://www.familysearch.org/Eng/Library/FHC/frameset_fhc.asp>

Genealogical Society of Utah; 35 North West Temple; Salt Lake City, Utah 84150

Harold B. Lee Library; Brigham Young University; Provo, Utah 84602; 801.378.2926; FHC 801.378.6200; Gen. Ref. 801.378.2927

Heritage Quest Lending Library; PO Box 329 Bountiful, Utah 84011-0329

Historical Department; The Church of Jesus Christ of Latter-day Saints; 50 East North Temple Street; Salt Lake City, Utah 84150; 801.240.3603

Icelandic Association of Utah; 84 N. 1120 E.; Spanish Fork, Utah 84660

Institute of Genealogy and History for Latin America; 2191 S. 2200 E.; Mt. Springs, Utah 84757; 435.674.5787; <http://www.genealogy.com/00000140.html?Welcome=1010690722>

Jewish Genealogical Society of Salt Lake City; 3510 Fleetwood Dr.; Salt Lake City, Utah 94109

Logan Public Library; 255 N. Main; Logan, Utah 84321

Marriott Library; University of Utah; Salt Lake City, Utah 84112; 801.581.8364; Fax 801.585.3464

Merrill Library; Utah State University; Logan, Utah 84322; 801.797.2678; Fax 801.797.2880

Methodist; Iliff School of Theology; Ira J. Taylor Library Archives; 2201 South University Blvd.; Denver, Colorado 80210; 303.744.1287; Fax 303.744.3387; Each congregation maintains its own records. The Ira J. Taylor Archives has the records for some of the discontinued congregations of Utah. They can also help you locate existing congregations.

National Archives & Records Administration; 7th Pennsylvania Ave.; Washington, D.C. 20408; 202.501.5400; Fax 202.501.5340; Mailing Address: General Branch; Civil Archives Division; National Archives; Washington, D.C. 20408; For Utah, the Washington National Records Center has the tract books of entries to about 1964, indexed case files from 1869 to 1908, indexed case files from 1908 to about 1973, patents from 1869 to 1908, and other records.

National Archives—Rocky Mountain Region (Denver); Building 48; West 6th Ave. & Kipling; Denver Federal Center; Denver, Colorado 80225; 303.236.0817; The Denver Branch has land office records for Utah, including correspondence, surveys, homestead and cash entry registers, receipts, and final certificates.

Presbyterian Historical Society; 425 Lombard St., Philadelphia, Pennsylvania 19147; Maintains records of discontinued congregations and some current congregations.

Presbytery of Utah; 342 West 200 South Street Suite 30; Salt Lake City, Utah 84101; 801.539.8446; Each Presbyterian congregation maintains its own records. The Presbytery of Utah can help you locate current congregations and will provide suggestions for finding records of discontinued congregations.

Rocky Mountain District, LCMS; 7000 North Broadway Street Suite 401; Denver, Colorado 80221-2907; 303.427.7553; Fax 303.426.5603; Each Lutheran congregation maintains its own records. The Rocky Mountain District office can help you locate current congregations and provide suggestions for finding the records of discontinued congregations.

Roman Catholic; Pastoral Center; Diocese of Salt Lake City; 27 C Street; Salt Lake City, Utah 84103; 801.328.8641; Diocese of Salt Lake City has records from the early 1870s to the present for all of Utah. The early records are incomplete. Each congregation presently keeps its records for a few years before sending them to the Pastoral Center.

Salt Lake City Family History Library of the Church of Jesus Christ of Latter-day Saints; 35 N. West Temple; Salt Lake City, Utah 84150

Salt Lake City Public Library; 209 East 500 South Street; Salt Lake City, Utah 84111; 801.524.8200; Fax 801.524.8289

Salt Lake County Records Management and Archives; 2001 South State Street N. 4400; Salt Lake City, Utah 84190; 801.468.2330; Fax 801.468.3987

Sons of the American Revolution, Utah Society; 5539 Capital Reef Dr.; West Jordan, Utah 84084

Sons of the Utah Pioneers; 3301 East 2920 South Street; Salt Lake City, Utah 84109; 801.484.4441; Fax 801.484.4442

Temple Area Gen. Library; Manti, Utah 84642

U.S. Mormon Batallion, Inc.; 7321 South State Street; Midvale, Utah 84047; 801.255.3591

Uintah and Ouray Agency; Uintah and Ouray Tribal Business Council; PO Box 190; Fort Duchesne, Utah 84026; 801.722.5141; Fax 801.722.2374

University of Utah Library; Salt Lake City, Utah 84112

Utah Chapter, AHSGR; 259 E. 500 North; Lehi, Utah 84043-1638; 801.731.3054

Utah Genealogical Association; PO Box 1144; Salt Lake City, Utah 84110; 1.888.463.6842 <http://www.infouga.org/>

Utah State Archives and Record Services; Archives Building; State Capitol; Salt Lake City, Utah 84114; 801.538.3013; Fax; 801.538.3354

Utah State Historical Society and Library; 300 South Rio Grande; Salt Lake City, Utah 84101-1143; 801.533.3503; <http://www.dced.state.ut.us/history/>

Westminster College Library; 1840 South 1300 East Street; Salt Lake City, Utah 84105; Includes miscellaneous collection of Utah Presbyterian records.

Bibliography and Record Sources

General Sources

A Guide to the Oral History Collection, Utah State Historical Society. Salt Lake City: Utah State Historical Society Library, 1980.

Allen, James B., and Glen M. Leonard. *The Story of the Latter-day Saints*. Salt Lake City: Deseret Book Co., 1976.

Alter, J. Cecil. *Early Utah Journalism*. Salt Lake City: Utah State Historical Society, 1938.

Alter, J. Cecil. *Utah, The Storied Domain, A Documentary History of Utah's Eventful Career*. 3 vol. Chicago & New York: American Historical Society, Inc, 1932.

Bennett, Archibald F., comp. *Family Genealogical Records Alphabetically Arranged. Research Notes By Benjamin F. Cummings Jr. on the Ancestry of Some Early Utah Families: Abt. 1898-1900*. (Salt Lake City: Filmed by the Genealogical Society of Utah, 1954). Microfilm, multiple rolls.

Bitton, Davis. *Guide to Mormon Diaries and Autobiographies*. Provo, Utah: Brigham Young University Press, 1977.

Carter, Kate B., comp. *Daughters of the Utah Pioneer Lessons*. 31 vols. Salt Lake City: Daughters of the Utah Pioneers, 1937-68.

Carter, Kate B., comp. *Heart Throbs of the West*. 12 vols. Salt Lake City: Daughters of the Utah Pioneers, 1939–.

Carter, Kate B., comp. *Our Pioneer Heritage*. 20 vols. Salt Lake City: Daughters of the Utah Pioneers, 1958-77.

Carter, Kate B., comp. *Treasures of Pioneer History*. 6 vols. Salt Lake City: Daughters of the Utah Pioneers, 1952-7

Church Almanac. Salt Lake City: Deseret News, 1974-. Annual 1974-1987, biannual 1989-.

Directory of Special Information Resources in Utah, 1982, Rev. Salt Lake City: Utah Library Association, 1987.

Episcopal Church. Diocese of Utah. *Episcopal Register of the Bishop of Utah (Bishop's Personal Register) 1899- 1946, 1951-1967*. (Salt Lake City: Filmed by the Genealogical Society of Utah, 1975). Microfilm, multiple rolls.

Esshom, Frank. *Pioneers and Prominent Men of Utah*. 1913. Reprint. Salt Lake City: Western Epics Inc, 1966.

Genealogical Society of Utah. *Genealogical Surveys of LDS Members: Autobiographies and Ancestors*. Salt Lake City: The Society, 1924-1929. Microfilm, multiple rolls.

Historical Records Survey (Utah). *Inventory of the Church Archives of Utah*. 3 vols. Salt Lake City: Utah Historical Records Survey, 1940.

Holley, Robert P., ed. *Utah's Newspapers-Traces of Her Past*. [Salt Lake City: University of Utah, 1984].

Jaussi, Laureen, and Gloria Chaston. *Genealogical Records of Utah*. Salt Lake City: Deseret Book Co., 1974.

Jenson, Andrew. *Encyclopedic History of the Church*. Salt Lake City: Deseret News Publishing Company, 1941.

Jenson, Andrew. *Latter-day Saint Biographical Encyclopedia*. Salt Lake City: A. Jenson History Co., 1901–36.

May, Dean L. *Utah: A People's History*. Salt Lake City: University of Utah Press, 1987.

Mooney, Bernice. *Salt of the Earth*. Salt Lake City: Catholic Diocese of Salt Lake City, 1987.

Name Index to the Library of Congress Collection of Mormon Diaries. Logan, Utah Utah State Univ., 1971.

Portrait, Genealogical and Biographical Record of the State of Utah. Chicago: National Historical Board, 1902.

Reorganized Church of Jesus Christ of Latter Day Saints. Utah District. *Church Records, 1868-1940*. (Salt Lake City: Filmed by the Genealogical Society of Utah, 1994). Microfilm, 2 rolls.

Smith, Joseph. *History of The Church of Jesus Christ of Latter-day Saints*. 7 vols. 1902 Reprint. Salt Lake City: Deseret Book Co., 1970.

Sutton, Wain, ed. Utah: *A Centennial History*. 3 vols. New York: Lewis Historical Publishing Co., 1949.

Thatcher, Linda. *Guide to Newspapers Located in the Utah State Historical Society Library*, [Salt Lake City: Utah State Historical Society, 1985].

Utah Pioneer Biographies. 44 vols. N.p., 1935-1964.

Utah State Historical Society. *Guide to Archives and Manuscript Collections in Selected Utah Repositories*. Salt Lake City: Utah State Historical Society, 1990. CD-ROM.

Utah State Historical Society. *A Guide to Unpublished Materials at the Utah State Historical Society Salt Lake City*: Utah State Historical Society Library, 1989;

Utah State Archives and Record Services. *Guide to Official Records of Genealogical Value in the State of Utah*. Salt Lake City: Utah State Archives and Record Services, 1980.

Utah State Archives and Record Services. *Municipal Records Manual, 1983*. Utah State Archives and Record Services, 1983.

Utah Research Outline. Series US-States, no.44. Salt Lake City: Family History Library, 1988.

Wasatch Presbyterian Church (Salt Lake City, Utah). *Wasatch Presbyterian Church Records, 1885-1955.* (Salt Lake City: Filmed by the Genealogical Society of Utah, 2000). Microfilm.

Wiggins, Marvin E. *Mormons and Their Neighbors: An Index of Over 75,000 Biographical Sketches from 1820 to the Present.* 2 vols., Provo, Utah: Brigham Young Univ., 1984.

Atlases, Maps and Gazetteers

Gallagher, John S. *The Post Offices of Utah.* Burtonsville, Maryland: The Depot, 1977.

Gannett, Henry A. *A Gazetteer of Utah.* Washington, D.C.: U.S. Government Printing Office, 1900.

Greer, Deon C., et al. *Atlas of Utah.* Ogden, Utah Weber State College, 1981.

Gruber, Ted. *Postal History of Utah, 1849-1976.* Crete, NB: J-B Publishing Co., 1978.

Leigh, Rufus Wood. *Five Hundred Utah Place Names.* Salt Lake City: Deseret News Press, 1961.

Miller, David E. *Utah History Atlas.* 2nd ed. n.p.: Miller, 1968.

Moffat, Riley Moore. *Printed Maps of Utah to 1900: An Annotated Cartobibliography.* Western Association of Map Librarians, 1981.

Sloan, Robert W. *Utah Gazetteer and Directory of Logan, Ogden, Provo and Salt Lake City for 1884.* Salt Lake City: Herald Printing and Publishing Co., 1884.

Utah: A Guide to the State. New York: Hastings House, 1941.

Utah Writer's Project. *Origins of Utah Place Names.* Salt Lake City: State Department of Instruction, 1940.

VanCott, John E., comp. *Utah Place Names: A Comprehensive Guide to the Origins of Geographic Names.* Salt Lake City: University of Utah Press, 1990.

Ward, Jill Anderson. *LDS Place Names Gazetteer.* Salt Lake City: Family History Library, 1986.

Census Records

Available Census Records and Census Substitutes

Federal Census 1850, 1860, 1870, 1880, 1900, 1910, 1920, 1930.

Federal Mortality Schedules 1870.

Union Veterans and Widows 1890.

State/Territorial Census 1851, 1856.

Church of Jesus Christ of Latter-day Saints. *Church Census Records, 1914-1960.* (Salt Lake City: Filmed by the Genealogical Society of Utah, 1962). Microfilm, multiple rolls.

Dollarhide, William. *The Census Book: A Genealogist's Guide to Federal Census Facts, Schedules and Indexes.* Bountiful, Utah Heritage Quest, 1999.

Lainhart, Ann S. *State Census Records.* Baltimore: Genealogical Publishing Co., Inc., 1992.

Kemp, Thomas Jay. *The American Census Handbook.* Wilmington, DE: Scholarly Resources, Inc., 2001.

Szucs, Loretto Dennis, and Matthew Wright. *Finding Answers in U.S. Census Records.* Ancestry Publishing, 2001.

Thorndale, William, and William Dollarhide. *Map Guide to the U.S. Federal Censuses, 1790-1920.* Baltimore: Genealogical Publishing Co., 1987.

United States. Bureau of Indian Affairs. *Indian Census Rolls, Fort Hall, 1885-1939.* Washington, D.C.: The National Archives, 1965.

Court Records, Probate and Wills

District Court (Utah County). *Appearance Docket Records 1859-1872.* (Salt Lake City: Filmed by the Genealogical Society of Utah, 1959).

Interior Department Territorial Papers, Utah, 1850-1902. Washington, D.C.: National Archives. Central Plains Region, 1963. Microfilm, 6 rolls.

Utah. District Court (Salt Lake County). *Probate Records; Estates and Guardianship, 1852-1910, and Index to Books A- F.* (Salt Lake City: Filmed by the Genealogical Society of Utah, 1966). Microfilm, multiple rolls.

United States. Supreme Court. *A Record of the Decisions of the United States Supreme Court for the Territory of Utah: Book A, 1861-1893.* Salt Lake City: Utah State Records and Archives Service, 1975.

Emigration, Immigration, Migration and Naturalization

Bashore, Melvin Lee. *Mormon Pioneer Companies Crossing the Plains (1847-1868) Narratives: Guide to Sources in Utah Libraries and Archives.* 3rd rev. ed. [Salt Lake City]: The Church of Jesus Christ of Latter-day Saints. Historical Dept., 1990.

Bashore, Melvin L., and Linda L. Haslam. *Mormons on the High Seas: Ocean Voyage Narratives to America (1840–1890).* Salt Lake City: Historical Department of The Church of Jesus Christ of Latter-day Saints, 1990.

Emigration Records, Scandinavian Mission (Denmark, Norway, Sweden) 1852- 1920. (Salt Lake City: Filmed by the Genealogical Society of Utah, 1951-1953). Microfilm, multiple rolls.

European Emigration Card Index, 1849-1925. (Salt Lake City: Filmed by the Genealogical Society of Utah, 1951). Microfilm, multiple rolls.

Hafen, LeRoy R., and Ann W. Hafen, *Handcarts to Zion: The Story of a Unique Western Migration, 1856-1860, with Contemporary Journals, Accounts, Reports, and Rosters of Members of the Ten Handcart Companies.* Glendale, California: Arthur H. Clark, 1960.

Naturalization Records, 1853-1936. Salt Lake City: Utah State Archives and Records Service, 1980-1981, 1989- 1990. Microfilm, multiple copies.

Naturalization Index, ca 1860-1989. Utah District Court (Utah County). Salt Lake City: Genealogical Society of Utah. 1989. Microfilm, multiple copies.

Perpetual Emigrating Fund Company. *Names of Persons and Sureties Indebted to the Perpetual Emigrating Fund Company from 1850 to 1877 Inclusive.* (Salt Lake City: Filmed by the Genealogical Society of Utah, 1950). Microfilm.

Sonne, Conway B. *Saints on the Seas: A Maritime History of Mormon Migration, 1830-1890.* Salt Lake City: University of Utah Press, 1983.

Sonne, Conway B. *Ships, Saints, and Mariners: A Maritime Encyclopedia of Mormon Migration, 1830-1890*. Salt Lake City: University of Utah Press, 1987.

Taylor, Margery. *Worldwide LDS Ship Register 1840–1913*. Salt Lake City: Family History Library, 1991.

United States. Supreme Court (Utah Territory). *Declarations of Intentions to Become Citizens, Vol. B-C, 1872-1893*. Salt Lake City: Utah State Archives and Records Service, 1982.

Utah Immigration Card Index, 1847-1868. (Salt Lake City: Filmed by the Genealogical Society of Utah, 1963). Microfilm, multiple rolls.

Land and Property

Barker, Joel. *Preliminary Inventory of Land Management – Utah*. Denver: Denver Archives and Records Center, 1979.

Fox, Feramorz Young. *The Mormon Land System, A Study of the Settlement and Utilization of Land Under the Direction of the Mormon Church*. Logan, Utah State Agricultural College, 1955.

Linford, Lawrence, L. "Establishing and Maintaining Land Ownership in Utah Prior to 1869." Salt Lake City: *Utah Historical Society Quarterly*, vol. 42 (1974): 126-43.

Nelson, Lowry. *The Mormon Village: A Pattern and Technique of Land Settlement*. Salt Lake City: University of Utah Press, 1952.

Military

Fisher, Margaret May Merrill. *Utah and the Civil War*. Salt Lake City: Deseret Book Co., 1929.

Hance, Watson, and Irene Warr. *Johnston, Connor and the Mormons: An Outline of Military History in Northern Utah*. [Salt Lake City]: n.p., 1962.

Larson, Carl V. *A Database of the Mormon Battalion*. Providence, Utah: K. W. Watkins, 1987.

Mabey, Charles R. *The Utah Batteries: A History*. [Spanish American War 1898] Salt Lake City: n.p., 1900.

Mexican Border Service, Muster Rolls, 1916-1917. Salt Lake City: Genealogical Society of Utah, 1966. Microfilm.

Prentiss, A., ed. *The History of the Utah Volunteers in the Spanish-American War and in the Philippine Islands*. Salt Lake City: W. F. Ford, 1900. (Salt Lake City: Filmed by the Genealogical Society of Utah, 1966).

United States. Bureau of Pensions. *Selected Pension Application Files for Members of the Mormon Battalion, Mexican War, 1846-48*. Washington: National Archives and Records Service, 1934.

United States. Record and Pension Office. *Compiled Service Records of Volunteer Soldiers Who Served During the Mexican War in Mormon Organizations*. Washington, D.C.: National Archives, 1961.

United States. Selective Service System. *Utah World War I Selective Service System Draft Registration Cards, 1917-1918*. Washington, D.C.: National Archives, 1987-1988.

Utah State Archives. *Card Index to Military Records of the Indian Wars, 1866-1867; A-Z*. (Salt Lake City: Filmed by the Genealogical Society of Utah, 1966). Microfilm, multiple rolls.

Utah State Archives. *Spanish-American War; Index to Utah Units*. (Salt Lake City: Filmed by the Genealogical Society of Utah, 1966). Microfilm.

Utah. Board of Commissioners of Indian War Records. *Service Records of Indian Wars in Utah, 1853-1868*. (Salt Lake City: Filmed by the Genealogical Society of Utah, 1966). Microfilm, multiple rolls.

Utah. Secretary of State. *Applications for Indian War Medals, 1905-1912*. Salt Lake City: Filmed by the Utah State Archives, 1980. Microfilm, multiple rolls.

Warrum, Noble. *Utah in the World War*. Salt Lake City: Utah State Council of Defense, 1924.

Vital and Cemetery Records

Cemetery Listing (Utah). Salt Lake City: Utah State Archives and Records Service, 1986.

Cemetery Records of Utah. 13 vols. Salt Lake City: Genealogical Society of Utah, 1953.

Church of Jesus Christ of Latter-day Saints. Church Historian's Office. *Obituary Index File to the Salt Lake Tribune and Deseret News as of 31 December 1970*. Salt Lake City: Church Historian's Office, 1971. Microfilm, 64 rolls.

Ellison, Marion. *An Inventory and Index to the Records of Carson County, Utah and Nevada Territories, 1855—1861*. Reno, Nevada: Grace Dangberg Foundation, 1984.

Guide to Public Vital Statistics of Utah. Salt Lake City: Utah Historical Records Survey, 1941.

Hansen, Judith Woolstenhulme. *Marriages in Utah Territory, 1850-1884: From the Deseret News, 1850-1872, and the Elias Smith Journals, 1850-1884*. Salt Lake City: Utah Genealogical Association, 1998.

Historical Records Survey (Utah). *Guide to Public Vital Statistics of Utah*. Salt Lake City: Historical Records Survey, 1941.

McClay, Irvin C. *Cemeteries in Utah*. Salt Lake City: Utah State Archives and Records Service, 1980

Miscellaneous Marriage Records Index: Compiled From Civil Records. Microfilm. 19 reels. Salt Lake City: Genealogical Society of Utah, 1972.

Salt Lake City (Utah). Office of Vital Statistics. *Birth Records, 1890-1950, 1953*. (Salt Lake City: Filmed by the Genealogical Society of Utah, 1950). Microfilm, multiple rolls.

Salt Lake City (Utah). Office of Vital Statistics. *Death Records of Salt Lake City, Utah, 1848 - Sept. 1950*. (Salt Lake City: Filmed by the Genealogical Society of Utah, 1950). Microfilm, multiple rolls.

Salt Lake County (Utah). County Clerk. *Alphabetic Marriage Listing, 1887-1987*. Salt Lake City: Management Information Systems, 1987 Microfilm, multiple rolls.

Territorial Vital Records: Births, Divorces, Guardianship, Marriages, Naturalization, Wills; 1800's thru 1906 Utah Territory, Arizona, Colorado, Idaho, Nevada, Wyoming, Indian Terr.; LDS Branches, Wards; Deseret News Vital Recs.; J.P. Marriages; Meth. Marriages. St. George, Utah Genealogical CD Publishing, 1994. CD-ROM.

United States. Bureau of Indian Affairs. Uintah and Ouray Agency. *Vital Records of the Ute Indians to 1946*. (Salt Lake City: Filmed by the Genealogical Society of Utah, 1953). Microfilm.

Utah Death Index: 1891-1905 (Excluding Salt Lake County).
Edited by Judith W. Hansen. Monograph Series, no. 2. Salt
Lake City: Professional Chapter, Utah Genealogical
Association, 1995.

Utah State Historical Society. *Burials Database.* Salt Lake City:
Utah State Historical Society, 2001. [Online Database
<www.dced.state.ut.us/history/Services/lcburials.html>.

Utah. Department of Health. Bureau of Vital Records. *Utah
Death Certificates, 1904-1943.* (Salt Lake City: Filmed by the
Genealogical Society of Utah, 2001). Microfilm, 127 rolls.

County Website	Map Index	Date Created	Parent County or Territory From Which Organized Address/Details
Beaver www.lofthouse.com/USA/Utah/ beaver/index.html	L2	1856	**Iron, Millard** Beaver County; 105 E Center; PO Box 392; Beaver, UT 84713-0392; Ph. 435.438.6463 Details: (Co Clk has b rec 1897-1905, m rec from 1887, d rec 1900-1905, div rec from 1871, pro rec from 1872 & ct rec from 1856; Beaver City Office has bur rec)
Box Elder* www.lofthouse.com/boxelder/	C2	5 Jan 1856	**Unorganized Territory Weber, Green River** Box Elder County; 1 S Main St; Brigham City, UT 84302; Ph. 435.734.3388 Details: (Co Clk has b & d rec 1898-1905, m rec from 1887, div, pro, ct & land rec from 1856)
Cache www.rootsweb.com/~utcache/	C6	5 Jan 1856	**Unorganized Territory Green River** Cache County; 170 N Main St; Logan, UT 84321-4541; Ph. 435.716.7150 Details: (Co Clk has m rec from 1888; Clk Dis Ct has div, pro & ct rec; Co Rcdr has land rec)
Carbon* www.co.carbon.ut.us/	I9	8 Mar 1894	**Emery** Carbon County; 120 E Main St; Price, UT 84501-3057; Ph. 435.636.3224 Details: (Co Clk has m rec; Clk Dis Ct has div, pro & ct rec; Co Rcdr has land rec)
Carson		17 Jan 1854	**Tooele, Juab, Millard, Iron** Details: (Transferred to Nevada Terr., 1861)
Cedar		1856	— Details: (Absorbed by Utah Co, 1862)
Daggett* www.rootsweb.com/~utdagget/ index.html	E11	4 Mar 1917	**Uintah** Daggett County; 95 N 1st St W; PO Box 219; Manila, UT 84046-0218; Ph. 435.784.3154 Details: (Co Clk has m, bur, div, pro, ct & land rec from 1918)
Davis www.co.davis.ut.us/	E5	1850	**Original county** Davis County; PO Box 618; Farmington, UT 84025-0618; Ph. 801.451.3420 Details: (Co Clk has m rec; Clk Dis Ct has div, pro & ct rec)
Desert		1852	— Details: (Absorbed by Tooele Co, 1862)
Duchesne www.duchesnegov.net/	G9	7 Mar 1913	**Uintah** Duchesne County; Drawer 910; Duchesne, UT 84021-0270; Ph. 435.738.1123 Details: (Co Clk has m, div, pro & ct rec from 1915; Co Rcdr has land rec from 1915)
Emery* www.co.emery.ut.us/	K8	12 Feb 1880	**Sanpete, Sevier** Emery County; 95 E Main St; Castle Dale, UT 84513; Ph. 435.381.5106 Details: (Co Clk has m rec from 1888; State Ct has div, pro & ct rec; Co Rcdr has land rec)
Garfield www.rootsweb.com/~utgarfie/ _Garfield_index.html	N7	1 Mar 1882	**Iron, Kane, Washington** Garfield County; 55 S Main St; PO Box 77; Panguitch, UT 84759-0077; Ph. 435.676.8826 Details: (Created in 1864 but not organized until 9 Mar 1882) (Co Clk has m rec from 1890, div, pro & ct rec from 1896; Co Rcdr has land rec from 1882 & d rec 1896-1905)
Grand* www.lofthouse.com/USA/Utah/ grand/index.html	J11	13 Mar 1890	**Emery, Uintah** Grand County; 125 E Center St; Moab, UT 84532-2449; Ph. 435.259.1321 Details: (Co Clk has m & pro rec from 1890, div & ct rec from 1896 & land rec)
Greasewood		1856	— Details: (Absorbed by Box Elder Co, 1862)
Great Salt Lake		3 Mar 1852	**Original county** Details: (see Salt Lake) (Name changed to Salt Lake 29 Jan 1868)
Green River		1852	**Original county** Details: (Transferred to Wyoming Terr., 1868)
Humboldt		1856	— Details: (Transferred to Nevada Terr., 1861)

County Website	Map Index	Date Created	Parent County or Territory From Which Organized Address/Details
Iron www.co.iron.ut.us/	**N2**	**31 Jan 1850**	**Original county** Iron County; 68 S 100 E; PO Box 429; Parowan, UT 84761; Ph. 435.477.8341 Details: (Formerly Little Salt Lake Co. Name changed to Iron 3 Dec 1850) (Co Clk has m rec from 1887; Co Rcdr has land rec from 1852; Clk Dis Ct has div, pro & ct rec)
Juab www.co.juab.ut.us/	**H4**	**3 Mar 1852**	**Original county** Juab County; 160 N Main St; Nephi, UT 84648-1412; Ph. 435.623.3410 Details: (Co Clk has b, m, d, div, pro, ct & land rec from 1898)
Kane www.kaneutah.com/	**O6**	**16 Jan 1864**	**Washington** Kane County; 76 N Main St; Kanab, UT 84741; Ph. 435.644.2458 Details: (Co Clk has m, div, pro & ct rec; Co Rcdr has land rec)
Little Salt Lake		**31 Jan 1850**	**Original county** Details: (see Iron) (Name changed to Iron 3 Dec 1850)
Malad		**1856**	— Details: (Absorbed by Box Elder Co, 1862)
Millard www.millardcounty.com/	**J3**	**4 Oct 1851**	**Iron** Millard County; 765 S Hwy 99; Fillmore, UT 84631; Ph. 435.743.6223 Details: (Co Clk has m rec from 1887, div, pro & ct rec from 1852; Co Rcdr has land & mil rec)
Morgan* www.rootsweb.com/~utmorgan/	**E6**	**17 Jan 1862**	**Summit, Weber, Cache** Morgan County; 48 W Young St; Morgan, UT 84050; Ph. 801.845.4011 Details: (Co Clk has m rec from 1888, div & ct rec from 1896 & pro rec from 1869; Co Rcdr has land rec)
Piute www.piute-county.org/	**L5**	**16 Jan 1865**	**Beaver** Piute County; 550 N Main St; PO Box 99; Junction, UT 84740; Ph. 435.577.2840 Details: (Co Clk has b & d rec from 1898, m rec from 1887, div, pro & ct rec from 1872)
Rich richcountyut.homestead.com/ genweb.html	**C7**	**16 Jan 1864**	**Original county** Rich County; 20 N Main St; PO Box 218; Randolph, UT 84064-0218; Ph. 435.793.2415 Details: (Formerly Richland Co. Name changed to Rich 29 Jan 1868) (Co Clk has m rec from 1888, div, pro & ct rec from 1872; Co Rcdr has land rec)
Richland		**16 Jan 1864**	**Original county** Details: (see Rich) (Name changed to Rich 29 Jan 1868)
Rio Virgin		**1869**	— Details: (Absorbed by Washington Co, 1872)
Salt Lake www.co.slc.ut.us/	**F6**	**1849**	**Original county** Salt Lake County; 2001 State St Rm S2200; Salt Lake City, UT 84190; Ph. 801.468.3519 Details: (Formerly Great Salt Lake Co. Name changed to Salt Lake 29 Jan 1868) (Co Clk has m rec from 1887, div & ct rec from 1896 & pro rec from 1852; Co Rcdr has land rec)
San Juan utahreach.usu.edu/sanjuan/index.htm	**N10**	**17 Feb 1880**	**Kane, Iron, Piute** San Juan County; 117 S Main St; PO Box 338; Monticello, UT 84535; Ph. 435.587.3223 Details: (Co Clk has m & pro rec from 1888, div & ct rec from 1891)
Sanpete* utahreach.usu.edu/sanpete/index.htm	**J6**	**3 Mar 1852**	**Original county** Sanpete County; 160 N Main St; Manti, UT 84642; Ph. 435.835.2131 Details: (Co Clk has b rec 1897-1905, d rec 1898-1905, m rec from 1888, div, pro & ct rec from 1878 & land rec from 1870)
Sevier utahreach.usu.edu/sevier/index.htm	**K6**	**16 Jan 1865**	**Sanpete** Sevier County; 250 N Main; PO Box 517; Richfield, UT 84701; Ph. 435.893.0401 Details: (Co Clk has b & d rec 1898-1905, m rec, nat rec 1850-1898; State Ct has div, pro & ct rec; Co Rcdr has land rec, mil dis rec from 1942)

County Website	Map Index	Date Created	Parent County or Territory From Which Organized Address/Details
Shambip		1856	—
			Details: (Absorbed by Tooele Co, 1862)
St. Marys		1856	—
			Details: (Transferred to Nevada Terr., 1861)
Summit www.co.summit.ut.us/ ct	E8	13 Jan 1854	**Salt Lake, Green River** Summit County; PO Box 128; Coalville, UT 84017; Ph. 435.336.3203 Details: (Co Clk has b rec 1898-1905, d rec 1898-1901, m rec from 1888, div, pro & rec from 1896; Co Rcdr has land rec)
Tooele* www.co.tooele.ut.us/	F3	3 Mar 1852	**Original county** Tooele County; 47 S Main St; Tooele, UT 84074; Ph. 435.843.3140 Details: (Co Clk has b & d rec 1897-1905 & m rec from 1887; Clk Dis Ct has div, pro & ct rec; Co Rcdr has land rec)
Uintah* utahreach.usu.edu/uintah/index.htm	H11	18 Feb 1880	**Wasatch** Uintah County; 147 E Main St; Vernal, UT 84078; Ph. 435.781.5360 Details: (Co Clk has m, div, pro & ct rec; Co Rcdr has land rec)
Utah* www.co.utah.ut.us/	G6	3 Mar 1852	**Original county** Utah County; 100 E Center #3600; Provo, UT 84606; Ph. 801.370.8108 Details: (Co Clk has m rec from 1887, div & pro rec from 1859 & ct rec from 1885; Co Rcdr has land rec)
Wasatch* www.co.wasatch.ut.us/	F7	17 Jan 1862	**Davis, Green River** Wasatch County; 25 N Main St; Heber City, UT 84032; Ph. 435.654.3211 Details: (Co Clk has b & d rec 1898-1905, m rec from 1879, div & ct rec from 1898, pro rec from 1897 & land rec from 1862)
Washington www.washco.state.ut.us/	O2	3 Mar 1852	**Unorganized Territory** Washington County; 197 E Tabernacle St; St. George, UT 84770; Ph. 435.634.5712 Details: (Co Clk has m rec from 1887, div rec from 1878, pro & ct rec from 1874; Co Rcdr has land rec)
Wayne www.rootsweb.com/~utwayne/ _Wayne_index.html	L8	10 Mar 1892	**Piute** Wayne County; 18 S Main; PO Box 189; Loa, UT 84747; Ph. 435.836.2731 Details: (Co Clk has some b & d rec 1898-1927 & m, div, ct & pro rec from 1898; Co Rcdr has land rec from 1898)
Weber* www.co.weber.ut.us/	D6	3 Mar 1852	**Original county** Weber County; 2380 Washington Blvd #320; Ogden, UT 84401; Ph. 801.399.8400 Details: (Co Clk has m rec from 1887; Clk Dis Ct has div, pro & ct rec; Co Rcdr has land rec)

Notes

Notes

Red Clover

VERMONT

CAPITAL: MONTPELIER – STATE 1791 (14TH)

The earliest European to explore Vermont was Samuel de Champlain, who discovered Lake Champlain in 1609. The French and English disputed the area for years. The French built forts at Isle La Motte in 1666, Crown Point in 1730, and Ticonderoga in 1755. The first permanent settlement made by the English was Fort Dummer in 1724, later named Brattleboro. When France finally gave up its claim to the area following the French and Indian War in 1763, there were fewer than 300 settlers in Vermont.

With the defeat of the French, settlement began in earnest. New Hampshire granted land for 129 towns in Vermont between 1749 and 1764. New York's claim to the area was validated by King George III, resulting in a nullification of all grants made by New Hampshire. Although some grantees obtained new grants from New York, the others banded together under Ethan Allen to form the Green Mountain Boys. They resisted New York's efforts to evict those who did not receive New York grants. The Revolutionary War prevented major conflicts between the Green Mountain Boys and New York. However, Ethan Allen and his men did fight for the colonies, capturing forts Ticonderoga and Crown Point from the British.

In 1776, Vermont held a convention and declared its independence from New York. The next year a constitution was approved making Vermont an independent republic. Vermont remained a republic until statehood was granted in 1791. The settlers in Vermont carried on substantial trade with Canada, most of it avoiding British revenue officers. The War of 1812 severely restricted this smuggling so Vermont was very antiwar. When the war ended, many Vermonters left the state to farm better lands in Ohio and a few New Englanders came to replace them.

The Champlain Canal opened in 1823, connecting Vermont with New York City. In 1825, the Erie Canal opened, carrying Vermont settlers to Ohio and other western areas. Irish laborers came to work on Vermont railroads, the first of which opened in 1848. During the Civil War, Vermont supplied more than 34,000 men to the Union armies.

Most of the early settlers came from the New England colonies. Other large groups of immigrants came from Ireland in the mid-1800's and French Canada later in the century. Farmers from Finland came into the Markham Mountain region in southwestern Windsor County and the Equinox Mountain section of northern Bennington County. Welsh came to the midwest section of Rutland County to work in the slate quarries. Scottish and Italian stonecutters came to the quarries southeast of Montpelier. Russians, Poles, Czechs, Austrians, and Swedes came to the granite quarries of Rutland County. About half of the foreign-born population in Vermont came from Canada.

Look for vital records in the following locations:

- **Birth, death, marriage and divorce records:** Town clerks have kept these records since 1760. Many of these records have been indexed for the entire state. The Vital Records Section, Department of Health will search these indexes for a fee. This office also has divorce records from 1861 to 1968. For birth, marriage, and death records since 1955 and divorce

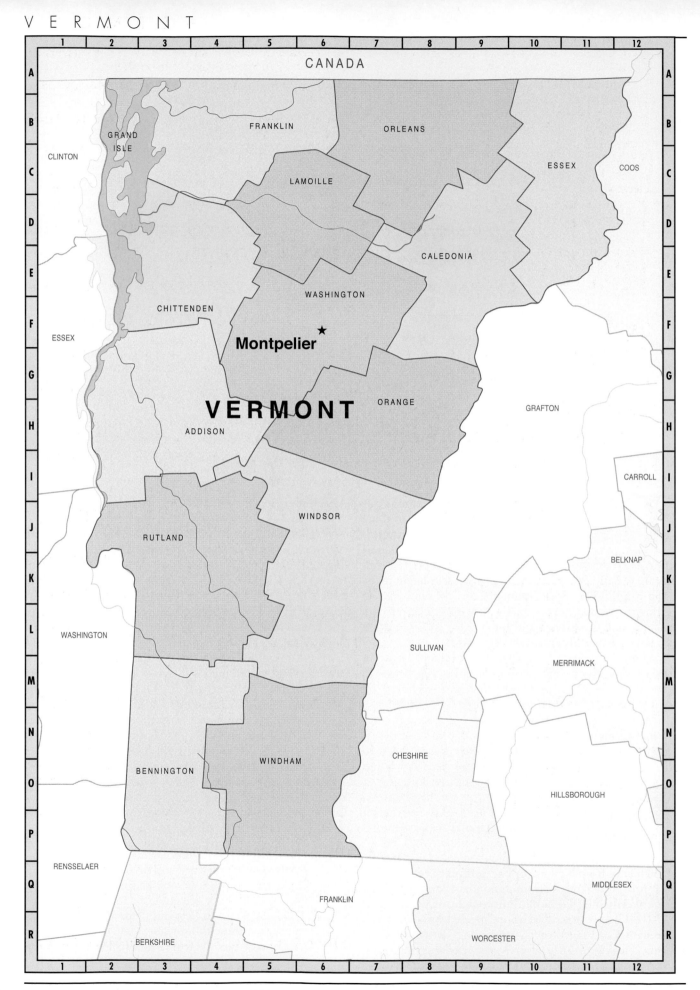

CANADA

CLINTON

GRAND ISLE

FRANKLIN

ORLEANS

ESSEX

COOS

LAMOILLE

ESSEX

CALEDONIA

CHITTENDEN

WASHINGTON

Montpelier ★

VERMONT

ORANGE

GRAFTON

ADDISON

CARROLL

WINDSOR

RUTLAND

BELKNAP

WASHINGTON

SULLIVAN

MERRIMACK

BENNINGTON

WINDHAM

CHESHIRE

HILLSBOROUGH

RENSSELAER

MIDDLESEX

FRANKLIN

BERKSHIRE

WORCESTER

records since 1968, contact the Division of Vital Statistics.

- **Census records:** The Vermont Historical Society Library has the largest genealogical collection in the state. Portions of some colonial censuses are available and have been published.
- **Land records:** Many colonial land records are at the Vermont State Archives, Division of State Papers. Later land transactions are kept by the town clerks.
- **Naturalization records:** Filed primarily in county and district courts.

Division of Vital Statistics
60 Main Street, PO Box 70
Burlington, Vermont 05402
802.863.7275

The Vital Records Section
Department of Health
PO Box 70
Montpelier, Vermont 05402

Vermont State Archives
Division of State Papers
Office of Secretary of State
109 State Street
Montpelier, Vermont 05602

Vermont Historical
Society Library
Pavilion Building
109 State Street
Montpelier, Vermont 05602

Societies and Repositories

Addison Town Historical Society; 288 Cedar Drive; Addison, Vermont 05491-8732

Alburgh Historical Society, Inc.; PO Box 453; Alburg, Vermont 05440

American Baptist. Samuel Colgate Historical Library; 1106 South Goodman; Street; Rochester, New York 14620; 716.473.1740

Archives of the Roman Catholic Diocese of Burlington; 351 North Avenue; Burlington, Vermont 05401; 802.658.6110

Assemblee des Eveques du Quebec; 1225 St. Joseph Blvd. East; Montreal, Quebec; Canada H2J 1L7

Bailey-Howe Library; University of Vermont; Burlington, Vermont 05405-0036; 802.656.2020; Fax 802.656.4038; Baptist records

Barnard Historical Society; Charles Danforth Public Library; Barnard, Vermont 05031

Barnet Historical Society; RR 1, Box 241; Barnet, Vermont 05821

Bennington Historical Society; West Main Street; Bennington, Vermont 05201; <www.benningtonmuseum.com/BHS.html>

Berlin Historical Society Inc.; 1921 Scott Hill Road; Berlin, Vermont 05602

Bethel Historical Society; Church Street; Bethel, Vermont 05032

Bradford Historical Society; PO Box 301; Bradford, Vermont 05033

Braintree Historical Society; RFD 1, Thayer Brook Road; Randolph, Vermont 05060;

Brattleboro Historical Society, Inc.; 23 West Street; Brattleboro, Vermont 05301

Bridport Historical Society; c/o Marjorie Huestis; 2947 Basin Harbor Road; Bridport, Vermont 05734

Bristol Historical Society Museum; Howden Hall Community Center; Main Street; Bristol, Vermont 05443

Brooks Memorial Library; 224 Main St.; Brattleboro, Vermont 05301

Burlington, Vermont Genealogical Group; 36 Franklin Square; Burlington, Vermont 05401

Cabot Historical Society; PO Box 63; Marshfield, Vermont 05658

Canaan Historical Society; PO Box 371; Canaan, Vermont 05903

Cavendish Historical Society; PO Box 110; Cavendish, Vermont 05142

Charleston Historical Society; 1896 VT Route 105; West Charleston, Vermont 05872

Charlotte Historical Society; 613 Hill's Point Road; Charlotte, Vermont 05445

Chelsea Historical Society; PO Box 206; Chelsea, Vermont 05038

Chester Historical Society; Main Street; Chester, Vermont 05143

Concord Historical Society; PO Box 195; Concord, Vermont 05824-0195

Congregational Library; 14 Beacon Street; Boston, Massachusetts 02108; 617.523.0470; Fax 617.523.0470

Crystal Lake Falls Historical Association; PO Box 253; Barton, Vermont 05822

Derby Historical Society; PO Box 357; Derby, Vermont 05829

Division of State Papers; Office of Secretary of State; 109 State Street; Montpelier, Vermont 05609-1103; 802.828.2308; Fax 802.828.5171

Dorset Historical Society; PO Box 52; Dorset, Vermont 05251;

Dover Historical Society; PO Box 53; East Dover, Vermont 05341-7705

Elmore Historical Society; PO Box 53; Lake Elmore, Vermont 05657

Enosburg Historical Society; PO Box 98; Enosburg Falls, Vermont 05450

Episcopal Diocesan Center; #5 Rock Point Road; Burlington, Vermont 05401-2735; 802.863.3431; Fax 802.860.1562

Essex Historical Society; 3 Browns River Road; Essex Jct., Vermont 05452; <www.essex.org/esxhs/esxhsfindex.htm>

Fairfax Historical Society; PO Box 145; Fairfax, Vermont 05454; 802.849.6638; <www.geocities.com/Heartland/Farm/9445/index.html>

Fairfield Historical Society; 1345 Northrup Road; Enosburg Falls, Vermont 05450

Fairlee Historical Society; PO Box 95; Fairlee, Vermont 05045

Family History Library; 35 North West Temple Street; Salt Lake City, Utah 84150; 800.346.6044 or 801.240.2584; <http://www.familysearch.org>; Find a Family History Center near you; <http://www.familysearch.org/Eng/Library/FHC/frameset_fhc.asp>

Fletcher Free Library; 235 College St.; Burlington, Vermont 05401

Genealogical Society of Vermont; PO Box 1553; St. Albans, Vermont 05478.1006; <www.rootsweb.com/~vtgsv>

General Services Center; Reference Research; US Route 2, Drawer 33; Middlesex, Vermont 05633.7601; 802.828.3286; Fax 802.828.3710

Georgia Historical Society Museum; PO Box 2072; Georgia, Vermont 05468

Glover Historical Society; Municipal Building; Glover, Vermont 05839; 802.525.8855

Grafton Historical Society; PO Box 202; Grafton, Vermont 05146

Green Mountain College Library; One College Circle; Poultney, Vermont 05764; 802.287.8225; Fax 802.287.8099 (Attention Library); (Methodist records)

Greensboro Historical Society; Highland Lodge; Greensboro, Vermont 05841

Groton Historical Society; PO Box 89; Groton, Vermont 05046; 802.584.3417

Guilford Historical Society; 236 School Road; Guilford, Vermont 05301

Halifax Historical Society; RR 4, Box 531; Brattleboro, Vermont 05301

Hartford Historical Society; PO Box 547; Hartford, Vermont 05047

Historical Society of Peru; PO Box 153; Peru, Vermont 05152

Historical Society of Windham County; PO Box 246; Newfane, Vermont 05345

Holland Historical Society; RD 1, Box 37, Derby Line; Holland, Vermont 05830

Huntington Historical Society; PO Box 147; Huntington, Vermont 05462

Hyde Park Historical Society; 97 Eden Street; Hyde Park, Vermont 05655

Island Pond Historical Society; PO Box 408; Island Pond, Vermont 05846

Isle La Motte Historical Society; Isle La Motte, Vermont 05463

Jamaica Historical Foundation; PO Box 287; Jamaica, Vermont 05343

Jericho Historical Society; PO Box 35; Jericho, Vermont 05465; <snowflakebentley.com/jhs.htm>

Lincoln Historical Society; c/o Town Clerk; Lincoln, Vermont 05443

Londonderry Historical Society; PO Box 114; So. Londonderry, Vermont 05155

Lowell Historical Society; 636 Irish Hill Road; Lowell, Vermont 05847

Lunenburg Historical Society; PO Box 5; Lunenburg, Vermont 05906

Lyndon Historical Society; PO Box 85; Lyndon Center, Vermont 05850; 802.626.8746; <www.sover.net/~boerad/historic.htm>

Manchester Historical Society; PO Box 363; Manchester, Vermont 05254

Marlboro Historical Society; PO Box 131; Marlboro, Vermont 05344

Memphremagog Historical Society; Goodrich Memorial Library; 70 Main Street; Newport, Vermont 05855

Middlesex Historical Society; 84 McCullough Hill Road; Middlesex, Vermont 05602

Milton Historical Society; PO Box 2; Milton, Vermont 05468

Missisquoi Valley Historical Society; East Main Street; North Troy, Vermont 05859

Montgomery Historical Society; PO Box 47; Montgomery, Vermont 05470

Moretown Historical Society; Moretown, Vermont 05660; 802.496.2090; <www.moretownvt.com/history3.html>

National Archives—Northeast Region (Boston); 380 Trapelo Road; Waltham, Massachusetts 02154; 617.647.8100; Fax 617.647.8460

New England Historic Genealogical Society; 101 Newbury Street; Boston, Massachusetts 02116-3007; 617.536.5740; Fax 617.536.7307

New Haven Historical Society; 70 East Street; New Haven, Vermont 05472

Northfield Historical Society; PO Box 88; Northfield, Vermont 05663

Norwich Historical Society; PO Box 1680; Norwich, Vermont 05055

Peacham Historical Association; 104 Thaddeus Stevens Road; Peacham, Vermont 05862; <www.peacham.net/historical/>

Pittsford Historical Society; PO Box 423; Pittsford, Vermont 05763;

Poultney Historical Society; 148 Upper Rd.; Poultney, Vermont 05764; <www.rootsweb.com/~vtphs/>

Pownal Historical Society, Inc.; PO Box 313; Pownal, Vermont 05261;

Publications Coordination; Family History Library; 35 N. West Temple; Salt Lake City, Utah 84150.3400

Randolph Historical Society; PO Box 15; Randolph Center, Vermont 05061

Reading Historical Society; Reading, Vermont 05062

Readsboro Historical Society; PO Box 158; Readsboro, Vermont 05350

Richford Historical Society; 186 So. Main St.; Richford, Vermont 05476

Rochester Historical Society; PO Box 7; Rochester, Vermont 05767

Royalton Historical Society; 4184 Route 14; Royalton, Vermont 05068

Rupert Historical Society; Box 2, Lewis Rd.; Rupert, Vermont 05768

Russell Collection, c/o The Dorothy Canfield Library; Main St.; Arlington, Vermont 05250

Rutland Historical Society; 96 Center Street; Rutland, Vermont 05701

Rutland Public Library; Court St.; Rutland, Vermont 05701

Salisbury Historical Society; 7 Forbes Circle; Middlebury, Vermont 05753

Saxtons River Historical Society; PO Box 18; Saxtons River, Vermont 05154

Shaftsbury Historical Society; PO Box 401; Shaftsbury, Vermont 05262

Shoreham Historical Society; Route 22-A; Shoreham, Vermont 05770; <steveworld.ksci.com/ShorehamHS/SHShome.htm>

Shrewsbury Historical Society; 996 Lincoln Hill Road; Cuttingsville, Vermont 05738

Sons of the American Revolution, Vermont Society; RFD Box 18; Norwich, Vermont 05055

Special Collections; Bailey/Howe Library; University of Vermont; Burlington, Vermont 05405-0036

Springfield Art & Historical Society; PO Box 313; Springfield, Vermont 05156

St. Albans Historical Society; PO Box 722; St. Albans, Vermont 05478

St. Johnsbury Historical Society; c/o Fairbanks Museum, Main St.; St. Johnsbury, Vermont 05819

Stannard Historical Society; 9 Willey Road; Greensboro Bend, Vermont 05842

Stowe Historical Society; Main Street; Stowe, Vermont 05672

Swanton Historical Society; 11 Lake St.; Swanton, Vermont 05488

Thetford Historical Society; PO Box 33; Thetford, Vermont 05074

Tinmouth Historical & Genealogical Society; 43 Chipmunk Crossing Dr.; Tinmouth, Vermont 05773.1179

Townshend Historical Society; PO Box 202; Townshend, Vermont 05353; <www.townshendvt.com>

Tunbridge Historical Society; 24 The Crossroad; Tunbridge, Vermont 05077

Univ. of Vermont Library; Burlington, Vermont 05401

Vermont Department of Health; PO Box 70; Burlington, Vermont 05402

Vermont Department of Libraries; 109 State Street; Montpelier, Vermont 05609-0601; 802.802.3268; Fax 802.828.2199

Vermont Finnish Society; RR1, Box 349A; Jamaica, Vermont 05343

Vermont French Canadian Genealogical Society; PO Box 65128; Burlington, Vermont 05406-5128; <members.aol.com/vtfcgs/genealogy/>

Vermont Genealogical Society; PO Box 422; Pittsford, Vermont 05763

Vermont Historical Society; Pavilion Office Bldg.; 109 State St.; Montpelier, Vermont 05609-0901; 802.828.3638; Fax 802.828.3638; <www.state.vt.us/vhs/>

Vermont Public Records Division; General Service Center; Reference Research; Drawer 33; Montpelier, Vermont 05633-7601; 802.828.3286; Fax 802.828.3710

Vermont State Archives; Office of the Secretary of State; State Office Building; 109 State Street Montpelier, Vermont 05609-1103; 802.828.2308; Fax 802.828.5171

Vernon Historians; PO Box 282; Vernon, Vermont 05354

Veterans' Affairs Office; Vermont Adjutant General; 120 State Street; Montpelier, Vermont 05620-4401; 802.828.3379; Fax 802.828.3381

Vital Records Office; Vermont Department of Health; 108 Cherry Street; Burlington, Vermont 05402; 802.863.7275; Fax 802.863.7425

Waitsfield Historical Society; PO Box 816; Waitsfield, Vermont 05673

Wallingford Historical Society; PO Box 327; Wallingford, Vermont 05773

Waterbury Historical Society; 28 North Main Street; Waterbury, Vermont 05676

Weathersfield Historical Society; PO Box 126; Weathersfield, Vermont 05151

Wells Historical Society; 8 Capron Lane; Wells, Vermont 05774

Welsh.American Genealogical Society; 60 Norton Ave.; Poultney, Vermont 05764.1011; <www.rootsweb.com/~vtwags>

West Haven Historical Society, Inc.; 834 Main St; West Haven, Vermont 05743

West Windsor Historical Society; PO Box 12; Brownsville, Vermont 05037; 802.484.7249

Westford Historical Society; PO Box 21; Westford, Vermont 05494; <www.geocities.com/westford_05494/>

Westminister Historical Society, Inc.; PO Box 2; Westminster, Vermont 05158-0002; <www.microserve.net/~rduffalo/wrhistsoc.html>

Whitingham Historical Society; PO Box 125; Jacksonville, Vermont 05342

Williamstown Historical Society; 498 Boyce Road; Williamstown, Vermont 05679

Williston Historical Society; PO Box 995; Williston, Vermont 05495

Woodstock Historical Society; 26 Elm Street; Woodstock, Vermont 05091; <www.uvm.edu/~histpres/vtiana/woodstockhs.html>

Bibliography and Record Sources

General Sources

A Guide to Newspaper Indexes in New England. [Holden, Mass.]: New England Library Association, 1978.

A Guide to Vermont's Repositories. Montpelier, Vermont: Vermont State Archives, 1986.

Basic Sources for Vermont Historical Research. Montpelier, Vermont: Office of the Secretary of State, 1981?

Bassett, T. D. Seymour, ed. Vermont: *A Bibliography of Its History.* Boston: G. K. Hall & Co. 1981.

Brigham, Loriman S. *A Calendar of Manuscripts in Certain Boxes at the Vermont Historical Society.* Montpelier, Vermont: [S.n.], 1970.

Brigham, Loriman S. *Guide to the "Miscellaneous File" of Uncatalogued Material in the Vermont Historical Society....* Montpelier, Vermont: [S.n.], 1969.

Carleton, Hiram. *Genealogical and Family History of the State of Vermont.* 2 vols. New York: Lewis Publishing Co., 1903.

Comstock, John Moore. *The Congregational Churches of Vermont and Their Ministry.* St. Johnsbury, Vermont: Caledonian Co., 1915.

Crandall, Ralph J., ed. *Genealogical Research in New England*. Baltimore: Genealogical Publishing Co., 1984.

Crocker, Henry. *History of the Baptists in Vermont*. Bellows Falls, Vermont: P. H. Gobie Press, 1913.

Cutter, William Richard. *New England Families, Genealogical and Memorial*. 4 vols. 1913. Reprinted and enlarged. New York: Lewis Historical Publishing Co., 1914.

Directory of Churches and Religious Organizations in the State of Vermont. Montpelier, Vermont: Historical Records Survey, 1939.

Dodge, Prentiss Cutler. *Encyclopedia, Vermont Biography*. Burlington, Vermont: Ullery Publishing Co., 1912.

Eichholz, Alice. *Collecting Vermont Ancestors*. Montpelier, Vermont: New Trails, 1986.

Final Report and Inventory of the Vermont Historical Records Survey, W.P.A.. Rutland, Vermont: Works Progress Administration, 1942.

Genealogist's Handbook for New England Research. 3rd. ed. Boston: New England Historic Genealogical Society, 1993.

Greenlaw, William Prescott. *The Greenlaw Index of the New England Historic Genealogical Society*. 2 vols. Boston: G. K. Hall, 1979.

Hall, Hiland. *The History of Vermont, from its Discovery to its Administration into the Union in 1791*. Albany, New York: J. Munsell, 1868.

Hall, Lu Verne V. *New England Family Histories and Genealogies: States of New Hampshire and Vermont*. Bowie, Maryland: Heritage Books, 2000.

Hemenway, Abby Maria, ed. *Vermont Historical Gazetteer: A Magazine Embracing a History of Each Town, Civil, Ecclesiastical, Biographical and Military*. 6 vols. Burlington, Vermont: A. M. Hemenway, 1868-91.

Historical Records Survey (Vermont). *A Directory of Churches and Religious Organizations in the State of Vermont*. Montpelier, Vermont: The Survey, 1939.

Historical Records Survey (Vermont). *Inventory of the Church Archives of Vermont, No. 1, Diocese of Vermont, Protestant Episcopal*. Montpelier, Vermont: The Survey, 1940.

Holbrook, Jay Mack. *Vermont's First Settlers*. Oxford, Massachusetts: Holbrook Research Institute, 1976. Alphabetically arranged land grants in Vermont, 1763 to 1803

Index to the Burlington Free Press. 6 vols. Montpelier, Vermont: Historical Records Survey, 1941.

Ireland, Norma Olin, and Winifred Irving. *Cutter Index: A Consolidated Index of Cutter's Nine Genealogy Series*. Fallbrook, California: Ireland Indexing Service, 197?.

Kent, Dorman B. E. *Vermonters*. Montpelier, Vermont: Vermont Historical Society, 1937.

New England Historic Genealogical Society. *English Origins of New England Families: From the New England Historical and Genealogical Register*. First Series, 3 vols. Boston, Massachusetts: The Society, 1984.

Rider, Fremont, ed. *American Genealogical-Biographical Index*. Vols. 1-186. Middletown, Connecticut: The Godfrey Memorial Library, 1952–.

Rising, Marsh Hoffman, *Vermont Newspaper Abstract: Vermont Gazette, The Vermont Gazette: Epitome of the World, The World, The Green-Mountain Farmer*. Boston: The New England Historic Genealogical Society, 2001.

Savage, James. *A Genealogical Dictionary of the First Settlers of New England: Showing Three Generations of Those Who Came Before May 1692*. 4 vols. 1860-62. Reprint. Baltimore: Genealogical Publishing Company, 1981.

The American Genealogical Index. Middletown, Connecticut: Published by a committee representing the cooperating subscribing libraries [at] Wesleyan University Station, 1942-51.

Thompson, Zadock. *History of Vermont*. Burlington, Vermont: Thompson, 1853.

Ullery, Jacob G. *Men of Vermont:* Brattleboro, Vermont: Transcript Publishing Co., 1894.

Vermont Research Outline. Series US-States, no. 45. Salt Lake City: Family History Library, 1988.

Atlases, Maps and Gazetteers

Graffagnino, J. Kevin. *The Shaping of Vermont: 1749-1877*. Rutland, Vermont: Vermont Heritage Press, 1983.

Hancock, William. *The Vermont Atlas and Gazetteer*. Yarmouth, Maine: D. Delorme, 1978.

Hayward, John. *A Gazetteer of Vermont: Containing Descriptions of all the Counties, Towns, and Districts in the State, and of its Principal Mountains, Rivers, Waterfalls, Harbors, Islands, and Curious Places*. Bowie, Maryland: Heritage Books, 1990.

Long, John H., ed. *Atlas of Historical County Boundaries: New Hampshire and Vermont*. New York: Simon & Schuster, 1993.

Slawson, George C., Arthur W. Bingham, and Sprague W. Drenan. *The Postal History of Vermont*. Collectors Club Handbook, no. 21. New York: Collectors Club, 1969.

Swift, Ester Munroe. *Vermont Place-Names: Footprints of History*. Brattleboro, Vermont: Stephen Greene Press, 1977.

Vermont Atlas and Gazetteer. 9th ed. Freeport, Maine: DeLorme Mapping Co., 1996.

Census Records

Available Census Records and Census Substitutes

Federal Census 1790, 1800, 1810, 1820, 1830, 1840, 1850, 1860, 1870, 1880, 1900, 1910, 1920, 1930.

Federal Mortality Schedules 1880.

Union Veterans and Widows 1890.

Dollarhide, William. *The Census Book: A Genealogist's Guide to Federal Census Facts, Schedules and Indexes*. Bountiful, Utah: Heritage Quest, 1999.

Holbrook, Jay Mack. *Vermont 1771 Census*. Oxford, Massachusetts: Holbrook Research Institute, 1982.

Kemp, Thomas Jay. *The American Census Handbook*. Wilmington, Delaware: Scholarly Resources, Inc., 2001.

Lainhart, Ann S. *State Census Records*. Baltimore: Genealogical Publishing Co., Inc., 1992.

Szucs, Loretto Dennis, and Matthew Wright. *Finding Answers in U.S. Census Records*. Ancestry Publishing, 2001.

Thorndale, William, and William Dollarhide. *Map Guide to the U.S. Federal Censuses, 1790-1920*. Baltimore: Genealogical Publishing Co., 1987.

Court Records, Probate and Wills

Note: Each county has one county court and one supreme court. Probate records are filed in a probate district. The probate district does not necessarily adhere to the county boundaries. Most records have not been microfilmed and each county must be contacted to search the court and probate records.

Vermont. Secretary of State. *State Papers of Vermont*. Montpelier, Vermont: Published by authority of Secretary of State, 1939-.

Emmigration, Immigration, Migration and Naturalization

Filby, P. William. *Passenger and Immigration Lists Index*.15 vols. Detroit: Gale Research, 1981–.

Stilwell, Lewis D. *Migration from Vermont*. Montpelier, Vermont: Vermont Historical Society, 1948.

United States. Bureau of Customs. *A Supplemental Index to Passenger Lists of Vessels Arriving At Atlantic & Gulf Coast Ports (Excluding New York) 1820-1874*. (Washington, D.C.: Filmed by the National Archives Record Services, 1960). National Archives Microfilm, M 334.

United States. Immigration and Naturalization Service. *Index to New England Naturalization Petitions, 1791-1906*. Washington, D.C.: National Archives, 1983. Microfilm.

United States. Immigration and Naturalization Service. *St. Albans District Manifest Records of Aliens Arriving from Foreign Contiguous Territory: Arrivals At Canadian Border Ports from January 1895 to June 30, 1954: Indexes (Soundex), 1895-1924*. Washington, D.C.: National Archives Records Service, 1986.

Land and Property

Bogart, Walter Thompson. *The Vermont Lease Lands*. Montpelier: Vermont Historical Society, 1950.

Charters Granted by the State of Vermont, 1779-1846. 2 vols. Vermont Public Records Division, 1974.

Denio, Herbert Williams. *Massachusetts Land Grants in Vermont*. Cambridge, Massachusetts: John Wilson and Son, University Press, 1920. Reprinted from *Publications of the Colonial Society of Massachusetts* 24 (March 1920): 35-99.

Holbrook, Jay Mack. *Vermont's First Settlers*. Oxford, Mass.: Holbrook Research Institute, 1976.

Index to the Papers of the Surveyors-General. 2nd ed.. Reprint. Montpelier, Vermont: Secretary of State, 1918. [S.l.: s.n., 1973].

State Papers of Vermont. 17 vols. Montpelier: Secretary of State 1918-69. Volumes have separate subjects. Vol. 5 is entitled *Petitions for Land Grants, 1778-1881*. Vol. 7 covers *New York Land Patents, 1668-1768, Covering Land and Included in the State of Vermont*.

Vermont. Secretary of State. *State Papers of Vermont*. Montpelier, Vermont: Published by authority of Secretary of State, 1939-.

Military

Clark, Byron N. *A List of Pensioners of the War of 1812. Vermont Claimants*. Baltimore: Genealogical Publishing Co., 1969.

Crockett, Walter Hill. *Revolutionary Soldiers Buried in Vermont*. 1903-1907. Reprint. Baltimore: Genealogical Publishing Co., 1959.

Daughters of the American Revolution (Vermont). *Genealogical Collection*. Microfilm. Washington, D.C.: Reproduction Systems for the Genealogical Society of Utah, 1971.

Fisher, Carleton E. *Soldiers, Sailors, and Patriots of the Revolutionary War, Vermont*. Camden, Maine: Picton Press, 1992

Goodrich, John E., comp. and ed. *Rolls of Soldiers in the Revolutionary War, 1775-1783*. Rutland, Vermont: Tuttle Co., 1904.

Johnson. Herbert T. *Vermont in the Spanish-American War*. Montpelier, Vermont: adjutant general. 1929.

Peck, Theodore S. *Revised Roster of Vermont Volunteers: and Lists of Vermonters Who Served in the Army and Navy of the United States During the War of the Rebellion, 1861-66*. Montpelier, Vermont: Watchman Publishing Co., 1892.

United States. Selective Service System. *Vermont, World War I Selective Service System Draft Registration Cards, 1917-1918*. National Archives Microfilm Publications, M1509. Washington, D.C.: National Archives, 1987-1988.

Vermont Adjutant General's Office. *Roster of Soldiers in the War of 1812-1814*. Montpelier, Vermont: Herbert T. Johnson, Adjutant General, 1933.

Vermont. Adjutant General. *Revised Roster of Vermont Volunteers and Lists of Vermonters Who Served in the Army and Navy of the United States during the War of the Rebellion, 1861-1866*. Montpelier, Vermont: Watchman, 1892.

Vital and Cemetery Records

Arnold, James N. *Index to James N. Arnold Tombstone Records' Collection*. [Knight Memorial Library] Providence, Rhode Island. (Salt Lake City: Filmed by the Genealogical Society of Utah, 1992). Microfilm.

Hyde, Arthur L. *Burial Grounds of Vermont*. [Townshend, Vermont]: Vermont Old Cemetery Association, 1991.

Jones, Gertrude H. *Cemetery Records, Eastern States Mission*. 11 vols. Typescript. [n.p.: n.p.]

Nichols, Joann H. *Index to Known Cemetery Listings in Vermont*. Brattleboro, Vermont: the author, 1976.

Proceedings of the Vermont Historical Society. – 1860-1929; New Ser., V. 1, No. 1 (Jan. 1930)-v. 11, No. 3-4 (Sept. 1943). Brattleboro, Vermont: The Society, 1860-1943.

Rollins, Alden M. *Vermont Warnings Out*. 2 vols. Camden, Maine: Picton Press, 1995-1997.

Vermont, Secretary of State. *General Index to Vital Records of Vermont, 1871-1908*. Salt Lake City: Genealogical Society of Utah, 1967. Microfilm, 120 rolls.

Vermont, Secretary of State. *General Index to Vital Records of Vermont, to 1870*. Salt Lake City: Genealogical Society of Utah, 1951. Microfilm, 287 rolls.

Vermont. Secretary of State. *State Records of Births, Marriages, and Deaths, 1909-1942*. (Salt Lake City: Filmed by the Genealogical Society of Utah, 1994-1997). Microfilm, 278 rolls.

Vermont. Secretary of State. *State Records of Births, Marriages, and Deaths, 1942-1954*. (Salt Lake City: Filmed by the Genealogical Society of Utah, 1994-1996). Microfilm, 133 rolls.

County Website	Map Index	Date Created	Parent County or Territory From Which Organized Address/Details
Addison home.att.net/~swaitela/Default.htm	H4	18 Oct 1785	**Rutland** Addison County; 5 Court St; Middlebury, VT 05753-1405; Ph. 802.388.4237 Details: (Twn Clks have b, m, d & bur rec; Co Clk has div & ct rec from 1797; Pro Judge has pro rec) Towns Organized Before 1800: Addison 1761, Bridport 1761, Cornwall 1761, Ferrisburgh 1762, Leicester 1761, Lincoln 1780, Middlebury 1761, Monkton 1762, New Haven 1761, Orwell 1763, Panton 1761, Ripton 1781, Salisbury 1761, Shoreham 1761, Starksboro 1780, Vergennes 1788, Waltham 1796, Weybridge 1761, Whiting 1763
Bennington www.rootsweb.com/~vtbennin/index.html	O3	11 Feb 1779	**Original county** Bennington County; 207 South St; Bennington, VT 05201; Ph. 802.447.2700 Details: (Twn Clks have b, m, d & bur rec; Co Clk has div rec from 1899 & ct rec from 1861; Pro Judge has pro rec) Towns Organized Before 1800: Arlington 1761, Bennington 1749, Dorset 1761, Glastenbury 1761, Landgrove 1780, Manchester 1761, Peru 1761, Pownal 1760, Rupert 1761, Sandgate 1761, Shaftsbury 1761, Sunderland 1761, Winhall 1761
Caledonia home.att.net/~local_history/ Caledonia-Co-VT.htm	E9	5 Nov 1792	**Orange** Caledonia County; 27 Main St; St. Johnsbury, VT 05819; Ph. 802.748.3813 Details: (Twn Clks have b, m, d, bur & land rec; Co Clk has div & ct rec from 1797; Pro Judge has pro rec) Towns Organized Before 1800: Barnet 1763, Burke 1782, Cabot 1780, Danville 1786, Groton 1789, Hardwick 1781, Lyndon 1780, Peacham 1763, Ryegate 1763, Sheffield 1793, St. Johnsbury 1785, Sutton 1782, Walden 1780, Waterford 1781, Wheelock 1785
Chittenden home.att.net/~local_history/ Chittenden-Co-VT.htm	F3	22 Oct 1787	**Addison** Chittenden County; 175 Main St; Burlington, VT 05401-8310; Ph. 802.863.7481 Details: (Twn Clks have b, m, d, bur, pro & land rec; Co Clk has div rec from 1829 & ct rec from 1798) Towns Organized Before 1800: Bolton 1763, Burlington 1763, Charlotte 1762, Colchester 1763, Essex 1763, Hinesburg, 1762, Huntington 1763, Jericho 1763, Milton 1763, Richmond 1794, Shelburne 1763, St. George 1763, Underhill 1763, Williston 1763.
Essex www.rootsweb.com/~vtessex/index.htm	C10	5 Nov 1792	**Orange** Essex County; PO Box 75; Guildhall, VT 05905; Ph. 802.676.3910 Details: (Co Clk has b & d rec from 1884, m & bur rec, a few div rec, ct rec from 1800 & land rec from 1762; Pro Judge has pro rec from 1800) Towns Organized Before 1800: Bloomfield 1762, Brunswick 1761, Canaan 1782, Concord 1780, Guildhall 1761, Lunenburg 1763, Maidstone 1761, Victory 1781.
Franklin www.rootsweb.com/~vtfrankl/ Franklin.html	B5	5 Nov 1792	**Chittenden** Franklin County; PO Box 808; St. Albans, VT 05478; Ph. 802.524.3863 Details: (Co Clk has div & ct rec from 1900; Twn Clks have b, m, d, bur & land rec; Pro Judge has pro rec) Towns Organized Before 1800: Bakersfield 1791, Berkshire 1781, Enosburg 1780, Fairfax 1763, Fairfield 1763, Fletcher 1781, Franklin 1789, Georgia 1763, Highgate 1763, Montgomery 1789, Richford 1780, Sheldon 1763, Swanton 1763, St. Albans 1763
Grand Isle d_larose.tripod.com/GrandIsleVT/	B2	9 Nov 1802	**Franklin, Chittenden** Grand Isle County; Rt 2; PO Box 7; North Hero, VT 05474; Ph. 802.372.8350 Details: (Pro Judge has pro rec; Twn Clks have b, m, d & land rec) Towns Organized Before 1800: Alburg 1781, Grand Isle 1779, Isles La Motte 1779, North Hero 1779, South Hero 1779
Jefferson		1 Nov 1810	**Addison, Orange, Caledonia, Orleans** Details: (see Washington) (Name changed to Washington 8 Nov 1814)

County Website	Map Index	Date Created	Parent County or Territory From Which Organized Address/Details
Lamoille www.usgennet.org/usa/vt/county/ lamoille1/index.htm	**C6**	**26 Oct 1835**	**Chittenden, Orleans, Franklin, Washington** Lamoille County; PO Box 303; Hyde Park, VT 05655-0303; Ph. 802.888.2207 Details: (Co Clk has div & ct rec from 1837; Twn Clks have b, m, d, bur & land rec; Pro Judge has pro rec) Towns Organized Before 1800: Cambridge 1781, Elmore 1781, Hyde Park 1781, Johnson 1792, Morristown 1763, Stowe 1763, Wolcott 1781
Orange www.usgennet.org/usa/vt/county/orange/	**H7**	**22 Feb 1781**	**Original county** Orange County; PO Box 95; Chelsea, VT 05038; Ph. 802.685.4610 Details: (Twn Clks have b, m, d, bur & land rec; Co Clk has div & ct rec from 1781 & land rec from 1771; Pro Judge has pro rec from 1771) Towns Organized Before 1800: Bradford 1770, Braintree 1781, Brookfield 1781, Chelsea 1781, Corinth 1764, Fairlee 1761, Newbury 1763, Orange 1781, Randolph 1781, Straford 1761, Thetford 1761, Topsham 1763, Turnbridge 1761, Vershire 1781, Washington 1781, West Fairlee 1779, Williamstown 1781
Orleans users.rootsweb.com/~vtorlean/ VTGenWeb.SM.htm	**B8**	**5 Nov 1792**	**Chittenden** Orleans County; PO Box 787; Newport, VT 05855-0787; Ph. 802.334.2711 Details: (Twn & City Clks have b, m, d & land rec; Dis Pro Ct has pro rec; Co Clk has div & ct rec from 1800) Towns Organized Before 1800: Barton 1789, Craftsbury 1781, Derby 1779, Glover 1783, Greensboro 1781, Holland 1779, Jay 1792, Westfield 1780
Rutland www.rootsweb.com/~vtrutlan/index.html	**J3**	**22 Feb 1781**	**Bennington** Rutland County; 83 Center St; Rutland, VT 05701; Ph. 802.775.4394 Details: (Secretary of State Office, Montpelier has b, m & d rec 1760-1955 & div rec 1760-1968; Twn Clks have land rec from 1826; Co Clk has land rec 1779-1826 & ct rec; Pro Ct has pro rec) Towns Organized Before 1800: Benson 1780, Brandon 1761, Castleton 1761, Chittenden 1780, Clarendon 1761, Danby 1761, Fair Haven 1779, Hubbardton 1764, Ira 1781, Mendon 1781, Middletown Springs 1784, Mt. Holly 1792, Mt. Tabor 1761, Pawlet 1761, Pittsford 1761, Poultney 1761, Rutland 1761, Sherburn 1761, Shrewsbury 1761, Sudbury 1763, Wallingford 1761, Wells 1761, West Haven 1792
Washington www.rootsweb.com/~vtwashin/index.htm	**E6**	**1 Nov 1810**	**Addison, Orange, Caledonia, Orleans** Washington County; PO Box 426; Montpelier, VT 05602-0426; Ph. 802.223.2091 Details: (Formerly Jefferson Co. Name changed to Washington 8 Nov 1814) (Secretary of State, Montpelier has b, m & d rec; Co Clk has div & ct rec; Pro Ct has pro rec; Twn & City Clks have land rec) Towns Organized Before 1800: Barre 1781, Berlin 1763, Calais 1781, Duxbury 1763, Marshfield 1782, Middlesex 1763, Montpelier 1781, Moretown 1763, Northfield 1781, Plainfield 1797, Roxbury 1781, Waitsfield 1782, Warren 1780, Waterbury 1763, Worcester 1763
Windham www.rootsweb.com/~vtwashin/index.htm	**O5**	**22 Feb 1781**	**Original county** Windham County; PO Box 207; Newfane, VT 05345-0207; Ph. 802.365.7979 Details: (Twn Clks have b, m, d, bur & land rec; Co Clk has div & ct rec from 1825; Pro Judge has pro rec) Towns Organized Before 1800: Athens 1780, Brattleboro 1753, Brookline 1794, Grafton 1754, Guilford 1754, Halifax 1750, Jamaica 1780, Londonderry 1780, Marlboro 1751, Newfane 1753, Putney 1753, Rockingham 1752, Townshend 1753, Woodbury 1781, Westminister 1752, Whitingham 1770, Wilmington 1751, Windham 1795
Windsor www.usgennet.org/usa/vt/county/windsor/	**J6**	**22 Feb 1781**	**Original county** Windsor County; 12 The Green; Woodstock, VT 05091-1212; Ph. 802.457.2121 Details: (Co Clk has div & ct rec from 1782; Twn Clks have b, m, d, bur & land rec; Pro Judge has pro rec) Towns Organized Before 1800: Andover 1761, Baltimore 1793, Barnard 1761, Bethel 1779, Bridgewater 1761, Cavendish 1761, Chester 1754, Hartford 1761, Hartland 1761, Ludlow 1761, Norwich 1761, Plymouth 1761, Pomfret 1761, Reading 1761, Royalton 1769, Sharon 1761, Springfield 1761, Stockbridge 1761, Weathersfield 1761, Weston 1799, Windsor 1761, Woodstock 1761

Notes

Dogwood

VIRGINIA

CAPITAL: RICHMOND — STATE 1788 (10TH)

James I granted a charter to the Virginia Company in 1606 to colonize Virginia. The first ships left in 1607 and formed the first permanent English settlement in the New World at Jamestown. Captain John Smith provided the strong leadership needed by the fledgling settlement. Through several harsh winters, the colony struggled to stay alive. New supplies and immigrants came each year, with the most crucial being in 1610, when the 65 surviving settlers were about to give up and return to England. In 1612, John Rolfe cultured the first commercial tobacco and later married Pocahontas. In 1618, the Virginia Company granted land to all free settlers and allowed a general assembly to be held. An Indian massacre in 1622 and internal disputes in the colony led James I to revoke the Virginia Company's charter and to make Virginia a royal colony in 1624.

Immigrants arrived nearly every month. By 1700, Virginia had 80,000 residents in the Tidewater area. Settlers began scattering over the coastal plain and the Piedmont Plateau before 1700. Between 1710 and 1740, passes were discovered across the Blue Ridge Mountains into the Shenandoah Valley. Emigrants from Pennsylvania and New Jersey began to enter the valley. In about 1730, there was a heavy immigration of Scotch-Irish, Germans, and Welsh from Pennsylvania into Virginia, most of whom settled in the upper valleys. They brought with them their religions–Presbyterian, Baptist, and Quaker. Methodist churches were established around 1800. By the mid-18th century, Virginia's population had grown to more than 280,000 people.

Between 1750 and 1784, land grants made to the Ohio Company encouraged exploration beyond the Alleghenies. Virginia organized the new area southeast of the Ohio River in 1775 and called it the District of West Augusta. Much of this area was ceded to Pennsylvania in 1779. In the 1770's the Wilderness Road across the Cumberland Gap opened up Kentucky. Kentucky County, which later became the state of Kentucky, was organized in 1776. Virginia was prominent in the Revolutionary War due to its great leaders like Thomas Jefferson, George Washington, Patrick Henry, George Mason, and Richard Henry Lee. Little fighting occurred on Virginian soil until the final years of the war and the final surrender at Yorktown.

In 1784, Virginia ceded its claims north of the Ohio River to the United States. Virginia entered the Union in 1788. Virginia seceded from the Union in 1861. Robert E. Lee was placed in command of the Confederate troops for Virginia, with Richmond as the capital of the Confederacy. The northwestern counties of the state refused to join in the secession and were admitted to the Union in 1863 as the state of West Virginia. Virginia was the central battlefield for the Civil War, with the first major battle at Bull Run (Manassas) and the final surrender at Appomattox. An estimated 155,000 men from Virginia fought for the Confederacy. Virginia was readmitted to the Union in 1870. The majority of foreign-born immigrants include Russians, English, Germans, Italians, Greeks, Polish, Czechs, Irish, Austrians, and Hungarians.

Look for vital records in the following locations:

- **Birth and death records:** Until 1786, the Anglican Church was the state church of Virginia. In accordance with English law, the church kept parish registers of vital statistics. Unfortunately, most of these are no longer in existence. Those that do exist have been photocopied and are in the Virginia State Library. The Archives Division of the Virginia State Library has copies of all existing Virginia birth and death records prior to 1896. Most have also been transcribed and published.
- **Land records:** In 1704, all Virginia landowners except those in Lancaster, Northumberland, Westmoreland, Richmond, and Stafford Counties

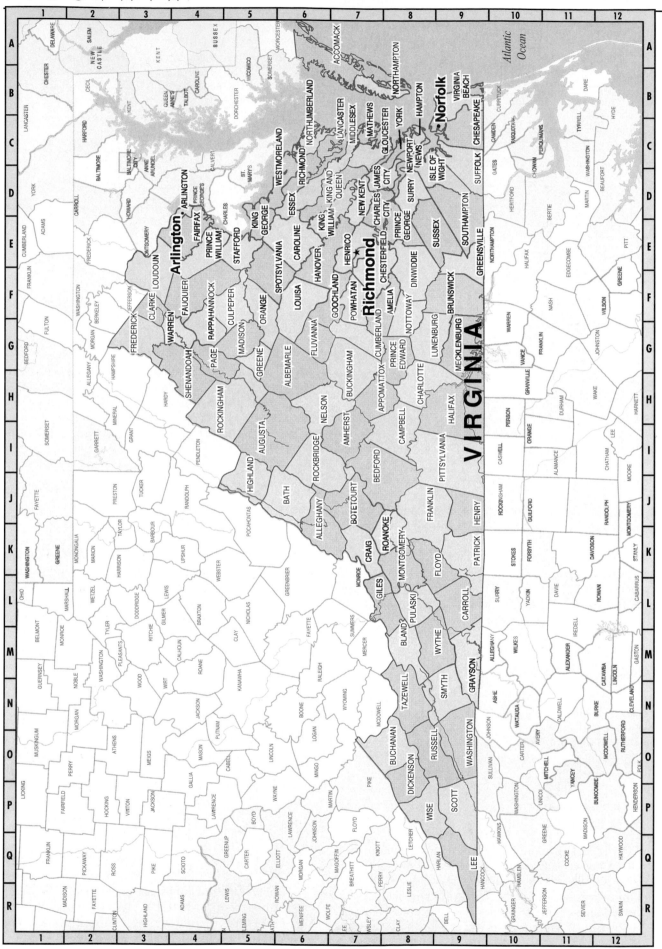

had to pay a Quit Rent to the king for every fifty acres. A Quit Rent list was made in 1704 for all who paid. Statewide registration of vital statistics began in 1912 and is at the Office of Vital Records.

- **Marriage records:** Archives Division of the Virginia State Library has copies of all existing Virginia marriage records 1853-1935. Beginning in 1660, a couple could marry by posting a bond with civil authorities or publishing banns at church. Reporting was required after 1780, but was sometimes done before that. Probate records are at the county level with the general court and at the county and circuit superior court. Independent cities have probates at the circuit court clerk's office. Lists of residents are available for some colonial years. Lists for 1624 and 1779 have been published.

Virginia State Library
11th Street at Capitol Square
Richmond, Virginia 23219
804.225.5000

Office of Vital Records
PO Box 1000
Richmond, Virginia 23208

Societies and Repositories

Albemarle County Historical Society; 220 Court Square; Charlottesville, Virginia 22901

Alderman Library; Univ. of Virginia; Charlottesville, Virginia 22903

Alexandria Library; 717 Queen St.; Alexandria, Virginia 22314

Alleghany Highlands Genealogical Society; 1011 N. Rockbridge St.; Covington, Virginia 24426

Arlington Central Library; 1015 N. Quincy St.; Arlington, Virginia 22201

Augusta County Genealogical Society; 2002 Lyndhurst Rd.; Waynesboro, Virginia 22980-5226

Augusta County, Virginia Historical Society; PO Box 686; Staunton, Virginia 24401

Bath County Historical Society, Inc.; PO Box 212; Warm Springs, Virginia 24484

Bedford Historical Society, Inc.; PO Box 602; Bedford, Virginia 24523

Blue Ridge Regional Library; 310 E. Church St.; Martinsville, Virginia 24112

Bristol Public Library; 701 Goode St.; Bristol, Virginia 24201

Caroline County Genealogical Society; PO Box 9; Bowling Green, Virginia 22427

Carroll Co. Hist. Soc. Museum; 307 N. Main St.; Hillsville, Virginia 24343

Carroll County Genealogical Club; PO Box 395; Hillsville, Virginia 24343

Carroll County Historical Society; PO Box 937; Hillsville, Virginia 24343

Central Virginia Genealogical Association; PO Box 5583; Charlottesville, Virginia 22905-5583

Chesterfield Historical Society of Virginia; PO Box 40; Chesterfield, Virginia 23832

Claiborne County Historical Society; Rt. 1, Box 589; Jonesville, Virginia 24263

Clinch Mountain Militia Chapter, SAR; 5 Windswept; Tazewell, Virginia 24651; 540.979.8251

Col. Fielding Lewis Chapter, SAR; 1314 Sophia Street; Fredericksburg, Virginia 22401-3742; 540.371.2370; <members.home.net/sarfielding/>

College of William and Mary; Earl Gregg Swem Library; PO Box 220; Williamsburg, Virginia 23187; 804.221.3500; Fax 804.221.3088

Colonel George Waller Chapter, SAR; 45 8th Street, Drawer A; Fieldale, Virginia 24089-0116; 540.673.6057

Culpeper Historical Society, Inc.; PO Box 785; Culpeper, Virginia 22701

Culpeper Minute Men Chapter, SAR; 11201 Springfield; Fredericksburg, Virginia 22408; 540.710.6764; <www.home.earthlink.net/~mmelyman/>

Culpeper Town and Co. Library; Main & Mason Sts.; Culpeper, Virginia 22701

Cumberland County Historical Society; Box 88; Cumberland, Virginia 23040

Dan River Chapter, SAR; 221 Weaver Street; Eden, Virginia 27266; 910.627.7966

Dan River Chapter, SAR; 4618 Black Stump Road; Weems, Virginia 22576.2003; 804.435.7088

Danville Public Library; 511 Patton St.; Danville, Virginia 24541

Division of Vital Records; State Health Department; PO Box 1000; Richmond, Virginia 23208-1000; 804.225.5000

Fairfax City Regional Library, Fairfax Co. Public Library System, Virginia Rm.; 3915 Chain Bridge Rd; Fairfax, Virginia 22030

Fairfax Genealogical Society; PO Box 2290; Merrifield, Virginia 22116-2290

Fairfax Historical Society; PO Box 415; Fairfax, Virginia 22030

Family History Library; 35 North West Temple Street; Salt Lake City, Utah 84150; 800.346.6044 or 801.240.2584; <www.familysearch.org>; Find a Family History Center near you; <http://www.familysearch.org/Eng/Library/FHC/frameset_fhc.asp>

Fauquier Heritage Society; PO Box 548; Marshall, Virginia 22115

Fincastle Resolutions Chapter, SAR; 3161 Stoneridge Rd., SW; Roanoke, Virginia 24014-4217; 540.345.8521

Fort Harrison Chapter, SAR; 879 Airport Road; Bridgewater, Virginia 22812.3500; 540.828.4669

Franklin County Genealogical Society; PO Box 316; Ferrum, Virginia 24088

Fredericksburg Regional Genealogical Society; PO Box 42013; Fredericksburg, Virginia 22404

Ft. Eustis Historical and Archaeological Association; PO Box 4408; Ft. Eustis, Virginia 23604

Gen. William Campbell Chapter, SAR; 19770 McCray Drive; Abingdon, Virginia 24211; 540.623.2442

Genealogical Research Institute of Virginia; PO Box 29178; Richmond, Virginia 23242-0178

Genealogical Society of Page County, Virginia; Page Public Library; 100 Zerkel St.; Luray, Virginia 22835

George Mason Chapter, SAR; 1740 Key West Lane; Vienna, Virginia 22182-2318; 703.281.5915

George Washington Chapter, SAR; 2202 Guildmore Road; Reston, Virginia 20191-4902; 703.620.9879

Goochland County Historical Society; Goochland, Virginia 23063

Grayson County Historical Society, Inc.; PO Box 529; Independence, Virginia 24348-0529

Greene County Historical Society; PO Box 185; Stanardsville, Virginia 22973

Hampton Public Library; 4205 Victoria Blvd.; Hampton, Virginia 23669

Handley Library; PO Box 58; Winchester, Virginia 22601; 540.662.9041; Fax 540.722.4769

Harrisonburg-Rockingham Hist. Soc. Library; 328 High St., PO Box 716; Dayton, Virginia 22821

Historical Society of Washington County, Virginia; Box 484; Abingdon, Virginia 24210

Holston Territory Genealogical Society; PO Box 433; Bristol, Virginia 24203-0433

Isle of Wight County Historical Society; PO Box 121; Smithfield, Virginia 23431

James Monroe Chapter, SAR; Route 2, Box 710; Montrose, Virginia 22520; 804.493.9522

James Monroe Museum & Memorial Library; 908 Charles St.; Fredericksburg, Virginia 22401

Jefferson / Madison Regional Library; 201 E. Market St.; Charlottesville, Virginia 22903

Jewish Genealogical Society of Tidewater; Jewish Community Center; 7300 Newport Ave.; Norfolk, Virginia 23505

Jones Memorial Library; 2311 Memorial Avenue; Lynchburg, Virginia 24501; 804.846.0501; Fax 804.846.0501

King George County Historical Society; PO Box 424; King George, Virginia 22485

Kirn Norfolk Public Library; 301 E. City Hall Ave.; Norfolk, Virginia 23510

Lee County Historical and Genealogical Society; PO Box 231; Jonesville, Virginia 24263

Library of Virginia (formerly Virginia State Library and Archives); 800 East Broad Street; Richmond, Virginia 23219-1905; 804.692.3500; Fax 804.692.3556;

Lt. David Cox Chapter, SAR; 1939 Englewood Road; Galax, Virginia 24333; 540.236-4682

Martha Woodroof Hiden Virginiana Rm., Main St. Library; 110 Main St.; Newport News, Virginia 23601

Martinsville Henry County Historical Society; PO Drawer 432; Martinsville, Virginia 24114

Mary Ball Washington Museum & Library; Inc. PO Box 97; Lancaster, Virginia 22503-0097

Mathews County Historical Society; PO Box 885; Mathews, Virginia 23109

Menno Simons Hist. Library / Archives; Eastern Mennonite College; Harrisonburg, Virginia 22801

Mount Vernon Genealogical Society; 1500 Shenandoah Rd.; Alexandria, Virginia 22308

National Archives-Mid-Atlantic Region; 5000 Wissahickon Avenue

National Gen. Soc. Library; 4527 17th St. North; Arlington, Virginia 22207; 703.525.0052; < genealogy.org/NGS/>

New River Historical Society; PO Box 373; Newbern, Virginia 24126

New River Valley Chapter, SAR; PO Box 638; Pembroke, Virginia 24136; 540.626.7193

Norfolk Chapter, SAR; 637 E. Lynn Shores Circle; Virginia Beach, Virginia 23452; 757.340.2536

Norfolk County Historical Society; Chesapeake Public Library; 298 Cedar Rd.; Chesapeake, Virginia 23320.5512

Norfolk Genealogical Society; PO Box 12813; Thomas Comer Sta.; Norfolk, Virginia 23502-5309

Northern Neck Historical Society; Westmoreland County; Montross, Virginia 22520

Northern Neck of Virginia Gen. Soc. Library; PO Box 511; Heathsville, Virginia 22473-0511

Orange County Historical Society; 130 Caroline St.; Orange, Virginia 22960

Page Public Library; 100 Zerkel St.; Luray, Virginia 22835

Palatines to America, Virginia Chapter; 3249 Cambridge Court; Fairfax, Virginia 22032-1942

Patrick County Genealogical Society; PO Drawer 1016; Stuart, Virginia 24171

Patrick Henry Chapter, SAR; 158 Rosecliff Farms; Amherst, Virginia 24521; 804.946.2050

Petersburg Public Library; 137 S. Sycamore St.; Petersburg, Virginia 23803

Pittsylvania Historical Society; PO Box 846; Chatham, Virginia 24531

Portsmouth Genealogical Society; PO Box 7062; Portsmouth, Virginia 23707-7062

Presbyterian Church Archives; Union Theological Seminary in Virginia; 3401 Brook Road; Richmond, Virginia 23227; 804.355.0671; Fax 804.355.3919

Prince William County Genealogical Society; PO Box 2019; Manassas, Virginia 20108-0812

Prince William Public Library System, RELIC, Bull Run Regional Library; 8051 Ashton Ave.; Manassas, Virginia 20109-2892; 703.792.4540; <www.pwcgov.org/library/services/relic>

Radford Public Library; Recreation Bldg.; Radford, Virginia 24141

Richmond Chapter, SAR; 5815 West Club Lane; Richmond, Virginia 23226; 804.288.2135

Roanoke City Public Library, Virginia Rm.; 706 S. Jefferson St.; Roanoke, Virginia 24016

Roanoke Valley Historical Society; PO Box 1904; Roanoke, Virginia 24008

Rockbridge Volunteers Chapter, SAR; Route 724, Box 76; Brownsburg, Virginia 24415; 540.348.5698

Rockingham County Historical Society; 301 S. Main St.; Dayton, Virginia 22812

Rockingham Public Library; 45 Newman Ave.; Harrisonburg, Virginia 22801

Sergeant-Major John Champe Chapter, SAR; 19433 Loudoun Orchard Road; Leesburg, Virginia 20175

Shenandoah Co. Library; 300 Stoney Creek Blvd.; Edinburg, Virginia 22824; 504.984.8200; Fax 540.984.8207; <www.shenandoah.co.lib.va.us>

Simpson Library, Mary Washington College; 1801 College Ave.; Fredericksburg, Virginia 22401-4664; 703.899.4594; Fax 703.899.4499

Society of the Old Creek Cross; 9501 4th Place; Lorton, Virginia 22079

Sons of the American Revolution, Virginia Society; 3600 West Broad, Suite 446; Richmond, Virginia 23230.4918

Southside Regional Library; PO Box 10; Boydton, Virginia 23917

Southwestern Virginia Genealogical Society; PO Box 12485; Roanoke, Virginia 24026

Surry County Historical Society and Museum; PO Box 262; Surry, Virginia 23883

Thomas Balch Library; 208 West Market St.; Leesburg, Virginia 22075; 703.777.0132

Thomas Jefferson Chapter, SAR; 3115 Dundee Road; Earlysville, Virginia 22936-9623; 804.975-0569; <monticello.avenue.org/tjcsar/>

Thomas Nelson, Jr. Chapter, SAR; 821 Sharpley Avenue; Hampton, Virginia 23666-2818; 757.826.8644

Tidewater Genealogical Society; PO Box 7650; Hampton, Virginia 23666

Tidewater, Afro-American Historical and Genealogical Society; 2200 Crossroad Trail; Virginia Beach, Virginia 23456

United Daughters of the Confederacy; UDC General Headquarters; 328 North Boulevard; Richmond, Virginia 23220-4057; 804.353.1396;

University of Virginia; Alderman Library; Charlottesville, Virginia 22903; 804.924.3021; Fax 804.924.1431

Virginia Baptist Historical Society; Boatwright Memorial Library; PO Box 34; University of Richmond; Richmond, Virginia 23173; 804.289.8434 (by appointment only)

Virginia Beach Genealogical Society; PO Box 62901; Virginia Beach, Virginia 23466-2901

Virginia Genealogical Society; 5001 W. Broad St. # 115; Richmond, Virginia 23230-3023;

Virginia Historical Library; PO Box 7311; Richmond, Virginia 23211

Virginia Historical Society; 428 North Boulevard; Richmond, Virginia 23220; <www.vahistorical.org/index.htm>

Virginia State Library; 11th St. at Capitol Square; Richmond, Virginia 23219-3491

Virginia-North Carolina, Piedmont Genealogical Society; PO Box 2272; Danville, Virginia 24541-2272

Waynesboro Public Library; 600 S. Waynes Ave.; Waynesboro, Virginia 22980

William & Mary College Library; Williamsburg, Virginia 23185

Williamsburg Chapter, SAR; 47 Whittaker's Mills Road; Williamsburg, Virginia 23185-5534; 757.229.0496

Winchester-Frederick County Historical Society; c/o Handley Regional Library; PO Box 58; Winchester, Virginia 22604

Bibliography and Record Sources

General Sources

A Key to Survey Reports and Microfilm of the Virginia Colonial Records Project. Richmond: Virginia State Library and Archives, 1990.

Axelson, Edith F. *A Guide to Episcopal Church Records in Virginia*. Athens, Georgia: Iberian Publishing, 1988.

Bible Records From Virginia. Salt Lake City: Genealogical Society of Utah, 1947. Microfilm, 4 rolls.

Brigham, Clarence Saunders. *History and Bibliography of American Newspapers, 1690-1820*. 2 vols. Worcester, Massachusetts: American Antiquarian Society, 1947, 1975.

Brock, Robert Alonza. *Virginia and Virginians*. 2 vols. Richmond, Virginia and Toledo, OH: H.H. Hardesty, 1888.

Brown, Stuart E., Jr. *Virginia Genealogies: A Trial List of Printed Books and Pamphlets*. 2 vols. Berryville, Virginia: Virginia Book, 1967, 1980.

Cappon, Lester J. *Virginia Newspapers 1821-1935: A Bibliography with Historical Introduction and Notes*. New York: D. Appleton Century, 1936.

Cerny, Johni, and Gary J. Zimmerman. *Before Germanna: The Origins and Ancestry of Those Affiliated with the Second Germanna Colony of Virginia*. Monograph series, 1-12. Bountiful, Utah: American Genealogical Lending Library, 1990.

Clark, Jewell T., and Elizabeth Terry Long. *A Guide to Church Records in the Archives Branch, Virginia State Library*. Richmond: Virginia State Library, Archives and Records Division, 1981.

Clay, Robert Young. *Virginia Genealogical Resources*. Detroit: Detroit Society of Genealogical Research, 1980.

Dabney Virginius. *Virginia: The New Dominion*. Charlottesville: University Press of Virginia, 1971

Daughters of the American Revolution. Virginia. Genealogical Records Committee. *Miscellaneous Bible, Tombstone and Court Records Submitted by Various Virginia Chapters of the Daughters of the American Revolution*. Salt Lake City: Genealogical Society of Utah, 1970. Microfilm.

Des Cognet, Louis, Jr., comp. *English Duplicates of Lost Virginia Records*. Baltimore: Genealogical Publishing Co., 1981.

Executive Journals of the Council of Colonial Virginia. 6 vols. Richmond: Virginia State Library, 1966-1978.

Finkelman, Paul. *State Slavery Statutes: Guide to the Microfiche Collection*. Frederick, Md.: University Publications of America, 1989.

Fleet, Beverley. *Virginia Colonial Abstracts*. 34 vols. 1937-1949. Reprint, Baltimore: Genealogical Publishing, 1988.

Foley, Louise Pledge Heath. *Early Virginia Families Along the James River:* 2 vols. 1978. Reprint. Baltimore: Genealogical Publishing Co., 1990.

Foote, William Henry. *Sketches of Virginia: Historical and Biographical*. 2 vols. Philadelphia: William S. Marten, 1850-56.

Greer, George C. *Early Virginia Immigrants, 1623-1666.* 1912. Reprint. Baltimore: Genealogical Publishing Co., 1982.

Hume, Robert. *Early Child Immigrants to Virginia, 1618-1642.* Baltimore: Magna Carta Book Co., 1986.

Stanard, William Glover. *Some Emigrants to Virginia: Memoranda in Regard to Several Hundred Emigrants to Virginia During the Colonial Period Whose Parentage is Shown or Former Residence Indicated by Authentic Records.* 1911. Reprint. Baltimore: Genealogical Publishing Co., 1979.

Withington, Lathrop. *Virginia Gleanings in England: Abstracts of 17th and 18th-Century English Wills and Administrations Relating to Virginia and Virginians.* Baltimore: Genealogical Publishing, 1980.

Land and Property

Auditor's Office. *Pay Rolls of Militia Entitled to Land Bounty Under Act of Congress of 1850.* Richmond, Virginia: Auditor's Office, 1851.

Brookes-Smith, Joan E. *Master Index Virginia Surveys and Grants 1774-1791.* Frankfort: Kentucky Historical Society, 1976.

Burgess, Louis A., comp. and ed. *Virginia Soldiers of 1776, Compiled from Documents on File in the Virginia Land Office; Together with Material Found in the Archives Department of the Virginia State Library and Other Reliable Sources.* 3 vols. Reprint. Spartanburg, SC: Reprint Co., 1973.

Cabell, Priscilla Harriss. *Turff and Twigg: The French Lands.* Richmond, Virginia: Priscilla Harriss Cabell, 1988.

Egle, William Henry. *Old Rights, Property Rights, Virginia Entries and Soldiers Entitled to Donation Lands.* Harrisburg, Virginia: C.M. Busch, State Printer, 1896.

Hone, Wade E. *Land and Property Research in the United States.* Salt Lake City: Ancestry Incorporated, 1997.

Hopkins, William Lindsay. *"Virginia Land Patent Books." Magazine of Virginia Genealogy.* Richmond: Virginia Genealogical Society, 1984-.

Hopkins, William Lindsay. *Virginia Revolutionary War Land Grant Claims 1783-1850 (Rejected).* Richmond: Gen-N-Dex, 1988.

Hudgins, Dennis, ed. *Cavaliers and Pioneers: Abstracts of Virginia Land Patents and Grants, 1732-1741.* Vol. 4 of 5. Richmond: Virginia Genealogical Society, 1994.

Hudgins, Dennis, ed. *Cavaliers and Pioneers: Abstracts of Virginia Land Patents and Grants, 1741-1749.* Vol. 5 of 5. Richmond: Virginia Genealogical Society, 1994.

Kaylor, Peter Cline. *Abstract of Land Grant Surveys, 1761-1791.* 1938. Baltimore: Clearfield Co., 1991.

Nugent, Nell Marion. *Cavaliers and Pioneers: Abstracts of Virginia Land Patents and Grants.* 5 vols. Richmond: Dietz Print: Virginia State Library: Virginia Genealogical Society, 1934, 1963, 1977-1979, 1994.

Parks, Gary. *Virginia Land Records: From the Virginia Magazine of History and Biography, the William and Mary College Quarterly, and Tyler's Quarterly.* Baltimore: Genealogical Publishing Co., 1982.

Robinson, W. Stitt. *Mother Earth—Land Grants in Virginia, 1607-1699.* Williamsburg: 350th Anniversary Celebration Corp., 1957.

Schreiner-Yantis, Netti. *Montgomery County, Virginia-Circa 1790: A Comprehensive Study, Including the 1789 Tax Lists, Abstracts of Over 800 Land Surveys and Data Concerning Migration.* Springfield, Virginia, 1972.

Smith, Annie Laurie Wright, comp. *The Quit Rents of Virginia, 1704.* Baltimore: Genealogical Publishing Co., 1980.

Wardell, Patrick G. *War of 1812 Virginia Bounty Land and Pension Applicants.* Bowie, Maryland: Heritage Books, 1987.

Military

Abercrombie, Janice L. *Virginia Publick Claims.* 3 vols. Athens, Georgia: Iberian Publishing Co., 1992.

Auditor's Office. *Muster Rolls of the Virginia Militia in the War of 1812.* Richmond, Virginia: Auditor's Office, 1852.

Bockstruck, Lloyd DeWitt. *Virginia's Colonial Soldiers.* Baltimore: Genealogical Publishing Co., 1988.

Brumbaugh, Gaius M. *Revolutionary War Records: Virginia Army and Navy Forces with bounty Land Warrants for Virginia Military District of Ohio and Virginia Scrip, From Federal and State Archives.* 1936. Reprint. Baltimore: Genealogical Publishing Co., 1967.

Butler, Stuart Lee. *Guide to Virginia Militia Units in the War of 1812.* Athens, Georgia: Iberian Publishing Co; 1988.

Butler, Stuart Lee. *Virginia Soldiers in the United States Army, 1800-1815.* Atlanta: Iberian Publishing Co., 1986.

Confederate Pension Applications, Virginia, Acts of 1888, 1900, 1902; Index, 1888-1934. Microreproduction of original records at the Virginia State Library and Archives in Richmond, Virginia. (Salt Lake City: Filmed by the Genealogical Society of Utah, 1988).

Crozier, William Armstrong. *Virginia Colonial Militia, 1651-1776.* 1905. Reprint. Baltimore: Genealogical Publishing Co., 1982.

Dorman, John Frederick, comp. *Virginia Revolutionary Pension Applications.* 51 vols. Washington, D.C.: n.p., 1958-1995.

Eckenrode, H. J. *List of the Colonial Soldiers of Virginia.* 1905. Reprint. Baltimore: Genealogical Publishing Co., 1974.

Eckenrode, H. J. *List of the Revolutionary Soldiers of Virginia.* Richmond: D. Bottom, 1912.

Egle, William Henry. *Old Rights, Property Rights, Virginia Entries and Soldiers Entitled to Donation Lands.* Harrisburg, Virginia: C.M. Busch, State Printer, 1896.

Gwathmey, John H. *Historical Register of Virginians in the Revolution: Soldiers, Sailors, Marines: 1775-1783.* Richmond, Virginia: Deitz Press, 1938. Reprint. Baltimore: Genealogical Publishing Co., 1973.

Haulsee, W. M., F. G. Howe, and A. C. Dayle, comps. *Soldiers of the Great War.* 3 vols. Washington, D.C.: Soldiers Record Publishing Association, 1920.

Hemphill, W. Edwin, ed. *Gold Star Honor Roll of Virginians in the Second World War.* Charlottesville, Virginia: Virginia World War II History Commission, 1947.

Howard, H. E. *Virginia Regimental History Series.* Lynchburg, Virginia: H. E. Howard, 1982-.

Lewis, Virgil A. *Soldiery of West Virginia in the French and Indian War: Lord Dunmore's War: The Revolution: The Later Indian Wars: The Whiskey Insurrection: The Second War with England:*

The War with Mexico, and Addenda Relating to West Virginians in the Civil War. Baltimore: Genealogical Publishing Co., 1967.

McCallister, Joseph T. *Index to Saffell's List of Virginia Soldiers in the Revolution.* Hot Springs, Virginia: McAllister Publishing Co., 1913.

Muster Rolls, Payrolls, and Index of the Virginia Militia in the War of 1812. Salt Lake City: Genealogical Society of Utah, 1955.

Taylor, Philip F. *A Calendar of the Warrants for Land in Kentucky, Granted for Service in the French and Indian War.* 1917. Reprint, Baltimore: Genealogical Publishing Company, 1967.

United States. Selective Service System. *Virginia, World War I Selective Service System Draft Registration Cards, 1917-1918.* Washington, D.C.: National Archives, 1987-1988.

Virginia Military Organizations in the World War: with Supplement of Distinguished Service. Richmond: n.p., 1927.

Virginia Military Records: From the Virginia Magazine of History and Biography, the William and Mary College Quarterly, and Tyler's Quarterly. Baltimore: Genealogical Publishing, 1983.

Virginia Regimental Histories Series. Lynchburg, Virginia: H. E. Howard, 1982–.

Virginia Revolutionary War State Pensions 1980; Reprint, Easley, South Carolina: Southern Historical Press, 1982.

Virginia. Office of the Secretary of Virginia Military Records. *Index to Confederate Service Records of Virginia; Confederate Service Records of Virginia, 1861-1865.* Microfilm of original at the State Library in Richmond, Virginia. (Salt Lake City: Filmed by the Genealogical Society of Utah, 1954).

Wallace, Lee A. *A Guide to Virginia Military Organizations, 1861-1865.* Lynchburg, Virginia: H. E. Howard, 1986.

Wardell, Patrick G. *War of 1812: Virginia Bounty Land and Pension Applications.* Bowie, Maryland: Heritage Books, 1987.

Wilson, Samuel Mackay. *Catalogue of Revolutionary Soldiers and Sailors of the Commonwealth of Virginia: To Whom Land Bounty Warrants Were Granted By Virginia for Military Service in the War for Independence.* Baltimore: Genealogical Publishing Co., 1967.

Vital and Cemetery Records

Borden, Duane L. *Tombstone Inscriptions (Virginia).* 9 vols. Ozark, Missouri: Yates Pub. Co., 1986.

Crozier, William A. *Early Virginia Marriages.* Baltimore: Genealogical Publishing Co., 1982.

Hall, Virginius Cornick. *Abstracts of Marriage and Obituary Notices in Virginia Newspapers Before 1820.* Salt Lake City: Genealogical Society of Utah, 1987.

Hogg, Anne M., and Dennis A. Tosh. *Virginia Cemeteries: A Guide to Resources.* Charlottesville: University of Virginia, 1986.

McDonald, Cecil D. *Some Virginia Marriages, 1800-1825.* 12 vols. In 1. Seattle: Cecil D. McDonald, 1973.

McDonald, Cecil D. *Some Virginia Marriages, 1700-1799.* 25 vols. In 2. Seattle: Cecil D. McDonald, 1972.

McIlwaine, H.R. *Index to Obituary Notices in the Richmond Enquirer from May 9, 1804 through 1828, and the Richmond Whig from January 1824 to 1838.* 1921. Reprint, Baltimore:

Genealogical Publishing, 1974.

Some Marriages in the Burned Record Counties of Virginia. Richmond: Virginia Genealogical Society, 1979.

True, Ransom B. *Some Virginia Marriages, 1826-1850.* 2 vols. In 1. Seattle: Cecil D. McDonald, 1975.

Virginia Marriage Records: From the Virginia Magazine of History and Biography, the William and Mary's College Quarterly, and the Tyler's Quarterly. Baltimore: Genealogical Publishing Co., 1982.

Virginia Vital Records: From the Virginia Magazine of History and Biography, the William and Mary's College Quarterly, and the Tyler's Quarterly. Baltimore: Genealogical Publishing Co., 1982.

Virginia. Bureau of Vital Statistics. *Birth Records, 1853-1941; Indexes, 1853-1950.* Microfilm of the original records at the Virginia State Library in Richmond, Virginia. (Salt Lake City: Filmed by the Genealogical Society of Utah, 1996). Microfilm, 99 rolls.

Vogt, John, and T. William Kethley. *Marriage Records in the Virginia State Library: A Researcher's Guide.* Athens, Georgia: Iberian Press, 1984.

Wulfeck, Dorothy F. *Marriages of Some Virginia Residents, 1607-1800.* 2 vols. Baltimore: Genealogical Publishing Co., 1986.

County Website	Map Index	Date Created	Parent County or Territory From Which Organized / Address/Details
Accawmack www.rootsweb.com/~vanortha/		1634	**Original Shire** Accawmack County; VA Details: (see Northampton) (Name changed to Northampton, 1643)
Accomack www.esva.net/~accomack/	B7	1634	**Northampton** Accomack County; County Courthouse; Accomac, VA 23301; Ph. 757.787.5776 Details: (Clk Cir Ct has m rec from 1784, div rec from 1850, pro, ct & land rec from 1663)
Albemarle www.albemarle.org/	H6	6 May 1744	**Goochland, Louisa** Albemarle County; 401 McIntire Rd; Charlottesville, VA 22902; Ph. 804.972.4084 Details: (Clk Cir Ct has m rec from 1870, land rec from 1748, div, pro & ct rec)
Alexandria (Ind. City) www.rootsweb.com/~vacalexa/alex1.htm		13 Mar 1847	**Fairfax** Alexandria (Ind. City); 520 King St Ste 307; Alexandria, VA 22314-3211; Ph. 703.838.4550 Details: (Co name changed to Arlington 16 Mar 1920; Part of District of Columbia 1791-1846; see District of Columbia for cen rec 1800-1840) (Alex. Hlth Center has b, d & bur rec; Clk Cir Ct has m & div rec from 1870, pro, ct & land rec from 1783)
Alleghany www.rootsweb.com/~vaallegh/	K6	5 Jan 1822	**Bath, Botetourt, Monroe** Alleghany County; 266 W Main St; Covington, VA 24426; Ph. 540.965.1730 Details: (Clk Cir Ct has m rec from 1845, div, pro, ct & land rec from 1822)
Amelia* www.rootsweb.com/~vaamelia/	F7	1 Feb 1734	**Brunswick, Prince George** Amelia County; 16441 Court St; Amelia Court House, VA 23002; Ph. 804.561.2128 Details: (Clk Cir Ct has m, div, land, pro, mil & ct rec from 1734)
Amherst www.amherstva.com/	I7	14 Sep 1758	**Albemarle** Amherst County; 100 E Court St; Amherst, VA 24521; Ph. 804.946.9321 Details: (Clk Cir Ct has m, div, pro, ct & land rec from 1761)
Appomattox www.appomattox.com/	H7	8 Feb 1845	**Buckingham, Campbell, Charlotte, Prince Edward** Appomattox County; PO Box 672; Appomattox, VA 24522; Ph. 804.352.5275 Details: (Clk Cir Ct has m, div & pro rec from 1892, ct & land rec)
Arlington www.co.arlington.va.us/scripts/default.asp	D4	13 Mar 1847	**Fairfax** Arlington County; 2100 Clarendon Blvd; Arlington, VA 22201-5445; Ph. 703.228.7010 Details: (Formerly Alexandria Co. Name changed to Arlington 16 Mar 1920) (Clk Cir Ct has b, m, d, pro, land & ct rec)
Augusta www.co.augusta.va.us/	I5	1 Aug 1738	**Orange** Augusta County; 6 E Johnson St; Staunton, VA 24401-4303; Ph. 540.245.5321 Details: (Clk Cir Ct has b & d rec 1853-1896, m rec from 1785, pro & land rec from 1745, property tax rec 1800-1851, land tax rec from 1786 & ct claims 1782-1785)
Barbour www.rootsweb.com/~wvgenweb/		—	Details: (See West Virginia)
Bath www.bathcountyva.org/	J6	14 Dec 1790	**Augusta, Botetourt, Greenbrier** Bath County; PO Box 180; Warm Springs, VA 24484-0180; Ph. 540.839.2361 Details: (Clk Cir Ct has b rec 1854-1880, d rec 1854-1870, div, pro, land & ct rec from 1791)
Bedford www.co.bedford.va.us/	I7	27 Feb 1752	**Albemarle, Lunenburg** Bedford County; 129 E Main St; Bedford, VA 24523-2034; Ph. 540.586.7601 Details: (Clk Cir Ct has b rec 1853-1897 & 1912-1918, d rec 1853-1918, m, div, pro, ct & land rec from 1754)
Bedford (Ind. City) www.rootsweb.com/~vabedfor/bedford.htm		1890	**Bedford** Bedford (Ind. City); 215 E Main St; Bedford, VA 24523-2012; Ph. 540.586.7102 Details: (Co seat of Bedford Co.) (Clk Cir Ct has m, pro & land rec)
Berkeley www.rootsweb.com/~wvgenweb/		—	Details: (See West Virginia)

County Website	Map Index	Date Created	Parent County or Territory From Which Organized Address/Details
Bland Future website at www.rootsweb.com/ ~vagenweb/	M8	30 Mar 1861	**Giles, Tazewell, Wythe** Bland County; 1 Courthouse Sq; Bland, VA 24315-0295; Ph. 540.688.4562 Details: (Clk Cir Ct has m, pro & land rec from 1861 & div rec from 1900)
Boone www.rootsweb.com/~wvgenweb/			— Details: (See West Virginia)
Botetourt co.botetourt.va.us/	J7	7 Nov 1769	**Augusta** Botetourt County; Box 219; Fincastle, VA 24090; Ph. 540.473.8274 Details: (Clk Cir Ct has b & d rec 1853-1870, m, div, pro, land, ct & cem rec from 1770)
Braxton www.rootsweb.com/~wvgenweb/			— Details: (See West Virginia)
Bristol (Ind. City) www.bristolva.org/		12 Feb 1890	**Washington** Bristol (Ind. City); 497 Cumberland St; Bristol, VA 24201-4394; Ph. 540.466.2221 Details: (Clk Cir Ct has m, div, land, pro, mil & ct rec from 1890)
Brooke www.rootsweb.com/~wvgenweb/			— Details: (See West Virginia)
Brunswick* www.tourbrunswick.org/	F9	2 Nov 1720	**Prince George, Isle of Wight, Surry** Brunswick County; 216 N Main St; Lawrenceville, VA 23868; Ph. 804.848.2215 Details: (Clk Cir Ct has m, div & pro rec from 1732 & land rec from 1900)
Buchanan www.silvermaple.net/buchanan/	O8	13 Feb 1858	**Russell, Tazewell** Buchanan County; Main and Walnut; PO Box 950; Grundy, VA 24614; Ph. 540.935.6575 Details: (Courthouse burned 1885) (Clk Cir Ct has m, div, pro, ct & land rec from 1885)
Buckingham www.rootsweb.com/~vabuckin/	H7	14 Sep 1758	**Albemarle** Buckingham County; PO Box 252; Buckingham, VA 23921-0252; Ph. 804.969.4734 Details: (Clk Cir Ct has b & d rec from 1896, m, div & pro rec from 1869)
Buena Vista (Ind. City)		1892	**Rockbridge** Buena Vista (Ind. City); 2039 Sycamore Ave; Buena Vista, VA 24416-3133; Ph. 540.261.6121 Details: (Clk Cir Ct has m, div, pro, ct, land & mil dis rec from 1892)
Cabell www.rootsweb.com/~wvgenweb/			— Details: (See West Virginia)
Calhoun www.rootsweb.com/~wvgenweb/			— Details: (See West Virginia)
Campbell www.co.campbell.va.us/index.htm	I8	5 Nov 1781	**Bedford** Campbell County; PO Box 7; Rustburg, VA 24588; Ph. 804.332.5161 Details: (Clk Cir Ct has b & d rec 1912-1918, m, div, pro, ct & land rec from 1782)
Caroline www.co.caroline.va.us/	E6	1 Feb 1727	**Essex, King and Queen, King William** Caroline County; PO Box 309; Bowling Green, VA 22427; Ph. 804.633.5800 Details: (Clk Cir Ct has m rec 1787-1853, land rec from 1836, div, pro & ct rec)
Carroll www.co.carroll.va.us/	L9	17 Jan 1842	**Grayson, Patrick** Carroll County; PO Box 218; Hillsville, VA 24343-0515; Ph. 540.728.3117 Details: (Clk Cir Ct has b rec 1842-1896, m, div, pro & land rec from 1842)
Charles City	D7	1634	**Original Shire** Charles City County; PO Box 128; Charles City, VA 23030; Ph. 804.829.9211 Details: (Clk Cir Ct has b, m, d, pro & land rec)

County Website	Map Index	Date Created	Parent County or Territory From Which Organized Address/Details
Charles River www.rootsweb.com/~vayork/		1634	**Original Shire** Details: (see York) (Name changed to York, 1643)
Charlotte www.co.charlotte.va.us/	H8	26 May 1764	**Lunenburg** Charlotte County; PO Box 38; Charlotte Court House, VA 23923-0038; Ph. 804.542.5147 Details: (Co Clk has b & d rec 1853-1870, m, pro, ct & land rec from 1765 & div rec)
Charlottesville (Ind. City)		1762	**Albemarle** Charlottesville (Ind. City); 605 E Main St; Charlottesville, VA 22901-5397; Ph. 804.971.3101 Details: (Co seat of Albemarle Co) (Clk Cir Ct has m, pro & land rec)
Chesapeake (Ind. City) www.rootsweb.com/~vanorfol/	C9	1 Jan 1963	**Norfolk** Chesapeake (Ind. City); 306 Cedar Rd; Chesapeake, VA 23320-5514; Ph. 757.547.6166 Details: (Formerly Norfolk Co. Changed to Chesapeake City 1 Jan 1963) (Clk Cir Ct, P.O. Box 15205, has b & d rec 1853-1870, m rec from 1706, div rec from 1800, pro & land rec from 1637)
Chesterfield* www.co.chesterfield.va.us/	F7	1 May 1749	**Henrico** Chesterfield County; 9500 Courthouse Rd; PO Box 125; Chesterfield, VA 23832; Ph. 804.748.1241 Details: (Clk Cir Ct has m rec from 1771, land rec from 1749, div, pro & ct rec)
Clarke www.co.clarke.va.us/	F3	8 Mar 1836	**Frederick** Clarke County; 102 N Church St; PO Box 189; Berryville, VA 22611; Ph. 540.955.5116 Details: (Clk Cir Ct has m, div, pro, ct & land rec from 1836)
Clay www.rootsweb.com/~wvgenweb/		—	Details: (See West Virginia)
Clifton Forge (Ind. City)		1906	**Alleghany** Clifton Forge (Ind. City); PO Box 631; Clifton Forge, VA 24422-0631; Ph. 540.863.5091 Details: (City Clk has m, div & land rec from 1906 & pro rec)
Colonial Heights (Ind. City)		1948	**Chesterfield** Colonial Heights (Ind. City); 1507 Boulevard; Colonial Heights, VA 23834-3049; Ph. 804.520.9265 Details: (Clk Cir Ct has m, div, pro, ct & land rec from 1961; Clk Cir Ct, Chesterfield Co, has div, pro ct & land rec to 1961)
Covington (Ind. City)		1952	**Alleghany** Covington (Ind. City); 158 N Court Ave; Covington, VA 24426-1534; Ph. 703.965.6300 Details: (Co seat of Alleghany Co) (Clk Cir Ct has m, pro & land rec)
Craig www.co.craig.va.us/	K7	21 Mar 1851	**Botetourt, Giles, Roanoke, Monroe** Craig County; 303 Main St; New Castle, VA 24127-0185; Ph. 540.864.6141 Details: (Clk Cir Ct has b rec 1864-1896, m, div, pro, ct & land rec from 1851)
Culpeper www.culpepercounty.gov/	F5	23 Mar 1748	**Orange** Culpeper County; 101 S W St; Culpeper, VA 22701; Ph. 540.727.3435 Details: (Clk Cir Ct has b rec 1864-1896 & 1912-1917, d rec 1864-1896, m rec from 1781, land & pro rec from 1749 & ct rec from 1831; Twn Clks have bur rec)
Cumberland www.rootsweb.com/~vacumber/	G7	1748	**Goochland** Cumberland County; County Courthouse; PO Box 8; Cumberland, VA 23040; Ph. 804.492.4442 Details: (Clk Cir Ct has m, div, pro & ct rec from 1749, b & d rec 1853-1870)
Danville (Ind. City)		1890	**Pittsylvania** Danville (Ind. City); 212 Lynn St; Danville, VA 24541-1208; Ph. 804.799.5168 Details: (Clk Cir Ct has m, div, land & ct rec from 1841, pro rec from 1857 & mil rec from 1942)

County Website	Map Index	Date Created	Parent County or Territory From Which Organized / Address/Details
Dickenson www.dickensonctyva.com/	P8	3 Mar 1880	**Buchanan, Russell, Wise** Dickenson County; PO Box 190; Clintwood, VA 24228-0190; Ph. 540.926.1616 Details: (Co Hlth Dept has b, d & bur rec; Clk Cir Ct has m, div, ct & land rec from 1880, pro & mil dis rec)
Dinwiddie* www.rootsweb.com/~vadinwid/	F8	27 Feb 1752	**Prince George** Dinwiddie County; PO Box 280; Dinwiddie, VA 23841-0280; Ph. 804.469.4540 Details: (Clk Cir Ct has b & d rec 1865-1896, m, pro, ct & land rec from 1833 & div rec from 1870)
Doddridge www.rootsweb.com/~wvgenweb/		—	Details: (See West Virginia)
Dunmore www.rootsweb.com/~vashenan/ vashenan.html		24 Mar 1772	**Frederick** Details: (see Shenandoah) Name changed to Shenandoah 1 Feb 1778
Elizabeth City www.rootsweb.com/~vaelizab/		1634	**Original Shire** Details: (see Hampton) Absorbed by Hampton Jul 1952
Essex www.essex-virginia.org/	D6	16 Apr 1692	**Rappahannock, old** Essex County; PO Box 445; Tappahannock, VA 22560; Ph. 804.443.3541 Details: (Clk Cir Ct has m rec from 1814, div & land rec from 1865, pro rec from 1656 & ct rec from 1692)
Fairfax www.rootsweb.com/~vafairfa/	E4	6 May 1742	**Prince William** Fairfax County; 4110 Chain Bridge Rd; Fairfax, VA 22030; Ph. 703.246.4168 Details: (Clk Cir Ct has b rec 1853-1912, m rec from 1853, div rec from 1850, pro, ct & land rec from 1742)
Fairfax (Ind. City)		1961	**Fairfax** Fairfax (Ind. City); 10455 Armstrong St; Fairfax, VA 22030-3630; Ph. 703.385.7855 Details: (Co seat of Fairfax Co) (Clk Cir Ct has m, pro & land rec)
Falls Church (Ind. City)		1948	**Fairfax** Falls Church (Ind. City); 300 Park Ave; Falls Church, VA 22046-3332; Ph. 703.241.5014 Details: (Fairfax Co Clk Cir Ct has b, m, div, pro, ct & land rec)
Fauquier www.co.fauquier.va.us/	F4	14 Sep 1758	**Prince William** Fauquier County; 40 Culpeper St; Warrenton, VA 22186; Ph. 540.347.8610 Details: (Clk Cir Ct has b rec 1853-1896, d rec 1853-1896 & 1912-1917, m, land & pro rec from 1759, div rec from 1831, ct rec from 1975 & mil dis rec from 1944)
Fayette www.rootsweb.com/~vagenweb/ kentucky.htm; www.rootsweb.com/ ~wvgenweb/		—	Details: (See West Virginia) (2 Counties, Fayette 1, split to Kentucky, & Fayette 2, split to West Virginia)
Fincastle		1772	**Botetourt** Details: (see Montgomery) (Discontinued 1777) (Divided into Kentucky, Montgomery, and Washington Co.)
Floyd www.fin.org/	K8	15 Jan 1831	**Montgomery, Franklin** Floyd County; 100 E Main St Rm 200; Floyd, VA 24091; Ph. 540.745.9330 Details: (Clk Cir Ct has b & d rec 1852-1872, m, div, pro, ct & land rec from 1831)
Fluvanna www.co.fluvanna.va.us/	G6	5 May 1777	**Albemarle** Fluvanna County; PO Box 299; Palmyra, VA 22963; Ph. 804.589.8011 Details: (Clk Cir Ct has b & d rec 1853-1896, m, div, pro, ct & land rec from 1777 & some bur rec)
Franklin www.franklincountyva.org/	J8	17 Oct 1785	**Bedford, Henry** Franklin County; Main St; Rocky Mount, VA 24151-1392; Ph. 540.483.3065 Details: (Clk Cir Ct has b, m, d, pro, land & ct rec)

County Website	Map Index	Date Created	Parent County or Territory From Which Organized Address/Details
Kanawah www.rootsweb.com/~wvgenweb/		—	Details: (See West Virginia)
Kentucky www.rootsweb.com/~vagenweb/ kentucky.htm		1776	**Fincastle** Details: (Discontinued 1780 and became Fayette, Jefferson & Lincoln Cos, Kentucky)
King & Queen www.iocc.com/~swright/kqmain.html	D6	16 Apr 1691	**New Kent** King & Queen County; County Courthouse; King & Queen Courthouse, VA 23085; Ph. 804.785.2460 Details: (Clk Cir Ct has b & d rec 1865-1898, m & div rec from 1864, pro & ct rec from 1865 & land rec from 1782)
King George www.rootsweb.com/~vakingge/ kinggeo.htm	E5	2 Nov 1720	**Richmond, Westmoreland** King George County; PO Box 105; King George, VA 22485; Ph. 540.775.3322 Details: (Clk Cir Ct has m rec from 1786, div, ct, land & pro rec from 1721)
King William www.co.king-william.va.us/	D7	5 Dec 1700	**King and Queen** King William County; PO Box 215; King William, VA 23086; Ph. 804.769.4927 Details: (Fire in 1855 burned most rec; some rec to 1702 have been photocopied) (Clk Cir Ct has m, div, pro & ct rec from 1885 & land rec)
Lancaster www.lancova.com/	C6	1652	**Northumberland, York** Lancaster County; PO Box 99; Lancaster, VA 22503; Ph. 804.462.5611 Details: (Co Hlth Dept has b rec; Clk Cir Ct has m rec from 1715, d, pro & land rec from 1652, div rec from 1800 & ct rec from 1910)
Lee lee.va-village.com/	Q9	25 Oct 1792	**Russell** Lee County; PO Box 326; Jonesville, VA 24263-0326; Ph. 540.346.7763 Details: (Clk Cir Ct has b & d rec 1853-1877, m rec from 1830, div rec from 1832, pro rec from 1800, ct & land rec from 1793)
Lewis www.rootsweb.com/~wvgenweb/		—	Details: (See West Virginia)
Lexington (Ind. City)		1778	**Rockbridge** Lexington (Ind. City); PO Box 922; Lexington, VA 24450-0922; Ph. 540.463.7133 Details: (Co seat ot Rockbridge Co) (Clk Cir Ct has m, pro & land rec)
Lincoln www.rootsweb.com/~vagenweb/ kentucky.htm		—	Details: (See West Virginia)
Logan www.rootsweb.com/~wvgenweb/		—	Details: (See West Virginia)
Loudoun www.co.loudoun.va.us/	F3	25 Mar 1757	**Fairfax** Loudoun County; 18 E Market St; Leesburg, VA 20176; Ph. 703.777.0270 Details: (Clk Cir Ct has b rec 1853-1859, 1864-1866 & 1869-1879, d rec 1853-1866, m rec from 1793, div, pro & land rec from 1757, ct rec from 1858 & tithables 1758-1786)
Louisa www.louisa-county.com/	F6	6 May 1742	**Hanover** Louisa County; PO Box 37; Louisa, VA 23093-0160; Ph. 540.967.5312 Details: (Clk Cir Ct has b rec 1867-1896, m, div & pro rec from 1742 & land rec)
Lower Norfolk		1637	**New Norfolk** Details: (See Princess Anne and Norfolk) (Abolished 1691 & divided between Princess Anne & Norfolk Cos)
Lunenburg www.rootsweb.com/~valunenb/	G8	6 May 1745	**Brunswick** Lunenburg County; County Courthouse; Lunenburg, VA 23952; Ph. 804.696.2230 Details: (Clk Cir Ct has m, div, pro, ct & land rec from 1746)

County Website	Map Index	Date Created	Parent County or Territory From Which Organized Address/Details
Lynchburg (Ind. City) www.rootsweb.com/~vaclynch/		1852	**Campbell** Lynchburg (Ind. City); 900 Church St; Lynchburg, VA 24504-1620; Ph. 804.847.1443 Details: (Clk Cir Ct has b & d rec 1853-1868, m, div, pro, ct & land rec from 1805, mil dis rec from 1919, mil rec from Civil War & slave register)
Madison www.summit.net/madison/	G5	4 Dec 1792	**Culpeper** Madison County; Main St; PO Box 220; Madison, VA 22727-0220; Ph. 540.948.6888 Details: (Clk Cir Ct has m, div, pro, ct & land rec from 1793)
Manassas Park (Ind. City)		1975	**Prince William** Manassas Park (Ind. City); 1 Park Center Pl; Manassas Park, VA 22111-1800; Ph. 703.335.8800 Details: (Co seat of Prince William Co) (Clk Cir Ct has m, pro & land rec)
Marion www.rootsweb.com/~wvgenweb/		—	Details: (See West Virginia)
Marshall www.rootsweb.com/~wvgenweb/		—	Details: (See West Virginia)
Martinsville (Ind. City) www.rootsweb.com/~vahenry/		1928	**Henry** Martinsville (Ind. City); PO Box 1112; Martinsville, VA 24114-1112; Ph. 540.656.5180 Details: (Co seat of Henry Co) (Clk Cir Ct has m, div, pro, ct & land rec from 1942)
Mason www.rootsweb.com/~wvgenweb/		—	Details: (See West Virginia)
Mathews www.co.mathews.va.us/	C7	16 Dec 1790	**Gloucester** Mathews County; 1 Court St; Mathews, VA 23109-0463; Ph. 804.725.2550 Details: (Clk Cir Ct has m, div, pro, ct & land rec from 1865)
McDowell www.rootsweb.com/~wvgenweb/		—	Details: (See West Virginia)
Mecklenburg www.msinets.com/meckco/	G9	26 May 1764	**Lunenburg** Mecklenburg County; Washington St; PO Box 307; Boydton, VA 23917; Ph. 804.738.6191 Details: (Clk Cir Ct has m, pro, land & ct rec)
Mercer www.rootsweb.com/~vagenweb/ kentucky.htm		—	Details: (See West Virginia)
Middlesex* www.co.middlesex.va.us/	C7	21 Sep 1674	**Lancaster** Middlesex County; Rts 17 & 33; PO Box 428; Saluda, VA 23149; Ph. 804.758.0061 Details: (Clk Cir Ct has b & m rec from 1840, pro, ct & land rec from 1673)
Monongalia www.rootsweb.com/~wvgenweb/		—	Details: (See West Virginia)
Monroe www.rootsweb.com/~wvgenweb/		—	Details: (See West Virginia)
Montgomery www.montva.com/	K8	7 Oct 1776	**Fincastle, Botetourt** Montgomery County; 1 E Main St; Christiansburg, VA 24073-3027; Ph. 540.382.5760 Details: (Clk Cir Ct has b & d rec 1853-1871, m, div, pro, ct & land rec from 1773)
Morgan www.rootsweb.com/~wvgenweb/		—	Details: (See West Virginia)

County Website	Map Index	Date Created	Parent County or Territory From Which Organized / Address/Details
Nansemond www.rootsweb.com/~vanansem/		1637	**Upper Norfolk** Details: (see Suffolk City) (Became an independent city, 1972. Nansemond Co and Suffolk City merged 1 Jan 1974)
Nelson www.nelsoncounty.com/	H6	25 Dec 1807	**Amherst** Nelson County; 84 Courthouse Sq; PO Box 55; Lovingston, VA 22949-0055; Ph. 804.263.4069 Details: (Clk Cir Ct has m, div, pro, ct & land rec from 1808)
New Kent www.co.new-kent.va.us/	D7	20 Nov 1654	**York, James City** New Kent County; PO Box 98; New Kent, VA 23124-0098; Ph. 804.966.9520 Details: (Clk Cir Ct has b & d rec 1865-1888, m, div, pro, ct & land rec from 1865)
New Norfolk		1636	**Elizabeth City** Details: Abolished 1637. Divided to Upper Norfolk (now Suffolk) & Lower Norfolk (now Chesapeake)
Newport News (Ind. City) www.rootsweb.com/~vanewpor/	C8	1896	**Warwick** Newport News (Ind. City); 2400 Washington Ave; Newport News, VA 23607-4300; Ph. 804.247.8411 Details: (Incorporated with Warwick 1 Jul 1958) (Clk Cir Ct has m, pro & land rec)
Nicholas www.rootsweb.com/~wvgenweb/		—	Details: (See West Virginia)
Norfolk www.rootsweb.com/~vanorfol/	C9	1691	**Lower Norfolk** Norfolk County; 810 Union St; Norfolk, VA 23510-2717; Ph. 757.441.2471 Details: (changed to Chesapeake City 1 Jan 1963) (Clk Cir Ct has m, pro, land & ct rec)
Northampton www.esva.net/northampton/	B7	1634	**Original Shire** Northampton County; 16404 Courthouse Rd; PO Box 36; Eastville, VA 23347; Ph. 757.678.5126 Details: (Formerly Accawmack Co. Name changed to Northampton, 1643) (Clk Cir Ct has m rec from 1706, pro, ct & land rec from 1632 & div rec from 1904)
Northumberland www.co.northumberland.va.us/	C6	12 Oct 1648	**Indian District. of Chickacoan** Northumberland County; PO Box 217; Heathsville, VA 22473-0217; Ph. 804.580.3777 Details: (Clk Cir Ct has m, div, pro, ct & land rec)
Norton (Ind. City)		1954	**Wise** Norton (Ind. City); PO Box 618; Norton, VA 24273-0618; Ph. 540.679.1160 Details: (All rec with Wise Co)
Nottoway www.nottoway-va.com/	F8	22 Dec 1788	**Amelia** Nottoway County; PO Box 25; Nottoway, VA 23955; Ph. 804.645.9043 Details: (Some rec were destroyed during the Civil War. Clk Cir Ct has m, div & ct rec from 1865, land, pro & mil rec from 1789)
Ohio www.rootsweb.com/~wvgenweb/		—	Details: (See West Virginia)
Orange www.rootsweb.com/~vaorange/index.htm	F5	1 Feb 1734	**Spotsylvania** Orange County; 109-A W Main St; Orange, VA 22960; Ph. 540.672.4066 Details: (Clk Cir Ct has b rec 1860-1895, m rec from 1757, pro, ct & land rec from 1734)
Page www.co.page.va.us/	G4	30 Mar 1831	**Rockingham, Shenandoah** Page County; 116 S Court St Ste A; Luray, VA 22835; Ph. 540.743.4142 Details: (Clk Cir Ct has m, div, land, pro & ct rec from 1831)
Patrick www.co.patrick.va.us/	K9	26 Nov 1790	**Henry** Patrick County; 101 Blue Ridge St; PO Box 148; Stuart, VA 24171-0148; Ph. 540.694.7213 Details: (Clk Cir Ct has b & d rec 1853-1896, m, div, pro, ct & land rec from 1791)

County Website	Map Index	Date Created	Parent County or Territory From Which Organized Address/Details
Pendleton www.rootsweb.com/~wvgenweb/			— Details: (See West Virginia)
Petersburg (Ind. City) www.rootsweb.com/~vacpeter/		16 Mar 1850	**Dinwiddie, Prince George, Chesterfield** Petersburg (Ind. City); Courthouse Hill; Petersburg, VA 23803; Ph. 804.733.2367 Details: (City Clk has b rec 1853-1896, d rec from 1853, m, div, pro & land rec from 1784)
Pittsylvania www.pittgov.org/pitt2.htm	19	6 Nov 1766	**Halifax** Pittsylvania County; 1 S Main St; Chatham, VA 24531; Ph. 804.432.2041 Details: (Clk Cir Ct has m, div, pro, ct & land rec from 1767)
Pleasants www.rootsweb.com/~wvgenweb/			— Details: (See West Virginia)
Pocahontas www.rootsweb.com/~wvgenweb/			— Details: (See West Virginia)
Poquoson (Ind. City) www.rootsweb.com/~vayork/		1952	**York** Poquoson (Ind. City); 830 Poquoson Ave; Poquoson, VA 23662-1797; Ph. 804.868.7151 Details: (Clk Cir Ct has m, pro & land rec)
Portsmouth (Ind. City)		1858	**Norfolk** Portsmouth (Ind. City); PO Box 820; Portsmouth, VA 23705-0820; Ph. 757.393.8746 Details: (Territory taken from Norfolk Co & annexed to Portsmouth in 1848, 1960 & 1968) (Clk Cir Ct has b & d rec 1858-1896, m, div, pro, ct & land rec from 1848; Portsmouth Pub Hlth Dept, P.O. Box 250, Portsmouth, VA 23705 has b, d & bur rec)
Powhatan* www.rootsweb.com/~vapowhat/	F7	5 May 1777	**Chesterfield, Cumberland** Powhatan County; PO Box 37; Powhatan, VA 23139; Ph. 804.598.5660 Details: (Clk Cir Ct has m, div, pro, ct & land rec from 1777)
Preston www.rootsweb.com/~wvgenweb/			— Details: (See West Virginia)
Prince Edward www.co.prince-edward.va.us/	G8	27 Feb 1752	**Amelia** Prince Edward County; PO Box 304; Farmville, VA 23901-0304; Ph. 804.392.5145 Details: (Clk Cir Ct has b rec 1853-1896, d rec 1853-1869, m, div, pro, ct & land rec from 1754)
Prince George* www.princegeorgeva.org/	E8	5 Dec 1700	**Charles City** Prince George County; 6400 Courthouse Rd; PO Box 68; Prince George, VA 23875; Ph. 804.733.2600 Details: (Clk Cir Ct has incomplete b rec 1865-1896, m, div & pro rec from 1865, ct rec from 1945 & land rec)
Prince William www.pwcgov.org/	E4	1 Feb 1727	**King George, Stafford** Prince William County; 9311 Lee Ave; Manassas, VA 22110; Ph. 703.792.6015 Details: (Clk Cir Ct has m rec from 1856, div & ct rec from 1823, pro rec from 1734 & land rec from 1731)
Princess Anne www.rootsweb.com/~vaprinc2/pa.htm		1691	**Lower Norfolk** Details: (see Virginia Beach) (Annexed to Norfolk Co, 1950. Now part of Ind. City of Virginia Beach; consolidated, 1963)
Pulaski www.pulaskicounty.org/	L8	30 Mar 1839	**Montgomery, Wythe** Pulaski County; 45 3rd St NW; Pulaski, VA 24301; Ph. 540.980.7825 Details: (Clk Cir Ct has m rec from 1882, div, pro, ct & land rec from 1839)

County Website	Map Index	Date Created	Parent County or Territory From Which Organized Address/Details
Putnam www.rootsweb.com/~wvgenweb/			— Details: (See West Virginia)
Radford (Ind. City)		1887	**Pulaski** Radford (Ind. City); 619 2nd St; Radford, VA 24141-1431; Ph. 540.731.3603 Details: (Clk Cir Ct has m, div, pro, ct & land rec from 1892)
Raleigh www.rootsweb.com/~wvgenweb/			— Details: (See West Virginia)
Randolph www.rootsweb.com/~wvgenweb/			— Details: (See West Virginia)
Rappahannock www.summit.net/rappahannock/	G4	8 Feb 1833	**Culpeper** Rappahannock County; 238 Gay St; PO Box 116; Washington, VA 22747; Ph. 540.675.3621 Details: (Clk Cir Ct has m, div, pro & ct rec from 1833, land rec from 1838 & some personal property rec from 1834)
Rappahannock, Old		1656	**Lancaster** Details: (see Essex) Abolished 1692
Richmond www.co.richmond.va.us/	D6	16 Apr 1692	**Rappahannock, old** Richmond County; 10 Court St; PO Box 1000; Warsaw, VA 22572; Ph. 804.333.3781 Details: (Clk Cir Ct has b & d rec 1853-1895, m rec from 1853, div, pro & land rec from 1693)
Richmond (Ind. City) www.rootsweb.com/~vahenric/		1782	**Henrico** Richmond (Ind. City); City Hall; Richmond, VA 23219-6115; Ph. 804.780.7970 Details: (Co seat of Henrico Co) (Dept of Hlth, Bureau of Vit Rec, Madison Bldg., Richmond, VA 23219, has div rec 1870-1954; Clk Chan Ct, City Hall, Richmond, VA 23219 has pro & land rec; Clk Civ Ct has ct rec)
Ritchie www.rootsweb.com/~wvgenweb/			— Details: (See West Virginia)
Roane www.rootsweb.com/~wvgenweb/			— Details: (See West Virginia)
Roanoke www.co.roanoke.va.us/	K8	30 Mar 1838	**Botetourt, Montgomery** Roanoke County; 305 E Main St; PO Box 1126; Salem, VA 24153-1126; Ph. 540.387.6205 Details: (Clk Cir Ct has m, div, pro, ct & land rec from 1838)
Roanoke (Ind. City) www.rootsweb.com/~varoanok/		1884	**Roanoke** Roanoke (Ind. City); 215 Church Ave SW; Roanoke, VA 24011-1517; Ph. 540.981.2333 Details: (Clk Cts has b rec 1884-1896, m, div, pro, ct & land rec from 1884)
Rockbridge webfeat-inc.com/rockbridge/	I6	20 Oct 1777	**Augusta, Botetourt** Rockbridge County; 2 S Main St; Lexington, VA 24450; Ph. 540.463.2232 Details: (Clk Cir Ct has b rec 1853-1896, d rec 1853-1870, m, div, pro, ct & land rec from 1778)
Rockingham www.co.rockingham.va.us/	H4	20 Oct 1777	**Augusta** Rockingham County; Circuit Ct; Harrisonburg, VA 22801; Ph. 540.564.3111 Details: (Clk Cir Ct has b rec 1862-1894, d rec 1890-1894, m, pro, ct & land rec from 1778 & div rec from 1833. Some rec burned in 1864)

County Website	Map Index	Date Created	Parent County or Territory From Which Organized Address/Details
Russell russellonline.com/	O8	17 Oct 1785	**Washington** Russell County; PO Box 435; Lebanon, VA 24266; Ph. 540.889.8023 Details: (Clk Cir Ct has m rec from 1853, div & ct rec from 1786, pro rec from 1803 & land rec from 1787)
Salem (Ind. City) www.rootsweb.com/~varoanok/		1802	**Roanoke** Salem (Ind. City); 114 N Broad St; Salem, VA 24153-3734; Ph. 540.375.3016 Details: (Co seat of Roanoke Co) (Clk Cir Ct has m, pro, land & ct rec)
Scott www.scottcountyva.com/	P9	24 Nov 1814	**Lee, Russell, Washington** Scott County; 104 E Jackson St Ste 2; Gate City, VA 24251; Ph. 540.386.3801 Details: (Clk Cir Ct has b rec 1853-1895, d rec 1853-1892, m, div, pro, ct & land rec from 1815)
Shenandoah www.co.shenandoah.va.us/	H4	24 Mar 1772	**Frederick** Shenandoah County; 112 S Main St; PO Box 406; Woodstock, VA 22664; Ph. 540.459.3791 Details: (Formerly Dunmore Co. Name changed to Shenandoah 1 Feb 1778) (Clk Cir Ct has m, div, pro, ct & land rec from 1772)
Smyth www.rootsweb.com/~vasmyth/	N8	23 Feb 1832	**Washington, Wythe** Smyth County; PO Box 1025; Marion, VA 24354-1025; Ph. 540.783.7186 Details: (Clk Cir Ct has m, div, pro, ct & land rec from 1832)
Southampton* www.rootsweb.com/~vasoutha/	E9	30 Apr 1749	**Isle of Wight, Nansemond** Southampton County; County Courthouse; PO Box 190; Courtland, VA 23837; Ph. 757.653.2200 Details: (Clk Cir Ct has m, ct, land & pro rec)
Spotsylvania www.spotsylvania.va.us/	F5	2 Nov 1720	**Essex, King and Queen, King William** Spotsylvania County; PO Box 96; Spotslyvania, VA 22553-0099; Ph. 540.582.7090 Details: (Clk Cir Ct has m & pro rec from 1722, b rec 1864-1895 & 1911-1915, d rec 1911-1915, ct rec from 1724, land rec from 1856, mil pension rec 1898-1926 & coroners inquests 1879-1912)
Stafford www.co.stafford.va.us/	E5	5 Jun 1666	**Westmoreland** Stafford County; PO Box 339; Stafford, VA 22554-0339; Ph. 540.658.8750 Details: (Clk Cir Ct has m rec from 1854, div & ct rec from 1664, pro & land rec from 1699)
Staunton (Ind. City)		16 Jan 1908	**Augusta** Staunton (Ind. City); 113 E Beverley St; Staunton, VA 24401-4390; Ph. 540.885.1251 Details: (Clk Cir Ct has b rec 1853-1896, d rec 1853-1892, m, div, pro, ct & land rec from 1802)
Suffolk (Ind. City) www.suffolk.va.us/	D9	1910	**Nansemond** Suffolk (Ind. City); 441 Market St; Suffolk, VA 23434-5237; Ph. 757.934.3111 Details: (Nansemond Co & Suffolk City merged 1 Jan 1974) (Clk City Ct has m, div, pro & land rec from 1866)
Surry www.rootsweb.com/~vasurry/	D8	1652	**James City** Surry County; 28 Colonial Trail E; Surry, VA 23883; Ph. 804.294.3161 Details: (Clk Cir Ct has b & d rec 1853-1896, m rec from 1768, pro & land rec from 1652, ct rec from 1671 & div rec)
Sussex www.sussex.k12.va.us/sussex_main.htm	E9	27 Feb 1752	**Surry** Sussex County; Rt 735; Sussex, VA 23884; Ph. 804.246.5511 Details: (Clk Cir Ct has b, m, pro, ct & land rec from 1754)
Taylor www.rootsweb.com/~wvgenweb/			**—** Details: (See West Virginia)
Tazewell www.tazewellcounty.org/	N8	17 Dec 1799	**Russell, Wythe** Tazewell County; 315 School St; PO Box 968; Tazewell, VA 24651; Ph. 540.988.7541 Details: (Clk Cir Ct has b & d rec 1853-1870, m, pro & land rec from 1800 & ct rec from 1832)

County Website	Map Index	Date Created	Parent County or Territory From Which Organized Address/Details

Tucker
www.rootsweb.com/~wvgenweb/   —
Details: (See West Virginia)

Tyler
www.rootsweb.com/~wvgenweb/   —
Details: (See West Virginia)

Upper Norfolk   1637   **New Norfolk**
Details: (see Nansemond) (Name changed to Nansemond 1642)

Upshur
www.rootsweb.com/~wvgenweb/   —
Details: (See W. Va.)

Virginia Beach   B9   1 Jan 1963   **Princess Anne**
(Ind. City)
Virginia Beach (Ind. City); Municipal Ctr; Virginia Beach, VA 23456-9099;
Ph. 757.427.4242
Details: (Clk Cir Ct has b & d rec 1864-1894, m rec from 1749 except m rec 1822-1852 which were destroyed in fire, div rec from 1814, pro, ct & land rec from 1691)

Warren   G4   9 Mar 1836   **Frederick, Shenandoah**
www.warrencounty.va.lgac.net/
Warren County; 1 E Main St; Front Royal, VA 22630; Ph. 540.635.2435
Details: (Clk Cir Ct has m, div, pro, ct & land rec from 1836)

Warrosquoyacke   1634   **Original Shire**
www.rootsweb.com/~vaisleof/
Details: (see Isle of Wight) Name changed to Isle of Wight 1637

Warwick   1634   **Original Shire**
www.rootsweb.com/~vawarwic/
Details: (see Newport News, Ind. City) Formerly Warwick River. Name changed to Warwick 1642. Incorporated as an independent city 1952. Merged with city of Newport News 1 Jul 1958

Warwick River   1634   **Original Shire**
www.rootsweb.com/~vawarwic/
   warwick.htm
Details: (Name changed to Warwick 1642; merged with city of Newport News 1 Jul 1958)

Washington   O9   7 Oct 1776   **Fincastle**
www.rootsweb.com/~vawashin/
Washington County; 216 Park St; Abingdon, VA 24210-3312; Ph. 540.628.8733
Details: (In 1974 nine sq. miles of Washington Co were annexed to the city of Bristol, which is an independent city with its own Clks office & rec) (Clk Cir Ct has m, div, pro, ct & land rec from 1777)

Wayne
www.rootsweb.com/~wvgenweb/   —
Details: (See West Virginia)

Waynesboro (Ind. City)   Feb 1948   **Augusta**
Waynesboro (Ind. City); 250 S Wayne Ave; Waynesboro, VA 22980-4622;
Ph. 540.942.6600
Details: (Clk Cir Ct has m, div, pro, ct & land rec from 1948)

Webster
www.rootsweb.com/~wvgenweb/   —
Details: (See West Virginia)

Westmoreland   D6   5 Jul 1653   **Northumberland**
www.co.westmoreland.va.us/
Westmoreland County; Polk St; PO Box 307; Montross, VA 22520; Ph. 804.493.0108
Details: (Clk Cir Ct has b & d rec 1855-1895, m rec from 1786, div rec from 1850, pro, ct & land rec from 1653)

Wetzel
www.rootsweb.com/~wvgenweb/   —
Details: (See West Virginia)

County Website	Map Index	Date Created	Parent County or Territory From Which Organized Address/Details
Williamsburg (Ind. City)		1884	**James City** Williamsburg (Ind. City); 401 Lafayette St; Williamsburg, VA 23185-3617; Ph. 804.220.6100 Details: (Clk Cir Ct has m, div, pro & land rec from 1865 & ct rec from 1953)
Winchester (Ind. City)		1874	**Frederick** Winchester (Ind. City); 5 N Kent St; Winchester, VA 22601-5037; Ph. 540.667.5770 Details: (City Clk has m, pro & land rec)
Wirt www.rootsweb.com/~wvgenweb/		—	Details: (See West Virginia)
Wise www.wisecounty.org/	P8	16 Feb 1856	**Lee, Russell, Scott** Wise County; 206 E Main St; PO Box 1248; Wise, VA 24293; Ph. 540.328.6111 Details: (Clk Cir Ct has m & div rec from 1856, pro & land rec)
Wood www.rootsweb.com/~wvgenweb/		—	Details: (See West Virginia)
Wyoming www.rootsweb.com/~wvgenweb/		—	Details: (See West Virginia)
Wythe www.wytheco.org/	M9	1 Dec 1789	**Montgomery** Wythe County; 225 S 4th St; PO Box 440; Wytheville, VA 24382; Ph. 540.223.6050 Details: (Clk Cir Ct has m, div, pro, ct & land rec from 1790)
Yohogania www.rootsweb.com/~vayohoga/		1776	**Augusta District** Details: (Discontinued & ceded to Pennsylvania 1786)
York www.co.york.va.us/	C8	1634	**Original Shire** York County; PO Box 532; Yorktown, VA 23690-0532; Ph. 757.890.3350 Details: (Formerly Charles River Co. Name changed to York 1642) (Clk Cir Ct has m, pro, land & ct rec)

Notes

WASHINGTON

CAPITAL: OLYMPIA – TERRITORY 1853 – STATE 1889 (42ND)

In 1775 Spaniards became the first non-natives to touch Washington soil. American fur traders came between 1789 and 1792, claiming much of the Northwest for America. The British explored Puget Sound in 1792, claiming the whole area for England. The first settlement of the area was at Astoria, a trading post established by John Jacob Astor. The British, however, controlled the area for the most part until the 1840's. Spain withdrew its claim in 1819. In 1836, Marcus Whitman established the second settlement near Walla Walla. Once Whitman and other missionaries had come, other settlers soon followed. The Willamette Valley and Columbia Valley were the main points of settlement. In 1846, the present boundary was established between the United States and Canada as Britain withdrew its claim to the area.

The Oregon Territory was created in 1848, including the present states of Oregon, Washington, Idaho, and parts of Montana and Wyoming. Settlers went farther north in 1849 to obtain food and lumber for the California gold fields. The Oregon Donation Act of 1850 guaranteed from 160 to 640 acres of land to those who settled and cultivated land before 1855. Some 30,000 settlers came as a result of this act, which prompted Congress to organize the Washington Territory in 1853. During the Civil War, Washington supplied nearly 1,000 men to the Union forces. Prospectors entered the area in 1860, when gold was discovered near Walla Walla. The Idaho Territory was created in 1863 from parts of eastern Washington Territory. In 1888, the transcontinental railroads reached Washington, bringing with them a new influx of settlers.

Washington became the forty-second state in 1889. Seattle was its largest city and the chief supply point for the Alaskan gold rush.

During its peak growth years, settlers from Wisconsin, Minnesota, and other western states came by the thousands. Canadian farmers came to obtain good land at a low price. Most of the newcomers were Canadian, Swedish, Norwegian, English, German, Finnish, Italian, Russian, Danish, and Scottish.

Look for vital records in the following locations:
- **Birth and death records:** State Department of Health, Center for Health Statistics since 1907. Records prior to that are in the offices of county auditors, and usually go back to 1891. City health departments in Seattle, Spokane, Bellingham, and Tacoma also have birth and death records.
- **Marriage and land records:** County auditors have marriage and land records. County clerks have wills and probate records.
- **Census records:** Territorial and state censuses exist for a few counties for various years prior to 1892. These partial censuses are available at the Washington State Library in Olympia.

State Department of Health
Center for Health Statistics
PO Box 9709
Olympia, Washington 98507
360.753.5936

Washington State Library
Capitol Campus
AJ-11
Olympia Washington 98504

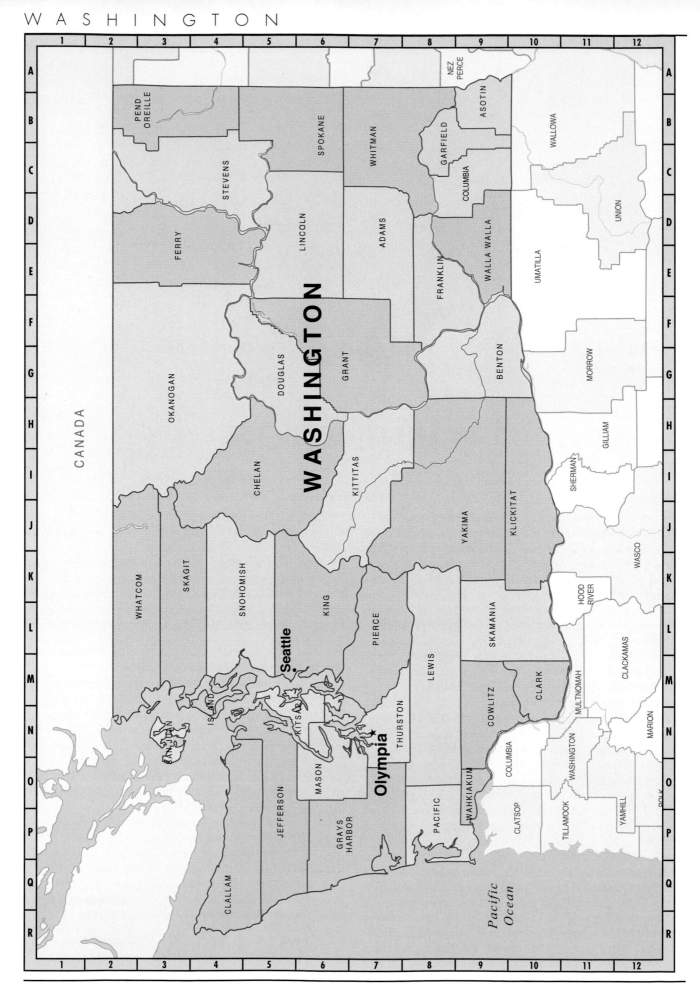

Societies and Repositories

American Baptist - Samuel Colgate Historical Library; 1106 South Goodman Street; Rochester, New York 14620-2532; 716.473.1740; Fax 716.473.1740

Archdiocese of Seattle; Chancery Office; 910 Marion Street; Seattle, Washington 98104; 206.382.4560; Fax 206.382.4840; (Roman Catholic records)

Bellevue Regional Library; NE 12th St. & 110th Ave. NE; Bellevue, Washington 98004; 425.450.1760

Bellingham Public Library; PO Box 1197; Bellingham, Washington 98225

Big Bend Chapter, AHSGR; 202 W 2nd; Ritzville, Washington 99169-1704; 509.659.1537

Big Bend Chapter, Germans from Russia; 202 West 2nd; Ritzville, Washington 99169

Blue Mountain Chapter, AHSGR; 2111 Gemstone; Walla Walla, Washington 99362; 509.529.2253

Blue Mountain Chapter, Germans from Russia; 240 Bald Rd.; Touchet, Washington 99360

Burlington Public Library; 900 Fairhaven St.; Burlington, Washington 98233

Central Washington Chapter, Germans from Russia; 3064 Alder St.; Toppenish, Washington 98958

Chehalis Valley Historical Society; 268-11 Oak Meadows Rd.; Oakville, Washington 98568

Chelan Valley Genealogical Society; PO Box "Y"; Chelan, Washington 98816

Clallam County Genealogical Society; c/o Genealogical Library, Clallam County Museum 223 E. Fourth St.; Port Angeles, Washington 98362

Clark Co. Gen. Society; 717 Grand Blvd.; Vancouver, Washington 98661; 360.750.5688; <www.ccgs-wa.org>

Clark Co. Museum; 1511 Main; Vancouver, Washington 98668

Collins Memorial Library; University of Puget Sound; 1500 North Warner; Tacoma, Washington 98416; 253.756.3669; Fax 253.756.3670; (United Methodist Church records. This library has records of ministers but not of church members.)

Columbia Basin Chapter, AHSGR; 1820 West Part St.; Pasco, Washington 99301; 509.545.9423

Columbia Basin Chapter, Germans from Russia; 1820 W. Park; Pasco, Washington 99301

Douglas County Genealogical Society; PO Box 580; Waterville, Washington 98858

Eastern Washington Genealogical Society; PO Box 1826; Spokane, Washington 99210-1826; <onlinepub.net/ewgs>

Eastside Genealogical Society; PO Box 374; Bellevue, Washington 98009

Ellensburg, Washington Genealogical Group; 507 E. Tacoma St.; Ellensburg, Washington 98926

Everett Public Library; 2702 Hoyt Ave.; Everett, Washington 98201

Family History Library; 35 North West Temple Street; Salt Lake City, Utah 84150; 800.346.6044 or 801.240.2584; <www.familysearch.org>; Find a Family History Center near you; <http://www.familysearch.org/Eng/Library/FHC/frameset_fhc.asp>

Fiske Gen. Foundation Library; 1644 43rd Ave. East; Seattle, Washington 98122-3222; 206.328.2716; <www.fiske.lib.wa.us>

Ft. Vancouver Historical Society; PO Box 1834; Vancouver, Washington 98663

Ft. Vancouver Regional Library; 1007 E. Mill Plain Blvd.; Vancouver, Washington 98660

Genealogical Society of Pierce County; PO Box 189; Dupont, Washington 98327-0189

Grant County Genealogical Society; c/o Ephrata Public Library; 45 Alder St. N.W.; Ephrata, Washington 98823

Grays Harbor Genealogical Society; PO Box 867; Cosmopolis, Washington 98537.0867

Greater Seattle Chapter, AHSGR; 7010 17th Avenue NE; Seattle, Washington 98115; 206.523.4136; <www.ahsgr.org/waseattl.html>

Greater Seattle Chapter, Germans from Russia; 7010 17th Ave., NE; Seattle, Washington 98115

Greater Spokane Chapter, AHSGR; 2936 Grandview Ave.; Spokane, Washington 99224-5525; 509.624.6947

Greater Spokane Chapter, Germans from Russia; 2936 W. Grandview; Spokane, Washington 99224

Heritage Center Museum and Library, Snohomish Co. Hist. Assoc.; PO Box 5203; Everett, Washington 98206

Heritage Quest Research Library; 909 Main St., Suite 5; Sumner, Washington 98390; 253.863.1806; <members.aol.com/hqrl/index.htm>

Issaquah Public Library; 140 E. Sunset Way; Bellevue, Washington 98004; 425.392.5430

Italian Interest Group of the Eastside Genealogical Society; PO Box 374; Bellevue, Washington 98009-0374

Jefferson County Genealogical Society; 210 Madison; Port Townsend, Washington 98368; 360.385.1003; <www.rootsweb.com/~wajcgs>

Jewish Genealogical Society of Washington; 14222 NE 1st Lane; Bellevue, Washington 98007

Kittitas County Genealogical Society; PO Box 1342; Ellensburg, Washington 98926; 509.925.5951

Lake Hills Library; 15528 Lake Hills Blvd., SE; Bellevue, Washington 98007; 425.747.3350

Lewis County Genealogical Society; PO Box 782; Chelalis, Washington 98532

Lower Columbia Genealogical Society; PO Box 472; Longview, Washington 98632

Maple Valley Historical Society; PO Box 123; Maple Valley, Washington 98038

Mason County Genealogical Society; PO Box 333; Hoodspont, Washington 98548

Mid-Columbia Library; 405 South Dayton; Kennewick, Washington 99336

National Archives—Pacific Northwest Region (Seattle); 6125 Sand Point Way, N.E.; Seattle, Washington 98115-7999; 206.526.6507; Fax 206.526.6545

Neill Public Library; N. 210 Grand Ave.; Pullman, Washington 99163

Newport Way Library; 14520 SE Newport Way; Bellevue, Washington 98006; 425.747.2390

North Bend Library; 115 E. Fourth St.; North Bend, Washington 98045; 425.888.0554

Northeast Washington Genealogical Society; c/o Colville Public Library; 195 S. Oak; Colville, Washington 99114

Okanogan County Genealogical Society; 263 Old Riverside Hwy.; Omak, Washington 98841

Olympia Genealogical Society; c/o Olympia Public Library; 8th and Franklin; Olympia, Washington 98501

Olympia Timberland Library; 313 8th Ave. SE; Olympia, Washington 98501; 206.352.0595

Olympic Peninsula Chapter, AHSGR; 30 Raccoon Rd.; Sequim, Washington 98382; 360.683.1765; <www.ahsgr.org/waolypen.html>

Olympic Peninsula Chapter, Germans from Russia; 2551 Fir Ave.; Bremerton, Washington 98310

Oregon State Office of the Bureau of Land Management (BLM); PO Box 2965; 1515 S.W. 5th Ave.; Portland; Oregon 97208-2965; 503.952.6287; Fax 503.952.6333. Other local land office records are at the National Archives—Pacific Northwest Region (Seattle).

Pacific County Genealogical Society; PO Box 843; Ocean Park, Washington 98640

Presbyterian Historical Society; Presbyterian Church U.S.A.; 425 Lombard Street; Philadelphia, Pennsylvania 19147-1516; 215.627.1852; Fax 215.627.0509

Puget Sound Genealogical Society; 1026 Sidney Ave., Suite 110; Port Orchard, Washington 98366-4298

Rainier Chapter, AHSGR; 1007 No. Meridian; Puyallup, Washington 98371; 253.845.0136; <www.ahsgr.org/warainer.html>

Redmond Historical Society; The Old Redmond Schoolhouse; 16600 NE 80 St., Rm. 106; Redmond, Washington 98052

Seattle Genealogical Society; 8511 15 Ave. NE; Seattle, Washington 98115

Seattle Public Library; 1000 Fourth Avenue; Seattle, Washington 98104; 206.386.4629; Fax 206.386.4632

Skagit Valley Genealogical Society; PO Box 715; Conway, Washington 98238

Sno-Isle Genealogical Society; PO Box 63; Edmonds, Washington 98020

Snoqualmie Public Library; 38580 SE River St.; Snoqualmie, Washington 98065; 425.888.1223

Sons of the American Revolution, Washington Society; 12233 9th Ave., NW; Seattle, Washington 98177

South King County Genealogical Society; PO Box 3174; Kent, Washington 98032

South Pierce County Historical Society; PO Box 537; Eatonville, Washington 98328

Spokane Public Library, Gen. Rm. (Eastern Washington Gen. Soc.); West 916 Main Ave.; Spokane, Washington 99201

State Capitol Historical Association; 211 W. 21st Ave.; Olympia, Washington 98501

Stillaguamish Valley Genealogical Society of North Snohomish County; PO Box 34; Arlington, Washington 98223

Suzzallo-Allen Library; University of Washington; PO Box 352900; Seattle, Washington 98195-2900; 206.543.9158; Fax 206.685.8049

Swan Creek Library; 3808 Portland Ave.; Tacoma, Washington 98404; 253.594.7805

Tacoma Public Library; 1102 Tacoma Ave. South; Tacoma, Washington 98402; 253.591.5666

Tacoma South Branch Library; 3711 S. 56th St.; Tacoma, Washington 98402; 253.591.5670

Tacoma, Anna Lemon Wheelock Library; 3722 North 26th St.; Tacoma, Washington 98402; 253.591.5640

Tacoma, Dr. Martin Luther King, Jr. Library; 1902 South Cedar St.; Tacoma, Washington 98402; 253.591.5166

Tacoma, Fern Hill Branch Library; 765 South 84th St.; Tacoma, Washington 98402; 253.591.5620

Tacoma, Kobetich Library; 212 Brown's Point Blvd. NE; Tacoma, Washington 98402; 253.591.5630

Tacoma, Moore Library; 215 South 56th St.; Tacoma, Washington 98402; 253.591.5650

Tacoma, Mottet Branch Library; 3523 East G Street; Tacoma, Washington 98404; 253.591.5660

Tacoma, Swasey Branch Library; 7001 Sixth Ave.; Tacoma, Washington 98402; 253.591.5680

Tacoma-Pierce County Genealogical Society; PO Box 1952; Tacoma, Washington 98401

Tonasket Genealogical Society; PO Box 84; Tonasket, Washington 98855

Tri-City Genealogical Society; PO Box 1410; Richland, Washington 99352.1410

Univ. of Washington Library; Seattle, Washington 98105

Vital Records; PO Box 9709; Olympia, Washington 98504-9709; 360.753.5936; Fax 360.753.4135

Walla Walla Valley Genealogical Society; PO Box 115; Walla Walla, Washington 99362.0115

Washington State Archives; 1120 Washington St. S.E.; PO Box 40238; Olympia, Washington 98504-0238: 360.586.1492; Fax 360.664.8814

Washington State Genealogical Society; PO Box 1422; Olympia, Washington 98507-1422; <www.rootsweb.com/~wasgs/>

Washington State Historical Society Library; Research Center; 315 North Stadium Way; Tacoma, Washington 98402; 253.798.5914; Fax 253.597.4186

Washington State Historical Society Library; State Historical Bldg.; 315 N. Stadium Way; Tacoma, Washington 98403;

Washington State Historical Society; 1911 Pacific Avenue; Tacoma, Washington 98402;

Washington State Library; PO Box 42460; Olympia, Washington 98504-2460; 360.753.5590; Fax 360.586.7575

Washington State Univ. Library; Holland Library; Pullman, Washington 99164-5610

Wenatchee Area Genealogical Society; 133 S. Mission St.; PO Box 5280; Wenatchee, Washington 98807.5280

Whatcom Genealogical Society; PO Box 1493; Bellingham, Washington 98227-1493

Whitman County Genealogical Society; PO Box 393; Pullman, Washington 99163; <www.completebbs.com/simonsen/wcgsindex.html>

Willapa Harbor Genealogical Society; c/o Raymond Public Library; 507 Duryea St.; Raymond, Washington 98577

Yakima Valley Genealogical Society; PO Box 445; Yakima, Washington 98907

Bibliography and Record Sources

General Sources

Abbott, Newton Carl. *The Evolution of Washington Counties.* [S.l.]: Yakima Valley Genealogical Society & Klickitat County Historical Society, 1978.

Avery, Mary Williamson. Washington: *A History of the Evergreen State.* Seattle: University of Washington Press, 1967.

Boyd, Robert. *History of the Synod of Washington of The Presbyterian Church in the United States of America 1835-1909.* Seattle: The Synod, [1910?].

Brulotte, Frieda Eichler. *Germans from Russia in the Yakima Valley, Prior to 1940.* Yakima, Washington: The Society, 1990.

Genealogical Resources in Washington State: A Guide to Genealogical Records Held at Repositories, Government Agencies, and Archives. Olympia, Washington: Office of the Secretary of State, Division of Archives and Records Management, 1983.

Clubb, Mrs. Robert Earl. *Family Records of Washington Pioneers Prior to 1891.* Daughters of the American Revolution of the State of Washington. Salt Lake City: Genealogical Society of Utah, 1960. Microfilm.

Dahlie, Jorgen. *A Social History of Scandinavian Immigration, Washington State, 1895-1910.* New York: Arno Press, 1980.

Evans, Elwood. *History of the Pacific Northwest: Oregon and Washington; Embracing an Account of the Original Discoveries on the Pacific Coast of North America, and a Description of the Conquest, Settlement and Subjugation of the…Original Territory of Oregon; also Interesting Biographies of the Earliest Settlers.* 2 vols. Portland, Oregon: North Pacific History Co., [1889].

Genealogical Resources in Washington State: A Guide to Genealogical Records Held at Repositories, Government Agencies and Archives. Olympia, Washington: Secretary of State, Division of Archives and Records Management, 1983.

Hines, Harvey K. *An Illustrated History of the State of Washington: Containing…Biographical Mention of…its Pioneers and Prominent Citizens….* Chicago: Lewis Pub. Co., 1893.

Hunt, Herbert. *Washington West of the Cascades: Historical and Descriptive, the Explorers, the Indians, the Modern.* Tucson, Arizona: W. C. Cox, 1974.

Missionary History of the Pacific Northwest: Containing the Wonderful Story of Jason Lee, with Sketches of Many of his Co-Laborers all Illustrating Life on the Plains and in the Mountains in Pioneer Days. Washington, D.C.: Library of Congress, 1990.

Historical Records of Washington State: Records and Papers Held at Repositories. Olympia, Washington: Washington State Historical Records Advisory Board, 1981.

Howell, Erle. *Methodisim in the Northwest.* Nashville, TN: Pacific Northwest Conference Historical Society, 1966.

Kirkham, E. Kay. *An Index to Some of the Bibles and Family Records of the United States.* vol. 2. Logan, Utah: Everton Publishers, 1984.

Miller, Frances Caldwell. *Celebrating the History of the Pioneer Families of Washington, 1853-1889.* Wenatchee, WA: Native Daughters of Washington Territorial Pioneers, 1989.

Newton Carl Abbott and Fred E. Carver, *The Evolution of Washington Counties.* [n.p.]: Yakima Valley Genealogical Society & Klickitat County Historical Society, 1978.

Osborn-Ryan, Sharon E. *Cumulative Baptism Index to the Catholic Church Records of the Pacific Northwest.* [S.l.]: Oregon Heritage Press, 1999.

Pollard, Lancaster. *A History of Washington.* 4 vols. New York: American Historical Society, 1937.

Preston, Ralph N. *Early Washington: Overland Stage Routes, Old Military Roads, Indian Battle Grounds, Old Forts, Old Gold Mines.* Corvallis, Oregon: Western Guide Publishers, 1974.

Prosch, Charles. *Reminiscences of Washington Territory.* Fairfield, WA: Ye Galleon Press, 1969.

Priestley, Marilyn. *Comprehensive Guide to the Manuscripts Collection and to the Personal Papers in the University Archives.* Seattle, WA: The Library, 1980.

Schoenberg, Wilfred P. *A History of the Catholic Church in the Pacific Northwest, 1743-1983.* Washington, D.C.: Pastoral Press, 1987.

Sketches of Washingtonians. Seattle: W.C. Wolfe & Co., 1906.

Swart, Shirley, comp. *Index to Washington State Daughters of the American Revolution.* Yakima, Wash.: Yakima Valley Genealogical Society, 1983.

Tacoma-Pierce County Genealogical Society. *Bibliography of Washington State Historical Society Library.* 3 vols. Tacoma, Wash.: The Society, 1986.

The Dictionary Catalog of the Pacific Northwest Collection of the University of Washington. 6 vols. Boston: G.K. Hall and Co., 1972.

Washington Research Outline. Series US-States, No. 47. Salt Lake City: Family History Library, 1988.

Washington State Division of Archives and Records Management. *Genealogical Resources in Washington State: A Guide to Genealogical Records Held at Repositories, Government Agencies, and Archives.* [Olympia, Wash.]: Sec. of State, Div. of Archives and Records Management, 1983.

Washington State Historical Records and Archives Projects. *Historical Records of Washington State: Records and Papers Held at Repositories.* [Olympia, WA:] Wash. State. Hist. Recds. Adv. Brd., 1981.

Washington State Union List of Newspapers: On Microfilm. Olympia, WA: Washington State Library, 1991. 11 microfiche.

Washington West of the Cascades. 3 vols. Chicago: S.J. Clarke, 1917.

Who's Who in Washington State: A Compilation of Biographical Sketches of Men and Women Prominent in the Affairs of Washington State. Seattle: H. Allen Pub., 1927.

Atlases, Maps and Gazetteers

Abbott, Newton Carl, Fred E. Carver, and J.W. Helm, comp. *The Evolution of Washington Counties.* Yakima, WA: Yakima Valley Genealogical Society and Klickitat County Historical Society, 1978.

Landes, Henry. *A Geographic Dictionary of Washington.* Washington Geological Survey. Bulletin no. 17. Olympic, Washington: F.M. Lamborn, 1917.

Meany, Edmond S. *Origin of Washington Geographic Names.* 1923. Reprint. Detroit: Gale Research Co., 1968.

Phillips, James W. *Washington State Place Names.* Seattle: University of Washington Press, 1971.

Preston, Ralph N. *Early Washington: Overland Stage Routes, Old Military Roads, Indian Battle Grounds, Old Forts, Old Gold Miners.* Corvallis, Oregon: Western Guide Publishers, 1974. Reprinted as *Early Washington Atlas.* 2nd Ed. Binford & Mort Publishers, 1974.

R. L. Polk & Co. Oregon & Washington Gazetteer and Business Directory , 1909-1910. Seattle: R.L. Polk, 1909.

Scott, James R. *Washington: A Centennial Atlas.* Bellingham: Western Washington University, 1989.

Scott, James R. and Roland L. DeLorme. *Historical Atlas of Washington.* Norman: University of Oklahoma Press, 1988.

Washington Atlas and Gazetteer. 3rd ed. Freeport, ME: DeLorme Mapping Co., 1996.

Census Records

Available Census Records and Census Substitutes

Federal Census 1860, 1870, 1880, 1900, 1910, 1920, 1930.

Federal Mortality Schedules 1850, 1860, 1870, 1880.

Union Veterans and Widows 1890.

State/Territorial Census 1857-1892, 1872-1888.

Dollarhide, William. *The Census Book: A Genealogist's Guide to Federal Census Facts, Schedules and Indexes.* Bountiful, UT: Heritage Quest, 1999.

Lainhart, Ann S. *State Census Records.* Baltimore: Genealogical Publishing Co., Inc., 1992.

Kemp, Thomas Jay. *The American Census Handbook.* Wilmington, DE: Scholarly Resources, Inc., 2001

Szucs, Loretto Dennis, and Matthew Wright. *Finding Answers in U.S. Census Records.* Ancestry Publishing, 2001.

Thorndale, William, and William Dollarhide. *Map Guide to the U.S. Federal Censuses, 1790-1920.* Baltimore: Genealogical Publishing Co., 1987.

United States. Bureau of Indian Affairs. Portland Area Office. *Tribal Census Information, 1877-1952.* Microfilm of originals at the Federal Record Center, Seattle, Washington. (Salt Lake City: Filmed by the Genealogical Society of Utah, 1978). 2 microfilm.

Washington. Secretary of State. *Washington Territorial Census Rolls, 1857-1892.* Olympia, Washington: Washington State Archives, 1987. Microfilm, 20 rolls.

Court Records, Probate and Wills

Frontier Justice Records Project (Washington State). *Frontier Justice: Guide to the Court Records of Washington Territory, 1853-1889.* 2 vols. Olympia, Washington: National Historical Publications and Records Commission, 1987.

Hopkins, Pat. *A Guide to the Records of Washington Territorial Supreme Court, 1853- 1889.* Olympia, Washington: Washington State Archives, 1983.

United States. Bureau of Indian Affairs. Portland Area Office. *Heirship and Probate Information, 1887-1952.* Microfilm of originals at the Federal Record Center, Seattle, Washington. (Salt Lake City: Filmed by the Genealogical Society of Utah, 1978). Microfilm, 10 rolls.

Emigration, Immigration, Migration and Naturalization

United States. District Court (Washington: Eastern District). *Declaration of Intention, 1890-1972; Petition for Naturalization, 1907-1 950; Repatriations, 1940-1942; Application for Citizenship, 1879-1906; Indexes, 1890-1947.* Microfilm of originals in the National Archives, Seattle Branch in Seattle, Washington. (Salt Lake City: Filmed by the Genealogical Society of Utah, 1988). Microfilm, 26 rolls.

United States. District Court (Washington: Western District: Southern Division). *Naturalization Indexes, 1896-1953.* Microfilm of originals at the Archives Branch of the Federal Archives and Records Center at Seattle, Washington. (Salt Lake City: Filmed by the Genealogical Society of Utah, 1984). Microfilm, 2 rolls.

United States. Immigration and Naturalization Service. *Passenger and Crew Lists of Vessels Arriving At Seattle, Washington, 1890- 1921.* Washington, D.C.: National Archives Records Service, 1957. Microfilm, multiple rolls.

United States. Immigration and Naturalization Service. *Crew Lists of Vessels Arriving at Seattle, Washington, 1903-1917.* Washington, D.C.: The National Archives, 1988. Microfilm, 15 rolls.

Land and Property

United States. Bureau of Indian Affairs. Tulalip Agency. *Allotment and Land Records, 1883-1932.* Microfilm of original records in the Federal Record Center, Seattle, Washington. (Salt Lake City: Filmed by the Genealogical Society of Utah, 1978). 4 microfilm.

United States. Land Office. *Donation Land Claims by Orphans in Oregon and Washington, 1867-1873.* Microfilm of originals in the National Archives Branch in Seattle, Washington. (Salt Lake City: Filmed by the Genealogical Society of Utah, 1989).

Washington Territory Donation Land Claims: An Abstract of Information in the Land Claim Papers of Persons Who Settled in Washington Territory Before 1856. Seattle: Seattle Genealogical Society, 1980.

Waugh, Kathleen. *Index to Mining Surveys, 1883-1964.* Olympia, Wash.: K. Waugh, 1985.

United States. General Land Office. *Abstracts of Washington Donation Land Claims, 1855-1902.* Washington, D.C.: The National Archives, 1951. Microfilm, multiple rolls.

United States. Land Office (Washington). *Land Records.* Microfilm of Originals in the National Archives Pacific Northwest Region Office in Seattle, Washington. (Salt Lake City: Filmed by the Genealogical Society of Utah, 1989). Microfilm 72 rolls.

United States. General Land Office. *Oregon and Washington Donation Land Files, 1851-1903.* Washington: The National Archives, 1970. Microfilm, 108 rolls.

Military

Field, Virgil F. *Washington National Guard Pamphlet: The Official History of the Washington National Guard.* 7 vols. in 3.Tacoma: Office of the Adjutant General, 1961.

Pompey, Sherman Lee. *Burial List of the Members of the 1st Washington Territory Infantry.* Kingsburg, California: Pacific Specialties, 1972.

Pompey, Sherman Lee. *Civil War Veteran Burials from the Arizona Territory, Nebraska, Nevada, New Mexico, Oregon, Utah and the Washington Territory.* (Salt Lake City: Filmed by the Genealogical Society of Utah, 1975). Microfilm.

Taylor, John. *Indian War Muster Rolls, 1855-1856.* Microfilm of originals in the Washington State Archives in Olympia, Washington. (Salt Lake City: Filmed by the Genealogical Society of Utah, 1991). Microfilm.

United States. Adjutant General's Office. *Index to Compiled Service Records of Volunteer Union Soldiers Who Served in Organizations from the Territory of Washington.* Washington, D.C.: The National Archives, 1964. Microfilm.

United States. Army. *Registers of Enlistments in the United States Army, 1798-1914.* Washington, D.C.: National Archives, 1956. Microfilm, Multiple rolls.

United States. Selective Service System. *Washington World War I Selective Service System Draft Registration Cards, 1917-1918.* National Archives Microfilm Publications, M1509. Washington, D.C.: National Archives, 1987-1988.

United States. Veterans Administration. *Pension Index Files, Indian Wars, 1892-1926.* Washington: Veterans' Administration, 1959. Microfilm, multiple rolls.

Vital and Cemetery Records

A Directory of Cemeteries and Funeral Homes in Washington State. Washington Interment Association and the Washington State Funeral Directors Association. Orting, WA: Heritage Quest, 1990.

Carter, John D., ed. *Washington's First Marriages of the Thirty-Nine Counties.* Spokane: Eastern Washington Genealogical Society, 1986.

Cemetery Records of Washington. 6 vols. Salt Lake City: Genealogical Society of Utah. 1957-1960.

Guide to Public Vital Statistics Records in Washington. Seattle, WS: Washington Historical Records Survey, 1941.

United States. Bureau of Indian Affairs. Northern Idaho Agency. *Agency Records, 1887-1947.* (Salt Lake City: Filmed by the Genealogical Society of Utah, 1979). 7 microfilm rolls.

Washington Bureau of Vital Statistics. *Index to Birth Certificates, 1907-1959.* Olympia, Washington: Bureau of Vital Statistics, 1960.

Washington Bureau of Vital Statistics. *Index to Death Certificates, 1907-1959, 1960-1979.* Olympia, Washington: Bureau of Vital Statistics, 1954-1960.

Washington. Department of Health. Bureau of Vital Statistics. *Index to Delayed Birth Records, 1900-1980.* Olympia, Washington: Bureau of Vital Statistics, 1996. 12 microfiche.

County Website	Map Index	Date Created	Parent County or Territory From Which Organized Address/Details
Adams* www.co.adams.wa.us/	D7	28 Nov 1883	**Whitman** Adams County; 210 W Broadway Ave; Ritzville, WA 99169-1860; Ph. 509.659.3257 Details: (Co Aud has b & d rec to 1907 & m rec; Co Clk has div & pro rec; Co Asr has land rec)
Asotin* www.palouse.org/asotin.htm	B9	27 Oct 1883	**Garfield** Asotin County; PO Box 159; Asotin, WA 99402-0159; Ph. 509.243.4181 Details: (Co Aud has b & m rec from 1891 & d rec 1891-1907; Co Clk has div & pro rec; Co Asr has land rec from 1891)
Benton* www.co.benton.wa.us/	G9	8 Mar 1905	**Yakima, Klickitat** Benton County; 600 Market St; Prosser, WA 99350-0190; Ph. 509.786.5624 Details: (Co Aud has b rec 1905-1907 & m rec from 1905; Co Clk has div, pro & ct rec; Co Asr has land rec)
Chehalis		14 Apr 1854	**Thurston** Details: (see Grays Harbor) (Name changed to Grays Harbor 15 Mar 1915)
Chelan* www.co.chelan.wa.us/	I5	13 Mar 1899	**Kittitas, Okanogan** Chelan County; 350 Douglas St; Wenatchee, WA 98801; Ph. 509.667.6380 Details: (Co Aud has b & d rec 1900-1907 & m rec from 1900; City Clk has bur rec; Co Clk has div, pro & ct rec)
Clallam www.clallam.net/	Q4	26 Apr 1854	**Jefferson** Clallam County; 223 E 4th St; PO Box 863; Port Angeles, WA 98362-3025; Ph. 360.417.2508 Details: (Co Aud has m & land rec; Co Clk has pro rec)
Clark www.co.clark.wa.us/	M10	27 Jun 1844	**Original county** Clark County; 1200 Franklin St; Vancouver, WA 98660; Ph. 360.397.2292 Details: (Formerly Vancouver Co. Name changed to Clark 3 Sep 1849) (Co Aud has b & d rec 1890-1906, m rec from 1890 & land rec from 1850; Co Clk has div, pro & ct rec from 1890)
Columbia www.columbiaco.com/	C9	11 Nov 1875	**Walla Walla** Columbia County; 341 E Main St; Dayton, WA 99328-1361; Ph. 509.382.4321 Details: (Co Clk has pro, div & ct rec from 1891; Co Aud has b & d rec 1891-1906, m rec from 1876, land rec from 1864 & mil dis rec)
Cowlitz* www.co.cowlitz.wa.us/	N9	21 Apr 1854	**Lewis** Cowlitz County; 207 4th Ave N; Kelso, WA 98626-1798; Ph. 360.577.3016 Details: (Co Aud has m rec from 1867, d rec 1891-1907 & land rec; Co Clk has div, pro & ct rec from 1874, nat & adoption rec from 1869)
Douglas www.douglascountywa.net/	G5	28 Nov 1883	**Lincoln** Douglas County; 213 S Rainier; Waterville, WA 98858; Ph. 509.745.8529 Details: (Co Aud has b rec to 1907, bur rec to 1909, land rec to 1925, m, d, div, pro & ct rec)
Ferry www.wa.gov/ferry/	E3	18 Feb 1899	**Stevens** Ferry County; 350 E Delaware; PO Box 302; Republic, WA 99166; Ph. 509.775.5232 Details: (Co Clk has div, pro & ct rec from 1899)
Franklin www.co.franklin.wa.us/	E8	28 Nov 1883	**Whitman** Franklin County; 1016 N 4th Ave; Pasco, WA 99301; Ph. 509.545.3525 Details: (Co Aud has b, d & bur rec 1891-1910, m rec from 1891 & land rec; Co Clk has div, pro & ct rec from 1891)
Garfield* www.palouse.org/garfield.htm	C8	29 Nov 1881	**Columbia** Garfield County; PO Box 915; Pomeroy, WA 99347-0915; Ph. 509.843.3731 Details: (Co Aud has b & d rec 1891-1907, m & land rec from 1891 & bur rec 1891-1918; Co Clk has div, pro & ct rec from 1882)
Grant www.grantcounty-wa.com/	G6	24 Feb 1909	**Douglas** Grant County; 35 C St NW; PO Box 37; Ephrata, WA 98823-0037; Ph. 509.754.2011 Details: (Co Aud has m & land rec from 1909; Co Clk has div, pro & ct rec)

County Website	Map Index	Date Created	Parent County or Territory From Which Organized Address/Details
Grays Harbor www.co.grays-harbor.wa.us/	P6	14 Apr 1854	**Thurston** Grays Harbor County; 102 W Broadway Rm 203; Montesano, WA 98563; Ph. 360.249.3842 Details: (Formerly Chehalis Co. Name changed to Grays Harbor 15 Mar 1915) (Co Clk has pro, div & ct rec from 1860; Co Aud has m rec from 1891; Co Asr has land rec from 1855; Co Hlth Dept has b & d rec)
Island www.islandcounty.net/	M4	6 Jan 1853	**Thurston** Island County; NE 6th & Main St; PO Box 5000; Coupeville, WA 98239-5000; Ph. 360.679.7359 Details: (Co Aud has b & d rec 1870-1907, m rec from 1855 & land rec from 1853; Co Clk has div, pro & ct rec)
Jefferson www.co.jefferson.wa.us/	P5	22 Dec 1852	**Thurston, Lewis** Jefferson County; 1820 Jefferson St; PO Box 1220; Port Townsend, WA 98368-0920; Ph. 360.385.9125 Details: (Co Clk has div rec from 1886, pro rec from 1891 & ct rec from 1890; Co Aud has b & d rec 1891-1907 & m rec from 1853)
King* www.metrokc.gov/	L6	22 Dec 1852	**Thurston** King County; 516 3rd Ave; Seattle, WA 98104; Ph. 206.296.1020 Details: (Rec & Elections Div, Rec Sec has b, m, d & land rec from 1853; Clk Sup Ct has div, pro & ct rec)
Kitsap www.kitsapgov.com/	N5	16 Jan 1857	**King, Jefferson** Kitsap County; 614 Division St; Port Orchard, WA 98366; Ph. 360.337.7164 Details: (Formerly Slaughter Co. Name changed to Kitsap 13 Jul 1857) (Co Aud has b rec 1891-1907, d rec 1892-1907 & m rec from 1892; Co Clk has div & ct rec from 1888, pro & adoption rec from 1861 & land rec from 1857)
Kittitas www.co.kittitas.wa.us/	I7	24 Nov 1883	**Yakima** Kittitas County; 205 W 5th Ave; Ellensburg, WA 98926; Ph. 509.962.7624 Details: (Co Aud has b & d rec 1891-1907, m rec from 1884 & land rec from 1882; Co Clk has div, pro & ct rec from 1890's)
Klickitat klickitatcounty.org/	J10	20 Dec 1859	**Skamania** Klickitat County; 205 S Columbus Ave Rm 204; Goldendale, WA 98620; Ph. 509.773.4559 Details: (Co Clk has div, pro & ct rec; Co Aud has m rec)
Lewis* www.co.lewis.wa.us/	M8	21 Dec 1845	**Original county** Lewis County; 351 NW North St; Chehalis, WA 98532; Ph. 360.740.2704 Details: (Co Aud has b & d rec 1891-1907 & m rec from 1850; Co Clk has div, pro & ct rec from 1870's)
Lincoln* www.rootsweb.com/~walincol/ lincoln.htm	E6	24 Nov 1883	**Spokane** Lincoln County; 450 Logan St; PO Box 369; Davenport, WA 99122; Ph. 509.725.1401 Details: (Co Aud has b & d rec 1891-1907, m & land rec from 1891; Co Clk has div, pro & ct rec)
Mason www.co.mason.wa.us/	O6	13 Mar 1854	**Thurston** Mason County; 411 N 5th; PO Box 340; Shelton, WA 98584; Ph. 360.427.9670 Details: (Formerly Sawamish Co. Name changed to Mason 8 Jan 1864) (Co Aud has m rec from 1892, d rec 1891-1906 & land rec from 1850's; Co Clk has div, pro & ct rec)
Okanogan www.okanogancounty.org/	H3	2 Feb 1888	**Stevens** Okanogan County; 149 3rd N; PO Box 72; Okanogan, WA 98840; Ph. 509.422.7275 Details: (Co Aud has b & d rec 1891-1908, m & land rec from 1891 & patents from 1892; Co Clk has div, pro & ct rec from 1896)
Pacific www.co.pacific.wa.us/	P8	4 Feb 1851	**Lewis** Pacific County; 300 Memorial Ave; PO Box 67; South Bend, WA 98586-0067; Ph. 360.875.9320 Details: (Co Aud has b & d rec 1891-1905 & m rec from 1868; Co Clk has div, pro & ct rec; Co Asr has land rec)

County Website	Map Index	Date Created	Parent County or Territory From Which Organized Address/Details
Pend Oreille www.usgennet.org/usa/wa/county/ pendoreille/	B3	1 Mar 1911	**Stevens** Pend Oreille County; 625 W 4th; PO Box 5020; Newport, WA 99156-5000; Ph. 509.447.2435 Details: (Co Aud has b, m & land rec from 1911; Co Clk has div, pro & ct rec from 1911)
Pierce www.co.pierce.wa.us/PC/	L7	22 Dec 1852	**Thurston** Pierce County; 930 Tacoma Ave S; Tacoma, WA 98402; Ph. 253.798.7455 Details: (Co Aud has m & land rec; Co Clk has div, pro & ct rec from 1890 & adoptions)
San Juan www.co.san-juan.wa.us/	N3	31 Oct 1873	**Whatcom** San Juan County; 350 Court St #7; Friday Harbor, WA 98250-1249; Ph. 360.378.2163 Details: (Co Clk has div, pro & ct rec; Co Aud has b rec 1892-1907, d rec 1890-1907 & m rec from 1878)
Sawamish		13 Mar 1854	**Thurston** Details: (see Mason) (Name changed to Mason 8 Jan 1864)
Skagit* www.skagitcounty.net/index.htm	K3	28 Nov 1883	**Whatcom** Skagit County; 700 S 2nd St; PO Box 837; Mount Vernon, WA 98273; Ph. 360.336.9440 Details: (Co Aud has b & d rec 1891-1907, m rec from 1884 & land rec from 1872; Co Clk has div, pro & ct rec from 1870)
Skamania Future website at usgenweb.com/	L9	9 Mar 1854	**Clark** Skamania County; 240 Vancouver Ave; Stevenson, WA 98648-0790; Ph. 509.427.9431 Details: (Co Aud has land rec; Co Clk has m, div, pro & ct rec from 1856)
Slaughter		16 Jan 1857	**King, Jefferson** Details: (see Kitsap) (Name changed to Kitsap 13 Jul 1857)
Snohomish* www.co.snohomish.wa.us/	K4	14 Jan 1861	**Island** Snohomish County; 3000 Rockefeller Ave MS 605; Everett, WA 98201-4046; Ph. 425.388.3583 Details: (Co Aud has b & d rec 1891-1907 & m rec from 1891; Co Clk has div, pro & ct rec)
Spokane* www.spokanecounty.org/	B6	29 Jan 1858	**Walla Walla** Spokane County; W 1116 Broadway; Spokane, WA 99260; Ph. 509.477.2245 Details: (Spokane Co was organized in 1858 from Walla Walla, then disorganized & reorganized in 1879 from Stevens Co) (Co Aud has b & d rec 1890-1907, m rec from 1890 & land rec; Co Clk has div, pro & ct rec)
Stevens* www.co.stevens.wa.us/	C4	20 Jan 1863	**Walla Walla** Stevens County; 215 S Oak St Rm 206; Colville, WA 99114; Ph. 509.684.7575 Details: (Co Aud has b & d rec 1891-1907, m rec from 1861 & land rec from 1883; Co Clk has pro, div & ct rec from 1889)
Thurston www.co.thurston.wa.us/	N7	12 Jan 1852	**Lewis** Thurston County; 2000 Lakeridge Dr SW; Olympia, WA 98502; Ph. 360.786.5438 Details: (Co Aud has b & d rec 1891-1907 & m rec from 1891; Co Clk has div, pro & ct rec)
Vancouver		27 Jun 1844	**Original county** Details: (see Clark) (Name changed to Clark 3 Sep 1849)
Wahkiakum www.cwcog.org/	O9	24 Apr 1854	**Pacific** Wahkiakum County; 64 Main St; PO Box 116; Cathlamet, WA 98612; Ph. 360.795.3558 Details: (Co Aud has b rec 1891-1907 & m rec from 1891; Co Clk has bur, div, pro, ct & land rec from 1868)
Walla Walla www.co.walla-walla.wa.us/	E9	25 Apr 1854	**Clark** Walla Walla County; 315 West Main St; PO Box 836; Walla Walla, WA 99362-0259; Ph. 509.527.3221 Details: (Co Clk has div, pro & ct rec from 1860)

County Website	Map Index	Date Created	Parent County or Territory From Which Organized Address/Details
Whatcom www.co.whatcom.wa.us/	L2	9 Mar 1854	**Island** Whatcom County; 311 Grand Ave; PO Box 1144; Bellingham, WA 98227; Ph. 360.676.6777 Details: (Co Aud has b & d rec 1891-1907, m rec from 1869 & land rec; Co Clk has div, pro & ct rec)
Whitman www.palouse.org/whitman.htm	C7	29 Nov 1871	**Stevens** Whitman County; N 404 Main St; Box 390; Colfax, WA 99111-2031; Ph. 509.397.6240 Details: (Co Clk has m rec 1872-1891, pro rec from 1870, div & ct rec from 1864 & nat rec 1862-1942; Co Aud has b & d rec 1891-1907 & land rec)
Yakima* co.yakima.wa.us/	J9	21 Jan 1865	**Walla Walla** Yakima County; 128 N 2nd St; Yakima, WA 98901; Ph. 509.574.1430 Details: (Co Aud had b & d rec 1891-1907, m rec from 1880 & land rec; Co Clk has pro, div & ct rec from 1882)

Notes

Rhododendron

WEST VIRGINIA

CAPITAL: CHARLESTON – STATE 1863 (35TH)

Fur traders entered western Virginia by the mid-1600's, with the first expedition across the Blue Ridge and Allegheny mountains occurring in 1671. In 1712, Baron de Graffenreid visited the eastern Panhandle to find land for Swiss families. Welsh, German, and Scotch-Irish settlers from Pennsylvania built the first settlements by 1734. Other early settlers came from Maryland to create Berkeley and Jefferson counties. In 1775, the west Augusta District was established by Virginia, which included all of present West Virginia and part of western Pennsylvania. Most of the northern part of the county was ceded to Pennsylvania in 1779 in exchange for Pennsylvania relinquishing its claims to the rest of the county.

When Virginia seceded from the Union in 1861, western counties objected. Fifty western counties united to form "The Restored Government of Virginia" and petitioned Congress for re-admittance to the Union. The state of West Virginia was admitted to the Union in 1863, after several Union victories in the area. During the Civil War, West Virginia had about 32,000 soldiers in the Union army and 9,000 in the Confederate army. In the 1870's industrial expansion in West Virginia attracted immigrants from the southern states and European immigrants, especially Italians, Poles, Hungarians, Austrians, English, Germans, Greeks, Russians, and Czechs.

Look for vital records in the following locations:

- **Birth and death records:** Contact the Division of Vital Statistics of the State Department of Health in Charleston, West Virginia. Statewide registration of births and deaths began in 1917.
- **Marriage and divorce records:** Although most state records were destroyed in a 1921 fire, most counties have records from 1853. Some counties also have marriage records from 1870. County clerks of individual circuit courts keep divorce records.
- **Probate records:** Contact individual county court administrations. These records are found in deed books and court order books.
- **Naturalization records:** Naturalization proceedings were recorded in the minutes and dockets of the courts until 1906. After 1929, only federal courts handled naturalizations.
- **Census records**: State censuses were taken in some counties between 1782 and 1785, and have been published along with tax records.

Division of Vital Statistics
State Department of Health
State Capitol Complex
Building 3, Room 513
Charleston, West Virginia 25305
304.558.2931.

West Augusta Historical & Genealogical Society; 251510th Ave.; Parkersburg, West Virginia 26101

West Virginia & Regional Hist. Collection; Colson Hall, West Virginia Univ. Library; Morgantown, West Virginia 26506

West Virginia Baptist Historical Society; Route #2 Box 304; Ripley, West Virginia 25271; 304.346.2036

West Virginia Collection, West Virginia University Library; Colson Hall, PO Box 6069; Morgantown, West Virginia 26506-6069; 304.293.3640; Fax 304.293.6923

West Virginia Genealogical Society; PO Box 172; Elkview, West Virginia 25071

West Virginia Historical Society; Cultural Center, Capitol Complex; Charleston, West Virginia 25305

West Virginia State Archives; Archives and History Library; The Cultural Center; 1900 Kanawha Boulevard, East; Charleston, West Virginia 25305.0300

Wetzel County Genealogical Society; PO Box 464; New Martinsville, West Virginia 26155-0464

Wheeling Area Genealogical Society; 2237 Marshall Ave.; Wheeling, West Virginia 26003.7444; <www.rootsweb.com/~wvwags/index.htm>

Wyoming County Genealogical Society; PO Box 1456; Pineville, West Virginia 24874

Bibliography and Record Sources

General Sources

Atkinson, George Wesley. *Prominent Men of West Virginia.* Wheeling, West Virginia: W. L. Callin, 1890.

Brown, Stuart E., Jr. *Virginia Genealogies, A Trial List of Printed Books and Pamphlets.* 3 vols. Berryville, Virginia: Virginia Book Co., 1967-89.

Butcher, Bernard Lee. *Genealogical and Personal History of the Upper Monongahela Valley, West Virginia.* 3 vols. New York: Lewis Historical Publishing Co., 1912.

Callaham, James Morton. *History of West Virginia, Old and New.* 3 vols. Chicago: American Historical Society, 1923.

Clark, Newell T., and Elizabeth Terry Long, *A Guide to Church Records in the Archives Branch of the Virginia State Library.* Richmond: Virginia State Library, 1981.

Comstock, Jim Comstock, comp. and ed. *The West Virginia Heritage Encyclopedia.* Richwood, West Virginia: Comstock, 1976. Microfiche.

Daughters of the American Revolution (West Virginia). *Genealogical Collection.* Microfilm. Salt Lake City: Genealogical Society of Utah, 1970.

Davis, Innis C. *A Bibliography of West Virginia.* Parts 1, 2, Charleston: West Virginia Department of Archives and History, 1939.

Ebert, Rebecca A. *Finding Your People in the Shenandoah Valley of Virginia and West Virginia.* Winchester, Virginia: The Rebecca Co., 1984.

Forbes, Harold M. *West Virginia History: A Guide to Research.* Morgantown: West Virginia University Press, 1981

Genealogies of WV Families. West Virginia Historical Magazine Quarterly. Reprint Clearfield Co 1992.

Ham, F. Gerald. *Guide to Manuscripts and Archives in the West Virginia Collection, Number II, 1958-1962.* Morgantown [West Virginia]: West Virginia University Library, 1965.

Hess, James W. *Guide to Manuscripts and Archives in the West Virginia Collection.* Morgantown, West Virginia: West Virginia University Library, 1974.

Historical Records Survey (West Virginia). *Church Records Survey, West Virginia, Episcopal.* (Salt Lake City: Filmed by the Genealogical Society of Utah, 1961).

Historical Records Survey (West Virginia). *An Inventory of the Records of the West Virginia Counties Which Have Been Deposited in the West Virginia University Library: Archives Section, at Morgantown, West Virginia.* [S.l.: s.n., 198-].

Historical Records Survey (West Virginia). *Church Records Survey, West Virginia, Methodist.* (Protestant). (Salt Lake City: Filmed by the Genealogical Society of Utah, 1961). 9 microfilm.

Historical Records Survey (West Virginia). *Inventory of the Church Archives of West Virginia: the Protestant Episcopal Church.* Wheeling, West Virginia: Diocese of West Virginia, 1939.

Historical Records Survey (West Virginia). *Survey of Baptist Churches, West Virginia.* (Salt Lake City: Filmed by the Genealogical Society of Utah, 1961).

Historical Records Survey (West Virginia). *Survey of Church Records, West Virginia, Presbyterian.* (Salt Lake City: Filmed by the Genealogical Society of Utah, 1961). 7 microfilm.

History of the Great Kanawha Valley: With Family History and Biographical Sketches. 2 vols. Madison, Wisconsin: Brant, Fuller & Co., 1891.

Lang, Theodore F. *Loyal West Virginia from 1861 to 1865.* Baltimore: Deutsch, 1895.

McGinnis, Carol. *West Virginia Genealogy: Sources and Resources.* Baltimore: Genealogical Publishing Co., 1988.

Men of West Virginia. 2 vols. Chicago: Biographical Publishing Co., 1903.

Miller, Thomas Condit, and Hu Maxwell. *West Virginia and Its People.* 3 vols. New York: Lewis Historical Publishing Co., 1913.

Peterkin, George W. *A History and Record of the Protestant Episcopal Church in the Diocese of West Virginia.* Charleston, West Virginia: Tribune Co., 1902.

Rice, Otis K. *West Virginia: A History.* Lexington, Kentucky: University Press of Kentucky, 1985.

Shetler, Charles. *Guide to the Study of West Virginia History.* Morgantown: West Virginia University Library, 1960.

Stewart, Robert Armistead. *Index to Printed Virginia Genealogies.* 1930. Reprint. Baltimore: Genealogical Publishing Co, 1970.

Stinson, Helen S. *A Handbook for Genealogical Research in West Virginia.* Rev. and exp. South Charleston, West Virginia: Kanawha Valley Genealogical Society. 1991.

Tetrick, W. Guy, comp. *Obituaries from Newspapers; Clarksburg Exponent, Clarksburg Telegram and Other Papers of Northern West Virginia.* Salt Lake City: Genealogical Society of Utah, 1958. Microfilm, multiple rolls.

Tetrick, W. Guy. *Obituaries from Newspapers of Northern West Virginia.* 2 vols. Clarksburg, West Virginia: W. G. Tetrick, 1933.

The West Virginia Heritage Encyclopedia. Richwood, West Virginia: Comstock, 1976. Microfiche.

Wardell, P. G. *Timesaving Aid to Virginia-West Virginia Ancestors: A Genealogical Index of Surnames from Published Sources.* 4 vols. Athens, Georgia: Iberian Publishing Co., 1990.

Wardell, Patrick G. *Virginians & West Virginians, 1607-1870.* Bowie, Maryland: Heritage Books, 1986-1992.

West Virginia Research Outline. Series US-States, no. 48. Salt Lake City: Family History Library, 1988.

Atlases, Maps and Gazetteers

Gannett, Henry. *Gazetteer of West Virginia.* Washington, D.C: U.S. Government Printing Office, 1904. Reprinted as *A Gazetteer of Virginia and West Virginia.* Baltimore: Genealogical Publishing Co., 1975.

Kenny, Hamill. *West Virginia Place Names, Their Origin and Meaning, Including the Nomenclature of the Streams and Mountains.* Piedmont, West Virginia: Place Name Press, 1945.

New Descriptive Atlas of West Virginia. Clarksburg, West Virginia: Clarksburg Publishing Co., 1933.

Puetz, C.J., comp. *West Virginia County Maps.* Lyndon Station, Wisconsin: Thomas Publishing Co., 1990.

Sims, Edgar B. *Making a State: Formation of West Virginia...* Charleston, West Virginia: Edgar B. Sims, 1956.

West Virginia historical Records Survey. *West Virginia County Formations and Boundary Changes.* Charleston, West Virginia: Historical Survey. 1938.

Census Records

Available Census Records and Census Substitutes

Federal Census 1870, 1880, 1900, 1910, 1920, 1930.

Federal Mortality Schedules 1850, 1860, 1870, 1880.

Union Veterans and Widows 1890.

Bridges, Steven A. *Virginians in 1800: Counties of West Virginia.* Trumbull, Conn.: Steven A. Bridges, 1987.

Dollarhide, William. *The Census Book: A Genealogist's Guide to Federal Census Facts, Schedules and Indexes.* Bountiful, Utah: Heritage Quest, 1999.

Fothergill, Augusta B., and John Mark Naugle. *Virginia Tax Payers, 1782-87, Other than Those Published by the United States Census Bureau.* 1940. Reprint. Baltimore: Genealogical Publishing Co., 1966.

Heads of Families...Records of the State Enumerations: 1782 to 1785, Virginia. 1908. Reprint. Baltimore: Southern Book Co., 1952.

Kemp, Thomas Jay. *The American Census Handbook.* Wilmington, Delaware: Scholarly Resources, Inc., 2001.

Schreiner-Yantis, Netti, and Florence Speakman Love, comps. *The 1787 Census of Virginia: An Accounting of the Names of Every White Male Tithable Over 21 Years.* 3 vols. Springfield, Virginia: Genealogical Books in Print, 1987.

Schreiner-Yantis, Netti. *A Supplement to the 1810 Census of Virginia. Tax Lists of the Counties for Which the Census is Missing.* Springfield, Virginia: Genealogical Books in Print, 1971.

Thorndale, William, and William Dollarhide. *Map Guides to the U.S. Federal Census, 1790-1920.* Baltimore: Genealogical Publishing Co., 1987.

Court, Probate and Wills

Chalkley, Lyman. *Chronicles of the Scots-Irish Settlement in Virginia: Extracted from the Original Court Records of Augusta County, 1754-1800.* 3 vols., 1912, Reprint. Baltimore: Genealogical Publishing Co., 1980.

Johnston, Ross B. *West Virginia Estate Settlements, 1753-1850: An Index to Wills, Inventories, Appraisements, Land Grants and Surveys to 1850.* Excerpted from West Virginia History, vols. 17-24. 1955-63. Reprint. Baltimore: Genealogical Publishing Co., 1977.

McFarland, K. T. H. *Early West Virginia Wills.* Apollo, Pennsylvania: Closson Press, 1993.

Torrence, Clayton. *Virginia Wills and Administrations, 1632-1800.* 1930. Reprint. Baltimore: Genealogical Publishing Co., 1965.

United States. District Court (West Virginia: Northern District). *Accounts: 1865-1880.* Microfilm of originals at the West Virginia University Library, Morgantown. (Salt Lake City: Filmed by the Genealogical Society of Utah, 1958). Microfilm.

Emigration, Immigration, Migration and Naturalization

Chalkley, Lyman. *Chronicles of the Scotch-Irish Settlement in Virginia: Extracted from the Original Court Records of Augusta County, 1754-1800.* Salt Lake City: Genealogical Society, 1958.

Filby, P. William, *Passenger and Immigration Lists Index.* 15 vols. Detroit: Gale Research, 1981-.

United States. District Court (West Virginia). *Naturalization Records, 1943-1954. Northern District.* Microfilm of originals at the federal building, Elkins. (Salt Lake City: Filmed by the Genealogical Society of Utah, 1987). 2 microfilm.

United States. District Court (West Virginia: Northern District*). Declarations of Intention, 1908-1938.* Microfilm copy of originals at federal building, Elkins. (Salt Lake City: Filmed by the Genealogical Society of Utah, 1987). 3 microfilm.

United States. District Court (West Virginia: Northern District). *Naturalization Records, 1844-1875.* Copies of original materials at the National Archives Record Center, Philadelphia. (Salt Lake City: Filmed by the Genealogical Society of Utah, 1990). 2 microfilm.

United States. District Court (West Virginia: Northern District). *Petitions Granted: 1929-1957.* Microfilm copy of originals at federal building, Elkins. (Salt Lake City: Filmed by the Genealogical Society of Utah, 1987).

Land and Property

Dyer, M. H. *Dyer's Index to Land Grants in West Virginia.* Salem, Massachusetts: Higginson Book Company, 1996.

Northern Neck Surveys, 1721-1779. Richmond: Virginia State Library, 1995. 36 microfilm.

Sims, Edgar B. *Sims Index to Land Grants in West Virginia.* Charleston: Auditor's Office, 1952. Supplement, 1963.

County Website	Map Index	Date Created	Parent County or Territory From Which Organized Address/Details
Hardy www.rootsweb.com/~wvhardy/	E6	17 Oct 1785	**Hampshire** Hardy County; 204 Washington St; Moorefield, WV 26836; Ph. 304.538.2929 Details: (Co Clk has b, m, d & bur rec from 1853, pro & land rec from 1786, ct rec from 1960 & div rec)
Harrison www.rootsweb.com/~wvharris/	J5	3 May 1784	**Monongalia** Harrison County; 301 W Main St; Clarksburg, WV 26301-2909; Ph. 304.624.8611 Details: (Co Clk has b & d rec from 1853, m rec from 1784, pro rec from 1788 & land rec from 1786)
Jackson www.rootsweb.com/~wvjackso/ JACK.HTM	M7	1 Mar 1831	**Kanawha, Mason, Wood** Jackson County; PO Box 800; Ripley, WV 25271; Ph. 304.372.2011 Details: (Co Clk has b & d rec from 1853, m rec from 1831, land rec from early 1800's, pro rec from 1861 & mil rec from 1918; Clk Cir Ct has div & ct rec from 1831)
Jefferson users.stargate.net/~commish/	B5	8 Jan 1801	**Berkeley** Jefferson County; PO Box 208; Charles Town, WV 25414; Ph. 304.728.3215 Details: (Co Clk has b & d rec from 1853 (except Civil War years), m, pro & land rec from 1801)
Kanawha www.kancocomm.com/	L8	14 Nov 1788	**Greenbrier, Montgomery, VA** Kanawha County; 409 Virginia St E; Charleston, WV 25301; Ph. 304.357.0130 Details: (Co Clk has b & d rec from 1853, m rec from 1824, pro rec from 1831 & land rec from 1790)
Lewis www.rootsweb.com/~wvlewis/	J6	18 Dec 1816	**Harrison** Lewis County; 110 Center Ave; Weston, WV 26452; Ph. 304.269.8215 Details: (Co Clk has b & d rec from 1853, m, pro & land rec from 1816; Clk Cir Ct has div rec)
Lincoln* www.rootsweb.com/~wvlincol/	N9	23 Feb 1867	**Boone, Cabell, Kanawha, Putnam** Lincoln County; 8000 Court Ave; Hamlin, WV 25523; Ph. 304.824.3336 Details: (Co Clk has b, m, d, pro & land rec from 1909)
Logan www.rootsweb.com/~wvlogan/logan.htm	N10	12 Jan 1824	**Kanawha & Cabell, WV; Giles & Tazewell, VA** Logan County; County Courthouse Rm 101; Logan, WV 25601; Ph. 304.792.8600 Details: (Co Clk has b, m & d rec from 1872, bur, pro, land & mil rec; Clk Cir Ct has div, ct & nat rec)
Marion* www.rootsweb.com/~wvmarion/l marion.htm	I4	14 Jan 1842	**Harrison, Monongalia** Marion County; 217 Adams St; Fairmont, WV 26554; Ph. 304.367.5440 Details: (Co Clk has b, m & d rec from 1872, pro & land rec)
Marshall www.rootsweb.com/~wvmarsha/ marsh.htm	J4	12 Mar 1835	**Ohio** Marshall County; 7th St; PO Box 459; Moundsville, WV 26041; Ph. 304.845.1220 Details: (Co Clk has b & d rec from 1853, m & land rec from 1835 & pro rec from 1850; Clk Cir Ct has div & ct rec)
Mason www.rootsweb.com/~wvmason/ mason.htm	N7	2 Jan 1804	**Kanawha** Mason County; 200 6th St; Point Pleasant, WV 25550; Ph. 304.675.1997 Details: (Co Clk has b & d rec from 1853, m, pro & land rec from 1804 & mil rec from 1918; Clk Cir Ct has div & ct rec)
McDowell www.geocities.com/mcdowellcounty/	M12	20 Feb 1858	**Tazewell, VA** McDowell County; 90 Wyoming St #109; Welch, WV 24801; Ph. 304.436.8344 Details: (Co seat was first Perryville; changed to Welch in 1892) (Co Clk has b rec from 1872, m rec from 1861, d rec from 1894, pro rec from 1897 & land rec; Clk Cir Ct has div rec)
Mercer www.rootsweb.com/~wvmercer/ mercer.htm	K11	17 Mar 1837	**Giles & Tazewell, VA** Mercer County; PO Box 1716; Princeton, WV 24740; Ph. 304.487.8311 Details: (Co Clk has b, m & d rec from 1853, pro & land rec from 1837; Clk Cir Ct has div & ct rec from 1837)
Mineral* www.mineralcountywv.com/	F5	1 Feb 1866	**Hampshire** Mineral County; 150 Armstrong St; Keyser, WV 26726-3505; Ph. 304.788.3924 Details: (Co Clk has b, m, d, pro & land rec from 1866)

County Website	Map Index	Date Created	Parent County or Territory From Which Organized Address/Details

Mingo   O10   30 Jan 1895
www.rootsweb.com/~wvmingo/
  mingo.htm

Logan
Mingo County; PO Box 1197; WIlliamson, WV 25661-1197; Ph. 304.235.0330
Details: (Co Clk has b, m, d & land rec from 1895 & bur rec from 1959; Clk Cir Ct has div, pro & ct rec)

Monongalia   I4   7 Oct 1776
www.co.monongalia.wv.us/

Dist. of W. Augusta
Monongalia County; 243 High St #123; Morgantown, WV 26505; Ph. 304.291.7230
Details: (Co Clk has b & d rec from 1853, m rec from 1796, pro rec from early 1800's & land rec from 1843; Clk Cir Ct has div & ct rec from 1845 & nat rec 1906-1953)

Monroe   J11   14 Jan 1799
www.rootsweb.com/~wvmonroe/

Greenbrier
Monroe County; Main St; Union, WV 24983; Ph. 304.772.3096
Details: (Co Clk has b & d rec from 1853, m & land rec from 1799 & pro rec)

Morgan   C4   9 Feb 1820
www.rootsweb.com/~wvmonroe/

Berkeley, Hampshire
Morgan County; 202 Fairfax St Ste 100; Berkeley Springs, WV 25411;
Ph. 304.258.8547
Details: (Co Clk has b, m, d & pro rec from 1865, land & some m & pro rec from 1820; Clk Cir Ct has div & ct rec)

Nicholas   K8   30 Jan 1818
www.rootsweb.com/~wvnichol/
  index.html

Greenbrier, Kanawha, Randolph
Nicholas County; 700 Main St; Summersville, WV 26651; Ph. 304.872.7820
Details: (Co Clk has b rec from 1855, m & land rec from 1812, d rec from 1890 & pro rec from 1880; Clk Cir Ct has div & ct rec)

Ohio   J3   7 Oct 1776
www.hostville.com/wvoh/

Dist. of W. Augusta
Ohio County; 1500 Chapline St; Wheeling, WV 26003; Ph. 304.234.3729
Details: (Co Clk has b & d rec from 1853, m rec from 1793, pro rec from 1777 & land rec from 1778; Clk Cir Ct has div & ct rec from 1884)

Pendleton*   F7   4 Dec 1787
franklinwv.com/

Augusta, Hardy & Rockingham, VA
Pendleton County; Main St; Franklin, WV 26807; Ph. 304.358.2505
Details: (Co Clk has b & d rec from 1853, m rec from 1800, pro & land rec from 1789)

Pleasants   L5   29 Mar 1851
www.geocities.com/CapitolHill/
  Lobby/3918/

Ritchie, Tyler, Wood
Pleasants County; 301 Court Ln #101; St. Marys, WV 26170; Ph. 304.684.3542
Details: (Co Clk has b, m, d & pro rec from 1853 & land rec from 1851; Clk Cir Ct has div & ct rec)

Pocahontas*   H8   21 Dec 1821
www.neumedia.net./~pocahontascc/

Pendleton & Randolph, WV & Bath, VA
Pocahontas County; 900 10th Ave; Marlinton, WV 24954; Ph. 304.799.4549
Details: (Co Clk has b rec from 1853, d rec from 1854, m, pro & land rec from 1822; Clk Cir Ct has div & ct rec)

Preston   H5   19 Jan 1818
www.rootsweb.com/~wvpresto/

Monongalia
Preston County; 101 W Main St #201; Kingwood, WV 26537; Ph. 304.329.0070
Details: (Co Clk has b, m, d, pro & land rec from 1869; Clk Cir Ct has div & ct rec)

Putnam*   N8   11 Mar 1848
www.putnamcounty.org/commission/

Kanawha, Mason, Cabell
Putnam County; 3389 Winfield Rd; Winfield, WV 25213; Ph. 304.586.0202
Details: (Co Clk has b rec from 1848, d rec from 1853, m & pro rec from 1849 & land rec from 1841; Clk Cir Ct has div & ct rec)

Raleigh   L10   23 Jan 1850
www.rootsweb.com/~wvraleig/

Fayette
Raleigh County; County Courthouse; 215 Main St; Beckley, WV 25801;
Ph. 304.255.9123
Details: (Co Clk has b, m, d, pro & land rec from 1850; Clk Cir Ct has div & ct rec)

Randolph*   H7   16 Oct 1786
www.randolphcountywv.com/core.htm

Harrison
Randolph County; 2 Randolph Ave; Elkins, WV 26241; Ph. 304.636.0543
Details: (Co Clk has b rec from 1856, m & pro rec from 1787, d rec from 1853 & land rec)

Ritchie*   K6   18 Feb 1843
www.rootsweb.com/~wvritchi/indexr.htm

Harrison, Lewis, Wood
Ritchie County; 115 E Main St Rm 201; Harrisville, WV 26362; Ph. 304.643.2164
Details: (Co Clk has b, m, d, pro, land & mil rec from 1853; Clk Cir Ct has div rec; Mag Ct has ct rec)

County Website	Map Index	Date Created	Parent County or Territory From Which Organized Address/Details
Roane* www.pa-roots.com/~roane/	L7	11 Mar 1856	**Kanawha, Jackson, Gilmer** Roane County; 200 Main St; Spencer, WV 25276-1497; Ph. 304.927.2860 Details: (Co Clk has b, m, d, pro & land rec from 1856)
Summers www.rootsweb.com/~wvsummer/ summers.htm	K11	27 Feb 1871	**Greenbrier, Monroe, Mercer, Fayette** Summers County; PO Box 97; Hinton, WV 25951; Ph. 304.466.7104 Details: (Co Clk has b, m, d, pro & land rec from 1871; Clk Cir Ct has div & ct rec)
Taylor* www.rootsweb.com/~wvtaylor/	I5	19 Jan 1844	**Barbour, Harrison, Marion** Taylor County; 214 W Main St; Grafton, WV 26354-1387; Ph. 304.265.1401 Details: (Co Clk has b, m, d, pro & land rec from 1853; Clk Cir Ct has div & ct rec)
Tucker www.tuckercounty.com/	G6	7 Mar 1856	**Randolph** Tucker County; 215 1st St; Parsons, WV 26287; Ph. 304.478.2414 Details: (Co Clk has b, m, d, pro & land rec from 1856; Clk Cir Ct has div, ct & nat rec)
Tyler www.tylercounty.net/Default.htm	K5	6 Dec 1814	**Ohio** Tyler County; Main St; PO Box 66; Middlebourne, WV 26149-0066; Ph. 304.758.2102 Details: (Co Clk has b, m & d rec from 1853 with incomplete m rec from 1815, pro & land rec from 1815; Clk Cir Ct has div & ct rec)
Upshur www.rootsweb.com/~wvupshur/	I7	26 Mar 1851	**Randolph, Barbour, Lewis** Upshur County; 40 W Main St #101; Buckhannon, WV 26201; Ph. 304.472.1068 Details: (Co Clk has b, m, d & land rec from 1853; Clk Cir Ct has div, pro & ct rec)
Wayne www.rootsweb.com/~wvwayne/ wayne.htm	O9	18 Jan 1842	**Cabell** Wayne County; 700 Hendricks St; Wayne, WV 25570; Ph. 304.272.6371 Details: (Co Clk has b & d rec from 1853, m rec from 1854, pro & land rec)
Webster www.websterwv.com/index1.html	J8	10 Jan 1860	**Braxton, Nicholas, Randolph** Webster County; 2 Court Sq #G1; Webster Springs, WV 26288; Ph. 304.847.2508 Details: (Co Clk has b, m, d, bur, pro & land rec from 1887)
Wetzel www.ovis.net/~billcham/	J4	10 Jan 1846	**Tyler** Wetzel County; PO Box 156; New Martinsville, WV 26155-0156; Ph. 304.455.8224 Details: (Co Clk has b, m, d, bur, pro, land & mil rec from 1846; Clk Cir Ct has div, ct & nat rec)
Wirt www.rootsweb.com/~wvwirt/index.htm	L6	19 Jan 1848	**Wood, Jackson** Wirt County; Washington St; PO Box 53; Elizabeth, WV 26143-0053; Ph. 304.275.4271 Details: (Co Clk has b & d rec from 1870, m rec from 1854, pro & land rec from 1848; Clk Cir Ct has div rec)
Wood www.rootsweb.com/~wvwood/index.htm	L6	21 Dec 1798	**Harrison** Wood County; 1 Court Sq; Parkersburg, WV 26101; Ph. 304.424.1844 Details: (Co Clk has b, m & d rec from 1850, pro rec, mil rec from 1900; Co Asr has land rec from 1798; Clk Cir Ct has div & ct rec)
Wyoming www.rootsweb.com/~wvwyomin/	M11	26 Jan 1850	**Logan** Wyoming County; Bank St; Pineville, WV 24874; Ph. 304.732.8000 Details: (Co Clk has b, m, d, pro & land rec, bond bks & co ct order bks from 1850; Clk Cir Ct has div & ct rec)

Violet

WISCONSIN

CAPITAL: MADISON – TERRITORY 1836 – STATE 1848 (30TH)

Jean Nicolet, a French explorer, first toured Wisconsin in 1634. Many other Frenchmen explored the area in the next few decades, leading to the first trading post at La Baye in 1648. The French gave up their claim to the area following the French and Indian War in 1763. A few settlers had come to the area by 1766. Wisconsin became part of the United States in 1783. It became part of the Northwest Territory in 1787. The British effectively controlled the area until after the War of 1812. Following inclusion in the Indiana Territory in 1800 and the Illinois Territory in 1809, Wisconsin became part of the Michigan Territory in 1818.

The first large-scale immigration took place in the 1820's, due to a lead-mining boom in the mines of southern Wisconsin. Following several Indian wars that eliminated Indian threats, settlers flocked to the southeastern areas of the state along Lake Michigan. The cities of Milwaukee, Racine, and Kenosha were settled during the 1830's. In 1836, Congress created the Wisconsin Territory, which included land west of the Mississippi River to the Missouri River. The creation of the Iowa Territory in 1838 took away much of the western portion.

In the 1840's many families arrived from Germany and New York. The biggest influx of people came in about 1848 when the last Indian lands were relinquished and Wisconsin became a state. They came from the northern European countries, doubling the population between 1850 and 1860. In the Civil War, Wisconsin provided about 90,000 men to the Union. The leading nationalities in Wisconsin are German (by nearly three to one), Polish, Norwegian, Russian, Austrian, Swedish, Czech, Italian, Danish, Hungarian, English, Finnish, Greek, Irish, and French.

Look for vital records in the following locations:

- **Birth and death records:** Contact the State Historical Society of Wisconsin in Madison. Statewide registration began in 1907. A few counties began keeping birth and death records in the 1850's. Both pre- and post- 1907 records are at the State Historical Society. To obtain copies write to Vital Records at the address below. Be sure to state the reason for your request.
- **Wills, deeds, land grants, and taxpayer lists:** Available at most county courthouses.
- **Military records:** Contact the Office of the Adjutant General in Madison.
- **Census records:** Residents of Wisconsin were included in the territorial censuses of Indiana in 1820, Michigan in 1830, and Wisconsin in 1849. Special censuses were taken by the territory or state in 1836, 1838, 1840, 1842, 1846, 1847, 1855, 1865, 1875, 1885, 1895, and 1905.

State Historical Society of Wisconsin
816 State Street
Madison, Wisconsin 53706

Vital Records
PO Box 309
Madison, Wisconsin 53702

Office of the Adjutant General
Madison, Wisconsin 53702

Societies and Repositories

Afro-American Genealogical Society of Milwaukee; 2620 W. Center St.; Milwaukee, Wisconsin 53206

Ancestors of Richland County Hills; 23783 Covered Bridge Dr.; Richland Center, Wisconsin 53581

Archdiocese of Milwaukee; 2000 West Wisconsin Avenue; Milwaukee, Wisconsin 53403; 414.769.3340;(Roman Catholic Church records)

Area Research Center, Superior Public Library; 1530 Tower Ave.; Superior, Wisconsin 54880; 715.394.8860

Ashland County Historical Society; Attn: Genealogical Dept.; PO Box 433; Ashland, Wisconsin 54806

Barron County Genealogical Society; 1122 Knapp St.; Chetek, Wisconsin 54728

Bay Area Genealogical Society; PO Box 283; Green Bay, Wisconsin 54305-0283

Beaver Dam Community Library; 311 S. Spring St.; Beaver Dam, Wisconsin 53916

Black River Falls Public Library, Jackson Co. History Room; 222 Fillmore St.; Black River Falls, Wisconsin 54615; 715.284.4112;

Brown Co. Library, Local Hist. & Gen. Dept.; 515 Pine St.; Green Bay, Wisconsin 54301

Bureau of Land Management, Eastern States Office; 7450 Boston Blvd.; Springfield, Virginia 22153; 703.440.1523; Fax 703.440.1599

Chalmer Davee Library, University of Wisconsin-River Falls; 410 South 3rd Street; River Falls, Wisconsin 54022; 715.425.3567

Charles & JoAnn Lester Memorial Library; 100 Park St.; Nekoosa, Wisconsin 54457; 715.886.7879; <www.rootsweb.com/~wiwood/Nekoosa>

Chippewa County Genealogical Society; 123 Allen St.; Chippewa Falls, Wisconsin 54729-2898; <www.chippewacounty.com/home/history.html>

Circus World Museum; Attention: Library and Research Center; 426 Water St.; Baraboo, Wisconsin 53913; 608.356.8341

Commissioner of Public Lands; 127 West Washington Avenue; Madison, Wisconsin 53703

Concordia Historical Institute; 801 DeMun Avenue; Wisconsin; St. Louis, Missouri 63105; 314.505.7900

Diocese of Green Bay; 1910 South Webster Avenue, PO Box 66; Green Bay, Wisconsin 54301; 414.435.4406; (Roman Catholic Church records)

Diocese of La Crosse; 421 Main Street, PO Box 982; La Crosse, Wisconsin 54601; 608.788.7700; (Roman Catholic Church records)

Diocese of Madison; 15 East Wilson Street, PO Box 111; Madison, Wisconsin 53701; 608.256.2677; (Roman Catholic Church records)

Diocese of Superior; 1201 Hughitt Avenue, PO Box 969; Superior, Wisconsin 54880; 715.392.2937; (Roman Catholic Church records)

Dodge and Jefferson Counties Genealogical Society; PO Box 91; Watertown, Wisconsin 53094-0091

Dunn County Genealogical Society; PO Box 633; Menomonie, Wisconsin 54751

Eagle River Historical Society; PO Box 2011; Eagle River, Wisconsin 54521

Elton E. Karrmann Library, University of Wisconsin-Platteville; 725 West Main Street; Platteville, Wisconsin 53818; 608.342.1719

Eugene W. Murphy Library, University of Wisconsin-La Crosse; 1631 West Pine Street; La Crosse, Wisconsin 54601; 608.785.8511

Evangelical Lutheran Church in America; 8765 West Higgins; Chicago, Illinois 60631; 773.380.2818; Fax 312.380.2977

Family History Library: 35 North West Temple Street: Salt Lake City, Utah 84150: 800.346.6044 or 801.240.2584: <www.familysearch.org>: Find a Family History Center near you: <www.familysearch.org/Eng/Library/FHC/ frameset_fhc.asp>

Fond du Lac County Genealogical Society; PO Box 1264; Fond du Lac, Wisconsin 54936.1264; <www.rootsweb.com/ ~wifonddu/resources/organizations/fdlgensoc.htm>

Fond du Lac County Historical Society; PO Box 1294; Fond du Lac, Wisconsin 54935

Fond du Lac Public Library; 32 Sheboygan St.; Fond du Lac, Wisconsin 54935

Forrest R. Polk Library, University of Wisconsin-Oshkosh; 800 Algoma Boulevard; Oshkosh, Wisconsin 54901; 414.424.3347

Fox Valley Genealogical Society; PO Box 1592; Appleton, Wisconsin 54913-1592

Fox Valley of Wisconsin Chapter, AHSGR; 945 Anchorage Court; Oshkosh, Wisconsin 54901; 920.235.7231

French Canadian/Acadian Genealogists of Wisconsin; PO Box 414; Hales Corners, Wisconsin 53130-0414;

Genealogical Research Society of Eau Claire; c/o Chippewa Valley Museum; PO Box 1204; Eau Claire, Wisconsin 54702.1204; <www.rootsweb.com/~wigrsec/>

Gilbert Simmons Library; 711-59th Place; Kenosha, Wisconsin 53140

Golda Meir Library, University of Wisconsin-Milwaukee; 2311 East Hartford Avenue; Milwaukee, Wisconsin 53201; 414.229.5402

Grant County, Wisconsin Genealogical Society; PO Box 281; Dickeyville, Wisconsin 53808.0281; <www.rootsweb.com/ ~wigrant/gcgensoc.htm>

Harold W. Anderson Library, University of Wisconsin–Whitewater; 800 West Main Street; Whitewater, Wisconsin 53190; 414.472.5520

Hartford Genealogical Society; c/o Hartford Public Library; 109 N. Main St.; Hartford, Wisconsin 53027

Heart O' Wisconsin Genealogical Society; PO Box 516; Wisconsin Rapids, Wisconsin 54494.0516; <www.rootsweb.com/~wiwood/HeartOWi/h.master.htm>

Huguenot Society of Wisconsin; 8920 North Lake Drive; Bayside, Wisconsin 53217-1940; 414.351.0644; <www.execpc.com/~drg/wihs.html>

Iowa County Wisconsin Genealogical Society; PO Box 321; Dodgeville, Wisconsin 53533-0321; <www.friendsnfamily.net/wiiowagensoc/index.html>

Irish Genealogical Society of Wisconsin, (I.G.S.W.); PO Box 13766; Wauwatosa, Wisconsin 53213-0766

Jackson County Historical Society; 13 South 1st St.; Black River Falls, Wisconsin 54615

Jackson County Wisconsin Footprints; W11770 Cty. Rd. P; Black River Falls, Wisconsin 54615-5926

Jewish Genealogical Society, Wisconsin; 9280 N. Fairway Dr.; Milwaukee, Wisconsin 53217

Kenosha County Genealogical Society; 4902 52nd St.; Kenosha, Wisconsin 53142

Kewaunee County Historical Society; Courthouse Square; Kewaunee, Wisconsin 54216

La Crosse Area Genealogical Society; PO Box 1782; La Crosse, Wisconsin 54602-1782; <www.rootsweb.com/~wilacgs/>

LaCrosse Area Genealogical Society; PO Box 1782; LaCrosse, Wisconsin 54601

LaCrosse Public Library, Archives & Local History; 800 Main St.; LaCrosse, Wisconsin 54601

Lafayette County Genealogical Society; PO Box 443; Shullsburg, Wisconsin 53586; <www.rootsweb.com/~wilafcgs/>

Langlade County Genealogical Society; PO Box 307; Antigo, Wisconsin 54409; <www.rootsweb.com/~wilcgs/index.html>

Learning Resources Center; University of Wisconsin-Stevens Point; Stevens Point, Wisconsin 54481; 715.346.2586

Letzebuerger Sprooch, Luxembourg Society of Wisconsin; PO Box 328; Port Washington, Wisconsin 53074-0328

Library Learning Center, University of Wisconsin-Green Bay; 2420 Nicolet Drive; Green Bay, Wisconsin 54311-7001; 414.465.2539

Library Learning Center; University of Wisconsin-Stout; Menomonie, Wisconsin 54751; 715.232.2300

Lower Wisconsin River Genealogical & Historical Research Center; PO Box 202; Wauzeka, Wisconsin 53826; <www.mwt.net/~bcobe/genealogy.html>

Manitowoc County Genealogical Society; PO Box 345; Manitowoc, Wisconsin 54220

Marathon Co. Historical Museum; 403 McIndoe; Wausau, Wisconsin 54401

Marathon Co. Public Library; 400 First St.; Wausau, Wisconsin 54401

Marathon County Genealogical Society; PO Box 1512; Wausau, Wisconsin 54402-1512; <www.geocities.com/mcgsociety/>

Marshfield Area Genealogical Group; PO Box 337; Marshfield, Wisconsin 54449

Maude Shunk Public Library; W156 N8447 Pilgrim Rd.; Menomonee Falls, Wisconsin 53051-3140

Max Kade Institute, German Research; 901 University Bay Dr.; Madison, Wisconsin 53705

Menomonee Falls Historical Society; PO Box 91; Menomonee Falls, Wisconsin 53051

Milwaukee County Genealogical Society; PO Box 27326; Milwaukee, Wisconsin 53227

Milwaukee County Historical Society; 910 North Third St.; Milwaukee, Wisconsin 53203; 414.273.8288

Milwaukee Public Library; 814 W. Wisconsin Ave.; Milwaukee, Wisconsin 53233-2385

Monroe Co. Local History Rm. & Library; 200 W. Main St., PO Box 419; Sparta, Wisconsin 54656

National Archives-Great Lakes Region; 7358 South Pulaski Road; Chicago, Illinois 60629; 773.581.7816; Fax 312.353.1294

National Archives-Reference Branch (Land Tracts, plats); Archives 1, 7th and Pennsylvania Ave. N. W.; Washington, DC 20408; 202.501.5395; Fax 202.219.6273

Northland College - Dexter Library Area Research Center; 1411 Ellis Ave.; Ashland, Wisconsin 54806

Northwoods Genealogical Society; PO Box 1132; Rhinelander, Wisconsin 54501

Oconomowoc Genealogical Club of Waukesha County; 733 E. Sherman Ave.; Oconomowoc, Wisconsin 53066

Oshkosh Public Library; 106 Washington Ave.; Oshkosh, Wisconsin 54901

Polish Genealogical Society of Wisconsin; 3731 Turnwood Dr.; Richfield, Wisconsin 53076

Pornmerscher Verein Freistadt Rundschreiben (Pomeranian Society of Freistadt); PO Box 204; Germantown, Wisconsin 53022

Portage Co. Library; 1001 Main St.; Stevens Point, Wisconsin 54481-2860

Racine Co. Hist. Soc. Gen. Library & Museum, Inc.; PO Box 1527, 701 S. Main St.; Racine, Wisconsin 53403

Rock County Genealogical Society; PO Box 711; Janesville, Wisconsin 53547; <www.rootsweb.com/~wircgs/index.html>

Saint Croix Valley Genealogical Society; PO Box 396; River Falls, Wisconsin 54022

Sauk County Historical Society; PO Box 651; Baraboo, Wisconsin 53913; <www.saukcounty.com/schs>

Seventh Day Baptist Historical Society; PO Box 1678; Janesville, Wisconsin 3547

Sheboygan Co. Historical Research Center; 518 Water St. #3; Sheboygan Falls, Wisconsin 53085-1455

Sons of the American Revolution, Wisconsin Society; 5677 N. Consaul Place; Milwaukee, Wisconsin 53217

South Central Chapter of WSGS; PO Box 5652; Madison, Wisconsin 53705-0652; <www.rootsweb.com/~wisccwsgs/>

Southeaster Wisconsin Chapter, AHSGR; 3121 Pioneer Rd.; Mequon, Wisconsin 53097-1620; <www.ahsgr.org/wisouthe.html>

Special Collections, William D. McIntyre Library; University of Wisconsin-Eau Claire; Eau Claire, Wisconsin 54702-5010; 715.836.3873

St. Croix Valley Genealogical Society; PO Box 396; River Falls, Wisconsin 54022; <www.pressenter.com/~scvgs/>

State Historical Society of Wisconsin; 816 State Street; Madison, Wisconsin 53706; 608.264.6460; Fax 608.264.6520;

Stevens Point Area Genealogical Society; c/o Portage County Library; 1001 Main St.; Stevens Point, Wisconsin 54481-2860

Taylor County Genealogical Society; 224 S. Second Street; Medford, Wisconsin 54451.1899; <www.rootsweb.com/~witcgs/>

University Archives–Parkside Library; Univ. of Wisconsin; Kenosha, Wisconsin 53141

University of Wisconsin / Eau Claire; William D. McIntyre Library; Eau Claire, Wisconsin 54701

University of Wisconsin / Green Bay; 7th Floor, Library Learning Center; Green Bay, Wisconsin 54301

University of Wisconsin / LaCrosse, Murphy Library; 1631 Pine St.; La Crosse, Wisconsin 54601

University of Wisconsin / Platteville, Karrmann Library; 725 W. Main St.; Platteville, Wisconsin 53818

University of Wisconsin / River Falls, Davee Library; 120 Cascade Ave.; River Falls, Wisconsin 54022

University of Wisconsin / Stevens Point; Learning Resources Center; Stevens Point, Wisconsin 54481

University of Wisconsin / Stout; Robert L. Pierce Library; Menomonie, Wisconsin 54751

University of Wisconsin / Superior; Jim Dan Hill Library; Superior, Wisconsin 54880

University of Wisconsin / Whitewater; Anderson Library, West Main St.; Whitewater, Wisconsin 53190

University of Wisconsin, Milwaukee Library; PO Box 604; Milwaukee, Wisconsin 53211

Vesterheim Genealogical Center and Naeseth Library (Norway); 415 W. Main St.; Madison, Wisconsin 54703; 608.255.2224; Fax 608.255.6842

Vesterheim Genealogical Center; Naeseth Library, 415 West Main St; Madison, Wisconsin 53703; 608.255.2224

Village of North Fond du Lac Public Library; 719 Wisconsin Ave.; North Fond du Lac, Wisconsin 54935

Vital Records; 1 West Wilson St., PO Box 309; Madison, Wisconsin 53701-0309; 608.266.1372

Walworth County Genealogical Society; PO Box 159; Delavan, Wisconsin 53115-0159; 608.752.8816; <www.rootsweb.com/~wiwalwor/wcgs.html>

Washburn County Genealogical Society; PO Box 366; Shell Lake, Wisconsin 54871

Washington County Historical Society Museum, Inc.; 340 S. 5th Ave.; West Bend, Wisconsin 53095

Waukesha County Genealogical Society; PO Box 1541; Waukesha, Wisconsin 53187-1541

Waupaca Area Genealogical Society (WAGS); PO Box 42; King, Wisconsin 54946-0042

White Pine Genealogical Society; PO Box 512; Marienette, Wisconsin 54143

Winnebagoland Genealogical Society; c/o Oshkosh Public Library; 106 Washington Ave.; Oshkosh, Wisconsin 54901-4985

Wisconsin Black Historical Society; 2620 West Center St.; Milwaukee, Wisconsin 53206; 414.372.7677

Wisconsin Conference United Methodist Church; 750 Windsor St.; Sun Prairie, Wisconsin 53590; 608.837.7328

Wisconsin Evangelical Lutheran Synod, Department of Archives and History; 2929 North Mayfair Rd.; Milwaukee, Wisconsin 53222; 414.256.3888

Wisconsin Genealogical Council, Inc.; N9307 Abitz Ln.; Luxemburg, Wisconsin 54217-9628

Wisconsin Genealogical Workshop; Rt. 3, Box 253; Black River Falls, Wisconsin 54615

Wisconsin Historical Society Library; 816 State St.; Madison, Wisconsin 53706

Wisconsin State Genealogical Society, Inc.; 2109 20th Ave.; Monroe, Wisconsin 53566; 608.325.2609; <www.wsgs.org>

Wisconsin State Old Cemetery Society; 1562 N 119th St.; Wauwatosa, Wisconsin 53226; 414.771.7781

Wisconsin State Old Cemetery Society; 6100 West Mequon Rd.; Mequon, Wisconsin 53092

Wyllie Library/Learning Center, University of Wisconsin-Parkside; PO Box 2000; Kenosha, Wisconsin 53141-2000; 414.595.2411

Bibliography and Record Sources

General Sources

Aikens, Andrew J. *Men of Progress, Wisconsin: A Selected List of Biographical Sketches and Portraits of the Leaders in Business, Professional and Official Life, Together with Short Notes on the History and Character of Wisconsin*. Milwaukee: Evening Wisconsin Co., 1897.

Alderson, Jo Bartels. *Wisconsin's Early French*. Bowie, Maryland: Heritage Books, 1998.

Bennett, Pansy S. *History of Methodism in Wisconsin*. Cincinnati: Cranston & Stowe, 1890.

Blake, William. *Cross and Flame in Wisconsin: The Story of United Methodism in the Badger State*. Sun Prairie, Wisconsin: United Methodist Church, Wisconsin Conference, 1973.

Cooper, Zachary. *Black Settlers in Rural Wisconsin*. Madison, Wisconsin: State Historical Society of Wisconsin, 1997.

Danky, James P. *Genealogical Research: An Introduction to the Resources of the State Historical Society of Wisconsin*. Rev. ed. Madison: State Historical Society of Wisconsin, 1986.

Danky, James P. *Newspapers in the State Historical Society of Wisconsin: A Bibliography with Holdings*. 2 vols. New York: Norman Ross, 1994.

Dexter, Frank N. *A Hundred Years of Congregational History in Wisconsin*. [S.l.]: Wisconsin Congregation Conference, 1933 (K & K Print Shop.)

Dictionary of Wisconsin Biography. Madison: State Historical Society, 1960.

Draper, Lyman Copeland. *Collections of the State Historical Society of Wisconsin*. 24 vols. Madison, Wisconsin: State Historical Society of Wisconsin, 1855–.

Draper, Lyman Copeland. *Draper Manuscript Collection*. (Chicago: Filmed by the University of Chicago Library, [197-?]). 147 microfilm.

Gleason, Margaret. *Printed Resources for Genealogical Searching in Wisconsin: A Selective Bibliography*. Detroit: Detroit Society for Genealogical Research, 1964.

Heckman, John. *Brethren in Northern Illinois and Wisconsin*. Elgin, Illinois: Brethren Publishing House, 1941.

Heming, Harry H. *The Catholic Church in Wisconsin: A History of the Catholic Church in Wisconsin from the Earliest Time to the Present Day Including an Account of the First Churches,*

Organization of Parishes, Dioceses and Archdiocese, Statement of Present Condition of the Church; Illustrated by Portraits of Archbishop, Bishops, Priests, Prominent Laymen an Pictures of Churches, Educational and Other Religious Institutions. Milwaukee, Wisconsin: Catholic Historical Publishing Co., 1895-1898.

Herrick, Linda M. *Wisconsin Genealogical Research.* Janesville, Wisconsin: Origins, 1996.

Historical Records Survey (Wisconsin*). Directory of Churches and Religious Organizations in Wisconsin.* Madison, Wisconsin: The Wisconsin Historical Records Survey, 1941.

Historical Records Survey (Wisconsin). *Guide to Church Vital Statistics Records in Wisconsin.* Madison, Wisconsin: Wisconsin Historical Records Survey, 1942.

History of Northern Wisconsin: Containing an Account of its Settlement, Growth, Development Resources; an Extensive Sketch of its Counties, Cities, Towns and Villages, Their Improvement, Industries, Manufactories; Biographical Sketches, Portraits of Prominent Men and Early Settlers; Views of County Seats, etc. Chicago, IL: Western Historical, 1881.

History of Wisconsin. Vols. 1–3, 5–6. Madison: State Historical Society, 1973–1988.

Lareau, Paul J., and Elmer Courteau. *French-Canadian Families of the North Central States: A Genealogical Dictionary.* 8 vols. St. Paul, Minn.: Northwest Territory French and Canadian Heritage Institute, 1980.

Lurie, Nancy Oestreich. *Wisconsin Indians.* Madison, Wisconsin: State Historical Society of Wisconsin, 1980.

Mason, Carol I. *Introduction to Wisconsin Indians: Prehistory to Statehood.* Salem, Wisconsin: Sheffield Publishing, 1988.

Nelke, David I. *Columbian Biographical Dictionary and Portrait Gallery....* Chicago: Lewis Publishing Co., 1895.

Nennett, Pansey S. F. *History of Methodism in Wisconsin.* Cincinnati: Cranston & Stowe, 1980.

Noonan, Barry Christopher. *Index to Green Bay Newspapers, 1833–1840.* Madison, Wisconsin: Wisconsin State Historical Society, 1987.

Notable Men of Wisconsin. Tucson, Arizona: W. C. Cox Co., 1974.

Oehlerts, Donald E. *Guide to Wisconsin Newspapers, 1833-1957.* Madison: State Historical Society of Wisconsin, 1958.

Patterson, Betty. *Some Pioneer Families of Wisconsin: An Index.* Madison: State Genealogical Society, 1977.

Paul, Barbara Dotts. *Wisconsin History: An Annotated Bibliography.* Westport Connecticut: Greenwood Press, 1999.

Peet, Stephen. *History of the Presbyterian and Congregational Churches and Ministers in Wisconsin.* Milwaukee: S. Chapman, 1851.

Quaife, Milo Milton. *Wisconsin: Its History and Its People, 1634-1924.* 4 vols. Chicago: S. J. Clarke Publishing Co., 1924.

Reed, Parker McCobb. *The Bench and Bar of Wisconsin: History and Biography.* Milwaukee: P.M. Reed, 1882.

Rentmeester, Les. *The Wisconsin Fur-Trade People.* [Melbourne, Florida]: L & J Rentmeester, 1991.

Rummel, Leo. *History of the Catholic Church in Wisconsin.* Madison, Wisconsin: Wisconsin State Council, Knights of Columbus, 1976.

Ryan, Carol Ward. *Searching for Your Wisconsin Ancestors in the Wisconsin Libraries.* 2nd ed. Green Bay, Wisconsin: Carol Ward Ryan, 1988

Schlinkert, Leroy. *Subject Bibliography of Wisconsin History.* Madison: State Historical Society of Wisconsin, 1947.

Smith, Alice E., ed. *Guide to the Manuscripts of the Wisconsin Historical Society.* Madison, Wisconsin: State Historical Society of Wisconsin, 1944, 1957.

Soldiers' and Citizens' Album of Biographical Record (of Wisconsin): Containing Personal Sketches of Army Men and Citizens Prominent in Loyalty of the Union: Also a Chronological and Statistical History of the Civil War and a History of the Grand Army of the Republic: With Portraits of Soldiers and Prominent Citizens. 2 vols. Bethesda, Maryland: University Publications of America, 1993. 19 microfiches.

Some Pioneer Families of Wisconsin: An Index, Volume 2. Madison: State Genealogical Society, 1987.

Stark, William F. *Ghost Towns of Wisconsin.* Sheboygan, Wisconsin: Zimmermann Press, 1977.

State Historical Society of Wisconsin. *Annotated Catalogue of Newspaper Files of the Library of the State Historical Society of Wisconsin.* Madison: Wisconsin State Historical Society, 1911.

Territorial Papers of the United States: The Territory of Wisconsin, 1836–1848: A Microfilm Supplement. Washington, D.C.: National Archives, 1959.

Tuttle, Charles Richard. *An Illustrated History of the State of Wisconsin: Being a Complete Civil, Political, and Military History of the State, from its First Exploration Down to 1875.* Boston: B.B. Russell, 1875.

United States Biographical Dictionary and Portrait: Gallery of Eminent and Self-made Men: Wisconsin Volume. Chicago: American Biographical Pub., 1877.

University of Wisconsin–Green Bay. *Guide to Archives and Manuscripts in the University of Wisconsin-Green Bay Area Research Center.* Rev. ed. Green Bay, Wisconsin: University of Wisconsin-Green Bay Area Research Center, 1992.

Usher, Ellis B. *Wisconsin: Its Story and Biography, 1848-1913.* 8 vols. Chicago: Lewis Publishing Co., 1914.

Waterstreet, Darlene E. *Biography Index to the Wisconsin Blue Books.* Milwaukee, Wisconsin: Badger Infosearch, 1974.

Wilcox, Pearl. *Regathering of the Scattered Saints in Wisconsin and Illinois.* Independence, MO: P. Wilcox, 1984.

Wisconsin Domesday Book: Town Studies. Publications of the State Historical Society of Wisconsin. Minasha, Wisconsin: George Santa Publishing Co., 1924.

Wisconsin Research Outline. Series US-States, no. 49. Salt Lake City: Family History Library, 1988.

Wisconsin. State Historical Society. *Guide to Archives and Manuscripts in the University of Wisconsin-Platteville Area Research Center.* Madison, Wisconsin: State Historical Society of Wisconsin, 1990.

Yearbook of the Wisconsin Evangelical Lutheran Synod. Milwaukee: Northwestern Publishing House, 1989–.

Atlases, Maps and Gazetteers

DeLorme Mapping Company. *Wisconsin Atlas & Gazetteer.* Freeport, Maine: DeLorme Mapping Co., 1988.

DenBoer, Gordon. *Wisconsin, Atlas of Historical County Boundaries*. New York: Charles Scribner's Sons, 1997.

Fox, Michael J., comp. *Maps and Atlases Showing Land Ownership in Wisconsin*. Madison: State Historical Society of Wisconsin, 1978.

Gard, Robert E., and L.G. Sorden. *The Romance of Wisconsin Place Names*. New York: October House, 1968. Reprint. Minocqua, Wisconsin: Heartland Press, 1988.

Hale, James B., comp. *Wisconsin Post Office Handbook, 1921-1971*. Wisconsin Postal History Society. Bulletin no. 10. Madison: Wisconsin Postal History Society, 1971.

Hunt, John W. *Wisconsin Gazetteer….* Madison, Wisconsin: P. Brown, 1853. Reprint. Microfiche. Louisville, Kentucky: Lost Cause Press, 1974. Ann Arbor, Michigan: University Microfilm.

Long, John H., ed. Historical *Atlas and Chronology of County Boundaries, 1788–1980*. vols. 1–5. Boston, Massachusetts: G.K. Hall, 1984.

Peck, George W., ed. *Wisconsin: Comprising Sketches of Counties, Towns, Events, Institutions and Persons Arranged in Cyclopedic Form*. Madison, Wisconsin: Western Historical Association, 1906.

Puetz, C.J., comp. *Wisconsin County Maps*. Lyndon Station, Wisconsin: Thomas Publishing Co., 1992.

Robinson, Arthur, and Jerry B. Culver. *Atlas of Wisconsin: General Maps and Gazetteers*. Madison: University of Wisconsin Press, 1974.

Snyder, Van Vechten & Co. *Historical Atlas of Wisconsin….* Janesville, Wisconsin: Origins, 1995.

Walling, H. F. *Atlas of the State of Wisconsin*. Detroit: Walling, Tackabury and Co., 1876.

Census Records

Available Census Records and Census Substitutes

Federal Census 1820 (with Michigan), 1830 (with Michigan), 1840, 1850, 1860, 1870, 1880, 1900, 1910, 1920, 1930.

Federal Mortality Schedules 1850, 1880.

Union Veterans and Widows 1890.

State/Territorial Census 1836, 1838, 1842, 1846, 1847, 1855, 1875, 1885 1895, 1905.

Dollarhide, William. *The Census Book: A Genealogist's Guide to Federal Census Facts, Schedules and Indexes*. Bountiful, Utah: Heritage Quest, 1999.

Kemp, Thomas Jay. *The American Census Handbook*. Wilmington, Delaware: Scholarly Resources, Inc., 2001.

Lainhart, Ann S. *State Census Records*. Baltimore: Genealogical Publishing Co., Inc., 1992.

Thorndale, William, and William Dollarhide. *Map Guide to the U.S. Federal Censuses, 1790-1920*. Baltimore: Genealogical Publishing Co., 1987.

Court Records, Probate and Wills

Note: Many court records are housed at the Wisconsin State Archives. Court records including probate, wills, inventories, guardianship and administrations are found in the individual county court records.

Delgado, David J. *Guide to the Wisconsin State Archives*. Madison, Wisconsin: State Historical Society of Wisconsin, 1966.

Emigration, Immigration, Migration and Naturalization

Current, Richard Nelson. *"A German State?" in Wisconsin: A Bicentennial History*. New York: W. W. Norton & Co., 1977.

Sachtjen, Maude. *Immigration to Wisconsin: A Thesis*. Madison: University of Wisconsin, 1928.

State Historical Society of Wisconsin (Madison, Wisconsin). *Index to Citizenship*. Microfilm of Original card index at the Wisconsin State Historical Society, Madison. (Salt Lake City: Filmed by the Genealogical Society of Utah, 1989).

United States. District Court. (Illinois: Northern District). *Soundex Index to Naturalization Petitions for U.S. District & Circuit Courts, Northern District of Illinois and Immigration and Naturalization Service District 9, 1840-1950*. (Salt Lake City: Filmed by the Genealogical Society of Utah, 1988). 183 microfilm.

Wisconsin. Circuit Court (Dane County). *Admission to Citizenship Records, 1855-1906*. (Salt Lake City: Filmed by the Genealogical Society of Utah, 1980). Microfilm.

Wisconsin. Circuit Court (Dane County). *Declarations of Intention, 1848-1906*. (Salt Lake City: Filmed by the Genealogical Society of Utah, 1980). Microfilm.

Wisconsin. Circuit Court (Dane County). *Petitions and Oaths, 1841-1905*. (Salt Lake City: Filmed by the Genealogical Society of Utah, 1980). Microfilm.

Wisconsin. Municipal Court (Madison). *Declarations of Intent, 1861-1906*. (Salt Lake City: Filmed by the Genealogical Society of Utah, 1980).

Wisconsin. Municipal Court (Madison). *Declarations of Intent, 1875-1906; Applications for Admission, 1906*. Salt Lake City: Filmed by the Genealogical Society of Utah, 1980. Microfilm.

Wisconsin. Supreme Court. *Naturalization Records, 1840-1900*. (Salt Lake City: Filmed by the Genealogical Society of Utah, 1979, 1984). 7 microfilm.

Land and Property

Bureau of Land Management. *Wisconsin, 1820–1908 Cash and Homestead Entries, Cadastral Survey Plats*. Springfield, Virginia: BLM Eastern States, 1994.

English, William Hayden. *Conquest of the Country Northwest of the River Ohio, 1778-1783, and Life of General George Rogers Clark: With Numerous Sketches of Men Who Served Under Clark and Full List of Those Allotted Lands in Clark's Grant for Service in the Campaigns Against the British Posts, Showing Exact Land Allotted Each*. 2 vols. Indiana: Bowen–Merrill, 1896.

Land Records: AL, AR, FL, LA, MI, MN, OH, WI. [S.l.]: Brøderbund, 1996. CD-ROM.

Military

Grand Army of the Republic. *Soldiers' and Citizens' Album*. 2 vols. Chicago, Illinois: Grand Army Publishing Co., 1888, 1890.

Miljat, Leslie Elizabeth. *Admission Applications, 1867–1872, National Home for Disabled Volunteer Soldiers, Northwestern Branch. Milwaukee, Wisconsin.* Wauwatosa, Wisconsin. L. E. Miljat, 1991.

Moore, Dennis R. *Researching Your Civil War Ancestors in Wisconsin.* Manitowoc, Wisconsin: Bivouac Publications, 1994.

Revolutionary War Veterans, 1775–1784, Buried in Wisconsin. (Salt Lake City: Filmed by the Genealogical Society of Utah, 1975).

Soldiers' and Citizens' Album of Biographical Record, 2 vols. Chicago: Grand Army Pub., 1888, 1890;

United States Veterans Administration. *Pension Index File, Alphabetical; of the Veterans Administration….* Washington: Veterans Administration, Publications Service, 1953.

United States. Adjutant General's Office. *Index to Compiled Service Records of Volunteer Union Soldiers Who Served in Organizations from the State of Wisconsin.* Washington, D.C.: The National Archives, 1964. Microfilm.

United States. Selective Service System. *Wisconsin, World War I Selective Service System Draft Registration Cards, 1917–1918.* Washington, D.C.: National Archives, 1987–1988.

Wisconsin Adjutant General's Office. *Annual Report of the Adjutant General, 1865.* Madison, Wisconsin: Democrat Printing. 1912.

Wisconsin. Adjutant General. *Roster of Wisconsin Volunteers, War of the Rebellion 1861-1865.* Madison: Democrat Print Co., 1886.

Wisconsin. Adjutant General's Office. *Military Records, 1861-1865.* (Salt Lake City: Filmed by the Genealogical Society of Utah, 1981). Microfilm.

Wisconsin's Gold Star List: Soldiers, Sailors, Marines and Nurses from the Badger State… Madison: State Historical Society of Wisconsin, 1925.

Vital and Cemetery Records

Bookstaff, Manning M. *Index to Deaths Reported in "The Wisconsin Jewish Chronicle," 1921–1961.* Milwaukee: M. M. Bookstaff, 1994.

Daughters of the American Revolution. Wisconsin. *Bible and Cemetery Inscriptions from Wisconsin.* Salt Lake City: Genealogical Society of Utah, 1970. Microfilm.

Daughters of the American Revolution. Wisconsin. *Bible and Cemetery Records, 1700-1940.* Microfilm. Salt Lake City: Genealogical Society of Utah, 1970.

Daughters of the American Revolution. Wisconsin. *Bible and Cemetery Records, 1800-1940.* Microfilm. Salt Lake City: Genealogical Society of Utah, 1970.

Herrick, Linda M. and Wendy K. Uncapher. *Cemetery Locations in Wisconsin.* Janesville, WI: Origins 1998.

Wisconsin, Bureau of Health Statistics. *Index to Registration of Births, 1852-1907.* 41 microfiche. Madison: Wisconsin State Historical Society, 1979.

Wisconsin, Bureau of Health Statistics. *Index to Registration of Marriages, 1852-1907.* Madison: Wisconsin State Historical Society, 1980. 77 microfiche.

Wisconsin, Bureau of Health Statistics. *Pre-1907 Death Index By Name.* Madison: Wisconsin State Historical Society, 1981. Microfiche.

Wisconsin, Bureau of Health Statistics. *Unedited Index to Registration of Births, 1852-1907.* 38 microfiche. Madison: Wisconsin State Historical Society, 1979.

Wisconsin. Bureau of Vital Statistics. *Delayed Births, Ca. 1937-1941; Affidavit Delayed Births, Ca. 1940-1942.* (Salt Lake City: Filmed by the Genealogical Society of Utah, 1981). Microfilm.

Wisconsin. Bureau of Vital Statistics. *Registration of Deaths, ca. 1862-1907.* Microfilm of original records of the Bureau of Health Statistics in Madison, Wisconsin. (Salt Lake City: Filmed by the Genealogical Society of Utah, 1981). 68 microfilm.

Wisconsin. Center for Health Statistics. *Death Records Index, 1959-1984.* [Madison, Wisconsin: Wisconsin Center for Health Statistics, 198-]. Microfilm.

County Website	Map Index	Date Created	Parent County or Territory From Which Organized Address/Details
Adams www.adamscountywi.com/	K7	11 Mar 1848	**Portage** Adams County; 400 N Main St; Friendship, WI 53934-0278; Ph. 608.339.4200 Details: (Reg of Deeds has b rec from 1860, m rec from 1859, d rec from 1873 & land rec from 1853; Clk Ct has div & ct rec; Reg in Pro has pro rec)
Ashland travelbayfieldcounty.com/	E5	27 Mar 1860	**LaPointe** Ashland County; 201 Main St W; Ashland, WI 54806-1652; Ph. 715.682.7000 Details: (Reg of Deeds has b rec from 1863, m rec from 1879, d rec from 1877 & land rec from 1860; Clk Cir Ct has div & ct rec from 1873; Reg in Pro has pro rec from 1890)
Bad Ax		1 Mar 1851	**Crawford** Details: (see Vernon) (Name changed to Vernon 22 Mar 1862)
Barron* www.co.barron.wi.us/	G3	19 Mar 1859	**Polk** Barron County; 330 E La Salle Ave; Barron, WI 54812-1591; Ph. 715.537.6200 Details: (Formerly Dallas Co. Name changed to Barron 4 Mar 1869) (Reg of Deeds has b, m, d & land rec; Reg in Pro has pro rec; Clk Cts has ct rec)
Bayfield travelbayfieldcounty.com/	E4	19 Feb 1845	**St. Croix** Bayfield County; 117 E 5th St; Washburn, WI 54891-9464; Ph. 715.373.6100 Details: (Formerly La Pointe Co. Name changed to Bayfield 12 Apr 1866) (Reg of Deeds has b, m & d rec, land rec from 1850; Clk Cir Ct has div rec from 1889, pro rec from 1870 & ct rec from 1888)
Brown www.co.brown.wi.us/	J10	26 Oct 1818	**Michigan Terr.** Brown County; 305 E Walnut St; PO Box 23600; Green Bay, WI 54305-3600; Ph. 920.448.4016 Details: (Reg of Deeds has b rec from 1846, m rec from 1821, d rec from 1834 & land rec; Clk Ct has div & ct rec from 1832; Reg in Pro has pro rec from 1828; see Mich for 1820-1830 cen)
Buffalo* www.buffalocounty.com/	J3	6 Jul 1853	**Jackson** Buffalo County; 407 S 2nd St; Alma, WI 54610; Ph. 608.685.6206 Details: (Reg of Deeds has b, m, d, bur & land rec; Clk Cir Ct has div & ct rec; Reg in Pro has pro rec)
Burnett www.mwd.com/burnett/	F2	31 Mar 1856	**Polk, Douglas** Burnett County; 7410 County Rd K; Siren, WI 54872; Ph. 715.349.2173 Details: (Reg of Deeds has b, m & d rec from 1861, bur rec, land rec from 1856 & mil dis rec from 1919; Clk Ct has div, ct & nat rec from 1856; Reg in Pro has pro rec from 1856)
Calumet www.co.calumet.wi.us/	J10	7 Dec 1836	**Brown** Calumet County; 206 Court St; Chilton, WI 53014-1198; Ph. 920.849.1458 Details: (Reg of Deeds has b rec from 1851, m rec from 1846, d rec from 1866 & land rec from 1840; Clk Cir Ct has div rec from 1880 & ct rec from 1877; Reg in Pro has pro rec from 1868)
Chippewa* www.co.chippewa.wi.us/	H4	3 Feb 1845	**Crawford** Chippewa County; 711 N Bridge St; Chippewa Falls, WI 54729-1876; Ph. 715.726.7980 Details: (Reg of Deeds has b rec from 1858, m rec from 1860, d rec from 1870, land rec from 1856, nat rec 1895-1955 & 1905 state cen; Reg in Pro has pro rec)
Clark* www.clark-cty-wi.org/	I5	6 Jul 1853	**Jackson** Clark County; 517 Court St; Neillsville, WI 54456-1992; Ph. 715.743.5148 Details: (Co Clk has b & d rec, m rec from 1866, land rec from 1855 & nat rec 1857-1954; Reg in Pro has pro rec from 1854)
Columbia www.co.columbia.wi.us/defaultt.asp	L8	3 Feb 1846	**Portage** Columbia County; PO Box 177; Portage, WI 53901-0177; Ph. 608.742.9654 Details: (Reg of Deeds has land, b, m, d & bur rec; Clk Cir Ct has div & ct rec; Reg in Pro has pro rec)

County Website	Map Index	Date Created	Parent County or Territory From Which Organized Address/Details
Crawford www.rootsweb.com/~wicrawfo/	L4	26 Oct 1818	**Michigan Terr.** Crawford County; 220 N Beaumont Rd; Prairie du Chien, WI 53821-1405; Ph. 608.326.0200 Details: (Co Clk has b rec from 1866, m rec from 1820, d & bur rec from 1880, div & ct rec from 1848 & pro rec from 1819; see Mich for 1820-1830 cen)
Dallas		19 Mar 1859	**Polk** Details: (see Barron) (Name changed to Barron 4 Mar 1869)
Dane www.co.dane.wi.us/	M7	7 Dec 1836	**Crawford, Iowa, Milwaukee** Dane County; 210 Martin Luther King Blvd; Madison, WI 53709; Ph. 608.266.4121 Details: (Reg of Deeds has b, m, d, land & mil rec; Clk Ct has div, pro & ct rec)
Dodge www.co.dodge.wi.us/	L9	7 Dec 1836	**Brown, Milwaukee** Dodge County; 127 E Oak St; Juneau, WI 53039; Ph. 920.386.3600 Details: (Reg of Deeds has b, m, d & land rec from 1877; Clk Ct has div & ct rec; Reg in Pro has pro rec from 1854)
Door www.co.door.wi.us/	H11	11 Feb 1851	**Brown** Door County; 421 Nebraska St; Sturgeon Bay, WI 54235-2204; Ph. 920.746.2200 Details: (Reg of Deeds has b, m, d & land rec from 1850; Clk Ct has div rec from 1900 & ct rec from 1860; Reg in Pro has pro rec from 1863)
Douglas* www.douglascountywi.org/	E3	9 Feb 1854	**LaPointe** Douglas County; 1313 Belknap St; Superior, WI 54880-2769; Ph. 715.395.1341 Details: (Reg of Deeds has b, m & d rec from 1878 & land rec; Clk Ct has div, pro & ct rec from 1878)
Dunn* www.rootsweb.com/~widunn/	H3	3 Feb 1854	**Chippewa** Dunn County; 800 Wilson Ave; Menomonie, WI 54751-2785; Ph. 715.232.1677 Details: (Reg of Deeds has b, m & d rec from 1860 & land rec)
Eau Claire* www.co.eau-claire.wi.us/	I4	6 Oct 1856	**Chippewa** Eau Claire County; 721 Oxford Ave; Eau Claire, WI 54703-5481; Ph. 715.839.4803 Details: (Reg of Deeds has b, m, d & land rec from 1856; Clk Ct has div rec from 1856 & ct rec from 1929)
Florence www.florencewisconsin.com/	F9	18 Mar 1882	**Marinette, Oconto** Florence County; 501 Lake Ave; Florence, WI 54121-0410; Ph. 715.528.3201 Details: (Reg of Deeds has b, m, d & land rec; Clk Cir Ct has div, pro & ct rec)
Fond du Lac www.rootsweb.com/~wifonddu/ index.htm	K9	7 Dec 1836	**Brown** Fond du Lac County; 160 S Macy St; Fond du Lac, WI 54935-4241; Ph. 920.929.3000 Details: (Reg of Deeds has b rec from 1847, m rec from 1844, d rec from 1868 & land rec; Clk Cts has div & ct rec; Pro Off has pro rec; Veterans Off has mil rec)
Forest www.rootsweb.com/~wiforest/	G9	11 Apr 1885	**Langlade** Forest County; 200 E Madison St; Crandon, WI 54520; Ph. 715.478.2422 Details: (Reg of Deeds has b, m, d & land rec from 1885; Clk Ct has div & ct rec; Reg in Pro has pro rec)
Gates		15 May 1901	**Chippewa** Details: (see Rusk) (Name changed to Rusk 19 Jun 1905)
Grant* grantcounty.org/	M5	8 Dec 1836	**Iowa** Grant County; 111 S Jefferson; Lancaster, WI 53813; Ph. 608.723.2675 Details: (Reg of Deeds has b & d rec from 1876, m rec from 1840 & land rec from 1837; Reg in Pro has pro rec from 1840; Clk Ct has div & ct rec; Veterans Service Officer has mil rec)
Green www.greencounty.org/	M7	8 Dec 1836	**Iowa** Green County; 1016 16th Ave; Monroe, WI 53566-2098; Ph. 608.328.9430 Details: (Reg of Deeds has b rec from 1907, m rec from 1846, d rec from 1878 & land rec; Clk Cir Ct has div & ct rec; Co Judge has pro rec)

County Website	Map Index	Date Created	Parent County or Territory From Which Organized Address/Details
Green Lake www.co.green-lake.wi.us/	**K8**	**5 Mar 1858**	**Marquette** Green Lake County; PO Box 3188; Green Lake, WI 54941; Ph. 920.294.4005 Details: (Reg of Deeds has b & d rec from 1876, m & land rec from 1852 & mil dis rec from 1945; Clk Cts has div & ct rec; Reg in Pro has pro rec)
Iowa www.iowacounty.org/	**M6**	**9 Oct 1829**	**Crawford** Iowa County; 222 N Iowa St; Dodgeville, WI 53533; Ph. 608.935.3024 Details: (Reg of Deeds has b & d rec from 1866, m rec from 1852 & land rec from 1835; Clk Cir Ct has div rec from 1860 & ct rec; Reg in Pro has pro rec from 1890; see Mich for 1830 cen)
Iron ironcountywi.com/	**E6**	**1 Mar 1893**	**Ashland** Iron County; 300 Taconite St; Hurley, WI 54534-1546; Ph. 715.561.3375 Details: (Reg of Deeds has b, m, d & land rec from 1893; Clk Cts has div & ct rec; Reg in Pro has pro rec)
Jackson* www.co.jackson.wi.us/	**J5**	**11 Feb 1853**	**LaCrosse** Jackson County; 307 Main St; Black River Falls, WI 54615; Ph. 715.284.0201 Details: (Reg of Deeds has b, m, d, bur & land rec; Clk Ct has div & ct rec; Reg in Pro has pro rec)
Jefferson www.co.jefferson.wi.us/	**M8**	**7 Dec 1836**	**Milwaukee** Jefferson County; 320 S Main St; Jefferson, WI 53549-1718; Ph. 920.674.7140 Details: (Reg of Deeds has b & m rec from 1850, d rec from 1840 & land rec from 1838; Clk Cir Ct has div rec from 1851 & ct rec from 1843; Reg in Pro has pro rec from 1840)
Juneau www.juneaucounty.com/	**K6**	**13 Oct 1856**	**Adams** Juneau County; 220 E State St; Mauston, WI 53948; Ph. 608.847.9300 Details: (Reg of Deeds has b, m & d rec from 1880 & land rec from 1854; Clk Ct has div & ct rec; Reg in Pro has pro rec)
Kenosha www.co.kenosha.wi.us/	**N10**	**30 Jan 1850**	**Racine** Kenosha County; 1010 56th St; Kenosha, WI 53140; Ph. 262.653.2552 Details: (Co Clk has m rec from 1900; Reg of Deeds has land rec; Reg in Pro has pro rec)
Kewaunee www.gokewaunee.net/	**I11**	**16 Apr 1852**	**Door** Kewaunee County; 613 Dodge St; Kewaunee, WI 54216; Ph. 920.388.7133 Details: (Reg of Deeds has b & land rec from 1873, m & d rec from 1874; Reg in Pro has pro rec from 1867)
La Crosse* www.co.la-crosse.wi.us./	**K4**	**1 Mar 1851**	**Crawford** La Crosse County; 400 4th St N; La Crosse, WI 54601-3200; Ph. 608.785.9577 Details: (Reg of Deeds has b, m, d & land rec from 1851; Clk Cir Ct has div & ct rec; Reg in Pro has pro rec from 1851)
La Pointe wicip.uwplatt.edu/lafayette/index.html		**19 Feb 1845**	**St. Croix** Details: (see Bayfield) (Name changed to Bayfield 12 Apr 1866)
Lafayette wicip.uwplatt.edu/lafayette/index.html	**N6**	**31 Jan 1846**	**Iowa** Lafayette County; 626 Main St; Darlington, WI 53530; Ph. 608.776.4850 Details: (Reg of Deeds has b rec from 1860, m rec from 1847, d rec from 1877 & land rec from 1840; Clk Ct has div & ct rec; Reg in Pro has pro rec)
Langlade www.rootsweb.com/~wilangl2/	**H8**	**27 Feb 1879**	**Oconto** Langlade County; 800 Clermont St; Antigo, WI 54409-1985; Ph. 715.627.6200 Details: (Formerly New Co. Name changed to Langlade 19 Feb 1880) (Reg of Deeds has b & d rec; Co Clk has m rec from 1918; Clk Cir Ct has div & ct rec; Reg in Pro has pro rec; Co Asr has land rec)
Lincoln www.co.lincoln.wi.us/	**G7**	**4 Mar 1874**	**Marathon** Lincoln County; 1110 E Main St; Merrill, WI 54452-2554; Ph. 715.536.0312 Details: (Reg of Deeds has m & land rec; Reg in Pro has pro rec; Clk Cts has ct rec)

County Website	Map Index	Date Created	Parent County or Territory From Which Organized / Address/Details
Manitowoc www.manitowoc-county.com/	J10	7 Dec 1836	**Brown** Manitowoc County; 1010 S 9th St; Manitowoc, WI 54220; Ph. 920.683.4000 Details: (Reg of Deeds has b, m & d rec from 1850, land & mil rec; Clk Cir Ct has div, pro & ct rec)
Marathon* www.co.marathon.wi.us/	I6	9 Feb 1850	**Portage** Marathon County; 500 Forest St; Wausau, WI 54403; Ph. 715.261.1500 Details: (Reg of Deeds has b, m & d rec from 1900 & land rec from 1850; Clk Cir Ct has div & ct rec from 1900; Co Ct has pro rec from 1900)
Marinette www.rootsweb.com/~wimarine/	G10	27 Feb 1879	**Oconto** Marinette County; 1926 Hall Ave; Marinette, WI 54143; Ph. 715.732.7532 Details: (Reg of Deeds has b, m, d & land rec from 1879; Clk Cir Ct has div & ct rec from 1879; Reg in Pro has pro rec from 1879)
Marquette co.marquette.wi.us/	K7	7 Dec 1836	**Brown** Marquette County; 77 W Park St; Montello, WI 53949; Ph. 608.297.9136 Details: (Reg of Deeds has b rec from 1876, m & d rec from 1869 & land rec; Clk Cir Ct has div & ct rec from 1878 & nat rec 1868-1936; Reg in Pro has pro rec from 1890)
Menominee www.rootsweb.com/~wimenomi/	H9	1 May 1961	**Oconto, Shawano** Menominee County; PO Box 279; Keshena, WI 54135; Ph. 715.799.3311 Details: (Co Clk has b, m, d & land rec; Reg in Pro has pro rec)
Milwaukee 204.194.250.11/	M10	6 Sep 1834	**Brown, Iowa** Milwaukee County; 901 N 9th St; Milwaukee, WI 53233; Ph. 414.278.4987 Details: (Reg of Deeds has b, m & d rec, land rec from 1835; Reg in Pro has pro rec from 1838)
Monroe www.co.monroe.wi.us/	K5	21 Mar 1854	**La Crosse** Monroe County; 202 S K St; Sparta, WI 54656; Ph. 608.269.8705 Details: (Reg of Deeds has b, m, d & land rec; Clk Ct has div, pro, ct & nat rec; Veterans Service Off has mil rec)
New		27 Feb 1879	**Oconto** Details: (see Langlade) (Name changed to Langlade 19 Feb 1880)
Oconto www.co.oconto.wi.us/	H9	6 Feb 1851	**Brown** Oconto County; 301 Washington St; Oconto, WI 54153-1621; Ph. 920.834.6800 Details: (Reg of Deeds has b, m, d, bur & land rec; Clk Cts has div & ct rec; Reg in Pro has pro rec; Oconto Hist Soc has hist rec)
Oneida* www.rootsweb.com/~wigenweb/oneida/	F8	11 Apr 1885	**Lincoln** Oneida County; 1 Courthouse Sq; Rhinelander, WI 54501; Ph. 715.369.6144 Details: (Reg of Deeds has b, m, d & land rec; Clk Cir Ct has div & ct rec; Reg in Pro has pro rec)
Outagamie www.co.outagamie.wi.us/	I9	17 Feb 1851	**Brown, Winnebago** Outagamie County; 410 S Walnut St; Appleton, WI 54911; Ph. 920.832.5077 Details: (Reg of Deeds has b, m & d rec from 1852; Clk Cts has div & ct rec from 1855; Reg in Pro has pro rec from 1855)
Ozaukee www.co.ozaukee.wi.us/	L10	7 Mar 1853	**Washington** Ozaukee County; 121 W Main St; PO Box 994; Port Washington, WI 53074; Ph. 262.284.8100 Details: (Reg of Deeds has b, m, d & land rec from 1853; Clk Cir Ct has div, pro & ct rec; Co Treas has tax rolls from 1851)
Pepin* www.co.pepin.wi.us/	I3	25 Feb 1858	**Dunn** Pepin County; 740 7th Ave W; Durand, WI 54736-1628; Ph. 715.672.8857 Details: (Reg of Deeds has b, m, d & land rec; Clk Cir Ct has div & ct rec; Reg in Pro has pro rec)
Pierce www.co.pierce.wi.us/	I2	25 Feb 1858	**Saint Croix** Pierce County; 414 W Main; PO Box 119; Ellsworth, WI 54011; Ph. 715.273.3531 Details: (Co Clk has b & d rec from 1876, m rec from 1855, div rec from 1875, pro rec from 1878 & ct rec from 1869)

County Website	Map Index	Date Created	Parent County or Territory From Which Organized Address/Details
Polk* www.co.polk.wi.us/	G2	14 Mar 1853	Saint Croix Polk County; 100 Polk County Plaza; Balsam Lake, WI 54810; Ph. 715.485.9226 Details: (Reg of Deeds has b rec from 1858, m rec from 1861, d rec from 1866 & land rec; Clk Ct has div & ct rec; Reg in Pro has pro rec)
Portage www.co.portage.wi.us/	J7	7 Dec 1836	Brown, Crawford, Iowa, Milwaukee Portage County; 1516 Church St; Stevens Point, WI 54481; Ph. 715.346.1351 Details: (Reg of Deeds has b rec from 1863, m rec from 1860, d rec from 1856 & land rec; Clk Cir Ct has div & ct rec from 1844; Co Judge has pro rec from 1890)
Price www.pricecounty.org/	G6	26 Feb 1879	Chippewa, Lincoln Price County; 126 Cherry St; Phillips, WI 54555; Ph. 715.339.3325 Details: (Reg of Deeds has b & m rec from 1880, d rec from 1884 & land rec from 1867; Clk Cir Ct has div & ct rec from 1882; Reg in Pro has pro rec from 1879; Co Clk has m applications)
Racine www.racineco.com/	M10	7 Dec 1836	Milwaukee Racine County; 730 Wisconsin Ave; Racine, WI 53403; Ph. 262.636.3121 Details: (Reg of Deeds has b rec from 1876, m & land rec from 1837, d rec from 1853 & veterans rec from 1918; Fam Ct has div rec from 1940; Pro Ct has pro rec from 1846; Clk Cts has ct rec from 1970)
Richland www.richlandcounty.com/	L5	18 Feb 1842	Crawford, Sauk Richland County; 181 W Seminary St; Richland Center, WI 53581; Ph. 608.647.2197 Details: (Reg of Deeds has b & d rec from 1870, m & land rec from 1850; Clk Ct has div & ct rec from 1860; Reg in Pro has pro rec from 1851; City Clks have bur rec)
Rock www.co.rock.wi.us/	M8	7 Dec 1836	Milwaukee Rock County; 51 S Main St; Janesville, WI 53545-3978; Ph. 608.757.5660 Details: (Reg of Deeds has b, m & d rec from 1849 & land rec from 1839; Reg in Pro has pro rec)
Rusk* www.ruskcounty.org/	G4	15 May 1901	Chippewa Rusk County; 311 Miner Ave E; Ladysmith, WI 54848-1862; Ph. 715.532.2100 Details: (Formerly Gates Co. Name changed to Rusk 19 Jun 1905) (Reg of Deeds has b, m, d & land rec from 1872; Co Ct has div, pro & ct rec)
Sauk www.co.sauk.wi.us/	L6	11 Jan 1840	Crawford, Dane, Portage Sauk County; 515 Oak St; Baraboo, WI 53913; Ph. 608.355.3286 Details: (Reg of Deeds has b rec from 1860, m rec from 1850, d rec from 1870 & land rec; Clk Cir Ct has div & ct rec; Reg in Pro has pro rec)
Sawyer www.sawyercountygov.org/	F4	10 Mar 1883	Ashland, Chippewa Sawyer County; 10610 Main; PO Box 273; Hayward, WI 54843; Ph. 715.634.4866 Details: (Reg of Deeds has b, m, d, bur, div, pro, ct & land rec)
Shawano* www.co.shawano.wi.us/	I8	16 Feb 1853	Oconto, Waupaca, Winnebago Shawano County; 311 N Main St; Shawano, WI 54166; Ph. 715.526.9150 Details: (Reg of Deeds has b, m, d & land rec; Reg in Pro has pro rec)
Sheboygan* www.rootsweb.com/~wisheboy/	K10	7 Dec 1836	Brown Sheboygan County; 615 N 6th St; Sheboygan, WI 53081; Ph. 920.459.3003 Details: (Reg of Deeds has b, m, d & land rec from 1872; Co Ct has div, ct & nat rec from 1850; Reg in Pro has pro rec from 1850)
St. Croix* www.co.saint-croix.wi.us/	H2	9 Jan 1840	Crawford St. Croix County; 1101 Carmichael Rd; Hudson, WI 54016; Ph. 715.386.4609 Details: (Reg of Deeds has b, m, d & land rec; Clk Cir Ct has div & ct rec; Reg in Pro has pro rec)
Taylor* www.taylor-county.com/	H5	4 Mar 1875	Clark, Lincoln, Marathon, Chippewa Taylor County; 224 S 2nd St; Medford, WI 54451; Ph. 715.748.1460 Details: (Reg of Deeds has b, m, d & land rec from 1875; Clk Ct has div & ct rec from 1875; Judge's Off has pro rec; Co Clk has cen rec; Historical Society has bur rec)

County Website	Map Index	Date Created	Parent County or Territory From Which Organized Address/Details
Trempealeau* www.tremplocounty.com/	J4	27 Jan 1854	**LaCrosse, Jackson, Buffalo, Chippewa** Trempealeau County; PO Box 67; Whitehall, WI 54773-0067; Ph. 715.538.2311 Details: (Reg of Deeds has b, m, d, bur & land rec; Clk Cir Ct has div & ct rec; Reg in Pro has pro rec)
Vernon* www.rootsweb.com/~wivernon/	L4	1 Mar 1851	**Crawford** Vernon County; 400 Courthouse Sq St; Viroqua, WI 54665; Ph. 608.637.5380 Details: (Formerly Bad Ax Co. Name changed to Vernon 22 Mar 1862) (Reg of Deeds has b, m, d & land rec; Clk Cir Ct has div & ct rec; Reg in Pro has pro rec)
Vilas co.vilas.wi.us/	F7	12 Apr 1893	**Oneida** Vilas County; 330 Court St; Eagle River, WI 54521; Ph. 715.479.3600 Details: (Reg of Deeds has b, m, d & land rec; Reg in Pro has pro rec)
Walworth www.walworthcounty.org/	N9	7 Dec 1836	**Milwaukee** Walworth County; 100 W Walworth; PO Box 1001; Elkhorn, WI 53121; Ph. 262.741.4241 Details: (Reg of Deeds has b rec from 1845, m & land rec from 1839, d rec from 1872, bur rec from 1969, div & ct rec from 1850 & pro rec from 1800's)
Washburn www.rootsweb.com/~wiwashbu/	F3	27 Mar 1883	**Burnett** Washburn County; 10 W 4th Ave; Shell Lake, WI 54871; Ph. 715.468.4600 Details: (Reg of Deeds has b, m, d & land rec from 1883; Clk Cts has div, pro & ct rec from 1883)
Washington www.co.washington.wi.us/	L9	7 Dec 1836	**Brown, Milwaukee** Washington County; 432 E Washington St; West Bend, WI 53095; Ph. 262.335.4301 Details: (Co Clk has b, m & d rec from 1850, div & ct rec from 1849; Reg in Pro has pro rec from 1851)
Waukesha www.waukeshacounty.gov/	M9	31 Jan 1846	**Milwaukee** Waukesha County; 1320 Pewaukee Rd; Waukesha, WI 53188; Ph. 262.548.7010 Details: (Reg of Deeds has b rec from 1860, m rec from 1846, d rec from 1879 & land rec; Clk Cts has div rec from 1847 & ct rec from 1962; Reg in Pro has pro rec from 1846; Co Clk has m applications from 1899)
Waupaca www.rootsweb.com/~wiwaupac/ index.htm	I8	17 Feb 1851	**Brown, Winnebago** Waupaca County; 811 Harding St; Waupaca, WI 54981; Ph. 715.258.6200 Details: (Reg of Deeds has b, m, d & land rec from 1852; Clk Ct has div rec from 1907 & ct rec from 1880; Clk Cir Ct has pro rec from 1857)
Waushara* www.1waushara.com/	J8	15 Feb 1851	**Marquette** Waushara County; 209 S Saint Marie St; PO Box 488; Wautoma, WI 54982; Ph. 920.787.0442 Details: (Reg of Deeds has b & d rec from 1876, m & land rec from 1852; Clk Ct has div & ct rec; Reg in Pro has pro rec)
Winnebago www.co.winnebago.wi.us/	J9	6 Jan 1840	**Brown, Calumet, Fond du Lac, Marquette** Winnebago County; 415 Jackson St; Oshkosh, WI 54901; Ph. 920.236.4888 Details: (Attached to Brown & Fond du Lac Cos prior to organization 1 Jan 1848) (Reg of Deeds has b & land rec from 1861, m rec from 1870 & d rec; Reg in Pro has pro rec)
Wood www.co.wood.wi.us/	I6	29 Mar 1856	**Portage** Wood County; 400 Market St; Wisconsin Rapids, WI 54494; Ph. 715.421.8460 Details: (Reg of Deeds has b, m & d rec from 1875 & land rec; Clk Cts has div & ct rec from 1875; Reg in Pro has pro rec from 1875)

Indian Paintbrush

WYOMING

CAPITAL: CHEYENNE – TERRITORY 1868 – STATE 1890 (44TH)

Before 1800, only a few fur traders and explorers entered the Wyoming region. After the Louisiana Purchase, Lewis and Clark and others explored the area. The American and Rocky Mountain Fur Companies explored the area extensively over the next three decades and opened the Overland Trail. In 1834, Fort Laramie became the first permanent settlement in Wyoming. In 1849, it became a supply depot on the Oregon Trail, with up to 50,000 individuals going through the fort in 1850 alone. The second settlement in the state was at Fort Bridger in 1842.

When the Dakota Territory was established in 1861, Wyoming was included in it. Laramie County was organized in 1867 and included all of the present state of Wyoming. Between 1867 and 1869, the transcontinental Union Pacific Railway was built through southern Wyoming, bringing the towns of Laramie, Cheyenne, Rawlins, Rock Springs, Green River, and Evanston into existence. Wyoming Territory was created in 1868 with 6,000 to 7,000 inhabitants. Yellowstone Park was established in 1872. Arapaho and Cheyenne Indians moved to reservations. The Sioux Indians were defeated in 1877, after which northern Wyoming was opened to cattle grazing. A cattle boom followed, which reached its peak in the 1880's.

In 1890, Wyoming became a state. The Carey Act of 1894 provided for the reclamation and homesteading of desert land, which stimulated new settlements in northern Wyoming. Mormons established towns in the Big Horn Basin. By 1940, Wyoming's foreign-born residents came from England, Germany, Sweden, Russia, Italy, Austria, Greece, Denmark, Norway, Ireland, Poland, Finland, Czechoslovakia, France, and Hungary.

Look for vital records in the following locations:

- **Birth, death and marriage records:** Contact Vital Records Services, Cheyenne, Wyoming. Birth and death records are available beginning in 1909. Marriage records start on 1 May 1941. Earlier records are filed with the county courts.
- **Probate, land and naturalization records:** Prior to statehood, probate records were kept by the territorial probate court. After statehood they were kept by the district court in each county, as were naturalization and land records.
- **Census records:** A state census exists for 1905, and is available at the Wyoming State Archives, Museums and Historical Department in Cheyenne.

Vital Records Services
Hathaway Building
Cheyenne, Wyoming 82002
307.777.7591

**Wyoming State Archives,
Museums and Historical Department**
Barrett Building, 2301 Central
Cheyenne, Wyoming 82002

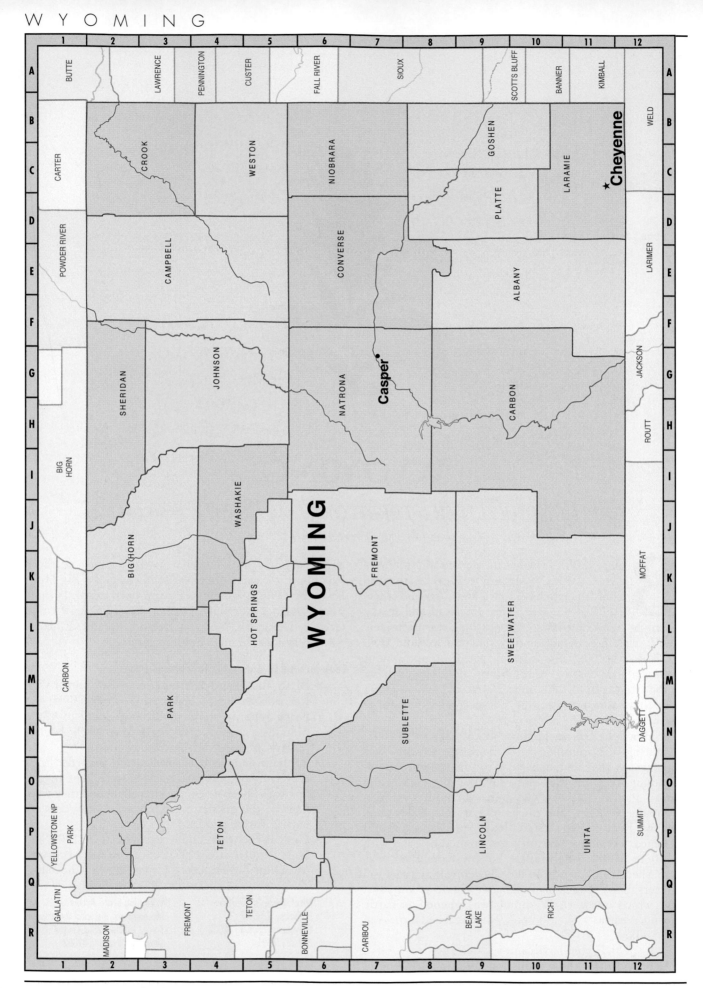

Societies and Repositories

Albany County Genealogical Society; PO Box 6163; Laramie, Wyoming 82070

Cheyenne Genealogical Society; Laramie County Library; Central Ave.; Cheyenne, Wyoming 82001

Congregational Library; 14 Beacon Street; Boston, Massachusetts 02108; 617.523.0470; Fax 617.523.0470

Department of Commerce, Division of Cultural Resources; Barrett Building, 2301 Central; Cheyenne, Wyoming 82002; 307.777.7016; Fax 307.777.7044

Fremont County Genealogical Society; c/o Riverton Branch Library; 1330 W. Park Ave.; Riverton, Wyoming 82501

Goshen Co. Public Library; 2001 East A Street; Torrington, Wyoming 82240

Land of Goshen Chapter, AHSGR; 100 E 23rd Ave; Torrington, Wyoming 82240; 307.532.2534

Lander Valley (Fremont County) Genealogical Society; 1015 Black Blvd.; Lander, Wyoming 82520; <www.fortunecity.com/millenium/bluepeter/119>

Laramie County Library, Cheyenne Genealogical Society; 2800 Central Avenue; Cheyenne, Wyoming 82001; 307.634.3561; Fax 307.634.2082

Laramie County Public Library; Cheyenne, Wyoming 82001

Laramie Peekers Genealogical Society of Platte County; 1108 21st St.; Wheatland, Wyoming 82201

National Archives-Rocky Mountain Region (Denver); Denver Federal Center Building 48; Denver, Colorado 80225; 303.236.0817; Fax 303.236.9354

Natrona County Genealogical Society; PO Box 50665; Casper, Wyoming 82605

Park County Genealogical Society; PO Box 3056; Cody, Wyoming 82414

Powell Valley Genealogical Club; PO Box 184; Powell, Wyoming 82435

Presbyterian Historical Society; United Presbyterian Church in the U.S.; 425 Lombard Street; Philadelphia, Pennsylvania 19147

Roman Catholic, Diocese of Cheyenne; Box 426; Cheyenne, Wyoming 82003; 307.638.1530; Fax 307.637.7936

Sheridan Genealogical Society, Inc.; Wyoming Rm., Sheridan County Library; 335 W. Alger St.; Sheridan, Wyoming 82801

Sons of the American Revolution, Wyoming Society; 1040 S. Thurmond; Sheridan, Wyoming 82801

Southeastern Wyoming Chapter, AHSGR; 2415 Van Lennen; Cheyenne, Wyoming 82001; 307.634.0309;

Sublette County Genealogical Society; PO Box 1186; Pindale, Wyoming 82941

United Methodist Archives Center; Drew University Library, PO Box 127; Madison, New Jersey 07940; 201.408.3189; Fax 201.408.3909

University of Wyoming Library; PO Box 3334, University Station; Laramie, Wyoming 82071-3334; 307.766.3279; Fax 307.766.3062

Vital Records Services; Hathaway Building; Cheyenne, Wyoming 82002; 307.777.7591; Fax 307.635.4103

Western History & Archives Dept.; Univ. of Wyoming; Laramie, Wyoming 82070

Weston County Genealogical Society; 23 W. Main; Newcastle, Wyoming 82701

Wyoming Room, Sheridan Co. Fulmer Public Library; 335 W. Alger St.; Sheridan, Wyoming 82801

Wyoming State Archives; Barrett Building; 2301 Central Avenue; Cheyenne, Wyoming 82002; 307.777.7044; <http://wyoarchives.state.wy.us/>

Wyoming State Historical Society; PMB #184; 1740H Dell Range Blvd.; Cheyenne, Wyoming 82009-4946; http://wyshs.org/

Wyoming State Library, Supreme Court and Library Building; 2301 Capitol Ave.; Cheyenne, Wyoming 82002-0006; 307.777.7281; Fax 307.777.6289

Wyoming State Office of the Bureau of Land Management; 2515 Warren Avenue, PO Box 1828; Cheyenne, Wyoming 82003; 307.775.6001; Fax 307.775.6082 Bibliography and Record Sources

Bibliography and Record Sources

General Sources

A Directory of Church and Religious Organizations in the State of Wyoming. Cheyenne: Historical Records Survey, 1939.

Bartlett, Ichabod S. *History of Wyoming*. 3 vols. Chicago: S.J. Clarke Publishing Co., 1918.

Beach, Cora May Brown. *Women of Wyoming: Including a Short History of Some of the Early Activities of Women of our State, Together with Biographies of those Women who were Our Early Pioneers as well as of Women Who Have Been Prominent in Public Affairs and in Civil Organizations and Service Work*. 2 vols. Casper, Wyoming: S. E. Boyer, 1927.

Beard, Frances B. *Wyoming from Territorial Days to the Present*. 3 vols. Chicago: American Historical Society, 1933.

Bird, Twila. *A Century of Saints: A Front Range History of the Church of Jesus Christ of Latter-day Saints*. [Aurora, CO: Front Range Centennial Committee], 1997.

Chaffin, Lorah. *Sons of the West: Biographical Account of Early-Day Wyoming*. Caldwell, Idaho: Caxton Printers, 1941.

Chamblin, Thomas S. *The Historical Encyclopedia of Wyoming*. 2 vols. Cheyenne, Wyoming: Published by Wyoming Historical Institute, 1970.

Donahue, Jim, ed. *Guide to the County Archives of Wyoming*. Cheyenne, Wyoming: Wyoming State Archives, 1991.

Donahue, Jim, ed. *Guide to the State Government and Municipal Archives of Wyoming*. Cheyenne, Wyoming: Wyoming State Archives, 1991.

Engebretson, Doug. *Empty Saddles, Forgotten Names: Outlaws of the Black Hills and Wyoming*. Aberdeen, South Dakota: North Plains Press, 1982.

Federal Postal Employees and Contractors in Wyoming, 1869–1911. Cheyenne, Wyoming: Medicine Bow Publications, 1985.

Gorzalka, Ann. *Wyoming's Territorial Sheriffs*. Glendo, Wyoming: High Plains Press, 1998.

Guide to Vital Statistics Records in Wyoming: Church Archives. Cheyenne: Historical Records Survey, 1942.

"Guide to Wyoming Frontier Newspapers," *Annals of Wyoming*, Vols. 33-35 (1961-1963). Cheyenne: Wyoming State Archives, 1923-.

Hendrickson, Gordon Olaf. *Peopling the High Plains: Wyoming's European Heritage*. Cheyenne, Wyoming: Wyoming State Archives and Historical Department, 1977.

Historical Records Survey (Wyoming). *Inventory of the Church Archives of Wyoming Presbyterian Churches*. (Salt Lake City: Filmed by the Genealogical Society of Utah, 1967).

Homsher, Lola. *Guide to Wyoming Newspapers, 1867-1967*. Cheyenne: Wyoming State Library, 1971.

Hoy, Billie. *A History of the Covenant Church in the Midwest and Southwest Conferences*. Salina, KS: Arrow Printing Co., 1961.

Inventory of the Church Archives of Wyoming Presbyterian Churches: (N.p.: Historical Records Survey, n.d.).

Lester, Margaret Moore. *From Rags to Riches: A History of Hilliard and Bear River, 1890-1990*. Evanston, Wyoming: 1st Impressions, 1992.

Peterson, C. S. *Men of Wyoming, the National Newspaper Reference Book of Wyoming: Containing Photographs and Biographies of over Three Hundred Men Residents*. Denver, CO: [s.n.], 1915.

Progressive Men of the State of Wyoming. Chicago: A. W. Bowen, 1903.

Sandahl, Charles Frederick. *The Nebraska Conference of the Augustana Synod: Survey of its Work with Sketches of its Congregations, Institutions, Organizations and Pioneers*. [S.l.]: Nebraska Conference, 1931.

Spiros, Joyce V. H. *Genealogical Guide to Wyoming*. Gallup. NM: Verlene Publisher, 1982.

Taft Alfred Larson. *History of Wyoming*. Lincoln: University of Nebraska Press, 1965.

Trenholm, Virginia Cole, ed. *Wyoming Blue Book*. 5 v. in 6. Cheyenne, Wyoming: Wyoming State Archives and Historical Department, 1991.

United States. Work Projects Administration. *Guide to Public Vital Statistics Records in Wyoming*. Cheyenne, Wyoming: [s.n.], 1941.

Welch, Charles Arthur. *History of the Big Horn Basin: With Stories of Early Days, Sketches of Pioneers and Writings of the Author*. Salt Lake City: Deseret News Press, 1940.

Wheeler, Denice. *The Feminine Frontier: Wyoming Women, 1850-1900*. [S.l.: s.n.], 1987.

Wiggins, Marvin E. *Mormons and Their Neighbors: An Index to Over 75,000 Biographical Sketches from 1820 to the Present*. 2 vols. [Provo, Utah]: Harold B. Lee Library, Brigham Young University, 1984.

Woods, Lawrence M. *Wyoming Biographies*. Worland, Wyoming: High Plains Pub. Co., 1991.

Wyoming Research Outline. Series US-States, no. 50. Salt Lake City: Family History Library, 1988.

Atlases, Maps and Gazetteers

Bishop, Loren C. *Maps of Wyoming Trails, Roads, Migration Routes and Forts*. [Cheyenne, Wyoming]: Wyoming State Archives & Historical Dept., 1963.

Gallagher, John S. *Wyoming Post Offices, 1850-1980*. Burtonsville, Maryland: The Depot, 1980.

Urbanek, Mae B. *Wyoming Place Names*. Reprint. Missoula, Montana: Mountain Press Publishing Co., 1988.

Wyoming Atlas and Gazetteer. Freeport, Maine: DeLorme Mapping Co., 1993.

Census Records
Available Census Records and Census Substitutes
Federal Census, 1860 (with Nebraska), 1870, 1880, 1900, 1910, 1920, 1930.
Federal Mortality Schedules 1870, 1880.
Union Veterans and Widows 1890.
State/Territorial Census 1905.

Dollarhide, William. *The Census Book: A Genealogist's Guide to Federal Census Facts, Schedules and Indexes*. Bountiful, Utah: Heritage Quest, 1999.

Kemp, Thomas Jay. *The American Census Handbook*. Wilmington, DE: Scholarly Resources, Inc., 2001.

Lainhart, Ann S. *State Census Records*. Baltimore: Genealogical Publishing Co., Inc., 1992.

Thorndale, William, and William Dollarhide. *Map Guide to the U.S. Federal Censuses, 1790-1920*. Baltimore: Genealogical Publishing Co., 1987.

Court Records Probate and Wills

Note: Court, probate and will records are kept at the county level. See county pages for individual references.

Emigration, Immigration, Migration and Naturalization

Cornwall, Rebecca. *Rescue of the 1856 Handcart Companies*. Provo, Utah: Brigham Young University Press, 1981.

Knight, Hal. *111 Days to Zion*. [Salt Lake City: Deseret News, 1978].

Land and Property

Bolger, Eile. *Preliminary Inventory of the Records of the Bureau of Land Management, Wyoming: Record Group 49*. Denver: Federal Archives and Records Center, 1983.

Stockmen's Gazateer [sic] of Wyoming, 1909. Cheyenne, Wyoming: State of Wyoming Microfilm Dept., 1959.

Military

Johnson, Dorothy M. *The Bloody Bozeman: The Perilous Trail to Montana's Gold*. Missoula, Montana: Mountain Press Pub. Co., 1998.

Murray, *Robert A. Military Posts of Wyoming*. [Fort Collins, CO]: The Old Army Press, [1974].

Sanchez, Leo R. *Reflections of World War II, 115th U.S. Cavalry Wyoming National Guard*. [Casper, Wyo.: The School, 1994?].

United States. Adjutant General's Office. *Index to Compiled Service Records of Volunteer Union Soldiers Who Served in Organizations From the Territory of Nebraska*. Washington, D.C.: The National Archives, 1964. 2 microfilm.

United States. Selective Service System. *Wyoming, World War I Selective Service System Draft Registration Cards, 1917-1918*.

Washington, D.C.: The National Archives, 1987-1988. 14 microfilm.

Vital and Cemetery Records

Lovell, Evelyn, and Marlys Albert Bias. *Davis Funeral Homes records for 1918-1951, Riverton, Wyoming: Master Index.* Riverton, Wyoming: Fremont County Genealogical Society, 1987.

Martin, Phyllis J. *Uinta County, Wyoming Cemetery Records.* Evanston, Wyoming: the author, 1982.

Territorial Vital Records: Births, Divorces, Guardianship, Marriages, Naturalization, Wills; 1800's thru 1906 Utah Territory, AZ, CO, ID, NV, WY, Indian Terr.; LDS Branches, Wards; Deseret News Vital Recs.; J.P. Marriages; Meth. Marriages. St. George, Utah: Genealogical CD Publishing, c1994. CD-ROM.

United States. Work Projects Administration. *Guide to Public Vital Statistics Records in Wyoming.* Cheyenne, Wyoming: [s.n.], 1941.

Whittlesey, Lee H. *Death in Yellowstone: Accidents and Foolhardiness in the First National Park.* Boulder, CO: Roberts Rinehart Pub., 1995.

Wyoming. State Hospital. *Burial Records.* Salt Lake City: Genealogical Society of Utah, 1969.

County / Website	Map Index	Date Created	Parent County or Territory From Which Organized / Address/Details
Albany www.rootsweb.com/~wyalbany/	E10	16 Dec 1868	**Original county** Albany County; County Courthouse Rm 202; Laramie, WY 82070; Ph. 307.721.2541 Details: (Co Clk has m rec from 1869, bur rec from 1885, land rec from 1868 & mil rec from 1919; Clk Dis Ct has div, pro, ct & nat rec)
Big Horn www.rootsweb.com/~wybighor/	K2	12 Mar 1890	**Fremont, Johnson, Sheridan** Big Horn County; 420 W C St; Basin, WY 82410; Ph. 307.568.2357 Details: (Co Clk has m & land rec from 1896; Clk Dis Ct has div, pro & ct rec from 1896)
Campbell ccg.co.campbell.wy.us/	E3	13 Feb 1911	**Crook, Weston** Campbell County; 500 S Gillette Ave Ste 220; Gillette, WY 82716; Ph. 307.682.7285 Details: (Co Clk has m & land rec from 1912 & election rec; Clk Ct has div, pro & ct rec)
Carbon www.rootsweb.com/~wycarbon/	H10	16 Dec 1868	**Original county** Carbon County; PO Box 6; Rawlins, WY 82301; Ph. 307.328.2668 Details: (Co Clk has m rec from 1876 & land rec from 1880; Clk Dis Ct has div, pro & ct rec; see Nebr for 1860 cen)
Carter		27 Dec 1867	**Original county** Details: (see Sweetwater) (Name changed to Sweetwater 13 Dec 1869)
Converse www.rootsweb.com/~wyconver/	E6	9 Mar 1888	**Laramie, Albany** Converse County; 107 N 5th St; PO Box 990; Douglas, WY 82633; Ph. 307.358.2244 Details: (Co Clk has m, land, mil dis & tax rec from 1888 & poll rec from 1930; Clk Ct has div, pro & ct rec from 1888)
Crook www.rootsweb.com/~wycrook/	C3	8 Dec 1875	**Laramie, Albany** Crook County; 309 Cleveland St; PO Box 37; Sundance, WY 82729-0037; Ph. 307.283.1323 Details: (Co Clk has m & land rec from 1855; Clk Ct has div, pro & ct rec)
Fremont www.rootsweb.com/~wyfremon/	K7	5 Mar 1884	**Sweetwater** Fremont County; 450 N 2nd St; Lander, WY 82520; Ph. 307.332.2405 Details: (Co Clk has m & land rec from 1884, bur & mil rec; Clk Dis Ct has div, pro & ct rec)
Goshen* www.prairieweb.com/goshen_cty_wy/ gc_home.htm	B9	9 Feb 1911	**Laramie** Goshen County; 2125 E A St; PO Box 160; Torrington, WY 82240; Ph. 307.532.4051 Details: (Co Clk has m & land rec; Clk Dis Ct has div, pro & ct rec)
Hot Springs www.rootsweb.com/~wyhotspr/	L5	9 Feb 1911	**Fremont, Park, Big Horn** Hot Springs County; 415 Arapahoe St; Thermopolis, WY 82443; Ph. 307.864.3515 Details: (Co Clk has m rec from 1913 & land rec; Clk Dis Ct has div, pro & ct rec; land rec transcribed from Fremont Co)
Johnson www.johnsoncountywyoming.org/	G4	8 Dec 1875	**Carbon** Johnson County; 76 N Main St; Buffalo, WY 82834; Ph. 307.684.7272 Details: (Formerly Pease Co. Name changed to Johnson 13 Dec 1879) (Co Clk has m & land rec; Clk Dis Ct has div, pro & ct rec)
Laramie* webgate.co.laramie.wy.us/	C11	9 Jan 1867	**Original county** Laramie County; 309 W 20th St; Cheyenne, WY 82001; Ph. 307.633.4268 Details: (Co Clk has m rec from 1868 & land rec; Clk Dis Ct has div, pro & ct rec; see Nebr for 1860 cen)
Lincoln www.co.lincoln.wy.us/	P9	20 Feb 1913	**Uinta** Lincoln County; PO Box 670; Kemmerer, WY 83101; Ph. 307.877.9056 Details: (Co Clk has m rec from 1913 & land rec; Clk Dis Ct has div & pro rec from 1913 & ct rec)
Natrona www.rootsweb.com/~wynatron/	G6	9 Mar 1888	**Carbon** Natrona County; 200 N Center St Rm 157; Casper, WY 82601; Ph. 307.235.9200 Details: (Co Clk has m & land rec from 1888, mil dis rec, power of attorney, notary & commissions tax license-state & fed; Clk Dis Ct has div, pro & ct rec)
Niobrara www.rootsweb.com/~wyniobra/	C6	14 Feb 1911	**Converse** Niobrara County; 424 S Elm; PO Box 420; Lusk, WY 82225; Ph. 307.334.2211 Details: (Co Clk has m & land rec from 1888; Clk Dis Ct has div, pro & ct rec)

County Website	Map Index	Date Created	Parent County or Territory From Which Organized / Address/Details
Park* www.rootsweb.com/~wypark/	N3	15 Feb 1909	**Big Horn** Park County; 1002 Sheridan Ave; PO Box 160; Cody, WY 82414; Ph. 307.587.5548 Details: (Co Clk has m & land rec from 1911; Clk Ct has div, pro & ct rec)
Pease		8 Dec 1875	**Carbon** Details: (see Johnson) (Name changed to Johnson 13 Dec 1879)
Platte* www.rootsweb.com/~wyplatte/	D9	9 Feb 1911	**Laramie** Platte County; 806 9th St; Wheatland, WY 82201; Ph. 307.322.3555 Details: (Co Clk has m & land rec from 1890; Clk Dis Ct has div, pro & ct rec)
Sheridan www.sheridancounty.com/	G2	9 Mar 1888	**Johnson** Sheridan County; 224 S Main St Ste B2; Sheridan, WY 82801; Ph. 307.674.2500 Details: (Co Clk has m & land rec from 1888; Clk Dis Ct has div, pro & ct rec)
Sublette www.rootsweb.com/~wysublet/	N8	15 Feb 1921	**Fremont, Lincoln** Sublette County; 21 S Tyler Ave; Pinedale, WY 82941; Ph. 307.367.4372 Details: (Co Clk has m rec from 1923 & land rec from 1910; Clk Dis Ct has div, pro & ct rec from 1923)
Sweetwater* www.co.sweet.wy.us/	L9	27 Dec 1867	**Original county** Sweetwater County; 80 W Flaming Gorge Way; PO Box 730; Green River, WY 82935; Ph. 307.872.6400 Details: (Formerly Carter Co. Name changed to Sweetwater 13 Dec 1869) (Co Clk has m rec from 1864 & land rec from 1876; Clk Dis Ct has div, pro & ct rec; see Nebr for 1860 cen)
Teton www.rootsweb.com/~wyteton/	P4	15 Feb 1921	**Lincoln** Teton County; 200 S Willow; PO Box 1727; Jackson, WY 83001; Ph. 307.733.4430 Details: (Co Clk has m, div, pro, land & ct rec)
Uinta www.uintacounty.com/	P11	1 Dec 1869	**Original county** Uinta County; 225 9th St; PO Box 810; Evanston, WY 82931; Ph. 307.783.0306 Details: (Co Clk has m rec from 1872, land rec from 1870 & mil dis rec from 1902; Clk Dis Ct has div & pro rec; see Nebr for 1860 cen)
Washakie www.rootsweb.com/~wywashak/	J4	9 Feb 1911	**Big Horn** Washakie County; 10th St & Big Horn Ave; Worland, WY 82401; Ph. 307.347.6491 Details: (Co Clk has m & land rec; Clk Dis Ct has div, pro & ct rec)
Weston www.rootsweb.com/~wyweston/	C5	12 Mar 1890	**Crook** Weston County; 1 W Main St; Newcastle, WY 82701; Ph. 307.746.4744 Details: (Co Clk has m rec from 1890 & land rec from 1886; Clk Dis Ct has div, pro & ct rec from 1890)

Notes

AUSTRALIA

CAPITAL CITY: CANBERRA

Dutch sailors saw Australia as early as the Seventeenth Century and Captain James Cook arrived in 1770. Australia was not considered for colonization until Britain lost its ability to transport criminals to the thirteen American colonies during the American Revolution. In 1788, the first British penal colony was established on the banks of Botany Bay in what would become Sydney.

Transportation of British criminals continued until the middle of the nineteenth century. During those years, over 150,000 persons were sent to Australia. One third were from Ireland, and one fifth were women. They were joined by a number of settlers who relocated by choice. After their terms of servitude, most transportees stayed in Australia.

By 1850, the population had risen to approximately 400,000. During the next decade, with the discovery of gold, the population tripled to 1.2 million. Many came from the United States and Canada. Restrictive immigration policies, known as the "White Australia Policy," barred most Asians from entering the country.

The regions of Australia unified and gained commonwealth status. In 1901, a constitution was created. Six states including New South Wales, Queensland, South Australia, Tasmania, Victoria and Western Australia were formed. The Northern Territory and the Australian Capital Territory were also formed at that time. The national capital, originally in Melbourne, was moved to Canberra in 1927.

The population of Australia surged again during the aftermath of World War II. Immigrants came from eastern and southern Europe. Some restrictions were lifted on Asian immigration also.

SOME MAJOR GENEALOGICAL RECORD SOURCES
Civil Registration

Government registration of births, marriages and deaths in Australia dates from 1856. Some earlier records were reconstituted from church records.

The vital records are in the custody of state and territorial registries. When requesting a certificate, include the date and place of the event. An extended ten-year search of indexes is undertaken for an additional fee. Some indexes to these certificates have been published on CD-ROM.

In general, a certificate shows:
- **Births**: Name of the infant; date and place of birth; parents' names, ages, occupations and residence.
- **Marriages**: Date and place of marriage, names of the bride and groom, their occupations, residences, prior marital statuses, birthplaces, ages, fathers' names and occupations.
- **Deaths**: Date and place of death, name of the deceased, gender, age, cause of death, parents' names and occupations, birthplace, and the names of the informant, minister and undertaker.

PASSENGER ARRIVAL LISTS

Convict arrivals are available from the original lists in 1788. Some are available online. The data is sparse, but shows the date, the name of the ship, the name of the transportee, where he or she was sentenced, and the term of the sentence (often 7 years, 14 years, or life).

Later arrival lists for non-penal passengers are available for various ports. Arrival lists from 1924 are in the custody of the National Archives of Australia. Arrival lists are in chronological order by port, with some indexes.

ARCHIVES, LIBRARIES AND SOCITIES

National Archives of Australia; Queen Victoria Terrace; Canberra ACT 2610; Australia; <http://www.naa.gov.au/.htm>

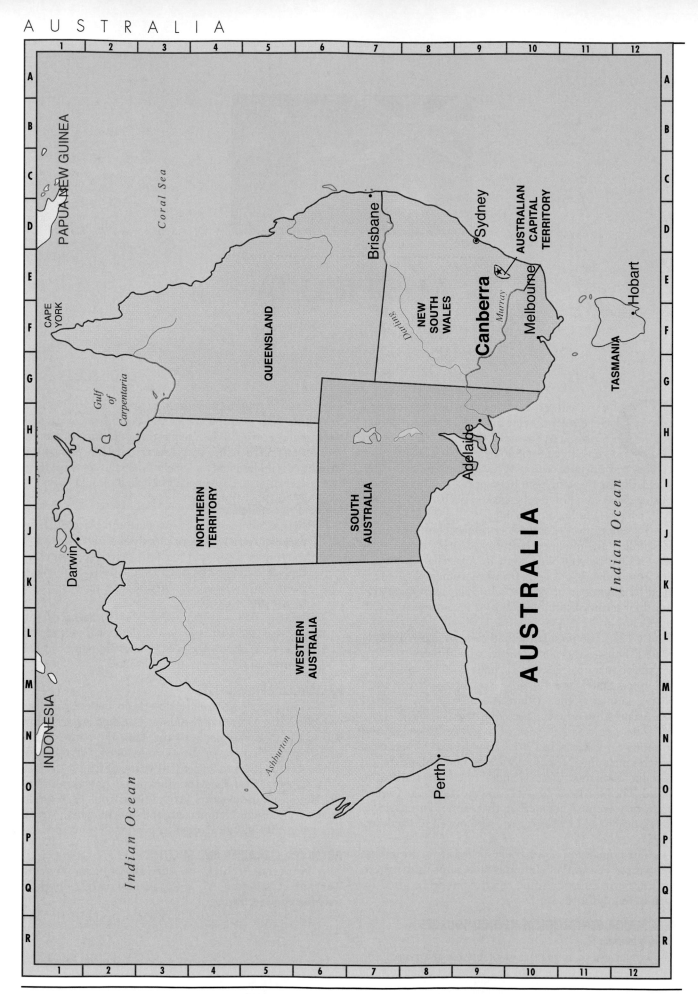

STATE AND TERRITORY ADDRESSES

Australian Capitol Territory

Australian Archives; PO Box 34; Dickson ACT 2602; 02.6209 9411

Australian Capital Territory Registry of Births, Deaths & Marriages; PO Box 788; Canberra, ACT 2601

Australian Institute of Aboriginal & Torres Strait: Islander Studies; GPO Box 553; Canberra ACT 2601; 02.6246.1111

Australian Jewish Historical Society; PO Box 105; Manuka ACT 2603

Australian War Memorial, Research Centre; Limestone Avenue; Campbell ACT 2601; 02.6243.4211

Fourth Fleet Families of Australia; PO Box 1011; Dickson ACT 2602

Heraldry & Genealogical Society of Canberra; GPO Box 585; Canberra ACT 2601; 02.6295.1141; E-mail: hagsoc@netspeed.com.au

Military Historical Society of Australia; PO Box 30; Garran ACT 2605

National Library of Australia; Canberra ACT 2600

Naval Historical Society of Australia; PO Box 117; Luneham ACT 2602

New South Wales

Anglican Archives, Diocese of Sydney; St. Andrew's Square; Sydney NSW 2000; 02.9269.0642

Archives Office of NSW, City Search Room; 2 Globe Street; The Rocks NSW 2000; 02.9237.0200

Australian Archives, NSW Regional Office; Level 4, 24 Campbell Street; Sydney NSW 2000; 02.9281.2500

Australian Jewish Genealogical Society; PO Box 154; Northbridge NSW 2065

Australian National Maritime Museum; Murray Street, Darling Harbour NSW 2009; 02.9552.7777

Baptist Historical Society of NSW; Morling College, 120 Herring Road; Eastwood NSW 2122

Catholic Archives, Archdiocese of Sydney; The Crypt, St. Mary's Cathedral; Sydney NSW 2000; 02.9232.3788

New South Wales Registry of Births, Deaths & Marriages; PO Box 30; Sydney, NSW 2001

Quaker Historical Society; 119 Devonshire Street; Surry Hills NSW 2010

Registry of Land Titles & Deeds; Queens Square; Sydney NSW 2000; 02.9228.6666

State Library of NSW/Mitchall Library; Macquarie Street; Sydney NSW 2000; 02.9273.1414

Supreme Court of NSW Probate Division; 5th Floor, Law Courts Building, Queens Square; Sydney NSW 2000; 02.9230.8111

Northern Territory

Anglican Archives, Diocese of Northern Territory; Christchurch Cathedral, Smith Street; Darwin NT 0800; 08.8981.6888

Australian Archives, NT Regional Office; Kelsey Crescent; Nightcliff NT 0810; 08.8943.8224

Catholic Archives, Diocese of Northern Territory; 90 Smith Street, Darwin NT 0800; 08.8981.2863

Genealogical Society of Northern Territory; 1st Floor, 25 Cavenagh Street; Darwin NT 0800; 08.8981.7363; E-mail: gsnt@austranet.com.au

Northern Territory Archives Service; Cnr Crowley & McMinn Streets; Darwin NT 0800; 08.8989.5188; <www.nt.gov.au/nta>

Northern Territory Registrar; PO Box 3021; Darwin, NT 0801

Registrar of Probates, Supreme Court of The; Northern Territory, Laws Courts Building, Mitchell Street; Darwin NT 0800; 08.8989.7953

State Library of the Northern Territory; 25 Cavenagh Street, Darwin NT 0800; 08.8989 7364

Queensland

Anglican Archives, Diocese of Brisbane; 439 Ann Street, Brisbane QLD 4000; 07.3229.4766

Australian Archives, QLD Regional Office; 996 Wynnum Road, Cannon Hill QLD 4170; 07.3249.4202

Australia's Immigration & Family History Centre; PO Box 937, Hervey Bay QLD 4655; 071.284.458 E-mail: jreakes@cyberalink.com.au

Baptist Historical Society of Queensland; PO Box 55, Broadway QLD 4006

Catholic Archives, Brisbane Archdiocese; 143 Edward Street, Brisbane QLD 4000; 07.3229.3744

Genealogical Society of Queensland; 1st Floor, Woolloongabba Post Office, Stanley Street; Woolloongabba QLD 4102; 07.38915085

Queensland State Archives; PO Box 1397; Sunnybank Hills QLD 4109; 07.3875.8755; <www.archives.qld.gov.au>

Queensland Registry of Births, Deaths & Marriages; PO Box 188; Brisbane, QLD 4002

South Australia

Aboriginal Family History; South Australian Museum, North Terrace; Adelaide SA 5000

Australasian Maritime Historical Society; PO Box 89; Lobethal SA 5241

Australian Archives; 11-13 Derlanger Avenue; Collinswood SA 5081

Catholic Archives; Catholic Church Office, 39 Wakefield Street; Adelaide SA 5000

Land Titles Office; 25 Pirie Street; Adelaide SA 5000

Lutheran Archives; 101 Archer Street; North Adelaide SA 5006

Pioneers' Association of South Australia; Aston House, 13 Leigh Street; Adelaide SA 5000

Polish Pioneers Descendents Group; 10 Scott Street; Firle SA 5070

South Aust. Genealogy & Heraldry Soc.; GPO Box 592, Adelaide 5001 SA; E-mail: saghs@dove.net.au; 08.8272.4222

Probate Office; 301 King William Street; Adelaide SA 5000

South Australian Principal Registrar; PO Box 1351; Adelaide, SA 5001

State Library of South Australia; GPO Box 419, North Terrace; Adelaide SA 5001; 08.8207.7360

State Records; PO Box 1056; Blair Athol West SA 5084; 08.8226.8000

Tasmania

Albany Branch - WAGS; PO Box 1267; Albany WA 6330; 08.9841.4965

Australian Archives, WA Regional Office; 348 Berwick Street; East Victoria Park WA 6101; 08.9361.8088

Probate Registry; 14th Floor, National Mutual Building, 111 St. George's Tce; Perth WA 6000; 08.9261.7699

Public Records Office of Western Australia; Alexander Library Building; Perth Cultural Centre; Perth WA 6000; 08.9427.3111

Registrar General's Office; PO Box 7720, Cloister's Square; Perth WA 6850; 08.9264.1555

Archives Office of Tasmania; 77 Murray Street, Hobart, TAS 7000; <www.tased.edu.au/archives/archives.hmm

Tasmanian Registrar General; PO Box 198; Hobart TAS 7000

Victoria

Administration & Probate; 2nd Floor, 436 Lonsdale Street; Melbourne Vic 3000; 03.9603 9296

Anglican Archives, Diocese of Melbourne; The Registrar, St. Paul's Cathedral; 209 Flinders Lane; Melbourne Vic 3000; 03.9650 3791

Australian Archives, Vic. Regional Office; Casselden Place, 2 Lonsdale Street; Melbourne Vic 3000; 03.9285.7999

Australian Churches of Christ Historical Soc. 40-60 Jacksons Road; Mulgrave Vic 3170

Australian Institute of Genealogical Studies; PO Box 339; Blackburn Vic 3130; 03.9877 3789; E-mail: aigs@alphalink.com.au

Genealogical Society of Victoria, Inc.; Level 6, 179 Queen Street; Melbourne Vic 3000; 03.9670 7033; Fax: 03.9670 4490

Land Titles Office; 283 Queen Street; Melbourne Vic 3000; 03.9603 5444

Public Records Office, City Search Room; 2nd Florr, Casseldon Place; 2 Lonsdale St.; Melbourne 2000 Vic; 03.9285.7999; <www.home.vicnet.net.au/~provic/>; E-mail: lavpro@vicnet.net.au

Victorian Registry of Births, Deaths & Marriages; PO Box 4332; Melbourne, VIC 3001

Western Australia

Australian Archives, WA Regional Office; 348 Berwick Street; East Victoria Park WA 6101; 08.9361 8088

Public Records Office of Western Australia; Alexander Library Building; Perth Cultural Centre; Perth WA 6000; 08.9427 3111; <www.liswa.wa.gov.au/archives.html>

Probate Registry, 14th Floor; National Mutual Building, 111 St. George's Tce, Perth WA 6000; 08.9261 7699

Registrar General's Office; PO Box 7720, Cloister's Square; Perth WA 6850; 08.9264 1555

State Archives, Alexander Library Building; Cultural Centre; Perth WA 6000

State Reference Library of WA; Alexander Library Building, Cultural Centre; Perth WA 6000

Uniting Church of Australia Archives; Synod of Western Australia, 3rd Floor; Westminster House, 10 Pier Street; Perth WA 6000

Western Australia Genealogical Society; 6/48 May Street; Bayswater WA 6053; 08.9271 4311; <www.wags.org.au>

WEB SITES

Australasian Genealogy: <home.vicnet.net.au/~AGWeb/agweb.htm>

Australian and New Zealand Genealogy Pages: <opax.swin.edu.au/andrew/aust_genealogy.html>

Australian Family History Compendium: <www.cohsoft.com.au/afhc/>

Central Register of Indexing Projects in Australia: <www.st.net.au/~judyweb/register.html>

Genealogy in Australia: <www.pcug.org.au/~mpahlow/welcome.html>

South Australian Family History & Genealogy: <www.adelaide.net/au/~bazle/>

SUGGESTED READING

Ancestors in Archives: A Guide to Family History Sources in the Official Records of South Australia. North Adelaide, SA: Research & Access Services, 1994.

Lay, Patricia. *A Guide to Genealogical and Family History Resources in the National Library of Australia.* Queanbeyan, NSW: Family History Services, 1988.

Reakes, Janet. *How to Trace Your Missing Ancestors Whether Living, Dead, or Adopted.* Sydney, NSW: Hale and Iremonger, 1994.

Reakes, Janet. *The A to Z of Genealogy: A Handbook.* Port Melbourne, VIC: Mandarin, 1995.

Smith, Diane. *Lookin for Your Mob: A Guide to Tracing Aboriginal Family Trees.* Canberra ACT: Aboriginal Studies Press, 1990.

Vine Hall, Nick. *Tracing Your Family History in Australia: A Guide to Sources.* Albert Park, Australia: Scriptorium Family History Center, 1994.

Webster, Judy. *Specialist Indexes in Australia: A Genealogist's Guide.* Brisbane QLD: J. Webster, 1996.

AUSTRIA (ÖSTERREICH)

CAPITAL CITY: VIENNA (WIEN)

Austria is a crossroads in Europe. Incursions by the Romans from the south, the Germans from the north and west, the Slavs from the east, and the Turks from the southeast have given it a colorful history. From the eighth century, Austria was affiliated with Germany and became known as the East Country, *Ost Reich*, which eventually became its German name.

Austria's position as a viable nation was established after the Battle of Lechfeld, in 955 AD, when the encroaching Magyars were beaten back by Germanic forces. With the rise of the Habsburgs during the fourteenth and fifteenth centuries, Austria became part of the Holy Roman Empire and acquired territories in other parts of Europe, largely through marriage alliances.

Austria is a Roman Catholic nation, but the 1555 Peace of Augsburg brought a certain amount of tolerance for Protestant denominations. An attempt by Ferdinand II to reinstate Roman Catholicism early in the seventeenth century led to the Thirty Years' War. The War brought the eventual defeat of the Holy Roman Empire in 1648. Although the Austrians were able to repel a Turkish invasion later that century, they lost many of their "remote" European possessions in the late eighteenth and early nineteenth centuries.

In a bid to hold itself together, the dual monarchy of Austria and Hungary was declared in 1867. The two nations were led by separate governments, but shared a common flag and head of state. A half-century later the dual monarchy was split by the turmoil of World War I. At that time they lost additional border territories to Poland, Czechoslovakia and other nations.

Germanic by tradition, Austria was declared part of Hitler's Third Reich in 1938. Although it was liberated by Allied troops in 1945, it was ten years before it again regained full sovereignty.

German is the official language of Austria. The ethnic heritage of a vast number of it residents remains Croatian, Magyars, Slovenes, Serbian and Italian. The majority of residents are Roman Catholics.

SOME MAJOR GENEALOGICAL RECORD SOURCES

The primary source for genealogical research in Austria is the parish register of the Roman Catholic Church. The registers list baptisms, marriages and deaths. By mandate, the Church began keeping the registers as early as the mid-sixteenth century. A civil order to maintain the records was formalized by Emperor Joseph II in 1784. The Catholic registers have added importance because of the lack of official tolerance of other denominations until the nineteenth century. Civil registration of vital events was not officially begun until 1939.

Some Protestant, Orthodox and Jewish records are available, but many of these records were kept with the Catholic records. The church registers are generally in local custody.

The Catholic parish registers include:

- **Baptisms** (*taufen*). The name of the infant, the date and place of baptism, the names of the parents, witnesses.
- **Marriages** (*heiraten*). The names and residences of bride and groom, parents, witnesses.
- **Deaths** (*toten*). The name of the deceased and the date and place of burial.

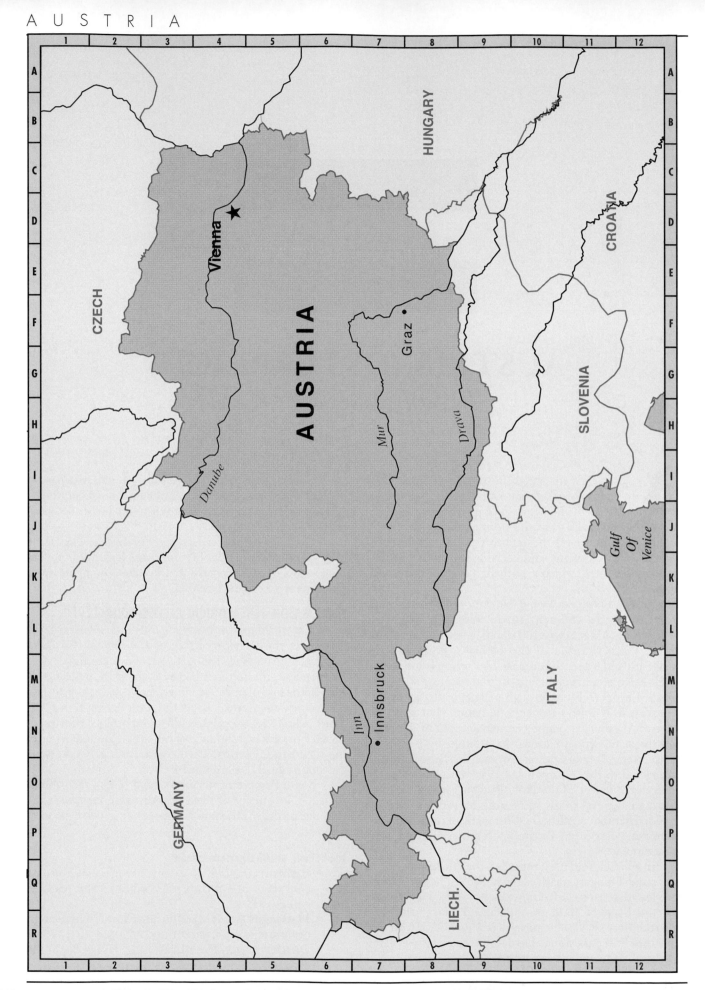

ARCHIVES, LIBRARIES AND SOCIETIES

Kriegsarchiv; Nottendorfergasse 2-4; 1030 Wien; Austria

Wiener Stadt und Landesarchiv; Doblhoffg 9; 1010 Wien; Austria

Vorarlberger Landesarchiv; Kirchstrasse 28; 6901 Bergenz; Austria; <www.vlr.gv.at/Landesregierung/iib/larchiv.htm>

Karntner Landesarchiv; St. Ruprechter Strasse 7; 9020 Klangenfurt; Austria

Tiroler Landesarchiv; Michael Gasmair Strasse 1; 6020 Innsbruck; Austria

Historischer Verein fur Steiermark; Hamerlingg 3; 8010 Graz; Austria

Oberosterreichisches Landesarchiv; Anzengruberstrasse 19; 4020 Linz; Austria

Niederosterreichisches Landesarchiv; Franz Schubert Platz 4; 3109 St. Polten; Austria

SUGGESTED READING

Baxter, Angus. *In Search of Your European Roots*. Baltimore: Genealogical Publishing Co., 1994.

Senekovic, Dagmar. *Handy Guide to Austrian Genealogical Records*. Logan, UT: Everton Publishers, 1979.

Thode, Ernest. *Address Book for Germanic Genealogy*. Baltimore: Genealogical Publishing Co., 1997.

WEB SITES

Austria GenWeb (World GenWeb): <www.rootsweb.com/~autwgw/>

Osterreich Alben:

Osterreichische Nationalbibliothek: <www.onb.ac.at/index.htm>

Starke Genealogy Index of German [and Austrian] Nobility: <www.rootsweb.com/~autwgw/sgi/index.htm>

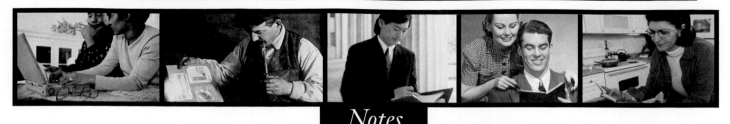

Notes

CANADA

CAPITAL CITY: OTTAWA

Early settlers of Canada may have come from Asia. Currently, many residents trace their ancestry through the immigration of Europeans. The French were first to settle on Canadian shores early in the seventeenth century. They settled in the maritime region known as Acadia, now Nova Scotia, New Brunswick, Prince Edward Island and Quebec. New France had about 8,000 residents by 1675.

During the same era, the British expanded their interests in that part of North America. Their presence resulted in American skirmishes that mirrored concurrent European wars. In 1713, the Treaty of Utrecht awarded the Hudson Bay region and Newfoundland to the British. The cultural conflict continued through a series of battles known as the French and Indian Wars from 1754 to 1763. During that time, the British expelled about 10,000 French Acadians whose loyalties were in question. Many moved to Louisiana, as it is known today. Some French Acadians returned to Acadia years later, while others remained. Although they were once know as "Acadian," they later became known as "Cajun."

The British eventually dominated Canada, but the Quebec Act of 1774 recognized the unique culture of the region and allowed its inhabitants to continue to use the French language and legal system. The Constitutional Act of 1791 created Upper Canada, also known as Canada West or Ontario. Lower Canada was known as Canada East or Quebec. The 1840 Act of Union united them into the Province of Canada.

Immigration increased during the eighteenth century when United Empire Loyalists fled their homes in the new United States to retain residence in a British colony. A similar influx occurred during the mid-nineteenth century when hundreds of thousands of Irish fled the effects of the Potato Famine. Confederation followed as a result of the 1867 British North America Act, which created the Dominion of Canada. Manitoba joined the Confederation in 1870, British Columbia in 1871, and Prince Edward Island in 1873. Alberta and Saskatchewan joined in 1905, and Newfoundland and Labrador in 1949. The Northwest Territories were defined in 1870, and the Yukon Territory was granted territorial status in 1898.

SOME MAJOR GENEALOGICAL RECORD SOURCES
Vital Records

Civil registration and vital records were compiled by the government. They date as early as the 1860s in some provinces. They were standardized nationwide in the 1920s. Vital statistics are found in Roman Catholic Church records in Quebec as early as the 1620s. Town clerks in Nova Scotia kept vital records as early as the late 1770s and early 1800s.

Among the vital records available for Canada:

- **Births**: Name, gender, date and place of birth, parents.
- **Marriages**: Marriage bonds are held by the district or county clerk and include names of groom and bride, date, location, and surety. Marriage registers (registres de marriage) contain the names of bride and groom, date, status prior to marriage (single, widowed, etc.), and witnesses. They also include age, residence, occupations, parents, and names of any previous spouses.
- **Divorces**: Prior to 1913 there were less than a thousand divorces registered in Canada. For information contact: Clerk of the Senate, Parliament Buildings, Ottawa, ON K1A 0NA, Canada.
- **Deaths (deces)**: originally the death records contained the name of the deceased and date of death. Later death records contained the age or birth date, race, residence, occupation, cause of death, burial information, name of spouse or parents, and name of informant.

Civil vital records are available from provincial vital records offices and provincial archives. Many are available on microfilm at the Family History Library in Salt Lake City.

National Archives of Canada – Information and Sources <www.archives.ca/02/02020202_e.html> –

Searchable database <olivetreegenealogy.com/ships/index.shtml> –

Web Ties – Genealogy Links Canada <genealogypro.com/links/Canada/>

ARCHIVES, LIBRARIES AND SOCIETIES

Alberta Vital Statistics; 10365 – 97th Street; Edmonton, AB T5K 2P2; Canada

Archives Nationales du Quebec; 1012, avenue du Seminaire; Sainte Foy, QC G1V 1W4; Canada

British Columbia Archives; 655 Belleville Street; Victoria, BC V8V 1X4; Canada; <www.bcarchives.gov.bc.ca/index.htm>

Genealogical Institute of the Maritimes; PO Box 3142; Halifax, NS B3J 3H5; Canada

Manitoba Vital Statistics; 254 Portage Avenue; Winnipeg, MB R3C 0B6; Canada

Maritime History Archive; Memorial University of Newfoundland; St. John's, NF A1C 5S7; Canada; <www.mun.ca/mha/>

National Archives of Canada; 395 Wellington Street; Ottawa, ON K1A 0N3; Canada; <www.archives.ca/MainMenu.html>

National Library of Canada; 395 Wellington Street; Ottawa, ON K1A 0N4; Canada; <nlc-bnc.ca/ehome.htm>

New Brunswick Vital Statistics Branch; Department of Health and Community Services; PO Box 6000; Fredericton, NB E3B 5H1; Canada

Newfoundland Vital Statistics; PO Box 8700; St. John's, NF A1B 4J6; Canada

Northwest Territorial Archives; Prince of Wales Northern Heritage Center; Yellowknife, NWT X1A 2L9; Canada

Northwest Territories Vital Records; PO Box 1320; Yellowknife, NWT X1A 2L9; Canada

Nova Scotia Provincial Library; 3770 Kempt Road; Halifax, NS B3K 4X8; Canada; <rs6000.nshpl.library.ns.ca>

Nova Scotia Vital Statistics; 1690 Hollis Street; Halifax, NS B3J 2M9; Canada; <www.gov.ns.ca/bacs/vstat/index.htm>

Ontario Archives; 77 Grenville Street; Toronto, ON M7A 1C7; Canada; <http://www.gov.on.ca/MCZCR/archives/>

Ontario Vital Statistics; PO Box 8700; St. John's, NF A1B 4J6; Canada

Prince Edward Island Public Archives and Records Office; Hon. George Coles Building; Richmond Street; Charlottetown, PEI; Canada

Prince Edward Island Vital Statistics; 35 Douses Road; Montague, PEI C0A 1R0; Canada

Provincial Archives of Alberta; 12845 – 102 Avenue; Edmonton, AB T5N 0M6; Canada

Provincial Archives of Manitoba; 200 Vaughan Street; Winnipeg, MB R3C 1T5; Canada; <www.gov.mb.ca/chc/archives/>

Provincial Archives of New Brunswick; 23 Dineen Drive; Fredericton, NB E3B 5H1; Canada

Provincial Archives of Newfoundland and Labrador; Colonial Building; Military Road St. John's, NF A1C 2C9; Canada

Quebec Vital Statistics; 205 Montagny Street; Quebec, QC G1N 2Z9; Canada

Saskatchewan Archives Board; Murray Building, University of Saskatchewan; 3 Campus Drive; Saskatoon, SK S7N 5A4; Canada

Saskatchewan Vital Statistics; 1942 Hamilton Street; Regina, SK S4P 3V7; Canada

Yukon Archives; PO Box 2703; Whitehorse, YT Y1A 2C6; Canada

Yukon Territory Vital Statistics; Department of Health and Human Resources; PO Box 2703; Whitehorse, YT X1A 2C6; Canada

SUGGESTED READING

Baxter, Angus. *In Search of Your Canadian Roots*. Baltimore: Genealogical Publishing Co., 1989.

Boudrou, Denis M. *Beginning Franco-American Genealogy*. Pawtucket, RI: American-French Genealogical Society, 1986.

Merriman, Brenda Dougall. *Genealogy in Ontario: Searching the Records*. Toronto: Ontario Genealogical Society, 1988.

Olivier, Reginald L. *Your Ancient Canadian Family Ties*. Logan, UT: Everton Publishers.

Punch, Terrence M. *Genealogist's Handbook for Atlantic Canada Research*. Boston: New England Historic Genealogical Society, 1989.

Roy, Janine. *Tracing Your Ancestors in Canada*. Ottawa: National Archives of Canada, 1991.

Smith, Marion L. "By Way of Canada: U.S. Records of Immigration across the U.S.–Canadian Border," 1895-1954 (St. Albans Lists). Prologue: Quarterly of the National Archives and Records Administration Fall 2000, vol. 32, no. 3.

Notes

Notes

DENMARK (DANMARK)

CAPITAL CITY: COPENHAGEN (KØBENHAVN)

The Danes came south from the Scandinavian Peninsula and spread their influence throughout Western Europe and the British Isles in the days of Vikings. By the thirteenth century, the Danes had established a system of *stavnsband,* or serfdom, where peasants were tied to specific plots of land, unable to move from place to place.

In 1397, Denmark, Norway and Sweden combined to form the Kalmar Union. The Union remained intact for over a century until Sweden left in 1523. In 1536, the National Assembly in Denmark acknowledged the Reformation and joined several other northern European and Scandinavian nations in changing the state religion from Catholic to Lutheran.

In 1788, the *stavnsband* system was abolished. The same year Denmark created an army and navy composed of their own people, rather than relying on foreign mercenaries. Following a failing alliance with French forces, the Treaty of Kiel separated Norway from Denmark and gave her to Sweden. In 1866, Denmark lost the southern duchies of Schleswig and Holstein in a war against Prussia and Austria. Later in 1920, the inhabitants of northern Schleswig voted to rejoin Denmark.

SOME MAJOR GENEALOGICAL RECORD SOURCES

Church Records

Early vital records were recorded by churches. In 1536, the state-supported Lutheran Church (Den Danske Folkekirke) was established. Registers of baptisms, marriages and burials became mandatory in 1645 and the Lutheran parishes began keeping duplicates of the registers in 1814. Copies of the registers are found in local parish offices and many have been filmed by the Family History Library. The Roman Catholic Church kept records from 1685, the Reformed Church from 1747, and the Jewish Church from 1814.

Civil Registration

Denmark did not begin nationwide civil registration of births, marriages and deaths until the nineteenth century. However, some localities do have civil records from that time. They are in the custody of the appropriate municipal or district office. Some are on microfilm at the Family History Library.

Copenhagen has civil registers dating from 1851, while other municipalities and districts began in 1863 or 1874.

Court Records

Courts are among the most important Danish institutions for recording information valuable to family historians. Court records are often not indexed but include criminal cases, land transactions, and probate proceedings.

Court records are in the custody of the local court, and many have been microfilmed by the Family History Library.

Land and Property Records

Land transactions were handled by the local courts and kept in separate registers from the criminal or probate proceedings. Court records of land transactions are found as early as 1738 and are found in the local court records. Transactions after 1844 are found in the provincial archives. The Family History Library has microfilm copies of some land transaction registers.

Land records available in Denmark include land tenure accounts, copyhold records, deeds, and mortgages. Contents vary, but may contain names of persons involved, date, and a description of the property. Some copyhold records include the birthplaces of the parties.

Probate Records

Local courts generally combined the records of probate matters with those of general interest until 1683 when they were kept separately. They include guardianship records as well as wills and other probate documents. A separate probate register was often kept for military officers, clergy, and teachers.

Local courts have custody of the probate records. Many have been microfilmed by the Family History Library.

Military Records

Denmark relied heavily on foreign troops for defense prior to 1788 when the monarchy placed a greater emphasis on using native forces. The Army levying rolls and the

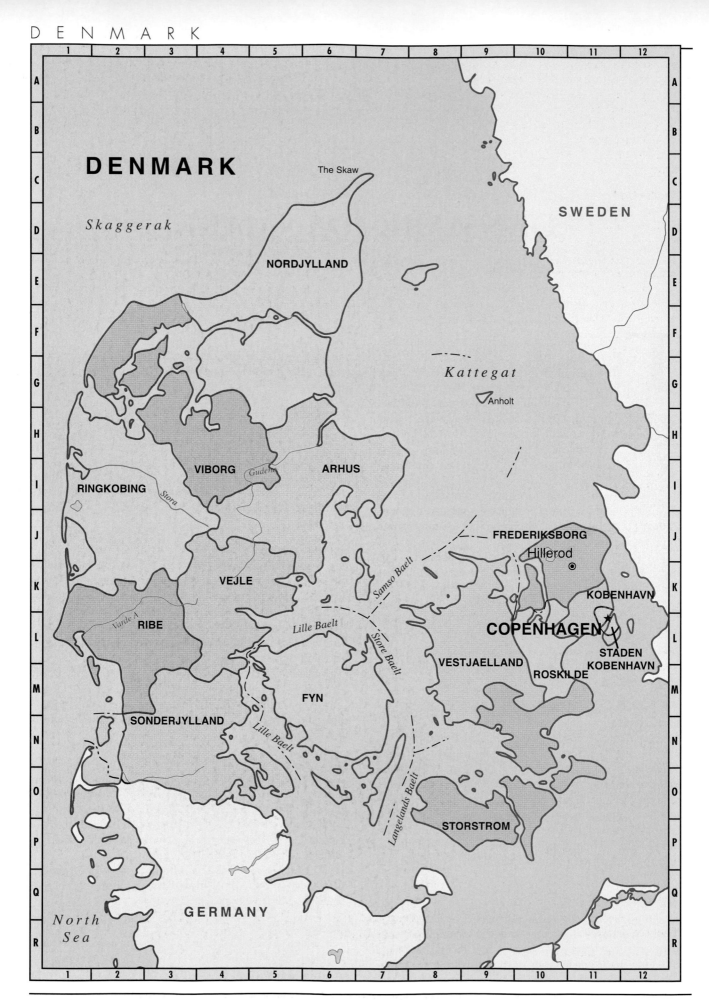

DENMARK

The Skaw

SWEDEN

Skaggerak

NORDJYLLAND

Kattegat

Anholt

VIBORG

Gudene

ARHUS

RINGKOBING

Stora

FREDERIKSBORG

Hillerod ⊙

VEJLE

KOBENHAVN

Varde A

RIBE

Samso Baelt

Lille Baelt

Store Baelt

COPENHAGEN

VESTJAELLAND

STADEN
KOBENHAVN

ROSKILDE

SONDERJYLLAND

Lille Baelt

FYN

Langelands Baelt

STORSTROM

GERMANY

North Sea

records of the Danish naval forces have considerable value to the family historian. They show the soldier's or sailor's name, age, birthplace, residence at the time he joined the military, previous occupation, physical description, rank, service record and conduct during his service

Military records are located in the *Haerens Arkiv* in Copenhagen, and some are on microfilm at the Family History Library.

Emigration Lists

During the nineteenth century many European ports did an enormous business of shipping goods and people to other ports in Europe, America, and elsewhere in the world. Unfortunately, the business of shipping emigrants was a goldmine for many unscrupulous agents. In 1869, in an attempt to cut down fraud, the port of Copenhagen devised a system for registering emigrants. These registers are separated into two departure lists. The *direct* lists show passengers traveling directly to their destination. The *indirect* lists show those whose vessels stopped at other ports on the way to their final destination. These departure lists were kept in chronological order and include the passenger's name, age, occupation, destination, and previous residence.

Microfiche copies of the emigration lists are available at the Family History Library. The Danish Emigration Archives in Aalborg hosts a website with a searchable database of the lists, and digitized images of individual pages can be downloaded (see "Archives, Libraries and Societies" below).

WEB SITES

Cyndi's List, Denmark - Information, Sources, Links and databases: <www.cyndislist.com/denmark.htm>

My Danish Roots – Information, History and Sources

Denmark Genealogy Links - Sources and Links <www.genealogylinks.net/europe/den.htm>

Denmark Genealogy – Sources, Information, History, Links and Databases <genealogy.about.com/cs/denmark/>

Danish Genealogy Resources - Information, Sources Databases <www.distantcousin.com/Links/Ethnic/Danish.html>

ARCHIVES, LIBRARIES AND SOCIETIES

Danish Data Archives; Islandsgade 10; DK-5000 Odense C.; Denmark; <www.dda.dk>

Danish Emigration Archives; Arkivstrade 1; Postbox 1731; DK-9100 Aalborg; Denmark; <users.cybercity.dk/~ccc13656/>

Frederiksburg Kommunebibliotek; Solbjergvej 25; DK-2000 Kobenhavn; Denmark

Harens Arkiv [Military Archive]; Slotsholmgade 4; DK-1216 Kovenhavn K.; Denmark

Kobenhavns Stadsarkiv [City Archives]; Kobenhavns Radhus; Radhuspladsen; Kobenhavn V.; Denmark

Landsarkivet for Fyn; Jernbanegade 36; DK-5000 Odense C.; Denmark; <www.sa.dk/lao>

Landsarkivet for Norrejylland; Lille Skt. Hansgade 5; DK-8800 Viborg; Denmark; <www.sa.dk/lav>

Landsarkivet for Sjaelland; Jagtvej 10; DK-2200 Kobenhavn K.; Denmark; <www.sa.dk/lak>

Landsarkivet for Sonderjylland; Haderslevvej 45; DK-6200 Aabenraa; Denmark; <www.sa.dk/laa>

Rigsarkivet [National Archives]; Rigsdagsgarden 9; DK-1218 Kobenhavn K.; Denmark

SUGGESTED READING

The Danish Genealogical Helper. Logan, UT: Everton Publishers, 1980.

Denmark Research Outline. Salt Lake City: Family History Library of The Church of Jesus Christ of Latter-day Saints, 1993.

Searching for Your Danish Ancestors. St. Paul, MN: Danish Genealogy Group of the Minnesota Genealogical Society, 1989.

Thomsen, Finn A. *The Beginner's Guide to Danish Genealogical Research*. Bountiful, UT: Thomsen's Genealogical Center, 1984.

Notes

ENGLAND and WALES

CAPITAL CITY: LONDON

England and Wales have experienced numerous cultural and political changes over the millennia. Iberians inhabited the country anciently and the Celts arrived about one thousand years BC. Rome invaded the country about 55 BC and was overthrown by the Anglos and Saxons three hundred years later. During the fifth century, Germanic Jutes arrived, and the Danes raided the British coasts as early as the eighth century. William brought other Normans with him when he fought to claim the throne in 1066.

Roman Catholicism was firmly established in the seventh century. In the 1530's, Henry VIII had a disagreement with Rome and reclaimed the kingly right of appointing his own bishops. Mary I briefly reestablished the Roman Church as the dominant religion between 1553 and 1558 but, over the years, the Church of England became Protestant. The Anglican Church is dominant in England and Wales today.

Civil authority in Britain has undergone changes as well. During its early history, numerous small local kingdoms were established. Attempts at unification brought about the signing of the Magna Charta in 1215. And later in the same century, parliament was established. These advances set the stage for wider acceptance of personal rights. The Black Death took a third of the population in the fourteenth century, which resulted in a labor shortage. This unfortunate situation strengthened the position of the common man, and led to the end of serfdom in the fifteenth century. The chain of responsibility held local leaders accountable to their own citizens. The Crown had to deal with a parliament rather than rule by decree, which gave Britain the civil stability it needed to handle the changes of global exploration and the industrial revolution. Conflict and suffering were not entirely avoided, but the social and political climate was less volatile than elsewhere in Europe.

SOME MAJOR GENEALOGICAL RECORD SOURCES
Church Records

The Church of England and the Church in Wales, also known as the Anglican Church, began keeping regular records of baptisms, marriages and burials in the early part of the sixteenth century. The mandate was first given in 1536 and reinforced in 1538, but relatively few parish registers date from that era. However, late sixteenth to mid-seventeenth century registers are common.

The parish registers were maintained locally. From about 1597, copies were made and sent to the diocesan office. Generically known as Bishops Transcripts (BTs), these copies provide a check on the accuracy of the original registers. Additional information may be included in the BTs that was not recorded in the local register. Both the original registers and transcript copies can often be found in the custody of the County Record Office. The Family History Library in Salt Lake City has microfilm copies of most of them in their collection.

Unlike Catholic registers common in Europe, the Anglican registers are brief, usually displaying the following data:
- **Baptisms:** Date, given name and gender of the child, full name of the father, and the mother's first name. Occasionally a residence may be given. Illegitimacy will usually be noted.
- **Marriages:** Date (if by banns, either the three dates they were read, or the final date of reading), whether by license or by banns, names and residence of bride and groom. Occasionally a previous marital status or occupation of the bride and groom is recorded.
- **Burials:** Date of burial and name of the deceased. Occasionally the name of the father is recorded, if the deceased was an infant, or the name of the surviving spouse.

Non-Anglican Protestants were known as "non-conformists" and maintained their own sets of registers. Many registers remain with the congregation and some have been deposited in the Public Record Office. The Family History Library has microfilmed the registers held in the Public Record Office. They are similar in form and substance to their Anglican counterparts, but are more likely to include the maiden name of the mother in the birth records. Transcript copies of non-conformist records were not generally made.

Neither Catholics nor Jews were considered non-conformists, but each kept their own set of records, often only at the local level.

Civil Registration

The civil registration of births, marriages and deaths began in England and Wales on 1 July 1837. The civil records include all persons, regardless of their religion. Data was collected in registration and sub-registration offices. Entries are arranged chronologically by the quarter of the year in which they were officially registered.

The indexes are also organized on the quarter system, with January through March being the first quarter, April through June the second, and so on. Each quarterly index entry includes the name, the registration or sub-registration office where the event was recorded, and the volume and page number on which the entry is found. Microfilm copies of these indexes are available at the Family History Library. To order a copy of the original certificate you must know all three items, plus the year and quarter.

The certificates include the following:

- **Birth:** Registration district, sub-registration district, county, certificate number, date and place of birth, given name(s), gender, father's full name, mother's full name (and maiden name), father's occupation, signature of the informant with his or her residence and description, the date of registration, the signature of the registrar, and any name given to the child after the date of registration.
- **Marriage:** Registration district, county, date of marriage, names of the bride and groom, their ages, previous marital status, occupations, residence, their fathers' names and occupations.
- **Death:** Registration district, sub-registration district, county, date and place of death, name of the deceased, gender, age, occupation, cause of death, signature of the informant with his or her residence and description, when registered, and the signature of the registrar.

Copies of the certificates can be obtained from the Family Records Centre in Islington.

Census Enumerations

Enumerations featuring the names of every resident of England and Wales began in 1841 and were conducted decennially from that time. The lists for 1841 through 1891 are available on microfilm at the Family History Library in Salt Lake City.

As with most enumerations, these are arranged geographically, generally by parish, and then by subdivisions. Some countywide indexes are beginning to appear, but unlike the United States federal censuses, there are as yet no comprehensive indexes to all of the available British censuses.

The 1841 schedule shows each person's full name, age, gender, occupation, and whether or not he or she was born in that county. Beginning with the 1851 census, the schedules also give the address, each person's relationship to the head of the household, marital status, and the town or parish of their birth. Knowledge of the birthplace is especially useful in tracking a person's mobility, and in locating the proper entries in civil registration records or parish registers.

Probate Records

Probate records deal with the distribution of an estate after its owner dies. They include not only large "plantation-type" estates, but also any earthly goods worth distributing. The records supply information about the deceased and his or her life, as well as identifying family relationships.

The Anglican Church handled most probate matters in England and Wales until 1858. The actions were handled by a variety of local jurisdictions, usually smaller than a county, and in some cases as small as a single parish. Each jurisdiction maintained their own records, and the Family History Library has microfilmed many. Probate matters involving property in more than one jurisdiction in the northern six counties of England were handled by the Prerogative Court of York, while those involving more than one probate jurisdiction elsewhere in England and Wales, or overseas, were handled by the Prerogative Court of Canterbury.

Generally, wills and other acts handled by ecclesiastical courts were filed chronologically with a "calendar" form of index. In this system, the entries for surnames beginning with each letter are listed together chronologically. To find a "Smith" in a calendar you would search all of the entries in the "S" section for each year.

Beginning on 11 January 1858, the two countries were divided into civil probate districts, with each handling probate matters in its own area. These districts maintained their own records, but sent copies of their records annually to the Principal Probate Registry, which is now known as the Probate Department of the Principal Registry of the Family Division. The Family History Library has microfilmed abstracts of some documents from this office.

Military Records

Regimental records of local militias are available as early as the eighteenth century. Regimental records are often filed in rough alphabetic order. They include the soldier's name, rank and service record. They may also include personal data, such as the date and place of his birth, his enlistment and discharge. Certificates of marriage and births of any children born to him while in military service, and a physical description are also included.

Regimental records are in the custody of the Public Record Office. In order to use them, one must know the regiment in which the ancestor served. If the regiment is known, using the regimental records is relatively easy. If the nickname of the regiment is all that is known, a reference book that identifies a regiment by its nickname should be consulted. If an ancestor was an officer, the annual Army Lists can be consulted to determine which regiment he served in. They are available at the Family History Library.

ADDITIONAL SOURCES

- Vital Records Index, British Isles: on CD-ROM, Family History Library
- 1881 British Census – Complete on microfiche and CD-ROM – Family History Library

•1871 British Census – Complete on microfiche – Family History Library

•1851 British Census – Three counties on CD-ROM – Family History Library

WEBSITES

Ancestry Databases <www.ancestry.com>

Birth Registrations <www.oz.net/~markhow/ukbirths.htm>

Census <www.gendocs.demon.co.uk/census.html>

Civil Registration <www.genuki.org.uk/big/eng/civreg/>

Family Search <www.familysearch.org/ Eng/Library/FHLC/ frameset_fhlc.asp>

Military Records <www.genuki.org.uk/big/BritMilRecs.html>

Probate Records <www.genuki.org.uk/big/eng/Probate.html>

UK Census <www.genuki.org.uk/big/eng/census.html>

UK Census <www.genuki.org.uk/big/eng/ ChurchRecords.html>

UK Census Transcriptions <www.mycensus.com>

ARCHIVES, LIBRARIES, AND SOCIETIES

Family Records Centre; 1 Mydlleton Street; Islington, London EC1R 1UW; United Kingdom

Guildhall Library; Manuscripts Section; Aldermanbury, London EC2P 2EJ; United Kingdom; <ihr.sas.ac.uk/ihr/ ghmnu.html>

John Rylands University Library of Manchester; Oxford Road; Manchester M13 9PP; United Kingdom;

National Library of Wales; Aberystwyth, Dyfed SY23 3BU; United Kingdom;

National Army Museum; Royal Hospital Road; Chelsea, London SW3 4HT; United Kingdom

National Maritime Museum; Romney Road; Greenwich, London SE10 9NF; United Kingdom;

Probate Department of the Principal Registry of the Family Division; First Avenue House; 42-49 High Holborn; London WC1V 6NP; United Kingdom

Public Record Office; Kew, Richmond; Surrey TW9 4DU; United Kingdom;

Society of Genealogists; 14 Charterhouse Buildings; Goswell Road; London EC1M 7BA; United Kingdom

The British Library; Oriental and India Office Collections; 197 Blackfriars Road; London SE1 8NG; United Kingdom;

The College of Arms; The Officer in Waiting; Queen Victoria Street; London EC4V 4BT; United Kingdom; <www.kwtelecom.com/heraldry/collarms/>

SUGGESTED READING

Baxter, Angus. *In Search of Your British & Irish Roots: A Complete Guide to Tracing Your English, Welsh, Scottish, and Irish Ancestors.* Baltimore: Genealogical Publishing Co., 1996.

Chapman, Colin. *Tracing Your British Ancestors.* Baltimore: Genealogical Publishing Co., 1996.

Cox, Jane. *Tracing Your Ancestors in the Public Record Office.* London: Her Majesty's Stationery Office, 1991.

Gibson, Jeremy Sumner Wycherley. *Record Offices: How to Find Them.* Baltimore: Genealogical Publishing Co., 1992.

Irvine, Sherry. *Your English Ancestry: A Guide for North Americans.* Salt Lake City: Ancestry, 1998.

Rawlins, Bert. J. *The Parish Churches and Nonconformist Chapels of Wales: Their Records and Where to Find Them.* Salt Lake City: Celtic Heritage Research, 1987.

Reid, Judith Prowse. *Genealogical Research in England's Public Record Office: A Guide for North Americans.* Baltimore: Genealogical Publishing Co., 1997.

Rowlands, John, et al. *Welsh Family History: A Guide to Research.* Baltimore: Genealogical Publishing Co., 1996.

FINLAND (SUOMI)

CAPITAL CITY: HELSINKI

Christianity was taken to Finland about 1050 by the Roman Catholic and Eastern Orthodox churches. With the assent of Rome, Finland came under Swedish domination in the late twelfth and early thirteenth centuries. As part of Sweden, Finland joined the Kalmar Union with Denmark and Norway in 1389.

The Kalmar Union dissolved in the early 1520s. The Protestant Reformation followed. The Roman Catholic Church was disenfranchised in 1524 when the Evangelical Lutheran Church became the state religion.

From 1695 to 1697, extreme famine from crop failure reduced the population. Then, from 1700 to 1721, Finland suffered from the Northern War and plague. It lost more than a quarter of its population at that time. During the Northern War, Russia invaded Finland. A series of battles were fought over the next century between the two countries. Russia succeeded in acquiring Finland in 1809. Finnish independence was proclaimed, and recognized by Russia in 1917, in the aftermath of the Russian Revolution.

SOME MAJOR GENEALOGICAL RECORD SOURCES

Evangelical Lutheran Church records are the main source of genealogical research in Finland. It was the established church for centuries and remains the denomination of choice for over 80 percent of the population. These records contain:

- **Births or baptisms:** date of event, name of infant, parents, and residence.
- **Marriages or banns:** date of event or reading of the banns, names of the bride and groom.
- **Deaths or burials:** date of event and name of the deceased.
- **Clerical surveys:** Beginning about 1686, parish ministers were required to keep a record of their annual examinations of parishioners on their knowledge of church principles. The surveys were kept in volumes covering five to ten years. They are organized geographically. A family entry is similar to a family group record and shows the father, mother and children, along with the birth date and place, marriage information, and death date. It also includes the results of the annual examination. A parish priest occasionally added personal notes including information on those who moved in and out of the parish or vaccinations.

All existing parish registers dating through the mid-1800s are available on microfilm at the Family History Library and at various Finnish locations. The Genealogical Society of Finland transcribed more recent registers, up through about 1900, and microfiche copies are available

ARCHIVES, LIBRARIES AND SOCIETIES

Genealogical Society of Finland; Liisankatu 16 A; FIN-00170 Helsinki; Finland

National Repository Library; PO Box 1710; SF-70421 Kuopio; Finland; <www.varasto.uku.fi/english/eng00000.htm>

Society for Computerized Genealogy; PO Box 264; FIN-00171 Helsinki; Finland

WEB SITES

Articles About Finland <www.genealogia.fi/emi/art/>

Beginner's Guide to Finnish Family History Research <members.aol.com/dssaari/guide.htm>

CHURCH RECORDS

Cyndi's List, Finland - Sources, Links, Databases <www.cyndislist.com/finland.htm>

Everton' s Genealogy Finland - Sources, Links <www.everton.com/reference/world/finland.php>

Family History Finland <www.open.org/rumcd/genweb/finn.html>

Finland Church Records

Finland GenWeb – Sources, Links, Databases <www.rootsweb.com/~finwgw/>

Finland Parish Records Database <www.genealogia.fi/hiski?en>

Genealogical Research in Finland <www.genealogia.fi/indexe.htm>

Genealogy Helplist Finland <jocke.twistercom.fi/suku.html>

SUGGESTED READING

Choquette, Margarita. *The Beginner's Guide to Finnish Genealogical Research*. Bountiful, UT: Thomsen's Genealogical Center, 1985.

Mether, Leif. Finnish Genealogy: Finnish Church Records. *The Finnish American Reporter*, July 2000.

Vincent, Timothy Laitila and Rick Tapio. *Finnish Genealogical Research*. New Brighton, MN: Finnish Americana, 1994.

Notes

FRANCE

CAPITAL CITY: PARIS

For over a thousand years, France experienced rule by monarchies. With the Revolution in 1789, a civil government was established, but a succession of monarchs (beginning with Napoleon Bonaparte) continued from 1799 until 1848. The Revolution affected vital records as much as it affected the government. Civil authorities took over registration of births, marriages and deaths–a task previously performed by churches. The government also assumed custody of the church-compiled vital records created before 1792. The official tie between the state and the Catholic Church was finally severed in 1905.

Like most central European nations, France has suffered a series of wars over the centuries, with numerous boundary changes. French is the dominant tongue, but other languages such as German in the east, Breton in the west, Basque and Catalan in the south, and Flemish in the northwest are used as well.

France is divided into 22 regions and 96 departments. Departments are composed of a number of *communes* (municipalities).

SOME MAJOR GENEALOGICAL RECORD SOURCES

Church Records

Historically, the Roman Catholic Church has been the most prominent religion in France. In 1539, the Catholic Church required its parish priests to record all births within their bounds. In 1579, they were required to record marriages and deaths. Protestants (*Huguenots*) began recording baptisms and marriages of their members in 1559.

In 1792, the government ruled that records belonged to the government, although various churches compiled them. All such vital records were ordered deposited in the departmental archives. Many are also available on microfilm through the Family History Library.

The basic church records are:
- **Baptisms** *(baptemes):* give the name of the infant, date of baptism, parents' names, child's legitimacy, and names of godparents. Some also show residence and father's occupation.
- **Marriages** *(mariages):* give the names of the bride and groom, date of the marriage, names of parents, whether each party was single or widowed before this marriage, and the names of witnesses.
- **Burials** *(sepultures):* give the name of the deceased, the date and place of burial, the age and residence of the deceased.

Civil Registration

Civil authorities took responsibility for registering the births, marriages and deaths for all people residing in France beginning in 1792. Contemporary records are kept in the local civil registration office (*bureau de l'etat civil*), usually in the town hall (*mairie*), and earlier records are in the departmental archives.

Records often include ten-year and annual indexes. Many pre-1860 civil registration records for Paris were destroyed by fire, although some have been reconstructed. The records include:
- **Births** *(naissances):* Date and place, name, gender, parents' names (including the mother's maiden name).
- **Marriages** *(mariages):* Date and place, names of bride and groom, names of parents.
- **Deaths** *(deces):* Date and place, name, age, birthplace, names of parents and informants.

Notarial Records

In France, notaries perform important legal roles. The *actes notaires* are usually filed in the departmental archives by the name of the notary and his town or towns. They are not usually indexed. Genealogists often find the

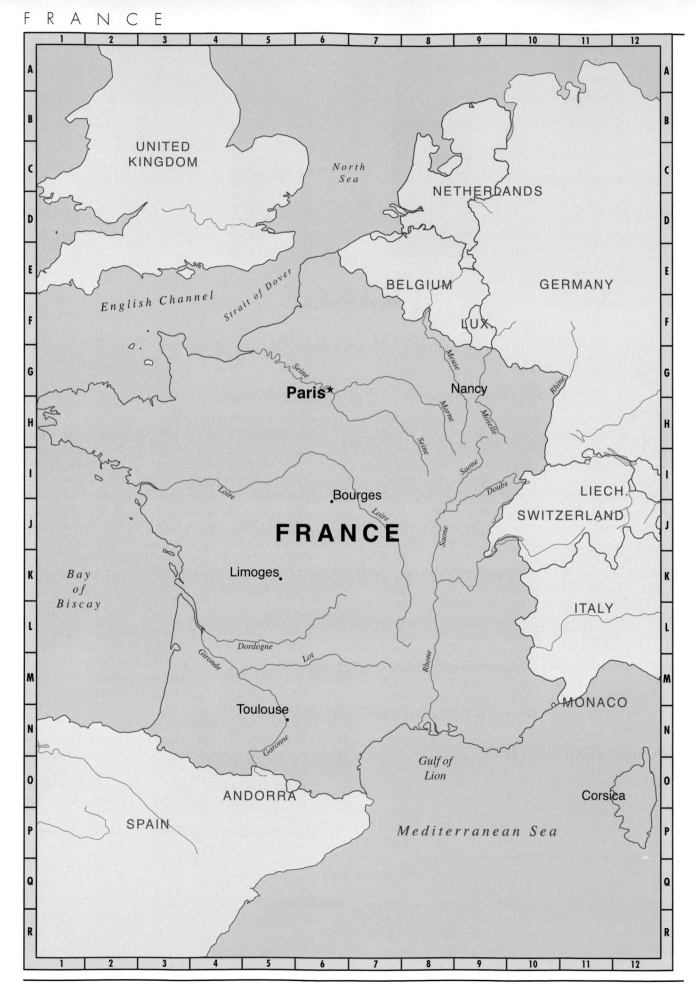

following notarial records useful:
- Marriage contracts (*contrats de mariage*)
- Wills (*testaments*)
- Division of property among heirs (*partages* and *successions*)
- Property inventories (*inventaires des biens* or *inventaires apres deces*)
- Guardianship agreements (*actes de tutelle*)

ARCHIVES AND LIBRARIES

Archives Nationales; 11, rue des Quatre-Fils; 75141 Paris; France

Bibliotheque Nationale; 58, rue de Richelieu; 75084 Paris; France

Office Departemental des Anciens Combattants; 295, rue St. Jacques; 75005 Paris; France

Tribunal de Grande Instance; 4, boulevard Palais; 75001 Paris; France

WEB SITES

Civil Registration <genealogy.about.com/library/weekly/aa070700b.htm>

Cyndi's List – France <www.cyndislist.com/france.htm>

Family History Library Catalog <www.familysearch.org/Eng/Library/FHLC/frameset_fhlc.asp>

France Genealogy Links – Regions <www.genealogylinks.net/europe/frenchregions.htm>

France GenWeb <www/francegenweb/org>

French Church Records <genealogy.about.com/library/weekly/aa070700d.htm>

French Church Records <genealogy.about.com/gi/dynamic/>

SUGGESTED READING

Aublet, Robert. *Nouveau Guide de Genealogie*. Evreaux, France: Ouest-France, 1986.

France: Research Outline. Salt Lake City: Family History Library, 1996.

Gautier, Valerie. *Genealogie:* Paris et Ile-de-France. Paris: Parigramme, 1996.

Valynseele, Joseph. *La Genealogies: Histoire et Pratique*. Paris: Larousse, 1992.

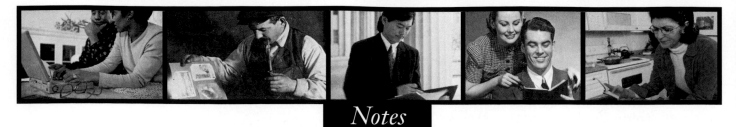

Notes

GERMANY (DEUTSCHLAND)

CAPITAL CITY: BERLIN

Germany dominates central Europe geographically, but in feudal times it was a patchwork of small states, independent cities and kingdoms. In 1871, the Prince Otto von Bismarck created the German Empire on the cornerstone of Prussia. For more than a century before that time, Prussia stretched from the Belgian border east into what is now Poland and Russia, and included the Alsace region of France.

Unification of various states making up Germany was more than a consolidation of territory. When Martin Luther broke away from the Roman Catholic Church, much of Europe was divided religiously and politically. Major conflicts, such as the Thirty Years War (1618-1648) and other minor skirmishes, pitted Protestants against Catholics. Catholics were powerful in the southern and western parts of Germany, while Protestants were stronger in the northern and eastern regions.

Political wars, both internal and external, also fractured the various German states. Napoleon pushed beyond the French borders, which meant that large portions of southern and western Germany were under French control from about 1792 to 1815. Both World War I and World War II had a dramatic effect on the western and eastern borders. Following World War II, modern-day Germany was split into two countries: East (the Democratic Republic) and West (the Federal Republic). They were reunited in 1990.

Boundary changes have effected the language of records kept by civil and church officials in Germanic areas. While most records are in German, many Catholic records are in Latin. Records on the western and eastern marches are often a mix. Alsatian records are in both German and French, while East Prussian registers are written in German, Polish and Russian.

SOME MAJOR GENEALOGICAL RECORD SOURCES
Church Records (*Kirchenbucher*)

Lutheran records began about 1540, Catholic records in 1563, and the Reformed Church records in 1650. Jewish records of births, marriages and deaths often were not compiled unless the law required it. Many church records were destroyed during wars, especially the Thirty Years War (1618-1648). While some records in southwestern Germany were written in French during the Napoleonic era (1792-1815), they were usually written in German (especially the Protestant registers), with Catholic records often written in Latin.

The local congregations kept church registers. Copies (known as *kirchenbuchduplikate*) were sent to church or state archives. Military parishes kept their own sets of registers. In some cases the predominant local church maintained records for other faiths. In some cases this meant that the local Catholic congregation would have records of Jewish vital events. Besides the parish, ecclesiastical and state archives, microfilm copies of many German church records are available in the Family History Library in Salt Lake City.

Among the church records of most value to the family historian are:

- **Baptisms** *(taufen):* name of infant, date of baptism, parents' names, legitimacy, names of witnesses. Often the death of the person is noted with a cross next to the baptismal entry and includes the date of death or burial.
- **Marriages** *(heiraten):* names of the bride and groom, date of wedding (or the three dates on which the banns were read), if single or widowed, names of the witnesses; could include the couples' ages, residences, occupations, birthplaces, and parents' names.
- **Burials** *(begrabnisse):* name of deceased, date and place of burial; could include the age at the time of death, residence, and cause of death.
- **Family registers** *(familienbucher):* similar to family group records, showing the father, mother and children, together with birth, marriage and death information. Often arranged in rough alphabetic

order by surname, they are more common in the southern states of Wurttemberg and Baden.

Civil Registration (*Zivilstandregister*)

France developed a form of civil registration in the southern and western parts of Germany in 1792, but formal civil registration did not begin until 1876. The records were kept locally in city archives, and copies were sent to state archives. The Family History Library has microfilmed many of the records.

- •**Births** (*geburten*): name of infant, gender, date and place of birth, father's name, age, occupation, residence; mother's name (including maiden name), age, marital status, and names of witnesses.
- •**Marriages** (*heiraten, ehen, trauungen*): usually recorded in the bride's home town; records the date of marriage, names of bride and groom, ages, birth dates and places, residences, occupations, single or widowed; parents' names, residence, occupations, marital status, living or deceased, and names of witnesses.
- •**Deaths** (*sterben, tote*): name of deceased, date, time and place of death, age at time of death, birthplace, occupation, residence, marital status, religion, and name of informant.

Emigration Records

War, adverse economic conditions, and religious persecution are among the reasons people left their European homes and emigrated to other countries. Those living in Germany had several ports from which to emigrate, including France, the Netherlands and Denmark. But the two main German ports for departure were Bremen and Hamburg, both in the north of Germany. The passenger departure lists for Bremen were destroyed during World War 2, but the lists for Hamburg survived.

Police authorities compiled the Hamburg passenger lists. They cover the time period of 1850 to 1934, with a break from 1915 to 1919 during World War 1. They are in the custody of the Staatsarchiv in Hamburg, and are on microfilm at the Family History Library in Salt Lake City.

From 1850 through 1910 two sets of lists were kept: the direct lists for vessels going directly to their destinations without a stop, and the indirect lists for ships that made stops on the way to a final port. The lists for 1850 through 1854 were arranged alphabetically and do not need an index. After 1854, each (direct and indirect) has its own index. The lists are an annual summary of passenger's names. Names appear in alphabetical order by the first letter of the surname, and are then listed chronologically. The ship's name and a page number are recorded next to each entry, allowing access to the full listing.

Military Records

German military records are filed by regiment, or by the name of the ship. They are found in the archives of the state from which the soldier or sailor served. The Family History Library has filmed a few regimental records.

Although the regimental records are most valuable for officers, there are also records for enlisted men also.

Among the various types of registers kept are personnel files (*stammrollen*), officer files (*offizier-stammlisten*), officer rolls (*ranglisten*) and regimental histories (*regimentsgeschichten*). Content varies, but generally they contain the name of the soldier or sailor, rank, service location, age, birthplace, residence, occupation, and a physical description.

One way to find the regiment of the soldier is to consult the military church books of the communities where he served. The register entry of his marriage record also shows his rank and regiment.

ARCHIVES, LIBRARIES AND SOCIETIES

Abteilung Militararchiv des Bundesarchivs; Wiesentalstrasse 10; 79115 Freiburg im Breisgau; Germany

Bistumsarchiv Berlin; Gotzstrasse 65; 12099 Berlin; Germany

Deutsche Zentralstelle fur Genealogie; Postfach 04002; 04109 Leipzig; Germany

Deutsches Adelsarchiv; Schwanelle 21; 35037 Marburg; Germany

Evangelisches Zentralarchiv in Berlin; Jebenstrasse 3; 10623 Berlin; Germany

Militarisches Zwischenarchiv; Zeppelinstrasse 127; 14471 Potsdam; Germany

WEB SITES

Archives in Germany – Information, Sources and Availability of Records <home.bawue.de/~hanacek/info/earchive.htm>

Cyndi's List – Germany – Links, Sources <home.bawue.de/~hanacek/info/earchive.htm>

Family History Library Catalog <www.familysearch.org/Eng/Library/FHLC/frameset_fhlc.asp>

German Emigrant Databases 18th & 19th Century – Searchable Database <http://ourworld.compuserve.com/homepages/German_Genealogy/sfemigr.htm>

German Emigration Databases, Several Ports <home.att.net/~wee-monster/emigration.html>

Germany GenWeb – Links and Sources: <www.rootsweb.com/~wggerman/>

Germans to America – Descriptions and Sources <www.genealogienetz.de/misc/emig/>

SUGGESTED READING

Baxter, Angus. *In Search of Your German Roots: A Complete Guide to Tracing Your Ancestors in the Germanic Areas of Europe.* Baltimore: Genealogical Publishing Co., 1991.

Germany Research Outline. Salt Lake City: Family History Library, 1997.

Glazier, Ira and P. William Filby. *Germans to America: Lists of Passengers Arriving at U.S. Ports.* Wilmington, DE: Scholarly Resources, 1988.

Hessische Truppen in Amerikanischen Unabhangigkeitskrieg (HETRINA). Marburg, Germany: Archivschule Marburg, 1987.

Jensen, Larry O. *A Genealogical Handbook of German Research.* Pleasant Grove, UT: Jensen, 1978-1983.

Schenk, Trudy, et al. *The Wuerttemberg Emigration Index.* Salt Lake City: Ancestry, 1986.

Smelzer, Ronald M. *Finding Your German Ancestors.* Salt Lake City: Ancestry, 1991.

Thode, Ernest. *Address Book for Germanic Genealogy.* Baltimore: Genealogical Publishing Co., 1994.

IRELAND (and NORTHERN IRELAND)

CAPITAL CITY: DUBLIN (AND BELFAST)

Native Celts were repeatedly invaded from the second through the twelfth centuries by the Scandinavians and Normans. The Welsh and Scots' attack during the seventeenth century was perhaps the most devastating. Many Irish were dispossessed of property ownership in favor of British landowners. Although they no longer owned land, many remained as renters and laborers.

Loss of land was not the only penalty endured by the Roman Catholic Irish. The British Penal Laws enacted late in the nineteenth century excluded Catholics from the political process as well. Even so, Irish agriculture fed a prosperous economy. The population of the island grew dramatically, especially in the first half of the nineteenth century. According to the 1841 census, it had risen to over eight million.

From 1845-1849, the Potato Famine destroyed crops. It is estimated that the devastation on the population between 1845 and 1855 resulted in as many as one million deaths and over two million emigrations. Eventually the population fell as low as four million.

Eventually, the Roman Catholics had many rights restored, but the Irish remained under British rule. The 1916 rebellion brought about the creation of the Republic of Ireland in 1921. The northern six counties remained in the United Kingdom as Northern Ireland. The capital of the Republic is Dublin. Belfast is the administrative center of Northern Ireland. Each retained its own collection of records after the 1921 split, although Dublin has many of the surviving records for Ireland before that time.

SOME MAJOR GENEALOGICAL RECORD SOURCES
Civil Registration

In 1845, centralized civil registration of marriages in the Church of Ireland began. Comprehensive registration of all births, marriages and deaths in Ireland did not begin until 1864. Vital events in Ireland were registered in local registration districts. Those offices made two copies of the registers, one of which was sent to the General Register Office in Dublin (or to the Public Record Office of Northern Ireland in Belfast for the six northern counties after 1921). Until 1878, the registers had annual indexes. From 1878, they have been indexed quarterly.

The Family History Library has microfilm of the indexes for both the Republic and Northern Ireland from 1845 to 1958, and copies of many certificates for both divisions. The certificates show:

- **Births:** name, date and place of birth, gender, names and residence of father and mother, father's occupation, when and where registered.
- **Marriages:** date and place of marriage, names, ages, prior marital statuses, residences and occupations of the bridegroom, their fathers' names and occupations.
- **Deaths:** date and place of death, name of deceased, age at time of death, gender, marital status, occupation, cause of death, informant, when and where registered.

Church Records

The Protestant Church of Ireland was the "established" church, but the majority of the Irish population worshipped in the Roman Catholic tradition. Church of Ireland parish boundaries conformed to the civil parish boundaries, while the boundaries of the Catholic parishes did not.

Each church kept registers in the local congregation, but the Church of Ireland parishes often sent copies of the registers to the Public Record Office. Much of the collection, covering about half of the parishes in Ireland, was burned in the 1922 fire. Currently the Representative Church Body Library in Dublin has custody of many remaining Church of Ireland registers. Catholic parishes retain their own records. Some church records from Ireland are also available on microfilm at the Family History Library. A valuable reference for locating the records of individual parishes is Ryan's *Irish Records: Sources for Family & Local History*.

The exact amount of data in each register entry can vary widely, but in general they tend to contain:

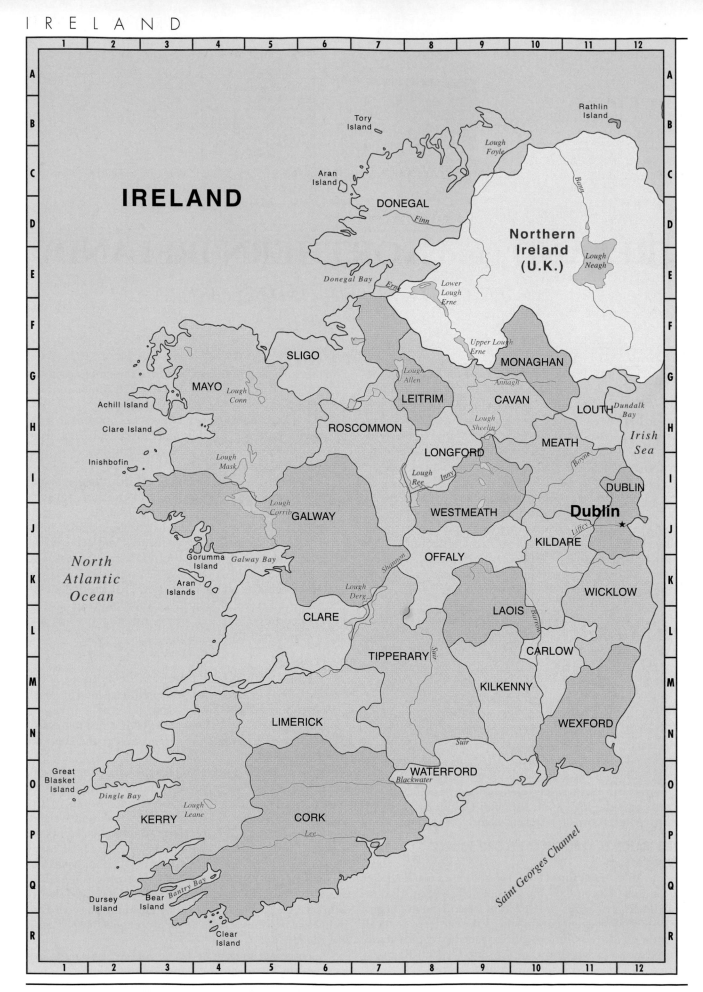

IRELAND

•**Baptisms:** name of infant, date of baptism, and parents' names; may also include the parents' residence, occupation, and legitimacy status of the child's birth.

•**Marriages:** names of the bride and groom, prior marital status, date of marriage or reading of banns, residence and fathers' names.

•**Burials:** name of deceased, date of burial; could include age at the time of death, residence, cause of death and occupation.

Probate Records

Prior to 1858, wills and other probate matters were handled by 28 ecclesiastical bodies known as diocesan (or consistory) courts, and by the Prerogative Court of Armagh. Unfortunately, the documents compiled by these courts were destroyed in a fire at the Public Record Office in Dublin in 1922, but an index to the wills and administrations survived. The entries in the index give the name and residence of the deceased along with the year of probate. The indexes are on microfilm at the Family History Library and some are published.

Beginning in 1858, Irish probate matters were handled by eleven (civil) district registries and by the Principal Probate Registry in Dublin. Many of these records were destroyed in the 1922 fire, but copies in other repositories were collected by the National Archives of Ireland and the Public Record Office of Northern Ireland. Microfilm copies of many probate records, as well as indexes and calendars, are available at the Family History Library.

Censuses

Population schedules were compiled in Ireland as they were in Britain. Unfortunately, enumerations for the nineteenth century were destroyed, either by the 1922 fire or by government decree. Researchers do have access to the 1901 and 1911 schedules. They record the name of each resident, his or her relationship to the head of household, religion, age, gender, occupation, marital status and birthplace. The 1911 census also shows the number of years a woman had been married, how many children she had delivered, and how many were alive.

These records are for the most part unindexed. The original enumerations are in the custody of the National Archives of Ireland and the Public Record Office of Northern Ireland. Microfilm copies are in the Family History Library.

Griffith's Valuation Lists

The Primary Valuation, taken between 1848 and 1864, is an excellent substitute for earlier censuses. The valuation is a survey of landholders and householders. It lists their names, residence and gives a brief property description, along with the name of the landlord and a valuation of his property.

Copies of the valuation lists and indexes are available in several libraries in Ireland as well as the Family History Library in Salt Lake City.

ARCHIVES, LIBRARIES AND SOCIETIES

General Register Office; Joyce House; 8-11 Lombard Street E; Dublin 2; Republic of Ireland

General Register Office; Oxford House; 49-55 Chichester Street; Belfast BT1 4HL; Northern Ireland

National Archives of Ireland; Bishop Street; Dublin 8; Republic of Ireland

National Library of Ireland; Kildare Street; Dublin 2; Republic of Ireland; <www.heanet.ie/natlib/homepage.html>

Public Record Office of Northern Ireland; 66 Balmoral Avenue; Belfast BT9 6NY; Northern Ireland;

Registry of Deeds; Henrietta Street; Dublin 1; Republic of Ireland

Representative Church Body Library; Braemor Park; Rathgar; Dublin 14; Republic of Ireland

WEB SITES

Cyndi's List, Ireland & Northern Ireland – Information, Sources, Links and Databases <www.cyndislist.com/ireland.htm>

Family History Library Catalog <www.familysearch.org/Eng/Library/FHLC/frameset_fhlc.asp>

FamilySearch – Searchable Databases <www.familysearch.org/Eng/Search/frameset_search.asp>

Ireland Genealogy and Family History – Information, Sources, Links and Databases <genealogy.about.com/cs/ireland/>

Ireland Genealogy– Links <www.genealogylinks.net/uk/ireland/index.html>

Ireland Genealogy Links – Sources and Links <www.genealogylinks.net/uk/ireland/>

Irish Ancestors – History of Religion in Ireland <scripts.ireland.com/ancestor/browse/records/church/>

Irish records – Searchable Databases, Parish Records and Census <www.ancestry.com>

Local Catholic Church History and Genealogy, Ireland – History, Sources, Links and Databases <home.att.net/~Local_Catholic/Catholic-Ireland.htm> –

NIDEX – Northern Ireland Genealogy – Links <www.nidex.com/genealogy.htm>

The Church of Ireland Genealogy and Family History – History, Sources, Links <www.ireland.anglican.org/library/libroots.html>

UK & Ireland – Sources and Databases <www.genuki.org.uk/big/>

SUGGESTED READING

Baxter, Angus. *In Search of Your British & Irish Roots: A Complete Guide to Tracing Your English, Welsh, Scottish and Irish Ancestors*. Baltimore: Genealogical Publishing Co., 1989.

Begley, Donald F. *Irish Genealogy: A Record Finder*. Dublin: Heraldic Artists, 1981.

Grehnam, John. *Tracing Your Irish Ancestors: The Complete Guide*. Dublin: Gill and Macmillan, 1992.

McCarthy, Tony. *The Irish Roots Guide*. Dublin: Lilliput Press, 1991.

Mitchell, Brian. *A Guide to Irish Parish Registers*. Baltimore: Genealogical Publishing Co., 1988.

Quinn, Sean E. *Trace Your Irish Ancestors*. Bray, Ireland: Magh Itha Teoranta, 1989.

Ryan, James G. *Irish Records: Sources for Family & Local History*. Salt Lake City: Ancestry Publishing, 1997).

Yurdan, Marilyn. *Irish Family History*. Baltimore: Genealogical Publishing Co., 1990.

ITALY (ITALIA)

CAPITAL CITY: ROME (ROMA)

From the fall of the Roman Empire, Italy experienced over a millennium of fracture. Until the nineteenth century it was a patchwork of independent cities, small states, duchies, kingdoms, and the Papal States. The region was unified briefly under Napoleon Bonaparte at the beginning of the nineteenth century, refractured, and then reunified in 1871. It operated as a nominal monarchy until 1946, when it became a democratic republic.

War was a recurring event in Italian history. All impacted the country, including the two World Wars as well as a series of battles from the medieval era to the present. War also impacted the availability of records of genealogical value, especially church registers.

The Roman Catholic Church is headquartered in Vatican City, an independent country inside Rome. Eighty percent of Italians are Catholic. Italian is the mother language, but German is spoken near the Austrian border.

Currently, Italy is organized into twenty regions; each is further divided into provinces (94 in all). Provinces are composed of municipalities (*comunes*).

SOME MAJOR GENEALOGICAL RECORD SOURCES
Church Records

From 1545, the Catholic Church required its local parishes to keep records of baptisms, marriages and burials. The local parishes keep the records. Some have been transferred to the diocesan archives (*archivio della diocesi*). The Family History Library in Salt Lake City has microfilmed some of the registers.

Some events registered at the parish level that are of value to genealogists are:

- **Baptisms** *(atti di battesimo):* date of the event, the name of the infant, gender, and names of the parents and godparents.
- **Marriages** *(atti di matrimonio):* date, names of the bride and groom, ages, birthplaces, addresses, parents names, and previous marital status.
- **Burials** *(atti di sepoltura):* date and place of death, name of the deceased, age, name of surviving spouse, date and place of burial.

Civil Records

Civil registration of births, marriages and deaths in southern Italy date from the early nineteenth century, but the practice did not become widespread until 1869.

Civil registration of vital events is under custody of the local archives (*archivio comunale*) and provincial state archives (*archivio di stato*). The oldest records (prior to 1870) are usually found in the state archives. The Family History Library has filmed vital records from some provincial archives.

Among the civil records of value to family historians:

- **Births** *(atti di nascita):* name of infant, gender, birth date, father's name, age, residence and occupation; mother's maiden name, age and residence; witnesses names, ages, residences.
- **Marriages** *(atti di matrimonio):* names of bride and groom, ages, previous marital status, residences, occupations, date of marriage, parents' names, residences and occupations.
- **Deaths** *(atti di morto):* name of deceased, age, date and place of death, birthplace, parents' names, ages (if still living), witnesses' names, ages and occupations.

ARCHIVES AND LIBRARIES

Archivio di Roma; Piazzale degli Archivi, 40; 00144 Roma; Italy

Archivio di Stato di Firenze; Viale Giovane Italie, 6; 50122 Firenze; Italy

Archivio di Stato di Milano; Via Senato, 10; 20121 Milano; Italy

Archivio di Stato di Napoli; Piazetta Grande Archivio, 5; 80138 Napoli; Italy

Archivio di Stato di Roma; Corso Rinascimento, 40; 00186 Roma; Italy

Archivio di Stato di Torino; Piazza Castello, 209; 10124 Torino; Italy

Centro de Fotoriproduzione, Legatoria e Restauro degli Archivi de Stato; Via C. Baudana Vaccolini, 14; 00153 Roma; Italy

WEB SITES

Cyndi' s List, Italy – Information, Links and Sources <www.cyndislist.com/italy.htm>

Family History Library Catalog – Collections <www.familysearch.org/Eng/Library/FHLC/ frameset_fhlc.asp>

ItalyWorldGenWeb – Information, Links and Sources <home.att.net/~Local_Catholic/Catholic-Italy.htm>

Local Catholic Church History and Genealogy <home.att.net/ ~Local_Catholic/Catholic-Italy.htm>

SUGGESTED READING

Cole, Trafford R. *Italian Genealogical Records: How To Use Italian Civil, Ecclesiastical, and Other Records in Family History Research*. Salt Lake City: Ancestry, 1995.

Colletta, John Philip. *Finding Italian Roots: The Complete Guide for Americans*. Baltimore: Genealogical Publishing Co., 1996.

DeAngelis, Priscilla Grindle. *Italian-American Genealogy: A Source Book*. Rockville, MD: Noteworthy Enterprises, 1994.

Nelson, Lynn. *A Genealogist's Guide to Discovering Your Italian Ancestors*. Cincinnati: Betterway Books, 1997.

Preece, Floren Stocks and Phyllis Pastore Preece. *Handy Guide to Italian Genealogical Records*. Logan, UT: Everton Publishers, 1978.

Notes

MEXICO
(ESTADOS UNIDOS DE MEXICO)

CAPITAL CITY: MEXICO CITY

The Spanish conquistadors first troubled the native Mayan and Aztec people early in the sixteenth century. By 1535, they had subdued the population and captured enough territory to warrant the first Spanish viceroy. Between 1535 and 1821, sixty-one viceroys governed Spain's Mexican colony.

The effects of the invasion were devastating on the native people. The population was estimated at about 11 million in the 1520s. That number fell dramatically, and a century later only about 1 million people lived in what is now Mexico. The population did rebound, reaching about 6.5 million by 1800.

After several attempts, Mexico declared its independence from Spain in 1821. Texas in turn declared its independence from Mexico in 1836. Following the Mexican American War, the Treaty of Guadeloupe Hidalgo set the border between Mexico and the United States using the Rio Grande River as a division line. In 1853, the United States made the Gadsden Purchase and the border that forms the southern parts of Arizona and New Mexico was set.

The Roman Catholic Church grew along with the European settlement. By 1859 the Church owned approximately one third of all property. During that time their holdings were nationalized, and the government decreed that only civil marriages would be recognized.

Subsequent to Napoleon III's wars in Europe, France attempted to assume control of Mexico in 1863. The Mexicans successfully removed the French influence four years later, but the political landscape remained turbulent until the 1920s and 1930s. Today Mexico is structured into 31 states plus the federal district.

SOME MAJOR GENEALOGICAL RECORD SOURCES
Church Records

The records of local Catholic congregations consist of separate registers of baptisms, confirmations, marriages, and deaths or burials.

- **Baptisms** *(bautismos):* name of infant, date, birthplace, parents, residence and birthplaces.
- **Confirmations** *(confirmaciones):* (12 or 15 years): name of person, date of event, parents' names, sometimes names of godparents.
- **Marriages** *(matrimonios):* names of bride and groom, date of marriage, birthplaces, residence, occupations, ages, names and residences of parents.
- **Deaths or burials** *(defunciones or entierros):* name of deceased, date of death or burial, and residence at time of death. Entries for small children may also give the names of the parents.

Church records are found with the local parish and in diocesan archives. Many have been microfilmed by the Family History Library.

Civil Registration

In 1857, civil authorities began keeping records of births, marriages and deaths. In general the records contain:
- **Births** *(nascimientos):* name of infant, date and time of birth, town, street address, parents' names and marital status, occupations, residence
- **Marriages** *(matrimonios):* names of bride and groom, ages, residence, birthplaces, parents' names and birthplaces.
- **Deaths** *(defunciones):* name of deceased, age, birthplace, marital status, occupation, cause of death, burial place; sometimes the names of parents, spouse, or children.

Civil registration records are found in state civil registration offices *(Registro Civil del Estado).*

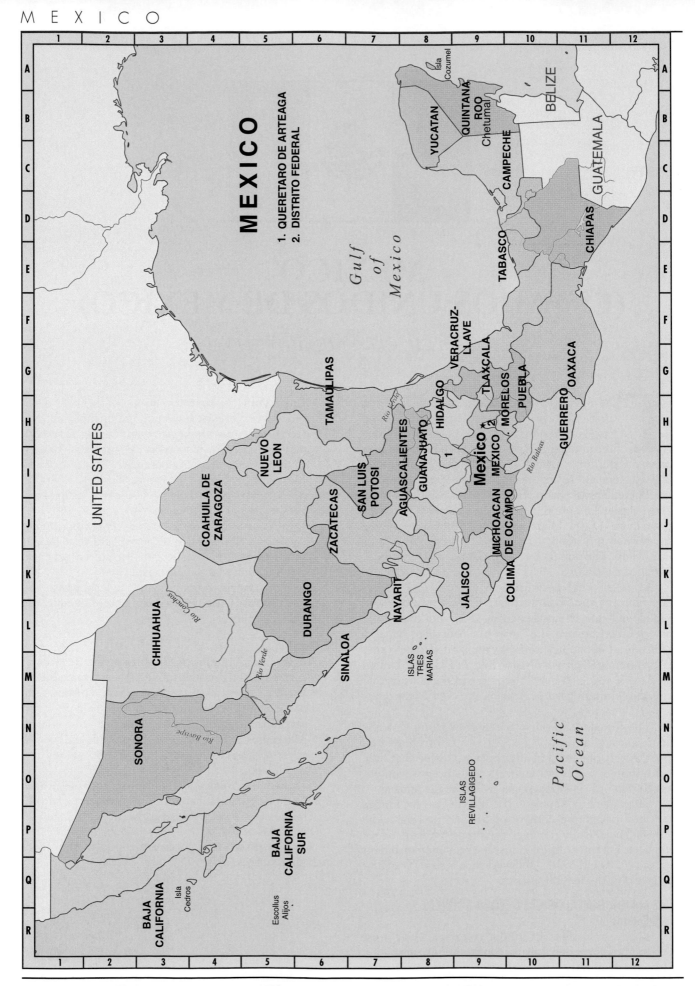

MEXICO

1. QUERETARO DE ARTEAGA
2. DISTRITO FEDERAL

Gulf of Mexico

BELIZE

Isla Cozumel

YUCATAN

QUINTANA ROO

Chetumal

CAMPECHE

GUATEMALA

TABASCO

CHIAPAS

VERACRUZ-LLAVE

TLAXCALA

HIDALGO

MORELOS

PUEBLA

Rio Tula

Rio Balsas

GUERRERO

OAXACA

UNITED STATES

TAMAULIPAS

NUEVO LEON

AGUASCALIENTES

GUANAJUATO

1

Mexico

2

MEXICO

SAN LUIS POTOSI

COAHUILA DE ZARAGOZA

ZACATECAS

MICHOACAN DE OCAMPO

Rio Conchos

DURANGO

NAYARIT

JALISCO

COLIMA

Rio Verde

CHIHUAHUA

SINALOA

ISLAS TRES MARIAS

SONORA

Rio Bavispe

Pacific Ocean

ISLAS REVILLAGIGEDO

BAJA CALIFORNIA SUR

BAJA CALIFORNIA

Isla Cedros

Escollus Alijos

ARCHIVES, LIBRARIES, AND SOCIETIES

Archivo General de la Nacion; Tacuba 8, 2o piso; Palacio
  Nacional; Mexico 1 Mexico;

Biblioteca Nacional de Mexico; Instituto de Investigaciones
  Bibliograficas; Universidade Nacional Autonoma de Mexico;
  Centro Cultural, Ciudad Universitaria; Delegacion
  Coyoacan; Apdo. 29-124; 04510 Mexico; Mexico

WEB SITES

Border Crossing Information and Addresses
  <www.maxpages.com/ourlostfamily/Research>

Catholic Church Parish Records in Mexico – Information,
  Links and Databases <home.att.net/~Local_Catholic/
  Catholic-Mexico.htm>

Cyndi's List, Mexico – Sources, Links, Databases
  <www.cyndislist.com/nm.htm>

Genealogy of Mexico – History, Sources, Databases and
  Information <PERLINK <http://members.tripod.com/
  ~GaryFelix/index1.htm>

Mexico GenWeb <www.rootsweb.com/~mexwgw/>

Mexican Sources – Sources, Links, and Information
  <www.genealogy.com/
  00000379.html?Welcome=1015278270>

SUGGESTED READING

Konrad, J. *Mexican and Spanish Family Research*. Munroe Falls,
  OH: Summit Publications, 1987.

Platt, Lyman. *Mexico: General Research Guide*. Salt Lake City:
  Instituto Genealogico e Historico Latinoamericano, 1989.

Research Outline: Latin America. Salt Lake City: Family History
  Library, 1992.

Notes

The NETHERLANDS (NEDERLAND)

CAPITAL CITY: AMSTERDAM

The Netherlands, or Holland, was part of the Spanish Empire as recently as the sixteenth century. In 1648, much of the territory broke away from Spain. It was known as the Dutch Republic of United Provinces and formalized in the Treaty of Munster. The United Provinces were successful in the shipping and international trade. They carried on trade with the colonies and two major enterprises, the Dutch East India Company and the Dutch West India Company.

For a time in the early nineteenth century, the Netherlands was briefly incorporated into Napoleon's France. They regained independence in 1815, along with Belgium. Belgium declared its independence from Holland in 1830, but the separation process was not completed until 1839.

The Netherlands is composed of twelve provinces with over 700 municipalities. The provinces are generally Roman Catholic in the south and Protestant in the north. The Netherlanders speak Dutch, although Frisian is the dominant language in Friesland.

SOME MAJOR GENEALOGICAL RECORD SOURCES

Church Records

The Dutch Reformed (*Nederhuits Hervormde Kerk*) and Evangelical Lutheran church records date back to the sixteenth century. Records of the Roman Catholic Church do not date before 1675. Copies of these registers are found in the original parish, in city archives, and in provincial archives. The Family History Library has microfilm copies of many parish registers from the Netherlands.

Among the most useful entries in church registers:
- **Births or baptisms:** date of event, name of infant and names of parents.
- **Marriages:** names and residence of the bride and groom, date of marriage or banns, and parents.
- **Deaths or burials:** date of event, name of deceased, names of parents of infant or name of a surviving spouse.

Civil Registration

Civil registration (*Burgelijke Stand*) of births, marriages and deaths began as early as 1793 in the southern provinces, and in 1811 for the entire country. The data is similar to church records. There are ten-year indexes to the civil records. The records are found in municipal register offices, district courts, and provincial archives. The Family History Library has microfilm copies of some civil records.

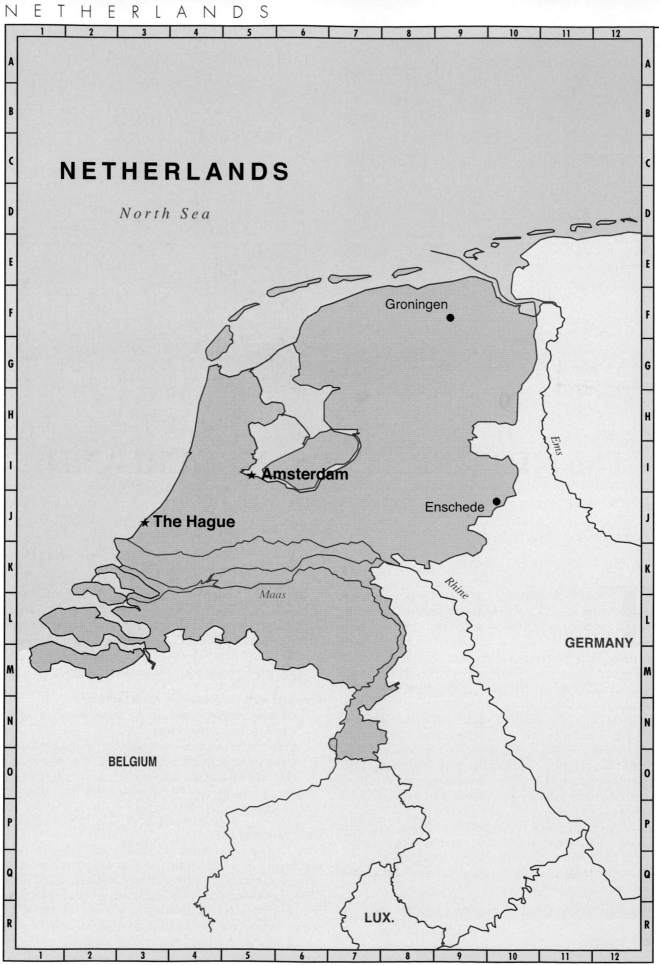

NETHERLANDS

North Sea

Groningen

Enschede

★ **Amsterdam**

★ **The Hague**

Maas

Ems

Rhine

GERMANY

BELGIUM

LUX.

ARCHIVES, LIBRARIES AND SOCIETIES

Algemeen Rijksarchief; Prins Willem-Alexanderhof 20; 2509 LM Den Haag; Netherlands; <www.archief.nl>

Central Bureau voor Genealogie; Prins Willem-Alexanderhof 22; 2502 AT Den Haag; Netherlands; <www.cbg.nl>

Koninklijke Biblitheck; Postbus 90407; 2509 LK Den Haag; Netherlands; <www.konbib.nl>

Rijksarchief in Drenthe; Brink 4; 9400 AN Assen; Netherlands

Rijksarchief in Flevoland; Visarenddreef 1; 8200 AB Lelystad; Netherlands

Rijksarchief in Friesland; Boterhoek 3; 8900 AB Leeuwarden; Netherlands

Rijksarchief in Gelderland; Markt 1; 6811 CG Arnheim; Netherlands

Rijksarchief in Groningen; St. Jansstraat 2; 9712 JN Groningen; Netherlands

Rijksarchief in Limburg; St. Pieterstraat 7; 6211 JM Maastricht; Netherlands

Rijksarchief in Noord-Brabant; De Citadel; Zuid-Willemsvaart 2; 5211 NW's-Hertogenbosch; Netherlands

Rijksarchief in Noord-Holland; Kleine Houtweg 18; 2012 CH Haarlem; Netherlands

Rijksarchief in Overijssel; Eikenstraat 20; 8021 WX Zwolle; Netherlands

Rijksarchief in Uthrecht; Alexander Numankande 201; 3572 KW Utrecht; Netherlands

Rijksarchief in Zeeland; St. Pieterstraat 38; 4331 EW Middelburg; Netherlands

Rijksarchief in Zuid-Holland; Prins Willem-Alexanderhof 20; 2509 LM 's-Gravenhage; Netherlands

WEB SITES

Dutch GenWeb <www.rootsweb.com/~nldwgw/>

Holland/Netherlands Genealogy–Sources, Links, Database <freepages.genealogy.rootsweb.com/~kemp/dutchlinks.html>

Dutch Genealogy Links <www.euronet.nl/users/mnykerk/genealog.htm>

The Dutch Heritage Site–Information, Sources, and Links <www.godutch.com>

Netherlands GenWeb <members.tripod.com/~westland/index.htm>

Netherlands Genealogy Link <www.genealogylinks.net/europe/net.htm>

Netherlands Genealogy Links–Provinces <www.genealogylinks.net/europe/netherlandprovinces.htm>

Cyndi's List, Netherlands–Sources, Links, and Databases <www.oz.net/~cyndihow/nether.htm>

SUGGESTED READING

Franklin, Charles M. *Dutch Genealogical Research*. C. M. Franklin, 1982.

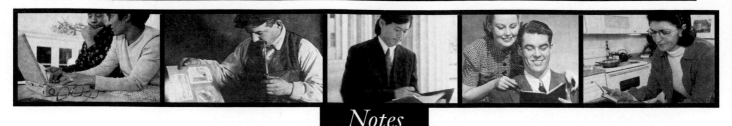

Notes

NEW ZEALAND

CAPITAL CITY: WELLINGTON

The Maori are among the earliest known inhabitants of New Zealand. They arrived by canoe from other Polynesian islands between the ninth and fourteenth centuries. Captain James Cook claimed the island group for Britain in 1769 and was followed by a few missionaries and settlers early in the nineteenth century. European immigration began in earnest in 1839 when the London-based New Zealand Company sponsored new immigrants.

In 1840, the British signed the Treaty of Waitangi, and gained assent of 50 Maori chiefs to purchase large tracts of their land in return for British protection. In 1841, the colonies of New Zealand and New South Wales were separated. Disagreement between the new immigrants and the native Maori flamed periodically, especially in the late 1840s and the 1860s. The Maori Wars finally ended with the promise of greater political participation for the Maori.

New Zealand formed a central government in the 1850s and became completely self-governing in 1907.

SOME MAJOR GENEALOGICAL RECORD SOURCES
Church Records

Church registers are the earliest records for the non-aboriginal peoples of New Zealand. The format of church records varies with each denomination. Generally they contain membership lists, births or baptisms, marriages, and deaths or burials.

The earliest churches in New Zealand were the Anglican Church (from 1814), Methodist (1822), Roman Catholic (1838), Presbyterian (1844), and Baptist (1851). The records are kept in local churches and church archives, although some copies are also available in local libraries.

Civil Registration

The civil government began registering European births, marriages and deaths in New Zealand in 1848. The process did not become mandatory until 1856. Maori registration was not required until early in the twentieth century (1911-1913).

The local registry offices handle civil registrations. Copies of civil registration records for New Zealand are housed in the Central Registry Office, in Lower Hutt. Indexes on microfiche are available for purchase, but the certificates must be purchased from a registry office.

Passenger Arrival Lists

Early arrival passenger lists beginning in 1839 through the mid-1880s consist of those immigrants who received some sort of assistance in their passage. They also show entries of former convicts who traded prison confinement for passage to New Zealand. Passenger lists for 1883 to 1973 are complete, covering all arrivals in the country.

Most passenger arrival lists are in the custody of the National Archives of New Zealand in Wellington. There are number of indexes to these passenger arrival lists.

WEB SITES

Cyndi's List - New Zealand – Information, Sources and Databases <www.cyndislist.com/austnz.htm>

Family History Library Catalog <www.familysearch.org/Eng/Library/FHLC/frameset_fhlc.asp>

New Zealand GenWeb Project <www.rootsweb.com/~nzlwgw/>

New Zealand Links and Information <www.benet.net.au/~brandis/links/nz.html>

New Zealand Society of Genealogists <homepages.ihug.co.nz/~nzsg/>

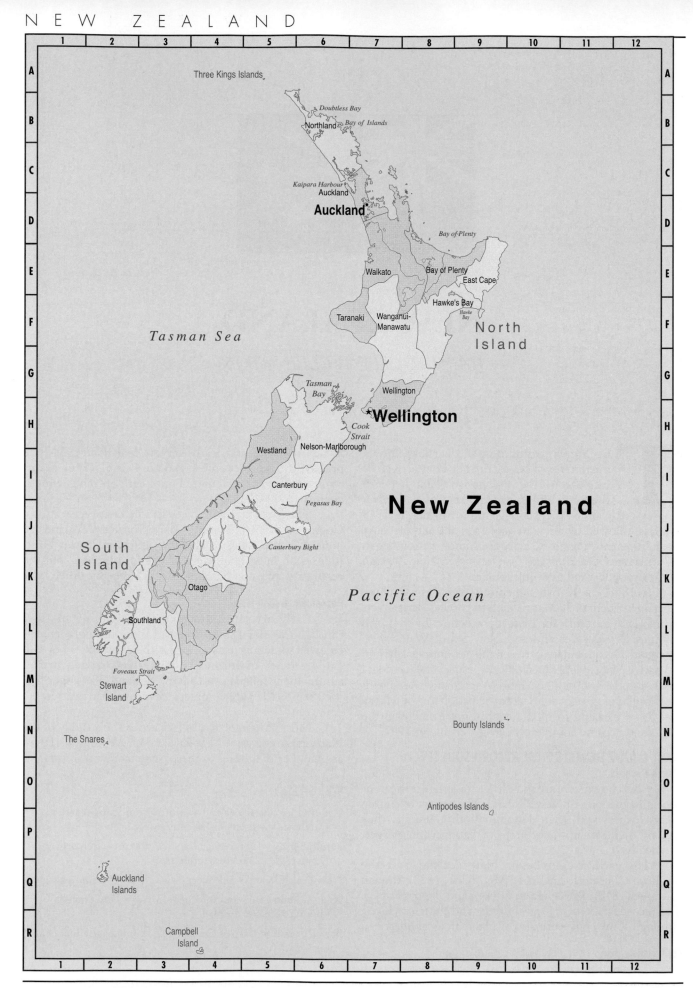

New Zealand

Presbyterian Church Archives of Aotearoa New Zealand –
Information and Searchable Databases
<www.archives.presbyterian.org.nz/index.htm>

Searchable On-line New Zealand Passenger Lists
<www.downtown.co.nz/genealogy/> –

Services-Births-Deaths-and-Marriages-Index. Open
Document> – New Zealand Births, Deaths and Marriages –
Information and SSources <www.bdm.govt.nz/
diawebsite.nsf/wpg_URL/

ARCHIVES, LIBRARIES AND SOCIETIES

Central Registry; Births, Deaths and Marriages; 191 High
Street; PO Box 31-115; Lower Hutt; New Zealand

National Archives of New Zealand, Auckland Regional Office;
525 Mt. Wellington Highway; Auckland; New Zealand

National Archives of New Zealand, Christchurch Regional
Office; 90 Peterborough Street; Christchurch; New Zealand

National Archives of New Zealand, Dunedin Regional Office;
556 George Street; Dunedin; New Zealand

National Archives of New Zealand; PO Box 12-050;
Wellington; New Zealand; <www.archives.govt.nz>

National Library of New Zealand; Molesworth and Aitken
Streets; PO Box 1467; Wellington; New Zealand;
<www.natlib.govt.nz>

SUGGESTED READING

Bromell, Anne. *Family History Research in New Zealand: A
Beginner's Guide*. Auckland, New Zealand: New Zealand
Society of Genealogists, 1984.

Bromell, Anne. *Tracing Your Family History in New Zealand*.
Auckland, New Zealand: Godwit, 1996.

Family History at National Archives. Wellington, New Zealand:
Bridget Williams Books, 1991.

Montague, R. H. *How to Trace Your Military Ancestors in
Australia and New Zealand*. Sydney, NSW, Australia: Hale &
Iremonger, 1989.

*Sources for New Zealand Pakeha Genealogy Available in the New
Zealand and Pacific Department, Auckland Central City Library*.
Auckland, New Zealand: Auckland City Libraries, 1994.

Notes

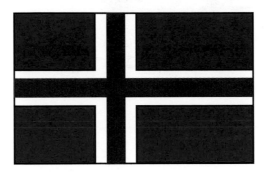

NORWAY (NORGE)

CAPITAL CITY: OSLO

Norway's history is tied to the sea. It boasts over 13,000 miles of coastline. Its waterways have always been more important to travelers than land routes, given the mountainous nature of the country. By the eighth century, Norway was already divided into 29 small kingdoms. King Harold the Fairhaired united the country in 1860, but it separated again after his death. In about 1035, Norway and Denmark united. In 1397, it became part of the Kalmar Union along with Denmark and Sweden. Denmark ceded Norway to Sweden in 1814, but Norway declared independence from both Denmark and Sweden. Sweden continued to maintain loose control for many years until Norway became fully independent in 1905.

Today Norway is divided in to 19 counties, which are composed of urban and rural municipalities. Approximately three-fourths of the population lives within 10 miles of the sea, and about the same percentage lives in urban areas. The capital city of Oslo took that name in 1924; before that time it was known as Kristiania or Christiania.

SOME MAJOR GENEALOGICAL RECORD SOURCES
Church Records

Norway became Protestant during the Reformation and the Lutheran Church (*Den Norske Kirke* or *Statskirken*) became the state church in 1536. In 1688, all parishes of the church were required to keep records of the baptisms, marriages and burials. By 1736, parishes also kept records of confirmations.

- **Baptismal records:** name of child, date, parents, legitimacy of the birth, godparents, and witnesses.
- **Confirmations:** *(14 to 20 years of age)*: name of confirmant, age, residence or birthplace, parents.
- **Marriage records:** date of marriage, names of groom and bride, status prior to marriage (bachelor,

widow, etc.), ages, residence, occupations, fathers' occupations, witnesses.
- **Burial records:** name, date, age, residence, occupation, father's name if deceased was an infant.

Church records are in the custody of the local parish and *landsarkivets*. Many are available on microfilm at the Family History Library.

Census

As early as 1664, an incomplete census of the rural areas in Norway was taken, listing the heads of households. An incomplete census of all males was taken in 1701. The 1801 census included everyone in the country, with names, residences, and occupations. Similar census enumerations in 1865, 1875 and 1900 were taken and contained birthplace and religion data.

Microfilm copies of the census are available at the Family History Library.

Probate Records

Probate matters were handled by local courts. Prior to 1687, the records were interfiled with the "regular" court records. They were usually kept in separate files after that time. A separate probate file was often kept for clergy, military officers and teachers, a practice that continued until 1812.

Most probate records are not indexed, but are a rich source of information such as, names of family members, relationships, date of death of deceased, and an inventory of property.

The records are housed in the local courts. Microfilm copies of many are available at the Family History Library.

Land Records

Land transactions were recorded in local courts. Such transactions include deeds, mortgages, leases, etc. Land

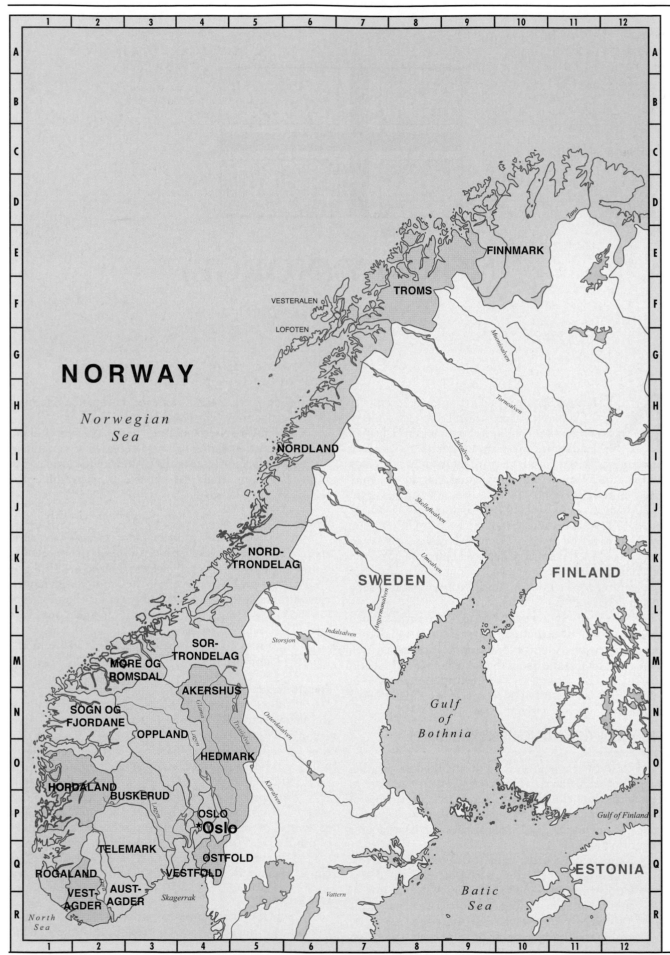

NORWAY

Norwegian Sea

FINNMARK

TROMS

VESTERALEN

LOFOTEN

NORDLAND

NORD-TRONDELAG

SWEDEN

FINLAND

SOR-TRONDELAG

MORE OG ROMSDAL

AKERSHUS

SOGN OG FJORDANE

OPPLAND

HEDMARK

Gulf of Bothnia

HORDALAND

BUSKERUD

OSLO
*Oslo

TELEMARK

ØSTFOLD

VESTFOLD

ROGALAND

Gulf of Finland

VEST-AGDER

AUST-AGDER

Skagerrak

Vattern

ESTONIA

Batic Sea

North Sea

records in Norway can contain family information, occupations, residences, and other data, along with the description of the property.

Land records created after 1865 are in the custody of the local magistrate, while earlier records are in the custody of the regional archives (*landsarkivet*). The Family History Library in Salt Lake City has microfilm copies of many Norwegian land records.

Passenger Departure Lists

Several Norwegian ports preserved lists of passengers departing from their facilities in the late nineteenth century and into the early years of the twentieth. Such lists typically include the names of passengers, date of departure, age, occupation, and residence.

Departure lists are available for the ports of:
Kristiania (Oslo), 1867-1902
Alesund, 1852-1923
Bergen, 1867-1926
Kristiansand, 1873-1911
Kristiansund, 1882-1959
Trondheim, 1867-1926

Copies of the lists are available at the Norwegian Emigration Center in Stavanger, and on microfilm at the Family History Library.

ARCHIVES, LIBRARIES, AND SOCIETIES

Norwegian Emigration Center; Bergjelandsgaten 30; N-4012 Stavanger; <www.utvandrersenteret.no/index.htm>

Norwegian Historical Data Center; University of Tromso; N-9037 Tromso; <www.isv.uit.no/seksjon/rhd/indexeng.htm>

Riksarkivet (National Archives); Folke Bernadottes vei 21; Postboks 4013 Ulleval Hageby; N-0806, Oslo; <www.riksarkivet.no/national.html>

Statsarkivet i Bergen; Arstadveien 22; N-5009 Bergen; <www.hist.uib.no/statsarkiv/>

Statsarkivet i Hamar; Lille Strandgate 3; Postboks 533; N-2301 Hamar

Statsarkivet i Kongsberg; Frogsvei 44; N-3600 Kongsberg

Statsarkivet i Kristiansand; Vesterveien 4; N-4613 Kristiansand

Statsarkivet i Oslo; Folke Bernadottes vei 21; Postboks 4013 Ulleval Hageby; N-0806, Oslo

Statsarkivet i Stavanger; Bergjelandsgate 30; N-4012 Stavanger

Statsarkivet i Tromso; Postboks 622; N-9005 Tromso

Statsarkivet i Trondheim; Hogskoleveien 12; N-7002 Trondheim

Universitetsbiblioteket; Drammensveien 42; N-0255 Oslo 2

WEB SITES

100 Years of Emigrant Ships from Norway Searchable Databases <www.norwayheritage.com/ships/index.asp>

1801, 1865 and 1900 Census Searchable Databases <www.rhd.uit.no/rhdfolketellinger_engelsk _britisk.html>

Cyndi's List, Norway – Sources, Links and Databases <www.cyndislist.com/norway.htm>

Family History Library Catalog <www.familysearch.org/Eng/ Library/FHLC/frameset_fhlc.asp>

Genealogy Norway – Sources, Links and Databases <genealogy.about.com/cs/norway/>

Norway Genealogy – Research Tips and Sources <www.rootsweb.com/~wgnorway/index.html>

Norway GenWeb – Sources, Links and Databases <www.rootsweb.com/~wgnorway/>

The Norwegian Emigration Center – information and sources

The oldest church registers in Norwegian Parishes – Information and Sources <www.nndata.no/home/jborgos/ register.htm>

SUGGESTED READING

Olstad, Jan H. and Gunvald Boe. *Research in Norway*. Burbank, CA: Southern California Genealogical Society, 1989.

Research Outline – Norway. Salt Lake City: Family History Library, 1992.

Smith, Frank and Finn A. Thomsen. *Genealogical Guidebook and Atlas of Norway*. Logan, UT: Everton Publishers, 1979.

Thomsen, Finn A. *The Beginner's Guide to Norwegian Genealogical Research*. Bountiful, UT: Thomsen's Genealogical Center, 1984.

Notes

POLAND (POLSKA)

CAPITAL CITY: WARSAW (WARSZAWA)

In 1386, Poland joined with Lithuania to become the third largest country in Europe, encompassing almost three times as much land as Poland claims today. Poland was an electoral commonwealth from 1577 to 1772. Repeated battles with Russia, Sweden and Turkey drastically cut its boundaries by about one fourth.

Between 1772 and 1795, Poland was divided three different times by Prussia, Austria and Russia. Russia claimed the largest portion of the former Polish territory. By 1795, the country of Poland ceased to exist. In 1806 a French protectorate, the Duchy of Warsaw, was created, but this small state only lasted until 1813 when the Russians again occupied the region. In 1815, the Duchy was distributed again to Russia, Prussia and Austria.

The independence of the modern Polish state was declared in November 1918, following World War 1. Its borders were reduced again in the aftermath of World War II. Polish eastern lands were then transferred to Russian control, while its western border with Germany was established along the banks of the Oder and Neisse rivers.

SOME MAJOR GENEALOGICAL RECORD SOURCES

Church Records

Church registers and civil registrations were kept in a wide variety of forms and languages.

The Roman Catholic, Russian Orthodox, Evangelical, Jewish and Mennonite churches dominated the area where Poland now exists. Catholic records date from the 1563 Council of Trent, although many early records (prior to the nineteenth century) have been lost. These Catholic records were written in Polish or Latin. Some Russian Orthodox registers date from the seventeenth century, but most no earlier than the late eighteenth century. The Russian Orthodox registers were written in Old Church Slavonic, Polish, Latin and Ukrainian. Evangelical Lutheran and Evangelical Reformed Churches were most popular in German areas and date as early as 1795. They are usually written in German. Several smaller religious groups, such as Jews and smaller Protestant denominations, often did not maintain their own registers until required by law.

Among the data you can find in church records:

- **Christenings:** date of baptism and sometimes date of birth, child's name, parents, and witnesses.
- **Marriages:** date, date of announcement, names of bride and groom, ages, residences, parents.
- **Burials:** date and place of death and burial, name of deceased, age, and residence; sometimes date and place of death, names of parents, if an infant, or the name of a spouse, if married.

Some Jewish communities kept circumcision registers, recording the Hebrew given name of the male child, date of circumcision according to the Hebrew calendar, and father's Hebrew name.

More recent church registers are found in the local parish. Earlier records are deposited in diocesan or state archives. The Family History Library has microfilmed many of the records.

Civil Registration

Vital records were compiled by state authorities and varied according to who was in control of Poland. Austrian territories began recording civil registration as early as 1784, the Russian areas from about 1808, and the Prussian regions from about 1874.

Currently the records are compiled and maintained by civil offices. Early records, referred to as Civil Transcripts of Church Records, were compiled from church records and used by civil authorities. The language of the records may be in Polish, German or Russian depending on the place and time in which they were kept.

Information found in the records includes:

- **Births:** date and place, child's name and gender, parents' names, residence and religion; some Austrian records include names of grandparents.
- **Marriages:** names of bride and groom, ages, residence, religion, date and place of marriage, witnesses and parents; some include bride's and groom's birth dates and places.
- **Deaths:** name of deceased, age, residence, religion, date and place of death and burial, and witnesses; also includes names of an infant's parents or name of a surviving spouse.

Recent civil registers are found in local civil records offices. Those records older than 100 years are located in state archives. The Family History Library has microfilm copies of many "older" civil records (those found in state archives, rather than local record offices).

ARCHIVES, LIBRARIES AND SOCIETIES

Archiwum Panstwowe w Bialymstoku; Rynek Kosciuski 41; 15-950 Bialystock; Poland

Archiwum Panstwowe m. st. Warszawy; ul. Krzywe Kolo 7; 00-270 Warszawa; Poland

Archiwum Panstwowe w Czestochowie; ul. Rejtana 13; 42-200 Czestochowa; Poland

Archiwum Panstwowe w Koazalinie; skr. poczt. 149; 75-950 Koszalin; Poland

Archiwum Panstwowe w Krakowie; ul. Sienna 16; 30-960 Krakow; Poland

Archiwum Panstwowe w Lublinie; skr. poczt. 113; 20-950 Lublin; Poland

Archiwum Panstwowe we Wroclawiu; ul. Pomorska 2; 50-215 Wroclaw; Poland

WEB SITES

Catholic Research in Poland – Information, Sources and Databases <www.maxpages.com/poland Catholic_Research>

Cyndi's List, Poland – Information, Sources, Links and Databases <www.cyndislist.com/poland.htm>

Genealogy and Poland: A Guide – Information and Sources <ourworld.compuserve.com/homepages/ German_Genealogy/kbak.htm>

Genealogy in Poland – Information, Sources, History, Databases <genealogy.about.com/cs/poland/>

Local Catholic Church History and Genealogy – Information, Sources and Databases <home.att.net/~Local_Catholic/ Catholic-Poland.htm>

Polish Genealogical Society of America – Information, Sources and Searchable Databases <www.pgsa.org>

Poland GenWeb – State Archives in Poland <www.rootsweb.com/~polwgw/polandgen.html>

The Polish Genealogy Home Page – Sources and Links <hum.amu.edu.pl/~rafalp/GEN/plgenhp.htm>

SUGGESTED READING

Hoskins, Janina W. *Polish Genealogy & Heraldry: An Introduction to Research*. Washington, DC: Library of Congress, 1987.

Konrad, J. *Polish Family Research*. Munroe Falls, OH: Summit Publications, 1977.

Schlyter, Daniel M. *Essentials in Polish Genealogical Research*. Chicago: Polish Genealogical Society of America, 1993.

Wynne, Suzan F. *Finding Your Jewish Roots in Galicia: A Resource Guide*. Teaneck, NJ: Avotaynu, 1998.

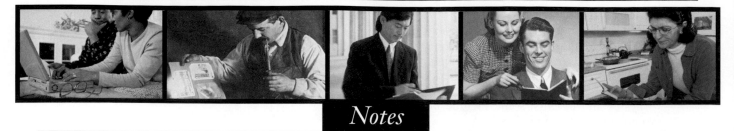

Notes

RUSSIA (ROSSIYA)

CAPITAL CITY: MOSCOW (MOSKVA)

The history of modern Russia goes back to Rurik, a ninth-century Scandinavian who founded a state centering on Kiev, which came to be known as "Rus". The influence of Rurik and his descendants grew through the next four centuries after the acceptance of Orthodox Christianity as the state religion in the tenth century. But the foundation was corroded by the Mongol Invasion in the thirteenth century and it devastated what remained of Rurik's legacy.

Expansion of the Russian state began again in the next century, with Moscow as the new center of power. In the sixteenth century, Ivan the Terrible declared himself the first Czar and absolute monarch of the realm. In 1597, serfdom was established, tying Russian peasants to specific tracts of land. That form of slavery persisted for almost three centuries.

Peter the Great expanded the Russian borders and moved the seat of government to his new capital, St. Petersburg. He established programs that created records of value to genealogists, such as conscriptions into his army and navy, registers in the Russian Orthodox Church, and census enumerations. Catherine the Great broadened the Russian borders on the south and west. Later Emperors expanded the borders to the east. By the end of the nineteenth century Russia reached east to the Pacific Ocean.

Alexander II abolished serfdom in 1861. The action required that serfs reimburse their owners for their freedom. This hardship contributed to the introduction of the industrial revolution to Russian society. Border conflicts continued, and an emerging democratic movement contributed to a long bloody struggle against the monarchy. The assassination of Alexander II in 1881 was followed by an abortive revolution in 1905, and finally by the overthrow of the Romanov monarchy in favor of communist rule in 1917.

Russia remained a socialist state as part of the Soviet Union until late in the twentieth century when it became a nominal democracy.

SOME MAJOR GENEALOGICAL RECORD SOURCES
Church Records

The Russian Orthodox Church, the state religion, began to keep records in 1722. Other Russian churches were required to keep similar records. The Roman Catholic records began in 1826, Islamic records in 1828, Protestant records in 1832, and Jewish records in 1835. Two copies of births, christenings, marriages, deaths and burials were kept; one remained in the local congregation and another was sent to a higher office. Today they are found in state and regional archives.

Civil Registration

Civil registration of births, marriages, divorces and deaths was organized in the aftermath of the 1917 revolution. The process was handled by local registry offices and village soviets, who retained custody of their records. This process, however, was largely ignored during the first years of soviet rule and was interrupted again during the Stalinist years. In addition, some registers were destroyed during World War II.

Serf Lists

From about 1650 until the official end of serfdom in 1861, estates kept lists of their serfs–both the household servants and the field servants. The records recognized the human "holdings" of the landed gentry by recording their names, ages and family relationships. Relationships were especially useful in establishing their hold on future generations of serfs. About one-third of the serfs were entered in the estate lists. Copies can be found in state, regional and central archives.

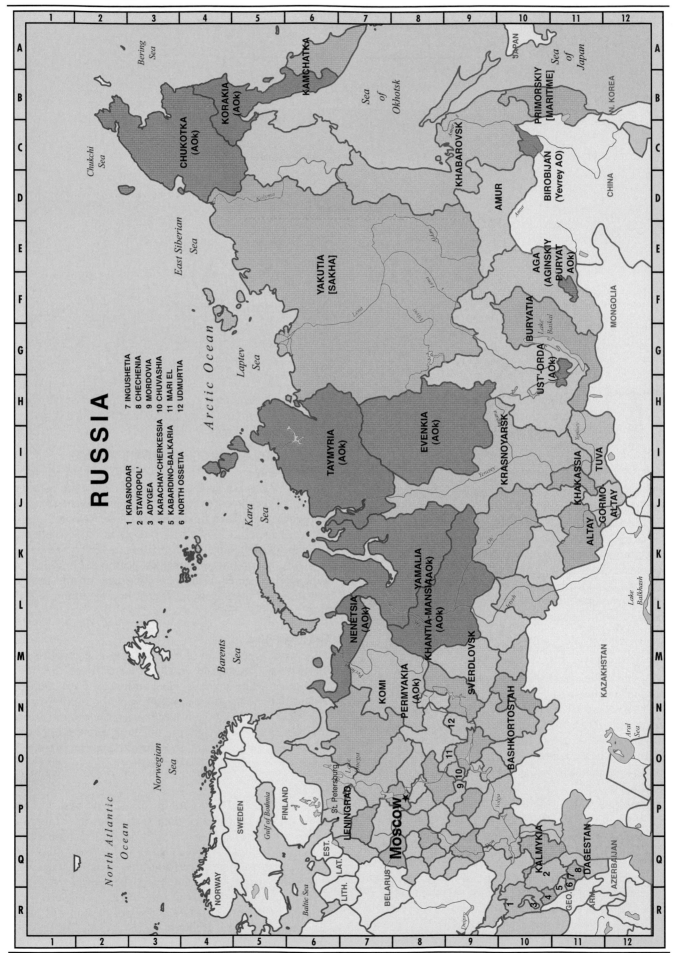

RUSSIA

1 KRASNODAR
2 STAVROPOL'
3 ADYGEA
4 KARACHAY-CHERKESSIA
5 KABARDINO-BALKARIA
6 NORTH OSSETIA
7 INGUSHETIA
8 CHECHENIA
9 MORDOVIA
10 CHUVASHIA
11 MARI EL
12 UDMURTIA

ARCHIVES, LIBRARIES AND SOCIETIES

Central State Archives; Vyborgskaya 3; 125212 Moscow; Russia

Central State Historical Archive of St. Petersburg; Pskovskaja str. 18; 190008 St. Petersburg; Russia; <www.ruslan.ru:8001/spb/assoc_csha.html>

Moscow Patriarchate of the Russian Orthodox Church; Danilov Monastery; 113191 Moscow; Russia

State Archives of the Russian Federation; Bolshaya Pirogovskaya ul. 17; 119817 Moscow; Russia

State Archival Service of Russia; Ilyinka 12; 103132 Moscow; Russia

WEB SITES

American Historical Society of Germans from Russia – Information, Sources and Databases <www.ahsgr.org>

Cyndi's List, Germans from Russia – Sources, Links and Databases <www.cyndislist.com/germruss.htm>

Jewish Religious Personnel in the Russian Empire, 1853-1854 <www.jewishgen.org/databases/deych.htm>

Odessa: A German–Russian Genealogical Library – Information and Sources <pixel.cs.vt.edu/library/odessa.html>

Russian-American Genealogical Archival Service (RAGAS) – Information and Sources <www.feefhs.org/ragas/frgragas.html>

Russia Genealogy and Family History – Information, Sources, Links and Databases <genealogy.about.com/cs/russia/>

Russia Genealogy Links – Information, Sources, Links and Databases <www.genealogylinks.net/europe/rus.htm>

Russia GenWeb – Sources, Links and Databases <www.rootsweb.com/~ruswgw/>

Russian Mennonite Genealogical Resources <www.mmhs.org/russia/mmhsgen4.htm>

Russian Research – Information, Sources, History, Databases <www.maxpages.com/poland/Russian_Research>

The Grodno Gubernia 1912 Voters List – Database <www.jewishgen.org/databases/grodno.htm>

SUGGESTED READING

Edlund, Thomas Kent. *The Lutherans of Russia*. St. Paul, MN: Germanic Genealogy Society, 1994.

Glazier, Ira A. *Migration from the Russian Empire: Lists of Passengers Arriving at the Port of New York, 1875-1889*. Baltimore: Genealogical Publishing Co., 1995-1997.

Mehr, Kahlile B. and Daniel Schlyter. *Sources for Genealogical Research in the Soviet Union*. Buffalo Grove, IL: Genun Publishers, 1983.

Sack, Sallyann Amdur and Suzan Fishl Wynne. *The Russian Consular Records Index and Catalog*. New York: Garland Publishing Co., 1987.

Notes

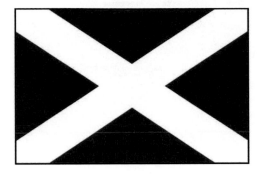

SCOTLAND

CAPITAL CITY: EDINBURGH

Upon their arrival to the island, the Romans pushed the natives, called Picts, into the north. The Romans constructed Hadrian's Wall in the second century AD in an effort to keep the Picts there. The Wall was not entirely successful, nor were the Romans, who were forced off the island in the next century. Christianity was introduced and largely accepted in the sixth and seventh centuries. The region was politically unified in the eighth century, but struggles between its component groups continued.

England annexed Scotland in 1296, but the country regained its independence in 1328. The two countries joined and separated several times before Scotland formally joined the United Kingdom in 1707. Perhaps the saddest chapter in Scottish history was the "Highland Clearances", occurring roughly between 1780 and 1854. A large portion of the Highlands population was forced to leave their land in favor of the sheep that were supposed to be the future of Scottish commerce.

Until 1975, Scotland was composed of 33 counties or shires. In that year its administrative areas were reorganized into nine regions and three island areas.

SOME MAJOR GENEALOGICAL RECORD SOURCES

Church Records

The records of the established church, the Presbyterian Church of Scotland, form the most important body of records available for genealogical research. Established as the state church in 1690, its registers often date to 1650. Among the church records most useful to family historians are:

- **Baptisms (or christenings):** date, name, father's name and occupation, mother's name, date of birth, legitimacy of birth, family residence, and witnesses.
- **Marriages:** names of bride and groom, date of marriage; also could give previous marital status, residence, occupations, name of father of the bride.
- **Burials:** name of deceased, date of burial; could also give age at time of death, name of spouse or parents. Sometimes a widow would take back her maiden name. Relatively few burial records were kept prior to 1855.

All church registers covering the years up to 1855 were sent to the General Register Office and are on microfilm at the Family History Library. The Family History Library has compiled a computer index to the christenings and marriages, known as the *Old Parochial Registers Index*, or OPR. This index is generally arranged by county, with separate indexes for christenings and marriages.

Civil Registration

The civil recording of every birth, marriage and death in Scotland was established on 1 January 1855. Local registration offices maintained two sets of registers, one was kept locally while the other was sent to the General Register Office in Edinburgh. They have annual indexes. While the General Register Office has the complete record, the Family History Library has microfilm copies of the indexes from 1855 through 1955, and of the original registers for 1855 through 1875, 1881 and 1891. The births and marriages for 1855 through 1875 have been added to the Family History Library's *International Genealogical Index*.

Scotland's civil records show:

- **Births:** date and place, name, gender, parents' names, father's occupation, name of the informant. After 1860 they also give the date and place of the parents' marriage.

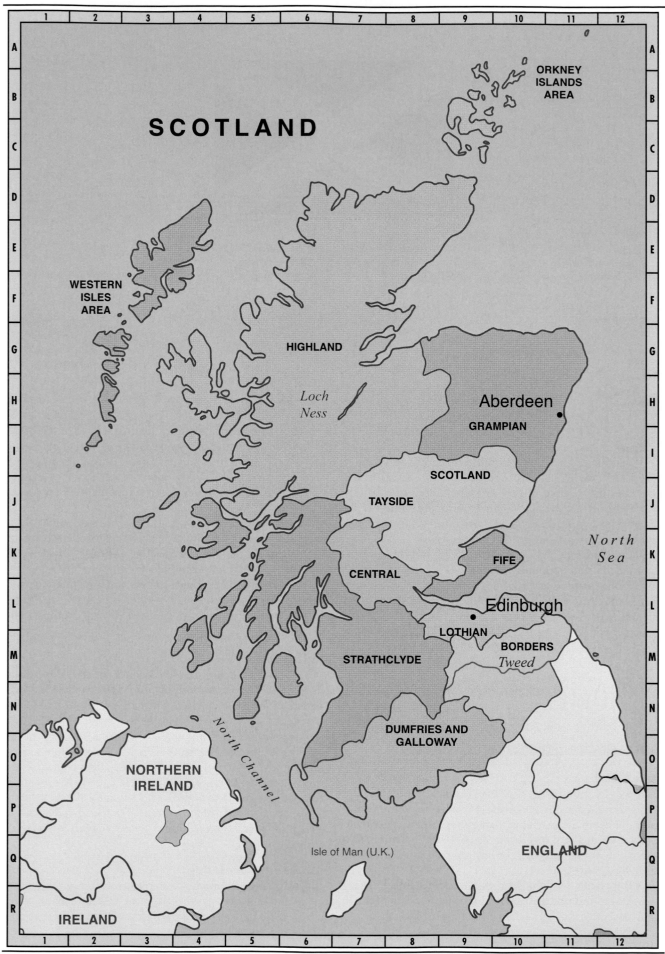

SCOTLAND

ORKNEY
ISLANDS
AREA

WESTERN
ISLES
AREA

HIGHLAND

*Loch
Ness*

Aberdeen
GRAMPIAN

SCOTLAND

TAYSIDE

*North
Sea*

FIFE

CENTRAL

Edinburgh
LOTHIAN

BORDERS
Tweed

STRATHCLYDE

DUMFRIES AND
GALLOWAY

North Channel

NORTHERN
IRELAND

Isle of Man (U.K.)

ENGLAND

IRELAND

- **Marriages:** date and place, names of bride and groom, previous marital status, ages, occupations, residence, fathers' names and occupations, whether their fathers were deceased, names and occupations of mothers, whether the marriage was by banns or by public notice, date and place of registration.
- **Deaths:** date and place, name of deceased, age, gender, occupation, marital status, father's name and occupation, mother's name, cause of death, name of informant, date and place the death was registered.

Census Schedules

Similar to censuses conducted in England and Wales, population schedules for Scotland began to show the name of each resident in 1841. Full enumerations were conducted every ten years thereafter. Copies of the schedules are in the custody of the General Register Office, and microfilm copies of the census schedules for 1841 through 1891 are available at the Family History Library. The Family History Library has an index to the 1881 census, and indexes for other censuses are being compiled.

The 1841 census recorded the name of each person, gender, address, occupation, and whether or not they were born in the county in which they were then residing. Beginning with the 1851 enumeration, the schedules included the relationship of each person to the head of the household and their birthplace.

Sasines

Transfer of land was originally registered by notaries in keeping with Roman law. In Scotland land could not be transferred by probate, as testaments could only be used to grant "moveable" property. Scottish "sasines" often performed a dual service for the genealogist, acting as a source of both probate and land information.

The sasines show the names of the parties involved, their relationship, a description of the land, the terms of transfer, and the date of the event.

The Scottish Record Office has sasines from about 1599, and some are available on microfilm at the Family History Library. Most are arranged by county, and are accessible through a series of indexes.

Testaments

A small percentage of the populace had sufficient moveable property to be handled via testament, making it an important resource for the genealogist.

Testaments were handled by regional commissariot courts, but it was also possible to have a testament from anywhere in Scotland handled by the principal commissariot court in Edinburgh. Scottish testaments are presently in the custody of the Scottish Record Office in Edinburgh, and the Family History Library has microfilm copies of them dating as early as 1560. The testaments are indexed up to 1800, and annual indexes exist for 1876 to 1959.

Testaments include the name of deceased, date of the testament, names of heirs, their relationships to the testator, and a description of the property transferred.

WEB SITES

Church of Scotland – Links and Databases <www.churchnet.org.uk/ukchurches/scotland/>

Church of Scotland – History <www.btinternet.com/~stnicholas.buccleuch/chart.htm>

Cyndi's List, Scotland – Sources, Links and Databases <www.cyndislist.com/scotland.htm>

Family History Library Catalog <www.familysearch.org/Eng/Library/FHLC/frameset_fhlc.asp>

FamilySearch – database <www.familysearch.org/Eng/Search/frameset_search.asp>

Scotland Genealogy links – Links and Sources <www.genealogylinks.net/uk/scotland/>

Scotland GenWeb – Sources, Links and Databases

Scotland – Information, Sources, Links and Databases <www.genuki.org.uk/big/sct/>

Scots Origins – Database

Tartans, Clans & Septs – History, Sources and Links: <www.infokey.com/hall/tartans.htm>

Tracing Your Scottish Genealogy – information, links and sources: <www.geo.ed.ac.uk/home/scotland/genealogy.html>

Vital Records <www.origins.net>

SUGGESTED READING

Cory, Kathleen B. *Tracing Your Scottish Ancestry*. Edinburgh: Polygon, 1990.

Hamilton-Edwards, Gerald K. *In Search of Scottish Ancestry*. Baltimore: Genealogical Publishing Co., 1986.

Irvine, Sherry. *Your Scottish Ancestors: A Guide for North Americans*. Salt Lake City: Ancestry, 1997.

Moody, David. *Scottish Family History*. Baltimore: Genealogical Publishing Co., 1994.

Scottish Research Outline. Salt Lake City: Family History Library, 1997.

Sinclair, Cecil. *Tracing Your Scottish Ancestors: A Guide to Ancestry Research in the Scottish Record Office*. Edinburgh: Her Majesty's Stationery Office, 1991.

Smith, Frank. *A Genealogical Gazetteer of Scotland*. Logan, UT: Everton Publishers.

Notes

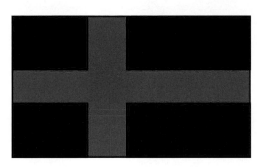

SWEDEN (SVERIGE)

CAPITAL CITY: STOCKHOLM

Sweden was united with Denmark and Norway in 1397 as part of the Kalmar Union under Margaret I. It was not until 1523 that Sweden regained independent control over much of its northern territory when the Union was dissolved during the reign of Gustav I. Sweden embraced Lutheranism along with the rest of Scandinavia at that time. Over the next century Sweden enlarged its political influence in territories bordering the Baltic Sea. Through a series of wars, Sweden gained land in the Baltic States, Poland, and northeastern Germany. In 1658, Sweden finally regained her southern territories from Denmark.

Following the war against France in 1814, Denmark ceded Norway to Sweden. Sweden slowly gave power back to Norway during the next century and declared complete independence for Norway in 1905.

Today Sweden has 24 counties. Each county is composed of towns, cities and rural districts. The *landsarkivet*, or regional archives, hold local records of genealogical value. National records are found in the *Riksarkivet* (National Archives) and *Krigsarkivet* (Military Archives), both located in Stockholm.

SOME MAJOR GENEALOGICAL RECORD SOURCES
Church Records

The state church is the Evangelical Lutheran Church (*Svenska Kyrkan*). In 1586, the parish priest was required to keep registers of the vital statistics. It was mandated again in 1608, and again by royal decree in 1686. The registers contain the following records:

- **Baptisms:** date, name of child, parents, legitimacy of child, witnesses and godparents.
- **Marriages:** date or dates of the reading of banns, groom and bride, marital status prior to ceremony, single, widowed, etc., witnesses; some entries include ages, occupations, birthplaces, and parents.
- **Deaths:** date of death or burial, name of deceased, age, residence, parents if the deceased was an infant; stillbirths are often recorded with other deaths in the parish.
- **Confirmations (between 14 to 16 years of age):** date of the event, name of confirmant, residence, and birth date or age.
- **Clerical Surveys:** similar to a census. They were updated annually and kept in books showing 5 or 10 years at a time. Families were listed together geographically. Each person's name, birth date and place, marriage date, occupation, and death date were recorded. The registers also list where people moved to when they left the parish, and where they came from when they moved into the parish.
- **In and Out Registers:** Many parishes have separate volumes showing the names of people moving into the parish from their previous residence, and those moving out of the parish and their destinations.

Church records are found in local parishes and in the regional archives. Many are available on microfilm at the Family History Library.

Court Records

City and district courts handled a variety of criminal and civil matters, including land transactions and probate matters. The probate records are similar to inventories compiled in the United States, and record the name of the deceased, date of death, date of inventory, residence, names of heirs, ages, residences, relationship to the deceased, and a description of the estate. An inventory often gives the names of daughter's husbands.

Swedish court records are found in regional archives. The Family History Library has microfilm of probate records in their collection.

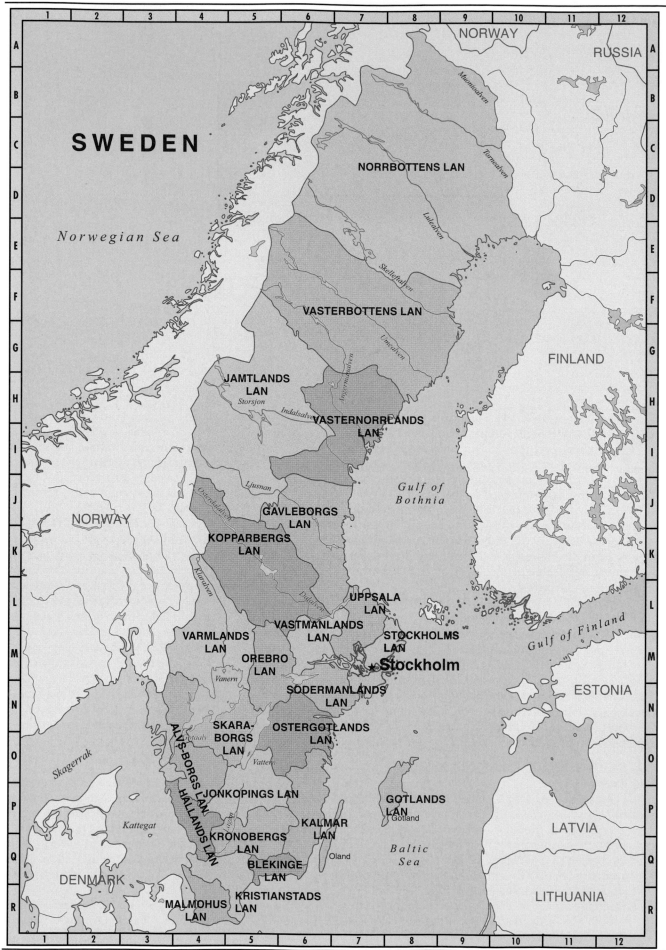

SWEDEN

NORWAY

RUSSIA

NORRBOTTENS LAN

Norwegian Sea

VASTERBOTTENS LAN

FINLAND

JAMTLANDS
LAN

Storsjon

VASTERNORRLANDS
LAN

Indalsalve

Ljusnan

*Gulf of
Bothnia*

GAVLEBORGS
LAN

KOPPARBERGS
LAN

NORWAY

UPPSALA
LAN

VASTMANLANDS
LAN

VARMLANDS
LAN

STOCKHOLMS
LAN

OREBRO
LAN

★ **Stockholm**

Vanern

Gulf of Finland

SODERMANLANDS
LAN

ESTONIA

SKARA-
BORGS
LAN

OSTERGOTLANDS
LAN

ALVS-BORGS LAN

Vattern

JONKOPINGS LAN

HALLANDS LAN

GOTLANDS
LAN

Gotland

Skagerrak

Kattegat

KALMAR
LAN

KRONOBERGS
LAN

Oland

*Baltic
Sea*

LATVIA

BLEKINGE
LAN

DENMARK

KRISTIANSTADS
LAN

LITHUANIA

MALMOHUS
LAN

Military Records

The government required each province to produce its own troops. Regimental records, especially the muster rolls, are important in finding information about the Swedish soldier.

The military muster rolls are arranged by regiment. Each entry shows the name of the soldier, province he came from, his age, height, marital status, length of service, and date of death or discharge.

The records are housed in the *Krigsarkivet* (Military Archives) in Stockholm, in the regional archives, and on microfilm at the Family History Center.

Passenger Departure Lists

During the second half of the nineteenth century, approximately one million Swedes left their homeland for North America. Police departments in port cities preserved chronological lists of those who left. Each list gave the name of the ship, date of departure, name of each passenger, their birthplace, age and destination.

Departure lists are found in regional archives and in the Family History Library for the cities of:

Goteborg (1869-1920)
Malmo (1874-1939)
Norrkoping (1861-1921)
Stockholm (1869-1920)

ARCHIVES, LIBRARIES AND SOCIETIES

Krigsarkivet (Military Archives); Banergatan 64; S-115 88 Stockholm

Kungliga Biblioteket (Royal Library); Box 5039; S-102 41 Stockholm; <www.kb.se>

Landsarkivet i Goteborg; Box 3009; S-400 10 Goteborg

Landsarkivet i Harnosand; Box 161; S-871 24 Harnosand

Landsarkivet i Lund; Box 2016; S-220 02 Lund <www.ra.se/lla/index.htm>

Landsarkivet i Ostersund; Arkivvagen 1; S-831 31 Ostersund

Landsarkivet i Uppsala; Box 135; S-751 04 Uppsala

Landsarkivet i Vadstena; Box 126; S-592 23 Vadstena

Landsarkivet i Visby; Box 2142; Visborgsgatan 1; S-621 57 Visby

Malmo Stadsarkiv; Stora Varvsgaten 11 N4; S-211 19 Malmo

Riksarkivet (National Archives); Box 12541; Fyrverkarbacken 13-17; S-102 29 Stockholm; <www.ra.se>

Stockholms Stadsarkiv; Box 22063; S-104 22 Stockholm; <www.ssa.stockholm.se>

Svenska Emigrantinstitutet; Box 201; S-351 04 Vaxjo

Svensk Arkivinformation; Box 160; Tingsvagen 5; S-880 40 Ramsele; <www.svar.ra.se>

Varmlandsarkivet; Box 475; Norra Strandgatan 4; S-651 11 Karlstad

WEB SITES

Cyndi's List, Sweden – Sources, Links and Databases: <www.cyndislist.com/sweden.htm>

Genline, Swedish Church Records – Searchable Database (in Swedish) <www.genline.se/>

Sweden Archives – Current Addresses <www.maxpages.com/ourlostfamily/Sweden>

Sweden Genealogy <www.rootsweb.com/~wgsweden/>

Sweden Genealogy links – Information, Sources, Links and Databases <www.genealogylinks.net/europe/swe.htm>

Sweden GenWeb – Sources, Links and Databases: <www.rootsweb.com/~swewgw/>

Swedish Emigration Institute – History, Information Databases <www.svenskaemigrantinstitutet.g.se/eng.html>

Swedish Federation of Genealogical Societies <www.genealogi.se>

Swedish Genealogy – Information, Sources, Links and Databases <genealogy.about.com/cs/sweden/>

Tracing your Swedish Roots – Links and Databases <www.sverigeturism.se/smorgasbord/smorgasbord/service/genealogy.html>

SUGGESTED READING

Johansson, Carl-Erik. *Cradled in Sweden*. Logan, UT: Everton Publishers, 1977.

Olsson, Nils William. *Tracing Your Swedish Ancestry*. Stockholm: Ministry for Foreign Affairs, 1985.

Olsson, Nils William and Erik Wiken. *Swedish Passenger Arrivals in the United States, 1820-1850*. Stockholm: Schmidts Boktryckeri AB, 1995.

Research Outline: Sweden. Salt Lake City: Family History Library, 1997.

Swedish Genealogical Resources. St. Paul, MN: Minnesota Genealogical Society, 1987.

Thomsen, Finn A. *The Beginner's Guide to Swedish Genealogical Research*. Bountiful, UT: Thomsen's Genealogical Center, 1984.

Notes

SWITZERLAND
(SCHWEIZ/SUISSE/SVIZZERA)

CAPITAL CITY: BERN (BERNE)

Parts of what would become Switzerland gained independence from the Holy Roman Empire as early as the fourteenth century, with the newly independent cities and cantons allying themselves in a loose confederation. The process was accelerated by the Protestant Reformation in the early sixteenth century and the 1648 Peace of Westphalia, which formally recognized Switzerland as an independent state.

French intrusion under Napoleon late in the eighteenth century and early in the nineteenth was repelled. The Swiss rejected the constitution that the French attempted to force on them, preferring to formulate their own. A brief civil war by Roman Catholic cantons in the southern region rocked Switzerland in 1847, but the uprising led to a new constitution the next year, followed by another rewrite in 1874.

Switzerland has 23 states, known as cantons, and three half-cantons. The main languages are German, French and Italian (spoken in the southern canton of Ticino).

SOME MAJOR GENEALOGICAL RECORD SOURCES
Parish Registers

Swiss church records (*pfarrbucher* in German, *registres paroissiaux* in French, *registri parrochiali* in Italian) date from about 1525 for some Protestant churches, and from about 1580 for the Roman Catholic Church. While the Catholic records are usually found in the local Catholic Church, Protestant records are usually in the custody of the local civil registrar or the state (canton) archive. The Family History Library in Salt Lake City has microfilm copies of some Swiss church records.

Among the items usually found in the parish registers:
- **Baptisms:** name of infant, date and place, name of father; the mother's name may be given.

- **Marriages:** date and place, names of bride and groom; after about 1700, names of parents may be included.
- **Burials:** name of deceased, date and place of death and burial, name of spouse, or names of parents, if a child.

Civil Registration

Civil registration (German: *Zivilstandregister*; French: *Etat civil*; Italian: *Stato civile*) officially dates from 1876 for the entire nation, although some cantons began the process decades earlier. The records are maintained by the local civil registrar, and have three main components:
- **Birth records:** name, date and place of birth, parents' names, residence, and occupation.
- **Marriage records:** date and place, bride and groom, ages, residence, occupations, parents' names, residence, occupations, witnesses.
- **Death records:** date and place, name and age of deceased, name of surviving spouse, or names of parents if a child, name and residence of informant; may include the deceased's birthplace.

Family Registers

As early as 1620, both Protestant and Catholic parishes preserved family registers (German: *familienregister*; French: *registres des familles*; Italian: *registri di famiglia*). The family registers vary widely in format and content. Generally they resemble a collection of family group records, and include names, dates of birth, marriage and death, and sometimes other residences of all family members.

Family registers, along with parish registers, have been filmed by the Family History Library.

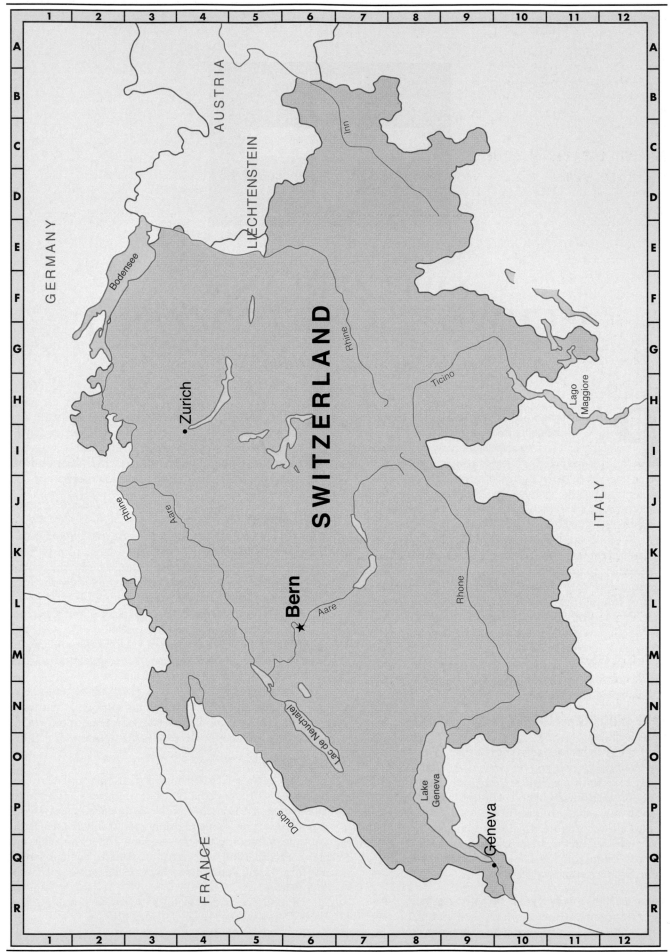

Court and Notarial Records

A variety of legal proceedings were handled by local courts in German cantons, or by notaries in French and Italian regions. The court records are usually in state (canton) archives. Notarial records are found in municipal and state archives. Orphan guardianships, property divisions among heirs, marriage contracts, and testaments are among the type of records kept by the courts.

ARCHIVES, LIBRARIES AND SOCIETIES

Federal Military Library; Bundeshaus Ost; CH-3003 Bern; Switzerland

Swiss Federal Archives; Archivstrasse 24; CH-3003 Bern; Switzerland

Swiss Genealogical Society; Case Postale 54; CH-3608 Thun; Switzerland

Swiss National Library; Hallwylstrasse 101; CH-3003 Bern; Switzerland;

WEB SITES

Catholic Church in Switzerland – Links <home.att.net/~Local_Catholic/Catholic-International.htm>

Cyndi's List, Switzerland – Information, Sources, Links and Databases <www.cyndislist.com/swiss.htm>

Genealogy in French-Speaking Switzerland – Information, Sources, Links <www.unige.ch/biblio/ses/jla/gen/swiss-e.html>

Swiss–American Genealogy – Sources and Links <www.usaswiss.org/swissweb/genealog.html>

Swiss Cross-Index at the Federation of East European Family History Societies – Sources and Links <www.feefhs.org/ch/indexch.html>

Switzerland Genealogy – Sources and Links <www.genealogylinks.net/europe/swi.htm>

Switzerland Genealogy – Sources and Links <genealogy.about.com/cs/switzerland/>

Switzerland Genealogy (World GenWeb) – Sources and Links: <www.rootsweb.com/~chewgw/>

SUGGESTED READING

Schrader-Muggenthaler, Cornelia. *The Swiss Emigration Book*. Apollo, PA: Closson Press, 1993.

Suess, Jared. *Handy Guide to Swiss Genealogical Records*. Logan, UT: Everton Publishers, 1978.

Wellauer, Maralyn A. *Tracing Your Swiss Roots*. Milwaukee: Wellauer, 1979.

Notes

MIGRATION TRAILS

ALABAMA-CHICKASAW TRAIL: From Montgomery, Alabama in a northwest direction to the Tombigbee River in Mississippi. Approximately 170 miles. **Map page 860.**
Alabama: Montgomery, Autauga, Chilton, Bibb, Tuscaloosa, Fayette, Lamar
Mississippi: Monroe

ALABAMA, CHOCTAW and NATCHEZ TRAIL: From Montgomery, Alabama west through Jackson, Mississippi to Vicksburg, Mississippi. Approximately 290 miles. **Map page 860.**
Alabama: Montgomery, Lowndes, Dallas, Marengo, Choctaw
Mississippi: Lauderdale, Newton, Scott, Rankin, Hinds, Warren

ALABAMA and MOBILE TRAIL: From Montgomery, Alabama southwest to Mobile, Alabama. Approximately 150 miles. **Map page 860.**
Alabama: Montgomery, Lowndes, Butler, Monroe, Clark, Baldwin

ALACHUA-TAMPA BAY TRAIL: From Alachua, Florida trailhead south to Tampa Bay, Florida. Approximately 140 miles. **Map page 860.**
Florida: Alachua, Marion, Sumter, Hernando, Pasco, Hillsborough, Pinellas

AUGUSTA and CHEROKEE TRAIL: Northwest on the west side of the Savannah River from Augusta, Georgia to where it intersects with the Lower Cherokee Traders Path, continues until it joins the trailhead at Tallulah Falls, Georgia with Coosa-Tugaloo Indian Path and Unicoi Turnpike. Approximately 100 miles. **Map page 859.**
Georgia: Richmond, Columbia, Lincoln, Wilkes, Elbert, Hart, Franklin, Stephens, Habersham

AUGUSTA-SAVANNAH TRAIL: South by southeast from Augusta, Georgia along the Savannah River on the Georgia side to Savannah, Georgia. Approximately 125 miles. **Map page 857.**
Georgia: Richmond, Burke, Screven, Effingham, Chatham

AUGUSTA-ST. AUGUSTINE TRAIL: From Augusta, Georgia south to join the Old Trading Path through several counties, then southeast to St. Augustine, Florida. Approximately 290 miles. **Map page 860.**
Georgia: Richmond, Burke, Jenkins, Candler, Evans, Taftnall, Appling, Bacon, Ware, Clinch, Echols
Florida: Hamilton, Columbia, Union, Bradford, Clay, St. Johns

BAY ROAD: From Boston to Taunton and New Bedford, Massachusetts traveling in a south direction. Approximately 60 miles. **Map page 856.**
Massachusetts: Suffolk, Norfolk, Bristol

BLACK FOX TRAIL: Northeast form the Hiwassee River in North Carolina to the Stone River in Tennessee, where it junctions with the Cisca and St. Augustine Trail. Approximately 140 miles. **Map page 859.**
North Carolina: Cherokee
Tennessee: Polk, Bradley, Hamilton, Bledsoe, Van Buren, Warren, Cannon, Rutherford

BOSTON POST ROAD: From Boston, Massachusetts to New York City. There are at least two different routes. One follows the Old Connecticut Path to Hartford, Connecticut continuing south to New Haven, then west by southwest through Bridgeport and Stamford, Connecticut to New York City. The other follows the Old Roebuck Road to Providence, Rhode Island, then continuing south by southwest, then following the coastal line across Connecticut to New Haven, west by southwest through Bridgeport and Stamford to New York City. Approximately 275 miles. **Map page 856.**

Route 1
Massachusetts: Suffolk, Middlesex, Worchester, Hampden
Connecticut: Hartford, Middlesex, New Haven, Fairfield
New York: Westchester, Bronx, New York, Kings, Queens

Route 2
Massachusetts: Suffolk, Norfolk, Bristol
Rhode Island: Providence, Kent, Washington
Connecticut: New London, Middlesex, New Haven, Fairfield
New York: Westchester, Bronx, New York, Kings, Queens

BOLIVAR and MEMPHIS TRAIL: West from Bolivar, Tennessee to Memphis and the Mississippi River. Approximately 60 miles. **Map Page 859.**
Tennessee: Hardeman, Fayette, Shelby

BRADDOCKS ROAD: West by northwest from Cumberland, Maryland along part of the Gist's Trace and on to Ft. Duquesne at Pittsburgh, Pennsylvania. Approximately 100 miles. **Map page 857.**
Maryland: Allegany, Garrett
Pennsylvania: Somerset, Fayette, Allegheny

BUFFALO TRACE: From Louisville, Kentucky west by northwest across southern Indiana to Vincennes, through Centralia, Illinois, then west by southwest to Kaskaskia, Illinois on the Missouri River. Approximately 320 Miles. **Map page 858.**
Kentucky: Jefferson
Indiana: Floyd, Harrison, Washington, Orange, Martin, Daviess, Knox
Illinois: Lawrence, Richland, Clay, Marion, Jefferson, Washington, Perry, Randolph

BURD'S ROAD: Northwest From Gist's Plantation to Ft. Burd and Brownsville on the Monongahela River, Pennsylvania. It became a link in the National Road. Approximately 35 miles. **Map page 855**.
Pennsylvania: Fayette

CAMDEN-CHARLESTON PATH: Southeast direction from Camden, to Charleston, South Carolina. Approximately 150 miles. **Map page 857**.
South Carolina: Kershaw, Sumter, Calhoun, Orangeburg, Dorchester, Charleston

CATAWBA and NORTHERN TRAIL: Starting in York County, South Carolina at the point where it intersects the lower Cherokee Traders Path running north along the Catawba River, then cross country to the Yadkin River in North Carolina to join the New River and Southern Trail. Approximately 100 miles. **Map page 857**.
South Carolina: York
North Carolina: Gaston, Lincoln, Catawba, Alexander, Wilkes

CATAWBA TRAIL: A continuation of the Old South Carolina State Road in a northwest direction across the small part of North Carolina, through the Great Smoky Mountains into the Great Valley of Tennessee, crossing the Great Indian Warpath and the Holston River at the western tip of Virginia, then to the Cumberland Gap, where it joins the Warrior's Path of Kentucky. Approximately 120 Miles. **Map page 859**.
North Carolina: Polk, Henderson, Buncombe, Madison
Tennessee: Cocke, Greene, Hamblen, Grainger, Claiborne, Hancock
Virginia: Lee

CATSKILL ROAD: West from Springfield, Massachusetts to Hudson River, then to Wattle's Ferry on the Susquehanna River. Approximately 90 miles. **Map page 856**.
Massachusetts: Hampden, Berkshire
New York: Columbia, Greene

CHARLESTON-FT. CHARLOTTE TRAIL: West by northwest from Charleston, South Carolina across southeast South Carolina to the Savannah River, where it joins the Ft. Charlotte and Cherokee Old Path. Approximately 105 miles. **Map page 855**.
South Carolina: Charleston, Dorchester, Orangeburg, Aiken, Edgefiele, McCormick

CHARLESTON-SAVANNAH TRAIL: Southwest along the cost from Charleston, South Carolina to Savannah, Georgia. Approximately 120 miles. **Map page 857**.
South Carolina: Charleston, Collection, Beaufort, Jasper
Georgia: Chatham

CHATTANOOGA-WILLSTOWN ROAD: North by northeast from the junction with the Tallapoosa Trail to Chattanooga, Tennessee. Approximately 70 miles. **Map page 860**.
Alabama: Etowah, DeKalb
Tennessee: Hamilton

CHICAGO-DUBUQUE HIGHWAY: West by northwest from Chicago, Illinois to the Mississippi River at Dubuque, Iowa. Approximately 170 miles. **Map page 858**.

Illinois: Cook, DuPage, Kane, McHenry, Boon, Winnebago, Stephenson, Jo Daviess
Iowa: Dubuque

CHICAGO-KASKASKIA ROAD: A road from Lake Michigan, south by southwest, through Peoria and Springfield, Illinois east of St. Louis to Kaskaskia on the Missouri River. Approximately 350 miles. **Map page 858**.
Illinois: Cook, Will, Grundy, Marshall, Woodford, Tazewell, Logan, Sangamon, Montgomery, Bond, Madison, St. Clair, Randolph

CHOCTAW-BAY ST. LOUIS TRAIL: From Meridian, Mississippi south by southwest to Bay St. Louis, Mississippi. Approximately 155 miles. **Map page 860**.
Mississippi: Lauderdale, Clarke, Jasper, Jones, Forest, Lamar, Pearl River, Hancock

CISCO and MIDDLE TENNESSEE TRAIL: A continuation of West Tennessee Chickasaw Trail, northeast from Bolivar, Tennessee to the Tennessee River in Benton County Tennessee. Approximately 65 miles. **Map page 859**.
Tennessee: Hardeman, Chester, Henderson, Carroll, Benton

CISCA and ST. AUGUSTINE TRAIL or NICKAJACK TRAIL: Northwest from Augusta, Georgia through Athens, Georgia and through Chattanooga to Nashville, Tennessee. Approximately 240 miles. **Map page 855**.
Georgia: Richmond, Columbia, McDuffie, Warren, Taliaferro, Greene, Morgan, Walton, Barrow, Hall, Forsyth, Cherokee, Bartow, Gordon, Whitfield, Catoosa
Tennessee: Hamilton, Marion, Franklin, Coffee, Bedford, Rutherford, Davidson

COASTAL PATH: Coastal road from Boston to Plymouth, Massachusetts, Traveling in a south by southeast direction. Approximately 35 miles. **Map page 856**.
Massachusetts: Suffolk, Norfolk, Plymouth

COOSA-TUGALOO INDIAN WARPATH: Northeast from Birmingham, Alabama through eastern Alabama then northern Georgia to the Tugaloo River between Georgia and South Carolina. Approximately 200 miles. **Map page 859**.
Alabama: Jefferson, St. Clair, Etowah, Cherokee
Georgia: Floyd, Bartow, Cherokee, Dawson, Hall, Banks, Stephens

CUMBERLAND and GREAT LAKES TRAIL: North by northwest from Nashville, Tennessee to near Lexington, Kentucky where it joins the Tennessee, Ohio, and Great Lakes Trail. Approximately 214 miles. **Map page 859**.
Tennessee: Davidson, Sumner, Macon
Kentucky: Monroe, Cumberland, Adair, Casey, Boyle, Mercer

CUMBERLAND and OHIO FALLS TRAIL: North by northwest from Nashville, Tennessee to Louisville, Kentucky on the Ohio River. Approximately 175 miles. **Map page 859**.
Tennessee: Davidson, Robertson
Kentucky: Logan, Warren, Edmonson, Hart, Hardin, Bullitt, Jefferson

CUMBERLAND ROAD: West from Brownsville, Pennsylvania to Ft. Henry at Wheeling, West Virginia.

Approximately 50 miles. **Map page 861.**
Pennsylvania: Fayette, Washington
West Virginia: Ohio

CUMBERLAND TRACE: West from Knoxville to Nashville, Tennessee. Approximately 180 miles. **Map page 859.**
Tennessee: Knox, Loudon, Roane, Cumberland, White, Putnam, Smith, Trousdale, Wilson, Davidson

DETROIT-CHICAGO ROAD: From Detroit, Michigan in a west by southwest direction to Chicago, Illinois. Approximately 275 miles. **Map page 858.**
Michigan: Wayne, Monroe, Lenawee, Hillsdale, Branch, St. Joseph, Cass, Berrien
Indiana: LaPorte, Porter, Luke
Illinois: Cook

FALL LINE or SOUTHERN ROAD: South by southwest form Philadelphia, Pennsylvania through Baltimore, Maryland, Richmond, Virginia, Raleigh and Fayetteville, North Carolina: Cheraw, Camden, and Columbia, South Carolina, and west Augusta, Georgia, passing through Macon and Columbus, Georgia to Montgomery, Alabama. Approximately 1,200 miles. **Map Page 855.**
Pennsylvania: Delaware, Philadelphia
Delaware: New Castle
Maryland: Cecil, Harford, Baltimore, Anne Arundel, Howard, Prince George's
Virginia: Arlington, Fairfax, Prince William, Stafford, Spotsylvania, Caroline, Hanover, Richmond, Henrico, Chesterfield, Dinwiddie, Brunswick
North Carolina: Warren, Franklin, Wake, Johnson, Harnett, Cumberland, Hoke, Scotland
South Carolina: Marlboro, Chesterfield, Kershaw, Richland, Lexington, Aiken
Georgia: Richmond, McDuffie, Warren, Hancock, Baldwin, Jones, Bibb, Crawford, Taylor, Talbot, Muscogee
Alabama: Russell, Lee, Macon, Montgomery

FAYETTEVILLE, ELIZABETHTOWN, and WILMINGTON TRAIL of NORTH CAROLINA: Southeast direction from Fayetteville through Elizabethville to Wilmington, North Carolina. Approximately 95 miles. **Map page 857.**
North Carolina: Cumberland, Bladen, Columbus, Brunswick

FORBIDEN PATH or CATSKILL TURNPIKE: West from Albany, New York across the state to Lake Erie, New York. Approximately 220 miles. **Map page 856.**
New York: Albany, Schoharie, Otsego, Chenango, Cortland, Tompkins, Schuyler, Steuben, Allegany, Cattaraugus, Erie

FT. CHARLOTTE and CHEROKEE OLD PATH: Northwest from Ft. Charlotte, South Carolina along the east side of the Savannah River where it intersects with the Lower Cherokee Traders Path, continuing on to the trailhead where Coosa-Tugaloo Path and Old Cherokee Path come together. Approximately 70 miles. **Map page 859.**
South Carolina: McCormick, Abbeville, Anderson, Oconee

FT. MOORE-CHARLESTON TRAIL: West by northwest from Charleston, South Carolina to Augusta, Georgia, where it joins a trailhead junction. Approximately 150 miles. **Map page 857.**

South Carolina: Charleston, Dorchester, Colleton, Bamberg, Barnwell, Aiken

GAINE'S TRACE: From the Tombigbee River in Monroe County, Mississippi northeast to the Tennessee River near Decatur, Alabama. Approximately 120 miles. **Map page 859.**
Mississippi: Monroe
Alabama: Lamar, Marion, Winston, Lawrence, Morgan

GIST'S TRACE or NEMACOLINIS PATH: West by northwest from Cumberland, Maryland to Christopher Gist's plantation between the Youghiogheny and Monongahela Rivers in Pennsylvania. Portions would become part of the Braddock's Road and the National Road. Approximately 60 miles. **Map page 857.**
Maryland: Allegany, Garrett
Pennsylvania: Somerset, Fayette

GREAT GENESEE ROAD: West from Utica, New York to the Genesee RIver and on to Fort Niagara, New York. Approximately 195 miles. **Map page 856.**
New York: Oneida, Madison, Onondaga, Cayuga, Wayne, Monroe, Genesee, Niagara

GREAT INDIAN WARPATH: Southwest direction from Philadelphia, through Lancaster, Pennsylvania; Hagerstown, Maryland; Martinsburg, West Virginia, Harrisonburg and Roanoke, Virginia, to Chattanooga, Tennessee. This great trunk trail has had many names for various sections and branches. Approximately 550 miles. **Map page 855.**
Pennsylvania: Philadelphia, Delaware, Chester, Lancaster, York, Adams
Maryland: Washington
West Virginia: Berkeley
Virginia: Frederick, Shenandoah, Rockingham, Augusta, Rockbridge, Botetourt, Roanoke, Montgomery, Pulaski, Wythe, Smyth, Washington
Tennessee: Sullivan, Washington, Greene, Cocke, Sevier, Blount, Monroe, McMinn, Bradley

GREAT SHAMOKIN PATH: Northwest from New York City through New Jersey to Susquehannah County, Pennsylvania, then west to Lake Erie. Approximately 440 miles. **Map page 856.**
New York: Kings, Queens, New York
New Jersey: Essex, Morris, Sussex
Pennsylvania: Pike, Wayne, Susquehanna, Bradford, Tioga, Potter, McKean, Warren, Erie

GREAT SOUTH TRAIL: From Nashville, Tennessee south through Huntsville and Birmingham, Alabama to Mobile, Alabama. Approximately 435 miles. **Map page 855.**
Tennessee: Davidson, Rutherford, Bedford, Lincoln
Alabama: Madison, Morgan, Cullman, Blount, Jefferson, Bibb, Perry, Marengo, Clarke, Washington, Mobile

GREAT TRADING PATH: Southwest direction from Roanoke, Virginia into northeast Tennessee (part of the Great Indian Warpath). The section from Roanoke to the Cumberland Gap was later part of the Wilderness Road. Approximately 190 miles. **Map page 857.**

Virginia: Roanoke, Montgomery, Pulaski, Wythe, Smyth, Washington
Tennessee: Sullivan, Hawkins, Hancock, Clairborne

GREAT TRAIL or GREAT PATH: From Pittsburgh, Pennsylvania in west by northwest direction to Detroit, Michigan. Approximately 270 miles. **Map page 858**.
Pennsylvania: Allegheny, Beaver, Lawrence
Ohio: Mahoning, Stark, Wayne, Ashland, Huron, Seneca, Sandusky, Ottawa, Lucas
Michigan: Monroe, Wayne

GREAT VALLEY ROAD or GREAT WAGON ROAD: Southwest direction from Hagerstown, Maryland though the Shenandoah Valley to Roanoke, Virginia (part of the Great Indian Warpath) Approximately 150 miles. **Map page 857.**
Maryland: Washington
West Virginia: Berkley
Virginia: Frederick, Shenandoah, Rockingham, Augusta, Rockbridge, Botetourt, Roanoke

GREENWOOD ROAD: Hartford, Connecticut to Albany, New York traveling in a northwest direction. Approximately 70 miles. **Map Page 856.**
Connecticut: Hartford, Litchfield
Massachusetts: Berkshire
New York: Columbia, Rensselaer, Albany

JACKSON'S MILITARY ROAD: From Nashville, Tennessee south by southwest through Florence, Alabama to Columbus, Mississippi, joining the Lake Ponchartrain Trail and ending at Lake Ponchartrain, Louisiana. Approximately 445 miles. **Map page 855.**
Tennessee: Davidson, Williamson, Maury, Giles, Lawrence
Alabama: Lauderdale, Colbert, Franklin, Marion
Mississippi: Monroe, Lowndes, Noxubee, Winston, Neshoba, Jasper, Smith, Covington, Jefferson, Davis, Marion, Walthall
Louisiana: Washington, St. Tammany

JACKSONVILLE-APALACHEE BAY TRAIL: From Jacksonville, Florida west across Florida to meet the Tugaloo-Apalachee Bay Trail, then south to Apalachee Bay. Approximately 170 miles. **Map page 860.**
Florida: Duval, Baker, Hamilton, Madison, Jefferson, Wakulla

JACKSONVILLE-ST. AUGUSTINE TRAIL: From Jacksonville, Florida south along the coastline to St. Augustine. Approximately 40 miles. **Map page 860.**
Florida: Duval, St. Johns

JONESBORO ROAD: Staring on the coast at the New Bern, North Carolina running in a northwest direction above Raleigh through Greensboro and Salem to the Catawba River, there joining Rutherford's War Trace to Asheville, then along the Broad River into Tennessee on the Catawba Trail to Knoxville, Tennessee. Approximately 345 miles. **Map page 857.**
North Carolina: Craven, Lenoir, Greene, Wilson, Nash, Durham, Orange, Allamance, Guilford, Forsyth, Davie, Iredell, Alexander, Catawba, Burke, McDowell, Buncombe, Madison
Tennessee: Cocke, Jefferson, Knox

KANAWHA BRANCH of the GREAT INDIAN WARPATH: Starting at Chillicothe, Ohio in a southeast direction crossing the Ohio River at Gallipolis, Ohio and following the Kanawha River past Charlestown, West Virginia, then following the New River of the Chiswets, and joining the main path. Approximately 205 miles. **Map page 857.**
Ohio: Ross, Jackson, Gallia
West Virginia: Mason, Putnam, Kanawha, Fayette, Raleigh, Summers, Mercer
Virginia: Giles, Pulaski

KELLOG TRAIL: A continuation of the Pecatonica Trail in a southeast direction from the Illinois River in Putnam County, Illinois to Terre Haute, Indiana. Approximately 160 miles. **Map page 858**.
Illinois: Putnam, Marshall, LaSalle, Livingston, Ford, Iroquois, Vermillion
Indiana: Parke, Vigo

KENNEBUNK ROAD: Coastal road from Boston, Massachusetts through Kennebunk and Portland to Augusta, Maine traveling in a north by northeast direction. Approximately 180 miles. **Map page 856**.
Massachusetts: Suffolk, Middlesex, Essex
New Hampshire: Rockingham
Maine: York, Cumberland, Sagadahoc, Kennebec

KITTANNING PATH: West by northwest form the Tuscarora Path through Altoona and Kittanning, to the Allegheny River, all in Pennsylvania. Approximately 115 miles. **Map page 856.**
Pennsylvania: Mifflin, Huntingdon, Blair, Cambria, Indiana, Armstrong

LAFAYETTE ROAD: South by southeast from Lafayette, Indiana to the Ohio River on Crawford County, Indiana. Approximately 170 miles. **Map page 858.**
Indiana: Tippecanoe, Montgomery, Putnam, Owen, Monroe, Lawrence, Orange, Crawford

LAKE CHAMPLAIN TRAIL: A continuation of the Hudson River Path from Albany, New York to the St. Lawrence River in Canada. Approximately 200 miles. **Map page 856.**
New York: Albany, Saratoga, Warren, Essex, Clinton
Canada: Quebec

LAKE PONCHARTRAIN TRAIL: Southeast from Wilkinson, Mississippi to Lake Pontchartrain, then northeast until the trail joins Jackson's Military Road. Approximately 80 miles. **Map page 860.**
Mississippi: Wilkinson
Louisiana: East Feliciana, St. Helena, Livingston, Tangipahoa, St. Tammany, Washington

LAKE TRAIL or LAKE SHORE PATH: West by southwest from Buffalo, New York along the shore of Lake Erie to Cleveland, Ohio, continuing west to Sandusky County, Ohio, where it joins and becomes part of the Great Trail or Great Path. Approximately 260 miles. **Map page 858**.
New York: Erie, Chautauqua
Pennsylvania: Erie
Ohio: Ashtabula, Lake, Cuyahoga, Lorain, Erie, Sandusky

LEHIGH and LACKAWANNA PATHS: South from the Forbidden Path or Catskill Turnpike in Otsego County, New York,

through Scranton, Pennsylvania to Northampton County, where it joins the Minsi Path. Approximately 90 miles. **Map page 856.**
New York: Otsego, Delaware
Pennsylvania: Wayne, Susquehanna, Lackawanna, Monroe, Northampton

LOWER CHEROKEE TRADERS' PATH: West by southwest from Charlotte, North Carolina across the northern section of South Carolina to the Tugaloo River, where it joins the Tugaloo-Apalachee Bay Trail. Approximately 215 miles. **Map page 859.**
South Carolina: York, Cherokee, Spartanburg, Greenville, Anderson, Oconee
North Carolina: Mecklenburg, Gaston

LOWER CREEK TRADING POST: West by southwest form Augusta, Georgia to Macon, Georgia, then west to Birmingham, Alabama; then west by northwest to the Tombigbee River in eastern Mississippi, continuing west by northwest to Oxford, Mississippi. Then west by southwest through Clarksdale to the Mississippi River. Approximately 540 miles. **Map page 855.**
Georgia: Richmond, McDuffie, Warren, Hancock, Baldwin, Jones, Bibb, Monroe, Upson, Meriwether, Troup
Alabama: Randolph, Clay, Talladega, Shelby, Jefferson, Walker, Fayette, Lamar
Mississippi: Monroe, Lee, Pontotoc, Lafayette, Panola, Quitman, Coahoma

LOWER WARPATH or WEST TENNESSEE TRAIL: West from Nashville, Tennessee to the Tennessee River. As the trail continues beyond the Tennessee River, it becomes the Mississippi and Tennessee River Trail. Approximately 60 miles. **Map page 859.**
Tennessee: Davidson, Cheatham, Dickson, Humphreys

MACON and MONTGOMERY TRAIL: From Montgomery, Alabama east through Columbus then east by northeast to Macon, Georgia. Approximately 120 miles. **Map page 860.**
Alabama: Montgomery, Macon, Russell, Lee
Georgia: Muskogee, Talbot, Taylor, Crawford, Bibb

MARYLAND ROAD: West from Baltimore, to Cumberland, Maryland. This was the first section of the National Road. Approximately 110 miles. **Map Page 857.**
Maryland: Baltimore, Carroll, Fredrick, Washington, Allegany

MAYSVILLE TURNPIKE: A continuation of Zane's Trace form Maysville, Kentucky southwest to Elizabethtown, Kentucky. Approximately 165 miles. **Map page 858.**
Kentucky: Mason, Robertson, Nicholas, Bourbon, Fayette, Woodford, Anderson, Washington, Nelson, Hardin.

MEMPHIS, PONTOTOC and MOBILE TRAIL: From Memphis, Tennessee south by southeast through Pontotoc, Mississippi, then southwest to Grenada, then south by southeast to Mobile, Alabama. Approximately 360 miles. **Map page 855.**
Tennessee: Shelby
Mississippi: DeSoto, Marshall, Union, Pontotoc, Calhoun, Grenada, Montgomery, Attala, Leake, Neshoba, Newton, Jasper, Clarke, Wayne, Greene
Alabama: Washington, Mobile

MIAMI PATH: North form Cincinnati, Ohio through western Ohio to Defiance, Ohio, where the trail joins the Vincennes and Indianapolis Road. Approximately 180 miles. **Map page 858.**
Ohio: Hamilton, Butler, Preble, Drake, Mercer, Van Wert, Paulding, Defiance

MICHIGAN ROAD: Straight south from South Bend, Indiana to Indianapolis, Indiana. Approximately 140 miles. **Map Page 858.**
Indiana: St. Joseph, Marshall, Fulton, Miami, Howard, Tipton, Hamilton, Marion

MIDDLE CREEK TRADING PATH: West by southwest from McCormack, South Carolina across Georgia to eastern Alabama. Approximately 230 miles. **Map page 855.**
South Carolina: McCormack
Georgia: Lincoln, Wilkes, Taliaferro, Greene, Morgan, Jasper, Buffs, Spalding, Pike, Meriwether, Troup
Alabama: Chambers

MIHOAUKEE TRAIL: North from Chicago, Illinois along the shore of Lake Michigan to Milwaukee, Wisconsin, then continuing north by northwest to Fond du Lac, Wisconsin. Approximately 110 miles. **Map page 858.**
Illinois: Cook. Lake
Wisconsin: Kenosha, Racine, Milwaukee, Washington, Fond du Lac

MINSI PATH: South by southwest from Kingston, New York to Port Jervis, then on the west side of the Delaware River to Philadelphia, Pennsylvania. Approximately 110 miles. **Map page 856.**
New York: Ulster, Sullivan, Orange
Pennsylvania: Pike, Monroe, Northampton, Bucks, Montgomery, Philadelphia

MISSISSIPPI and TENNESSEE RIVER TRAIL: West from the Tennessee River to the Mississippi River. Approximately 90 miles. **Map page 859.**
Tennessee: Benton, Carroll, Gibson, Dyer

MOBILE and NATCHEZ TRAIL: From Mobile, Alabama across lower Mississippi in a west by northwest direction to Natchez, Mississippi. Approximately 220 miles. **Map page 860.**
Alabama: Mobile
Mississippi: George, Perry, Forest, Lamar, Marion, Walthall, Pike, Amite, Franklin, Adams

MOHAWK or IROQUOIS TRAIL: West by northwest from Albany, New York along the Mohawk River Utica and Rome, diverging with a branch to Fort Oswego on Lake Ontario. Approximately 190 miles. **Map page 856.**
New York: Albany, Schenectady, Herkimer, Oneida, Oswego

NASHVILLE ROAD: West by northwest from Knoxville, Tennessee to near Monterey, where it joins the Cumberland Trace. Approximately 86 miles. **Map page 859.**
Tennessee: Knox, Anderson, Morgan, Fentress, Overton, Putnam

NASHVILLE-SALINE RIVER TRAIL: Northwest from Nashville, Tennessee through the small part of Kentucky, crossing the Ohio River near Paducah into Illinois, then to

Allegany, Garrett
Pennsylvania: Somerset, Fayette, Washington
West Virginia: Ohio
Ohio: Belmont, Guernsey, Muskingum. Licking, Franklin, Madison, Clark, Montgomery, Preble
Indiana: Wayne, Henry, Hancock, Marion, Hendricks, Morgan, Putnam, Clay, Vigo
Illinois: Clark, Cumberland, Jasper, Effingham, Fayette, Bond, Madison
Missouri: St. Louis

TOMBIGBEE and ARKANSAS RIVER TRAIL: West from the Tombigbee River in Monroe County, Mississippi across the state to the mouth of the Arkansas River. Approximately 180 miles. **Map page 860.**
Mississippi: Monroe, Chickasaw, Calhoun, Yalobusha, Tallahatchie, Sunflower, Bolivar

TUGALOO – APALACHEE BAY TRAIL: South by southwest from the Tugaloo River in Georgia across the Florida panhandle to the Gulf of Mexico. Approximately 310 miles. **Map page 855.**
Georgia: Stephens, Franklin, Madison, Jackson, Clarke, Oconee, Walton, Newton, Buffs, Lamar, Upson, Taylor, Schley, Sumter, Lee, Dougherty, Baker, Mitchell, Grady
Florida: Leon, Wakulla

TUSCARORA PATH: Southwest from Scranton, Pennsylvania to Bedford, Pennsylvania. Approximately 215 miles. **Map page 856**.
Pennsylvania: Lackawanna, Luzerne, Columbia, Northumberland, Snyder, Mifflin, Huntingdon, Bedford

TUSCARORA PATH: Southwest from Scranto, Pennsylvania to Bedford, Pennsylvania. Approximately 106 miles. **Map Page 856.**
New York: Kings, Queens, New York
New Jersey: Hudson, Union, Middlesex, Mercer, Burlington
Pennsylvania: Philadelphia

UNICOI TURNPIKE: Northwest from the trailhead at Tallulah Falls, to the trailhead in North Carolina, intersects with Black Fox Trail and Rutherford War Trace on the Hiwassee River. Approximately 60 miles. **Map page 859.**
Georgia: Rabun, Towns
North Carolina: Clay, Cherokee

UPPER CREEKS-PENSCOLA TRAIL: From Montgomery, Alabama in a southwesterly direction around the boundary of the panhandle of Florida, then turning southeast to Pensacola Bay, Florida. Approximately 235 miles. **Map page 860.**
Alabama: Montgomery, Lowndes, Butler, Conecuh, Escambia, Baldwin
Florida: Escambia

VENANGO PATH: North from Kittanning, to the Great Shamokin Path, Joining together near Corry, Pennsylvania, then turning west to Erie, Pennsylvania. Approximately 110 miles. **Map page 858.**
Pennsylvania: Butler, Venango, Forest, Warren, Erie.

VINCENNES AND INDIANAPOLIS ROAD: South by southwest from Detroit, Michigan through Defiance, Ohio, Ft. Wayne and Indianapolis to Vincennes, Indiana. Approximately 360 miles. **Map page 858.**
Michigan: Wayne, Monroe
Ohio: Lucas, Wood, Henry, Defiance, Paulding
Indiana: Allen, Wells, Huntington, Grant, Madison, Hamilton, Marion, Morgan, Monroe, Greene, Knox

WARRIORS PATH of KENTUCKY: A continuation of the Scioto Trail in a southern direction from the Ohio River at Portsmouth, Ohio, to the Cumberland Gap, Kentucky. Approximately 190 miles. **Map page 859.**
Kentucky: Greenup, Carter, Rowan, Bath, Montgomery, Powell, Estell, Jackson, Laurel, Knox, Bell

WEST TENNESSEE CHICKASAW TRAIL: South from Bolivar, Tennessee to the junction point with Natchez Trace Trail in Mississippi. Approximately 160 miles. **Map page 859.**
Tennessee: Hardeman
Mississippi: Tippah, Union, Pontotoc

WILDERNESS ROAD: Cleared by Daniel Boone and 30 ax-men, followed the Great Indian Warpath on the North Fork of the Holston River on the Virginia-Tennessee border, west to the Cumberland Gap, then taking the Warriors Path into Kentucky. From there continuing northwest through Harrodsburg, on to Louisville, Kentucky. Approximately 180 miles. **Map page 859**.
Tennessee: Sullivan, Hawkins, Hancock, Clairborne
Kentucky: Bell, Knox, Laurel, Rockcastle, Lincoln, Boyle, Mercer, Washington, Spencer, Jefferson

WIMINGTON, HIGHPOINT and NORTHERN TRAIL: Starting at Wilmington, North Carolina running in a northwest direction to the Greensboro aea, then north into Virginia where it joins the Great Indian Warpath near Roanoke, Virginia. Approximately 255 miles. **Map page 857**.
North Carolina: Brunswick, Columbus, Robeson, Scotland, Richmond, Moore, Randolph, Guilford, Rockingham
Virginia: Henry, Franklin, Roanoke

ZANE'S TRACE: In general southwest direction from Wheeling, West Virginia through Chillicothe, Ohio to Maysville, Kentucky. Approximately 255 miles. **Map page 858.**
West Virginia: Ohio
Ohio: Belmont, Guernsey, Muskingum, Perry, Fairfield, Hocking, Ross, Pike, Adams, Brown
Kentucky: Maso

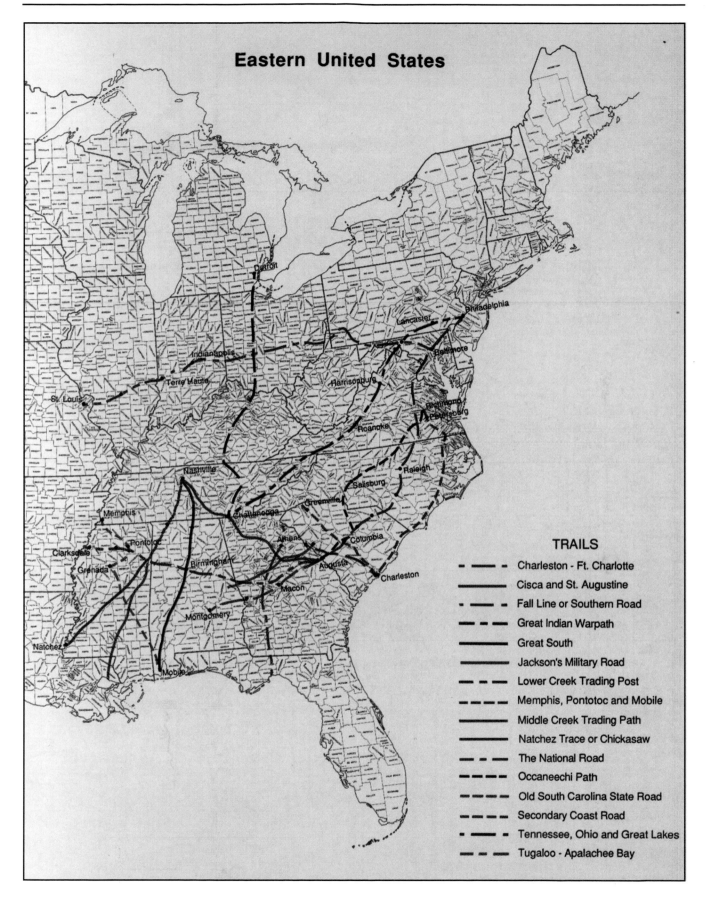

Eastern United States

TRAILS

- – · – · – Charleston - Ft. Charlotte
- ———— Cisca and St. Augustine
- – · – · – Fall Line or Southern Road
- – – – – Great Indian Warpath
- ———— Great South
- ———— Jackson's Military Road
- – – – – Lower Creek Trading Post
- – – – – Memphis, Pontotoc and Mobile
- ———— Middle Creek Trading Path
- ———— Natchez Trace or Chickasaw
- – – – The National Road
- – – – – Occaneechi Path
- – – – – Old South Carolina State Road
- – – – – Secondary Coast Road
- – · – · – Tennessee, Ohio and Great Lakes
- – – – Tugaloo - Apalachee Bay

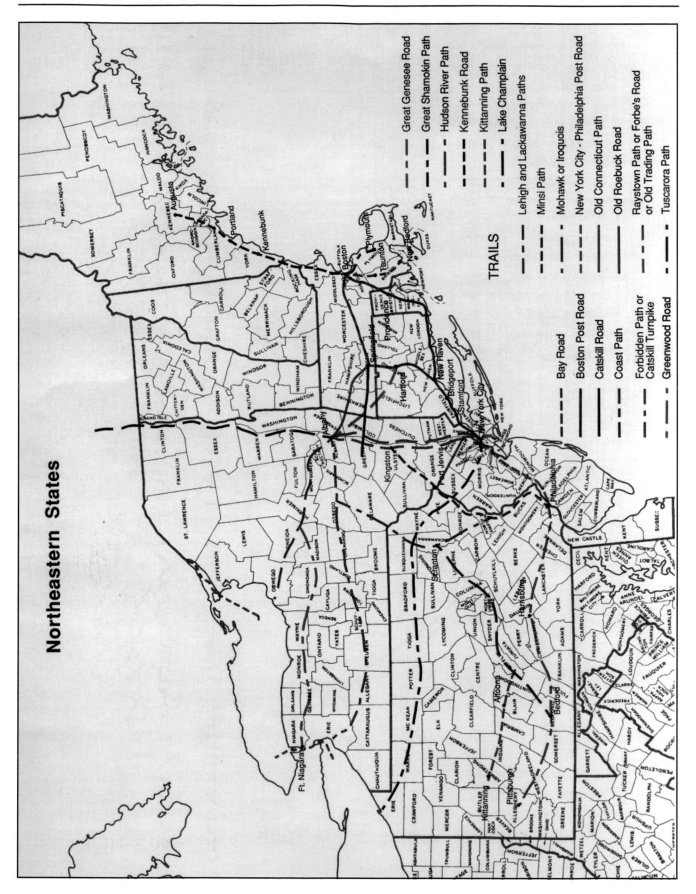

Northeastern States

TRAILS

- – – – Great Genesee Road
- – – – Great Shamokin Path
- – – – Hudson River Path
- – – – Kennebunk Road
- – – – Kittanning Path
- – – – Lake Champlain
- – – – Lehigh and Lackawanna Paths
- – – – Minsi Path
- – – – Mohawk or Iroquois
- – – – New York City - Philadelphia Post Road
- – – – Old Connecticut Path
- – – – Old Roebuck Road
- – – – Raystown Path or Forbe's Road or Old Trading Path
- – – – Tuscarora Path
- – – – Bay Road
- – – – Boston Post Road
- – – – Catskill Road
- – – – Coast Path
- – – – Forbidden Path or Catskill Turnpike
- – – – Greenwood Road

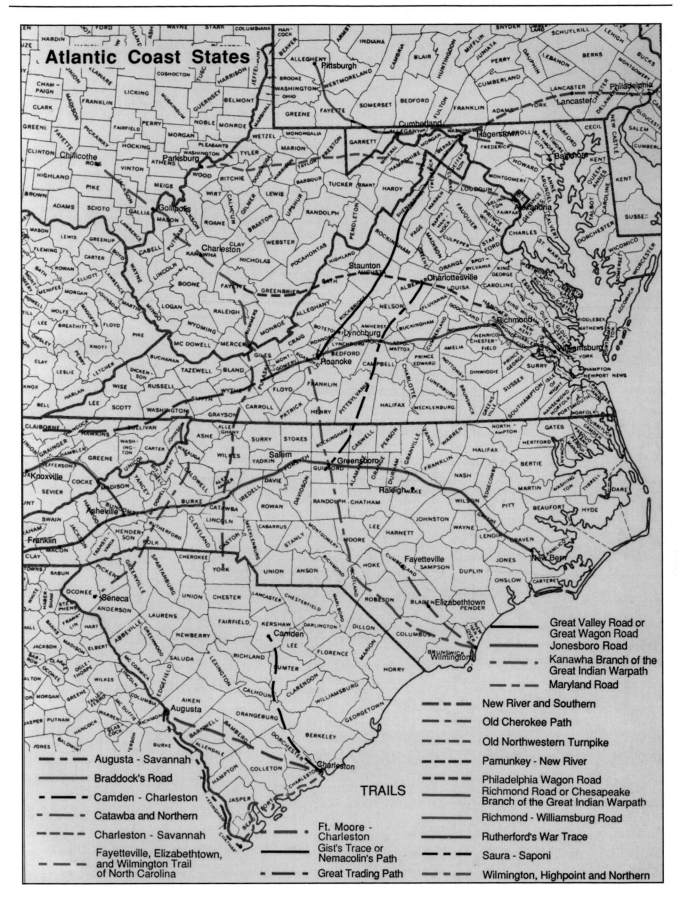

Atlantic Coast States

TRAILS

Great Valley Road or Great Wagon Road
Jonesboro Road
Kanawha Branch of the Great Indian Warpath
Maryland Road
New River and Southern
Old Cherokee Path
Old Northwestern Turnpike
Pamunkey - New River
Philadelphia Wagon Road
Richmond Road or Chesapeake Branch of the Great Indian Warpath
Richmond - Williamsburg Road
Rutherford's War Trace
Saura - Saponi
Wilmington, Highpoint and Northern

Augusta - Savannah
Braddock's Road
Camden - Charleston
Catawba and Northern
Charleston - Savannah
Fayetteville, Elizabethtown, and Wilmington Trail of North Carolina
Ft. Moore - Charleston
Gist's Trace or Nemacolin's Path
Great Trading Path

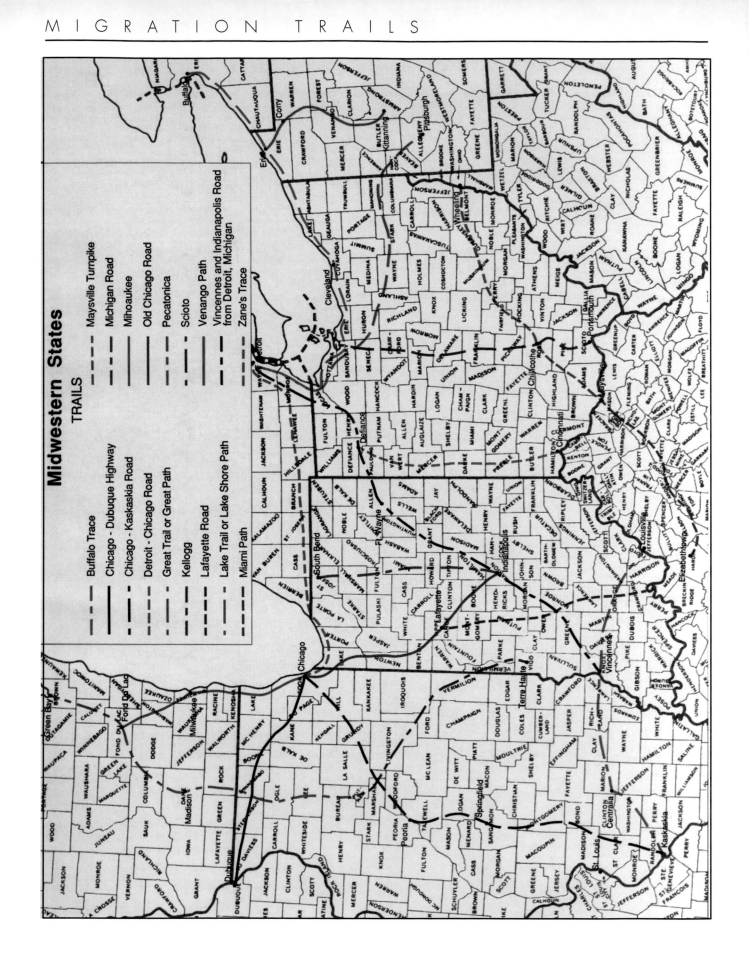

Midwestern States
TRAILS

Buffalo Trace	Maysville Turnpike
Chicago - Dubuque Highway	Michigan Road
Chicago - Kaskaskia Road	Mihoaukee
Detroit - Chicago Road	Old Chicago Road
Great Trail or Great Path	Pecatonica
Kellogg	Scioto
Lafayette Road	Venango Path
Lake Trail or Lake Shore Path	Vincennes and Indianapolis Road from Detroit, Michigan
Miami Path	Zane's Trace

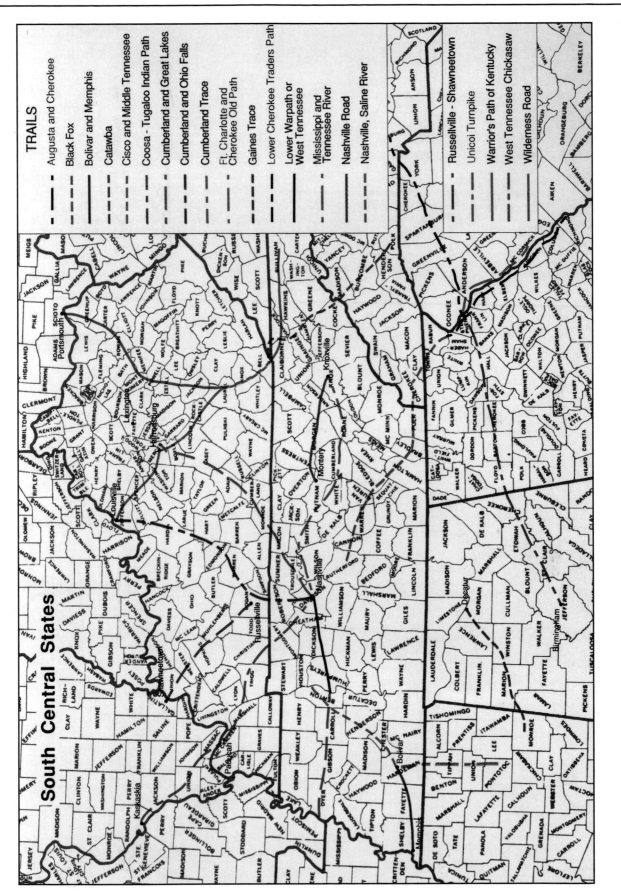

TRAILS

Augusta and Cherokee

Black Fox

Bolivar and Memphis

Catawba

Cisco and Middle Tennessee

Coosa - Tugaloo Indian Path

Cumberland and Great Lakes

Cumberland and Ohio Falls

Cumberland Trace

Ft. Charlotte and Cherokee Old Path

Gaines Trace

Lower Cherokee Traders Path

Lower Warpath or West Tennessee

Mississippi and Tennessee River

Nashville Road

Nashville, Saline River

Russellville - Shawneetown

Unicoi Turnpike

Warrior's Path of Kentucky

West Tennessee Chickasaw

Wilderness Road

South Central States

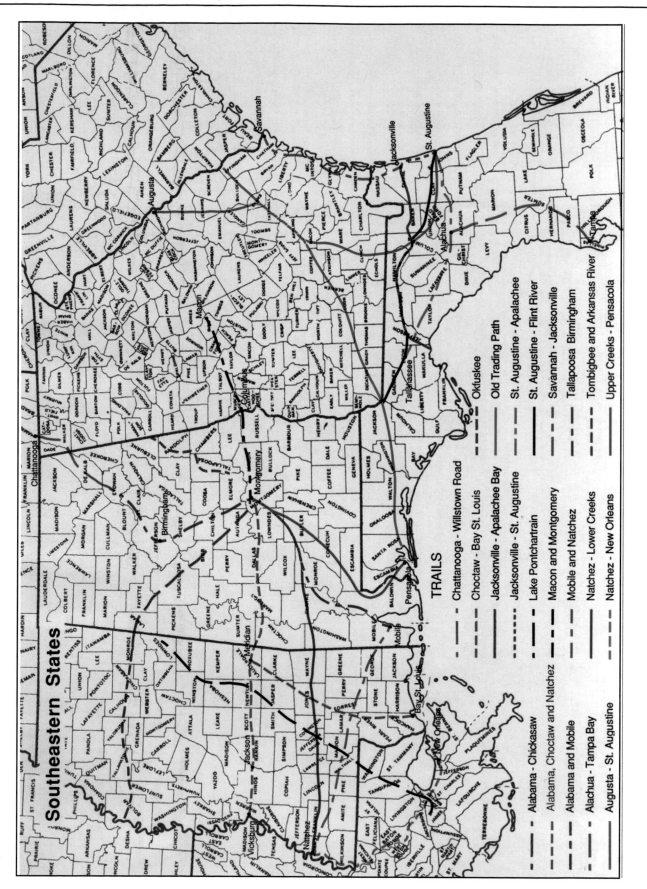

Southeastern States

TRAILS

- - - Chattanooga - Willstown Road
- - - Choctaw - Bay St. Louis
——— Jacksonville - Apalachee Bay
——— Jacksonville - St. Augustine
- - - Lake Pontchartrain
- - - Macon and Montgomery
- - - Mobile and Natchez
——— Natchez - Lower Creeks
- - - Natchez - New Orleans

- - - Oktuskee
- - - Old Trading Path
——— St. Augustine - Apalachee
——— St. Augustine - Flint River
——— Savannah - Jacksonville
——— Tallapoosa - Birmingham
- - - Tombigbee and Arkansas River
- - - Upper Creeks - Pensacola

- - - Alabama - Chickasaw
- - - Alabama, Choctaw and Natchez
- - - Alabama and Mobile
- - - Alachua - Tampa Bay
——— Augusta - St. Augustine

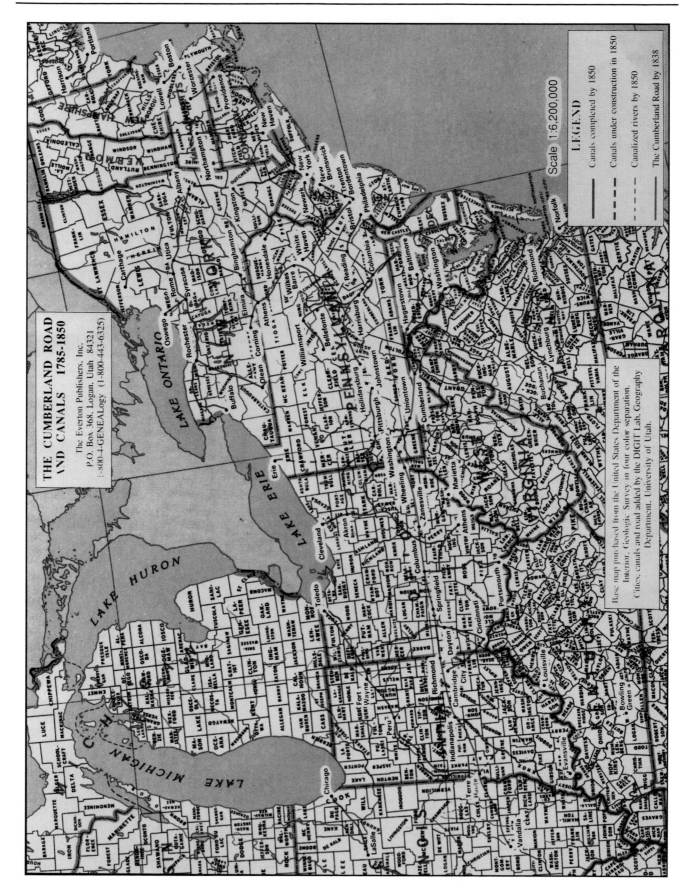

Scale 1:6,200,000

LEGEND

————	Canals completed by 1850
- - - -	Canals under construction in 1850
· · · ·	Canalized rivers by 1850
————	The Cumberland Road by 1838

THE CUMBERLAND ROAD AND CANALS 1785-1850

The Everton Publishers, Inc.
P.O. Box 368, Logan, Utah 84321
1-800-4-GENEALogy (1-800-443-6325)

Base map purchased from the United States Department of the Interior, Geologic Survey in four color separation. Cities, canals and road added by the DIGIT Lab, Geography Department, University of Utah.

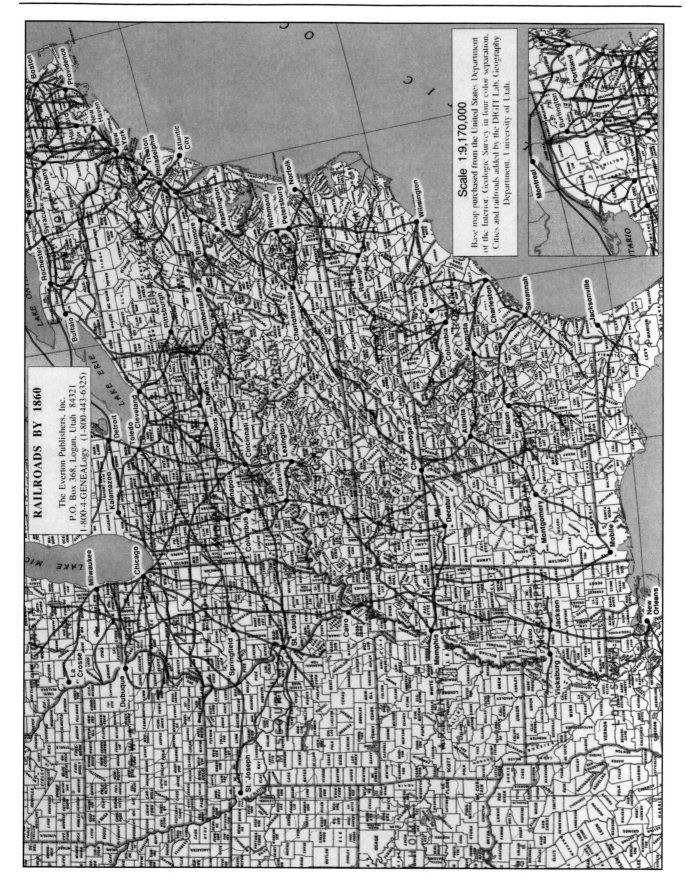

Scale 1:9,170,000

Base map purchased from the United States Department of the Interior, Geologic Survey in four color separation. Cities and railroads added by the DIGIT Lab, Geography Department, University of Utah.

RAILROADS BY 1860

The Everton Publishers, Inc.
P.O. Box 368, Logan, Utah 84321
1-800-4-GENEALogy (1-800-443-6325)

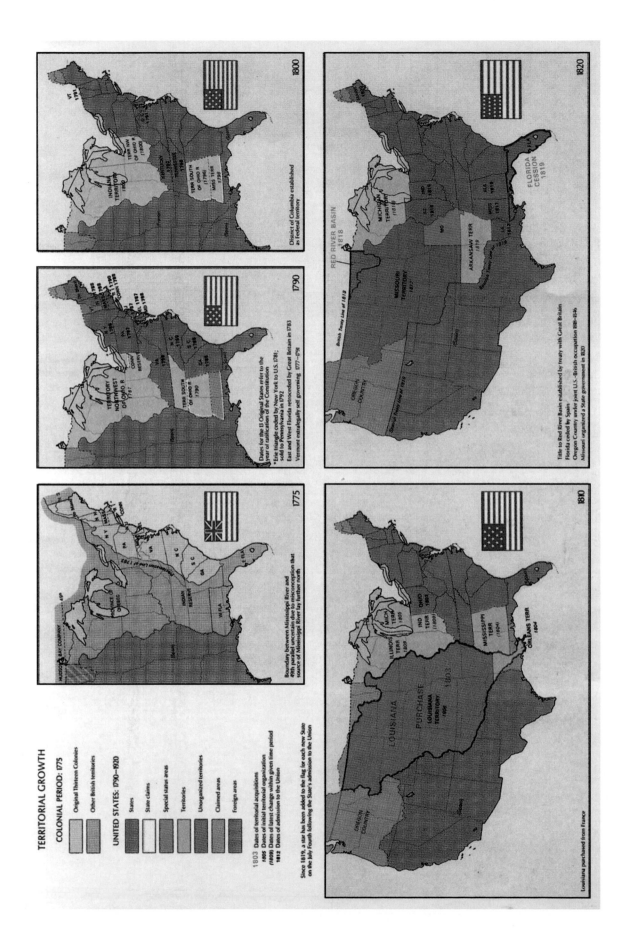

TERRITORIAL GROWTH

COLONIAL PERIOD: 1775

Original Thirteen Colonies
Other British territories

UNITED STATES: 1790–1920

States
State claims
Special status areas
Territories
Unorganized territories
Claimed areas
Foreign areas

1803 Dates of territorial acquisitions
1805 Dates of initial territorial organization
(1809) Dates of latest change within given time period
1812 Dates of admission to the Union

Since 1819, a star has been added to the flag for each new State on the July Fourth following the State's admission to the Union

1775
Boundary between Mississippi River and 49th parallel uncertain due to misconception that source of Mississippi River lay further north

1790
Dates for the 13 Original States refer to the year of ratification of the Constitution

*Erie triangle ceded by New York to U.S. 1781; sold to Pennsylvania in 1792

East and West Florida retroceded by Great Britain in 1783

Vermont extralegally self governing 1777–1791

1800
District of Columbia established as Federal territory

1810
Louisiana purchased from France

1820
Title to Red River Basin established by treaty with Great Britain
Florida ceded by Spain
Oregon Country under joint U.S.–British occupation 1818–1846
Missouri organized a State government in 1820

Territorial Growth, 1830–1860

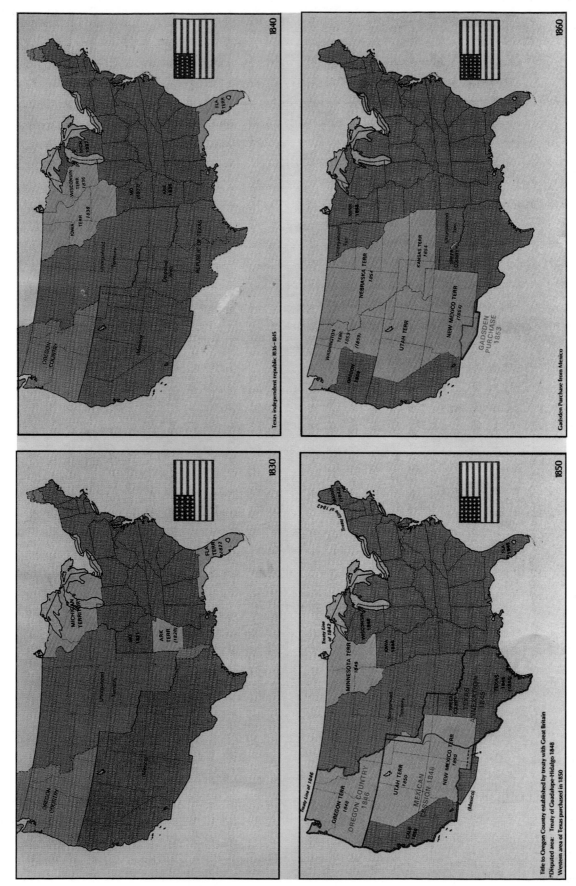

1840

Texas independent republic 1836–1845

1860

Gadsden Purchase from Mexico

1830

1850

Title to Oregon Country established by treaty with Great Britain
*Disputed area: Treaty of Guadalupe-Hidalgo 1848
Western area of Texas purchased in 1850

A, Oklahoma, 557
Abbeville, South Carolina, 611
Acadia County, Louisiana, 289
Acadia Parish, Louisiana, 289
Accawmack, Virginia, 710
Accomack, Virginia, 710
Ada, Idaho, 177
Adair, Iowa, 230
Adair, Kentucky, 268
Adair, Missouri, 397
Adair, Oklahoma, 557
Adams, Colorado, 97
Adams, Idaho, 177
Adams, Illinois, 192
Adams, Indiana, 211
Adams, Iowa, 230
Adams, Mississippi, 378
Adams, Nebraska, 428
Adams, North Dakota, 522
Adams, Ohio, 540
Adams, Pennsylvania, 588
Adams, Washington, 732
Adams, Wisconsin, 755
Addison, Vermont, 698
Aiken, South Carolina, 611
Aishcum, Michigan, 343
Aitkin, Minnesota, 362
Alachua, Florida, 133
Alamance, North Carolina, 506
Alameda, California, 84
Alamosa, Colorado, 97
Albany, New York, 488
Albany, Wyoming, 766
Albemarle, North Carolina, 506
Albemarle, Virginia, 710
Alcona, Michigan, 343
Alcorn, Mississippi, 378
Aleutians East Borough, Alaska, 48
Aleutians West Census Area, Alaska, 48
Alexander, Illinois, 192
Alexander, North Carolina, 506
Alexandria (Ind. City), Virginia, 710
Alfalfa, Oklahoma, 557
Alger, Michigan, 343
Allamakee, Iowa, 230
Allegan, Michigan, 343
Allegany, Maryland, 317
Allegany, New York, 488
Alleghany, North Carolina, 506
Alleghany, Virginia, 710
Allegheny, Pennsylvania, 588
Allen, Indiana, 211
Allen, Kansas, 248
Allen, Kentucky, 268
Allen, Missouri, 397
Allen, Ohio, 540
Allen Parish, Louisiana, 289
Allendale, South Carolina, 611
Allred, North Dakota, 522
Alpena, Michigan, 343

Alpine, California, 84
Alturas, Idaho, 177
Amador, California, 84
Amelia, Virginia, 710
Amherst, Virginia, 710
Amite, Mississippi, 378
Anamickee, Michigan, 343
Anchorage Borough, Alaska, 48
Anderson, Kansas, 248
Anderson, Kentucky, 268
Anderson, South Carolina, 611
Anderson, Tennessee, 638
Anderson, Texas, 658
Andrew, Missouri, 397
Andrews, Texas, 658
Androscoggin, Maine, 304
Andy Johnson, Minnesota, 362
Angelina, Texas, 658
Anne Arundel, Maryland, 317
Anoka, Minnesota, 362
Anson, North Carolina, 506
Antelope, Nebraska, 428
Antrim, Michigan, 343
Apache, Arizona, 56
Appanoose, Iowa, 230
Appling, Georgia, 151
Appomattox, Virginia, 710
Aransas, Texas, 658
Arapahoe, Colorado, 97
Arapahoe, Kansas, 248
Archdale, North Carolina, 506
Archer, Texas, 658
Archuleta, Colorado, 97
Arenac, Michigan, 343
Arenac, old, Michigan, 343
Arkansas, Arkansas, 66
Arkansas, Missouri, 397
Arlington, Virginia, 710
Armstrong, Pennsylvania, 588
Armstrong, South Dakota, 622
Armstrong, Texas, 658
Armstrong, old, South Dakota, 622
Aroostook, Maine, 304
Arthur, Nebraska, 428
Ascension Parish, Louisiana, 289
Ashe, North Carolina, 506
Ashland, Ohio, 540
Ashland, Wisconsin, 755
Ashley, Arkansas, 66
Ashley, Missouri, 397
Ashmore, South Dakota, 622
Ashtabula, Ohio, 540
Asotin, Washington, 732
Assumption Parish, Louisiana, 289
Atascosa, Texas, 658
Atchison, Kansas, 248
Atchison, Missouri, 397
Athens, Ohio, 540
Atkinson, Georgia, 151
Atlantic, New Jersey, 464
Atoka, Oklahoma, 557

Attakapas County, Louisiana, 289
Attala, Mississippi, 378
Audrain, Missouri, 397
Audubon, Iowa, 230
Auglaize, Ohio, 540
Augusta, Virginia, 710
Aurora, South Dakota, 622
Austin, Texas, 658
Autauga, Alabama, 35
Avery, North Carolina, 506
Avoyelles Parish, Louisiana, 289
B, Oklahoma, 557
Baca, Colorado, 97
Bacon, Georgia, 151
Bad Ax, Wisconsin, 755
Bailey, Texas, 658
Bainbridge, Mississippi, 378
Baine, Alabama, 35
Baker, Alabama, 35
Baker, Florida, 133
Baker, Georgia, 151
Baker, Oregon, 572
Baldwin, Alabama, 35
Baldwin, Georgia, 151
Ballard, Kentucky, 268
Baltimore, Maryland, 317
Baltimore City, Maryland, 317
Bamberg, South Carolina, 611
Bancroft, Iowa, 230
Bandera, Texas, 658
Banks, Georgia, 151
Banner, Nebraska, 428
Bannock, Idaho, 177
Baraga, Michigan, 343
Barber, Kansas, 248
Barbour, Alabama, 35
Barbour, Virginia, 710
Barbour, West Virginia, 743
Barnes, North Dakota, 522
Barnstable, Massachusetts, 329
Barnwell, South Carolina, 611
Barren, Kentucky, 268
Barron, Wisconsin, 755
Barrow, Georgia, 151
Barry, Michigan, 343
Barry, Missouri, 397
Bartholomew, Indiana, 211
Barton, Kansas, 248
Barton, Missouri, 397
Bartow, Georgia, 151
Bastrop, Texas, 658
Bates, Missouri, 397
Bath, Kentucky, 268
Bath, North Carolina, 506
Bath, Virginia, 710
Baton Rouge Parish, Louisiana, 289
Baxter, Arkansas, 66
Bay, Florida, 133
Bay, Michigan, 343
Bayfield, Wisconsin, 755
Baylor, Texas, 658
Beadle, South Dakota, 622

Beadle, old, South Dakota, 622
Bear Lake, Idaho, 177
Beaufort, North Carolina, 506
Beaufort, South Carolina, 611
Beauregard Parish, Louisiana, 289
Beaver, Oklahoma, 557
Beaver, Pennsylvania, 588
Beaver, Utah, 686
Beaverhead, Montana, 415
Becker, Minnesota, 362
Beckham, Oklahoma, 557
Bedford, Pennsylvania, 588
Bedford, Tennessee, 638
Bedford, Virginia, 710
Bedford (Ind. City), Virginia, 710
Bee, Texas, 658
Belknap, New Hampshire, 452
Bell, Kentucky, 268
Bell, Texas, 659
Belmont, Ohio, 540
Beltrami, Minnesota, 362
Ben Hill, Georgia, 151
Benewah, Idaho, 177
Bennett, South Dakota, 622
Bennington, Vermont, 698
Benson, North Dakota, 522
Bent, Colorado, 97
Benton, Alabama, 35
Benton, Arkansas, 66
Benton, Florida, 133
Benton, Indiana, 211
Benton, Iowa, 230
Benton, Minnesota, 362
Benton, Mississippi, 378
Benton, Missouri, 397
Benton, Oregon, 572
Benton, Tennessee, 638
Benton, Washington, 732
Benzie, Michigan, 343
Bergen, New Jersey, 464
Berkeley, North Carolina, 506
Berkeley, South Carolina, 611
Berkeley, Virginia, 710
Berkeley, West Virginia, 743
Berkeley, old, South Carolina, 611
Berks, Pennsylvania, 588
Berkshire, Massachusetts, 329
Bernalillo, New Mexico, 473
Berrien, Georgia, 151
Berrien, Michigan, 344
Bertie, North Carolina, 506
Bethel Census Area, Alaska, 48
Bexar, Texas, 659
Bibb, Alabama, 35
Bibb, Georgia, 151
Bienville Parish, Louisiana, 289
Big Horn, Montana, 415
Big Horn, Wyoming, 766
Big Sioux, Minnesota, 362
Big Sioux, South Dakota, 622
Big Stone, Minnesota, 362

Howard, Iowa, 234
Howard, Kansas, 251
Howard, Maryland, 318
Howard, Missouri, 401
Howard, Nebraska, 431
Howard, North Dakota, 524
Howard, Texas, 666
Howell, Missouri, 401
Hubbard, Minnesota, 364
Hudson, New Jersey, 464
Hudspeth, Texas, 666
Huerfano, Colorado, 99
Hughes, Oklahoma, 559
Hughes, South Dakota, 625
Humboldt, California, 84
Humboldt, Iowa, 234
Humboldt, Nevada, 442
Humboldt, Utah, 686
Humboldt, old, Iowa, 234
Humphreys, Mississippi, 379
Humphreys, Tennessee, 641
Hunt, Texas, 666
Hunter, Kansas, 251
Hunterdon, New Jersey, 464
Huntingdon, Pennsylvania, 590
Huntington, Indiana, 213
Huron, Michigan, 346
Huron, Ohio, 543
Hutchinson, South Dakota, 625
Hutchinson, Texas, 666
Hyde, North Carolina, 509
Hyde, South Dakota, 625
I, Oklahoma, 559
Iberia Parish, Louisiana, 290
Iberville Parish, Louisiana, 290
Ida, Iowa, 234
Idaho, Idaho, 178
Illinois, Virginia, 715
Imperial, California, 84
Independence, Arkansas, 68
Indian River, Florida, 135
Indiana, Pennsylvania, 590
Ingham, Michigan, 346
Inyo, California, 85
Ionia, Michigan, 346
Iosco, Michigan, 346
Iowa, Iowa, 234
Iowa, Wisconsin, 757
Iredell, North Carolina, 510
Irion, Texas, 666
Iron, Michigan, 346
Iron, Missouri, 401
Iron, Utah, 687
Iron, Wisconsin, 757
Iroquois, Illinois, 194
Irwin, Georgia, 156
Isabella, Michigan, 346
Isanti, Minnesota, 364
Island, Washington, 733
Isle of Wight, Virginia, 715
Isle Royal, Michigan, 346
Issaquena, Mississippi, 379
Itasca, Minnesota, 364

Itawamba, Mississippi, 380
Izard, Arkansas, 68
Izard, Nebraska, 431
Jack, Texas, 667
Jackson, Alabama, 37
Jackson, Arkansas, 68
Jackson, Colorado, 99
Jackson, Florida, 135
Jackson, Georgia, 156
Jackson, Illinois, 194
Jackson, Indiana, 213
Jackson, Iowa, 234
Jackson, Kansas, 251
Jackson, Kentucky, 271
Jackson, Michigan, 346
Jackson, Minnesota, 365
Jackson, Mississippi, 380
Jackson, Missouri, 401
Jackson, Nebraska, 431
Jackson, North Carolina, 510
Jackson, Ohio, 543
Jackson, Oklahoma, 559
Jackson, Oregon, 573
Jackson, South Dakota, 625
Jackson, Tennessee, 641
Jackson, Texas, 667
Jackson, Virginia, 715
Jackson, West Virginia, 744
Jackson, Wisconsin, 757
Jackson Parish, Louisiana, 290
James City, Virginia, 715
Jasper, Georgia, 157
Jasper, Illinois, 195
Jasper, Indiana, 213
Jasper, Iowa, 234
Jasper, Mississippi, 380
Jasper, Missouri, 401
Jasper, South Carolina, 613
Jasper, Texas, 667
Jay, Indiana, 213
Jayne, South Dakota, 625
Jeff Davis, Georgia, 157
Jeff Davis, Texas, 667
Jefferson, Alabama, 38
Jefferson, Arkansas, 68
Jefferson, Colorado, 99
Jefferson, Florida, 135
Jefferson, Georgia, 157
Jefferson, Idaho, 178
Jefferson, Illinois, 195
Jefferson, Indiana, 213
Jefferson, Iowa, 234
Jefferson, Kansas, 252
Jefferson, Kentucky, 271
Jefferson, Mississippi, 380
Jefferson, Missouri, 401
Jefferson, Montana, 416
Jefferson, Nebraska, 431
Jefferson, New York, 489
Jefferson, Ohio, 543
Jefferson, Oklahoma, 559
Jefferson, Oregon, 573
Jefferson, Pennsylvania, 590

Jefferson, Tennessee, 641
Jefferson, Texas, 667
Jefferson, Vermont, 698
Jefferson, Virginia, 715
Jefferson, Washington, 733
Jefferson, West Virginia, 744
Jefferson, Wisconsin, 757
Jefferson Davis, Mississippi, 380
Jefferson Davis Parish,
    Louisiana, 291
Jefferson Parish, Louisiana, 291
Jenkins, Georgia, 157
Jennings, Indiana, 213
Jerauld, South Dakota, 625
Jerome, Idaho, 178
Jersey, Illinois, 195
Jessamine, Kentucky, 271
Jewell, Kansas, 252
Jim Hogg, Texas, 667
Jim Wells, Texas, 667
Jo Daviess, Illinois, 195
Johnson, Arkansas, 68
Johnson, Georgia, 157
Johnson, Illinois, 195
Johnson, Indiana, 214
Johnson, Iowa, 234
Johnson, Kansas, 252
Johnson, Kentucky, 271
Johnson, Missouri, 401
Johnson, Nebraska, 431
Johnson, Tennessee, 641
Johnson, Texas, 667
Johnson, Wyoming, 766
Johnston, North Carolina, 510
Johnston, Oklahoma, 559
Jones, Alabama, 38
Jones, Georgia, 157
Jones, Iowa, 234
Jones, Mississippi, 380
Jones, Nebraska, 431
Jones, North Carolina, 510
Jones, South Dakota, 625
Jones, Texas, 667
Josephine, Oregon, 573
Juab, Utah, 687
Judith Basin, Montana, 416
Juneau, City and Bourough,
    Alaska, 48
Juneau, Wisconsin, 757
Juniata, Pennsylvania, 590
K, Oklahoma, 560
Kalamazoo, Michigan, 346
Kalawao, Hawaii, 168
Kalkaska, Michigan, 346
Kanabec, Minnesota, 365
Kanawah, Virginia, 716
Kanawha, West Virginia, 744
Kandiyohi, Minnesota, 365
Kane, Illinois, 195
Kane, Utah, 687
Kankakee, Illinois, 195
Kanotin, Michigan, 346
Kansas, Kansas, 252

Karnes, Texas, 667
Kauai, Hawaii, 168
Kaufman, Texas, 667
Kautawaubet, Michigan, 347
Kay, Oklahoma, 560
Kaykakee, Michigan, 347
Kearney, Nebraska, 432
Kearny, Kansas, 252
Keith, Nebraska, 432
Kemper, Mississippi, 380
Kenai Peninsula Borough,
    Alaska, 48
Kendall, Illinois, 195
Kendall, Texas, 667
Kenedy, Texas, 667
Kennebec, Maine, 304
Kenosha, Wisconsin, 757
Kent, Delaware, 121
Kent, Maryland, 318
Kent, Michigan, 347
Kent, Rhode Island, 602
Kent, Texas, 667
Kenton, Kentucky, 271
Kentucky, Virginia, 716
Keokuk, Iowa, 234
Kern, California, 85
Kerr, Texas, 668
Kershaw, South Carolina, 613
Keskkauko, Michigan, 347
Ketchikan Gateway Borough,
    Alaska, 48
Kewaunee, Wisconsin, 757
Keweenaw, Michigan, 347
Keya Paha, Nebraska, 432
Kidder, North Dakota, 524
Kimball, Nebraska, 432
Kimble, Texas, 668
Kinchafoonee, Georgia, 157
Kinderhook, Missouri, 401
King, Texas, 668
King, Washington, 733
King & Queen, Virginia, 716
King George, Virginia, 716
King William, Virginia, 716
Kingfisher, Oklahoma, 560
Kingman, Kansas, 252
King's, Rhode Island, 602
Kings, California, 85
Kings, New York, 489
Kingsbury, South Dakota, 625
Kinney, Texas, 668
Kiowa, Colorado, 99
Kiowa, Kansas, 252
Kiowa, Oklahoma, 560
Kiowa, old, Kansas, 252
Kishkekosh, Iowa, 235
Kit Carson, Colorado, 99
Kitsap, Washington, 733
Kittitas, Washington, 733
Kittson, Minnesota, 365
Kittson, North Dakota, 524
Klamath, California, 85
Klamath, Oregon, 573

Macon, Missouri, 402
Macon, North Carolina, 510
Macon, Tennessee, 641
Macoupin, Illinois, 196
Madera, California, 85
Madison, Alabama, 38
Madison, Arkansas, 69
Madison, Florida, 135
Madison, Georgia, 158
Madison, Idaho, 179
Madison, Illinois, 196
Madison, Iowa, 235
Madison, Indiana, 214
Madison, Kansas, 253
Madison, Kentucky, 272
Madison, Mississippi, 381
Madison, Missouri, 402
Madison, Montana, 416
Madison, Nebraska, 432
Madison, New York, 490
Madison, North Carolina, 510
Madison, Ohio, 543
Madison, Tennessee, 642
Madison, Texas, 669
Madison, Virginia, 717
Madison Parish, Louisiana, 291
Magoffin, Kentucky, 272
Mahaska, Iowa, 235
Mahnomen, Minnesota, 366
Mahoning, Ohio, 544
Major, Oklahoma, 560
Malad, Utah, 687
Malheur, Oregon, 573
Manassas Park (Ind. City),
  Virginia, 717
Manatee, Florida, 135
Mandan, South Dakota, 626
Manistee, Michigan, 348
Manitou, Michigan, 348
Manitowoc, Wisconsin, 758
Mankahto, Minnesota, 366
Manomin, Minnesota, 366
Marathon, Wisconsin, 758
Marengo, Alabama, 38
Maricopa, Arizona, 56
Maries, Missouri, 402
Marin, California, 85
Marinette, Wisconsin, 758
Marion, Alabama, 38
Marion, Arkansas, 69
Marion, Florida, 135
Marion, Georgia, 158
Marion, Illinois, 196
Marion, Indiana, 214
Marion, Iowa, 235
Marion, Kansas, 253
Marion, Kentucky, 273
Marion, Mississippi, 381
Marion, Missouri, 402
Marion, Ohio, 544
Marion, Oregon, 573
Marion, South Carolina, 614
Marion, Tennessee, 642

Marion, Texas, 669
Marion, Virginia, 717
Marion, West Virginia, 744
Mariposa, California, 85
Marlboro, South Carolina, 614
Marquette, Michigan, 348
Marquette, Wisconsin, 758
Marshall, Alabama, 38
Marshall, Illinois, 196
Marshall, Indiana, 214
Marshall, Iowa, 235
Marshall, Kansas, 253
Marshall, Kentucky, 273
Marshall, Minnesota, 366
Marshall, Mississippi, 381
Marshall, Oklahoma, 560
Marshall, South Dakota, 626
Marshall, Tennessee, 642
Marshall, Virginia, 717
Marshall, West Virginia, 744
Martin, Florida, 135
Martin, Indiana, 214
Martin, Kentucky, 273
Martin, Minnesota, 366
Martin, North Carolina, 510
Martin, South Dakota, 626
Martin, Texas, 669
Martinsville (Ind. City), Virginia,
  717
Mason, Illinois, 196
Mason, Kentucky, 273
Mason, Michigan, 348
Mason, Texas, 669
Mason, Virginia, 717
Mason, Washington, 733
Mason, West Virginia, 744
Massac, Illinois, 196
Matagorda, Texas, 669
Matanuska-Susitna Borough,
  Alaska, 48
Mathews, Virginia, 717
Maui, Hawaii, 168
Maury, Tennessee, 642
Maverick, Texas, 669
Mayes, Oklahoma, 560
McClain, Oklahoma, 560
McCone, Montana, 417
McCook, South Dakota, 626
McCormick, South Carolina, 614
McCracken, Kentucky, 273
McCreary, Kentucky, 273
McCulloch, Texas, 669
McCurtain, Oklahoma, 561
McDonald, Missouri, 402
McDonough, Illinois, 196
McDowell, North Carolina, 510
McDowell, Virginia, 717
McDowell, West Virginia, 744
McDuffie, Georgia, 158
McGee, Kansas, 253
McHenry, Illinois, 196
McHenry, North Dakota, 524
McIntosh, Georgia, 158

McIntosh, North Dakota, 524
McIntosh, Oklahoma, 561
McKean, Pennsylvania, 591
McKenzie, North Dakota, 524
McKenzie, old, North Dakota,
  525
McKinley, New Mexico, 474
McLean, Illinois, 196
McLean, Kentucky, 273
McLean, North Dakota, 525
McLennan, Texas, 670
McLeod, Minnesota, 366
McMinn, Tennessee, 642
McMullen, Texas, 670
McNairy, Tennessee, 642
McNeale, Nebraska, 432
McPherson, Kansas, 253
McPherson, Nebraska, 432
McPherson, South Dakota, 626
Meade, Kansas, 253
Meade, Kentucky, 273
Meade, South Dakota, 626
Meagher, Montana, 417
Mecklenburg, North Carolina,
  510
Mecklenburg, Virginia, 717
Mecosta, Michigan, 348
Medina, Ohio, 544
Medina, Texas, 670
Meegisee, Michigan, 348
Meeker, Minnesota, 366
Meigs, Ohio, 544
Meigs, Tennessee, 642
Mellette, South Dakota, 626
Menard, Illinois, 196
Menard, Texas, 670
Mendocino, California, 85
Menifee, Kentucky, 273
Menominee, Michigan, 348
Menominee, Wisconsin, 758
Merced, California, 85
Mercer, Illinois, 196
Mercer, Kentucky, 273
Mercer, Missouri, 403
Mercer, New Jersey, 464
Mercer, North Dakota, 525
Mercer, Ohio, 544
Mercer, Pennsylvania, 591
Mercer, Virginia, 717
Mercer, West Virginia, 744
Meriwether, Georgia, 158
Merrick, Nebraska, 433
Merrimack, New Hampshire,
  452
Mesa, Colorado, 100
Metcalfe, Kentucky, 273
Meyer, South Dakota, 626
Miami, Indiana, 214
Miami, Kansas, 253
Miami, Ohio, 544
Miami-Dade, Florida, 136
Michilimackinac, Michigan, 348
Middlesex, Connecticut, 113

Middlesex, Massachusetts, 330
Middlesex, New Jersey, 464
Middlesex, Virginia, 717
Midland, Michigan, 348
Midland, Texas, 670
Midway, South Dakota, 626
Mifflin, Pennsylvania, 591
Mikenauk, Michigan, 348
Milam, Texas, 670
Millard, Utah, 687
Mille Lacs, Minnesota, 366
Miller, Arkansas, 69
Miller, Georgia, 158
Miller, Missouri, 403
Miller, old, Arkansas, 69
Mills, Iowa, 235
Mills, South Dakota, 627
Mills, Texas, 670
Milton, Georgia, 158
Milwaukee, Wisconsin, 758
Miner, South Dakota, 627
Mineral, Colorado, 100
Mineral, Montana, 417
Mineral, Nevada, 442
Mineral, West Virginia, 744
Mingo, West Virginia, 745
Minidoka, Idaho, 179
Minnehaha, South Dakota, 627
Missaukee, Michigan, 348
Mississippi, Arkansas, 69
Mississippi, Missouri, 403
Missoula, Montana, 417
Mitchell, Georgia, 158
Mitchell, Iowa, 235
Mitchell, Kansas, 253
Mitchell, North Carolina, 511
Mitchell, Texas, 670
Mobile, Alabama, 38
Modoc, California, 85
Moffat, Colorado, 100
Mohave, Arizona, 56
Moniteau, Missouri, 403
Monmouth, New Jersey, 464
Mono, California, 85
Monona, Iowa, 236
Monongalia, Minnesota, 366
Monongalia, Virginia, 717
Monongalia, West Virginia, 745
Monroe, Alabama, 39
Monroe, Arkansas, 69
Monroe, Florida, 136
Monroe, Georgia, 158
Monroe, Illinois, 197
Monroe, Indiana, 214
Monroe, Iowa, 236
Monroe, Kentucky, 273
Monroe, Michigan, 348
Monroe, Mississippi, 381
Monroe, Missouri, 403
Monroe, Nebraska, 433
Monroe, New York, 490
Monroe, Ohio, 544
Monroe, Pennsylvania, 591

Ozaukee, Wisconsin, 758
P, Oklahoma, 561
Pacific, Washington, 733
Page, Iowa, 236
Page, Virginia, 718
Pahute, Nevada, 443
Palm Beach, Florida, 136
Palo Alto, Iowa, 236
Palo Pinto, Texas, 671
Pamlico, North Carolina, 511
Pamptecough, North Carolina, 511
Panola, Mississippi, 381
Panola, Texas, 671
Park, Colorado, 100
Park, Montana, 417
Park, Wyoming, 767
Parke, Indiana, 215
Parker, Texas, 671
Parmer, Texas, 671
Pasco, Florida, 136
Pasquotank, North Carolina, 511
Passaic, New Jersey, 465
Patrick, Virginia, 718
Patuxent, Maryland, 318
Paulding, Georgia, 159
Paulding, Ohio, 545
Pawnee, Kansas, 254
Pawnee, Nebraska, 433
Pawnee, Oklahoma, 561
Payette, Idaho, 179
Payne, Oklahoma, 561
Peach, Georgia, 159
Pearl River, Mississippi, 381
Pease, Wyoming, 767
Pecos, Texas, 671
Pembina, Minnesota, 367
Pembina, North Dakota, 525
Pemiscot, Missouri, 404
Pend Oreille, Washington, 734
Pender, North Carolina, 512
Pendleton, Kentucky, 274
Pendleton, South Carolina, 614
Pendleton, Virginia, 719
Pendleton, West Virginia, 745
Pennington, Minnesota, 367
Pennington, South Dakota, 627
Penobscot, Maine, 305
Peoria, Illinois, 197
Pepin, Wisconsin, 758
Perkins, Nebraska, 433
Perkins, South Dakota, 627
Perquimans, North Carolina, 512
Perry, Alabama, 39
Perry, Arkansas, 69
Perry, Illinois, 197
Perry, Indiana, 215
Perry, Kentucky, 274
Perry, Mississippi, 382
Perry, Missouri, 404
Perry, Ohio, 545
Perry, Pennsylvania, 592

Perry, Tennessee, 642
Pershing, Nevada, 443
Person, North Carolina, 512
Petersburg (Ind. City), Virginia, 719
Petroleum, Montana, 417
Pettis, Missouri, 404
Phelps, Missouri, 404
Phelps, Nebraska, 433
Philadelphia, Pennsylvania, 592
Phillips, Arkansas, 69
Phillips, Colorado, 100
Phillips, Kansas, 254
Phillips, Montana, 417
Piatt, Illinois, 197
Pickaway, Ohio, 545
Pickens, Alabama, 39
Pickens, Georgia, 159
Pickens, South Carolina, 614
Pickering, Mississippi, 382
Pickett, Tennessee, 643
Pickney District, South Carolina, 614
Pierce, Georgia, 159
Pierce, Minnesota, 367
Pierce, Nebraska, 433
Pierce, North Dakota, 525
Pierce, Washington, 734
Pierce, Wisconsin, 758
Pierce, old, Nebraska, 433
Pike, Alabama, 39
Pike, Arkansas, 69
Pike, Georgia, 159
Pike, Illinois, 197
Pike, Indiana, 215
Pike, Kentucky, 274
Pike, Mississippi, 382
Pike, Missouri, 404
Pike, Ohio, 545
Pike, Pennsylvania, 592
Pima, Arizona, 56
Pinal, Arizona, 56
Pine, Minnesota, 367
Pinellas, Florida, 136
Pipestone, Minnesota, 367
Piscataquis, Maine, 305
Pitkin, Colorado, 100
Pitt, North Carolina, 512
Pittsburgh, Oklahoma, 562
Pittsylvania, Virginia, 719
Piute, Utah, 687
Placer, California, 86
Plaquemines Parish, Louisiana, 291
Platte, Missouri, 404
Platte, Nebraska, 433
Platte, Wyoming, 767
Pleasants, Virginia, 719
Pleasants, West Virginia, 745
Plumas, California, 86
Plymouth, Iowa, 236
Plymouth, Massachusetts, 330
Pocahontas, Iowa, 236

Pocahontas, Virginia, 719
Pocahontas, West Virginia, 745
Poinsett, Arkansas, 69
Pointe Coupee Parish, Louisiana, 292
Polk, Arkansas, 70
Polk, Florida, 136
Polk, Georgia, 159
Polk, Iowa, 236
Polk, Minnesota, 367
Polk, Missouri, 404
Polk, Nebraska, 433
Polk, North Carolina, 512
Polk, Oregon, 573
Polk, Tennessee, 643
Polk, Texas, 672
Polk, Wisconsin, 759
Pondera, Montana, 417
Pontotoc, Mississippi, 382
Pontotoc, Oklahoma, 562
Pope, Arkansas, 70
Pope, Illinois, 197
Pope, Minnesota, 367
Poquoson (Ind. City), Virginia, 719
Portage, Ohio, 545
Portage, Wisconsin, 759
Porter, Indiana, 215
Portsmouth (Ind. City), Virginia, 719
Posey, Indiana, 215
Pottawatomie, Kansas, 254
Pottawatomie, Oklahoma, 562
Pottawattamie, Iowa, 237
Potter, Pennsylvania, 592
Potter, South Dakota, 627
Potter, Texas, 672
Powder River, Montana, 417
Powell, Kentucky, 274
Powell, Montana, 417
Power, Idaho, 179
Poweshiek, Iowa, 237
Powhatan, Virginia, 719
Prairie, Arkansas, 70
Prairie, Montana, 417
Pratt, Kansas, 255
Pratt, South Dakota, 627
Preble, Ohio, 545
Prentiss, Mississippi, 382
Presho, South Dakota, 627
Presidio, Texas, 672
Presque Isle, Michigan, 350
Preston, Virginia, 719
Preston, West Virginia, 745
Price, Wisconsin, 759
Prince Edward, Virginia, 719
Prince George, Virginia, 719
Prince George's, Maryland, 318
Prince of Wales-Outer Ketchika, Alaska, 49
Prince William, Virginia, 719
Princess Anne, Virginia, 719
Providence, Rhode Island, 602

Providence Plantations, Rhode Island, 602
Prowers, Colorado, 100
Pueblo, Colorado, 101
Pulaski, Arkansas, 70
Pulaski, Georgia, 159
Pulaski, Illinois, 197
Pulaski, Indiana, 215
Pulaski, Kentucky, 274
Pulaski, Missouri, 404
Pulaski, Virginia, 719
Pulaski, old, Missouri, 404
Pushmataha, Oklahoma, 562
Putnam, Florida, 136
Putnam, Georgia, 159
Putnam, Illinois, 197
Putnam, Indiana, 216
Putnam, Missouri, 404
Putnam, New York, 491
Putnam, Ohio, 545
Putnam, Tennessee, 643
Putnam, Virginia, 720
Putnam, West Virginia, 745
Pyatt, South Dakota, 627
Q, Oklahoma, 562
Quay, New Mexico, 474
Queen Anne's, Maryland, 318
Queens, New York, 491
Quitman, Georgia, 160
Quitman, Mississippi, 382
Rabun, Georgia, 160
Racine, Wisconsin, 759
Radford (Ind. City), Virginia, 720
Rains, Texas, 672
Raleigh, Virginia, 720
Raleigh, West Virginia, 745
Ralls, Missouri, 404
Ramsey, Minnesota, 367
Ramsey, North Dakota, 525
Randall, Texas, 672
Randolph, Alabama, 39
Randolph, Arkansas, 70
Randolph, Georgia, 160
Randolph, Illinois, 197
Randolph, Indiana, 216
Randolph, Missouri, 404
Randolph, North Carolina, 512
Randolph, Virginia, 720
Randolph, West Virginia, 745
Randolph, old, Georgia, 160
Rankin, Mississippi, 382
Ransom, North Dakota, 525
Rapides Parish, Louisiana, 292
Rappahannock, Virginia, 720
Rappahannock, Old, Virginia, 720
Ravalli, Montana, 417
Rawlins, Kansas, 255
Ray, Missouri, 405
Reagan, Texas, 672
Real, Texas, 672
Red Lake, Minnesota, 368
Red River, Texas, 672

A Genealogical and Historical Atlas of the United States of America

Cemetery Record Compendium

Immigrants to America Appearing in English Records

Index to Some of the Bibles and Family Records of the United States Vol. 2

Index to Some of the Family Records of the Southern States Vol. 1

Locating Your Immigrant Ancestors: A Guide to Naturalization Records

Migration, Emigration, Immigration Vol. 1

Migration, Emigration, Immigration Vol. 2

Our Native Americans: Their Records of Genealogical Value Vol. 1

Our Native Americans: Their Records of Genealogical Value Vol. 2

The Compass Vol. 1

The Compass Vol. 2

The Handwriting of American Records for a Period of 300 Years

Central European Genealogical Terminology

Handy Guide to Austrian Genealogical Records

A Genealogical Gazetteer of Scotland

A Genealogical Guide and Atlas of Silesia

A Genealogical Handbook for England and Wales

The Lives and Times of Our English Ancestors Vol. 1

The Lives and Times of Our English Ancestors Vol. 2

Your Ancient Canadian Family Ties

Atlantic Bridge to Germany, Vol. 1 - Baden-Wuerttemberg

Atlantic Bridge to Germany, Vol. 2 - Hessen, Rheinland-Pfalz

Atlantic Bridge to Germany, Vol. 3 - Bavaria

Atlantic Bridge to Germany, Vol. 4 - Saarland, Alsace-Lorraine and Switzerland

Atlantic Bridge to Germany, Vol. 5 - Bremen, Hamburg, and Schleswig-Holstein

Atlantic Bridge to Germany, Vol. 6 - Mecklenburg

Atlantic Bridge to Germany, Vol. 7 - Nordhein-Westfalen; Northrhine-Westphalia

Atlantic Bridge to Germany, Vol. 8 - Prussia (Brandenburg, East and West Prussia, Pommerania, Posen)

Atlantic Bridge to Germany, Vol. 9 - Saxony-Sachsen, (Kingdom province, Thuringen/Thuringia, Nine Duchies)

Atlantic Bridge to Germany, Vol. 10 - Hannover (Niedereschen/Lower Saxony, Braunschweig/Brunswick, Schaumburg-Lippe, Oldenburg)

Handy Guide to Hungarian Genealogical Records

Handy Guide to Italian Genealogical Research

Genealogical Guidebook and Atlas of Norway

Handy Guide to Swiss Genealogical Records